THE GUINNESS ENCYCLOPEDIA OF INTERNATIONAL SPORTS RECORDS & RESULTS

C000089948

PETER MATTHEWS AND IAN MORRISON

GUINNESS PUBLISHING

The authors Peter Matthews (general editor) and
Ian Morrison are well-known sports experts.

Peter Matthews, sports consultant to the *Guinness Book of Records*, commentates on his speciality, athletics, for ITV and Channel 4. Guinness published his *Track & Field Athletics – The Records* in 1986 and *Cricket Firsts* (with Robert Brooke) in 1988. He is editor of the *International Athletics Annual*, and his other works include the *Piccolo Encyclopaedia of Sport* (1974), *Who's Who in British Athletics* (1990), and the sports section of the *Guinness Book of Winners & Champions* (1981).

Ian Morrison, an established Guinness author and professional sports statistician, has written books on Motor Racing, Horse Racing, Rugby League, Golf, Snooker, Soccer, Cycling and Boxing. His two most recent books published by Guinness in their 'Records' series are *World Championship Boxing* (1990) and *Motor Racing* (1989). He has also provided biographical information on sports personalities, from sports as far apart as Archery and Weightlifting, for many publications.

Editor: Simon Duncan
Design and layout: Ken Vail Graphic Design, Cambridge

© Peter Matthews, Ian Morrison and Guinness Publishing Ltd 1987, 1990

Published in Great Britain by Guinness Publishing Ltd, 33 London Road, Enfield, Middlesex

Typeset in Frutiger
Printed and bound in Great Britain by The Bath Press

'Guinness' is a registered trade mark of Guinness Superlatives `Ltd

British Library Cataloguing in Publication Data

Matthews, Peter *1945–*
The Guinness encyclopedia of international
sports records and results – 2nd ed.
1. Sports & games, history
I. Title II. Morrison, Ian *1947–*
796.09

ISBN 0-85112-910-2

CONTENTS

INTRODUCTION

In the introduction to the first edition of this book, published in 1987, Ian Morrison and I stated that our aim was to gather together a comprehensive collection of the statistics of international sport. That remained the basis for this new edition, but we have not only updated the text with the myriad happenings in the world of sport over the past three years, but have made extensive additions to the contents, so that even with the greater density of text this new edition is 54 pages longer than the first.

Despite the increased size we have still had to face difficult decisions as to where to draw the line in determining what went in and what had to be left out. As before, lists of world champions and world records at all major sports were our first priority, and we endeavoured to include all major events at each sport. We have taken a very international viewpoint, so that sports enthusiasts from most nations will find their major interests covered. In particular we have substantially increased our coverage of the major American sports.

We have tried to pack in as much data as possible. For instance we have saved space in many of the lists of team champions by bringing together the wins by each team. For these and other annual events, consecutive wins have been shown in the style 1984-90, meaning wins each year from 1984 to 1990 inclusive. Country abbreviations have been used throughout.

In compiling this book, Ian and I split the sports between us. Both of us are sports 'nuts' with very wide-ranging interests, but such a division meant that we could each concentrate on our own particular favourites. So Ian initiated the text on such sports as boxing, motor racing, snooker and all the codes of football, and I did the same for athletics, cricket, swimming and many of the other Olympic sports. On golf, horse racing and tennis we each contributed sections.

It has been great fun to compile this book, and we trust that readers will continue to find its contents of value. We know that we make the work of those who set pub sports quiz questions both easier and harder. Easier as they have an authoritative reference source, harder because the contestants study it avidly!

I would like to pay tribute to the encouragement of Simon Duncan and Charles Richards at Guinness Publishing and to the excellent typesetting and design work of Ken Vail Graphic Design of Cambridge, who took all the data from me on computer disks. Their efforts have enabled me to make this book as up-to-date as publishing deadlines permit. Career figures are generally updated to the end of a season, which might be spring 1990 or the end of 1989, and we have event winners included for the first half of 1990, with a final cut-off set at 8 July 1990, the date of the final of the World Cup at soccer as well as the Wimbledon Tennis Championships.

Peter Matthews
June 1990

ABBREVIATIONS

av.   average
cc   cubic capacity
d   days
hr   hours
kg   kilograms
km   kilometres
km/h   kilometres per hour
m   metres
min   minutes
mph   miles per hour
m/s   metres per second
sec   seconds
y   yards
yr   years

In dates, months are usually abbreviated to their first three digits.

COUNTRIES

Alb   Albania
Alg   Algeria
Ant   Antigua
Arg   Argentina
Aus   Australia
Aut   Austria
Bah   Bahamas
Ban   Bangladesh
Bar   Barbados
Bel   Belgium
Ber   Bermuda
Bhn   Bahrain * (BRN)
Bra   Brazil
Bul   Bulgaria
Bur   Burma (Myanmar) * (MYA)
Cam   Cameroon * (CMR)
Can   Canada
Chl   Chile * (CHI)
Chn   China (People's Republic)
Col   Colombia
Con   Congo * (CGO)
Cs   Czechoslovakia * (TCH)
Cub   Cuba
Cyp   Cyprus
Den   Denmark
Dji   Djibouti
Dom   Dominican Republic
Ecu   Ecuador
Egy   Egypt
Eng   England
Est   Estonia
Eth   Ethiopia
Fij   Fiji
Fin   Finland
Fra   France
FRG   Federal Republic of Germany
Gab   Gabon
Gam   The Gambia
GDR   German Democratic Republic
Ger   Germany (pre-1945)
Gha   Ghana
Gre   Greece
Gua   Guatemala
Guy   Guyana
Haw   Hawaii
HK   Hong Kong * (HKG)
Hol   Holland/Netherlands
Hun   Hungary
Ice   Iceland * (ISL)
Ina   Indonesia
Ind   India
IOM   Isle of Man
Ire   Ireland * (IRL)
Irn   Iran
Irq   Iraq
Isr   Israel
Ita   Italy
IvC   Ivory Coast * (CIV)

Jam   Jamaica
Jap   Japan * (JPN)
Ken   Kenya
Kuw   Kuwait
Lat   Latvia
Lie   Liechtenstein
Lux   Luxembourg
Mal   Malaysia
Maw   Malawi
Mex   Mexico
Mgl   Mongolia
Mlt   Malta
Mon   Monaco
Mor   Morocco * (MAR)
NI   Northern Ireland
Nic   Nicaragua * (NCA)
Nig   Nigeria * (NGR)
NKo   North Korea (Korean DPR) * (PRK)
Nor   Norway
NZ   New Zealand * (NZL)
Pak   Pakistan
Pan   Panama
Par   Paraguay
Per   Peru
Phi   Philippines
PNG   Papua New Guinea
Pol   Poland
Por   Portugal
PR   Puerto Rico * (PUR)
Qat   Qatar
Rho   Rhodesia
Rom   Romania
Rus   Russia (USSR from 1917)
SAf   South Africa (RSA)
Sco   Scotland
Sen   Sénégal
Sin   Singapore
SKo   Korea (South) * (KOR)
Som   Somalia
Spa   Spain * (ESP)
SRho   Southern Rhodesia (now Zimbabwe)
Sri   Sri Lanka
Sud   Sudan
SVI   St Vincent
Swe   Sweden
Swi   Switzerland * (SUI)
Syr   Syria
Tai   Taiwan (Chinese Taipeh) * (TPE)
Tan   Tanzania
Tha   Thailand
Tri   Trinidad & Tobago
Tun   Tunisia
Tur   Turkey
Uga   Uganda
UK   United Kingdom of Great Britain & N.Ireland * (GBR)
Uru   Uruguay
USA   United States
USSR   Soviet Union * (URS)
Ven   Venezuela
Wal   Wales
WI   West Indies
Yug   Yugoslavia
Zai   Zaire
Zam   Zambia
Zim   Zimbabwe (formerly Rhodesia)

* These abbreviations differ in some cases from those used by the IOC (which are shown in brackets). The latter are always three digits and often French language based; we have preferred English or those of the countries concerned.

GOVERNING BODIES OF SPORT

Specified here in English – see relevant sports for actual titles and dates of founding.

AAA   Amateur Athletic Association (UK)
AAU   Amateur Athletic Union (USA)
AIBA   International Amateur Boxing Federation
FAI   International Aeronautics Federation
FEI   International Equestrian Federation
FIA   International Automobile Association
FIAC   International Amateur Cycling Federation
FIBA   International Basketball Federation
FIBT   International Bobsleigh and Tobogganing Federation
FIC   International Canoeing Federation
FIDE   International Chess Federation
FIE   International Fencing Federation
FIFA   International Association Football Federation
FIG   International Gymnastic Federation
FIH   International Hockey Federation
FIL   International Luge Federation
FILA   International Amateur Wrestling Federation
FIM   International Motorcycling Federation
FINA   International Amateur Swimming Federation
FIQ   International Bowling Federation
FIRA   International Amateur Rugby Federation
FIRS   International Roller Skating Federation
FIS   International Ski Federation
FISA   International Rowing Federation
FIT   International Trampoline Federation
FITA   International Archery Federation
FIVB   International Volleyball Federation
GAA   Gaelic Athletic Association
IAAF   International Amateur Athletic Federation
IBA   International Baseball Federation
IBF   International Badminton Federation
       International Boxing Federation
IBSF   International Billiards & Snooker Federation
ICF   International Curling Federation
IHF   International Handball Federation
IIHF   International Ice Hockey Federation
IJF   International Judo Federation
IOF   International Orienteering Federation
IRF   International Racketball Federation
IRFB   International Rugby Football Board
ISF   International Softball Federation
ISRF   International Squash Racquets Federation
ISU   International Skating Union
ITF   International Tennis Federation
ITTF   International Table Tennis Federation
IWF   International Weightlifting Federation
IWSF   International Water Ski Federation
IYRU   International Yacht Racing Union
LPGA   Ladies Professional Golfers Association
MCC   Marylebone Cricket Club
NBA   National Basketball Federation (USA)
NBL   National Basketball League (USA)
NCAA   National Collegiate Athletic Association (USA)
NFL   National Football League (USA)
NHL   National Hockey League (USA)
PGA   Professional Golfers Association
PRCA   Professional Rodeo Cowboys Association
TCCB   Test and County Cricket Board
UCI   International Cycling Union
UIPMB International Union of Modern Pentathlon and Biathlon
UIT   International Shooting Union
WBA   World Boxing Association
WBC   World Boxing Council
WBO   World Boxing Organisation
WTF   World Taekwondo Federation
WWSU   World Water Skiing Union

Other abbreviations for sports bodies are given under their respective sports.

ACKNOWLEDGEMENTS

The authors acknowledge with grateful thanks the assistance of the following experts and officials of governing bodies:

All England Women's Lacrosse Association
Maria Elena Assenza, Fédération Internationale de Tir à l'Arc
Jörg Bahrke, International Handball Federation
Max Bangereter, International Gymnastics Federation
Howard Bass, winter sports
Gisele Bertrand, International Motorcycling Federation
Dennis Bird, ice and roller skating
Arnold Böstrom, International Powerlifting Federation
Glenna Brouse, The Thoroughbred Record, USA
Chong Woo Lee, World Taekwondo Federation
Marion Collin, women's cricket
Peter Craft, The Tug-of-War Association
Mike Cunningham, British Surfing Association
Pat Davis, Badminton
Kevin Desmond, Powerboating
Domenico Di Gianfrancesco, Federazione Italiana Hockey e Pattinaggio
Pat Dombrowski, American Power Boat Association

Terry Dooris, British Orienteering Federation
Albert Dormer, World Bridge Federation
Gavin Ehringer, Professional Rodeo Cowboys Association
Keith Escott, CHESS magazine
Ron Ferguson, Australian Water Ski Association
David Ford, Billiards & Snooker Control Council
Mike Getty, British Darts Organisation
Rulan Hancock, United States National Archery Association
Col. Harper, the Hurlingham Polo Association
Gillian Hill, British Water Ski Federation
Vic Isaacs, One Day Cricket
Naoshi Ito, Japan
Ove Karlsson, Idrottsbøken
Darren P. Kingsley, US Squash Racquets Association
Rodney Knight, Eton Fives Association
Chong Woo Lee, World Taekwondo Federation
Graham Lester, lacrosse
Paula McMartin, Women's International Bowling Congress
Bob Mason, hockey
Andy Milroy, ultra-distance running
Linda Mojer, American Amateur Racquetball Association
John Moody, British Amateur Weight Lifters' Association

Anthony Needell, powerboating
Joseph and Pauline New, National Skating Association of Great Britain
Keith Osmin, Autosport
Tony Pawson, fly fishing
David Pickup, trampolining
Bill Plummer III, Amateur Softball Federation, USA
Mike Price, cycling
P.J. Reeder, Rugby Fives Association
Jack Richmond, The Camanachd Association
Vern Roberts, Handball Magazine, USA
Barry Rolfe, British Gliding Association
Jack Rollin, soccer
George Sarahete, International Federation of Tenpin Bowling
Renee Schlitz, Women's International Bowling Congress
Len Smith, Australian harness racing
William Stephens, Rackets Association
Lance Tingay, lawn tennis
Steve Trew, triathlon
Mel Welch, English Basket Ball Association
Dr. Roy Wheatley, National Roller Hockey Association of Great Britain
Rick Wilson, British Hang Gliding Association
Anne Woodley, Powerboat secretary, Royal Yachting Association
Hugh Wrampling, pétanque
Ian Wright, recketball and squash

AMERICAN FOOTBALL

American Football evolved from the British games of soccer and rugby in the latter part of the 19th century. There were conflicting versions of football, but an important development was the first match under Harvard Rules by Harvard University against McGill University, Montreal in May 1874. In 1876 the Intercollegiate Football Association was formed, and in that year Harvard agreed to reduce the number of players per side from 15 to 11, which it is today. The first professional game was between Latrobe and Jeanette in Pennsylvania on 31 Aug 1895, and by the end of the century it had become the national game, although exceptionally rough at the time. After many fatalities in the early part of the 20th century considerable modifications were made to the rules, including the introduction of the forward pass in 1906. The first Rose Bowl game between the leading college teams was held in 1902.

The American Professional Football Association was formed in 1920 and twelve teams contested the first league season. The association became the National Football League (NFL) in 1922.

NATIONAL FOOTBALL LEAGUE CHAMPIONS

From 1921-32 there was just one league.

Champions:

1921	Chicago Staleys
1922	Canton Bulldogs (Ohio)
1923	Canton Bulldogs (Ohio)
1924	Cleveland Bulldogs
1925	Chicago Cardinals
1926	Frankford Yellowjackets
1927	New York Giants
1928	Providence Steamroller
1929	Green Bay Packers
1930	Green Bay Packers
1931	Green Bay Packers
1932	Chicago Bears

From 1933 the NFL was divided into two divisions, Eastern and Western, with the respective winners playing off for the NFL Championship. Between 1950-52 the divisions were renamed American Conference (Eastern) and National Conference (Western). Between 1953-59 they were known as the Eastern and Western Conferences.

	Eastern	Western	Championship Game
1933	New York Giants	Chicago Bears	Chicago 23 New York 21
1934	New York Giants	Chicago Bears	New York 30 Chicago 13
1935	New York Giants	Detroit Lions	Detroit 26 New York 7
1936	Boston Redskins	Green Bay Packers	Green Bay 21 Boston 6
1937	Washington Redskins	Chicago Bears	Washington 28 Chicago 21
1938	New York Giants	Green Bay Packers	New York 23 Green Bay 17
1939	New York Giants	Green Bay Packers	Green Bay 27 New York 0
1940	Washington Redskins	Chicago Bears	Chicago 73 Washington 0
1941	New York Giants	Chicago Bears	Chicago 37 New York 9
1942	Washington Redskins	Chicago Bears	Washington 14 Chicago 6
1943	Washington Redskins	Chicago Bears	Chicago 41 Washington 21
1944	New York Giants	Green Bay Packers	Green Bay 14 New York 7
1945	Washington Redskins	Cleveland Rams	Cleveland 15 Washington 14
1946	New York Giants	Chicago Bears	Chicago 24 New York 14
1947	Philadelphia Eagles	Chicago Cardinals	Chicago Card. 28 Philadelphia 21
1948	Philadelphia Eagles	Chicago Cardinals	Philadelphia 7 Chicago Card. 0
1949	Philadelphia Eagles	Los Angeles Rams	Philadelphia 14 Los Angeles 0
1950	Cleveland Browns	Los Angeles Rams	Cleveland 30 Los Angeles 28
1951	Cleveland Browns	Los Angeles Rams	Los Angeles 24 Cleveland 17
1952	Cleveland Browns	Detroit Lions	Detroit 17 Cleveland 7
1953	Cleveland Browns	Detroit Lions	Detroit 17 Cleveland 16
1954	Cleveland Browns	Detroit Lions	Cleveland 56 Detroit 10
1955	Cleveland Browns	Los Angeles Rams	Cleveland 38 Los Angeles 14
1956	New York Giants	Chicago Bears	New York 47 Chicago 7
1957	Cleveland Browns	Detroit Lions	Detroit 59 Cleveland 14
1958	New York Giants	Baltimore Colts	Baltimore 23 New York 17
1959	New York Giants	Baltimore Colts	Baltimore 31 New York 16

The American Football League (AFL) was formed in 1960 as a rival to the NFL. It had Eastern and Western Divisions while the NFL still had its Eastern and Western Conferences. Both the AFL and NFL had end of season Championships and at the end of the 1966 season the AFL and NFL champions met for the first Super Bowl (played January 1967). Divisional winners and championship game results 1960-69

American Football League

Year	Eastern winners	Western winners	Playoff
1960	Houston Oilers	Los Angeles Chargers	Houston 24 Los Angeles 16
1961	Houston Oilers	San Diego Chargers	Houston 10 San Diego 3
1962	Houston Oilers	Dallas Texans	Dallas 20 Houston 17
1963	Boston Patriots	San Diego Chargers	San Diego 51 Boston 10
1964	Buffalo Bills	San Diego Chargers	Buffalo 20 San Diego 7
1965	Buffalo Bills	San Diego Chargers	Buffalo 23 San Diego 0
1966	Buffalo Bills	Kansas City Chiefs	Kansas City 31 Buffalo 7
1967	Houston Oilers	Oakland Raiders	Oakland 40 Houston 7
1968	New York Jets	Oakland Raiders	New York Jets 27 Oakland 23
1969	New York Jets	Oakland Raiders	Kansas City Chiefs 17 Oakland 7

In 1969 the top two in each division qualified for AFL play-offs

National Football League

Year	Eastern winners	Western winners	Playoff
1960	Philadelphia Eagles	Green Bay Packers	Philadelphia 17 Green Bay 13
1961	New York Giants	Green Bay Packers	Green Bay 37 New York 0
1962	New York Giants	Green Bay Packers	Green Bay 16 New York 7
1963	New York Giants	Chicago Bears	Chicago 14 New York 10
1964	Cleveland Browns	Baltimore Colts	Cleveland 27 Baltimore 0
1965	Cleveland Browns	Green Bay Packers	Green Bay 23 Cleveland 12
1966	Dallas Cowboys	Green Bay Packers	Green Bay 34 Dallas 27
1967	(a) Dallas Cowboys	(c) Los Angeles Rams	
	(b) Cleveland Browns	(d) Green Bay Packers	Green Bay 21 Dallas 17
1968	(a) Dallas Cowboys	(c) Baltimore Colts	
	(b) Cleveland Browns	(d) Minnesota Vikings	Baltimore 34 Cleveland 0
1969	(a) Dallas Cowboys	(c) Los Angeles Rams	
	(b) Cleveland Browns	(d) Minnesota Vikings	Minnesota 27 Cleveland 7

(a) Capitol Division (b) Century Division (c) Coastal Division (d) Central Division

In 1970 the NFL and AFL merged under the National Football League banner and divided into two conferences, American (AFC) and National (NFC), each with three divisions, Eastern, Central and Western. End of season play-offs culminate in the American and National Conference Championship games with the two winners meeting in the Super Bowl.

AFC Divisional champions

	Eastern	Central	Western
1970	Baltimore Colts	Cincinnati Bengals	Oakland Raiders
1971	Miami Dolphins	Cleveland Browns	Kansas City Chiefs
1972	Miami Dolphins	Pittsburgh Steelers	Oakland Raiders
1973	Miami Dolphins	Cincinnati Bengals	Oakland Raiders
1974	Miami Dolphins	Pittsburgh Steelers	Oakland Raiders
1975	Baltimore Colts	Pittsburgh Steelers	Oakland Raiders
1976	Baltimore Colts	Pittsburgh Steelers	Oakland Raiders
1977	Baltimore Colts	Pittsburgh Steelers	Denver Broncos
1978	New England Patriots	Pittsburgh Steelers	Denver Broncos
1979	Miami Dolphins	Pittsburgh Steelers	San Diego Chargers
1980	Buffalo Bills	Cleveland Browns	San Diego Chargers
1981	Miami Dolphins	Cincinnati Bengals	San Diego Chargers
1983	Miami Dolphins	Pittsburgh Steelers	Los Angeles Raiders
1984	Miami Dolphins	Pittsburgh Steelers	Denver Broncos
1985	Miami Dolphins	Cleveland Browns	Los Angeles Raiders
1986	New England Patriots	Cleveland Browns	Denver Broncos
1987	Indianapolis Colts	Cleveland Browns	Denver Broncos
1988	Buffalo Bills	Cincinatti Bengals	Seattle Seahawks
1989	Buffalo Bills	Cleveland Browns	Denver Broncos

AFC Championship Games

1970	Baltimore 27 Oakland 17	1982	Miami 14 New York Jets 0
1971	Miami 21 Baltimore 0	1983	Los Angeless 30 Seattle 14
1972	Miami 21 Pittsburgh 17	1984	Miami 45 Pittsburgh 28
1973	Miami 27 Oakland 10	1985	New England 31 Miami 14
1974	Pittsburgh 24 Oakland 13	1986	Denver 23 Cleveland 20
1975	Pittsburgh 16 Oakland 10	1987	Denver 38 Cleveland 33
1976	Oakland 24 Pittsburgh 7	1988	Cincinnati 21 Buffalo 10
1977	Denver 20 Oakland 17	1989	Denver 37 Cleveland 21
1978	Pittsburgh 34 Houston 5		
1979	Pittsburgh 27 Houston 13		
1980	Oakland 34 San Diego 27		
1981	Cincinnati 27 San Diego 7		

In 1982 a players' strike shortened the season and the top eight teams in each Conference played-off to decide the championship

NFC Divisional champions

	Eastern	*Central*	*Western*
1970	Dallas Cowboys	Minnesota Vikings	San Francisco 49ers
1971	Dallas Cowboys	Minnesota Vikings	San Francisco 49ers
1972	Washington Redskins	Green Bay Packers	San Francisco 49ers
1973	Dallas Cowboys	Minnesota Vikings	San Francisco 49ers
1974	St Louis Cardinals	Minnesota Vikings	Los Angeles Rams
1975	St Louis Cardinals	Minnesota Vikings	Los Angeles Rams
1976	Dallas Cowboys	Minnesota Vikings	Los Angeles Rams
1977	Dallas Cowboys	Minnesota Vikings	Los Angeles Rams
1978	Dallas Cowboys	Minnesota Vikings	Los Angeles Rams
1979	Dallas Cowboys	Tampa Bay Buccaneers	Los Angeles Rams
1980	Philadelphia Eagles	Minnesota Vikings	Atlanta Falcons
1981	Dallas Cowboys	Tampa Bay Buccaneers	San Francisco 49ers
1983	Washington Redskins	Detroit Lions	San Francisco 49ers
1984	Washington Redskins	Chicago Bears	San Francisco 49ers
1985	Dallas Cowboys	Chicago Bears	Los Angeles Rams
1986	New York Giants	Chicago Bears	San Francisco 49ers
1987	Washington Redskins	Chicago Bears	San Francisco 49ers
1988	Philadelphia Eagles	Chicago Bears	San Francisco 49ers
1989	New York Giants	Minnesota Vikings	San Francisco 49ers

NFC Championship Games

1970	Dallas 17 San Francisco 10
1971	Dallas 14 San Francisco 3
1972	Washington 26 Dallas 3
1973	Minnesota 27 Dallas 10
1974	Minnesota 14 Los Angeles 10
1975	Dallas 37 Los Angeles 7
1976	Minnesota 24 Los Angeles 13
1977	Dallas 23 Minnesota 6
1978	Dallas 28 Los Angeles 0
1979	Los Angeles 9 Tampa Bay 0
1980	Philadelphia 20 Dallas 7
1981	San Francisco 28 Dallas 27
1982	Washington 31 Dallas 17
1983	Washington 24 San Francisco 21
1984	San Francisco 23 Chicago 0
1985	Chicago 24 LA Rams 0
1986	New York 17 Washington 0
1987	Washington 17 Minnesota 10
1988	San Francisco 28 Chicago 3
1989	San Francisco 30 LA Rams 3

SUPER BOWL

Inaugurated in 1966 Superbowl, the contest between the AFC and NFC champions, has become America's greatest sporting event. Tickets for the game are highly prized and record television audiences are regularly attracted to the game, held in January each year at the end of the regular season.

Results

Year	Winners	Runners-up
1967	Green Bay Packers 35	Kansas City Chiefs 10
1968	Green Bay Packers 33	Oakland Raiders 14
1969	New York Jets 16	Baltimore Colts 7
1970	Kansas City Chiefs 23	Minnesota Vikings 7
1971	Baltimore Colts 16	Dallas Cowboys 13
1972	Dallas Cowboys 24	Miami Dolphins 3
1973	Miami Dolphins 14	Washington Redskins 7
1974	Miami Dolphins 24	Minnesota Vikings 7
1975	Pittsburgh Steelers 16	Minnesota Vikings 6
1976	Pittsburgh Steelers 21	Dallas Cowboys 17
1977	Oakland Raiders 32	Minnesota Vikings 14
1978	Dallas Cowboys 27	Denver Broncos 10
1979	Pittsburgh Steelers 35	Dallas Cowboys 31
1980	Pittsburgh Steelers 31	Los Angeles Rams 19
1981	Oakland Raiders 27	Philadelphia Eagles 10
1982	San Francisco 49ers 26	Cincinnati Bengals 21
1983	Washington Redskins 27	Miami Dolphins 17
1984	Los Angeles Raiders 38	Washington Redskins 9
1985	San Francisco 49ers 38	Miami Dolphins 16
1986	Chicago Bears 46	New England Patriots 10
1987	New York Giants 39	Denver Broncos 20
1988	Washington Redskins 42	Denver Broncos 10
1989	San Francisco 49ers 20	Cincinnati Bengals 16
1990	San Francisco 49ers 55	Denver Broncos 10

Super Bowl career records

Most games (player):
5 Marv Fleming (Green Bay 1967-8, Miami 1972-4)
5 Larry Cole (Dallas 1971-2, 1976, 1978-9)
5 Cliff Harris (Dallas 1971-2, 1976, 1978-9)
5 D.D.Lewis (Dallas 1971-2, 1976, 1978-9)
5 Preston Pearson (Baltimore 1969, Pittsburgh 1975, Dallas 1976, 1978-9)
5 Charlie Waters (Dallas 1971-2, 1976, 1978-9)
5 Rayfield Wright (Dallas 1971-2, 1976, 1978-9)
Most games (coach): 6 Don Schula (Baltimore 1969, Miami 1972-4, 1983, 1985)
Most points : 24 Franco Harris (Pittsburgh), Roger Craig, Jerry Rice (San Francisco)
Most touchdowns: 4 Franco Harris (Pittsburgh), Roger Craig, Jerry Rice (San Francisco)
Most field goals : 5 Ray Wersching (San Francisco)

Super Bowl single game records

Most points: 18 Roger Craig (San Francisco 1985), Jerry Rice (San Francisco 1990)
Most touchdowns : 3 Roger Craig (San Francisco 1985), Jerry Rice (San Francisco 1990)

Most field goals : 4 Don Chandler (Green Bay v Oakland, 1968), Ray Wersching (San Francisco v Cincinnati, 1982)
Yards gained rushing:
204 Timmy Smith (Washington Redskins 1988)
Yards gained passing:
357 Joe Montana (San Francisco 49ers 1989)
Yards gained receiving:
215 Jerry Rice (San Francisco 49ers 1989)
Passes completed:
29 Dan Marino (Miami Dolphins 1985)
Touchdown passes:
5 Joe Montana (San Francisco 49ers 1990)
Pass receptions: 11 Dan Ross (Cincinnati Bengals 1982), Jerry Rice (San Francisco 49ers 1989)

Super Bowl MVPs

1967	Bart Starr (QB), Green Bay Packers
1968	Bart Starr (QB), Green Bay Packers
1969	Joe Namath (QB), New York Jets
1970	Len Dawson (QB), Kansas City
1971	Chuck Howley (LB), Dallas Cowboys
1972	Roger Staubach (QB), Dallas Cowboys
1973	Jake Scott (S), Miami Dolphins
1974	Larry Csonka (RB), Miami Dolphins
1975	Franco Harris (RB) Pittsburgh Steelers
1976	Lynn Swann (WR), Pittsburgh Steelers
1977	Fred Biletnikoff (WR), Oakland Raiders
1978	Randy White (DT) & Harvey Martin (DE), Dallas
1979	Terry Bradshaw (QB), Pittsburgh Steelers
1980	Terry Bradshaw (QB), Pittsburgh Steelers
1981	Jim Plunkett (QB), Oakland Raiders
1982	Joe Montana (QB), San Francisco 49ers
1983	Joe Riggins (RB), Washington Redskins
1984	Marcus Allen (RB), Los Angeles Raiders
1985	Joe Montana (QB), San Francisco 49ers
1986	Richard Dent (DE), Chicago Bears
1987	Phil Simms (QB), New York Giants
1988	Doug Williams (QB), Washington Redskins
1989	Jerry Rice (WR), San Francisco 49ers
1990	Joe Montana (QB), San Francisco 49ers

Best Super Bowl teams

1 point for winning a Division, 2 for being the Super Bowl runners-up and 3 for winning the Super Bowl.
26 Dallas Cowboys
22 Oakland/Los Angeles Raiders
21 Miami Dolphins
21 Pittsburgh Steelers
19 Minnesota Vikings
16 San Francisco 49ers
14 Washington Redskins
13 Green Bay Packers
12 Baltimore/Indianapolis Colts
11 Denver Broncos
11 Los Angeles Rams
10 Cleveland Browns
9 Chicago Bears
8 Cincinnati Bengals

8 Dallas Texans/Kansas City Chiefs
8 Los Angeles/San Diego Chargers
7 New York Giants
5 Buffalo Bills
5 Boston/New England Patriots
5 Philadelphia Eagles
4 Houston Oilers
3 New York Jets
2 Chicago/St Louis/Phoenix Cardinals
2 Tampa Bay Buccaneers
1 Seattle Seahawks
1 Detroit Lions
1 Atlanta Falcons
0 New Orleans Saints

MAJOR NFL RECORDS

General

Most games: 340 George Blanda (Chicago Bears, Baltimore, Houston, Oakland) 1949-75
Most season as head coach: 40 George Halas (Chicago Bears) 1920-9, 1933-42, 1946-55, 1958-67

Scoring

Most points (career): 2,002 George Blanda (Chicago Bears, Baltimore, Houston, Oakland) 1949-75
Most points (season): 176 Paul Hornung (Green Bay) 1960
Most points (game): 40 Ernie Nevers (Chicago Cardinals v Chicago Bears) 28 Nov 1929
Most touchdowns (career): 126 Jim Brown (Cleveland) 1957-65
Most touchdowns (season): 24 John Riggins (Washington) 1983
Most touchdowns (game):
6 Ernie Nevers (Chicago Cardinals v Chicago Bears) 28 Nov 1929
6 William Jones (Cleveland v Chicago Bears) 25 Nov 1951
6 Gale Sayers (Chicago v San Francisco) 12 Dec 1965
Most field goals (career): 373 Jan Stenerud (Kansas City, Green Bay, Minnesota) 1967-85
Most field goals (season): 35 Ali Haji-Sheikh (New York Giants) 1983
Most field goals (game): 7 Jim Bakken (St.Louis v Pittsburgh) 24 Sep 1967

Rushing

Most yards gained (career): 16,726 Walter Payton (Chicago) 1975-87
Most yards gained (season): 2,105 Eric Dickerson (Los Angeles Rams) 1984
Most yards gained (game): 275 Walter Payton (Chicago v Minnesota) 20 Nov 1977

Passing

Most passes completed (career): 3,686 Fran Tarkenton (Minnesota, New York Giants) 1961-78
Most passes completed (season): 378 Dan Marino (Miami) 1986
Most passes completed (game): 42 Richard Todd (New York Jets v San Francisco) 21 Sep 1980
Most yards gained (career): 47,003 Fran Tarkenton (Minnesota, New York Giants) 1961-78
Most yards gained (season): 5,084 Dan Marino (Miami) 1984
Most yards gained (game): 554 Norm Van Brocklin (Los Angeles v New York Yankees) 28 Sep 1951

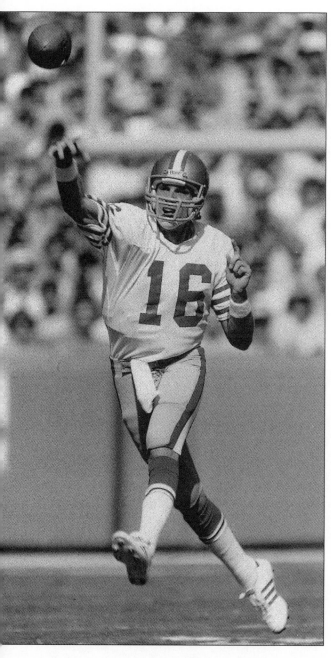

Joe Montana has helped the San Francisco 49ers to three Superbowl victories and has Superbowl career records of 1142 yards gained passing, 83 passes completed and 11 touchdown passes in his four games (All-Sport)

ALL-TIME TOP TENS

Most Points

George Blanda	2,002
Jan Stenerud	1,699
Jim Turner	1,439
Mark Moseley	1,382
Jim Bakken	1,380
Fred Cox	1,365
Lou Groza	1,349
Pat Leahy	1,261
Chris Bahr	1,213
Gino Cappelletti	1,130

Most Touchdowns

Jim Brown	126
Walter Payton	125
John Riggins	116
Lenny Moore	113
Don Hutson	105
Steve Largent	101
Franco Harris	100
Jim Taylor	93
Bobby Mitchell	91
Tony Dorsett	91

Most Passes Completed

Fran Tarkenton	3,686
Dan Fouts	3,297
Johnny Unitas	2,830
Ken Anderson	2,654
Joe Montana	2,593
Jim Hart	2,593
John Brodie	2,489
Sonny Jurgensen	2,433
Y A Tittle	2,427
Joe Ferguson	2,367

Most Yards Gained Passing

Fran Tarkenton	47,003
Dan Fouts	43,040
Johnny Unitas	40,239
Jim Hart	34,665
John Hadl	33,513
Y A Tittle	33,070
Ken Anderson	32,838
Sonny Jurgensen	32,224
John Brodie	31,548
Joe Montana	31,054

Most Yards Gained Rushing

Walter Payton	16,726
Tony Dorsett	12,739
Jim Brown	12,312
Franco Harris	12,120
John Riggins	11,352
O J Simpson	11,236
Eric Dickerson	11,226
Earl Campbell	9,407
Ottis Anderson	9,317
Jim Taylor	8,597

Fewest games to reach 10,000 yards rushing: 91 Eric Dickerson, 110 O.J.Simpson, 113 Walter Payton

Franchise changes

Since the formation of the AFL in 1960 the following teams have changed their franchise:

	From	To
1960	Chicago Cardinals	St Louis Cardinals
1961	Los Angeles Chargers	San Diego Chargers
1963	Dallas Texans	Kansas City Chiefs
1981	Oakland Raiders	Los Angeles Raiders
1984	Baltimore Colts	Indianapolis Colts
1988	St Louis Cardinals	Phoenix Cardinals

COLLEGE FOOTBALL

More than 650 colleges, affiliated to the National Collegiate Athletic Association compete throughout the United States each year. The ultimate aim of them all is to reach one of the many Bowl finals held at the end of the season.

National College Football Champions

At the end of December each year journalists throughout the United States engage in a national poll to vote for the outstanding college team of the year. The poll has been conducted since 1936.

1936 Minnesota
1937 Pittsburgh
1938 Texas Christian
1939 Texas A & M
1940-1 Minnesota
1942 Ohio State
1943 Notre Dame
1944-5 Army
1946-7 Notre Dame
1948 Michigan
1949 Notre Dame
1950 Oklahoma
1951 Tennessee
1952 Michigan State
1953 Maryland
1954 Ohio State & UCLA
1955-6 Oklahoma
1957 Auburn & Ohio State
1958 Louisiana State
1959 Syracuse
1960 Minnesota
1961 Alabama
1962 South Carolina
1963 Texas
1964 Alabama
1965 Alabama & Michigan State
1966 Notre Dame
1967 South Carolina
1968 Ohio State
1969 Texas
1970 Texas & Nebraska
1971 Nebraska
1972 South Carolina
1973 Notre Dame
1974 Oklahoma & South Carolina
1975 Oklahoma
1976 Pittsburgh
1977 Notre Dame
1978 Alabama & South Carolina
1979 Alabama
1980 Georgia
1981 Clemson
1982 Penn State
1983 Miami (Florida)
1984 Brigham Young
1985 Oklahoma
1986 Penn State
1987 Miami (Florida)
1988 Notre Dame
1989 Miami (Florida)

Most wins: 8 Notre Dame

BOWL GAMES

The highlight of the College season are the end-of-season Bowl Games and the 'Big Four' are the Rose Bowl, Orange Bowl, Sugar Bowl, and Cotton Bowl. Most wins in each have been as follows:

Rose Bowl

19 Southern California (USC), 6 Michigan, 5 Alabama, Stanford, Ohio State, UCLA; 4 Washington, 3 Illinois, Michigan State

Orange Bowl

11 Oklahoma, 5 Miami, Nebraska; 4 Alabama, 3 Georgia Tech, Penn State; 2 Duquesne, Georgia, Louisiana State,

Texas, Clemson, Notre Dame
Sugar Bowl
7 Alabama, 5 Mississippi, 4 Georgia Tech, Oklahoma; 3 Tennessee, Louisiana State, Nebraska; 2 Texas Christian, Santa Clara, Georgia, Pittsburgh, Auburn
Cotton Bowl
9 Texas, 4 Texas A & M, 3 Rice, Louisiana State, Southern Methodist, Notre Dame; 2 Texas Christian, Alabama, Arkansas, Georgia, Penn State, Houston, Tennessee

Alabama, Georgia and Notre Dame have won all four major Bowls
Most Bowl appearances: 42 Alabama, 33 USC, 32 Texas, 30 Tennessee, 29 Oklahoma, 28 Georgia, 27 Louisiana State
Most wins: 23 USC, 21 Alabama, 17 Oklahoma, 15 Texas, Georgia Tech, Penn State, Tennessee; 13 Nebraska
Most 'Big Four' appearances: 31 Alabama, 26 USC, 22 Texas, 19 Oklahoma, 17 Georgia, Nebraska
Most 'Big Four' wins: 20 USC, 18 Alabama, 15 Oklahoma, 12 Texas

Major College career records:
Most points scored: 393 Derek Schmidt (Florida State) 1984-7
Most touchdowns: 59 Glenn Davis (Army) 1943-6, 59 Tony Dorsett (Pittsburgh) 1973-6
Most field goals: 79 John Lee (UCLA) 1982-5
Most yards gained rushing: 6,082 Tony Dorsett (Pittsburgh) 1973-6
Most yards gained passing: 11,425 Todd Santos (San Diego State) 1984-7

Most passes completed: 910 Todd Santos (San Diego State) 1984-7

HEISMAN TROPHY
Awarded annually since 1935 by the Downtown Athletic Club of New York to the top college footballer as determined by a poll of journalists. It was originally called the D.A.C. Trophy but changed its name in 1936. Its full title is the John W.Heisman Memorial Trophy and is named after the first athletic director of the Downtown club.
Winners:
1935 Jay Berwanger (Chicago)
1936 Larry Kelley (Yale)
1937 Clint Frank (Yale)
1938 Davey O'Brien (Texas Christian)
1939 Nile Kinnick (Iowa)
1940 Tom Harmon (Michigan)
1941 Bruce Smith (Minnesota)
1942 Frank Sinkwich (Georgia)
1943 Angelo Bertelli (Notre Dame)
1944 Les Horvath (Ohio State)
1945 Doc Blanchard (Army)
1946 Glenn Davis (Army)
1947 John Lujack (Notre Dame)
1948 Doak Walker (Southern Methodist)
1949 Leon Hart (Notre Dame)
1950 Vic Janowicz (Ohio State)
1951 Dick Kazmaier (Princeton)
1952 Billy Vessels (Oklahoma)
1953 John Lattner (Notre Dame)
1954 Alan Ameche (Wisconsin)
1955 Howard Cassady (Ohio State)
1956 Paul Hornung (Notre Dame)
1957 John Crow (Texas A & M)
1958 Pete Dawkins (Army)
1959 Billy Cannon (Louisiana State)
1960 Joe Bellino (Navy)

1961 Ernie Davis (Syracuse)
1962 Terry Baker (Oregon State)
1963 Roger Staubach (Navy)
1964 John Huarte (Notre Dame)
1965 Mike Garrett (USC)
1966 Steve Spurrier (Florida)
1967 Gary Beban (UCLA)
1968 O.J.Simpson (USC)
1969 Steve Owens (Oklahoma)
1970 Jim Plunkett (Stanford)
1971 Pat Sullivan (Auburn)
1972 Johnny Rogers (Nebraska)
1973 John Cappelletti (Penn State)
1974 Archie Griffin (Ohio State)
1975 Archie Griffin (Ohio State)
1976 Tony Dorsett (Pittsburgh)
1977 Earl Campbell (Texas)
1978 Billy Sims (Oklahoma)
1979 Charles White (USC)
1980 George Rogers (South Carolina)
1981 Marcus Allen (USC)
1982 Herschel Walker (Georgia)
1983 Mike Rozier (Nebraska)
1984 Doug Flutie (Boston College)
1985 Bo Jackson (Auburn)
1986 Vinny Testaverde (Miami)
1987 Tim Brown (Notre Dame)
1988 Barry Sanders (Oklahoma)
1989 Andre Ware (Houston)

BUDWEISER BOWL
Winners of the British American Football Championship for the Budweiser Bowl have been:
1986-7 London Ravens, 1988 Birmingham Bulls, 1989 Manchester Spartans.

EUROPEAN CHAMPIONSHIPS
Winners: 1983 Italy, 1985 Finland, 1987 Italy, 1989 Great Britian

ANGLING

Angling is the art of catching fish with rod, line and hook. Such an activity naturally dates back to civilised man's earliest days. The oldest club still in existence is the Ellem fishing club in Scotland, formed in 1829. English national championships were first held in 1906 and the International Confederation of Anglers (CIPS - see below) was formed in Rome in 1952.

WORLD CHAMPIONSHIPS
The first World Fresh Water Championship was held in 1957, three years after the staging of the first European championships.
Winners:

	Individual	Team
1957	Mandeli (Ita)	Italy
1958	Garroit (Bel)	Belgium
1959	Robert Tesse (Fra)	France
1960	Robert Tesse (Fra)	Belgium
1961	Ramon Legogue (Fra)	GDR
1962	Raimondo Tedasco (Ita)	Italy
1963	William Lane (Eng)	France
1964	Joseph Fontanet (Fra)	France

1965	Robert Tesse (Fra)	Romania
1966	Henri Guiheneuf (Fra)	France
1967	Jacques Isenbaert (Bel)	Belgium
1968	Günter Grebenstein (FRG)	France
1969	Robin Harris (Eng)	Holland
1970	Marcel Van den Eynde (Bel)	Belgium
1971	Dino Bassi (Ita)	Italy
1972	Hubert Levels (Hol)	France
1973	Pierre Michiels (Bel)	Belgium
1974	Aribert Richter (FRG)	France
1975	Ian Heaps (Eng)	France
1976	Dino Bassi (Ita)	Italy
1977	Jean Mainil (Bel)	Luxembourg
1978	Jean-Pierre Fouquet (Fra)	France
1979	Gérard Heulard (Fra)	France
1980	Wolf-Rüdiger Kremkus (FRG)	FR Germany
1981	Dave Thomas (Eng)	France
1982	Kevin Ashurst (Eng)	Holland
1983	Wolf-Rüdiger Kremkus (FRG)	Belgium
1984	Bobby Smithers (Ire)	Luxembourg
1985	Dave Roper (Eng)	England
1986	Lud Wever (Hol)	Italy
1987	Clive Branson (Wal)	England
1988	Jean-Pierre Fouquet (Fra)	England
1989	Tom Pickering (Eng)	Wales

Most Individual wins: 3 Robert Tesse
Most team wins: 11 France

WORLD FLY FISHING CHAMPIONSHIPS

The first world fly fishing championship was held in 1981, organised by the Confédération Internationale de la Pêche Sportive (CIPS).

Year	Venue	Individual winner	Team winner
1981	Lake Echter-nach (Lux)	C.Wittkamp (Hol)	Netherlands
1982	Narcea River (Spa)	Viktor Diez y Diez (Spa)	Italy
1983	Sesia River (Ita)	Segismondo Fernandez (Spa)	Italy
1984	Tormes River (Spa)	Tony Pawson (Eng)	Italy
1985	San River (Pol)	Leslaw Frasik (Pol)	Poland
1986	Ourthe River (Bel)	Slivoj Svoboda (Cs)	Italy
1987	Various locations (Eng)	Brian Leadbetter (Eng)	England
1988	Various locations in Tasmania (Aus)	John Pawson (Eng)	England
1989	Kuusinski and Kitka Rivers (Fin)	Wladyslaw Trzebuinia (Pol)	Poland

ARCHERY

From the use of bow and arrow in hunting and in warfare, archery developed as one of man's earliest known organized sports. The world governing body is the Fédération Internationale de Tir á l'Arc (FITA), which was founded in 1931. Practitioners can remain at the top for a long time. A most notable example is that of Alice Blanche Legh who won a record 23 British ladies' titles between 1881 and 1922, when she was 67.

WORLD CHAMPIONSHIPS

World target archery championships were first staged in 1931 and are now held bienially. From 1957 to 1985 the contests were over Double FITA rounds of 36 arrows at 90m, 70m, 50m and 30m for men; 70m, 60m, 50m and 30m for women; scores are given for these. From 1987 the championships have been conducted on a knockout basis with scores not being accumulated over the rounds, and the scores given are for the final round of 36 arrows.

Winners:
Men's Individual
1931 Michal Sawicki (Pol)
1932 Laurent Reith (Bel)
1933 Donald Mackenzie (USA)
1934 Henry Kjellson (Swe)
1935 Adriaan van Kohlen (Bel)
1936 Emil Heilborn (Swe)
1937 George De Rons (Bel)
1938 Frantisek Hadas (Cs)
1939 Roger Beday (Fra)
1946 Einar Tang Holbek (Den)
1947-50 Hans Deutgen (Swe)
1952 Stellan Andersson (Swe)
1953 Bror Lundgren (Swe)
1955 Nils Andersson (Swe)
1957 Ozziek Smathers (USA) 2231
1958 Stig Thysell (Swe) 2101
1959 James Caspers (USA) 2247
1961 Joseph Thornton (USA) 2310
1963 Charles Sandlin (USA) 2332
1965 Matti Haikonen (Fin) 2313
1967 Ray Rogers (USA) 2298
1969 Hardy Ward (USA) 2423
1971 John Williams (USA) 2445
1973 Viktor Sidoruk (USSR) 2185

1975 Darrell Pace (USA) 2548
1977 Richard McKinney (USA) 2501
1979 Darrell Pace (USA) 2474
1981 Kyösti Laasonen (Fin) 2541
1983 Richard McKinney (USA) 2617
1985 Richard McKinney (USA) 2601
1987 Vladimir Yesheyev (USSR) 329
1989 Stanislav Zabrodskiy (USSR) 332

Most wins: 4 Hans Deutgen, 3 Richard McKinney

Men's Team wins:

14 USA	1957, each championship 1959-83
5 Sweden	1934, 1948, 1952-3, 1955
4 Czechoslovakia	1936, 1938, 1947, 1949
2 France	1931, 1939
2 Poland	1932, 1937
2 Belgium	1933, 1935
2 Denmark	1946, 1950
1 Finland 1958, South Korea 1985, F.R.Germany 1987,USSR 1989	

Record score: 7812 USA 1983

Women's Individual
1931-4 Janina Kurkowska (Pol)
1935 Ina Catani (Swe)
1936 Janina Kurkowska (Pol)
1937 Ingo Simon (UK)
1938 Nora Weston Martyr (UK)
1939 Janina Kurkowska (Pol)
1946 Nilla de Wharton Burr (UK)
1947 Janina Kurkowska (Pol)
1948 Nilla de Wharton Burr (UK)
1949 Barbara Waterhouse (UK)
1950 Jean Lee (USA)
1952 Jean Lee (USA)
1953 Jean Richards (USA)
1955 Katarzyna Wisniowska (Pol)
1957 Carole Meinhart (USA) 2120
1958 Sigrid Johansson (Swe) 2053
1959 Ann Corby (née Weber) (USA) 2023
1961 Nancy Vanderheide (USA) 2173
1963 Victoria Cook (USA) 2253
1965 Maire Lindholm (Fin) 2214
1967 Maria Maczynska (Pol) 2240
1969 Dorothy Lidstone (Can) 2361
1971 Emma Gapchenko (USSR) 2380
1973 Linda Myers (USA) 2204
1975 Zebiniso Rustamova (USSR) 2465
1977 Luann Ryon (USA) 2515
1979 Kim Jin-ho (SKo) 2507
1981 Natalya Butuzova (USSR) 2514
1983 Kim Jin-ho (SKo) 2616
1985 Irina Soldatova (USSR) 2595
1987 Ma Xiagjun (Chn) 330
1989 Kim Soo-nyung (SKo) 338

Most wins: 7 Janina Kurkowska (née Spychajowa) (Pol)

Women's Team wins:
8 USA	1952, 1957-9, 1961, 1963, 1965, 1977
7 Poland	1933-4, 1936, 1938-9, 1967, 1971
6 USSR	1969, 1973, 1975, 1981, 1985, 1987
5 United Kingdom	1935, 1937, 1946, 1949, 1955
3 South Korea	1979, 1983, 1989
2 Finland	1950, 1953
1 Denmark 1947, Czechoslovakia 1948	

Record score: 7721 USSR 1985

OLYMPIC GAMES
The sport was included in the Olympic Games from 1900 to 1908, then again in 1920 (at the Belgian style of shooting) and was re-introduced in 1972. Olympic archery is now contested at double FITA rounds, and as for the World Championships there is a final round of 36 arrows. *Winners:*

Year	Men	Women
1972	John Williams (USA) 2528	Doreen Wilber (USA) 2424
1976	Darrell Pace (USA) 2571	Luann Ryon (USA) 2499
1980	Tomi Poikolainen (Fin) 2455	Keto Lossaberidze (USSR) 2491
1984	Darrell Pace (USA) 2616	Seo Hyang-soon (SKo) 2568
1988	Jay Barrs (USA) 338	Kim Soo-nyung (SKo) 344

Team events for men and women were contested from 1988. *Winners:*
1988 South Korea 986   South Korea 982
Olympic records for Double FITA rounds:
Men   Darrell Pace (USA) 2616 in 1984 Women: Kim Soo-nyung (SKo) 2683 in 1988
Hubert van Innis (Bel) won a record six gold and three silver medals: two gold, one silver 1900, the rest in 1920.

WORLD RECORDS
For single FITA rounds (maximum 360 points for each set)
MEN
FITA	1342	Stanislav Zabrobskiy (USSR) 1989
90m	329	Yuriy Leontyev (USSR) 1989
70m	344	Hiroshi Yamamoto (Jap) 1990
50m	345	Richard McKinney (USA) 1982
Final	342	Stanislav Zabrobskiy (USSR) 1989
Team	3963	USSR (Stanislav Zabrobskiy, Vadim Shikarev, Vladimir Yesheyev) 1989
Final	999	USSR (Stanislav Zabrobskiy, Vadim Shikarev, Vladimir Yesheyev) 1989

WOMEN
FITA	1368	Kim Soo-nyung (SKo) 1989
70m	341	Kim Soo-nyung (SKo) 1990
60m	347	Kim Soo-nyung (SKo) 1989
50m	336	Kim Soo-nyung (SKo) 1988
30m	356	Kim Soo-nyung (SKo) 1987
Final	343	Kim Soo-nyung (SKo) 1989
Team	4025	South Korea (Kim Soo-nyung, Wang Hee-nyung, Kim Kyung-wook) 1989
Final	1010	South Korea (Kim Soo-nyung, Wang Hee-nyung, Kim Kyung-wook) 1989

WORLD INDOOR RECORDS
Indoor FITA Rounds , maximum score 600
MEN
18m	591	Vladimir Yesheyev (USSR) 1989
25m	591	Erwin Verstegen (Hol) 1989

WOMEN
18m	587	Denise Parker (USA) 1989
25m	588	Yelena Marfel (USSR) 1985

WORLD FIELD ARCHERY CHAMPIONSHIPS
Held in 1969, 1971 and biennially from 1972 at bare bow and freestyle categories for men and women.
Most wins: 3 Anders Rosenberg (Swe) men's bare bow 1978, 1980, 1982.

WORLD FLIGHT RECORDS

The following have been recognised as records by the United States National Archery Association at unlimited weight categories (or at weight categories shown in brackets if superior):

Regular Flight

Bow type	Metres	Name	Year
MEN			
Recurve Bow	1222.01	Don Brown	1987
Compound Bow	1060.55	Bert McCune Jr.	1987
Longbow	325.87	Don Brown	1989
Primitive Bow	259.56	Daniel Perry	1988
Unlimited Footbow	1854.40	Harry Drake	1971
Conventional Footbow	1410.87	Harry Drake	1979
Crossbow	1871.84	Harry Drake	1988
WOMEN			
Recurve Bow	950.39	April Moon	1981
Compound Bow (25kg)	826.73	April Moon	1989
Longbow	199.11	April Moon	1989
Conventional Footbow	1018.48	Arylne Rhode	1978

Broadhead Flight

Bow type	Metres	Name	Year
MEN			
Compound Bow	601.78	Roy Rodgers	1989
Recurve Bow	481.10	Don Brown	1988
Longbow	278.49	Don Brown	1988
Primitive Bow	183.16	Daniel Perry	1989
WOMEN			
Compound Bow	440.01	April Moon	1989
Recurve Bow	332.95	April Moon	1987
Longbow	187.88	April Moon	1987

Longbows are of a minimum length of 68 inches for men and 66 inches for women.
Primitive bows are totally constructed of natural materials, plant or animal.
Standard recurve bows are of the type normally used for hunting purposes or field events.
Compound bows are so constructed that a mechanical advantage is obtained by the use of accessory limbs, levers, pulleys etc..

ASSOCIATION FOOTBALL

The Chinese played a form of football, *Tsu chu* (meaning 'to kick a ball of stuffed leather'), over 2500 years ago. Other versions may have been played in various parts of the world, but much of the game's development came in England. An early reference to the sport came in 1314 when Edward II issued a prohibition on the game due to the excessive noise people were making hustling over footballs in the streets of London. Three subsequent British monarchs also banned the sport, for one reason or another, until it became organised in the 19th century. The first rules were drawn up at Cambridge University in 1848 and there were various modifications over the next decades. The Sheffield club, the oldest club still in existence, was formed in 1855, and the Football Association was founded in 1863. The sport grew rapidly in popularity world-wide, and the Fédération Internationale de Football Association (FIFA), the world governing body, was formed in Paris in 1904. It now has over 160 members.

WORLD CUP

The first World Cup for the Jules Rimet Trophy was held in Uruguay in 1930. The competition has been staged every four years since then, with the exception of the war years. Brazil won the trophy outright in 1970 following their third win and teams now compete for the FIFA World Cup.

Johan Cruyff (left) in action for Holland against Sweden in the 1974 World Cup (**All-Sport**)

Finals:
(Goalscorers are shown beneath each team)

Year	Winners		Runners-up		Venue	Attendance
1930	URUGUAY Dorado, Cea, Iriarte, Castro	4	ARGENTINA Peucelle, Stabile	2	Montevideo, Uruguay	90,000
1934	ITALY Orsi, Schiavio	2	CZECHOSLOVAKIA Puc	1 *	Rome, Italy	55,000
1938	ITALY Colaussi (2), Piola (2)	4	HUNGARY Titkos, Sarosi	2	Paris, France	50,000
1950	URUGUAY Schiaffino, Ghiggia	2	BRAZIL Friaca	1 **	Rio de Janeiro, Brazil	199,854
1954	F.R.GERMANY Rahn (2), Morlock	3	HUNGARY Puskas, Czibor	2	Berne, Switzerland	55,000
1958	BRAZIL Vava (2), Pele (2), Zagalo	5	SWEDEN Liedholm, Simonsson	2	Stockholm, Sweden	49,737
1962	BRAZIL Amarildo, Zito, Vava	3	CZECHOSLOVAKIA Masopust	1	Santiago, Chile	69,068
1966	ENGLAND Hurst (3), Peters	4	F.R.GERMANY Haller, Weber	2 *	Wembley, London, England	93,000
1970	BRAZIL Gerson, Jairzinho, Pele, Carlos Alberto	4	ITALY Boninsegna	1	Mexico City, Mexico	110,000
1974	F.R.GERMANY Breitner (pen), Muller	2	HOLLAND Neeskens (pen)	1	Munich, F.R.Germany	77,833
1978	ARGENTINA Kempes (2), Bertoni	3	HOLLAND Nanninga	1 *	Buenos Aires, Argentina	77,000
1982	ITALY Rossi, Tardelli, Altobelli	3	F.R.GERMANY Breitner	1	Madrid, Spain	92,000
1986	ARGENTINA Brown, Valdano, Burruchaga	3	F.R.GERMANY Rummenigge, Voller	2	Mexico City, Mexico	114,580
1990	F.R.GERMANY Brehme (pen)	1	ARGENTINA	O	Rome, Italy	73,603

* after extra time, ** deciding match of final pool

WORLD CUP RECORDS
Individual
MOST APPEARANCES IN FINALS
21 Uwe Seeler (FRG) 1958-70
21 Wladislaw Zmuda (Pol) 1974-86
20 Grzegorz Lato (Pol) 1974-82
19 Wolfgang Overath (FRG) 1966-74
19 Berti Vogts (FRG) 1970-78
19 Karl-Heinz Rummenigge (FRG)
     1978-86
19 Diego Maradona (Arg) 1982-90
Most by a British Isles player:
17 Peter Shilton (Eng) 1982-90

Alfred Bickel (Swi) and Erik Nilsson (Swe) are the only players to have appeared in the final stages both before and after World War II. They both played in 1938 and 1950.

MOST FINAL TOURNAMENTS
5 Antonio Carbajal (Mex) 1950-66
4 Djalma Santos (Bra) 1954-66
4 Pele (Bra) 1958-70
4 Uwe Seeler (FRG) 1958-70
4 Karl-Heinz Schnellinger (FRG)
    1958-70
4 Gianni Rivera (Ita) 1962-74
4 Pedro Rocha (Uru) 1962-74
4 Wladislaw Zmuda (Pol) 1974-86
Most by a British Isles player:
3 Tom Finney, Billy Wright (Eng)
    1950-58, Bobby Moore, Bobby
    Charlton (Eng) 1962-70, Kenny
    Dalglish, Joe Jordan (Sco) 1974-82,
    Graeme Souness (Sco) 1978-86,
    Peter Shilton, Bryan Robson, Terry
    Butcher (Eng) 1982-90, Alex
    McLeish (Sco) 1982-90

Uwe Seeler

PLAYED FOR TWO WINNING TEAMS
Giovanna Ferrari, Giuseppe Meazza (Ita) 1934,1938
Didi, Garrincha, Gilmar dos Santos, Djalma Santos, Nilton
Santos, Vava, Mario Zagalo*, Zito (Bra) 1958, 1962
Pele (Bra) 1958, 1970
*Zagalo was the first man to play in and manage a
World Cup winning team. His feat was emulated in
1990 by Franz Beckenbauer, who uniquely became the
first man to captain and manage winning teams.*

MOST GOALS IN FINALS
14 Gerd Müller (FRG) 1970-74
13 Juste Fontaine (Fra) 1958
12 Pele (Bra) 1958-70
11 Sandor Kocsis (Hun) 1954
10 Helmut Rahn (FRG) 1954-58
10 Grzegorz Lato (Pol) 1974-82
10 Gary Lineker (England) 1986

MOST GOALS IN ONE TOURNAMENT
13 Juste Fontaine (Fra) 1958
11 Sandor Kocsis (Hun) 1954
10 Gerd Müller (FRG) 1970
 9 Ademir (Bra) 1950
 9 Eusebio (Por) 1966
 8 Guillermo Stabile (Arg) 1930
 8 Leonidas (Bra) 1938
Most by a British Isles player:
 6 Gary Lineker (England) 1986

Most goals in one game: 4 Leonidas (Bra) v Poland 1938,
Ernst Willimowski (Pol) v Brazil 1938, Gustav Wetterström
(Swe) v Cuba 1938, Juan Schiaffino (Uru) v Bolivia 1950,
Ademir (Bra) v Sweden 1950, Sándor Kocsis (Hun) v
F.R.Germany 1954, Just Fontaine (Fra) v F.R.Germany
1958, Eusebio (Por) v North Korea 1966, Emilio
Butragueno (Spa) v Denmark 1986

Team

THE LEADING TEAMS

	Tourn-aments	P	W	D	L	For	Agt	Pts	Win	Final	SF
Brazil	14	66	44	11	11	148	65	99	3	4	7
Germany/F.R.Germany	12	68	39	15	14	145	90	93	3	6	9
Italy	12	54	31	12	11	89	54	74	3	4	6
Argentina	10	48	24	9	15	82	59	57	2	4	4
England	9	41	18	12	11	55	38	48	1	1	2
Uruguay	9	37	15	8	14	61	52	38	2	2	4
USSR	7	31	15	6	10	53	34	36	–	–	1
France	9	34	15	5	14	71	56	35	–	–	3
Yugoslavia	8	33	14	7	12	55	42	35	–	–	2
Hungary	9	32	15	3	14	87	57	33	–	2	2
Spain	8	32	13	7	12	43	38	33	–	–	1
Poland	5	25	13	5	7	39	29	31	–	–	2
Sweden	8	31	11	6	14	51	52	28	–	1	3
Czechoslovakia	8	30	11	5	14	44	45	27	–	2	2
Austria	6	26	12	2	12	40	41	26	–	–	2
Holland	5	20	8	6	6	35	23	22	–	2	2
The other teams with one semi-final appearance are:											
Belgium	8	25	7	4	14	33	49	18	–	–	1
Chile	6	21	7	3	11	26	32	17	–	–	1
Portugal	2	9	6	0	3	19	12	12	–	–	1
United States	4	10	3	0	7	14	23	6	–	–	1

MOST GOALS IN ONE TOURNAMENT
27 Hungary (1954)
25 F.R.Germany (1954)
23 France (1958)
22 Brazil (1950)
19 Brazil (1970)
18 Argentina (1930)
17 Austria (1954)
17 Portugal (1966)
17 F.R.Germany (1970)

HIGHEST SCORES (Final Stages)
10-1 Hungary v El Salvador,
    15 Jun 1982
 9-0 Hungary v South Korea,
    17 Jun 1954
 9-0 Yugoslavia v Zaire, 18 Jun 1974
 8-0 Sweden v Cuba, 12 Jun 1938
 8-0 Uruguay v Bolivia, 2 Jul 1950
 8-3 Hungary v F.R.Germany,
    20 Jun 1954
Highest aggregate:
12 goals Austria (7) v Switzerland (5),
    26 Jun 1954

HIGHEST SCORE (all matches)
13-0 New Zealand v Fiji,
    15 Aug 1981 Q
12-0 F.R.Germany v Cyprus,
    21 May 1969 Q
11-1 Hungary v Greece,
    25 Mar 1938 Q
11-1 Trinidad v Antigua,
    10 Nov 1972 Q
10-0 USSR v Finland, 15 Aug 1957 Q
    (Soviet Union were away)
10-0 Australia v Fiji, 14 Aug 1981 Q
10-1 Hungary v El Salvador,
    15 Jun 1982
Q denotes qualifying match

OLYMPIC GAMES

Soccer was unofficially played in the first modern Olympics in 1896. It was included in the Paris Games four years later but some sources still regard it as an unofficial competition, as with those of 1904 and 1906. Soccer has been an official sport at all Olympics from 1908, except for 1932, when it was not staged at Los Angeles. Because of the strength of the so called 'non-professional' Eastern-bloc nations, FIFA ruled that all players who had competed in the 1982 World Cup could not compete in the Los Angeles Olympics two years later. As it transpired, the ban had no effect on the eastern European nations because of their boycott of the Games.

Leading medal winning nations

	Gold	Silver	Bronze	Total
Hungary	3	1	1	5
Yugoslavia	1	3	1	5
Denmark	1	3	1	5
USSR	1	-	3	4
Great Britain	3	-	-	3
GDR	1	1	1	3
Sweden	1	-	2	3
Holland	-	-	3	3

Biggest win: 17-1 Denmark v France 'A' 1908
Most goals in an Olympic tournament:
12 Ferenc Bene (Hun) 1964
Olympic champions/World Cup holders simultaneously:
Uruguay 1928 Olympics, 1930 World Cup
Italy 1934 World Cup, 1936 Olympics, 1938 World Cup

Finals:

Year	Winner		Runner-up	
1900	Upton Park FC (UK)	4	UFSA (Fra)	0
1904	Galt FC, Ontario (Can)	7	Christian Brothers College (USA)	2
1906	Denmark	5	Smyrna (Gre)	2
1908	Great Britain	2	Denmark	0
1912	Great Britain	4	Denmark	2
1920	Belgium	2	Czechoslovakia	0

(Czechoslovakia disqualified after walking off the pitch as a protest against refereeing decisions. Spain were awarded the silver medal)

Year	Winner		Runner-up	
1924	Uruguay	3	Switzerland	0
1928	Uruguay	2	Argentina	2
	(after 1-1 draw)			
1936	Italy	2	Austria	2*
1948	Sweden	3	Yugoslavia	2
1952	Hungary	2	Yugoslavia	0
1956	USSR	2	Yugoslavia	0
1960	Yugoslavia	3	Denmark	2
1964	Hungary	2	Czechoslovakia	2
1968	Hungary	4	Bulgaria	2
1972	Poland	2	Hungary	2
1976	GDR	3	Poland	2
1980	Czechoslovakia	2	GDR	0
1984	France	2	Brazil	0
1988	USSR	2	Brazil	2*

* after extra time

EUROPEAN CHAMPIONSHIP

Held every four years, the championship is played over a two-year period. Originally called the European Nations Cup it changed to its present name in 1968. Competing nations contest the Henri Delaunay Cup, named after the former General Secretary of the Union of European Football Associations (UEFA).

Finals:

Year	Winners		Runners-up		Venue	Attendance
1960	USSR Metreveli, Ponedelnik	2	YUGOSLAVIA Netto (og)	1 *	Paris	17,966
1964	SPAIN Pereda, Marcellino	2	USSR Khusainov	1	Madrid	120,000
1968	ITALY Domenghini	1	YUGOSLAVIA Dzajic	1 *	Rome	75,000
Replay	ITALY Riva, Anastasi	2	YUGOSLAVIA	0	Rome	60,000
1972	F.R.GERMANY G Müller (2), Wimmer	3	USSR	0	Brussels	43,437
1976	CZECHOSLOVAKIA Svehlik, Dobias	2	F.R.GERMANY D Müller, Holzenbein	2 *	Belgrade	45,000
	(Czechoslovakia won 5-3 on penalties)					
1980	F.R.GERMANY Hrubesch (2)	2	BELGIUM Van der Eycken	1	Rome	47,864
1984	FRANCE Platini, Bellone	2	SPAIN	0	Paris	48,000
1988	HOLLAND Gullit, Van Basten	2	USSR	0	Munich	72,308

* after extra time

Most wins: 2 F.R.Germany   *Most finals:* 4 USSR

EUROPEAN CHAMPION CLUBS' CUP

Popularly known as the European Cup it is an annual knockout competition for the league champions of all UEFA affiliated countries. It was first held in 1955/6, shortly after the formation of UEFA, and was the idea of Gabriel Hanot, the soccer editor of the French daily newspaper *L'Equipe*.

Finals:

Year	Winners		Runners-up		Venue	Attendance
1956	REAL MADRID Rial(2), Di Stefano, Marquitos	4	STADE DE REIMS Leblond, Templin, Hidalgo	3	Paris	38,000
1957	REAL MADRID Di Stefano (pen), Gento	2	FIORENTINA	0	Madrid	124,000
1958	REAL MADRID Di Stefano, Rial, Gento	3	AC MILAN Schiaffino, Grillo	2	Brussels	67,000
1959	REAL MADRID Mateos, Di Stefano	2	STADE DE REIMS	0	Stuttgart	80,000
1960	REAL MADRID Puskas (4), Di Stefano (3)	7	EINTRACHT FRANKFURT Stein (2), Kress	3	Glasgow	127,621
1961	BENFICA Aguas, Coluna, Ramallets (og)	3	BARCELONA Kocsis, Czibor	2	Berne	28,000
1962	BENFICA Eusebio (2, 1 pen), Aguas, Cavem, Coluna	5	REAL MADRID Puskas (3)	3	Amsterdam	65,000
1963	AC MILAN Altafini (2)	2	BENFICA Eusebio	1	London	45,000
1964	INTER MILAN Mazzola (2), Milani	3	REAL MADRID Felo	1	Vienna	74,000
1965	INTER MILAN Jair	1	BENFICA	0	Milan	80,000
1966	REAL MADRID Amancio, Serena	2	PARTIZAN BELGRADE Vasovic	1	Brussels	55,000
1967	GLASGOW CELTIC Gemmell, Chalmers	2	INTER MILAN Mazzola (pen)	1	Lisbon	56,000
1968	MANCHESTER UNITED Charlton (2), Best, Kidd	4	BENFICA Graca	1 *	London	100,000
1969	AC MILAN Prati (3), Sormani	4	AJAX Vasovic (pen)	1	Madrid	50,000
1970	FEYENOORD Israel, Kindvall	2	GLASGOW CELTIC Gemmell	1 *	Milan	50,000
1971	AJAX van Dijk, Haan	2	PANATHINAIKOS	0	London	90,000
1972	AJAX Cruyff (2)	2	INTER MILAN	0	Rotterdam	67,000
1973	AJAX Rep	1	JUVENTUS	0	Belgrade	93,500
1974	BAYERN MÜNCHEN Schwarzenbeck	1	ATLETICO MADRID Luis	1 *	Brussels	65,000
Replay	BAYERN MÜNCHEN Hoeness (2), Müller (2)	4	ATLETICO MADRID	0	Brussels	65,000
1975	BAYERN MÜNCHEN Roth, Müller	2	LEEDS UNITED	0	Paris	48,000
1976	BAYERN MÜNCHEN	1	ST.ETIENNE	0	Glasgow	54,864
1977	LIVERPOOL McDermott, Smith, Neal (pen)	3	BORUSSIA MÖNCHENGLADBACH Simonsen	1	Rome	57,000
1978	LIVERPOOL Dalglish	1	FC BRUGES	0	London	92,000
1979	NOTTINGHAM FOREST Francis	1	MALMÖ	0	München	57,500

Year	Winners		Runners-up		Venue	Attendance
1980	NOTTINGHAM FOREST Robertson	1	SV HAMBURG	0	Madrid	50,000
1981	LIVERPOOL A.Kennedy	1	REAL MADRID	0	Paris	48,360
1982	ASTON VILLA Withe	1	BAYERN MÜNCHEN	0	Rotterdam	46,000
1983	SV HAMBURG Magath	1	JUVENTUS	0	Athens	80,000
1984	LIVERPOOL (Liverpool won 4-2 on penalties) Neal	1	AS ROMA Pruzzo	1 *	Rome	69,693
1985	JUVENTUS Platini (pen)	1	LIVERPOOL	0	Brussels	58,000
1986	STEAUA BUCHAREST (Steau won 2-0 on penalties)	0	BARCELONA	0 *	Seville	70,000
1987	FC PORTO Madjer, Juary	2	BAYERN MÜNCHEN Kögl	1	Vienna	59,000
1988	PSV EINDHOVEN (Eindhoven won 6-5 on penalties)	0	BENFICA	0 *	Stuttgart	70,000
1989	AC MILAN Van Basten (2), Gullit (2)	4	STEAUA BUCHAREST	0	Barcelona	97,000
1990	AC MILAN Rijkaard	1	BENFICA	0	Vienna	57,500

* after extra time

Biggest win: 12-2 Feyenoord v Reykjavik (1st round) 17 Sep 1969
Biggest win (final): 7-3 Real Madrid v Eintracht 18 May 1960
Biggest win (aggregate): 18-0 (8-0 & 10-0) Benfica v Stade
Dudelange (preliminary round) Sep & Oct 1965

Marco van Basten of AC Milan, who was voted European Footballer of the Year in both 1988 and 1989. He scored in the finals of three major European competitions in successive seasons: in the European Cup-winners' Cup for Ajax in 1987, in the European Championships for Holland in 1988, and in the European Champion Clubs' Cup for AC Milan in 1989
(All-Sport/Roger Labrosse)

Ruud Gullitt, who moved from PSV Eindhoven for a record transfer fee to AC Milan, where he was European Footballer of the Year in 1987
(All-Sport/David Cannon)

EUROPEAN CUP-WINNERS' CUP

The second most important European club competition after the Champions' Cup, the Cup-Winners' Cup is open to winners of domestic senior cup competitions in UEFA-affiliated countries. The first final in 1961 was over two legs, but all subsequent finals have been played as a single game.

Finals:

Year	Winners		Runners-up		Venue	Attendance
1961	FIORENTINA	2	GLASGOW RANGERS	0	Glasgow	80,000
	Milan (2)					
	FIORENTINA	2	GLASGOW RANGERS	1	Florence	50,000
	Milan, Hamrin		Scott			
	(Fiorentina won 4-1 on aggregate)					
1962	ATLETICO MADRID	1	FIORENTINA	1	Glasgow	27,289
	Peiro		Hamrin			
Replay	ATLETICO MADRID	3	FIORENTINA	0	Stuttgart	38,120
	Jones, Mendonca, Peiro					
1963	TOTTENHAM HOTSPUR	5	ATLETICO MADRID	1	Rotterdam	49,143
	Greaves (2), Dyson (2), White		Collar (pen)			
1964	SPORTING LISBON	3	MTK BUDAPEST	3 *	Brussels	3,208
	Figueiredo (2), Dansky (og)		Sándor (2), Kuti			
Replay	SPORTING LISBON	1	MTK BUDAPEST	0	Antwerp	19,924
	Morais					
1965	WEST HAM UNITED	2	MÜNCHEN 1860	0	London	97,974
	Sealey (2)					
1966	BORUSSIA DORTMUND	2	LIVERPOOL	1 *	Glasgow	41,657
	Held, Yeats (og)		Hunt			
1967	BAYERN MÜNCHEN	1	GLASGOW RANGERS	0 *	Nürnberg	69,480
	Roth					
1968	AC MILAN	2	SV HAMBURG	0	Rotterdam	53,276
	Hamrin (2)					
1969	SLOVAN BRATISLAVA	3	BARCELONA	2	Basle	19,478
	Cvetler, Hrivnak, Jan Capkovich		Zaluda, Rexach			
1970	MANCHESTER CITY	2	GORNIK ZABRZE	1	Vienna	7,968
	Young, Lee (pen)		Ozlizlo			
1971	CHELSEA	1	REAL MADRID	1 *	Athens	42,000
	Osgood		Zoco			
Replay	CHELSEA	2	REAL MADRID	1	Athens	24,000
	Dempsey, Osgood		Fleitas			
1972	GLASGOW RANGERS	3	DYNAMO MOSCOW	2	Barcelona	24,701
	Johnston (2), Stein		Yestrekov, Makovikov			
1973	AC MILAN	1	LEEDS UNITED	0	Salonika	45,000
	Chiarugi					
1974	FC MAGDEBURG	2	AC MILAN	0	Rotterdam	4,641
	Lanzi (og), Seguin					
1975	DYNAMO KIEV	3	FERENCVAROS	0	Basle	10,897
	Onischenko (2), Blokhin					
1976	ANDERLECHT	4	WEST HAM UNITED	2	Brussels	58,000
	Rensenbrink (2,1 pen) Van der Elst (2)		Holland, Robson			
1977	SV HAMBURG	2	ANDERLECHT	0	Amsterdam	65,000
	Volkert (pen), Magath					
1978	ANDERLECHT	4	AUSTRIA WAC	0	Paris	48,679
	Rensenbrink (2), Van Binst (2)					
1979	BARCELONA	4	FORTUNA DÜSSELDORF	3 *	Basle	58,000
	Sanchez, Asensi, Rexach, Krankl		Seel (2), K.Allofs			
1980	VALENCIA	0	ARSENAL	0 *	Brussels	40,000
	(Valencia won 5-4 on penalties)					

Year	Winners		Runners-up		Venue	Attendance
1981	DYNAMO TBILISI Gutsayev, Daraselia	2	CARL ZEISS JENA Hoppe	1	Düsseldorf	9,000
1982	BARCELONA Simonsen, Quini	2	STANDARD LIEGE Vandermissen	1	Barcelona	100,000
1983	ABERDEEN Black, Hewitt	2	REAL MADRID Juanito (pen)	1 *	Göteborg	17,804
1984	JUVENTUS Vignola, Boniek	2	FC PORTO Sousa	1	Basle	60,000
1985	EVERTON Gray, Steven, Sheedy	3	RAPID VIENNA Krankl	1	Rotterdam	35,000
1986	DYNAMO KIEV Zavarov, Blokhin, Yevtushenko	3	ATLETICO MADRID	0	Lyon	39,300
1987	AJAX AMSTERDAM Van Basten	1	LOKOMOTIV LEIPZIG	0	Athens	35,000
1988	MECHELEN Den Boer	1	AJAX AMSTERDAM	0	Strasbourg	40,000
1989	BARCELONA Salinas, Recarte	2	SAMPDORIA	0	Berne	45,000
1990	SAMPDORIA Vialli (2)	2	ANDERLECHT	0 *	Göteborg	20,103

* after extra time
Biggest win: 16-1 Sporting Lisbon v Apoel Nicosia (1st round) 13 Nov 1963
Biggest win (final): 5-1 Tottenham Hotspur v Atletico Madrid 15 May 1963
Biggest win (aggregate): 21-0 (8-0 & 13-0) Chelsea v Jeunesse Hautcharage (1st round) 15 & 29 Sep 1971

UEFA CUP

Initially intended, when established in 1955, as a tournament for European cities that sponsored international industrial fairs, hence the competition's original name, the International Industries Fairs Inter- Cities Cup, commonly known as the Fairs Cup. The first tournament took three years to complete. The second Fairs Cup predominently involved club sides and from 1960/1 the competition became an annual event. It became known as the European Fairs Cup in 1966 and in 1971 the UEFA Cup. The competition is open to leading sides not eligible for the other two main European competitions. The final, unlike the other European tournaments, is played over two legs on a home and away basis. The matches are shown in the order in which they were played:
Finals:

Year	Home team		Away team		Attendance
1958	LONDON Greaves, Langley (pen)	2	BARCELONA Tejada, Martinez	2	45,466
	BARCELONA Suarez (2), Evaristo (2), Martinez, Verges (Barcelona won 8-2 on aggregate)	6	LONDON	0	62,000
1960	BIRMINGHAM CITY	0	BARCELONA	0	40,500
	BARCELONA Czibor (2), Martinez, Coll (Barcelona won 4-1 on aggregate)	4	BIRMINGHAM CITY Hooper	1	70,000
1961	BIRMINGHAM CITY Hellawell, Orritt	2	AS ROMA Manfredini (2)	2	21,005
	AS ROMA Farmer (og), Pestrin (AS Roma won 4-2 on aggregate)	2	BIRMINGHAM CITY	0	60,000
1962	VALENCIA Guillot (3), Yosu (2), H.Nunez	6	BARCELONA Kocsis (2)	2	65,000
	BARCELONA Kocsis (Valencia won 7-3 on aggregate)	1	VALENCIA Guillot	1	60,000

Year	Home team		Away team		Attendance
1963	**DYNAMO ZAGREB** Zambata	1	**VALENCIA** Waldo, Urtiaga	2	40,000
	VALENCIA Mano, Nunez (Valencia won 4-1 on aggregate)	2	**DYNAMO ZAGREB**	0	55,000
1964	**REAL ZARAGOZA** Villa, Marcelino (Played over one leg at Barcelona)	2	**VALENCIA** Urtiaga	1	50,000
1965	**FERENCVAROS** Fenyvesi (Played over one leg, at Turin)	1	**JUVENTUS**	0	25,000
1966	**BARCELONA**	0	**REAL ZARAGOZA** Canario	1	70,000
	REAL ZARAGOZA Marcelino (2) (Barcelona won 4-3 on aggregate)	2	**BARCELONA** Pujol (3), Zaballa	4 *	70,000
1967	**DYNAMO ZAGREB** Cercer (2)	2	**LEEDS UNITED**	0	40,000
	LEEDS UNITED (Dynamo Zagreb won 2-0 on aggregate)	0	**DYNAMO ZAGREB**	0	35,604
1968	**LEEDS UNITED** Jones	1	**FERENCVAROS**	0	25,368
	FERENCVAROS (Leeds United won 1-0 on aggregate)	0	**LEEDS UNITED**	0	70,000
1969	**NEWCASTLE UNITED** Moncur (2), Scott	3	**UJPEST DOZSA**	0	60,000
	UJPEST DOZSA Bene, Gorocs (Newcastle United won 6-2 on aggregate)	2	**NEWCASTLE UNITED** Moncur, Arentoft, Foggon	3	37,000
1970	**ANDERLECHT** Mulder (2), Devrindt	3	**ARSENAL** Kennedy	1	37,000
	ARSENAL Kelly, Radford, Sammels (Arsenal won 4-3 on aggregate)	3	**ANDERLECHT**	0	51,612
1971	**JUVENTUS** (abandoned after 51 minutes, waterlogged pitch)	0	**LEEDS UNITED**	0	40,000
Replay	**JUVENTUS** Bettega, Capello	2	**LEEDS UNITED** Madeley, Bates	2	42,000
	LEEDS UNITED Clarke (Leeds United won on the away-goals rule)	1	**JUVENTUS** Anastasi	1	42,483
1972	**WOLVERHAMPTON W** McCalliog	1	**TOTTENHAM HOTSPUR** Chivers (2)	2	38,362
	TOTTENHAM HOTSPUR Mullery (Tottenham Hotspur won 3-2 on aggregate)	1	**WOLVERHAMPTON W** Wagstaffe	1	54,303
1973	**LIVERPOOL** (abandoned after 27 minutes waterlogged pitch)	0	**BORUSSIA MöNCHENGLADBACH**	0	44,967
Replay	**LIVERPOOL** Keegan (2), Lloyd	3	**BORUSSIA MöNCHENGLADBACH**	0	41,169
	BORUSSIA MöNCHENGLADBACH Heynckes (2) (Liverpool won 3-2 on aggregate)	2	**LIVERPOOL**	0	35,000
1974	**TOTTENHAM HOTSPUR** England, van Daele (og)	2	**FEYENOORD** van Hanegem, De Jong	2	46,281

Year	Home team		Away team		Attendance
	FEYENOORD Rijsbergen, Ressel (Feyenoord won 4-2 on aggregate)	2	TOTTENHAM HOTSPUR	0	59,317
1975	BORUSSIA MöNCHENGLADBACH	0	TWENTE ENSCHEDE	0	42,368
	TWENTE ENSCHEDE Drost	1	BORUSSIA MöNCHENGLADBACH Heynckes (3), Simonsen (2, 1 pen)	5	21,767
	(Borussia Mönchengladbach won 5-1 on aggregate)				
1976	LIVERPOOL Kennedy, Case, Keegan (pen)	3	FC BRUGES Lambert, Cools	2	49,981
	FC BRUGES Lambert (pen)	1	LIVERPOOL Keegan	1	32,000
	(Liverpool won 4-3 on aggregate)				
1977	JUVENTUS Tardelli	1	ATHLETIC BILBAO	0	75,000
	ATHLETIC BILBAO Irureta, Carlos	2	JUVENTUS Bettega	1	43,000
	(Juventus won on the away-goals rule)				
1978	BASTIA	0	PSV EINDHOVEN	0	15,000
	PSV EINDHOVEN W.van der Kerkhof, Deykers, van der Kuylen	3	BASTIA	0	27,000
	(Eindhoven won 3-0 on aggregate)				
1979	RED STAR BELGRADE Sestic	1	BORUSSIA MöNCHENGLADBACH Juristic (og)	1	87,500
	BORUSSIA MöNCHENGLADBACH Simonsen (pen)	1	RED STAR BELGRADE	0	45,000
	(Borussia Mönchengladbach won 2-1 on aggregate)				
1980	BORUSSIA MöNCHENGLADBACH Kulik (2), Matthaus	3	EINTRACHT FRANKFURT Karger, Holzenbein	2	25,000
	EINTRACHT FRANKFURT Schaub	1	BORUSSIA MöNCHENGLADBACH	0	60,000
	(Eintracht won on the away-goals rule)				
1981	IPSWICH TOWN Wark(pen), Thijssen, Mariner	3	AZ 67 ALKMAAR	0	27,532
	AZ 67 ALKMAAR Welzl, Metgod, Tol, Jonker	4	IPSWICH TOWN Thijssen, Wark	2	28,500
	(Ipswich Town won 5-4 on aggregate)				
1982	IFK GÖTEBORG Tord Holmgren	1	SV HAMBURG	0	42,548
	SV HAMBURG	0	IFK GÖTEBORG Corneliusson, Nilsson, Fredriksson (pen)	3	60,000
	(Göteborg won 4-0 on aggregate)				
1983	ANDERLECHT Brylle	1	BENFICA	0	60,000
	BENFICA Sheu	1	ANDERLECHT Lozano	1	80,000
	(Anderlecht won 2-1 on aggregate)				
1984	ANDERLECHT Olsen	1	TOTTENHAM HOTSPUR Miller	1	40,000
	TOTTENHAM HOTSPUR Roberts	1	ANDERLECHT Czerniatynski	1 *	46,205
	(Tottenham H won 4-3 on penalties)				

Year	Home team		Away team		Attendance
1985	**VIDEOTON**	0	**REAL MADRID**	3	30,000
			Michel, Santillana, Juanito		
	REAL MADRID	0	**VIDEOTON**	1	90,000
			Majer		
	(Real Madrid won 3-1 on aggregate)				
1986	**REAL MADRID**	5	**FC COLOGNE**	1	80,000
	Valdano (2), Sanchez,		K.Allofs		
	Gordillo, Santillana				
	FC COLOGNE	2	**REAL MADRID**	0	15,000
	Bein, Geilenkirchen				
	(Real Madrid won 5-3 on aggregate)				
1987	**IFK GÖTEBORG**	1	**DUNDEE UNITED**	0	50,023
	Petterson				
	DUNDEE UNITED	1	**IFK GÖTEBORG**	1	20,911
	Clark		Nilsson		
	(Göteborg won 2-1 on aggregate)				
1988	**ESPAÑOL**	3	**BAYER LEVERKUSEN**	0	42,000
	Losada (2), Soler				
	BAYER LEVERKUSEN	3	**ESPAÑOL**	0 *	22,000
	Tita, Goetz, Cha-Bum Kun				
	(Leverkusen won 3-2 on penalties)				
1989	**NAPOLI**	2	**STUTTGART**	1	83,000
	Maradona (Pen), Careca		Gaudino		
	STUTTGART	3	**NAPOLI**	3	67,000
	Klinsmann, O Schmaler,		Alemao, Ferrara, Careca		
	Gaudino				
	(Napoli won 5-4 on aggregate)				
1990	**JUVENTUS**	3	**FIORENTINA**	1	45,000
	Galia, Casiraghi, De Agostini		Buso		
	FIORENTINA	0	**JUVENTUS**	0	38,000
	(Juventus won 3-1 on aggregate)				

* after extra time
Biggest win: 13-0 Cologne v Union Luxembourg (1st round) 5 Oct 1965
Biggest win (final/aggregate): 8-2 (2-2 & 6-0) Barcelona v London 5 Mar & 1 May 1958
Biggest win (aggregate): 21-0 (9-0 & 12-0) Feyenoord v US Rumelange (1st round) 13 & 27 Sep 1972

Above *The great Russian goalkeeper
Lev Yashin, who died in 1990*
(Hulton-Deutsch)
Right *Denis Law, in action for Scotland
at Wembley in 1967* **(Popperfoto)**

EUROPE'S LEADING TEAMS

The following is a table of all teams that have won two or more major European tournaments:
Ch = Champion's Cup, CW = Cup Winners Cup, UEFA = Fairs/UEFA Cup

	Ch	CW	UEFA	Total
Real Madrid	6	-	2	8
AC Milan	4	2	-	6
Liverpool	4	-	2	6
Barcelona	-	3	3	6
Bayern München	3	1	-	4
Ajax	3	1	-	4
Juventus	1	1	2	4
Anderlecht	-	2	1	3
Tottenham Hotspur	-	1	2	3
Valencia	-	1	2	3
Benfica	2	-	-	2
Inter Milan	2	-	-	2
Nottingham Forest	2	-	-	2
SV Hamburg	1	1	-	2
Feyenoord	1	-	1	2
PSV Eindhoven	1	-	1	2
Dynamo Kiev	-	2	-	2
Borussia Mönchengladbach	-	-	2	2
Leeds United	-	-	2	2

By nations

The following countries have provided winners of the three main European competitions

	Ch	CW	UEFA	Total
England	8	5	9	22
Spain	6	5	8	19
Italy	7	5	4	16
F.R.Germany	4	3	4	11
Holland	5	1	2	8
Portugal	3	1	-	4
Belgium	-	3	1	4
Scotland	1	2	-	3
USSR	-	3	-	3
Sweden	-	-	2	2
Romania	1	-	-	1
Czechoslovakia	-	1	-	1
GDR	-	1	-	1
Hungary	-	-	1	1
Yugoslavia	-	-	1	1

EUROPEAN SUPER CUP

After Ajax won the European Cup for the second successive year in 1972 the Dutch newspaper *De Telegraaf* suggested they play the winners of the Cup-winners Cup for a Super Cup. They played, and beat, Glasgow Rangers over two legs and became the first winners. UEFA did not officially recognise the event until 1974. There was no competition in 1981 and 1985. In 1984 and 1986 the cup was decided on one match.

Year	Winners	Runners-up	Result(s)
1972[1]	Ajax *	Glasgow Rangers	3-1, 3-2
1973[1]	Ajax *	AC Milan	0-1, 6-0
1974[2]	Bayern München *	FC Magdeburg	3-2, 2-1
1975	Dynamo Kiev	Bayern München *	1-0, 2-0
1976	Anderlecht	Bayern München *	1-2, 4-1
1977	Liverpool *	SV Hamburg	1-1, 6-0
1978	Anderlecht	Liverpool *	3-1, 1-2
1979	Nottingham Forest*	Barcelona	1-0, 1-1
1980	Valencia	Nottingham Forest*	1-2, 1-0
	(Valencia won on the away goals rule)		
1982	Aston Villa *	Barcelona	0-1, 3-0
1983	Aberdeen	SV Hamburg *	0-0, 2-0
1984	Juventus	Liverpool *	2-0
1986[1]	Steaua Bucharest *	Dynamo Kiev	1-0
1987	FC Porto *	Ajax	1-0, 1-0
1988[1]	Mechelen	PSV Eindhoven	3-0, 0-1
1989	AC Milan	Barcelona	1-1, 1-0

* indicates European Cup holders,
[1] *played the following year*
[2] The two scheduled clubs, Bayern München and Magdeburg, were drawn together in the second round of the 1974-75 European Champions Cup. They decided the results of that match would decide that season's Super Cup winners.

EUROPEAN FOOTBALLER OF THE YEAR

Le Ballon D'Or (Golden Ball) is awarded each year by the French newspaper *France Football* who ask various journalists in UEFA affiliated countries to draw up a list of their five nominees. *Winners:*

1956 Stanley Matthews (Blackpool)
1957 Alfredo di Stefano (Real Madrid)
1958 Raymond Kopa (Real Madrid)
1959 Alfredo di Stefano (Real Madrid)
1960 Luis Suarez (Barcelona)
1961 Omar Sivori (Juventus)
1962 Josef Masopust (Dukla Prague)
1963 Lev Yashin (Dynamo Moscow)
1964 Denis Law (Manchester United)
1965 Eusebio (Benfica)
1966 Bobby Charlton (Manchester United)
1967 Florian Albert (Ferencvaros)
1968 George Best (Manchester United)
1969 Gianni Rivera (AC Milan)
1970 Gerd Müller (Bayern München)
1971 Johan Cruyff (Ajax)
1972 Franz Beckenbauer (Bayern München)
1973 Johan Cruyff (Barcelona)
1974 Johan Cruyff (Barcelona)
1975 Oleg Blokhin (Dynamo Kiev)
1976 Franz Beckenbauer (Bayern München)
1977 Allan Simonsen (B.Mönchengladbach)
1978 Kevin Keegan (SV Hamburg)
1979 Kevin Keegan (SV Hamburg)
1980 Karl-Heinz Rummenigge (Bayern München)
1981 Karl-Heinz Rummenigge (Bayern München)
1982 Paolo Rossi (Juventus)
1983 Michel Platini (Juventus)

1984 Michel Platini (Juventus)
1985 Michel Platini (Juventus)
1986 Igor Belanov (Dynamo Kiev)
1987 Ruud Gullit (AC Milan)
1988 Marco Van Basten (AC Milan)
1989 Marco Van Basten (AC Milan)

Most wins: 3 Johan Cruyff, Michel Platini; 2 Alfredo di Stefano, Franz Beckenbauer, Kevin Keegan, Karl-Heinz Rummenigge, Marco Van Basten
Most wins (clubs): 5 Bayern München, 4 Juventus, AC Milan; 3 Real Madrid, Barcelona, Manchester United

ADIDAS GOLDEN BOOT AWARD
An annual award made by the sportswear manufacturers who present a Golden Boot to the European player who scores the most goals in the domestic League season. *Winners:*

Year Player (Club)	Goals
1968 Eusebio (Benfica)	43
1969 Petar Jekov (CSKA Sofia)	36
1970 Gerd Müller (Bayern München)	38
1971 Josip Skoblar (Marseille)	44
1972 Gerd Müller (Bayern München)	40
1973 Eusebio (Benfica)	40
1974 Hector Yazalde (Sporting Lisbon)	46
1975 Dudu Georgescu (Dinamo Bucharest)	33
1976 Sotiris Kaiafas (Omonia Nicosia)	39
1977 Dudu Georgescu (Dinamo Bucharest)	47
1978 Hans Krankl (Rapid Vienna)	41
1978 Kees Kist (AZ 67 Alkmaar)	34
1980 Erwin van den Bergh (Lierse)	39
1981 Georgi Slavkov (Trakia)	31
1982 Wim Kieft (Ajax)	32
1983 Fernando Gomes (FC Porto)	36
1984 Ian Rush (Liverpool)	32
1985 Fernando Gomes (FC Porto)	39
1986 Marco van Basten (Ajax)	37
1987 Rodion Camataru (Dinamo Bucharest)	44
1988 Tanjn Colak (Galatasaray)	39
1989 Dorin Mateut (Dinamo Bucharest)	43
1990 Hugo Sanchez (Real Madrid)	38
Christo Stoichkov (CSKA Sofia)	

SOUTH AMERICAN CHAMPIONSHIP
In 1910 an Argentine national side, composed mainly of British exiles, suggested a tournament against Uruguay and Chile. This was the forerunner of the South American Championship which was inaugurated in 1916, the year of the formation of the South American Football Confederation. Organisation has left a lot to be desired over the years and the popularity of the event dropped considerably in the 1960s, particularly after the introduction of the Copa Libertadores, when club soccer was regarded as more important than the international game in some countries. The championship was revived in 1975, after a gap of eight years, and is now played on a home and away league basis with the ten competing nations split into three groups. It becomes a

knockout competition from the semi-final stage. Held every four years 1975-87 and now every two years. *Winners:*

12	Uruguay	1916-7, 1920, 1923-4, 1926, 1935*, 1942, 1956*, 1959*,1967, 1983, 1987
12	Argentina	1921, 1925, 1927, 1929, 1937, 1941*, 1945*, 1946*, 1947, 1955, 1957, 1959
4	Brazil	1919, 1922, 1949, 1989
2	Peru	1939, 1975
2	Paraguay	1953, 1979
1	Bolivia	1963

* extraordinary tournament

SOUTH AMERICAN CUP
First contested in 1960 as the South American Champion's Club Cup. Like the European Cup it was open to national league champions of countries affiliated to the South American Confederation. In 1965 league runners-up were also allowed to enter the competition and, that year, it changed its name to the Copa Libertadores. *Winners:*

1960-1 Penarol (Uru)	1979 Olimpia (Par)
1962-3 Santos (Bra)	1980 Nacional (Uru)
1964-5 Independiente (Arg)	1981 Flamengo (Bra)
1966 Penarol (Uru)	1982 Penarol (Uru)
1967 Racing Club (Arg)	1983 Gremio (Bra)
1968-70 Estudiantes (Arg)	1984 Independiente (Arg)
1971 Nacional (Uru)	1985 Argentinos Juniors (Arg)
1972-5 Independiente (Arg)	1986 River Plate (Arg)
1976 Cruzeiro (Bra)	1987 Penarol (Uru)
1977-8 Boca Juniors (Arg)	1988 Nacional (Uru)
	1989 Nacional (Col)

Most wins:
7 Independiente, 5 Penarol,
3 Estudiantes, Nacional (Uru)

WORLD CLUB CHAMPIONSHIP
The World Club Championship was first held in 1960 and was a meeting between the winners of the European Champions Cup and the South American Champions Cup. The two competing teams played each other on a home and away basis (with the exception of 1973) but since 1980 the winners have been decided by one match (for the Intercontinental Cup) played in Tokyo. There were no championship matches in 1975 and 1978. During the 1970s many of the matches became very physical affairs and on five occasions the European Cup holders refused to take part; their places were taken by the runners-up. Prior to 1969, if both sides won a match each, a third match was played to decide the winner. *Results:*

Year	Winners	Runners-up	Result(s)	Play-off
1960	Real Madrid (Spa)	Penarol (Uru)	0-0, 5-1	
1961	Penarol (Uru)	Benfica (Por)	0-1, 5-0	2-1
1962	Santos (Bra)	Benfica (Por)	3-2, 5-2	
1963	Santos (Bra)	AC Milan (Ita)	2-4, 4-2	1-0
1964	Inter Milan (Ita)	Independiente (Arg)	0-1, 2-0	1-0
1965	Inter Milan (Ita)	Independiente (Arg)	3-0, 0-0	
1966	Penarol (Uru)	Real Madrid (Spa)	2-0, 2-0	

1967	Racing Club (Arg)	Glasgow Celtic (Sco)	0-1, 2-1	1-0
1968	Estudiantes (Arg)	Manchester U (Eng)	1-0, 1-1	
1969	AC Milan (Ita)	Estudiantes (Arg)	3-0, 1-2	
1970	Feyenoord (Hol)	Estudiantes (Arg)	2-2, 1-0	
1971	Nacional (Uru)	Panathinaikos (Gre)	1-1, 2-1	
1972	Ajax (Hol)	Independiente (Arg)	1-1, 3-0	
1973	Independiente (Arg)	Juventus (Ita)	1-0	
1974	Atletico Madrid (Spa)	Independiente (Arg)	0-1, 2-0	
1976	Bayern München (FRG)	Cruzeiro (Bra)	2-0, 0-0	
1977	Boca Juniors (Arg)	Borussia Mönchengladbach (FRG)	2-2, 3-0	
1979	Olimpia (Par)	Malmö (Swe)	1-0, 2-1	
1980	Nacional (Uru)	Nottingham Forest (Eng)	1-0	
1981	Flamengo (Bra)	Liverpool (Eng)	3-0	
1982	Penarol (Uru)	Aston Villa (Eng)	2-0	
1983	Gremio (Bra)	SV Hamburg (FRG)	2-1	
1984	Independiente (Arg)	Liverpool (Eng)	1-0	
1985	Juventus (Ita)	Argentinos Juniors (Arg)	2-2	

(Juventus won 4-2 on penalties)

1986	River Plate (Arg)	Steaua Bucharest (Rom)	1-0
1987	FC Porto (Por)	Penarol (Uru)	2-1
1988	Nacional (Uru)	PSV Eindhoven (Hol)	2-2

(Nacional won 7-6 on penalties)

1989	AC Milan (Ita)	Atletico Nacional (Col)	1-0

Most wins: 3 Penarol, Nacional (Uru). European wins: 11, South American wins: 17
No European team has won a match in South America. Real Madrid (1960), Inter Milan (1965), Feyenoord (1970), Ajax (1972) and Bayern München (1976) all managed to draw.
Biggest attendance: 150,000 Santos v AC Milan (2nd leg 1963) at Rio de Janeiro

INTERNATIONAL CAPS
England's Billy Wright was the first player to reach the milestone of making 100 senior international appearances. His 100th match was against Scotland at Wembley on 11 April 1959. Since then many players have passed the 100 mark. The most capped players have been:
150 * Hector Chumpitaz (Per) 1963-82
125 Peter Shilton (Eng) 1970-90
120 * Rivelino (Bra) 1968-79
119 Pat Jennings (NI) 1964-86
115 Björn Nordqvist (Swe) 1963-78
112 Dino Zoff (Ita) 1968-83
111 * Pele (Bra) 1957-71
In addition to Jennings and Shilton, the following British players have won 100 caps:
108 Bobby Moore (Eng) 1962-73
106 Bobby Charlton (Eng) 1958-70
105 Billy Wright (Eng) 1946-59
102 Kenny Dalglish (Sco) 1971-86
* *Includes matches against club sides and other representative selections.*

MOST EXPENSIVE TRANSFERS
£7.7 million Roberto Baggio, Fiorentina to Juventus, May 1990
£6.9 million Diego Maradona, Barcelona to Napoli, June 1984
£5.5 million Ruud Gullit, PSV Eindhoven to AC Milan, June 1987
£5.5 million Karl-Heinz Riedle, Werder Bremen to Lazio, June 1990
£5.5 million Thomas Hässler, FC Cologne to Juventus, June 1990
£4.8 million Dragan Stojkovic, Red Star Belgrade to Marseille, June 1990
£4.8 million Diego Maradona, Boca Juniors to Barcelona, June 1982
£4.5 million Chris Waddle, Tottenham Hotspur to Marseille, July 1989
£4 million Rui Barros, FC Porto to Juventus, July 1988
£4 million Ronald Koeman, PSV Eindhoven to Barcelona, July 1989
£3.5 million Ruggi Rizzitelli, Cesena to Roma, May 1988
£3.4 million Karl-Heinz Rummenigge, Bayern München to Inter Milan, July 1984
£3.2 million Ian Rush, Liverpool to Juventus, June 1987

INDIVIDUAL GOALSCORING RECORDS
For first class matches

Most goals in one game
World record: 16 Stephan Stanis (Racing Club Lens v Aubry-Asturies) 13 Dec 1942
International: 10 Sofus Nielsen (Denmark v France) 1908 Olympics, 10 Gottfried Fuchs (Germany v Russia) 1912 Olympics
British international record: 6 Joe Bambrick (N Ireland v Wales) 1 Feb 1930
World Cup: several players have scored four goals in one game (see page 18)
Major European competition: 6 Lothar Emmerich (Borussia Dortmund v Floriana) Cup-winners'Cup 1st round 13 Oct 1965
FA Cup (proper): 9 Ted MacDougall (Bournemouth v Margate) 1st round 20 Nov 1971
F.A.Cup (preliminary round): 10 Chris Marron (South Shields v Radcliffe) 20 Sep 1947
Football League/Milk/Littlewoods Cup: 6 Frankie Bunn (Oldham A v. Scarborough) 25 Oct 1989

Football League: 10 Joe Payne (Luton T v Bristol R) Div.3S 13 Apr 1936
Scottish Cup: 13 John Petrie (Arbroath v Bon Accord) Cup 5 Sep 1885
Scottish League: 8 Jimmy McGrory (Celtic v Dunfermline A) Div 1 14 Jan 1928

Most goals in a career

World record: 1329 Artur Friedenreich (Germania, CA Ipiranga, Americano, CA Paulistano, São Paulo, Flamengo) 1909-35
Full Internationals: 97 Pele (Bra) 1957-70, (British record): 49 Bobby Charlton (Eng) 1958-70
World Cup: 14 Gerd Müller (FRG) 1970-74
European Cup: 49 Alfredo di Stefano (Real Madrid) 1955-64
Football League: 434 Arthur Rowley (West Bromwich A, Fulham, Leicester, Shrewsbury T) 1946-65
Scottish League: 410 Jimmy McGrory (Celtic, Clydebank) 1922-38

Hat tricks in major finals

World Cup: Geoff Hurst (England v F.R.Germany) 30 Jul 1966
European Championship and European Cup-winners' Cup: none
European Cup: Ferenc Puskas (4 goals) (Real Madrid v Eintracht) 18 May 1960, Alfredo di Stefano (Real Madrid v Eintracht) 18 May 1960, Ferenc Puskas (Real Madrid v Benfica) 2 May 1962, Pierino Prati (AC Milan v Ajax) 28 May 1969
UEFA/Fairs Cup: Vicente Guillot (Valencia v Barcelona) 8 Sep 1962, Luis Pujol (Barcelona v Real Zaragoza) 21 Sep 1966, Jupp Heynckes (B.Mönchengladbach v Twente Enschede) 21 May 1975
FA Cup: William Townley (Blackburn R v Sheffield W) 29 Mar 1890, Jimmy Logan (Notts County v Bolton Wanderers) 31 Mar 1894, Stan Mortensen (Blackpool v Bolton Wanderers) 2 May 1953
Football League/Milk/Littlewoods Cup: none
Scottish FA Cup: Jimmy Quinn (Celtic v Rangers) 16 Apr 1904, Dixie Deans (Celtic v Hibernian) 6 May 1972
Scottish League Cup: , Davie Duncan (East Fife v Falkirk) 1 Nov 1948, Willie Bauld (Hearts v Motherwell) 23 Oct 1954, John McPhail (Celtic v Rangers) 19 Oct 1957, Jim Forrest (4 goals) (Rangers v Morton) 26 Oct 1963, Bobby Lennox (Celtic v Hibernian) 5 Apr 1969, Dixie Deans (Celtic v Hibernian) 26 Oct 1974, Joe Harper (Hibernian v Celtic) 26 Oct 1974, Ally McCoist (Rangers v Celtic) 25 Mar 1984
Most hat tricks in a career:
92 Pele 1956-77. British record: 37 Dixie Dean 1924-39

BRITISH INTERNATIONAL CHAMPIONSHIP

The oldest international championship in the world, the four home countries of England, Scotland, Wales and Northern Ireland (formerly Ireland) contested the series annually from 1883-84 until 1983-84. The four countries played each other once with two points for a win and one for a draw. If two or more nations obtained the same number of points they shared the title. From 1979-80 however, goal difference decided the champions in case of a tie. With a decline in interest in the 1960s and 70s, the championship, often referred to as the Home International Championship, ended after the 1983-4 season. Only the England v Scotland fixture remains on a regular basis. The championship was not completed in 1980-81 and no champions were declared. Outright Wins:

34 England	1888, 1891-3, 1895, 1898-9, 1901, 1904-5, 1909, 1911, 1913, 1930, 1932, 1938, 1947-8, 1950, 1954-5, 1957, 1961, 1965-6, 1968-9, 1971, 1973, 1975, 1978-9, 1982-3
24 Scotland	1884-5, 1887, 1889, 1894, 1896-7, 1900, 1902, 1910, 1921-3, 1925-6, 1929, 1936, 1949, 1951, 1962-3, 1967, 1976-7
7 Wales	1907, 1920, 1924, 1928, 1933-4, 1937
3 N.Ireland/Ireland	1914, 1980, 1984

In 1955-6 all four nations shared the title with three points each.

FOOTBALL LEAGUE

The Football League was the brainchild of William McGregor of Aston Villa who called the first meeting of interested clubs to the Anderton's Hotel, Fleet Street, London on 22 March 1888. The first formal meeting took place less than a month later, on 17 April, at the Royal Hotel, Manchester when 12 members agreed to form the Football League. The first matches were played the following September, and Preston North End emerged as the inaugural champions. A Second Division was formed in 1892 when most members of the old Football Alliance joined the League. A Third Division was added in 1920 and when 20 northern clubs joined the League in 1921 the Third Division was constituted into two sections, Northern and Southern. The current complement of 92 clubs was reached in 1950 and in 1958 the geographically divided Third Divisions were split into Third and Fourth Divisions.

The first ever fixtures of the Football League, on 8 September 1888, were as follows:

Bolton Wanderers	3	Derby County	6
Everton	2	Accrington	1
Preston North End	5	Burnley	2
Stoke City	0	West Bromwich Albion	2
Wolverhampton W	1	Aston Villa	1

(Blackburn Rovers and Notts County did not play)

First Division champions

Season	Champions	Pts
1888/9	Preston North End	40
1889/90	Preston North End	33
1890/1	Everton	29
1891/2	Sunderland	42

Season	Champions	Pts
1892/3	Sunderland	48
1893/4	Aston Villa	44
1894/5	Sunderland	47
1895/6	Aston Villa	45

Season	Champions	Pts
1896/7	Aston Villa	47
1897/8	Sheffield United	42
1898/9	Aston Villa	45
1899/00	Aston Villa	50
1900/1	Liverpool	45
1901/2	Sunderland	44
1902/3	Sheffield Wednesday	42
1903/4	Sheffield Wednesday	47
1904/5	Newcastle United	48
1905/6	Liverpool	51
1906/7	Newcastle United	51
1907/8	Manchester United	52
1908/9	Newcastle United	53
1909/10	Aston Villa	53
1910/1	Manchester United	52
1911/2	Blackburn Rovers	49
1912/3	Sunderland	54
1913/4	Blackburn Rovers	51
1914/5	Everton	46
1919/20	West Bromwich Albion	60
1920/1	Burnley	59
1921/2	Liverpool	57
1922/3	Liverpool	60
1923/4	Huddersfield Town	57
1924/5	Huddersfield Town	58
1925/6	Huddersfield Town	57
1926/7	Newcastle United	56
1927/8	Everton	53
1928/9	Sheffield Wednesday	52
1929/30	Sheffield Wednesday	60
1930/1	Arsenal	66
1931/2	Everton	56
1932/3	Arsenal	58
1933/4	Arsenal	59
1934/5	Arsenal	58
1935/6	Sunderland	56
1936/7	Manchester City	57
1937/8	Arsenal	52
1938/9	Everton	59
1946/7	Liverpool	57
1947/8	Arsenal	59
1948/9	Portsmouth	58
1949/50	Portsmouth	56
1950/1	Tottenham Hotspur	60
1951/2	Manchester United	57
1952/3	Arsenal	54
1953/4	Wolverhampton W.	57
1954/5	Chelsea	52
1955/6	Manchester United	60
1956/7	Manchester United	64
1957/8	Wolverhampton W.	64
1958/9	Wolverhampton W.	61
1959/60	Burnley	55
1960/1	Tottenham Hotspur	66
1961/2	Ipswich Town	56
1962/3	Everton	61
1963/4	Liverpool	57

Liverpool manager Bob Paisley (All-Sport/Mike Powell)

1964/5	Manchester United	61
1965/6	Liverpool	61
1966/7	Manchester United	60
1967/8	Manchester City	58
1968/9	Leeds United	67
1969/70	Everton	66
1970/1	Arsenal	65
1971/2	Derby County	58
1972/3	Liverpool	60
1973/4	Leeds United	62
1974/5	Derby County	53
1975/6	Liverpool	60
1976/7	Liverpool	57
1977/8	Nottingham Forest	64
1978/9	Liverpool	68
1979/80	Liverpool	60
1980/1	Aston Villa	60
1981/2	Liverpool	87
1982/3	Liverpool	82
1983/4	Liverpool	80
1984/5	Everton	90
1985/6	Liverpool	88
1986/7	Everton	86
1987/8	Liverpool	90
1988/9	Arsenal	76
1989/90	Liverpool	79

Maximum points available: 44 1888/9 to 1890/1, 52 1891/2, 60 1892/3 to 1897/8, 68 1898/9 to 1904/5, 76 1905/6 to 1914/5, 84 1919/20 to 1980/1, 126 1981/2 to 1986/7, 120 1987/8, 114 from 1988/9

Most titles
Division 1:   18 Liverpool
Division 2:   6 Leicester City, Manchester City
Division 3:   2 Portsmouth, Oxford United
Division 3(S): 3 Bristol City
Division 3(N): 3 Barnsley, Doncaster Rovers, Lincoln City
Division 4:   2 Chesterfield, Doncaster Rovers, Peterborough United

Most points in a season

Division	Old system - two points for win	System from 1981 - three points for win
1	68 Liverpool 1978/9	90 Everton 1984/5, Liverpool 1987/8
2	70 Tottenham Hotspur 1919/20	99 Chelsea 1988/9
3	70 Aston Villa 1971/2	95 Oxford United 1983/4
4	74 Lincoln City 1975/6	102 Swindon Town 1985/6

*Most goals scored in a season (42 games except for * (46 games))*
Division 1:   128 Aston Villa 1930/1
Division 2:   122 Middlesbrough 1926/7
Division 3:   111* Queen's Park Rangers 1961/2
Division 4:   134* Peterborough United 1960/1
Division 3(S): 127 Millwall 1927/8
Division 3(N): 128 Bradford City 1928/9

Highest scores
13-0 Stockport County v Halifax Town, Div.3N - 6 Jan 1934
13-0 Newcastle United v Newport County, Div.2 - 5 Oct 1946
13-4 Tranmere Rovers v Oldham Athletic, Div.3N - 26 Dec 1935
12-0 West Bromwich Albion v Darwen, Div.1 - 4 Apr 1892
12-0 Small Heath (later Birmingham City) v Walsall Town Swifts, Div.2 - 17 Dec 1892
12-0 Arsenal v Loughborough Town, Div.2 - 12 Mar 1900
12-0 Small Heath (later Birmingham City) v Doncaster Rovers, Div.2 - 11 Apr 1903
12-0 Nottingham Forest v Leicester Fosse, Div.1 - 21 Apr 1909
12-0 Chester v York City, Div.3N - 1 Feb 1936
12-0 Luton Town v Bristol Rovers, Div.3S - 13 Apr 1936
Other divisional records:
11-0 Oldham Athletic v Southport, Div.4 - 26 Dec 1962
 9-0 Tranmere Rovers v Accrington Stanley, Div.3 - 18 Apr 1959
 9-0 Brentford v Wrexham, Div.3 - 15 Oct 1963
Most individual goals in a game
10 Joe Payne, Luton Town v Bristol Rovers, Div.3S - 13 Apr 1936
 9 Robert Bell, Tranmere Rovers v Oldham Athletic, Div.3N - 26 Dec 1935
 7 Arthur Whitehurst, Bradford City v Tranmere Rovers, Div.3N - 6 Mar 1929
 7 Ted Drake, Arsenal v Aston Villa, Div.1 - 14 Dec 1935
 7 Ted Harston, Mansfield Town v Hartlepools United, Div.3N - 23 Jan 1937
 7 Eric Gemmell, Oldham Athletic v Chester, Div.3N - 19 Jan 1952
 7 Tommy Briggs, Blackburn Rovers v Bristol Rovers, Div.2 - 5 Feb 1955
 7 Neville Coleman, Stoke City v Lincoln City, Div.2 - 23 Feb 1957
Most individual goals in a season:
60 Dixie Dean, Everton, Div.1 - 1927-8
59 George Camsell, Middlesbrough, Div.2 - 1926-7
55 Joe Payne, Luton Town, Div.3S - 1936-7
55 Ted Harston, Mansfield Town, Div.3N - 1936-7
52 Terry Bly, Peterborough United, Div.4 - 1960-1

FA CUP

The idea for the Football Association Challenge Cup came from the secretary of the Football Association, Charles Alcock, who put forward his plans at a meeting attended by 12 clubs on 18 October 1871. The following 15 teams eventually entered the first competition: Wanderers, Harrow Chequers, Clapham Rovers, Upton Park, Crystal Palace, Hitchin, Maidenhead, Great Marlow, Barnes, Civil Service, Royal Engineers, Reigate Priory, Donington School, Hampstead Heathens, Queen's Park (Glasgow). Contested annually on a knock-out basis. *Finals:*

Year	Winners		Runners-up		Venue	Attendance
1872	WANDERERS	1	ROYAL ENGINEERS	0	Kennington Oval	2,000
	Betts					
1873	WANDERERS	2	OXFORD UNIVERSITY	0	Lillie Bridge	3,000
	Kinnaird, Wollaston					
1874	OXFORD UNIVERSITY	2	ROYAL ENGINEERS	0	Kennington Oval	2,000
	Mackarness, Patton					
1875	ROYAL ENGINEERS	1	OLD ETONIANS	1 *	Kennington Oval	3,000
	Renny-Tailyour		Bonsor			
Replay	ROYAL ENGINEERS	2	OLD ETONIANS	0	Kennington Oval	3,000
	Renny-Tailyour, Stafford					
1876	WANDERERS	1	OLD ETONIANS	1	Kennington Oval	3,000
	Edwards		Bonsor			
Replay	WANDERERS	3	OLD ETONIANS	0	Kennington Oval	3,500
	Hughes (2), Wollaston					
1877	WANDERERS	2	OXFORD UNIVERSITY	1 *	Kennington Oval	3,000
	Lindsay, Kenrick		Kinnaird (og)			
1878	WANDERERS	3	ROYAL ENGINEERS	1	Kennington Oval	4,500
	Kenrick (2), Kinnaird		unknown			
1879	OLD ETONIANS	1	CLAPHAM ROVERS	0	Kennington Oval	5,000
	Clerke					
1880	CLAPHAM ROVERS	1	OXFORD UNIVERSITY	0	Kennington Oval	6,000
	Lloyd-Jones					
1881	OLD CARTHUSIANS	3	OLD ETONIANS	0	Kennington Oval	4,500
	Wyngard, Parry, Todd					
1882	OLD ETONIANS	1	BLACKBURN ROVERS	0	Kennington Oval	6,500
	Macauley					
1883	BLACKBURN OLYMPIC	2	OLD ETONIANS	1 *	Kennington Oval	8,000
	Matthews, Crossley		Goodhart			
1884	BLACKBURN ROVERS	2	QUEEN'S PARK	1	Kennington Oval	4,000
	Sowerbutts, Forrest		Christie			
1885	BLACKBURN ROVERS	2	QUEEN'S PARK	0	Kennington Oval	12,500
	Forrest, Brown					
1886	BLACKBURN ROVERS	0	WEST BROMWICH ALBION	0	Kennington Oval	15,000
Replay	BLACKBURN ROVERS	2	WEST BROMWICH ALBION	0	Racecourse Ground, Derby	12,000
	Brown, Sowerbutts					
1887	ASTON VILLA	2	WEST BROMWICH ALBION	0	Kennington Oval	15,500
	Hunter, Hodgetts					
1888	WEST BROMWICH ALBION	2	PRESTON NORTH END	1	Kennington Oval	19,000
	Woodhall, Bayliss		Dewhurst			
1889	PRESTON NORTH END	3	WOLVERHAMPTON W	0	Kennington Oval	22,000
	Dewhurst, Ross, Thomson					
1890	BLACKBURN ROVERS	6	SHEFFIELD WEDNESDAY	1	Kennington Oval	20,000
	Townley (3), Walton John Southworth, Lofthouse		Bennett			
1891	BLACKBURN ROVERS	3	NOTTS COUNTY	1	Kennington Oval	23,000
	Southworth, Dewar, Townley		Oswald			
1892	WEST BROMWICH ALBION	3	ASTON VILLA	0	Kennington Oval	32,810
	Nicholls, Geddes, Reynolds					
1893	WOLVERHAMPTON W.	1	EVERTON	0	Fallowfield	45,000
	Allen					
1894	NOTTS COUNTY	4	BOLTON WANDERERS	1	Goodison Park	37,000
	Logan (3), Watson		Cassidy			
1895	ASTON VILLA	1	WEST BROMWICH ALBION	0	Crystal Palace	42,560
	Devey					
1896	SHEFFIELD WEDNESDAY	2	WOLVERHAMPTON W	1	Crystal Palace	48,836
	Spiksley (2)		Black			

Year	Winners		Runners-up		Venue	Attendance
1897	ASTON VILLA Devey, Campbell, Crabtree	3	EVERTON Bell, Hartley	2	Crystal Palace	65,891
1898	NOTTINGHAM FOREST Capes (2), McPherson	3	DERBY COUNTY Bloomer	1	Crystal Palace	62,017
1899	SHEFFIELD UNITED Bennett, Priest, Beers, Almond	4	DERBY COUNTY Boag	1	Crystal Palace	73,833
1900	BURY McLuckie (2), Wood, Plant	4	SOUTHAMPTON	0	Crystal Palace	68,945
1901	TOTTENHAM HOTSPUR Brown(2)	2	SHEFFIELD UNITED Bennett, Priest	2	Crystal Palace	110,820
Replay	TOTTENHAM HOTSPUR Cameron, Smith, Brown	3	SHEFFIELD UNITED Priest	1	Burnden Park	20,470
1902	SHEFFIELD UNITED Common	1	SOUTHAMPTON Wood	1	Crystal Palace	76,914
Replay	SHEFFIELD UNITED Hedley, Barnes	2	SOUTHAMPTON Brown	1	Crystal Palace	33,068
1903	BURY Leeming (2), Ross, Sagar, Plant, Wood	6	DERBY COUNTY	0	Crystal Palace	63,102
1904	MANCHESTER CITY Meredith	1	BOLTON WANDERERS	0	Crystal Palace	61,374
1905	ASTON VILLA Hampton (2)	2	NEWCASTLE UNITED	0	Crystal Palace	101,117
1906	EVERTON Young	1	NEWCASTLE UNITED	0	Crystal Palace	75,609
1907	SHEFFIELD WEDNESDAY Stewart, Simpson	2	EVERTON Sharp	1	Crystal Palace	84,584
1908	WOLVERHAMPTON W Hunt, Hedley, Harrison	3	NEWCASTLE UNITED Howie	1	Crystal Palace	74,967
1909	MANCHESTER UNITED A.Turnbull	1	BRISTOL CITY	0	Crystal Palace	71,401
1910	NEWCASTLE UNITED Rutherford	1	BARNSLEY Tuffnell	1	Crystal Palace	77,747
Replay	NEWCASTLE UNITED Shepherd (2-1 pen)	2	BARNSLEY	0	Goodison Park	69,000
1911	BRADFORD CITY	0	NEWCASTLE UNITED	0	Crystal Palace	69,098
Replay	BRADFORD CITY Spiers	1	NEWCASTLE UNITED	0	Old Trafford	58,000
1912	BARNSLEY	0	WEST BROMWICH ALBION	0	Crystal Palace	54,556
Replay	BARNSLEY Tuffnell	1	WEST BROMWICH ALBION	0 *	Bramall Lane	38,555
1913	ASTON VILLA Barber	1	SUNDERLAND	0	Crystal Palace	120,081
1914	BURNLEY Freeman	1	LIVERPOOL	0	Crystal Palace	72,778
1915	SHEFFIELD UNITED Simmons, Kitchen, Fazackerley	3	CHELSEA	0	Old Trafford	49,557
1920	ASTON VILLA Kirton	1	HUDDERSFIELD TOWN	0 *	Stamford Bridge	50,018
1921	TOTTENHAM HOTSPUR Dimmock	1	WOLVERHAMPTON W	0	Stamford Bridge	72,805
1922	HUDDERSFIELD TOWN Smith (pen)	1	PRESTON NORTH END	0	Stamford Bridge	53,000
1923	BOLTON WANDERERS Jack, J.R.Smith	2	WEST HAM UNITED	0	Wembley	126,047
1924	NEWCASTLE UNITED Harris, Seymour	2	ASTON VILLA	0	Wembley	91,695

Year	Winners		Runners-up		Venue	Attendance
1925	SHEFFIELD UNITED Tunstall	1	CARDIFF CITY	0	Wembley	91,763
1926	BOLTON WANDERERS Jack	1	MANCHESTER CITY	0	Wembley	91,447
1927	CARDIFF CITY Ferguson	1	ARSENAL	0	Wembley	91,206
1928	BLACKBURN ROVERS Roscamp (2), McLean	3	HUDDERSFIELD TOWN Jackson	1	Wembley	92,041
1929	BOLTON WANDERERS Butler, Blackmore	2	PORTSMOUTH	0	Wembley	92,576
1930	ARSENAL James, Lambert	2	HUDDERSFIELD TOWN	0	Wembley	92,488
1931	WEST BROMWICH ALBION W.G.Richardson (2)	2	BIRMINGHAM Bradford	1	Wembley	92,406
1932	NEWCASTLE UNITED Allen (2)	2	ARSENAL John	1	Wembley	92,298
1933	EVERTON Stein, Dean, Dunn	3	MANCHESTER CITY	0	Wembley	92,950
1934	MANCHESTER CITY Tilson (2)	2	PORTSMOUTH Rutherford	1	Wembley	93,258
1935	SHEFFIELD WEDNESDAY Rimmer (2), Hooper, Palethorpe	4	WEST BROMWICH ALBION Boyes, Sandford	2	Wembley	93,204
1936	ARSENAL Drake	1	SHEFFIELD UNITED	0	Wembley	93,384
1937	SUNDERLAND Gurney, Carter, Burbanks	3	PRESTON NORTH END F.O'Donnell	1	Wembley	93,495
1938	PRESTON NORTH END Mutch (pen)	1	HUDDERSFIELD TOWN	0 *	Wembley	93,497
1939	PORTSMOUTH Parker (2), Barlow, Anderson	4	WOLVERHAMPTON W Dorsett	1	Wembley	99,370
1946	DERBY COUNTY Stamps (2), Doherty, H.Turner(og)	4	CHARLTON ATHLETIC H.Turner	1 *	Wembley	98,215
1947	CHARLTON ATHLETIC Duffy	1	BURNLEY	0 *	Wembley	99,000
1948	MANCHESTER UNITED Rowley (2), Pearson, Anderson	4	BLACKPOOL Shimwell (pen), Mortensen	2	Wembley	99,000
1949	WOLVERHAMPTON W Pye (2), Smyth	3	LEICESTER CITY Griffiths	1	Wembley	99,500
1950	ARSENAL Lewis (2)	2	LIVERPOOL	0	Wembley	100,000
1951	NEWCASTLE UNITED Milburn (2)	2	BLACKPOOL	0	Wembley	100,000
1952	NEWCASTLE UNITED G.Robledo	1	ARSENAL	0	Wembley	100,000
1953	BLACKPOOL Mortensen (3), Perry	4	BOLTON WANDERERS Lofthouse, Moir, Bell	3	Wembley	100,000
1954	WEST BROMWICH ALBION Allen (2,1 pen), Griffin	3	PRESTON NORTH END Morrison, Wayman	2	Wembley	100,000
1955	NEWCASTLE UNITED Milburn, Mitchell, Hannah	3	MANCHESTER CITY Johnstone	1	Wembley	100,000
1956	MANCHESTER CITY Hayes, Dyson, Johnstone	3	BIRMINGHAM CITY Kinsey	1	Wembley	100,000
1957	ASTON VILLA McParland (2)	2	MANCHESTER UNITED Taylor	1	Wembley	100,000
1958	BOLTON WANDERERS Lofthouse (2)	2	MANCHESTER UNITED	0	Wembley	100,000

Year	Winners		Runners-up		Venue	Attendance
1959	NOTTINGHAM FOREST Dwight, Wilson	2	LUTON TOWN Pacey	1	Wembley	100,000
1960	WOLVERHAMPTON W McGrath (og), Deeley (2)	3	BLACKBURN ROVERS	0	Wembley	100,000
1961	TOTTENHAM HOTSPUR Smith, Dyson	2	LEICESTER CITY	0	Wembley	100,000
1962	TOTTENHAM HOTSPUR Greaves, Smith, Blanchflower (pen)	3	BURNLEY Robson	1	Wembley	100,000
1963	MANCHESTER UNITED Herd (2), Law	3	LEICESTER CITY Keyworth	1	Wembley	100,000
1964	WEST HAM UNITED Sissons, Hurst, Boyce	3	PRESTON NORTH END Holden, Dawson	2	Wembley	100,000
1965	LIVERPOOL Hunt, St.John	2	LEEDS UNITED Bremner	1 *	Wembley	100,000
1966	EVERTON Trebilcock (2), Temple	3	SHEFFIELD WEDNESDAY McCalliog, Ford	2	Wembley	100,000
1967	TOTTENHAM HOTSPUR Robertson, Saul	2	CHELSEA Tambling	1	Wembley	100,000
1968	WEST BROMWICH ALBION Astle	1	EVERTON	0 *	Wembley	100,000
1969	MANCHESTER CITY Young	1	LEICESTER CITY	0	Wembley	100,000
1970	CHELSEA Houseman, Hutchinson	2	LEEDS UNITED Charlton, Jones	2 *	Wembley	100,000
Replay	CHELSEA Osgood, Webb	2	LEEDS UNITED Jones	1 *	Old Trafford	62,078
1971	ARSENAL Kelly, George	2	LIVERPOOL Heighway	1 *	Wembley	100,000
1972	LEEDS UNITED Clarke	1	ARSENAL	0	Wembley	100,000
1973	SUNDERLAND Porterfield	1	LEEDS UNITED	0	Wembley	100,000
1974	LIVERPOOL Keegan (2), Heighway	3	NEWCASTLE UNITED	0	Wembley	100,000
1975	WEST HAM UNITED A.Taylor (2)	2	FULHAM	0	Wembley	100,000
1976	SOUTHAMPTON Stokes	1	MANCHESTER UNITED	0	Wembley	100,000
1977	MANCHESTER UNITED Pearson, J.Greenhoff	2	LIVERPOOL Case	1	Wembley	100,000
1978	IPSWICH TOWN Osborne	1	ARSENAL	0	Wembley	100,000
1979	ARSENAL Talbot, Stapleton, Sunderland	3	MANCHESTER UNITED McQueen, McIlroy	2	Wembley	100,000
1980	WEST HAM UNITED Brooking	1	ARSENAL	0	Wembley	100,000
1981	TOTTENHAM HOTSPUR Hutchison (og)	1	MANCHESTER CITY Hutchison	1 *	Wembley	100,000
Replay	TOTTENHAM HOTSPUR Villa (2), Crooks	3	MANCHESTER CITY Mackenzie, Reeves (pen)	2	Wembley	92,000
1982	TOTTENHAM HOTSPUR Hoddle	1	QUEEN'S PARK RANGERS Fenwick	1 *	Wembley	100,000
Replay	TOTTENHAM HOTSPUR Hoddle (pen)	1	QUEEN'S PARK RANGERS	0	Wembley	90,000
1983	MANCHESTER UNITED Stapleton, Wilkins	2	BRIGHTON & HOVE A Smith, Stevens	2 *	Wembley	100,000

Year	Winners		Runners-up		Venue	Attendance
Replay	MANCHESTER UNITED Robson (2), Whiteside, Muhren (pen)	4	BRIGHTON & HOVE A	0	Wembley	92,000
1984	EVERTON Sharp, Gray	2	WATFORD	0	Wembley	100,000
1985	MANCHESTER UNITED Whiteside	1	EVERTON	0 *	Wembley	100,000
1986	LIVERPOOL Rush (2), Johnston	3	EVERTON Lineker	1	Wembley	98,000
1987	COVENTRY CITY Bennett, Houchen, Mabbutt (og)	3	TOTTENHAM HOTSPUR C.Allen, Mabbutt	2 *	Wembley	98,000
1988	WIMBLEDON Sanchez	1	LIVERPOOL	0	Wembley	98,203
1989	LIVERPOOL Rush (2), Aldridge	3	EVERTON McCall (2)	2 *	Wembley	82,800
1990	MANCHESTER UNITED Robson, Hughes (2)	3	CRYSTAL PALACE O'Reilly, Wright (2)	3 *	Wembley	80,000
Replay	MANCHESTER UNITED Martin	1	CRYSTAL PALACE	0	Wembley	80,000

* after extra time

Most wins: 7 Aston Villa, Tottenham Hotspur, Manchester United; 6 Blackburn Rovers, Newcastle United
Most finals: 11 Arsenal, Newcastle United, Everton, Manchester United; 10 West Bromwich Albion
Most semi-finals: 22 Everton, 19 West Bromwich Albion, 18 Liverpool, Manchester United
Most winners' medals: 5 James Forrest (Blackburn Rovers) 1884-86, 1890-1, Hon.A.F.Kinnaird (Wanderers) 1873, 1877-8 (Old Etonians) 1879, 1882, Charles Wollaston (Wanderers) 1872-3, 1876-8
Biggest win: 26-0 Preston North End v Hyde United (1st round) 15 Oct 1887
Biggest win (final): 6-0 Bury v Derby County 18 Apr 1903

Second Division Finalists The following clubs from the second division (formed 1892-3) of the Football League have reached the FA Cup final:

1894 Notts County *	1921 Wolverhampton Wanderers	1964 Preston North End
1904 Bolton Wanderers	1923 West Ham United	1973 Sunderland *
1908 Wolverhampton Wanderers *	1931 West Bromwich Albion *	1975 Fulham
1910 Barnsley	1936 Sheffield United	1976 Southampton *
1912 Barnsley *	1947 Burnley	1980 West Ham United *
1920 Huddersfield Town	1949 Leicester City	1982 Queen's Park Rangers

No clubs from the 3rd or 4th divisions have reached the FA Cup final but non-league clubs, since the formation of the the League, to have reached the final have been Southampton 1900 and 1902, Tottenham Hotspur 1901*
* Indicates winners

FOOTBALL LEAGUE CUP

Instituted in 1960-1, but it was not until the 1969/70 season that all 92 Football League teams took part. All finals up to 1966 were played on a two-leg basis but since then they have been played at Wembley Stadium. With sponsorship from the Milk Marketing Board in 1982 the Cup's name was changed to the Milk Cup, and from 1986 to 1990 it was the Littlewoods Cup.

Year	Home team		Away team		Attendance
1961	ROTHERHAM UNITED Webster, Kirkman	2	ASTON VILLA	0	12,226
	ASTON VILLA O'Neill, Burrows, McParland (Aston Villa won 3-2 on aggregate)	3	ROTHERHAM UNITED	0 *	31,202
1962	ROCHDALE	0	NORWICH CITY Lythgoe (2), Punton	3	11,123
	NORWICH CITY Hill (Norwich City won 4-0 on aggregate)	1	ROCHDALE	0	19,708

Year	Home team		Away team		Attendance
1963	**BIRMINGHAM CITY**	3	**ASTON VILLA**	1	31,850
	Leek (2), Bloomfield		Thomson		
	ASTON VILLA	0	**BIRMINGHAM CITY**	0	37,920
	(Birmingham City won 3-1 on aggregate)				
1964	**STOKE CITY**	1	**LEICESTER CITY**	1	22,309
	Bebbington		Gibson		
	LEICESTER CITY	3	**STOKE CITY**	2	25,372
	Stringfellow, Gibson, Riley		Viollet, Kinnell		
	(Leicester City won 4-3 on aggregate)				
1965	**CHELSEA**	3	**LEICESTER CITY**	2	20,690
	Tambling, McCreadie,		Appleton, Goodfellow		
	Venables (pen)				
	LEICESTER CITY	0	**CHELSEA**	0	26,958
	(Chelsea won 3-2 on aggregate)				
1966	**WEST HAM UNITED**	2	**WEST BROMWICH ALBION**	1	28,341
	Moore, Byrne		Astle		
	WEST BROMWICH ALBION	4	**WEST HAM UNITED**	1	31,925
	Kaye, Brown, Clark, Williams		Peters		
	(West Bromwich Albion won 5-3 on aggregate)				

Year	Winners		Runners-up		Venue	Attendance
1967	**QUEEN'S PARK RANGERS**	3	**WEST BROMWICH ALBION**	2	Wembley	97,952
	R.Morgan, Marsh, Lazarus		Clark (2)			
1968	**LEEDS UNITED**	1	**ARSENAL**	0	Wembley	97,887
	Cooper					
1969	**SWINDON TOWN**	3	**ARSENAL**	1	Wembley	98,189
	Rogers (2), Smart		Gould			
1970	**MANCHESTER CITY**	2	**WEST BROMWICH ALBION**	1	Wembley	97,963
	Doyle, Pardoe		Astle			
1971	**TOTTENHAM HOTSPUR**	2	**ASTON VILLA**	0	Wembley	100,000
	Chivers (2)					
1972	**STOKE CITY**	2	**CHELSEA**	1	Wembley	100,000
	Conroy, Eastham		Osgood			
1973	**TOTTENHAM HOTSPUR**	1	**NORWICH CITY**	0	Wembley	100,000
	Coates					
1974	**WOLVERHAMPTON W**	2	**MANCHESTER CITY**	1	Wembley	100,000
	Hibbitt, Richards		Bell			
1975	**ASTON VILLA**	1	**NORWICH CITY**	0	Wembley	100,000
	Graydon					
1976	**MANCHESTER CITY**	2	**NEWCASTLE UNITED**	1	Wembley	100,000
	Barnes, Tueart		Gowling			
1977	**ASTON VILLA**	0	**EVERTON**	0	Wembley	100,000
Replay	**ASTON VILLA**	1	**EVERTON**	1 *	Hillsborough	55,000
	Kenyon (og)		Latchford			
Replay	**ASTON VILLA**	3	**EVERTON**	2 *	Old Trafford	54,749
	Little (2), Nicholl		Latchford, Lyons			
1978	**NOTTINGHAM FOREST**	0	**LIVERPOOL**	0 *	Wembley	100,000
Replay	**NOTTINGHAM FOREST**	1	**LIVERPOOL**	0	Old Trafford	54,375
	Robertson (pen)					
1979	**NOTTINGHAM FOREST**	3	**SOUTHAMPTON**	2	Wembley	100,000
	Birtles (2), Woodcock		Peach, Holmes			
1980	**WOLVERHAMPTON W**	1	**NOTTINGHAM FOREST**	0	Wembley	100,000
	Gray					
1981	**LIVERPOOL**	1	**WEST HAM UNITED**	1 *	Wembley	100,000
	A.Kennedy		Stewart (pen)			
Replay	**LIVERPOOL**	2	**WEST HAM UNITED**	1	Villa Park	36,693
	Dalglish, Hansen		Goddard			

Year	Winners		Runners-up		Venue	Attendance
1982	LIVERPOOL Whelan (2), Rush	3	TOTTENHAM HOTSPUR Archibald	1 *	Wembley	100,000
1983	LIVERPOOL Kennedy, Whelan	2	MANCHESTER UNITED Whiteside	1 *	Wembley	100,000
1984	LIVERPOOL	0	EVERTON	0 *	Wembley	100,000
Replay	LIVERPOOL Souness	1	EVERTON	0	Maine Road	52,089
1985	NORWICH CITY Chisholm (og)	1	SUNDERLAND	0	Wembley	100,000
1986	OXFORD UNITED Hebberd, Houghton, Charles	3	QUEEN'S PARK RANGERS	0	Wembley	90,396
1987	ARSENAL Nicholas (2)	2	LIVERPOOL Rush	1	Wembley	96,000
1988	LUTON TOWN B.Stein (2), Wilson	3	ARSENAL Hayes, Smith	2	Wembley	95,732
1989	NOTTINGHAM FOREST Clough (2, 1 pen), Webb	3	LUTON TOWN Harford	1	Wembley	76,130
1990	NOTTINGHAM FOREST Jemson	1	OLDHAM ATHLETIC	0	Wembley	74,343

* after extra time

Most wins: 4 Liverpool, Nottingham Forest; 3 Aston Villa
Most finals: 6 Liverpool, 5 Aston Villa, Nottingham Forest; 4 Norwich City, Arsenal
Most semi-finals: 8 Aston Villa, Liverpool; 7 Tottenham H
Most winners' medals: 4 Phil Neal, Alan Kennedy, Kenny Dalglish, Sammy Lee, Ian Rush, Graeme Souness (all Liverpool)
Biggest win: 10-0 West Ham United v Bury (2nd round, 2nd leg) 25 Oct 1983, 10-0 Liverpool v Fulham (2nd round, 1st leg) 23 Sep 1986
Biggest win (final): 4-1 West Bromwich A v West Ham United (2nd leg) 23 Mar 1966
The following non-first division sides have reached the final:
Div.2: 1961 Rotherham United, 1962 Norwich City *, 1975 Aston Villa * and Norwich City, 1981 West Ham United, 1990 Oldham Athletic
Div.3: 1967 Queen's Park Rangers *, 1969 Swindon Town *, 1971 Aston Villa
Div.4: 1962 Rochdale
* winners

THE LEADING FOOTBALL LEAGUE CLUBS

Number of divisional titles, FA Cup Final wins and Football League/Milk/Littlewoods Cup Final wins.

	Football League.Divisions						FA	FL	
	1	2	3	4	3N	3S	Cup	Cup	TOTAL
Liverpool	18	4	-	-	-	-	4	4	30
Aston Villa	7	2	1	-	-	-	7	3	20
Manchester U	7	2	-	-	-	-	7	-	16
Arsenal	9	-	-	-	-	-	5	1	15
Everton	9	1	-	-	-	-	4	-	14
Wolverhampton W	3	2	1	1	1	-	4	2	14
Manchester C	2	6	-	-	-	-	4	2	14
Tottenham H	2	2	-	-	-	-	7	2	13
Sheffield W	4	5	-	-	-	-	3	-	12
Newcastle U	4	1	-	-	-	-	6	-	11
Sunderland	6	1	1	-	-	-	2	-	10
Blackburn R	2	1	1	-	-	-	6	-	10
Most divisional titles by clubs that have not won the 1st division:									
Leicester City	-	6	-	-	-	-	-	1	7
Notts County	-	3	-	1	2	-	-	-	6
Grimsby Town	-	2	1	1	-	2	-	-	6
Doncaster Rovers	-	-	-	2	-	3	-	-	5

Clubs that have been champions of Divisions 1, 2 and 3 (incl. 3N or 3S):
Aston Villa, Blackburn R, Wolverhampton W., Preston North End, Burnley, Derby County, Ipswich Town, Nottingham Forest, Sunderland
Champions of Divisions 1 and 4:
Huddersfield Town, Sheffield United
Champions of most divisions:
Wolverhampton Wanderers have been champions of Divisions 1,2, 3, 4 and 3 (North). Grimsby Town have been champions of the 2nd, 3rd, 4th and 3rd Division (North)
Dual FA Cup/League Cup winners:
Liverpool, Aston Villa, Wolverhampton W, Manchester City, Tottenham Hotspur, Leeds United, Chelsea, West Bromwich A, Nottingham Forest, Arsenal

All-time League table

Our own league table based on a points system of 12 points for winning the 1st Division title, 10 for winning the FA Cup and 8 for winning the League/Milk/Littlewoods Cup, with half those points for finishing runners-up.

	Club	points		Club	points
1	Liverpool	361	7	Tottenham Hotspur	138
2	Aston Villa	250	8	Newcastle United	137
3	Manchester United	232	9	Sunderland	131
4	Everton	221	10	Manchester City	122
5	Arsenal	218	11	West Bromwich A	115
6	Wolverhampton W	142	12	Preston North End	105

AWARDS

FOOTBALL WRITERS' PLAYER OF THE YEAR

The Football Writers Association was founded in 1947 and since 1947-48 its members have voted for their Player of the Year. *Winners:*

1948 Stanley Matthews (Blackpool)
1949 Johnny Carey (Manchester United)
1950 Joe Mercer (Arsenal)
1951 Harry Johnston (Blackpool)
1952 Billy Wright (Wolverhampton Wanderers)
1953 Nat Lofthouse (Bolton Wanderers)
1954 Tom Finney (Preston North End)
1955 Don Revie (Manchester City)
1956 Bert Trautmann (Manchester City)
1957 Tom Finney (Preston North End)
1958 Danny Blanchflower (Tottenham Hotspur)
1959 Syd Owen (Luton Town)
1960 Bill Slater (Wolverhampton Wanderers)
1961 Danny Blanchflower (Tottenham Hotspur)
1962 Jimmy Adamson (Burnley)
1963 Stanley Matthews (Stoke City)
1964 Bobby Moore (West Ham United)
1965 Bobby Collins (Leeds United)

John Barnes beats Prusik of Poland in a World Cup qualifying match, which England won 3-0 in 1989
(All-Sport/Ben Radford)

1966 Bobby Charlton (Manchester United)
1967 Jackie Charlton (Leeds United)
1968 George Best (Manchester United)
1969 Tony Book (Manchester City) &
     Dave Mackay (Derby County)
1970 Billy Bremner (Leeds United)
1971 Frank McLintock (Arsenal)
1972 Gordon Banks (Stoke City)
1973 Pat Jennings (Tottenham Hotspur)
1974 Ian Callaghan (Liverpool)
1975 Alan Mullery (Fulham)
1976 Kevin Keegan (Liverpool)
1977 Emlyn Hughes (Liverpool)
1978 Kenny Burns (Nottingham Forest)
1979 Kenny Dalglish (Liverpool)
1980 Terry McDermott (Liverpool)
1981 Frans Thijssen (Ipswich Town)
1982 Steve Perryman (Tottenham Hotspur)
1983 Kenny Dalglish (Liverpool)
1984 Ian Rush (Liverpool)
1985 Neville Southall (Everton)
1986 Gary Lineker (Everton)
1987 Clive Allen (Tottenham Hotspur)
1988 John Barnes (Liverpool)
1989 Steve Nicol (Liverpool)
1990 John Barnes (Liverpool)

Tom Finney, Footballer of the Year 1957
(Popperfoto)

Most wins: 2 Tom Finney, Danny Blanchflower, Stanley Matthews, Kenny Dalglish, John Barnes
Most wins (clubs): 10 Liverpool, 4 Tottenham Hotspur, 3 Leeds United, Manchester City, Manchester United
The following winners of the award never won a full international cap: Bert Trautmann (1956), Jimmy Adamson (1962), Tony Book (1969)
The only players to win the award while with a second division club were: Stanley Matthews (Stoke City, 1963), Dave McKay (Derby County, 1969), Alan Mullery (Fulham, 1975)

PROFESSIONAL FOOTBALLERS' ASSOCIATION PLAYER OF THE YEAR

At the end of each season the professional players vote for their Player of the Year, a trophy much cherished by its winners. The first such award was made in 1974. A Young Player award is also presented annually, as well as a Merit Award. *Winners:*

Player of the Year
1974 Norman Hunter (Leeds United)
1975 Colin Todd (Derby County)
1976 Pat Jennings (Tottenham Hotspur)
1977 Andy Gray (Aston Villa)
1978 Peter Shilton (Nottingham Forest)
1979 Liam Brady (Arsenal)
1980 Terry McDermott (Liverpool)
1981 John Wark (Ipswich Town)
1982 Kevin Keegan (Southampton)
1983 Kenny Dalglish (Liverpool)
1984 Ian Rush (Liverpool)
1985 Peter Reid (Everton)
1986 Gary Lineker (Everton)
1987 Clive Allen (Tottenham Hotspur)
1988 John Barnes (Liverpool)
1989 Mark Hughes (Manchester United)
1990 David Platt (Aston Villa)

Young Player of the Year
1974 Kevin Beattie (Ipswich Town)
1975 Mervyn Day (West Ham United)
1976 Peter Barnes (Manchester City)
1977 Andy Gray (Aston Villa)
1978 Tony Woodcock (Nottingham Forest)
1979 Cyrille Regis (West Bromwich Albion)
1980 Glenn Hoddle (Tottenham Hotspur)
1981 Gary Shaw (Aston Villa)
1982 Steve Moran (Southampton)
1983 Ian Rush (Liverpool)
1984 Paul Walsh (Luton Town)
1985 Mark Hughes (Manchester United)
1986 Tony Cottee (West Ham United)
1987 Tony Adams (Arsenal)
1988 Paul Gascoigne (Newcastle United)
1989 Paul Merson (Arsenal)
1990 Matthew Le Tissier (Southampton)

Merit Award

1974	Bobby Charlton & Cliff Lloyd
1975	Denis Law
1976	George Eastham
1977	Jack Taylor
1978	Bill Shankly
1979	Tom Finney
1980	Sir Matt Busby
1981	John Trollope
1982	Joe Mercer
1983	Bob Paisley
1984	Bill Nicholson
1985	Ron Greenwood
1986	Alf Ramsey, Harold Shepherdson & the 1966 England World Cup winning squad
1987	Sir Stanley Matthews
1988	Billy Bonds
1989	Nat Lofthouse
1990	Peter Shilton

Dual winners:
The following players have won the Player of the Year and Young Player of the Year awards: Andy Gray (uniquely both in the same year), Ian Rush, Mark Hughes

The most honoured English players
The following players have been honoured by three or more awards from the three main associations.

		FWA	PFA	Europe
4	Kevin Keegan	1	1	2
3	Stanley Matthews	2	-	1
3	Tom Finney	2	1	-
3	Kenny Dalglish	2	1	-
3	Bobby Charlton	1	1	1
3	Ian Rush	1	2	-
3	John Barnes	2	1	-

BARCLAYS BANK MANAGER OF THE YEAR

Instituted in 1965-6 the trophy and accompanying cheque is presented to the Manager of the Season. In addition to the annual prize, monthly awards are made to the Manager of the Month, and divisional awards are also made monthly. Known as the Bell's Scotch Whisky Manager of the Year until 1989. *Annual winners:*

1966	Jock Stein (Glasgow Celtic)
1967	Jock Stein (Glasgow Celtic)
1968	Matt Busby (Manchester United)
1969	Don Revie (Leeds United)
1970	Don Revie (Leeds United)
1971	Bertie Mee (Arsenal)
1972	Don Revie (Leeds United)
1973	Bill Shankly (Liverpool)
1974	Jack Charlton (Middlesbrough)
1975	Ron Saunders (Aston Villa)
1976	Bob Paisley (Liverpool)
1977	Bob Paisley (Liverpool)
1978	Brian Clough (Nottingham Forest)
1979	Bob Paisley (Liverpool)
1980	Bob Paisley (Liverpool)
1981	Ron Saunders (Aston Villa)
1982	Bob Paisley (Liverpool)
1983	Bob Paisley (Liverpool)
1984	Joe Fagan (Liverpool)
1985	Howard Kendall (Everton)
1986	Kenny Dalglish (Liverpool)
1987	Howard Kendall (Everton)
1988	Kenny Dalglish (Liverpool)
1989	George Graham (Arsenal)
1990	Kenny Dalglish (Liverpool)

Most wins: 6 Bob Paisley, 3 Don Revie, Kenny Dalglish
Bob Paisley's nine-year reign as Liverpool's manager was the most successful ever in the history of English football. His complete record was:

	League Champs	League/ Milk Cup	FA Cup	European Cup	UEFA Cup	European Super Cup
Wins	6	3	-	3	1	1
Runners-up	2	1	1	-	-	-

SCOTTISH FOOTBALL LEAGUE

The Scottish League was formed in 1890, two years after the Football League. A second division was added in 1893 and the biggest re-organisation in the League since its formation came in 1975-6 when it was completely re-structured. The leading ten teams formed a new Premier division while the remaining teams were divided into Divisions 1 and 2. The number of teams in the Premier Division was extended to twelve in 1986-7, but reduced back to ten from 1988-9.

First Division/Premier Division champions

Season	Champions	Pts	Max
1890/1	Dumbarton & Rangers	29	36
1891/2	Dumbarton	37	44
1892/3	Celtic	29	36
1893/4	Celtic	29	36
1894/5	Hearts	31	36
1895/6	Celtic	30	36
1896/7	Hearts	28	36
1897/8	Celtic	33	36
1898/9	Rangers	36	36
1899/00	Rangers	32	36
1900/1	Rangers	35	40
1901/2	Rangers	28	36
1902/3	Hibernian	37	44
1903/4	Third Lanark	43	52
1904/5	Celtic	41	52
1905/6	Celtic	49	60
1906/7	Celtic	55	68
1907/8	Celtic	55	68
1908/9	Celtic	51	68
1909/10	Celtic	54	68
1910/1	Rangers	52	68
1911/2	Rangers	51	68
1912/3	Rangers	53	68
1913/4	Celtic	65	76

Season	Champions	Pts	Max
1914/5	Celtic	65	76
1915/6	Celtic	67	76
1916/7	Celtic	64	76
1917/8	Rangers	56	68
1918/9	Celtic	58	68
1919/20	Rangers	71	84
1920/1	Rangers	76	84
1921/2	Celtic	67	84
1922/3	Rangers	55	76
1923/4	Rangers	59	76
1924/5	Rangers	60	76
1925/6	Celtic	58	76
1926/7	Rangers	56	76
1927/8	Rangers	60	76
1928/9	Rangers	67	76
1929/30	Rangers	60	76
1930/1	Rangers	60	76
1931/2	Motherwell	66	76
1932/3	Rangers	62	76
1933/4	Rangers	66	76
1934/5	Rangers	55	76
1935/6	Celtic	66	76
1936/7	Rangers	61	76
1937/8	Celtic	61	76
1938/9	Rangers	59	76
1946/7	Rangers	46	68
1947/8	Hibernian	48	68
1948/9	Rangers	46	68
1949/50	Rangers	50	68
1950/1	Hibernian	48	68
1951/2	Hibernian	45	68
1952/3	Rangers	43	68
1953/4	Celtic	43	68
1954/5	Aberdeen	49	68
1955/6	Rangers	52	68
1956/7	Rangers	55	68
1957/8	Hearts	62	68
1958/9	Rangers	50	68
1959/60	Hearts	54	68
1960/1	Rangers	51	68
1961/2	Dundee	54	68
1962/3	Rangers	57	68
1963/4	Rangers	55	68
1964/5	Kilmarnock	50	68
1965/6	Celtic	57	68
1966/7	Celtic	58	68
1967/8	Celtic	63	68
1968/9	Celtic	54	68
1969/70	Celtic	57	68
1970/1	Celtic	56	68
1971/2	Celtic	60	68
1972/3	Celtic	57	68
1973/4	Celtic	53	68
1974/5	Rangers	56	68

Premier Division

Season	Champions	Pts	Max
1975/6	Rangers	54	72
1976/7	Celtic	55	72

Season	Champions	Pts	Max
1977/8	Rangers	55	72
1978/9	Celtic	48	72
1979/80	Aberden	48	72
1980/1	Celtic	56	72
1981/2	Celtic	55	72
1982/3	Dundee United	56	72
1983/4	Aberdeen	57	72
1984/5	Aberdeen	59	72
1985/6	Celtic	50	72
1986/7	Rangers	69	88
1987/8	Celtic	72	88
1988/9	Rangers	56	72
1989/90	Rangers	51	72

Most wins: 40 Rangers, 35 Celtic

Biggest win: 13-2 East Fife v Edinburgh City (Division 2 - 11 Dec 1937)

Biggest win (Division 1/Premier Division): 11-0 Celtic v Dundee 26 Oct 1895

Most individual goals in a match:
8 Owen McNally (Arthurlie v Armadale) Division 2 - 1 Oct 1927
8 Jimmy McGrory (Celtic v Dunfermline Athletic) Division 1 - 14 Jan 1928
8 Jim Dyet (King's Park v Forfar Athletic) Division 2 - 2 Jan 1930
8 John Calder (Morton v Raith Rovers) Division 2- 18 Mar 1936

Most individual goals in a season:
66 Jim Smith (Ayr United) Division 2 - 1927/8
53 Robert Skinner (Dunfermline Athletic) Division 2 - 1925/6
52 Bill McFadyen (Motherwell) Division 1 - 1931/2
50 Jimmy McGrory (Celtic) Division 1 - 1935/6

SCOTTISH FA CUP

When Queen's Park called a meeting of clubs on 13 March 1873 it was with the intention of organising a cup competition, similar to the FA Cup. Seven clubs attended that first meeting and Queen's Park's wishes were granted but, at the same meeting, it was decided to form the Scottish Football Association and so the new cup competition was called the Scottish Football Association Cup.

The venue of the Final has been Hampden Park, except for: Hamilton Crescent 1876-7, Cathkin Park 1880, 1882, 1886; Kinning Park 1881, Ibrox Park 1890, 1892-3, 1895, 1900-1, 1906, 1910-12, 1914, 1924; Logie Green 1896, Celtic Park 1902-3, 1913, 1921.

Year	Winners		Runners-up		Attendance
1874	Queen's Park	2	Clydesdale	0	3,500
1875	Queen's Park	3	Renton	0	7,000
1876	Queen's Park	1	Third Lanark	1	10,000
Replay	Queen's Park	2	Third Lanark	0	6,000
1877	Vale of Leven	0	Rangers	0	10,000
Replay	Vale of Leven	1	Rangers	1	15,000

Year	Winners		Runners-up		Attendance
Replay	Vale of Leven	3	Rangers	2	12,000
1878	Vale of Leven	1	Third Lanark	0	5,000
1879	Vale of Leven	1	Rangers	1	9,000
	awarded trophy as Rangers refused to appear for the replay				
1880	Queen's Park	3	Thornlibank	0	4,000
1881	Queen's Park	2	Dumbarton	1	15,000
	replayed due to spectator invasion of pitch				
Replay	Queen's Park	3	Dumbarton	1	7,000
1882	Queen's Park	2	Dumbarton	2	12,500
Replay	Queen's Park	4	Dumbarton	1	14,000
1883	Dumbarton	2	Vale of Leven	2	9,000
Replay	Dumbarton	2	Vale of Leven	1	12,000
1884	*Queen's Park awarded cup as Vale of Leven failed to appear*				
1885	Renton	0	Vale of Leven	0	2,500
Replay	Renton	3	Vale of Leven	1	3,500
1886	Queen's Park	3	Renton	1	7,000
1887	Hibernian	2	Dumbarton	1	12,000
1888	Renton	6	Cambuslang	1	11,000
1889	Third Lanark	3	Celtic	1	18,000
	game declared void due to snowstorm				
Replay	Third Lanark	2	Celtic	1	13,000
1890	Queen's Park	1	Vale of Leven	1	11,000
Replay	Queen's Park	2	Vale of Leven	1	14,000
1891	Hearts	1	Dumbarton	0	10,836
1892	Celtic	1	Queen's Park	0	40,000
	replayed due to spectator disruption				
Replay	Celtic	5	Queen's Park	1	26,000
1893	Queen's Park	0	Celtic	1	18,771
	replayed due to frosty pitch				
Replay	Queen's Park	2	Celtic	1	13,239
1894	Rangers	3	Celtic	1	17,000
1895	St.Bernard's	2	Renton	1	15,000
1896	Hearts	3	Hibernian	1	17,034
1897	Rangers	5	Dumbarton	1	14,000
1898	Rangers	2	Kilmarnock	0	13,000
1899	Celtic	2	Rangers	0	25,000
1900	Celtic	4	Queen's Park	3	15,000
1901	Hearts	4	Celtic	3	12,000
1902	Hibernian	1	Celtic	0	16,000
1903	Rangers	1	Hearts	1	40,000
Replay	Rangers	0	Hearts	0	35,000
Replay	Rangers	2	Hearts	0	32,000
1904	Celtic	3	Rangers	2	65,000
1905	Third Lanark	0	Rangers	0	54,000
Replay	Third Lanark	3	Rangers	1	55,000
1906	Hearts	1	Third Lanark	0	25,000
1907	Celtic	3	Hearts	0	50,000
1908	Celtic	5	St.Mirren	1	55,000
1909	Celtic	2	Rangers	2	70,000
Replay	Celtic	1	Rangers	1	61,000
	Owing to a riot, cup withheld after two drawn games				
1910	Dundee	2	Clyde	2	62,300
Replay	Dundee	0	Clyde	0	24,500
Replay	Dundee	2	Clyde	1	25,400
1911	Celtic	0	Hamilton A	0	45,000
Replay	Celtic	2	Hamilton A	0	24,700
1912	Celtic	2	Clyde	0	46,000
1913	Falkirk	2	Raith Rovers	0	45,000
1914	Celtic	0	Hibernian	0	56,000
Replay	Celtic	4	Hibernian	1	40,000
1920	Kilmarnock	3	Albion Rovers	2	95,000
1921	Partick Thistle	1	Rangers	0	28,300
1922	Morton	1	Rangers	0	75,000
1923	Celtic	1	Hibernian	0	80,100
1924	Airdrieonians	2	Hibernian	0	59,218
1925	Celtic	2	Dundee	1	75,137
1926	St.Mirren	2	Celtic	0	98,620
1927	Celtic	3	East Fife	1	80,070
1928	Rangers	4	Celtic	0	118,115
1929	Kilmarnock	2	Rangers	0	114,708
1930	Rangers	0	Partick Thistle	0	107,475
Replay	Rangers	2	Partick Thistle	1	103,686
1931	Celtic	2	Motherwell	2	105,000
Replay	Celtic	4	Motherwell	2	98,579
1932	Rangers	1	Kilmarnock	1	111,982
Replay	Rangers	3	Kilmarnock	0	104,965
1933	Celtic	1	Motherwell	0	102,339
1934	Rangers	5	St.Mirren	0	113,403
1935	Rangers	2	Hamilton A	1	87,286
1936	Rangers	1	Third Lanark	0	88,859
1937	Celtic	2	Aberdeen	1	147,365
1938	East Fife	1	Kilmarnock	1	80,091
Replay	East Fife	4	Kilmarnock	2	92,716
1939	Clyde	4	Motherwell	0	94,799
1947	Aberdeen	2	Hibernian	1	82,140
1948	Rangers	1	Morton	1	129,176
Replay	Rangers	1	Morton	0	133,570
1949	Rangers	4	Clyde	1	108,435
1950	Rangers	3	East Fife	0	118,262
1951	Celtic	1	Motherwell	0	131,943
1952	Motherwell	4	Dundee	0	136,274
1953	Rangers	1	Aberdeen	1	129,681
Replay	Rangers	1	Aberdeen	0	112,619
1954	Celtic	2	Aberdeen	1	129,926
1955	Clyde	1	Celtic	1	106,111
Replay	Clyde	1	Celtic	0	68,735
1956	Hearts	3	Celtic	1	133,339
1957	Falkirk	1	Kilmarnock	1	83,000
Replay	Falkirk	2	Kilmarnock	1	79,785
1958	Clyde	1	Hibernian	0	95,124
1959	St.Mirren	3	Aberdeen	1	108,591
1960	Rangers	2	Kilmarnock	0	108,017
1961	Dunfermline A	0	Celtic	0	113,618
Replay	Dunfermline A	2	Celtic	0	87,866
1962	Rangers	2	St.Mirren	0	126,930
1963	Rangers	1	Celtic	1	129,527
Replay	Rangers	3	Celtic	0	120,263
1964	Rangers	3	Dundee	1	120,982
1965	Celtic	3	Dunfermline A	2	108,800
1966	Rangers	0	Celtic	0	126,552
Replay	Rangers	1	Celtic	0	98,202
1967	Celtic	2	Aberdeen	0	127,117
1968	Dunfermline A	3	Hearts	1	56,366

Year	Winners		Runners-up		Attendance
1969	Celtic	4	Rangers	0	132,874
1970	Aberdeen	3	Celtic	1	108,434
1971	Celtic	1	Rangers	1	120,092
Replay	Celtic	2	Rangers	1	103,332
1972	Celtic	6	Hibernian	1	106,102
1973	Rangers	3	Celtic	2	122,714
1974	Celtic	3	Dundee United	0	75,959
1975	Celtic	3	Airdrieonians	1	75,457
1976	Rangers	3	Hearts	1	85,354
1977	Celtic	1	Rangers	0	54,252
1978	Rangers	2	Aberdeen	1	61,563
1979	Rangers	0	Hibernian	0	50,610
Replay	Rangers	0	Hibernian	0	33,506
Replay	Rangers	3	Hibernian	2	30,602
1980	Celtic	1	Rangers	0	70,303
1981	Rangers	0	Dundee United	0	55,000
Replay	Rangers	4	Dundee United	1	43,009
1982	Aberdeen	4	Rangers	1 *	53,788
1983	Aberdeen	1	Rangers	0 *	62,979
1984	Aberdeen	2	Celtic	1 *	58,900
1985	Celtic	2	Dundee United	1	60,346
1986	Aberdeen	3	Hearts	0	62,841

Year	Winners		Runners-up		Attendance
1987	St Mirren	1	Dundee United	0 *	51,792
1988	Celtic	2	Dundee United	1	74,000
1989	Celtic	1	Rangers	0	72,069
1990	Aberdeen	0	Celtic	0 *	60,493

Aberdeen won 9-8 on penalties

* after extra time

Most wins: 29 Celtic, 24 Rangers
Biggest win: 36-0 Arbroath v Bon Accord (1st round) 12 Sep 1885
Biggest win (final): 6-1 Renton v Cambuslang 4 Feb 1888, 6-1 Celtic v Hibernian 6 May 1972
Most individual goals in one match: 13 John Petrie (Arbroath v Bon Accord) 1st round 5 Sep 1885
Most winner's medals: 8 Charles Campbell (Queen's Park) 1874-6, 1880-2, 1884, 1886

Graeme Souness played for Middlesbrough, Liverpool and Sampdoria before becoming player-manager of Glasgow Rangers. He made 54 international appearances for Scotland from 1975-86 (**All-Sport/David Cannon**)

SCOTTISH LEAGUE CUP

The Scottish League Cup was first contested in 1946/7, replacing the Southern League Cup that had been played during the war. Prior to 1977/8 the teams were split into eight or nine groups, with the winners going through to a knockout competition. Since 1977, however, it has been run on a strict knockout basis. The Cup became known as the Skol Cup in 1984/5. All finals have been at Hampden Park, unless otherwise stated. Year shown is second half of the season, although the matches have often been contested the previous year.

Year	Winners		Runners-up		
1947	Rangers	4	Aberdeen	0	
1948	East Fife	1	Falkirk	1	*
Replay	East Fife	4	Falkirk	1	
1949	Rangers	2	Raith Rovers	0	
1950	East Fife	3	Dunfermline A	0	
1951	Motherwell	3	Hibernian	0	
1952	Dundee	3	Rangers	2	
1953	Dundee	2	Kilmarnock	0	
1954	East Fife	3	Partick Thistle	2	
1955	Hearts	4	Motherwell	2	
1956	Aberdeen	2	St.Mirren	1	
1957	Celtic	0	Partick Thistle	0	*
Replay	Celtic	3	Partick Thistle	0	
1958	Celtic	7	Rangers	1	
1959	Hearts	5	Partick Thistle	1	
1960	Hearts	2	Third Lanark	1	
1961	Rangers	2	Kilmarnock	0	
1962	Rangers	1	Hearts	1	*
Replay	Rangers	3	Hearts	1	
1963	Hearts	1	Kilmarnock	0	
1964	Rangers	5	Morton	0	
1965	Rangers	2	Celtic	1	
1966	Celtic	2	Rangers	1	
1967	Celtic	1	Rangers	0	
1968	Celtic	5	Dundee	3	
1969	Celtic	6	Hibernian	2	
1970	Celtic	1	St.Johnstone	0	
1971	Rangers	1	Celtic	0	
1972	Partick Thistle	4	Celtic	1	
1973	Hibernian	2	Celtic	1	
1974	Dundee	1	Celtic	0	
1975	Celtic	6	Hibernian	3	
1976	Rangers	1	Celtic	0	
1977	Aberdeen	2	Celtic	1	
1978	Rangers	2	Celtic	1	
1979	Rangers	2	Aberdeen	1	
1980	Dundee United	0	Aberdeen	0	
Replay	Dundee United	3	Aberdeen	0	**
1981	Dundee United	3	Dundee	0	**
1982	Rangers	2	Dundee United	1	
1983	Celtic	2	Rangers	1	
1984	Rangers	3	Celtic	2	*
1985	Rangers	1	Dundee United	0	
1986	Aberdeen	3	Hibernian	0	
1987	Rangers	2	Celtic	1	

Year	Winners		Runners-up		
1988	Rangers	3	Aberdeen	3	*
	(Rangers won 5-3 on penalties)				
1989	Rangers	3	Aberdeen	2	
1990	Aberdeen	2	Rangers	1	*

* after extra time   ** Played at Dens Park, Dundee

Most wins: 16 Rangers, 9 Celtic
Biggest win (final): 7-1 Celtic v Rangers 19 Oct 1957

Most successful Scottish clubs - domination of Celtic and Rangers

Wins in the Scottish League, Cup and League Cup:

	League	Cup	Lg.Cup	Total
Rangers	40	24	16	80
Celtic	34	29	9	72
Aberdeen	4	7	4	15
Hearts	5	5	4	14
Queen's Park	-	10	-	10

NORTH AMERICAN SOCCER LEAGUE (NASL)

The North American Soccer League (NASL) was formed in 1968 through the merger of the United States Soccer Association and the National Professional Soccer League. The recruiting of such big international names as Pele and Franz Beckenbauer in the 1970s resulted in crowds topping the 70,000 mark. After that, however, the league declined and from a peak of 24 teams in 1979, the numbers dwindled until the NASL folded in 1985.

Champions:

1968 Atlanta Chiefs	1977 New York Cosmos
1969 Kansas City Spurs	1978 New York Cosmos
1970 Rochester Lancers	1979 Vancouver Whitecaps
1971 Dallas Tornados	1980 New York Cosmos
1972 New York Cosmos	1981 Chicago Sting
1973 Philadelphia Atoms	1982 New York Cosmos
1974 Los Angeles Aztecs	1983 Tulsa Roughnecks
1975 Tampa Bay Rowdies	1984 Chicago Sting
1976 Toronto Metro-Croatia	

Most wins: 5 New York Cosmos

MAJOR INDOOR SOCCER LEAGUE (MISL)

Founded in 1978 at a time when outdoor soccer in the USA was enjoying a boom. The NASL collapsed in 1985 and in 1988 the MISL was reduced from eleven to seven teams. The champions each year are decided by an end-of-season best-of-seven match. *Winners:*

1979-82 New York Arrows
1983   San Diego Sockers
1984   Baltimore Blast
1985-6   San Diego Sockers
1987   Dallas Sidekicks
1988-90 San Diego Sockers

ATHLETICS

Competition in running, jumping or throwing naturally dates back into pre-history. The earliest evidence we have of organised running is from about 3800BC in Egypt, and athletic achievements were particularly prized at the ancient Olympic Games in Greece. Those Games were more than just sporting contests for they were also great artistic and cultural festivals maintaining the Greek ideal of perfection of mind and body. They provided the inspiration for the modern Olympic Games, which have provided the focus for athletics since their re-introduction in 1896. At least that is until recently, for separate world championships for all events were instituted in 1983, and nowadays there is a plethora of top-class competition. The first national championships were those of England in 1866, organised by the Amateur Athletic Club. These preceded the formation of the Amateur Athletic Association in 1880.

International governing body: The International Amateur Athletic Federation (IAAF), formed in 1912 initially with 17 members. It ratified the first list of world records in 1914. The IAAF now has 187 nations affiliated to it, more than any other international organisation, sporting or otherwise.

Harrison Dillard was the world's greatest high hurdler of the 1940s but missed the team for the 1948 Olympics when he hit three hurdles in the US Trials. So he turned to the flat 100 metres, qualified, and won the Olympic gold. In 1952 he added the 110m hurdles gold medal (Hulton-Deutsch)

OLYMPIC GAMES

The first Olympic Games of the modern era were staged in Athens, Greece, 6 – 15 April 1896, when just 59 athletes from ten nations contested the athletics events. The 1900 and 1904 Games were also small-scale affairs, with just over 100 athletes at each, but from 1908 the Games grew rapidly in importance to true world championships. Women's events were first included in 1928, and the number of contestants in athletics passed 1000 for the first time at the 1960 Games.

Note that automatic timing was first used at the Olympic Games in 1932. In this list of champions, automatic times are given, where known, for proper comparisons. OR indicates Olympic record.

Note that times are given in minutes : seconds, distances in metres.

MEN

100 metres
1896	Thomas Burke (USA)	12.0
1900	Francis Jarvis (USA)	11.0
1904	Archie Hahn (USA)	11.0
1906	Archie Hahn (USA)	11.2
1908	Reginald Walker (SAf)	10.8
1912	Ralph Craig (USA)	10.8
1920	Charles Paddock (USA)	10.8
1924	Harold Abrahams (UK)	10.6
1928	Percy Williams (Can)	10.8
1932	Eddie Tolan (USA)	10.38
1936	Jesse Owens (USA)	10.3
1948	Harrison Dillard (USA)	10.3
1952	Lindy Remigino (USA)	10.79
1956	Bobby Morrow (USA)	10.62
1960	Armin Hary (FRG)	10.32
1964	Robert Hayes (USA)	10.06
1968	James Hines (USA)	9.95
1972	Valeriy Borzov (USSR)	10.14
1976	Hasely Crawford (Tri)	10.06
1980	Allan Wells (UK)	10.25
1984	Carl Lewis (USA)	9.99
1988	Carl Lewis (USA)	9.92 OR

200 metres
1900	Walter Tewksbury (USA)	22.2
1904	Archie Hahn (USA)	21.6
1908	Robert Kerr (Can)	22.6
1912	Ralph Craig (USA)	21.7
1920	Allen Woodring (USA)	22.0
1924	Jackson Scholz (USA)	21.6
1928	Percy Williams (Can)	21.8
1932	Eddie Tolan (USA)	21.12
1936	Jesse Owens (USA)	20.7
1948	Melvin Patton (USA)	21.1

1952	Andrew Stanfield (USA) 20.81
1956	Bobby Morrow (USA) 20.75
1960	Livio Berruti (Ita) 20.62
1964	Henry Carr (USA) 20.36
1968	Tommie Smith (USA) 19.83
1972	Valeriy Borzov (USSR) 20.00
1976	Donald Quarrie (Jam) 20.22
1980	Pietro Mennea (Ita) 20.19
1984	Carl Lewis (USA) 19.80
1988	Joe DeLoach (USA) 19.75 OR

400 metres

1896	Thomas Burke (USA) 54.2
1900	Maxie Long (USA) 49.4
1904	Harry Hillman (USA) 49.2
1906	Paul Pilgrim (USA) 53.2
1908	Wyndham Halswelle (UK) 50.0
1912	Charles Reidpath (USA) 48.2
1920	Bevil Rudd (SAf) 49.6
1924	Eric Liddell (UK) 47.6
1928	Ray Barbuti (USA) 47.8
1932	Bill Carr (USA) 46.28
1936	Archie Williams (USA) 46.66
1948	Arthur Wint (Jam) 46.2
1952	George Rhoden (Jam) 46.09
1956	Charles Jenkins (USA) 46.86
1960	Otis Davis (USA) 45.07
1964	Michael Larrabee (USA) 45.15
1968	Lee Evans (USA) 43.86 OR
1972	Vincent Matthews (USA) 44.66
1976	Alberto Juantorena (Cub) 44.26
1980	Viktor Markin (USSR) 44.60
1984	Alonzo Babers (USA) 44.27
1988	Steve Lewis (USA) 43.87

800 metres

1896	Edwin Flack (Aus) 2:11.0
1900	Alfred Tysoe (UK) 2:01.2
1904	James Lightbody (USA) 1:56.0
1906	Paul Pilgrim (USA) 2:01.5
1908	Mel Sheppard (USA) 1:52.8
1912	James Meredith (USA) 1:51.9
1920	Albert Hill (UK) 1:53.4
1924	Douglas Lowe (UK) 1:52.4
1928	Douglas Lowe (UK) 1:51.8
1932	Tom Hampson (UK) 1:49.70
1936	John Woodruff (USA) 1:52.9
1948	Malvin Whitfield (USA) 1:49.2
1952	Malvin Whitfield (USA) 1:49.34
1956	Thomas Courtney (USA) 1:47.75
1960	Peter Snell (NZ) 1:46.48
1964	Peter Snell (NZ) 1:45.1
1968	Ralph Doubell (Aus) 1:44.40
1972	David Wottle (USA) 1:45.86
1976	Alberto Juantorena (Cub) 1:43.50
1980	Steven Ovett (UK) 1:45.40
1984	Joaquim Cruz (Bra) 1:43.00 OR
1988	Paul Ereng (Ken) 1:43.45

1500 metres

1896	Edwin Flack (Aus) 4:33.2
1900	Charles Bennett (UK) 4:06.2
1904	James Lightbody (USA) 4:05.4
1906	James Lightbody (USA) 4:12.0
1908	Mel Sheppard (USA) 4:03.4
1912	Arnold Jackson (UK) 3:56.8
1920	Albert Hill (UK) 4:01.8
1924	Paavo Nurmi (Fin) 3:53.6
1928	Harri Larva (Fin) 3:53.2
1932	Luigi Beccali (Ita) 3:51.20
1936	Jack Lovelock (NZ) 3:47.8
1948	Henry Eriksson (Swe) 3:49.8
1952	Josef Barthel (Lux) 3:45.28
1956	Ron Delany (Ire) 3:41.49
1960	Herbert Elliott (Aus) 3:35.6
1964	Peter Snell (NZ) 3:38.1
1968	Kipchoge Keino (Ken) 3:34.91
1972	Pekka Vasala (Fin) 3:36.33
1976	John Walker (NZ) 3:39.17
1980	Sebastian Coe (UK) 3:38.40
1984	Sebastian Coe (UK) 3:32.53 OR
1988	Peter Rono (Ken) 3:35.96

5000 metres

1912	Hannes Kolehmainen (Fin) 14:36.6
1920	Joseph Guillemot (Fra) 14:55.6
1924	Paavo Nurmi (Fin) 14:31.2
1928	Ville Ritola (Fin) 14:38.0
1932	Lauri Lehtinen (Fin) 14:29.91
1936	Gunnar Höckert (Fin) 14:22.2
1948	Gaston Reiff (Bel) 14:17.6
1952	Emil Zátopek (Cs) 14:06.72
1956	Vladimir Kuts (USSR) 13:39.86
1960	Murray Halberg (NZ) 13:43.4
1964	Robert Schul (USA) 13:48.8
1968	Mohamed Gammoudi (Tun) 14:05.0
1972	Lasse Viren (Fin) 13:26.42
1976	Lasse Viren (Fin) 13:24.76
1980	Miruts Yifter (Eth) 13.20.91
1984	Saïd Aouita (Mor) 13:05.59 OR
1988	John Ngugi (Ken) 13:11.70

10 000 metres

1912	Hannes Kolehmainen (Fin) 31:20.8
1920	Paavo Nurmi (Fin) 31:45.8
1924	Ville Ritola (Fin) 30:23.2
1928	Paavo Nurmi (Fin) 30:18.8
1932	Janusz Kusocinski (Pol) 30:11.4
1936	Ilmari Salminen (Fin) 30:15.4
1948	Emil Zátopek (Cs) 29:59.6
1952	Emil Zátopek (Cs) 29:17.0
1956	Vladimir Kuts (USSR) 28:45.60
1960	Pyotr Bolotnikov (USSR) 28:32.18
1964	William Mills (USA) 28:24.4
1968	Naftali Temu (Ken) 29:27.4
1972	Lasse Viren (Fin) 27:38.35
1976	Lasse Viren (Fin) 27:40.38

1980	Miruts Yifter (Eth) 27:42.69
1984	Alberto Cova (Ita) 27:47.54
1988	Brahim Boutayeb (Mor) 27:21.46 OR

Marathon (42.295km)

1896	Spyridon Louis (Gre) 2:58:50.0 (40km)
1900	Michel Théato (Fra) 2:59:45.0 (40.26km)
1904	Thomas Hicks (USA) 3:28:35.0 (40km)
1906	William Sherring (Can) 2:51:23.6 (41.86km)
1908	John Hayes (USA) 2:55:18.4
1912	Kenneth McArthur (SAf) 2:36:54.8 (40.2km)
1920	Hannes Kolehmainen (Fin) 2:32:35.8 (42.75km)
1924	Albin Stenroos (Fin) 2:41:22.6
1928	Mohamed Boughéra El Ouafi (Fra) 2:32:57.0
1932	Juan Carlos Zabala (Arg) 2:31:36.0
1936	Kitei Son (Jap)* 2:29:19.2
1948	Delfo Cabrera (Arg) 2:34:51.6
1952	Emil Zátopek (Cs) 2:23:03.2
1956	Alain Mimoun (Fra) 2:25:00.0
1960	Abebe Bikila (Eth) 2:15:16.2
1964	Abebe Bikila (Eth) 2:12:11.2
1968	Mamo Wolde (Eth) 2:20:26.4
1972	Frank Shorter (USA) 2:12:19.8
1976	Waldemar Cierpinski (GDR) 2:09:55
1980	Waldemar Cierpinski (GDR) 2:11:03
1984	Carlos Lopes (Por) 2:09:21 OR
1988	Gelindo Bordin (Ita) 2:10:32

* Actually the Korean Sohn Kee-chung

110 metres hurdles

1896	Thomas Curtis (USA) 17.6
1900	Alvin Kraenzlein (USA) 15.4
1904	Fred Schule (USA) 16.0
1906	Robert Leavitt (USA) 16.2
1908	Forrest Smithson (USA) 15.0
1912	Fred Kelly (USA) 15.1
1920	Earl Thomson (Can) 14.8
1924	Daniel Kinsey (USA) 15.0
1928	Sydney Atkinson (SAf) 14.8
1932	George Saling (USA) 14.57
1936	Forrest Towns (USA) 14.2
1948	William Porter (USA) 13.9
1952	Harrison Dillard (USA) 13.91
1956	Lee Calhoun (USA) 13.70
1960	Lee Calhoun (USA) 13.98
1964	Hayes Jones (USA) 13.67
1968	Willie Davenport (USA) 13.33
1972	Rodney Milburn (USA) 13.24
1976	Guy Drut (Fra) 13.30
1980	Thomas Munkelt (GDR) 13.39
1984	Roger Kingdom (USA) 13.20
1988	Roger Kingdom (USA) 12.98 OR

400 metres hurdles

1900	Walter Tewksbury (USA) 57.6
1904	Harry Hillman (USA) 53.0
1908	Charles Bacon (USA) 55.0
1920	Frank Loomis (USA) 54.0
1924	Morgan Taylor (USA) 52.6
1928	Lord Burghley (UK) 53.4
1932	Robert Tisdall (Ire) 51.67
1936	Glenn Hardin (USA) 52.4
1948	Roy Cochran (USA) 51.1
1952	Charles Moore (USA) 51.06
1956	Glenn Davis (USA) 50.29
1960	Glenn Davis (USA) 49.51
1964	Rex Cawley (USA) 49.69
1968	David Hemery (UK) 48.12
1972	John Akii-Bua (Uga) 47.82
1976	Edwin Moses (USA) 47.63
1980	Volker Beck (GDR) 48.70
1984	Edwin Moses (USA) 47.75
1988	Andre Phillips (USA) 47.19 OR

Steeplechase

1900	George Orton (Can) 7:34.4 (2500m)
1900	John Rimmer (UK) 12:58.4 (4000m)
1904	James Lightbody (USA) 7:39.6 (2590m)
1908	Arthur Russell (UK) 10:47.8 (3200m)

3000 metres steeplechase

1920	Percy Hodge (UK) 10:00.4
1924	Ville Ritola (Fin) 9:33.6
1928	Toivo Loukola (Fin) 9:21.8
1932	Volmari Iso-Hollo (Fin) 10:33.4*
1936	Volmari Iso-Hollo (Fin) 9:03.8
1948	Tore Sjöstrand (Swe) 9:04.6
1952	Horace Ashenfelter (USA) 8:45.68
1956	Christopher Brasher (UK) 8:41.35
1960	Zdzislaw Kryszkowiak (Pol) 8:34.31
1964	Gaston Roelants (Bel) 8:30.8
1968	Amos Biwott (Ken) 8:51.0
1972	Kipchoge Keino (Ken) 8:23.64
1976	Anders Gärderud (Swe) 8:08.02
1980	Bronislaw Malinowski (Pol) 8:09.70
1984	Julius Korir (Ken) 8:11.80
1988	Julius Kariuki (Ken) 8:05.51 OR

* due to lap counting error distance was 3460 metres

High jump

1896	Ellery Clark (USA) 1.81
1900	Irving Baxter (USA) 1.90
1904	Samuel Jones (USA) 1.80
1906	Con Leahy (UK/Ire) 1.77
1908	Harry Porter (USA) 1.90
1912	Alma Richards (USA) 1.93
1920	Richard Landon (USA) 1.94
1924	Harold Osborn (USA) 1.98
1928	Robert King (USA) 1.94
1932	Duncan McNaughton (Can) 1.97
1936	Cornelius Johnson (USA) 2.03
1948	John Winter (Aus) 1.98
1952	Walter Davis (USA) 2.04
1956	Charles Dumas (USA) 2.12
1960	Robert Shavlakadze (USSR) 2.16
1964	Valeriy Brumel (USSR) 2.18

1968	Dick Fosbury (USA) 2.24	1904	Myer Prinstein (USA) 14.35
1972	Jüri Tarmak (USSR) 2.23	1906	Peter O'Connor (UK/Ire) 14.07
1976	Jacek Wszola (Pol) 2.25	1908	Tim Ahearne (UK/Ire) 14.91
1980	Gerd Wessig (GDR) 2.36	1912	Gustaf Lindblom (Swe) 14.76
1984	Dietmar Mögenburg (FRG) 2.35	1920	Vilho Tuulos (Fin) 14.50
1988	Gennadiy Avdeyenko (USSR) 2.38 OR	1924	Anthony Winter (Aus) 15.52

Pole vault

1896	William Hoyt (USA) 3.30	1928	Mikio Oda (Jap) 15.21
1900	Irving Baxter (USA) 3.30	1932	Chuhei Nambu (Jap) 15.72
1904	Charles Dvorak (USA) 3.50	1936	Naoto Tajima (Jap) 16.00
1906	Fernand Gonder (Fra) 3.40	1948	Arne Åhman (Swe) 15.40
1908	Edward Cooke & Alfred Gilbert (USA) 3.71	1952	Adhemar Ferreira da Silva (Bra) 16.22
1912	Harry Babcock (USA) 3.95	1956	Adhemar Ferreira da Silva (Bra) 16.35
1920	Frank Foss (USA) 4.09	1960	Jozef Schmidt (Pol) 16.81
1924	Lee Barnes (USA) 3.95	1964	Jozef Schmidt (Pol) 16.85
1928	Sabin Carr (USA) 4.20	1968	Viktor Saneyev (USSR) 17.39
1932	Bill Miller (USA) 4.31	1972	Viktor Saneyev (USSR) 17.35
1936	Earle Meadows (USA) 4.35	1976	Viktor Saneyev (USSR) 17.29
1948	Guinn Smith (USA) 4.30	1980	Jaak Uudmäe (USSR) 17.35
1952	Robert Richards (USA) 4.55	1984	Al Joyner (USA) 17.26
1956	Robert Richards (USA) 4.56	1988	Khristo Markov (Bul) 17.61 OR
1960	Donald Bragg (USA) 4.70		

Shot

1964	Frederick Hansen (USA) 5.10	1896	Robert Garrett (USA) 11.22
1968	Bob Seagren (USA) 5.40	1900	Richard Sheldon (USA) 14.10
1972	Wolfgang Nordwig (GDR) 5.50	1904	Ralph Rose (USA) 14.80
1976	Tadeusz Slusarski (Pol) 5.50	1906	Martin Sheridan (USA) 12.32
1980	Wladyslaw Kozakiewicz (Pol) 5.78	1908	Ralph Rose (USA) 14.21
1984	Pierre Quinon (Fra) 5.75	1912	Patrick McDonald (USA) 15.34
1988	Sergey Bubka (USSR) 5.90 OR	1920	Ville Pörhölä (Fin) 14.81
		1924	Clarence Houser (USA) 14.99

Long jump

1896	Ellery Clark (USA) 6.35	1928	John Kuck (USA) 15.87
1900	Alvin Kraenzlein (USA) 7.18	1932	Leo Sexton (USA) 16.00
1904	Myer Prinstein (USA) 7.34	1936	Hans Woellke (Ger) 16.20
1906	Myer Prinstein (USA) 7.20	1948	Wilbur Thompson (USA) 17.12
1908	Francis Irons (USA) 7.48	1952	Parry O'Brien (USA) 17.41
1912	Albert Gutterson (USA) 7.60	1956	Parry O'Brien (USA) 18.57
1920	William Pettersson (Swe) 7.15	1960	William Nieder (USA) 19.68
1924	William De Hart Hubbard (USA) 7.44	1964	Dallas Long (USA) 20.33
1928	Edward Hamm (USA) 7.73	1968	Randy Matson (USA) 20.54
1932	Edward Gordon (USA) 7.64	1972	Wladyslaw Komar (Pol) 21.18
1936	Jesse Owens (USA) 8.06	1976	Udo Beyer (GDR) 21.05
1948	William Steele (USA) 7.82	1980	Vladimir Kiselyov (USSR) 21.35
1952	Jerome Biffle (USA) 7.57	1984	Alessandro Andrei (Ita) 21.26
1956	Gregory Bell (USA) 7.83	1988	Ulf Timmermann (GDR) 22.47 OR
1960	Ralph Boston (USA) 8.12		

Discus

1964	Lynn Davies (UK) 8.07	1896	Robert Garrett (USA) 29.15
1968	Bob Beamon (USA) 8.90 OR	1900	Rudolf Bauer (Hun) 36.04
1972	Randy Williams (USA) 8.24	1904	Martin Sheridan (USA) 39.28
1976	Arnie Robinson (USA) 8.35	1906	Martin Sheridan (USA) 41.46
1980	Lutz Dombrowski (GDR) 8.54	1908	Martin Sheridan (USA) 40.89
1984	Carl Lewis (USA) 8.54	1912	Armas Taipale (Fin) 45.21
1988	Carl Lewis (USA) 8.72	1920	Elmer Niklander (Fin) 44.68
		1924	Clarence Houser (USA) 46.15

Triple jump

1896	James Connolly (USA) 13.71	1928	Clarence Houser (USA) 47.32
1900	Myer Prinstein (USA) 14.47	1932	John Anderson (USA) 49.49
		1936	Ken Carpenter (USA) 50.48
		1948	Adolfo Consolini (Ita) 52.78

1952	Sim Iness (USA) 55.03
1956	Al Oerter (USA) 56.36
1960	Al Oerter (USA) 59.18
1964	Al Oerter (USA) 61.00
1968	Al Oerter (USA) 64.78
1972	Ludvik Danek (Cs) 64.40
1976	Mac Wilkins (USA) 67.50
1980	Viktor Rashchupkin (USSR) 66.64
1984	Rolf Danneberg (FRG) 66.60
1988	Jürgen Schult (GDR) 68.82 OR

Hammer

1900	John Flanagan (USA) 49.73
1904	John Flanagan (USA) 51.23
1908	John Flanagan (USA) 51.92
1912	Matt McGrath (USA) 54.74
1920	Patrick Ryan (USA) 52.87
1924	Fred Tootell (USA) 53.29
1928	Patrick O'Callaghan (Ire) 51.39
1932	Patrick O'Callaghan (Ire) 53.92
1936	Karl Hein (Ger) 56.49
1948	Imre Németh (Hun) 56.07
1952	József Csermak (Hun) 60.34
1956	Harold Connolly (USA) 63.19
1960	Vasiliy Rudenkov (USSR) 67.10
1964	Romuald Klim (USSR) 69.74
1968	Gyula Zsivótzky (Hun) 73.36
1972	Anatoliy Bondarchuk (USSR) 75.50
1976	Yuriy Sedykh (USSR) 77.52
1980	Yuriy Sedykh (USSR) 81.80

Jürgen Schult, world record holder and Olympic champion in the discus (**All-Sport/Gray Mortimore**)

| 1984 | Juha Tiainen (Fin) 78.08 |
| 1988 | Sergey Litvinov (USSR) 84.80 OR |

Javelin

1906	Erik Lemming (Swe) 53.90
1908	Erik Lemming (Swe) 54.82
1912	Erik Lemming (Swe) 60.64
1920	Jonni Myyrä (Fin) 65.78
1924	Jonni Myyrä (Fin) 62.96
1928	Erik Lundkvist (Swe) 66.60
1932	Matti Järvinen (Fin) 72.71
1936	Gerhard Stöck (Ger) 71.84
1948	Tapio Rautavaara (Fin) 69.77
1952	Cyrus Young (USA) 73.78
1956	Egil Danielsen (Nor) 85.71
1960	Viktor Tsibulenko (USSR) 84.64
1964	Pauli Nevala (Fin) 82.66
1968	Janis Lusis (USSR) 90.10
1972	Klaus Wolfermann (FRG) 90.48
1976	Miklós Németh (Hun) 94.58 OR
1980	Dainis Kula (USSR) 91.20
1984	Arto Harkönen (Fin) 86.76
1988	Tapio Korjus (Fin) 84.28

Decathlon (points re-scored on 1984 tables)

1912	Jim Thorpe (USA) 6564 #
1920	Helge Lövland (Nor) 5804
1924	Harold Osborn (USA) 6476
1928	Paavo Yrjölä (Fin) 6587*
1932	James Bausch (USA) 6735*
1936	Glenn Morris (USA) 7254
1948	Robert Mathias (USA) 6628
1952	Robert Mathias (USA) 7592
1956	Milton Campbell (USA) 7614
1960	Rafer Johnson (USA) 7926
1964	Willi Holdorf (FRG) 7794 est
1968	Bill Toomey (USA) 8144
1972	Nikolay Avilov (USSR) 8466
1976	Bruce Jenner (USA) 8634
1980	Daley Thompson (UK) 8522
1984	Daley Thompson (UK) 8847 OR
1988	Christian Schenk (GDR) 8488

 # disqualified for professionalism, and gold given to Hugo Weislander (Swe) 5965, but posthumously re-instated in 1982.
* On the 1984 tables, the second placed Akilles Järvinen scored 6645 in 1928 and 6879 in 1932!

20 000 metres walk

1956	Leonid Spirin (USSR) 1:31:27.4
1960	Vladimir Golubnichiy (USSR) 1:34:07.2
1964	Kenneth Matthews (UK) 1:29:34.0
1968	Vladimir Golubnichiy (USSR) 1:33:58.4
1972	Peter Frenkel (GDR) 1:26:42.4
1976	Daniel Bautista (Mex) 1:24:40.6
1980	Maurizio Damilano (Ita) 1:23:35.5
1984	Ernesto Canto (Mex) 1:23:13
1988	Jozef Pribilinec (Cs) 1:19:57 OR

50 000 metres walk

1932	Thomas Green (UK) 4:50:10.0
1936	Harold Whitlock (UK) 4:30:41.1
1948	John Ljunggren (Swe) 4:41:52.0
1952	Giuseppe Dordoni (Ita) 4:28:07.8
1956	Norman Read (NZ) 4:30:42.8
1960	Don Thompson (UK) 4:25:30.0
1964	Abdon Pamich (Ita) 4:11:12.4
1968	Christophe Höhne (GDR) 4:20:13.6
1972	Bernd Kannenberg (GDR) 3:56:11.6
1980	Hartwig Gauder (GDR) 3:49:24
1984	Raúl Gonzales (Mex) 3:47:26
1988	Vyacheslav Ivanenko (USSR) 3:38.29 OR

4x100 metres relay

1912	UK 42.4
1920	USA 42.2
1924	USA 41.0
1928	USA 41.0
1932	USA 40.1
1936	USA 39.8
1948	USA 40.6
1952	USA 40.26
1956	USA 39.59
1960	F.R Germany 39.66
1964	USA 39.06
1968	USA 38.23
1972	USA 38.19
1976	USA 38.83
1980	USSR 38.26
1984	USA 37.83 OR
1988	USSR 38.19

Medley relay

(200m, 200m, 400m, 800m)

1908	USA 3:29.4

4x400 metres relay

1912	USA 3:16.6
1920	UK 3:22.2
1924	USA 3:16.0
1928	USA 3:14.2
1932	USA 3:08.14
1936	UK 3:09.0
1948	USA 3:10.4
1952	Jamaica 3:04.04
1956	USA 3:04.80
1960	USA 3:02.37
1964	USA 3:00.71
1968	USA 2:56.16 OR
1972	Kenya 2:59.83
1976	USA 2:58.66
1980	USSR 3:01.08
1984	USA 2:57.91
1988	USA 2:56.16 OR

WOMEN

100 metres

1928	Elizabeth Robinson (USA) 12.2
1932	Stanislawa Walasiewicz (Pol) 11.9
1936	Helen Stephens (USA) 11.5
1948	Fanny Blankers-Koen (Hol) 11.9
1952	Marjorie Jackson (Aus) 11.65
1956	Betty Cuthbert (Aus) 11.82
1960	Wilma Rudolph (USA) 11.08
1964	Wyomia Tyus (USA) 11.49
1968	Wyomia Tyus (USA) 11.08
1972	Renate Stecher (GDR) 11.07
1976	Annegret Richter (FRG) 11.08
1980	Lyudmila Kondratyeva (USSR) 11.06
1984	Evelyn Ashford (USA) 10.97
1988	Florence Griffith-Joyner (USA) 10.54w (10.62 OR in quarter-final)

200 metres

1948	Fanny Blankers-Koen (Hol) 24.4
1952	Marjorie Jackson (Aus) 23.89
1956	Betty Cuthbert (Aus) 23.55
1960	Wilma Rudolph (USA) 24.03
1964	Edith Maguire (USA) 23.05
1968	Irena Szewinska (Pol) 22.58
1972	Renate Stecher (GDR) 22.40
1976	Bärbel Eckert (GDR) 22.37
1980	Bärbel Wöckel (née Eckert) (GDR) 22.03
1984	Valerie Brisco-Hooks (USA) 21.81
1988	Florence Griffith-Joyner (USA) 21.34 OR

400 metres

1964	Betty Cuthbert (Aus) 52.01
1968	Colette Besson (Fra) 52.03
1972	Monika Zehrt (GDR) 51.08
1976	Irena Szewinska (Pol) 49.29
1980	Marita Koch (GDR) 48.88
1984	Valerie Brisco-Hooks (USA) 48.83
1988	Olga Bryzgina (USSR) 48.65 OR

800 metres

1928	Lina Radke (Ger) 2:16.8
1960	Lyudmila Shevtsova (USSR) 2:04.50
1964	Ann Packer (UK) 2:01.1
1968	Madeline Manning (USA) 2:00.92
1972	Hildegard Falck (FRG) 1:58.55
1976	Tatyana Kazankina (USSR) 1:54.94
1980	Nadezhda Olizarenko (USSR) 1:53.43 OR
1984	Doina Melinte (Rom) 1:57.60
1988	Sigrun Wodars (GDR) 1:56.10

1500 metres

1972	Lyudmila Bragina (USSR) 4:01.38
1976	Tatyana Kazankina (USSR) 4:05.48
1980	Tatyana Kazankina (USSR) 3:56.56
1984	Gabriella Doria (Ita) 4:03.25
1988	Paula Ivan (Rom) 3:53.96 OR

Paula Ivan leads Doina Melinte at Pescara in 1989. Both Romanians have won Olympic gold medals, and are the world's fastest women milers, Ivan outdoors and Melinte indoors (All-Sport/Gray Mortimore)

3000 metres
1984   Maricica Puica (Rom) 8:35.96
1988   Tatyana Samolenko (USSR) 8:26.53 OR

10 000 metres
1988   Olga Bondarenko (USSR) 31:05.21 OR

Marathon
1984   Joan Benoit (USA) 2:24:52 OR
1988   Rosa Mota (Por) 2:25:40

80 metres hurdles
1932   Mildred Didrikson (USA) 11.7
1936   Trebisonda Valla (Ita) 11.75
1948   Fanny Blankers-Koen (Hol) 11.2
1952   Shirley Strickland (Aus) 11.03
1956   Shirley Strickland (Aus) 10.96
1960   Irina Press (USSR) 10.94
1964   Karin Balzer (GDR) 10.54
1968   Maureen Caird (Aus) 10.39

100 metres hurdles
1972   Annelie Ehrhardt (GDR) 12.59
1976   Johanna Schaller (GDR) 12.77
1980   Vera Komisova (USSR) 12.56
1984   Benita Fitzgerald-Brown (USA) 12.84
1988   Yordanka Donkova (Bul) 12.38 OR

400 metres hurdles
1984   Nawal El Moutawakil (Mor) 54.61
1988   Debbie Flintoff-King (Aus) 53.17 OR

High jump
1928   Ethel Catherwood (Can) 1.59
1932   Jean Shiley (USA) 1.65
1936   Ibolya Csák (Hun) 1.60
1948   Alice Coachman (USA) 1.68
1952   Esther Brand (SAf) 1.67
1956   Mildred McDaniel (USA) 1.76
1960   Iolanda Balas (Rom) 1.85
1964   Iolanda Balas (Rom) 1.90
1968   Miloslava Rezková (Cs) 1.82
1972   Ulrike Meyfarth (FRG) 1.92
1976   Rosemarie Ackermann (GDR) 1.93
1980   Sara Simeoni (Ita) 1.97
1984   Ulrike Meyfarth (FRG) 2.02
1988   Louise Ritter (USA) 2.03 OR

Long jump
1948   Olga Gyarmati (Hun) 5.69
1952   Yvette Williams (NZ) 6.24
1956   Elzbieta Krzesinska (Pol) 6.35
1960   Vyera Krepkina (USSR) 6.37
1964   Mary Rand (UK) 6.76
1968   Viorica Viscopoleanu (Rom) 6.82
1972   Heide Rosendahl (FRG) 6.78
1976   Angela Voigt (GDR) 6.72
1980   Tatyana Kolpakova (USSR) 7.06
1984   Anisoara Stanciu (Rom) 6.96
1988   Jackie Joyner-Kersee (USA) 7.40 OR

Shot
1948   Micheline Ostermeyer (Fra) 13.75
1952   Galina Zybina (USSR) 15.28
1956   Tamara Tishkyevich (USSR) 16.59
1960   Tamara Press (USSR) 17.32
1964   Tamara Press (USSR) 18.14
1968   Margitta Gummel (GDR) 19.61
1972   Nadezhda Chizhova (USSR) 21.03
1976   Ivanka Khristova (Bul) 21.16
1980   Ilona Slupianek (GDR) 22.41 OR
1984   Claudia Losch (FRG) 20.48
1988   Natalya Lisovskaya (USSR) 22.24

Discus
1928   Helena Konopacka (Pol) 39.62
1932   Lillian Copeland (USA) 40.58
1936   Gisela Mauermayer (Ger) 47.63
1948   Micheline Ostermeyer (Fra) 41.92
1952   Nina Ponomaryeva (USSR) 51.42
1956   Olga Fikotová (Cs) 53.69
1960   Nina Ponomaryeva (USSR) 55.10
1964   Tamara Press (USSR) 57.27
1968   Lia Manoliu (Rom) 58.28
1972   Faina Melnik (USSR) 66.62
1976   Evelin Schlaak (GDR) 69.00

1980   Evelin Jahl (née Schlaak) (GDR) 69.96
1984   Ria Stalmach (Hol) 65.36
1988   Martina Hellmann (GDR) 72.30 OR

Javelin
1932   Mildred Didrikson (USA) 43.68
1936   Tilly Fleischer (Ger) 45.18
1948   Herma Bauma (Aut) 45.57
1952   Dana Zátopková (Cs) 50.47
1956   Inese Jaunzeme (USSR) 53.86
1960   Elvira Ozolina (USSR) 55.98
1964   Mihaela Penes (Rom) 60.54
1968   Angéla Németh (Hun) 60.36
1972   Ruth Fuchs (GDR) 63.88
1976   Ruth Fuchs (GDR) 65.94
1980   Maria C.Colón (Cub) 68.40
1984   Tessa Sanderson (UK) 69.56
1988   Petra Felke (GDR) 74.68 OR

Pentathlon
80m hurdles, high jump, shot, long jump, 200m 1964-8.
100m hurdles replaced 80m hurdles from 1972 and 800m
replaced 200m from 1976. All scored on 1971 tables.
1964   Irina Press (USSR) 4702
1968   Ingrid Becker (FRG) 4559
1972   Mary Peters (UK) 4801
1976   Sigrun Siegl (GDR) 4745
1980   Nadezhda Tkachenko (USSR) 5083

Heptathlon
1984   Glynis Nunn (Aus) 6387
1988   Jackie Joyner-Kersee (USA) 7291 OR

4x100 metres relay
1928	Canada 48.4	1964	Poland 43.69
1932	USA 46.86	1968	USA 42.87
1936	USA 46.9	1972	FR Germany 42.81
1948	Netherlands 47.5	1976	GDR 42.55
1952	USA 46.14	1980	GDR 41.60 OR
1956	Australia 44.65	1984	USA 41.65
1960	USA 44.72	1988	USA 41.98

4x400 metres relay
1972	GDR 3:22.95	1984	USA 3:18.29
1976	GDR 3:19.23	1988	USSR 3:15.18 OR
1980	USSR 3:20.12		

Other discontinued events
60 metres
1900   Alvin Kraenzlein (USA) 7.0
1904   Archie Hahn (USA) 7.0
5 miles
1906   Henry Hawtrey (UK) 26:11.8
1908   Emil Voigt (UK) 25:11.2
Team race
1900   Great Britain (5000m)
1908   Great Britain (3 Miles)
1912   USA (3000m)

1920   USA (3000m)
1924   Finland (3000m)
Cross-country individual
1912   Hannes Kolehmainen (Fin) 45:11.6 (12 000m)
1920   Paavo Nurmi (Fin) 27:15.0 (8000m)
1924   Paavo Nurmi (Fin) 32:54.8 (10 000m)
Cross-country team
1904   USA
1912   Sweden
1920   Finland
1924   Finland
200 metres hurdles
1900   Alvin Kraenzlein (USA) 25.4
1904   Harry Hillman (USA) 24.6
Pentathlon
1906: standing long jump, Greek style discus, javelin,
192m race and Greco-Roman wrestling.
1912-24: long jump, javelin, 200m, discus and 1500m.
1906   Hjalmar Mellander (Swe)
1912   Jim Thorpe (USA)*
        Ferdinand Bie (Nor)
1920   Eero Lehtonen (Fin)
1924   Eero Lehtonen (Fin)
* posthumously reinstated as winner
Standing high jump
1900   Ray Ewry (USA) 1.655
1904   Ray Ewry (USA) 1.50
1906   Ray Ewry (USA) 1.565
1908   Ray Ewry (USA) 1.575
1912   Platt Adams (USA) 1.63
Standing long jump
1900   Ray Ewry (USA) 3.21
1904   Ray Ewry (USA) 3.476
1906   Ray Ewry (USA) 3.30
1908   Ray Ewry (USA) 3.335
1912   Konstantin Tsiklitiras (Gre) 3.37
Standing triple jump
1900   Ray Ewry (USA) 10.58
1904   Ray Ewry (USA) 10.55
56lb weight
1904   Etienne Desmarteau (Can) 10.465
1920   Patrick McDonald (USA) 11.265
Stone (6.4kg) put
1906   Nicolaos Georgantas (Gre) 19.925
Shot - both hands
(aggregate of throws with right and left hands)
1912   Ralph Rose (USA) 27.70
Discus - Greek style
1906   Werner Järvinen (Fin) 35.17
1908   Martin Sheridan (USA) 38.00
Discus - both hands
1912   Armas Taipale (Fin) 82.86
Javelin - free style
1908   Erik Lemming (Swe) 54.445
Javelin - both hands
1912   Julius Saaristo (Fin) 109.42
1500 metres walk
1906   George Bonhag (USA) 7:12.6

3000 metres walk
1906   György Sztantics (Hun) 15:13.2
1920   Ugo Frigerio (Ita) 13:14.2
3500 metres walk
1908   George Larner (UK) 14:55.0

10 000 metres walk
1912   George Goulding (Can) 46:28.4
1920   Ugo Frigerio (Ita) 48:06.2
1924   Ugo Frigerio (Ita) 47:49.0
1948   John Mikaelsson (Swe) 45:13.2
1952   John Mikaelsson (Swe) 45:02.8
10 miles walk
1908   George Larner (UK) 1:15:57.4

Most Medals G - Gold, S - Silver, B - Bronze

MEN		G	S	B	Years
12	Paavo Nurmi (Fin)	9	3	-	1920-8
10	Raymond Ewry (USA)	10	-	-	1900-8
9	Martin Sheridan (USA)	5	3	1	1906-8
8	Ville Ritola (Fin)	5	3	-	1924-8
7	Carl Lewis (USA)	6	1	-	1984-8
7	Eric Lemming (Swe)	4	-	3*	1906-12

* including one for tug of war

Others to win four gold medals:
James Lightbody (USA) 1904-6
Alvin Kraenzlein (USA) 1900
Archie Hahn (USA) 1904-06
James Lightbody (USA) 1904-06
Myer Prinstein (USA) 1900-06
Erik Lemming (Swe) 1906-12
Mel Sheppard (USA) 1908-12
Hannes Kolehmainen (Fin) 1912-20
Jesse Owens (USA) 1936
Emil Zátopek (Cs) 1948-52
Harrison Dillard (USA) 1948-52
Al Oerter (USA) 1956-68
Lasse Viren (Fin) 1972-76
Most Games contested: 6 Lia Manoliu (Rom) 1952-72, *women's discus, successively 6th, 9th, 3rd, 3rd, 1st, 9th.*

WOMEN		G	S	B	Years
7	Shirley de la Hunty (Aus)	3	1	3	1948-56
7	Irena Szewinska (Pol)	3	2	2	1964-76

Four gold medals:
Fanny Blankers-Koen (Hol) 1948
Betty Cuthbert (Aus) 1956-64
Bärbel Wöckel (GDR) 1976-80
Most gold medals at one Games
MEN: 5 Paavo Nurmi (Fin) 1924; 4 Alvin Kraenzlein (USA) 1900, Ville Ritola (Fin) 1924, Jesse Owens (USA) 1936, Carl Lewis (USA) 1984.
WOMEN: 4 Fanny Blankers-Koen (Hol) 1948.
Most medals at one Games
6 Ville Ritola (Fin) 4 gold, 2 silver 1924
Oldest gold medallists: MEN 42 years 23 days Pat McDonald (USA) 56lb weight 1920; **WOMEN:** 36 years 176 days Lia Manoliu (Rom) discus 1968.
Oldest medallists: MEN 48y 115d Tebbs Lloyd Johnson (UK) 3rd 50km walk 1948; WOMEN 37 years 348 days Dana Zátopková (Cs) 2nd javelin 1960.
Youngest gold medallists: MEN 17y 263d Bob Mathias (USA) decathlon 1948;
WOMEN: 15y 123d Barbara Pearl Jones (USA) 4x100m relay 1952.

Medal table of leading nations (including 1906 Games)

	MEN			WOMEN			TOTAL
NATION	*Gold*	*Silver*	*Bronze*	*Gold*	*Silver*	*Bronze*	*Medals*
USA	241	178	152	32	21	11	635
USSR	34	35	40	30	20	34	193
United Kingdom	41	54	38	4	20	12	169
GDR	14	19	14	25	28	24	124
Finland	47	32	29	-	2	-	110
F.R.Germany *	11	24	34	11	13	12	105
Sweden	17	24	41	-	-	3	85
Australia	6	9	11	11	8	11	56
France	7	19	17	3	1	2	49
Canada	9	9	16	2	5	6	47
Italy	13	7	18	3	4	2	47
Poland	9	7	4	6	8	7	41
Hungary	6	13	16	3	1	2	41
Romania	-	-	1	9	8	6	24
Czechoslovakia	6	7	3	3	2	2	23
Greece	3	8	12	-	-	-	23
Kenya	10	8	6	-	-	-	22
Jamaica	4	9	4	-	1	3	21

In all 62 nations have won medals at track and field sports, with Djibouti and Sénégal added to the list in 1988.
* Germany 1896-1952, since then the Federal Republic of Germany. Medals won by the combined German teams of 1956, 1960 and 1964 have been allocated to FRG or GDR according to the athlete's origin.

WORLD CHAMPIONSHIPS

Athletics events at the Olympic Games have had world championship status, but the first championships for athletics alone were staged in the Olympic Stadium, Helsinki, Finland in 1983. The second world championships were held in Rome in September 1987, and the third will be in Tokyo in 1991. *Champions:*

MEN	1983	1987
100m	Carl Lewis (USA) 10.07	Ben Johnson (Can) 9.83
200m	Calvin Smith (USA) 20.14	Calvin Smith (USA) 20.16
400m	Bert Cameron (Jam) 45.05	Thomas Schönlebe (GDR) 44.33
800m	Willi Wülbeck (FRG) 1:43.65	Billy Konchellah (Ken) 1:43.06
1500m	Steve Cram (UK) 3:41.59	Abdi Bile (Som) 3:36.80
5000m	Eamonn Coghlan (Ire) 13:28.53	Saïd Aouita (Mor) 13:26.44
10 000m	Alberto Cova (Ita) 28:01.04	Paul Kipkoech (Ken) 27:38.63
Marathon	Rob de Castella (Aus) 2:10:03	Douglas Wakiihuri (Ken) 2:11:48
3000m steeple	Patriz Ilg (FRG) 8:15.06	Francesco Panetta (Ita) 8:08.57
110m hurdles	Greg Foster (USA) 13.42	Greg Foster (USA) 13.21
400m hurdles	Edwin Moses (USA) 47.50	Edwin Moses (USA) 47.46
High jump	Gennadiy Avdeyenko (USSR) 2.32	Patrik Sjöberg (Swe) 2.38
Pole vault	Sergey Bubka (USSR) 5.70	Sergey Bubka (USSR) 5.85
Long jump	Carl Lewis (USA) 8.55	Carl Lewis (USA) 8.67
Triple jump	Zdzislaw Hoffmann (Pol) 17.42	Khristo Markov (Bul) 17.92
Shot	Edward Sarul (Pol) 21.39	Werner Günthör (Swi) 22.23
Discus	Imrich Bugár (Cs) 67.72	Jürgen Schult (GDR) 68.74
Hammer	Sergey Litvinov (USSR) 82.68	Sergey Litvinov (USSR) 83.06
Javelin	Detlef Michel (GDR) 89.48 (old spec.)	Seppo Räty (Fin) 83.54
Decathlon	Daley Thompson (UK) 8714	Torsten Voss (GDR) 8680
4x100m relay	USA 37.86	USA 37.90
4x400m relay	USSR 3:00.79	USA 2:57.29
20km walk	Ernesto Canto (Mex) 1:20:49	Maurizio Damilano (Ita) 1:20:45
50km walk	Ronald Weigel (GDR) 3:43:08	Hartwig Gauder (GDR) 3:40:53

WOMEN		
100m	Marlies Göhr (GDR) 10.97	Silke Gladisch (GDR) 10.90
200m	Marita Koch (GDR) 22.13	Silke Gladisch (GDR) 21.74
400m	Jarmila Kratochvílová (Cs) 47.99	Olga Bryzgina (USSR) 49.38
800m	Jarmila Kratochvílová (Cs) 1:54.68	Sigrun Wodars (GDR) 1:55.26
1500m	Mary Decker (USA) 4:00.90	Tatyana Samolenko (USSR) 3:58.56
3000m	Mary Decker (USA) 8:34.62	Tatyana Samolenko (USSR) 8:38.73
10 000m	not held	Ingrid Kristiansen (Nor) 31:05.85
Marathon	Grete Waitz (Nor) 2:28:09	Rosa Mota (Por) 2:25:17
100m hurdles	Bettina Jahn (GDR) 12.35	Ginka Zagorcheva (Bul) 12.34
400m hurdles	Yekaterina Fesenko (USSR) 54.14	Sabine Busch (GDR) 53.62
High jump	Tamara Bykova (USSR) 2.01	Stefka Kostadinova (Bul) 2.09
Long jump	Heike Daute (GDR) 7.27w	Jackie Joyner-Kersee (USA) 7.36
Shot	Helena Fibingerová (Cs) 21.05	Natalya Lisovskaya (USSR) 21.24
Discus	Martina Opitz (GDR) 68.94	Martina Hellmann* (GDR) 71.62
Javelin	Tiina Lillak (Fin) 70.82	Fatima Whitbread (UK) 76.64
Heptathlon	Ramona Neubert (GDR) 6770	Jackie Joyner-Kersee (USA) 7128
10km walk	not held	Irina Strakhova (USSR) 44:12
4x100m relay	GDR 41.76	USA 41.58
4x400m relay	GDR 3:19.73	GDR 3:18.63

* (née Opitz), w = wind assisted

Winners of the most medals

6 Carl Lewis (USA) gold 100m, long jump & 4x100m relay 1983; long jump & 4x100m relay 1987; silver 100m 1987.
4 Marita Koch (GDR) gold 200m, 4x100m & 4x400m, silver 100m 1983.

4 Silke Gladisch (GDR) gold 4x100m relay 1983, 100m & 200m 1987; silver 4x100m relay 1987.
4 Calvin Smith (USA) gold 200m & 4x100m relay 1983, 200m 1987; silver 100m 1983.

WORLD INDOOR CHAMPIONSHIPS

First held as World Indoor Games at Bercy, Paris, France 19-20 January 1985. Official Championships are now staged biennially. *Winners:*

MEN

60 metres
1985   Ben Johnson (Can) 6.62
1987   Ben Johnson (Can) 6.41 WR
1989   Andrés Simon (Cub) 6.52

200 metres
1985   Aleksandr Yakovlyev (USSR) 20.95
1987   Kirk Baptiste (USA) 20.73
1989   John Regis (UK) 20.54

400 metres
1985   Thomas Schönlebe (GDR) 45.60
1987   Antonio McKay (USA) 45.98
1989   Antonio McKay (USA) 45.59

800 metres
1985   Colomán Trabado (Spa) 1:47.42
1987   José Luiz Barbosa (Bra) 1:47.49
1989   Paul Ereng (Ken) 1:44.84 WR

1500 metres
1985   Mike Hillardt (Aus) 3:40.27
1987   Marcus O'Sullivan (Ire) 3:39.04
1989   Marcus O'Sullivan (Ire) 3:36.64

3000 metres
1985   João Campos (Por) 7:57.63
1987   Frank O'Mara (Ire) 8:03.32
1989   Saïd Aouita (Mor) 7:47.94

60 metres hurdles
1985   Stéphane Caristan (Fra) 7.67
1987   Tonie Campbell (USA) 7.51
1989   Roger Kingdom (USA) 7.43

High jump
1985   Patrik Sjöberg (Swe) 2.32
1987   Igor Paklin (USSR) 2.38
1989   Javier Sotomayor (Cub) 2.43 WR

Pole vault
1985   Sergey Bubka (USSR) 5.75
1987   Sergey Bubka (USSR) 5.85
1989   Rodion Gataullin (USSR) 5.85

Long jump
1985   Jan Leitner (Cs) 7.96
1987   Larry Myricks (USA) 8.23
1989   Larry Myricks (USA) 8.37

Triple jump
1985   Khristo Markov (Bul) 17.22
1987   Mike Conley (USA) 17.54
1989   Mike Conley (USA) 17.65

Shot
1985   Remigius Machura (Cs) 21.22
1987   Ulf Timmermann (GDR) 22.24
1989   Ulf Timmermann (GDR) 21.75

5000 metres walk
1985   Gérard Lélièvre (Fra) 19:06.22
1987   Mikhail Shchennikov (USSR) 18:27.79 WR
1989   Mikhail Shchennikov (USSR) 18:27.10
WR World indoor record

Roger Kingdom (left) and Colin Jackson (right) were gold and silver medallists at the 1989 World Indoor championships
(All-Sport/Gray Mortimore)

Kerry Saxby on her way to victory in the 1989 World Indoor championships. Her world record was one of more than 20 she has set, indoors and out (All-Sport/Pascal Rondeau)

WOMEN

60 metres
1985	Silke Gladisch (GDR)	7.20
1987	Nellie Fiere-Cooman (Hol)	7.08
1989	Nellie Cooman (Hol)	7.05

200 metres
1985	Marita Koch (GDR)	23.09
1987	Heike Drechsler (GDR)	22.27 WR
1989	Merlene Ottey (Jam)	22.34

400 metres
1985	Diane Dixon (USA)	53.35
1987	Sabine Busch (GDR)	51.66
1989	Helga Arendt (FRG)	51.52

800 metres
1985	Cristieana Cojocaru (Rom)	2:04.22
1987	Christine Wachtel (GDR)	2:01.31
1989	Christine Wachtel (GDR)	1:59.24

1500 metres
1985	Elly van Hulst (Hol)	4:11.41
1987	Doina Melinte (Rom)	4:05.68
1989	Doina Melinte (Rom)	4:04.79

3000 metres
1985	Debbie Scott (Can)	9:04.99
1987	Tatyana Samolenko (USSR)	8:46.52
1989	Elly van Hulst (Hol)	8:33.82 WR

60 metres hurdles
1985	Xénia Siska (Hun)	8.03
1987	Cornelia Oschkenat (GDR)	7.82
1989	Yelisaveta Chernyshova (USSR)	7.82

High jump
1985	Stefka Kostadinova (Bul)	1,97
1987	Stefka Kostadinova (Bul)	2.05 WR
1989	Stefka Kostadinova (Bul)	2.02

Long jump
1985	Helga Radtke (GDR)	6.86
1987	Heike Drechsler (GDR)	7.10
1989	Galina Chistyakova (USSR)	6.98

Shot
1985	Natalya Lisovskaya (USSR)	20.07
1987	Natalya Lisovskaya (USSR)	20.52
1989	Claudia Losch (FRG)	20.45

3000 metres walk
1985	Giuliana Salce (Ita)	12:53.42
1987	Olga Krishtop (USSR)	12:05.49 WR
1989	Kerry Saxby (Aus)	12:01.65 WR

Most wins: 3 Stefka Kostadinova (high jump)

IAAF WORLD CUP

First held in 1977. The competing teams represent each of the five continents, with national teams from the USA and the top two men's and women's teams from the European Cup. Host nations Italy and Spain competed as ninth teams in 1981 and 1989. Each team enters one competitor per event. *Winners:*

Year	Men	Women
1977	GDR	Europe
1979	USA	GDR
1981	Europe	GDR
1985	USA	GDR
1989	USA	GDR

Individual event winners

MEN
100 metres
1977	Steve Williams (USA)	10.13
1979	James Sanford (USA)	10.17
1981	Allan Wells (Eur/UK)	10.20
1985	Ben Johnson (Ame/Can)	10.00
1989	Linford Christie (UK)	10.10

200 metres
1977	Clancy Edwards (USA)	20.17
1979	Silvio Leonard (Ame/Cub)	20.34
1981	Mel Lattany (USA)	20.21
1985	Robson Caetano Da Silva (Ame/Bra)	20.44
1989	Robson da Silva (Ame/Bra)	20.00

400 metres
1977	Alberto Juantorena (Ame/Cub)	45.36
1979	Hassan El Kashief (Afr/Sud)	45.39
1981	Cliff Wiley (USA)	44.88
1985	Mike Franks (USA)	44.47
1989	Roberto Hernández (Ame/Cub)	44.58

800 metres
1977	Alberto Juantorena (Ame/Cub)	1:44.04
1979	James Maina (Afr/Ken)	1:47.69
1981	Sebastian Coe (Eur/UK)	1:46.16
1985	Sammy Koskei (Afr/Ken)	1:45.14
1989	Tom McKean (UK)	1:44.95

1500 metres
1977	Steve Ovett (Eur/UK)	3:34.45
1979	Thomas Wessinghage (Eur/FRG)	3:46.00
1981	Steve Ovett (Eur/UK)	3:34.95
1985	Omer Khalifa (Afr/Sud)	3:41.16
1989	Abdi Bile (Afr/Som)	3:35.56

5000 metres
1977	Miruts Yifter (Afr/Eth)	13:13.82
1979	Miruts Yifter (Afr/Eth)	13:35.9
1981	Eamonn Coghlan (Eur/Ire)	14:08.39
1985	Doug Padilla (USA)	14:04.11
1989	Saïd Aouita (Afr/Mor)	13:23.14

10 000 metres
1977	Miruts Yifter (Afr/Eth)	28:32.3
1979	Miruts Yifter (Afr/Eth)	27:53.07
1981	Werner Schildhauer (GDR)	27:38.43
1985	Woldajo Bulti (Afr/Eth)	29:22.96
1989	Salvatore Antibo (Eur/Ita)	28:05.26

3000 metres steeplechase
1977	Michael Karst (FRG)	8:21.6
1979	Kiprotich Rono (Afr/Ken)	8:25.97
1981	Boguslaw Maminski (Eur/Pol)	8:19.89
1985	Julius Kariuki (Afr/Ken)	8:39.51
1989	Julius Kariuki (Afr/Ken)	8:20.84

110 metres hurdles
1977	Thomas Munkelt (GDR)	13.41
1979	Renaldo Nehemiah (USA)	13.39
1981	Greg Foster (USA)	13.32
1985	Tonie Campbell (USA)	13.35w
1989	Roger Kingdom (USA)	12.87w

400 metres hurdles
1977	Ed Moses (USA)	47.58
1979	Ed Moses (USA)	47.53
1981	Ed Moses (USA)	47.37
1985	Andre Phillips (USA)	48.42
1989	David Patrick (USA)	48.74

High jump
1977	Rolf Beilschmidt (GDR)	2.30
1979	Franklin Jacobs (USA)	2.27
1981	Tyke Peacock (USA)	2.28
1985	Patrik Sjöberg (Eur/Swe)	2.31
1989	Patrik Sjöberg (Eur/Swe)	2.34

Pole vault
1977	Mike Tully (USA)	5.60
1979	Mike Tully (USA)	5.45
1981	Konstantin Volkov (USSR)	5.70
1985	Sergey Bubka (USSR)	5.85
1989	Philippe Collet (Eur/Fra)	5.75

Long jump
1977	Arnie Robinson (USA)	8.19
1979	Larry Myricks (USA)	8.52
1981	Carl Lewis (USA)	8.15
1985	Mike Conley (USA)	8.20
1989	Larry Myricks (USA)	8.29

Triple jump
1977	João de Oliveira (Ame/Bra)	16.68
1979	João de Oliveira (Ame/Bra)	17.02
1981	João de Oliveira (Ame/Bra)	17.37
1985	Willie Banks (USA)	17.58
1989	Mike Conley (USA)	17.49

Shot
1977	Udo Beyer (GDR)	21.74
1979	Udo Beyer (GDR)	20.45
1981	Udo Beyer (GDR)	21.40
1985	Ulf Timmermann (GDR)	22.00
1989	Ulf Timmermann (GDR)	21.68

Discus
1977	Wolfgang Schmidt (GDR)	67.14
1979	Wolfgang Schmidt (GDR)	66.02
1981	Armin Lemme (GDR)	66.38
1985	Gennadiy Kolnootchenko (USSR)	69.08
1989	Jürgen Schult (GDR)	67.12

Hammer
1977	Karl-Hans Riehm (FRG)	75.64

1979	Sergey Litvinov (USSR) 78.70
1981	Yuriy Sedykh (USSR) 77.42
1985	Jüri Tamm (USSR) 82.12
1989	Heinz Weis (Eur/FRG) 77.68

Javelin

1977	Michael Wessing (FRG) 87.46
1979	Wolfgang Hanisch (GDR) 86.48
1981	Dainis Kula (USSR) 89.74
1985	Uwe Hohn (GDR) 96.96
1989	Steve Backley (UK) 85.90

4 x 100 metres relay

1977	USA 38.03
1979	Americas 38.70
1981	Europe 38.73
1985	USA 38.10
1989	USA 38.29

4 x 400 metres relay

1977	F.R.Germany 3:01.34
1979	USA 3:00.70
1981	USA 2:59.12
1985	USA 3:00.71
1989	Americas 3:00.65

WOMEN

100 metres

1977	Marlies Oelsner (GDR) 11.16
1979	Evelyn Ashford (USA) 11.06
1981	Evelyn Ashford (USA) 11.02
1985	Marlies Göhr (née Oelsner) (GDR) 11.10
1989	Sheila Echols (USA) 11.18

200 metres

1977	Irena Szewinska (Eur/Pol) 22.72
1979	Evelyn Ashford (USA) 21.83
1981	Evelyn Ashford (USA) 22.18
1985	Marita Koch (GDR) 21.90
1989	Silke Möller (GDR) 22.46

400 metres

1977	Irena Szewinska (Eur/Pol) 49.52
1979	Marita Koch (GDR) 48.97
1981	Jarmila Kratochvílová (Eur/Cs) 48.61
1985	Marita Koch (GDR) 47.60
1989	Ana F.Quirot (Ame/Cub) 51.6

800 metres

1977	Totka Petrova (Eur/Bul) 1:59.20
1979	Nikolina Shtereva (Eur/Bul) 2:00.52
1981	Lyudmila Veselkova (USSR) 1:57.48
1985	Christine Wachtel (GDR) 2:01.57
1989	Ana F.Quirot (Ame/Cub) 1:54.44

1500 metres

1977	Tatyana Kazankina (USSR) 4:12.7
1979	Totka Petrova (Eur/Bul) 4:06.46*
1981	Tamara Sorokina (USSR) 4:03.33
1985	Hildegard Körner (GDR) 4:10.86
1989	Paula Ivan (Eur/Rom) 4:18.60

3000 metres

1977	Grete Waitz (Eur/Nor) 8:43.5
1979	Svyetlana Ulmasova (USSR) 8:36.32
1981	Angelika Zauber (GDR) 8:54.89

1985	Ulrike Bruns (GDR) 9:14.65
1989	Yvonne Murray (Eur/UK) 8:44.32

10 000 metres

1985	Aurora Cunha (Por) 32:07.50
1989	Kathrin Ullrich (GDR) 31:33.92

100 metres hurdles

1977	Grazyna Rabsztyn (Eur/Pol) 12.70
1979	Grazyna Rabsztyn (Eur/Pol) 12.67
1981	Tatyana Anisimova (USSR) 12.85
1985	Cornelia Oschkenat (GDR) 12.71
1989	Cornelia Oschkenat (GDR) 12.60

400 metres hurdles

1979	Barbara Klepp (GDR) 55.83
1981	Ellen Neumann (GDR) 54.82
1985	Sabine Busch (GDR) 54.45
1989	Sandra Patrick (USA) 53.84

High jump

1977	Rosemarie Ackermann (GDR) 1.98
1979	Debbie Brill (Ame/Can) 1.96
1981	Ulrike Meyfarth (Eur/FRG) 1.96

Ana Quirot achieved a unique treble in the 1989 World Cup, at 400m, 800m and on the America's 4 x 400m relay team **(All-Sport/Bob Martin)**

| 1985 | Stefka Kostadinova (Eur/Bul) 2.00 |
| 1989 | Silvia Costa (Ame/Cub) 2.04 |

Long jump

1977	Lynette Jacenko (Oce/Aus) 6.54
1979	Anita Stukane (USSR) 6.64
1981	Sigrid Ulbricht (GDR) 6.80
1985	Heike Drechsler (GDR) 7.27
1989	Galina Chistyakova (USSR) 7.10

Shot

1977	Ilona Slupianek (GDR) 20.93 *
1979	Ilona Slupianek (GDR) 20.98
1981	Ilona Slupianek (GDR) 20.60
1985	Natalya Lisovskaya (USSR) 20.69
1989	Huang Zhihong (Asi/Chn) 20.73

Discus

1977	Faina Melnik (USSR) 68.10
1979	Evelin Jahl (GDR) 65.18
1981	Evelin Jahl (GDR) 66.70
1985	Martina Opitz (GDR) 69.78
1989	Ilke Wyludda (GDR) 71.54

Javelin

1977	Ruth Fuchs (GDR) 62.36
1979	Ruth Fuchs (GDR) 66.10
1981	Antoaneta Todorova (Eur/Bul) 70.08
1985	Olga Gavrilova (USSR) 66.80
1989	Petra Felke (GDR) 70.32

4 x 100 metres relay

1977	Europe 42.51
1979	Europe 42.19
1981	GDR 42.22
1985	GDR 41.37
1989	GDR 42.21

4 x 400 metres relay

1977	GDR 3:24.04
1979	GDR 3:20.38
1981	GDR 3:20.62
1985	GDR 3:19.49
1989	Americas 3:23.05

Most individual event wins
MEN: 4 Miruts Yifter (Afr/Eth), 3 Ed Moses (USA), João de Oliveira (Ame/Bra), Udo Beyer (GDR)
WOMEN: 4 Evelyn Ashford (USA); 3 Ilona Slupianek* (GDR), Marita Koch (GDR)
* subsequently disqualified for infringing the doping regulations, Slupianek at the preceding European Cup.

IAAF WORLD RACE WALKING CUP

This competition is held biennially for the Lugano Trophy (men) and the Eschborn Cup (women). It has been officially recognised by the IAAF with the above name since 1977.

Lugano Cup

Contested by men's national teams walking over 20km and 50 km **Wins:**
5 GDR 1965, 1967, 1970, 1973, 1985
4 USSR 1975, 1983, 1987, 1989
2 United Kingdom 1961, 1963

2 Mexico 1977, 1979
1 Italy 1981
Best performances

20km:	1:19:24 Carlos Mercenario (Mex) 1987
	1:18:49 (short) Daniel Bautista (Mex) 1979
50km:	3:42:26 Ronald Weigel (GDR) 1987

Eschborn Cup

Contested by women's national teams walking over 10km (5km 1979-81). **Wins:**
3 USSR 1981, 1987, 1989
2 China 1983, 1985
1 United Kingdom 1979
Best performance

| 10km: | 43:08 Beate Anders (GDR) 1989 |

IAAF WORLD CUP MARATHON

Staged biennially from the first at Hiroshima, Japan in 1985. **Winners:**
Men's team: 1985 Djibouti, 1987 Italy, 1989 Ethiopia
Men's individual
1985 Ahmed Salah (Dji) 2:08:09
1987 Ahmed Salah (Dji) 2:10:55
1989 Metaferia Zeleke (Eth) 2:10:28

Women's team: 1985 Italy, 1987 USSR, 1989 USSR
Women's individual
1985 Katrin Dörre (GDR) 2:33:30
1987 Zoya Ivanova (USSR) 2:30:39
1989 Sue Marchiano (USA) 2:30:48

IAAF WOMEN'S WORLD ROAD RACE CHAMPIONSHIP

Held annually, at 15km (10km 1983-4). Winners:

	Team	Individual
1983	USA	Wendy Sly (UK) 32:23
1984	UK	Aurora Cunha (Por) 33:04
1985	UK	Aurora Cunha (Por) 49:17
1986	USSR	Aurora Cunha (Por) 48:31
1987	Portugal	Ingrid Kristiansen (Nor) 47:17
1988	USSR	Ingrid Kristiansen (Nor) 48:24
1989	China	Wang Xiuting (Chn) 49:34

COMMONWEALTH GAMES

See Commonwealth Games section for all winners.

Most gold medals:
MEN
6 Don Quarrie (Jam) 1970-78
WOMEN
7 Marjorie Nelson (née Jackson) (Aus) 1950-54
7 Raelene Boyle (Aus) 1970-82
6 Pam Kilborn/Ryan (Aus) 1962-70

Most wins at one event
MEN
3 Howard Payne (Eng) Hammer 1962, 1966, 1970
3 Don Quarrie (Jam) 100m 1970, 1974, 1978

3 Daley Thompson (Eng) Decathlon 1978, 1982, 1986
WOMEN
3 Valerie Young (NZ) Shot 1962, 1966, 1970
3 Pam Ryan (Aus) 80mh 1962, 1966, 100mh 1970
3 Jennifer Lamy (Aus) 4x100m relay 1966, 1970, 1974
3 Kathy Cook (Eng) 4x100m relay 1978, 1982, 1986
3 Tessa Sanderson (Eng) Javelin 1978, 1986, 1990

Most Medals G - Gold, S - Silver, B - Bronze

MEN	G	S	B	Years
6 Don Quarrie (Jam)	6	-	-	1970-78
6 Harry Hart (SAf)	4	1	1	1930-34
6 Allan Wells (Sco)	4	1	1	1978-82
WOMEN				
9 Raelene Boyle (Aus)	7	2	-	1970-82
8 Denise Boyd (Aus)	2	3	3	1974-82
7 Marjorie Jackson (Aus)	7	-	-	1950-54
7 Valerie Young (NZ)	5	1	1	1958-74
7 Kathy Cook (Eng)	3	3	1	1978-86
7 Debbie Flintoff (Aus)	3	3	1	1982-90
7 Angella Issajenko (Can)	3	2	2	1982-86
6 Pam Ryan (Aus)	6	-	-	1962-70

Boyd née Robertson, Young née Sloper, Cook née Smallwood, Issajenko née Taylor, Ryan née Kilborn

Most medals at one Games:

5 Decima Norman (Aus)	5	-	-	1938
5 Shirley Strickland (Aus)	3	2	-	1950

Debbie Flintoff-King, Commonwealth champion at 400m hurdles in 1982 and 1986 and at 400m in 1986
(All-Sport/Michael King)

EUROPEAN CUP

The European Cup is contested biennially by European nations, with each team entering one athlete per event and one team in each relay. The Cup is dedicated to the memory of Dr Bruno Zauli, the former President of the European Committee of the IAAF, who died suddenly in 1963 soon after the decision had been made to start this competition. With the temporary switch to biennial European Championships in 1969 and 1971, the European Cup was held in 1970, rather than those years.

From 1965 until 1981 the competition was staged with a qualifying round, semifinals and final, but from 1983 the nations have been arranged into groups according to strength, with eight men's and eight women's teams in A and B groups, with additional nations in C1 and C2 groups. There is two up and two down promotion and relegation system between the groups (one up and down between A and B.prior to 1989).

Men's final wins:
6 GDR 1970, 1975, 1977, 1979, 1981, 1983
5 USSR 1965, 1967, 1973, 1985, 1987
1 UK 1989

Women's final wins:
9 GDR 1970, 1973, 1975, 1977, 1979, 1981, 1983, 1987, 1989
3 USSR 1965, 1967, 1985

Most individual event wins in finals
MEN
5 Harald Schmid (FRG) 400m 1979, 400mh 1979, 1983, 1985, 1987
WOMEN
6 Marlies Göhr (GDR) 100m 1977, 1979, 1981, 1983, 1985, 1987
5 Renate Stecher (GDR) 100m 1973, 1975, 200m 1970, 1973, 1975
4 Irena Szewinska (Pol) 100m 1967, 200m 1967, 1977, 400m 1975
4 Ruth Fuchs (GDR) JT 1970, 1973, 1975, 1977
4 Marita Koch (GDR) 200m 1985, 400m 1977, 1979, 1981

European Combined Events Cup
Held biennially at decathlon for men and heptathlon (pentathlon 1973-9) for women since 1973. As with the European Cup, nations are now divided into A, B, C1 and C2 groups. **Wins:**
MEN
3 USSR 1975, 1977, 1985
3 GDR 1979, 1987, 1989
2 FR Germany 1981, 1983
1 Poland 1973
WOMEN
6 GDR 1973, 1975, 1979, 1981, 1983, 1985
3 USSR 1977, 1987, 1989

European Marathon Cup
Held biennially, moving forward a year in 1988. **Winners:**
Men's individual
1981 Massimo Magnani (Ita) 2:13:29
1983 Waldemar Cierpinski (GDR) 2:12:26
1985 Michael Heilmann (GDR) 2:11:28
1988 Ravil Kashapov (USSR) 2:11:30

Men's team: 1981 Italy, 1983 GDR, 1985 GDR, 1988 USSR

Women's individual
1981 Zoya Ivanova (USSR) 2:38:58
1983 Nadezhda Gumerova (USSR) 2:38:36
1985 Katrin Dörre (GDR) 2:30:11
1988 Katrin Dörre (GDR) 2:28:28

Women's team: 1985 GDR, 1988 USSR

IAAF/MOBIL GRAND PRIX
Introduced in 1986, half the standard men's and women's events are contested each year for individual events Grand Prix and an overall Grand Prix over a series of 15-16 international meetings (expanded to 20 in 1990) throughout the world. **Overall champions:**

Year	Men	Women
1985	Doug Padilla (USA)	Mary Slaney (USA)
1986	Saïd Aouita (Mor)	Yordanka Donkova (Bul)
1987	Tonie Campbell (USA)	Merlene Ottey (Jam)
1988	Saïd Aouita (Mor)	Paula Ivan (Rom)
1989	Saïd Aouita (Mor)	Paula Ivan (Rom)

EUROPEAN CHAMPIONSHIPS
The first European Championships were staged at the Stadio Communale, Turin in 1934 for men only. Women's championships were held separately in 1938, but men's and women's events were combined at one venue from 1946. The championships are held at four-yearly intervals, although there was a break in that pattern when they were held in 1969 and 1971.

Winners at the last two championships (1982 and 1986), championships bests (CBP), and athletes to have won a particular event twice:

MEN
100 metres
1982   Frank Emmelmann (GDR) 10.21
1986   Linford Christie (UK) 10.15 CBP
Most: 3 Valeriy Borzov (USSR) 1969, 1971, 1974
200 metres
1982   Olaf Prenzler (GDR) 20.46
1986   Vladimir Krylov (USSR) 20.52
Most: 2 Pietro Mennea (Ita) 1974, 1978 (20.16 CBP)
400 metres
1982   Hartmut Weber (FRG) 44.72
1986   Roger Black (UK) 44.59 CBP
800 metres
1982   Hans-Peter Ferner (FRG) 1:46.33
1986   Sebastian Coe (UK) 1:44.50
CBP: 1:43.84 Olaf Beyer (GDR) 1978
Most: 2 Manfred Matuschewski (GDR) 1962, 1966
1500 metres
1982   Steve Cram (UK) 3:36.49
1986   Steve Cram (UK) 3:41.09
CBP: 3:35.59 Steve Ovett (UK) 1978
Most: 2 Steve Cram
5000 metres
1982   Thomas Wessinghage (FRG) 13:28.90

1986   Jack Buckner (UK) 13:10.15 CBP
10 000 metres
1982   Alberto Cova (Ita) 27:41.03
1986   Stefano Mei (Ita) 27:56.79
CBP: 27:30.99 Martti Vainio (Fin) 1978
Most: 2 Ilmari Salminen (Fin) 1934, 1938;
2 Emil Zátopek (Cs) 1950, 1954;
2 Jürgen Haase (GDR) 1966, 1969
Marathon
1982   Gerard Nijboer (Hol) 2:15:16
1986   Gelindo Bordin (Ita) 2:10:54 CBP
3000 metres steeplechase
1982   Patriz Ilg (FRG) 8:18.52
1986   Hagen Melzer (GDR) 8:16.65
Most: 2 Bronislaw Malinowski (Pol) 1974 (8:15.04 CBP), 1978
110 metres hurdles
1982   Thomas Munkelt (GDR) 13.41
1986   Stéphane Caristan (Fra) 13.20 CBP
Most: 2 Eddy Ottoz (Ita) 1966, 1969;
2 Thomas Munkelt 1978, 1982
400 metres hurdles
1982   Harald Schmid (FRG) 47.48 CBP
1986   Harald Schmid (FRG) 48.65
Most: 3 Harald Schmid 1978, 1982, 1986
4 x 100 metres relay
1982   USSR 38.60
1986   USSR 38.29 CBP
4 x 400 metres relay
1982   FR Germany 3:00.51
1986   United Kingdom 2:59.84 CBP
20 kilometres walk
1982   José Marin (Spa) 1:23:43
1986   Jozef Pribilinec (Cs) 1:21:15 CBP
50 kilometres walk
1982   Reima Salonen (Fin) 3:55:29
1986   Hartwig Gauder (GDR) 3:40:55 CBP
Most: 2 Abdon Pamich (Ita) 1962, 1966;
2 Christoph Höhne (GDR) 1969, 1974
High jump
1982   Dietmar Mögenburg (FRG) 2.30
1986   Igor Paklin (USSR) 2.34 CBP
Pole vault
1982   Aleksandr Krupskiy (USSR) 5.60
1986   Sergey Bubka (USSR) 5.85 CBP
Most: 3 Wolfgang Nordwig (GDR) 1966, 1969, 1971;
2 Eeles Landström (Fin) 1954, 1958
Long jump
1982   Lutz Dombrowski (GDR) 8.41w
1986   Robert Emmiyan (USSR) 8.41 CBP
Most: 3 Igor Ter-Ovanesyan (USSR) 1958, 1962, 1969;
2 Wilhelm Leichum (Ger) 1934, 1938
Triple jump
1982   Keith Connor (UK) 17.29
1986   Khristo Markov (Bul) 17.66 CBP
Most: 2 Leonid Shcherbakov (USSR) 1950, 1954;
2 Jozef Schmidt (Pol) 1958, 1962;
2 Viktor Saneyev (USSR) 1969, 1974

Shot
1982   Udo Beyer (GDR) 21.50
1986   Werner Günthör (Swi) 22.22 CBP
Most: 2 Gunnar Huseby (Ice) 1946, 1950;
2 Vilmos Varju (Hun) 1962, 1966; Hartmut Briesenick (GDR) 1971, 1974; Udo Beyer (GDR) 1978, 1982
Discus
1982   Imrich Bugár (Cs) 66.64
1986   Romas Ubartas (USSR) 67.08
CBP: 67.20 Wolfgang Schmidt (GDR) 1978 (qualifying round)
Most: 3 Adolfo Consolini (Ita) 1946, 1950, 1954
Hammer
1982   Yuriy Sedykh (USSR) 81.66
1986   Yuriy Sedykh (USSR) 86.74 CBP
Most: 3 Yuriy Sedykh 1978, 1982, 1986
Javelin
1982   Uwe Hohn (GDR) 91.34
1986   Klaus Tafelmeier (FRG) 84.76 CBP (new javelin)
Most: 4 Janis Lusis (USSR) 1962, 1966, 1969 (CBP old javelin 91.52), 1971; 2 Matti Järvinen (Fin) 1934, 1938; Janusz Sidlo (Pol) 1954, 1958
Decathlon
1982   Daley Thompson (UK) 8774
1986   Daley Thompson (UK) 8811 CBP
Most: 3 Vasiliy Kuznetsov (USSR) 1954, 1958, 1962; 2 Joachim Kirst (GDR) 1969, 1971; Daley Thompson

WOMEN
100 metres
1982   Marlies Göhr (GDR) 11.01
1986   Marlies Göhr (GDR) 10.91 CBP
Most: 3 Marlies Göhr 1978, 1982, 1986
200 metres
1982   Bärbel Wöckel (GDR) 22.04
1986   Heike Drechsler (GDR) 21.71 CBP
Most: 2 Irena Szewinska (Pol) 1966, 1974
400 metres
1982   Marita Koch (GDR) 48.15 CBP
1986   Marita Koch (GDR) 48.22
Most: 3 Marita Koch 1978, 1982, 1986;
2 Mariya Itkina (USSR) 1958, 1962
800 metres
1982   Olga Mineyeva (USSR) 1:55.41 CBP
1986   Nadezhda Olizarenko (USSR) 1:57.15
Most: 2 Vera Nikolic (Yug) 1966, 1971
1500 metres
1982   Olga Dvirna (USSR) 3:57.80 CBP
1986   Ravilya Agletdinova (USSR) 4:01.19
3000 metres
1982   Svetlana Ulmasova (USSR) 8:30.28 CBP
1986   Olga Bondarenko (USSR) 8:33.99
Most: 2 Svetlana Ulmasova 1978, 1982
10 000 metres
1986   Ingrid Kristiansen (Nor) 30:23.25 CBP

On the first lap of the 1987 World Marathon championships. Rosa Mota (475) won by over seven minutes. Lisa Martin (16) did not finish, but in 1988 took the Olympic silver medal behind Mota **(All-Sport)**

Marathon
1982   Rosa Mota (Por) 2:36:04
1986   Rosa Mota (Por) 2:28:38 CBP
Most: 2 Rosa Mota
100 metres hurdles
1982   Lucyna Kalek (Pol) 12.45
1986   Yordanka Donkova (Bul) 12.38 CBP
Most: 3 Karin Balzer (GDR) 1966 (80mh), 1969, 1971; 2
Fanny Blankers-Koen (Hol) 1946, 1950 (both at 80mh)
400 metres hurdles
1982   Ann-Louise Skoglund (Swe) 54.58
1986   Marina Styepanova (USSR) 53.32 CBP
4 x 100 metres relay
1982   GDR 42.19
1986   GDR 41.84 CBP
4 x 400 metres relay
1982   GDR 3:19.05
1986   GDR 3:16.87 CBP
10 kilometres walk
1986   Maria Cruz Diaz (Spa) 46:09 CBP
High jump
1982   Ulrike Meyfarth (FRG) 2.02 CBP
1986   Stefka Kostadinova (Bul) 2.00
Most: 2 Iolanda Balas (Rom) 1958, 1962
Long jump
1982   Vali Ionescu (Rom) 6.79
1986   Heike Drechsler (GDR) 7.27 CBP
Shot
1982   Ilona Slupianek (GDR) 21.59 CBP
1986   Heidi Krieger (GDR) 21.10
Most: 4 Nadezhda Chizhova (USSR) 1966, 1969, 1971,
1974; 2 Ilona Slupianek 1978, 1982
Discus
1982   Tsvetanka Khristova (Bul) 68.34
1986   Diane Sachse (GDR) 71.36 CBP
Most: 2 Nina Dumbadze (USSR) 1946, 1950; Tamara Press
(USSR) 1958, 1962; Faina Melnik (USSR) 1971, 1974
Javelin
1982   Anna Verouli (Gre) 70.02
1986   Fatima Whitbread (UK) 76.32 (77.44 CBP in
        qualifying)
Most: 2 Dana Zátopková (Cs) 1954, 1958; Ruth Fuchs
(GDR) 1974, 1978
Heptathlon
1982   Ramona Neubert (GDR) 6664
1986   Anke Behmer (GDR) 6717 CBP
Most (at pentathlon): 2 Galina Bystrova (USSR) 1958, 1962

Most gold medals at all events:
MEN
5 Harald Schmid (FRG) 1978-86
4 Janis Lusis (USSR) 1962-71
4 Valeriy Borzov (USSR) 1969-74
WOMEN
6 Marita Koch (GDR) 1978-86
5 Fanny Blankers-Koen (Hol) 1946-50
5 Irena Szewinska (Pol) 1966-74
5 Marlies Göhr (GDR) 1978-86

4 Maria Itkina (USSR) 1954-62
4 Nadezhda Chizhova (USSR) 1966-74
4 Renate Stecher (GDR) 1969-74

Most medals: G - Gold, Silver, Bronze

MEN		G	S	B	Years
6	Harald Schmid (FRG)	5	1	-	1978-86
6	Pietro Mennea (Ita)	3	2	1	1971-74
WOMEN					
10	Irena Szewinska (Pol)	5	1	4	1966-78
8	Fanny Blankers-Koen (Hol)	5	1	2	1938-50
8	Renate Stecher (GDR)	4	4	-	1969-74
7	Marlies Göhr (GDR)	5	1	1	1978-86
6	Yevgeniya Sechenova (USSR)	2	2	2	1946-50
6	Marita Koch (GDR)	6	-	-	1978-86

Most medals at one event: (long jump)

5	Igor Ter-Ovanesyan (USSR)	3	2	-	1966-71

Most medals at one Championships:

4	Fanny Blankers-Koen (Hol)	3	1	-	1950
4	Irena Kirszenstein* (Pol)	3	1	-	1966
* later Szewinska					
4	Stanislawa Walasiewicz (Pol)	2	2	-	1938

EUROPEAN INDOOR CHAMPIONSHIPS
European Indoor Games were held for the first time on 27
Mar 1966 at the Westfallenhalle in Dortmund. From 1970
they received IAAF sanction as the official European Indoor
Championships. Held annually to date but biennially from
1990. **Most wins:**
MEN
7 Valeriy Borzov (USSR) 60m 1970-1, 1974-7; 50m 1972
6 Viktor Saneyev (USSR) triple jump 1970-2, 1975-7
5 Marian Woronin (Pol) 60m 1979-82, 1987
5 José Luis González (Spa) 1500m 1982, 1985-6; 3000m
  1987-8
5 Dietmar Mögenburg (FRG) high jump 1980, 1982, 1984,
  1986, 1989
WOMEN
8 Helena Fibingerová (Cs) shot 1973-4, 1977-8, 1980,
  1983-5
5 Karin Balzer (GDR) 50m hurdles 1967-9, 60m hurdles
  1970-1
5 Nadezhda Chizhova (USSR) shot 1967-8, 1970-2
5 Marlies Göhr (GDR) 60m 1977-9, 1982-3
5 Nellie Cooman/Fiere (Hol) 60m 1985-9

WORLD RECORDS
World records for athletics were first officially recognised
by the IAAF in 1913. Initially records were accepted for 96
men's events, and this list has been reduced at various
times, including the elimination of Imperial distances,
except the 1 mile, in 1977. From 1977 all records at sprint
distances up to 400 metres have been accepted only if
timed fully automatically. Prior to that date the best hand
times have been listed.
Records are shown for each of the currently recognised

events, with the records at 15-year intervals. Pre-1900 performances and those indicated by (u) were not, for various reasons, ratified by the IAAF, but they are considered as the best acceptable. Also listed are those athletes to have set most records at each event.
A set at high altitude (over 1000m).

MEN
100 metres

1900	10.8	Luther Cary (USA) 4 Jul 1891
	10.8	eight other men
1915	10.5 u	Emil Ketterer (Ger) 9 Jul 1911
	10.5 u	Richard Rau (Ger) 13 Aug 1911
1930	10.2 u	Charles Paddock (USA) 18 Jun 1921
1945	10.2	also Jesse Owens (USA) 20 Jun 1936
	10.2	Hal Davis (USA) 6 Jun 1941
	10.2u	Lloyd La Beach (Pan) 8 Aug 1943
1960	10.0	Armin Hary (FRG) 21 Jun 1960
		(10.25 auto)
	10.0	Harry Jerome (Can) 15 Jul 1960
1975	9.9 hand	by seven men
	9.95A	Jim Hines (USA) 14 Oct 1968
1990	9.92	Carl Lewis (USA) 24 Sep 1988
	9.83	Ben Johnson (Can) 30 Aug 1987

Johnson's time was officially ratified but later dropped after his admission of taking steroids for many years. He ran 9.79 in the Olympic Games at Seoul on 24 Sep 1988 but was disqualified on that occasion for a positive drugs test.

Most officially ratified
4 Steve Williams (USA) all at 9.9 1974-6

200 metres (y = 220 yards)

1900	21.2y #	Bernie Wefers (USA) 30 May 1896
1915	21.2y	William Applegarth (UK) 4 Jul 1914
	20.8y #	Albert Robinson (USA) 2 May 1913
1930	21.0 u	Helmut Körnig (Ger) 26 Aug 1928
	20.6 #	Roland Locke (USA) 1 May 1926
1945	20.6y	James Carlton (Aus) 18 Jun 1932 (u)
	20.3y #	Jesse Owens (USA) 25 May 1935
1960	20.5y	Peter Radford (UK) 28 May 1960
	20.5	Stonewall Johnson (USA) 2 Jul 1960
	20.5	Ray Norton (USA) 2 Jul 1960
	20.5	Livio Berruti (Ita) 3 Sep 1960
		(20.62 auto)
	20.0 #	Dave Sime (USA) 9 Jun 1956
1975	19.83A	Tommie Smith (USA) 16 Oct 1968
	19.5 #	Tommie Smith (USA) 7 May 1966
1990	19.72A	Pietro Mennea (Italy) 12 Sep 1979

Best time at low altitude:
19.75 Carl Lewis (USA) 19 Jun 1983.
 # straight track (c.0.3 - 0.4.sec faster) - prior to 1951 records could be set on any type of course, from 1951 to 1975 separate records were maintained for straight and turn, thereafter all records must be made around a full turn.
Most   5 Ray Norton (USA) 20.6 - 20.5 (1959-60)

400 metres (y = 440 yards)

1900	47.8y	Maxie Long (USA) 29 Sep 1900
1915	47.8y	as above
1930	47.0	Emerson Spenser (USA) 12 May 1928
1945	46.0	Rudolf Harbig (Ger) 12 Aug 1939

Carl Lewis was well beaten in this 100m race at San Jose in 1986 by Ben Johnson (right) but gained the world record when the latter was banned for drug abuse (All-Sport/Mike Powell)

Butch Reynolds, who at Zürich in 1988 smashed the world record for 400metres, which had stood for nearly 20 years (All-Sport/Bob Martin)

	46.0	Grover Klemmer (USA) 29 Jun 1941
1960	44.9	Otis Davis (USA) 6 Sep 1960
	44.9	Carl Kaufmann (FRG) 6 Sep 1960

(auto times: 45.07 Davis, 45.08 Kaufmann)

1975	43.86A	Lee Evans (USA) 18 Oct 1968
1990	43.29	Butch Reynolds (USA) 17 Aug 1988
Most	4 Herb McKenley (Jam) 46.2y - 45.9 (1946-8)

800 metres   (y = 880 yards)

1900	1:53.4y	Charles Kilpatrick (USA) 21 Sep 1895
1930	1:50.6	Séraphin Martin (Fra) 14 Jul 1928
1945	1:46.6	Rudolf Harbig (Ger) 15 Jul 1939
1960	1:45.7	Roger Moens (Bel) 3 Aug 1955
1975	1:43.7	Marcello Fiasconaro (Ita) 27 Jun 1973
	1:44.1y	Rick Wohlhuter (USA) 8 Jun 1974
1990	1:41.73	Sebastian Coe (UK) 10 Jun 1981

Most   7 Lawrence 'Lon' Myers (USA) 1:56.2y - 1:55.4y (1880-5)

1000 metres

1900	2:36.8	Henri Deloge (Fra)10 Jun 1900
1915	2:31.0 u	Emilio Lunghi (Ita) 31 May 1908
1930	2:23.6	Jules Ladoumègue (Fra) 19 Oct 1930
1945	2:21.5	Rudolf Harbig (Ger) 24 May 1941
1960	2:16.7	Siegfried Valentin (GDR) 29 Jul 1960
1975	2:13.9	Rick Wohlhuter (USA) 30 Jul 1974
1990	2:12.18	Sebastian Coe (UK) 11 Jul 1981

Most   3 Auden Boysen (Nor) 2:20.4 - 2:19.0 (1953-5)

1500 metres

1900	4:06.2	Charles Bennett (UK) 15 Jul 1900
1915	3:55 est	Norman Taber (USA) 16 Jul 1915
1930	3:49.2	Jules Ladoumègue (Fra) 5 Oct 1930
1945	3:43.0	Gunder Hägg (Swe) 7 Jul 1944
1960	3:35.6	Herb Elliott (Aus) 6 Sep 1960
1975	3:32.16	Filbert Bayi (Tan) 2 Feb 1974
1990	3:29.46	Saïd Aouita (Mor) 23 Aug 1985

Most   3 Abel Kiviat (USA) 3:59.2 - 3:55.8 (1912)
       3 Gunder Hägg (Swe) 3:47.6 - 3:43.0 (1941-4)
       3 Steve Ovett (UK) 3:32.09 - 3:30.77 (1980-3)

1 mile

1900	4:12 3/4	Walter George (UK) 23 Aug 1886 (professional)
	4:15.6	Thomas Conneff (USA) 30 Aug 1895
1915	4:12.6	Norman Taber (USA) 16 Jul 1915
1930	4:10.4	Paavo Nurmi (Fin) 23 Aug 1923
1945	4:01.3	Gunder Hägg (Swe) 17 Jul 1945
1960	3:54.5	Herb Elliott (Aus) 6 Aug 1958
1975	3:49.4	John Walker (NZ) 12 Aug 1975
1990	3:46.32	Steve Cram (UK) Oslo 27 Jul 1985

Most   3 Gunder Hägg (Swe) 4:06.1 - 4.01.3 (1942-5)
       3 Arne Andersson (Swe) 4:06.2 - 4:01.6 (1942-4)
       3 Sebastian Coe (UK) 3:48.95 - 3:47.33 (1979-81)

2000 metres

1900	5:38.8*	Thomas Conneff (USA) 2 Sep 1895
1915	5:37.0*	Alfred Shrubb (UK) 11 Jun 1904

Saïd Aouita, uniquely a world record holder simultaneously at 1500m, 2000m, 3000m and 5000m (All-Sport/Bob Martin)

1930	5:23.4	Eino Borg (Purje) (Fin) 9 Aug 1927
1945	5:11.8	Gunder Hägg (Swe) 23 Aug 1942
1960	5:02.2	István Rozsavölgyi (Hun) 2 Oct 1955
1975	4:56.2	Michel Jazy (Fra) 12 Oct 1966
1990	4:50.81	Saïd Aouita (Mor) 16 Jul 1987

* time at 1 1/4 mile (2011.68m)

3000 metres

1900	9:18.2	Henri Deloge (Fra) Paris 22 Oct 1895
1915	8:36.9	Hannes Kolehmainen (Fin) 12 Jul 1912
1930	8:20.4	Paavo Nurmi (Fin) 13 Jul 1926
1945	8:01.2	Gunder Hägg (Swe) 28 Aug 1942
1960	7:52.8	Gordon Pirie (UK) 4 Sep 1956
1975	7:35.2	Brendan Foster (UK) 3 Aug 1974
1990	7:29.45	Saïd Aouita (Mor) 20 Aug 1989

Most   4 Paavo Nurmi (Fin) 8:28.6 - 8:20.4 (1922-6)

5000 metres

1900	15:20.0	Charles Bennett (UK) 22 Jul 1900
1915	14:36.6	Hannes Kolehmainen (Fin) 10 Jul 1912
1930	14:28.2	Paavo Nurmi (Fin) 19 Jun 1924
1945	13:58.1	Gunder Hägg (Swe) 20 Sep 1942
1960	13:35.0	Vladimir Kuts (USSR) 13 Oct 1957
1975	13:13.0	Emiel Puttemans (Bel) 20 Sep 1972
1990	12:58.39	Saïd Aouita (Mor) 22 Jul 1987

Most: 4 Vladimir Kuts (USSR) 13:56.6-13:35.0 (1954-7)
       4 Ron Clarke (Aus) 13:34.4 - 13:16.6 (1965-6)

10 000 metres
1900	31:40.0	Walter George (UK) 28 Jul 1884
1915	30:58.8	Jean Bouin (Fra) 16 Nov 1911
1930	30:06.1	Paavo Nurmi (Fin) 31 Aug 1924
1945	29:35.4	Viljo Heino (Fin) 25 Aug 1944
1960	28:18.8	Pyotr Bolotnikov (USSR) 5 Oct 1960
1975	27:30.80	David Bedford (UK) 13 Jul 1973
1990	27:08.23	Arturo Barrios (Mex) 18 Aug 1989
Most	5 Emil Zátopek (Cs) 29:28.2 - 28:54.2 (1949-54)	

Marathon
Note that records are not officially recognised for the marathon, for which times are affected by the nature of the road courses. The distance of 26 miles 385 yards (42.195 km) was that used for the race at the 1908 Olympic Games, run from Windsor to the White City stadium, and which became standard from 1924.

Best times:
1915	2:36:06.6	Alexis Ahlgren (Swe) 31 May 1913
1930	2:29:01.8	Al Michelsen (USA) 12 Oct 1925
1945	2:26:42	Sohn Kee-chung (Kor) 3 Nov 1935
1960	2:15:16.2	Abebe Bikila (Eth) 10 Sep 1960
1975	2:08:33.6	Derek Clayton (Aus) 30 May 1969
1990	2:06:50	Belayneh Dinsamo (Eth) 17 Apr 1988
Most	4 Jim Peters (UK) 2:20:42.2 - 2:17:39.4 (1952-4)	

3000 metres steeplechase
1930	9:21.8 u	Toivo Loukola (Fin) 4 Aug 1928
1945	8:59.6 u	Erik Elmsäter (Swe) 4 Aug 1944
1960	8:31.4	Zdzislaw Krzyszkowiak (Pol) 26 Jun 1960
1975	8:09.70	Anders Gärderud (Swe) 1 Jul 1975
1990	8:05.35	Peter Koech (Ken) 4 Jul 1989
Most:	4 Anders Gärderud (Swe) 8:20.7 - 8:08.02 (1972-6)	

110 metres hurdles   (y = 120 yards, 109.73m time)
1900	15.4y	Stephen Chase (USA) 28 Sep 1895
1915	15.0	Forrest Smithson (USA) 25 Jul 1908
1930	14.4y	Earl Thomson (USA) 29 May 1920
	14.4	Eric Wennström (Swe) 25 Aug 1929
	14.4y	Stephen Anderson (USA) 23 Aug 1930
1945	13.7	Forrest Towns (USA) 27 Aug 1936
	13.7	Fred Wolcott (USA) 29 Jun 1941
1960	13.2	Martin Lauer (FRG) 7 Jul 1959 (13.56 auto)
	13.2	Lee Calhoun (USA) 21 Aug 1960
1975	13.0y	Rod Milburn (USA) 25 Jun 1971
		Rod Milburn (USA) 20 Jun 1973
	13.0	Guy Drut (Fra) 22 Aug 1975
	13.24	Rod Milburn (USA) 7 Sep 1972
1990	12.92	Roger Kingdom (USA) 16 Aug 1989
Most	6 Forrest Towns (USA) 14.1 - 13.7 (1936)	
	6 Rod Milburn (USA) 13.2 - 13.0y/13.24 (1971-5)	

400 metres hurdles   (y = 440 yards time)
1900	57.2	Godfrey Shaw (UK) 12 Aug 1891
1915	54.6y u	William Meanix (USA) 16 Jul 1915
1930	52.0	F.Morgan Taylor (USA) 5 Jul 1928
1945	50.6	Glenn Hardin (USA) 26 Jul 1934
1960	49.2	Glenn Davis (USA) 6 Aug 1958
	49.3y	Gert Potgieter (SAf) 16 Apr 1960
1975	47.82	John Akii-Bua (Uga) 2 Sep 1972
1990	47.02	Edwin Moses (USA) 31 Aug 1983
Most	4 Edwin Moses (USA) 47.63 - 47.02 (1976-83)	

High jump
1900	1.97m	Michael Sweeney (USA) 21 Sep 1895
1915	2.01m	Edward Beeson (USA) 2 May 1914
1930	2.03m	Harold Osborn (USA) 27 May 1924
1945	2.11m	Lester Steers (USA) 17 Jun 1941
1960	2.22m	John Thomas (USA) 1 Jul 1960
1975	2.30m	Dwight Stones (USA) 11 Jul 1973
1990	2.44m	Javier Sotomayor (Cub) 29 Jul 1989
Most	6 Valeriy Brumel (USSR) 2.23 - 2.28 (1961-3)	
	4 John Thomas (USA) 2.17 - 2.22 (1960)	

Pole vault
1900	3.62m	Raymond Clapp (USA) 16 Jun 1898
1915	4.02m	Marcus Wright (USA) 8 Jun 1912
1930	4.30m	Lee Barnes (USA) 28 Apr 1930
1945	4.77m	Cornelius Warmerdam (USA) 23 May 1942 (and 4.78m indoors 20 Mar 1943)
1960	4.82m u	Bob Gutowski (USA) 15 Jun 1957
	4.80m	Don Bragg (USA) 2 Jul 1960
1975	5.65m	Dave Roberts (USA) 28 Mar 1975
1990	6.06m	Sergey Bubka (USSR) 10 Jul 1988
Most	9 Sergey Bubka (USSR) 5.85 - 6.06 (1984-8)	
	9 John Pennel (USA) 4.95 - 5.44 (1963-9) (five u)	
	7 Cornelius Warmerdam (USA) 4.57 - 4.77 (1940-2)	
	6 Bob Seagren (USA) 5.32 - 5.63 (1966-72)	
	5 Thierry Vigneron (Fra) 5.75 - 5.91 (1980-4)	

Long jump
1900	7.51m	Peter O'Connor (Ire) 29 Aug 1900
1915	7.61m	Peter O'Connor (Ire) 5 Aug 1901
1930	7.93m	Silvio Cator (Haiti) 9 Sep 1928
1945	8.13m	Jesse Owens (USA) 25 May 1935
1960	8.21m	Ralph Boston (USA) 12 Aug 1960
1975	8.90mA	Bob Beamon (USA) 18 Oct 1968
1990	as above.	

Beamon's 8.90m was set at the 2240m altitude of Mexico City. The best low altitude jump is 8.79m by Carl Lewis (USA) at Indianapolis 19 Jun 1983

Most	6 Ralph Boston (USA) 8.21 - 8.35 (1960-5)	
	5 Peter O'Connor (Ire) 7.51 - 7.61 (1900-1)	

Triple jump
1900	14.78m	Edwin Bloss (USA) 16 Sep 1893
1915	15.52m	Daniel Ahearne (USA) 30 May 1911
1930	15.52m	also Anthony Winter (Aus) 12 Jul 1924
1945	16.00m	Naoto Tajima (Jap) 6 Aug 1936
1960	17.03m	Jozef Schmidt (Pol) 5 Aug 1960

1975	17.89mA	João Carlos de Oliveira (Bra) 15 Oct 1975
1990	17.97m	Willie Banks (USA) 16 Jun 1985
Most	5 Adhemar Ferreira da Silva (Bra) 16.00 - 16.56 (1951-5)	

Shot

1900	14.75m	George Gray (Can) 1 Aug 1898
1915	15.54m	Ralph Rose (USA) 21 Aug 1909
1930	16.04m	Emil Hirschfeld (Ger) 26 Aug 1928
1945	17.40m	Jack Torrance (USA) 5 Aug 1934
1960	20.06m	Bill Nieder (USA) 12 Aug 1960
1975	22.86m	Brian Oldfield (USA) 10 May 1975 (professional)
	22.02m	George Woods (USA) 8 Feb 1974 (indoors)
	21.82m	Al Feuerbach (USA) 5 May 1973
1990	23.12m	Randy Barnes (USA) 19 May 1990
Most	14 Parry O'Brien (USA) 18.00 - 19.30 (1953-9)	
	9 Dallas Long (USA) 19.25 - 20.68 (1959-64)	
	7 George Gray (USA) 13.76 - 14.75 (1889-98)	
	7 Ralph Rose (USA) 14.81 - 15.54 (1904-9)	
	5 Jack Torrance (USA) 16.30 - 17.40 (1934)	

Discus

1915	47.85mu	Armas Taipale (Fin) 20 Jul 1913
1930	51.73m	Paul Jessup (USA) 23 Aug 1930
1945	53.34m	Adolfo Consolini (Ita) 26 Oct 1941
1960	59.91m	Edmund Piatkowski (Pol) 14 Jun 1959
	59.91m	Rink Babka (USA) 12 Aug 1960
1975	69.08m	John Powell (USA) 4 May 1975
	70.38mu	Jay Silvester (USA) 16 May 1971
1990	74.08m	Jürgen Schult (GDR) 6 Jun 1986
Most	6 Jay Silvester (USA) 60.56 - 70.38 (1961-71)	
	5 Martin Sheridan (USA) from 2.5m circle 36.77 - 43.69 (1901-5)	
	4 Fortune Gordien (USA) 56.46 - 59.28 (1949-53)	
	4 Al Oerter (USA) 61.10 - 62.94 (1962-4)	
	4 Mac Wilkins (USA) 69.18 - 70.86 (1976)	

Hammer

1900	51.61m	John Flanagan (USA) 29 Sep 1900
1915	57.77m	Pat Ryan (USA) 17 Aug 1913
1930	as above	
1945	59.00m	Erwin Blask (Ger) 27 Aug 1938
	59.55mu	Pat O'Callaghan (Ire) 22 Aug 1937
1960	70.33m	Hal Connolly (USA) 12 Aug 1960
1975	79.30m	Walter Schmidt (FRG) 14 Aug 1975
1990	86.74m	Yuriy Sedykh (USSR) 30 Aug 1986
Most	18 John Flanagan (USA) 44.46 - 56.19 (1895-1909)	
	7 Hal Connolly (USA) 66.71 - 71.26 (1956-65)	
	7 Mikhail Krivonosov (USSR) 63.34 - 67.32 (1954-6)	
	7 James Mitchell (USA) 36.40 - 44.21 (1886-92)	
	6 Yuriy Sedykh (USSR) 80.38 - 86.74 (1980-6)	

Javelin - old specification

1900	49.32m	Eric Lemming (Swe) 18 Jun 1899
1915	64.81mu	Jonni Myyrä (Fin) 18 Jul 1915
1930	72.93m	Matti Järvinen (Fin) 14 Sep 1930
1945	78.70m	Yrjö Nikkanen (Fin) 11 Oct 1938
1960	86.04m	Albert Cantello (USA) 5 Jun 1959
1975	94.08m	Klaus Wolfermann (FRG) 5 May 1973
Last	104.80m	Uwe Hohn (GDR) 20 Jul 1984
Most	10 Matti Järvinen (Fin) 71.57 - 77.23 (1930-6)	
	9 Eric Lemming (Swe) 49.32 - 62.32 (1899-1912)	
	5 Jonni Myrrä(Fin) 63.29 - 68.56 (1914-25)	

- *new specification introduced 1987*

1990	89.58m	Steve Backley (UK) 2 Jul 1990

Decathlon - all rescored on the 1984 Tables

1915	6564u	Jim Thorpe (USA) 13/15 Jul 1912
1930	6865	Akilles Järvinen (Fin) 19/20 Jul 1930
1945	7254	Glenn Morris (USA) 7/8 Aug 1936
1960	7982	Rafer Johnson (USA) 8/9 Jul 1960
1975	8420	Bruce Jenner (USA) 9/10 Aug 1975
1987	8847	Daley Thompson (UK) 8/9 Aug 1984

(100m: 10.44, long jump: 8.01m, shot: 15.72m, high jump: 2.03m, 400m: 46.97, 110m hurdles: 14.33, discus: 46.56m, pole vault: 5.00m, javelin: 65.24m, 1500m: 4:35.00)

Most	4 Paavo Yrjöla (Fin) 6460 - 6700 (1926-30)	
	4 Daley Thompson (UK) 8648 - 8847 (1980-4)	

4 x 100 metres relay

1915	42.3	Germany 8 Jul 1912
1930	40.8	Germany 2 Sep 1928
	40.8	four other times
1945	39.8	USA 9 Aug 1936
1960	39.59	USA 1 Dec 1956
1975	38.19	USA 10 Sep 1972
1990	37.83	USA 11 Aug 1984

(Sam Graddy, Ron Brown, Calvin Smith, Carl Lewis)

4 x 400 metres relay

1915	3:16.6	USA 15 Jul 1912
1930	3:14.2	USA 5 Aug 1928
1945	3:08.2	USA 7 Aug 1932
1960	3:02.37	USA 8 Sep 1960
1975	2:56.16A	USA 20 Oct 1968

(Vince Matthews, Ron Freeman II, Larry James, Lee Evans)

1990	2:56.16	USA 1 Oct 1988

(Danny Everett, Steve Lewis, Kevin Robinzine, Butch Reynolds)

Other current relay world records

4 x 200m	1:19.38	Santa Monica Track Club (USA) 23 Aug 1989 (Danny Everett, Leroy Burrell, Floyd Heard, Carl Lewis)
4 x 800m	7:03.89	UK 30 Aug 1982 (Peter Elliott, Garry Cook, Steve Cram, Sebastian Coe)
4 x 1500m	14:38.8	FR Germany 17 Aug 1977 (Thomas Wessinghage, Harald Hudak, Michael Lederer, Karl Fleschen)

WOMEN

Women's athletics really started in the 1920s, but 1915 'records' are shown for some events, recognising the efforts of dedicated early pioneers. Women's records were first accepted by the Féderation Sportive Féminine Internationale (FSFI), from its formation in 1921. The FSFI merged with the IAAF in 1936. Women's records at distances from 1500m upwards have only been added to the official lists over the past two decades. The years that the IAAF first officially recognised records for such events are shown as IAAF 19...

100 metres

1915	13.1	Nina Popova (Russia) 22 Aug 1913
1930	12.0	Elizabeth Robinson (USA) 2 Jun 1928
	12.0	Myrtle Cook(Can) 2 Jul 1928
	12.0	Tollien Schuurman (Hol) 31 Aug 1930
1945	11.5 u	Helen Stephens (USA) 15 May 1936
	11.5	Helen Stephens (USA) 10 Aug 1936
1960	11.3	Shirley Strickland (Aus) 4 Aug 1955
	11.3	Vera Krepkina (USSR) 13 Sep 1958
1975	10.8	Renate Stecher (GDR) 20 Jul 1973
	11.07	Renate Stecher (GDR) 2 Sep 1972
1990	10.49	Florence Griffith-Joyner (USA) 16 Jul 1988
Most	10 Stanislawa Walasiewicz* (Pol) 11.9 - 11.6 (1932-7)	
	9 Renate Stecher (née Meissner) (GDR) 11.0 - 10.8 (1970-3)	

* Note that Walasiewicz's femininity has subsequently been questioned.

200 metres   (y = 220 yards time)

1930	25.2y	Nellie Halstead (UK) 16 Aug 1930
	24.7 #	Kitomi Hitomi (Jap) 19 May 1929
1945	24.1	Helen Stephens (USA) 19 Aug 1936
	23.6	Stanislawa Walasiewicz* (Pol) 4 Aug 1935
1960	22.9	Wilma Rudoplh (USA) 9 Jul 1960
1975	22.21	Irena Szewinska (Pol) 13 Jun 1974 (22.0 hand)
1990	21.34	Florence Griffith-Joyner (USA) 29 Sep 1988
Most	4 Irena Szewinska (née Kirszenstein) (Pol) 22.7 - 22.21 1965-74	
	4 Marita Koch (GDR) 22.06 - 21.71 (1978-84)	
	4 Eileen Edwards (UK) 26.2y = 25.3 (1924-7)	

straight track

400 metres   IAAF 1957   (y = 440 yards time)

1930	59.0 #	Kinue Hitomi (Jap) 5 May 1928
	59.2y	Marion King (USA) 13 Jul 1929
1945	56.8y	Nellie Halstead (UK) 9 Jul 1932
1960	53.0 u	Shin Keum Dan (NKo) 22 Oct 1960
	53.4	Maria Itkina (USSR) 12 Sep 1959
1975	49.9	Irena Szewinska (Pol) 22 Jun 1974
	50.14	Riitta Salin (Fin) 4 Sep 1974
1990	47.60	Marita Koch (GDR) 6 Oct 1985
Most	7 Marita Koch (GDR) 49.19 - 47.60 (1978-85)	
	5 Shin Keum Dan (NKo) 53.0 - 51.2 (1962-4)	

nearly straight track

800 metres   (y = 880 yards time)

1930	2:18.2y	Gladys Lunn (UK) 16 Aug 1930
1945	2:12.0 u	Yekdokiya Vasilyeva (USSR) 5 Aug 1943
1960	2:04.3	Lyudmila Lysenko/Shevtsova (USSR) 3 Jul 1960 and 7 Sep 1960
1975	1:57.48	Svetla Zlateva (Bul) 24 Aug 1973
1990	1:53.28	Jarmila Kratochvílová (Cs) 26 Jul 1983
Most	7 Nina Otkalenko (née Pletnyova) 2:12.0 - 2:05.0 (1951-5)	

1000 metres   IAAF 1984

1990	2:30.6	Tatyana Providokhina (USSR) 20 Aug 1978

1500 metres   IAAF 1967

1930	5:18.2	Anna Mushkina (USSR) 19 Aug 1927
1945	4:38.0	Yevdokiya Vasilyeva (USSR) 17 Aug 1944
1960	4:25.0 u	Diane Leather (UK) 21 Sep 1955
1975	4:01.38	Lyudmila Bragina (USSR) 9 Sep 1972
1990	3:52.47	Tatyana Kazankina (USSR) 13 Aug 1980
Most	4 Lyudmila Bragina (USSR) 4:06.9 - 4:01.38 (1972)	

1 mile   IAAF 1967

1945	5:15.3	Evelyne Forster (UK) 22 Jul 1939
1960	4:45.0	Diane Leather (UK) 21 Sep 1955
1975	4:28.5 ind	Francie Larrieu (USA) 3 Mar 1975
	4:28.8 u	Adrienne Beames (Aus) 7 Jan 1972
	4:29.5	Paola Pigni (Ita) 8 Aug 1973
1990	4:15.61	Paula Ivan (Rom) 10 Jul 1989
Most	5 Diane Leather (UK) 5:07.6 - 4:45.0 (1953-5)	

2000 metres   IAAF 1984

1990	5:28.69	Maricica Puica (Rom) 11 Jul 1986

3000 metres   IAAF 1974

1975	8:46.6	Grete Waitz (Nor) 24 Jun 1975
1990	8:22.62	Tatyana Kazankina (USSR) 26 Aug 1984
Most	4 Paola Cacchi (née Pigni) (Ita) 9:42.8- 9:09.4 (1969-72)	
	3 Lyudmila Bragina (USSR) 8:53.0 - 8:27.12 (1972-6)	

5000 metres   IAAF 1981

1975	15:48.5u	Adrienne Beames (Aus) 5 Jan 1972
1990	14:37.33	Ingrid Kristiansen (Nor) 5 Aug 1986
Most	3 Ingrid Kristiansen (Nor) 15:28.43 - 14:37.33 (1981-6)	

10 000 metres   IAAF 1981

1975	34:01.4	Christa Vahlensieck (FRG) 20 Aug 1975
1990	30:13.74	Ingrid Kristiansen (Nor) 5 Jul 1986

Marathon

Note that records are not officially recognised for the marathon, for which times are affected by the nature of the road courses.

Best times:

1960	3:40:22	Violet Piercy (UK) 3 Oct 1926
1975	2:38:19	Jackie Hansen (USA) 1 Dec 1974
1990	2:21:06	Ingrid Kristiansen (Nor) 21 Apr 1985
Most	4 Grete Waitz (Nor) 2:32:30 - 2:25:29 (1978-83)	

80 metres hurdles

The standard women's hurdles distance was 80 metres, over seven flights of 2ft 6in (76cm) hurdles from 1927 until replaced by the 100m over eight flights of 2ft 9in (84cm) hurdles in 1969.

1930	12.1	Maj Jacobsson (Swe) 2 Sep 1930
1945	11.3	Claudia Testoni (Ita) 23 Jul 1939
	11.3	Claudia Testoni (Ita) 13 Aug 1939
	11.3	Fanny Blankers-Koen (Hol) 20 Sep 1942
1960	10.5	Gisela Birkmeyer (GDR) 24 Jul 1960
1969	10.2	Vera Korsakova (USSR) 16 Jun 1968
	10.39	Maureen Caird (Aus) 18 Oct 1968 (auto)
Most	6 Irina Press (USSR) 10.6 - 10.3 (1960-5)	
	5 Claudia Testoni (Ita) 11.6 - 11.3 (1938-9)	

100 metres hurdles

Replaced the 80 metres hurdles in 1969

1975	12.3	Annelie Ehrhardt (GDR) 22 Jul 1973 (12.68 auto)
	12.59	Annelie Ehrhardt (GDR) 8 Sep 1972
1990	12.21	Yordanka Donkova (Bul) 20 Aug 1988
Most	6 Karin Balzer (GDR) 13.3 - 12.6 (1969-71)	
	5 Yordanka Donkova (Bul) 12.36 - 12.21 (1986-8)	

400 metres hurdles   IAAF 1974

1975	56.51	Krystyna Kacperczyk (Pol) 13 Jul 1974
1990	52.94	Marina Styepanova (USSR) 17 Sep 1986
Most	3 Marina Styepanova (née Makeyeva) (USSR) 54.78 - 52.94 1979-86	

High jump

1915	1.47m *	Margaret Belasco (UK) 6 Jun 1914
1930	1.625m *	Joan Belasco (UK) 27 May 1920
	1.60m	Carolina Gisolf (Hol) 18 Aug 1929
1945	1.71m	Fanny Blankers-Koen (Hol) 30 May 1943
1960	1.86m	Iolanda Balas (Rom) 10 Jul 1960
1975	1.95m	Rosemarie Witschas (GDR) 8 Sep 1974
1990	2.09m	Stefka Kostadinova (Bul) 30 Aug 1987
Most	14 Iolanda Balas (Rom) 1.75 - 1.91 (1956-61)	
	7 Rosemarie Ackermann (née Witschas) (GDR) 1.94 - 2.00 (1974-7)	

* in schools meetings, not subject to official measurements

Long jump

1915	5.00m	Ellen Hayes (USA) 7 Apr 1913
1930	5.98m	Kinue Hitomi (Jap) 20 May 1928
1945	6.25m	Fanny Blankers-Koen (Hol) 19 Sep 1943
1960	6.40m	Hildrun Claus (FRG) 7 Aug 1960
1975	6.84m	Heide Rosendahl (FRG) 3 Sep 1970
1990	7.52m	Galina Chistyakova (USSR) 11 Jun 1988
Most	4 Tatyana Shchelkanova (USSR) 6.48 - 6.70 (1962-4)	
	4 Anisoara Cusmir (Rom) 7.15 - 7.43 (1982-3)	

Triple jump

Official recognition from 1990.

1990	14.52m	Galina Chistyakova (USSR) 3 Jul 1989

Shot

1930	12.85m	Grete Heublein (Ger) 21 Jul 1929
1945	14.89m	Tatyana Sevryukova (USSR) 14 Oct 1945
1960	17.78m	Tamara Press (USSR) 13 Aug 1960
1975	21.60m	Marianne Adam (GDR) 6 Aug 1975
1990	22.63m	Natalya Lisovskaya (USSR) 7 Jun 1987
Most	15 Galina Zybina (USSR) 15.19 - 16.76 (1952-6)	
	10 Nadezhda Chizhova (USSR) 18.67 - 21.45 (1968-73)	
	9 Grete Heublein (Ger) 10.86 - 13.70 (1927-31)	
	6 Tamara Press (USSR) 17.25 - 18.59 (1959-65)	
	5 Ruth Lange (Ger) 10.84 - 11.52 (1927-8)	

Discus

1930	39.62m	Halina Konopacka (Pol) 31 Jul 1928
1945	49.88m	Nina Dumbadze (USSR) 14 Aug 1944
1960	57.15m	Tamara Press (USSR) 12 Sep 1960
1975	70.20m	Faina Melnik (USSR) 20 Aug 1975
1990	76.80m	Gabriele Reinsch (GDR) 9 Jul 1988
Most	11 Faina Melnik (USSR) 64.22 - 70.50 (1971-6)	
	9 Jadwiga Wajsowna (Pol) 40.34 - 44.19 (1932-4)	
	9 Gisela Mauermayer (Ger) 44.34 - 48.31 (1935-6)	
	7 Nina Dumbadze (USSR) 49.11 - 57.04 (1939-52)	
	6 Halina Konopacka (Pol) 31.24 - 39.62 (1925-8)	
	6 Tamara Press (USSR) 57.15 - 59.70 (1960-5)	

Javelin

1930	42.32m	Elisabeth Schumann (Ger) 8 Aug 1930
1945	48.39mu	Lyudmila Anokina (USSR) 15 Sep 1945
1960	59.55m	Elvira Ozolina (USSR) 4 Jun 1960
1975	67.22m	Ruth Fuchs (GDR) 3 Sep 1974
1990	80.00m	Petra Felke (GDR) 9 Sep 1988
Most	6 Ruth Fuchs (GDR) 65.06 - 69.96 (1972-80)	
	4 Elvira Ozolina (USSR) 57.92 - 61.38 (1960-4)	

Heptathlon - scored on the 1984 Tables

1990	7291	Jackie Joyner (USA) 23/24 Sep 1988

(100m hurdles: 12.69, high jump: 1.86m, shot: 15.80m, 200m: 22.56, long jump: 7.27m, javelin: 45.66m, 800m: 2:08.51)

Most	4 Ramona Neubert (GDR) 6670 - 6935 (1981-3)
	4 Jackie Joyner-Kersee (USA) 7148 - 7291 (1986-8)

The heptathlon has been the standard women's multi-event competition since 1981. Until 1980 the pentathlon was the standard competition. The events changed several times, and the scores given are all rescored on the 1984 tables.

Most 8 Irina Press (USSR) 4121 - 4602 (1959-64)
       5 Aleksandra Chudina (USSR) 3564 - 4024
          (1947-55)

4 x 100 metres relay

1930	48.4	Canada 5 Aug 1928
1945	46.4	Germany 8 Aug 1936
1960	44.51	USA 7 Sep 1960
1975	42.51	GDR 8 Sep 1974
1990	41.37	GDR 6 Oct 1985

(Silke Gladisch, Sabine Rieger, Ingrid Auerswald, Marlies Göhr)

4 x 400 metres relay   IAAF 1969

| 1975 | 3:22.95 | GDR 10 Sep 1972 |
| 1990 | 3:15.17 | USSR 1 Oct 1988 |

(Tatyana Ledovskaya, Olga Nazarova, Maria Pinigina, Olga Bryzgina)

Other current relay world records

| 4 x 200m | 1:28.15 | GDR 9 Aug 1980 |

(Marlies Göhr, Romy Müller, Bärbel Wöckel, Marita Koch)

| 4 x 800m | 7:50.17 | USSR 5 Aug 1984 |

(Nadezhda Olizarenko, Lyubov Gurina, Lyudmila Borisova, Irina Podyalovskaya)

Africans dominate the Grand Prix 800 metres race at Lausanne in 1989. Paul Ereng (126) won from Abdi Bile (172)
(All-Sport/Gary Mortimore)

WORLD INDOOR RECORDS

World indoor records have been recognized by the IAAF since 1 Jan 1987. Track performances around a turn must be made on a track no larger than 200 metres.

Event	Mark	Athlete (Nation)	Venue	Date
MEN				
50 metres	5.55	Ben Johnson # (Can)	Ottawa	31 Jan 1987
	5.61	Manfred Kokot (GDR)	East Berlin	4 Feb 1973
	5.61	James Sanford (USA)	San Diego	20 Feb 1981
60 metres	6.41	Ben Johnson # (CAN)	Indianapolis	7 Mar 1987
	6.50	Lee McRae (USA)	Indianapolis	7 Mar 1987
200 metres	20.36	Bruno Marie-Rose (Fra)	Liévin	22 Feb 1987
400 metres	45.05	Thomas Schönlebe (GDR)	Sindelfingen	5 Feb 1988
	45.05*	Danny Everett (USA)	Stuttgart	4 Feb 1990

* not recognised – run in lanes all the way; IAAF rules specify breaking after 2 turns

800 metres	1:44.84	Paul Ereng (Ken)	Budapest	4 Mar 1989
1000 metres	2:16.4*	Rob Druppers (Hol)	The Hague	20 Feb 1988

* auto time of 2:16.62 declared to be faulty, and hand time ratified

1500 metres	3:34.21	Peter Elliott (UK)	Seville	27 Feb 1990
1 mile	3:49.78	Eamonn Coghlan (Ire)	East Rutherford	27 Feb 1983
3000 metres	7:39.2	Emiel Puttemans (Bel)	Berlin	18 Feb 1973
5000 metres	13:20.4	Suleiman Nyambui (Tan)	New York	6 Feb 1981
50 metres hurdles	6.25	Mark McKoy (Can)	Kobe	5 Mar 1986
60 metres hurdles	7.36	Greg Foster (USA)	Los Angeles	16 Jan 1987
High jump	2.43	Javier Sotomayor (Cub)	Budapest	4 Mar 1989
Pole vault	6.05	Sergey Bubka (USSR)	Donyetsk	17 Mar 1990
Long jump	8.79	Carl Lewis (USA)	New York	27 Jan 1984
Triple jump	17.76	Mike Conley (USA)	New York	27 Feb 1987
Shot	22.66	Randy Barnes (USA)	Los Angeles	20 Jan 1989
5000m walk	18:11.41u	Ronald Weigel (GDR)	Vienna	13 Feb 1988
	18:27.10	Mikhail Shchennikov (USSR)	Budapest	5 Mar 1989
4 x 200m relay	1:22.32	Italy	Turin	11 Feb 1984
		(Pierfrancesco Pavoni, Stefano Tilli, Giovanni Bongiorni, Carlo Simionato)		
4 x 400m relay	3:05.21	USA	Glasgow	10 Mar 1989
		(Clarence Daniel, Chip Jenkins, Ken Lowery, Mark Rowe)		
Octathlon	7084	Christian Plaziat (Fra)	Vittel	11/12 Feb 1989

(60m: 6.78, SP: 14.73, HJ: 2.10, 400m: 49.38, LJ: 7.64, 60mh: 7.91, PV: 4.80, 1000m: 2:48.08)

WOMEN				
50 metres	6.06	Angella Issajenko (Can) #	Ottawa	31 Jan 1987
	6.11	Marita Koch (GDR)	Grenoble	6 Feb 1980
60 metres	7.00	Nellie Cooman (Hol)	Madrid	23 Feb 1986
200 metres	22.27	Heike Drechsler (GDR)	Indianapolis	7 Mar 1987
400 metres	49.59	Jarmila Kratochvílová (Cs)	Milan	7 Mar 1982
800 metres	1:56.40	Christine Wachtel (GDR)	Vienna	13 Feb 1988
1000 metres	2:34.8	Brigitte Kraus (FRG)	Dortmund	19 Feb 1978
1500 metres	4:00.27	Doina Melinte (Rom)	East Rutherford	9 Feb 1990
1 mile	4:17.13	Doina Melinte (Rom)	East Rutherford	9 Feb 1990
3000 metres	8:33.82	Elly van Hulst (Hol)	Budapest	4 Mar 1989
5000 metres	15:22.64	Lynn Jennings (USA)	Hanover, NH	7 Jan 1990
	15:19.84mx	Lesley Welch (USA)	Boston	25 Jan 1986
50 metres hurdles	6.58	Cornelia Oschkenat (GDR)	East Berlin	20 Feb 1988
60 metres hurdles	7.71	Lyudmila Narozhilenko (USSR)	Chelyabinsk	4 Feb 1990
High jump	2.06	Stefka Kostadinova (Bul)	Piraeus	20 Feb 1988
Long jump	7.37	Heike Drechsler (GDR)	Vienna	13 Feb 1988
Triple jump	14.45	Galina Christyakova (USSR)	Lipetsk	29 Jan 1989
Shot	22.20	Helena Fibingerová (Cs)	Jablonec	19 Feb 1977
3000m walk	11:59.36	Beate Anders (GDR)	Glasgow	4 Mar 1990

Event	Mark	Athlete (Nation)	Venue	Date
4 x 200m relay	1:32.55	SC Eintracht Hamm (FRG)	Dortmund	20 Feb 1988
		(Helga Arendt, Silke-Beate Knoll, Mechthild Kluth, Gisela Kinzel)		
4 x 400m relay	3:34.38	F.R.Germany	Dortmund	30 Jan 1981
		(Heide-Elke Gaugel, Christina Sussiek, Christiane Brinkmann, Gaby Bussmann)		
Pentathlon	4705	Liliana Nastase (Rom)	Sofia	24/25 Feb 1990
		(8.19 60mh, 1.72 HJ, 13.71 SP, 6.77 LJ, 2:16.60 800m)		

u - unratified mark, mx - mixed race
The IAAF stripped Johnson and Issajenko of their records in January 1990, after both had admitted long-term steroid use

WORLD RECORDS and BESTS - LONG DISTANCE TRACK EVENTS - MEN

	hr:min:sec	Name	Venue	Date
15 km	0:42:54.8	Jos Hermens (Hol)	Papendal	14 Sep 1975
10 miles	0:45:57.6	Jos Hermens (Hol)	Papendal	14 Sep 1975
20 km	0:57:18.4	Dionisio Castro (Por)	La Flèche	31 Mar 1990
15 miles	1:11:43.1	Bill Rodgers (USA)	Saratoga, Cal.	21 Feb 1979
25 km	1:13:55.8	Toshihiko Seko (Jap)	Christchurch, NZ	22 Mar 1981
30 km	1:29:18.8	Toshihiko Seko (Jap)	Christchurch, NZ	22 Mar 1981
20 miles	1:39:14.4	Jack Foster (NZ)	Hamilton, NZ	15 Aug 1971
30 miles	2:42:00	Jeff Norman (UK)	Timperley, Cheshire	7 Jun 1980
50 km	2:48:06	Jeff Norman (UK)	Timperley, Cheshire	7 Jun 1980
40 miles	3:48:35	Don Ritchie (UK)	Hendon, London	16 Oct 1982
50 miles	4:51:49	Don Ritchie (UK)	Hendon, London	12 Mar 1983
100 km	6:10:20	Don Ritchie (UK)	Crystal Palace	28 Oct 1978
150 km	10:36:42	Don Ritchie (UK)	Crystal Palace	15 Oct 1977
100 miles	11:30:51	Don Ritchie (UK)	Crystal Palace	15 Oct 1977
200 km	15:11:10#	Yiannis Kouros (Gre)	Montauban, Fra	15-16 Mar 1985
200 miles	27:48:35	Yiannis Kouros (Gre)	Montauban, Fra	15-16 Mar 1985
500 km	60:23:00	Yiannis Kouros (Gre)	Colac, Aus	26-29 Nov 1984
500 miles	105:42:09	Yiannis Kouros (Gre)	Colac, Aus	26-30 Nov 1984
1000 km	136:17:00	Yiannis Kouros (Gre)	Colac, Aus	26-31 Nov 1984
1500 km	13d 08:58:04	Tony Rafferty (Aus)	Granville, NSW	12-25 Aug 1989
1000 mile	14d 11:59:04	Tony Rafferty (Aus)	Granville, NSW	12-26 Aug 1989

	kilometres			
1 hour	20.944	Jos Hermens (Hol)	Papendal	1 May 1976
2 hrs	37.994	Jim Alder (UK)	Walton-on-Thames	17 Oct 1964
24 hrs	283.600	Yiannis Kouros (Gre)	Montauban, Fra	15-16 Mar 1985
48 hrs	452.270	Yiannis Kouros (Gre)	Montauban, Fra	15-17 Mar 1985
6 days	1023.200	Yiannis Kouros (Gre)	Colac, Aus	26 Nov-1 Dec 1984

Running watch time, no stopped times taken.

LONG DISTANCE ROAD BESTS   Where superior to track bests and run on properly measured road courses.

	hr:min:sec	Name	Venue	Date
15 km	0:42:27.6	Mike Musyoki (Ken)	Portland, Oregon	26 Jun 1983
10 miles	0:45:13	Ian Stewart (UK)	Stoke-on-Trent	8 May 1977
Half mar	1:00:43	Mike Musyoki (Ken)	Newcastle	8 Jun 1986
30 km	1:28:40	Steve Jones (UK)	Chicago	10 Oct 1985
20 miles	1:35:22	Steve Jones (UK)	Chicago	10 Oct 1985
50km	2:43:38	Thompson Magawana (RSA)	Claremont-Kirstenbosch	12 Apr 1988
40 miles	3:46:31	Barney Klecker (USA)	Chicago	5 Oct 1980
50 miles	4:50:21	Bruce Fordyce (RSA)	London-Brighton	25 Sep 1983
1000 miles	10d:10:30:35	Yiannis Kouros (Gre)	New York	21-30 May 1988

	kilometres			
24 hours	286.463	Yiannis Kouros (Gre)	New York	28-29 Sep 1985
6 days	1028.370	Yiannis Kouros (Gre)	New York	21-26 May 1988

It should be noted that road times must be assessed with care as course conditions can vary considerably.

WORLD RECORDS and BESTS- LONG DISTANCE TRACK EVENTS - WOMEN

	hr:min:sec	Name	Venue	Date
15 km	0:49:44.0	Silvana Cruciata (Ita)	Rome	4 May 1981
10 miles	0:55:58.0	Nancy Conz (USA)	Amherst	25 Jun 1981
20 km	1:06:55.5	Rosa Mota (Por)	Lisbon	14 May 1983
25 km	1:29:30	Karolina Szabó (Hun)	Budapest	23 Apr 1988
30 km	1:47:06	Karolina Szabó (Hun)	Budapest	23 Apr 1988
20 miles	1:59:09#	Chantal Langlacé (Fra)	Amiens	3 Sep 1983
30 miles	3:28:12	Ann Franklin (UK)	Barry, Wales	9 Mar 1986
50 km	3:36:58	Ann Franklin (UK)	Barry, Wales	9 Mar 1986
40 miles	4:47:27	Ann Franklin (UK)	Barry, Wales	9 Mar 1986
50 miles	6:17:30#	Monika Kuno (FRG)	Vogt	8-9 Jul 1983
100 km	8:01:01	Monika Kuno (FRG)	Vogt	8-9 Jul 1983
100 miles	14:29:44	Ann Trason (USA)	Santa Rosa, USA	18-19 Mar 1989
200 km	19:28:48	Eleanor Adams (UK)	Melbourne	19-20 Aug 1989
200 miles	39:09:03	Hilary Walker (UK)	Blackpool	5-7 Nov 1988
500 km	77:50:56	Eleanor Adams (UK)	Colac, Aus.	13-15 Nov 1989
500 miles	133:57:53	Eleanor Adams (UK)	Colac, Aus.	13-19 Nov 1989
	kilometres			
1 hour	18.084	Silvana Cruciata (Ita)	Rome	4 May 1981
2 hrs	32.652	Chantal Langlacé (Fra)	Amiens	3 Sep 1983
24 hrs	240.169	Eleanor Adams (UK)	Melbourne	19-20 Aug 1989
48 hrs	366.512	Hilary Walker (UK)	Blackpool	5-7 Nov 1988
6 days	866.360	Eleanor Adams (UK)	Colac, Aus.	13-19 Nov 1989

Timed on one running watch only

Indoors where superior to track best

200 km	19:00:31	Eleanor Adams (UK)	Milton Keynes	3/4 Feb 1990

LONG DISTANCE ROAD BESTS   Run on properly measured road courses.

	hr:min:sec	Name	Venue	Date
10 km	0:30:38	Liz McColgan (UK)	Orlando	12 Feb 1989
15 km	0:47:17	Ingrid Kristiansen (Nor)	Monaco	21 Nov 1987
10 miles	0:51:47	Cathy O'Brien (USA)	Flint	26 Aug 1989
	0:50:31u	Ingrid Kristiansen (Nor)	Amsterdam	11 Oct 1989
Half mar	1:06:40	Ingrid Kristiansen (Nor)	Sandnes	5 Apr 1987
25 km	1:21:21	Ingrid Kristiansen (Nor)	London	10 May 1987
30 km	1:38:27	Ingrid Kristiansen (Nor)	London	10 May 1987
20 miles	1:46:04	Ingrid Kristiansen (Nor)	London	10 May 1987
30 miles	3:01:16	Frith van der Merwe (SAf)	Claremont - Kirstenbosch	25 Mar 1989
50 km	3:08:13	Frith van der Merwe (SAf)	Claremont - Kirstenbosch	25 Mar 1989
40 miles	4:43:22	Marcy Schwam (USA)	Chicago	3 Oct 1982
50 miles	5:54:17	Ann Trason (USA)	Duluth	28 Oct 1989
100 km	7:18:57	Birgit Lennartz (FRG)	Hanau	28 Apr 1990
100 miles	13:55:02	Ann Trason (USA)	New York	16-17 Sep 1989
200 km	19:22:05*	Ann Trason (USA)	New York	16-17 Sep 1989
500 km	82:10 #	Annie Van Der Meer (Hol)	Paris-Colmar	8-11 Jun 1983
1000 miles	14d 20:18:24	Suprabha Schecter (USA)	New York	20 Sep - 5 Oct 1989
	kilometres			
24 hours	236.453 km	Hilary Walker (UK)	Blackpool	5-6 Nov 1988

* time at 125 miles (201.16km) on one running watch, # for 518km
It should be noted that road times must be assessed with care as course conditions can vary considerably.

WALKING

The IAAF currently ratify records at just four track walking events - at 20, 30 and 50 kilometres and at 2 hours. At one time their list embraced a large number of distances, but the shorter distance records were dropped due in particular to difficulties in judging whether walkers were maintaining the strict disciplines of the event. The standard road walking events have become established at 20 and 50 kilometres.

World Records and Bests - Track Walks

	hr:min:sec			
1500m	5:13.53i	Tim Lewis (USA)	East Rutherford	13 Feb 1988
1 mile	5:33.53i	Tim Lewis (USA)	New York	5 Feb 1988
3000m	10:47.11	Giovanni di Benedictis	San Giovanni Valdermo	19 May 1990
5000m	18:11.41i	Ronald Weigel (GDR)	Vienna	13 Feb 1988
	18:28.80	Roman Mrazek (Cs)	Bratislava	14 Jun 1989
10 km	38:02.60	Jozef Pribilinec (Cs)	Banská Bystrica	30 Aug 1985
15 km	58:22.4	Jozef Pribilinec (Cs)	Hildesheim	6 Sep 1986
20 km	1:18:40.0	Ernesto Canto (Mex)	Fana	5 May 1984
25 km	1:44:54.0	Maurizio Damilano (Ita)	San Donato Milanese	5 May 1985
30 km	2:07:59.8	José Marin (Spa)	Barcelona	8 Apr 1979
	2:06:07.3 u	Maurizio Damilano (Ita)	San Donato Milanese	5 May 1985
40 km	2:55:54.0	Raúl Gonzales (Mex)	Fana	2 May 1980
50 km	3:41:38.4	Raúl Gonzales (Mex)	Fana	25 May 1979
100 km	9:16:32.3	Fréderic Marie (Fra)	Etrechy	19 Apr 1987
	kilometres			
1 hour	15.447	Jozef Pribilinec (Cs)	Hildesheim	6 Sep 1986
2 hrs	28.165	José Marin (Spa)	Barcelona	8 Apr 1979
	28.565 u	Maurizio Damilano (Ita)	San Donato Milanese	5 May 1985

*i indoors, * unratified*

World Bests - Road Walks   Where superior to track bests and walked on properly measured road courses.

	hr:min:sec			
25 km	1:42:14	Andrey Perlov (USSR)	Sochi	19 Feb 1989
30 km	2:02:41	Andrey Perlov (USSR)	Sochi	19 Feb 1989
40 km	2:53:59	Andrey Perlov (USSR)	Leningrad	5 Aug 1989
50 km	3:37:41	Andrey Perlov (USSR)	Leningrad	5 Aug 1989
100 km	8:53:30	François Charcellay (Fra)	Bourges	11 Oct 1987
	kilometres			
24 hours	228.930	Jesse Casteneda (USA)	Albuquerque	18-19 Sep 1976

Women's World Records and Bests - Track Walks

The IAAF have ratified records for women's track walking at 5000m and 10 000m since 1981.

	hr:min:sec			
1500m	6:01.16i	Maryanne Torrellas (USA)	East Rutherford	14 Feb 1987
	6:03.3	Kerry Saxby (Aus)	Sydney	23 Nov 1985
1 mile	6:28.46i	Giuliana Salce (Ita)	Genoa	16 Feb 1985
3000m	11:59.36	Beate Anders (GDR)	Glasgow	4 Mar 1990
	12:01.61	Beate Anders (GDR)	Jessheim	31 May 1990
5000m	20:07.52	Beate Anders (GDR)	Rostock	23 Jun 1990
10 000m	42:14.2 #	Kerry Saxby (Aus)	Canberra	26 Jan 1988
	42:25.2	Kerry Saxby (Aus)	Fana	26 May 1990
15 000m	1:15:37.9	Ann Jansson (Swe)	Stockholm	25 Oct 1987
20 000m	1:41:33.9	Ann Jansson (Swe)	Stockholm	25 Oct 1987
	kilometres			
1 hour	12.644	Giuliana Salce (Ita)	Ostia	25 Apr 1986
2 hours	22.239	Jana Zarubová (Cs)	Prague	12 Oct 1985

i indoors, # in mixed race (men and women), disallowed for record purposes

Women's World Bests - Road Walks   Where superior to track bests

10 km	41:30	Kerry Saxby (Aus)	Canberra	27 Aug 1988
15 km	1:09:33	Kerry Saxby (Aus)	Canberra	13 Jul 1985
20 km	1:29:40	Kerry Saxby (Aus)	Värnamo	13 May 1988
25 km	2:12:38	Sue Cook (Aus)	Canberra	20 Jun 1981
30 km	2:45:52	Sue Cook (Aus)	Melbourne	5 Sep 1982
40 km	3:39:43	Ann Jansson (Swe)	New York	27 Oct 1985
50 km	5:01:52	Lilian Millen (UK)	York	16 Apr 1983
100 km	10:57:50	Annie van den Meer (Hol)	Rouen	10 May 1986
	kilometres			
24 hours	211.250	Annie van den Meer (Hol)	Rouen	10-11 May 1986

MAJOR MARATHON RACES

The marathon distance is 26 miles 385 yards (42.195km), the distance for the race at the 1908 Olympic Games, run from Windsor to the White City Stadium, London. That distance became standard from 1924.

BOSTON

The Boston marathon is the world's oldest annual race. It was first run by 15 men on 19 Apr 1897 over a distance of 24 miles 1232 yards (39.75km). Since then it has been run every year on or about the 19th April, Patriot's Day, which honours the famed ride of Paul Revere through Boston. The full marathon distance was first run in 1927.
Kathy Switzer (USA) contested the race in 1967, although the race director tried to prevent her, but her pioneering efforts helped force the acceptance of women runners, and they were admitted officially for the first time in 1972. *Winners from 1970:*

MEN
1970	Ron Hill (UK) 2:10:30
1971	Alvaro Mejia (Col) 2:18:45
1972	Olavi Suomalainen (Fin) 2:15:39
1973	Jon Anderson (USA) 2:16:03
1974	Neil Cusack (Ire) 2:13:39
1975	Bill Rodgers (USA) 2:09:55
1976	Jack Fultz (USA) 2:20:19
1977	Jerome Drayton (Can) 2:14:46
1978	Bill Rodgers (USA) 2:10:13
1979	Bill Rodgers (USA) 2:09:27
1980	Bill Rodgers (USA) 2:12:11
1981	Toshihiko Seko (Jap) 2:09:26
1982	Alberto Salazar (USA) 2:08:51
1983	Greg Meyer (USA) 2:09:01
1984	Geoff Smith (UK) 2:10:34
1985	Geoff Smith (UK) 2:14:05
1986	Rob de Castella (Aus) 2:07:51
1987	Toshihiko Seko (Jap) 2:11:50
1988	Ibrahim Hussein (Ken) 2:08:43
1989	Abebe Mekonnen (Eth) 2:09:06
1990	Gelindo Bordin (Ita) 2:08:19

Most wins: 7 Clarence De Mar (USA) 1911, 1922-4, 1927-8, 1930; 4 Gérard Coté (Can) 1940, 1943-4, 1948; 4 Bill Rodgers (USA) 1975, 1978-80

WOMEN
1972	Nina Kuscsik (USA) 3:08:58
1973	Jackie Hansen (USA) 3:05:59
1974	Miki Gorman (USA) 2:47:11
1975	Liane Winter (FRG) 2:42:24
1976	Kim Merritt (USA) 2:47:10
1977	Miki Gorman (USA) 2:48:33
1978	Gayle Barron (USA) 2:44:52
1979	Joan Benoit (USA) 2:35:15
1980	Jacqueline Gareau (Can) 2:34:28
1981	Allison Roe (NZ) 2:26:46
1982	Charlotte Teske (FRG) 2:29:33
1983	Joan Benoit (USA) 2:22:43
1984	Lorraine Moller (NZ) 2:29:28
1985	Lisa Weidenbach (USA) 2:34:06
1986	Ingrid Kristiansen (Nor) 2:24:55
1987	Rosa Mota (Por) 2:25:21
1988	Rosa Mota (Por) 2:24:30
1989	Ingrid Kristiansen (Nor) 2:24:35
1990	Rosa Mota (Por) 2:25:24

Most wins: 3 Rosa Mota, 2 Miki Gorman, Joan Benoit, Ingrid Kristiansen

CHICAGO

First held in 1977 as the Mayor Daley Marathon, world class fields have been attracted annually since 1983, and there have been large prize funds, especially rewarding for the world records for both men and women in 1985. Not held in 1987. *Winners from 1983:*

MEN
1983	Joseph Nzau (Ken) 2:09:45
1984	Steve Jones (UK) 2:08:05
1985	Steve Jones (UK) 2:07:13
1986	Toshihiko Seko (Jap) 2:08:27
1988	Alejandro Cruz (Mex) 2:08:57
1989	Paul Davies-Hale (UK) 2:11:25

WOMEN
1983	Rosa Mota (Por) 2:31:12
1984	Rosa Mota (Por) 2:26:01
1985	Joan Benoit (USA) 2:21:21
1986	Ingrid Kristiansen (Nor) 2:27:08
1988	Lisa Weidenbach (USA) 2:29:17
1989	Lisa Weidenbach (USA) 2:28:15

FUKUOKA

The Asahi marathon was first run in 1947 at Kumamoto. It was first held at Fukuoka in 1951, and the race has been held there every year since 1964 in early December. Over the past 20 years it has consistently attracted world class men's fields. *Winners from 1967, when Derek Clayton set a world record to win the race:*

1967	Derek Clayton (Aus)	2:09:37
1968	Bill Adcocks (UK)	2:10:48
1969	Jerome Drayton (Can)	2:11:13
1970	Akio Usami (Jap)	2:10:38
1971	Frank Shorter (USA)	2:12:51
1972	Frank Shorter (USA)	2:10:30
1973	Frank Shorter (USA)	2:11:45
1974	Frank Shorter (USA)	2:11:32
1975	Jerome Drayton (Can)	2:10:09
1976	Jerome Drayton (Can)	2:12:25
1977	Bill Rodgers (USA)	2:10:56
1978	Toshihiko Seko (Jap)	2:10:21
1979	Toshihiko Seko (Jap)	2:10:35
1980	Toshihiko Seko (Jap)	2:09:45
1981	Rob de Castella (Aus)	2:08:18
1982	Paul Ballinger (NZ)	2:10:15
1983	Toshihiko Seko (Jap)	2:08:52
1984	Takeyuki Nakayama (Jap)	2:10:00
1985	Masanari Shintaku (Jap)	2:09:51
1986	Juma Ikangaa (Tan)	2:10:06
1987	Takeyuki Nakayama (Jap)	2:08:18
1988	Toshihiru Shibutani (Jap)	2:11:04
1989	Manuel Matias (Por)	2:12:54

Most wins: 4 Frank Shorter, Toshihiko Seko

LONDON

The first London marathon was run on 29 Mar 1981. Organised and inspired by the 1956 Olympic steeplechase gold medallist, Chris Brasher, it caught the public's imagination and was a great success, 7055 runners started and 6418 finished. Numbers increased each year to a record 24,871 finishers in 1990. *Winners:*

MEN

1981	Dick Beardsley (USA) & Inge Simonsen (Nor)	2:11:48
1982	Hugh Jones (UK)	2:09:24
1983	Mike Gratton (UK)	2:09:43
1984	Charlie Spedding (UK)	2:09:57
1985	Steve Jones (UK)	2:08:16
1986	Toshihiko Seko (Jap)	2:10:02
1987	Hiromi Taniguchi (Jap)	2:09:50
1988	Henrik Jørgensen (Den)	2:10:20
1989	Douglas Wakiihuri (Ken)	2:09:03
1990	Allister Hutton (UK)	2:10:10

WOMEN

1981	Joyce Smith (UK)	2:29:57
1982	Joyce Smith (UK)	2:29:43
1983	Grete Waitz (Nor)	2:25:29
1984	Ingrid Kristiansen (Nor)	2:24:26
1985	Ingrid Kristiansen (Nor)	2:21:06
1986	Grete Waitz (Nor)	2:24:54
1987	Ingrid Kristiansen (Nor)	2:22:48
1988	Ingrid Kristiansen (Nor)	2:25:41
1989	Véronique Marot (UK)	2:25:56
1990	Wanda Panfil (Pol)	2:26:31

NEW YORK

Fred Lebow has organised the New York marathon annually from 1970. The race was run in Central Park until 1976, when, to celebrate the US Bicentennial the course was changed to a route through all five boroughs of the city. From that year, when there were 2090 runners, the race has become one of the world's great sporting occasions, and in 1989 there were a record 24,996 runners, of which 24,588 finished. *Winners since 1976:*

MEN

1976	Bill Rodgers (USA)	2:10:10
1977	Bill Rodgers (USA)	2:11:29
1978	Bill Rodgers (USA)	2:12:12
1979	Bill Rodgers (USA)	2:11:42
1980	Alberto Salazar (USA)	2:09:41
1981	Alberto Salazar (USA)	2:08:13
1982	Alberto Salazar (USA)	2:09:29
1983	Rod Dixon (NZ)	2:08:59
1984	Orlando Pizzolato (Ita)	2:14:53
1985	Orlando Pizzolato (Ita)	2:11:34.
1986	Gianni Poli (Ita)	2:11:06
1987	Ibrahim Hussein (Ken)	2:11:01
1988	Steve Jones (UK)	2:08:20
1989	Juma Ikangaa (Tan)	2:08:01

WOMEN

1976	Miki Gorman (USA)	2:39:11
1977	Miki Gorman (USA)	2:43:10
1978	Grete Waitz (Nor)	2:32:30
1979	Grete Waitz (Nor)	2:27:33
1980	Grete Waitz (Nor)	2:25:41
1981	Allison Roe (NZ)	2:25:29
1982	Grete Waitz (Nor)	2:27:14
1983	Grete Waitz (Nor)	2:27:00
1984	Grete Waitz (Nor)	2:29:30
1985	Grete Waitz (Nor)	2:28:34
1986	Grete Waitz (Nor)	2:28:06
1987	Priscilla Welch (UK)	2:30:17
1988	Grete Waitz (Nor)	2:28:07
1989	Ingrid Kristiansen (Nor)	2:25:30

Note that the course used from 1981 to 1983 was found to be 170 yards (155m) short of the full marathon distance, equivalent to about 30 seconds at top men's pace. That sadly meant that the world best times set by Alberto Salazar and Alison Roe in 1981 were invalidated.

ROTTERDAM

Since its inception in 1981 Rotterdam has attracted élite fields for men. Women also run, but apart from the first couple of years the field has not matched the men's for quality. *Winners:*

MEN

1981	John Graham (UK)	2:09:28
1982	Rodolfo Gomez (Mex)	2:11:57
1983	Rob de Castella (Aus)	2:08:37

1984 Gidamis Shahanga (Tan) 2:11:12
1985 Carlos Lopes (Por) 2:07:12
1986 Abebe Mekonnen (Eth) 2:09:08
1987 Belayneh Dinsamo (Eth) 2:12:58
1988 Belayneh Dinsamo (Eth) 2:06:50
1989 Belayneh Dinsamo (Eth) 2:08:39
1990 Hiromi Taniguchi (Jap) 2:10:56

WOMEN
1983 Rosa Mota (Por) 2:32:27
1984 Carla Beurskens (Hol) 2:34:56
1985 Wilma Rusman (Hol) 2:35:32
1986 Ellinor Ljungros (Swe) 2:41:06
1987 Nelly Aerts (Bel) 2:41:24
1988 Xiao Hong-yan (Chn) 2:37:46
1989 Elena Murgoci (Rom) 2:32:03
1990 Carla Beurskens (Hol) 2:29:47

CROSS-COUNTRY RUNNING

WORLD CROSS-COUNTRY CHAMPIONSHIPS
The International Cross-Country Championships were first held at Hamilton Park Racecourse, Glasgow in 1903 over 8 miles (12.87km), contested by the four countries from the British Isles. The race was held annually, with France first entering in 1907, Belgium in 1923, and thereafter the event steadily gained in international prestige. A junior race was first added in 1961, although there had been an international race for juniors between England, France and Belgium in 1940, and the first women's race held in 1967. There were two women's races in 1970; included here is the one in the USA, the other, in France, was won by Paula Pigni (Ita), with the Netherlands team winners. The event has had official world championship status from 1973, when the IAAF took control of the event from the International Cross-Country Union. A junior women's race was run for the first time in 1989. The distances raced now are: men 12km, women 5km, junior men 8km, junior women 4km. Men's teams are of nine runners, with six to score; women and juniors of six runners, four to score.

Winning senior teams
MEN
45 England	1903-14, 1920-1, 1924-5, 1930-8, 1951, 1953-5, 1958-60, 1962, 1964-72, 1976, 1979-80
14 France	1922-3, 1926-9, 1939, 1946-7, 1949-50, 1952, 1956, 1978
7 Belgium	1948, 1957, 1961, 1963, 1973-4, 1977
5 Ethiopia	1981-5
5 Kenya	1986-90
1 New Zealand	1975

WOMEN
8 USA	1968-9, 1975, 1979, 1983-5, 1987
8 USSR	1976-7, 1980-2, 1988-90
7 England	1967, 1970-74, 1986
1 Romania	1978

There were record fields in 1986, when the number of finishers were: 328 men, 171 junior men and 161 women; with 39, 29 and 28 teams respectively placing.

Individual winners
International Championships 1903-72
MEN
1903-4	Alfred Shrubb (Eng)
1905	Albert Aldridge (Eng)
1906	Charles Straw (Eng)
1907	Adam Underwood (Eng)
1908	Archie Robertson (Eng)
1909-10	Edward Wood (Eng)
1911-3	Jean Bouin (Fra)
1914	Arthur Nicholls (Eng)
1920	James Wilson (Sco)
1921	Walter Freeman (Eng)
1922	Joseph Guillemot (Fra)
1923	Charles Blewitt (Eng)
1924	William 'Joe' Cotterell (Eng)
1925	Jack Webster (Eng)
1926	Ernest Harper (Eng)
1927	Lewis Payne (Eng)
1928	Harry Eckersley (Eng)
1929	William 'Joe' Cotterell (Eng)
1930	Thomas Evenson (Eng)
1931	Tim Smythe (Ire)
1932	Thomas Evenson (Eng)
1933-5	Jack Holden (Eng)
1936	William Eaton (Eng)
1937	James Flockhart (Sco)
1938	John Emery (Eng)
1939	Jack Holden (Eng)
1946-7	Raphael Pujazon (Fra)
1948	John Doms (Bel)
1949	Alain Mimoun (Fra)
1950	Lucien Theys (Bel)
1951	Geoffrey Saunders (Eng)
1952	Alain Mimoun (Fra)
1953	Franjo Mihalic (Yug)
1954	Alain Mimoun (Fra)
1955	Frank Sando (Eng)
1956	Alain Mimoun (Fra)
1957	Frank Sando (Eng)
1958	Stan Eldon (Eng)
1959	Fred Norris (Eng)
1960	Rhadi ben Abdesselem (Mor)
1961	Basil Heatley (Eng)
1962	Gaston Roelants (Bel)
1963	Roy Fowler (Eng)
1964	Francesco Arizmendi (Spa)
1965	Jean Fayolle (Fra)
1966	Ben Assou El Ghazi (Mor)
1967	Gaston Roelants (Bel)
1968	Mohammed Gammoudi (Tun)
1969	Gaston Roelants (Bel)
1970	Michael Tagg (Eng)
1971	David Bedford (Eng)
1972	Gaston Roelants (Bel)

WOMEN
1967-71	Doris Brown (USA)
1972	Joyce Smith (Eng)

World Championships from 1973

MEN		WOMEN	
1973	Pekka Paivarinta (Fin)	1973	Paola Cacchi (Ita)
1974	Eric De Beck (Bel)	1974	Paola Cacchi (Ita)
1975	Ian Stewart (Sco)	1975	Julie Brown (USA)
1976	Carlos Lopes (Por)	1976	Carmen Valero (Spa)
1977	Leon Schots (Bel)	1977	Carmen Valero (Spa)
1978	John Treacy (Ire)	1978	Grete Waitz (Nor)
1979	John Treacy (Ire)	1979	Grete Waitz (Nor)
1980	Craig Virgin (USA)	1980	Grete Waitz (Nor)
1981	Craig Virgin (USA)	1981	Grete Waitz (Nor)
1982	Mohamed Kedir (Eth)	1982	Maricica Puica (Rom)
1983	Bekele Debele (Eth)	1983	Grete Waitz (Nor)
1984	Carlos Lopes (Por)	1984	Maricica Puica (Rom)
1985	Carlos Lopes (Por)	1985	Zola Budd (Eng)
1986	John Ngugi (Ken)	1986	Zola Budd (Eng
1987	John Ngugi (Ken)	1987	Annette Sergent (Fra)
1988	John Ngugi (Ken)	1988	Ingrid Kristiansen (Nor)
1989	John Ngugi (Ken)	1989	Annette Sergent (Fra)
1990	Khalid Skah (Mor)	1990	Lynn Jennings (USA)

MEN
Most wins: 4 Jack Holden (Eng), Alain Mimoun (Fra), Gaston Roelants (Bel), John Ngugi (Ken).
Most placings in first three: 7 Gaston Roelants four wins, three second 1960-72
Most placings in first ten: 10 Jack Holden 1930-46
Most appearances: 20 Marcel Van de Wattyne 1946-65

WOMEN
Most wins: 5 Doris Brown (USA), Grete Waitz (Nor).
Most placings in first three: 7 Grete Waitz five wins, two third 1978-84
Most placings in first ten: 7 Grete Waitz 1978-84
Most appearances: 16 Jean Lochhead (Wal) 1967-84
Greatest winning margins:
MEN: 56 sec Jack Holden (Eng) 1934
WOMEN: 40 sec Grete Waitz (Nor) 1980

English National Cross-Country Championship
The 'National' is the oldest and largest of all national cross-country championships. It was first held in 1876, when all 32 runners went off course and the race was declared void. Held annually since then, apart from the war years, there was a peak field in the senior race in 1990, when 2195 men finished and 250 teams of six runners scored. *Recent winners:*

Year	Individual	Team
1980	Nick Rose	Tipton Harriers
1981	Julian Goater	Tipton Harriers
1982	David Clarke	Tipton Harriers
1983	Tim Hutchings	Aldershot, Farnham & D
1984	Eamonn Martin	Aldershot, Farnham & D
1985	David Lewis	Aldershot, Farnham & D
1986	Tim Hutchings	Tipton Harriers
1987	David Clarke	Gateshead Harriers
1988	David Clarke	Birchfield Harriers
1989	David Lewis	Tipton Harriers
1990	Richard Nerurkar	Valli Harriers

Most wins (individual): 4 Percy Stenning 1877-80, Alfred Shrubb 1901-4; 3 Edward Parry 1888-9, 1891; Jack Holden 1938-9, 1946; Frank Aaron 1949-51; Gordon Pirie 1953-5; Basil Heatley 1960-1, 1963.
Most wins (team): 29 Birchfield Harriers, 7 Tipton Harriers, 6 Salford Harriers, Gateshead Harriers.

The English women's cross-country championships were first held in 1927. *Recent winners:*

Year	Individual	Team
1980	Ruth Smeeth	Birchfield
1981	Wendy Smith	Sale Harriers
1982	Paula Fudge	Sale Harriers
1983	Christine Benning	Sale Harriers
1984	Jane Furniss	Aldershot, Farnham & D
1985	Angela Tooby	Crawley
1986	Carole Bradford	Sale Harriers
1987	Jane Shields (née Furniss)	Sale Harriers
1988	Helen Titterington	Birchfield
1989	Angela Pain	Parkside
1990	Andrea Whitcombe	Parkside

Most wins (individual): 6 Lillian Styles 1928-30, 1933-4, 1937; 5 Rita Ridley 1969-72, 1974; 4 Diane Leather 1953-6; Pam Davies 1965-8.
Most wins (team): 13 Birchfield Harriers, 7 London Olympiades, 6 Ilford, Sale Harriers

John Ngugi on the way to the first of his four successive World Cross-country titles (**All-Sport/Bob Martin**)

AUSTRALIAN RULES FOOTBALL

A predominantly kicking game, played by teams of 18-a-side. Its principal initiators were Henry Colden Harrison and Thomas Wills, who helped to form the Melbourne Football Club in 1858. In 1877 the Victorian Football Association was founded, from which eight clubs broke away to form the Victorian Football League (VFL). Four more teams had been admitted by 1925, and in 1987 teams from Queensland and Western Australia joined the league to now make it the Australian Football League.

Victorian Football League

Australia's premier game is the VFL Grand Final, played annually since 1897 at the Melbourne Cricket Ground, except in 1945 when it was staged at North Carlton. The attendance record is 121,696 in 1970.
Most premierships (winning Grand Final):

15	Carlton	1906-8, 1914-5, 1938, 1945, 1947, 1968, 1970, 1972, 1979, 1981-2, 1987
14	Essendon	1897, 1901, 1911-2, 1923-4, 1942, 1946, 1949-50, 1962, 1965, 1984-5
13	Collingwood	1902-3, 1910, 1917, 1919, 1927-30, 1935-6, 1953, 1958
12	Melbourne	1900, 1926, 1939-41, 1948, 1955-7, 1959-60, 1964
10	Richmond	1920-1, 1932, 1934, 1943, 1967, 1969, 1973-4, 1980
8	Hawthorn	1961, 1971, 1976, 1978, 1983, 1986, 1988-9
8	Fitzroy	1898-9, 1904-5, 1913, 1916, 1922, 1944
6	Geelong	1925, 1931, 1937, 1951-2, 1963
3	South Melbourne	1909, 1918, 1933
2	North Melbourne	1975, 1977
1	Footscray	1954
1	St Kilda	1966

VFL Records:

Highest aggregate score: 345 St Kilda beat Melbourne 204-141, 6 May 1978
Team score: 238 (36 goals, 22 behinds) Fitzroy v. Melbourne 28 Jul 1979
Record margin in Grand Final: 96 Hawthorn beat Melbourne 152 to 56 on 24 Sep 1988
Goals in career: 2191 Peter Hudson 1963-81
Goals in season: 150 Bob Pratt (South Melbourne) 1934, Peter Hudson (Hawthorn) 1971
Goals in Grand Final: 9 Gordon Coventry for Collingwood v Richmond 1928
Most games: 403 Kevin Bartlett (Richmond) 1965-83
Greatest attendance: 121,696 for the Grand Final on 26 Sep 1970.

Australian National Football League Championship

The first inter-state game was between Victoria and South Australia in 1879 and the first inter-state carnival in 1908.

Winners:
Victoria 1908, 1914, 1924, 1927, 1930, 1933, 1937, 1947, 1950, 1953, 1956, 1958, 1966, 1969, 1972, 1980, 1989
South Australia 1911, 1985, 1987-8
Western Australia 1921, 1961, 1979, 1983, 1984, 1986

National Football League

Contested by the leading teams from all over Australia. Held from 1976 to 1986, but Victoria withdrew in 1977-8, when it ran its own Premiership series (winners: 1977 Hawthorn, 1978 Fitzroy). *Winners:*
1976 Hawthorn (Vic)
1977 Norwood (SA)
1978 South Adelaide (SA)
1979 Collingwood (Vic)
1980 North Melbourne (Vic)
1981 Essendon (Vic)
1982 Sydney Swans (NSW)
1983 Carlton (Vic)
1984 Essendon (Vic)
1985-6 Hawthorn (Vic)

Most premierships:

South Australia: 29 Port Adelaide 1884-1989
Western Australia: 26 East Fremantle 1900-85

BADMINTON

The name of the game comes from its playing at Badminton House in England by the family and guests of the Duke of Beaufort in the 19th century. Its origins, however, are most directly from the children's game of battledore and shuttlecock, and a similar game was played in China over two thousand years ago. Badminton was played considerably by Army officers in the 1870s in India, where the first modern rules were codified.

The Badminton Association was founded in England in 1893. The world governing body is the International Badminton Federation, formed in 1934, with 94 affiliated member nations in 1989.

THOMAS CUP

The international team competition for men's teams of six players who play five singles and four doubles in each contest, held every three years until 1982 when it became a biennial event. The cup was donated in 1940 by Sir George Thomas, winner of 21 All-England titles, but the competition could not start until after the war. *Winners:*

1949	Malaya	1973	Indonesia
1952	Malaya	1976	Indonesia
1955	Malaya	1979	Indonesia
1958	Indonesia	1982	China
1961	Indonesia	1984	Indonesia
1964	Indonesia	1986	China
1967	Malaysia	1988	China
1970	Indonesia	1990	China

Most wins: 8 Indonesia

UBER CUP

The women's equivalent of the Thomas Cup, it was also contested triennially until 1984 when it became a biennial event. The cup was presented by Betty Uber who represented England a then record 37 times between 1926 and 1951. Each tie consists of three singles and four doubles. *Winners:*

1957	United States	1975	Indonesia
1960	United States	1978	Japan
1963	United States	1981	Japan
1966	Japan	1984	China
1969	Japan	1986	China
1972	Japan	1988	China
		1990	China

Most wins: 5 Japan

WORLD CHAMPIONSHIPS

Instituted in 1977 and initially held every three years, but now staged biennially. *Winners:*

Men's singles
1977	Flemming Delfs (Den)
1980	Rudy Hartono (Ina)
1983	Icuk Sugiarto (Ina)
1985	Han Jian (Chn)
1987	Yang Yang (Chn)
1989	Yang Yang (Chn)

Women's singles
1977	Lene Köppen (Den)
1980	Wiharjo Verawaty (Ina)
1983	Li Lingwei (Chn)
1985	Han Aiping (Chn)
1987	Han Aiping (Chn)
1989	Li Lingwei (Chn)

Men's doubles
1977	Johan Wahjudi & Tjun Tjun (Ina)
1980	Ade Chandra & Hadinata Christian (Ina)
1983	Steen Fladberg & Jesper Helledie (Den)
1985	Park Joo-bong & Kim Moon-soo (SKo)
1987	Li Yongbo & Tian Bingyi (Chn)
1989	Li Yongbo & Tian Bingyi (Chn)

Women's doubles
1977	Etsuko Tuganoo & Emiko Vero (Jap)
1980	Nora Perry & Jane Webster (UK)
1983	Lin Ying & Wu Dixi (Chn)
1985	Han Aiping & Li Lingwei (Chn)
1987	Lin Ying & Guan Weizhen (Chn)
1989	Lin Ying & Guan Weizhen (Chn)

Mixed doubles
1977	Steen Stovgaard & Lene Köppen (Den)
1980	Hadinata Christian & Imelda Wigoeno (Ina)
1983	Thomas Kihlström (Swe) & Nora Perry (UK)
1985	Park Joo-bong & Yoo Sang-hee (SKo)
1987	Wang Pengrin & Shi Fagjing (Chn)
1989	Park Joo-bong & Chung Myung-hee (SKo)

ALL ENGLAND CHAMPIONSHIPS

First played in 1899, until the advent of the World Championships this was the premier tournament in the world.

Men's singles
1900	Sydney Smith (Eng)
1901	H Davies (Eng)
1902-3	Ralph Watling (Eng)
1904-5	Henry Marrett (Eng)
1906-7	Norman Wood (Eng)
1908	Henry Marrett (Eng)
1909-10	Frank Chesterton (Eng)
1911-2	George Sautter (Eng)
1920-3	George Thomas (Eng)
1924	'Curly' Mack (Ire)
1925-9	Frank Devlin (Ire)
1930	Donald Hume (Eng)
1931	Frank Devlin (Ire)
1932	Ralph Nichols (Eng)
1933	Raymond White (Eng)
1934	Ralph Nichols (Eng)
1935	Raymond White (Eng)
1936-8	Ralph Nichols (Eng)

1939	Tage Madsen (Den)
1947	Conny Jepsen (Swe)
1948	Jørn Skaarup (Den)
1949	Dave Freeman (USA)
1950-2	Wong Peng Soon (Mal)
1953-4	Eddie Choong (Mal)
1955	Wong Peng Soon (Mal)
1956-7	Eddie Choong (Mal)
1958	Erland Kops (Den)
1959	Tan Joe Hok (Ina)
1960-3	Erland Kops (Den)
1964	Knud Nielsen (Den)
1965	Erland Kops (Den)
1966	Tan Aik Huang (Mal)
1967	Erland Kops (Den)
1968-74	Rudy Hartono (Ina)
1975	Svend Pri (Den)
1976	Rudy Hartono (Ina)
1977	Flemming Delfs (Den)
1978-9	Liem Swie King (Ina)
1980	Prakash Padukone (Ina)
1981	Liem Swie King (Ina)
1982	Morten Frost (Den)
1983	Luan Jin (Chn)
1984	Morten Frost (Den)
1985	Zhao Jianhua (Chn)
1986-7	Morten Frost (Den)
1988	Ib Frederiksen (Den)
1989	Yang Yang (Chn)
1990	Zhao Jianhua (Chn)

Most wins: 8 Rudy Hartono (Ina)

Men's doubles

1899	D Oakes & S Massey (Eng)
1900-2	H Mellersh & F Collier (Eng)
1903	Stewart Massey & E Huson (Eng)
1904	Albert Prebble & Henry Marrett (Eng)
1905	Stewart Massey & C Barnes (Eng)
1906	George Thomas & Henry Marrett (Eng)
1907	Albert Prebble & Norman Wood (Eng)
1908	George Thomas & Henry Marrett (Eng)
1909	Albert Prebble & Frank Chesterton (Eng)
1910	George Thomas & Henry Marrett (Eng)
1911	P Fitton & Edward Hawthorn (Eng)
1912	George Thomas & Henry Marrett (Eng)
1913-4	George Thomas & Frank Chesterton (Eng)
1920	Alfred Engelbach & Robert du Roveray (Eng)
1921	George Thomas & Francis Hodge (Eng)
1922	Frank Devlin (Ire) & George Sautter (Eng)
1923	Frank Devlin & 'Curly' Mack (Ire)
1924	George Thomas & Francis Hodge (Eng)
1925	Herbert Huber & A Jones (Eng)
1926-7	Frank Devlin & 'Curly' Mack (Ire)
1928	George Thomas & Francis Hodge (Eng)
1929-31	Frank Devlin & 'Curly' Mack (Ire)
1932-5	Donald Hume & Raymond White (Eng)
1936-8	Ralph Nichols & Leslie Nichols (Eng)

Morten Frost, three times All-England singles champion
(All-Sport)

1939	Tom Boyle & James Rankin (Ire)
1947	Tage Madsen & Poul Holm (Den)
1948	Preben Dabelsteen & Borge Fredricksen (Den)
1949	Ooi Teik Hock & Teoh Seng Khoon (Mal)
1950	Preben Dabelsteen & Jørn Skaarup (Den)
1951-3	Eddie Choong & David Choong (Mal)
1954	Ooi Teik Hock & Ong Poh Lim (Mal)
1955-6	Finn Kobbero & Jørgen Hammergaard Hansen (Den)
1957	Joseph Alston (USA) & Hock Aun Heah (Mal)
1958	Erland Kops & Per Nielsen (Den)
1959	Lim Say Hup & Teh Kew San (Mal)
1960	Finn Kobbero & Per Neilsen (Den)
1961-4	Finn Kobbero & Jørgen Hammergaard Hansen (Den)
1965-6	Ng Boon Bee & Tan Yee Khan (Mal)
1967-9	Erland Kops & Henning Borch (Den)
1970	Tom Backer & Paul Petersen (Den)
1971	Ng Boon Bee & Punch Gunalan (Mal)
1972-3	Hadinata Christian & Ade Chandra (Ina)
1974-5	Tjun Tjun & Johan Wahjudi (Ina)
1976	Bengt Froman & Thomas Kihlström (Swe)
1977-80	Tjun Tjun & Johan Wahjudi (Ina)
1981	Hariamanto Kartono & Rudy Heryanto (Ina)
1982	Razif Sidek & Jalaini Sidek (Mal)
1983	Stefan Karlsson & Thomas Kihlström (Swe)
1984	Hariamanto Kartono & Rudy Heryanto (Ina)
1985-6	Kim Moon-soo & Park Joo-bong (SKo)
1987-8	Li Yongbo & Tian Bingyi (Chn)
1989	Lee Sang-bok & Park Joo-bong (SKo)
1990	Kim Moon-soo & Park Joo-bong (SKo)

Women's singles

1900-1	Ethel Thomson (Eng)
1902	Meriel Lucas (Eng)
1903-4	Ethel Thomson (Eng)
1905	Meriel Lucas (Eng)
1906	Ethel Thomson (Eng)
1907-10	Meriel Lucas (Eng)
1911	Margaret Larminie (Eng)
1912	Margaret Tragett (née Larminie) (Eng)
1913-4	Lavinia Radeglia (Eng)
1920-2	Kitty McKane (Eng)
1923	Lavinia Radeglia (Eng)
1924	Kitty McKane (Eng)
1925	Margaret Stocks (Eng)
1926-7	Marjorie Barrett (Eng)
1928	Margaret Tragett (Eng)
1929-31	Marjorie Barrett (Eng)
1932	Leonie Kingsbury (Eng)
1933	Alice Woodroffe (Eng)
1934	Leonie Kingsbury (Eng)
1935	Betty Uber (Eng)
1936-7	Thelma Kingsbury (Eng)
1938	Daphne Young (Eng)
1939	Dorothy Walton (Can)
1947	Marie Ussing (Den)
1948	Kirsten Thorndahl (Den)
1949	Aase Jacobsen (Den)
1950	Tonny Olsen-Ahm (Den)
1951	Aase Jacobsen (Den)
1952	Tonny Olsen-Ahm (Den)
1953	Marie Ussing (Den)
1954	Judy Devlin (USA)
1955-6	Margaret Varner (USA)
1957-8	Judy Devlin (USA)
1959	Heather Ward (Eng)
1960	Judy Devlin (USA)
1961-4	Judy Hashman (née Devlin) (USA)
1965	Ursula Smith (Eng)
1966-7	Judy Hashman (USA)
1968	Eva Twedberg (Swe)
1969	Hiroe Yuki (Jap)
1970	Etsuko Takenaka (Jap)
1971	Eva Twedberg (Swe)
1972	Noriko Nakayama (Jap)
1973	Margaret Beck (Eng)
1974-5	Hiroe Yuki (Jap)
1976	Gillian Gilks (Eng)
1977	Hiroe Yuki (Jap)
1978	Gillian Gilks (Eng)
1979-80	Lene Köppen (Den)
1981	Sun Ai-hwang (SKo)
1982-3	Zang Ailing (Chn)
1984	Li Lingwei (Chn)
1985	Han Aiping (Chn)
1986	Kim Yun-ja (SKo)
1987	Kirsten Larsen (Den)
1988	Gu Jiaming (Chn)
1989	Li Lingwei (Chn)
1990	Susi Susanti (Ina)

Most wins: 10 Judy Hashman (née Devlin) (USA)

Women's doubles

1899-1900	Meriel Lucas & Miss Graeme (Eng)
1901	Miss St.John & E Moseley (Eng)
1902	Meriel Lucas & Ethel Thomson (Eng)
1903	M Hardy & Dorothea Douglass (Eng)
1904-6	Meriel Lucas & Ethel Thomson (Eng)
1907-9	Meriel Lucas & G Murray (Eng)
1910	Mary Bateman & Meriel Lucas (Eng)
1911-2	Alice Gowenlock & Dorothy Cundall (Eng)
1913	Hazel Hogarth & Mary Bateman (Eng)
1914	Margaret Tragett (née Larminie) & Eveline Peterson (Eng)
1920	Lavinia Radeglia & Violet Elton (Eng)
1921	Kitty McKane & Margaret McKane (Eng)
1922-3	Margaret Tragett & Hazel Hogarth (Eng)
1924	Margaret Stocks (née McKane) & Kitty McKane (Eng)
1925	Margaret Tragett & Hazel Hogarth (Eng)
1926	A Head & Violet Elton (Eng)
1927	Margaret Tragett & Hazel Hogarth (Eng)
1928-30	Marjorie Barrett & Violet Elton (Eng)
1931	Betty Uber & Marianne Horsley (Eng)
1932	Marjorie Barrett & Leonie Kingbury (Eng)
1933-6	Thelma Kingsbury & Marjorie Bell-Henderson (Eng)
1937-8	Betty Uber & Diana Doveton (Eng)
1939	Ruth Dalsgard & Tonny Olsen (Den)

Han Aiping celebrates her 1985 All-England win
(All-Sport)

1947-8	Tonny Olsen-Ahm & Kirsten Thorndahl (Den)
1949	Betty Uber & Queenie Allen (Eng)
1950-1	Tonny Olsen-Ahm & Kirsten Thorndahl (Den)
1952	Tonny Olsen-Ahm & Aase Jacobsen (Den)
1953	Iris Cooley & June White (Eng)
1954	Judy Devlin & Susan Devlin (USA)
1955	Iris Cooley & June White (Eng)
1956	Judy Devlin & Susan Devlin (USA)
1957	Kirsten Granlund (née Thorndahl) & Ami Hammergaard Hansen (Den)
1958	Margaret Varner & Heather Ward (Eng)
1959	Iris Cooley-Rogers & June White-Timperley (Eng)
1960	Judy Devlin & Susan Devlin (USA)
1961	Judy Hashman (née Devlin) (USA) & Susan Peard (née Devlin) (Ire)
1962	Judy Hashman (USA) & Tonny Holst-Christensen (Den)
1963	Judy Hashman (USA) & Susan Peard (Ire)
1964-5	Karen Jorgensen & Ulla Rasmussen (Den)
1966	Judy Hashman (USA) & Susan Peard (Ire)
1967	Irme Rietveld (Hol) & Ulla Strand (née Rasmussen) (Den)
1968	Retno Koestijah & Miss Minarni (Ina)
1969-70	Margaret Boxall & Sue Whetnall (Eng)
1971	Noriko Takagi & Hiroe Yuki (Jap)
1972-3	Machiko Aizawa & Etsuko Takenaka (Jap)
1974	Margaret Beck & Gillian Gilks (Eng)
1975	Machiko Aizawa & Etsuko Takenaka (Jap)
1976	Gillian Gilks & Sue Whetnall (Eng)
1977	Etsuko Tuganoo (née Takenaka) & Emiko Ueno (Jap)
1978	Atsuko Tokuda & Mikiko Takada (Jap)
1979	Wiharjo Verawaty & Imelda Wigoeno (Ina)
1980	Gillian Gilks & Nora Perry (Eng)
1981	Nora Perry & Jane Webster (Eng)
1982	Lin Ying & Wu Dixi (Chn)
1983	Xu Rong & Wu Jianqiu (Chn)
1984	Liu Ying & Wu Dixi (Chn)
1985	Li Lingwei & Han Aiping (Chn)
1986-7	Chung Myung-hee & Hwang Hye-young (SKo)
1988	Chung So-young & Kim Jun-ja (SKo)
1989	Chung Myung-hee & Chung So-young (SKo)
1990	Chung Myung-hee & Hwang Hye-young (SKo)

Mixed doubles

1899-1900	D Oakes & Miss St.John (Eng)
1901	F Collier & Miss E Stawell-Brown (Eng)
1902	L Ransford & Miss E Moseley (Eng)
1903	George Thomas & Ethel Thomson (Eng)
1904	Henry Marrett & Dorothea Douglass (Eng)
1905	Henry Marrett & Hazel Hogarth (Eng)
1906	George Thomas & Ethel Thomson (Eng)
1907	George Thomas & Miss G Murray (Eng)
1908	Norman Wood & Meriel Lucas (Eng)
1909	Albert Prebble & Dora Boothby (Eng)
1910	George Sautter & Dorothy Cundall (Eng)
1911	George Thomas & Margaret Larminie (Eng)
1912	Edward Hawthorn & Hazel Hogarth (Eng)

1913	George Sautter & Miss M Mayston (Eng)
1914	George Thomas & Hazel Hogarth (Eng)
1920-2	George Thomas & Hazel Hogarth (Eng)
1923	'Curly' Mack (Ire) & Margaret Tragett (née Larminie) (Eng)
1924-5	Frank Devlin (Ire) & Kitty McKane (Eng)
1926-7	Frank Devlin (Ire) & Eveline Peterson (Eng)
1928	A Harbot & Margaret Tragett (Eng)
1929	Frank Devlin (Ire) & Marianne Horseley (Eng)
1930-2	Herbert Uber & Betty Uber (Eng)
1933-6	Donald Hume & Betty Uber (Eng)
1937	Ian Maconachie (Ire) & Thelma Kingsbury (Eng)
1938	Raymond White & Betty Uber (Eng)
1939	Ralph Nichols & Bessie Staples (Eng)
1947	Poul Holm & Tonny Olsen-Ahm (Den)
1948	Jørn Skaarup & Kirsten Thorndahl (Den)
1949	Cliton Stephens & Patsey Stephens (USA)
1950-2	Poul Holm & Tonny Olsen-Ahm (Den)
1953	Eddie Choong (Mal) & June White (Eng)
1954	John Best & Iris Cooley (Eng)
1955	Finn Kobbero & Kirsten Thorndahl (Den)
1956	Tony Jordan & June Timperley (née White) (Eng)
1957	Finn Kobbero & Kirsten Granlund (née Thorndahl) (Den)
1958	Tony Jordan & June Timperley (Eng)
1959	Per Nielsen & Mrs.I Hansen (Den)
1960-1	Finn Kobbero & Kirsten Granlund (Den)
1962-3	Finn Kobbero & Ulla Ramussen (Den)
1964	Tony Jordan & Jennifer Pritchard (Eng)
1965-6	Finn Kobbero & Ulla Strand (née Ramussen) (Den)
1967	Svend Andersen & Ulla Strand (Den)
1968	Tony Jordan & Sue Pound (Eng)
1969	Roger Mills & Gillian Perrin (Eng)
1970	Per Walsöe & Pernille Mölgaard Hansen (Den)
1971-2	Svend Pri & Ulla Strand (Den)
1973	Derek Talbot & Gillian Gilks (Eng)
1974	David Eddy & Sue Whetnall (Eng)
1975	Elliott Stuart & Nora Gardner (Eng)
1976-7	Derek Talbot & Gillian Gilks (Eng)
1978	Mike Tredgett & Nora Perry (née Gardner) (Eng)
1979	Hadinata Christian & Imelda Wigoeno (Ina)
1980-1	Mike Tredgett & Nora Perry (Eng)
1982	Martin Dew & Gillian Gilks (Eng)
1983	Thomas Kihlstrom (Swe) & Nora Perry (Eng)
1984	Martin Dew & Gillian Gilks (Eng)
1985	Billy Gillibrand & Nora Perry (Eng)
1986	Park Joo-bong & Chung Myung-hee (SKo)
1987	Lee Deuk-choon & Chung Myung-hee (SKo)
1988	Wang Pengren & Shi Fangjiing (Chn)
1989-90	Park Joo-bong & Chung Myung-hee (SKo)

Most titles:

MEN

21 George Thomas 1903-28 4 singles, 9 men's doubles, 8 mixed doubles

18 Frank Devlin 1922-31 6 singles, 7 men's doubles, 5 mixed doubles

WOMEN
17 Meriel Lucas 1899-1910 6 singles, 10 women's
   doubles, 1 mixed doubles
17 Judy Hashman (née Devlin) 1954-67 10 singles, 7
   women's doubles

**Badminton champions who won Wimbledon titles at
Lawn Tennis:**
Men: Sydney Smith 1900-6
Women: Ethel Larcombe (née Thomson) 1900-14;
Dorothea Lambert Chambers (née Douglass) 1903-14;
Dora Boothby 1909-13; Kitty Godfree (née McKane)
1920-6

EUROPEAN CHAMPIONSHIPS
The European Badminton Union was formed in 1967, and
has staged biennial championships from 1968.

Men's Singles Champions
1968	Sture Johnsson (Swe)
1970	Sture Johnsson (Swe)
1972	Wolfgang Bochow (FRG)
1974	Sture Johnsson (Swe)
1976	Flemming Delfs (Den)
1978	Flemming Delfs (Den)
1980	Flemming Delfs (Den)
1982	Jens Peter Nierhoff (Den)
1984	Morten Frost (Den)
1986	Morten Frost (Den)
1988	Darren Hall (Eng)
1990	Steve Baddeley (Eng)

Women's Singles Champions
1968	Irmgard Latz (FRG)
1970	Eva Twedberg (Swe)
1972	Margaret Beck (Eng)
1974	Gillian Gilks (Eng)
1976	Gillian Gilks (Eng)
1978	Lene Köppen (Den)
1980	Liselotte Blumer (Swi)
1982	Lene Köppen (Den)
1984	Helen Troke (Eng)
1986	Helen Troke (Eng)
1988	Kirsten Larsen (Den)
1990	Pernille Nedergaard (Den)

Most doubles titles
10 Gillian Gilks (Eng) Women's 1972, 1974, 1976, 1982,
   Mixed 1972, 1974, 1976, 1982, 1984, 1986
6 Mike Tredgett (Eng) Men's 1976, 1978, 1984, Mixed
   1978, 1980
5 Sue Whetnall (Eng) Women's 1968, 1970, 1976, Mixed
   1968, 1970

European Team Champions
England 1974, 1978, 1982, 1984
Denmark 1976, 1980, 1986, 1988

BANDY

An 11-a-side game similar to hockey, but played on an ice
rink, 90-110 metres long and 45-65 metres wide. Unlike
ice hockey, however, bandy is played with a ball rather
than a puck. It may have originated in England c.1790,
and Bury Fen Bandy Club in the North East of England is
the original home of the modern game. Some well-known
soccer clubs, such as Sheffield United and Nottingham
Forest originally had Bandy in their titles as well as
Football. The game is now played principally in the Baltic
regions, with more than half a million players in the USSR,
Finland, Norway and Sweden.

The National Bandy Association was formed in England
in 1891, but at the turn of the century the game was
forced into the background by ice hockey. The game was
introduced into Sweden in 1894 by C.G.Tebbutt of Bury
Fen, who had also organised the first international match,
between Bury Fen and Haarlem (Hol) in 1891. The first
Swedish club was established in Stockholm in 1895. Bandy
was first played in Russia in 1898. The International Bandy
Federation was formed in 1955.

World Championships are held for men's teams, first in
1957, then every two years from 1961. The USSR have
won 13 titles to 1989, every one except for 1981, 1983
and 1987 when the winners were Sweden.

The record score in a World Championship match:
USSR beat USA 21-1 at Skövde, Sweden on 1 Feb 1987.
Most gold medals by an individual: 8 Valeriy Maslov (USSR)
1961, 1963, 1965, 1967, 1971, 1973, 1975, 1977.

Olympic Games
Bandy was included as a demonstration sport at the 1952
Winter Olympics in Oslo. Sweden won the tournament
from Finland and Norway.

BASEBALL

The English believe that baseball is derived from the very
English game of rounders. The Americans, however, are
adamant that Abner Doubleday, a West Point cadet, laid
out the first 'diamond' at Cooperstown in 1839. A special
commission was set up in the United States in 1905 to
establish the true 'birth' of baseball, and their findings
credited it to Doubleday. The first rules were drawn up by
Alexander Cartwright Jr in 1845 and the first match under
the Cartwright rules was a year later between the New
York Base Ball Club and the sport's first organised club, the
New York Knickerbockers.

WORLD SERIES
There are two baseball leagues in America, the National
League (NL) which was formed in 1876 and the American
League (AL) which was formed in 1901. A total of 26

teams make up the two leagues and after a regular season of 162 matches against other teams in their own league, a series of play-offs decides which team shall represent each league in the best-of-seven game World Series played each October.

Year	Winners	Runners-up	Score
1903	Boston Red Sox (AL)	Pittsburgh Pirates (NL)	5-3
1904	Not held		
1905	New York Giants (NL)	Philadelphia Athletics (AL)	4-1
1906	Chicago White Sox (AL)	Chicago Cubs (NL)	4-2
1907	Chicago Cubs (NL)	Detroit Tigers (AL)	4-0*
1908	Chicago Cubs (NL)	Detroit Tigers (AL)	4-1
1909	Pittsburgh Pirates (NL)	Detroit Tigers (AL)	4-3
1910	Philadelphia Athletics (AL)	Chicago Cubs (NL)	4-1
1911	Philadelphia Athletics (AL)	New York Giants (NL)	4-2
1912	Boston Red Sox (AL)	New York Giants (NL)	4-3*
1913	Philadelphia Athletics (AL)	New York Giants (NL)	4-1
1914	Boston Braves (NL)	Philadelphia Athletics (AL)	4-0
1915	Boston Red Sox (AL)	Philadelphia Phillies (NL)	4-1
1916	Boston Red Sox (AL)	Brooklyn Dodgers (NL)	4-1
1917	Chicago White Sox (AL)	New York Giants (NL)	4-2
1918	Boston Red Sox (AL)	Chicago Cubs (NL)	4-2
1919	Cincinnati Reds (NL)	Chicago White Sox (AL)	5-3
1920	Cleveland Indians (AL)	Brooklyn Dodgers (NL)	5-2
1921	New York Giants (NL)	New York Yankees (AL)	4-3
1922	New York Giants (NL)	New York Yankees (AL)	4-0*
1923	New York Yankees (AL)	New York Giants (NL)	4-2
1924	Washington Senators (AL)	New York Giants (NL)	4-3
1925	Pittsburgh Pirates (NL)	Washington Senators (AL)	4-3
1926	St.Louis Cardinals (NL)	New York Yankees (AL)	4-3
1927	New York Yankees (AL)	Pittsburgh Pirates (NL)	4-0
1928	New York Yankees (AL)	St.Louis Cardinals (NL)	4-0
1929	Philadelphia Athletics (AL)	Chicago Cubs (NL)	4-1
1930	Philadelphia Athletics (AL)	St.Louis Cardinals (NL)	4-2
1931	St.Louis Cardinals (NL)	Philadelphia Athletics (AL)	4-3
1932	New York Yankees (AL)	Chicago Cubs (NL)	4-0
1933	New York Giants (NL)	Washington Senators (AL)	4-1
1934	St.Louis Cardinals (NL)	Detroit Tigers (AL)	4-3
1935	Detroit Tigers (AL)	Chicago Cubs (NL)	4-2
1936	New York Yankees (AL)	New York Giants (NL)	4-2
1937	New York Yankees (AL)	New York Giants (NL)	4-1
1938	New York Yankees (AL)	Chicago Cubs (NL)	4-0
1939	New York Yankees (AL)	Cincinnati Reds (NL)	4-0
1940	Cincinnati Reds (NL)	Detroit Tigers (AL)	4-3
1941	New York Yankees (AL)	Brooklyn Dodgers (NL)	4-1
1942	St.Louis Cardinals (NL)	New York Yankees (AL)	4-1
1943	New York Yankees (AL)	St.Louis Cardinals (NL)	4-1
1944	St.Louis Cardinals (NL)	St.Louis Browns (AL)	4-2
1945	Detroit Tigers (AL)	Chicago Cubs (NL)	4-3
1946	St.Louis Cardinals (NL)	Boston Red Sox (AL)	4-3
1947	New York Yankees (AL)	Brooklyn Dodgers (NL)	4-3
1948	Cleveland Indians (AL)	Boston Braves (NL)	4-2
1949	New York Yankees (AL)	Brooklyn Dodgers (NL)	4-1
1950	New York Yankees (AL)	Philadelphia Phillies (NL)	4-0
1951	New York Yankees (AL)	New York Giants (NL)	4-2
1952	New York Yankees (AL)	Brooklyn Dodgers (NL)	4-3
1953	New York Yankees (AL)	Brooklyn Dodgers (NL)	4-2
1954	New York Giants (NL)	Cleveland Indians (AL)	4-0
1955	Brooklyn Dodgers (NL)	New York Yankees (AL)	4-3
1956	New York Yankees (AL)	Brooklyn Dodgers (NL)	4-3

Year	Winners	Runners-up	Score
1957	Milwaukee Braves (NL	New York Yankees (AL)	4-3
1958	New York Yankees (AL)	Milwaukee Braves (NL)	4-3
1959	Los Angeles Dodgers (NL)	Chicago White Sox (AL)	4-2
1960	Pittsburgh Pirates (NL)	New York Yankees (AL)	4-3
1961	New York Yankees (AL)	Cincinnati Reds (NL)	4-1
1962	New York Yankees (AL)	San Francisco Giants (NL)	4-3
1963	Los Angeles Dodgers (NL)	New York Yankees (AL)	4-0
1964	St.Louis Cardinals (NL)	New York Yankees (AL)	4-3
1965	Los Angeles Dodgers (NL)	Minnesota Twins (AL)	4-3
1966	Baltimore Orioles (AL)	Los Angeles Dodgers (NL)	4-0
1967	St.Louis Cardinals (NL)	Boston Red Sox (AL)	4-3
1968	Detroit Tigers (AL)	St.Louis Cardinals (NL)	4-3
1969	New York Mets (NL)	Baltimore Orioles (AL)	4-1
1970	Baltimore Orioles (AL)	Cincinnati Reds (NL)	4-1
1971	Pittsburgh Pirates (NL)	Baltimore Orioles (AL)	4-3
1972	Oakland 'A's (AL)	Cincinnati Reds (NL)	4-3
1973	Oakland 'A's (AL)	New York Mets (NL)	4-3
1974	Oakland 'A's (AL)	Los Angeles Dodgers (NL)	4-1
1975	Cincinnati Reds (NL)	Boston Red Sox (AL)	4-3
1976	Cincinnati Reds (NL)	New York Yankees (AL)	4-0
1977	New York Yankees (AL)	Los Angeles Dodgers (NL)	4-3
1978	New York Yankees (AL)	Los Angeles Dodgers (NL)	4-2
1979	Pittsburgh Pirates (NL)	Baltimore Orioles (AL)	4-3
1980	Philadelphia Phillies (NL)	Kansas City Royals (AL)	4-2
1981	Los Angeles Dodgers (NL)	New York Yankees (AL)	4-2
1982	St.Louis Cardinals (NL)	Milwaukee Brewers (AL)	4-3
1983	Baltimore Orioles (AL)	Philadelphia Phillies (NL)	4-1
1984	Detroit Tigers (AL)	San Diego Padres (NL)	4-1
1985	Kansas City Royals (AL)	St.Louis Cardinals (NL)	4-3
1986	New York Mets (NL)	Boston Red Sox (AL)	4-3
1987	Minnesota Twins (AL)	St.Louis Cardinals (NL)	4-3
1988	Los Angeles Dodgers (NL)	Oakland Athletics (AL)	4-1
1989	Oakland Athletics (AL)	San Francisco Giants (NL)	4-0
*	Includes one drawn game		

(AL) American League, (NL) National League

Most wins: 22 New York Yankees, 9 St.Louis Cardinals, 5 Boston Red Sox, Pittsburgh Pirates, Philadelphia Athletics, New York Giants, Los Angeles Dodgers; 4 Cincinnati Reds, Detroit Tigers, Oakland A's; 3 Baltimore Orioles

Most Appearances: 33 New York Yankees; 15 St Louis Cardinals; 14 New York Giants; 10 Chicago White Sox; 9 Boston Red Sox, Detroit Tigers, Los Angeles Dodgers, Brooklyn Dodgers

Most individual appearances: 14 Lawrence 'Yogi' Berra (New York Yankees) 1947, 1949-53, 1955-8, 1960-3 (he was on the winning team 10 times)

Most home runs in one game: 3 'Babe' Ruth (New York Yankees v St.Louis Cardinals, 4th game) 6 Oct 1926; Reggie Jackson (New York Yankees v Los Angeles Dodgers, 6th game) 18 Oct 1977 (Jackson hit three consecutive pitches out of the park for his homers)

Most runs in a series: 10 Reggie Jackson (New York Yankees, 1977)

Most home runs in a series: 5 Reggie Jackson (New York Yankees, 1977)

Perfect pitch (9 innings): Don Larsen (New York Yankees v Brooklyn Dodgers, 5th game) 8 Oct 1956

Record attendance (series): 420,784 Los Angeles Dodgers v Chicago White Sox 1-8 Oct 1959

Record attendance (single game): 92,706 Los Angeles Dodgers v Chicago White Sox (5th game) at Memorial Coliseum, Los Angeles, 6 Oct 1959

Most valuable player award

The only men to have won the coveted award twice are: Sandy Koufax (Los Angeles, NL 1963, 1965), Bob Gibson (St.Louis NL, 1964, 1967), Reggie Jackson (Oakland AL, New York AL, 1973, 1977)

MAJOR LEAGUE RECORDS

Most National League titles (from 1876):
17 New York Giants, 16 Chicago Cubs, 14 St.Louis Cardinals, 12 Brooklyn Dodgers, 9 Boston Braves, Pittsburgh Pirates, Los Angeles Dodgers
Most American League titles (from 1901):
33 New York Yankees, 10 Boston Red Sox, 9 Detroit Tigers, Philadelphia Athletics

BATTING
Career
Best batting average: .367 Ty Cobb (Detroit AL, Philadelphia AL) 1905-28
Most runs: 2245 Ty Cobb (Detroit AL, Philadelphia AL) 1905-28
Most home runs: 755 Hank Aaron (Milwaukee NL, Atlanta NL, Milwaukee AL) 1954-76
Most runs batted in: 2297 Hank Aaron (Milwaukee NL, Atlanta NL, Milwaukee AL) 1954-76
Most base hits: 4256 Pete Rose (Cincinatti NL, Philadelphia NL) 1963-86
Total bases: 6856 Hank Aaron (Milwaukee NL, Atlanta NL, Milwaukee AL) 1954-76
Stolen bases: 938 Louis Brock (Chicago NL, St.Louis NL) 1961-79

Season

Best batting average: .438 Hugh Duffy (Boston NL) 1894
Most runs: 196 William Hamilton (Philadelphia NL) 1894
Most home runs: 61 Roger Maris (New York AL) 1961
Most runs batted in: 190 Hack Wilson (Chicago NL) 1930
Most base hits: 257 George Sisler (St.Louis AL) 1920
Total bases: 457 Babe Ruth (New York AL) 1921
Stolen bases: 130 Rickey Henderson (Oakland AL) 1982

General

Consecutive hits: 12 Pinky Higgins (Boston AL) 19-21 Jun 1938; Moose Dropo (Detroit AL) 14-15 Jul 1952
Consecutive games batted safely: 56 Joe DiMaggio (New York AL) 15 May-16 Jul 1941
Consecutive games played: 2130 Lou Gehrig (New York AL) 1 Jun 1925-30 Apr 1939

PITCHING

Career

Games won: 511 Cy Young (Cleveland NL, St.Louis AL, Boston NL, Boston AL, Cleveland AL) 1890-1911
Shutouts: 110 Walter Johnson (Washington AL) 1907-27
Strikeouts: 5076 Nolan Ryan (New York NL, California AL, Houston NL, Texas AL) 1968-89
No-hit games: 5 Nolan Ryan
Complete games: 751 Cy Young (Cleveland NL, St.Louis AL, Boston NL, Boston AL, Cleveland AL) 1890-1911

Season

Games won: 60 Charles Radbourne (Providence NL) 1884
Shutouts: 16 George Bradley (St.Louis NL) 1876; Grover Alexander (Philadelphia NL) 1916
Strikeouts: 383 Nolan Ryan (California AL) 1973
General
Consecutive games won: 24 Carl Owen Hubbell (New York NL) 1936-7

ALL-TIME TOP TENS

Batting - Most Runs

Ty Cobb	2245
Babe Ruth	2174
Hank Aaron	2174
Pete Rose	2165
Willie Mays	2062
Stan Musial	1949
Lou Gehrig	1888
Tristram Speaker	1881
Melvin Ott	1859
Frank Robinson	1829

Batting - Most Hits

Pete Rose	4256
Ty Cobb	4191
Hank Aaron	3771
Stan Musial	3630
Tristram Speaker	3515
John P.Wagner	3430
Carl Yastrzemski	3419
Ted Collins	3309
Willie Mays	3283
Napolean Lajoie	3252

Batting - Most Home Runs

Hank Aaron	755
Babe Ruth	714
Willie Mays	660
Frank Robinson	586
Harmon Killibrew	573
Reggie Jackson	563

Michael Schmidt	548*
Mickey Mantle	536
James Foxx	534
Ted Williams	521
Willie McCovey	521

Pitching - Most Wins

Cy Young	511
Walter Johnson	416
Chris Matthewson	373
Grover Alexander	373
Warren Spahn	363
Charles Nichols	361
James Galvin	361
Timothy Keefe	342
Steve Carlton	329
John Clarkson	327

Pitching - Most Strikeouts

Nolan Ryan	5076*
Steve Carlton	4136
Tom Seaver	3640
Don Sutton	3574
Bart Blyleven	3562*
Gaylord Perry	3534
Walter Johnson	3508
Phil Niekro	3342
Ferguson Jenkins	3192
Robert Gibson	3117

* Denotes current player

Ty Cobb, the 'Georgia Peach', still holds baseball career records for batting average and most hits (Hulton-Deutsch)

LEAGUE LEADERS

Post-war leaders - taking the best of the AL or NL each year:

Best batting average

1946	Stan Musial (St.Louis)	NL	.365
1947	Harry Walker (St.Louis/Philadelphia)	NL	.363
1948	Stan Musial (St.Louis)	NL	.376
1949	George Kell (Detroit)	AL	.343
1950	Billy Goodman (Boston)	AL	.354
1951	Stan Musial (St.Louis)	NL	.355
1952	Stan Musial (St.Louis)	NL	.336
1953	Carl Furillo (Brooklyn)	NL	.344
1954	Willie Mays (New York Giants)	NL	.345
1955	Al Kaline (Detroit)	AL	.340
1956	Mickey Mantle (New York Yankees)	AL	.353
1957	Ted Williams (Boston)	AL	.388
1958	Richie Ashburn (Philadelphia)	NL	.350
1959	Hank Aaron (Milwaukee)	NL	.355
1960	Dick Groat (Pittsburgh)	NL	.325
1961	Norm Cash (Detroit)	AL	.361
1962	Tommy Davis (Los Angeles)	NL	.346
1963	Tommy Davis (Los Angeles)	NL	.326
1964	Roberto Clemente (Pittsburgh)	NL	.339
1965	Roberto Clemente (Pittsburgh)	NL	.329
1966	Maria Alou (Pittsburgh)	NL	.342
1967	Roberto Clemente (Pittsburgh)	NL	.357
1968	Pete Rose (Cincinatti)	NL	.335
1969	Pete Rose (Cincinatti)	NL	.348
1970	Rico Carty (Atlanta)	NL	.366
1971	Joe Torre (St.Louis)	NL	.363
1972	Billy Williams (Chicago)	NL	.333
1973	Rod Carew (Minnesota)	AL	.350
1974	Rod Carew (Minnesota)	AL	.364
1975	Rod Carew (Minnesota)	AL	.359
1976	Bill Madlock (Chicago)	NL	.339
1977	Rod Carew (Minnesota)	AL	.388
1978	Dave Parker (Pittsburgh)	NL	.334
1979	Keith Hernandez (St.Louis)	NL	.344
1980	George Brett (Kansas City)	AL	.390
1981	Bill Madlock (Pittsburgh)	NL	.341
1982	Willie Watson (Kansas City)	AL	.332
1983	Wade Boggs (Boston)	AL	.361
1984	Tony Gwynn (San Diego)	NL	.341
1985	Wade Boggs (Boston)	AL	.368
1986	Wade Boggs (Boston	AL	.357
1987	Tony Gwynne (San Diego)	NL	.370
1988	Wade Boggs (Boston)	AL	.366
1989	Kirby Puckett (Minnesota)	AL	.339

Highest ever average: .438 Hugh Duffy (Boston NL) 1894

AL best: .421 Napolean Lajoie (Philadelphia) 1901

Most seasons with best average:

AL 9 Ty Cobb (Detroit) 1907-15

7 Rod Carew (Minnesota) 1969, 1972-5, 1977-8

6 Ted Williams (Boston) 1941-2, 1947-8, 1957-8

NL 8 John P.Wagner (Pittsburgh) 1900, 1903-4, 1906-9, 1911

7 Rogers Hornsby (St.Louis) 1920-5, 1928

7 Stan Musial (St.Louis) 1943, 1946, 1948, 1950-2, 1957

Most home runs

1946	Hank Greenberg (Detroit)	AL	44
1947	Ralph Kiner (Pittsburgh)	NL &	
	Johnny Mize (New York Giants)	NL	51
1948	Ralph Kiner (Pittsburgh)	NL &	
	Johnny Mize (New York Giants)	NL	40
1949	Ralph Kiner (Pittsburgh)	NL	54
1950	Ralph Kiner (Pittsburgh)	NL	47
1951	Ralph Kiner (Pittsburgh)	NL	42
1952	Ralph Kiner (Pittsburgh)	NL &	
	Hank Sauer (Chicago)	NL	37
1953	Eddie Mathews (Milwaukee)	NL	47
1954	Ted Kluszewski (Cincinnati)	NL	49
1955	Willie Mays (New York Giants)	NL	51
1956	Mickey Mantle (New York Yankees)	NL	52
1957	Hank Aaron (Milwaukee)	NL	44
1958	Ernie Banks (Chicago)	NL	47
1959	Eddie Mathews (Milwaukee)	NL	46
1960	Ernie Banks (Chicago)	NL	41
1961	Orlando Cepeda (San Francisco)	NL	46
1962	Willie Mays (San Francisco)	NL	49
1963	Harmon Killebrew (Minnesota)	AL	45
1964	Harmon Killebrew (Minnesota)	AL	49
1965	Willie Mays (San Francisco)	NL	52
1966	Frank Robinson (Baltimore)	AL	49
1967	Carl Yastrzemski (Boston)	AL &	
	Harmon Killebrew (Minnesota)	AL	44
1968	Frank Howard (Washington)	AL	44
1969	Harmon Killebrew (Minnesota)	AL	49
1970	Johnny Bench (Cincinnati)	NL	45
1971	Willie Stargel (Pittsburgh)	NL	48
1972	Johnny Bench (Cincinnati)	NL	40
1973	Willie Stargel (Pittsburgh)	NL	44
1974	Mike Schmidt (Philadelphia)	NL	36
1975	Mike Schmidt (Philadelphia)	NL	38
1976	Mike Schmidt (Philadelphia)	NL	38
1977	George Foster (Cincinnati)	NL	52
1978	Jim Rice (Boston)	AL	46
1979	Dave Kingman (Chicago)	NL	48
1980	Mike Schmidt (Philadelphia)	NL	48
1981	Mike Schmidt (Philadelphia)	NL	31
1982	Gorman Thomas (Milwaukee)	AL &	
	Reggie Jackson (California)	AL	39
1983	Mike Schmidt (Philadelphia)	NL	40
1984	Tony Armas (Boston)	AL	43
1985	Darrell Evans (Detroit)	AL	60
1986	Jesse Barfield (Toronto)	AL	40
1987	Mark McGwire (Oakland)	AL	
	& Andre Dawson (Chicago)	NL	49
1988	Jose Canseco (Oakland)	AL	42
1989	Kevin Mitchell (San Francisco)	NL	47

Most seasons leading

AL 12 Babe Ruth (New York) 1918-21, 1923-4, 1926-31

6 Harmon Killebrew 1959, 1962-4, 1967, 1969

NL 8 Mike Schmidt 1974-6, 1980-1, 1983-4, 1986

7 Ralph Kiner (Pittsburgh) 1946-52

6 Melvin Ott (New York) 1932, 1934, 1936-8, 1942

Earned run average

Year	Player	League	ERA
1946	Hal Newhouser (Detroit)	AL	1.94
1947	Warren Spahn (Boston)	NL	2.33
1948	Harry Brecheen (St.Louis)	NL	2.24
1949	Dave Koslo (New York)	NL	2.50
1950	Jim Hearn (St.Louis/New York)	NL	2.49
1951	Saul Rogovin (Detroit/Chicago)	AL	2.78
1952	Allie Reynolds (New York)	AL	2.07
1953	Warren Spahn (Milwaukee)	NL	2.10
1954	John Antonelli (New York)	NL	2.29
1955	Billy Pierce (Chicago)	AL	1.57
1956	Whitey Ford (New York)	AL	2.47
1957	Bobby Schantz (New York)	AL	2.45
1958	Whitey Ford (New York)	AL	2.01
1959	Hoyt Wilhelm (Baltimore)	AL	2.19
1960	Frank Baumann (Chicago)	AL	2.68
1961	Richard Donovan (Washington)	AL	2.40
1962	Hank Aguirre (Detroit)	AL	2.21
1963	Sandy Koufax (Los Angeles)	NL	1.88
1964	Dean Chance (Los Angeles)	AL	1.64
1965	Sandy Koufax (Los Angeles)	NL	2.04
1966	Sandy Koufax (Los Angeles)	NL	2.04
1967	Phil Niekro (Atlanta)	NL	1.87
1968	Bob Gibson (St.Louis)	NL	1.12
1969	Juan Marichal (San Francisco)	NL	2.10
1970	Diego Segui (Oakland)	AL	2.56
1971	Tom Seaver (New York)	NL	1.76
1972	Luis Tiant (Boston)	AL	1.91
1973	Tom Seaver (New York)	NL	2.07
1974	Buzz Capra (Atlanta)	NL	2.28
1975	Jim Palmer (Baltimore)	AL	2.09
1976	Mark Fidrych (Detroit)	AL	2.34
1977	John Candelaria (Pittsburgh)	NL	2.34
1978	Ron Guidry (New York)	AL	1.74
1979	J.R.Richard (Houston)	NL	2.71
1980	Don Sutton (Los Angeles)	NL	2.21
1981	Nolan Ryan (Houston)	NL	1.69
1982	Steve Rogers (Montreal)	NL	2.40
1983	Atlee Hammaker (San Francisco)	NL	2.25
1984	Alejandro Pena (Los Angeles)	NL	2.56
1985	Dwight Gooden (New York)	NL	1.53
1986	Mike Scott (Houston)	AL	2.22
1987	James E.Key (Toronto)	AL &	2.76
	Nolan Ryan (Houston)	NL	2.76
1988	Allan Anderson (Minnesota)	AL &	
	Teodoro Higuera (Milwaukee)	AL	2.45
1989	Scott Garrelts (San Francisco)	NL	2.28

Most times leader:
AL 8 Lefty Grove (Philadelphia, Boston) 1926, 1930-2, 1935-6, 1938-9
4 Barney Johnson (Washington) 1913, 1918-9, 1924
NL 5 Pete Alexander (Philadelphia, Chicago) 1915-7, 1919-20
5 Sandy Koufax (Los Angeles) 1962-6
3 Dazzy Vance (Brooklyn) 1924, 1928, 1930
3 Carl Hubbell (New York) 1933-4, 1936
3 Tom Seaver (New York) 1970-1, 1973

MOST VALUABLE PLAYER OF THE YEAR

At the end of each season the Baseball Writers' Association vote for the Most Valuable Player of the Year in both the American and National leagues. The award was instituted in 1931. *Post-war winners:*

Year	AMERICAN LEAGUE	NATIONAL LEAGUE
1946	Ted Williams (Boston)	Stan Musial (St.Louis)
1947	Joe DiMaggio (New York)	Bob Elliott (Boston)
1948	Louis Boudreau (Cleveland)	Stan Musial (St.Louis)
1949	Ted Williams (Boston)	Jack Robinson (Brooklyn)
1950	Philip Rizzuto (New York)	Jim Konstanty (Philadelphia)
1951	'Yogi' Berra (New York)	Roy Campanella (Brooklyn)
1952	Robert Shantz (Philadelphia)	Hank Sauer (Chicago)
1953	Albert Rosen (Cleveland)	Roy Campanella (Brooklyn)
1954	'Yogi' Berra (New York)	Willie Mays (New York)
1955	'Yogi' Berra (New York)	Roy Campanella (Brooklyn)
1956	Mickey Mantle (New York)	Don Newcombe (Brooklyn)
1957	Mickey Mantle (New York)	Hank Aaron (Milwaukee)
1958	Jack Jensen (Boston)	Ernest Banks (Chicago)
1959	Nelson Fox (Chicago)	Ernest Banks (Chicago)
1960	Roger Maris (New York)	Dick Groat (Pittsburgh)
1961	Roger Maris (New York)	Frank Robinson (Cincinnati)
1962	Mickey Mantle (New York)	Maurice Wills (Los Angeles)
1963	Elston Howard (New York)	Sandy Koufax (Los Angeles)
1964	Brooks Robinson (Baltimore)	Kenton Boyer (St.Louis)
1965	Zoilo Versalles (Minnesota)	Willie Mays (San Francisco)
1966	Frank Robinson (Baltimore)	Roberto Clemente (Pittsburgh)
1967	Carl Yastrzemski (Boston)	Orlando Cepeda (St.Louis)
1968	Dennis McLain (Detroit)	Robert Gibson (St.Louis)
1969	Harmon Killebrew (Minnesota)	Willie McCovey (San Francisco)
1970	John Powell (Baltimore)	Johnny Bench (Cincinnati)
1971	Vida Blue (Oakland)	Joe Torre (St.Louis)
1972	Dick Allen (Chicago)	Johnny Bench (Cincinnati)
1973	Reggie Jackson (Oakland)	Pete Rose (Cincinnati)
1974	Jeffrey Burroughs (Texas)	Steve Garvey (Los Angeles)
1975	Fredric Lynn (Boston)	Joe Morgan (Cincinnati)
1976	Thurman Munson (New York)	Joe Morgan (Cincinnati)
1977	Rod Carew (Minnesota)	George Foster (Cincinnati)

1978	Jim Rice (Boston)	Dave Parker (Pittsburgh)
1979	Donald Baylor (California)	Keith Hernandez (St.Louis) & Willie Stargell (Pittsburgh)
1980	George Brett (Kansas City)	Mike Schmidt (Philadelphia)
1981	Rollie Fingers (Milwaukee)	Mike Schmidt (Phildaelphia)
1982	Robin Yount (Milwaukee)	Dale Murphy (Atlanta)
1983	Cal Ripken Jr (Baltimore)	Dale Murphy (Atlanta)
1984	Willie Hernandez (Detroit)	Ryne Sandberg (Chicago)
1985	Don Mattingly (New York)	Willie McGee (St.Louis)
1986	Roger Clemmens (Boston)	Mike Schmidt (Philadelphia)
1987	George Bell (Toronto)	Andre Dawson (Chicago)
1988	Jose Canseco (Oakland)	Kirk Gibson (Los Angeles)
1989	Robin Yount (Milwaukee)	Kevin Mitchell (San Francisco)

Most selections:
NL: 3 Stan Musial 1943, 1946, 1948; Roy Campanella, Mike Schmidt
AL: 3 James E.Foxx (Philadelphia) 1932-3, 1938; Joe Di Maggio 1939, 1941, 1947; Yogi Berra, Mickey Mantle

CY YOUNG AWARD

Awarded from 1956 to the outstanding pitcher on the major leagues. From 1967 awards have been made for both American and National leagues. *Recent winners:*

	AMERICAN LEAGUE	NATIONAL LEAGUE
1980	Steve Stone (Baltimore)	Steve Carlton (Philadelphia)
1981	Rollie Fingers (Milwaukee)	Fernando Valenzuela (Los Angeles)
1982	Pete Vukovich (Milwaukee)	Steve Carlton (Philadelphia)
1983	LaMarr Hoyt (Chicago)	John Denny (Philadelphia)
1984	Willie Hernandez (Detroit)	Rick Sutcliffe (Chicago)
1985	Bret Saberhagen (Kansas City)	Dwight Gooden (New York)
1986	Roger Clemens (Boston)	Mike Scott (Houston)
1987	Roger Clemens (Boston)	Steve Bedrosian (Philadelphia)
1988	Frank Viola (Minnesota)	Orel Hershiser (Los Angeles)
1989	Bret Saberhagen (Kansas City)	Mark Davis (San Diego)

Most wins: 3 Sandy Koufax (Los Angeles AL) 1963, 1965-6; James Palmer (Baltimore AL) 1973, 1975-6; Tom Seaver (New York NL) 1969, 1973, 1975; Steve Carlton (Philadelphia NL) 1977, 1980, 1982

Joe DiMaggio of the New York Yankees, perhaps the game's greatest ever centrefield, became almost as famous for his marriage to Marilyn Monroe as for his hitting (Hulton-Deutsch)

Mike Schmidt led the National League for home runs in a record eight seasons (All-Sport)

NCAA CHAMPIONSHIP

Held annually since 1947. Since 1950 every championship final has been played at Omaha, Nebraska.

Recent winners		
1980	Arizona	1984 Cal St.Fullerton
1981	Arizona State	1985 Miami (Florida)
1982	Miami (Florida)	1986 Arizona
1983	Texas	1987-8 Stanford
		1989 Wichita State

The Arizona State v. Ohio State match in 1965 was not resolved until the 15th innings. Arizona won 2-1.
Most wins: 11 Southern California, 5 Arizona State, 4 Texas, 3 Arizona, Minnesota

WORLD AMATEUR CHAMPIONSHIP

Instituted 1938. Coordinated by the International Baseball Association (IBA), membership of which reached 66 nations in 1989. Held biennially since 1974. *Winners:*
19 Cuba   1939-40, 1942-3, 1950, 1952-3, 1961,
                1969-73*, 1976, 1978, 1980, 1984, 1986, 1988
3 Venezuela 1941, 1944-5,
2 Colombia 1947, 1965, USA 1973*-4
1 United Kingdom 1938, Dominican Republic 1948,
   Puerto Rico 1951, South Korea 1982
*1973, Cuba and USA shared title

OLYMPIC GAMES

American baseball has appeared at six Olympic Games as a demonstration sport. In addition, Finnish baseball was included in 1952. *Winners:*
1912 USA
1936 'World Amateurs'
1956 American Services team
1964 USA
1984 Japan
1988 USA

BASKETBALL

The modern game of basketball was invented by Dr James Naismith at the Training School of the International YMCA College at Springfield, Massachussets, USA in December 1891. Games bearing a resemblance to basketball have been played for thousands of years, the earliest being perhaps 'Pok-ta-Pok', played by the Olmecs in Mexico in the 10th century BC.

The early games of basketball had large numbers of players, but five-a-side as standard was agreed in 1895. The AAU organised the first national tournament in the USA in 1897. The first profesional league was the National Basketball League (NBL), founded in 1898. This organization merged with the Basketball Association of America in 1949 to form the National Basketball Association (NBA).

The world governing body, the Fédération Internationale de Basketball (FIBA) was founded in 1932 and the sport added to the Olympic programme in 1936. FIBA membership reached 178 in 1989.

OLYMPIC GAMES

First played by men in 1936 and by women in 1976. *Winners:*
MEN
1936 USA
1948 USA
1952 USA
1956 USA
1960 USA
1964 USA
1968 USA
1972 USSR
1976 USA
1980 Yugoslavia
1984 USA
1988 USSR

WOMEN
1976 USSR
1980 USSR
1984 USA
1988 USA

WORLD CHAMPIONSHIPS

First held for men in Buenos Aires in 1950, and for women in 1953. They are each now held quadrenially. *Winners:*
MEN
1950 Argentina
1954 USA
1959 Brazil
1963 Brazil
1967 USSR
1970 Yugoslavia
1974 USSR
1978 Yugoslavia
1982 USSR
1986 USA
WOMEN
1953 USA
1957 USA
1959 USSR
1964 USSR
1967 USSR
1971 USSR
1975 USSR
1979 USA
1983 USSR
1986 USA

EUROPEAN CHAMPIONSHIPS

Contested by European nations. Held biennially. *Wins:*
MEN
14 USSR 1947, 1951, 1953, 1957, 1959, 1961, 1963,
       1965, 1967, 1969, 1971, 1979, 1981, 1985
4 Yugoslavia 1973, 1975, 1977, 1989
2 Lithuania 1937, 1939
1 Latvia 1935, Czechoslovakia 1946, Egypt 1949
1 Hungary 1955, Italy 1983, Greece 1987

WOMEN
20 USSR 1950, 1952, 1954, 1956, 1960, 1962, 1964, 1966, 1968, 1970, 1972, 1974, 1976, 1978, 1980, 1981, 1983, 1985, 1987, 1989
1 Italy 1938, Bulgaria 1958

EUROPEAN CHAMPIONS' CUP
First held in 1958 for men and 1959 women. *Wins:*
MEN
7 Real Madrid (Spa) 1964-5, 1967-8, 1974, 1978, 1980
5 Varese (Ita) 1970, 1972-3, 1975-6
4 CSKA Moskva (USSR) 1961, 1963, 1969, 1971
3 ASK Riga (USSR) 1958-60
3 Milan (Ita) 1966, 1987-8
2 Cantu (Ita) 1982-3
2 Maccabi Tel Aviv (Isr) 1977, 1981
2 Cibona Zagreb (Yug) 1985-6
2 Jugoplastika Split (Yug) 1989
1 Dynamo Tbilisi (USSR) 1962, Bosna Sarajevo (Yug) 1979, Banco di Roma (Ita) 1984
WOMEN
18 Daugawa Riga (USSR) 1960-2, 1964-75, 1977, 1981-2
5 AS Vicenza (Ita) 1983, 1985-8
2 Slavia Sofia (Bul) 1959, 1963, 1984
1 CKD Praha (Cs) 1976, Sesto San Giovanni (Ita) 1978, Red Star Belgrade 1979, Turin (Ita) 1980, Levski Spartak Sofia 1984, Jedinstvo Aida (Yug) 1989, Enimont Priolo (Ita) 1990

NBA CHAMPIONS
The 23 American professional teams are divided into two conferences, the Eastern, subdivided into the Atlantic Division and the Central Division, and the Western, subdivided into the Midwest Division and the Pacific Division. The best teams contest play-offs annually to determine the champions. The American Basketball Association, which had begun in 1967, merged with the NBA in 1976.
National League Champions:
1938 Goodyears
1939-40 Firestones
1941-2 Oshkosh
1943-5 Fort Wayne Pistons
1946 Rochester Royals
1947 Chicago Stags
1948 Minneapolis Lakers
1949 Anderson Packers
NBA Champions:
1947 Philadelphia Warriors
1948 Baltimore Bullets
1949-50 Minneapolis Lakers
1951 Rochester Royals
1952-4 Minneapolis Lakers
1955 Syracuse Nationals
1956 Philadelphia Warriors
1957 Boston Celtics
1958 St Louis Hawks
1959-66 Boston Celtics
1967 Philadelphia 76ers

1968-9 Boston Celtics
1970 New York Knicks
1971 Milwaukee Bucks
1972 Los Angeles Lakers
1973 New York Knicks
1974 Boston Celtics
1975 Golden State Warriors
1976 Boston Celtics
1977 Portland Trail Blazers
1978 Washington Bullets
1979 Seattle Supersonics
1980 Los Angeles Lakers
1981 Boston Celtics
1982 Los Angeles Lakers
1983 Philadelphia 76ers
1984 Boston Celtics
1985 Los Angeles Lakers
1986 Boston Celtics
1987-8 Los Angeles Lakers
1989-90 Detroit Pistons

Most wins: 16 Boston Celtics

NBA Records
Highest match aggregate: 370 Detroit Pistons beat Denver Nuggets 186-184, Denver, 13 Dec 1983. Extra time was played following a 145-145 tie in regulation time.
Most points in game: 100 Wilt Chamberlain, Philadelphia v New York, 2 Mar 1962.
Most points in playoffs game: 63 Michael Jordan, Chicago v Boston, 20 Apr 1986.
Season's record points: 4029 Wilt Chamberlain, Philadelphia, 1962 (at a record average 50.4 points per game).
Career record points:
38,387 Kareem Abdul-Jabbar for Milwaukee Bucks & Los Angeles Lakers 1969-89 (in 1560 games, average 24.61 points per game, with a record 15,837 field goals. He also scored a record 5762 points, including 2396 field goals, in play-off games).

Leading career scorers (NBA and ABA)

Points	Name	Years	Games	Ave.
38,387	Kareem Abdul-Jabbar	1970-89	1560	24.6
31,419	Wilt Chamberlain	1960-73	1045	30.1
30,026	Julius Erving	1972-87	1243	24.2
27,482	Dan Issel	1971-85	1218	22.6
27,313	Elvin Hayes	1969-84	1303	21.0
27,039	Moses Malone	1975-90	1208	22.4
26,710	Oscar Robertson	1961-74	1040	25.7
26,595	George Gervin	1973-86	1061	25.1
26,395	John Havlicek	1963-78	1270	20.8
25,279	Rick Barry	1966-80	1020	24.8
25,192	Jerry West	1961-74	932	27.0
24,941	Artis Gilmore	1972-88	1329	18.8
24,850	Alex English	1977-90	1114	22.3
23,149	Elgin Baylor	1959-72	846	27.4
22,458	Adrian Dantley	1977-89	900	25.0

Other averages over 25.0 for more than 10,000 points

20,880	Bob Pettit	1955-65	792	26.4
19,719	Larry Bird	1980-90	792	24.9
16,665	Dominique Wilkins	1983-90	641	26.0
14,016	Michael Jordan	1984-90	427	32.8

Leading career scorers in NBA Playoffs (Pre – 1990)

Points	Name	Games	Average
5762	Kareem Abdul-Jabbar	237	24.3
4457	Jerry West	153	29.1
3776	John Havlicek	172	22.0
3623	Elgin Baylor	134	27.0
3607	Wilt Chamberlain	160	22.5
3559	Larry Bird	145	24.5
3088	Julius Irving	141	21.9
3047	Dennis Johnson	175	17.4

Other averages over 25.0 for more than 1500 points

2240	Bob Pettit	88	25.5
2202	George Gervin	59	27.0

NBA Leading Scorers each season

Year	Name (Club)	Games	Points
1950	George Mikan (Minneapolis)	68	1865
1951	George Mikan (Minneapolis)	68	1932
1952	Paul Arizin (Philadelphia)	66	1674
1953	Neil Johnston (Philadelphia)	70	1564
1954	Neil Johnston (Philadelphia)	72	1759
1955	Neil Johnston (Philadelphia)	72	1631
1956	Bob Pettit (St Louis)	72	1849
1957	Paul Arizin (Philadelphia)	71	1817
1958	George Yardley (Detroit)	72	2001
1959	Bob Pettit (St Louis)	72	2105
1960	Wilt Chamberlain (Philadelphia)	72	2707
1961	Wilt Chamberlain (Philadelphia)	79	3033
1962	Wilt Chamberlain (Philadelphia)	80	4029
1963	Wilt Chamberlain (San Francisco)	80	3586
1964	Wilt Chamberlain (San Francisco)	80	2948
1965	Wilt Chamberlain (Philadelphia)	80	2534
1966	Wilt Chamberlain (Philadelphia)	79	2649
1967	Rick Barry (San Francisco)	78	2775
1968	Dave Bing (Detroit)	79	2142
1969	Elvin Hayes (San Diego)	82	2327
1970	Jerry West (Los Angeles)	74	2309
1971	Lew Alcindor* (Milwaukee)	82	2596
1972	Kareem Abdul-Jabbar (Milwaukee)	81	2822
1973	Nate Archibald (Kansas City/Omaha)	80	2719
1974	Bob McAdoo (Buffalo)	74	2261
1975	Bob McAdoo (Buffalo)	82	2831
1976	Bob McAdoo (Buffalo)	78	2427
1977	Pete Maravich (New Orleans)	73	2273
1978	George Gervin (San Antonio)	82	2232
1979	George Gervin (San Antonio)	80	2365
1980	George Gervin (San Antonio)	78	2585
1981	Adrian Dantley (Utah)	80	2452
1982	George Gervin (San Antonio)	79	2551
1983	Alex English (Denver)	82	2326
1984	Adrian Dantley (Utah)	79	2418
1985	Bernard King (New York)	55	1809
1986	Dominique Wilkins (Atlanta)	78	2366
1987	Michael Jordan (Chicago)	82	3041
1988	Michael Jordan (Chicago)	82	2868
1989	Michael Jordan (Chicago)	81	2633
1990	Michael Jordan (Chicago)	82	2753

* *took name of Kareem Abdul-Jabbar from 1971/2 season*

Highest scoring runners-up

1963	Elgin Baylor (Los Angeles)	80	2719
1990	Karl Malone (Utah Jazz)	82	2540
1961	Elgin Baylor (Los Angeles)	73	2538
1982	Moses Malone (Houston)	81	2520

Most seasons leading:
7 Wilt Chamberlain, 3 Neil Johnston, Bob McAdoo
Most seasons over 2000 points:
9 Kareem Abdul-Jabbar 1970-4, 1976-7, 1980-1
8 Alex English 1982-9
7 Wilt Chamberlain 1960-6, Oscar Robertson 1961-7
6 George Gervin 1978-83, Dominique Wilkins 1985-90
Years shown are those of second half of the season.

NBA Most Valuable Player
Voted annually by NBA players from 1956:
1956 Bob Pettit (St Louis)
1957 Bob Cousy (Boston)
1958 Bill Russell (Boston)

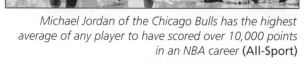

Michael Jordan of the Chicago Bulls has the highest average of any player to have scored over 10,000 points in an NBA career **(All-Sport)**

1959 Bob Pettit (St Louis)
1960 Wilt Chamberlain (Philadelphia)
1961-3 Bill Russell (Boston)
1964 Oscar Robertson (Cincinnati)
1965 Bill Russell (Boston)
1966-8 Wilt Chamberlain (Philadelphia)
1969 Wes Unseld (Baltimore)
1970 Willis Reed (New York)
1971-2 Kareem Abdul-Jabbar* (Milwaukee)
1973 Dave Cowens (Boston)
1974 Kareem Abdul-Jabbar (Milwaukee)
1975 Bob McAdoo (Buffalo)
1976-7 Kareem Abdul-Jabbar (Los Angeles)
1978 Bill Walton (Portland)
1979 Moses Malone (Houston)
1980 Kareem Abdul-Jabbar (Los Angeles)
1981 Julius Erving (Philadelphia)
1982 Moses Malone (Houston)
1983 Moses Malone (Philadelphia)
1984-6 Larry Bird (Boston)
1987 Earvin 'Magic' Johnson (Los Angeles)
1988 Michael Jordan (Chicago)
1989-90 Earvin 'Magic' Johnson (Los Angeles)

Most wins: 6 Kareem Abdul-Jabbar; 5 Bill Russell;
4 Wilt Chamberlain; 3 Moses Malone, Larry Bird, Earvin
'Magic' Johnson
* still known as Lew Alcindor in 1971

NCAA CHAMPIONSHIPS
The most important inter-collegiate competition in the
USA, first contested in 1939. *Division One Wins:*
10 UCLA 1964-5, 1967-73, 1975
5 Kentucky 1948-9, 1951, 1958, 1978
5 Indiana 1940, 1953, 1976, 1981, 1987
2 Oklahoma A&M 1945-6
2 Kansas 1952, 1988
2 San Francisco 1955-6
2 North Carolina 1957, 1982
2 Cincinnati 1961-2
2 North Carolina State 1974, 1983
2 Louisville 1980, 1986
1 Oregon 1939, Wisconsin 1941, Stanford 1942, Wyoming
1943, Utah 1944, Holy Cross 1947, City College of New
York 1950, LaSalle 1954, California 1959, Ohio State 1960,
Loyola (Ill) 1963, Texas Western 1966, Marquette 1977,
Michigan State 1979, Georgetown 1984, Villanova 1985,
Michigan 1989, Nevada-Las Vegas 1990

One player was been voted the Most Valuable Player in
the NCAA final three times: Lew Alcindor of UCLA
(University College of Los Angeles) 1967-9. He
subsequently changed his name to Kareem Abdul-Jabbar.

Highest match aggregate:
331 Loyola Marymount Lions beat US International Gulls
181-150 in Los Angeles on 31 Jan 1989
Most points in game:
100 Frank Selvy for Furman v Newberry 1954

NCAA Division I career scoring average leaders

Points	Name (College)	Years	Games	Ave.
3667	Pete Maravich (LSU)	1968-70	83	44.2
2560	Austin Carr (Notre Dame)	1969-71	74	34.6
2973	Oscar Robertson (Cincinnati)	1958-60	88	33.8
2548	Calvin Murphy (Niagara)	1968-70	77	33.1

Scoring over 3200 points in four years

3249	Freeman Williams (Portland ST) 1975-8		106	30.7

Maravich averaged over 40 points in each season of his
college career: 1968 - 1138 pts av.43.8, 1969- 1148 pts
av.44.2, 1970 - 1381 pts av.44.5.

NCAA Women's championship
First contested 1982. *Division I winners:*
1982 Louisiana Tech
1983-4 Un. Southern California
1985 Old Dominion
1986 Texas
1987 Tennessee
1988 Louisiana Tech
1989 Tennessee
1990 Stanford
Highest match aggregate: 261 St Joseph's (Indiana) beat
Northern Kentucky 131-130 on 27 Feb 1988

*Earvin 'Magic' Johnson led the Los Angeles Lakers to five
NBA titles in the 1980s* (All-Sport)

BIATHLON

Combined cross-country skiing and rifle shooting. Competitors ski over prepared courses carrying a small-bore rifle. Men compete individually over 10km or 20km distances. During the former they have two shooting competitions and in the latter four, prone and standing, at a target 50 metres away. The relay event is four by 7.5km, each member shooting once prone and once standing. Penalties are imposed for missing the target. The women's equivalent distances are 5km, 10km and 3 by 5km relay. The sport's governing body is L'Union Internationale de Pentathlon Moderne et Biathlon, the UIPMB, which took on the administration of biathlon in 1957, and which staged the first world championships the following year.

OLYMPIC GAMES

Men's biathlon has been on the Olympic programme since 1960. Women's events at 7.5km, 15km and 3 x 7.5km relay are being added at the 1992 Winter Games. *Winners:*

Men's 10 kilometres
1980 Frank Ullrich (GDR) 32:10.69
1984 Eirik Kvalfoss (Nor) 30:53.8
1988 Frank-Peter Rötsch (GDR) 25:08.1

Men's 20 kilometres
1960 Klas Lestander (Swe) 1:33:21.6
1964 Vladimir Melanin (USSR) 1:20:26.8
1968 Magnar Solberg (Nor) 1:13:45.9
1972 Magnar Solberg (Nor) 1:15:55.5
1976 Nikolay Kruglov (USSR) 1:14:12.26
1980 Anatoliy Alyabyev (USSR) 1:08:16.31
1984 Peter Angerer (FRG) 1:11:52.7
1988 Frank-Peter Rötsch (GDR) 56:33.33

Men's 4 x 7.5 kilometres relay
1968 USSR 2:13:02.4
1972 USSR 1:51:44.92
1976 USSR 1:57:55.64
1980 USSR 1:34:03.27
1984 USSR 1:38:51.70
1988 USSR 1:22:30.0

Most gold medals:
4 Aleksandr Tikhonov (USSR) relay 1968, 1972, 1976, 1980.
Most medals:
5 Aleksandr Tikhonov 4 relay gold, 20km silver 1968

WORLD CHAMPIONSHIPS

Held annually from 1958 for men and 1984 for women, with the exception of Olympic years. *Winners:*

Men's 20 kilometres
1958 Alosh Wiklund (Swe) 1:33:44
1959 Vladimir Melanin (USSR) 1:41:05
1961 Kalevi Huuskonen (Fin) 1:32:11
1962 Vladimir Melanin (USSR) 1:23:30
1963 Vladimir Melanin (USSR) 1:32:06.8
1965 Olav Jordet (Nor) 1:23:34.9
1966 Jon Istad (Nor) 1:38:21.8
1967 Viktor Mamatov (USSR) 1:28:34.1
1969 Aleksandr Tikhonov (USSR) 1:22:46.2
1970 Aleksandr Tikhonov (USSR) 1:23:42.1
1971 Dieter Speer (GDR) 1:18:20.2
1973 Aleksandr Tikhonov (USSR) 1:26:30.20
1974 Juhani Suutarinen (Fin) 1:12:04.74
1975 Heikki Ikola (Fin) 1:13:52.3
1977 Heikki Ikola (Fin) 1:10:51.8
1978 Odd Lirhus (Nor) 1:05:26.39
1979 Klaus Siebert (GDR) 1:07:40.13
1981 Heikki Ikola (Fin) 1:13:07.29
1982 Frank Ullrich (GDR) 1:07:17.03
1983 Frank Ullrich (GDR) 1:05:00.09
1985 Yuriy Kashkarov (USSR) 57:50.3
1986 Valeriy Medvetsev (USSR) 57:05
1987 Frank-Peter Rötsch (GDR) 1:00:00.40
1989 Eirik Kvalfoss (Nor) 58:14
1990 Valeriy Medvetsev (USSR) 1:06:39

Men's team
Sweden 1958
USSR 1959, 1962-3
Finland 1961
Norway 1965

Men's 10 kilometres
1974 Juhani Suutarinen (Fin) 37:42.43
1975 Nikolay Kruglov (USSR) 35:27.7
1977 Aleksandr Tikhonov (USSR) 32:47.8
1978 Frank Ullrich (GDR) 32:17.44
1979 Frank Ullrich (GDR) 40:35.37
1981 Frank Ullrich (GDR) 33:08.57
1982 Eirik Kvalfoss (Nor) 33:03.26
1983 Eirik Kvalfoss (Nor) 31:12.03
1985 Frank-Peter Rötsch (GDR) 30:25.2
1986 Valeriy Medvetsev (USSR) 28:02
1987 Frank-Peter Rötsch (GDR) 29:49.60
1989 Frank Luck (GDR) 28:08.07
1990 Mark Kirchner (GDR) 25:48.09

Men's 4 x 7.5 kilometres relay
Norway 1965-7
USSR 1969-71, 1973-4, 1977, 1983, 1985-6
Finland 1975
GDR 1978-9, 1981-2, 1987, 1989
Italy 1990

Men's 20 kilometres Team
USSR 1989
GDR 1990

Women's 5 kilometres
1984 Venera Chernyshova (USSR) 23:00.1
1985 Sanna Grönlid (Nor) 21:58.90

1986 Kaya Parve (USSR) 20:07
1987 Yelena Golovina (USSR) 21:14.7
1988 Petra Schaar (FRG) 19:33.0

Women's 7.5 kilometres
1989 Anne-Elinor Elvebakk (Nor) 27:12.03
1990 Anne-Elinor Elvebakk (Nor) 27:12.8

Women's 10 kilometres
1984 Venera Chernyshova (USSR) 44:21.7
1985 Kaya Parve (USSR) 43:31.40
1986 Eva Korpela (Swe) 41:56
1987 Sanna Grönlid (Nor) 42:42.0
1988 Anne-Elinor Elvebakk (Nor) 36:53.0

Women's 15 kilometres
1989 Petra Schaaf (FRG) 1:06:11.2
1990 Svetlana Davydova (USSR)

Women's relay (3 x 5km 1984-9, 3 x 7.5km 1990)
7 wins USSR 1984-90

Women's 15 kilometres team
USSR 1989-90

Most World and Olympic titles
MEN
14 Aleksandr Tikhonov (USSR) 4 individual, 10 relay 1968-80
10 Frank Ullrich (GDR) 6 individual, 4 relay 1978-83
7 Vladimir Melanov (USSR) 4 individual, 3 team 1959-63
WOMEN
6 Kaya Parve (USSR) 2 individual, 4 relay 1984-6, 1988.

WORLD CUP
Contested at 10km and 20km over a series of five events during each winter. *Winners:*
MEN
1978 Frank Ullrich (GDR)
1979 Klaus Siebert (GDR)
1980-2 Frank Ullrich (GDR)
1983 Peter Angerer (FRG)
1984-5 Frank-Peter Rötsch (GDR)
1986 André Sehmisch (GDR)
1987-8 Frank-Peter Rötsch (GDR)
1989 Eirik Kvalfoss (Nor)
1990 Sergey Chepikov (USSR)
WOMEN (7.5km)
1988 Anne-Elinor Elvebakk (Nor)
1989 Yelena Golovina (USSR)
1990 Jirina Adamichkova (Cs)

Frank-Peter Rötsch (All-Sport)

BILLIARDS

The earliest reference to billiards, which is related to the outdoor game of paille-malle, played on grass, was in the early 15th-century. Louis XI, King of France (1461-83) is believed to have had a billiard table. The game became popular in Britain at the turn of the 19th century and the governing body, the Billiards Association (now the Billiards & Snooker Control Council), was formed in 1885.

WORLD PROFESSIONAL CHAMPIONSHIPS
First held in 1870, the championship was organised on a challenge basis until 1909. From 1909 it was run on a knockout basis under Billiard Control Club rules, until becomming dormant in 1934. It was revived on a challenge basis in 1951. In 1980 it was restored to a tournament event and, since 1982, has been held annually. *Winners:*
1870 William Cook (Eng)
1870 John Roberts, Jnr (Eng)
1870 Joseph Bennett (Eng)
1871 John Roberts, Jnr (Eng)
1871 William Cook (Eng)
1875 John Roberts, Jnr (Eng)
1880 Joseph Bennett (Eng)
1885 John Roberts Jnr (Eng)
1889 Charles Dawson (Eng)
1901 H.W.Stevenson (Eng)
1901 Charles Dawson (Eng)
1901 H.W.Stevenson (Eng)
1903 Charles Dawson (Eng)
1908 Melbourne Inman (Eng)
1909-11 H.W.Stevenson (Eng)
1912-4 Melbourne Inman (Eng)
1919 Melbourne Inman (Eng)
1920 Willie Smith (Eng)
1921-2 Tom Newman (Eng)
1923 Willie Smith (Eng)
1924-7 Tom Newman (Eng)
1928-30 Joe Davis (Eng)
1931 no competition
1932 Joe Davis (Eng)
1933-4 Walter Lindrum (Aus)
1951 Clark McConachy (NZ)
1968 Rex Williams (Eng)
1971 Leslie Driffield (Eng)
1971 Rex Williams (Eng)
1980 Fred Davis (Eng)
1982 Rex Williams (Eng)
1983 Rex Williams (Eng)
1984 Mark Wildman (Eng)
1985 Ray Edmonds (Eng)
1986 Robbie Foldvari (Aus)
1987-8 Norman Dagley (Eng)
1989 Mike Russell (Eng)

Most wins (pre-1909): John Roberts, Jnr made 8 successful defences of his title 1870-85
(post-1909): 7 Rex Williams 1968-76 (including 5 successful challenges). Tom Newman won a record six titles under knockout conditions, 1921-7

WORLD AMATEUR CHAMPIONSHIPS
Inaugurated in 1926 it is now scheduled to be held every two years and is organised by the International Billiards & Snooker Federation (IBSF). The 1989 tournament was cancelled. It is a round-robin event with the four leading players then competing in a knockout tournament. *Winners:*
1926 Joe Earlham (Eng)
1927 Allan Prior (SAf)
1929 Les Hayes (Aus)
1931 Laurie Steeples (Eng)
1933 Sydney Lee (Eng)
1935 Horace Coles (Wal)
1936 Robert Marshall (Aus)
1938 Robert Marshall (Aus)
1951 Robert Marshall (Aus)
1952 Leslie Driffield (Eng)
1954 Tom Cleary (Aus)
1958 Wilson Jones (Ind)
1960 Herbert Beetham (Eng)
1962 Robert Marshall (Aus)
1964 Wilson Jones (Ind)
1967 Leslie Driffield (Eng)
1969 Jack Karnehm (Eng)
1971 Norman Dagley (Eng)
1973 Mohammed Lafir (Sri)
1975 Norman Dagley (Eng)
1977 Michael Ferreira (Ind)
1979 Paul Mifsud (Malta)
1981 Michael Ferreira (Ind)
1983 Michael Ferreira (Ind)
1985 Geet Sethi (Ind)
1987 Geet Sethi (Ind)
Most wins: 4 Robert Marshall

UNITED KINGDOM PROFESSIONAL CHAMPIONSHIPS
Instituted in 1934 it was discontinued in 1951 but was revived from 1979 to 1983, when it was taken off the professional calender. It was revived once more in 1987. *Winners:*
1934-9 Joe Davis
1946 John Barrie
1947 Joe Davis
1948 Sidney Smith

1950 John Barrie
1951 Fred Davis
1979 Rex Williams
1980 Jack Karnehm
1981 Rex Williams
1983 Mark Wildman
1987 Norman Dagley
1988 Ian Williamson (Eng)
1989-90 Mike Russell (Eng)
Most wins: 7 Joe Davis

RECORD BREAKS
Highest break including the now outlawed cradle cannon: 499,135 Tom Reece 3 Jun-6 Jul 1907
Highest certified break using the anchor cannon:
42,746 William Cook 29 May-7 Jun 1907
Official world record break (since introduction of the 25-hazard rule in 1926): 4,137 Walter Lindrum 1932
Highest break under the baulk-line rule: 1,784 Joe Davis 29 May 1936
Highest official break in amateur competition: 1,149 Michael Ferreira 15 Dec 1978
Highest break under current 'two pot' rule: 962 (unfinished) Michael Ferreira 29 Apr 1986

THREE CUSHION BILLIARDS
Played on a table without pockets, this variation of billiards dates to 1878. The governing body, the Union Mondiale de Billiard (UMB), was formed in 1928. Popular in the USA and Europe, the lack of pockets makes it a 'cannons-only' game, but there are several variations which demand a high level of skill. In Europe is it known as Carom.

The greatest American exponent, Willie Hoppe, won a total of 51 three-cushion championships throughout the United States.

UMB WORLD THREE CUSHION BILLIARDS CHAMPIONSHIPS
First held in 1928, annually to 1938, then in 1948, 1952-3, 1958 and annually from 1960. Raymond Ceulemans (Bel) won a record 19 world titles: 1963-73, 1975-80, 1983, 1985
Other world champions since 1963:
1974 Nobuaki Kobayashi (Jap)
1981 Ludo Dielis (Bel)
1982 Rini van Bracht (Hol)
1984 Nobuaki Kobayashi (Jap)
1986 Avelino Rico (Spa)
1987-8 Torbjörn Blomdahl (Swe)
1989 Ludo Dielis (Bel)

Raymond Ceulemans, Belgian master of the three-cushion game (All-Sport)

BOBSLEIGH & TOBOGGANING

The first known bobsleigh races were run by British enthusiasts in Switzerland in the 1880s, when improvements were made to sleighs to make them go faster. Luge races had been held a few years earlier, and two special luge runs were constructed at Davos, Switzerland in 1879. The earliest known sledge is dated c.6500 BC and was found at Heinola, Finland.

The first purpose-built bobsleigh run was constructed at St Moritz in 1902. There are now Olympic bobsleigh events for two- and four-man teams, who sit in the bob. Skeleton one-man toboggans are used on the Cresta Run, and there was an Olympic event for them in 1924 and 1948. In the skeleton toboggans the riders lie face down, but this form of tobogganing has been superseded in the Olympics by Luge Tobogganing, in which the rider sits up or lies back.

International governing bodies: Fédération Internationale de Bobsleigh et de Togogganing (FIBT), founded in 1923. Luge tobogganing originally came under the auspices of the FIBT, but from 1957 has had its own governing body, the Fédération Internationale de Luge (FIL).

Bobsleigh runs are between 1100m and 1600m in length. The two-man bob has a maximum length of 2.7m and a maximum weight of bob and crew of 390kg; for a four-man bob the maxima are 3.8m and 630kg; luges are about 1.50m in length, and the maximum weight of the luge is 20kg for a single-seater or 22kg for a two-seater. Luge runs are over a minimum of 1000m. Women are not permitted to contest international bobsleigh events, but contest single-seater luge races, an Olympic event since 1964.

OLYMPIC GAMES
A bob competition for four-man sleds was first held in 1924. The two-man event was introduced in 1932, and both events have been staged at each subsequent Games except for those of 1960, when no run was built at Squaw Valley. *Winners:*

Two-man bob
1932 Hubert Stevens & Curtis Stevens (USA)
1936 Ivan Brown & Alan Washbond (USA)
1948 Felix Endrich & Friedrich Waller (Swi)
1952 Andreas Ostler & Lorenz Nieberl (FRG)
1956 Lamberto Dalla Costa & Giacomo Conti (Ita)
1964 Tony Nash & Robin Dixon (UK)
1968 Eugenio Monti & Luciano de Paolis (Ita)
1972 Wolfgang Zimmerer & Peter Utzschneider (FRG)
1976 Meinhard Nehmer & Bernhard Germeshausen (GDR)
1980 Erich Schärer & Josef Benz (Swi)
1984 Wolfgang Hoppe & Dietmar Schauerhammer (GDR)
1988 Janis Kipurs & Vladimir Kozlov (USSR)

Four-man bob
1924 Switzerland
1928 USA
1932 USA
1936 Switzerland
1948 USA
1952 Germany (FRG)
1956 Switzerland
1964 Canada
1968 Italy
1972 Switzerland
1976 GDR
1980 GDR
1984 GDR
1988 Switzerland

Skeleton bob winners:
1928 Jennison Heaton (USA)
1948 Nino Bibbia (Ita)

Wolfgang Hoppe and Dietmar Schauerhammer (GDR) won Olympic golds at both 2-man and 4-man bob in 1984
(All-Sport)

Most gold medals by an individual: 3 Meinhard Nehmer & Bernhard Germeshausen (GDR) 2-man 1976, 4-man 1976 and 1980.
Most medals: 6 Eugenio Monti (Ita) two gold 1968, two silver 1956, two bronze 1964.

Luge tobogganning - single-seater winners:
MEN
1964 Thomas Köhler (GDR)
1968 Manfred Schmid (Aut)
1972 Wolfgang Scheidel (GDR)
1976 Detlef Günther (GDR)
1980 Bernhard Glass (GDR)
1984 Paul Hildgartner (Ita)
1988 Jens Müller (GDR)
WOMEN
1964 Ortrun Enderlein (GDR)
1968 Erica Lechner (Ita)
1972 Anna-Maria Müller (GDR)
1976 Margit Schumann (GDR)
1980 Vera Sosulya (USSR)
1984 Steffi Martin (GDR)
1988 Steffi Walter (née Martin) (GDR)

Luge - men's two-seater
1964 Josef Feistmantl & Manfred Stengl (Aut)
1968 Thomas Köhler & Klaus Bonsack (GDR)
1972 Paul Hildgartner & Walter Plaikner (Ita) and
        Horst Hörnlein & Reinhard Bredow (GDR)
1976 Hans Rinn & Norbert Hahn (GDR)
1980 Hans Rinn & Norbert Hahn (GDR)
1984 Hans Stanggasinger & Franz Wembacher (FRG)
1988 Jörg Hoffmann & Jochen Pietzsch (GDR)

BOBSLEIGH WORLD CHAMPIONSHIPS
Held annually from 1930 for the four-man bob and 1931 for the two-man bob. The Olympic events (qv) are the world championships in those years. *Winners:*
Two-man bob
1931 Hanns Killian & Sebastian Huber (Ger)
1933 Alexandru Papana & Dumitru Hubert (Rom)
1934 Alexandru Frim & Vasile Dumitrescu (Rom)
1935 Reto Capadrutt & Emil Diener (Swi)
1937 Frederic McEnvoy & B.H.Black (UK)
1938 Bibo Fischer & Rolf Thielacke (Ger)
1939 René Lundnen & J.Kuffer (Bel)
1947 Fritz Feierabend & Stephan Waser (Swi)
1949 Felix Endrich & Friedrich Waller (Swi)
1950 Fritz Feierabend & Stephan Waser (Swi)
1951 Andreas Osterl & Lorenz Nieberl (FRG)
1953 Felix Endrich & Fritz Stoeckli (Swi)
1954 Guglielmo Scheibmeier & Andrea Zambelli (Ita)
1955 Fritz Feierabend & Harry Warburton (Swi)
1957-9 Eugenio Monti & Renzo Alverà (Ita)
1961 Eugenio Monti & Sergio Siorpaes (Ita)
1962 Rinaldo Ruatti & Enrico De Lorenzo (Ita)
1963 Eugenio Monti & Sergio Siorpaes (Ita)
1965 Tony Nash & Robin Dixon (UK)

1966 Eugenio Monti & Sergio Siorpaes (Ita)
1967 Erwin Thaler & Reinhold Durnthaler (Aut)
1969 Nevio de Zordo & Adriano Frassinelli (Ita)
1970 Horst Floth & Pepi Bader (FRG)
1971 Gianfranco Gaspari & Mario Armano (Ita)
1973-4 Wolfgang Zimmerer & Peter Utzschneider (FRG)
1975 Giorgio Alverà & Franco Perruquet (Ita)
1977 Hans Hiltebrand & Heinz Meier (Swi)
1978-9 Erich Schärer & Josef Benz (Swi)
1981 Bernhard Germeshausen & Hans-Jürgen Gerhardt (GDR)
1982 Erich Schärer & Josef Benz (Swi)
1983 Ralf Pichler & Urs Leuthold (Swi)
1985-6 Wolfgang Hoppe & Dietmar Schauerhammer (GDR)
1987 Ralf Pichler & Celest Poltera (Swi)
1989 Wolfgang Hoppe & Bogdan Musiol (GDR)
1990 Gustav Weber & Bruno Gerber (Swi)

Four-man bob
14 Switzerland 1939, 1947, 1954-5, 1957, 1971, 1973, 1975, 1982-3, 1986-7, 1989-90
6 FR Germany   1951, 1958, 1962, 1969, 1974, 1979
4 Italy   1930, 1961, 1963, 1970
4 USA   1949-50, 1953, 1959
4 GDR   1977-8, 1981, 1985
3 Germany   1931, 1934-5
2 United Kingdom 1937-8
1 Canada   1965
Not decided in 1966 due to a fatal accident and in 1967 because of a thaw.

Most Bobsleigh World and Olympic titles : 2-man/4-man
11 Eugenio Monti (Ita) 8/3
8 Erich Schärer (Swi) 4/4
6 Fritz Feierabend (Swi) 3/3
6 Bernhard Germeshausen (GDR) 2/4

BOBSLEIGH WORLD CUP
First held over a series of events in 1984. *Winners:*
1985 Anton Fischer (FRG)
1986 Ekkehard Fasser (Swi)
1987 Matt Roy (USA)
1988 Ingo Appelt (Aut)
1989 Gustav Weder (Swi)
1990 Maris Poikans (USSR)

LUGE WORLD CHAMPIONSHIPS
Held annually from 1955, with the exception of years in which luge events were included in the Olympics, with which they are now merged, to 1981 and now biennially on artificial runs. Separate world championships on natural runs were held in 1979 and biennially from 1980. *Winners:*
Single seater
MEN
1955 Anton Salvesen (Nor)
1957 Hans Schaller (FRG)
1958 Jerzy Wojnar (Pol)

1959 Herbert Thaler (Aut)
1960 Helmuth Berndt (FRG)
1961 Jerzy Wojnar (Pol)
1962 Thomas Köhler (GDR)
1963 Fritz Nachmann (FRG)
1965 Hans Plenk (FRG)
1967 Thomas Köhler (GDR)
1969 Josef Feistmantl (Aut)
1970 Josef Fendt (FRG)
1971 Karl Brunner (Ita)
1973 Hans Rinn (GDR)
1974 Josef Fendt (FRG)
1975 Wolfram Fiedler (GDR)
1977 Hans Rinn (GDR)
1978 Paul Hildgartner (Ita)
1979 Detlef Günther (GDR)
1981 Sergey Danilin (USSR)
1983 Miroslav Zajonc (Can)
1985 Michael Walter (GDR)
1987 Markus Prock (Aut)
1989 Georg Hackl (FRG)

WOMEN
1955 Karla Kienzl (Aut)
1956 Maria Isser (Aut)
1957 Maria Semczyszak (Pol)
1959 Elly Lieber (Aut)
1960 Maria Isser (Aut)
1961 Elisabeth Nagele (Swi)
1962-3 Ilse Geisler (GDR)
1965 Ortrun Enderlein (GDR)
1967 Ortrun Enderlein (GDR)
1969 Petra Tierlich (GDR)
1970 Barbara Piecha (Pol)
1971 Elisabeth Demleitner (FRG)
1973-5 Margrit Schumann (GDR)
1977 Margrit Schumann (GDR)
1978 Vera Sosulya (USSR)
1979 Melitta Sollmann (GDR)
1980 Vera Sosulya (USSR)
1981 Melitta Sollmann (GDR)
1983 Steffi Martin (GDR)
1985 Steffi Martin (GDR)
1987 Cerstin Schmidt (GDR)
1989 Susi Erdmann (GDR)

Event cancelled in 1966

Men's two-seater
1955 Hans Krausner & Herbert Thaler (Aut)
1957-8 Josef Strillinger & Fritz Nachmann (FRG)
1960 Reinhold Frosch & Ewald Walch (Aut)
1961 Roman Pichler & Raimondo Prinoth (Ita)
1962 Giovanni Graber & Gianpoulo Ambrosi (Ita)
1963 Ryszard Pedrak & Lucjan Kudzia (Pol)
1965 Wolfgang Scheidel & Thomas Köhler (GDR)
1967 Klaus Bonsack & Thomas Köhler (GDR)
1969-70 Manfred Schmid & Ewald Walch (Aut)

1971 Paul Hildgartner & Walter Plaikner (Ita)
1973 Horst Hörnlein & Reinhard Bredow (GDR)
1974-5 Bernd Hann & Ulrich Hann (GDR)
1977 Hans Rinn & Norbert Hahn (GDR)
1978 Dainis Bremse & Aigars Krikis (USSR)
1979 Hans Brandner & Balthasar Schwarm (FRG)
1980 Hans Rinn & Norbert Hahn (GDR)
1981 Bernd Hann & Ulrich Hann (GDR)
1983 Jörg Hoffmann & Jochen Pietzsch (GDR)
1985 Jörg Hoffmann & Jochen Pietzsch (GDR)
1987 Jörg Hoffmann & Jochen Pietzsch (GDR)
1989 Stefan Krausse & Jan Behrendt (GDR)

Cancelled in 1959 and 1966

Most Luge World and Olympic titles
MEN 6 Thomas Köhler (GDR), Hans Rinn (GDR).
WOMEN: 5 Margrit Schumann (GDR).

LUGE WORLD CUP
Held over a series of events annually from the 1977/8
season. *Winners:*
Single-seater
MEN
1978 Anton Winkler (GDR)
1979 Paul Hildgartner (Ita)
1980 Ernst Haspinger (Ita)
1981 Ernst Haspinger (Ita) & Paul Hildgartner (Ita)
1982 Ernst Haspinger (Ita)
1983 Paul Hildgartner (Ita)
1984 Michael Walter (GDR)
1985-7 Norbert Huber (Ita)
1988 Markus Prock (Aut)
1989-90 Georg Hackl (FRG)

WOMEN
1978 Regina König (FRG)
1979-81 Angelika Schafferer (Aut)
1982 Vera Sosulya (USSR)
1983 Ute Weiss (GDR)
1984 Steffi Martin (GDR) & Bettina Schmidt (GDR)
1985 Cerstin Schmidt (GDR)
1986 Maria Rainer (Ita)
1987 Cerstin Schmidt (GDR)
1988 Gerda Weissensteiner (Ita)
1989 Ute Oberhoffner (GDR)
1990 Yuliya Antipova (USSR)

Men's two-seater
1978-9 Peter Gschnitzer & Karl Brunner (Ita)
1980-2 Günther Lemmerer & Reinhold Sulzbacher (Aut)
1983 Hansjörg Raffl & Norbert Huber (Ita)
1984 Jörg Hoffmann & Jochen Pietzsch (GDR)
1985-6 Hansjörg Raffl & Norbert Huber (Ita)
1987 Thomas Schwab & Wolfgang Staudinger (FRG)
1988 Yevgeniy Belousov & Aleksandr Belyukov (USSR)
1989 Hansjörg Raffl & Norbert Huber (Ita)
1990 Hansjörg Raffl & Norbert Huber (Ita)

BOWLING (TENPIN)

Bowling at 'pins' has existed as a pastime since 5200 BC, but it only started to take shape in its present form in the early 19th century. Dutch or German migrants took the game of ninepins to the United States and the game became immensely popular - so popular it attracted much gambling and consequently the game was banned. To get round the law, a tenth pin was added, and they were laid out in a diamond shape. The new game, once again, became very popular. The American Bowling Congress was formed in 1895, and they standardised the rules. The Women's International Bowling Congress (WIBC) was formed in 1916. The world governing body of the amateur game is the Fédération Internationale des Quilleurs (FIQ). Prior to the last war the International Bowling Association (IBA) governed the sport.

WORLD CHAMPIONSHIPS

The IBA organised four world championships between 1923 and 1936. Since 1954 the championships have been organised by the FIQ, and since 1963 have been held every four years. Women took part for the first time in 1963. *Winners:*

MEN
Individual

Year	Winner	Score	Games	Ave.
1923	Thure Sandström (Swe)	414	2	207.00
1926	Hugo Lillier (Swe)	829	4	207.25
1929	Schirgio (USA)	836	4	209.00
1936	Goldtammer (Ger)	921	4	230.25
1954	Gösta Algeskog (Swe)	4932	25	197.28
1955	Nils Böckström (Swe)	4838	25	193.52
1958	Kaarlo Asukas (Fin)	5034	25	201.36
1960	Tito Reynolds (Mex)	4963	25	198.52
1963	Les Zikes (USA)	5519	28	197.11
1967	David Pond (UK)	5708	28	203.86
1971	Ed Luther (USA)	5963	28	212.96
1975	Bud Staudt (USA)	5816	28	207.71
1979	Ollie Ongtawco (Phi)	1278	6	213.00
1983	Armando Marino (Col)	1357	6	226.17
1987	Rolland Patrick (Fra)	1332	6	222.00

Doubles
4 Sweden 1923, 1955, 1958, 1987
3 Great Britain 1967, 1975, 1983*
2 Finland 1926, 1954
2 United States 1936, 1963
2 Australia 1979, 1983*
1 Mexico 1960, Puerto Rico 1971
* *Shared title*
Best average score: 219.83 Sweden (1987) 2638 pts from 6 games

Trios
1 Malaysia 1979, Sweden 1983, United States 1987
Best average score: 216.61 Sweden (1983) 3899 pts from 6 games

Teams of five players
4 Finland 1958, 1967, 1975, 1983
4 Sweden 1923, 1926, 1954, 1987
3 United States 1936, 1963, 1971
1 FR Germany 1955, Venezuela 1960, Australia 1979
Best average score: 211.83 Finland (1983) 6355 pts from 6 games

All-Events
Score from all four events, singles, doubles, trios & team:
1983 Mats Karlsson (Swe) 5242 pts (av. 218.42)
1987 Rick Steelsmith (USA) 5261 pts (av.219.21)

Teams of eight players (discontinued 1975)
3 United States 1963, 1967, 1971
2 Sweden 1954, 1958
1 Finland 1955, Mexico 1960, FR Germany 1975
Best average score: 198.30 United States (1971) 12,691 pts from 8 games

Masters
1979 Gerry Bugden (UK)
1983 Tony Cariello (USA)
1987 Roger Pieters (Bel)

WOMEN
Individual

Year	Winner	Score	Games	Ave.
1963	Helen Shablis (USA)	4535	24	188.96
1967	Helen Weston (USA)	4585	24	191.04
1971	Ashie Gonzales (PR)	4535	24	188.96
1975	Annedore Haefker (FRG)	4615	24	192.29
1979	Lita de la Rosa (Phi)	1220	6	203.33
1983	Lena Sulkanen (Swe)	1293	6	215.50
1987	Edda Piccini (Ita)	1259	6	209.83

Doubles
2 United States 1963, 1987
1 Mexico 1960, Japan 1971, Sweden 1975, Philippines 1979, Denmark 1983
Best average score: 213.83 United States (1987) 2566 pts from 6 games

Trios
2 USA 1979, 1987; 1 FR Germany 1983
Best average score: 200.17 United States (1987) 3603 pts from 6 games

Teams of five players
3 USA 1971, 1979, 1987
1 Finland 1967, Japan 1975, Sweden 1983
Best average score: 200.37 United States (1987) 6011 pts from 6 games

All-Events
1983 Bong Coo (Phi) 4806 pts (av.200.25)
1987 Sandra Jo Shiery (USA) 4894 pts (av.203.92)

Teams of four players (discontinued 1975)
2 United States 1963*, 1971
1 Mexico 1963*, Finland 1967, Japan 1975
* *There were two titles in 1963*
Best average score: 194.00 United States (1971) 4656 pts from 6 games

Masters
1979 Lita de la Rosa (Phi)
1983 Lena Sulkanen (Swe)
1987 Annette Hagre (Swe)

The only perfect game (300) in the world championships was rolled by Rick Steelsmith (USA) during the Trios event at the 1987 championships.

US BOWLING

The American Bowling Congress
The most important event run by the ABC is the annual Masters Bowling Tournament. *Winners:*

1951 Lee Jouglard	1972 Bill Beach
1952 Willard Taylor	1973 Dave Soutar
1953 Rudy Habetler	1974 Paul Colwell
1954 Eugene Elkins	1975 Ed Ressler Jr.
1955 Buzz Fazio	1976 Nelson Burton Jr.
1956-7 Dick Hoover	1977 Earl Anthony
1958 Tom Hennessey	1978 Frank Ellenburg
1959 Ray Bluth	1979 Doug Meyers
1960 Bill Golembiewski	1980 Neil Burton
1961 Don Carter	1981 Randy Lightfoot
1962 Bill Golembiewski	1982 Joe Berardi
1963 Harry Smith	1983 Mike Lastowski
1964-5 Billy Welu	1984 Earl Anthony
1966 Bob Strampe	1985 Steve Wunderlich
1967 Lou Scalia	1986 Mark Fahy
1968 Pete Tountas	1987 Rick Steelsmith
1969 Jim Chestney	1988 Del Ballard Jr.
1970 Don Glover	1989 Mike Aulby
1971 Jim Godman	

Most wins: 2 Hoover, Golembiewski, Welu, Anthony

ABC Champions
Held annually from 1901 at the following categories: all-events, singles, doubles and five-man team.

All-events champions from 1970:
1970 Mike Berlin 2004
1971 Al Cohn 2063
1972 Mac Lowry 2026
1973 Ron Woolet 2104
1974 Bob Hart 2087
1975 Bobby Meadows 2033
1976 Jim Lindquist 2071
1977 Bub Debenham 2117
1978 Chris Cobus 1994
1979 Bob Basacchi 2097
1980 Steve Fehr 2076
1981 Rod Toft 2107
1982 Rich Wonders 2076
1983 Tony Cariello 2059
1984 Bob Goike 2142
1985 Barry Asher 2033
1986 Ed Marzka 2116
1987 Ryan Shafer 2044
1988 Rick Steelsmith 2053
1989 George Hall 2227

Most wins: 2 Barney Spinella 1922, 1927; Joe Wilman 1939, 1946; Frank Santore 1950, 1953

ABC records for League and Tournament play
Team series (5 men)	3858	Budweiser Beer, St Louis 12 Mar1958
Team game (5 men)	1382	Sunset Bowl, Kansas City, Kansas, 8 Sep 1987
Doubles series	1655	Thomas Jordan & Ken Yonker Jr., Union, NJ 7 Mar 1989
Doubles game	600	John Cotta & Steve Larsen, Manteca, Cal. 1 May 1981
	600	Jeff Mraz & Dave Roney, Canton, Ohio 8 Nov 1987
Individual series	899	Thomas Jordan, Union, NJ 7 Mar 1989

A perfect score, strikes in all ten frames of a game, is 300. Thus the singles total maximum for three sanctioned games is 900.

The most 300 games in ABC sanctioned play:
33 Bob Learn Jr., Jim Johnson Jr., 32 John Wilcox Jr., 29 Ron Woolet, 27 Elvin Mesger

Most scores of over 800 in ABC sanctioned play: 21 Elvin Mesger.

The Professional Bowlers Association
The PBA was formed in the USA in 1958. Its annual Tournament of Champions is held at its home in Akron, Ohio, and is sponsored by Firestone.

Year	Tournament of Champions winners	PBA leading money winners	$
1962	Joe Joseph	Don Carter	22,525
1963	Not held	Dick Weber	26,280
1964	Not held	Don Carter	49,972
1965	Billy Hardwick	Dick Weber	46,333
1966	Wayne Zahn	Bob Strampe	33,592
1967	Jim Stefanich	Dick Weber	47,674
1968	Dave Davis	Jim Stefanich	54,720
1969	Jim Godman	Billy Hardwick	64,160
1970	Don Johnson	Mike McGrath	52,049
1971	Johnny Petraglia	Johnny Petraglia	85,065
1972	Mike Durbin	Don Johnson	56,648
1973	Jim Godman	Don McCune	69,000
1974	Earl Anthony	Earl Anthony	99,585
1975	Dave Davis	Earl Anthony	107,585
1976	Marshall Holman	Earl Anthony	110,833
1977	Mike Berlin	Mark Roth	105,583
1978	Earl Anthony	Mark Roth	134,500
1979	George Pappas	Mark Roth	124,517
1980	Wayne Webb	Wayne Webb	116,700
1981	Steve Cook	Earl Anthony	164,735
1982	Mike Durbin	Earl Anthony	134,760
1983	Joe Berardi	Earl Anthony	135,605
1984	Mike Durbin	Mark Roth	158,712
1985	Mark Williams	Mike Aulby	201,200
1986	Marshall Holman	Walter Williams	145,550
1987	Pete Weber	Pete Weber	179,516

Year	Tournament of Champions winners	PBA leading money winners	$
1988	Mark Williams	Brian Voss	225,485
1989	Del Ballard Jr.	Mike Aulby	298,237
1990	Dave Ferraro		

Pro Career Earnings and most PBA (and other) tournaments won:
(to end of 1989 season)

Name	Earnings	Titles
Marshall Holman	$1,429,756	21
Mark Roth	1,378,756	37
Earl Anthony	1,302,226	41
Mike Aulby	1,079,740	17
Pete Weber	1,071,850	13
Wayne Webb	907,176	18
Dick Weber	812,584	64
Joe Berardi	780,579	10
George Pappas	779,684	14
Dave Husted	763,496	6

Others with more than 18 titles
Don Johnson 26, Dick Ritger 20, Camen Salvino 18

The Women's International Bowling Congress
WIBC Championships have been held annually from 1916, except for 1943-5. Their tournament attracted a record 75,480 entrants in 1983 for the event held over a three-month period.

All-events winners from 1970:
1970 Dorothy Fothergill 1984
1971 Lorrie Nichols 1840
1972 Mildred Ignizio 1877
1973 Toni Starin 1910
1974 Judy Soutar 1944
1975 Virginia Norton 1821
1976 Betty Morris 1866
1977 Akiko Yamaga (Jap) 1895
1978 Annese Kelly 1896
1979 Betty Morris 1945
1980 Cheryl Robinson 1945
1981 Virginia Norton 1905
1982 Aleta Sill 1905
1983 Virginia Norton 1922
1984 Shinobu Saitoh (Jap) 1921
1985 Aleta Sill 1900
1986 Robin Romeo & Maria Lewis 1877
1987 Leanne Barrette 1972
1988 Lisa Wagner 1871
1989 Nancy Fehr 1911

Most wins: 4 Emma Jaeger 1918, 1921, 1928-9; 3 Virginia Norton

WIBC Queens Tournament
WIBC's most prestigious event, winners from its inception in 1961:
1961 Janet Harman
1962 Dorothy Wilkinson
1963 Irene Monterosso
1964 D.D.Jacobson
1965 Betty Kuczynski
1966 Judy Lee
1967 Mildred Ignizio
1968 Phyllis Massey
1969 Ann Feigel
1970-1 Mildred Ignizio
1972-3 Dorothy Fothergill
1974 Judy Soutar
1975 Cindy Powell
1976 Pamela Buckner
1977 Dana Stewart
1978 Loa Boxberger
1979-80 Donna Adamek
1981-2 Katsuko Sugimoto (Jap)
1983 Aleta Sill
1984 Kazue Inahashi (Jap)
1985 Aleta Sill
1986 Cora Fiebig
1987 Cathy Almeida
1988 Wendy Macpherson
1989 Carol Gianotti (Aus)

Queen's leading money winners: $67,785 Aleta Sill, $37,420 Katsuko Sugimoto, $36,730 Donna Adamek

WIBC Records:

Team series (5 women)	3437	Goebel Beer, Detroit, 1988/9
Team game (5 women)	1244	Chamberlain Wholesale, Detroit 1987/8
Doubles series	1508	Pat Mercetanti & Lisa Wagner 1986/7
Doubles game	553	Jean Reeder & Janice James, Cleveland 1982/3
Individual series (3 game)	864	Jeanne Maiden, Solon, Ohio, 23 Nov 1986

Most sanctioned 300 games: 17 Jeanne Maiden; 10 Vicki Fischel, 9 Betty Morris, Cindy Coburn, Aleta Still, Tish Johnson; 8 Donna Adamek, Robin Romeo

US Opens
First held in 1941 for men and 1949 for women and run by the Bowling Proprietors' Association of America (BPAA). It became the US Open in 1971. *Most wins:*
MEN
4 Don Carter 1952, 1954, 1956, 1958
4 Dick Weber 1962-3, 1965-6
WOMEN
8 Marion Ladewig 1949-52, 1954, 1956, 1959, 1963
3 Pat Costello 1974, 1976, 1980

BOWLS

The ancient Egyptians are believed to have played a game similar to bowls around 5200 BC but the earliest recorded green is at Southampton in 1299, although one was claimed in Chesterfield in 1294. The modern rules for bowls were drawn up in Scotland in 1848-9 by Glasgow solicitor William Mitchell. The English Bowling Association was founded in 1903 with Test cricketer W.G.Grace as its first president, although this was preceded by the founding of the International (later Imperial) Bowling Association in 1899, but this lasted only until 1905, when the present world governing body the International Bowling Board was formed. The Women's International Bowling Board was formed in 1969.

WORLD OUTDOOR CHAMPIONSHIPS

Instituted in 1966 for men and 1969 for women the championships are now held every four years. The Leonard Trophy for men is presented to the winning team based on performances in all categories at the world championship. *Winners:*

Men's Singles
1966 David Bryant (Eng)
1972 Malwyn Evans (Wal)
1976 Doug Watson (SAf)
1980 David Bryant (Eng)
1984 Peter Belliss (NZ)
1988 David Bryant (Eng)

Men's Pairs
1966 Geoff Kelly & Bert Palm (Aus)
1972 Clementi Delgado & Eric Liddell (HK)
1976 Doug Watson & William Moseley (SAf)
1980 Alf Sandercock & Peter Rheuben (Aus)
1984 George Adrain*(Sco) & Skippy Arculli (USA)
1988 Rowan Brassey & Peter Bellis (NZ)
* substituted for Jim Candelet

Men's Triples	Men's Fours	Leonard Trophy
1966 Australia	1966 New Zealand	1966 Australia
1972 United States	1972 England	1972 Scotland
1976 South Africa	1976 South Africa	1976 South Africa
1980 England	1980 Hong Kong	1980 England
1984 Ireland	1984 England	1984 Scotland
1988 New Zealand	1988 Ireland	1988 England

Most wins overall: 5 David Bryant (singles 1966, 1980; 1988 triples and team 1980)

Women's Singles
1969 Gladys Doyle (PNG)
1973 Elsie Wilke (NZ)
1977 Elsie Wilke (NZ)
1981 Norma Shaw (Eng)
1985 Merle Richardson (Aus)
1988 Janet Ackland (Wal)

Women's Pairs
1969 E.McDonald & M.Cridlan (SAf)
1973 Lorna Lucas & Dot Jenkinson (Aus)
1977 Helen Wong & Elvie Chok (HK)
1981 Eileen Bell & Nan Allely (Ire)
1985 Merle Richardson & Fay Craig (Aus)
1988 Margaret Johnston & Phyllis Nolan (Ire)

Women's Triples	Women's Fours	Women's Team
1969 South Africa	1969 South Africa	1969 South Africa
1973 New Zealand	1973 New Zealand	1973 New Zealand
1977 Wales	1977 Australia	1977 Australia
1981 Hong Kong	1981 England	1981 England
1985 Australia	1985 Scotland	1985 Australia
1988 Australia	1988 Australia	1988 England

Most wins overall: 3 Merle Richardson (fours 1977, singles and pairs 1985)

WORLD INDOOR CHAMPIONSHIP

Instituted 1979 for singles and 1986 for pairs and sponsored by Embassy. *Winners:*

Singles
1979 David Bryant (Eng)	1985 Terry Sullivan (Wal)
1980 David Bryant (Eng)	1986-7 Tony Allcock (Eng)
1981 David Bryant (Eng)	1988 Hugh Duff (Sco)
1982 John Watson (Sco)	1989 Richard Corsie (Sco)
1983 Bob Sutherland (Sco)	1990 John Price (Wal)
1984 Jim Baker (Ire)	

Most wins: 3 David Bryant

Pairs
1986-7 David Bryant & Tony Allcock (Eng)
1988 Ian Schubak & Jim Yates (Aus)
1989-90 David Bryant & Tony Allcock (Eng)

WOMEN'S WORLD INDOOR CHAMPIONSHIP

First held in 1988. *Winners:*
1988-9 Margaret Johnston (Ire)
1990 Fleur Bougourd (UK)

INTERNATIONAL CHAMPIONSHIP

First held in 1903 and contested by the four Home Countries of the British Isles. There was no championship in 1976. *Wins:*

34 Scotland	1904, 1907-10, 1912-4, 1919, 1921-3, 1928, 1932, 1935-6, 1950, 1952-3, 1963, 1965-75, 1977, 1979-80
26 England	1903, 1906, 1911, 1924, 1926-7, 1929, 1939, 1947, 1949, 1954-6, 1958-62, 1964, 1983-9
13 Wales	1920, 1925, 1930-1, 1933-4, 1937-8, 1946, 1948, 1957, 1978, 1982
3 Ireland	1905, 1951, 1981

ENGLISH BOWLING ASSOCIATION CHAMPIONSHIP

First held in 1903, the year of the formation of the EBA. The most titles won is 16 by David Bryant between 1957 and 1985. He won six singles, three pairs, three triples, and four fours titles. *Recent winners:*

Singles

1981 Andy Thomson
1982 Chris Ward
1983 John Bell
1984 Wynne Richards
1985 Roy Keating
1986 Wynne Richards
1987 David Holt
1988 Richard Bray
1989 John Ottaway
Most wins: 6 David Bryant 1960, 1966, 1971-3, 1975; 4 Percy Baker 1932, 1946, 1952, 1955

Triples

1981 St.Peter's, Hunts.
1982 Lenham, Kent
1983 Marlborough, Suffolk
1984 Clevedon, Avon
1985 Clevedon, Avon
1986 Poole Park, Dorset

1987 Worcester County
1988 Belgrave, Leicester
1989 Southbourne, Sussex

Fours

1981 Owton Lodge, Durham
1982 Castle, Notts
1983 Bolton, Lancs
1984 Boscombe Cliff, Hants
1985 Aldersbrook, Essex
1986 Stony Stratford, Bucks
1987 Aylesbury Town, Bucks
1988 Summertown, Oxfordshire
1989 Blackheath & Greenwich, Kent

Pairs

1981 Burton House, Lincs (Alan Bates & Richard White)
1982 Bedford Borough, Bucks (David Hurst & John McConnell)
1983 Eldon Grove, Durham (George Turley & Mal Hughes)
1984 Lenham, Kent (Ollie Jones & Len Hayes)
1985 Haxby Road, Yorks (Peter Richardson & Frank Maxwell)
1986 Owton Lodge, Durham (Dave Kilner & Cliff Simpson)
1987 Bolton, Lancs (David Holt & Tom Armstrong)
1988 Leicester (John Stephenson & Paul Clarke)
1989 Essex County (Paul Maynard & David McCathie)

WOOLWICH MASTERS

A popular spring tournament played at Worthing annually since 1978. Originally sponsored by Kodak, Gateway were sponsors 1984-7 and the Woolwich Building Society from 1988. *Winners:*
1978-9 David Bryant (Eng)
1980-1 William Moseley (SAf)
1982 David Bryant (Eng)
1983 George Souza (HK)
1984-9 David Bryant (Eng)

WATERLOO CUP

Crown Green bowling's premier tournament the Waterloo Handicap has been held since 1907 and has its home at Blackpool's Waterloo Hotel. *Recent winners:*
1977 Len Barrett
1978 Arthur Murray
1979 Brian Duncan
1980 Vernon Lee
1981 Roy Nicholson
1982 Dennis Mercer
1983 Stan Frith
1984 Steve Ellis
1985 Tommy Johnstone
1986 Brian Duncan
1987 Brian Duncan
1988 Ingham Gregory
1989 Brian Duncan
Most wins: 4 Brian Duncan, 2 Bernard Kelly 1953-4, Arthur Murray 1973, 1978

Tony Allcock became at age 24 the youngest world champion, when he teamed up with Jim Hobday and David Bryant to win the triples in 1980. Since then many further titles have come his way (All-Sport)

BOXING

From the beginning of time man has fought his fellow man, but the first record of a boxing match was in 1681 when the Duke of Albemarle organised a match between his butler and his butcher. In 1719 James Figg of Oxfordshire, regarded as the first boxing champion, set up his school of arms in London. The earliest prize-ring code of rules was formulated in England in 1743 by the champion pugilist Jack Braughton, and in 1865 the 8th Marquess of Queensberry drew up his famous rules for boxing, directed to fighting with gloves rather than the earlier bare-knuckle fighters.

WORLD CHAMPIONS

The first world championship fight with gloves and conducted under the Queensberry Rules was on 30 July 1884, when Irish-born Jack Dempsey beat George Fulljames of the USA in New York for the middleweight title. There has been a proliferation of world champions, with a increase in recent years in the number of weight divisions, and now, the curious situation of four different governing bodies recognising "world champions".

The National Boxing Association (NBA) was formed in the USA in 1920. The title was changed to World Boxing Association (WBA) in 1962. In Britain the British Boxing Board of Control (BBBC) was formed in 1929, earlier title fights having been largely under the control of the National Sporting Club.

The WBA recognise world champions, but rather closer to an international governing body is the World Boxing Council (WBC), founded in Mexico City in 1963. Neither body has been able to agree on fight regulations, and the situation has been further complicated by the formation of the International Boxing Federation (IBF) in the USA in 1983 and the World Boxing Organisation (WBO) in 1988. All titleholders recognised by these various bodies are shown in the following lists of champions. For each weight the current weight limits (generally in force from 1970) are indicated. The names for the new intermediate weight categories vary, but the WBC versions have been shown in bold print, with the WBA, IBF and WBO titles beneath.

The following weight limits had been established following discussions in 1910 between boxing authorities in the UK and USA:

Heavyweight	over 175lb	Featherweight	122lb
Light-heavy	175lb	Bantamweight	116lb
Middleweight	154lb	Flyweight	112lb
Welterweight	142lb	Paperweight	105lb
Lightweight	133lb		

HEAVYWEIGHT
Over 190lb (86.2kg)
Undisputed
1882 John L.Sullivan (USA)
1892 James J.Corbett (USA)
1897 Bob Fitzsimmons (UK)
1899 James J.Jefferies (USA)
1905 Marvin Hart (USA)

'Iron' Mike Tyson, the youngest ever world heavyweight champion at 20 years 144 days in 1986, sensationally lost his title in 1990 to 'Buster' Douglas (All-Sport/Bob Martin)

1906 Tommy Burns (Can)
1908 Jack Johnson (USA)
1915 Jess Willard (USA)
1919 Jack Dempsey (USA)
1926 Gene Tunney (USA)
1930 Max Schmeling (Ger)
1932 Jack Sharkey (USA)
1933 Primo Carnera (Ita)
1934 Max Baer (USA)
1935 James J.Braddock (USA)
1937 Joe Louis (USA)
1949 Ezzard Charles (USA)
1951 Jersey Joe Walcott (USA)
1952 Rocky Marciano (USA)
1956 Floyd Patterson (USA)
1959 Ingemar Johansson (Swe)
1960 Floyd Patterson (USA)
1962 Sonny Liston (USA)
1964 Cassius Clay (USA)
1970 Joe Frazier (USA)
1973 George Foreman (USA)
1974 Muhammad Ali (USA)
1978 Leon Spinks (USA)
1987 Mike Tyson (USA)
WBA
1965 Ernie Terrell (USA)
1968 Jimmy Ellis (USA)
1978 Muhammad Ali (USA)
1979 John Tate (USA)
1980 Mike Weaver (USA)

1982 Mike Dokes (USA)
1983 Gerrie Coetzee (SAf)
1984 Greg Page (USA)
1985 Tony Tubbs (USA)
1986 Tim Witherspoon (USA)
1986 James Smith (USA)
1987 Mike Tyson (USA)
1989 Mike Tyson (USA)
1990 James 'Buster' Douglas (USA)
WBC
1978 Ken Norton (USA)
1978 Larry Holmes (USA)
1984 Tim Witherspoon (USA)
1984 Pinklon Thomas (USA)
1986 Trevor Berbick (Jam)
1989 Mike Tyson (USA)
1990 James 'Buster' Douglas (USA)
IBF
1984 Larry Holmes (USA)
1985 Michael Spinks (USA)
1987 Tony Tucker (USA)
1989 James 'Buster' Douglas (USA)
WBO
1989 Francesco Damiani (Ita)

CRUISERWEIGHT
JUNIOR HEAVYWEIGHT WBO
Limit 190lb (86.2kg)
Undisputed
1988 Evander Holyfield (USA)

WBA
1982 Ossie Ocasio (PR)
1984 Piet Crous (SAf)
1985 Dwight Muhammad Qawi (USA)
1986 Evander Holyfield (USA)
1989 Taoufik Belbouli (Fra)
1989 Robert Daniels (USA)
WBC
1979 Marvin Camel (USA)
1980 Carlos de Leon (PR)
1982 S.T.Gordon (USA)
1983 Carlos de Leon (PR)
1985 Alfonso Ratliff (USA)
1985 Bernard Benton (USA)
1986 Carlos de Leon (PR)
1989 Carlos de Leon (PR)
IBF
1983 Marvin Camel (USA)
1984 Lee Roy Murphy (USA)
1986 Rickey Parkey (USA)
1987 Evander Holyfield (USA)
1989 Glenn McCrory (UK)
1990 Jeff Lampkin (USA)
WBO
1989 Richard Pultz (USA)
1990 Magne Havnaa (Nor)

LIGHT HEAVYWEIGHT
Limit 175lb (79.4kg)
Undisputed
1903 Jack Root (Aut)
1903 George Gardner (Ire)
1903 Bob Fitzsimmons (Eng)
1905 Jack O'Brien (USA)
1912 Jack Dillon (USA)
1916 Battling Levinsky (USA)
1920 Georges Carpentier (Fra)
1922 Battling Siki (Sen)
1923 Mike McTigue (Ire)
1925 Paul Berlenbach (USA)
1926 Jack Delaney (Can)
1927 Jim Slattery (USA)
1927 Tommy Loughran (USA)
1930 Jim Slattery (USA)
1930 Maxie Rosenbloom (USA)
1934 Bob Olin (USA)
1935 John Henry Lewis (USA)
1939 Melio Bettina (USA)
1939 Billy Conn (USA)
1941 Anton Christoforidis (Gre)
1941 Gus Lesnevich (USA)
1948 Freddie Mills (UK)
1950 Joey Maxim (USA)
1952 Archie Moore (USA)
1962 Harold Johnson (USA)
1963 Willie Pastrano (USA)
1965 José Torres (PR)
1966 Dick Tiger (Nig)

1968 Bob Foster (USA)
1983 Michael Spinks (USA)
WBA
1971 Vicente Rondon (Ven)
1974 Victor Galindez (Arg)
1978 Mike Rossman (USA)
1979 Victor Galindez (Arg)
1979 Marvin Johnson (USA)
1980 Eddie Mustafa Muhammad (USA)
1981 Michael Spinks (USA)
1986 Marvin Johnson (USA)
1987 Leslie Stewart (Jam)
1987 Virgil Hill (USA)
WBC
1974 John Conteh (UK)
1977 Miguel Cuello (Arg)
1978 Mate Parlov (Yug)
1978 Marvin Johnson (USA)
1979 Matthew Saad Muhammad
    (USA)
1981 Dwight Muhammah Qawi (USA)
1985 J.B.Williamson (USA)
1986 Dennis Andries (UK)
1987 Thomas Hearns (USA)
1988 Donny Lalonde (Can)
1988 Sugar Ray Leonard (USA)
1989 Dennis Andries (UK)
1989 Jeff Harding (Aus)
IBF
1985 Slobodan Kacar (Yug)
1986 Bobby Czyz (USA)
1987 Prince Charles Williams (USA)
WBO
1988 Michael Moorer (USA)

SUPER MIDDLEWEIGHT
Limit 168lb (76.2kg).
WBA
1984 Park Chong-pal (SKo)
1988 Fulgencio Obelmejias (Ven)
1989 Baek In-chul (SKo)
1990 Christophe Tiozzo (Fra)
WBC
1988 Sugar Ray Leonard (USA)
IBF
1984 Murray Sutherland (Can)
1988 Graciano Rocchigiani (FRG)
1990 Lindell Holmes (USA)
WBO
1988 Thomas Hearns (USA)

MIDDLEWEIGHT
Limit 160lb (72.6kg)
Undisputed
1891 Nonpareil Jack Dempsey (Ire)
1891 Bob Fitzsimmons (UK)
1897 Kid McCoy (USA)
1898 Tommy Ryan (USA)

1908 Stanley Ketchel (USA)
1908 Billy Papke (USA)
1908 Stanley Ketchel (USA)
1910 Billy Papke (USA)
1911 Cyclone Thompson (USA)
1911 Billy Papke (USA)
1912 Frank Mantell (USA)
1912 Billy Papke (USA)
1913 Frank Klaus (USA)
1913 George Chip (USA)
1914 Al McCoy (USA)
1917 Mike O'Dowd (USA)
1920 Johnny Wilson (USA)
1923 Harry Greb (USA)
1926 Tiger Flowers (USA)
1926 Mickey Walker (USA)
1931 Gorilla Jones (USA)
1932 Marcel Thil (Fra)
1937 Fred Apostoli (USA)
1939 Ceferino Garcia (Phi)
1940 Ken Overlin (USA)
1941 Billy Soose (USA)

Thomas 'The Hitman' Hearns was the first boxer to win world titles at four weight catagories (**All-Sport/Dave Cannon**)

1941 Tony Zale (USA)
1947 Rocky Graziano (USA)
1948 Tony Zale (USA)
1948 Marcel Cerdan (Alg)
1949 Jake la Motta (USA)
1951 Sugar Ray Robinson (USA)
1951 Randolph Turpin (UK)
1951 Sugar Ray Robinson (USA)
1953 Carl Bobo Olsen (Haw)
1955 Sugar Ray Robinson (USA)
1957 Gene Fullmer (USA)
1957 Sugar Ray Robinson (USA)
1957 Carmen Basilio (USA)
1958 Sugar Ray Robinson (USA)
1960 Paul Pender (USA)

1961 Terry Downes (UK)
1962 Paul Pender (USA)
1962 Dick Tiger (Nig)
1963 Joey Giardello (USA)
1965 Dick Tiger (Nig)
1966 Emile Griffith (USA)
1968 Nino Benvenuti (Ita)
1970 Carlos Monzon (Arg)
1976 Carlos Monzon (Arg)
1977 Rodrigo Valdez (Col)
1978 Hugo Corro (Arg)
1979 Vito Antuofermo (Ita)
1980 Alan Minter (UK)
1980 Marvin Hagler (USA)

WBA
1987 Sambu Kalambay (Zai)
1989 Mike McCallum (USA)

WBC
1974 Rodrigo Valdez (Col)
1987 Sugar Ray Leonard (USA)
1987 Thomas Hearns (USA)
1988 Iran Barkley (USA)
1989 Roberto Duran (Pan)

IBF
1987 Frank Tate (USA)
1988 Michael Nunn (USA)

WBO
1989 Doug De Witt (USA)
1990 Nigel Benn (UK)

SUPER WELTERWEIGHT
JUNIOR MIDDLEWEIGHT WBA, IBF,
WBO *Limit 154lb (69.9kg)*
Undisputed
1962 Denny Moyer (USA)
1963 Ralph Dupas (USA)
1963 Sandro Mazzinghi (Ita)
1965 Nino Benvenuti (Ita)
1966 Kim Ki-soo (SKo)
1968 Sandro Mazzinghi (Ita)
1969 Freddie Little (USA)
1970 Carmelo Bossi (Ita)
1971 Koichi Wajima (Jap)
1974 Oscar Albarado (USA)
1975 Koichi Wajima (Jap)

WBA
1975 Yuh Jae-do (SKo)
1976 Koichi Wajima (Jap)
1976 José Duran (Spa)
1976 Angel Castellini (Arg)
1977 Eddie Gazo (Nic)
1978 Masashi Kudo (Jap)
1979 Ayube Kalule (Uga)
1981 Sugar Ray Leonard (USA)
1981 Tadashi Mihara (Jap)
1982 Davey Moore (USA)
1983 Roberto Duran (Pan)
1984 Mike McCallum (Jam)

1988 Julian Jackson (USA)
WBC
1975 Miguel de Oliviera (Bra)
1975 Elisha Obed (Bah)
1976 Eckhard Dagge (FRG)
1977 Rocky Mattioli (Ita)
1979 Maurice Hope (UK)
1981 Wilfred Benitez (USA)
1982 Thomas Hearns (USA)
1986 Duane Thomas (USA)
1987 Lupe Aquino (Mex)
1988 Gianfranco Rosi (Ita)
1988 Don Curry (USA)
1989 René Jacquot (Fra)
1989 John Mugabi (Uga)
1990 Terry Norris (USA)

IBF
1984 Mark Medal (USA)
1984 Carlos Santos (PR)
1986 Buster Drayton (USA)
1987 Matthew Hilton (Can)
1988 Robert Hines (USA)
1989 Darrin Van Horn (USA)
1989 Gianfranco Rosi (Ita)

WBO
1988 John David Jackson (USA)

WELTERWEIGHT
Limit 147lb (66.7kg)
Undisputed
1892 Billy Smith (USA)
1894 Tommy Ryan (USA)
1898 Billy Smith (USA)
1900 Rube Ferns (USA)
1900 Matty Matthews (USA)
1901 Rube Ferns (USA)
1901 Joe Walcott (Bar)
1904 Dixie Kid (USA)
1905 Joe Walcott (Bar)
1906 Honey Mellody (USA)
1907 Mike Sullivan (USA)
1908 Harry Lewis (USA)
1914 Waldemar Holberg (Den)
1914 Tom McCormick (Ire)
1914 Matt Wells (UK)
1915 Mike Glover (USA)
1915 Jack Britton (USA)
1915 Ted Kid Lewis (UK)
1916 Jack Britton (USA)
1917 Ted Kid Lewis (UK)
1919 Jack Britton (USA)
1922 Mickey Walker (USA)
1926 Pete Latzo (USA)
1927 Joe Dundee (Ita)
1928 Jack Thompson (USA)
1929 Jackie Fields (USA)
1930 Jack Thompson (USA)
1930 Tommy Freeman (USA)

1931 Jack Thompson (USA)
1931 Lou Brouillard (Can)
1932 Jackie Fields (USA)
1933 Young Corbett III (Ita)
1933 Jimmy McLarnin (Ire)
1934 Barney Ross (USA)
1934 Jimmy McLarnin (Ire)
1935 Barney Ross (USA)
1938 Henry Armstrong (USA)
1940 Fritzie Zivic (USA)
1941 Red Cochrane (USA)
1946 Marty Servo (USA)
1946 Sugar Ray Robinson (USA)
1951 Johnny Bratton (USA)
1951 Kid Gavilan (Cub)
1954 Johnny Saxton (USA)
1955 Tony de Marco (USA)
1955 Carmen Basilio (USA)
1956 Johnny Saxton (USA)
1956 Carmen Basilio (USA)
1958 Virgil Atkins (USA)
1958 Don Jordon (Dom)
1960 Benny Kid Paret (Cub)
1961 Emile Griffith (USA)
1961 Benny Kid Paret (Cub)
1962 Emile Griffith (USA)
1963 Louis Rodriguez (Cub)
1963 Emile Griffith (USA)
1966 Curtis Cokes (USA)
1969 José Napoles (Cub)
1970 Billy Backus (USA)
1971 José Napoles (Cub)
1981 Sugar Ray Leonard (USA)
1985 Don Curry (USA)
1986 Lloyd Honeyghan (UK)

WBA
1975 Angel Espada (PR)
1976 Pipino Cuevas (Mex)
1980 Thomas Hearns (USA)
1983 Don Curry (USA)
1987 Mark Breland (USA)
1987 Marlon Starling (USA)
1988 Tomas Molinares (Col)
1989 Mark Breland (USA)

WBC
1975 John H.Stracey (UK)
1976 Carlos Palomino (Mex)
1979 Wilfred Benitez (USA)
1979 Sugar Ray Leonard (USA)
1980 Roberto Duran (Pan)
1980 Sugar Ray Leonard (USA)
1983 Milton McCrory (USA)
1987 Lloyd Honeyghan (UK)
1987 Jorge Vaca (Mex)
1988 Lloyd Honeyghan (UK)
1989 Marlon Starling (USA)

IBF
1984 Don Curry (USA)

1987 Lloyd Honeyghan (UK)
1988 Simon Brown (Jam)
WBO
1989 Genaro Leon (Mex)

SUPER LIGHTWEIGHT
JUNIOR-WELTERWEIGHT WBA, IBF,
WBO *Limit 140lb (63.5kg)*
Undisputed
1922 Pinky Mitchell (USA)
1926 Mushy Callahan (USA)
1930 Jackie Kid Berg (UK)
1931 Tony Canzoneri (USA)
1932 Johnny Jaddick (USA)
1933 Battling Shaw (Mex)
1933 Tony Canzoneri (USA)
1933 Barney Ross (USA)
1946 Tippy Larkin (USA)
1959 Carlos Ortiz (PR)
1960 Duilio Loi (Ita)
1962 Eddie Perkins (USA)
1962 Duilio Loi (Ita)
1963 Roberto Cruz (Phi)
1963 Eddie Perkins (USA)
1965 Carlos Hernandez (Ven)
1966 Sandro Lopopolo (Ita)
1967 Paul Fujii (Haw)
WBA
1968 Nicolino Loche (Arg)
1972 Alfonso Frazer (Pan)
1972 Antonio Cervantes (Col)
1976 Wilfred Benitez (USA)
1977 Antonio Cervantes (Col)
1980 Aaron Pryor (USA)
1984 Johnny Bumphus (USA)
1984 Gene Hatcher (USA)
1985 Ubaldo Sacco (Arg)
1986 Patrizio Oliva (Ita)
1987 Juan Martin Coggi (Arg)
WBC
1968 Pedro Adigue (Phi)
1970 Bruno Acari (Ita)
1974 Perico Fernandez (Spa)
1975 Saensak Muangsurin (Tha)
1976 Miguel Velasquez (Spa)
1976 Saensak Muangsurin (Tha)
1978 Kim Sang-hyun (SKo)
1980 Saoul Mamby (USA)
1982 Leroy Haley (USA)
1983 Bruce Curry (USA)
1984 Billy Costello (USA)
1985 Lonnie Smith (USA)
1986 Tsuyoshi Hamada (Jap)
1986 René Arredondo (Mex)
1987 René Arredondo (Mex)
1988 Roger Mayweather (USA)
1989 Julio César Chávez (Mex)
IBF

1983 Aaron Pryor (USA)
1986 Gary Hinton (USA)
1986 Joe Louis Manley (USA)
1987 Terry Marsh (UK)
1988 James Buddy McGirt (USA)
1988 Meldrick Taylor (USA)
1990 Julio César Chávez (Mex)
WBO
1989 Hector Camacho (PR)

LIGHTWEIGHT
Limit 135lb (61.2kg)
Undisputed
1896 George Lavigne (USA)
1899 Frank Erne (Swi)
1902 Joe Gans (USA)
1908 Battling Nelson (Den)
1910 Ad Wolgast (USA)
1912 Willie Ritchie (USA)
1914 Freddie Welsh (UK)
1917 Benny Leonard (USA)
1925 Jimmy Goodrich (USA)
1925 Rocky Kansas (USA)
1926 Sammy Mandell (USA)
1930 Al Singer (USA)
1930 Tony Canzeroni (USA)
1933 Barney Ross (USA)
1935 Tony Canzeroni (USA)
1936 Lou Ambers (USA)
1938 Henry Armstrong (USA)
1939 Lou Ambers (USA)
1940 Lew Jenkins (USA)
1941 Sammy Angott (USA)
1942 Beau Jack (USA)
1943 Bob Montgomery (USA)
1943 Sammy Angott (USA)
1944 Juan Zurita (Mex)
1945 Ike Williams (USA)
1951 Jimmy Carter (USA)
1952 Lauro Salas (Mex)
1952 Jimmy Carter (USA)
1954 Paddy de Marco (USA)
1954 Jimmy Carter (USA)
1955 Wallace Bud Smith (USA)
1956 Joe Brown (USA)
1962 Carlos Ortiz (PR)
1965 Ismael Laguna (Pan)
1965 Carlos Ortiz (PR)
1968 Carlos Teo Cruz (Dom)
1969 Mando Ramos (USA)
1970 Ismael Laguna (Pan)
1978 Roberto Duran (Pan)
WBA
1970 Ken Buchanan (UK)
1972 Roberto Duran (Pan)
1979 Ernesto Espana (Ven)
1980 Hilmer Kenty (USA)
1981 Sean O'Grady (USA)

1981 Claude Noel (Tri)
1981 Arturo Frias (USA)
1982 Ray Mancini (USA)
1984 Livingstone Bramble (USA)
1986 Edwin Rosario (PR)
1987 Julio César Chávez (Mex)
1989 Edwin Rosario (USA)
1990 Juan Nazario (PR)
WBC
1971 Pedro Carrasco (Spa)
1972 Mando Ramos (USA)
1972 Chango Carmona (Mex)
1972 Rodolfo Gonzalez (Mex)
1974 Guts Ishimatsu (Jap)
1976 Esteban de Jesús (PR)
1979 Jim Watt (UK)
1981 Alexis Arguello (Nic)
1983 Edwin Rosario (PR)
1984 José Luis Ramirez (Mex)
1985 Hector Camacho (PR)
1987 José Luis Ramirez (Mex)
1988 Julio César Chávez (Mex)
1989 Pernell Whitaker (USA)
IBF
1984 Charlie Brown (USA)
1984 Harry Arroyo (USA)
1985 Jimmy Paul (USA)
1986 Greg Haugen (USA)
1987 Vinny Pazienza (USA)
1988 Greg Haugen (USA)
1989 Pernell Whitaker (USA)
WBO
1989 Amancio Castro (Col)
1989 Mauricio Aceves (Mex)

SUPER FEATHERWEIGHT
JUNIOR LIGHTWEIGHT WBA, IBF,
WBO *Limit 130lb (59kg)*
Undisputed
1921 Johnny Dundee (Ita)
1923 Jack Bernstein (USA)
1923 Johnny Dundee (Ita)
1924 Kid Sullivan (USA)
1925 Mike Ballerino (USA)
1925 Tod Morgan (USA)
1929 Benny Bass (USA)
1931 Kid Chocolate (Cub)
1933 Frankie Klick (USA)
1959 Harold Gomes (USA)
1960 Flash Elorde (Phi)
1967 Yoshiaki Numata (Jap)
1967 Hiroshi Kobayashi (Jap)
WBA
1971 Alfredo Marcano (Ven)
1972 Ben Villaflor (Phi)
1973 Kuniaki Shibata (Jap)
1973 Ben Villaflor (Phi)
1976 Sam Serrano (PR)

1980 Yasutsune Uehara (Jap)
1981 Sam Serrano (PR)
1983 Roger Mayweather (USA)
1984 Rocky Lockridge (USA)
1985 Wilfredo Gomez (PR)
1986 Alfredo Layne (Pan)
1986 Brian Mitchell (SAf)

WBC
1969 René Barrientos (Phi)
1970 Yoshiaki Numata (Jap)
1971 Ricardo Arredondo (Mex)
1974 Kuniaki Shibata (Jap)
1975 Alfredo Escalera (PR)
1978 Alexis Arguello (Nic)
1980 Rafael Limon (Mex)
1981 Cornelius Boza Edwards (Uga)
1981 Rolando Navarette (Phi)
1982 Rafael Limon (Mex)
1982 Bobby Chacon (USA)
1983 Hector Camacho (PR)
1984 Julio César Chávez (Mex)
1988 Azumah Nelson (Gha)

IBF
1984 Yuh Hwan-kil (SKo)
1985 Lester Ellis (Aus)
1985 Barry Michael (Aus)
1987 Rocky Lockridge (USA)
1988 Tony Lopez (USA)
1989 Juan Molina (PR)
1990 Tony Lopez (USA)

WBO
1989 Juan Molina (PR)
1989 Kamel Bou Ali (Tun)

FEATHERWEIGHT
Limit 126lb (57.2kg)
Undisputed
1891 Young Griffo (Aus)
1892 George Dixon (Can)
1897 Solly Smith (USA)
1898 Dave Sullivan (Ire)
1898 George Dixon (Can)
1900 Terry McGovern (USA)
1901 Young Corbett II (USA)
1904 Jimmy Britt (USA)
1904 Tommy Sullivan (USA)
1906 Abe Attell (USA)
1912 Johnny Kilbane (USA)
1923 Eugene Criqui (Fra)
1923 Johnny Dundee (Ita)
1925 Kid Kaplan (USA)
1927 Benny Bass (USA)
1928 Tony Canzoneri (USA)
1928 Andre Routis (Fra)
1929 Battling Battalino (USA)
1932 Kid Chocolate (Cub)
1933 Freddie Miller (USA)
1936 Petey Sarron (USA)

1937 Henry Armstrong (USA)
1938 Joey Archibald (USA)
1940 Harry Jeffra (USA)
1941 Joey Archibald (USA)
1941 Chalky Wright (Mex)
1942 Willie Pep (USA)
1948 Sandy Saddler (USA)
1949 Willie Pep (USA)
1950 Sandy Sadler (USA)
1957 Hogan Kid Bassey (Nig)
1959 Davey Moore (USA)
1963 Sugar Ramos (Cub)
1964 Vicente Saldivar (Mex)

WBA
1968 Raul Rojas (USA)
1968 Shozo Saijyo (Jap)
1971 Antonio Gomez (Ven)
1972 Ernesto Marcel (Pan)
1974 Ruben Olivares (Mex)
1974 Alexis Arguello (Nic)
1977 Rafael Ortega (Pan)
1977 Cecilio Lastra (Spa)
1978 Eusebio Pedroza (Pan)
1985 Barry McGuigan (Ire)
1986 Steve Cruz (USA)
1987 Antonio Esparragoza (Ven)

WBC
1968 Howard Winstone (UK)
1968 José Legra (Cub)
1969 Johnny Famechon (Fra)
1970 Vicente Saldivar (Mex)
1970 Kuniaki Shibata (Jap)
1972 Clemente Sanchez (Mex)

1972 José Legra (Cub)
1973 Eder Jofre (Bra)
1974 Bobby Chacon (USA)
1975 Ruben Olivares (Mex)
1975 David Kotey (Gha)
1976 Danny Lopez (USA)
1980 Salvador Sanchez (Mex)
1982 Juan Laporte (PR)
1984 Wilfredo Gomez (PR)
1984 Azumah Nelson (Gha)
1988 Jeff Fenech (Aus)
1990 Marcos Villasana (Mex)

IBF
1984 Oh Min-keum (SKo)
1985 Chung Ki-young (SKo)
1986 Antonio Rivera (PR)
1988 Calvin Grove (USA)
1988 Jorge Paez (Mex)

WBO
1989 Maurizio Stecca (Ita)
1989 Louie Espinoza (USA)

SUPER-BANTAMWEIGHT
JUNIOR-FEATHERWEIGHT WBA,
IBF, WBO *Limit 122lb (55.3kg)*
Undisputed
1922 Jack Kid Wolfe (USA)
1923 Carl Duane (USA)

WBA
1977 Hong Soo-hwan (SKo)
1978 Ricardo Cardona (Col)
1980 Leo Randolph (USA)
1980 Sergio Palma (Arg)

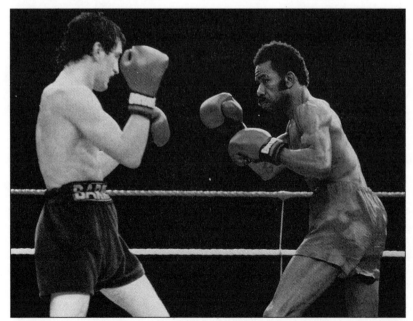

Barry McGuigan (left) ended the seven-year reign as WBA world featherweight champion of Eusebio Pedroza (right) with a 15-rounds points decision at Queen's Park Rangers' football ground in 1985 (All-Sport)

1982 Leo Cruz (Dom)
1984 Loris Stecca (Ita)
1984 Victor Callejas (PR)
1987 Louis Espinoza (USA)
1987 Julio Gervacio (Dom)
1988 Bernardo Pinango (Ven)
1988 Juan José Estrada (Mex)
1989 Jesús Saled (USA)

WBC
1976 Rigoberto Riasco (Pan)
1976 Royal Kobayashi (Jap)
1976 Yum Dong-kyun (SKo)
1977 Wilfredo Gomez (PR)
1983 Jaime Garza (USA)
1984 Juan Meza (Mex)
1985 Lupe Pintor (Mex)
1986 Samart Payakarun (Tha)
1987 Jeff Fenech (Aus)
1988 Daniel Zaragoza (Mex)
1990 Paul Banks (USA)

IBF
1983 Bobby Berna (Phi)
1984 Suh Seung-il (SKo)
1985 Kim Ji-won (SKo)
1987 Lee Seung-hoon (SKo)
1988 José Sanabria (Ven)
1989 Fabrice Benichou (Fra)
1990 Welcome Ncita (SAf)

WBO
1989 Kenny Mitchell (USA)
1989 Valerio Nati (Ita)
1990 Orlando Fernandez (PR)

BANTAMWEIGHT
Limit 118lb (53.5kg)
Undisputed
1891 George Dixon (Can)
1892 Billy Plimmer (UK)
1895 Pedlar Palmer (UK)
1899 Terry McGovern (USA)
1901 Harry Forbes (USA)
1903 Frankie Neil (USA)
1904 Joe Bowker (UK)
1905 Jimmy Walsh (USA)
1907 Owen Moran (UK)
1908 Johnny Coulon (Can)
1914 Kid Williams (Den)
1917 Pete Herman (USA)
1920 Joe Lynch (USA)
1921 Pete Herman (USA)
1921 Johnny Buff (USA)
1922 Joe Lynch (USA)
1924 Abe Goldstein (USA)
1924 Eddie Martin (USA)
1925 Charlie Rosenberg (USA)
1927 Bud Taylor (USA)
1928 Bushy Graham (Ita)
1929 Al Brown (Pan)
1935 Baltazar Sangchilli (Spa)
1936 Tony Marino (USA)
1936 Sixto Escobar (Spa)
1937 Harry Jeffra (USA)
1938 Sixto Escobar (Spa)
1940 Lou Salica (USA)
1942 Manuel Ortiz (USA)
1947 Harold Dade (USA)

1947 Mauel Ortiz (USA)
1950 Vic Toweel (SAf)
1952 Jimmy Carruthers (Aus)
1954 Robert Cohen (Alg)
1956 Mario D'Agata (Ita)
1957 Alphonse Halimi (Alg)
1959 Joe Becerra (Mex)
1960 Eder Jofre (Bra)
1965 Fighting Harada (Jap)
1968 Lionel Rose (Aus)
1969 Ruben Olivares (Mex)
1970 Chucho Castillo (Mex)
1971 Ruben Olivares (Mex)
1972 Rafael Herrera (Mex)
1972 Enrique Pinder (Pan)

WBA
1973 Romeo Anaya (Mex)
1973 Arnold Taylor (SAf)
1974 Hong Soo-hwan (SKo)
1975 Alfonso Zamora (Mex)
1977 Jorge Lujan (Pan)
1980 Julian Solis (PR)
1980 Jeff Chandler (USA)
1984 Richard Sandoval (USA)
1986 Gaby Canizales (USA)
1986 Bernardo Pinango (Ven)
1987 Takuya Muguruma (Jap)
1987 Park Chang-young (SKo)
1987 Wilfredo Vasquez (PR)
1988 Khaokor Galaxy (Tha)
1988 Moon Sung-kil (SKo)
1989 Khaokor Galaxy (Tha)
1989 Luisito Espinosa (Phi)

WBC
1973 Rafael Herrera (Mex)
1974 Rodolfo Martinez (Mex)
1976 Carlos Zarate (Mex)
1979 Lupe Pintor (Mex)
1983 Alberto Davila (USA)
1985 Daniel Zaragoza (Mex)
1985 Miguel Lora (Col)
1988 Raul Perez (Mex)

IBF
1984 Satoshi Shingaki (Jap)
1985 Jeff Fenech (Aus)
1987 Kelvin Seabrooks (USA)
1988 Orlando Canizales (USA)

WBO
1989 Israel Contreras (Ven)

SUPER FLYWEIGHT
JUNIOR-BANTAMWEIGHT WBA, IBF, WBO *Limit 115lb (52.2kg)*
WBA
1981 Gustavo Ballas (Arg)
1981 Rafael Pedroza (Pan)
1982 Jiro Watanabe (Jap)
1984 Khaosai Galaxy (Tha)

Azumah Nelson, like Barry McGuigan, was a Commonwealth gold medallist in 1978 and went on to be world featherweight champion
(All-Sport/Simon Bruty)

WBC
1980 Rafael Orono (Ven)
1981 Kim Chul-ho (SKo)
1982 Rafael Orono (Ven)
1983 Payao Poontarat (Tha)
1984 Jiro Watanabe (Jap)
1986 Gilberto Roman (Mex)
1987 Santos Laciar (Arg)
1987 Jesús Rojas (Col)
1988 Gilberto Roman (Mex)
1989 Nana Yaw Konadu (Gha)
1990 Moon Sung-kil (SKo)
IBF
1983 Chun Joo-do (SKo)
1985 Ellyas Pical (Ina)
1986 Cesar Polanco (Dom)
1986 Chang Tae-il (SKo)
1987 Ellyas Pical (Ina)
1989 Juan Polo Perez (Col)
1990 Robert Quirogo (USA)
WBO
1989 José Ruiz (PR)

FLYWEIGHT
Limit 112lb (50.8kg)
Undisputed
1913 Sid Smith (UK)
1913 Bill Ladbury (UK)
1914 Percy Jones (UK)
1915 Joe Symonds (UK)
1916 Jimmy Wilde (UK)
1923 Pancho Villa (Phi)
1925 Fidel La Barba (USA)
1928 Frankie Genaro (USA)
1929 Emile Pladner (Fra)
1929 Frankie Genaro (USA)
1931 Young Perez (Tun)
1932 Jackie Brown (UK)
1935 Benny Lynch (UK)
1938 Peter Kane (UK)
1943 Jackie Paterson (UK)
1948 Rinty Monaghan (UK)
1950 Terry Allen (UK)
1950 Dado Marino (Haw)
1952 Yoshio Shirai (Jap)
1954 Pascual Perez (Arg)
1960 Pone Kingpetch (Tha)
1962 Fighting Harada (Jap)
1963 Pone Kingpetch (Tha)
1963 Hiroyuki Ebihara (Jap)
1964 Pone Kingpetch (Tha)
1965 Salvatore Burruni (Ita)
WBA
1966 Horacio Accavallo (Arg)
1969 Hiroyuki Ebihara (Jap)
1969 Bernabe Villacampo (Phi)
1970 Berkrerk Chartvanchai (Tha)
1970 Masao Ohba (Jap)

1973 Chartchai Chionoi (Tha)
1974 Susumu Hanagata (Jap)
1975 Erbito Salavarria (Phi)
1976 Alfonso Lopez (Pan)
1976 Guty Espadas (Mex)
1978 Betulio Gonzalez (Ven)
1979 Luis Ibarra (Pan)
1980 Kim Tae-shik (SKo)
1980 Shoji Oguma (Jap)
1980 Peter Mathebula (SAf)
1981 Santos Laciar (Arg)
1981 Luis Ibarra (Pan)
1981 Juan Herrera (Mex)
1982 Santos Laciar (Arg)
1985 Hilario Zapata (Pan)
1987 Fidel Bassa (Col)
1989 Jesús Rojas (Ven)
1990 Lee Yul-woo (SKo)
WBC
1966 Walter McGowan (UK)
1966 Chartchai Chionoi (Tha)
1969 Efren Torres (Mex)
1970 Chartchai Chionoi (Tha)
1970 Erbito Salavarria (Phi)
1972 Venice Borkorsor (Tha)
1973 Betulio Gonzalez (Ven)
1974 Shoji Oguma (Jap)
1975 Miguel Canto (Mex)
1979 Park Chan-hee (SKo)
1981 Antonio Avelar (Mex)
1982 Prudencio Cardona (Col)
1982 Freddie Castillo (Mex)
1982 Eleoncio Mercedes (Dom)
1983 Charlie Magri (UK)
1983 Frank Cedeno (Phi)
1984 Koji Kobayashi (Jap)
1984 Gabriel Bernal (Mex)
1984 Sot Chitalada (Tha)
1988 Kim Yung-kang (SKo)
1989 Sot Chitalda (Tha)
IBF
1983 Kwon Soon-chun (SKo)
1985 Chung Chong-kwan (SKo)
1986 Chung Bi-won (SKo)
1986 Shin Hi-sup (SKo)
1987 Dodie Penalosa (Phi)
1987 Choi Chang-ho (SKo)
1988 Rolando Bohol (Phi)
1988 Duke McKenzie (UK)
1989 Dave McAuley (UK)
WBO
1989 Elvis Alvarez (Col)

LIGHT FLYWEIGHT
JUNIOR-FLYWEIGHT WBA, IBF, WBO
Limit 108lb (49kg)
WBA
1975 Jaime Rios (Pan)

1976 Juan José Guzman (Dom)
1976 Yoko Gushiken (Jap)
1981 Pedro Flores (Mex)
1981 Kim Hwan-jin (SKo)
1981 Katsuo Takashiki (Jap)
1983 Lupe Madera (Mex)
1984 Francisco Quiroz (Dom)
1985 Joey Olivo (USA)
1985 Yuh Myung-woo (SKo)
WBC
1975 Franco Udella (Ita)
1975 Luis Estaba (Ven)
1978 Freddie Castillo (Mex)
1978 Netrnoi Vorasingh (Tha)
1978 Kim Sung-jun (SKo)
1980 Shigeo Nakajima (Jap)
1980 Hilario Zapata (Pan)
1982 Amado Ursua (Mex)
1982 Tadashi Tomori (Jap)
1982 Hilario Zapata (Pan)
1983 Chang Jung-koo (Kor)
1988 German Torres (Mex)
1989 Lee Yul-woo (SKo)
1989 Humberto Gonzalez (Mex)
IBF
1983 Dodie Penalosa (Phi)
1986 Choi Chong-hwan (SKo)
1988 Tacy Macalos (Phi)
1989 Muancgchai Kittikasem (Tha)
WBO
1989 José de Jesús (PR)

STRAWWEIGHT
MINI-FLYWEIGHT WBA, IBF, WBO
Limit 105lb (47.6kg)
WBA
1988 Leo Gamez (Dom)
1989 Kim Bong-jun (SKo)
WBC
1987 Lee Kyung-yung (SKo)
1988 Hiroki Ioka (Jap)
1988 Napa Kiatwanchai (Tha)
1989 Choi Jeum-hwan (SKo)
1990 Hideyuki Ohashi (Jap)
IBF
1988 Samuth Sithnaruepol (Tha)
1989 Nico Thomas (Ina)
1989 Eric Chavez (Phi)
1990 Fahlan Lookmingkwan (Tha)
WBO
1989 Rafael Torres (Dom)

MOST WORLD TITLES
5 Sugar Ray Leonard
  WBC Welterweight 1979
  WBA Junior middleweight 1981
  WBC Middleweight 1987
  WBC Super middleweight 1988

WBC Light-heavyweight 1988
5 Thomas Hearns
   WBA Welterweight 1980
   WBC Junior middleweight 1982
   WBC Light-heavyweight 1987
   WBC Middleweight 1987
   WBO Super middleweight 1988
4 Roberto Duran
   WBA Lightweight 1972
   Welterweight 1980
   WBA Junior middleweight 1983
   WBC Middleweight 1989
3 Bob Fitzsimmons
   Middleweight 1891
   Heavyweight 1897
   Light-heavyweight 1903
3 Tony Canzoneri
   Featherweight 1928
   Lightweight 1930
   Junior welterweight 1931
3 Barney Ross
   Lightweight 1933
   Junior welterweight 1933
   Welterweight 1934
3 Henry Armstrong
   Featherweight 1937
   Welterweight 1938
   Lightweight 1938
3 Alexis Arguello
   WBA Featherweight 1974
   WBC Junior lightweight 1978
   WBC Lightweight 1981
3 Wilfredo Gomez
   WBC Junior featherweight 1977
   WBC Featherweight 1984
   WBA Junior lightweight 1985
3 Julio César Chávez
   WBC Junior lightweight 1984
   WBA Lightweight 1987
   WBC Junior welterweight 1989
3 Jeff Fenech
   IBF Bantamweight 1985
   WBC Junior featherweight 1987
   WBC Featherweight 1988

Emile Griffith won the welterweight title in 1961 and the middleweight title in 1966. He also claimed to be the first junior-middleweight champion in 1962 but his title was recognised in Austria only.

MOST WORLD TITLE FIGHTS

27 Joe Louis, 26 Henry Armstrong, 25 Muhammad Ali, 24 Larry Holmes, 23 Wilfredo Gomez, Manuel Ortiz, Hilario Zapata; 22 Alexis Arguello, Tony Canzoneri, George Dixon, Emile Griffith, Eusebio Pedroza, Sugar Ray Robinson; 21 Antonio Cervantes, Roberto Duran

Most World Title Fight Wins

26 Joe Louis, 22 Muhammad Ali, Henry Armstrong; 21 Larry Holmes, Manuel Ortiz; 20 Wilfredo Gomez. Louis made a record 25 defences of his heavyweight title, the most in any weight division
Longest reigning champion: Joe Louis (USA), heavyweight 11 years 252 days
Oldest world champion: 48 years 59 days Archie Moore (USA), light-heavyweight. (Moore may have been only 45 years because of a doubt over his date of birth. But either way, he is still the oldest champion.)
Youngest world champion: 17 years 176 days Wilfred Benitez (USA), light welterweight
Heaviest world champion: 270lb (122kg) Primo Carnera (Ita)
Tallest world champion: 6ft 6in (1.98m) Ernie Terrell (USA), heavyweight
Jess Willard is often incorrectly quoted as being 6ft 6½ in

OLYMPIC CHAMPIONS

Boxing was included on the Olympic programme in 1904 and 1908 and has been at each Games since 1920. Weight limits shown are those currently in use, followed by previous limits on the following line.

Super-heavyweight - over 91kg
1984 Tyrell Biggs (USA)
1988 Lennox Lewis (Can)

Heavyweight - 91kg
Over 156lb (71.7kg) 1904-08, over 175lb (79.4kg) 1920-36, over 80kg 1948, over 81kg 1952-80
1904 Samuel Berger (USA)
1908 Albert Leonard Oldham (UK)
1912 Not held
1920 Ronald Rawson (UK)
1924 Otto von Porat (Nor)
1928 Arturo Rodriguez Jurado (Arg)
1932 Santiago Lovell (Arg)
1936 Herbert Runge (Ger)
1948 Rafael Iglesias (Arg)
1952 Edward Sanders (USA)
1956 Peter Rademacher (USA)
1960 Franco de Piccoli (Ita)
1964 Joe Frazier (USA)
1968 George Foreman (USA)
1972 Teofilo Stevenson (Cub)
1976 Teofilo Stevenson (Cub)
1980 Teofilo Stevenson (Cub)
1984 Henry Tillman (USA)
1988 Ray Mercer (USA)

Light-heavyweight - 81 kg
Limit 175lb (79.4kg) 1920-36, 80kg 1948
1920 Eddie Eagan (USA)
1924 Harry Mitchell (UK)
1928 Victor Avendano (Arg)
1932 David Carstens (SAf)
1936 Roger Michelot (Fra)
1948 George Hunter (SAf)
1952 Norvel Lee (USA)
1956 James Boyd (USA)
1960 Cassius Clay (USA)
1964 Cosimo Pinto (Ita)
1968 Dan Poznyak (USSR)
1972 Mate Parlov (Yug)
1976 Leon Spinks (USA)
1980 Slobodan Kacar (Yug)
1984 Anton Jospovic (Yug)
1988 Andrew Maynard (USA)

Middleweight - 75kg
Limit 158lb (71.7kg) 1904-08, 160lb (72.6kg) 1920-36, 73kg 1948
1904 Charles Mayer (USA)
1908 John Douglas (UK)
1920 Harry Mallin (UK)
1924 Harry Mallin (UK)
1928 Piero Toscani (Ita)
1932 Carmen Barth (USA)
1936 Jean Despeaux (Fra)
1948 László Papp (Hun)
1952 Floyd Patterson (USA)
1956 Gennadiy Schatkov (USSR)
1960 Edward Crook (USA)
1964 Valeriy Popenchenko (USSR)
1968 Chris Finnegan (UK)
1972 Vyacheslav Lemechev (USSR)
1976 Michael Spinks (USA)
1980 José Gomez (Cub)
1984 Shin Joon-sup (Sko)
1988 Henry Maske (GDR)

Light middleweight - 71kg
1952 László Papp (Hun)
1956 László Papp (Hun)
1960 Wilbert McClure (USA)
1964 Boris Lagutin (USSR)
1968 Boris Lagutin (USSR)
1972 Dieter Kottysch (FRG)
1976 Jerzy Rybicki (Pol)

1980 Armando Martinez (Cub)
1984 Frank Tate (USA)
1988 Park Si-hun (Kor)

Welterweight - 67kg
Limit 143.75lb (65.3kg) 1904, 147lb (66.7kg) 1920-36
1904 Albert Young (USA)
1908 not held
1920 Albert Schneider (Can)
1924 Jean Delarge (Bel)
1928 Edward Morgan (NZ)
1932 Edward Flynn (USA)
1936 Sten Suvio (Fin)
1948 Julius Torma (Cs)
1952 Zygmunt Chychla (Pol)
1956 Nicolae Linca (Rom)
1960 Giovanni Benvenuti (Ita)
1964 Marian Kasprzyk (Pol)
1968 Manfred Wolke (GDR)
1972 Emilio Correa (Cub)
1976 Jochen Bachfeld (GDR)
1980 Andrés Aldama (Cub)
1984 Mark Breland (USA)
1988 Robert Wangila (Ken)

Light-welterweight - 63.5kg
1952 Charles Adkins (USA)
1956 Vladimir Yengibaryan (USSR)
1960 Bohumil Nemecek (Cs)
1964 Jerzy Kulej (Pol)
1968 Jerzy Kulej (Pol)
1972 Ray Seales (USA)
1976 Ray Leonard (USA)
1980 Patrizio Oliva (Ita)
1984 Jerry Page (USA)
1988 Vyacheslav Janovskiy (USSR)

Lightweight - 60kg
Limit 135lb (61.2kg) 1904, 1920-36, 140lb (63.5kg) 1908, 62kg 1948
1904 Harry Spanger (USA)
1908 Frederick Grace (UK)
1920 Samuel Mosberg (USA)
1924 Hans Neilsen (Den)
1928 Carlo Orlando (Ita)
1932 Lawrence Stevens (SAf)
1936 Imre Harangi (Hun)
1948 Gerald Dreyer (SAf)
1952 Aureliano Bolognesi (Ita)
1956 Dick McTaggart (UK)
1960 Kazimierz Pazdzior (Pol)
1964 Józef Grudzien (Pol)
1968 Ron Harris (USA)
1972 Jan Szczepanski (Pol)
1976 Howard Davis (USA)
1980 Angel Herrera (Cub)
1984 Pernell Whitaker (USA)

Mark Breland beat the Korean An Young-su to take the 1984 Olympic welterweight gold medal. Three years later he was WBA world professional champion **(All-Sport)**

László Papp beat John Wright of Britain in London in 1948 for the first of his three Olympic medals **(All-Sport)**

1988 Andreas Zuelow (GDR)

Featherweight - 57kg
Limit 125lb (56.7kg) 1904, 126lb (57.1kg) 1908-36, 58kg 1948
1904 Oliver Kirk (USA)
1908 Richard Gunn (UK)
1920 Paul Fritsch (Fra)
1924 John Fields (USA)

1928 Lambertus van Klaveren (Hol)
1932 Carmelo Robledo (Arg)
1936 Oscar Casanovas (Arg)
1948 Ernesto Formenti (Ita)
1952 Jan Zachara (Cs)
1956 Vladimir Safronov (USSR)
1960 Francesco Musso (Ita)
1964 Stanislav Stepashkin (USSR)
1968 Antonio Roldan (Mex)

1972 Boris Kuznetsov (USSR)
1976 Angel Herrera (Cub)
1980 Rudi Fink (GDR)
1984 Meldrick Taylor (USA)
1988 Giovanni Parisi (Ita)

Bantamweight - 54kg
*Limit 114lb (52.2kg) 1904, 116lb
(52.6kg) 1908, 118lb (53.5kg) 1920-36*
1904 Oliver Kirk (USA)
1908 Henry Thomas (UK)
1920 Clarence Walker (SAf)
1924 William Smith (SAf)
1928 Vittorio Tamagnini (Ita)
1932 Horace Gwynne (Can)
1936 Ulderico Sergo (Ita)
1948 Tibor Csik (Hun)
1952 Pentti Hämäläinen (Fin)
1956 Wolfgang Behrendt (FRG)
1960 Oleg Grigoryev (USSR)
1964 Takao Sakurai (Jap)
1968 Valeriy Sokolov (USSR)
1972 Orlando Martinez (Cub)
1976 Gu Yung-jo (NKo)
1980 Juan Hernández (Cub)
1984 Maurizio Stecca (Ita)
1988 Kennedy McKinney (USA)

Flyweight - 51kg
*Limit 105lb (47.6kg) 1904, 112lb
(50.8kg) 1920-36*
1904 George Finnegan (USA)
1908 not held
1920 Frankie Genaro (USA)
1924 Fidel La Barba (USA)
1928 Antal Kocsis (Hun)
1932 István Énekes (Hun)
1936 Willi Kaiser (Ger)
1948 Pascual Perez (Arg)
1952 Nathan Brooks (USA)
1956 Terry Spinks (UK)
1960 Gyula Török (Hun)
1964 Fernando Atzori (Ita)
1968 Ricardo Delgado (Mex)
1972 Georgi Kostadinov (Bul)
1976 Leo Randolph (USA)
1980 Petar Lessov (Bul)
1984 Steve McCrory (USA)
1988 Kim Kwang-sun (SKo)

Light-flyweight - 48kg
1968 Francisco Rodriguez (Ven)
1972 György Gedo (Hun)
1976 Jorge Hernandez (Cub)
1980 Shamil Sabirov (USSR)
1984 Paul Gonzales (USA)
1988 Ivailo Khristov (Bul)

Leading medal-winning nations

	Gold	Silver	Bronze	Total
United States	46	19	28	93
USSR	14	19	17	50
United Kingdom	12	10	20	42
Poland	8	9	25	42
Italy	14	12	13	39
Cuba	12	8	5	25
Argentina	7	7	9	23
FR Germany	4	10	9	23

Most individual gold medals: 3 László Papp (Hun) middleweight 1948, light-middleweight 1952, 1956; Teofilo Stevenson (Cub) heavyweight 1972, 1976, 1980
Oldest champion: 37 years 254 days Richard Gunn (UK) featherweight 1908
Youngest champion: 16 years 162 days Jackie Fields (USA) featherweight 1924

Olympic champions who went on to win professional world titles

	Olympic title	First professional
Fidel LaBarba (USA)	1924 fly	1925 fly
Willie Smith (SAf)	1924 bantam	1927 bantam *
Frankie Genaro (USA)	1920 fly	1928 fly
Jackie Fields (USA)	1924 feather	1929 welter
Pascual Perez (Arg)	1948 fly	1954 fly
Floyd Patterson (USA)	1952 middle	1956 heavy
Cassius Clay (USA)	1960 light-heavy	1964 heavy
Nino Benvenuti (Ita)	1960 welter	1965 light middle
Joe Frazier (USA)	1964 heavy	1968 heavy
George Foreman (USA)	1968 heavy	1973 heavy
Mate Parlov (Yug)	1972 light-heavy	1978 light-heavy
Leon Spinks (USA)	1976 light-heavy	1978 heavy
Sugar Ray Leonard (USA)	1976 light welter	1979 junior middle
Leo Randolph (USA)	1976 fly	1980 junior fly
Michael Spinks (USA)	1976 middle	1981 light-heavy
Slobodan Kacar (Yug)	1980 light-heavy	1985 middle
Patrizio Oliva (Ita)	1980 light welter	1986 junior welter
Mark Breland (USA)	1984 welter	1987 welter
Frank Tate (USA)	1984 light middle	1987 middle
Meldrick Taylor (USA)	1984 feather	1988 junior welter
Maurizio Stecca (Ita)	1984 bantam	1989 feather
Pernell Whittaker (USA)	1984 welter	1989 light

* *Smith won the British version of the world title only*

WORLD AMATEUR CHAMPIONSHIPS

First held in Havana in 1974 they have subsequently been staged in between Olympic Games at Belgrade in 1978, Munich 1982, Reno 1986 and Moscow 1989. A challenge series, involving seven of the 1982 champions, was organised in Reno in March 1983, and a second series of challenge bouts for the remaining champions took place in Tokyo two months later - these winners have been included in the tables below.

SUPER-HEAVYWEIGHT - 91kg +
1982 Tyrell Biggs (USA)
1983 Tyrell Biggs (USA)
1986 Teofilo Stevenson (Cub)
1989 Roberto Balado (Cub)

HEAVYWEIGHT - 91kg
1974 Teofilo Stevenson (Cub)
1978 Teofilo Stevenson (Cub)
1982 Aleksandr Lagubkin (USSR)
1983 Willie DeWitt (Can)
1986 Félix Savon (Cub)
1989 Félix Savon (Cub)

LIGHT-HEAVYWEIGHT - 81kg
1974 Mate Parlov (Yug)
1978 Sixto Soria (Cub)
1982 Pablo Romero (Cub)
1983 Pablo Romero (Cub)
1986 Pablo Romero (Cub)
1989 Henry Maske (GDR)

MIDDLEWEIGHT - 75kg
1974 Rufat Riskiyev (USSR)
1978 José Gomez (Cub)
1982 Bernardo Comas (Cub)
1983 Bernardo Comas (Cub)
1986 Darin Allen (USA)
1989 Andrey Kurnyavka (USSR)

LIGHT MIDDLEWEIGHT - 71kg
1974 Rolando Garbey (Cub)
1978 Viktor Savchenko (USSR)
1982 Aleksandr Koshkin (USSR)
1983 Shawn O'Sullivan (Can)
1986 Angel Espinosa (Cub)
1989 Israel Akopkokhyan (USSR)

WELTERWEIGHT - 67kg
1974 Emilio Correa (Cub)
1978 Valeriy Rachkov (USSR)
1982 Mark Breland (USA)
1983 Mark Breland (USA)
1986 Kenneth Gould (USA)
1989 Francisc Vastag (Rom)

LIGHT WELTERWEIGHT - 63.5kg
1974 Ayub Kalule (Uga)
1978 Valeriy Lvov (USSR)
1982 Carlos Garcia (Cub)
1983 Carlos Garcia (Cub)
1986 Vasiliy Shishov (USSR)
1989 Igor Ruzhnikov (USSR)

LIGHTWEIGHT - 60kg
1974 Vasiliy Solomin (USSR)
1978 Andeh Davison (Nig)
1982 Angel Herrera (Cub)
1983 Pernell Whitaker (USA)
1986 Adolfo Horta (Cub)
1989 Julio González (Cub)

FEATHERWEIGHT - 57kg
1974 Howard Davis (USA)
1978 Angel Herrera (Cub)
1982 Adolfo Horta (Cub)
1983 Adolfo Horta (Cub)
1986 Kelcie Banks (USA)
1989 Airat Khamatov (USSR)

BANTAMWEIGHT - 54kg
1974 Wilfredo Gomez (PR)
1978 Adolfo Horta (Cub)
1982 Floyd Favors (USA)
1983 Floyd Favors (USA)
1986 Moon Sung-kil (SKo)
1989 Enrique Carrion (Cub)

FLYWEIGHT - 51kg
1974 Douglas Rodriguez (Cub)
1978 Henryk Srednicki (Pol)
1982 Yuriy Aleksandrov (USSR)
1983 Steve McCrory (USA)
1986 Pedro Reyes (Cub)
1989 Yuriy Arbachakov (USSR)

LIGHT FLYWEIGHT - 48kg
1974 Jorge Hernández (Cub)
1978 Stephen Muchoki (Ken)
1982 Ismail Mustafov (Bul)
1983 Rafael Saiz (Cub)
1986 Juan Torres (Cub)
1989 Eric Griffin (USA)

Most titles: 3 Teofilo Stevenson, Adolfo Horta (and 1983 world challenge). Pablo Romero won two and the world challenge in 1983.

BRIDGE (CONTRACT)

This card game was developed from Whist, with the extra dimension of a competititive auction added. Auction Bridge, in which the highest bidder names trumps was first played in about 1903. It was superseded by Contract, in which no tricks won in the play are counted towards game unless contracted for in the bidding, a principle used earlier in Plafond. Contract Bridge developed erratically until the present scoring table was devised in 1925 by Harold S.Vanderbilt (USA). Highly publicised matches staged brilliantly by Ely Cuthbertson against Lt-Col.Walter Buller's British team in 1930 and Sydney Lenz's 'official' US team in 1931 attracted worldwide publicity and made Cuthbertson the supreme authority.

The ruling body is the World Bridge Federation.

WORLD TEAM CHAMPIONSHIP
Contested by international teams for the Bermuda Bowl; first held in 1951, at first annually and now biennially. The women's competition for the Venice Trophy is now held concurrently. *Wins:*

Men – Bermuda Bowl
13 Italy   1957-9, 1961-3, 1965-7, 1969, 1973-5
13 USA*   1950-1, 1953-4, 1970-1, 1976-7, 1979, 1981, 1983, 1985, 1987
               (* as North America 1970)
1 Great Britain 1955, France 1956, Brazil 1989

Women – Venice Trophy
5 USA   1974, 1976, 1978, 1987, 1989
2 Great Britain 1981, 1985

WORLD TEAM OLYMPIAD
First held in 1960, winners have been:

Year	Open	Women
1960	France	United Arab Republic
1964	Italy	Great Britain
1968	Italy	Sweden
1972	Italy	Italy
1976	Brazil	USA
1980	France	USA
1984	Poland	USA
1988	USA	Denmark

WORLD PAIRS OPEN CHAMPIONS
1962	Pierre Jais & Roger Trézel (Fra)
1966	Cornelius Slavenburg & Hans Kreyns (Hol)
1970	Fritz Babsch & Peter Manhardt (Aut)
1974	Robert Hamman & Robert Wolff (USA)
1978	Marcello Branco & Gabino Cintra (Bra)
1982	Chip Martel & Lew Stansby (USA)
1986	Jeff Meckstroth & Eric Rodwell (USA)

Women's champions:
1962	Rixi Markus & Fritzi Gordon (UK)

| 1966 | Joan Durran & Jane Priday (UK) |
1970 Mary Jane Farrell & Marilyn Johnson (USA)
1974 Rixi Markus & Fritzi Gordon (UK)
1978 Kathie Wei & Judi Radin (USA)
1982 Carol Sanders & Betty Ann Kennedy (USA)
1986 Jacqui Mitchell & Amalya Kearse (USA)

WORLD KNOCKOUT TEAMS
Held with the World Pairs event. *Winners:*
1978 Poland, 1982 France, 1986 USA

The most successful individual at world championship play has been Giorgio Belladonna who played on all 13 Italian Bermuda Bowl winning teams and their three Olympiad wins.

EPSON WORLDWIDE BRIDGE CONTEST
Inaugurated in 1986 and based on the use of computer technology. It attracted 66,338 entrants playing exactly the same hands at more than 1000 centres in 76 countries. The 1987 event was contested by 73,256 players at 1537 centres, 1988 by 84,352 players at 1731 centres, and that of 1989 by 85,100 players in 90 countries. *Winners*

1986 Fraisnais & Bouteille (Fra)
1987 Peter Thompson & Robin Stretch (UK)
1988 Jan Horwitz & Barbara Norante (USA)
1989 Wojciech Blegajlo & Dariusz Zembrzuski (Pol)
1990 Sorin Lupan & Soren Godtfredsen (Den)

MASTER POINTS
The World Bridge Federation regularly produces a Master Points ranking list. The all-time leading scorer is Giorgio Belladonna (Ita) with 1821 1/4 points, and the top woman is Jacqui Mitchell (USA) with 347 points.

The American Contract Bridge League award master points to their players. The first to pass 10,000 points was Oswald Jacoby in 1967. The most points is 35,137.6 by Barry Crane at the time of his murder in 1985. The current leader is Paul Soloway with 32,832 to 1990.

CANOEING

International canoe racing is practised in kayaks or Canadian canoes over flat water or, for canoe slalom, on wild water. Kayak is the Eskimo word for a canoe made of sealskin, originally stretched over a whalebone frame. Kayak canoeists use a paddle with a blade at each end but Canadian canoes are propelled by a paddle with a single blade, from a half-kneeling position. Races are designated with K for kayak and C for Canadian canoes followed by the number of canoeists, e.g. K1, K2, K4, C1, C2.

The most important pioneer of canoeing as a sport was John MacGregor, who founded the Canoe Club in Surrey, England in 1866. The sport's governing body is the International Canoe Federation, founded in 1924. From then until 1946 its official title was the 'Internationale Representantschaft für Kanusport'. European Championships were first held in 1933, with racing at six categories: K1, C1 and C2 over 1000m; K1 and C1 and C2 for folding crafts over 10,000m. Olympic recognition followed in 1936. Wild water and slalom canoeing were introduced in the 1930s.

Speed races on still water are contested at 500m and 1000m in a straight line and 10,000m on a circuit. Slalom competitions are contested over a rapid river course of maximum extent 600m, through a series of 25 gates with scoring both for time and as penalty points for faults in negotiating the course. Wild water competitions are contested on a course of at least 3km length.

OLYMPIC GAMES
The sport has been held at each Olympic Games from 1936, with slalom events also in 1972. *Winners:*

Canoe racing – MEN
K1 500m
1976 Vasile Diba (Rom) 1:46.41
1980 Vladimir Parfenovich (USSR) 1:43.43
1984 Ian Ferguson (NZ) 1:47.84
1988 Zsolt Gyulay (Hun) 1:44.82
K1 1000m
1936 Gregor Hradetzky (Aut) 4:22.9
1948 Gert Fredriksson (Swe) 4:33.2
1952 Gert Fredriksson (Swe) 4:07.9
1956 Gert Fredriksson (Swe) 4:12.8
1960 Erik Hansen (Den) 3:53.00
1964 Rolf Peterson (Swe) 3:57.13
1968 Mihály Hesz (Hun) 4:02.63
1972 Aleksandr Shaparenko (USSR) 3:48.06
1976 Rüdiger Helm (GDR) 3:48.20
1980 Rüdiger Helm (GDR) 3:48.77
1984 Alan Thompson (NZ) 3:45.73
1988 Greg Barton (USA) 3:55.27
K1 10 000m
1936 Ernst Krebs (Ger) 46:01.6
1948 Gert Fredriksson (Swe) 50:47.7
1952 Thorvald Strömberg (Fin) 47:22.8
1956 Gert Fredriksson (Swe) 47:43.4
K1 4 x 500m relay
1960 Germany 7:39.43
K2 500m
1976 Joachim Mattern & Bernd Olbricht (GDR) 1:35.87
1980 Vladimir Parfenovich & Sergey Chukrai (USSR) 1:32.38
1984 Ian Ferguson & Paul McDonald (NZ) 1:34.21
1988 Ian Ferguson & Paul McDonald (NZ) 1:33.98

K2 1000m
1936 Adolf Kainz & Alfons Dorfner (Aut) 4:03.8
1948 Hans Berglund & Lennart Klingström (Swe) 4:07.3
1952 Kurt Wires & Yrjö Hietanen (Fin) 3:51.1
1956 Michel Scheuer & Meinrad Miltenberger (FRG)
    3:49.6
1960 Gert Fredriksson & Sven-Olov Sjödelius (Swe)
    3:34.7
1964 Sven-Olov Sjödelius & Nils Utterberg (Swe) 3:38.4
1968 Aleksandr Shaparenko & Vladimir Morozov (USSR)
    3:37.54
1972 Nikolay Gorbachev & Viktor Kratassyuk (USSR)
    3:31.23
1976 Sergey Nagorny & Vladimir Romanovsky (USSR)
    3:29.01
1980 Vladimir Parfenovich & Sergey Chukrai (USSR)
    3:26.72
1984 Hugh Fisher & Alwyn Morris (Can) 3:24.22
1988 Greg Barton & Norman Bellingham (USA) 3:32.42

K2 10 000m
1936 Paul Weavers & Ludwig Landen (Ger) 41:45.0
1948 Gunnar Åkerlund & Hans Wetterström (Swe)
    46:09.4
1952 Kurt Wires & Yrjö Hietanen (Fin) 44:21.3
1956 János Urányi & László Fábián (Hun) 43:37.0

K4 1000m
1964 USSR 3:14.67
1968 Norway 3:14.38
1972 USSR 3:14.02
1976 USSR 3:08.69
1980 GDR 3:13.76
1984 New Zealand 3:02.28
1988 Hungary 3:00.20

C1 500m
1976 Aleksandr Rogov (USSR) 1:59.23
1980 Sergey Postrekhin (USSR) 1:53.37
1984 Larry Cain (Can) 1:57.01
1988 Olaf Heukrodt (GDR) 1:56.42

C1 1000m
1936 Francis Amyot (Can) 5:32.1
1948 Josef Holecek (Cs) 5:42.0
1952 Josef Holecek (Cs) 4:56.3
1956 Leon Rotman (Rom) 5:05.3
1960 János Parti (Hun) 4:33.93
1964 Jürgen Eschert (GDR) 4:35.14
1968 Tibor Tatai (Hun) 4:36.14
1972 Ivan Patzaichin (Rom) 4:08.94
1976 Matija Ljubek (Yug) 4:09.51
1980 Lubomir Lubenov (Bul) 4:12.38
1984 Ulrich Eicke (FRG) 4:06.32
1988 Ivan Klementyev (USSR) 4:12.78

C1 10 000m
1948 Frantisek Capek (Cs) 62:05.2
1952 Frank Havens (USA) 57:41.1
1956 Leon Rotman (Rom) 56:41.0

C2 500m
1976 Sergey Petrenko & Aleksandr Vinogradov (USSR)
    1:45.81

1980 Laszlo Foltan & Istvan Vaskuti (Hun) 1:43.39
1984 Matija Ljubek & Mirko Nisovic (Yug) 1:43.67
1988 Viktor Reneyskiy & Nikolay Zhuravskiy (USSR)
    1:41.77

C2 1000m
1936 Vladimir Syrovátka & Jan-Felix Brzák (Cs) 4:50.1
1948 Jan-Felix Brzák & Bohumil Kudrna (Cs) 5:07.1
1952 Bent Peder Rasch & Finn Haunstoft (Den) 4:38.3
1956 Alexe Dumitru & Simion Ismailciuc (Rom) 4:47.4
1960 Leonid Geyshtor & Sergey Makarenko (USSR)
    4:17.94
1964 Andrey Khimich & Stepan Oschepkov (USSR)
    4:04.64
1968 Ivan Patzaichin & Serghei Covaliov (Rom) 4:07.18
1972 Vladas Chessyunas & Yuriy Lobanov (USSR) 3:52.60
1976 Sergey Petrenko & Aleksandr Vinogradov (USSR)
    3:52.76
1980 Ivan Patzaichin & Toma Simionov (Rom) 3:47.65
1984 Ivan Patzaichin & Toma Simionov (Rom) 3:40.60
1988 Viktor Reneyskiy & Nikolay Zhuravskiy (USSR)
    3:48.36

C2 10 000m
1936 Václav Mottl & Zdenek Skrdlant (Cs) 50:33.5
1948 Stephen Lysack & Stephen Macknowski (USA)
    55:55.4
1952 Georges Turlier & Jean Laudet (Fra) 54:08.3
1956 Pavel Kharin & Gratsian Botev (USSR) 54:02.4

Folding kayak 1936
K1: Gregor Hradetzky (Aut) 50:01.2
K2: Sven Johansson & Eric Bladström (Swe) 45:48.9

Slalom racing 1972
K1: Siegbert Horn (GDR) 268.56 pts
C1: Reinhard Eiben (GDR) 315.84
C2: Walter Hofmann & Rolf-Dieter Amend (GDR) 310.68
Most gold medals: 6 Gert Fredriksson (Swe) 1948-60; 4
Ivan Patzaichin (Rom) 1968-84, Ian Ferguson (NZ) 1984-8.
Most gold medals at one Games: 3 Vladimir Parfenovich
(USSR) 1980, Ian Ferguson (NZ) 1984.
Most medals: 8 Gert Fredriksson 6 gold as above, silver K1
10 000m 1952, bronze K1 1000m 1960; 7 Ivan Patzaichin
4 gold as above, 3 silver C2 500m 1980-84, C2 1000m
1972.

Canoe racing winners – WOMEN
K1 500m
1948 Karen Hoff (Den) 2:31.9
1952 Sylvi Saimo (Fin) 2:18.4
1956 Yelisaveta Dementyeva (USSR) 2:18.9
1960 Antonina Seredina (USSR) 2:08.08
1964 Lyudmila Khvedosyuk (USSR) 2:12.87
1968 Lyudmila Pinayeva (USSR) 2:11.09
1972 Yulia Ryabchinskaya (USSR) 2:03.17
1976 Carola Zirzow (GDR) 2:01.05
1980 Birgit Fischer (GDR) 1:57.96
1984 Agneta Andersson (Swe) 1:58.72
1988 Vania Gecheva (Bul) 1:55.19

K2 500m
1960 Maria Zhubina & Antonina Seredina (USSR) 1:54.76

1964 Anne-Marie Zimmermann & Roswitha Esser (FRG)
   1:56.95
1968 Anne-Marie Zimmermann & Roswitha Esser (FRG)
   1:56.44
1972 Lyudmila Pinayeva & Yekaterina Kuryshko (USSR)
   1:53.50
1976 Nina Gopova & Galina Kreft (USSR) 1:51.15
1980 Carsta Genäuss & Martina Bischof (GDR) 1:43.88
1984 Agneta Andersson & Anna Olsson (Swe) 1:45.25
1988 Birgit Schmidt & Anke Nothnagel (GDR) 1:43.46

K4 500m
1984 Romania 1:38.54
1988 GDR 1:40.78

K1 Canoe slalom
1972 Angelika Bahmann (GDR) 364.50 pts
Most gold medals:
3 Lyudmila Pinayeva (née Khevedosyuk) 1964-8, 3 Birgit
Schmidt (née Fischer) 1980-8
Most medals:
4 Birgit Schmidt (née Fischer), 3 gold as above and silver
K1 500m 1988
4 Lyudmila Pinayeva, 3 gold as above, bronze K2 500m
1968

Richard Fox won a record four individual and four team gold medals at K1 in the canoe slalom world championships (All-Sport)

4 Vanya Gecheva gold K1 500m 1988, silver K1 500m
1980 & K2 500m 1988, bronze K4 500m 1988

CANOE RACING WORLD CHAMPIONSHIPS
First held in 1938, then in 1948, 1950, 1954, 1958, 1963,
1966 and annually from 1970 with the exception of
Olympic years.

1989 winners
MEN

K1 500m	Martin Hunter (Aus) 1:41.65
K1 1000m	Zsolt Gyulay (Hun) 3:38.87
K1 10 000m	Attila Szabó (Hun) 42:48.94
K2 500m	Kay Bluhm & Torsten Gütsche (GDR) 1:31.58
K2 1000m	Kay Bluhm & Torsten Gütsche (GDR) 3:11.62
K4 5000m	USSR 1:22.50
K4 1000m	Hungary 2:55.30
K4 10 000m	USSR 35:58.54
C1 500m	Mikhail Slivinsky (USSR) 1:53.17
C1 1000m	Ivan Klementyev (USSR) 4:00.04
C1 10 000m	Ivan Klementyev (USSR) 46:49.96
C2 500m	Nikolay Zhuravsky & Viktor Reneisky (USSR) 1:40.90
C2 1000m	Christian Fredriksen & Arne Nielsson (Den) 3:37.08
C2 10 000m	Christian Fredriksen & Arne Nielsson (Den) 42:42.59
C4 500m	USSR 1:31.10
C4 1000m	USSR 3:19.94

WOMEN

K1 500m	Katrin Borchert (GDR) 1:53.38
K1 5000m	Katrin Borchert (GDR) 22:15.80
K2 500m	Anke Nothnagel & Heike Singer (GDR) 1:43.17
K2 5000m	Monike Bünke & Ramona Portwich (GDR) 20:27.05
K4 500m	GDR 1:32.90

Most wins at World Championships and Olympic Games
MEN
13 Gert Fredriksson (Swe) K1 500m 1948, 1954; K1
   1000m 1948, 1950, 1952, 1954, 1956; K1 10 000m
   1948, 1956; K1 4x500m relay 1948, 1950, 1954; K2
   1000m 1960
13 Rüdiger Helm (GDR) K1 1000m 1976, 1978-83; K2
   500m 1978; K4 500m 1983; K4 10 000m 1978-81
13 Ivan Patzaichin (Rom) C1 1000m 1972-3, 1977; C1
   10,000m 1978; C2 500m 1979; C2 1000m 1968,
   1970, 1972, 1980-1, 1983-4; C2 10 000m 1982
12 Vladimir Parfenovich (USSR) K1 500m 1979-83; K2
   500m 1979-82; K2 1000m 1980-2
11 Yuriy Lobanov (USSR) C2 500m 1974-5, C2 1000m
   1972, 1974, 1977, 1979; C2 10 000m 1973-5, 1977,
   1979
WOMEN
22 Birgit Schmidt (née Fischer) (GDR) K1 500m 1980-3,
   1985, 1987; K2 500m 1977-8, 1981-3, 1985, 1987-8;
   K4 500m 1978-9, 1981-3, 1985, 1987-8

Most individual wins at one event
MEN
7   Tamas Wichmann (Hun) C1 10,000m 1970-1, 1974, 1977, 1979, 1981-2
6   Rüdiger Helm (GDR) K1 1000m 1976, 1978-83
5   Vladimir Parfenovich (USSR) K1 500m 1979-83
WOMEN
6   Birgit Fischer (GDR) K1 500m 1980-3, 1985, 1987
5   Lyudmila Pinayeva (USSR) K1 500m 1964, 1966, 1968, 1970-1

CANOE SLALOM WORLD CHAMPIONSHIPS
Held biennially since 1949.
MEN *Most individual wins:*
5   Jon Lugbill (USA) C1 1979, 1981, 1983, 1987, 1989 (also 6 at C1 team 1979-89)
4   Richard Fox (UK) K1 1981, 1983, 1985, 1989 (also 4 at K1 team 1981-7)
3   Manfred Schubert (GDR) C1 1957, 1961, 1963 (also C1 team 1963, C2 team 1959)
1987 K1 winner was Anton Prijon (FRG)
WOMEN *recent K1 winners:*
1985   Margit Messelhäuser (FRG)
1987   Elizabeth Sharman (UK)
1989   Myriam Jerusalmi (Fra)
Other 1989 winners:
C2: Frank Hemmer & Thomas Loose (FRG). Team: C1 – USA, C2 – France, K1 – Yugoslavia, women's K1 – France

WILD WATER WORLD CHAMPIONSHIPS
Held biennially since 1959. Most individual wins:
MEN
4   Jean-Pierre Burny (Bel) K1 1969, 1973, 1975, 1979

4   Gilles Zok (Fra) C1 1981, 1983, 1985, 1987 (also 5 at C1 team 1977-85)
WOMEN
3   Gisela Grothaus (FRG) K1 1973, 1975, 1977 (also 4 K1 team 1973-83)
1989 individual winners:
MEN K1 – Marco Prevido-Massara (Ita), C1 – Andrej Jelenc (Yug), C2 – Andrej Grobisa & Srecko Maslé (Yug); WOMEN K1 – Sabine Kleinhentz (Fra)
1989 team winners:
MEN K1 – France, C1 – France, C2 – FRG, WOMEN K1 – France, C1 – France

CANOE MARATHON WORLD CHAMPIONSHIPS
Held at Holme Pierrepont, Nottingham, England in *1988.*
Winners:
MEN
K1: John Jacoby (Aus)
K2: Thor Nielsen & Lars Koch (Den)
C1: Pál Pétervári (Hun)
C2: Steve Train & Andrew Train (UK)
WOMEN
K1: Jane Hall (Aus)
K2: Gayle Mayes & Denise Cooper (Aus)

CANOE SAILING WORLD CHAMPIONSHIPS
First held in 1938, and then every 3/4 years from 1961.*Recent winners:*
1984 Steve Clark (USA)
1987 Robin Wood (UK)
Most wins: 3 Alain Emus (UK) 1961, 1965, 1969.

CHESS

A board game played by two players, each with 16 pieces on a 64-square board. Its origins are uncertain, but it is thought to have originated in the Punjab, India. The earliest definite references are to Chaturanga, the Indian war game imported into Persia. This game evolved into Shatranj, and thence to the modern game of chess. The current pieces have been standard for the past 500 years. The world governing body is the Fédération Internationale des Echecs (FIDE), formed in 1924.

WORLD CHAMPIONS
The first officially accepted match for the world championship was in 1886 when Wilhelm Steinitz beat Johannes Zukertort. However champions had been generally accepted since Adolf Anderssen won the world's first international tournament, held in London in 1851. The FIDE took control of the championship in 1948, and there is now a triennial cycle of eliminating contests culminating in a contender to challenge the current champion.

Champions:

1851-8	Adolf Anderssen (Ger)
1858-62	Paul Morphy (USA)
1862-6	Adolf Anderssen (Ger)
1866-94	Wilhelm Steinitz (Aut)
1894-1921	Emanuel Lasker (Ger)
1921-7	José Capablanca (Cub)
1927-35	Alexandre Alekhine (Fra)
1935-7	Max Euwe (Hol)
1937-46	Alexandre Alekhine (Fra)
1948-57	Mikhail Botvinnik (USSR)
1957-8	Vasiliy Smyslov (USSR)
1958-60	Mikhail Botvinnik (USSR)
1960-1	Mikhail Tal (USSR)
1961-3	Mikhail Botvinnik (USSR)
1963-9	Tigran Petrosian (USSR)
1969-72	Boris Spassky (USSR)
1972-5	Robert Fischer (USA)
1975-85	Anatoliy Karpov (USSR)
1985-	Gary Kasparov (USSR)

Youngest champion: Gary Kasparov won in 1985 at the age of 22 years 210 days.

Oldest champion: Wilhelm Steinitz was 58 years 10 days when he lost to Lasker in 1894.

Women's World Champions

1927-44	Vera Menchik (UK)
1950-3	Lyudmila Rudenko (USSR)
1953-6	Yelizaveta Bykova (USSR)
1956-8	Olga Rubtsova (USSR)
1958-62	Yelizaveta Bykova (USSR)
1962-78	Nona Gaprindashvili (USSR)
1978-	Maya Chiburdanidze (USSR)

Youngest champion: Maya Chiburdanidze was aged 17 when she won the title in 1978.

CHESS OLYMPIADS

These world team events, which were first held in 1927, are now held biennially. *Wins:*

17 USSR	1952, 1954, 1956, 1958, 1960, 1962, 1964, 1966, 1968, 1970, 1972, 1974, 1980, 1982, 1984, 1986, 1988
5 USA	1931, 1933, 1935, 1937, 1976
3 Hungary	1927, 1928, 1978
1 Poland 1930, Germany 1939, Yugoslavia 1950	

Although women may play in the Olympiads, a separate competition for women only was introduced in 1957, and this event has been held concurrently with the men's from 1972. *Wins:*

11 USSR	1957, 1963, 1966, 1969, 1972, 1974, 1978, 1980, 1982, 1984, 1986
1 Israel 1976, Hungary 1988	

USSR teams have dominated the tournaments since they first competed in 1952. The only time that a Soviet team has been other than first was second place in 1978 and the women's loss in 1988, on both occasions to Hungary. The USSR did not contest in 1976, when the Olympiad was held in Haifa, Israel.

An élite event for Continental champions and other top teams was been held in 1985 and 1989, the USSR won on both occasions.

WORLD CUP

The first World Cup was staged over a series of six tournaments between April 1988 and September 1989 and contested by the top 25 grandmasters. The inaugural winner was Gary Kasparov (USSR) with Anatoliy Karpov (USSR) second.

ELO RATINGS

FIDE issues a list of Elo ratings for the world's leading players twice yearly. The system is named after Professor Elo. Grandmaster level is 2500, a rating currently attained by about 100 players. The highest rating ever achieved is 2800 by the current world champion Gary Kasparov, reached in January 1990. He has surpassed the previous best, 2785 of Robert Fischer.

Bobby Fischer one step away from the world title, as he convincingly beat Tigran Petrosyan 6^1/$_2$ to 2^1/$_2$ in the final of the Candidates competition in 1971 **(Hulton-Deutsch)**

COMMONWEALTH GAMES

The Commonwealth Games are multi-sport competitions, held every four years, and contested by representatives of the nations of the British Commonwealth. They were first staged as the British Empire Games at Hamilton, Canada, opening on 16 August 1930. The eleven nations participating were Australia, Bermuda, British Guiana, Canada, England, Ireland, Newfoundland, New Zealand, Scotland, South Africa and Wales. Six sports were included, but there were women's events only in swimming. Women first competed in athletics in 1934.

The idea of staging such an event was first put forward by a Yorkshireman, Rev. J.Astley Cooper in the magazine Greater Britain in 1891. The first Inter-Empire Sports meeting was held at Crystal Palace, London in 1911, forming part of the celebrations for the Coronation of King George V. Competitors from Britain, Canada, Australia and New Zealand contested four sports – athletics (five events), heavyweight boxing, swimming (two events) and middleweight wrestling. Canadians won four gold medals, Britain three, and Australia two.

The Games became the British Empire and Commonwealth Games in 1954, and simply the British Commonwealth Games in 1970, in which year the Games went metric for distances and weights.

Ten sports are held at each Games – athletics and swimming are obligatory, and the others are selected from 15 recognised sports, with additionally two demonstration sports. The recognised sports yet to be included officially at any Games are canoeing, table tennis and yachting. Judo was included for the first time in 1990.

Venues

1930 Hamilton, Canada
1934 London, England
1938 Sydney, Australia
1950 Auckland, New Zealand
1954 Vancouver, Canada
1958 Cardiff, Wales
1962 Perth, Australia

1966 Kingston, Jamaica
1970 Edinburgh, Scotland
1974 Christchurch, New Zealand
1978 Edmonton, Canada
1982 Brisbane, Australia
1986 Edinburgh, Scotland
1990 Auckland, New Zealand
1994 Victoria, Canada

A pair of Commonwealth sprint champions. Here Don Quarrie (26) beats Allan Wells (25) in the 1976 AAA 100 metres **(Hulton-Deutsch)**

COMMONWEALTH GAMES WINNERS

ARCHERY 1982 only
Men Mark Blenkarne (Eng) 2446
Women Neroli Fairhall (NZ) 2373

ATHLETICS
Imperial distances run 1930 to 1966. *Note that where known fully-automatic times are given as per the current regulations (original official hand times may well have differed). w = wind assisted performance.*

MEN

100 yards (91.4m)
1930 Percy Williams (Can) 9.9
1934 Arthur Sweeney (Eng) 10.0
1938 Cyril Holmes (Eng) 9.7
1950 John Treloar (Aus) 9.7
1954 Mike Agostini (Tri) 9.6
1958 Keith Gardner (Jam) 9.66
1962 Seraphino Antao (Ken) 9.5
1966 Harry Jerome (Can) 9.41

100 metres
1970 Don Quarrie (Jam) 10.24w
1974 Don Quarrie (Jam) 10.38
1978 Don Quarrie (Jam) 10.03w
1982 Allan Wells (Sco) 10.05w
1986 Ben Johnson (Can) 10.07
1990 Linford Christie (Eng) 9.93w
        (10.02 semi – Games record)

220 yards (201.17m)
1930 Stanley Engelhart (Eng) 21.8
1934 Arthur Sweeney (Eng) 21.9
1938 Cyril Holmes (Eng) 21.2
1950 John Treloar (Aus) 21.5
1954 Donald Jowett (NZ) 21.5
1958 Tom Robinson (Bah) 21.08
1962 Seraphino Antao (Ken) 21.28
1966 Stanley Allotey (Gha) 20.65

200 metres
1970 Don Quarrie (Jam) 20.56
1974 Don Quarrie (Jam) 20.73
1978 Allan Wells (Sco) 20.12w
1982 Allan Wells (Sco)
        & Mike McFarlane (Eng) 20.43
1986 Atlee Mahorn (Can) 20.31w
1990 Marcus Adam (Eng) 20.10w

440 yards (402.34m)
1930 Alex Wilson (Can) 48.8
1934 Godfrey Rampling (Eng) 48.0
1938 Bill Roberts (Eng) 47.9
1950 Edwin Carr (Aus) 47.9
1954 Kevan Gosper (Aus) 47.2
1958 Milkha Singh (Ind) 46.71

1962 George Kerr (Jam) 46.74
1966 Wendell Mottley (Tri) 45.08
400 metres
1970 Charles Asati (Ken) 45.01
1974 Charles Asati (Ken) 46.04
1978 Rick Mitchell (Aus) 46.34
1982 Bert Cameron (Jam) 45.89
1986 Roger Black (Eng) 45.57
1990 Darren Clark (Aus) 44.60

880 yards (804.67m)
1930 Thomas Hampson (Eng) 1:52.4
1934 Phil Edwards (Guy) 1:54.2
1938 Vernon Boot (NZ) 1:51.2
1950 John Parlett (Eng) 1:53.1
1954 Derek Johnson (Eng) 1:50.7
1958 Herb Elliott (Aus) 1:49.32
1962 Peter Snell (NZ) 1:47.64
1966 Noel Clough (Aus) 1:46.9
800 metres
1970 Robert Ouko (Ken) 1:46.89
1974 John Kipkurgat (Ken) 1:43.85
1978 Mike Boit (Ken) 1:46.39
1982 Peter Bourke (Aus) 1:45.18
1986 Steve Cram (Eng) 1:43.22
1990 Sammy Tirop (Ken) 1:45.98

1 mile (1609.35m)
1930 Reg Thomas (Eng) 4:14.0
1934 Jack Lovelock (NZ) 4:12.8
1938 Jim Alford (Wal) 4:11.6
1950 William Parnell (Can) 4:11.0
1954 Roger Bannister (Eng) 3:58.8
1958 Herb Elliott (Aus) 3:59.03
1962 Peter Snell (NZ) 4:04.58
1966 Kipchoge Keino (Ken) 3:55.34
1500 metres
1970 Kipchoge Keino (Ken) 3:36.6
1974 Filbert Bayi (Tan) 3:32.16
1978 David Moorcroft (Eng) 3:35.48
1982 Steve Cram (Eng) 3:42.37
1986 Steve Cram (Eng) 3:50.87
1990 Peter Elliott (Eng) 3:33.39

3 miles (4820.04m)
1930 Stan Tomlin (Eng) 14:27.4
1934 Walter Beavers (Eng) 14:32.6
1938 Cecil Matthews (NZ) 13:59.6
1950 Len Eyre (Eng) 14:23.6
1954 Chris Chataway (Eng) 13:35.2
1958 Murray Halberg (NZ) 13:14.96
1962 Murray Halberg (NZ) 13:34.15
1966 Kipchoge Keino (Ken) 12:57.4
5000 metres
1970 Ian Stewart (Sco) 13:22.8
1974 Ben Jipcho (Ken) 13:14.4
1978 Henry Rono (Ken) 13:23.04
1982 David Moorcroft (Eng) 13:33.00

Kip Keino, a triple Commonwealth Games gold medallist, winning at the White City, London (Hulton-Deutsch)

1986 Steve Ovett (Eng) 13:24.11
1990 Andrew Lloyd (Aus) 13:24.86

6 miles (9656.07m)
1930 John Savidan (NZ) 30:49.6
1934 Arthur Penny (Eng) 31:00.6
1938 Cecil Matthews (NZ) 30:14.5
1950 Harold Nelson (NZ) 30:29.6
1954 Peter Driver (Eng) 29:09.4
1958 David Power (Aus) 28:48.16
1962 Bruce Kidd (Can) 28:26.13
1966 Naftali Temu (Ken) 27:14.21
10 000 metres
1970 Lachie Stewart (Sco) 28:11.71
1974 Richard Tayler (NZ) 27:46.4
1978 Brendan Foster (Eng) 28:13.65
1982 Gidamis Shahanga (Tan)
    28:10.15
1986 Jonathan Solly (Eng) 27:57.42
1990 Eamonn Martin (Eng) 28:08.57

**Marathon (26 miles 385 yards
    42.195km)**
1930 Duncan McL.Wright (Sco)
    2:43:43
1934 Harold Webster (Can) 2:40:36
1938 Johannes Coleman (SAf)
    2:30:49.8
1950 Jack Holden (Eng) 2:32:57
1954 Joseph McGhee (Sco) 2:39:36
1958 David Power (Aus) 2:22:45.6
1962 Brian Kilby (Eng) 2:21:17
1966 Jim Alder (Sco) 2:22:07.8
1970 Ron Hill (Eng) 2:09:28
1974 Ian Thompson (Eng) 2:09:12
1978 Gidamis Shahanga (Tan)
    2:15:39.8
1982 Rob de Castella (Aus) 2:09:18
1986 Rob de Castella (Aus) 2:10:15
1990 Douglas Wakiihuri (Ken)
    2:10:27

3000 metres steeplechase

Held over 8 laps in 1930 and at 2 miles (3218.7m) in 1934
1930 George Bailey (Eng) 9:52.0
1934 Stanley Scarsbrook (Eng) 10:23.4
1962 Trevor Vincent (Aus) 8:43.4
1966 Peter Welsh (NZ) 8:29.44
1970 Tony Manning (Aus) 8:26.2
1974 Ben Jipcho (Ken) 8:20.8
1978 Henry Rono (Ken) 8:26.54
1982 Julius Korir (Ken) 8:23.94
1986 Graeme Fell (Can) 8:24.49
1990 Julius Kariuki (Ken) 8:20.64

120 yards hurdles (109.73m)

1930 Lord Burghley (Eng) 14.6
1934 Don Finlay (Eng) 15.2
1938 Tom Lavery (SAf) 14.0w
1950 Peter Gardner (Aus) 14.3
1954 Keith Gardner (Jam) 14.2
1958 Keith Gardner (Jam) 14.20w
1962 Ghulam Raziq (Pak) 14.34
1966 David Hemery (Eng) 14.1

110 metres hurdles

1970 David Hemery (Eng) 13.66w
1974 Fatwel Kimaiyo (Ken) 13.69
1978 Berwyn Price (Wal) 13.70w
1982 Mark McKoy (Can) 13.37
1986 Mark McKoy (Can) 13.31w
1990 Colin Jackson (Wal) 13.08

440 yards hurdles (402.34m)

1930 Lord Burghley (Eng) 54.4
1934 Alan Hunter (Sco) 55.2
1938 John Loaring (Can) 52.9
1950 Duncan White (Sri) 52.5
1954 David Lean (Aus) 52.4
1958 Gerhardus Potgieter (SAf) 49.73
1962 Ken Roche (Aus) 51.5
1966 Ken Roche (Aus) 50.95

400 metres hurdles

1970 John Sherwood (Eng) 50.03
1974 Alan Pascoe (Eng) 48.83
1978 Daniel Kimaiyo (Ken) 49.48
1982 Garry Brown (Aus) 49.37
1986 Phil Beattie (NI) 49.60
1990 Kriss Akabusi (Eng) 48.89

4 x 110 yards relay (4 x 100.54m)

1930 Canada 42.2
1934 England 42.2
1938 Canada 41.6
1950 Australia 42.2
1954 Canada 41.3
1958 England 40.72
1962 England 40.62
1966 Ghana 39.8

4 x 100 metres relay

1970 Jamaica 39.46
1974 Australia 39.31
1978 Scotland 39.24
1982 Nigeria 39.15
1986 Canada 39.15
1990 England 38.67

4 x 440 yards relay

1930 England 3:19.4
1934 England 3:16.8
1938 Canada 3:16.9
1950 Australia 3:17.8
1954 England 3:11.2
1958 South Africa 3:08.21
1962 Jamaica 3:10.2
1966 Trinidad & Tobago 3:02.8

4 x 400 metres relay

1970 Kenya 3:03.63
1974 Kenya 3:04.4
1978 Kenya 3:03.54
1982 England 3:05.45
1986 England 3:07.19
1990 Kenya 3:02.48

High jump

1930 Johannes Viljoen (SAf) 1.90
1934 Edwin Thacker (SAf) 1.90
1938 Edwin Thacker (SAf) 1.96
1950 John Winter (Aus) 1.98
1954 Emmanuel Ifeajuna (Nig) 2.03
1958 Ernest Haisley (Jam) 2.06
1962 Percy Hobson (Aus) 2.11
1966 Lawrie Peckham (Aus) 2.08
1970 Lawrie Peckham (Aus) 2.14
1974 Gordon Windeyer (Aus) 2.16
1978 Claude Ferragne (Can) 2.20
1982 Milt Ottey (Can) 2.31
1986 Milt Ottey (Can) 2.30
1990 Nick Saunders (Ber) 2.36

Pole vault

1930 Victor Pickard (Can) 3.73
1934 Sylvanus Apps (Can) 3.81 (3.88 jump-off)
1938 Andries du Plessis (SAf) 4.11
1950 Tim Anderson (Eng) 3.97
1954 Geoff Elliott (Eng) 4.26
1958 Geoff Elliott (Eng) 4.16
1962 Trevor Bickle (Aus) 4.49
1966 Trevor Bickle (Aus) 4.80
1970 Mike Bull (NI) 5.10
1974 Don Baird (Aus) 5.05
1978 Bruce Simpson (Can) 5.10
1982 Ray Boyd (Aus) 5.20
1986 Andrew Ashurst (Eng) 5.20
1990 Simon Arkell (Aus) 5.35

Long jump

1930 Leonard Hutton (Can) 7.20
1934 Sam Richardson (Can) 7.17
1938 Harold Brown (Can) 7.43
1950 Neville Price (SAf) 7.31
1954 Ken Wilmshurst (Eng) 7.54
1958 Paul Foreman (Jam) 7.47
1962 Michael Ahey (Gha) 8.05w
1966 Lynn Davies (Wal) 7.99
1970 Lynn Davies (Wal) 8.06w
1974 Alan Lerwill (Eng) 7.94
1978 Roy Mitchell (Eng) 8.06
1982 Gary Honey (Aus) 8.13
1986 Gary Honey (Aus) 8.08
1990 Yusuf Alli (Nig) 8.39w

Triple jump

1930 Gordon Smallacombe (Can) 14.76
1934 Jack Metcalfe (Aus) 15.63
1938 Jack Metcalfe (Aus) 15.49
1950 Brian Oliver (Aus) 15.61
1954 Ken Wilmshurst (Eng) 15.28
1958 Ian Tomlinson (Aus) 15.74
1962 Ian Tomlinson (Aus) 16.20
1966 Samuel Igun (Nig) 16.40
1970 Phil May (Aus) 16.72
1974 Joshua Owusu (Gha) 16.50
1978 Keith Connor (Eng) 17.21
1982 Keith Connor (Eng) 17.81w
1986 John Herbert (Eng) 17.27w
1990 Marios Hadjiandreou (Cyp) 16.95

Shot

1930 Hendrik Hart (SAf) 14.58
1934 Hendrik Hart (SAf) 14.67
1938 Louis Fouche (SAf) 14.48
1950 Maitaika Tuicakau (Fiji) 14.64
1954 John Savidge (Eng) 16.77
1958 Arthur Rowe (Eng) 17.57
1962 Martyn Lucking (Eng) 18.08
1966 David Steen (Can) 18.79
1970 David Steen (Can) 19.21
1974 Geoff Capes (Eng) 20.74
1978 Geoff Capes (Eng) 19.77
1982 Bruno Pauletto (Can) 19.55
1986 Billy Cole (Eng) 18.16
1990 Simon Williams (Eng) 18.54

Discus

1930 Hendrik Hart (SAf) 41.44
1934 Hendrik Hart (SAf) 41.54
1938 Eric Coy (Can) 44.76
1950 Ian Reed (Aus) 47.72
1954 Stephanus du Plessis (SAf) 51.70
1958 Stephanus du Plessis (SAf) 55.94
1962 Warwick Selvey (Aus) 56.48
1966 Les Mills (NZ) 56.18

1970 George Puce (Can) 59.02
1974 Robin Tait (NZ) 63.08
1978 Borys Chambul (Can) 59.70
1982 Brad Cooper (Bah) 64.04
1986 Raymond Lazdins (Can) 58.86
1990 Adewale Olokoju (Nig) 62.62

Hammer
1930 Malcolm Nokes (Eng) 47.12
1934 Malcolm Nokes (Eng) 48.24
1938 George Sutherland (Can) 48.70
1950 Duncan Clark (Sco) 49.94
1954 Muhammad Iqbal (Pak) 55.38
1958 Mike Ellis (Eng) 62.90
1962 Howard Payne (Eng) 61.64
1966 Howard Payne (Eng) 61.98
1970 Howard Payne (Eng) 67.80
1974 Ian Chipchase (Eng) 69.56
1978 Peter Farmer (Aus) 71.10
1982 Robert Weir (Eng) 75.08
1986 David Smith (Eng) 74.06
1990 Sean Carlin (Aus) 75.66

Javelin
1930 Stanley Lay (NZ) 63.12
1934 Robert Dixon (Can) 60.02
1938 James Courtwright (Can) 62.80
1950 Leo Roininen (Can) 57.10
1954 James Achurch (Aus) 68.52
1958 Colin Smith (Eng) 71.28
1962 Alfred Mitchell (Aus) 78.10
1966 John FitzSimons (Eng) 79.78
1970 David Travis (Eng) 79.50
1974 Charles Clover (Eng) 84.92
1978 Phil Olsen (Can) 84.00
1982 Michael O'Rourke (NZ) 89.48
1986 David Ottley (Eng) 80.62
1990 Steve Backley (Eng) 86.02

Decathlon
All scored on the 1984 Scoring Tables
1966 Roy Williams (NZ) 7133
1970 Geoff Smith (Aus) 7420
1974 Mike Bull (NI) 7363
1978 Daley Thompson (Eng) 8470w
1982 Daley Thompson (Eng) 8424
1986 Daley Thompson (Eng) 8663
1990 Mike Smith (Can) 8525

20 miles road walk
1966 Ron Wallwork (Eng) 2:44:42.8
1970 Noel Freeman (Aus) 2:33:33
1974 John Warhurst (Eng) 2:35:23.0
30 kilometres road walk
1978 Ollie Flynn (Eng) 2:22:03.7
1982 Steve Barry (Wal) 2:10:16
1986 Simon Baker (Aus) 2:07:47
1990 Guillaume LeBlanc (Can) 2:08:28

WOMEN
100 yards (91.4m)
1934 Eileen Hiscock (Eng) 11.3
1938 Decima Norman (Aus) 11.1
1950 Marjorie Jackson (Aus) 10.8
1954 Marjorie Jackson (Aus) 10.7
1958 Marlene Willard (Aus) 10.70
1962 Dorothy Hyman (Eng) 11.2
1966 Dianne Burge (Aus) 10.6
100 metres
1970 Raelene Boyle (Aus) 11.26w
1974 Raelene Boyle (Aus) 11.27
1978 Sonia Lannaman (Eng) 11.27w
1982 Angella Taylor (Can) 11.00
1986 Heather Oakes (Eng) 11.20w
1990 Merlene Ottey (Jam) 11.02w

220 yards (201.17m)
1934 Eileen Hiscock (Eng) 25.0
1938 Decima Norman (Aus) 24.7
1950 Marjorie Jackson (Aus) 24.3
1954 Marjorie Nelson (née Jackson)
      (Aus) 24.0
1958 Marlene Willard (Aus) 23.65
1962 Dorothy Hyman (Eng) 24.00
1966 Dianne Burge (Aus) 23.73
200 metres
1970 Raelene Boyle (Aus) 22.75w
1974 Raelene Boyle (Aus) 22.50
1978 Denise Boyd (Aus) 22.82w
1982 Merlene Ottey (Jam) 22.19w
1986 Angella Issajenko (Can) 22.91w
1990 Merlene Ottey (Jam) 22.76

440 yards (402.34m)
1966 Judy Pollock (Aus) 53.0
400 metres
1970 Marilyn Neufville (Jam) 51.02
1974 Yvonne Saunders (Can) 51.67
1978 Donna Hartley (Eng) 51.69
1982 Raelene Boyle (Aus) 51.26
1986 Debbie Flintoff (Aus) 51.29
1990 Fatima Yusuf (Nig) 51.08

880 yards (804.67m)
1934 Gladys Lunn (Eng) 2:19.4
1962 Dixie Willis (Aus) 2:03.85
1966 Abigail Hoffman (Can) 2:04.3
800 metres
1970 Rosemary Stirling (Sco) 2:06.24
1974 Charlene Rendina (Aus) 2:01.1
1978 Judy Peckham (Aus) 2:02.82
1982 Kirsty McDermott (Wal) 2:01.31
1986 Kirsty Wade (Wal) 2:00.94
1990 Diane Edwards (Eng) 2:00.25

1500 metres
1970 Rita Ridley (Eng) 4:18.8

1974 Glenda Reiser (Can) 4:07.8
1978 Mary Stewart (Eng) 4:06.34
1982 Christina Boxer (Eng) 4:08.28
1986 Kirsty Wade (Wal) 4:10.91
1990 Angela Chalmers (Can) 4:08.41

3000 metres
1978 Paula Fudge (Eng) 9:12.98
1982 Anne Audain (NZ) 8:45.53
1986 Lynn Williams (Can) 8:54.29
1990 Angela Chalmers (Can) 8:38.38

10 000 metres
1986 Liz Lynch (Sco) 31:41.42
1990 Liz McColgan (née Lynch) (Sco)
      32:23.56

Marathon
1986 Lisa Martin (Aus) 2:26:07
1990 Lisa Martin (Aus) 2:25:28

80 metres hurdles
1934 Marjorie Clark (SAf) 11.8
1938 Barbara Burke (SAf) 11.7
1950 Shirley Strickland (Aus) 11.6
1954 Edna Maskell (Zam) 10.9
1958 Norma Thrower (Aus) 10.72w
1962 Pam Kilborn (Aus) 11.07
1966 Pam Kilborn (Aus) 10.9
100 metres hurdles
1970 Pam Kilborn (Aus) 13.27
1974 Judy Vernon (Eng) 13.45
1978 Lorna Boothe (Eng) 12.98w
1982 Shirley Strong (Eng) 12.78w
1986 Sally Gunnell (Eng) 13.29
1990 Kay Morley (Wal) 12.91

400 metres Hurdles
1982 Debbie Flintoff (Aus) 55.89
1986 Debbie Flintoff (Aus) 54.94
1990 Sally Gunnell (Eng) 55.38

Sprint Relay – 2 x 220 yards, 2 x 110 yards
1934 Canada 1:14.4
1938 Australia 1:15.2
1950 Australia 1:13.4

4 x 110 yards relay
1954 Australia 46.8
1958 England 45.37
1962 Australia 46.71
1966 Australia 45.3
4 x 100 metres relay
1970 Australia 44.14
1974 Australia 43.51
1978 England 43.70
1982 England 43.15

1986 England 43.39
1990 Australia 43.87

4 x 400 metres relay
1974 England 3:29.2
1978 England 3:27.19
1982 Canada 3:27.70
1986 Canada 3:28.92
1990 England 3:28.08

High jump
1934 Marjorie Clark (SAf) 1.60
1938 Dorothy Odam (Eng) 1.60
1950 Dorothy Tyler (née Odam) (Eng) 1.60
1954 Thelma Hopkins (NI) 1.67
1958 Michele Mason (Aus) 1.70
1962 Robyn Woodhouse (Aus) 1.78
1966 Michele Brown (née Mason) (Aus) 1.73
1970 Debbie Brill (Can) 1.78
1974 Barbara Lawton (Eng) 1.84
1978 Katrina Gibbs (Aus) 1.93
1982 Debbie Brill (Can) 1.88
1986 Christine Stanton (Aus) 1.92
1990 Tania Murray (NZ) 1.88

Debbie Brill was the first woman to use the 'flop' style successfully as she pioneered the Brill Bend in the late 1960s. In 1970 she was the youngest female Commonwealth athletics champion at 17 years 137 days, and here she competes in her fourth Games in 1986 (All-Sport)

Long jump
1934 Phyllis Bartholomew (Eng) 5.47
1938 Decima Norman (Aus) 5.80
1950 Yvette Williams (NZ) 5.90
1954 Yvette Williams (NZ) 6.08
1958 Sheila Hoskin (Eng) 6.02
1962 Pam Kilborn (Aus) 6.27
1966 Mary Rand (Eng) 6.36
1970 Sheila Sherwood (Eng) 6.73
1974 Modupe Oshikoya (Nig) 6.46
1978 Sue Reeve (Eng) 6.59
1982 Shonel Ferguson (Bah) 6.91w
1986 Joyce Oladapo (Eng) 6.43
1990 Jane Flemming (Aus) 6.78

Shot
1954 Yvette Williams (NZ) 13.96
1958 Valerie Sloper (NZ) 15.54
1962 Valerie Young (née Sloper) (NZ) 15.23
1966 Valerie Young (NZ) 16.50
1970 Mary Peters (NI) 15.93
1974 Jane Haist (Can) 16.12
1978 Gael Mulhall (Aus) 17.31
1982 Judy Oakes (Eng) 17.92
1986 Gael Martin (Aus) 19.00
1990 Myrtle Augee (Eng) 18.48

Discus
1954 Yvette Williams (NZ) 45.02
1958 Suzanne Allday (Eng) 45.91
1962 Valerie Young (NZ) 50.20
1966 Valerie Young (NZ) 49.78
1970 Rosemary Payne (Sco) 54.46
1974 Jane Haist (Can) 55.52

1978 Carmen Ionescu (Can) 62.16
1982 Margaret Ritchie (Sco) 62.98
1986 Gael Martin (Aus) 56.42
1990 Lisa-Marie Vizaniari (Aus) 56.38

Javelin
1934 Gladys Lunn (Eng) 32.18
1938 Robina Higgins (Can) 38.28
1950 Charlotte MacGibbon-Weeks (Aus) 38.84
1954 Magdalena Swanepoel (SAf) 43.82
1958 Anna Pazera (Aus) 57.40
1962 Susan Platt (Eng) 50.24
1966 Margaret Parker (Aus) 51.38
1970 Petra Rivers (Aus) 52.00
1974 Petra Rivers (Aus) 55.48
1978 Tessa Sanderson (Eng) 61.34
1982 Suzanne Howland (Aus) 64.46
1986 Tessa Sanderson (Eng) 69.80
1990 Tessa Sanderson (Eng) 65.72

Pentathlon (Scored on 1971 tables)
1970 Mary Peters (NI) 4515 (5148 on tables used)
1974 Mary Peters (NI) 4455
1978 Diane Konihowski (Can) 4768

Heptathlon (Scored on 1984 tables)
1982 Glynis Nunn (Aus) 6254
1986 Judy Simpson (Eng) 6282w
1990 Jane Flemming (Aus) 6695

10 kilometres walk
1990 Kerry Saxby (Aus) 45:03

BADMINTON
Men's singles
1966 Tan Aik Huang (Mal)
1970 Jamie Paulson (Can)
1974 Punch Gunalan (Mal)
1978 Padukone Prakash (Ind)
1982 Syed Modi (Ind)
1986 Steve Baddeley (Eng)
1990 Rashid Sidek (Mal)

Men's doubles
1966 Tan Aik Huang & Yew Cheng
    Hoe (Mal)
1970 Ng Boon Bee & Punch Gunalam
    (Mal)
1974 Derek Talbot & Elliot Stuart (Eng)
1978 Ray Stevens & Michael Tredgett
    (Eng)
1982 Razif Sidek & Beng Teong Ong
    (Mal)
1986 Billy Gilliland & Dan Travers (Sco)
1990 Jalani Sidek & Razif Sidek (Mal)

Women's singles
1966 Angela Bairstow (Eng)
1970 Margaret Beck (Eng)
1974 Gillian Gilks (Eng)
1978 Sylvia Ng (Mal)
1982 Helen Troke (Eng)
1986 Helen Troke (Eng)
1990 Fiona Smith (Eng)

Women's doubles
1966 Helen Horton & Ursula Smith
    (Eng)
1970 Margaret Boxall & Susan
    Whetnall (Eng)
1974 Margaret Beck & Gillian Gilks
    (Eng)
1978 Nora Perry & Anne Statt (Eng)
1982 Claire Backhouse & Johanne
    Falardeau (Can)
1986 Gillian Clark & Gillian Gowers
    (Eng)
1990 Fiona Smith & Sara Sankey (Eng)

Mixed doubles
1966 Roger Mills & Angela Bairstow
    (Eng)
1970 Derek Talbot & Margaret Boxall
    (Eng)
1974 Derek Talbot & Gillian Gilks (Eng)
1978 Michael Tredgett & Nora Perry
    (Eng)
1982 Martin Dew & Karen Chapman
    (Eng)
1986 Mike Scandolera & Audrey
    Tuckey (Aus)

Helen Troke, the only badminton player to win two Commonwealth singles gold medals (All-Sport)

1990 Chan Chi Choi & Amy Chan (HK)

Team
1978 England
1982 England
1986 England
1990 England

BOWLS

MEN
Singles
1930 Robert Colquhoun (Eng)
1934 Robert Sprot (Sco)
1938 Horace Harvey (SAf)
1950 James Pirret (NZ)
1954 Ralph Hodges (Zim)
1958 Phineas Danilowitz (SAf)
1962 David Bryant (Eng)
1970 David Bryant (Eng)
1974 David Bryant (Eng)
1978 David Bryant (Eng)
1982 William Wood (Sco)
1986 Ian Dickison (NZ)
1990 Rob Parella (Aus)

Pairs
1930 Tommy Hills & George Wright
    (Eng)
1934 Tommy Hills & George Wright
    (Eng)
1938 Lance Macey & William Denison
    (NZ)
1950 Robert Henry & Phil Exelby (NZ)
1954 William Rosbotham & Percy
    Watson (NI)
1958 John Morris & Richard
    Pilkington (NZ)
1962 Robert McDonald & Hugh
    Robson (NZ)

1970 Norman King & Peter Line (Eng)
1974 John Christie & Alex McIntosh (Sco)
1978 Eric Liddell & Clementi Delgado (HK)
1982 John Watson & David Gourlay (Sco)
1986 George Adrain & Grant Knox (Sco)
1990 Trevor Morris & Ian Schuback (Aus)

Fours
1930 England
1934 England
1938 New Zealand
1950 South Africa
1954 South Africa
1958 England
1962 England
1970 Hong Kong
1974 New Zealand
1978 Hong Kong
1982 Australia
1986 Wales
1990 Scotland

WOMEN
Singles
1986 Wendy Line (Eng)
1990 Geva Vada Tau (PNG)
Pairs
1986 Freda Elliott & Margaret Johnstone (NI)
1990 Marie Watson & Judy Howat (NZ)
Triples
1982 Zimbabwe
Fours
1986 Wales
1990 Australia

BOXING
48kg – Light Flyweight
1970 James Odwori (Uga)
1974 Stephen Muchoki (Ken)
1978 Stephen Muchoki (Ken)
1982 Abraham Wachire (Ken)
1986 Scott Olson (Can)
1990 Justin Juko (Uga)
51kg – Flyweight
1930 Jacob Smith (SAf)
1934 Patrick Palmer (Eng)
1938 Johannes Joubert (SAf)
1950 Hugh Riley (Sco)
1954 Richard Currie (Sco)
1958 Jackie Brown (Sco)
1962 Robert Mallon (Sco)
1966 Sulley Shittu (Gha)

1970 David Needham (Eng)
1974 David Larmour (NI)
1978 Michael Irungu (Ken)
1982 Michael Mutua (Ken)
1986 John Lyon (Eng)
1990 Wayne McCullough (NI)
54kg – Bantamweight
1930 Hyman Mizler (Eng)
1934 Freddy Ryan (Eng)
1938 William Butler (Eng)
1950 Johannes van Rensburg (SAf)
1954 John Smillie (Sco)
1958 Howard Winstone (Wal)
1962 Jeffery Dynevor (Aus)
1966 Edward Ndukwu (Nig)
1970 Sulley Shittu (Gha)
1974 Pat Cowdell (Eng)
1978 Barry McGuigan (NI)
1982 Joe Orewa (Nig)
1986 Sean Murphy (Eng)
1990 Sabo Mohammed (Nig)
57kg – Featherweight
1930 F.R.Meachem (Eng)
1934 Charles Catterall (SAf)
1938 Anadale Henricus (Sri)
1950 Henry Gilliland (Sco)
1954 Leonard Leisching (SAf)
1958 Wally Taylor (Aus)
1962 John McDermott (Sco)
1966 Philip Waruinge (Ken)
1970 Philip Waruinge (Ken)
1974 Edward Ndukwa (Nig)
1978 Azumah Nelson (Gha)
1982 Peter Konyegwachie (Nig)
1986 Billy Downey (Can)
1990 John Irwin (Eng)
60kg – Lightweight
1930 James Rolland (Sco)
1934 Leslie Cook (Aus)
1938 Harry Groves (Eng)
1950 Ronald Latham (Eng)
1954 Piet van Staden (Zim)
1958 Dick McTaggart (Sco)
1962 Eddie Blay (Gha)
1966 Anthony Andeh (Nig)
1970 Abayomi Adeyemi (Nig)
1974 Ayub Kalule (Uga)
1978 Gerard Hamil (NI)
1982 Hussein Khalili (Ken)
1986 Asif Dar (Can)
1990 Godfrey Nyakana (Uga)
63.5kg Light-Welterweight
1954 Mickey Bergin (Can)
1958 Henry Loubscher (SAf)
1962 Clement Quartey (Gha)
1966 James McCourt (NI)
1970 Muhamad Muruli (Uga)
1974 Obisia Nwakpa (Nig)

1978 Winfield Braithwaite (Guy)
1982 Christopher Ossai (Nig)
1986 Howard Grant (Can)
1990 Charlie Kane (Sco)
67kg – Welterweight
1930 Leonard Hall (SAf)
1934 David McCleave (Eng)
1938 Bill Smith (Aus)
1950 Terence Ratcliffe (Eng)
1954 Nicholas Gargano (Eng)
1958 Joseph Greyling (SAf)
1962 Wallace Coe (NZ)
1966 Eddie Blay (Gha)
1970 Emma Ankudey (Gha)
1974 Muhamad Muruli (Uga)
1978 Michael McCallum (Jam)
1982 Christopher Pyatt (Eng)
1986 Darren Dyer (Eng)
1990 David Defiagbon (Nig)
71kg – Light-Middleweight
1954 Wilfred Greaves (Can)
1958 Grant Webster (SAf)
1962 Harold Mann (Can)
1966 Mark Rowe (Eng)
1970 Tom Imrie (Sco)
1974 Lotti Mwale (Zam)
1978 Kelly Perlette (Can)
1982 Shawn O'Sullivan (Can)
1986 Dan Sherry (Can)
1990 Richie Woodhall (Eng)
75kg – Middleweight
1930 Frederick Mallin (Eng)
1934 Alf Shawyer (Eng)
1938 Denis Reardon (Wal)
1950 Theunis van Schalkwyk (SAf)
1954 Johannes van der Kolff (SAf)
1958 Terry Milligan (NI)
1962 Cephas Colquhoun (Jam)
1966 Joe Darkey (Gha)
1970 John Conteh (Eng)
1974 Frankie Lucas (SVI)
1978 Philip McElwaine (Aus)
1982 Jimmy Price (Eng)
1986 Rod Douglas (Eng)
1990 Christopher Johnson (Can)
81kg – Light-Heavyweight
1930 Joe Goyder (Eng)
1934 George Brennan (Eng)
1938 Nicholaas Wolmarans (SAf)
1950 Donald Scott (Eng)
1954 Piet Van Vuuren (SAf)
1958 Tony Madigan (Aus)
1962 Tony Madigan (Aus)
1966 Roger Tighe (Eng)
1970 Fatai Ayinla (Nig)
1974 William Knight (Eng)
1978 Roger Fortin (Can)
1982 Fine Sani (Fiji)

1986 James Moran (Eng)
1990 Joseph Akhasamba (Nig)
Over 81kg – Heavyweight
1930 Victor Stuart (Eng)
1934 Pat Floyd (Eng)
1938 Thomas Osborne (Can)
1950 Frank Creagh (NZ)
1954 Brian Harper (Eng)
1958 Daniel Bekker (SAf)
1962 George Oywello (Uga)
1966 William Kini (NZ)
1970 Benson Masanda (Uga)
1974 Neville Meade (Eng)
1978 Julius Awome (Eng)
1982 Willie DeWit (Can)
91kg – Heavyweight
1986 James Peau (NZ)
1990 George Onyango (Ken)
Over 91kg – Super-Heavyweight
1986 Lennox Lewis (Can)
1990 Michael Kenny (NZ)

CYCLING
Sprint
1934 Ernest Higgins (Eng)
1938 Edgar Gray (Aus)
1950 Russell Mockridge (Aus)
1954 Cyril Peacock (Eng)
1958 Dick Ploog (Aus)
1962 Thomas Harrison (Aus)
1966 Roger Gibbon (Tri) and
1970 John Nicholson (Aus)
1974 John Nicholson (Aus)
1978 Kenrick Tucker (Aus)
1982 Kenrick Tucker (Aus)
1986 Gary Neiwand (Aus)
1990 Gary Neiwand (Aus)

1000 metres time trial
1934 Edgar Gray (Aus) 1:16.4
1938 Robert Porter (Aus) 1:15.2
1950 Russell Mockridge (Aus) 1:13.4
1954 Dick Ploog (Aus) & Alfred Swift
    (SAf) 1:12.5
1958 Neville Tong (Eng) 1:12.1
1962 Peter Bartels (Aus) 1:12.9
1966 Roger Gibbon (Tri) 1:09.6
1970 Harry Kent (NZ) 1:08.69
1974 Dick Paris (Aus) 1:11.85
1978 Jocelyn Lovell (Can) 1:06.00
1982 Craig Adair (NZ) 1:06.954
1986 Martin Vinnicombe (Aus)
    1:06.23
1990 Martin Vinnicombe (Aus)
    1:05.572

4000 metres individual pursuit
1950 Cyril Cartwright (Eng) 5:16.3

1954 Norman Sheil (Eng) 5:03.5
1958 Norman Sheil (Eng) 5:10.2
1962 Maxwell Langshaw (Aus) 5:08.2
1966 Hugh Porter (Eng) 4:56.6
1970 Ian Hallam (Eng) 5:01.41
1974 Ian Hallam (Eng) 5:05.46
1978 Michael Richards (NZ) 4:49.74
1982 Michael Turtur (Aus) 4:50.990
1986 Dean Woods (Aus) 4:43.92
1990 Garry Anderson (NZ) 4:44.610

4000 metres team pursuit
1974 England 4:40.50
1978 Australia 4:29.43
1982 Australia 4:26.090
1986 Australia 4:26.94
1990 New Zealand 4:22.76

Tandem sprint
1970 Gordon Johnson & Ron Jonker
    (Aus) 11.43
1974 Geoffrey Cooke & Ernest
    Crutchlow (Eng) 10.74
1978 Jocelyn Lovell & Gordon
    Singleton (Can) 15.52

10 miles track
1934 Robert McLeod (Can) 24:26.2
1938 William Maxfield (Eng) 24:44.0
1950 William Heseltine (Aus) 23:23.4
1954 Lindsay Cocks (Aus) 21:59.5
1958 Ian Browne (Aus) 21:40.2
1962 Douglas Adams (Aus) 22:10.8
1966 Ian Alsop (Eng) 21:46.0
1970 Jocelyn Lovell (Can) 20:46.72
1974 Stephen Heffernan (Eng)
    20:51.25
1978 Jocelyn Lovell (Can) 20:05.81
1982 Kevin Nichols (Aus) 19:56.559
1986 Wayne McCarney (Aus) 19:40.61
1990 Garry Anderson (NZ) 19:44.20

Points
1990 Robert Burns (Aus)

100 kilometres road team time trial
1982 England 2:09:27
1986 England 2:13:16
1990 New Zealand 2:06:46.5

Road race
Raced over 100km 1938-54, 120
miles *193 km* 1958-66, 164.6 km
1970, 183km 1974, 117 miles *188
km* 1978, 184km 1982, 105 miles
169 km 1986, 173km 1990.
1938 Hendrik Binneman (SAf)
    2:53:29.6

1950 Hector Sutherland (Aus)
    3:13:06.4
1954 Eric Thompson (Eng) 2:44:08.1
1958 Ray Booty (Eng) 5:16:33.7
1962 Wesley Mason (Eng) 5:20:26.2
1966 Peter Buckley (IOM) 5:07:52.5
1970 Bruce Biddle (NZ) 4:38:05.8
1974 Clyde Sefton (Aus) 5:07:16.87
1978 Philip Anderson (Aus) 4:22:34.41
1982 Malcolm Elliott (Eng) 4:34:40.06
1986 Paul Curran (Eng) 4:08:50
1990 Graeme Miller (NZ) 4:34:00.19

Women's sprint
1990 Louise Jones (Wal)
Women's 3000m individual pursuit
1990 Madonna Harris (NZ) 3:54.67
Women's road race (72km)
1990 Kathryn Watt (Aus) 1:55:11.60

FENCING
Individual
Men's foil
1950 René Paul (Eng)
1954 René Paul (Eng)
1958 Raymond Paul (Eng)
1962 Alexander Leckie (Sco)
1966 Allan Jay (Eng)
1970 Mike Breckin (Eng)

Men's epée
1950 Charles-Louis de Beaumont (Eng)
1954 Ivan Lund (Aus)
1958 William Hoskyns (Eng)
1962 Ivan Lund (Aus)
1966 William Hoskyns (Eng)
1970 William Hoskyns (Eng)

Men's sabre
1950 Arthur Pilbrow (Eng)
1954 Michael Amberg (Eng)
1958 William Hoskyns (Eng)
1962 Ralph Cooperman (Eng)
1966 Ralph Cooperman (Eng)
1970 Alexander Leckie (Sco)

Women's foil – individual
1950 Mary Glen-Haig (Eng)
1954 Mary Glen-Haig (Eng)
1958 Gillian Sheen (Eng)
1962 Melody Coleman (NZ)
1966 Janet Wardell-Yerburgh (Eng)
1970 Janet Wardell-Yerburgh (Eng)

Team
Men's foil
1950 England
1954 England

1958 England
1962 England
1966 England
1970 England
Men's epée
1950 Australia
1954 England
1958 England
1962 England
1966 England
1970 England
Men's sabre
1950 England
1954 Canada
1958 England
1962 England
1966 England
1970 England
Women's foil – team
1966 England
1970 England

GYMNASTICS
Men's all-round
1978 Philip Delesalle(Can)
1990 Curtis Hibbert (Can)
Men's team
1978 Canada
1990 Canada
Women's all-round
1978 Elfi Schlegel (Can)
1990 Lori Strong (Can)
Women's team
1978 Canada
1990 Canada
Individual apparatus gold medal winners 1990
MEN: Curtis Hibbert (Can) won rings, parallel bars, horizontal bars, the latter with Alan Nolet (Can)
Neil Thomas (Eng) won floor exercises, Brennon Dowrick (Aus) won pommel horse, James May (Eng) won vault.
WOMEN: Lori Strong (Can) won beam and floor, Nicky Jenkins (NZ) won vault, Monique Allen (Aus) won asymmetrical bars
Rhythmic Gymnastics 1990 winners
Mary Fuzesi (Can) won overall, ribbon and hoop; Angela Walker (NZ) won rope.

JUDO
Men all 1990
60kg: Carl Finney (Eng)
65kg: Brent Cooper (NZ)
71kg: Roy Stone (Eng)
78kg: David Southby (Eng)

86kg: Densign White (Eng)
95kg: Ray Stevens (Eng)
Over 95kg: Elvis Gordon (Eng)
Open: Elvis Gordon (Eng)
Women all 1990
48kg: Karen Briggs (Eng)
52kg: Sharon Rendle (Eng)
56kg: Loretta Cusack (Sco)
61kg: Diane Bell (Eng)
66kg: Sharon Mills (Eng)
72kg: Jane Morris (Eng)
Over 72kg: Sharon Lee (Eng)
Open: Sharon Lee (Eng)

ROWING
Single sculls
1930 Bobby Pearce (Aus) 8:03.6
1938 Herbert Turner (Aus) 8:24.0
1950 Mervyn Wood (Aus) 7:46.8
1954 Donald Rowlands (NZ) 8:28.2
1958 Stuart Mackenzie (Aus) 7:20.1
1962 James Hill (NZ) 7:39.7
1986 Steven Redgrave (Eng) 7:28.29

Double sculls
1930 Elswood Bole & Bob Richards
      (Can) 7:48.0
1938* William Bradley & Cecil Pearce
      (Aus) 7:29.4
1950 Mervyn Wood & Murray Riley
      (Aus) 7:22.0
1954 Mervyn Wood & Murray Riley
      (Aus) 7:54.5
1958 Michael Spracklen & Geoffrey
      Baker (Eng) 6:54.4
1962 George Justice & Nicholas
      Birkmyre (Eng) 6:52.4
1986 Pat Walter & Bruce Ford (Can)
      6:19.43
* *no medals awarded*

Coxless pairs
1950 Walter Lambert & Jack Webster
      (Aus) 7:58.0
1954 Robert Parker & Reginald
      Douglas (NZ) 8:23.9
1958 Robert Parker & Reginald
      Douglas (NZ) 7:11.1
1962 Stewart Farquharson & James
      Lee-Nicholson (Eng) 7:03.7
1986 Steven Redgrave & Andrew
      Holmes (Eng) 6:40.48

Coxless fours
1930 England 7:04.6
1958 England 6:34.4
1962 England 6:31.1
1986 Canada 6:00.56

Coxed fours
1930 New Zealand 8:02.0
1938 Australia 7:16.8
1950 New Zealand 7:17.2
1954 Australia 7:58.3
1958 England 6:46.5
1962 New Zealand 6:48.2
1986 England 6:08.13

Eights
1930 England 6:37.0
1938 England 6:29.0
1950 Australia 6:27.0
1954 Canada 6:59.0
1958 Canada 5:51.1
1962 Australia 5:53.4
1986 Australia 5:44.42

Lightweight single sculls
1986 Peter Antonie (Aus) 7:16.43
Lightweight coxless Fours
1986 England 6:25.86

Women's single sculls
1986 Stephanie Foster (NZ) 7:43.22
Women's double sculls
1986 Stephanie Foster & Robin Clarke
      (NZ) 7:21.52
Women's coxless pairs
1986 Kathryn Barr & Andrea
      Schreiner (Can) 7:34.51
Women's coxed fours
1986 Canada 6:50.13
Women's eights
1986 Australia 6:43.69
Women's lightweight single sculls
1986 Adair Ferguson (Aus) 7:45.49
Women's Lightweight Coxless Fours
1986 England 6:54.70

SHOOTING
Small bore rifle *(.22 rifle)*
1966 Gilmour Boa (Can) 587
1974 Yvonne Gowland (Aus) 594
1978 Alister Allan (Sco) 1194

Small bore rifle – prone
1982 Alan Smith (Aus) 1184
1986 Alan Smith (Aus) 599
1990 Roger Harvey (NZ) 591

Small bore rifle – prone – pairs
1982 Malcolm Cooper & Mike
      Sullivan (Eng) 1187
1986 Michael Ashcroft & Gale
      Stewart (Can) 1175
1990 Stephen Pettersson & Roger
      Harvey (NZ) 1185

Small bore rifle- three positions
1982 Alister Allan (Sco) 1146
1986 Malcolm Cooper (Eng) 1170
1990 Mart Klepp (Can) 1157

Small bore rifle – three positions – pairs
1982 Malcolm Cooper & Barry
      Dagger (Eng) 2301
1986 Malcolm Cooper & Sarah
      Cooper (Eng) 2278
1990 Jean-François Senecal & Mart
      Klepp (Can) 2272

Full bore rifle
.303 rifle 1966, 7.62mm rifle from 1974
1966 Lord (John) Swansea (Wal) 394
1974 Maurice Gordon (NZ) 387.26
1978 Desmond Vamplew (Can) 391
1982 Arthur Clarke (Sco) 387
1986 Stan Golinski (Aus) 396
1990 Colin Mallett (Jersey) 394

Full bore rifle – pairs
1982 Keith Affleck & Geoffrey Ayling
      (Aus) 572
1986 Alain Marion & William Baldwin
      (Can) 583
1990 Simon Belither & Andrew Tucker
      (Eng) 580

Sarah and Malcolm Cooper achieved a unique husband-and-wife achievement when they took the small bore rifle three positions pairs gold in 1986 (Hulton-Deutsch)

Free pistol *(.22 single shot)*
1966 Charles Sexton (Eng) 544
1974 Jules Sobrian (Can) 549
1978 Yvon Trempe (Can) 543
1982 Tom Guinn (Can) 553
1986 Greg Yelavich (NZ) 551
1990 Phillip Adams (Aus) 554

Free pistol – pairs
1982 Phillip Adams & John Tremelling
      (Aus) 1077
1986 Tom Guinn & Claude Beaulieu
      (Can) 1099
1990 Phillip Adams & Bengt
      Sandström (Aus) 1106

Centre fire pistol
1966 James Lee (Can) 576
1982 John Cooke (Eng) 580
1986 Robert Northover (Eng) 583
1990 Ashok Pandit (Ind) 583

Centre fire pistol – pairs
1982 Noel Ryan & Alexander Taransky
      (Aus) 1151
1986 Phillip Adams & Roderick Hack
      (Aus) 1165
1990 Phillip Adams & Bruce Quick
      (Aus) 1155

Rapid fire pistol *.22 semi automatic*
1966 Anthony Clark (Eng) 585
1974 William Hare (Can) 586
1978 Jules Sobrian (Can) 587
1982 Solomon Lee (HK) 583
1986 Pat Murray (Aus) 591
1990 Adrian Breton (Guernsey) 583

Rapid fire pistol – pairs
1982 Peter Heuke & Alexander
      Taransky (Aus) 1160
1986 Brian Girling & Terry Turner
      (Eng) 1169
1990 Bruce Farrell & Patrick Murray
      (Aus) 1153

Air pistol
1982 George Darling (Eng) 576
1986 Greg Yelavich (NZ) 575
1990 Bengt Sandström (Aus) 580

Air pistol – pairs
1982 Phillip Adams & Gregory
      Colbert (Aus) 1128
1986 Paul Leatherdale & Ian Reid
      (Eng) 1143
1990 Atteequr Rahman & Abdus
      Sattar (Ban) 1138

Air rifle
1982 Jean-Francois Senecal (Can) 574
1986 Guy Lorion (Can) 588
1990 Guy Lorion (Can) 583

Air rifle – pairs
1982 Alister Allan & Bill McNeil (Sco)
      1137
1986 Guy Lorion & Sharon Bowes
      (Can) 1167
1990 Guy Lorion & Mart Klepp (Can)
      1163

Olympic trap (Clay pigeon)
1974 John Primrose (Can) 196
1978 John Primrose (Can) 186
1982 Peter Boden (Eng) 191
1986 Ian Peel (Eng) 195
1990 John Maxwell (Aus) 184

Olympic trap – pairs
1982 Jim Ellis & Terry Rumbel (Aus)
      190
1986 Ian Peel & Peter Boden (Eng)
      185
1990 Kevin Gill & Ian Peel (Eng) 181

Skeet
1974 Harry Willsie (Can) 194
1978 John Woolley (NZ) 193
1982 John Woolley (NZ) 197
1986 Nigel Kelly (IOM) 196
1990 Kenneth Harman (Eng) 187

Skeet – pairs
1982 Brian Gabriel & Fred Altmann
      (Can) 191
1986 Joe Neville & Kenneth Harman
      (Eng) 195

1990 Ian Marsden & James Dunlop (Sco) 189

Running boar
1990 Colin Robertson (Aus) 539

SWIMMING
Men
50 metres freestyle
1990 Andrew Baildon (Aus) 22.76
100 yards freestyle (91.44m)
1930 Munroe Bourne (Can) 56.0
1934 George Burleigh (Can) 55.0
110 yards freestyle (100.58m)
1938 Bob Pirie (Can) 59.6
1950 Peter Salmon (Can) 1:00.4
1954 Jon Henricks (Aus) 56.5
1958 John Devitt (Aus) 56.6
1962 Richard Pound (Can) 55.8
1966 Mike Wenden (Aus) 54.0
100 metres freestyle
1970 Mike Wenden (Aus) 53.06
1974 Mike Wenden (Aus) 52.73
1978 Mark Morgan (Aus) 52.70
1982 Neil Brooks (Aus) 51.14
1986 Greg Fasala (Aus) 50.95
1990 Andrew Baildon (Aus) 49.80

200 metres freestyle
1970 Mike Wenden (Aus) 1:56.69
1974 Stephen Badger (Aus) 1:56.72
1978 Ron McKeon (Aus) 1:52.06
1982 Andrew Astbury (Eng) 1:51.52
1986 Robert Gleria (Aus) 1:50.57
1990 Martin Roberts (Aus) 1:49.58

400 yards freestyle (365.76m)
1930 Noel Ryan (Aus) 4:39.8
440 yards freestyle (402.34m)
1934 Noel Ryan (Aus) 5:03.0
1938 Bob Pirie (Can) 4:54.6
1950 Garrick Agnew (Aus) 4:49.4
1954 Gary Chapman (Aus) 4:39.8
1958 John Konrads (Aus) 4:25.9
1962 Murray Rose (Aus) 4:20.0
1966 Robert Windle (Aus) 4:15.0
400 metres freestyle
1970 Graham White (Aus) 4:08.48
1974 John Kulasalu (Aus) 4:01.44
1978 Ron McKeon (Aus) 3:54.43
1982 Andrew Astbury (Eng) 3:53.29
1986 Duncan Armstrong (Aus) 3:52.25
1990 Ian Brown (Aus) 3:49.91

1500 yards freestyle (1371.6m)
1930 Noel Ryan (Aus) 18:55.4
1934 Noel Ryan (Aus) 18:25.4

1650 yards freestyle (1508.76m)
1938 Robert Leivers (Eng) 19:46.4
1950 Graham Johnston (SAf) 19:55.7
1954 Graham Johnston (SAf) 19:01.4
1958 John Konrads (Aus) 17:45.4
1962 Murray Rose (Aus) 17:18.1
1966 Ron Jackson (Aus) 17:25.9
1500 metres freestyle
1970 Graham Windeatt (Aus) 16:23.82
1974 Steve Holland (Aus) 15:34.73
1978 Max Metzker (Aus) 15:31.92
1982 Max Metzker (Aus) 15:23.94
1986 Jason Plummer (Aus) 15:12.62
1990 Glen Housman (Aus) 14:55.25

4 x 110 yards freestyle relay
1962 Australia 3:43.9
1966 Australia 3:35.6
4 x 100 metres freestyle relay
1970 Australia 3:36.02
1974 Canada 3:33.79
1978 Canada 3:27.94
1982 Australia 3:24.17
1986 Australia 3:21.58
1990 Australia 3:20.05

4 x 200 yards freestyle relay
1930 Canada 8:42.4
1934 Canada 8:40.6
4 x 220 yards freestyle relay
1938 England 9:19.0
1950 New Zealand 9:27.7
1954 Australia 8:47.6
1958 Australia 8:33.4
1962 Australia 8:13.4
1966 Australia 7:59.5
4 x 200 metres freestyle relay
1970 Australia 7:50.77
1974 Australia 7:50.13
1978 Australia 7:34.83
1982 Australia 7:28.81
1986 Australia 7:23.49
1990 Australia 7:21.17

100 yards backstroke (91.44m)
1930 John Trippett (Eng) 1:05.4
1934 Willie Francis (Sco) 1:05.2
110 yards backstroke (100.58m)
1938 Percy Oliver (Aus) 1:07.9
1950 Jacobus Wiid (SAf) 1:07.7
1954 John Brockway (Wal) 1:06.5
1958 John Monckton (Aus) 1:01.7
1962 Graham Sykes (Eng) 1:04.5
1966 Peter Reynolds (Aus) 1:02.4
100 metres backstroke
1970 Bill Kennedy (Can) 1:01.65
1974 Mark Tonelli (Aus) 59.65

1978 Glenn Patching (Aus) 57.90
1982 Michael West (Can) 57.12
1986 Mark Tewksbury (Can) 56.45
1990 Mark Tewksbury (Can) 56.07

220 yards backstroke (201.17m)
1962 Julian Carroll (Aus) 2:20.9
1966 Peter Reynolds (Aus) 2:12.0
200 metres backstroke
1970 Mike Richards (Wal) 2:14.53
1974 Brad Cooper (Aus) 2:06.31
1978 Gary Hurring (NZ) 2:04.37
1982 Cameron Henning (Can) 2:02.88
1986 Sandy Goss (Can) 2:02.55
1990 Gary Anderson (Can) 2:01.69

110 yards breaststroke (100.58m)
1962 Ian O'Brien (Aus) 1:11.4
1966 Ian O'Brien (Aus) 1:08.2
100 metres breaststroke
1970 Bill Mahony (Can) 1:09.0
1974 David Leigh (Eng) 1:06.52
1978 Graham Smith (Can) 1:03.81
1982 Adrian Moorhouse (Eng) 1:02.93
1986 Victor Davis (Can) 1:03.01
1990 Adrian Moorhouse (Eng) 1:01.49

200 yards breaststroke (182.88m)
1930 Jack Aubin (Can) 2:38.4
1934 Norman Hamilton (Sco) 2:41.4
220 yards breaststroke (201.17m)
1938 John Davies (Eng) 2:51.9
1950 David Hawkins (Aus) 2:54.1
1954 John Doms (NZ) 2:52.6
1958 Terry Gathercole (Aus) 2:41.6
1962 Ian O'Brien (Aus) 2:38.2
1966 Ian O'Brien (Aus) 2:29.3
200 metres breaststroke
1970 Bill Mahony (Can) 2:30.29
1974 David Wilkie (Sco) 2:24.42
1978 Graham Smith (Can) 2:20.86
1982 Victor Davis (Can) 2:16.25
1986 Adrian Moorhouse (Eng) 2:16.35
1990 John Cleveland (Can) 2:14.96

110 yards butterfly (100.59m)
1962 Kevin Berry (Aus) 59.5
1966 Ron Jacks (Can) 1:00.3
100 metres butterfly
1970 Byron MacDonald (Can) 58.44
1974 Neil Rogers (Aus) 56.58
1978 Dan Thompson (Can) 55.04
1982 Dan Thompson (Can) 54.71
1986 Andrew Jameson (Eng) 54.07
1990 Andrew Baildon (Aus) 53.98

220 yards butterfly (201.17m)
1958 Ian Black (Sco) 2:22.6
1962 Kevin Berry (Aus) 2:10.8
1966 David Gerrard (NZ) 2:12.7
200 metres butterfly
1970 Tom Arusoo (Can) 2:08.97
1974 Brian Brinkley (Eng) 2:04.51
1978 George Nagy (Can) 2:01.99
1982 Phil Hubble (Eng) 2:00.98
1986 Anthony Mosse (NZ) 1:57.27
1990 Anthony Mosse (NZ) 1:57.33

200 metres individual medley
1970 George Smith (Can) 2:13.72
1974 David Wilkie (Sco) 2:10.11
1978 Graham Smith (Can) 2:05.25
1982 Alex Baumann (Can) 2:02.25
1986 Alex Baumann (Can) 2:01.80
1990 Gary Anderson (Can) 2:02.94

440 yards individual medley
(402.34m)
1962 Alex Alexander (Aus) 5:15.3
1966 Peter Reynolds (Aus) 4:50.8
400 metres individual medley
1970 George Smith (Can) 4:48.87
1974 Mark Treffers (NZ) 4:35.90
1978 Graham Smith (Can) 4:27.34
1982 Alex Baumann (Can) 4:23.53
1986 Alex Baumann (Can) 4:18.29
1990 Rob Bruce (Aus) 4:20.26

3 x 100 yards medley relay
1934 Canada 3:11.2
3 x 110 yards medley relay
1938 England 3:28.2
1950 England 3:26.6
1954 Australia 3:22.0
4 x 110 yards medley relay
Butterfly leg added
1958 Australia 4:14.2
1962 Australia 4:12.4
1966 Canada 4:10.5
4 x 100 metres medley relay
1970 Canada 4:01.10
1974 Canada 3:52.93
1978 Canada 3:49.76
1982 Australia 3:47.34
1986 Canada 3:44.00
1990 Canada 3:42.45

Springboard Diving
1930 Alfred Phillips (Can)
1934 J.Briscoe Ray (Eng)
1938 Ron Masters (Aus)
1950 George Athans (Can)
1954 Peter Heatly (Sco)
1958 Keith Collin (Eng)

1962 Brian Phelps (Eng)
1966 Brian Phelps (Eng)
1970 Donald Wagstaff (Aus)
1974 Donald Wagstaff (Aus)
1978 Chris Snode (Eng)
1982 Chris Snode (Eng)
1986 Shaun Panayi (Aus)
1990 **3m** Craig Rogerson (Aus)
     1m Russell Butler (Aus)

Highboard Diving
1930 Alfred Phillips (Can)
1934 Tommy Mather (Eng)
1938 Doug Tomalin (Eng)
1950 Peter Heatly (Sco)
1954 William Patrick (Can)
1958 Peter Heatly (Sco)
1962 Brian Phelps (Eng)
1966 Brian Phelps (Eng)
1970 Donald Wagstaff (Aus)
1974 Donald Wagstaff (Aus)
1978 Chris Snode (Eng)
1982 Chris Snode (Eng)
1986 Craig Rogerson (Aus)
1990 Robert Morgan (Wal)

Water Polo
1950 Australia

Women
50 metres freestyle
1990 Lisa Curry-Kenny (Aus) 25.80

100 yards freestyle (91.44m)
1930 Joyce Cooper (Eng) 1:07.0
1934 Phyllis Dewar (Can) 1:03.0
110 yards freestyle (100.58m)
1938 Evelyn de Lacy (Aus) 1:10.1
1950 Marjorie McQuade (Aus) 1:09.0
1954 Lorraine Crapp (Aus) 1:05.8
1958 Dawn Fraser (Aus) 1:01.4
1962 Dawn Fraser (Aus) 59.5
1966 Marion Lay (Can) 1:02.3
100 metres freestyle
1970 Angela Coughlan (Can) 1:01.22
1974 Sonya Gray (Aus) 59.13
1978 Carol Klimpel (Can) 57.78
1982 June Croft (Eng) 56.97
1986 Jane Kerr (Can) 57.62
1990 Karen Van Wirdum (Aus) 56.48

200 metres freestyle
1970 Karen Moras (Aus) 2:09.78
1974 Sonya Gray (Aus) 2:04.27
1978 Rebecca Perrott (NZ) 2:00.63
1982 June Croft (Eng) 1:59.74
1986 Susie Baumer (Aus) 2:00.61
1990 Hayley Lewis (Aus) 2:00.79

400 yards freestyle (365.76m)
1930 Joyce Cooper (Eng) 5:25.4
440 yards freestyle (402.34m)
1934 Phyllis Dewar (Can) 5:45.6
1938 Dorothy Green (Aus) 5:39.7
1950 Joan Harrison (SAf) 5:26.4
1954 Lorraine Crapp (Aus) 5:11.4
1958 Ilsa Konrads (Aus) 4:49.4
1962 Dawn Fraser (Aus) 4:51.4
1966 Kathy Wainwright (Aus) 4:38.8
400 metres freestyle
1970 Karen Moras (Aus) 4:27.38
1974 Jenny Turrall (Aus) 4:22.09
1978 Tracey Wickham (Aus) 4:08.45
1982 Tracey Wickham (Aus) 4:08.82
1986 Sarah Hardcastle (Eng) 4:07.68
1990 Hayley Lewis (Aus) 4:08.89

800 metres freestyle
1970 Karen Moras (Aus) 9:02.45
1974 Jaynie Parkhouse (NZ) 8:58.49
1978 Tracey Wickham (Aus) 8:24.62
1982 Tracey Wickham (Aus) 8:29.05
1986 Sarah Hardcastle (Eng) 8:24.77
1990 Julie McDonald (Aus) 8:30.27

4 x 100 yards freestyle relay
1930 England 4:32.8
1934 Canada 4:21.8
4 x 110 yards freestyle relay
1938 Canada 4:48.3
1950 Australia 4:44.9
1954 South Africa 4:33.9
1958 Australia 4:17.4
1962 Australia 4:11.0
1966 Canada 4:10.8
4 x 100 metres freestyle relay
1970 Australia 4:06.41
1974 Canada 3:57.14
1978 Canada 3:50.28
1982 England 3:54.23
1986 Canada 3:48.45
1990 Australia 3:46.85

4 x 200 metres freestyle relay
1986 Australia 8:12.09
1990 Australia 8:08.95

100 yards backstroke (91.44m)
1930 Joyce Cooper (Eng) 1:15.0
1934 Phyllis Harding (Eng) 1:13.8
110 yards backstroke (100.58m)
1938 Pat Norton (Aus) 1:19.5
1950 Judy-Joy Davies (Aus) 1:18.6
1954 Joan Harrison (SAf) 1:15.2
1958 Judy Grinham (Eng) 1:11.9
1962 Linda Ludgrove (Eng) 1:11.1
1966 Linda Ludgrove (Eng) 1:09.2

100 metres backstroke
1970 Lynne Watson (Aus) 1:07.10
1974 Wendy Cook (Can) 1:06.37
1978 Debra Forster (Aus) 1:03.97
1982 Lisa Forrest (Aus) 1:03.48
1986 Sylvia Hume (NZ) 1:04.00
1990 Nicole Livingstone (Aus)
    1:02.46

220 yards backstroke (201.17m)
1962 Linda Ludgrove (Eng) 2:35.2
1966 Linda Ludgrove (Eng) 2:28.5
200 metres backstroke
1970 Lynne Watson (Aus) 2:22.86
1974 Wendy Cook (Can) 2:20.37
1978 Cheryl Gibson (Can) 2:16.57
1982 Lisa Forrest (Aus) 2:13.36
1986 Georgina Parkes (Aus) 2:14.88
1990 Anna Simcic (NZ) 2:12.32

110 yards breaststroke (100.58m)
1962 Anita Lonsbrough (Eng) 1:21.3
1966 Diana Harris (Eng) 1:19.7
100 metres breaststroke
1970 Beverley Whitfield (Aus)
    1:17.40
1974 Catherine Gaskell (Eng) 1:16.42
1978 Robin Corsiglia (Can) 1:13.56
1982 Kathy Bald (Can) 1:11.89
1986 Allison Higson (Can) 1:10.84
1990 Keltie Duggan (Can) 1:10.74

200 yards breaststroke (182.88m)
1930 Celia Wolstenholme (Eng)
    2:54.8
1934 Claire Dennis (Aus) 2:50.2
220 yards breaststroke (201.17m)
1938 Doris Storey (Eng) 3:06.3
1950 Elenor Gordon (Sco) 3:01.7
1954 Elenor Gordon (Sco) 2:59.2
1958 Anita Lonsbrough (Eng) 2:53.5
1962 Anita Lonsbrough (Eng) 2:51.7
1966 Jill Slattery (Eng) 2:50.3
200 metres breaststroke
1970 Beverley Whitfield (Aus) 2:44.12
1974 Pat Beavan (Wal) 2:43.11
1978 Lisa Borsholt (Can) 2:37.70
1982 Anne Ottenbrite (Can) 2:32.07
1986 Allison Higson (Can) 2:31.20
1990 Nathalia Giguere (Can) 2:32.16

110 yards butterfly (100.59m)
1958 Beverley Bainbridge (Aus)
    1:13.5
1962 Mary Stewart (Can) 1:10.1
1966 Elaine Tanner (Can) 1:06.8
100 metres butterfly
1970 Diane Lansley (Eng) 1:07.90

1974 Patti Stenhouse (Can) 1:05.38
1978 Wendy Quirk (Can) 1:01.92
1982 Lisa Curry (Aus) 1:01.22
1986 Caroline Cooper (Eng) 1:02.12
1990 Lisa Curry-Kenny (Aus) 1:00.66

220 yards butterfly (201.17m)
1966 Elaine Tanner (Can) 2:29.9
200 metres butterfly
1970 Maree Robinson (Aus) 2:24.67
1974 Sandra Yost (Aus) 2:20.57
1978 Michelle Ford (Aus) 2:11.29
1982 Michelle Ford (Aus) 2:11.89
1986 Donna McGinnis (Can) 2:11.97
1990 Hayley Lewis (Aus) 2:11.15

200 metres individual medley
1970 Denise Langford (Aus) 2:28.89
1974 Leslie Cliff (Can) 2:24.13
1978 Sharron Davies (Eng) 2:18.37
1982 Lisa Curry (Aus) 2:16.94
1986 Suzanne Landells (Aus) 2:17.02
1990 Nancy Sweetnam (Can) 2:15.61

440 yards individual medley
(402.34m)
1962 Anita Lonsbrough (Eng) 5:38.6
1966 Elaine Tanner (Can) 5:26.3
400 metres individual medley
1970 Denise Langford (Aus) 5:10.74
1974 Leslie Cliff (Can) 5:01.35
1978 Sharron Davies (Eng) 4:52.44
1982 Lisa Curry (Aus) 4:51.95
1986 Suzanne Landells (Aus) 4:45.82
1990 Hayley Lewis (Aus) 4:42.65

3 x 100 yards medley relay
1934 Canada 3:42.0
3 x 110 yards medley relay
1938 England 3:57.7
1950 Australia 3:53.8
1954 Scotland 3:51.0
4 x 110 yards medley relay
Butterfly leg added
1958 England 4:54.0
1962 Australia 4:45.9
1966 England 4:40.6
4 x 100 metres medley relay
1970 Australia 4:30.66
1974 Canada 4:24.77
1978 Canada 4:15.26
1982 Canada 4:14.33
1986 England 4:13.48
1990 Australia 4:10.87

Springboard Diving
1930 Oonagh Whitsett (SAf)
1934 Judy Moss (Can)

1938 Irene Donnett (Aus)
1950 Edna Child (Eng)
1954 Ann Long (Eng)
1958 Charmian Welsh (Eng)
1962 Susan Knight (Aus)
1966 Kathy Rowlatt (Eng)
1970 Beverley Boys (Can)
1974 Cindy Shatto (Can)
1978 Janet Nutter (Can)
1982 Jenny Donnet (Aus)
1986 Debbie Fuller (Can)
1990 **3m** Jenny Donnet (Aus)
    1m Mary De Piero (Can)

Highboard Diving
1930 Pearl Stoneham (Can)
1934 Elizabeth Macready (Eng)
1938 Lurline Hook (Aus)
1950 Edna Child (Eng)
1954 Barbara McAulay (Aus)
1958 Charmian Welsh (Eng)
1962 Susan Knight (Aus)
1966 Joy Newman (Eng)
1970 Beverley Boys (Can)
1974 Beverley Boys (Can)
1978 Linda Cuthbert (Can)
1982 Valerie Beddoe (Aus)
1986 Debbie Fuller (Can)
1990 Anna Dacyshyn (Can)

Synchronised swimming – solo
1986 Sylvie Frechette (Can)
1990 Sylvie Frechette (Can)

Synchronised swimming – duet
1986 Carolyn Waldo & Michelle
    Cameron (Can)
1990 Katherine Glen & Christine
    Larsen (Can)

Synchronised swimming – team
1986 Canada

WEIGHTLIFTING
Three lifts 1950-70, two from 1974.
Separate medals also awarded for
each lift – snatch, clean and jerk in
1990. All weights are for totals in
kilograms (originally measured in
pounds 1950-66).

Flyweight – up to 52kg
1970 George Vasiliades (Aus) 290
1974 Precious McKenzie (Eng) 215
1978 Ekambaram Karunakaran (Ind)
    205
1982 Nick Voukelatos (Aus) 207.5
1986 Greg Hayman (Aus) 212.5

1990 Chandersekaran Raghavan (Ind) 232.5

Bantamweight – up to 56kg
1950 Tho Fook Hung (Mal) 297
1954 Maurice Megennis (Eng) 281
1958 Reginald Gaffley (SAf) 299
1962 Chua Phung Kim (Sin) 322
1966 Precious McKenzie (Eng) 319.5
1970 Precious McKenzie (Eng) 335
1974 Michael Adams (Aus) 222.5
1978 Precious McKenzie (NZ) 220
1982 Geoffrey Laws (Eng) 235
1986 Nick Voukelatos (Aus) 245
1990 Rangaswamy Punnuswamy (Ind) 247.5

Featherweight – up to 60kg
1950 Koh Eng Tong (Mal) 310.5
1954 Rodney Wilkes (Tri) 313
1958 Tan Ser Cher (Sin) 310.5
1962 George Newton (Eng) 326.5
1966 Kum Weng Chung (Wal) 337
1970 George Perrin (Eng) 342.5
1974 George Vasiliades (Aus) 237.5
1978 Michel Mercier (Can) 237.5
1982 Dean Willey (Eng) 267.5
1986 Raymond Williams (Wal) 252.5
1990 Chandra Sharma (Ind) 257.5

Lightweight – up to 67.5kg
1950 James Halliday (Eng) 344.5
1954 Verdi Barberis (Aus) 347
1958 Tan Howe Liang (Sin) 358
1962 Carlton Goring (Eng) 351.5
1966 Hugo Gittens (Tri) 367
1970 George Newton (Eng) 372.5
1974 George Newton (Eng) 260
1978 Bill Stellios (Aus) 272.5
1982 David Morgan (Wal) 295
1986 Dean Willey (Eng) 315
1990 Paramjit Sharma (Ind) 295

Middleweight – up to 75kg
1950 Gerard Gratton (Can) 360.5
1954 James Halliday (Eng) 362.5
1958 Blair Blenman (Bar) 360.5
1962 Tan Howe Laing (Sin) 390
1966 Pierre St Jean (Can) 404.5
1970 Russell Perry (Aus) 412.5
1974 Tony Ebert (NZ) 275
1978 Sam Castiglione (Aus) 300
1982 Stephen Pinsent (Eng) 312.5
1986 Bill Stellios (Aus) 302.5
1990 Ron Laycock (Aus) 310

Light-Heavyweight – up to 82.5kg
1950 James Varaleau (Can) 369.5
1954 Gerry Gratton (Can) 403.5
1958 Phil Caira (Sco) 396.5
1962 Phil Caira (Sco) 408
1966 George Vakakis (Aus) 419.5
1970 Nicolo Ciancio (Aus) 447.5

1974 Tony Ford (Eng) 302.5
1978 Robert Kabbas (Aus) 322.5
1982 Newton Burrowes (Eng) 325
1986 David Morgan (Wal) 350
1990 David Morgan (Wal) 347.5

Middle-Heavyweight – up to 90kg
1954 Keevil Daly (Can) 399
1958 Manoel Santos (Aus) 403.5
1962 Louis Martin (Eng) 469.5
1966 Louis Martin (Eng) 462
1970 Louis Martin (Eng) 457.5
1974 Nicolo Ciancio (Aus) 330
1978 Gary Langford (Eng) 335
1982 Robert Kabbas (Aus) 337.5
1986 Keith Boxell (Eng) 350
1990 Duncan Dawkins (Eng) 357.5

Sub-Heavyweight – up to 100kg
1978 John Burns (Wal) 340
1982 Oliver Orok (Nig) 350
1986 Denis Garon (Can) 360
1990 Andrew Saxton (Eng) 362.5

Heavyweight – up to 110kg
1950 Harold Cleghorn (NZ) 408
1954 Doug Hepburn (Can) 471.5
1958 Ken McDonald (Eng) 455.5
1962 Arthur Shannos (Aus) 465
1966 Donald Oliver (NZ) 497
1970 Russell Prior (Can) 490
1974 Russell Prior (Can) 352.5
1978 Russell Prior (Can) 347.5
1982 John Burns (Wal) 347.5
1986 Kevin Roy (Can) 375
1990 Mark Thomas (Eng) 357.5

Super Heavyweight – over 110kg
1970 Ray Rigby (Aus) 500
1974 Graham May (NZ) 342.5
1978 Jean-Marc Cardinal (Can) 365
1982 Dean Lukin (Aus) 377.5
1986 Dean Lukin (Aus) 392.5
1990 Andrew Davies (Wal) 402.5

WRESTLING
48kg – Light-Flyweight
1970 Ved Prakash (Ind)
1974 Mitchell Kawasaki (Can)
1978 Ashok Kumar (Ind)
1982 Ram Chander Sarang (Ind)
1986 Ron Moncur (Can)

52kg – Flyweight
1950 Bert Harris (Aus)
1954 Louis Baise (SAf)
1958 Ian Epton (SAf)
1962 Mohammad Niaz (Pak)
1966 Mohammad Nazir (Pak)
1970 Sudesh Kumar (Ind)
1974 Sudesh Kumar (Ind)
1978 Ray Takahashi (Can)

1982 Mahabir Singh (Ind)
1986 Chris Woodcroft (Can)

57kg – Bantamweight
1930 James Trifunov (Can)
1934 Edward Melrose (Sco)
1938 Ted Purcell (Aus)
1950 Douglas Mudgeway (NZ)
1954 Geoffrey Jameson (Aus)
1958 Muhammad Akhtar (Pak)
1962 Siraj-ud-Din (Pak)
1966 Bishambar Singh (Ind)
1970 Sadar Mohd (Pak)
1974 Premnath (Ind)
1978 Satbir Singh (Ind)
1982 Brian Aspen (Eng)
1986 Mitch Ostberg (Can)

62kg – Featherweight
1930 Clifford Chilcott (Can)
1934 Robert McNab (Can)
1938 Roy Purchase (Aus)
1950 John Armitt (NZ)
1954 Abraham Geldenhuys (SAf)
1958 Abraham Geldenhuys (SAf)
1962 Ala-ud-Din (Pak)
1966 Mohammad Akhtar (Pak)
1970 Mohammad Saeed (Pak)
1974 Egon Beiler (Can)
1978 Egon Beiler (Can)
1982 Bob Robinson (Can)
1986 Paul Hughes (Can)

68kg – Lightweight
1930 Howard Thomas (Can)
1934 Richard Garrard (Aus)
1938 Richard Garrard (Aus)
1950 Richard Garrard (Aus)
1954 Godfrey Pienaar (SAf)
1958 Muhammad Ashraf (Pak)
1962 Muhammad Akhtar (Pak)
1966 Mukhtiar Singh (Ind)
1970 Udey Chand (Ind)
1974 Jagrup Singh (Ind)
1978 Zsigmund Kelevitz (Aus)
1982 Jagminder Singh (Ind)
1986 David McKay (Can)

74kg – Welterweight
1930 Reg Priestley (Can)
1934 Joseph Schleimer (Can)
1938 Thomas Trevaskis (Aus)
1950 Henry Hudson (Can)
1954 Nicholas Laubscher (SAf)
1958 Muhammad Bashir (Pak)
1962 Muhammad Bashir (Pak)
1966 Muhammad Bashir (Pak)
1970 Mukhtiar Singh (Ind)
1974 Raghunath Pawar (Ind)
1978 Rajinder Singh (Ind)
1982 Rajinder Singh (Ind)
1986 Gary Holmes (Can)

82kg – Middleweight
1930 Mike Chepwick (Can)
1934 Terry Evans (Can)
1938 Terry Evans (Can)
1950 Maurice Vachon (Can)
1954 Hermanus van Zyl (SAf)
1958 Hermanus van Zyl (SAf)
1962 Muhammad Faiz (Pak)
1966 Muhammad Faiz (Pak)
1970 Harish Rajindra (Ind)
1974 David Aspin (NZ)
1978 Richard Deschatelets (Can)
1982 Chris Rinke (Can)
1986 Chris Rinke (Can)

90kg – Light-Heavyweight
1930 Bill McIntyre (Can)
1934 Mick Cubbin (SAf)
1938 Edward Scarf (Aus)
1950 Patrick Morton (SAf)
1954 Jacob Theron (SAf)
1958 Jacob Theron (SAf)
1962 Anthony Buck (Eng)
1966 Robert Chamberot (Can)
1970 Muhammad Faiz (Pak)
1974 Terry Paice (Can)
1978 Stephen Danier (Can)
1982 Clark Davis (Can)
1986 Noel Loban (Eng)

100kg – Heavyweight
1930 Earl McCready (Can)
1934 Jack Knight (Aus)
1938 Jack Knight (Aus)
1950 James Armstrong (Aus)
1954 Kenneth Richmond (Eng)
1958 Lila Ram (Ind)
1962 Muhammad Niaz (Pak)
1966 Bhim Singh (Ind)
1970 Edward Millard (Can)
1974 Claude Pilon (Can)
1978 Wyatt Wishart (Can)
1982 Richard Deschatelets (Can)
1986 Clark Davis (Can)

Over 100kg – Super-Heavyweight
Limit 130kg from 1986
1970 Ikram Ilahi (Pak)
1974 Bill Benko (Can)
1978 Robert Gibbons (Can)
1982 Wyatt Wishart (Can)
1986 Wayne Brightwell (Can)

Most gold medals
9 Bill Hoskyns (Eng) fencing – 3 individual épée and 6 team golds 1958-70
9 Michael Wenden (Aus) swimming – 4 individual and 5 relay golds 1966-74

Most gold medals won at 1 Games
6 Graham Smith (Can) swimming – 4 individual and 2 relay 1978
5 Hayley Lewis (Aus) swimming – 4 individual and 1 relay 1990
5 Decima Norman (Aus) athletics – 3 individual and 2 relay 1938

Most medals
14 Phillip Adams (Aus) shooting – 6 gold, 7 silver, 1 bronze 1982-90
13 Michael Wenden (Aus) swimming – 9 gold, 3 silver, 1 bronze 1966-74
13 Ivan Lund (Aus) fencing – 3 gold, 6 silver, 4 bronze 1950-62

Women's record
9 Raelene Boyle (Aus) athletics – 7 gold, 2 silver 1970-82

Most medals won at one Games
8 Ralph Hutton (Can) swimming – 1 gold, 5 silver, 2 bronze 1966
7 Elaine Tanner (Can) swimming – 4 gold, 3 silver 1966

COMMONWEALTH GAMES MEDALS BY NATION 1930-90
Gold – G, Silver – S, Bronze – B

Rank	Nation	G	S	B	Total
1	England	420	368	368	1156
2	Australia	397	374	322	1093
3	Canada	287	301	299	887
4	New Zealand	94	121	161	376
5	Scotland	56	74	109	239
6	South Africa *	60	44	47	151
7	Wales	32	39	60	131
8	India	37	36	31	104
9	Kenya	35	25	33	93
10	Nigeria	19	25	26	70
11	Northern Ireland #	15	20	34	69
12	Jamaica	20	14	18	52
13	Pakistan	20	13	10	43
14	Ghana	12	16	12	40
15	Uganda	8	13	13	34
16	Trinidad & Tobago	7	11	11	29
	Malaysia	10	10	9	29
18	Zambia	2	10	16	28
19	Zimbabwe	3	7	14	24
20	Bahamas	3	6	4	13
	Tanzania	3	5	5	13
	Guyana	2	5	6	13
23	Hong Kong	5	2	5	12
24	Singapore	4	1	4	9
	Fiji	2	2	5	9
26	Western Samoa	-	1	6	7
27	Barbados	1	3	2	6
28	Sri Lanka	2	2	1	5
	Isle of Man	2	-	3	5
	Guernsey	1	3	1	5
31	Papua-New Guinea	1	2	1	4
	Jersey	1	-	3	4
33	Nauru	1	2	-	3
	Bermuda	1	1	1	3
	Malawi	-	-	3	3
36	St.Vincent	1	-	1	2
	Bangladesh	1	-	1	2
	Cyprus	1	1	-	2
	Swaziland	-	1	2	3
40	Gambia	-	-	1	1
	Botswana	-	-	1	1
	Malta	-	-	1	1
	TOTAL	**1566**	**1558**	**1650**	**4774**

* no longer a member of the Commonwealth   # Ireland in 1930

CRICKET

Cricket originated in England in the Middle Ages. Its exact origins are obscure, but bat and ball games were played from the 13th century and games similar to the modern one from around 1550. The earliest major match for which the full score survives was that when England played Kent in London in 1744. In that year the first known Laws of the game were issued. The Marylebone Cricket Club (MCC) was founded in 1787, and until the formation of the Cricket Council in 1968 was accepted as the ruling body of the game from its headquarters at Lord's Cricket Ground, London. The MCC remains responsible for the Laws of Cricket. The Imperial (International from 1965) Cricket Conference was formed by representatives of England, Australia and South Africa in 1909. India, New Zealand and West Indies were elected members in 1926, Pakistan in 1953 and Sri Lanka in 1981.

South Africa ceased to be a member in 1961. Other, non-Test playing nations have been admitted: 18 as associate members and five as affiliate members.

TEST CRICKET

The first Test match was played at Melbourne on 15-19 Mar 1877 between Australia and England, represented by James Lillywhite's touring side. Neither side was truly representative of their countries and indeed such was the case for many matches, now accepted as Test matches, played over the next fifty years or so. The first match in England was against Australia at the Oval on 6-8 Sep 1880. First Tests by other nations were as follows: South Africa 1889, West Indies 1928, New Zealand 1930, India 1932, Pakistan 1952, Sri Lanka 1982.

Summary of Test match results at 1 June 1990

The first figure is number of wins by the team on the left over the team in that column, the second figure is number of draws, Thus in England v Australia Tests, England have won 88, Australia 101, with 80 Tests left drawn.

	A	E	I	NZ	P	SA	SL	WI	Wins	Tests
Australia	-	101/80	20/16*	10/10	12/13	29/13	3/1	28/16*	202	498
England	88/80	-	30/34	30/32	13/29	46/38	2/1	22/36	231	661
India	8/16*	11/34	-	12/13	4/37	-	2/4	6/30	43	268
New Zealand	6/10	4/32	6/13	-	3/16	2/6	4/2	4/12	28	199
Pakistan	9/13	5/29	7/37	10/16	-	-	5/3	6/10	42	192
South Africa	11/13	18/38	-	9/6	-	-	-	-	38	172
Sri Lanka	0/1	0/1	1/4	0/2	1/3	-	-	-	2	29
West Indies	22/16*	41/36	26/30	8/12	9/10	-	-	-	106	277

* plus one tie. There have been two tied Tests:
9-14 Dec 1960 at Brisbane, Australia v West Indies, 18-22 Sep 1986 at Madras, Australia v India

Team Records

Highest innings totals

903-7 dec	England	v A	The Oval	20-23 Aug 1938
849	England	v WI	Kingston	3-5 Apr 1930
790-3 dec	West Indies	v P	Kingston	27 Feb – 1 Mar 1958
758-8 dec	Australia	v WI	Kingston	13-15 Jun 1955
729-6 dec	Australia	v E	Lord's	28-30 Jun 1930
708	Pakistan	v E	The Oval	6-8 Aug 1987
701	Australia	v E	The Oval	18-20 Aug 1934

Highest match aggregates
1981 runs South Africa (530 & 481) v England (316 & 654-5) at Durban 3-14 Mar 1939. This was the 'Timeless Test'. The total playing time was 43 hours 16 minutes, over 10 days, and was left drawn because England had to catch the boat home at the end of their tour.
1815 runs West Indies (286 & 408-5) v England (849 & 272-9 dec) at Kingston 3-12 Apr 1930.

1764 runs Australia (533 & 339-9) v West Indies (276 & 616) at Adelaide 24-29 Jan 1969. This is the record for a five day Test.
All the above three Tests were left drawn.
Highest winning margin
Innings and 579 runs England (903-7 dec) beat Australia (201 & 123) at the Oval 20-24 Aug 1938.

Lowest completed innings totals

26	New Zealand	v E	Auckland	28 Mar 1955
30	South Africa	v E	Port Elizabeth	14 Feb 1896
30	South Africa	v E	Birmingham	16 Jun 1924

Lowest match aggregate: 234 runs Australia (153) beat South Africa (36 & 45) 12-15 Feb 1932

Individual Test records

Most Tests

125	Sunil Gavaskar (Ind)	1971-87
115	Allan Border (Aus)	1978-90
114	Colin Cowdrey (Eng)	1954-75
111	Vivian Richards (WI)	1974-90
110	Clive Lloyd (WI)	1966-85
108	Geoffrey Boycott (Eng)	1964-82
107	Dilip Vengsarkar (Ind)	1976-90
106	David Gower (Eng)	1978-89
106	Kapil Dev (Ind)	1978-90
104	Javed Miandad (Pak)	1976-90
100	Gordon Greenidge (WI)	1974-90
97	Ian Botham (Eng)	1977-89
96	Rodney Marsh (Aus)	1970-84
95	Alan Knott (Eng)	1967-81
93	Garfield Sobers (WI)	1954-74
91	Godfrey Evans (Eng)	1946-59
91	Gundappa Viswanath (Ind)	1969-83
90	Bob Willis (Eng)	1971-84
89	Desmond Haynes (WI)	1978-90
88	Syed Kirmani (Ind)	1976-86
87	Greg Chappell (Aus)	1970-84
86	Derek Underwood (Eng)	1977-82
85	Walter Hammond (Eng)	1927-47

Youngest player: 15 yr 124 days Mushtaq Mohammed (Pak) v WI Lahore 26 Mar 1959.
Oldest player: 52 yr 165 days Wilfred Rhodes (Eng) v WI Kingston 12 Apr 1930.
Longest Test career: 30 yr 314 days Wilfred Rhodes (Eng) 1 Jun 1899 to 12 Apr 1930.

Allan Border took over the Australian captaincy in 1985 and despite initially playing with a poor team, he maintained a Test batting average of over 50. He has played in a record number of one-day internationals, captaining Australia in well over 100 of these matches and leading them to victory in the World Cup in 1987 (All-Sport/Adrian Murrell)

Most Test appearances as captain
(no. matches won in brackets)

74 (36)	Clive Lloyd (WI)	1974-85	39 (12)	Bobby Simpson (Aus)	1963-78
52 (13)	Allan Border (Aus)	1984-90	39 (9)	Garfield Sobers (WI)	1965-72
48 (21)	Greg Chappell (Aus)	1975-83	38 (23)	Vivian Richards (WI)	1980-90
47 (9)	Sunil Gavaskar (Ind)	1976-85		Other captains to have won 15 or more Tests:	
42 (12)	Imran Khan (Pak)	1982-90	31 (18)	Mike Brearley (Eng)	1977-81
41 (20)	Peter May (Eng)	1955-61	30 (15)	Ian Chappell (Aus)	1971-5
40 (9)	Nawab of Pataudi Jnr (Ind)	1962-75	24 (15)	Don Bradman (Aus)	1936-48

TEST MATCH BATTING

Highest individual innings scores (over 300)

365*	Garfield Sobers (WI)	v P	Kingston	27 Feb- 1 Mar 1958
364	Leonard Hutton (Eng)	v A	The Oval	20-23 Aug 1938
337	Hanif Mohammad (Pak)	v WI	Bridgetown	20-23 Jan 1958
336*	Walter Hammond (Eng)	v NZ	Auckland	31 Mar- 1 Apr 1933
334	Don Bradman (Aus)	v E	Leeds	11-12 Jul 1930
325	Andrew Sandham (Eng)	v WI	Kingston	3-4 Apr 1930
311	Bobby Simpson (Aus)	v E	Manchester	23-25 Jul 1964
310*	John Edrich (Eng)	v NZ	Leeds	8-9 Jul 1965
307	Bob Cowper (Aus)	v E	Melbourne	12-16 Feb 1966
304	Don Bradman (Aus)	v E	Leeds	21-23 Jul 1934
302	Lawrence Rowe (WI)	v E	Bridgetown	7-10 Mar 1974

Fastest Scoring

100	70 minutes (67 balls) Jack Gregory , Aus v SA, Johannesburg, 12 Nov 1921
	56 balls (81 minutes) Vivian Richards WI v E, St John's, 15 Apr 1986
200	214 minutes (259 balls) Don Bradman Aus v E, Leeds, 11 Jul 1930
	219 balls (268 minutes) Ian Botham Eng v I, The Oval, 8-9 Jul 1982
300	288 minutes Walter Hammond Eng v NZ, Auckland, 31 Mar – 1 Apr 1933

During his innings of 336 not out in 318 minutes Hammond hit ten sixes, a record for a Test innings. His third hundred took just 47 minutes, the fastest in Test cricket.

Most Test hundreds (double hundreds in brackets)

34 (4)   Sunil Gavaskar (Ind)
29 (12) Don Bradman (Aus)
26 (2)   Garfield Sobers (WI)
24 (4)   Greg Chappell (Aus)
24 (3)   Vivian Richards (WI)
23 (1)   Allan Border (Aus)
22 (7)   Walter Hammond (Eng)
22 (1)   Geoffrey Boycott (Eng)
22 (-)   Colin Cowdrey (Eng)
22 (6)   Javed Miandad (Pak)
21 (2)   Neil Harvey (Aus)
20 (1)   Ken Barrington (Eng)
19 (4)   Leonard Hutton (Eng)
19 (1)   Clive Lloyd (WI)

also scoring 4 double hundreds:
12 (4)   Zaheer Abbas (Pak)

Most runs in a Test career

Runs	Name	Ave.	Tests	Years
10122	Sunil Gavaskar (Ind)	51.12	125	1971-87
8701	Allan Border (Aus)	53.38	115	1978-90
8114	Geoffrey Boycott (Eng)	47.72	108	1964-82
8032	Garfield Sobers (WI)	57.78	93	1954-74
7990	Vivian Richards (WI)	51.21	111	1974-90
7891	Javed Miandad (Pak)	56.36	104	1976-90
7624	Colin Cowdrey (Eng)	44.06	114	1954-75
7515	Clive Lloyd (WI)	46.67	110	1966-85
7363	David Gower (Eng)	43.42	106	1978-89
7249	Walter Hammond (Eng)	58.45	85	1927-47
7134	Gordon Greenidge (WI)	46.02	100	1974-90
7110	Greg Chappell (Aus)	53.86	87	1970-84
6996	Don Bradman (Aus)	99.94	52	1928-48
6971	Leonard Hutton (Eng)	56.67	79	1937-55
6806	Ken Barrington (Eng)	58.67	82	1955-68
6545	Dilip Vengsarkar (Ind)	44.22	107	1976-90
6227	Rohan Kanhai (WI)	47.53	79	1957-74
6149	Neil Harvey (Aus)	48.41	79	1948-63
6080	Gundappa Viswanath (Ind)	41.93	91	1969-83
5807	Denis Compton (Eng)	50.06	78	1937-57
5711	Desmond Haynes (WI)	41.99	89	1978-90
5410	Jack Hobbs (Eng)	56.94	61	1908-30
5357	Doug Walters (Aus)	48.26	74	1965-81
5345	Ian Chappell (Aus)	42.42	75	1964-80
5234	Bill Lawry (Aus)	47.15	67	1961-71
5138	John Edrich (Eng)	43.54	77	1963-76
5119	Ian Botham (Eng)	34.35	97	1977-89
5062	Zaheer Abbas (Pak)	44.79	78	1969-85
4882	Tom Graveney (Eng)	44.38	79	1951-69

Sir Leonard Hutton at the Oval, 50 years after his record innings of 364 against Australia in 1938 **(All-Sport/Adrian Murrell)**

The easy grace of David Gower, at Lord's in 1989 when he scored his fifteenth Test century, his sixth against Australia **(All-Sport/Adrian Murrell)**

Runs	Name	Ave.	Tests	Years
4869	Bobby Simpson (Aus)	46.81	62	1957-78
4862	Graham Gooch (Eng)	37.11	75	1975-90
4737	Ian Redpath (Aus)	43.45	66	1964-76
4555	Herbert Sutcliffe (Eng)	60.73	54	1924-35
4537	Peter May (Eng)	46.77	66	1951-61
4502	Edward Dexter (Eng)	47.89	62	1958-68
4455	Everton Weekes (WI)	58.61	48	1948-58

Don Bradman at 99.94 has the highest average in Test cricket. In addition to those in the table above the following have averages of over 55 for more than 10 Tests:

Runs	Name	Ave.	Tests	Years
3798	Clyde Walcott (WI)	56.68	44	1948-60
2256	Graeme Pollock (SAf)	60.97	23	1963-70
2190	George Headley (WI)	60.83	22	1930-54
1618	Mark Taylor (Aus)	64.72	15	1989-90
1540	Edward Paynter (Eng)	59.23	20	1931-39
1072	Sidney Barnes (Aus)	63.05	13	1938-48
995	K.S.Duleepsinhji (Eng)	58.52	12	1929-31
990	Ernest Tyldesley (Eng)	55.00	14	1921-29
910	Charles Russell (Eng)	56.87	10	1920-23
723	Stewart Dempster (NZ)	65.72	10	1930-33

Fewest innings to reach:
1000 runs: 12 Herbert Sutcliffe, Everton Weekes
2000/3000/4000/5000/6000 runs:
           22/33/48/56/68 Don Bradman
7000 runs: 131 Walter Hammond
8000 runs: 157 Garfield Sobers
9000 runs: 192 Sunil Gavaskar
10000 runs: 212 Sunil Gavaskar

Most runs in a Test series

Runs	average		Tests	Season
974	139.14	Don Bradman (Aus)	5 v E	1930
905	113.12	Walter Hammond (Eng)	5 v A	1928-9
839	83.90	Mark Taylor (Aus)	6 v E	1989
834	92.66	Neil Harvey (Aus)	5 v SA	1952-3
829	118.42	Vivian Richards (WI)	4 v E	1976
827	82.70	Clyde Walcott (WI)	5 v A	1955
824	137.33	Garfield Sobers (WI)	5 v P	1958
810	90.00	Don Bradman (Aus)	5 v E	1936-7
806	201.50	Don Bradman (Aus)	5 v SA	1931-2

The most runs in a series of three Tests or less:

Runs	average		Tests	Season
583	194.33	Zaheer Abbas (Pak)	3 v I	1978
563	563.00	Walter Hammond (Eng)	2 v NZ	1933
558	111.60	Seymour Nurse (WI)	3 v NZ	1969

Most series scoring 500 runs
7 Don Bradman; 6 Sunil Gavaskar, Garfield Sobers
Most centuries in a Test series
5 Clyde Walcott (WI) v A 1955

Desmond Haynes, the most prolific century-maker in one-day internationals, batting for Middlesex in 1989, his first season in county cricket (All-Sport/Adrian Murrell)

TEST MATCH BOWLING

Nine wickets in an innings

10-53	Jim Laker (Eng)	v A	Manchester	30-31 Jul 1956
9-28	George Lohmann (Eng)	v SA	Johannesburg	3 Mar 1896
9-37	Jim Laker (Eng)	v A	Manchester	27-30 Jul 1956
9-52	Richard Hadlee (NZ)	v A	Brisbane	8-9 Nov 1985
9-56	Abdul Qadir (Pak)	v E	Lahore	25 Nov 1987
9-69	Jasubhai Patel (Ind)	v A	Kanpur	20 Dec 1959
9-83	Kapil Dev (Ind)	v WI	Ahmedabad	14-16 Nov 1983
9-86	Sarfraz Nawaz (Pak)	v A	Melbourne	14-15 Mar 1979
9-95	John Noreiga (WI)	v I	Port-of-Spain	7-9 Mar 1971
9-102	Subhash Gupte (Ind)	v WI	Kanpur	12 Dec 1958
9-103	Sydney Barnes (Eng)	v SA	Johannesburg	29-30 Dec 1913
9-113	Hugh Tayfield (SAf)	v E	Johannesburg	19-20 Feb 1957
9-121	Arthur Mailey (Aus)	v E	Melbourne	14-16 Feb 1921

Most wickets in a match

19-90	Jim Laker (Eng)	v A	Manchester	26-31 Jul 1956
17-159	Sydney Barnes (Eng)	v SA	Johannesburg	26-30 Dec 1913
16-136	Narendra Hirwani (Ind)	v WI	Madras	11-15 Jan 1988
16-137	Bob Massie (Aus)	v E	Lord's	22-26 Jun 1972

Both Hirwani (8-81 & 8-75) and Massie (8-84 and 8-53) achieved their feats on their Test début.

Five wickets in an innings most times in Tests

(No. of times ten wickets in match shown in brackets)

35 (9) Richard Hadlee (NZ)
27 (4) Ian Botham (Eng)
24 (7) Sydney Barnes (Eng)
23 (7) Dennis Lillee (Aus)
23 (6) Imran Khan (Pak)
22 (4) Malcolm Marshall (WI)
21 (7) Clarence Grimmett (Aus)
21 (2) Kapil Dev (Ind)
18 (2) Lance Gibbs (WI)
17 (6) Derek Underwood (Eng)
17 (3) Fred Trueman (Eng)
16 (3) Graham McKenzie (Aus)
16 (2) Bhagwant Chandrasekhar (I)
16 (1) Richie Benaud (Aus)
16 (-) Bob Willis (Eng)

Most wickets in a Test career

Wkts	Name	Ave.	Tests	Years
415	Richard Hadlee (NZ)	22.23	83	1973-90
376	Ian Botham (Eng)	28.27	97	1977-89
364	Kapil Dev (Ind)	29.54	106	1978-90
358	Imran Khan (Pak)	22.87	82	1971-90
355	Dennis Lillee (Aus)	23.92	70	1971-84
329	Malcolm Marshall (WI)	20.76	68	1978-90
325	Bob Willis (Eng)	25.20	90	1971-84
309	Lance Gibbs (WI)	29.09	79	1958-76
307	Fred Trueman (Eng)	21.57	67	1952-65
297	Derek Underwood (Eng)	25.83	86	1966-82
266	Bishen Bedi (Ind)	28.71	67	1966-79
259	Joel Garner (WI)	20.97	58	1977-87
252	Brian Statham (Eng)	24.84	70	1951-65

Richard Hadlee, the great New Zealand fast-medium bowler during the 1988 series against India when he passed Ian Botham's record tally of wickets in a Test career
(All-Sport/Simon Bruty)

Wkts	Name	Ave.	Tests	Years
249	Michael Holding (WI)	23.68	60	1975-87
248	Richie Benaud (Aus)	27.03	63	1952-64
246	Graham McKenzie (Aus)	29.78	60	1961-71
242	Bhagwant Chandrasekhar (Ind)			
		29.74	58	1964-79
236	Alec Bedser (Eng)	24.89	51	1946-55
235	Garfield Sobers (WI)	34.03	93	1954-74
230	Abdul Qadir (Pak)	32.42	63	1977-89
228	Ray Lindwall (Aus)	23.03	61	1946-60
216	Clarrie Grimmett (Aus)	24.21	37	1925-36
202	John Snow (Eng)	26.66	49	1965-76
202	Andy Roberts (WI)	25.61	47	1974-83
200	Jeff Thomson (Aus)	28.00	51	1972-85
193	Jim Laker (Eng)	21.24	46	1948-59
192	Wes Hall (WI)	26.38	48	1958-69
189	Sydney Barnes (Eng)	16.43	27	1901-14
189	Erapalli Prasanna (Ind)	30.38	49	1962-78
186	Alan Davidson (Aus)	20.53	44	1953-63
180	Geoff Lawson (Aus)	30.56	46	1980-89
177	Sarfraz Nawaz (Pak)	32.75	55	1969-84
174	Tony Lock (Eng)	25.58	49	1952-68
171	Iqbal Qasim (Pak)	28.11	50	1976-89
170	Keith Miller (Aus)	22.97	55	1946-56
170	Hugh Tayfield (SAf)	25.91	37	1949-60

Fewest Tests to reach:
100 wickets: 16 George Lohmann (Eng)
200 wickets: 35 Clarrie Grimmett (Aus)
300 wickets: 56 Dennis Lillee (Aus)
In his Test career Lohmann took 112 wickets 1886-96 at 10.75, the lowest average for any bowler taking 25 or more wickets in a Test career. At 34.11 balls per wicket he also has the best striking rate. The next best for both these categories: John Ferris (Eng/Aus) 61 wickets av.12.70, 36.9 balls/wkt; Michael Proctor (SAf) 41 wickets av.15.02, 37.7 balls/wkt.

Most wickets in a Test series

Wkts	Tests		Tests	Season
49	10.93	Sydney Barnes (Eng)	4 v SA	1913-4
46	9.60	Jim Laker (Eng)	5 v A	1956
44	14.59	Clarrie Grimmett (Aus)	5 v SA	1935-6
42	21.26	Terry Alderman (Aus)	6 v E	1981
41	12.85	Rodney Hogg (Aus)	6 v E	1978-9
41	17.36	Terry Alderman (Aus)	6 v E	1989
40	13.95	Imran Khan (Pak)	6 v I	1982-3

The most in a three Test series:

35	5.80	George Lohmann (Eng)	3 v SA	1896
34	8.29	Sydney Barnes (Eng)	3 v SA	1912
33	12.15	Richard Hadlee (NZ)	3 v A	1985

Most series taking 20 wickets
9 Fred Trueman, Dennis Lillee; 8 Malcolm Marshall, 7 Lance Gibbs, 6 Clarrie Grimmett, Alan Davidson, Jeff Thomson, Imran Khan.

Alan Knott, who not only took more dismissals in Tests than any other England wicket-keeper, but who also scored 4389 runs, averaging 32.75 (All-Sport/Adrian Murrell)

TEST MATCH WICKET-KEEPING
(ct – caught, st – stumped)

Most dismissals in an innings
7 (all ct) Wasim Bari, Pak v NZ, Auckland, 23 Feb 1979
7 (all ct) Bob Taylor Eng v I, Bombay, 15 Feb 1980

Most dismissals in a Test career

Dis		ct	st	Tests	Years
355	Rodney Marsh (Aus)	343	12	96	1970-84
269	Alan Knott (Eng)	250	19	95	1967-81
228	Wasim Bari (Pak)	201	27	81	1967-84
223	Jeffrey Dujon (WI)	218	5	68	1981-90
219	Godfrey Evans (Eng)	173	46	91	1946-59
198	Syed Kirmani (Ind)	160	38	88	1976-86
189	Deryck Murray (WI)	181	8	62	1963-80
187	Wally Grout (Aus)	163	24	51	1957-66
174	Bob Taylor (Eng)	167	7	57	1971-84
148	Ian Smith (NZ)	140	8	52	1980-90
141	John Waite (SAf)	124	17	50	1951-65
130	Bert Oldfield (Aus)	78	52	54	1920-37

Most dismissals in a Test series

Dis	ct	st		Tests	season
28	28	-	Rodney Marsh (Aus)	5 v E	1982-3
26	23	3	John Waite (SAf)	5 v NZ	1961-2
26	26	-	Rodney Marsh (Aus)	6 v WI	1975-6
24	22	2	Deryck Murray (WI)	5 v E	1963
24	24	-	Denis Lindsay (SAf)	5 v A	1966-7
24	21	3	Alan Knott (Eng)	6 v A	1970-1

The most in a three Test series

22	21	1	Amal Silva (Sri)	3 v I	1985

TEST MATCH CATCHES
(By fielders, not wicket-keepers)

Most catches in an innings
5 Victor Richardson Aus v SA, Durban, 3 Mar 1936
5 Yajurvindra Singh Ind v E, Bangalore, 29-30 Jan 1977
5 Mohammad Azharuddin Ind v I, Karachi, 15-16 Nov
  1989

Most catches in a Test career

Ct		Tests	Years
125	Allan Border (Aus)	115	1978-90
122	Greg Chappell (Aus)	87	1970-84
120	Colin Cowdrey (Eng)	114	1954-75
116	Vivian Richards (WI)	111	1974-90
112	Ian Botham (Eng)	97	1977-89
110	Bobby Simpson (Aus)	62	1957-78
110	Walter Hammond (Eng)	85	1927-47
109	Garfield Sobers (WI)	93	1954-74
108	Sunil Gavaskar (Ind)	125	1971-87
105	Ian Chappell (Aus)	75	1964-80
93	Gordon Greenidge (WI)	100	1974-90
90	Clive Lloyd (WI)	110	1966-85
87	Tony Greig (Eng)	58	1972-77
86*	Javed Miandad (Pak)	104	1976-90
83	Ian Redpath (Aus)	66	1964-76
80	Tom Graveney (Eng)	79	1951-69

* and 1 stumping

Most catches in a Test series

Ct	Tests	Tests	Season
15	Jack Gregory (Aus)	5 v E	1920-1
14	Greg Chappell (Aus)	6 v E	1974-5
13	Bobby Simpson (Aus)	5 v SA	1957-8
13	Bobby Simpson (Aus)	5 v WI	1960-1

The most in a three Test series

11	Tony Greig (Eng)	3 v P	1974

ALL-ROUNDERS

Best Test career records – over 2000 runs and 150 wickets: The final column is the ratio of batting average to bowling average, a good test of ability.

	Tests	Runs	Wkts	Catches	Ratio
Ian Botham (Eng)	97	5119	376	112	1.22
Garfield Sobers (WI)	93	8032	235	109	1.70
Kapil Dev (Ind)	106	4301	364	54	1.03

Imran Khan, who by his example and inspiration as captain unified the Pakistan Test team, has compiled an all-round Test record surpassed only by Gary Sobers
(All-Sport/Gray Mortimore)

Imran Khan (Pak)	82	3541	358	28	1.61
Richard Hadlee (NZ)	83	3017	415	37	1.22
Richie Benaud (Aus)	63	2201	248	65	0.90
Keith Miller (Aus)	55	2958	170	38	1.61
Vinoo Mankad (Ind)	44	2109	162	33	0.97

Others with ratios of 1.5 or more, and 1000 runs/50 wickets

Walter Hammond (Eng)	85	7249	83	110	1.55
Aubrey Faulkner (SAf)	25	1754	82	20	1.53

Fewest Tests to reach:
1000 runs 100 wickets: 21 Ian Botham, 23 Vinoo Mankad, 25 Kapil Dev
2000 runs 200 wickets: 42 Ian Botham, 50 Kapil Dev, Imran Khan
3000 runs 300 wickets: 71 Ian Botham, 75 Imran Khan, 83 Kapil Dev, Richard Hadlee

300 runs and 20 wickets in a Test series

Runs	Wkts	Name	v.	season
475	34	George Giffen (Aus)	5 v E	1894-5
399	34	Ian Botham (Eng)	6 v A	1981
329	30	Richie Benaud (Aus)	5 v SA	1957-8
545	29	Aubrey Faulkner (SAf)	5 v E	1909-10
430	24	Tony Greig (Eng)	5 v WI	1974
442	23	Jack Gregory (Aus)	5 v E	1920-1

Runs	Wkts	Name	v.	season
424	23	Garfield Sobers (WI)	5 v I	1962
318	22	Kapil Dev (Ind)	6 v E	1981-2
301	21	Richard Hadlee (NZ)	4 v E	1983
722	20	Garfield Sobers (WI)	5 v E	1966
439	20	Keith Miller (Aus)	5 v WI	1955
362	20	Keith Miller (Aus)	5 v WI	1951-2
322	20	Garfield Sobers (WI)	5 v E	1963

ONE-DAY INTERNATIONALS

The first ever one-day international match was played at Melbourne on 5 Jan 1971 when Australia beat England by 5 wickets. They have proliferated in recent years, especially in Australia.

WORLD CUP

The first World Cup was held in England in 1975, contested by the six Test playing nations plus Sri Lanka and East Africa at 60-over matches. This tournament was sponsored by the Prudential Assurance Company as were the next World Cup competitions held in England in 1979 and 1983. From 1979 the non-Test playing members of the International Cricket Conference (ICC) have played-off in England for the ICC Trophy and the right to enter the following World Cup tournament. The 1987 World Cup was held in India and Pakistan, where the matches were contested at 50 overs per innings.

World Cup Finals

Year	Venue	Result
1975	Lord's	West Indies (291-8) beat Australia (274) by 17 runs
1979	Lord's	West Indies (286-9) beat England (194) by 92 runs
1983	Lord's	India (183) beat West Indies (140) by 43 runs
1987	Calcutta	Australia (253-5) beat England (246-8) by 7 runs

World Cup Innings Records
Total: 360-4 West Indies v Sri Lanka at Karachi 13 Oct 1987
Lowest: 45 Canada v England at Manchester 14 Jun 1979
Individual: 181 Vivian Richards, West Indies v Sri Lanka at Karachi 13 Oct 1987
Best bowling: 7-51 Winston Davis, West Indies v Australia at Leeds 11-12 Jun 1983
Dismissals: 5 Syed Kirmani, India v Zimbabwe at Leicester 11 Jun 1983
Economical bowling: 1-6 in 12 overs Bishen Bedi, India v East Africa at Leicester 11 Jun 1975
Hat-trick: Chetan Sharma, India v New Zealand at Nagpur 31 Oct 1987

World Cup Career Records
Most runs: 1013 (av. 63.31) Vivian Richards (WI)
Most wickets: 27 (av. 14.96) Imran Khan (Pak)
Most dismissals: 22 (18 ct, 4 st) Wasim Bari (Pak)

ICC Trophy winners

1979 Sri Lanka
1982 Zimbabwe
1986 Zimbabwe
1990 Zimbabwe
Highest innings total: 455-9 off 60 overs Papua New Guinea v Gibraltar at Rugeley 18 Jun 1986.

Benson & Hedges World Series Cup

Contested annually since 1979-80 in Australia between the home country and two other teams. At 50 overs per innings.

Year	Winners	2nd	3rd
1980	West Indies	England	Australia
1981	Australia	New Zealand	India
1982	West Indies	Australia	Pakistan
1983	Australia	New Zealand	England
1984	West Indies	Australia	Pakistan
1985	West Indies	Australia	Sri Lanka
1986	Australia	India	New Zealand
1987	England	Australia	West Indies
1988	Australia	New Zealand	Sri Lanka
1989	West Indies	Australia	Pakistan
1990	Australia	Pakistan	Sri Lanka

ONE-DAY INTERNATIONAL RECORDS

Innings Records

Total: 360-4 West Indies v Sri Lanka at Karachi 13 Oct 1987
Lowest: 45 Canada v England at Manchester 14 Jun 1979
Lowest between Test nations: 55 Sri Lanka v West Indies at Sharjah 3 Dec 1986
Individual: 189* Vivian Richards, West Indies v England at Manchester 31 May 1984
Best bowling: 7-51 Winston Davis, West Indies v Australia at Leeds 11-12 Jun 1983

Career Records   to June 1990

Most runs		Ave.	100s	Games
6501	Vivian Richards (WI)	47.80	11	179
6471	Desmond Haynes (WI)	43.14	16	174
5610	Javed Miandad (Pak)	43.15	3	169
5263	Allan Border (Aus)	31.70	3	210
4981	Gordon Greenidge (WI)	46.55	11	120
3857	Dean Jones (Aus)	48.82	6	100
3795	Richie Richardson (WI)	35.80	3	126
3541	Krishnamachari Srikkanth (Ind)	29.02	4	126
3454	Dilip Vengsarkar (Ind)	34.54	1	127
3416	John Wright (NZ)	27.32	1	127
3253	Graham Gooch (Eng)	42.80	8	83
3246	Allan Lamb (Eng)	42.15	4	97
3147	Geoff Marsh (Aus)	38.85	7	87
3145	Salim Malik (Pak)	32.76	4	117
3092	Sunil Gavaskar (Ind)	35.13	1	108
3088	Ramiz Rama (Pak)	31.83	4	105
3082	Kapil Dev (Ind)	26.57	1	155
3041	Imran Khan (Pak)	32.35	1	149
3035	David Gower (Eng)	31.61	7	107

Most dismissals

		Ct	St	Games
188	Jeffrey Dujon (WI)	170	18	155
124	Rodney Marsh (Aus)	120	4	92
90	Salim Yousuf (Pak)	73	17	79
65	Ian Smith (NZ)	60	5	73

Most catches by fielder

		Games
99	Vivian Richards (WI)	179
94	Allan Border (Aus)	210

Most wickets

		Average	Games
181	Kapil Dev (Ind)	27.00	155
165	Imran Khan (Pak)	24.62	149
158	Richard Hadlee (NZ)	21.56	115
146	Joel Garner (WI)	18.84	98
142	Michael Holding (WI)	21.36	102
140	Ewen Chatfield (NZ)	25.86	114
137	Malcolm Marshall (WI)	24.91	113
131	Abdul Qadir (Pak)	25.49	100
130	Wasim Akram (Pak)	23.63	97
118	Ian Botham (Eng)	29.75	98
118	Vivian Richards (WI)	35.17	179

All-round *over 2000 runs and 100 wickets*

	Games	Runs	Wkts	Ct	Ratio
Kapil Dev (Ind)	155	3082	181	56	0.98
Imran Khan (Pak)	148	3041	165	33	1.31
Vivian Richards (WI)	179	6501	118	99	1.36
Mudassar Nazar (Pak)	122	2654	111	21	0.81
Ravi Shastri (Ind)	121	2335	111	33	0.81

Ratio is batting average to bowling average

Most consecutive matches: 81 Steve Waugh (Aus) every one played by Australia from his début on 9 Jan 1986 to 4 Jan 1990.

Steve Waugh was already an established one-day international player when he scored brilliant maiden Test centuries of 177 not out and 152 not out in the first two Tests against England in 1989 (All-Sport/Adrian Murrell)

FIRST-CLASS CRICKET

First-class matches are contested over three or more days. Such matches are now specified by the members of the ICC, but prior to 1947 when the term was first defined, there are doubts about the first-class status of many matches. The Association of Cricket Statisticians (ACS) has done much work in studying the problem and deciding about the status of such matches. They have drawn up lists of matches and, as a consequence, consistency can be achieved in statistical compilations. However there is still some disagreement about the status of various matches, and figures compiled as a result are sometimes at variance with traditional figures. We have respected tradition although incorporating corrections agreed by leading statisticians. First-class cricket is taken as having originated in 1815.

Abdul Qadir, keeping the leg-spinner's art alive (All-Sport/Adrian Murrell)

Team Records

Highest innings totals

1107   Victoria v New South Wales at Melbourne 27-28 Dec 1926
1059   Victoria v Tasmania at Melbourne 2-5 Feb 1923
951-7 dec Sind v Baluchistan at Karachi 18-20 Feb 1974
918   New South Wales v South Australia at Sydney 5-8 Jan 1901
912-8 dec Holkar v Mysore at Indore 2-4 Mar 1946
910-6 dec Railways v Dera Ismail Khan at Lahore 2-4 Dec 1964
903-7 dec England v Australia at The Oval 20-23 Aug 1938

Highest match aggregate
2376 runs Bombay (651 & 714-8 dec) beat Maharashtra (407 & 604) at Poona over 7 days on 5-11 Mar 1949.

Largest margin of victory
Innings & 851 runs Railways (910-6 dec) beat Dera Ismail Khan (32 & 27) at Lahore on 2-4 Dec 1964.

Lowest completed innings totals

12 Oxford University (batted one short) v MCC and Ground at Oxford 24 May 1877
12 Northamptonshire v Gloucestershire at Gloucester 11 Jun 1907
13 Auckland v Canterbury at Auckland 31 Dec 1877
13 Nottinghamshire v Yorkshire at Nottingham 20-21 Jun 1901
Lowest aggregate in a completed first-class match
105 runs Australians (41 & 12-1) beat MCC (33 & 19) at Lord's 27 May 1878.

Individual Records

BATTING

Highest innings (scores of over 400)

499   Hanif Mohammed   Karachi v Bahawalpur at Karachi 8-11 Jan 1959
452* Don Bradman   New South Wales v Queensland at Sydney 4-6 Jan 1930
443* Bhausahib Nimbalkar Maharashtra v Kathiawar at Poona 16-18 Dec 1948
437   Bill Ponsford   Victoria v Queensland at Melbourne 16-17 Dec 1927
429   Bill Ponsford   Victoria v Tasmania at Melbourne 3-5 Feb 1923
428   Aftab Baloch   Sind v Baluchistan at Karachi 18-20 Feb 1974
424   Archie McLaren   Lancashire v Somerset at Taunton 15-16 Jul 1895
405* Graeme Hick   Worcestershire v Somerset at Taunton 5-6 May 1988

Fastest scoring

Either minutes or balls received to reach the following scores:

Score	Mins	Balls	
50	8	13	Clive Inman, Leicestershire v Notts at Nottingham 20 Aug 1965
100	35	40-46	Percy Fender, Surrey v Northants at Northampton 26 Aug 1920
	35	54	Steven O'Shaughnessy, Lancashire v Leics at Manchester 13 Sep 1983
	43	34	David Hookes, South Australia v Victoria at Adelaide 25 Oct 1982
200	113	123	Ravi Shastri, Bombay v Baroda at Bombay 10 Jan 1985
	120	121	Clive Lloyd, West Indians v Glamorgan at Swansea 9 Aug 1976
	120	?	Gilbert Jessop, Gloucestershire v Sussex at Hove 1 Jun 1903
300	181	?	Denis Compton, MCC v N.E.Transvaal at Benoni 3-4 Dec 1948

Edwin Alletson scored 189 runs in 90 mins for Nottinghamshire v Sussex at Hove 20 May 1911, his final 142 runs being hit off 51 balls in 40 minutes. Gilbert Jessop scored 191 in 90 minutes (passing 150 in 63 mins) for the Gentlemen of the South v Players at Hastings 3 Sep 1907.

Six sixes from a six-ball over
Garfield Sobers (Notts) off Malcolm Nash (Glamorgan) at Swansea 31 Aug 1968
Ravi Shastri (Bombay) off Tilak Raj (Baroda) at Bombay on 10 Jan 1985
Playing in a Shell Trophy match for Wellington v Canterbury at Christchurch on 20 Feb 1990, in a deliberate attempt to give away runs Bert Vance bowled an over containing 22 balls, 17 of which were deliberate no-balls (the umpire losing count and declaring over one ball early!). From this over Lee German of Canterbury hit 70 runs, including eight sixes and five fours, Richard Petrie five runs including one four, and with two runs from no-balls off which no runs were hit, a total of 77 runs was conceded.

Most sixes in an innings
15 John Reid in an innings of 296 for Wellington v Northern Districts at Wellington 14-15 Jan 1963.

Most runs in a first-class career *and most 100s, 200s, 300s*
To the end of the 1989 English season. All English unless stated. The final column shows innings per century

Runs	Name	Average	Years	100s	200s	300s	Inns/100
61237*	Jack Hobbs	50.65	1905-34	197	16	1	6.7
58959	Frank Woolley	40.77	1906-38	145	9	1	10.6
57611	Patsy Hendren	50.80	1907-38	170	22	1	7.6
55061	Philip Mead	47.67	1905-36	153	13	-	8.8
54896*	W.G.Grace	39.55	1865-1908	126	13	3	11.8
50551	Walter Hammond	56.10	1920-51	167	36	4	6.0
50138*	Herbert Sutcliffe	51.95	1919-45	149	17	1	7.3
48426	Geoffrey Boycott	56.83	1962-86	151	10	1	6.7
47793	Tom Graveney	44.91	1948-72	122	7	-	10.0
43551	Tom Hayward	41.79	1893-1914	104	8	1	10.3
43423	Dennis Amiss	42.86	1960-87	102	3	-	11.2
42719	Colin Cowdrey	42.89	1950-76	107	3	2	10.6
41284	Andrew Sandham	44.82	1911-38	107	11	1	9.3
40140	Len Hutton	55.51	1934-60	129	11	1	6.3
39832	Mike Smith	41.84	1951-75	66	3	-	16.5
39802*	Wilfred Rhodes	30.83	1896-1930	58	3	-	26.3
39790	John Edrich	45.47	1956-78	103	4	1	9.5
39405	Bob Wyatt	40.04	1923-57	85	2	-	13.4
38942	Denis Compton	51.85	1936-64	123	9	1	6.8
38874	Ernest Tyldesley	45.46	1909-36	102	7	-	9.4
37897	Johnny Tyldesley	40.66	1895-1923	86	13	-	11.6
37665	Keith Fletcher	37.77	1962-88	63	2	-	18.5
37252	Jack (J.W.) Hearne	40.98	1909-36	96	11	-	10.7
37248	Leslie Ames	43.51	1926-51	102	9	-	9.0
37002	Don Kenyon	33.63	1946-67	74	7	-	15.7
36965	Bill Edrich	42.39	1934-58	86	9	-	11.2
36673	Jim Parks	34.76	1949-76	51	1	-	24.1
36440	David Denton	33.40	1894-1920	69	3	-	16.8
36323	George Hirst	34.13	1891-1929	60	4	1	20.2
36049	Alan Jones	32.89	1957-83	56	1	-	20.9
36012	Billy Quaife	35.38	1894-1928	72	4	-	16.7
35725	Roy Marshall	35.95	1945-72	68	3	-	15.5
35513	Gordon Greenidge (WI)	46.00	1971-89	86	11	-	9.8
35208	George Gunn	35.96	1902-32	62	1	-	17.1

Others with career averages over 50 and 20 000 runs, or 80 100s or 10 200s

Runs	Name	Average	Years	100s	200s	300s	Inns/100
34843	Zaheer Abbas (Pak)	51.54	1965-87	108	10	-	7.1
34346	Glenn Turner (NZ)	49.70	1964-83	103	10	1	7.7
33660	Maurice Leyland	40.50	1920-48	80	5	-	11.6
32429	Alvin Kallicharan (WI)	43.88	1966-89	87	6	-	9.5
31847	Joe Hardstaff Jnr	44.35	1930-55	83	10	-	9.8
31409	Vivian Richards (WI)	50.01	1971-89	102	9	1	6.6
30886	Charles Fry	50.22	1892-1921	94	16	-	7.0
30574	Percy Holmes	42.11	1913-35	67	12	2	12.1
30546	Reg Simpson	38.32	1944-63	64	10	-	13.3
28774	Rohan Kanhai (WI)	49.01	1955-82	83	7	-	8.1
28358	Barry Richards (SAf)	54.74	1964-83	80	6	1	7.2
28315	Garfield Sobers (WI)	54.87	1953-74	86	6	1	7.1
28067	Don Bradman (Aus)	95.14	1927-49	117	37	6	2.9
27592	Peter May	51.00	1948-63	85	5	-	7.3
26439	Arthur Shrewsbury	36.66	1875-1902	59	10	-	13.7
26409	Javed Miandad (Pak)	54.67	1973-89	76	11	1	7.5
25834	Sunil Gavaskar (Ind)	51.46	1966-87	81	10	1	7.0

24692	K.S.Ranjitsinhji (Ind)	56.37	1893-1920	72	14	-	6.9
24535	Greg Chappell (Aus)	52.20	1966-84	74	4	-	7.3
21699	Neil Harvey (Aus)	50.93	1946-63	67	7	-	6.9
21029	Bobby Simpson (Aus)	56.22	1952-78	60	12	2	7.3
20940	Graeme Pollock (SAf)	54.67	1960-87	64	5	-	6.8
20561	Allan Border (Aus)	52.99	1976-89	60	2	-	7.6

Others with career averages over 55 and 10000 runs, or a century more often than every six innnings

18635	Vijay Hazare (Ind)	57.87	1934-67	60	10	2	6.1
16890	Lindsay Hassett (Aus)	58.24	1932-54	59	8	-	5.5
13819	Bill Ponsford (Aus)	65.18	1920-35	47	13	4	5.0
13923	Martin Crowe (NZ)	56.82	1979-89	49	2	-	5.9
13392	Bill Woodfull (Aus)	65.00	1921-35	49	7	-	5.0
13248	Vijay Merchant (Ind)	71.22	1929-51	44	11	1	5.2
12762	Alan Kippax (Aus)	57.22	1918-36	43	7	1	6.0
12733	Graeme Hick	60.92	1983-89	46	5	1	5.1
12614	Arthur Morris (Aus)	53.67	1940-64	46	4	-	5.4
12010	Everton Weekes (WI)	55.34	1944-64	36	9	1	6.7
11820	Clyde Walcott (WI)	56.55	1941-64	40	4	1	5.9
9921	George Headley (WI)	69.80	1928-54	33	9	1	5.0

* *ACS figures which are at considerable variance:*
Hobbs 61760 runs (av.50.66), 199 100s; W.G.Grace 54211 runs av. 39.45,
124 centuries (11.9 inns per 100); Sutcliffe 50670 runs (av.52.02), 150 100s;
Rhodes 39969 runs (av.30.81).

Least innings to reach 100 centuries:
295 Don Bradman, 552 Denis Compton,
619 Len Hutton, 645 Geoffrey Boycott,
658 Zaheer Abbas, 658 Vivian Richards,
680 Walter Hammond, 700 Herbert Sutcliffe.
Most times scoring two centuries in a match
8 Zaheer Abbas (including 200 and 100 four times);
7 Walter Hammond; 6 Jack Hobbs, Glenn Turner;
5 Charles Fry.
Uniquely Arthur Fagg scored two double centuries in
a match, 244 and 202* Kent v Essex at Colchester
13-15 Jul 1938.
Most centuries in successive innings
6 Charles Fry for Sussex (5) and Rest of England 1901
6 Don Bradman for his XI and for South Australia (5)
    1938-9
6 Mike Proctor for Rhodesia 1970-1

Most runs in an English season

Runs		100s	Average	Year
3816	Denis Compton	18	90.85	1947
3539	Bill Edrich	12	80.43	1947
3518	Tom Hayward	13	66.37	1906
3429	Len Hutton	12	68.58	1949
3352	Frank Woolley	12	60.94	1928
3336	Herbert Sutcliffe	14	74.13	1932
3323	Walter Hammond	13	67.81	1933
3311	Patsy Hendren	13	70.44	1928
3309	Bobby Abel	7	55.15	1901
also 14 or more centuries				
3024	Jack Hobbs	16	70.32	1925
3011	Walter Hammond	15	75.27	1938
highest average				
2429	Don Bradman	13	115.66	1938
1538	Geoffrey Boycott	6	102.53	1979

*Qualified for England in 1991, Graeme Hick, formerly of
Zimbabwe, now of Worcestershire, is scoring hundreds at a rate
unsurpassed since Don Bradman's retirement*
(All-Sport/Ben Radford)

Most seasons scoring 3000 runs:
3 Herbert Sutcliffe 1928, 1931, 1932; Patsy Hendren 1923, 1928, 1933; Walter Hammond 1933, 1937, 1938.
Most seasons scoring 2000 runs:
17 Jack Hobbs; 15 Patsy Hendren, Herbert Sutcliffe; 13 Frank Woolley; 12 Walter Hammond; 11 James Langridge, Philip Mead; 10 Tom Hayward; 9 Bill Edrich, Len Hutton, Jack Robertson.
Most seasons (English or overseas) scoring 1000 runs:
28 W.G.Grace, Frank Woolley; 27 Colin Cowdrey, Philip Mead; 26 Geoffrey Boycott, Jack Hobbs; 25 Patsy Hendren; 24 Billy Quaife, Herbert Sutcliffe, Dennis Amiss; 23 Alan Jones.

Most sixes in a season: 80 Ian Botham 1985 (in 1530 runs, av. 69.54)

BOWLING

Best bowling
The taking of all ten wickets in an innings by a single bowler has been recorded more than 70 times in first-class cricket. Bowlers to have achieved this feat more than once are:
3 Alfred 'Tich' Freeman, Kent 1929, 1930, 1931
2 Vyell Walker, England 1859 and Middlesex 1865
2 W.G.Grace, MCC 1873, 1886
2 Hedley Verity, Yorkshire 1931, 1932
2 Jim Laker, Surrey and England 1956
The least expensive ten wickets analyses:
10-10 Hedley Verity, Yorkshire v Nottinghamshire at Leeds 12 Jul 1932
10-18 George Geary, Leicestershire v Glamorgan at Pontypridd 15 Aug 1929
10-20 Premansu Chatterjee, Bengal v Assam at Jorhat 28 Jan 1957
10-26 Bert Vogler, Eastern Province v Griqualand West at Johannesburg 28 Dec 1906
10-28 A.E.Moss, Canterbury v Wellington at Christchurch 27-28 Dec 1889 (on his first-class debut)
10-28 William Howell, Australians v Surrey at The Oval 15 May 1899
10-30 Colin Blythe, Kent v Northants at Northampton 1 Jun 1907
10-32 Henry Pickett, Essex v Leicestershire at Leyton 3 Jun 1895

Most wickets in a match: 19 (9-37, 10-53) Jim Laker, England v Australia 26-31 Jul 1956. 17 wickets in a match has been achieved on 18 occasions; the least expensive being for 48 runs by Colin Blythe, 10-30 and 7-18, Kent v Northants 1 Jun 1907.
Most successive wickets
The feat of taking four wickets with consecutive balls has been achieved on 27 occasions. The only man to do this twice has been Bob Crisp for Western Province in Currie Cup matches in 1931-2 and 1934. The most notable spell was by Pat Pocock for Surrey v Sussex at Eastbourne 15 Aug 1972; his records included five wickets in one over, six wickets in nine balls and seven in eleven.
Most hat-tricks (three wickets with consecutive balls): 7 Douglas Wright (Eng) 1937-49; 6 Charlie Parker (Eng) 1922-30, Tom Goddard (Eng) 1924-47.

Most wickets in a first-class career
All English unless stated. The final two columns show the number of occasions on which the bowler has taken 5 wickets in an innings and 10 wickets in a match.

Wkts	Name	Average	Years	5wi	10wm
4187*	Wilfred Rhodes	16.71	1898-1930	287	67
3776	Alfred 'Tich' Freeman	18.42	1914-36	386	140
3278	Charlie Parker	19.46	1903-35	277	91
3061	Jack (J.T.) Hearne	17.75	1888-1923	255	64
2979	Tom Goddard	19.84	1922-52	251	86
2876*	W.G.Grace	17.92	1865-1908	240	64
2874	Alex Kennedy	21.43	1907-36	225	45
2857	Derek Shackleton	18.65	1948-69	194	38
2844	Tony Lock	19.23	1946-71	196	50
2830	Fred Titmus	22.37	1949-82	168	26
2784	Maurice Tate	18.16	1912-37	195	44
2739*	George Hirst	18.72	1891-1929	184	40

2506	Colin Blythe	16.81	1899-1914	218	71
2431	Ewart Astill	23.76	1906-39	140	22
2420	Derek Underwood	20.12	1963-86	152	47
2356	Jack White	18.57	1909-37	193	58
2323	Eric Hollies	20.94	1932-57	182	40
2304	Fred Trueman	18.29	1949-69	126	25
2260	Brian Statham	18.36	1950-68	123	11
2233	Reg Perks	24.07	1930-55	143	24
2221	Johnny Briggs	15.93	1879-1900	200	52
2218	Don Shepherd	21.32	1950-72	123	28
2151	George Dennett	19.82	1903-26	211	57
2105	Tom Richardson	18.42	1892-1904	200	72

Others with career average below 15 and 1500 wickets, or more than 50 times taking 10 wickets in a match

2028	Alfred Shaw	12.12	1864-97	177	44
1956	Hedley Verity	14.90	1930-39	164	54
1841	George Lohmann	13.74	1884-98	176	57
1681	James Southerton	14.46	1854-79	192	59
1673	Arthur Mold	15.54	1889-1901	152	56
1571	Tom Emmett	13.56	1866-88	121	29

The best non-English players

1674	Albert Trott (Aus)	21.09	1893-1911	131	41
1571	Intikhab Alam (Pak)	27.67	1957-82	85	13
1560	Bishen Bedi (Ind)	21.69	1961-82	106	20
1424	Clarrie Grimmett (Aus)	22.28	1911-41	127	33
1417	Mike Proctor (SAf)	19.53	1965-89	70	15

* ACS figures: Rhodes 4204 wickets (av.16.72), W.G.Grace 2808 (av 18.15), Hirst 2742 (av.18.73)

Least matches to reach 1000 wickets:
134 Tom Richardson 1892-6, 147 George Dennett 1903-9, 149 Arthur Mold 1899-1905, 156 Jack (J.T.) Hearne 1888-96, 159 George Lohmann 1884-8.

Least matches to reach 2000 wickets:
327 Tom Richardson 1892-1903, 347 Jack (J.T.) Hearne 1888-1902, 349 George Dennett 1903-24, 350 Colin Blythe 1899-1912, 350 'Tich' Freeman 1914-29.

Most wickets in an English season

Wickets		Average	Year
304	Alfred 'Tich' Freeman	18.05	1928
298	Alfred 'Tich' Freeman	15.26	1933
290	Tom Richardson	14.37	1895
283	Charlie Turner	11.68	1888
276	Alfred 'Tich' Freeman	15.60	1931
275	Alfred 'Tich' Freeman	16.84	1930
273	Tom Richardson	14.45	1897

200 wickets in a season most often: 8 'Tich' Freeman, 5 Charlie Parker, 4 Tom Goddard, 3 Jack (J.T.) Hearne, George Lohmann, Wilfred Rhodes, Tom Richardson, Maurice Tate, Hedley Verity.
100 wickets in a season most often 23 Wilfred Rhodes, 20 Derek Shackleton, 17 'Tich' Freeman, 16 Tom Goddard, Charlie Parker, Reg Perks, Fred Titmus; 15 Jack (J.T.) Hearne, George Hirst, Alex Kennedy.
The best average while taking at least 100 wickets in a season: 8.54 Alfred Shaw, 186 wkts in 1880.

ALL-ROUNDERS
Best Career Figures
Determined by the best ratios of batting average divided by bowling average (the figure in the first column), for those with at least 10000 runs and 1000 wickets:

	Ratio	Runs	Ave.	Wkts	Ave.	Years
W.G.Grace (Eng)	2.21	54896	39.55	2876	17.92	1865-1908
Frank Tarrant (Aus)	2.06	17857	36.36	1489	17.66	1898-1936
Frank Woolley (Eng)	2.05	58959	40.77	2068	19.85	1906-38
Garfield Sobers (WI)	1.98	28315	54.87	1043	27.74	1953-74

	Ratio	Runs	Ave.	Wkts	Ave.	Years
Wilfred Rhodes (Eng)	1.85	39802	30.83	4187	16.71	1895-1930
Mike Proctor (SAf)	1.84	21936	36.01	1417	19.53	1965-89
George Hirst (Eng)	1.82	36272	34.12	2742	18.73	1891-1929
Jack (J.W.) Hearne (Eng)	1.68	37252	40.98	1839	24.43	1909-36
Imran Khan (Pak)	1.65	16881	36.22	1266	22.00	1969-89
Other with 25000 runs and 2000 wickets:						
Trevor Bailey (Eng)	1.44	28642	33.42	2082	23.13	1945-67

Best season's figures in England

	Ratio	Runs	Ave.	Wkts	Ave.	Years
2000 runs and 150 wickets in a season						
George Hirst	2.78	2385	45.86	208	16.50	1906
Frank Woolley	2.66	2101	42.87	167	16.14	1921
Frank Woolley	2.50	2022	45.95	163	18.37	1922
3000 runs and 100 wickets in a season						
James Parks	1.97	3003	50.89	101	25.83	1937
Ratios of over 3.00 for 1000 runs and 100 wickets						
W.G.Grace	4.09	1664	52.00	140	12.71	1875
Richard Hadlee (NZ)	3.65	1179	51.26	117	14.05	1981
W.G.Grace	3.30	2622	62.42	130	18.90	1876
Wilfred Rhodes	3.26	1511	39.76	119	12.19	1922
George Hirst	3.16	1844	47.28	128	14.94	1903
W.G.Grace	3.11	1474	39.83	179	12.81	1877
Jack (J.W.) Hearne	3.09	2148	55.07	142	17.83	1920

Best match: George Giffen (Aus) scored 271 and took 9-96 and 7-70, South Australia v Victoria 7-11 Nov 1891.

WICKET-KEEPING DISMISSALS   (ct - caught, st - stumped)

Most dismissals in an innings
8 (all ct) Wally Grout, Queensland v Western Australia at Brisbane 15 Feb 1960
8 (all ct) David East, Essex v Somerset at Taunton 27 Jul 1985
Most stumpings in an innings
6 Hugo Yarnold, Worcestershire v Scotland at Broughty Ferry 2 Jul 1951
Most dismissals in a match
12 (8ct, 4st) Edward Pooley, Surrey v Sussex at The Oval 6-7 Jul 1868
12 (9ct, 3st) Don Tallon, Queensland v New South Wales at Sydney 2-4 Jan 1939
12 (9ct, 3st) Brian Taber, New South Wales v South Australia at Adelaide 13-17 Dec 1968

Most dismissals in a first-class career
All English

Dis	ct	st	Name	Per match	Career
1649	1473	176	Bob Taylor	2.6	1960-88
1527	1270	257	John Murray	2.4	1952-75
1496	1242	254	Herbert Strudwick	2.2	1902-27
1344	1211	133	Alan Knott	2.6	1965-85
1310	933	377	Frederick Huish	2.6	1895-1914
1294	1081	213	Brian Taylor	2.3	1949-73
1263	913	350	David Hunter	2.3	1889-1909
1228	953	275	Harry Butt	2.3	1890-1912
1207	852	355	Jack Board	2.3	1891-1915
1206	904	302	Harry Elliott	2.3	1920-47
1181	1088	93	Jim Parks	1.6	1949-76
1126	949	177	Roy Booth	2.4	1951-70
1121	703	418	Les Ames	1.9	1926-51
1095	754	341	George Duckworth	2.2	1923-47
1086	948	138	David Bairstow	2.4	1970-89
1082	748	334	Harold Stephenson	2.3	1948-64

Dis	ct	st	Name	Per match	Career
1071	895	176	Jimmy Binks	2.1	1955-69
1066	816	250	Godfrey Evans	2.3	1939-69
Best non-English					
869	804	65	Rodney Marsh (Aus)	3.4	1968-84
849	741	108	Deryck Murray (WI)	2.3	1961-80
824	703	121	Farokh Engineer (Ind)	2.5	1958-76
812	667	145	Wasim Bari (Pak)	2.9	1964-83
Over 350 dismissals and 3 per match					
587	473	114	Wally Grout (Aus)	3.2	1946-66
492	447	45	Ray Jennings (SAf)	3.9	1973-89
395	345	50	Brian Taber (Aus)	3.1	1964-74
385	354	31	John Maclean (Aus)	3.6	1968-79
369	292	77	Gil Langley (Aus)	3.0	1945-57

Most dismissals in an English season

Dis	ct	st	Name	Year
127	79	48	Leslie Ames	1929
122	70	52	Leslie Ames	1928
110	62	48	Hugo Yarnold	1949
107	77	30	George Duckworth	1928
107	96	11	Jimmy Binks	1960
104	40	64	Leslie Ames	1932
104	82	22	John Murray	1957
102	70	32	Frederick Huish	1913
102	95	7	John Murray	1960

CATCHES BY FIELDERS
Most catches in an innings: 7 Micky Stewart, Surrey v Northants at Northampton 7 Jun 1957, Tony Brown, Gloucestershire v Notts at Nottingham 26 Jul 1966
Most catches in a match
10 (4 & 6) Walter Hammond, Gloucestershire v Surrey at Cheltenham 16-17 Aug 1928

Most catches in a first-class career All English unless stated

Catches	Name	Per match	Career
1018	Frank Woolley	1.04	1906-38
887	W.G.Grace (874 ACS)	1.00	1865-1908
831	Tony Lock	1.27	1946-71
819	Walter Hammond	1.29	1920-51
813	Brian Close	1.04	1949-86
784	John Langridge	1.37	1928-55
764	Wilfred Rhodes	0.61	1896-1930
758	Arthur Milton	1.22	1948-74
754	Patsy Hendren	0.91	1907-38
697	Peter Walker	1.49	1956-72
695	John Tunnicliffe	1.40	1891-1907
675	James Seymour	1.22	1900-26
671	Philip Mead	0.82	1905-36
644	Keith Fletcher	0.88	1962-88
638	Colin Cowdrey	0.92	1950-76
634	Micky Stewart	1.19	1954-72

Highest averages per match of those taking 300 or more:

602	Graham Roope	1.50	1964-86
383	Bobby Simpson (Aus)	1.49	1952-78
328	Hugh Trumble (Aus)	1.54	1887-1904

Most catches in an English season

78	Walter Hammond	1928
77	Micky Stewart	1957
73	Peter Walker	1961
71	Philip Sharpe	1962
70	John Tunnicliffe	1901

COUNTY CHAMPIONSHIP
The first recorded inter-county match was contested in 1709 between Kent and Surrey, and the first county to be acclaimed as champions were Sussex in 1827. Such references became more frequent from 1864, the year in which overarm bowling was legalised, but it was not until the 1890 season that the County Championship was officially recognised and a points system introduced.

From 1827 to 1862 the Southern counties of Kent, Surrey and Sussex generally proved the best, with an occasional challenge from Nottinghamshire. From 1864, when eight counties took part in inter-county matches, to 1889 the following champion counties were proclaimed, principally on the basis of fewest matches lost (* shared):

Surrey	1864, 1887-8, 1889*
Gloucestershire	1873*, 1874, 1876-7
Nottinghamshire	1865, 1868, 1869*, 1871-2, 1873*, 1875, 1879*, 1880, 1882*, 1883-6, 1889*
Middlesex	1866
Yorkshire	1867, 1869*, 1870
Lancashire	1879*, 1881, 1882*, 1889*

Undecided in 1878

COUNTY CHAMPIONS FROM 1890
The Championship was sponsored by Schweppes in 1977-83 and by Britannic Assurance from 1984. *Wins:*

30*	Yorkshire	1893, 1896, 1898, 1900-2, 1905, 1908, 1912, 1919, 1922-5, 1931-3, 1935, 1937-9, 1946, 1949*, 1959-60, 1962-3, 1966-8
16*	Surrey	1890-2, 1894-5, 1899, 1914, 1950*, 1952-8, 1971
10#	Middlesex	1903, 1920-1, 1947, 1949*, 1976, 1977*, 1980, 1982, 1985
8*	Lancashire	1897, 1904, 1926-8, 1930, 1934, 1950*
7*	Kent	1906, 1909-10, 1913, 1970, 1977*, 1978
5	Worcestershire	1964-5, 1974, 1988-9
4	Essex	1979, 1983-4, 1986
4	Nottinghamshire	1907, 1929, 1981, 1987
3	Warwickshire	1911, 1951, 1972
2	Glamorgan	1948, 1969
2	Hampshire	1961, 1973
1	Derbyshire	1936
1	Leicestershire	1975

* *including 1 tie, # including two ties*
Most appearances: 763 Wilfred Rhodes (Yorkshire) 1898-1930, 707 Frank Woolley (Kent) 1906-38.

GILLETTE CUP / NATWEST BANK TROPHY

Introduced as the Gillette Cup in 1963 as a one-day knock-out event contested by the first-class counties over one innings per side of 65 overs (60 overs from 1964). From 1981 it has been contested for the NatWest Bank Trophy, and Ireland, Scotland and the leading minor counties also take part. *Wins:*

4 Lancashire	1970-2, 1975
4 Sussex	1963-4, 1978, 1986
4 Middlesex	1977, 1980, 1984, 1988
3 Warwickshire	1966, 1968, 1989
2 Yorkshire	1965, 1969
2 Kent	1967, 1974
2 Somerset	1979, 1983
1 Gloucestershire	1973
1 Northamptonshire	1976
1 Derbyshire	1981
1 Surrey	1982
1 Essex	1985
1 Nottinghamshire	1987

Team Records (all 60 overs per innings)
Highest innings: 413-4 Somerset v Devon at Torquay 27 Jun 1990
Highest in final: 317-4 Yorkshire v Surrey at Lord's 4 Sep 1965
Lowest completed innings: 39 Ireland v Sussex at Hove 3 Jul 1985
Largest runs margin: 244 Sussex (283-6) beat Ireland (39) at Hove 3 Jul 1985

Individual Innings Records
Highest innings: 206 Alvin Kallicharan, Warwickshire v Oxfordshire at Birmingham 4 Jul 1984
Best bowling: 8-21 Michael Holding, Derbyshire v Sussex at Hove 22 June 1988
Most economical bowling: 1-3 in 12 overs Jack Simmons, Lancashire v Suffolk at Bury St Edmunds 3 Jul 1985
Most dismissals: 6 (5ct 1st) Bob Taylor, Derbyshire v Essex at Derby 19 Aug 1981; 6 (4ct 2st) Terry Davies, Glamorgan v Staffordshire at Stone 25 Jun 1986

Individual Career Records 1963-89
Most runs: 1950 Dennis Amiss (Warwicks) 1963-87, 1920 Clive Lloyd (Lancs) 1969-86, 1573 Clive Radley (Middx) 1965-87, 1573 Graham Gooch (Essex) 1973-89
Most wickets: 81 Geoff Arnold (Surrey/Sussex) 1963-80, 79 Jack Simmons (Lancs) 1970-89, 78 Peter Lever (Lancs) 1963-76, 77 Derek Underwood (Kent) 1963-87
Most dismissals: 66 Bob Taylor (Derby) 1963-84, 65 Alan Knott (Kent) 1965-85, 57 Arnold Long (Surrey/Sussex) 1963-80

BENSON & HEDGES CUP

A one-day competition played at 55 overs per innings, and contested by 20 teams, the 17 first-class counties and teams representing the Minor Counties, Scotland and the Combined Universities. Played on a zonal basis of four groups of five and then by knock-out. *Wins:*

3 Kent	1973, 1976, 1978
3 Leicestershire	1972, 1975, 1985
2 Somerset	1981-2
2 Middlesex	1983, 1986

1 Surrey 1974, Gloucestershire 1977, Essex 1979, Northamptonshire 1980, Lancashire 1984, Yorkshire 1987, Hampshire 1988, Nottinghamshire 1989

Team Records
Highest innings: 352-6 Lancashire v Hampshire at Old Trafford 9 May 1990 (match abandoned)
Lowest completed innings: 56 Leicestershire v Minor Counties at Wellington 22 May 1982

Individual Innings Records
Highest innings: 198* Graham Gooch, Essex v Sussex at Hove 25 May 1982
Best bowling: 7-12 Wayne Daniel, Middlesex v Minor Counties (East) at Ipswich 22 Apr 1978
Most economical bowling: 1-3 in 11 overs Chris Old, Yorkshire v Middlesex at Lord's 6 Jun 1979
Most dismissals: 8 (all ct) Derek Taylor, Somerset v Combined Universities at Taunton 8 May 1982

Individual Career Records 1972-89
Most runs: 3669 Graham Gooch (Essex) 1973-89, 2363 Derek Randall (Notts) 1972-89, 2315 Alvin Kallicharan (Warwicks)
Most wickets: 149 John Lever (Essex) 1972-89, 112 Ian Botham (Somerset, Worcs), 107 Stuart Turner (Essex, Minor C) 1972-88, 107 Derek Underwood (Kent) 1972-87
Most dismissals: 121 David Bairstow (Yorks) 1972-89, 88 Alan Knott (Kent) 1972-85, 77 Bob Taylor (Derby) 1972-84

SUNDAY LEAGUE

Introduced in 1969 and played on Sundays by the first-class counties in matches of 40 overs per innings. John Player League 1969-86, Refuge Assurance League from 1987. *Wins:*

3 Kent	1972-3, 1976
3 Essex	1981, 1984-5
3 Hampshire	1975, 1978, 1986
3 Worcestershire	1971, 1987-8
3 Lancashire	1969-70, 1989
2 Leicestershire	1974, 1977

1 Somerset 1979, Warwickshire 1980. Sussex 1982, Yorkshire 1983

Refuge Assurance Cup
From 1988 the first four teams in the Refuge Assurance League met in semi-finals, and then a final for this new competition. *Winners:* 1988 Lancashire, 1989 Essex

Team Records
Highest innings: 310-5 Essex v Glamorgan at Southend 17 Jul 1983
Lowest completed innings: 23 Middlesex v Yorkshire at

Leeds 23 Jun 1974
Largest runs margin: 190 runs Kent (257-7) beat Northants (67) at Brackley 22 Jul 1973

Individual Innings Records

Highest innings: 176 Graham Gooch, Essex v Glamorgan at Southend 17 Jul 1983
Best bowling: 8-26 Keith Boyce, Essex v Lancashire at Manchester 30 May 1971; 4 wickets in 4 balls Alan Ward, Derbyshire v Sussex, Derby 7 Jun 1970
Most economical bowling: 0-0 in 8 overs Brian Langford, Somerset v Essex at Yeovil 27 Jul 1969
Most dismissals: 7 (6 ct, 1 st) Bob Taylor, Derbyshire v Lancashire at Manchester 4 May 1975

Season's Records

Most runs: 818 (av.58.14) Clive Rice (Notts) 1977
Most wickets: 34 (av.13.17) Bob Clapp (Somerset) 1974, Clive Rice (Notts) 1986
Most dismissals: 29 (26 ct 3 st) Steven Rhodes (Worcs) 1987

Individual Career Records 1969-88

Most runs: 7040 Dennis Amiss (Warwicks) 1969-87, 6650 Clive Radley (Middlesex) 1969-87, 6639 David Turner (Hants) 1969-89, 6348 Gordon Greenidge (Hants) 1970-87, 6265 Clive Rice (Notts) 1975-87, 6144 Glenn Turner (Worcs) 1969-82, 6094 Peter Willey (Northants, Leics) 1969-89
Most wickets: 386 John Lever (Essex) 1969-89, 346 Derek Underwood (Kent) 1969-87, 307 Jack Simmons (Lancs) 1969-89, 303 Stuart Turner (Essex) 1969-86, 284 Norman Gifford (Worcs/Warwicks) 1969-88, 267 John Shepherd (Kent/Glos) 1969-87
Most dismissals: 252 David Bairstow (Yorkshire) 1970-89, 236 Bob Taylor (Derby) 1969-84, 223 Eifion Jones (Glamorgan) 1969-83, 218 Alan Knott (Kent) 1969-85

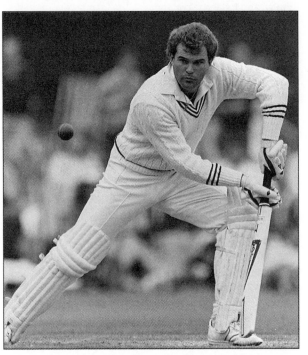

Martin Crowe has played a major rôle in establishing New Zealand as a force to be reckoned with in Test cricket
(All-Sport/Adrian Murrell)

FIRST-CLASS COUNTIES

Placings in the first three in the County Championship 1890-1989 and John Player League/Refuge Assurance League (JPL/RA) 1969-89, and wins (W), runners-up (RU) or losing semi-finalists (SF) in the Gillette Cup/Nat West Bank Trophy (GC/NW) 1963-89 and Benson & Hedges Cup (B&H) 1972-89. The final column shows the year in which the counties first took part in the Championship or in its preceding inter-county matches from 1864.

County	COUNTY CHAMPS			GC/NW			B&H			JPL/RA			First
	1st	2nd	3rd	W	RU	SF	W	RU	SF	1st	2nd	3rd	Year
Derbyshire	1	1	3	1	1	1	-	2	1	-	-	1	1871
Essex	4	2	2	1	-	2	1	4	2	3	4'	3	1895
Glamorgan	2	2	2	-	1	-	-	-	1	-	-	-	1921
Gloucestershire	-	6	7	1	-	3	1	-	1	-	1	1	1870
Hampshire	2	3	4	-	-	7	1	-	2	3	1	2	1864
Kent	7'	8	9"	2	3	1	3	2	5	3	2	3	1864
Lancashire	8'	13'	10'	4	3	5	1	-	4	3	-	2	1865
Leicestershire	1	1	3'	-	-	2	3	1	1	2	1	2	1895
Middlesex	10"	11	13	4	2	6	2	1	2	-	1	2	1864
Northamptonshire	-	4	3	1	3	2	1	1	1	-	-	-	1905
Nottinghamshire	4	5	4	1	1	1	1	1	2	-	2	1	1864
Somerset	-	-	5	2	2	4	2	-	3	1	6'	-	1882
Surrey	16'	7	11	1	2	4	1	2	2	-	-	-	1864
Sussex	-	7	2'	4	3	4	-	-	1	1	1	1	1864
Warwickshire	3	2	1	3	3	4	-	1	4	1	-	1	1895
Worcestershire	5	4'	1	-	3	6	-	2	2	3	2	1	1899
Yorkshire	30'	13"	11'	2	-	2	1	1	2	1	1	-	1864

' Including one tie for place, " including two ties for place

CRICKET IN AUSTRALIA

Most Runs in an Australian Season

Runs	Player	Average	Season
1690	Don Bradman (NSW)	93.88	1928-9
1659	Neil Harvey (Vic)	63.80	1952-3
1586	Don Bradman (NSW)	113.28	1929-30
1553	Walter Hammond (Eng)	91.35	1928-9
1552	Don Bradman (SA)	86.22	1936-7

Don Bradman exceeded 1000 runs in a record 12 Australian seasons

Most Wickets in an Australian Season

Wkts	Player	Average	Season
106	Charlie Turner (NSA)	13.59	1887-8
93	George Giffen (SA) *	22.54	1894-5
82	Clarrie Grimmett (SA)	23.69	1929-30
82	Richie Benaud (NSW)	19.25	1958-9
81	Arthur Mailey (NSW)	22.53	1920-1

* George Giffen also scored 902 runs (av.50.11) in 1894-5 for the best ever all-round figures.

Most Dismissals in an Australian Season: 67 (63ct 4 st) Rodney Marsh 1975-6.

Sheffield Shield

The annual first-class inter-state competition has been contested for the shield, purchased with money donated by the 3rd Earl of Sheffield, from 1891-2. The original three states were joined by Queensland in 1926-7, Western Australia 1947-8 and Tasmania 1977-8. From 1983 the Shield winner has been determined by a final between the top two teams. *Winners: year shown is that of second half of the season*

40 New South Wales	1896-7, 1900, 1902-7, 1909, 1911-2, 1914, 1920-1, 1923, 1926, 1929, 1932-3, 1938, 1940, 1949-50, 1952, 1954-62, 1965-6, 1983, 1985-6, 1990
24 Victoria	1893, 1895, 1898-9, 1901, 1908, 1915, 1922, 1924-5, 1928, 1930-1, 1934-5, 1937, 1947, 1951, 1963, 1967, 1970, 1974, 1979-80
12 South Australia	1894, 1910, 1913, 1927, 1936, 1939, 1953, 1964, 1969, 1971, 1976, 1982
10 Western Australia	1948, 1968, 1972-3, 1975, 1977-8, 1981, 1984, 1987-9

Limited Overs Competitions

The Australian states currently contest a knock-out competition for the FAI Insurance Cup at matches of 50 overs per innings. Prior to FAI, sponsors were V&G two years from 1969/70, Coca-Cola two years from 1971/2, Gillette six years from 1973/4, McDonald's nine years from 1978/9. New Zealand also took part in the first six years. *Winners: (year shown is second half of the season):*

7 Western Australia	1971, 1974, 1977-8, 1983, 1986, 1990
4 Queensland	1976, 1981-2, 1989
3 New Zealand	1970, 1973, 1975
2 Victoria	1972, 1980
2 South Australia	1984, 1987
2 New South Wales	1985, 1988
1 Tasmania	1979

Innings records

Highest team score: 325-6 S.Australia v Tasmania in final at Hobart 15 Mar 1987
Highest individual innings: 164 Rick McCosker, NSW v S.Australia at Sydney 3 Dec 1981
Best bowling: 6-18 Jeff Thomson, Queensland v S.Australia at Brisbane 28 Oct 1978
Most economical bowling: 1-8 in 10 overs Graham Porter, W.Australia v Victoria at Perth 10 Oct 1986
Most dismissals: 6 (6 ct) Ken Wadsworth, New Zealand v NSW at Sydney 30 Dec 1969

INDIA

Most runs in a season: 1604 (av.64.16) Chandu Borde 1964-5. Vijay Hazare scored 1423 runs in 1943-4 at an average of 177.87, the highest ever recorded for 1000 runs in a season.
Most wickets in a season: 88 (av.15.02) Bishen Bedi 1974-5 and 88 (av.19.30) Bishen Bedi 1976-7.
Most dismissals in a season: 43 (32ct 11st) Farokh Engineer 1964-5
In the Indian sub-continent (India, Pakistan, Sri Lanka and Burma):
Most runs in a season: 2121 (av.88.37), including a record 10 centuries, Sunil Gavaskar (Ind) 1978-9
Most wickets in a season: 116 (av.13.78) Maurice Tate (Eng) 1926-7

Ranji Trophy

The annual Indian first-class inter-state competition was instituted in 1934 in memory of K.S.Ranjitsinhji. It is contested on a zonal basis, culminating in a knock-out competition. *Winners: year given is that of the second half of the season*

30 Bombay	1935-6, 1942, 1945, 1949, 1952, 1954, 1956-7, 1959-73, 1975-7, 1981, 1984-5
5 Delhi	1979-80, 1982, 1986, 1989
4 Baroda	1943, 1947, 1950, 1958
4 Holkar	1946, 1948, 1951, 1953
3 Karnatka	1974, 1978, 1983
2 Maharashtra	1940-1
2 Hyderabad	1938, 1987
2 Bengal	1939, 1990
1 Nawanagar	1937, Western India 1944, Madras 1955, Tamil Nadu 1988

NEW ZEALAND

Most runs in season: 1676 (av.93.11) Martin Crowe 1986-7
Most wickets in season: 66 (av.16.48) Stephen Boock 1977-8

Most dismissals in season: 41 (31ct 10st) Ervin McSweeney 1984-5

Plunket Shield

This first-class competition was run on a challenge basis from 1906 to 1921, and then annually on a league basis from 1921-2 to 1974-5. The Shield was presented by Lord Plunket, Governor-General of New Zealand.
Challenge holders: 1906-7 Canterbury, 1907-11 Auckland, 1911-2 Canterbury, 1912-3 Auckland, 1913-8 Canterbury, 1918-9 Wellington, 1919-20 Canterbury, 1920-1 Auckland, 1921 Wellington.

League wins: *year given is that of second half of the season*

14 Wellington	1924, 1926, 1928, 1930, 1932, 1936, 1950, 1955, 1957, 1961-2, 1966, 1973-4
12 Auckland	1922, 1927, 1929, 1934, 1937-40, 1947, 1959, 1964, 1969
9 Canterbury	1923, 1931, 1935, 1946, 1949, 1952, 1956, 1960, 1965,
9 Otago	1925, 1933, 1948, 1951, 1953, 1958, 1970, 1972, 1975
4 Central Districts	1954, 1967-8, 1971
1 Northern Districts	1963

Shell Series

From 1975-6 the first-class provincial competition has been sponsored by Shell. In the first four years the Shell Cup was awarded to the League winners and the Shell Trophy to winners of a knock-out competition. From 1979-80 the Shell Trophy has been won by the league winners, and the Shell Cup by the winners of the limited-overs competition.
Cup winners 1976-9: 1976 Canterbury, 1977 Northern Districts, 1978 Canterbury, 1979 Otago.
Trophy winners:

4 Otago	1977, 1979, 1986, 1988
4 Wellington	1982, 1983, 1985, 1990
3 Auckland	1978, 1981, 1989
2 Canterbury	1976, 1984
1 Northern Districts 1980, Central Districts 1987	

Limited Overs Competition

Now contested for the Shell Cup, but previously sponsored by the NZ Motor Corporation, 1971-7 and Gillette 1977-9.
Winners:

7 Auckland	1973, 1979, 1981, 1983-4, 1987, 1990
5 Canterbury	1972, 1976-8, 1986
4 Wellington	1974-5, 1982, 1989
1 Northern Districts 1980, Central Districts 1985, Otago 1988	

PAKISTAN

Most runs in season: 1649 (av.63.42) Saadat Ali 1983-4
Most wickets in season: 107 (av.16.06) Ijaz Faqih 1985-6
Most dismissals in season: 70 (62ct 8st) Ashraf Ali 1986-7

Quaid-e-Azam Trophy

Pakistan's annual national first-class championship is named after Mohammad Ali Jinnah, who was known as Quaid-e-Azam, or 'Great Leader'. From its inception in 1953-4 to 1979-80 it was organised by a zonal basis culminating in a knock-out stage, but it is now run on a league system. *Winners: year given is that of second half of the season*

6 Karachi	1955, 1959-60, 1963 (Karachi A), 1968, 1986
5 National Bank	1976, 1979, 1982, 1984, 1987
4 Karachi Blues	1962, 1964, 1966, 1971
4 United Bank	1977, 1981, 1983, 1985
3 PIA	1970, 1980, 1990
2 Bahawalpur	1954, 1958
2 Punjab	1957, 1975 (Punjab A)
2 Railways	1973-4
2 Habib Bank	1978, 1988
1 Lahore 1969, ADBP 1989	

SOUTH AFRICA

Most runs in a season: 1915 (av.68.39) John Reid (NZ) 1961-2
Most wickets in a season: 106 (av.19.39) Richie Benaud (Aus) 1957-8
Most dismissals in a season: 65 (57ct 8st) Ray Jennings 1982-3

Currie Cup

The annual first-class competition for the South African provinces. The Cup was presented by Sir Donald Currie and first contested in the 1889/90 season. Until 1966 it was not normally contested in the seasons when a touring team visited South Africa. *Winners (* shared wins): year given is that of second half of the season*

28 (4*) Transvaal	1890, 1895, 1903-5, 1907, 1922*, 1924, 1926-7, 1930, 1935, 1938*, 1951, 1959, 1966*, 1969, 1970*, 1971-3, 1979-80, 1983-5, 1987-8
21 (3*) Natal	1911, 1913, 1922*, 1934, 1937, 1938*, 1947-8, 1952, 1955, 1960-1, 1963-4, 1966*, 1967-8, 1974, 1976-7, 1981
16 (3*) Western Province	1893-4, 1897-8, 1909, 1921, 1922*, 1932, 1953, 1956, 1970*, 1975, 1978, 1982, 1986, 1990*
2 (1*) Eastern Province	1989, 1990*
1 Kimberley (now Griqualand West) 1891	

Nissan Shield

The South African limited overs competition was contested for the Gillette Cup from 1969-70 to 1976-7, for the Datsun Shield 1977-8 to 1982-3 and for the Nissan Shield from 1983-4. *Winners:*

8 Transvaal	1974, 1979-81, 1983-6
5 Western Province	1970-1, 1973, 1982, 1989

The West Indian fast bowler Malcolm Marshall took most Test wickets (323) in the 1980s
(All-Sport/Adrian Murrell)

4 Eastern Province   1972, 1976, 1988, 1990
3 Natal   1975, 1977, 1987
1 Rhodesia   1978

Benson & Hedges Trophy
A limited overs competition played at night under floodlights, which was introduced in 1981/2. Winners:
3 Transvaal   1982-3, 1985
3 Western Province   1986-8
1 Natal 1984, Orange Free State 1989, Eastern Province 1990

WEST INDIES
Most runs in a season: 1765 (av.135.76) Patsy Hendren (Eng) 1929-30
Most wickets in a season: 80 (av. 12.46) Edward Dowson (Eng) 1901-2
Most dismissals in a season: 33 (31ct 2 st) Jeffrey Dujon 1983 and 1986

Red Stripe Cup (Shell Shield from 1966 to 1987)
This annual first-class competition for the West Indian teams has been contested annually from 1966, except in 1968. *Winners (* shared):*
12 Barbados   1966-7, 1972, 1974, 1976*,
                     1977-80, 1982, 1984, 1986
4 Trinidad & Tobago 1970-1, 1976*, 1985
4 Guyana   1973, 1975, 1983, 1987
3 Jamaica   1969, 1988-9
1 Combined Islands 1981, Leeward Islands 1990

There was a triangular Inter-Colonial tournament first held in 1893, up to 1939, but not resumed after the war. Wins: Trinidad 11, Barbados 10, Demerara/British Guiana 5. Other post-war tournaments prior to the Shell Shield were won by British Guiana in 1957, 1962 and 1964.

WOMEN'S CRICKET

The first women's cricket match recorded was at Gosden Common in Surrey, England in 1745. The first women's club was the White Heather Club, founded at Nun Appleton, Yorkshire in 1887 and the first women's Test match was played between England and Australia at Brisbane on 28-31 December 1934.
The Women's Cricket Association (WCA) was formed in England in 1926 and the International Women's Cricket Council (IWCC) in 1958.

World Cup
First held in 1973. *Winners:* 1973 England, 1978 Australia, 1982 Australia, 1988 Australia
Highest team score: 297 New Zealand v Netherlands 1988
Highest individual scores:
143* Lindsay Reeler (Australia) v Netherlands 29 Nov 1988
138* Jeanette Brittin, England v International XI, Hamilton (NZ) 14 Jan 1982
134* Lynne Thomas (England) v International XI 23 Jun 1973

Best bowling:
6-10 Jackie Lord (New Zealand) v India 14 Jan 1982
6-20 Glenys Page (New Zealand) v Trinidad & Tobago 23
　　Jun 1973

Test records

Highest innings: 503-5 dec. England v New Zealand,
Christchurch, 16-18 Feb 1935
Lowest innings: 35 England v Australia, St.Kilda,
Melbourne, 22 Feb 1958
INDIVIDUAL
Highest innings:
193 Denise Annetts, Australia v England, Collingham, 23-
　　24 Aug 1987 (381 min)
190 Sandiya Aggarwal, India v England, Worcester, 14 July
　　1986 (563 min)
189 Betty Snowball, England v New Zealand,
　　Christchurch, 16 Feb 1935 (222 min)
Best bowling:
7-6　Mary Duggan, England v Australia, St.Kilda,
　　Melbourne, 22 Feb 1958
7-7　Betty Wilson, Australia v England, St.Kilda,
　　Melbourne, 22 Feb 1958 (including the only hat trick
　　in women's Test cricket)
Best match analysis:
11-16 Betty Wilson, 7-7 and 4-9, as above 22 Feb 1958
11-63 Julia Greenwood, 6-46 and 5-17, England v West
　　Indies, Canterbury, 16-18 June 1979

Test career records:

Most Tests: 25 Rachael Heyhoe-Flint, England 1960-79
Most runs: 1814 Rachael Heyhoe-Flint (Eng) in 25 Tests,
av.49.02 1960-79
Highest average: 59.88 Enid Bakewell (Eng), 1078 runs in
12 Tests 1968-79
Most centuries: 4 Enid Bakewell (Eng) and Rachel Heyhoe-
Flint (Eng)
Most wickets: 77 Mary Duggan (Eng) in 17 Tests, av.13.49
1949-63

England have played Australia in 33 Tests from 1934 to
1987, England have won 6, Australia 6, one match was
abandoned and 20 have been drawn.

National Club League Competition
Run annually by the WCA from 1988, with English clubs
playing in area competitions leading to national semi-finals
and final. The 1988 Finals were abandoned due to bad
weather, with Somerset Wanderers, Wakefield,
Redoubtables and Vagabonds reaching semi-finals. In
1989 Wakefield beat Gunnersbury in the final.

Club Knockout Competition
Organised annually by the WCA.Winners
1974　　Edgbaston
1975　　Wallington
1977　　Wallington
1978　　Riverside
1979-82 Gunnersbury
1983　　Vagabonds
1984　　Invicta
1985　　Somerset Wanderers
1987　　Vagabonds
1988　　Wolverhampton
1989　　Wakefield
not held in 1976, 1986

Area Championships
Organised annually since 1980 (except for 1983-4, 1987)
by the WCA. *Wins:*
Middlesex 1980-1, 1985, 1986 (tied with Kent)
East Midlands 1988-9
West Midlands 1982

*Denise Annetts hit the highest ever score in women's Test
cricket for Australia against England in 1987. Her stand of
309 with Lindsay Reeler was also a Test record*
(All-Sport/Adrian Murrell)

CROQUET

Croquet is played with ball and mallet and six hoops with a peg laid out on a grass lawn 35 yd (31.9m) long by 28 yd (25.6m) wide. While its exact origins are obscure, it was probably derived from the French game Jeu de Mail, played from the 12th century. A game resembling croquet, probably of foreign origin, was played in Ireland in the 1830s. Jean Jaques, the sports goods manufacturers, made the first croquet sets in England in the 1850s and published a book on the game in 1857. Ten years later the first championships were held at Evesham, Worcestershire.

The All-England Croquet Club was founded at Wimbledon in 1869 and the current governing body, the Croquet Association was formed in 1896. The game was played at the 1900 Olympic Games, when all the contestants were French.

Continental Airways World Singles Championships
First held at Hurlingham in 1989, when Joe Hogan (NZ) beat Mark Avery (Eng) in the final.

MacRobertson International Shield
Contested by Australia, Great Britain and New Zealand, first in 1925. *Wins:*
8 Great Britain 1925, 1937, 1956, 1963, 1969, 1974, 1982, 1990
3 Australia   1928, 1930, 1935
3 New Zealand 1950, 1979, 1986

The Croquet Championship
First held in 1867. Recent champions and most wins:
OPEN CHAMPIONSHIP
1977	Michael Heap
1978	Nigel Aspinall
1979	David Openshaw
1980	William de R.Prichard
1981	David Openshaw
1982-4	Nigel Aspinall
1985	David Openshaw
1986	Joe Hogan (NZ)
1987	Mark Avery
1988	Stephen Mulliner
1989	Joe Hogan (NZ)

Most wins:
10 John W.Solomon 1953, 1956, 1959, 1961, 1963-8
8 Nigel Aspinall 1969, 1974-6, 1978, 1982-4
7 Humphrey Hicks 1932, 1939, 1947-50, 1952
5 Cyril Corbally 1902-3, 1906, 1908, 1913
Most wins by a woman:
4 Dorothy Steel 1925, 1933, 1935-6

OPEN DOUBLES
First played in 1924.
1977-8	Nigel Aspinall & William Ormerod
1979	Bernard Neal & S.R.Hemsted
1980	William de B.Prichard & Stephen Mulliner
1981	Stephen Mulliner & M.Ormerod
1982	Martin Murray & A.B.Hope
1983	John McCullough & Phil Cordingley
1984	Nigel Aspinall & Stephen Mulliner
1985	David Openshaw & Mark Avery
1986	Nigel Aspinall & Stephen Mulliner
1987	David Openshaw & Mark Avery
1988	Nigel Aspinall & Stephen Mulliner
1989	Joe Hogan & Bob Jackson (NZ)

Most wins:
10 John W. Solomon & Edmond Cotter 1954-5, 1958-9, 1961-5, 1969
10 Nigel Aspinall with William Ormerod 1971-2, 1975-6, 1977-8, with J.W.Simon 1966, 1968, 1970, with Stephen Mulliner 1984, 1986, 1988

MEN'S CHAMPIONSHIP
First played in 1925.
1977	Edgar Jackson
1978	Paul Hands
1980	Martin Murray
1981	David Openshaw
1982	Martin Murray
1983	Nigel Aspinall
1984-5	Stephen Mulliner
1986	David Foulser
1987	Keith Aiton
1988	Mark Saurin
1989	Keith Aiton

Most wins:
10 John W.Solomon 1951, 1953, 1958-60, 1962, 1964-5, 1971-2
9 Humphrey Hicks 1930, 1932, 1948-50, 1955-6, 1961, 1966

WOMEN'S CHAMPIONSHIP
First played in 1869.
1980	B.Meachem
1981	Veronica Carlisle
1982-3	Mrs. Wiggins (NZ)
1984	Veronica Carlisle
1985	Mary Collin
1986	Mrs. Wiggins (NZ)
1987	Mary Collin
1988	Debbie Cornelius
1989	Bo Harris

Most wins:
15 Dorothy Steel 1919, 1922, 1925-7, 1929-30, 1932-9
6 Miss Walsh 1871-3, 1878-80
6 E.J.Warwick 1960, 1962, 1965-6, 1968-9
6 Mrs. E.Rotherham 1952-3, 1955, 1959, 1963-4

MIXED DOUBLES
First played in 1899.

1980	Brian Sykes & Mrs. Sykes
1981	Martin Murray & Mrs. B.Meacham
1982	Nigel Aspinall & Mrs. C.Knox
1983	Martin Murray & Mrs. K.G.Yeoman
1984	Ian Bond & Veronica Carlisle
1985	Keith Aiton & Mary Collin
1986	T.Griffith & Jan Macleod
1987	Nigel Aspinall & Debbie Cornelius
1988	Paul Smith & Lady Carmen Bazley
1989	Ian Maugham & Bo Harris

Most titles at all events:
31 John W.Solomon 10 open, 10 men's, 10 doubles, 1 mixed doubles
31 Dorothy Steel 4 open, 15 women's, 5 doubles, 7 mixed doubles
27 Humphrey Hicks 7 open, 9 men's, 7 doubles, 4 mixed doubles

President's Cup
An annual invitation event for the best eight players, first held in 1934.

Most wins:
12 Nigel Aspinall 1969-70, 1973-6, 1978, 1980-2, 1984-5
9 John W.Solomon 1955, 1957-9, 1962-4, 1968, 1971
6 Edmond Cotter 1949-50, 1952-3, 1956, 1960
5 Humphrey Hicks 1947-8, 1951, 1954, 1961
4 Stephen Mulliner 1981, 1983, 1986, 1987
Other recent winners:
1988 Chris Clarke
1989 Robert Fulford

The lowest ever handicap was minus 5.5 by Humphrey Hicks. The limit is now fixed at minus 5.

CURLING

Curling resembles bowls on ice and is known as the 'roaring game', due to the noise made by the curling stone (which weighs about 40lb/18kg) as it runs over the ice rink. The curlers use brooms to sweep the rink ahead of their stone to remove impediments and smooth the ice. The game became popular in Scotland, but it may have originated in the Netherlands more than 400 years ago. The Grand Caledonian Curling Club was formed in Edinburgh in 1838. Five years later it added Royal to its title and eventually became the international governing body of the sport.

Scots introduced curling to Canada, where the first club was the Royal Montreal Curling Club, founded in 1807. The first club in the USA was the Orchard Lake Club, formed in Michigan in 1832.

The first international match was between Canada and the USA in 1884, the start of the Gordon International Medal series, now contested annually by clubs representing the Canadian branch of the Royal Caledonian Curling Club and the Grand National Curling Club of America. The Strathcona Cup series between Canada and Scotland started in 1903. The International Curling Federation was founded in 1966.

WORLD CHAMPIONSHIPS

Men
Played annually for the Scotch Whisky Cup 1959-67 and for the Air Canada Silver Broom 1968-86. *Winners:*

Year	Nation	Skip
1959-60	Canada	Ernie Richardson
1961	Canada	Hec Gervais
1962-3	Canada	Ernie Richardson
1964	Canada	Lyall Dagg
1965	USA	Bud Somerville
1966	Canada	Ron Northcott
1967	Scotland	Chuck Hay
1968-9	Canada	Ron Northcott
1970-1	Canada	Don Duguid
1972	Canada	Orest Meleschuk
1973	Sweden	Kjell Oscarius
1974	USA	Bud Somerville
1975	Switzerland	Otto Danielli
1976	USA	Bruce Roberts
1977	Sweden	Ragnar Kamp
1978	USA	Bob Nichols
1979	Norway	Kristian Sørum
1980	Canada	Rick Falk
1981	Switzerland	Jürg Tanner
1982	Canada	Al Hackner
1983	Canada	Ed Werenich
1984	Norway	Eigel Ramsfjell
1985	Canada	Al Hackner
1986	Canada	Ed Lukovich
1987	Canada	Russ Howard
1988	Norway	Eigel Ramsfjell
1989	Canada	Pat Ryan
1990	Canada	Ed Werenich

Most wins: 20 Canada, 4 USA
Most times as winning skip:
4 Ernie Richardson, 3 Ron Northcott

Women
Played annually from 1979. *Winners:*

1979	Switzerland	Gaby Casanova
1980	Canada	Mary Mitchell
1981	Sweden	Elisabeth Högström
1982	Denmark	Marianne Jørgensen
1983	Switzerland	Erika Müller
1984	Canada	Connie Laliberte
1985	Canada	Linda Moore
1986	Canada	Marilyn Darte
1987	Canada	Pat Saunders
1988	FR Germany	Andrea Schöpp
1989	Canada	Heather Euston
1990	Norway	Djordy Nordby

Most wins: 6 Canada

Olympic Games

Curling was included as a demonstration sport at the Games of 1924, 1932 and 1964, and again in 1988. A specialised German version of the game was demonstrated in 1936.

1988 winners: MEN Norway (skip – Eigil Ramsfjell),
WOMEN Canada (skip – Linda Moore)

The Canadian women on their way to another world title at curling (All-Sport)

CYCLING

The forerunner of the bicycle, the célerifère was demonstrated in the garden of the Palais Royale, Paris in 1791. The first treadle-propelled bicycle was designed by Scottish blacksmith Kirkpatrick Macmillan in 1839, but the first practical bicycle was the vélocipède built in March 1861 by Pierre and his son Ernest Michaux of Paris. The first cycling club, the Liverpool Velocipede Club, was formed in 1867 and the first race took place the following year, over 1200 metres at the Parc St.Cloud, Paris, and was won by Englishman James Moore. The first international organisation was the International Cyclist Association (ICA), founded in 1892, which promoted the first world championships the following year. The current governing body, the Union Cycliste International (UCI) was founded in 1900. In 1965 two federations were formed within the UCI – the Fédération de Cyclisme Amateur (FIAC) and the Fédération Internationale de Cyclisme Professional (FICP).

OLYMPIC GAMES

Cycling was included in the first Olympics of 1896 and at every Games since except 1904 when there were no official events. A women's road races was introduced in 1984, and the sprint added in 1988 *Winners:*

MEN
Sprint

1896 and 1900 over 2000 metres, since then at 1000 metres. Now raced over the best of three races with the time for the last 200 metres shown from 1924.

1896 Paul Masson (Fra) 4:56.0
1900 Georges Taillandier (Fra) 2:52.0 *2000m* (13.0)
1906 Francesco Verri (Ita) 1:42.2
1908 *declared void as riders exceeded time limit*
1920 Maurice Peeters (Hol) 1:38.3
1924 Lucien Michard (Fra) 12.8
1928 Roger Beaufrand (Fra) 13.2
1932 Jacobus van Egmond (Hol) 12.6
1936 Toni Merkens (Ger) 11.8
1948 Mario Ghella (Ita) 12.0
1952 Enzo Sacchi (Ita) 12.0
1956 Michel Rousseau (Fra) 11.4
1960 Sante Gaiardoni (Ita) 11.1
1964 Giovanni Pettenella (Ita) 13.69
1968 Daniel Morelon (Fra) 10.68
1972 Daniel Morelon (Fra) 11.25
1976 Anton Tkác (Cs) 10.78
1980 Lutz Hesslich (GDR) 11.40
1984 Mark Gorski (USA) 10.49
1988 Lutz Hesslich (GDR) 11.82

1000 metres time trial

1896 and 1906 raced over 333.33 metres
1896 Paul Masson (Fra) 24.0
1906 Francesco Verri (Ita) 22.8
1928 Willy Falck-Hansen (Den) 1:14.4
1932 Edgar Gray (Aus) 1:13.0
1936 Arie van Vliet (Hol) 1:12.0
1948 Jacques Dupont (Fra) 1:13.5
1952 Russell Mockridge (Aus) 1:11.1
1956 Leandro Faggin (Ita) 1:09.8
1960 Sante Gaiardoni (Ita) 1:07.27
1964 Patrick Sercu (Bel) 1:09.59
1968 Pierre Trentin (Fra) 1:03.91
1972 Niels-Christian Fredborg (Den) 1:06.44
1976 Klaus-Jurgen Grünke (GDR) 1:05.93
1980 Lothar Thoms (GDR) 1:02.955
1984 Freddy Schmidtke (FRG) 1:06.10
1988 Aleksandr Kirichenko (USSR) 1:04.499

4000 metres individual pursuit

1964 Jiri Daler (Cs) 5:04.75
1968 Daniel Rebillard (Fra) 4:41.71
1972 Knut Knudsen (Nor) 4:45.74
1976 Gregor Braun (GDR) 4:47.61
1980 Robert Dill-Bundi (Swi) 4:35.66
1984 Steve Hegg (USA) 4:39.55
1988 Gintautas Umaras (USSR) 4:32.00

Points race

Introduced 1984
1984 Roger Ilegems (Bel) 37 pts
1988 Dan Frost (Den) 38 pts

Individual road race

Distance in kilometres shown for each year

1896   87 km   Aristidis Konstantinidis (Gre) 3:22:31.0
1906   84   Fernand Vast (Fra) 2:41:28.0
1912   320   Rudolph Lewis (SAf) 10:42:39.0
1920   175   Harry Stenqvist (Swe) 4:40:01.8
1924   188   Armand Blanchonnet (Fra) 6:20:48.0
1928   168   Henry Hansen (Den) 4:47:18.0
1932   100   Attilio Pavesi (Ita) 2:28:05.6
1936   100   Robert Charpentier (Fra) 2:33:05.0
1948   194.63   José Beyaert (Fra) 5:18:12.6
1952   190.4   André Noyelle (Bel) 5:06:03.4
1956   187.73   Ercole Baldini (Ita) 5:21:17.0
1960   175.38   Viktor Kapitonov (USSR) 4:20:37.0
1964   194.83   Mario Zanin (Ita) 4:39:51.63
1968   196.2   Pierfranco Vianelli (Ita) 4:41:25.24
1972   182.4   Hennie Kuiper (Hol) 4:14:37.0
1976   175   Bernt Johansson (Swe) 4:46:52.0
1980   189   Sergey Sukhoruchenkov (USSR) 4:48:28.9
1984   196   Alexi Grewal (USA) 4:59:57.0
1988   196.8   Olaf Ludwig (GDR) 4:32:22.0

4000 metres team pursuit

Held over 1810.5 metres in 1908

1908 Great Britain 2:18.6
1920 Italy 5:20.0
1924 Italy 5:15.0
1928 Italy 5:01.8
1932 Italy 4:53.0
1936 France 4:45.0
1948 France 4:57.8
1952 Italy 4:46.1
1956 Italy 4:37.4
1960 Italy 4:30.90
1964 FR Germany 4:35.67
1968 Denmark 4:22.44
1972 FR Germany 4:22.14
1976 FR Germany 4:21.06
1980 USSR 4:15.70
1984 Australia 4:25.99
1988 USSR 4:13.31

Team road race

1912-20 combined times of best four riders in the individual race. 1924-52 combined times of best three. 1956 based on placings.

1912 Sweden 44:35:33.6
1920 France 19:16:43.2
1924 France 19:13:14.0
1928 Denmark 15:09:14.0
1932 Italy 7:27:15.2
1936 France 7:39:16.2
1948 Belgium 15:58:17.4
1952 Belgium 15:20:46.6
1956 France 22 points

100km team time trial

1960 Italy 2:14:33.53
1964 Netherlands 2:26:31.19
1968 Netherlands 2:07:49.06
1972 USSR 2:11:17.8
1976 USSR 2:08:53.0
1980 USSR 2:01:21.7
1984 Italy 1:58:28.0
1988 GDR 1:57:47.7

WOMEN
Road race

1984   79.2km   Connie Carpenter-Phinney (USA) 2:11:11.0
1988   82km   Monique Knol (Hol) 2:00:52.0

Sprint (1000m)

1988 Erika Salumyae (USSR) 12.00

SUPERSEDED MEN'S TRACK EVENTS

660yd   1908 Victor Johnson (UK) 51.2
5km   1906 Francesco Verri (Ita) 8:35.0
      1908 Benjamin Jones (UK) 8:36.2
10km   1896 Paul Masson (Fra) 17:54.2
20km   1906 William Pett (UK) 29:00.0
      1908 Charles Kingsbury (UK) 34:13.6
50km   1920 Henry George (Bel) 1:16:43.2
      1924 Jacobus Willems (Hol) 1:18:24.0
100km   1896 Léon Flameng (Fra) 3:08:19.2
      1908 Charles Bartlett (UK) 2:41:48.6
12hrs   1896 Adolf Schmal (Aut) 314.997km

In 1904 track races were won by: Marcus Hurley (USA) at 1/4, 1/3, 1/2 and 1 mile; Burton Downing (USA) at 2 and 25 miles, Charles Schlee (USA) at 5 miles.

Men's 2000 metres tandem

From 1924-72 times recorded only over last 200m

1906 John Matthews & Arthur Rushen (UK) 2:57.0
1908 Maurice Schilles & André Auffray (Fra) 3:07.8
1920 Harry Ryan & Thomas Lance (UK) 2:49.4
1924 Lucien Choury & Jean Cugnot (Fra) 12.6
1928 Bernhard Leene & Daan van Dijk (Hol) 11.8
1932 Maurice Perrin & Louis Chaillot (Fra) 12.0
1936 Ernst Ihbe & Carl Lorenz (Ger) 11.8
1948 Renato Perona & Ferdinando Terruzzi (Ita) 11.3
1952 Lionel Cox & Russell Mockridge (Aus) 11.0
1956 Ian Browne & Anthony Marchant (Aus) 10.8
1960 Giuseppe Beghetto & Sergio Bianchetto (Ita) 10.7
1964 Sergio Bianchetto & Angelo Damiano (Ita) 10.75
1968 Daniel Morelon & Pierre Trentin (Fra) 9.83
1972 Vladimir Semenets & Igor Tselovalnikov (USSR) 10.52

All events

Most gold medals: 3 Paul Masson (Fra) 1896, Francisco Verri (Ita) 1906, Robert Charpentier (Fra) 1936, Daniel Morelon (Fra) 1968-72.
Most medals: 5 Morelon, who also won a silver in 1976 and bronze in 1964, both in the sprint.

WORLD CHAMPIONSHIPS

World Championships were first held in 1893 in Chicago, with two events: the sprint and the motor-paced race over 100km. A road race was first held in 1921 and women's events were introduced in 1959. Separate world championships are not contested in Olympic years for events on the Olympic programme (qv).

Events currently contested, with those to have won most often, and winners from 1970 are as follows:

Amateur sprint – first held 1893

1969-71	Daniel Morelon (Fra)
1973	Daniel Morelon (Fra)
1974	Anton Tkac (Cs)
1975	Daniel Morelon (Fra)
1977	Hans-Jürgen Geschke (GDR)
1978	Anton Tkac (Cs)
1979	Lutz Hesslich (GDR)
1981-2	Sergey Kopylov (USSR)
1983	Lutz Hesslich (GDR)
1985	Lutz Hesslich (GDR)
1986	Michael Hübner (GDR)
1987	Lutz Hesslich (GDR)
1989	Bill Huck (GDR)

Most wins: 7 Daniel Morelon (Fra) 1966-7, 1969-71, 1973, 1975; 4 William Bailey (UK) 1909-11, 1913; Lutz Hesslich as above.

The Irishman Sean Kelly (below) was the inaugural winner of the World Cup in 1989 **(All-Sport/Vandystadt)**

Amateur 1km time trial

First held 1966

1970	Niels Fredborg (Den)
1971	Eduard Rapp (USSR)
1973	Janusz Kierzkowski (Pol)
1974	Eduard Rapp (USSR)
1975	Klaus Grünke (GDR)
1977-9	Lothar Thoms (GDR)
1981	Lothar Thoms (GDR)
1982	Fredy Schmidtke (FRG)
1983	Sergey Kopylov (USSR)
1985	Jens Glücklich (GDR)
1986	Maik Malchow (GDR)
1987	Martin Vinnicombe (Aus)
1989	Jens Glücklich (GDR)

Most wins: 4 Lothar Thoms (GDR) as above; 3 Niels Fredborg (Den) 1967-8, 1970.

Amateur 4km pursuit

First held 1946

1970	Xavier Kurmann (Swi)
1971	Martin-Emilio Rodriguez (Col)
1973	Knut Knudsen (Nor)
1974	Hans Lutz (FRG)
1975	Thomas Huschke (GDR)
1977	Norbert Durpisch (GDR)
1978	Detlef Macha (GDR)
1979	Nikolay Makarov (USSR)
1981-2	Detlef Macha (GDR)
1983	Viktor Kupovets (USSR)
1985-6	Vyacheslav Yekimov (USSR)

| 1987 | Gintautas Umaras (USSR) |
| 1989 | Vyacheslav Yekimov (USSR) |

Most wins: 3 Tiemen Groen (Hol) 1964-6; Detlef Macha (GDR) as above; Vyacheslav Yekimov (USSR) as above.

Amateur team pursuit – first held 1962. Wins:
7 FR Germany 1962, 1964, 1970, 1973-5, 1983
6 USSR 1963, 1965, 1967, 1969, 1982, 1987
5 GDR 1977-9, 1981, 1989
4 Italy 1966, 1968, 1971, 1985
1 Czechoslovakia 1986

Amateur tandem sprint – first held 1966
1970	Jürgen Barth & Rainer Müller (FRG)
1971	Jürgen Geschke & Werner Otto (GDR)
1973-4	Vladimir Vackar & Miroslav Vymazal (Cs)
1976	Benedykt Kocot & Janusz Kotlinski (Pol)
1977-8	Vladimir Vackar & Miroslav Vymazal (Cs)
1979	Yave Cahard & Frank Depine (Fra)
1980-2	Ivan Kucirek & Pavel Martinek (Cs)
1983	Philippe Vernet & Frank Depine (Fra)
1984	Jürgen Greil & Frank Weber (FRG)
1985-6	Vitezlav Voboril & Roman Rehousek (Cs)
1987-9	Fabrice Colas & Frédéric Magné (Fra)

Most wins: 4 Vackar & Vymazal as above

Amateur 50km points race
First held 1976
1976	Walter Baumgartner (Swi)
1977	Constant Tourne (Bel)
1978	Noel de Jonckheere (Bel)
1979	Jiri Slama (Cs)
1980	Gary Sutton (Aus)
1981	Lutz Haueisen (GDR)
1982	Hans-Joachim Pohl (GDR)
1983	Michael Marcussen (Den)
1985	Martin Penc (Cs)
1986	Dan Frost (Den)
1987	Marat Ganeeyev (USSR)
1989	Marat Satybyldiev (USSR)

Amateur motor-paced
Held at 100km 1893-1914, for 1 hour 1958-71, at 50km from 1972
1970	Cees Stam (Hol)
1971-3	Horst Gnas (FRG)
1974	Jean Breuer (FRG)
1975-7	Gaby Minneboo (Hol)
1978	Rainer Podlesch (GDR)
1979	Matthe Pronk (Hol)
1980	Gaby Minneboo (Hol)
1981	Matthe Pronk (Hol)
1982	Gaby Minneboo (Hol)
1983	Rainer Podlesch (GDR)
1984	Jan de Nijs (Hol)
1985	Roberto Dotti (Ita)

1986-7	Mario Gentili (Ita)
1988	Vincenzo Colamartino (Ita)
1989	Roland Königshofer (Aut)

Most wins: 7 Leon Meredith (UK) 1904-5, 1907-9, 1911, 1913; 5 Gaby Minneboo (Hol) as above; 3 Horst Gnas (FRG) as above.

Amateur road race
1970	Jørgen Schmidt (Den)
1971	Regis Ovion (Fra)
1973	Ryszard Szurkowski (Pol)
1974	Janusz Kowalski (Pol)
1975	André Gevers (Hol)
1977	Claudio Corti (Ita)
1978	Gilbert Glaus (Swi)
1979	Gianni Giacomini (Ita)
1981	Andrey Vedernikov (USSR)
1982	Bernd Drogan (GDR)
1983	Uwe Raab (GDR)
1985	Lech Piasecki (Pol)
1986	Uwe Ampler (GDR)
1987	Richard Vivien (Fra)
1989	Joachim Halupczok (Pol)

Most wins: 2 Giuseppe Martano (Ita) 1930, 1932; Gustav Adolf Schur (GDR) 1958-9.

Amateur team time trial
First held 1962. Contested on the roads at approximately 100km
Wins:
4 USSR 1970, 1977, 1983, 1985
4 Italy 1962, 1964-5, 1987
3 Sweden 1967-9, 1974
3 Netherlands 1978, 1982, 1986
3 GDR 1979, 1981, 1989
2 Poland 1973, 1975
1 France 1963, Denmark 1966
1 Belgium 1971

Professional sprint
1970	Gordon Johnson (Aus)
1971	Leijin Loevesijn (Hol)
1972-3	Robert van Lancker (Bel)
1974	Peder Pedersen (Den)
1975-6	John Nicholson (Aus)
1977-86	Koichi Nakano (Jap)
1987	Noboyuki Tawara (Jap)
1988	Stephen Pate (Aus)
1989	Claudio Golinelli (Ita)

Most wins: 10 Koichi Nakano (Jap) as above; 7 Jeff Scherens (Bel) 1932-7, 1947; Antonio Maspes (Ita) 1955-6, 1959-62, 1964; 6 Thorvald Ellegaard (Den) 1901-3, 1906, 1908, 1911; 5 Piet Moeskops (Hol) 1921-4, 1926; 4 Lucien Michard (Fra) 1927-30; Reg Harris (UK) 1949-51, 1954.

Professional 5km pursuit
First held in 1939, when it was left unfinished, and then 1946.

1970	Hugh Porter (UK)
1971	Dirk Baert (Bel)
1972-3	Hugh Porter (UK)
1974-5	Roy Schuiten (Hol)
1976	Francesco Moser (Ita)
1977-8	Gregor Braun (FRG)
1979	Bert Osterbosch (Hol)
1980	Tony Doyle (UK)
1981-2	Alain Bondue (Fra)
1983	Steele Bishop (Aus)
1984-5	Hans-Henrik Oersted (Den)
1986	Tony Doyle (UK)
1987	Hans-Henrik Oersted (Den)
1988	Lech Piasecki (Pol)
1989	Colin Sturgess (UK)

Most wins: 4 Hugh Porter (UK) 1968, 1970, 1972-3; 3 Guido Messina (Ita) 1954-6; 3 Roger Rivière 1957-9; 3 Leando Faggin (Ita) 1963, 1965-6, 3 Hans-Henrik Oersted as above

Professional keirin – first held 1980

1980-1	Danny Clark (Aus)
1982	Gordon Singleton (Can)
1983	Urs Freuler (Swi)
1984	Robert Dill-Bundi (Swi)
1985	Urs Freuler (Swi)
1986	Michel Vaarten (Bel)
1987	Harumi Honda (Jap)
1988	*vacant*, winner Claudio Golinelli (Ita) failed drugs test
1989	Claudio Golinelli (Ita)

Professional points pace
First held 1980

1980	Stan Tourne (Bel)
1981-7	Urs Freuler (Swi)
1988	Daniel Wyder (Swi)
1989	Urs Freuler (Swi)

Most wins: 8 Urs Freuler

Professional motor-paced
First held 1895. Held at 100km 1895-1971, over 1 hour from 1972.

1970	Ehrenfried Rudolph (FRG)
1971-2	Theo Verschueren (Bel)
1973-4	Cees Stam (Hol)
1975	Dieter Kemper (FRG)
1976	Wilfried Peffgen (FRG)
1977	Cees Stam (Hol)
1978	Wilfried Peffgen (FRG)
1979	Martin Venix (Hol)
1980	Wilfried Peffgen (FRG)
1981	René Kos (Hol)
1982	Martin Venix (Hol)
1983	Bruno Vicini (Ita)

1984	Horst Schütz (FRG)
1985-6	Bruno Vicini (Ita)
1987	Max Hürtzler (Swi)
1988	Danny Clark (Aus)
1989	Giovanni Renosto (Ita)

Most wins: 6 Guillermo Timoner (Spa) 1955, 1959-60, 1962, 1964-5;
4 Victor Linart (Bel) 1921, 1924, 1926-7

Professional road race
First held 1927

1970	Jean-Pierre Monseré (Bel)
1971	Eddy Merckx (Bel)
1972	Marino Basso (Ita)
1973	Felice Gimondi (Ita)
1974	Eddy Merckx (Bel)
1975	Hennie Kuiper (Hol)
1976	Freddy Maertens (Bel)
1977	Francesco Moser (Ita)
1978	Gerrie Knetemann (Hol)
1979	Jan Raas (Hol)
1980	Bernard Hinault (Fra)
1981	Freddy Maertens (Bel)
1982	Giuseppe Saronni (Ita)
1983	Greg LeMond (USA)
1984	Claude Criquielion (Bel)
1985	Joop Zoetemelk (Hol)
1986	Moreno Argentin (Ita)
1987	Stephen Roche (Ire)
1988	Maurizio Fondriest (Ita)
1989	Greg LeMond (USA)

Most wins: 3 Alfredo Binda (Ita) 1927, 1930, 1932; Rik van Steenbergen (Bel) 1949, 1956-7; Eddy Merckx (Bel) as above.

Women's sprint – first held 1958

1969-71	Galina Tsareva (USSR)
1972	Galina Yermolayeva (USSR)
1973	Sheila Young (USA)
1974	Tamara Piltsikova (USSR)
1975	Sue Novarra (USA)
1976	Sheila Young (USA)
1977-9	Galina Tsareva (USSR)
1980	Sue Reber (née Novarra) (USA)
1981	Sheila Ochowitz (née Young) (USA)
1982-4	Connee Paraskevin (USA)
1985	Iasabelle Nicoloso (Fra)
1986	Christa Rothenburger (GDR)
1987	Erika Salumyae (USSR)
1989	Erika Salumyae (USSR)

Most wins: 6 Galina Yermolayeva (USSR) 1958-61, 1963, 1972; Galina Tsareva (USSR) as above.

Women's 3km pursuit

1970-4	Tamara Garkushina (USSR)
1975-6	Keetie van Oosten-Hage (Hol)
1977	Vera Kuznetsova (USSR)
1978-9	Keetie van Oosten-Hage (Hol)

1980-1   Nadezhda Kibardina (USSR)
1982   Rebecca Twigg (USA)
1983   Connie Carpenter (USA)
1984-5   Rebecca Twigg (USA)
1986   Jeannie Longo (Fra)
1987   Rebecca Twigg (USA)
1988-9   Jeannie Longo (Fra)
Most wins: 6 Tamara Garkushina (USSR) 1967, 1970-4; 5 Beryl Burton (UK) 1959-60, 1962-3, 1966; 4 Keetie van Oosten-Hage (Hol) and Rebecca Twigg (USA) as above.

Women's 30km points
1987   (demonstration event) Sally Hodge (UK)
1989   Jeannie Longo (Fra)

Women's road race – first held 1958
1970-1   Anna Konkina (USSR)
1972   Geneviève Gambillon (Fra)
1973   Nicole Vandenbroeck (Bel)
1974   Geneviève Gambillon (Fra)
1975   Trijntje Fopma (Hol)
1976   Keetie van Oosten-Hage (Hol)
1977   Josiane Bost (Fra)
1978   Beate Habetz (FRG)
1979   Petra de Bruin (Hol)

1980   Beth Heiden (USA)
1981   Ute Enzenauer (FRG)
1982   Mandy Jones (UK)
1983   Marianne Berglund (Swe)
1985-7   Jeannie Longo (Fra)
1989   Jeannie Longo (Fra)
Most wins: 4 Yvonne Reynders (Bel) 1959, 1961, 1963, 1966

Women's 50 km team trial
First held 1987
1987 USSR
1988 Italy
1989 USSR

Jeannie Longo uniquely won three events in one year in 1989.
Note that three women's cycling world champions, Beth Heiden, Sheila Young and Christa Rothenburger, have also been world champions at speed skating.

Jeannie Longo on her way to the first of a record three successive victories in the women's Tour de France in 1987
(All-Sport)

TOUR DE FRANCE

Without doubt, the Tour de France is the greatest cycle race in the world and its popularity attracts the largest audience of any sporting event with more than 10 million people watching the annual race. It was first held in 1903 and the successful riders have to cover 4800km/3,000 miles of mixed terrain over a three week period. *Winners:*

1903	Maurice Garin (Fra)
1904	Henri Cornet (Fra)
1905	Louis Trousselier (Fra)
1906	René Pottier (Fra)
1907-8	Lucien Petit-Breton (Fra)
1909	François Faber (Lux)
1910	Octave Lapize (Fra)
1911	Gustave Garrigou (Fra)
1912	Odile Defraye (Bel)
1913-4	Philippe Thys (Bel)
1919	Firmin Lambot (Bel)
1920	Philippe Thys (Bel)
1921	Léon Scieur (Bel)
1922	Firmin Lambot (Bel)
1923	Henri Pélissier (Fra)
1924-5	Ottavio Bottecchia (Ita)
1926	Lucien Buysse (Bel)
1927-8	Nicholas Frantz (Lux)
1929	Maurice De Waele (Bel)
1930	André Leducq (Fra)
1931	Antonin Magne (Fra)
1932	André Leducq (Fra)
1933	Georges Speicher (Fra)
1934	Antonin Magne (Fra)
1935	Romain Maës (Bel)
1936	Sylvere Maës (Bel)
1937	Roger Lapébie (Fra)
1938	Gino Bartali (Ita)
1939	Sylvere Maës (Bel)
1947	Jean Robic (Fra)
1948	Gino Bartali (Ita)
1949	Fausto Coppi (Ita)
1950	Ferdinand Kübler (Swi)
1951	Hugo Koblet (Swi)
1952	Fausto Coppi (Ita)
1953-5	Louison Bobet (Fra)
1956	Roger Walkowiak (Fra)
1957	Jacques Anquetil (Fra)
1958	Charly Gaul (Lux)
1959	Federico Bahamontès (Spa)
1960	Gastone Nencini (Ita)
1961-4	Jacques Anquetil (Fra)
1965	Felice Gimondi (Ita)
1966	Lucien Aimar (Fra)
1967	Roger Pingeon (Fra)
1968	Jan Janssen (Hol)
1969-72	Eddy Merckx (Bel)
1973	Luis Ocana (Spa)
1974	Eddy Merckx (Bel)
1975	Bernard Thevenet (Fra)
1976	Lucien van Impe (Bel)

Jaques Anquetil turns to commentating after his phenomenally successful racing career **(All-Sport)**

1977	Bernard Thevenet (Fra)
1978-9	Bernard Hinault (Fra)
1980	Joop Zoetemelk (Hol)
1981-2	Bernard Hinault (Fra)
1983-4	Laurent Fignon (Fra)
1985	Bernard Hinault (Fra)
1986	Greg LeMond (USA)
1987	Stephen Roche (Ire)
1988	Pedro Delgado (Spa)
1989	Greg LeMond (USA)

Fastest average speed: 38.88 km/h (24.16 mph) Pedro Delgado 1988
Longest race: 5745 km (3569 miles) 1926

Most successful Tour de France riders:

five points for a win, 4-3-2-1 for 2nd to 5th places

Name	Years	1st	2nd	3rd	4th	5th	Points
Joop Zoetemilk	1970-82	1	6	-	3	1	36
Bernard Hinault	1978-86	5	2	-	-	-	33
Lucien van Impe	1971-83	1	3	3	2	1	31
Eddy Merckx	1969-75	5	1	-	-	-	29
Jacques Anquetil	1957-64	5	-	1	-	-	28
Raymond Poulidor	1962-76	-	3	5	-	-	27
Louison Bobet	1948-55	3	-	1	1	-	20
Greg LeMond	1984-9	2	1	1	-	-	17
Bernard Thévenet	1971-7	2	1	-	1	-	16

TOUR OF ITALY

After the Tour de France, the Tour of Italy (Giro d'Italia) is the second most presitigous of the continental tours. It was first held in 1909 and until 1950 when Switzerland's Hugo Koblet won, all winners had been Italian. *Recent winners:*

1977	Michel Pollentier (Bel)
1978	Johan De Muynck (Bel)
1979	Giuseppe Saronni (Ita)
1980	Bernard Hinault (Fra)
1981	Giovani Battaglin (Ita)
1982	Bernard Hinault (Fra)
1983	Giuseppe Saronni (Ita)
1984	Francesco Moser (Ita)
1985	Bernard Hinault (Fra)
1986	Roberto Visentini (Ita)

1987   Stephen Roche (Ire)
1988   Pedro Delgado (Spa)
1989   Greg LeMond (USA)
1990   Gianni Bugno (Ita)

Most wins: 5 Alfredo Binda (Ita) 1925, 1927-9, 1933; Fausto Coppi (Ita) 1940, 1947, 1949, 1952-3; Eddy Merckx (Bel) 1968. 1970, 1972-4

TOUR OF SPAIN

The Tour of Spain (Vuelta de España) is the third major tour of the continental season. It was first held in 1935, and annually from 1955. *Recent winners:*

1977   Freddie Maertens (Bel)
1978   Bernard Hinault (Fra)
1979   Joop Zoetemelk (Hol)
1980   Faustino Ruperez (Spa)
1981   Giovani Battaglin (Ita)
1982   Marino Lejaretta (Spa)
1983   Bernard Hinault (Fra)
1984   Eric Caritoux (Fra)
1985   Pedro Delgado (Spa)
1986   Alvaro Pino (Spa)
1987   Luis Herrera (Col)
1988   Sean Kelly (Ire)
1989   Pedro Delgado (Spa)
1990   Marco Giovannetti (Ita)

Most wins: 2 Gustave Deloor (Bel) 1935-6, Julio Berrendero (Spa) 1941-2, José Manuel Fuente (Spa) 1972, 1974, Bernard Hinault (Fra) 1978, 1983, Pedro Delgado, as above

THE CLASSICS

The following races make up the major classic races on the continent:

Milan – San Remo (MR)

The first major classic of the season, it the longest unpaced of all the classics. First held in 1907 it is known as the *Primavera* in Italy.

Most wins: 7 Eddy Merckx (Bel) 1966-7, 1969, 1971-2, 1975-6; 6 Constante Girardengo (Ita) 1918, 1921, 1923, 1925-6, 1928

Tour of Flanders (Fl)

First held in 1913 the race takes place around Ghent and one of the major features of the race are the steep cobbled climbs, notably the Koppenberg Hill.

Most wins: 3 Achiel Buysse (Bel) 1940-1, 1943; Fiorenzo Magni (Ita) 1949-51; Erik Leman (Bel) 1970, 1972-3

Paris-Roubaix (PR)

Regarded as the toughest one-day race in the world, hence its nickname, 'The Hell of the North'. The latter stages of the race take place over farm tracks and cobbled roads. It was first held in 1896.

Most wins: 4 Roger de Vlaeminck (Bel) 1972, 1974-5, 1977

Flèche Wallonne (FW)

There is no fixed course for the Flèche Wallonne but it takes place around the Ardennes district of Belgium and is approximately 250 km (155 miles) in length. It was first held in 1936.

Most wins: 4 Eddy Merckx (Bel) 1967, 1970, 1972, 1975

Liège-Bastogne-Liège

First held in 1891 it is the oldest of the Belgian classics. Until 1912 it was for amateurs only. Like the Flèche Wallonne it takes place around the Ardennes district.

Most wins: 5 Eddy Merckx (Bel) 1969, 1971-3, 1975

Paris-Brussels (PB)

First held in 1893, but not again until 1906 when professionals were allowed to compete. The race was discontinued in 1966 and replaced on the 'Classics' list by the Frankfurt Grand Prix, but it returned in 1973.

Most wins: 3 Octave Lapize (Fra) 1911-3, Felix Sellier (Bel) 1922-4

Tour of Lombardy (TL)

The Tour of Lombardy is one of the Autumn Classics and traditionally marks the end of the road-racing season on the continent. It was first held in 1905 and is often referred to as 'The Race of the Falling Leaves'.

Most wins: 5 Fausto Coppi (Ita) 1946-9, 1954

Other major continental races include:

Bordeaux-Paris (BP)

The longest continuous cycle race in the world it is normally around 600 km (375 miles) in length. First held in 1891 it is known as the 'Derby' of road races. The first part of the race, up to Chattellerault, is staged in darkness. Thereafter, the riders are paced by Derny motorcycle riders.

Most wins: 7 (incl.one shared) Herman Van Springel (Bel) 1970, 1974-5, 1977-8, 1980-1

Grand Prix des Nations (GN)

The world's premier time trial, it is regarded as the time-trialists 'unofficial' world championship. The venue for the race has varied over the years but has always been held in France. It was first held in 1932.

Most wins: 9 Jacques Anquetil (Fra) 1953-8, 1961, 1965-6; 5 Bernard Hinault (Fra) 1977-9, 1982, 1984

Paris-Nice (PN)

An gruelling early-season stage race, the riders cover more than 1100km in six days.

Most wins: 7 Sean Kelly (Ire) 1982-8

Most wins in a season

54 Eddy Merckx (Bel) 1971
53 Freddy Maertens (Bel) 1977
52 Freddy Maertens 1976; Eddy Merckx 1970
51 Eddy Merckx 1973
50 Eddy Merckx 1972
42 Rik Van Looy (Bel) 1965

The Classic riders

The riders to have had most wins in the Classic races (MR to BP as shown in text), the Grand Prix des Nations (GN), the World Road Race Championship (WC) and the three prestigious Continental tours: Tour de France (Fr), Tour of Italy (It), Tour of Spain (Sp).

Name	MR	Fl	PR	FW	LB	PB	TL	BP	GN	WC	Fr	It	Sp	Total
Eddy Merckx	7	2	3	4	5	1	2	-	1	3	5	5	1	39
Bernard Hinault	-	-	1	2	2	-	2	-	5	1	5	3	2	23
Fausto Coppi	3	-	1	1	-	-	5	-	2	1	2	5	-	20
Jacques Anquetil	-	-	-	-	1	-	-	1	9	-	5	2	1	19
Alfredo Binda	2	-	-	-	-	-	4	-	-	3	-	5	-	14
Roger de Vlaeminck	3	1	4	1	1	1	3	-	-	-	-	-	-	14
Rik van Looy	1	2	3	1	1	2	1	-	-	2	-	-	-	13
Gino Bartali	4	-	-	-	-	-	3	-	-	-	2	3	-	12
Felice Gimondi	1	-	1	-	-	1	2	-	2	1	1	2	1	12
Rik van Steenbergen	1	2	2	2	-	1	-	-	-	3	-	-	-	11
Herman van Springel	-	-	-	-	-	-	1	7	2	-	-	-	-	10
Louison Bobet	1	1	1	-	-	-	1	1	1	1	3	-	-	10

WORLD CUP

The first World Cup, sponsored by Perrier, was introduced in 1989. Riders amassed points in 12 major races, including six classics, throughout the year. The inaugural winner was Sean Kelly (Ire).

SUPER PRESTIGE PERNOD COMPETITION

Various European races were designated as counting towards a season-long competition with varying points depending upon status of the race, and the rider's finishing position. The rider with the most points at the end of the season won the Super Prestige Pernod Trophy. The first award was made in 1959, and won by Henri Anglade(Fra). *Recent winners:*

1977	Freddie Maertens (Bel) 326 pts	
1978	Francesco Moser (Ita) 323	
1979	Bernard Hinault (Fra) 421	
1980	Bernard Hinault (Fra) 315	
1981	Bernard Hinault (Fra) 325	
1982	Bernard Hinault (Fra) 266	
1983	Greg LeMond (USA) 245	
1984	Sean Kelly (Ire) 435	
1985	Sean Kelly (Ire) 309	
1986	Sean Kelly (Ire) 910	
1987	Stephen Roche (Ire) 800	

TOUR OF BRITAIN (Milk Race)

Until 1983 the Milk Race was an amateur-only event but it has since gone open. First held in 1951 it was originally sponsored by the Daily Express, but has been sponsored by the Milk Marketing Board since 1958 when the race resumed after a two year lay-off. *Winners:*

1951	Ian Steel (UK)
1952	Ken Russell (UK)
1953	Gordon Thomas (UK)
1954	Eugene Tamburlini (Fra)
1955	Anthony Hewson (UK)
1958	Richard Durlacher (Aut)
1959-60	Bill Bradley (UK)
1961	Billy Holmes (UK)
1962	Eugen Pokorny (Pol)
1963	Peter Chisman (UK)
1964	Arthur Metcalfe (UK)
1965	Les West (UK)
1966	Josef Gawliczek (Pol)
1967	Les West (UK)
1968	Gösta Pettersson (Swe)
1969	Fedor Den Hertog (Hol)
1970	Jiri Mainus (Cs)
1971	Fedor Den Hertog (Hol)
1972	Hennie Kuiper (Hol)
1973	Piet van Katwijk (Hol)
1974	Roy Schuiten (Hol)
1975	Bernt Johansson (Swe)
1976	Bill Nickson (UK)
1977	Said Gusseinov (USSR)
1978	Jan Brzezny (Pol)
1979	Yuriy Kashirin (USSR)
1980	Ivan Mitchtenko (USSR)
1981	Sergey Krivocheyev (USSR)
1982	Yuriy Kashirin (USSR)
1983	Matt Eaton (USA)
1984	Oleg Czougeda (USSR)
1985	Eric van Lancker (Bel)
1986	Joey McLoughlin (UK)
1987	Malcolm Elliott (UK)
1988	Vasiliy Zhdanov (USSR)
1989	Brian Walton (Can)
1990	Shane Sutton (Aus)

Most wins: 2 Bill Bradley, Les West, Fedor Den Hertog, Yuriy Kashirin

SPEED RECORDS

Records are recognised for both professionals and amateurs on open air and indoor tracks for a variety of distances at unpaced flying and standing starts and for motor-paced. In this selection only the best (amateur or professional) is shown.

MEN – WORLD RECORDS – OPEN-AIR TRACKS
UNPACED STANDING START

Distance	hr:min:sec			
1km	1:02.091	Maic Malchow (GDR)	Colorado Springs	28 Aug 1986
4km	4:31.160	Gintautas Umaras (USSR)	Seoul	18 Sep 1987
5km	5:44.700	Gregor Braun (FRG)	La Paz	12 Jan 1986
10km	11:39.720	Francesco Moser (Ita)	Mexico City	19 Jan 1984
20km	23:21.592	Francesco Moser (Ita)	Mexico City	23 Jan 1984
100km	2hr 09:11.312	Kent Bostick (USA)	Colorado Springs	13 Oct 1989
51.15135km	*1 hour*	Francesco Moser (Ita)	Mexico City	23 Jan 1984

UNPACED FLYING START

200m	10.118	Michael Hübner (GDR)	Colorado Springs	28 Aug 1986
500m	26.776	Philippe Boyer (Fra)	La Paz	Jun 1989
1km	58.269	Domingo Rueda (Col)	La Paz	13 Dec 1986

MOTOR-PACED

50km	35:21.108	Aleksandr Romanov (USSR)	Tbilisi	6 May 1987
100km	1hr 10:29.42	Giovanni Renosto (Ita)	Bassano del Grappa	16 Sep 1988
85.067 km	1 hour	Giovanni Renosto (Ita)	Bassano del Grappa	16 Sep 1988

MEN – WORLD RECORDS – INDOOR TRACKS
UNPACED STANDING START

Distance	hr:min:sec			
1km	1:02.576	Aleksandr Kirichenko (USSR)	Moscow	2 Aug 1989
4km	4:28.900	Vyacheslav Yekimov (USSR)	Moscow	20 Sep 1986
5km	5:39.316	Vyacheslav Yekimov (USSR)	Moscow	25 Apr 1990
10km	11:31.968	Vyacheslav Yekimov (USSR)	Moscow	7 Jan 1989
20km	23:14.553	Vyacheslav Yekimov (USSR)	Moscow	3 Feb 1989
100km	2hr 10:08.287	Beat Meister (Swi)	Stuttgart	22 Sep 1989
50.644km	*1 hour*	Francesco Moser (Ita)	Stuttgart	21 May 1988
4km team	4:10.877	USSR	Moscow	4 Aug 1989
		(Vyacheslav Yekimov, Dmitriy Nelyubin, Mikhail Orlov, Yevgeniy Berzin)		

UNPACED FLYING START

200m	10.117	Nikolay Kovch (USSR)	Moscow	5 Feb 1988
500m	26.649	Aleksandr Kirichenko (USSR	Moscow	29 Oct 1988
1km	57.260	Aleksandr Kirichenko (USSR	Moscow	25 Apr 1989

MOTOR-PACED

50km	32:56.746	Aleksandr Romanov (USSR)	Moscow	21 Feb 1987
100km	1hr 05:58.031	Aleksandr Romanov (USSR)	Moscow	21 Feb 1987
91.131 km	*1 hour*	Aleksandr Romanov (USSR)	Moscow	21 Feb 1987

WOMEN – WORLD RECORDS – OPEN-AIR TRACKS

UNPACED STANDING START

Distance	hr:min:sec			
1km	1:14.249	Erika Salumyae (USSR)	Tashkent	17 May 1984
3km	3:38.190	Jeannie Longo (Fra)	Mexico City	5 Oct 1989
5km	6:14.135	Jeannie Longo (Fra)	Mexico City	27 Sep 1989
10km	12:59.435	Jeannie Longo (Fra)	Mexico City	1 Oct 1989
20km	25:59.883	Jeannie Longo (Fra)	Mexico City	1 Oct 1989
100km	2hr 28:26.259	Francesco Galli (Ita)	Milan	26 Oct 1987
46.35270km	*1 hour*	Jeannie Longo (Fra)	Mexico City	1 Oct 1989

UNPACED FLYING START

200m	0:11.383	Isabelle Gautheron (Fra)	Colorado Springs	16 Aug 1986
500m	0:30.59	Isabelle Gautheron (Fra)	Cali	14 Sep 1986
1km	1:10.463	Erika Salumyae (USSR)	Tashkent	15 May 1984

WOMEN – WORLD RECORDS – INDOOR TRACKS
UNPACED STANDING START

Distance	hr:min:sec			
1km	1:13.377	Erika Salumyae (USSR)	Moscow	21 Sep 1983
3km	3:43.490	Jeannie Longo (Fra)	Paris (Bercy)	14 Nov 1986
5km	6:22.713	Jeannie Longo (Fra)	Grenoble	2 Nov 1986
10km	12:54.26	Jeannie Longo (Fra)	Paris (Bercy)	19 Oct 1989
20km	26:51.22	Jeannie Longo (Fra)	Moscow	29 Oct 1989
100km	2hr 31:30.043	Mieke Havik (Hol)	Rotterdam	19 Sep 1983
45.016km	1 hour	Jeannie Longo (Fra)	Moscow	29 Oct 1989

UNPACED FLYING START

200m	0:11.170	Erika Salumyae (USSR)	Moscow	1 Aug 1989
500m	0:29.655	Erika Salumyae (USSR)	Moscow	6 Aug 1987
1km	1:05.232	Erika Salumyae (USSR)	Moscow	31 May 1987

1 HOUR

The classic speed record is that for 1 hour. The current record as in the table above was set at high altitude by Francesco Moser. He also holds the best distance set at sea level: 49.80193 km at Milan on 3 Oct 1986. Similarly Jeannie Longo also holds the women's sea-level best: 43.58789 km at Milan on 30 Sep 1986.

The men's 1 hour record at the end of each decade has progressed:

km			
40.781	M.W.Hamilton (USA)	Denver	9 Jul 1898
41.520	Marcel Berthet (Fra)	Paris	20 Jun 1907
44.247	Oscar Egg (Swi)	Paris	18 Jun 1914
45.767	Maurice Archambaud (Fra)	Milan	3 Nov 1937
45.848	Fausto Coppi (Ita)	Milan	7 Nov 1942
47.346	Roger Rivière (Fra)	Milan	23 Nov 1958
48.653	Ole Ritter (Den)	Mexico City	10 Dec 1968
49.431	Eddy Merckx (Bel)	Mexico City	25 Oct 1972
51.151	Francesco Moser (Ita)	Mexico City	23 Jan 1984

The women's record has progressed:

41.347	Elsy Jacobs (Lux)	Milan	9 Nov 1958
41.471	Maria Cressari (Ita)	Mexico City	25 Nov 1972
43.082	Cornelia Van Oosten (Hol)	Munich	16 Sep 1978
46.352	Jeannie Longo (Fra)	Mexico City	1 Oct 1989

Francesco Moser in training at Mexico City, where in January 1984 he twice smashed the world record for one hour, with 50.80937 km on the 19th and 51.15135 km four days later. He set new records at 10km en route in the first race and at 20km in the second **(Popperfoto)**

CYCLO-CROSS

The first world cross-country cycling world championships were held in 1950.
From 1967 they have been split into amateur and professional categories.

Open and Professional champions

1950	Jean Robic (Fra)
1951-3	Roger Rondeaux (Fra)
1954-8	André Dufraisse (Fra)
1959	Renato Longo (Ita)
1960-1	Rolf Wolfshohl (FRG)
1962	Renato Longo (Ita)
1963	Rolf Wolfshohl (FRG)
1964-5	Renato Longo (Ita)
1966	Eric de Vlaeminck (Bel)
1967	Renato Longo (Ita)
1968-73	Eric de Vlaeminck (Bel)
1974	Albert van Damme (Bel)
1975	Roger de Vlaeminck (Bel)
1976-9	Albert Zweifel (Swi)
1980	Roland Liboton (Bel)
1981	Johannes Stamsnijder (Hol)
1982-4	Roland Liboton (Bel)
1985	Klaus-Peter Thaler (FRG)
1986	Albert Zweifel (Swi)
1987	Klaus-Peter Thaler (FRG)
1988	Pascal Richard (Swi)
1989	Danny de Bie (Bel)
1990	Henk Baars (Hol)

Most wins: 7 Eric de Vlaeminck; 5
André Dufraisse, Renato Longo

Amateur champions

1967	Michel Pelchat (Fra)
1968	Roger de Vlaeminck (Bel)
1969	René Declercq (Bel)
1970-1	Robert Vermeire (Bel)
1972	Norbert de Deckere (Bel)
1973	Klaus-Peter Thaler (FRG)
1974-5	Robert Vermeire (Bel)
1976	Klaus-Peter Thaler (FRG)
1977	Robert Vermeire (Bel)
1978	Roland Liboton (Bel)
1979	Vito di Tano (Ita)
1980	Fritz Saladin (Swi)
1981-2	Milos Fisera (Cs)
1983-4	Radomir Simunek (Cs)
1985	Mike Kluge (FRG)
1986	Vito di Tano (Ita)
1987	Mike Kluge (FRG)
1988	Karel Camrda (Cs)
1989	Ondrej Glajza (Cs)
1990	Andreas Brüsser (Swi)

Most wins: 5 Robert Vermeire

Amateur Team (from 1979)

1979	Poland
1980	Switzerland
1981	Italy
1982-4	Czechoslovakia
1985	Switzerland
1986	Belgium
1987	Czechoslovakia
1988	Switzerland
1989	Czechoslovakia
1990	Switzerland

Eric de Vlaeminck at Crystal Palace in 1973, on his way to his sixth successive world cyclo-cross title (Hulton-Deutsch)

DARTS

Darts, or *Dartes*, were first used as a means of self defence during battles in Ireland in the 16th century. The Pilgrim Fathers played darts aboard the *Mayflower* on their way to discovering the New World in 1620. The modern game, however, dates to 1896 when Brian Gamlin of Bury, Lancashire, devised the present numbering system. The National Darts Association was formed in 1924 and the British Darts Organisation (BDO) was established in 1973. Since then it has developed into a popular television sport, and today more than 6 million people play darts in Britain alone.

WORLD PROFESSIONAL CHAMPIONSHIP

The world professional championship, sponsored by Embassy, is the professional players' leading tournament. It was instituted at the Heart of the Midlands Night Club, Nottingham in 1978. Between 1979 and 1985 all tournaments were held at Jollees Night Club, Stoke-on-Trent. Since 1986 the Lakeside Country Club, Frimley Green, Surrey, has been host to the championship.

Year	Winner	Runner-up	Score
1978	Leighton Rees (Wal)	John Lowe (Eng)	11-7
1979	John Lowe (Eng)	Leighton Rees (Wal)	5-0
1980	Eric Bristow (Eng)	Bobby George (Eng)	5-3
1981	Eric Bristow (Eng)	John Lowe (Eng)	5-3
1982	Jocky Wilson (Sco)	John Lowe (Eng)	5-3
1983	Keith Deller (Eng)	Eric Bristow (Eng)	6-5
1984	Eric Bristow (Eng)	Dave Whitcombe (Eng)	7-1
1985	Eric Bristow (Eng)	John Lowe (Eng)	6-2
1986	Eric Bristow (Eng)	Dave Whitcombe (Eng)	6-0
1987	John Lowe (Eng)	Eric Bristow (Eng)	6-4
1988	Bob Anderson (Eng)	John Lowe (Eng)	6-4
1989	Jocky Wilson (Sco)	Eric Bristow (Eng)	6-4
1990	Phil Taylor (Eng)	Eric Bristow (Eng)	6-1

1977 best of 21 legs, 1978-82 best of 9 sets, 1983 best of 11 sets, 1984 best of 13 sets, 1985-90 best of 11 sets

WORLD MASTERS

The first World Masters took place at the West Centre Hotel, Fulham in 1974. *Winners:*

1974	Cliff Inglis (Eng)
1975	Alan Evans (Wal)
1976	John Lowe (Eng)
1977	Eric Bristow (Eng)
1978	Ronnie Davis (Eng)
1979	Eric Bristow (Eng)
1980	John Lowe (Eng)
1981	Eric Bristow (Eng)
1982	Dave Whitcombe (Eng)
1983-4	Eric Bristow (Eng)
1985	Dave Whitcombe (Eng)
1986-8	Bob Anderson (Eng)
1989	Peter Evison (Eng)

WORLD CUP

A biennial event, the first World Cup was at Wembley in 1977. The winning nation is the team with the most points after a singles, pairs and fours competition. The United States hosted the event in 1979, New Zealand in 1981, Scotland in 1983, Australia in 1985, Denmark in 1987, and Canada in 1989. The women's competition was introduced in 1983.

Team winners		*Runners-up*
1977	Wales	England
1979	England	USA
1981	England	Scotland
1983	England	Scotland
1985	England	USA
1987	England	Canada
1989	England	Canada

Individual title:

1977	Leighton Rees (Wal)
1979	Nicky Virachkul (USA)
1981	John Lowe (Eng)
1983	Eric Bristow (Eng)
1985	Eric Bristow (Eng)
1987	Eric Bristow (Eng)
1989	Eric Bristow (Eng)

Most winning teams: 6 John Lowe, Eric Bristow (both England)

NATIONS CUP

A tournament for three-man teams, the first Nations Cup was organised in 1977. *Winners:*

1977	Scotland
1978	Sweden
1979-80	England
1981	Scotland
1982-4	England
1985	Finland
1986-8	England
1989	Not held

Most wins: 8 England.   *Most winning teams:* 8 John Lowe, Eric Bristow (both England)

BRITISH OPEN

Inaugurated 1975 *Winners:*

1975	Alan Evans (Wal)
1976	Jack North (Eng)
1977	John Lowe (Eng)
1978	Eric Bristow (Eng)
1979	Tony Brown (Eng)
1980	Cliff Lazarenko (Eng)
1981	Eric Bristow (Eng)
1982	Jocky Wilson (Sco)
1983	Eric Bristow (Eng)
1984	John Cusnett (Eng)
1985-6	Eric Bristow (Eng)
1987	Bob Anderson (Eng)
1988	John Lowe (Eng)

1989   Brian Cairns (Wal) *
1990   Alan Warriner (Eng) *
* Held previous December

WORLD PAIRS CHAMPIONSHIP
Instituted 1986 *Winners:*
1986   John Lowe & Bob Anderson (Eng)
1987   Eric Bristow (Eng) & Peter Locke (Wal)
1988   Jocky Wilson (Sco) & Ritchie Gardner (Eng)
1989   Not held

WORLD MATCH-PLAY   Instituted 1984
Winners:
1984   John Lowe (Eng)
1985   Eric Bristow (Eng)
1986   Mike Gregory (Eng)
1987   Bob Anderson (Eng)
1988   Eric Bristow (Eng)
1989   Not held

Bob Anderson ended the supremacy of John Lowe and Eric Bristow when he took the World darts title in 1988 as well as the World Masters titles in 1986, 1987 and 1988 (All-Sport/Pascal Rondeau)

BRITISH MATCH-PLAY
Instituted 1976 *Winners:*
1976   Bill Lennard (Eng)
1977   Rab Smith (Sco)
1978   John Lowe (Eng)
1979   Cliff Lazarenko (Eng)
1980-1 Jocky Wilson (Sco)
1982-3 Eric Bristow (Eng)
1984   Mike Gregory (Eng)
1985   John Lowe (Eng)
1986   Eric Bristow (Eng)
1987   Dave Whitcombe (Eng)
1988-9 Bob Anderson (Eng)

BRITISH PROFESSIONAL CHAMPIONSHIP
First contested 1981 *Winners:*
1981   Jocky Wilson (Sco)
1982   Eric Bristow (Eng)
1983   Jocky Wilson (Sco)
1984   Mike Gregory (Eng)
1985   Eric Bristow (Eng)
1986   Jocky Wilson (Sco)
1987   Keith Deller (Eng)
1988   Jocky Wilson (Sco)
1989   Not held

THE SUPER CHAMPIONS

EWC – Embassy World Championship, WM – World Masters, WCI – World Cup Individual, BO – British Open, WP – World Pairs, WMP – World Match-play, BMP – British Match-Play, BP – British Professional, NOW – News of the World. *Players winning three or more:*

	Total	EWC	WM	WCI	BO	WP	WMP	BMP	BP	NOW
Eric Bristow	29	5	5	4	5	1	2	3	2	2
John Lowe	12	2	2	1	2	1	1	2	-	1
Jocky Wilson	10	2	-	-	1	1	-	2	4	-
Bob Anderson	9	1	3	-	1	1	1	2	-	-
Mike Gregory	5	-	-	-	-	-	1	1	1	2
Dave Whitcombe	4	-	2	-	-	-	-	1	-	1

NEWS OF THE WORLD CHAMPIONSHIP

Prior to the World Professional championship the News of the World title was the most prestigious in darts. Because of the thousands of entrants from all over the British Isles it remains the most difficult title to win, and is one still sought after by even the best of the professionals. The first championship was in the London Area only in 1928. Other areas had their own News of the World Championships but it was not until 1948 that it became a national event. *Winners (all British unless otherwise stated):*

1948	Harry Leadbetter	1969	Barry Twomlow
1949	Jack Boyce	1970	Henry Barney
1950	Dixie Newberry	1971	Dennis Filkins
1951	Harry Perryman	1972	Brian Netherton
1952	Tommy Gibbons	1973	Ivor Hodgkinson
1953	Jimmy Carr	1974	Peter Chapman
1954	Oliver James	1975	Derek White
1955	Tom Reddington	1976	Bill Lennard
1956	Trevor Peachey	1977	Mick Norris
1957	Alwyn Mullins	1978	Stefan Lord (Swe)
1958	Tommy Gibbons	1979	Bobby George
1959	Albert Welch	1980	Stefan Lord (Swe)
1960	Tom Reddington	1981	John Lowe
1961	Alec Adamson	1982	Roy Morgan
1962	Eddie Brown	1983-4	Eric Bristow
1963	Robbie Rumney	1985	Dave Lee
1964-5	Tom Barrett	1986	Bobby George
1966	Wilf Ellis	1987-8	Mike Gregory
1967	Wally Seaton	1989	Dave Whitcombe
1968	Bill Duddy	1990	Paul Cook

WOMEN'S DARTS

WORLD CUP

Instituted in 1983 and played at the same time as the men's competition.

	Team winners	Runners-up	Individual
1983	England	USA	Sandy Reitan (USA)
1985	England	Scotland	Linda Batten (UK)
1987	USA	Holland	Valerie Maycum (Hol)
1989	England	USA	Eva Grigsby (USA)

WORLD MASTERS

1982	Ann-Marie Davies (Wal)
1983	Sonja Ralphs (Eng)
1984	Kathy Wones (Eng)
1985	Lilian Barnett (NZ)
1986	Kathy Wones (Eng)
1987	Ann Thomas (Wal)
1988-9	Mandy Solomons (Eng)

BRITISH OPEN   First held 1979. *Winners:*

1979	Judy Campbell (Sco)
1980	Linda Batten (Eng)
1981	Ann Marie-Davies (Wal)
1982	Maureen Flowers (Eng)
1983	Sandy Earnshaw (Eng)
1984	Ann Marie Davies (Wal)
1985	Linda Batten (Eng)
1986	Gwen Sutton (Eng)
1987	Sharon Colclough (Eng)
1988	Jane Stubbs (Eng)
1989	Cathie McCullough (Sco)
1990	Sharon Colclough (Eng)

EQUESTRIANISM

The earliest known show jumping competition was in Ireland when the Royal Dublin Society held its first 'Horse Show' on 15 Apr 1864. The Societé Hippique Française was founded in 1865 and held its first Concours Hippique in Paris in 1866. The first event in England was at the Agricultural Hall, London in 1869.

Dressage competition derived from the exercises taught at 16th century Italian and French horsemanship academies, while the three-day event developed from cavalry endurance rides. One of the earliest known three-day event competitions was from Vienna to Berlin in 1892. The international governing body, the Fédération Equestre Internationale (FEI), was founded in Brussels in 1921, initially with eight member nations. The current president is HRH Princess Anne, who succeeded her father, HRH Prince Philip in 1986, and membership reached 91 nations in 1989.

SHOW JUMPING

OLYMPIC GAMES

Although not connected with events staged with the World Fair, what is regarded now as the first Olympic show jumping were the three days of international competition staged by the Societé Hippique Française in Paris in 1900, with jumping, high jump and long jump events. Two equestrian events were planned for 1908, but not held due to the paucity of entries, so show jumping was officially introduced in 1912. The 1956 competition took place in Stockholm, Sweden, because of quarantine restriction in force in Australia at the time. *Winners:*

Individual

	Rider	Horse
1900	Aimé Haegeman (Bel)	Benton II
1912	Jean Cariou (Fra)	Mignon
1920	Tommaso Lequio (Ita)	Trebecco
1924	Alphonse Gemuseus (Swi)	Lucette
1928	Frantisek Ventura (Cs)	Eliot
1932	Takeichi Nishi (Jap)	Uranus
1936	Kürt Hasse (Ger)	Tora
1948	Humberto Mariles Cortés (Mex)	Arete
1952	Pierre Jonquères d'Oriola (Fra)	Ali Baba
1956	Hans-Günter Winkler (Ger)	Halla
1960	Raimondo d'Inzeo (Ita)	Posillipo
1964	Pierre Jonquères d'Oriola (Fra)	Lutteur B
1968	William Steinkraus (USA)	Snowbound
1972	Graziano Mancinelli (Ita)	Ambassador
1976	Alwin Schockemöhle (FRG)	Warwick Rex
1980	Jan Kowalczyk (Pol)	Artemor
1984	Joe Fargis (USA)	Touch of Class
1988	Pierre Durand (Fra)	Jappeloup

Team

6 FR Germany 1936 (as Germany), 1956, 1960, 1964, 1972, 1988
3 Sweden 1912, 1920, 1924
1 Spain 1928, Mexico 1948, Great Britain 1952, Canada 1968, France 1976, USSR 1980, USA 1984

No medals awarded 1932, when event not completed as no nation completed the course with three riders.

Most gold medals: 5 Hans-Günter Winkler (FRG) team 1956, 1960, 1964, 1972; individual 1956
Most medals:
7 Hans-Günter Winkler 5 gold, team silver 1976, team bronze 1968; 6 Raimondo d'Inzeo (Ita) 1 gold (ind. 1960), 2 silver (team and ind. 1956), 3 bronze team 1960, 1964, 1972); 6 Piero d'Inzeo (Ita) 2 silver, 4 bronze (ind. silver 1960, bronze 1960, 1 team silver and 3 team bronze as for his younger brother Raimondo).

WORLD CHAMPIONSHIPS

Instituted in 1953, the championships are now held every four years. In the individual final each rider has to ride not only his own horse but also those of the other finallists. In 1965, 1970 and 1974, women had a separate competition on their own horses only, but now compete equally with their male counterparts. A team competition was introduced in 1978. *Winners:*

Individual

	Rider	Horse
1953	Francisco Goyoago (Spa)	Quorum
1954	Hans-Günter Winkler (FRG)	Halla
1955	Hans-Günter Winkler (FRG)	Halla
1956	Raimondo d'Inzeo (Ita)	Merano

Raimondo d'Inzeo, here riding Fiorello *at Wembley in 1970, competed in eight Olympic Games between 1948 and 1976, winning medals at four of them* (Hulton-Deutsch)

1960	Raimondo d'Inzeo (Ita)	Gowran Girl
1966	Pierre Jonquères d'Oriola (Fra)	Pomone B
1970	David Broome (UK)	Beethoven
1974	Hartwig Steenken (FRG)	Simona
1978	Gerd Wiltfang (FRG)	Roman
1982	Norbert Koof (FRG)	Fire II
1986	Gail Greenhough (Can)	Mr.T

Women

1965	Marion Coakes (UK)	Stroller
1970	Janou Lefèbvre (Fra)	Rocket
1974	Janou Tissot (née Lefèbvre) (Fra)	Rocket

Team
Great Britain 1978, France 1982, USA 1986
Most titles: 2 Hans-Günter Winkler, Raimondo d'Inzeo, Janou Tissot (née Lefèbvre)

VOLVO WORLD CUP
Instituted by the FEI in 1979 and contested over a series of primarily indoor competitions held between October and April with an annual final. *Winners:*

1979	Hugo Simon (Aut)	Gladstone
1980	Conrad Homfeld (USA)	Balbuco
1981	Michael Matz (USA)	Jet Run
1982	Melanie Smith (USA)	Calypso
1983	Norman Dello Joio (USA)	I Love You
1984	Mario Deslauriers (Can)	Aramis
1985	Conrad Homfeld (USA)	Abdullah
1986	Leslie Burr-Lenehan (USA)	McLain
1987	Katharine Burdsall (USA)	The Natural
1988-9	Ian Millar (Can)	Big Ben
1990	John Whitaker (UK)	Henderson Milton

NATION'S CUP
The President's Cup was introduced by the FEI in 1965 for Nations Cup teams. The performances by national teams of four at selected meetings count towards the Cup, with different countries staging just one Nations Cup meeting, which must be at its official International Horse Show. Renamed the Prince Philip Trophy in 1985, to mark his 21st year in office as FEI President, and the Gucci Cup from 1989.
Winning nations:
13 Great Britain 1965, 1967, 1970, 1972-4, 1977-9, 1983, 1985-6, 1989
7 FR Germany 1969, 1971, 1975-6, 1981-2, 1984
3 France 1980, 1987-8
2 USA 1966, 1968

EUROPEAN CHAMPIONSHIPS
Inaugurated in 1957, and staged bienially from 1963, men and women had separate competitions (and were allowed to ride two horses) until 1975, when the FEI introduced a team event as well as an individual competition open to both men and women. In 1957 and 1959 they were conducted with a change-horse final, as per the World Championships, but that was then abandoned. *Winners (with first horses prior to 1975):*

Men

	Rider	*Horse*
1957	Hans-Günter Winkler (FRG)	Sonnenglanz
1958	Fritz Thiedemann (FRG)	Meteor
1959	Piero d'Inzeo (Ita)	Uruguay
1961	David Broome (UK)	Sunsalve
1962	David Barker (UK)	Mister Softee
1963	Graziano Mancinelli (Ita)	Rockette
1965	Hermann Schridde (FRG)	Dozent
1966	Nelson Pessoa (Bra)	Gran Geste
1967	David Broome (UK)	Mister Softee
1969	David Broome (UK)	Mister Softee
1971	Hartwig Steenken (FRG)	Simona
1973	Paddy McMahon (UK)	Pennwood Forge Mill
1975	Alwin Schockemöhle (FRG)	Warwick
1977	Johan Heins (Hol)	Seven Valleys
1979	Gerhard Wiltfang (FRG)	Roman
1981	Paul Schockemöhle (FRG)	Deister
1983	Paul Schockemöhle (FRG)	Deister
1985	Paul Schockemöhle (FRG)	Deister
1987	Pierre Durand (Fra)	Jappeloup
1989	John Whitaker (UK)	Next Milton

Team
4 Great Britain 1979, 1985, 1987, 1989
2 FR Germany 1975, 1981
1 Netherlands 1977, Switzerland 1983

Women

1957	Pat Smythe (UK)	Flanagan
1958	Guilia Serventi (Ita)	Doly
1959	Ann Townsend (UK)	Bandit IV
1960	Susan Cohen (UK)	Clare Castle
1961	Pat Smythe (UK)	Scorchin
1962	Pat Smythe (UK)	Flanagan
1963	Pat Smythe (UK)	Flanagan
1966	Janou Lefèbvre (Fra)	Kenavo
1967	Kathy Kusner (USA)	Untouchable
1968	Anneli Drummond-Hay (UK)	Merely-a-Monarch
1969	Iris Kellett (Ire)	Morning Light
1971	Ann Moore (UK)	Psalm
1973	Ann Moore (UK)	Psalm

Flanagan is the only horse to have won four European Championships, the three above and in 1961 when he was Pat Smythe's second horse.

ROYAL INTERNATIONAL HORSE SHOW
First staged as the International Horse Show in the Grand Hall at Olympia in 1907. The world's first Nations Cup for teams was staged in 1909. The Show is now held annually at Wembley. The two most famous events are the:
King George V Gold Cup
A gold international challenge trophy presented by King George V to be perpetually contested. It was first contested in 1911, and is regarded as the principle show

jumping competition for male riders. Any rider winning the event three times keeps the trophy. *Post war winners:*

1947	Pierre Jonquères d'Oriola (Fra)	Marquis III
1948	Harry Llewellyn (UK)	Foxhunter
1949	Brian Butler (UK)	Tankard
1950	Harry Llewellyn (UK)	Foxhunter
1951	Kevin Barry (Ire)	Ballyneety
1952	Carlos Figueroa (Spa)	Gracieux
1953	Harry Llewellyn (UK)	Foxhunter
1954	Fritz Thiedemann (FRG)	Meteor
1955	Luigi Cartesegna (Ita)	Brando
1956	William Steinkraus (USA)	First Boy
1957	Piero d'Inzeo (Ita)	Uruguay
1958	Hugh Wiley (USA)	Master William
1959	Hugh Wiley (USA)	Nautical
1960	David Broome (UK)	Sunsalve
1961-2	Piero d'Inzeo (Ita)	The Rock
1963	Thomas Wade (Ire)	Dundrum
1964	William Steinkraus (USA)	Sinjon
1965	Hans-Günter Winkler (FRG)	Fortun
1966	David Broome (UK)	Mister Softee
1967	Peter Robeson (UK)	Firecrest
1968	Hans-Günter Winkler (FRG)	Enigk
1969	Ted Edgar (UK)	Uncle Max
1970	Harvey Smith (UK)	Mattie Brown
1971	Gerd Wiltfang (FRG)	Askan
1972	David Broome (UK)	Sportsman
1973	Paddy McMahon (UK)	Pennwood Forge Mill
1974	Frank Chapot (USA)	Main Spring
1975	Alwin Schockemöhle (FRG)	Rex the Robber
1976	Michael Saywell (UK)	Chain Bridge
1977	David Broome (UK)	Philco
1978	Jeff McVean (Aus)	Claret
1979	Robert Smith (UK)	Video
1980	David Bowen (UK)	Scorton
1981	David Broome (UK)	Mr.Ross
1982	Michael Whitaker (UK)	Disney Way
1983	Paul Schockemöhle (FRG)	Deister
1984	Nick Skelton (UK)	St.James
1985	Malcolm Pyrah (UK)	Towerlands Anglezark
1986	John Whitaker (UK)	Next Ryan's Son
1987	Malcolm Pyrah (UK)	Towerlands Anglezark
1988	Robert Smith (UK)	Brook Street Boysie
1989	Michael Whitaker (UK)	Next Didi
1990	John Whitaker (UK)	Henderson Milton

Most wins: Rider: 5 David Broome, 3 Jack Talbot-Ponsonby 1930, 1932, 1934; Harry Llewellyn, Piero d'Inzeo, David Broome.
Horse: 3 Foxhunter 1948, 1950, 1953

Queen Elizabeth II Cup
The Queen Elizabeth II Cup is the women's equivalent of the King George V Gold Cup. It was inaugurated in 1949. *Winners:*

1949	Iris Kellett (Ire)	Rusty
1950	Gill Palethorpe (UK)	Silver Cloud
1951	Iris Kellett (Ire)	Rusty
1952	Gill Rich (UK)	Quicksilver III
1953	Marie Delfosse (UK)	Fanny Rosa
1954	Josée Bonnaud (Fra)	Charleston
1955-6	Dawn Palethorpe (UK)	Earlsrath Rambler
1957	Elizabeth Anderson (UK)	Sunsalve
1958	Pat Smythe (UK)	Mr.Pollard
1959	Anna Clement (FRG)	Nico
1960	Susan Cohen (UK)	Clare Castle
1961	Lady Sarah FitzAlan Howard (UK)	Oorskiet
1962	Judy Crago (UK)	Spring Fever
1963	Julie Nash (UK)	Trigger Hill
1964	Gillian Makin (UK)	Jubilant
1965	Marion Coakes (UK)	Stroller
1966	Althea Roger Smith (UK)	Havana Royal
1967	Betty Jennaway (UK)	Grey Leg
1968	Mary Chapot (USA)	White Lightning
1969	Alison Westwood (UK)	The Maverick VII
1970	Anneli Drummond-Hay (UK)	Merely-a-Monarch
1971	Marion Mould (née Coakes) (UK)	Stroller
1972	Ann Moore (UK)	Psalm
1973	Ann Moore (UK) &	Psalm
	Alison Dawes (née Westwood)	Mr.Banbury
1974	Jean Davenport (née Goodwin) (UK)	All Trumps
1975	Jean Davenport (UK)	Hang On
1976	Marion Mould (UK)	Elizabeth Ann
1977	Liz Edgar (UK	Everest Wallaby
1978	Caroline Bradley (UK)	Marius
1979	Liz Edgar (UK)	Forever
1980	Caroline Bradley (UK)	Tigre
1981-2	Liz Edgar (UK)	Everest Forever
1983	Jean Germany (UK)	Mandingo
1984	Véronique Whitaker (UK)	Next's Jingo
1985	Sue Pountain (UK)	Ned Kelly VI
1986	Liz Edgar (UK)	Everest Rapier
1987	Gillian Greenwood (UK)	Monsanta
1988-9	Janet Hunter (UK)	Everest Lisnamarrow
1990	Emma-Jane Mac	Everest Oyster

Most wins: 5 Liz Edgar, 3 Marion Mould (née Coakes)
The only horse to win the King George V Gold Cup and Queen Elizabeth II Cup is Sunsalve, 1957, 1960.

BRITISH SHOW JUMPING DERBY
Held annually at the All-England Jumping Centre Hickstead in Sussex, the first Derby was in 1961. A Derby is contested over a course of c.1300m, about 500m longer than an Olympic Nations Cup course.

1961	Seamus Hayes (Ire)	Goodbye III
1962	Pat Smythe (UK)	Flanagan
1963	Nelson Pessoa (Bra)	Gran Geste
1964	Seamus Hayes (Ire)	Goodbye III
1965	Nelson Pessoa (Bra)	Gran Geste

1966	David Broome (UK)	Mister Softee
1967	Marion Coakes (UK)	Stroller
1968	Alison Westwood (UK)	The Maverick VII
1969	Anneli Drummond-Hay (UK)	Xanthos II
1970	Harvey Smith (UK)	Mattie Brown
1971	Harvey Smith (UK)	Mattie Brown
1972	Hendrick Snoek (FRG)	Shirokko
1973	Alison Dawes (née Westwood)	Mr.Banbury
1974	Harvey Smith (UK)	Salvador
1975	Paul Darragh (Ire)	Pele
1976-9	Eddie Macken (Ire)	Boomerang
1980	Michael Whitaker (UK)	Owen Gregory
1981	Harvey Smith (UK)	Sanyo Video
1982	Paul Schockemöhle (FRG)	Deister
1983	John Whitaker (UK)	Ryan's Son
1984	John Ledingham (Ire)	Gabhran
1985	Paul Schockemöhle (FRG)	Lorenzo
1986	Paul Schockemöhle (FRG)	Deister
1987	Nick Skelton (UK)	Raffles
1988-9	Nick Skelton (UK)	Apollo

Most wins: 4 Eddie Macken, Harvey Smith; 3 Paul Schockemöhle, Nick Skelton

JUMPING RECORDS
The official high jump world record is 2.47m (8 ft 1 1/4 in) by *Huasó*, ridden by Capt.Alberto Larraguibel (Chl) on 5 Feb 1949. The world long jump record is 8.40m (27 ft 6 3/4in) by *Something*, ridden by André Ferreira (SAf) on 26 Apr 1975

THREE-DAY EVENTING
Competitors ride the same horse in a) a dressage test, b) endurance competition of four phases: roads and track 16-20 km in Games and championships, steeplechase of 3105-3450m, roads and track again, cross country of 7410-7980m, c) jumping test.

OLYMPIC GAMES
Both individual and team competitions were first held at the 1912 Games. *Winners:*

Individual
1912	Axel Nordlander (Swe)	Lady Artist
1920	Helmer Mörner (Swe)	Germania
1924	Adolph v.d.Voort van Zijp (Hol)	Silver Piece
1928	Charles Pahud de Mortanges (Hol)	Marcroix
1932	Charles Pahud de Mortanges (Hol)	Marcroix
1936	Ludwig Stubbendorff (Ger)	Nurmi
1948	Bernard Chevallier (Fra)	Aiglonne
1952	Hans von Blixen-Finecke Jr (Swe)	Jubal
1956	Petrus Kastenman (Swe)	Iluster
1960	Lawrence Morgan (USA)	Salad Days
1964	Mauro Checcoli (Ita)	Surbean
1968	Jean-Jacques Gùyon (Fra)	Pitou
1972	Richard Meade (UK)	Laurieston
1976	Edmund Coffin (USA)	Bally-Cor
1980	Federico Roman (Ita)	Rossinan
1984	Mark Todd (NZ)	Charisma
1988	Mark Todd (NZ)	Charisma

Team
4 USA 1932, 1948, 1976, 1984
3 Sweden 1912, 1920, 1952
3 Great Britain 1956, 1968, 1972
3 Germany/FR Germany 1936, 1938, 1988
2 Holland 1924, 1928
1 Australia 1960, Italy 1964, USSR 1980
Most gold medals: 4 Charles Pahud de Mortanges (Hol) team 1924, 1928; individual 1928, 1932 (also won team silver 1932 for a record five medals)

WORLD CHAMPIONSHIPS
Instituted in 1966, men and women have competed together at all championships.

Individual
1966	Carlos Moratorio (Arg)	Chalon
1970	Mary Gordon-Watson (UK)	Cornishmàn V
1974	Bruce Davidson (USA)	Irish Cap
1978	Bruce Davidson (USA)	Might Tango
1982	Lucinda Green (UK	Regal Realm
1986	Virginia Leng (UK)	Priceless

Virginia Leng and Master Craftsman, *three-day event winners at Badminton and in the Europeans in 1989*
(All-Sport/Bob Martin)

Bruce Davidson on J.J.Babu at the 1984 Olympics, when he was a member of the winning US three-day event team, but well out of the running in the individual event (All-Sport)

Team *wins*
3 Great Britain 1970, 1982, 1986
1 Ireland 1966, USA 1974, Canada 1978
Most gold medals: 3 Bruce Davidson ind. 1974, 1978, team 1974; 3 Virginia Leng ind. 1986, team 1982, 1986

EUROPEAN CHAMPIONSHIPS

Individual
1953	Lawrence Rook (UK)	Starlight
1954	Albert Hill (UK)	Crispin
1955	Frank Weldon (UK)	Kilbarry
1957	Sheila Willcox (UK)	High and Mighty
1959	Hans Schwarzenbach (Swi)	Burn Trout
1962	James Templar (UK)	M'Lord Connolly
1965	Marian Babirecki (Pol)	Volt
1967	Eddie Boylan (Ire)	Durlas Eile
1969	Mary Gordon-Watson (UK)	Cornishman V
1971	HRH Princess Anne (UK)	Doublet
1973	Aleksandr Yevdokimov (USSR)	Jeger
1975	Lucinda Prior-Palmer (UK)	Be Fair
1977	Lucinda Prior-Palmer (UK)	George
1979	Nils Haagensen (Den)	Monaco
1981	Hansueli Schmutz (Swi)	Oran
1983	Rachel Bayliss (UK)	Mystic Minstrel
1985	Virginia Holgate (UK)	Priceless
1987	Virginia Leng (née Holgate) (UK)	Night Cap
1989	Virginia Leng (UK)	Master Craftsman

Team *wins*
12 Great Britain 1953-5, 1957, 1967, 1969, 1971, 1977, 1981, 1985, 1987, 1989
3 USSR 1962, 1965, 1975
2 FR Germany 1959, 1973
1 Ireland 1979; Sweden 1983

BADMINTON
One of the classic Three-Day events, the Badminton Horse Trials take place in the grounds of Badminton House in Gloucestershire, home of the Beaufort family. The first event was in 1949. *Winners:*
1949	John Shedden (UK)	Golden Willow
1950	Tony Collings (UK)	Remus
1951	Hans Schwarzenbach (Swi)	Vae Victus

1952	Mark Darley (Ire)	Emily Little
1953	Lawrence Rook (UK)	Starlight
1954	Margaret Hough (UK)	Bambi
1955-6	Frank Weldon (UK) #	Kilbarry
1957-8	Sheila Willcox (UK)	High and Mighty
1959	Sheila Waddington (née Willcox)	Airs and Graces
1960	Bill Roycroft (Aus)	Our Solo
1961	Lawrence Morgan (Aus)	Salad Days
1962	Anneli Drummond-Hay (UK)	Merely-a-Monarch
1963	Susan Fleet (UK) *	Gladiator
1964	James Templer (UK)	M'Lord Connolly
1965	Eddie Boylan (Ire)	Durlas Eile
1966	Not held	
1967	Celia Ross-Taylor (UK)	Jonathan
1968	Jane Bullen (UK)	Our Nobby
1969	Richard Walker (UK)	Pasha
1970	Richard Meade (UK)	The Poacher
1971-2	Mark Phillips (UK)	Great Ovation
1973	Lucinda Prior-Palmer (UK)	Be Fair
1974	Mark Phillips (UK)	Columbus
1975	Cancelled after dressage	
1976	Lucinda Prior-Palmer (UK)	Wideawake
1977	Lucinda Prior-Palmer (UK)	George
1978	Jane Holderness-Roddam (née Bullen) (UK)	Warrior
1979	Lucinda Prior-Palmer (UK)	Killaire
1980	Mark Todd (NZ)	Southern Comfort
1981	Mark Phillips (UK)	Lincoln
1982	Richard Meade (UK)	Speculator III
1983	Lucinda Green (née Prior-Palmer)	Regal Realm
1984	Lucinda Green (UK)	Beagle Bay
1985	Virginia Holgate (UK)	Priceless
1986	Ian Stark (UK)	Sir Wattie
1987	Not held	
1988	Ian Stark (UK)	Sir Wattie
1989	Virginia Leng (née Holgate) (UK)	Master Craftsman
1990	Nicola McIrvine (UK)	Middle Road

Most wins: 6 Lucinda Green (née Prior-Palmer), 4 Mark Phillips, 3 Sheila Waddington (née Willcox)
Held at Windsor, * reduced to a one day event because of the weather

BURGHLEY HORSE TRIALS
Held each September on the estate surrounding Burghley House in Lincolnshire, this is the major event of the autumn trials season. Burghley House was the home of the former Olympic athletics gold medallist, David Burghley, the Marquess of Exeter. *Winners:*

1961	Anneli Drummond-Hay (UK)	Merely-a-Monarch
1963	Harry Freeman-Jackson (Ire)	St.Finbar
1964	Richard Meade (UK)	Barberry
1965	Jeremy Beale (UK)	Victoria Bridge
1967	Lorna Sutherland (UK)	Popadom

1968	Sheila Willcox (UK)	Fair and Square
1969	Gillian Watson (UK)	Shaitan
1970	Judy Bradwell (UK)	Don Camillo
1972	Janet Hodgson (UK)	Larkspur
1973	Mark Phillips (UK)	Maid Marion
1975	Aly Pattinson (UK)	Carawich
1976	Jane Holderness-Roddam (UK)	Warrior
1977	Lucinda Prior-Palmer (UK)	George
1978	Lorna Clarke (UK	Greco
1979	Andrew Hoy (Aus)	Davy
1980	Richard Walker (UK)	John of Gaunt
1981	Lucinda Prior-Palmer (UK)	Beagle Bay
1982	Richard Walker (UK)	Ryan's Cross
1983	Virginia Holgate (UK)	Priceless
1984	Virginia Holgate (UK)	Night Cap
1986	Virginia Leng (née Holgate) (UK)	Murphy Himself
1987	Mark Todd (NZ)	Wilson Fair
1988	Jane Thelwall (UK)	King's Jester

1962, 1971, 1985, 1989 see European Championship
1966, 1974 see World Championship
Most wins: 3 Virginia Leng (née Holgate), 2 Lorna Clarke (née Sutherland), Lucinda Prior-Palmer, Richard Walker

DRESSAGE

OLYMPIC GAMES
The individual competition was included in the 1912 Games, but the team competition was not introduced until 1928.
Individual

1912	Carl Bonde (Swe)	Emperor
1920	Janne Lundblad (Swe)	Uno
1924	Ernst Linder (Swe)	Piccolomini
1928	Carl von Langen (Ger)	Draufgänger
1932	Xavier Lesage (Fra)	Taine
1936	Heinz Pollay (Ger)	Kronos
1948	Hans Moser (Swi)	Hummer
1952	Henri St.Cyr (Swe)	Master Rufus
1956	Henri St.Cyr (Swe)	Juli
1960	Sergey Filatov (USSR)	Absent
1964	Henri Chammartin (Swi)	Woermann
1968	Ivan Kizimov (USSR)	Ichor
1972	Liselott Linsenhoff (FRG)	Piaff
1976	Christine Stückelberger (Swi)	Granat
1980	Elisabeth Theurer (Aut)	Mon Cherie
1984	Reiner Klimke (FRG)	Ahlerich
1988	Nicole Uphoff (FRG)	Rembrandt

Team (not held 1960)
7 FR Germany 1928 & 1936 (as Germany), 1964, 1968, 1976, 1984, 1988
2 France 1932, 1948; Sweden 1952, 1956; USSR 1972, 1980

Most gold medals: 6 Reiner Klimke (FRG) team gold 1964, 1968, 1976, 1984, 1988, individual 1984; 4 Henri St.Cyr (Swe) team 1952, 1956; individual 1952, 1956
Most medals: 7 Klimke, six gold, individual bronze 1976

WORLD CHAMPIONSHIPS
Inaugurated 1966. *Winners:*

Individual
1966	Josef Neckermann (FRG)	Mariano
1970	Yelena Petuchkova (USSR)	Pepel
1974	Reiner Klimke (FRG)	Mehmed
1978	Christine Stückelberger (Swi)	Granat
1982	Reiner Klimke (FRG)	Ahlerich
1986	Anne Grethe Jensen (Den)	Marzog

Team
5 FR Germany 1966, 1974, 1978, 1982, 1986
1 USSR 1970
Most gold medals: 6 Reiner Klimke, 2 individual, 4 team
1966, 1974, 1982, 1986

FEI WORLD CUP
First held in 1986. *Winners:*
1986	Anne Grethe Jensen (Den)	Marzog
1987-8	Christine Stückelberger (Swi)	Gauguin de Lully
1989	Margrit Otto-Crepin (Fra)	Corlandus

EUROPEAN CHAMPIONSHIPS
Inaugurated 1963. *Winners:*

Individual
1963	Henri Chammartin (Swi)	Wolfdietrich
1965	Henri Chammartin (Swi)	Wolfdietrich
1967	Reiner Klimke (FRG)	Dux
1969	Liselott Linsenhoff (FRG)	Piaff
1971	Liselott Linsenhoff (FRG)	Piaff
1973	Reiner Klimke (FRG)	Mehmed
1975	Christine Stückelberger (Swi)	Granat
1977	Christine Stückelberger (Swi)	Granat
1979	Elisabeth Theurer (Aut)	Mon Cherie
1981	Uwe Schulten-Baumer (FRG)	Madras
1983	Anne Grethe Jensen (Den)	Marzog
1985	Reiner Klimke (FRG)	Ahlerich
1987	Margrit Otto-Crepin (Fra)	Corlandus
1989	Nicole Uphoff (FRG)	Rembrandt

Team
13 FR Germany 1965, 1967, 1969, 1971, 1973, 1975,
1977, 1979, 1981, 1983, 1985, 1987, 1989
1 Great Britain 1963

CARRIAGE DRIVING
Rules for driving events were established by the FEI in 1970. Combined driving for teams of four horses or for pairs consists of a) presentation and dressage, b) endurance marathon of 23-27 km, c) obstacle driving.

WORLD CHAMPIONSHIPS
Instituted in 1972 and subsequently held every two years. *Winners:*
Individual
1972	August Dubey (Swi)
1974	Sándor Fülöp (Hun)
1976	Imre Abonyi (Hun)
1978	György Bárdos (Hun)
1980	György Bárdos (Hun)
1982	Tjeerd Velstra (Hol)
1984	László Juhász (Hun)
1986	Tjeerd Velstra (Hol)
1988	Ijsbrand Chardon (Hol)

Team
3 Great Britain 1972, 1974, 1980; Hungary 1976, 1978, 1984; Netherlands 1982, 1986, 1988
Members of three winning teams: György Bárdos and Sándor Fülöp (Hun), Ijsbrand Chardon (Hol)

WORLD PAIRS
First held in 1983. *Winners:*
	Team	Individual
1983	Netherlands	Paul Gregory (UK)
1985	Switzerland	Ekkert Meinecke (FRG)
1987	FR Germany	László Kecskerneti (Hun)
1989	Hungary	Udo Hochgeschorz (Can)

Women's name changes
First name	Single	Married
Jane	Bullen	Holderness-Roddam
Marion	Coakes	Mould
Jean	Goodwin	Davenport
Virginia	Holgate	Leng
Janou	Lefèbvre	Tissou
Lucinda	Prior-Palmer	Green
Lorna	Sutherland	Clarke
Sheila	Willcox	Waddington
Alison	Westwood	Dawes

FENCING

Fencing, the sport of fighting with a sword, is one of man's oldest pastimes, obviously related to the use of swords in war or single combat. There is evidence of swordsmanship in Egypt as early as 1360 BC. Fencing was widespread in the Middle Ages, and the rapier had been developed as the principal weapon by the end of the 16th century.

Modern weapons are the épée, foil and sabre. With the épée (weighing 770 grams) the conditions closely follow those that once appertained to duelling and the whole body is a target area. With the lighter weapons, for the foil (maximum weight 500 grams) the target area is the metallic jacket covering the top half of the body, and for the sabre (500 grams) above the waist, including the head. For the two latter weapons a hit must follow prescribed movements – the "phrase".

The world governing body, the Fédération Internationale d'Escrime (FIE), was founded in Paris in 1913.

OLYMPIC GAMES

Fencing has been included at all Olympic Games, and these tournaments count as world championships in Olympic years. At the Games between 1896 and 1906, in addition to the competitions, of which the winners are shown below, there were also events for Fencing Masters, at which these professionals competed against the other contestants. Women first competed in 1924 (with the foil); electronic scoring was introduced for the épée in 1936 and for the foil in 1956. *Winners:*

Men	Foil	Epée	Sabre
1896	Emile Gravelotte (Fra)	Not held	Jean Georgiadis (Gre)
1900	Emile Coste (Fra)	Ramón Fonst (Cub)	Georges de la Falaise (Fra)
1904	Ramón Fonst (Cub)	Ramón Fonst (Cub)	Manuel Diaz (Cub)
1906	Georges Dillon-Kavanagh (Fra)	Georges de la Falaise (Fra)	Jean Georgiadis (Gre)
1908	Not held	Gaston Alibert (Fra)	Jenö Fuchs (Hun)
1912	Nedo Nadi (Ita)	Paul Anspach (Bel)	Jenö Fuchs (Hun)
1920	Nedo Nadi (Ita)	Armand Massard (Fra)	Nedo Nadi (Ita)
1924	Roger Ducret (Fra)	Charles Delporte (Bel)	Sándor Posta (Hun)
1928	Lucien Gaudin (Fra)	Lucien Gaudin (Fra)	Odön Tersztyanszky (Hun)
1932	Gustavo Marzi (Ita)	Giancarlo Cornaggia-Medici (Ita)	György Piller (Hun)
1936	Giulio Gaudini (Ita)	Franco Riccardi (Ita)	Endre Kabos (Hun)
1948	Jean Buhan (Fra)	Luigi Cantone (Ita)	Aladár Gerevich (Hun)
1952	Christian d'Oriola (Fra)	Edoardo Mangiarotti (Ita)	Pál Kovács (Hun)
1956	Christian d'Oriola (Fra)	Carlo Pavesi (Ita)	Rudolf Kárpáti (Hun)
1960	Viktor Zhdanovich (USSR)	Giuseppe Delfino (Ita)	Rudolf Kárpáti (Hun)
1964	Egon Franke (Pol)	Grigoriy Kriss (USSR)	Tibor Pézsa (Hun)
1968	Ion Drimba (Rom)	Gyözö Kulcsár (Hun)	Jerzy Pawlowski (Pol)
1972	Witold Woyda (Pol)	Csaba Fenyvesi (Hun)	Viktor Sidiak (USSR)
1976	Fabio Dal Zotto (Ita)	Alexander Pusch (FRG)	Viktor Krovopuskov (USSR)
1980	Vladimir Smirnov (USSR)	Johan Harmenberg (Swe)	Viktor Krovopuskov (USSR)
1984	Mauro Numa (Ita)	Philippe Boisse (Fra)	Jean François Lamour (Fra)
1988	Stefano Cerioni (Ita)	Arnd Schmitt (FRG)	Jean François Lamour (Fra)

Men's Team *Wins*
Foil
6 France   1924, 1932, 1948, 1952, 1968, 1980
5 Italy   1920, 1928, 1936, 1956, 1984
3 USSR   1960, 1964, 1988
1 Cuba 1904, Poland 1972, FR Germany 1976
Epée
7 France   1906, 1908, 1924, 1932, 1948, 1980, 1988
6 Italy   1920, 1928, 1936, 1952, 1956, 1960
3 Hungary   1964, 1968, 1972
1 Belgium 1912, Sweden 1976, FR Germany 1984
Sabre
10 Hungary 1908, 1912, 1928, 1932, 1936, 1948, 1952, 1956, 1960, 1988
4 Italy   1920, 1924, 1972, 1984
4 USSR   1964, 1968, 1976, 1980
1 Germany 1906

Women's Foil

1924 Ellen Osiier (Den)
1928 Helène Mayer (Ger)
1932 Ellen Preis (Aut)
1936 Ilona Elek (Hun)
1948 Ilona Elek (Hun)
1952 Irene Camber (Ita)
1956 Gillian Sheen (UK)
1960 Heidi Schmid (FRG)
1964 Ildikó Ujlaki-Rejtö (Hun)
1968 Yelena Novikova (USSR)
1972 Antonella Ragno-Lonzi (Ita)
1976 Ildikó Schwarczenberger (Hun)
1980 Pascale Trinquet (Fra)
1984 Luan Jujie (Chn)
1988 Anja Fichtel (FRG)

Women's Foil Team *Wins*

4 USSR   1960, 1968, 1972, 1976
2 FR Germany 1984, 1988
1 Hungary 1964, France 1980

Anja Fichtel became world fencing champion in 1986 a few days before her 18th birthday, and won two Olympic gold medals, individual foil and team in 1988. She is coached by 1976 Olympic gold medallist Alexander Pusch **(All-Sport)**

Most Olympic medals – individual (I) and team (T):

Name	GOLD	SILVER	BRONZE	TOTAL	
Men	I/T	I/T	I /T		
Edoardo Mangiarotti (Ita)	1/5	1/4	2/-	13	1936-60
Aladár Gerevich (Hun)	1/6	1/-	1/1	10	1932-60
Giulio Gaudini (Ita)	1/2	1/3	2/-	9	1928-36
Roger Ducret (Fra)	1/2	2/2	1/-	8	1920-28
Philippe Cattiau (Fra)	-/3	2/2	-/1	8	1920-36
Pál Kovács (Hun)	1/5	-/-	1/-	7	1936-60
Others with five or more including four gold medals:					
Christian d'Oriola (Fra)	2/2	1/1	-/-	6	1948-56
Rudolf Kárpáti (Hun)	2/4	-/-	-/-	6	1948-60
Nedo Nadi (Ita)	3/3	-/-	-/-	6	1912-20
Giuseppe Delfino (Ita)	1/3	1/1	-/-	6	1952-64
Gyözö Kulcsár (Hun)	1/3	-/-	2/-	6	1964-76
Viktor Sidiak (USSR)	1/3	-/1	1/-	6	1968-80
Ramón Fonst (Cub)	3/1	1/-	-/-	5	1900-04
Lucien Gaudin (Fra)	2/2	-/1	-/-	5	1920-28
Nadi won a record five gold medals at one Games in 1920.					
Women					
Ildikó Sagi-Ujlaki-Rejtö (Hun)	1/1	-/3	1/1	7	1960-76
Yelena Byelova (née Novikova) (USSR)	1/3	-/1	1/-	6	1968-80

WORLD CHAMPIONSHIPS

Held annually except in Olympic years (see above). From 1921 to 1935 they were styled as European championships.
Winners

Men	Foil	Epée	Sabre
1921	-	Lucien Gaudin (Fra)	-
1922	-	Raoul Herde (Nor)	Adrianus de Jong (Hol)
1923	-	Wouter Brouwer (Hol)	Adrianus de Jong (Hol)
1925	-	-	János Garay (Hun)
1926	Giorgio Chiavacci (Ita)	Georges Tainturier (Fra)	Sándor Gambos (Hun)
1927	Oreste Puliti (Ita)	Georges Buchard (Fra)	Sándor Gambos (Hun)
1929	Oreste Puliti (Ita)	Philippe Cattiau (Fra)	Gyula Glykais (Hun)
1930	Giulio Gaudini (Ita)	Philippe Cattiau (Fra)	György Piller (Hun)
1931	René Lemoine (Fra)	Georges Buchard (Fra)	György Piller (Hun)
1933	Gioacchino Guaragna (Ita)	Georges Buchard (Fra)	Endre Kabos (Hun)
1934	Giulio Gaudini (Ita)	Pál Dunay (Hun)	Endre Kabos (Hun)
1935	shared by four men	Hans Drakenberg (Swe)	Aladár Gerevich (Hun)
1937	Gustavo Marzi (Ita)	Bernard Schmetz (Fra)	Pál Kovács (Hun)
1938	Gioacchino Guaragna (Ita)	Michel Pécheux (Fra)	Aldo Montano (Ita)
1947	Christian d'Oriola (Fra)	Edouard Artigas (Fra)	Aldo Montano (Ita)
1949	Christian d'Oriola (Fra)	Dario Mangiarotti (Ita)	Gastone Daré (Fra)
1950	Renzo Nostino (Ita)	Mogens Luchow (Den)	Jean Levavasseur (Fra)
1951	Manlio Di Rosa (Ita)	Edoardo Mangiarotti (Ita)	Aladár Gerevich (Hun)
1953	Christian d'Oriola (Fra)	Jozsef Sakovics (Hun)	Pál Kovács (Hun)
1954	Christian d'Oriola (Fra)	Edoardo Mangiarotti (Ita)	Rudolf Kárpáti (Hun)
1955	Jozsef Gyuricza (Hun)	Giorgio Anglesio (Ita)	Aladár Gerevich (Hun)
1957	Mihaly Fülöp (Hun)	Armand Mouyal (Fra)	Jerzy Pawlowski (Pol)
1958	Giancarlo Bergamini (Ita)	Bill Hoskyns (UK)	Yakov Rylsky (USSR)
1959	Allan Jay (UK)	Bruno Khabarov (USSR)	Rudolf Kárpáti (Hun)
1961	Ryszard Parulski (Pol)	Jack Guittet (Fra)	Yakov Rylsky (USSR)
1962	German Sveshnikov (USSR)	Istvan Kausz (Hun)	Zoltan Horvath (Hun)
1963	Jean-Claude Magnan (Fra)	Roland Losert (Aut)	Yakov Rylsky (USSR)
1965	Jean-Claude Magnan (Fra)	Zoltan Nemere (Hun)	Jerzy Pawlowski (Pol)
1966	German Sveshnikov (USSR)	Aleksey Nikanchikov (USSR)	Jerzy Pawlowski (Pol)
1967	Viktor Putyatin (USSR)	Aleksey Nikanchikov (USSR)	Mark Rakita (USSR)
1969	Friedrich Wessel (FRG)	Bogdan Andrzejewski (Pol)	Viktor Sidiak (USSR)
1970	Friedrich Wessel (FRG)	Aleksey Nikanchikov (USSR)	Tibor Pézsa (Hun)
1971	Vasiliy Stankovich (USSR)	Grigoriy Kriss (USSR)	Michele Maffei (Ita)
1973	Christian Noël (Fra)	Rolf Edling (Swe)	Mario Aldo Monttano (Ita)
1974	Aleksandr Romankov (USSR)	Rolf Edling (Swe)	Mario Aldo Monttano (Ita)
1975	Christian Noël (Fra)	Alexander Pusch (FRG)	Vladimir Nazlimov (USSR)
1977	Aleksandr Romankov (USSR)	Johan Harmenberg (Swe)	Pál Gerevich (Hun)
1978	Didier Flament (Fra)	Alexander Pusch (FRG)	Viktor Krovopuskov (USSR)
1979	Aleksandr Romankov (USSR)	Philippe Riboud (Fra)	Vladimir Nazlimov (USSR)
1981	Vladimir Smirnov (USSR)	Zoltan Szekely (Hun)	Mariusz Wodke (Pol)
1982	Aleksandr Romankov (USSR)	Jenö Pap (Hun)	Viktor Krovopuskov (USSR)
1983	Aleksandr Romankov (USSR)	Ellmar Bormann (FRG)	Vasiliy Etropolski (Bul)
1985	Mauro Numa (Ita)	Philippe Boisse (Fra)	György Nebald (Hun)
1986	Andrea Borella (Ita)	Philippe Riboud (Fra)	Sergey Mindirgassov (USSR)
1987	Mathias Gey (FRG)	Volker Fischer (FRG)	Jean François Lamour (Fra)
1989	Alexander Koch (FRG)	Manuel Pereira (Spa)	Grigoriy Kirienko (USSR)
MOST	5 Aleksandr Romankov (USSR)	3 Georges Buchard (Fra)	3 Aladár Gerevich (Hun)
WINS	4 Christian d'Oriola (Fra)	3 Aleksey Nikanchikov (USSR)	3 Jerzy Pawlowski (Pol)
			3 Yakov Rylsky (USSR)

Men's Team Foil *Wins*

14 Italy	1929-31, 1933-5, 1937-8, 1949-50, 1954-5, 1985-6	
14 USSR	1959, 1961-3, 1965-6, 1969-70, 1973-4, 1979, 1981-2, 1989	

6 France	1947, 1951, 1953, 1958, 1971, 1975
3 FR Germany	1977, 1983, 1987
1 Hungary 1957, Romania 1967, Poland 1978	

Men's Team Epée *Wins*

11 Italy	1931, 1933, 1937, 1949-50, 1953-5, 1957-8, 1989
10 France	1934-5, 1938, 1947, 1951, 1962, 1965-6, 1982-3
6 USSR	1961, 1967, 1969, 1979, 1981, 1987
4 Hungary	1959, 1970-1, 1978
3 FR Germany	1973, 1985-6
3 Sweden	1974-5, 1977
1 Belgum 1930, Poland 1963	

Men's Team Sabre *Wins*

17 Hungary	1930-1, 1933-5, 1937, 1951, 1953-5, 1957-8, 1966, 1973, 1978, 1981-2
14 USSR	1965, 1967, 1969-71, 1974-5, 1977, 1979, 1983, 1985-7, 1989
4 Italy	1938, 1947, 1949-50
4 Poland	1959, 1961-3

Women's Foil

1929	Helène Mayer (Ger)
1930	Jenny Addams (Bel)
1931	Helène Mayer (Ger)
1933	Gwen Neligan (UK)
1934	Ilona Elek (Hun)
1935	Ilona Elek (Hun)
1937	Helène Mayer (Ger)
1938	Marie Sediva (Cs)
1947	Ellen Müller-Preiss (Aut)
1949	Ellen Müller-Preiss (Aut)
1950	Ellen Müller-Preiss (Aut) & Renée Garilhe (Fra)
1951	Ilona Elek (Hun)
1953	Irene Camber (Ita)
1954	Karen Lachman (Den)
1955	Lidia Dömölki (Hun)
1957	Aleksandra Zabelina (USSR)
1958	Valentina Kiselyeva (USSR)
1959	Yelina Yefimova (USSR)
1961	Heidi Schmid (FRG)
1962	Olga Szabo-Orban (Rom)
1963	Ildikó Rejtö (Hun)
1965	Galina Gorokhova (USSR)
1966	Tatyana Samusenko (USSR)
1967	Aleksandra Zabelina (USSR)
1969	Yelena Novikova (USSR)
1970	Galina Gorokhova (USSR)
1971	Marie-Chantal Demaille (Fra)
1973	Valentina Nikonova (USSR)
1974	Ildikó Bóbis (Hun)
1975	Ecaterina Stahl (Rom)
1977	Valentina Sidorova (USSR)
1978	Valentina Sidorova (USSR)
1979	Cornelia Hanisch (FRG)

1981	Cornelia Hanisch (FRG)
1982	Naila Giliazova (USSR)
1983	Dorina Vaccaroni (Ita)
1985	Cornelia Hanisch (FRG)
1986	Anja Fichtel (FRG)
1987	Elisabeta Tufan (Rom)
1989	Olga Velichko (USSR)

Most wins: 3 Helène Mayer, Ilona Elek, Ellen Müller-Preiss, Cornelia Hanisch

Women's Team Foil *Wins*

15 USSR	1956, 1958, 1961, 1963, 1965-6, 1970-1, 1974-5, 1977-9, 1981, 1986
13 Hungary	1933-5, 1937, 1952-5, 1959, 1962, 1967, 1973, 1987
3 Denmark	1932, 1947-8
3 Italy	1957, 1982-3
2 France	1950-1
2 FR Germany	1985, 1989
1 Germany 1936, Romania 1969	

Women's Epée

1989	Anja Straub (Swi)

Women's Team Epée

1 Hungary	1989

FIVES (ETON)

The game of Eton Fives as now known originated at Eton College in 1840, when courts were built which incorporated features of the area where a handball game had been played before (first recorded in 1825). The courts had a distinctive built-in buttress, which had been used by boys playing against the outside of the chapel.

The Amateur Championship

Played, as doubles, annually for the Kinnaird Cup. First held in 1928. *Most wins by one pair:*

10 Brian Matthews & John Reynolds 1981-90
8 Anthony Hughes and Arthur Campbell 1958, 1965-8, 1971, 1973, 1975. Hughes also won in 1963 with D.J.S.Guilford.
3 A.H.Fabian & J.K.G.Webb 1937, 1939, 1948
3 Peter May & John May 1951-3
3 J.W.Biggs & J.C.Wallis 1961-2, 1964

FIVES (RUGBY)

This court game was first played around 1850. The court differs from that used for Eton Fives in that there is no buttress. The Rugby Fives Association was formed in 1927. It drew up a standard set of rules in 1930 and in the following year established the standard court dimensions, 28ft (8.54m) long and 18ft (5.49m) wide).

Amateur Singles Championship

Contested annually for the Jesters' Club Cup from 1932, except for the war years 1940-7. *Most wins:*
16 Wayne Enstone 1973-8, 1980-9
4 John Pretlove 1953, 1955-6, 1958
4 Eric Marsh 1960-3
3 Philip Malt 1933-5
Wayne Enstone has thus dominated in recent years. The winner in 1979 was David Hebden.

Amateur Doubles Championship

Contested annually for the Cyriax Cup, first in 1926, then annually 1930-9 and from 1947. *Most wins:*
10 Ian Fuller & David Hebden 1980-5, 1987-90
7 John Pretlove 1952, 1954, 1956-9, 1961 (4 with Dennis Silk 1956-9)
7 David Gardner 1960, 1965-6, 1970-2, 1974
6 Wayne Enstone 1975-9 (with John East), 1986 (with Steve Ashton)
5 John East 1975-9

Invitation World Championships

Held each year from 1983 to 1985, winners each time: singles: Wayne Enstone, doubles: Wayne Enstone & Steve Ashton.

GAELIC FOOTBALL

A 15-a-side game, Gaelic football has common features with soccer, rugby and Australian Rules football. The first reference of a game resembling Gaelic football was in 1712 when a match between Meath and Louth took place at Slane. The rules were standardized following the formation of the Gaelic Athletic Association, the governing body in Ireland for handball, hurling and rounders as well as for Gaelic football, in 1884. The number of players per team was fixed at 21 in 1884, but reduced to 17 in 1892 and to 15 in 1913.

All Ireland Championships

The sport's principal championship; the final is played at Dublin's Croke Park on the third Sunday in September each year for the Sam Maguire Trophy. Held annually from 1887, except for 1888 when this inter-county event was unfinished. *Most wins:*

30 Kerry	1903-4, 1909, 1913-4, 1924, 1926, 1929-32, 1937, 1939-41, 1946, 1953, 1955, 1959, 1962, 1969-70, 1975, 1978-81, 1984-6
21 Dublin	1891-2, 1894, 1897-9, 1901-2, 1906-8, 1921-3, 1942, 1958, 1963, 1974, 1976-7, 1983
7 Galway	1925, 1934, 1938, 1956, 1964-6
5 Wexford	1893, 1915-8
5 Cavan	1933, 1935, 1947-8, 1952
5 Cork	1890, 1911, 1945, 1973, 1989
5 Meath	1949, 1954, 1967, 1987-8
4 Tipperary	1889, 1895, 1900, 1920
4 Kildare	1905, 1919, 1927-8
3 Louth	1910, 1912, 1957
3 Mayo	1936, 1950-1
3 Down	1960-1, 1968
3 Offaly	1971-2, 1982
2 Limerick	1887, 1896
2 Roscommon	1943-4

Highest team score in a final: 27 Dublin (5 goals, 12 points) beat Armagh 15 (3, 6) in 1977
Highest aggregate score in a final: 45 Cork (26) beat Galway (19) in 1973.
Most individual appearances: 10, including a record 8 wins by the Kerry players Pat Spillane, Paudie O'Shea, Denis Moran, 1975-86.

GLIDING

There is some evidence of the use of gliders in Ancient Egypt about four thousand years ago, and the ability to float in the air like a bird has long been of fascination for man. Gliding (or soaring) as a sport began to gain popular appeal in the 1930s in Europe and the USA.

RECORDS

A wide variety of world records are maintained for single-seater and for multi-seater gliders, for both men and women pilots. There are also records for motor gliders.

SINGLE-SEATERS

(Category: Record, Pilot, Glider, Venue, Date*)*
Straight distance: 1460.8km Hans-Werner Grosse (FRG), ASW-12, Lübeck (FRG) to Biarritz (Fra), 25 Apr 1972
Declared goal distance: 1254.26km Bruce Drake, David Speight, Dick Georgeson (NZ), all in Nimbus 2s, Te Anau to Te Araroa, New Zealand, 14 Jan 1978
Goal and return distance: 1646.68km Tom Knauff (USA), Nimbus 3, Williamsport, Pa. to Knoxville, Tn. USA, 25 Apr 1983
Triangular distance: 1362.68km Tom Knauff (USA), Nimbus 3; L.R.McMaster, J.C.Seymour, K-H.Striedick (USA), ASW-20B; R.L.Robertson (UK), Ventus A, all on 2 May 1986
Height gain: 12849m Paul Bikle (USA), Schweizer SGS 1-23E, Mojave, Cal., USA, 25 Feb 1961
Absolute altitude: 14938m Robert Harris (USA), Grob G102, California, 17 Feb 1986
Speed over triangular course:

100km	195.30km/h	Ingo Renner (Aus), Nimbus 3, 14 Dec 1982
300km	170.06km/h	Beat Bunzli (Swi), Nimbus 3, 18 Dec 1987
500km	164.11km/h	Jean-Paul Castel (Fra), Nimbus 3, 10 Dec 1986
750km	158.40km/h	Hans-Werner Grosse (FRG), ASW-22, 8 Jan 1985

1000km	145.32km/h	Hans-Werner Grosse (FRG), ASW-17, 3 Jan 1979
1250km	133.24km/h	Hans-Werner Grosse (FRG), ASW-17, 9 Dec 1980

WOMEN'S SINGLE-SEATERS

Straight distance: 949.7km Karla Karel (UK), LS-3, Australia, 20 Jan 1980
Goal distance: 748.37km Joann Shaw (USA), Nimbus 2, 17 Aug 1983
Goal and return distance: 1126.68km Doris Grove (USA), Nimbus 2, 28 Sep 1981
Triangular distance: 847.27km Joanne Shaw (USA), Nimbus 2, 5 Aug 1984
Height gain: 10212m Yvonne Loader (NZ), Omarama, NZ 12 Jan 1988
Absolute altitude: 12637m Sabrina Jackintell (USA), Astir GS, 14 Feb 1979
Speed over triangular course:

100km	139.45km/h	Susan Martin (Aus), LS-3, 2 Feb 1979
300km	138.71km/h	Inge Müller (FRG), Ventus B, 8 Dec 1984
500km	133.14km/h	Susan Martin (Aus), LS-3, 29 Jan 1979
750km	110.53km/h	Pamela Hawkins (UK), ASW-17, 17 Nov 1984

WORLD CHAMPIONSHIPS

First held in 1937 and now staged biennially. *Winners:*

Open Category

1937 Heini Dittmar (Ger)
1948 Per Persson (Swe)
1950 Billy Nilsson (Swe)
1952 Philip Wills (UK)
1954 Gérard Pierre (Fra)
1956 Paul MacCready (USA)
1958 Ernst Haase (FRG)
1960 Rudolf Hossinger (Arg)
1963 Eduard Makula (Pol)
1965 Jan Wroblewski (Pol)
1968 Harro Wödl (Aut)
1970 George Moffat (USA)
1972 Göran Ax (Swe)
1974 George Moffat (USA)
1976 George Lee (UK)
1978 George Lee (UK)
1981 George Lee (UK)
1983 Ingo Renner (Aus)
1985 Ingo Renner (Aus)
1987 Ingo Renner (Aus)
1989 Claude Lopitaux (Fra)

Two-seater

1952 Luis Juez & J.Ara (Spa)
1954 Z.Rain & P.Komac (Yug)
1956 Nick Goodhart & Frank Foster (UK)

Standard Class

1958 Adam Witek (Pol)
1960 Heinz Huth (FRG)
1963 Heinz Huth (FRG)
1965 Francois Henry (Fra)
1968 A.J.Smith (USA)
1970 Helmut Reichmann (FRG)
1972 Jan Wroblewski (Pol)
1974 Helmut Reichmann (FRG)
1976 Ingo Renner (Aus)
1978 Baer Selen (Hol)
1981 Marc Schroeder (Fra)
1983 Stig Oye (Den)
1985 Leonardo Brigliadori (Ita)
1987 Markku Kuittinen (Fin)
1989 Jacques Aboulin (Fra)

15 Metres Class

1978 Helmut Reichmann (FRG)
1981 Göran Ax (Swe)
1983 Kees Musters (Hol)
1985 Doug Jacobs (USA)
1987 Brian Speckley (UK)
1989 Bruno Gartenbrink (FRG)

Most titles: 4 Ingo Renner, 3 Helmut Reichmann, George Lee

GOLF

The exact origins of golf are uncertain, as with so many sports. The Chinese played a form of golf 1800 years ago, and the French, Dutch and Belgians played something resembling the sport in the middle ages. Scotland, must however be regarded as the home of golf. The game was banned in 1457 but golf was later played by Scottish royalty such as James IV and Mary. The world's first golf club, the Honourable Company of Edinburgh golfers, was founded in 1744. The ruling body of the sport, in the eyes of most countries, is the Royal & Ancient situated at St.Andrews. The Society of St.Andrews Golfers, the forerunner of the R&A, played its first game of golf over the famous St.Andrews links on 14 May 1754. The first international federation was founded in 1989 when the World Golf Association was formed with the purpose of gaining Olympic status for the sport.

BRITISH OPEN

The Open first took place at Prestwick on 17 October 1860. Eight competitors took part and the lowest score over three 12-hole rounds was recorded by Willie Park senior. Prestwick hosted the first twelve Opens and all subsequent championships have been played over seaside links. The original prize was a Championship Belt but this was won outright by Tom Morris junior in 1870 and there was no event the following year. When it resumed in 1872 the prize was the silver claret jug, still awarded to the champion today. Played over 36 holes 1860-91 and thereafter at 72 holes. Prize money (totalling £10) was introduced in 1863. The total grew at first steadily and in recent years rapidly: some landmarks being £110 in 1892, £500 1931, £1000 1946, £5000 1959, £10,000 1965, £50,000 1972, £200,000 1980, £771,300 1989.

Winners, with scores and venue:

		Score	Venue
1860	Willie Park, Snr (UK)	174	Prestwick
1861	Tom Morris, Snr (UK)	163	Prestwick
1862	Tom Morris, Snr (UK)	163	Prestwick
1863	Willie Park, Snr (UK)	168	Prestwick
1864	Tom Morris, Snr (UK)	167	Prestwick
1865	Andrew Strath (UK)	162	Prestwick
1866	Willie Park, Snr (UK)	169	Prestwick
1867	Tom Morris, Snr (UK)	170	Prestwick
1868	Tom Morris, Jnr (UK)	157	Prestwick
1869	Tom Morris, Jnr (UK)	154	Prestwick
1870	Tom Morris, Jnr (UK)	149	Prestwick
1872	Tom Morris, Jnr (UK)	166	Prestwick
1873	Tom Kidd (UK)	179	St.Andrews
1874	Mungo Park (UK)	159	Musselburgh
1875	Willie Park, Snr (UK)	166	Prestwick
1876	Bob Martin (UK)	176	St.Andrews
1877	Jamie Anderson (UK)	160	Musselburgh
1878	Jamie Anderson (UK)	157	Prestwick
1879	Jamie Anderson (UK)	169	St.Andrews
1880	Robert Ferguson (UK)	162	Musselburgh
1881	Robert Ferguson (UK)	170	Prestwick
1882	Robert Ferguson (UK)	171	St.Andrews
1883	Willie Fernie (UK)	159*	Musselburgh
1884	Jack Simpson (UK)	160	Prestwick
1885	Bob Martin (UK)	171	St.Andrews
1886	David Brown (UK)	157	Musselburgh
1887	Willie Park, Jnr (UK)	161	Prestwick
1888	Jack Burns (UK)	171	St.Andrews
1889	Willie Park, Jnr (UK)	155*	Musselburgh
1890	John Ball (UK) #	164	Prestwick
1891	Hugh Kirkaldy (UK)	166	St.Andrews
1892	Harold H.Hilton (UK) #	305	Muirfield
1893	William Auchterlonie (UK)	322	Prestwick
1894	John H.Taylor (UK)	326	Sandwich
1895	John H.Taylor (UK)	322	St.Andrews
1896	Harry Vardon (UK)	316*	Muirfield
1897	Harold H.Hilton (UK) #	314	Hoylake
1898	Harry Vardon (UK)	307	Prestwick
1899	Harry Vardon (UK)	310	Sandwich
1900	John H.Taylor (UK)	309	St.Andrews
1901	James Braid (UK)	309	Muirfield
1902	Sandy Herd (UK)	307	Hoylake
1903	Harry Vardon (UK)	300	Prestwick
1904	Jack White (UK)	296	Sandwich
1905	James Braid (UK)	318	St.Andrews
1906	James Braid (UK)	300	Muirfield
1907	Arnaud Massy (Fra)	312	Hoylake
1908	James Braid (UK)	291	Prestwick
1909	John H.Taylor (UK)	295	Deal
1910	James Braid (UK)	299	St.Andrews
1911	Harry Vardon (UK)	303	Sandwich
1912	Edward Ray (UK)	295	Muirfield
1913	John H.Taylor (UK)	304	Hoylake
1914	Harry Vardon (UK)	306	Prestwick
1920	George Duncan (UK)	303	Deal
1921	Jock Hutchinson (USA)	296*	St.Andrews
1922	Walter Hagen (USA)	300	Sandwich
1923	Arthur Havers (UK)	295	Troon
1924	Walter Hagen (USA)	301	Hoylake
1925	Jim Barnes (USA)	300	Prestwick
1926	Bobby Jones (USA) #	291	Royal Lytham
1927	Bobby Jones (USA) #	285	St.Andrews
1928	Walter Hagen (USA)	292	Sandwich
1929	Walter Hagen (USA)	292	Muirfield
1930	Bobby Jones (USA) #	291	Hoylake
1931	Tommy Armour (USA)	296	Carnoustie
1932	Gene Sarazen (USA)	283	Prince's
1933	Densmore Shute (USA)	292*	St.Andrews
1934	Henry Cotton (UK)	283	Sandwich
1935	Alfred Perry (UK)	283	Muirfield
1936	Alfred Padgham (UK)	287	Hoylake
1937	Henry Cotton (UK)	290	Carnoustie
1938	Reg Whitcombe (UK)	295	Sandwich
1939	Dick Burton (UK)	290	St.Andrews
1946	Sam Snead (USA)	290	St.Andrews
1947	Fred Daly (UK)	293	Hoylake
1948	Henry Cotton (UK)	284	Muirfield
1949	Bobby Locke (SAf)	283*	Sandwich
1950	Bobby Locke (SAf)	279	Troon
1951	Max Faulkner (UK)	285	Portrush
1952	Bobby Locke (SAf)	287	Royal Lytham
1953	Ben Hogan (USA)	282	Carnoustie
1954	Peter Thomson (Aus)	283	Royal Birkdale
1955	Peter Thomson (Aus)	281	St.Andrews
1956	Peter Thomson (Aus)	286	Hoylake
1957	Bobby Locke (SAf)	279	St.Andrews
1958	Peter Thomson (Aus)	278*	Royal Lytham
1959	Gary Player (SAf)	284	Muirfield
1960	Kel Nagle (Aus)	278	St.Andrews
1961	Arnold Palmer (USA)	284	Royal Birkdale
1962	Arnold Palmer (USA)	276	Troon
1963	Bob Charles (NZ)	277*	Royal Lytham
1964	Tony Lema (USA)	279	St.Andrews
1965	Peter Thomson (Aus)	285	Royal Birkdale
1966	Jack Nicklaus (USA)	282	Muirfield
1967	Roberto de Vicenzo (Arg)	278	Hoylake
1968	Gary Player (SAf)	289	Carnoustie
1969	Tony Jacklin (UK)	280	Royal Lytham
1970	Jack Nicklaus (USA)	283*	St.Andrews
1971	Lee Trevino (USA)	278	Royal Birkdale
1972	Lee Trevino (USA)	278	Muirfield
1973	Tom Weiskopf (USA)	276	Troon
1974	Gary Player (SAf)	282	Royal Lytham
1975	Tom Watson (USA)	279*	Carnoustie
1976	Johnny Miller (USA)	279	Royal Birkdale
1977	Tom Watson (USA)	268	Turnberry
1978	Jack Nicklaus (USA)	281	St.Andrews
1979	Seve Ballesteros (Spa)	283	Royal Lytham

1980	Tom Watson (USA)	271	Muirfield
1981	Bill Rogers (USA)	276	Sandwich
1982	Tom Watson (USA)	284	Troon
1983	Tom Watson (USA)	275	Royal Birkdale
1984	Seve Ballesteros (Spa)	276	St.Andrews
1985	Sandy Lyle (UK)	282	Sandwich
1986	Greg Norman (Aus)	280	Turnberry
1987	Nick Faldo (UK)	279	Muirfield
1988	Seve Ballesteros (Spa)	273	Royal Lytham
1989	Mark Calcavecchia (USA)	275*	Troon

after play-off, # amateur champions

Most wins: 6 Harry Vardon; 5 James Braid, John H.Taylor, Peter Thomson, Tom Watson
Most top 3 placings: 13 Jack Nicklaus, 12 Vardon, Taylor; 11 Braid
Most top 6 placings: 18 Taylor, 17 Nicklaus, 16 Vardon, Braid; 12 Thomson

UNITED STATES OPEN

First played on a 9-hole course at Newport, Rhode Island on 4 October 1895, when English-born Horace Rawlins won and collected a cheque for $150 (from a total of $335). Played over 72 holes (36 in 1895-7). Prize money reached $1200 in 1916, $5000 1929, $15,000 1950, $131,690 1965, $506,184 1983 and $1 milion in 1990. Winners (all USA unless otherwise stated)

		Score	Venue
1895	Horace Rawlins	173	Newport
1896	James Foulis	152	Shinnecock Hills
1897	Joe Lloyd	162	Chicago
1898	Fred Herd	328	Myopia Hunt
1899	Willie Smith	315	Baltimore
1900	Harry Vardon (UK)	313	Chicago
1901	Willie Anderson	331*	Myopia Hunt
1902	Laurie Auchterlonie	307	Garden City
1903	Willie Anderson	307*	Baltusrol
1904	Willie Anderson	303	Glen View
1905	Willie Anderson	314	Myopia Hunt
1906	Alex Smith	295	Onwentsia
1907	Alex Ross	302	Philadelphia
1908	Fred McLeod	322*	Myopia Hunt
1909	George Sargent	290	Englewood
1910	Alex Smith	298*	Philadelphia
1911	John McDermott	307*	Chicago
1912	John McDermott	294	Buffalo
1913	Francis Ouimet #	304*	Brookline
1914	Walter Hagen	290	Midlothian
1915	Jerome Travers #	297	Baltusrol
1916	Charles Evans, Jnr #	286	Minikahda
1919	Walter Hagen	301*	Brae Burn
1920	Edward Ray (UK)	295	Inverness
1921	Jim Barnes	289	Columbia
1922	Gene Sarazen	288	Skokie
1923	Bobby Jones #	296*	Inwood
1924	Cyril Walker	297	Oakland Hills
1925	Willie Macfarlane	291*	Worcester

1926	Bobby Jones #	293	Scioto
1927	Tommy Armour	301*	Oakmont
1928	Johnny Farrell	294*	Olympia Fields
1929	Bobby Jones #	294*	Winged Foot
1930	Bobby Jones #	287	Interlachen
1931	Billy Burke	292*	Inverness
1932	Gene Sarazen	286	Fresh Meadow
1933	Johnny Goodman #	287	North Shore
1934	Olin Dutra	293	Merion
1935	Sam Parks, Jnr	299	Oakmont
1936	Tony Manero	282	Baltusrol
1937	Ralph Guldahl	281	Oakland Hills
1938	Ralph Guldahl	284	Cherry Hills
1939	Byron Nelson	284*	Philadelphia
1940	Lawson Little	287*	Canterbury
1941	Craig Wood	284	Colonial
1946	Lloyd Mangrum	284*	Canterbury
1947	Lew Worsham	282*	St.Louis
1948	Ben Hogan	276	Riviera
1949	Cary Middlecoff	286	Medinah
1950	Ben Hogan	287*	Merion
1951	Ben Hogan	287	Oakland Hills
1952	Julius Boros	281	Northwood
1953	Ben Hogan	283	Oakmont

Ben Hogan, who in 1953 became the only man to win the US Masters, US Open and British Open in the same season
(All-Sport)

1954	Ed Furgol	284	Baltusrol	1978	Andy North	285	Cherry Hills
1955	Jack Fleck	287*	Olympic	1979	Hale Irwin	284	Inverness
1956	Cary Middlecoff	281	Oak Hill	1980	Jack Nicklaus	272	Baltusrol
1957	Dick Mayer	282*	Inverness	1981	David Graham (Aus)	273	Merion
1958	Tommy Bolt	283	Southern Hills	1982	Tom Watson	282	Pebble Beach
1959	Billy Casper	282	Winged Foot	1983	Larry Nelson	280	Oakmont
1960	Arnold Palmer	280	Cherry Hills	1984	Fuzzy Zoeller	276*	Winged Foot
1961	Gene Littler	281	Oakland Hills	1985	Andy North	279	Oakland Hills
1962	Jack Nicklaus	283*	Oakmont	1986	Raymond Floyd	279	Shinnecock Hills
1963	Julius Boros	293*	Brookline	1987	Scott Simpson	277	Olympic Club
1964	Ken Venturi	278	Congressional	1988	Curtis Strange	278	Brookline
1965	Gary Player (SAf)	282*	Bellerive	1989	Curtis Strange	278	Oak Hill
1966	Billy Casper	278*	Olympic	1990	Hale Irwin	280*	Medinah
1967	Jack Nicklaus	275	Baltusrol				
1968	Lee Trevino	275	Oak Hill				
1969	Orville Moody	281	Champions				
1970	Tony Jacklin (UK)	281	Hazeltine				
1971	Lee Trevino	280*	Merion				
1972	Jack Nicklaus	290	Pebble Beach				
1973	Johnny Miller	279	Oakmont				
1974	Hale Irwin	287*	Winged Foot				
1975	Lou Graham	287	Medinah				
1976	Jerry Pate	277	Atlanta				
1977	Hubert Green	278	Southern Hills				

after play-off, # amateur champions

Most wins: 4 Willie Anderson, Bobby Jones, Ben Hogan, Jack Nicklaus

Most top 3 placings: 9 Nicklaus, 7 Hogan, Gene Sarazen; 6 Anderson, Arnold Palmer

Most top 6 placings: 12 Hogan, 11 Anderson, Walter Hagan, Sarazen, Palmer, Nicklaus

US MASTERS

Held annually at the Augusta National course in Georgia, the Masters was introduced in 1934. Both the course and the tournament were the idea of the legendary golfer Bobby Jones. Entry to the Masters is by invitation only and the eventual winner is presented with the coveted green jacket. Contested over 72 holes of strokeplay. Winners (all USA unless otherwise stated):

1934	Horton Smith	284
1935	Gene Sarazen	282*
1936	Horton Smith	285
1937	Byron Nelson	283
1938	Henry Picard	285
1939	Ralph Guldahl	279
1940	Jimmy Demaret	280
1941	Craig Wood	280
1942	Byron Nelson	280*
1946	Herman Keiser	282
1947	Jimmy Demaret	281
1948	Claude Harmon	279
1949	Sam Snead	282
1950	Jimmy Demaret	283
1951	Ben Hogan	280
1952	Sam Snead	286
1953	Ben Hogan	274
1954	Sam Snead	289*
1955	Cary Middlecoff	279
1956	Jack Burke, Jnr	289
1957	Doug Ford	282
1958	Arnold Palmer	284
1959	Art Wall, Jnr	284
1960	Arnold Palmer	282*
1961	Gary Player (SAf)	280
1962	Arnold Palmer	280*
1963	Jack Nicklaus	286
1964	Arnold Palmer	276

In 1989 Curtis Strange became the first man for 38 years to retain the US Open title
(All-Sport)

1965	Jack Nicklaus	271
1966	Jack Nicklaus	288*
1967	Gay Brewer	280
1968	Bob Goalby	277
1969	George Archer	281
1970	Billy Casper	279*
1971	Charles Coody	279
1972	Jack Nicklaus	286
1973	Tommy Aaron	283
1974	Gary Player (SAf)	278
1975	Jack Nicklaus	276
1976	Raymond Floyd	271
1977	Tom Watson	276
1978	Gary Player (SAf)	277
1979	Fuzzy Zoeller	280*
1980	Seve Ballesteros (Spa)	275
1981	Tom Watson	280

1982	Craig Stadler	284*
1983	Seve Ballesteros (Spa)	280
1984	Ben Crenshaw	277
1985	Bernhard Langer (FRG)	282
1986	Jack Nicklaus	279
1987	Larry Mize	285*
1988	Sandy Lyle (UK)	281
1989	Nick Faldo (UK)	283*
1990	Nick Faldo (UK)	278*

* after play-off

Most wins: 6 Jack Nicklaus, 4 Arnold Palmer
Most top 5 placings: 16 Nicklaus, 9 Snead, Ben Hogan, Arnold Palmer

Nick Faldo at Augusta in 1989; he emulated Jack Nicklaus as the only man to win two successive US Masters titles **(All-Sport/David Cannon)**

UNITED STATES PGA CHAMPIONSHIP

First held in 1916, the championship was a match-play event until 1958, when it became a stroke-play competition over four rounds. Entry is based on qualification from the PGA tour; it is the least publicised of the four majors. Winners (all USA unless otherwise stated)

Year	Winner	Score	Venue
1916	Jim Barnes	1 up	Siwanoy
1919	Jim Barnes	6 & 5	Engineers
1920	Jock Hutchison	1 up	Flossmoor
1921	Walter Hagen	3 & 2	Inwood
1922	Gene Sarazen	4 & 3	Oakmont
1923	Gene Sarazen	at 38th	Pelham
1924	Walter Hagen	2 up	French Lick
1925	Walter Hagen	6 & 5	Olympia Fields
1926	Walter Hagen	5 & 3	Salisbury
1927	Walter Hagen	1 up	Cedar Crest
1928	Leo Diegel	6 & 5	Five Farms
1929	Leo Diegel	6 & 4	Hill Crest
1930	Tommy Armour	1 up	Fresh Meadow
1931	Tom Creavy	2 & 1	Wannamoisett
1932	Olin Dutra	4 & 3	Keller
1933	Gene Sarazen	5 & 4	Blue Mound
1934	Paul Runyan	at 38th	Park
1935	Johnny Revolta	5 & 4	Twin Hills
1936	Densmore Shute	3 & 2	Pinehurst
1937	Densmore Shute	at 37th	Pittsburgh
1938	Paul Runyan	8 & 7	Shawnee
1939	Henry Picard	at 37th	Pomonok
1940	Byron Nelson	1 up	Hershey
1941	Vic Ghezzi	at 38th	Cherry Hills
1942	Sam Snead	2 & 1	Sea View
1944	Bob Hamilton	1 up	Manito
1945	Byron Nelson	4 & 3	Morraine
1946	Ben Hogan	6 & 4	Portland
1947	Jim Ferrier	2 & 1	Plum Hollow
1948	Ben Hogan	7 & 6	Norwood Hills
1949	Sam Snead	3 & 2	Hermitage
1950	Chandler Harper	4 & 3	Scioto
1951	Sam Snead	7 & 6	Oakmont
1952	Jim Turnesa	1 up	Big Spring
1953	Walter Burkemo	2 & 1	Birmingham
1954	Chick Harbert	4 & 3	Keller
1955	Doug Ford	4 & 3	Meadowbrook
1956	Jack Burke	3 & 2	Blue Hill
1957	Lionel Hebert	2 & 1	Miami Valley
1958	Dow Finsterwald	276	Llanerch
1959	Bob Rosburg	277	Minneapolis
1960	Jay Hebert	281	Firestone
1961	Jerry Barber	277*	Olympia Fields
1962	Gary Player (SAf)	278	Aronomink
1963	Jack Nicklaus	279	Dallas
1964	Bobby Nichols	271	Columbus
1965	Dave Marr	280	Laurel Valley
1966	Al Geiberger	280	Firestone
1967	Don January	281*	Columbine
1968	Julius Boros	281	Pecan Valley
1969	Raymond Floyd	276	NCR, Dayton
1970	Dave Stockton	279	Southern Hills
1971	Jack Nicklaus	281	PGA National
1972	Gary Player (SAf)	281	Oakland Hills
1973	Jack Nicklaus	277	Canterbury
1974	Lee Trevino	276	Tanglewood
1975	Jack Nicklaus	276	Firestone
1976	Dave Stockton	281	Congressional
1977	Lanny Wadkins	282*	Pebble Beach
1978	John Mahaffey	276*	Oakmont
1979	David Graham (Aus)	272*	Oakland Hills
1980	Jack Nicklaus	274	Oak Hill
1981	Larry Nelson	273	Atlanta
1982	Raymond Floyd	272	Southern Hills
1983	Hal Sutton	274	Riviera
1984	Lee Trevino	273	Shoal Creek
1985	Hubert Green	278	Cherry Hills
1986	Bob Tway	276	Toledo
1987	Larry Nelson	287*	Palm Beach
1988	Jeff Sluman	272	Oak Tree
1989	Payne Stewart	276	Kemper Lakes

* after play-off

Most wins: 5 Walter Hagen, Jack Nicklaus; 3 Gene Sarazen, Sam Snead

THE MAJORS – Records

Lowest four round total

The Open	268	Tom Watson 1977
US Open	272	Jack Nicklaus 1980
US PGA	271	Bobby Nichols 1964
US Masters	271	Jack Nicklaus 1965
	271	Raymond Floyd 1976

Lowest single round

The Open	63 Mark Hayes (USA) 2nd Rd 1977
	63 Isao Aoki (Jap) 3rd Rd 1980
	63 Greg Norman (Aus) 2nd Rd 1986
US Open	63 Johnny Miller (USA) 4th Rd 1973
	63 Tom Weiskopf (USA) 1st Rd 1980
	63 Jack Nicklaus (USA) 1st Rd 1980
US PGA	63 Bruce Crampton (Aus) 2nd Rd 1975
	63 Raymond Floyd (USA) 1st Rd 1982
	63 Gary Player (SAf) 2nd Rd 1984
US Masters	63 Nick Price (SAf) 3rd Rd 1986

Oldest winners

The Open	46y 99d Tom Morris, Snr. 1867
US Open	43y 284d Raymond Floyd 1986
US PGA	48y 140d Julius Boros 1968
US Masters	46y 82d Jack Nicklaus 1986

Youngest winners

The Open	17y 249d Tom Morris, Jnr. 1868
US Open	19y 318d John McDermott 1911
US PGA	20y 173d Gene Sarazen 1922
US Masters	23y 4d Severiano Ballesteros 1980

Most wins

A British Open, B US Open, C US PGA, D US Masters

	A	B	C	D	Total
Jack Nicklaus	3	4	5	6	18
Walter Hagen	4	2	5	-	11

Ben Hogan	1	4	2	2	9
Gary Player	3	1	2	3	9
Tom Watson	5	1	-	2	8
Harry Vardon	6	1	-	-	7
Bobby Jones	3	4	-	-	7
Gene Sarazen	1	2	3	1	7
Sam Snead	1	-	3	3	7
Arnold Palmer	2	1	-	4	7

When he won the Masters in 1935 Gene Sarazen became the first man to have won all four majors.

No man has won all four in one year, but in 1953 Ben Hogan won three (British Open, US Open and Masters); he did not contest the PGA. In 1986 Greg Norman led going into the final round of all four championships; he won only one, the British Open.

Jack Nicklaus also won two US Amateur titles and Bobby Jones won five US Amateur and one British Amateur. Jones uniquely won the Open and Amateur Championships of the USA and Britain in one year, 1930.

WORLD MATCH-PLAY CHAMPIONSHIP

An annual end-of-season knockout competition held at Wentworth, Surrey. The number of entrants was originally eight but has since been increased to 12 (16 in 1977-8). Each match consists of two rounds, one in the morning and one in the afternoon. Sponsored by Piccadilly 1964-76, Colgate 1977-8, Suntory from 1979.

Year	Winner	Runner-up	Score
1964	Arnold Palmer (USA)	Neil Coles (UK)	2 & 1
1965	Gary Player (SAf)	Peter Thomson (Aus)	3 & 2
1966	Gary Player (SAf)	Jack Nicklaus (USA)	6 & 4
1967	Arnold Palmer (USA)	Peter Thomson (Aus)	1 up
1968	Gary Player (SAf)	Bob Charles (NZ)	1 up
1969	Bob Charles (NZ)	Gene Littler (USA)	at 37th
1970	Jack Nicklaus (USA)	Lee Trevino (USA)	2 & 1
1971	Gary Player (SAf)	Jack Nicklaus (USA)	5 & 4
1972	Tom Weiskopf (USA)	Lee Trevino (USA)	4 & 3
1973	Gary Player (SAf)	Graham Marsh (Aus)	at 40th
1974	Hale Irwin (USA)	Gary Player (SAf)	3 & 1
1975	Hale Irwin (USA)	Al Geiberger (USA)	4 & 2
1976	David Graham (Aus)	Hale Irwin (USA)	at 38th
1977	Graham Marsh (Aus)	Raymond Floyd (USA)	5 & 3
1978	Isao Aoki (Jap)	Simon Owen (NZ)	3 & 2
1979	Bill Rogers (USA)	Isao Aoki (Jap)	1 up
1980	Greg Norman (Aus)	Sandy Lyle (UK)	1 up
1981	Seve Ballesteros (Spa)	Ben Crenshaw (USA)	1 up
1982	Seve Ballesteros (Spa)	Sandy Lyle (UK)	at 37th
1983	Greg Norman (Aus)	Nick Faldo (UK)	3 & 2
1984	Seve Ballesteros (Spa)	Bernhard Langer (FRG)	2 & 1
1985	Seve Ballesteros (Spa)	Bernhard Langer (FRG)	6 & 5
1986	Greg Norman (Aus)	Sandy Lyle (UK)	2 & 1
1987	Ian Woosnam (UK)	Sandy Lyle (UK)	1 up
1988	Sandy Lyle (UK)	Nick Faldo (UK)	2 & 1
1989	Nick Faldo (UK)	Ian Woosnam (UK)	1 up

Most wins: 5 Gary Player, 4 Severiano Ballesteros, 3 Greg Norman

Biggest winning margin: 11 & 9 Tom Watson (USA) v Dale Hayes (SAf), 1st round 1979

TOURNAMENT PLAYERS CHAMPIONSHIP

Introduced into the US tour at Atlanta in 1974, with the intention of being a fifth 'major', a status it has not really achieved, although its $1.5 million total purse was the highest on the 1990 PGA tour. Open only to players who have won official PGA Tour events in the previous year. From 1977 it has been played on the TPC's own course at Sawgrass, Ponte Vedra, Florida. Winners (all USA unless stated):

1974	Jack Nicklaus	272
1975	Al Geiberger	270
1976	Jack Nicklaus	269
1977	Mark Hayes	289
1978	Jack Nicklaus	289
1979	Lanny Wadkins	283
1980	Lee Trevino	278
1981	Raymond Floyd	285
1982	Jerrry Pate	280
1983	Hal Sutton	283
1984	Fred Couples	277
1985	Calvin Peete	274
1986	John Mahaffey	275
1987	Sandy Lyle (UK)	274
1988	Mark McCumber	273
1989	Tom Kite	279
1990	Jodie Mudd	278

Arnold Palmer swings to victory in the 1967 World Match-play (**Popperfoto**)

WORLD CUP

The World Cup was the idea of American industrialist Jay Hopkins. He saw the need for an international team competition for male professionals, other than for those of Great Britain and the United States. Contested annually over 72 holes of strokeplay by two-man teams. Interest has fallen in the competition in recent years and it was not played in 1981 or 1986.

Year	Winning Team		Leading Individual	
1953	Argentina (Roberto de Vicenzo & Antonio Cerda)	287*	Antonio Cerda (Arg)	140*
1954	Australia (Peter Thomson & Kel Nagle)	556	Stan Leonard (Can)	275
1955	USA (Ed Furgol & Chick Harbert)	560	Ed Furgol (USA)	279
1956	USA (Ben Hogan & Sam Snead)	567	Ben Hogan (USA)	277
1957	Japan (Torakichi Nakamura & Koichi Ono)	557	Torakichi Nakamura (Jap)	274
1958	Ireland (Harry Bradshaw & Christy O'Connor)	579	Angel Miguel (Spa)	286
1959	Australia (Kel Nagle & Peter Thomson)	563	Stan Leonard (Can)	275
1960	USA (Arnold Palmer & Sam Snead)	565	Flory van Donck (Bel)	279
1961	USA (Jimmy Demaret & Sam Snead)	560	Sam Snead (USA)	272
1962	USA (Arnold Palmer & Sam Snead)	557	Roberto de Vicenzo (Arg)	276
1963	USA (Jack Nicklaus & Arnold Palmer)	482*	Jack Nicklaus (USA)	237*
1964	USA (Jack Nicklaus & Arnold Palmer)	554	Jack Nicklaus (USA)	276
1965	South Africa (Harold Henning & Gary Player)	571	Gary Player (SAf)	281
1966	USA (Jack Nicklaus & Arnold Palmer)	548	George Knudson (Can)	272
1967	USA (Jack Nicklaus & Arnold Palmer)	557	Arnold Palmer (USA)	276
1968	Canada (Al Balding & George Knudson)	569	Al Balding (Can)	274
1969	USA (Orville Moody & Lee Trevino)	552	Lee Trevino (USA)	275
1970	Australia (Bruce Devlin & David Graham)	544	Roberto de Vicenzo (Arg)	269
1971	USA (Jack Nicklaus & Lee Trevino)	555	Jack Nicklaus (USA)	271
1972	Taiwan (Hsieh Min-nan & Lu Liang-huan)	438*	Hsieh Min-nan (Tai)	217*
1973	USA (Johnny Miller & Jack Nicklaus)	558	Johnny Miller (USA)	277
1974	South Africa (Bobby Cole & Dale Hayes)	554	Bobby Cole (SAf)	271
1975	USA (Lou Graham & Johnny Miller)	554	Johnny Miller (USA)	275
1976	Spain (Severiano Ballesteros & Manuel Pinero)	574	Ernesto Perez Acosta (Mex)	282
1977	Spain (Severiano Ballesteros & Antonio Garrido)	591	Gary Player (SAf)	289
1978	USA (John Mahaffey & Andy North)	564	John Mahaffey (USA)	281
1979	USA (John Mahaffey & Hale Irwin)	575	Hale Irwin (USA)	285
1980	Canada (Dan Halldorson & Jim Nelford)	572	Sandy Lyle (Sco)	282
1982	Spain (José-Maria Canizares & Manuel Pinero)	563	Manuel Pinero (Spa)	281
1983	USA (Rex Caldwell & John Cook)	565	Dave Barr (Can)	276
1984	Spain (José-Maria Canizares & José Rivero)	414*	José-Maria Canizares	205*
1985	Canada (Dan Halldorson & Dave Barr)	559	Howard Clark (Eng)	272
1987	Wales (Ian Woosnam & David Llewellyn)	574	Ian Woosnam (Wal)	274
1988	USA (Ben Crenshaw & Mark McCumber)	560	Ben Crenshaw (USA)	275
1989	Australia (Peter Fowler & Wayne Grady)	278*	Peter Fowler (Aus)	137*

Most team wins: 17 USA *Team wins by individuals:* 6 Jack Nicklaus, Arnold Palmer
Most Individual titles: 3 Jack Nicklaus
Lowest four rounds scores: team 544 Australia 1970; *individual* 269 Roberto de Vicenzo 1970
* played over 36 holes in 1953, 63 holes in 1963, 54 holes in 1972 and 1984. Rain reduced play to 36 holes in 1989

RYDER CUP

The Ryder Cup started as a result of the efforts of wealthy businessman Samuel Ryder. It was launched in 1927, the year after a successful match between Great Britain and the United States at Wentworth. Held every two years the countries take it in turn to play host. Opposing the USA were Great Britain 1927-71, Great Britain and Ireland 1973-77, Europe from 1979. The current format is for four foursomes and four fourball matches on each of the first two days, and 12 singles on the third and final day.

Year	Venue	Winners	Score	Year	Venue	Winners	Score
1927	Worcester, Massachusetts	USA	9½-2½	1935	Ridgewood, New Jersey	USA	9-3
1929	Moortown, Yorkshire	GB	7-5	1937	Southport & Ainsdale, Lancs.	USA	8-4
1931	Scioto, Ohio	USA	9-3	1947	Portland, Oregan	USA	11-1
1933	Southport & Ainsdale, Lancs.	GB	6½-5½	1949	Ganton, Yorkshire	USA	7-5

Year	Venue	Winners	Score
1951	Pinehurst, North Carolina	USA	9½-2½
1953	Wentworth, Surrey	USA	6½-5½
1955	Thunderbird G&CC, California	USA	8-4
1957	Lindrick, Yorkshire	GB	7½-4½
1959	Eldorado CC, California	USA	8½-3½
1961	Royal Lytham, Lancs.	USA	14½-9½
1963	Atlanta, Georgia	USA	23-9
1965	Royal Birkdale, Lancs.	USA	19½-12½
1967	Houston, Texas	USA	23½-8½
1969	Royal Birkdale, Lancs.	Drawn	16-16
1971	St.Louis, Missouri	USA	18½-13½
1973	Muirfield, Scotland	USA	19-13
1975	Laurel Valley, Pennsylvania	USA	21-11
1977	Royal Lytham, Lancs.	USA	12½-7½
1979	Greenbrier, West Virginia	USA	17-11
1981	Walton Heath, Surrey	USA	18½-9½
1983	PGA National, Florida	USA	14½-13½
1985	The Belfry, Sutton Coldfield	Europe	16½-11½
1987	Muirfield Village, Ohio	Europe	15-13
1989	The Belfry, Sutton Coldfield	Drawn	14-14

Most wins: 21 United States
Most selections: 10 Christy O'Connor (Ire), 1955-73
Oldest player: 50y 66d Edward Ray (GB), 1927
Youngest player: 20y 59d Nick Faldo (GB&I), 1977

Leading players records

Golfers who have played 20 or more matches. pts = points as 1 for win, ½ for halved match

Name	Years	Cups	played	won	lost	halved	pts
GB/GB&I/EUROPE							
Nick Faldo	1977-89	7	27	16	9	2	17
Tony Jacklin	1967-79	7	35	13	14	8	17
Neil Coles	1961-77	8	40	12	21	7	15½
Bernard Gallacher	1969-83	8	31	13	13	5	15½
Peter Oosterhuis	1971-81	6	28	14	11	3	15½
Severiano Ballesteros	1979-89	5	25	13	8	4	15
Christy O'Connor	1955-73	10	35	11	20	4	13
Peter Alliss	1953-69	8	30	10	15	5	12½
Bernhard Langer	1981-9	5	22	10	8	4	12
Brian Barnes	1969-79	6	26	11	14	1	11½
Brian Huggett	1963-75	6	24	8	10	6	11
Bernard Hunt	1953-69	8	28	6	16	6	9
UNITED STATES							
Billy Casper	1961-75	8	37	20	10	7	23½
Arnold Palmer	1961-73	6	32	22	8	2	23
Lee Trevino	1969-81	6	30	17	7	6	20
Jack Nicklaus	1969-81	6	28	17	8	3	18½
Gene Littler	1961-75	7	27	14	5	8	18
Lanny Wadkins	1977-89	6	25	15	9	1	15½
Tom Kite	1979-89	6	24	13	7	4	15
Raymond Floyd	1969-85	6	23	7	13	3	8½
Also with 10 or more wins							
Hale Irwin	1975-81	4	16	11	4	1	11½
Sam Snead *	1937-59	7	13	10	2	1	10½

* Snead was also selected for 1939 and 1941 teams when the match was not contested

DUNHILL CUP

International knockout team tournament for teams of three professionals. Inaugurated in 1985 and played at St.Andrews, Scotland. *Finals:*

1985	Australia 3	USA 0
1986	Australia 3	Japan 0
1987	England 2	Scotland 1
1988	Ireland 2	Australia 1
1989	USA 3	Japan 2

LEADING MONEY WINNERS

The following is a list of leading money winners, season-by-season, on the tours in Europe and the USA.

Europe

		£
1961	Bernard Hunt (UK)	4,492
1962	Peter Thomson (Aus)	5,764
1963	Bernard Hunt (UK)	7,209
1964	Neil Coles (UK)	7,890
1965	Peter Thomson (Aus)	7,011
1966	Bruce Devlin (Aus)	13,205
1967	Gay Brewer (USA)	20,235
1968	Gay Brewer (USA)	23,107
1969	Billy Casper (USA)	23,483
1970	Christy O'Connor (Ire)	31,532
1971	Gary Player (SAf)	11,281
1972	Bob Charles (NZ)	18,538
1973	Tony Jacklin (UK)	24,839
1974	Peter Oosterhuis (UK)	32,127
1975	Dale Hayes (SAf)	20,507
1976	Seve Ballesteros (Spa)	39,504
1977	Seve Ballesteros (Spa)	46,436
1978	Seve Ballesteros (Spa)	54,348
1979	Sandy Lyle (UK)	49,233
1980	Greg Norman (Aus)	74,829
1981	Bernhard Langer (FRG)	95,991
1982	Sandy Lyle (UK)	86,141
1983	Nick Faldo (UK)	140,761
1984	Bernhard Langer (FRG)	160,883
1985	Sandy Lyle (UK)	199,020
1986	Seve Ballesteros (Spa)	242,208
1987	Ian Woosnam (UK)	253,717*
1988	Seve Ballesteros (Spa)	451,559
1989	Ronan Rafferty (Ire)	400,311

Most times leading:
5 Severiano Ballesteros

* Woosnam's total worldwide earnings in 1987 were a record £1,042,662

USA

All winners from USA unless otherwise stated. Total winnings shown in dollars:

1934	Paul Runyan	6,767
1935	Johnny Revolta	9,543
1936	Horton Smith	7,682
1937	Harry Cooper	14,138
1938	Sam Snead	19,534
1939	Henry Picard	10,303
1940	Ben Hogan	10,655
1941	Ben Hogan	18,358
1942	Ben Hogan	13,143
1943	*statistics not compiled*	
1944	Byron Nelson	37,967*
1945	Byron Nelson	63,335*
1946	Ben Hogan	42,556
1947	Jimmy Demaret	27,936
1948	Ben Hogan	32,112
1949	Sam Snead	31,593
1950	Sam Snead	35,758
1951	Lloyd Mangrum	26,088
1952	Julius Boros	37,032
1953	Lew Worsham	34,002
1954	Bob Toski	65,819
1955	Julius Boros	63,121
1956	Ted Kroll	72,835
1957	Dick Mayer	65,835
1958	Arnold Palmer	42,607
1959	Art Wall, Jnr	53,167
1960	Arnold Palmer	75,262
1961	Gary Player (SAf)	64,450
1962	Arnold Palmer	81,448
1963	Arnold Palmer	128,230
1964	Jack Nicklaus	113,284
1965	Jack Nicklaus	140,752
1966	Billy Casper	121,944
1967	Jack Nicklaus	188,998
1968	Billy Casper	205,168
1969	Frank Beard	164,707
1970	Lee Trevino	157,037
1971	Jack Nicklaus	244,490
1972	Jack Nicklaus	320,542
1973	Jack Nicklaus	308,362
1974	Johnny Miller	353,021
1975	Jack Nicklaus	298,149
1976	Jack Nicklaus	266,438
1977	Tom Watson	310,653
1978	Tom Watson	362,428
1979	Tom Watson	462,636
1980	Tom Watson	530,808
1981	Tom Kite	375,698
1982	Craig Stadler	446,462
1983	Hal Sutton	426,668
1984	Tom Watson	476,260
1985	Curtis Strange	542,321
1986	Greg Norman	653,296
1987	Curtis Strange	925,941
1988	Curtis Strange	1,147,644
1989	Tom Kite	1,395,278

* Nelson received War Bonds.

Most times leading:
8 Jack Nicklaus

HARRY VARDON TROPHY

Europe
Awarded annually from 1937, when the first winner was Charles Whitcombe, to the leading player in the Order of Merit. *Most wins:*
5 Severiano Ballesteros (Spa) 1976-8, 1986, 1988
4 Peter Oosterhuis (UK) 1971-4
3 Bobby Locke (SAf) 1946, 1950, 1954
3 Bernard Hunt (UK) 1958, 1960, 1965
3 Sandy Lyle (UK) 1979-80, 1985

USA
Awarded annually by the USPGA to the player who has the lowest stroke average in PGA Tournaments in that year. *Most wins:*
5 Billy Casper 1960, 1963, 1965-6, 1968
5 Lee Trevino 1970-2, 1974, 1980
4 Sam Snead 1938, 1949-50, 1955
4 Arnold Palmer 1961-2, 1964, 1967

ALL-TIME EARNINGS

European Tour
Amount		Years	Wins
£1,956,588	Severiano Ballesteros (Spa)	1974-89	45
£1,505,372	Nick Faldo (UK)	1976-89	17
£1,344,895	Ian Woosnam (UK)	1978-89	13
£1,306,081	Sandy Lyle (UK)	1977-89	15
£1,144,023	Bernhard Langer (FRG)	1976-89	20
£1,007,165	Sam Torrance (UK)	1971-89	12

United States Tour
Amount		Years	Wins
$5,600,691	Tom Kite (USA)	1972-89	13
$5,160,243	Tom Watson (USA)	1971-89	32
$5,102,420	Jack Nicklaus (USA)	1962-89	71
$5,015,720	Curtis Strange (USA)	1977-89	17
$4,115,074	Ben Crenshaw (USA)	1973-89	14
$3,940,949	Lanny Wadkins (USA)	1971-89	18
$3,616,587	Raymond Floyd (USA)	1963-89	21
$3,606,707	Payne Stewart (USA)	1981-9	5
$3,460,416	Lee Trevino (USA)	1966-89	27
$3,227,831	Hale Irwin (USA)	1968-89	17

Most tournament wins:
84 Sam Snead (1937-65), 71 Jack Nicklaus, 62 Ben Hogan, 61 Arnold Palmer, 54 Byron Nelson, 51 Billy Casper, 37 Cary Middlecoff, 34 Lloyd Mangrum, 32 Jimmy Demaret, Tom Watson, 30 Horton Smith.

RECORDS

European Tour
Most wins in a season: 7 Norman Von Nida (Aus) 1947, Flory Van Donck (Bel) 1953
Most consecutive wins: 4 Alf Padgham (UK) 1935-6, Severiano Ballesteros (Spa) 1986
Lowest score (72 holes): 260 Kel Nagle (Aus) 1961 Irish Hospital's, Mike Clayton (Aus) 1984 Timex Open
Lowest score (18 holes): 60 Baldovino Dassu (Ita) 1971 Swiss Open
Oldest winner: 58y Sandy Herd (UK) 1926 News of the World
Youngest winner: 19y 121d Severiano Ballesteros (Spa) 1976 Dutch Open

US PGA Tour
Most wins in a season: 18 Byron Nelson (USA) 1945
Most consecutive wins: 11 Byron Nelson 1945
Lowest score (72 holes): 257 Mike Souchak (USA) 1955 Tournament Texas Open
Lowest score (18 holes): 59 Al Geiberger (USA) 1977 Memphis Classic
Oldest winner: 52y 312d Sam Snead 1965 Greater Greensboro Open
Youngest winner: 19y 10m John McDermott (USA) 1911 US Open

SONY WORLD RANKINGS
Introduced in 1986 in an attempt to rank players on their achievements worldwide. The leader at the end of the first year was Greg Norman (Aus). He remained on top at the end of 1989.

US AMATEUR CHAMPIONSHIP
Although unofficial US Amateur championships had been held previously, the first official championship was at Newport, Rhode Island in 1895. They were held during the same week, and at the same venue, as the inaugural US Open. Originally a match-play competition, it changed to being stroke-play in 1965, but reverted back to match-play in 1973 *Recent winners (all USA):*

1977	John Fought
1978	John Cook
1979	Mark O'Meara
1980	Hal Sutton
1981	Nathaniel Crosby
1982-3	Jay Sigel
1984	Scott Verplank
1985	Sam Randolph
1986	Buddy Alexander
1987	Bill Mayfair
1988	Eric Meeks
1989	Chris Patton

Most wins: 5 Bobby Jones 1924-5, 1927-8, 1930; 4 Jerome Travers 1907-8, 1912-3; Walter Travis 1900-01, 1903
Lowest score (stroke-play): 279 Lanny Wadkins , 1970
Biggest winning margin – final (match-play): 12 & 11 Charles Blair Macdonald, 1895

THE AMATEUR CHAMPIONSHIP
In 1885 Thomas Owen Potter of Hoylake organised the first British Amateur Championship at his home course – eight years after the Royal & Ancient showed little interest in running such a competition. Since 1886, however, the

championships have been run by the R&A. It has always been a knockout match-play competition and since 1983 all competitors have to play two medal rounds to reduce the field to 64. *Recent winners:*

1977-8 Peter McEvoy (UK)
1979 Jay Sigel (USA)
1980 Duncan Evans (UK)
1981 Phillipe Ploujoux (Fra)
1982 Martin Thompson (UK)
1983 Andrew Parkin (UK)
1984 José-Maria Olazabal (Spa)
1985 Garth McGimpsey (UK)
1986 David Curry (UK)
1987 Paul Mayo (UK)
1988 Christian Hardin (Swe)
1989 Stephen Dodd (UK)
1990 Rolf Muntz (Hol)

Most wins: 8 John Ball (UK) 1888, 1890, 1892, 1894, 1899, 1907, 1910, 1912; 5 Michael Bonallack (UK) 1961, 1965, 1968-70; 4 Harold Hilton (UK) 1900-1, 1911, 1913; 3 Joe Carr (Ire) 1953, 1958, 1960

Biggest winning margin (final): 14 & 13 W.Lawson Little (USA) beat Jack Wallace (UK), 1934

WALKER CUP

Following the success of an international match between amateur teams from the USA and Great Britain (Great Britain and Ireland from 1981) at Hoylake in 1921 the first official series of Walker Cup matches took place the following year. The trophy was donated by George Herbert Walker, a former president of the USA Golf Association. It is a biennial event, held alternately in the British Isles and the USA.

Year	Venue	Winners	Score
1922	Long Island, New York	USA	8 – 4
1923	St.Andrews, Scotland	USA	6½ - 5½
1924	Garden City, New York	USA	9 – 3
1926	St.Andrews, Scotland	USA	6½ - 5½
1928	Chicago GC, Illinois	USA	11 – 1
1930	Royal St.George's, Sandwich	USA	10 – 2
1932	Brookline, Massachusetts	USA	9½ - 2½
1934	St.Andrews, Scotland	USA	9½ - 2½
1936	Pine Valley, New Jersey	USA	10½ - 1½
1938	St.Andrews, Scotland	GB	7½ - 4½
1947	St.Andrews, Scotland	USA	8 – 4
1949	Winged Foot, New York	USA	10 – 2
1951	Royal Birkdale, Southport	USA	7½ - 4½
1953	Kittansett, Massachusetts	USA	9 – 3
1955	St.Andrews, Scotland	USA	10 – 2
1957	Minikhada, Minnesota	USA	8½ - 3½
1959	Muirfield, Scotland	USA	9 – 3
1961	Seattle, Washington	USA	11 – 1
1963	Turnberry, Scotland	USA	14 -10
1965	Baltimore, Maryland	Drawn	12 -12
1967	Royal St.George's, Sandwich	USA	15 – 9
1969	Milwaukee, Wisconsin	USA	13 -11
1971	St.Andrews, Scotland	GB	13 -11
1973	Brookline, Massachusetts	USA	14- 10
1975	St.Andrews, Scotland	USA	15½ - 8½

1977	Shinnecock Hills, New York	USA	16 – 8
1979	Muirfield, Scotland	USA	15½ - 8½
1981	Cypress Point, California	USA	15 – 9
1983	Royal Liverpool, Hoylake	USA	13½ -10½
1985	Pine Valley, Philadelphia	USA	13 -11
1987	Sunnindgdale, Berkshire	USA	16½ -7½
1989	Peachtree, Georgia	GB & I	12½ -11½

Most wins: 28 USA

Most appearances: 10 Joe Carr (GB) 1947-67

Leading players records
Golfers who have played 15 or more matches or who have won 10 or more matches, note that some men were also selected on other occasions, but these records include only those Cups in which they actually played. Pts = points as 1 for win, ½ for halved match

Name	Years	Cups	played	won	lost	halved	pts
GB/GB&I							
Michael Bonnallack	1959-73	8	25	8	14	3	9½
Peter McEvoy	1977-89	5	18	5	11	2	6
Joe Carr	1947-67	10	20	5	14	1	5½
UNITED STATES							
Jay Sigel	1977-89	7	27	14	8	5	16½
William Campbell	1951-75	7	18	11	4	3	12½
William Patton	1955-65	5	14	11	3	0	11
Francis Ouimet	1922-34	7	16	9	5	2	10
Bob Lewis Jr	1981-7	4	14	10	4	0	10

WORLD AMATEUR TEAM CHAMPIONSHIP

An international team competiition for four-man teams. It has been held biennially from 1958. The winning team receives the Eisenhower Trophy, named after the former USA President Dwight D.Eisenhower. The best three scores by members of the four-man teams, each playing four rounds of strokeplay determines the result.

Year	Winning Team		Leading Individual	
1958	Australia	918	Bruce Devlin (Aus)	301
			Reid Jack (Sco)	301
			Bill Hyndman (USA)	301
1960	USA	834	Jack Nicklaus (USA)	269
1962	USA	854	Gary Cowan (Can)	280
1964	GB & Ireland	895	Hsieh Min-nan (Tai)	294
1966	Australia	877	Ronnie Shade (UK)	281
1968	USA	868	Michael Bonallack (UK)	286
			Vinnie Giles (USA)	286
1970	USA	854	Victor Regalado (Mex)	280
1972	USA	865	Tony Gresham (Aus)	285
1974	USA	888	Jerry Pate (USA)	294
			Jaime Gonzalez (Bra)	294
1976	GB & Ireland	892	Ian Hutcheon (UK)	293
			Chen Tze Ming (Tai)	293
1978	USA	873	Bob Clampett (USA)	287
1980	USA	848	Hal Sutton (USA)	276
1982	USA	859	Luis Carbonetti (Arg)	284
1984	Japan	870	Luis Carbonetti (Arg)	286
1986	Canada	838	Eduardo Herrera (Col)	275
1988	GB & Ireland	882	Peter McEvoy (GB)	284

Most wins: 9 USA
Lowest team score: 834 USA, 1960
Lowest individual score: 269 Jack Nicklaus (USA), 1960

WOMEN'S GOLF

The Women's Professional Golf Association (WPGA) was formed in the USA in 1944 and reformed in 1948 as the LPGA (Ladies for Women's).

US WOMEN'S OPEN

First held in 1946 at Spokane, Washington at match-play, but at 72 holes of stroke-play annually on different courses from 1947. Winners *(all USA, unless stated) Score*

1946	Patty Berg	5 & 4
1947	Betty Jameson	295
1948	Mildred Zaharias	300
1949	Louise Suggs	291
1950	Mildred Zaharias	291
1951	Betsy Rawls	293
1952	Louise Suggs	284
1953	Betsy Rawls	302
1954	Mildred Zaharias	291
1955	Fay Crocker	299
1956	Kathy Cornelius	302
1957	Betsy Rawls	299
1958	Mickey Wright	290
1959	Mickey Wright	287
1960	Betsy Rawls	292
1961	Mickey Wright	293
1962	Murle Lindstrom	301
1963	Mary Mills	289
1964	Mickey Wright	290
1965	Carol Mann	290
1966	Sandra Spuzich	297
1967	Catherine Lacoste (Fra)	294
1968	Susie Berning	289
1969	Donna Caponi	294
1970	Donna Caponi	287
1971	JoAnne Carner	288
1972	Susie Berning	299
1973	Susie Berning	290
1974	Sandra Haynie	295
1975	Sandra Palmer	295
1976	JoAnne Carner	292
1977	Hollis Stacy	292
1978	Hollis Stacy	289
1979	Jerilyn Britz	284
1980	Amy Alcott	280
1981	Pat Bradley	279
1982	Janet Alex	283
1983	Jan Stephenson	290
1984	Hollis Stacy	290
1985	Kathy Baker	280
1986	Jane Geddes	287
1987	Laura Davies (UK)	285
1988	Liselotte Neumann (Swi)	277
1989	Betsy King	278

Most wins: 4 Mickey Wright, Betsy Rawls

Lowest aggregate: 279 Pat Bradley 1981; Lowest round: 65 Sally Little 4th 1978, Judy Dickinson 3rd 1985
Biggest margin of victory: 14 strokes Louise Suggs 1949
Oldest winner: Fay Crocker 40yr 11 months 1955;
Youngest winner: Catherine Lacoste 22 yr 5 days 1967

US LPGA Championship

First held in 1955. 72 holes except for 1955, when it was match-play. *Winners (all USA)*

1955	Beverly Hanson	4&3
1956	Marlene Hagge	291
1957	Louise Suggs	285
1958	Mickey Wright	288
1959	Betsy Rawls	288
1960	Mickey Wright	292
1961	Mickey Wright	287
1962	Judy Kimball	282
1963	Mickey Wright	294
1964	Mary Mills	278
1965	Sandra Haynie	279
1966	Gloria Ehret	282
1967	Kathy Whitworth	284
1968	Sandra Post	294
1969	Betsy Rawls	293
1970	Shirley Englehorn	285
1971	Kathy Whitworth	288
1972	Kathy Ahem	293
1973	Mary Mills	288
1974	Sandra Haynie	288
1975	Kathy Whitworth	288
1976	Betty Burfeindt	287
1977	Chako Higuchi	279
1978	Nancy Lopez	275

Nancy Lopez first won the US LPGA title at the age of 21
(All-Sport/Dave Cannon)

1979	Donna Caponi	279
1980	Sally Little	285
1981	Donna Caponi	280
1982	Jan Stephenson	279
1983	Patty Sheehan	279
1984	Patty Sheehan	272
1985	Nancy Lopez	273
1986	Pat Bradley	277
1987	Jane Geddes	275
1988	Sherri Turner	281
1989	Nancy Lopez	274

Most wins: 4 Mickey Wright

In 1984 Patty Sheehan set records for: *Biggest margin of victory*, 10 strokes; *Lowest aggregate* 272, *Lowest round* 63

THE WOMEN'S 'MAJORS'

The four majors in US women's golf are:
A US Women's Open, first held 1946
B LPGA Championship, inaugurated 1955
C Nabisco Dinah Shore, inaugurated 1972 as the Colgate-Dinah Shore until name change in 1983. It was designated major status in 1983
D the du Maurier Classic which was granted Major status in 1979. First held in 1973 as the La Canadienne, and known as the Peter Jackson Classic 1974-82.

The Western Open (E) and Titleholders Championship (F) both used to be Majors.

Most wins (since formation of the US LPGA in 1950):

		A	B	C	D	E	F
12	Mickey Wright	4	4	-	-	2	2
8	Betsy Rawls	4	2	-	-	-	2
7	Patty Berg	-	-	-	-	3	4
6	Louise Suggs	1	1	-	-	3	1
6	Kathy Whitworth	-	3	-	-	2	1
6	Pat Bradley	1	1	1	3	-	-
5	Mildred Zaharias	2	-	-	-	2	1
4	Susie Berning	3	-	-	-	-	1
4	Donna Caponi	2	2	-	-	-	-
4	Sandra Haynie	1	2	-	1	-	-
4	Hollis Stacey	3	-	-	1	-	-
4	Amy Alcott	1	-	2	1	-	-

BRITISH WOMEN'S OPEN CHAMPIONSHIP

Contested annually at stroke-play from 1976, except for 1983. *Winners (UK unless stated)*

1976	Jennifer Lee Smith	299
1977	Vivien Saunders	306
1978	Janet Melville	310
1979	Alison Sheard (SAf)	301
1980	Debbie Massey (USA)	294
1981	Debbie Massey (USA)	295
1982	Marta Figueras-Dotti (Spa)	296
1984	Ayako Okamoto (Jap)	289
1985	Betsy King (USA)	300
1986	Laura Davies	283
1987	Alison Nicholas	296
1988	Corinne Dibnah (Aus)	295
1989	Jane Geddes (USA)	274

LADIES' BRITISH OPEN AMATEUR CHAMPIONSHIP

First held in 1893 and contested annually at match-play.
Recent winners (UK unless stated):

1977	Angela Uzielli
1978	Edwina Kennedy (Aus)
1979	Maureen Madill (Ire)
1980	Anne Sander (USA)
1981	Belle Robertson
1982	Katrina Douglas
1983	Jill Thornhill
1984	Jody Rosenthal (USA)
1985	Lilian Behan (Ire)
1986	Marnie McGuire (NZ)
1987	Janet Collingham
1988	Joanne Furby
1989	Helen Dobson
1990	Julie Hall

Most wins: 4 Cecil Leitch 1914, 1920-1, 1926; 4 Joyce Wethered 1922, 1924-5, 1929; 3 Lady Margaret Scott 1893-5; 3 May Hezlet 1899, 1902, 1907; 3 Enid Wilson 1931-3, Jesse Valentine (née Anderson) 1937, 1955, 1958
Most finals: 6 Cecil Leitch, also runner-up 1922, 1925
Biggest winning margin in final: 9 & 7 Joyce Wethered beat Cecil Leitch 1922
Oldest winner: Belle Robertson 45y 56d 1981. Youngest winner: May Hezlet 17y 7 days 1899.

US WOMEN'S AMATEUR CHAMPIONSHIP

Held at stroke-play in 1895, and annually at match-play from 1896, except for the war years of 1917-8, 1942-5.
Most wins: 6 Glenna Vare (née Collett) 1922, 1925, 1928-30, 1935: 5 JoAnne Carner (née Gunderson) 1957, 1960, 1962, 1966, 1968; 3 Beatrix Hoyt 1896-8; Margaret Curtis 1907, 1911-12; 3 Alexa Stirling 1916, 1919-20; 3 Dorothy Campbell Hurd 1909-10, 1924; 3 Virginia van Wie 1932-4; 3 Anne Quast (later Decker, Welts, Sander) 1958, 1961, 1963; 3 Juli Inkster 1980-2.
Biggest winning margin in final: 14 & 13 Anne Quast beat Phyllis Preuss 1961.
Oldest winner: Dorothy Campbell Hurd, 41 years 4 months 1924
Youngest winner: Laura Baugh 16 years 82 days 1971

WOMEN'S WORLD AMATEUR TEAM CHAMPIONSHIP

Contested bienially from 1964 by teams of three for the Espirito Santo Trophy. *Wins:*
10 USA 1966, 1968, 1970, 1972, 1974, 1976, 1980, 1982, 1984, 1988
1 France 1964, Australia 1978, Spain 1986
Lowest aggregate total (72 holes): 579 USA 1982
Lowest individual aggregate: 284 Marie-Laure de Lorenzi (Fra) 1986

US LPGA TOURNAMENT RECORDS

Lowest score – 72 holes: 268 Nancy Lopez 1985 Henredon Classic, Willow Creek GC, NC
Lowest score – 18 holes: 62 Mickey Wright 1964 Tall City Open, Hogan Park CC, Texas; 62 Vicki Fergon 1984 San Jose Classic
Most consecutive wins: 4 Mickey Wright 1962 and in 1963, Kathy Whitworth 1969. Nancy Lopez won five successive tournaments that she contested 1978
Most wins in a season: 13 Mickey Wright 1963
Oldest winner: 46yr 163d Joanne Carner 1985 Safeco Classic
Youngest winner: 18yr 14d Marlene Hagge 1952 Sarasota Open

ALL-TIME CAREER MONEY LEADERS on

US LPGA circuit as at 1 Jan 1990

Money		Wins	Years
$2,866,029	Pat Bradley	23	1974-89
$2,725,208	Nancy Lopez	42	1977-89
$2,469,694	Betsy King	20	1977-89
$2,469,693	Amy Alcott	28	1975-89
$2,299,699	JoAnne Carner	42	1970-89
$2,097,846	Patty Sheehan	20	1980-89
$2,029,905	Beth Daniel	18	1979-89
$1,801,035	Jan Stephenson (Aus)	16	1974-89
£1,739,582	Ayoko Okamoto (Jap)	15	1981-89
$1,713,152	Kathy Whitworth	88	1959-89
$1,406,579	Hollis Stacey	17	1974-89
$1,387,235	Donna Caponi	24	1965-88

Pat Bradley, the leading money winner in women's golf, passing $3 million in 1990 (All-Sport/Simon Miles)

Progressive record for the amount won in a season from $20,000 to over $500,000

$20,235	Marlene Hagge 1956
26,774	Betsy Rawls 1959
31,269	Mickey Wright 1963
33,517	Kathy Whitworth 1966
48,379	Kathy Whitworth 1968
65,063	Kathy Whitworth 1972
82,854	Kathy Whitworth 1973
87,094	JoAnne Carner 1974
94,805	Sandra Palmer 1975
150,734	Judy Rankin 1976
189,813	Nancy Lopez 1978
215,987	Nancy Lopez 1979
231,000	Beth Daniel 1980
310,399	JoAnne Carner 1982
416,472	Nancy Lopez 1985
492,021	Pat Bradley 1986
654,132	Betsy King 1989

Most seasons as leading money winner
8 Kathy Whitworth 1965-8, 1970-3; 4 Mildred 'Babe' Zaharias 1948-51; 4 Mickey Wright 1961-4.

Others with more than 30 LPGA wins: 82 Mickey Wright, 57 Patty Berg (inc.13 pre LPGA), 55 Betsy Rawls, 50 Louise Suggs, 42 Sandra Haynie, 38 Carol Mann, 31 Mildred 'Babe' Zaharias.

Women's PGA European Tour

Money leaders from the formalisation of the WPGA tour in 1979:

Year	Top money winner	£
1979	Alison Sheard (UK)	4,965
1980	Muriel Thomson (UK)	8,008
1981	Jenny Lee Smith (UK)	13,519
1982	Jenny Lee Smith (UK)	12,551
1983	Beverly Huke (UK)	9,226
1984	Dale Reid (UK)	28,239
1985	Laura Davies (UK)	21,736
1986	Laura Davies (UK)	37,500
1987	Dale Reid (UK)	53,815
1988	Marie-Laure de Lorenzi (Fra)	99,360
1989	Marie-Laure de Lorenzi (Fra)	77,534

The Order of Merit winners have been the same as the leading money winner except for: 1979 Catherine Panton (UK), 1983 Muriel Thomson (UK)

CURTIS CUP

A biennial team competition involving women's team from the United States and Great Britain and Ireland. It was first held at Wentworth in 1932 and is named after American sisters Margaret and Harriot Curtis.

Year	Venue	Winners	Score
1932	Wentworth, Surrey	USA	5½-3½
1934	Chevy Chase, Maryland	USA	6½-2½
1936	Gleneagles, Scotland	Drawn	4½-4½

1938	Essex, Massachusetts	USA	5½-3½
1948	Royal Birkdale, Southport	USA	6½-2½
1950	Buffalo CC, New York	USA	7½-1½
1952	Muirfield, Scotland	GB&I	5-4
1954	Merion, Pennsylvania	USA	6-3
1956	Prince's, Sandwich	GB&I	5-4
1958	Brae Burn, Massachusetts	Drawn	4½-4½
1960	Lindrick, Sheffield	USA	6½-2½
1962	Broadmoor, Colorado Springs	USA	8-1
1964	Royal Porthcawl, Wales	USA	10½-7½
1966	Hot Springs, Virginia	USA	13-5
1968	Royal County Down, Ireland	USA	10½-7½
1970	Brae Burn, Massachusetts	USA	11½-6½
1972	Western Gailes, Scotland	USA	10-8
1974	San Francisco, California	USA	13-5
1976	Royal Lytham, Lancashire	USA	11½-6½
1978	Apawamis, New York	USA	12-6
1980	St.Pierre, Chepstow	USA	13-5
1982	Denver, Colorado	USA	14½-3½
1984	Muirfield, Scotland	USA	9½-8½
1986	Prairie Dunes, Kansas	GB&I	13-5
1988	Royal St.George's, Sandwich	GB&I	11-7

Most wins: 19 USA
Most appearances: 9 Mary McKenna (GB&I) 1970-86

Leading players records
Golfers who have played 20 or more matches or won 10 or more. pts = points as 1 for win, ½ for halved match

Name	Years	Cups	played	won	lost	halved	pts
GB/GB&I							
Mary McKenna	1970-86	9	30	10	16	4	12
Belle Robertson	1960-86	7	24	5	12	7	8½
UNITED STATES							
Anne Quast Sander	1958-84	7	20	9	7	4	11
Phyllis Preuss	1962-70	5	15	10	4	1	10½

GREYHOUND RACING

The first greyhound meeting took place at Hendon, North London in September 1876, but the sport became popular following the perfecting of the mechanical hare by Owen Patrick Smith in the USA in 1919. Smith and George Sawyer formed the International Greyhound Racing Association at Tulsa in 1920. The oldest greyhound track in the world, still in operation, is the St. Petersburg Kennel Club, at St. Petersburg, Florida, opened on 3 Jan 1925. The first meeting with a mechanical hare in Great Britain was at Belle Vue, Manchester, on 24 July 1926, in which year the Greyhound Racing Association was formed.

DERBY

The most prestigious race in British greyhound racing, the Derby was instituted in 1927 and run over 500 yards at the White City. Between 1928-74 it was over 525 yards, between 1975-84 over 500 metres and since 1986 over 480 metres. The 1940 race was at Harringay and since 1985, following the closure of White City, all races have been at Wimbledon.

Winners:

1927	Entry Badge	1931	Seldom Led
1928	Bother Ash	1932	Wild Woolley
1929-30	Mick the Miller	1933	Future Cutlet

1934	Davesland	1949	Narrogar Ann
1935	Greta Ranee	1950	Ballmac Ball
1936	Fine Jubilee	1951	Ballylanigan Tanist
1937	Wattle Bark	1952	Endless Gossip
1938	Lone Keel	1953	Daws Dancer
1939	Highland Rum	1954	Pauls Fun
1940	G. R. Archduke	1955	Rushton MAck
1945	Ballyhennessy Seal	1956	Dunmore King
1946	Mondays News	1957	Ford Spartan
1947	Trevs Perfection	1958	Pigalle Wonder
1948	Priceless Border	1959	Mile Bush Pride

1960	Duleek Dandy
1961	Palm's Printer
1962	The Grand Canal
1963	Lucky Boy Boy
1964	Hack Up Chieftain
1965	Chittering Clapton
1966	Faithful Hope
1967	Tric-Trac
1968	Camera Flash
1969	Sand Star
1970	John Silver
1971	Dolores Rocket
1972-3	Patricia's Hope
1974	Jimsum
1975	Tartan Khan
1976	Mutts Silver
1977	Balliniska Band
1978	Lacca Champion
1979	Sarah's Bunny
1980	Indian Joe
1981	Parkdown Jet
1982	Laurie's Panther
1983	I'm Slippy
1984	Whisper Wishes
1985	Pagan Swallow
1986	Tico
1987	Signal Spark
1988	Hit the Lid
1989	Lartigue Note
1990	Slippy Blue

Most wins: 2 Mick the Miller, Patricia's Hope
Shortest priced winner: 1-4 Entry Badge (1927) the very first winner
Longest priced winner: 25-1 Duleek Dandy (1960); Tartan Khan (1975)

GRAND NATIONAL

The first of the year's classics, for hurdlers, was first run in 1927 at the White City. Since 1985 it has been run at Hall Green, Birmingham. 1927-74 run over 500 yards, since 1975 over 474 metres (five flights).
Winners:

1927	Bonzo
1928	Cormorant
1929	Lavator
1930	Stylish Cutlet
1931	Rule the Roost
1932	Long Hop
1933	Scapegoat
1934	Lemonition
1935	Quarter Day
1936	Kilganny Bridge
1937	Flying Wedge
1938	Juvenile Classic
1939	Valiant Bob

1940	Juvenile Classic
1946	Barry from Limerick
1947	Baytown Pigeon
1948	Joves Reason
1949-50	Blossom of Annagura
1951	XPDNC
1952	Whistling Laddie
1953	Denver Berwick
1954	Prince Lawrence
1955	Barrowside
1956	Blue Sand
1957	Tanyard Tulip
1958	Fodda Champion
1959	Prince Poppit
1960	Bruff Chariot
1961	Ballinatona Special
1962	Corsica Reward
1963	Indoor Sport
1964	Two Aces
1965	I'm Crazy
1966	Halfpenny King
1967	The Grange Santa
1968	Ballintore Tiger
1969	Tony's Friend
1970-2	Sherry's Price
1973	Killone Flash
1974	Shanney's Darkie
1975	Pier Hero
1976	Weston Pete
1977	Salerno
1978-9	Top O' The Tide
1980	Gilt Edge Flyer
1981	Bobcol
1982	Face The Nutt
1983	Sir Winston
1984	Kilcoe Foxy
1985	Seaman's Star
1986	Castelyons Cash
1987	Cavan Town
1988	Breek's Rocket
1989	Lemon Chip

Most wins: 3 Sherry's Prince; 2 Juvenile Classic, Blossom Annagura, Top O' The Tide

THE LAURELS

An early-season flat race classic it was first held at Wimbledon over 525 yards in 1930. When distances went metric in 1975 it was reduced to 460 metres.
Winners:

1930	Kilbrean Boy
1931	Future Cutlet
1932	Beef Cutlet
1933	Wild Woolley
1934	Brilliant Bob
1935	Kitshine
1936	Top O' The Carlow Road

1937-8	Balleyhennessy Sandhills
1939	Musical Duke
1940	April Burglar
1945	Burhill Moon
1946	Shannon Shore
1947	Rimmels Black
1948	Good Worker
1949-50	Ballymac Ball
1951	Ballylanigan Tansit
1952	Endless Gossip
1953	Polonius
1954	Coolkill Chieftain
1955-6	Duet Leader
1957	Ford Spartan
1958	Granthamian
1959	Mighty Hassan
1960	Dunstown Paddy
1961	Clonalvy Pride
1962	Turturama
1963	Dalcassion Son
1964-5	Conna Count
1966	Super Fame
1967	Carry on Oregon
1968	Ambiguous
1969	Ardine Flame
1970	Sole Aim
1971	Black Andrew
1972	Cricket Bunny
1973	Black Banjo
1974	Over Protected
1975	Pineapple Grand
1976	Xmas Holiday
1977	Greenfield Fox
1978	Jet Control
1979	Another Splatter
1980	Flying Pursuit
1981	Echo Spark
1982	Lauries Panther
1983	Darkie Fli
1984	Amenhotet
1985	Ballygroman Jim
1986	Mollifrend Lucky
1987	Flashy Sir
1988	Commeragh Boy
1989	Parquet Pal

Most wins: 2 Ballyhennessy Sandhills, Ballymac Ball, Duet Leader, Conna Count

SCURRY GOLD CUP

Known as the 'Sprinter's Classic'. It was first run in 1928 and immediately accorded 'Classic' status. Run at Clapton over 440 yards 1928-73 it moved to Slough in 1974 and was run over 475 yards. 1975-7 run over 434 metres and 1978-86 over 442 metres. It was moved to Catford in 1987 and is

now run over 385 metres.
Winners:

1928	Cruiseline Boy	1953	Rolling Mike	1977	Wired to Moon
1929	Loose Card	1954	Demon King	1978	Greenfield Fox
1930	Barlock	1955	Chance Me Paddy	1979	Northway Point
1931	Brave Enough	1956	Belinga's Customer	1980	Willing Slave
1932	Experts Boast	1957	Lisbrook Chieftain	1981	Smokey
1933	Creamery Border	1958	Beware Champ	1982-4	Yankee Express
1934	Brilliant Bob	1959-60	Gorey Airways	1985	Daley's Gold
1935	Jack's Joke	1961	Palm's Printer	1986	Mollifrend Lucky
1936	Mitzvah	1962	Hi Darkie	1987	Rapid Mover
1937	Hexham Bridge	1963	Lucky Joan	1988	Sarncombe Black
1938	Orluck's Best	1964	Salthill Sand	1989	Nan's Brute
1939	Silver Wire	1965	After You		
1945	Country Life	1966	Geddy's Blaze		
1946	Mischievous Manhattan	1967	Carry On Oregan		
1947	Rimmell's Black	1968	Foyle Tonic		
1948	Local Interprize	1969	Ace of Trumps		
1949	Burndennett Brook	1970-1	Don't Gambol		
1950	Gortnagory	1972	Cricket Bunny		
1951	Defence Leader	1973	Casa Miel		
1952	Monachdy Girlie	1974	Westmead Valley		
		1975	Langor Lad		
		1976	Xmas Holiday		

Most wins: 3 Yankee Express; 2 Gorey Airways, Don't Gambol

Greyhound Records
Highest speed: 41.72 mph (67.14 km/h) by The Shoe at Richmond, NSW, Australia, 25 Apr 1968
Most career wins: 143 by JR's Ripper (USA) 1982-6
Most consecutive wins: 32 Ballyregan Bob (UK) 1985-6

GYMNASTICS

The ancient Greeks and Romans were exponents of gymnastics and excelled at the Ancient Olympic Games over 2000 years ago. Modern techniques, however, were developed in Germany towards the latter part of the 18th-century and the first teacher of modern gymnastics was Johann Friedrich Simon at Basedow's School, Dessau, in 1776. Regarded as the father figure of modern gymnastics was Friedrich Jahn, who founded the Turnverein in Berlin in 1811. In Britain the Amateur Gymnastics Association was formed in 1888. The International Gymnastics Federation (IGF) was formed in 1891.

Apparatus

MEN
Parallel bars – two bars of round cross section, 350 cm long, set 42 cm apart, and supported 160 cm above the floor on uprights fixed to a broad stable base.
Horizontal bar – bar 240 cm long supported 255 cm above the ground by an upright at each end and braced with wires.
Pommel horse – similar to vaulting horse; 110 cm high, 163 cm long, but with two raised handles at the centre.
Rings – two rigid rings 18 cm in diameter suspended 250 cm from the floor by two wires 50 cm apart attached to a frame, braced with wires, 550 cm high.
Horse vault – Horse is 163 cm long, 135 cm high. Springboard is 120 cm long, placed in line with the long side of the horse.

MEN & WOMEN
Floor exercises – on a 12m square area.

WOMEN
Asymmetrical bars – two horizontal bars 350 cm long, arranged parallel to one another but at different heights. Lower is 150 cm and upper 230 cm above the floor. Each is supported by an upright at each end, and these two frames are placed 43 cm apart.
Beam – rigid beam of wood 5m long mounted horizontally, 10 cm wide at 120 cm above the floor.
Horse vault – Horse is 163 cm long 120 cm high. Springboard as for men's.

Modern Rhythmic Gymnastics
In this women's sport the disciplines are characterized by the handling of light portable objects, skipping ropes, hoops, clubs, ribbons and balls, to musical accompaniment. The IGF recognised Rhythmic gymnastics in 1962, world championships were first held in 1963 and the sport was added to the Olympics in 1984.

OLYMPIC GAMES

Gymnastics was included in the first Modern Olympics of 1896. A women's competition was first included in 1928. *Winners:*

MEN
Team
5 Japan 1960, 1964, 1968, 1972, 1976
4 Italy 1912, 1920, 1924, 1932,
4 USSR 1952, 1956, 1980, 1988
2 USA 1904 (TG Philadelphia), 1984
1 Norway 1906, Sweden 1908,
Switzerland 1928, Germany 1936,
Finland 1948

Individual
Combined exercises
1900 Gustave Sandras (Fra)
1904 Julius Lenhart (Aut) #
1906 Pierre Payssé (Fra) *
1908 Alberto Braglia (Ita)
1912 Alberto Braglia (Ita)
1920 Giorgio Zampori (Ita)
1924 Leon Stukelj (Yug)
1928 Georges Miez (Sui)
1932 Romeo Neri (Ita)
1936 Alfred Schwarzmann (Ger)
1948 Veikko Huhtanen (Fin)
1952 Viktor Chukarin (USSR)
1956 Viktor Chukarin (USSR)
1960 Boris Shakhlin (USSR)
1964 Yukio Endo (Jap)
1968 Sawao Kato (Jap)
1972 Sawao Kato (Jap)
1976 Nikolay Andrianov (USSR)
1980 Aleksandr Ditiatin (USSR)
1984 Koji Gushiken (Jap)
1988 Vladimir Artemov (USSR)
* won two competitions in 1906 – 5 events and 6 events
# member of USA Philadelphia Club who won team event

Floor exercises
1932 István Pelle (Hun)
1936 Georges Miez (Swi)
1948 Ferenc Pataki (Hun)
1952 William Thoresson (Swe)
1956 Valentin Muratov (USSR)
1960 Nobuyuki Aihara (Jap)
1964 Franco Menichelli (Ita)
1968 Sawao Kato (Jap)
1972 Nikolay Andrianov (USSR)
1976 Nikolay Andrianov (USSR)
1980 Roland Brückner (GDR)
1984 Li Ning (Chn)
1988 Sergey Kharikov (USSR)

Eight members of the Soviet Olympic gymnastics team in 1956 joined by swimmer Lyudmila Klipova (top left). The gymnasts: top row l-r: Sofia Muratova, Lydia Kalinina, Tamara Manina. Bottom row l-r: Valentin Muratov, Boris Shakhlin, Viktor Chukarin, Albert Azaryan and Grant Shaginyan (Hulton-Deutsch)

Parallel bars
1896 Alfred Flatow (Ger)
1904 George Eyser (USA)
1924 August Güttinger (Swi)
1928 Ladislav Vácha (Cs)
1932 Romeo Neri (Ita)
1936 Konrad Frey (Ger)
1948 Michael Reusch (Swi)
1952 Hans Eugster (Swi)
1956 Viktor Chukarin (USSR)
1960 Boris Shakhlin (USSR)
1964 Yukio Endo (Jap)
1968 Akinori Nakayama (Jap)
1972 Sawao Kato (Jap)
1976 Sawao Kato (Jap)
1980 Aleksandr Tkachev (USSR)
1984 Bart Conner (USA)
1988 Vladimir Artemov (USSR)

Pommel horse
1896 Louis Zutter (Swi)
1904 Anton Heida (USA)
1924 Josef Wilhelm (Swi)
1928 Hermann Hänggi (Swi)
1932 István Pelle (Hun)
1936 Konrad Frey (Ger)
1948 Paavo Aaltonen (Fin), Veikko Huhtanen (Fin) & Heikki Savolainen (Fin)
1952 Viktor Chukarin (USSR)
1956 Boris Shakhlin (USSR)
1960 Eugen Ekman (Fin) & Boris

Shakhlin (USSR)
1964 Miroslav Cerar (Yug)
1968 Miroslav Cerar (Yug)
1972 Viktor Klimenko (USSR)
1976 Zoltán Magyar (Hun)
1980 Zoltán Magyar (Hun)
1984 Li Ning (Chn) & Peter Vidmar (USA)
1988 Dmitriy Belozerchev (USSR), Zsolt Borkai (Hun) & Lyubomir Gueraskov (Bul)

Rings
1896 Ioannis Mitropoulos (Gre)
1904 Hermann Glass (USA)
1924 Francesco Martino (Ita)
1928 Leon Skutelj (Yug)
1932 George Gulack (USA)
1936 Alois Hudec (Cs)
1948 Karl Frei (Swi)
1952 Grant Shaginyan (USSR)
1956 Albert Azaryan (USSR)
1960 Albert Azaryan (USSR)
1964 Takuji Hayata (Jap)
1968 Akinori Nakayama (Jap)
1972 Akinori Nakayama (Jap)
1976 Nikolay Andrianov (USSR)
1980 Aleksandr Ditiatin (USSR)
1984 Koji Gushiken (Jap) & Li Ning (Chn)
1988 Holger Behrendt (GDR) & Dmitriy Belozerchev (USSR)

Horizontal Bar
1896 Hermann Weingärtner (Ger)
1904 Anton Heida (USA) & Edward
     Hennig (USA)
1924 Leon Stukelj (Yug)
1928 Georges Miez (Swi)
1932 Dallas Bixler (USA)
1936 Aleksanteri Saarvala (Fin)
1948 Josef Stadler (Swi)
1952 Jack Günthard (Swi)
1956 Takashi Ono (Jap)
1960 Takashi Ono (Jap)
1964 Boris Shakhlin (USSR)
1968 Mikhail Voronin (USSR) &
     Akinori Nakayama (Jap)
1972 Mitsuo Tsukahara (Jap)
1976 Mitsuo Tsukahara (Jap)
1980 Stoyan Deltchev (Bul)
1984 Shinji Morisue (Jap)
1988 Vladimir Artemov (USSR) &
     Valeriy Lyukin (USSR)

Horse vault
1896 Carl Schuhmann (Ger)
1904 Anton Heida (USA) & George
     Eyser (USA)
1924 Frank Kriz (USA)
1928 Eugen Mack (Swi)
1932 Savino Guglielmetti (Ita)
1936 Alfred Schwarzmann (Ger)
1948 Paavo Aaltonen (Fin)
1952 Viktor Chukarin (USSR)
1956 Helmuth Bantz (Ger) & Valentin
     Muratov (USSR)
1960 Takashi Ono (Jap) & Boris
     Shakhlin (USSR)
1964 Haruhiro Yamashita (Jap)
1968 Mikhail Voronin (USSR)
1972 Klaus Köste (GDR)
1976 Nikolay Andrianov (USSR)
1980 Nikolay Andrianov (USSR)
1984 Lou Yun (Chn)
1988 Lou Yun (Chn)

WOMEN
Team
9 USSR 1952, 1956, 1960, 1964,
1968, 1972, 1976, 1980, 1988
1 Netherlands 1928, Germany 1936,
Czechoslovakia 1948, Romania 1984

Individual
Combined exercises
1952 Maria Gorokhovskaya (USSR)
1956 Larisa Latynina (USSR)
1960 Larisa Latynina (USSR)
1964 Vera Cáslavská (Cs)
1968 Vera Cáslavská (Cs)
1972 Lyudmila Tourischeva (USSR)
1976 Nadia Comaneci (Rom)
1980 Yelena Davydova (USSR)
1984 Mary Lou Retton (USA)
1988 Yelena Shushunova (USSR)

Asymmetrical bars
1952 Margit Korondi (Hun)
1956 Agnes Keleti (Hun)
1960 Polina Astakhova (USSR)
1964 Polina Astakhova (USSR)
1968 Vera Cáslavská (Cs)
1972 Karin Janz (GDR)
1976 Nadia Comaneci (Rom)
1980 Maxi Gnauck (GDR)
1984 Ma Yanhong (Chn) & Julianne
     McNamara (USA)
1988 Daniela Silivas (Rom)

Balance beam
1952 Nina Bocharova (USSR)
1956 Agnes Keleti (Hun)
1960 Eva Bosáková (Cs)
1964 Vera Cáslavská (Cs)
1968 Natalya Kuchinskaya (USSR)
1972 Olga Korbut (USSR)
1976 Nadia Comaneci (Rom)
1980 Nadia Comaneci (Rom)
1984 Simona Pauca (Rom) &
     Ecaterina Szabo (Rom)
1988 Daniela Silivas (Rom)

Floor exercises
1952 Agnes Keleti (Hun)
1956 Larisa Latynina (USSR) & Agnes
     Keleti (Hun)
1960 Larisa Latynina (USSR)
1964 Larisa Latynina (USSR)
1968 Larisa Petrik (USSR) & Vera
     Cáslavská (Cs)
1972 Olga Korbut (USSR)
1976 Nelli Kim (USSR)

Daniela Silivas admitted in 1990 that she had been 14, a year younger than specified at the time, when she won a gold medal at balance beam in the 1985 world championships (All-Sport)

1980 Nelli Kim (USSR) & Nadia
     Comaneci (Rom)
1984 Ecaterina Szabo (Rom)
1988 Daniela Silivas (Rom)

Horse vault
1952 Yekaterina Kalinchuk (USSR)
1956 Larisa Latynina (USSR)
1960 Margarita Nikolayeva (USSR)
1964 Vera Cáslavská (Cs)
1968 Vera Cáslavská (Cs)
1972 Karin Janz (GDR)
1976 Nelli Kim (USSR)
1980 Natalya Shaposhnikova (USSR)
1984 Ecaterina Szabo (Rom)
1988 Svetlana Boginskaya (USSR)

Rhythmic Gymnastics
1984 Lori Fung (Can)
1988 Marina Lobach (USSR)

Discontinued events
MEN
Parallel bars (Team)
1896 Germany
Horizontal bars (Team)
1896 Germany
Rope climbing
1896 Nicolaos Andriakopoulos (Gre)
1904 George Eyser (USA)
1906 Georgios Aliprantis (Gre)
1924 Bedrich Supcik (Cs)
1932 Raymond Bass (USA)
Club swinging
1904 Edward Hennig (USA)
1932 George Roth (USA)
Seven event competition
1904 Anton Heida (USA)
Nine event competition
1904 Adolf Spinnler (Swi)
Triathlon (100 yards, long jump, shot)
1904 Max Emmerich (USA)
Sidehorse vault
1924 Albert Séguin (Fra)
Tumbling
1932 Rowland Wolfe (USA)
Swedish event (team)
1912 Sweden
1920 Sweden
Free system (team)
1912 Norway
1920 Denmark

WOMEN
Portable apparatus (team)
1952 Sweden
1956 Hungary

Most Olympic medals (G gold, S silver, B bronze)

Total	Gymnast	G	S	B	Years
	MEN				
15	Nikolay Andrianov (USSR)	7	5	3	1972-80
13	Boris Shakhlin (USSR)	7	4	2	1956-64
13	Takashi Ono (Jap)	5	4	4	1956-64
12	Sawao Kato (Jap)	8	3	1	1968-76
11	Viktor Chukarin (USSR)	7	3	1	1952-6
10	Akinori Nakayama (Jap)	6	2	2	1968-72
10	Aleksandr Ditiatin (USSR)	3	6	1	1976-80
9	Mitsuo Tsukahara (Jap)	5	1	3	1968-76
9	Elizo Kenmotsu (Jap)	3	3	3	1968-76
9	Mikhail Voronin (USSR)	2	6	1	1968-72
9	Yuriy Titov (USSR)	1	5	3	1956-64
	WOMEN				
18	Larisa Latynina (USSR)	9	5	4	1956-64
11	Vera Cáslavská (Cs)	7	4	0	1964-8
10	Agnes Kaleti (Hun)	5	3	2	1952-6
10	Polina Astakhova (USSR)	5	2	3	1956-64
9	Nadia Comaneci (Rom)	5	3	1	1976-80
9	Lyudmila Tourescheva (USSR)	4	3	2	1968-76

Also 4 gold medals:
MEN Georges Miesz (Swi), Anton Heida (USA), Yukio Endo (Jap), Giorgio Zampori (Ita), Valentin Muratov (USSR), Vladimir Artemov (USSR)
WOMEN Olga Korbut (USSR), Nelli Kim (USSR)

WORLD CHAMPIONSHIPS
First held for men at Antwerp in 1903 and every two years until 1913. They were re-introduced in 1922 and held every four years with the Olympic champions also being the world champions. Since 1979 they have reverted to being held biennially. The first women's championships were held in 1934. *Winners:*

MEN
Team
7 Czechoslovakia 1907, 1911, 1913, 1922, 1926, 1930, 1938
7 USSR 1954, 1958, 1979, 1981, 1985, 1987, 1989
5 Japan 1962, 1966, 1970, 1974, 1978
3 France 1903, 1905, 1909
1 Switzerland 1950, China 1983
There was no team competition in 1934.

Combined exercises
1903 Joseph Martinez (Fra/Alg)
1905 Marcel Lalu (Fra)
1907 Josef Cada (Cs)
1909 Marco Torrès (Fra)
1911 Ferdinand Steiner (Cs)
1913 Marco Torrès (Fra)
1922 Peter Sumi (Yug) & Frantisek Pechacek (Cs)
1926 Peter Sumi (Yug)
1930 Josip Primozic (Yug)
1934 Eugen Mack (Swi)
1938 Jan Gajdos (Cs)
1950 Walter Lehmann (Swi)
1954 Viktor Chukarin (USSR)
1958 Boris Shakhlin (USSR)
1962 Yuriy Titov (USSR)
1966 Mikhail Voronin (USSR)
1970 Eizo Kenmotsu (Jap)
1974 Shigeru Kasamatsu (Jap)
1978 Nikolay Andrianov (USSR)
1979 Aleksandr Ditiatin (USSR)
1981 Yuriy Korolev (USSR)
1983 Dmitriy Belozerchev (USSR)
1985 Yuriy Korolev (USSR)
1987 Dmitriy Belozerchev (USSR)
1989 Igor Korobchinskiy (USSR)

Floor exercises
1913 Giorgio Zampori (Ita) & V Rabic (Cs)
1930 Josip Primozic (Yug)
1934 Georges Miesz (Swi)
1938 Jan Gajdos (Cs)
1950 Josef Stadler (Swi)
1954 Valentin Muratov (USSR) &

Masao Takemoto (Jap)
1958 Masao Takemoto (Jap)
1962 Nobuyuki Aihara (Jap) & Yukio Endo (Jap)
1966 Akinori Nakayama (Jap)
1970 Akinori Nakayama (Jap)
1974 Shigeru Kasamatsu (Jap)
1978 Kurt Thomas (USA)
1979 Kurt Thomas (USA) & Roland Brückner (GDR)
1981 Yuriy Korolev (USSR) & Li Yuejiu (Chn)
1983 Tong Fei (Chn)
1985 Tong Fei (Chn)
1987 Lou Yun (Chn)
1989 Igor Korobchinskiy (USSR)

Horizontal Bar
1903 Joseph Martinez (Fra/Alg) & Pierre Payssé (Fra)

Dmitriy Belozerchev, who had been the youngest ever male world champion at 16 years 315 days in 1983, returned from serious injury to win again in 1987 **(All-Sport)**

1905 Marcel Lalu (Fra)
1907 Georges Charmoille (Fra) & Frantisek Erben (Cs)
1909 Joseph Martinez (Fra), Josef Cada (Cs) & Frantisek Erben (Fra)
1911 Josef Cada (Cs)
1913 Josef Cada (Cs)
1922 Miroslav Klinger (Cs)
1926 Leon Stukelj (Yug)
1930 István Pelle (Hun)
1934 Ernst Winter (Ger)
1950 Paavo Aaltonen (Fin)
1954 Valentin Muratov (USSR)
1958 Boris Shakhlin (USSR)
1962 Takashi Ono (Jap)
1966 Akinori Nakayama (Jap)
1970 Eizo Kenmotsu (Jap)
1974 Eberhard Gienger (FRG)
1978 Shigeru Kasamatsu (Jap)
1979 Kurt Thomas (USA)
1981 Aleksandr Tkachev (USSR)
1983 Dmitriy Belozerchev (USSR)
1985 Tong Fei (Chn)
1987 Dmitriy Belozerchev (USSR)
1989 Li Chunyang (Chn)

Parallel bars
1903 Joseph Martinez (Fra) & Francois Hentges (Lux)
1905 Joseph Martinez (Fra/Alg)
1907 Jos Lux (Fra)
1909 Joseph Martinez (Fra/Alg)
1911 Giorgio Zampori (Ita)
1913 Giorgio Zampori (Ita) & Guido Boni (Ita)
1922 Leon Stukelj (Yug), Stane Derganc (Yug), N Jindrich (Cs), Miroslav Klinger (Cs), & Vlado Simoncic (Yug)
1926 Ladislav Vácha (Cs)
1930 Josip Primozic (Yug)
1934 Eugen Mack (Swi)
1938 Michael Reusch (Swi)
1950 Hans Eugster (Swi)
1954 Viktor Chukarin (USSR)
1958 Boris Shakhlin (USSR)
1962 Miroslav Cerar (Yug)
1966 Sergey Diomidov (USSR)
1970 Akinori Nakayama (Jap)
1974 Eizo Kenmotsu (Jap)
1978 Eizo Kenmotsu (Jap)
1979 Bart Conner (USA)

1981 Aleksandr Ditiatin (USSR) & Koji Gushiken (Jap)
1983 Vladimir Artemov (USSR) & Lou Yun (Chn)
1985 Silvio Kroll (GDR) & Valentin Mogilnyi (USSR)
1987 Vladimir Artemov (USSR)
1989 Li Jing (Chn) & Vladimir Artemov (USSR)

Horse vault
1903 G De Jaeghere (Fra), Jos Lux (Fra) & N Thysen (Hol)
1905 G De Jaeghere (Fra)
1907 Frantisek Erben (Cs)
1913 Karel Stary (Cs), Ben Sadoun (Fra), Osvaldo Palazzi (Ita) & Stane Vidmar (Yug)
1934 Eugen Mack (Swi)
1950 Ernst Gebendinger (Swi)
1954 Leo Sotornik (Cs)
1958 Yuriy Titov (USSR)
1962 Premysel Krbec (Cs)
1966 Haruhiro Matsuda (Jap)
1970 Mitsuo Tsukahara (Jap)
1974 Shigeru Kasamatsu (Jap)
1978 Junichi Shimizu (Jap)
1979 Aleksandr Ditiatin (USSR)
1981 Ralf-Peter Hemmann (GDR)
1983 Artur Akopian (USSR)
1985 Yuriy Korolev (USSR)
1987 Silvio Kroll (GDR) & Lou Yun (Chn)
1989 Jörg Behrendt (GDR)

Rings
1903 Joseph Martinez (Fra/Alg) & Jos Lux (Lux)
1909 Guido Romano (Ita) & Marco Torres (Fra)
1911 Ferdinand Steiner (Cs), Dominique Follacci (Fra) & Pietro Bianchi (Ita)
1913 Laurent Grech (Fra), Marco Torres (Fra), Giorgio Zampori (Ita) & Guido Boni (Ita)
1922 Laurent Karasek (Cs), Josef Maly (Cs), Leon Stukelj (Yug) & Peter Sumi (Yug)
1926 Leon Stukelj (Yug)
1930 Emanuel Löffler (Cs)
1934 Alois Hudec (Cs)
1938 Alois Hudec (Cs)
1950 Walter Lehmann (Swi)
1954 Albert Azarian (USSR)
1958 Albert Azarian (USSR)
1962 Yuriy Titov (USSR)
1966 Mikhail Voronin (USSR)

1970 Akinori Nakayama (Jap)
1974 Nikolay Andrianov (USSR) & Dan Grecu (Rom)
1978 Nikolay Andrianov (USSR)
1979 Aleksandr Ditiatin (USSR)
1981 Aleksandr Ditiatin (USSR)
1983 Dmitriy Belozerchev (USSR) & Koji Gushiken (Jap)
1985 Li Ning (Chn) & Yuriy Korolev (USSR)
1987 Yuriy Korolev (USSR)
1989 Andreas Aguilar (FRG)

Pommel horse
1911 Osvaldo Palazzi (Ita)
1913 Giorgio Zampori (Ita), N Aubrey (Fra) & Osvaldo Palazzi (Ita)
1922 Miroslav Klinger (Cs), N Jindrich (Cs) & Leon Stukelj (Yug)
1926 Jan Karafiát (Cs)
1930 Josip Primozic (Yug)
1934 Eugène Mack (Swi)
1938 Michael Reusch (Swi) & Vratislav Petracek (Cs)
1950 Josef Stalder (Swi)
1954 Grant Chaginyan (USSR)
1958 Boris Shakhlin (USSR)
1962 Miroslav Cerar (Yug)
1966 Miroslav Cerar (Yug)
1970 Miroslav Cerar (Yug)
1974 Zoltán Magyar (Hun)
1978 Zoltán Magyar (Hun)
1979 Zoltán Magyar (Hun)
1981 Michael Nikolay (GDR) & Li Xiaoping (Chn)
1983 Dmitriy Belozerchev (USSR)
1985 Valentin Mogilnyi (USSR)
1987 Dmitriy Belozerchev (USSR) & Zsolt Borkai (Hun)
1989 Valentin Mogilnyi (USSR)

WOMEN
Team
10 USSR 1954, 1958, 1962, 1970, 1974, 1978, 1981, 1983, 1985, 1989
3 Czechoslovakia 1934, 1938, 1966
2 Romania 1979, 1987
1 Sweden 1950

Combined exercises
1934 Vlasta Dekanová (Cs)
1938 Vlasta Dekanová (Cs)
1950 Helena Rakoczy (Pol)
1954 Galina Roudiko (USSR)
1958 Larisa Latynina (USSR)
1962 Larisa Latynina (USSR)
1966 Vera Cáslavská (Cs)
1970 Lyudmila Tourischeva (USSR)

1974 Lyudmila Tourischeva (USSR)
1978 Yelena Mukhina (USSR)
1979 Nelli Kim (USSR)
1981 Olga Bicherova (USSR)
1983 Natalya Yurchenko (USSR)
1985 Oksana Omelianchik (USSR) & Yelena Shushunova (USSR)
1987 Aurelia Dobre (Rom)
1989 Svetlana Boginskaya (USSR)

Parallel bars
1938 Vlasta Dekanová (Cs)

Horse vault
1938 Matylda Pálfyová (Cs) & Marta Majowska (Pol)
1950 Helena Rakoczy (Pol)
1954 Tamara Manina (USSR) & Anna Petersson (Swe)
1958 Larisa Latynina (USSR)
1962 Vera Cáslavská (Cs)
1966 Vera Cáslabská (Cs)
1970 Erika Zuchold (GDR)
1974 Olga Korbut (USSR)
1978 Nelli Kim (USSR)
1979 Dumitrata Turner (Rom)
1981 Maxi Gnauck (GDR)
1983 Boriana Stoyanova (Bul)
1985 Yelena Shushunova (USSR)
1987 Yelena Shushunova (USSR)
1989 Olessia Dudnik (USSR)

Balance beam
1938 Vlasta Dekanová (Cs)
1950 Helena Rakoczy (Pol)
1954 Keiko Tanaka (Jap)
1958 Larisa Latynina (USSR)
1962 Eva Bosáková (Cs)
1966 Natalya Kuchinskaya (USSR)
1970 Erika Zuchold (GDR)
1974 Lyudmila Tourischeva (USSR)
1978 Nadia Comaneci (Rom)
1979 Vera Cerna (Cs)
1981 Maxi Gnauck (GDR)
1983 Olga Mostepanova (USSR)
1985 Daniela Silivas (Rom)
1987 Aurelia Dobre (Rom)
1989 Daniela Silivas (Rom)

Floor exercises
1938 Matylda Pálfyová (Cs)
1950 Helena Rakoczy (Pol)
1954 Tamara Manina (USSR)
1958 Eva Bosáková (Cs)
1962 Larisa Latynina (USSR)
1966 Natalya Kuchinskaya (USSR)
1970 Lyudmila Tourischeva (USSR)
1974 Lyudmila Tourischeva (USSR)

1978 Nelli Kim (USSR) & Yelena
     Mukhina (USSR)
1979 Emilia Eberle (Rom)
1981 Natalya Ilyenko (USSR)
1983 Ecaterina Szabo (Rom)
1985 Oksana Omelianchik (USSR)
1987 Yelena Shushunova (USSR) &
     Daniela Silivas (Rom)
1989 Daniela Silivas (Rom) & Svetlana
     Boginskaya (USSR)

Asymmetrical bars
1950 Helena Rakoczy (Pol)
1954 Agnes Kaleti (Hun)
1958 Larisa Latynina (USSR)
1962 Irina Pervuschina (USSR)
1966 Natalya Kuchinskaya (USSR)
1970 Karin Janz (GDR)
1974 Annelore Zinke (GDR)
1978 Marcia Frederick (USA)
1979 Ma Yanhong (Chn) & Maxi
     Gnauck (GDR)
1981 Maxi Gnauck (GDR)
1983 Maxi Gnauck (GDR)
1985 Gabriela Fahnrich (GDR)
1987 Daniela Silivas (Rom) & Dörte
     Thümmler (GDR)
1989 Fan Di (Chn) & Daniela Silivas
     (Rom)

Modern Rhythmic Gymnastics
Team winners:
8 Bulgaria 1969, 1971, 1981, 1983,
  1985, 1987, 1989 (tie)
5 USSR 1967, 1973, 1977, 1979,
  1989 (tie)
1 Italy 1975
Individual overall winners
1963 Lyudmila Savinkova (USSR)
1965 Hana Micechová (Cs)
1967 Yelena Karpukhina (USSR)
1969 Maria Gigova (Bul)
1971 Maria Gigova (Bul)
1973 Maria Gigova (Bul) & Galina
     Shugarova (USSR)
1975 Carmen Rischer (FRG)
1977 Irina Deryugina (USSR)
1979 Irina Deryugina (USSR)
1981 Anelia Ralenkova (Bul)
1983 Diliana Georgieva (Bul)
1985 Diliana Georgieva (Bul)
1987 Bianka Panova (Bul) *
1989 Aleksandra Timoschenko (USSR)

** Bianka Panova won all four
disciplines in 1987, all with maximum
scores, a unprecedented
achievement.*

MOST INDIVIDUAL GOLD MEDALS, OLYMPICS & WORLD CHAMPIONSHIPS

MEN
10 Boris Shakhlin (USSR) 1956-64
9 Leon Stukelj (Yug) 1922-8
9 Akinori Nakayama (Jap) 1966-72
9 Nikolay Andrianov (USSR) 1972-80
9 Dmitriy Belozerchev (USSR) 1983-8
7 Joseph Martinez (Fra) 1903-9
6 Eugen Mack (Swi) 1928-38
6 Yuriy Korolev (USSR) 1981-7
6 Vladimir Artemov (USSR) 1983-9

WOMEN
12 Larisa Latynina (USSR) 1956-64
10 Vera Cáslavská (Cs) 1962-8
9 Daniela Silivas (Rom) 1985-9
6 Lyudmila Tourischeva (USSR) 1968-76
6 Nadia Comaneci (Rom) 1976-80
6 Nelli Kim (USSR) 1976-80
6 Maxi Gnauck (GDR) 1979-83

World Championships only
MEN
Most gold medals – individual:
7 Dmitriy Belozerchev; 6 Yuriy
Korolev; 5 Eugen Mack, Akinori
Nakayama, Aleksandr Ditiatin (USSR)
Most medals: 12 Eizo Kenmotsu (Jap);
10 Akinori Nakayama, Boris Shakhlin,
Nikolay Andrianov
WOMEN
Most gold medals – individual: 6
Daniela Silivas; 5 Larisa Latynina,
Lyudmila Tourischeva
Most medals: 9 Larisa Latynina,
Lyudmila Tourischeva, Eva Bosáková
(Cs)

WORLD CUP
First held 1975

Overall Champions
MEN
1975 Nikolay Andrianov (USSR)
1977 Nikolay Andrianov (USSR) &
     Vladimir Markelov (USSR)
1978 Aleksandr Ditiatin (USSR)
1979 Aleksandr Ditiatin (USSR)
1982 Li Ning (Chn)
1986 Yuriy Korolev (USSR) & Li Ning
     (Chn)

WOMEN
1975 Lyudmila Tourescheva (USSR)
1977 Maria Filatova (USSR

1978 Maria Filatova (USSR)
1979 Stella Zakharova (USSR)
1982 Olga Bicherova (USSR) &
     Natalya Yurchenko (USSR)
1986 Yelena Shushunova (USSR)

EUROPEAN CHAMPIONSHIPS
First held 1955. *Overall Champions:*

MEN
1955 Boris Shakhlin (USSR)
1957 Joachim Blume (Spa)
1959 Yuriy Titov (USSR)
1961 Miroslav Cerar (Yug)
1963 Miroslav Cerar (Yug)
1965 Franco Menichelli (Ita)
1967 Mikhail Voronin (USSR)
1969 Mikhail Voronin (USSR)
1971 Viktor Klimenko (USSR)
1973 Viktor Klimenko (USSR)
1975 Nikolay Andrianov (USSR)
1977 Vladimir Markelov (USSR)
1979 Stoyan Deltchev (Bul)
1981 Aleksandr Tkachev (USSR)
1983 Dmitriy Belozerchev (USSR)
1985 Dmitriy Belozerchev (USSR)
1987 Valeriy Lyukin (USSR)
1989 Igor Korobchinsky (USSR)
1990 Valentin Mogilnyi (USSR)

WOMEN
1957 Larisa Latynina (USSR)
1959 Natalie Kot (Pol)
1961 Larisa Latynina (USSR)
1963 Mirjana Bilic (Yug)
1965 Vera Cáslavská (Cs)
1967 Vera Cáslavská (Cs)
1969 Karin Janz (GDR)
1971 Lyudmila Tourischeva (USSR) &
     Tamara Lazakovich (USSR)
1973 Lyudmila Tourischeva (USSR)
1975 Nadia Comaneci (Rom)
1977 Nadia Comaneci (Rom)
1979 Nadia Comaneci (Rom)
1981 Maxi Gnauck (GDR)
1983 Olga Bicherova (USSR)
1985 Yelena Shushunova (USSR)
1987 Daniela Silivas (Rom)
1989-90 Svetlana Boginskaya (USSR)

RHYTHMIC GYMNASTICS WORLD CUP
First held 1983, then 1986 and
quadrenially from 1990.
Individual overall winners: 1983 Lilia
Ignatova (Bul), 1986 Lilia Ignatova (Bul)
Team: 1983 USSR, 1986 Bulgaria

HANDBALL

The modern game, similar to association football, with hands substituted for feet, was first played in Germany around 1890. The first international match was played on 3 Sep 1925 when Austria beat Germany 6-3 at Halle/Salle. Germany has long been a stronghold of the game, and it was introduced to the Olympic Games at Berlin in 1936 as an 11-a-side outdoor game. When reintroduced in 1972, again in Germany, at Munich, it was as an indoor 7-a-side game, and this version of the game has been predominant since 1952. The indoor court is 40m long by 20m wide; the goals are 2m high and 3m wide.

Prior to 1928 the International Amateur Athletic Federation looked after the interests of handball, but in that year the International Amateur Handball Federation (FIHA) was founded with Avery Brundage (USA), later the President of the International Olympic Committee, as its first president. The current governing body, the International Handball Federation (IHF) was founded in 1946, replacing the FIHA. The growth of the game is demonstrated by the fact that the IHF comprised 101 member federations by 1988.

OLYMPIC GAMES

Played outdoors at 11-a-side in 1936, indoors at 7-a-side from 1972 (men) and 1976 (women). *Winners:*

MEN	WOMEN
1936 Germany	–
1972 Yugoslavia	–
1976 USSR	1976 USSR
1980 GDR	1980 USSR
1984 Yugoslavia	1984 Yugoslavia
1988 USSR	1988 South Korea

The following USSR players won two gold medals in 1976 and 1980: Larissa Karlova, Zinaida Turchina, Tatyana Kochergina, Lyudmila Poradnik, Aldona Nenenene, Lyubov Odinokova.

WORLD CHAMPIONSHIPS

First held outdoors in 1938 for men and 1949 for women. Men's nations are now divided into three groups A, B and C; and the women into A and B groups. *Winners:*

MEN OUTDOORS	WOMEN OUTDOORS
1938 Germany	1949 Hungary
1948 Sweden	1956 Romania
1952 FR Germany	1960 Romania
1955 FR Germany	
1959 FR Germany/GDR	**WOMEN INDOORS (A)**
1963 GDR	1957 Czechoslovakia
1966 FR Germany	1962 Romania
	1965 Hungary
MEN INDOORS (A group)	1971 GDR
1938 Germany	1973 Yugoslavia
1954 Sweden	1975 GDR
1958 Sweden	1979 GDR
1961 Romania	1982 USSR
1964 Romania	1986 USSR
1967 Czechoslovakia	
1970 Romania	
1974 Romania	
1978 FR Germany	
1982 USSR	
1986 Yugoslavia	
1990 Sweden	

EUROPEAN CUP

Contested by national champions. First held in 1957 (men), 1961 (women). *Winners:*

MEN
1957 Stadtmannschaft Prague (Cs)
1959 RIK Göteborg (Swe)
1961-2 Frischauf Göppongen (FRG)
1963 Dukla Prague (Cs)
1965 Dinamo Bucharest (Rom)
1966 DHfK Leipzig (GDR)
1967 Vfl Gummersbach (FRG)
1968 Steaua Bucharest (Rom)
1970-1 Vfl Gummersbach (FRG)
1972 Partizan Bjelovar (Yug)
1973 MAI Moscow (USSR)
1974 Vfl Gummersbach (FRG)
1975 ASK Vorwärts Frankfurt/Oder (GDR)
1976 Borac Banjalukar (Yug)
1977 Steaua Bucharest (Rom)
1978 SC Magdeburg (GDR)
1979-80 TV Grosswallstadt (FRG)
1981 SC Magdeburg (GDR)
1982 Honved SE, Budapest (Hun)
1983 VfL Gummersbach (FRG)
1984 Dukla Prague (Cs)
1985-6 Metaloplastika Sabac (Yug)
1987 SKA Minsk (USSR)
1988 CSKA Moscow (USSR)
1989-90 SKA Minsk (USSR)

Most wins: 5 Vfl Gummersbach

WOMEN
1961 Stiinta Bucharest (Rom)
1962 Spartak Prague (Cs)
1963 Trud Moscow (USSR)
1964 Rapid Bucharest (Rom)
1965 HG København (Den)
1966 SC Leipzig (GDR)
1967-8 Zalgiris Kaunas (USSR)
1970-3 Spartak Kiev (USSR)
1974 SC Leipzig (GDR)
1975 Spartak Kiev (USSR)

1976 Radnicki Belgrad (Yug)
1977 Spartak Kiev (USSR)
1978 TSC Berlin (GDR)
1979 Spartak Kiev (USSR)
1980 RK Radnicki Belgrad (Yug)
1981 Spartak Kiev (USSR)
1982 Vasas SC, Budapest (Hun)
1983 Spartak Kiev (USSR)
1984 Radnicki Belgrad (Yug)
1985-8 Spartak Kiev (USSR)
1989-90 Hyperbank Sudstadt (Aut)
Most wins: 13 Spartak Kiev

EUROPEAN CUP WINNERS CUP
First held 1976 (men), 1977 (women). *Winners:*

MEN
1976 Balonmano Granollers (Spa)
1977 MAI Moskva (USSR)
1978-9 VfL Gummersbach (FRG)
1980 Calpisa Alicante (Spa)
1981 TuS Nettelstedt (FRG)
1982 SC Empor Rostock (GDR)
1983 SKA Minsk (USSR)
1984-6 FC Barcelona (Spa)
1987 CSKA Moscow (USSR)
1988 SKA Minsk (USSR)
1989 Tusam Essen (FRG)
1990 Santander (Spa)
Most wins: 3 FC Barcelona

WOMEN
1977 TSC Berlin (GDR)
1978 Ferencvarosi Budapest (Hun)
1979 TSC Berlin (GDR)
1980 Iskra Partizanske (Cs)
1981 Spartacus Budapest (Hun)
1982-3 RK Osiejek (Yug)
1984 Dalma Split (Yug)
1985 Budocnost Titograd (Yug)
1986 Radnicki Belgrad (Yug)
1987-8 Kuban Krasnodar (USSR)
1989 Stiinta Bacau (Rom)
1990 Rostov (USSR)
Most wins: 2 Kuban Krasnodar,
RK Osiejek

IHF CUP
First held in the 1982. *Winners:*

MEN
1982 Vfl Gummersbach (FRG)
1983 IL Saporozhye (USSR)
1984 TV Grosswallstadt (FRG)
1985 Minaur Baia Mare (Rom)
1986 Raba Vasas Etö Györ (Hun)
1987 Granitas Kaunas (USSR)
1988 Minaur Baia Mare (Rom)

1989 Düsseldorf (FRG)
1990 Kuban Krasnodar (USSR)

WOMEN
1982 IHK Tresnjevka, Zagreb (Yug)
1983 Automobilist Baku (USSR)
1984 Chimistul Vilcea (Rom)
1985 ASK Vorwärts Frankfurt/Oder (GDR)
1986 SC Leipzig (GDR)
1987 Budocnost Tiitograd (Yug)
1988 Egle Vilnius (USSR)
1989 Chimistul Vilcea (Rom)
1990 ASK Vorwärts Frankfurt (GDR)

A unique achievement in winning all possible competitions in one year was when Vfl Gummersbach (FRG) in 1983 won the FRG national championship and cup, the European Champions Cup and the IHF Super Cup, contested by the winners of the two European Cup competitions.

SCORING ROUNDS
Highest score in an international match: USSR beat Afghanistan 86-2 in the 'Friendly Army Tournament' at Miskolc, Hungary, August 1981.

Strong pressure on the Soviet Union by two members of the South Korean women's team, who won this tense final match 21-19 to take the Olympic title **(All-Sport)**

COURT HANDBALL

Handball played against walls or in a court is a game of ancient Celtic origin. The game has been particularly prominent in Ireland and the USA, and the first ever international match was between the champions of these nations in 1887, when Phil Casey (USA) beat Bernard McQuade (Ire). In Ireland and Australia the court is 60 ft (18.3m) long and 30 ft (9.1m) wide, but a smaller court of 40 ft (12m) long and 20ft (6.1m) wide is used in North America.

The first US Championships under the suspices of the AAU were held in 1919 at four-wall singles and doubles. The United States Handball Association (USHA) was founded in 1951.

USHA Professional Championships were first held in 1951. *Most wins:*
Singles: 10 Naty Alvarado 1977, 1979-80, 1982-7; 6 Jim Jacobs 1955-7, 1960, 1964-5; 6 Fred Lewis 1972, 1974-6, 1978, 1981
Doubles: 8 Marty Decatur 1962-3, 1965, 1967-8, 1975, 1978-9 (the first five with Jim Jacobs), 6 Jim Jacobs 1960, 1962-3, 1965, 1967-8; 5 John Sloan 1957-9, 1961, 1964 1989 four-wall winners: *pro singles:* Alfonso 'Poncho' Monreal, *open doubles:* Danny Bell and Charlie Kalil.

HANG GLIDING

An elementary form of hang glider is reputed to have been used by the monk, Eilmer, to fly from the top of Malmesbury Abbey, Wiltshire. The first modern pioneer of hang gliding was Otto Lilienthal in Germany in the 1890s. Duration and distance records have increased substantially in recent years as pilots have utilised optimum conditions and improved designs.

Records officially recognised by the FAI:
(Category: Record, Pilot, Glider, Venue, Date)
FLEXWING – MEN
Straight line distance: 462.604m Paul Christopherson (USA), Whiskey Peak, Wyoming, USA, 3 Aug 1989
Height gain: 4343.4m Larry Tudor (USA), Owens Valley, Cal., USA, 4 Aug 1985
Declared goal distance: 348.7km Larry Tudor (USA), Owens Valley, Cal., USA, 30 Jan 1988
Out and return distance: 310.302km Geoffrey R.Loyns (UK) & Larry Tudor (USA), Owens Valley, Cal., USA 26 Jun 1988
Distance over triangular course: 161km Drew Cooper (Aus), Kössen, Aut., 10 Jun 1989
RIGIDWING – MEN
Straight line distance: 223.70km William T.Reynolds (USA), Lone Pine, Cal., USA 27 Jun 1988
Height gain: 3820m Rainer Scholl (FRG), Owens Valley, Cal., USA 5 Aug 1985

FLEXWING – WOMEN
Straight line distance: 263.627km Kathrine Yardley (USA), Owens Valley, Cal., USA, 13 Jul 1989
Height gain: 3657m Tover Buas-Hansen (Nor), Owens Valley, Cal., USA, 6 Jul 1989
Out and return distance: 131.96km Tover Buas-Hansen (Nor), Owens Valley, Cal., USA, 6 Jul 1989
Declared goal distance: 201.123km Liavan Mallin (Ire), Owens Valley, Cal., USA, 6 Jul 1989
Distance over triangular course: 101km Jenney Canderton (Aus), Forbes, Aus., 22 Jan 1990

WORLD CHAMPIONSHIPS

An unofficial world championship was held in 1975, won by David Cronk (USA), and the first official championships the following year at Kössen in Austria. *Winners have been:*

Team Champions:
1976 Austria
1979 France
1981 Great Britain
1983 Australia
1985 Great Britain
1988 Australia
1989 Great Britain
Individual Champions:
1976   Class I – Standard: Christian Steinbach (Aut)
        Class II – High Aspect Ratio: Terry Dolore (NZ)
        Class III – Open: Ken Battle (Aus)
1979   Class I – Weight Shift: Josef Guggenmos (FRG)
        Class II – Movable Surfaces: Rex Miller (USA)
1981   Class I – Weight Shift: Pepe Lopes (Bra)
        Class II – Movable Surfaces: Graeme Bird (NZ)
1983   Steve Moyes (Aus)
1985   John Pendry (UK)
1988   Rick Duncan (Aus)
1989   Robbie Whittall (UK)
Women's World Championships
Held separately in 1987, when the winners were:
Individual: Judy Leden (UK), *Team:* UK.

MICROLIGHT RECORDS

The Fédération Aéronautique Internationale recognise records for two classes of aircraft: C1 a/o and R 1-2-3, The following, the overall best of the two classes are all for C1 a/o, except Altitude – R1:
Altitude: 9144m Eric Winton (Aus), Taygareh Aerodrome, NSW, Aus.,11 Apr 1989
Distance in a straight line without landing: 1627.78km Wilhem Lischak (Aut), Voslau to Brest, France 8 Jun 1988
Distance over a closed circuit: 2702.16km Wilhem Lischak (Aut), Wels, Austria 18 Jun 1988
Speed over 100km closed circuit: 297.72km/h C.T.Andrews (USA) 3 Aug 1982
Speed over 500km closed circuit: 293.04km/h C.T.Andrews (USA) 3 Aug 1982
Speed over 1000km closed circuit: 178.19km/h Wilhem Lischak (Aut), Wels, Austria 18 Jun 1988

HARNESS RACING

A form of horse racing in which the horses trot or pace while being driven in a light two-wheeled cart, the sulky. Pacers have a lateral gait, as they move their fore and hind legs in unison on one side and then the other, whereas trotters have a diagonal gait, in that their off fore and near hind legs are brought together in unison, followed by their near fore and off hind legs. Standardbred horses (which race up to a certain standard of speed) are raced as opposed to thoroughbreds in horse racing. Race tracks are of dirt surface, oval in shape, of a half-a-mile to a mile in circumference.

Trotting races were first held in the Netherlands in 1554, and the sulky first appeared in harness racing in 1829. The sport became very popular in the USA in the 19th century, and the National Trotting Association was founded, originally as the National Association for the Promotion of the Interests of the Trotting Turf in 1870. It brought needed controls to a sport that had been threatened by gambling corruption.

1 mile records

Trotting race record	1:52.2 Mack Lobell (driver, John Campbell) at Springfield, Illinois 21 Aug 1987
Pacing record	1:48.4 Matt's Scooter (driver, Michel Lachance) at Lexington, Kentucky 23 Sep 1988
Pacing race record	1:49.6 Nihilator (driver, Bill O'Donnell) at East Rutherford, New Jersey 3 Aug 1985
	1:49.6 Call For Rain (driver Clint Galbraith) at Lexington, Kentucky 1 Oct 1988

The Hambletonian

The most famous race in North America is the Hambletonian Stakes, run annually for three-year-olds. It was first staged at Syracuse, New York in 1926. Previously run at Syracuse, Lexington, and the New York tracks of Yonkers and Goshen, since 1956 it has been run at Du Quoin, Illinois. Hambletonian, born in 1849, although only an ordinary racer, had a most notable influence on the breeding of American trotters. Winners since 1970:

Year	Horse	Driver
1970	Timothy T	John Simpson Jr.
1971	Speedy Crown	Howard Beissinger
1972	Super Bowl	Stanley Dancer
1973	Flirth	Ralph Baldwin
1974	Christopher T	Bill Haughton
1975	Bonefish	Stanley Dancer
1976	Steve Lobell	Bill Haughton
1977	Green Speed	Bill Haughton
1978	Speedy Somolli	Howard Beissinger
1979	Legend Hanover	George Sholty
1980	Burgomeister	Bill Haughton
1981	Shiaway St.Pat	Ray Remmen
1982	Speed Bowl	Tommy Haughton
1983	Duenna	Stanley Dancer
1984	Historic Freight	Ben Webster
1985	Prakas	Bill O'Donnell
1986	Nuclear Kosmos	Ulf Thoresen
1987	Mack Lobell	John Campbell
1988	Armbro Goal	John Campbell
1989	Park Avenue	Ron Wables
	Joe Probe tied	Bill Fahy

Race record: 1:53.3 Mack Lobell 1987

The prize purse first passed $100,000 with $117,118 in 1953, when the winner was Helicopter; $200,000 in 1975 when it was $232,192; $500,000 in 1981 when it was $838,000 and the million dollars in 1983 at $1,080,000. A record $1,272,000 was paid in 1985.

The Little Brown Jug

Pacing's three-year-old classic has been held annually at Delaware, Ohio from 1946. The name honours a great 19th century pacer. Winners from 1970:

Year	Horse	Driver
1970	Most Happy Fella	Stanley Dancer
1971	Nansemond	Herve Filion
1972	Strike Out	Keith Waples
1973	Melvin's Woe	Joe O'Brien
1974	Ambro Omaha	Bill Haughton
1975	Seatrain	Ben Webster
1976	Keystone Ore	Stanley Dancer
1977	Governor Skipper	John Chapman
1978	Happy Escort	Bill Popfinger
1979	Hot Hitter	Herve Filion
1980	Niatross	Clint Galbraith
1981	Fan Hanover (filly)	Glen Garnsey
1982	Merger	John Campbell
1983	Ralph Hanover	Ron Waples
1984	Colt Forty Six	Chris Boring
1985	Nihilator	Bill O'Donnell
1986	Barbery Spur	Bill O'Donnell
1987	Jaguar Spur	Dick Stillings
1988	B.J.Scott	Bill Fahey
1989	Goalie Jeff	Michel Lachance

Race record: 1:52.1 Nihilator 1985

Leading Drivers

Most wins in a year: 814 Herve Filion 1989, 798 Herve Filion 1988, 770 Michel Lachance 1986.

The all-time money winning drivers to 1 Jan 1990:

Driver	Winnings	Races (with position on all-time list)
John Campbell	$79,862,806	4593 (13)
Bill O'Donnell	$66,799,441	4195 (17)
Herve Filion	$66,698,471	12 007 (1)
Carmine Abbatiello	£47,691,101	6944 (2)
Michel Lachance	$46,564,866	5562 (3)
Buddy Gilmour	$42,842,404	5329 (4)
Billy Haughton	$40,160,336	4910 (7)
Ron Waples	$40,113,510	4894 (8)
Ben Webster	$38,235,801	3934 (21)
Joe Marsh Jr	$30,110,255	4986 (6)
Walter Paisley	$28,486,559	4995 (5)

The first driver to win $1 million in a year was Stanley Dancer, $1,051,538 in 1964; $2 million was passed by Herve Filion with $2.473,265 in 1972 and $10 million in 1985.

Top money winning drivers from 1980:

1980	John Campbell	$3,732,306
1981	Bill O'Donnell	$4,065,608
1982	Bill O'Donnell	$5,755,067
1983	John Campbell	$6,104,082
1984	Bill O'Donnell	$9,059,184
1985	Bill O'Donnell	$10,207,372
1986	John Campbell	$9,515,055
1987	John Campbell	$10,186,495
1988	John Campbell	$11,148,565
1989	John Campbell	$9,738,450

Most years as leading money-winning driver from 1948:
12 Bill Haughton 1952-9, 1963, 1965, 1967-8
7 Herve Filion 1970-4, 1976-7
7 John Campbell 1979-80, 1983, 1986-9

Top money winning horses
The leading all-time money winners in North America have been the pacer Nihilator with $3,225,653 in 1984-5 and Matt's Scooter with $2,944,591 in 1988-9. The most by a trotting horse is $2,753,666 by Idéal de Gazeau (France).

The first to win $1 million in a year and current record:
Pacer: Niatross $1,414,313 in 1980, record now $1,864,286 Nihilator in 1985
Trotter: Joie De Vie $1,007,705 in 1983, record $1,878,798 Mack Lobell in 1987

The largest ever purse was $2,161,000 for the Woodrow Wilson two-year-old race for pacers at Meadowlands, New Jersey on 16 Aug 1984. The winner, Nihilator, driven by Bill O'Donnell, earned a record $1,080,500.

Harness Horse of the Year
Chosen annually by the US Trotting Association and the US Harness Writers Association: *Most wins:*
3 Bret Hanover 1964-6, Nevele Pride 1967-9; 2 Scott Frost 1955-6, Adios Butler 1960-1, Albatross 1971-2, Niatross 1980-1, Cam Fella 1982-3, Mack Lobell 1987-8

AUSTRALIAN HARNESS RACING

The Inter-Dominion Championship
The first trotting race in Australia was at Parramatta in 1810. The most important race in the Southern Hemisphere is the Inter-Dominion Championship, first held in 1936. Held annually at various venues in Australia and New Zealand. Run at varying distances between 1 1/2 and 2 miles (2414-3218m), at 2500m in 1989.
Winners from 1970 (shown in brackets is the Australian state or New Zealand ownership

Year	Horse	Driver
1970	Bold David (Vic)	Alf Simons
1971	Stella Frost (NZ)	Dinny Townley
1972	Welcome Advice (NSW)	Alan Harpley
1973	Hondo Grattan (NSW)	Tony Turnbull
1974	Hondo Grattan (NSW)	Tony Turnbull
1975	Young Quinn (NZ)	John Langdon
1976	Carclew (SA)	Chris Lewis
1977	Stanley Rio (NZ)	John Noble
1978	Markovina (SA)	Bruce Gath
1979	Rondel (NZ)	Peter Wolfenden
1980	Koala King (NSW)	Brian Hancock
1981	San Simeon (WA)	Lyle Austin
1982	Rhett's Law (WA)	Colin Warwick
1983	Gammalite (Vic)	Bill Clarke
1984	Gammalite (Vic)	Bill Clarke
1985	Preux Chevalier (WA)	Barry Perkins
1986	Village Kid (WA)	Chris Lewis
1987	Lightning Blue (Vic)	Jim O'Sullivan
1988	Our Maestro (Qld)	John Binskin
1989	Jodie's Babe (Vic)	Scott Stewart
1990	Thorate (Tas)	Howard Wilson

Most wins: 2 Captain Sandy (NZ) 1950, 1953; Hondo Grattan 1973-4; Gammalite 1983-4.

Records
Drivers – most wins in a season: 203 Andrew Peace 1988/9
Top money-winning horse: Village Kid (WA) $1,937,338 in 1984-9
Highest stakewinner in a season: Village Kid (WA) $574,561 1987/8
Most wins in a season: 34 Cane Smoke (Qld) 1985/6
Most wins in a career: 119 Cane Smoke 1981-90

HOCKEY

Stick and ball games date back some 4000 years, with modern hockey, which is played by teams of 11-a-side, becoming established in the 19th century. The sport's first governing body was an English Hockey Association, formed in London in 1875. The current English men's governing body, the Hockey Association was founded in 1886 and the All-England Women's Hockey Association in 1895, a year after the Irish Ladies' Hockey Union.

The current international governing body, the Fédération Internationale de Hockey (FIH) was formed in 1924. A separate body governed women's hockey until both men's and women's games were united under the auspices of the IHF in 1982. The number of member nations of the IHF reached 103 in 1989.

The sport was long dominated by India and Pakistan, who won every Olympic tournament from 1928 to 1968. From then, however, success has been more widespread, with the amazing result at the 1986 World Cup of India and Pakistan in 11th and 12th places.

OLYMPIC GAMES
Men's winners:

England	1908, 1920
India	1928, 1932, 1936, 1948, 1952, 1956, 1964, 1980
Pakistan	1960, 1968, 1984
F.R.Germany	1972
New Zealand	1976
Great Britain	1988

Highest score: India beat USA 24-1 at Los Angeles 1932
Most gold medals: seven Indian players have won three gold medals: Richard Allen 1928-36, Dhyan Chand 1928-36, Randhir Singh Gentle 1948-56, Leslie Claudius 1948-56, Ranganandan Francis 1948-56, Udham Singh 1952-64. Claudius and Udham Singh also won silver medals in 1960.

Women's winners: 1980 Zimbabwe, 1984 Netherlands, 1988 Australia

IHF WORLD CUP
First contested in 1971 for men, 1974 for women, 1979 for junior women.*Winners:*

Jubilation for Steve Batchelor as the British team have beaten FR Germany 3-1 to win the 1988 Olympic title **(All-Sport)**

MEN

Pakistan	1971, 1978, 1982
Netherlands	1973, 1990
India	1975
Australia	1986

JUNIOR MEN

Pakistan	1979
FR Germany	1982, 1985, 1989

WOMEN

Netherlands	1974, 1978, 1983, 1986, 1990
F.R.Germany	1976, 1981

WOMEN'S WORLD CHAMPIONSHIPS
Organised by the International Federation of Women's Hockey Association twice.
Winners: 1975 England, 1979 Netherlands.

CHAMPIONS TROPHY
First held in 1978, the leading six men's teams contest this trophy annually. *Winners:*
1978 Pakistan
1980 Pakistan
1981-2 Netherlands
1983-5 Australia
1986-8 FR Germany
1989 Australia

The first women's Champion's Trophy was contested in 1987. *Winners:* 1987 Netherlands, 1989 South Korea

EUROPEAN CHAMPIONSHIPS
Contested by men's national teams at four-yearly intervals from 1970, and by women's from 1984. Winners:
MEN
1970 FR Germany
1974 Spain
1978 FR Germany
1983 Netherlands
1987 Netherlands
WOMEN
1984 Netherlands
1987 Netherlands

EUROPEAN CUP FOR CLUB CHAMPIONS
First held unofficially in 1969 and 1970 and officially from 1971. *Winners:*
1969-70 Club Egara de Tarrasa (Spa)
1971-5 Frankfurt 1880 (FRG)
1976-8 Southgate (Eng)
1979 Klein Zwitserland (Hol)
1980 Slough (Eng)
1981 Klein Zwitserland (Hol)
1982-3 Dynamo Alma-Ata (USSR)
1984 TG 1846 Frankental (FRG)
1985 Atletico Tarrasa (Spa)
1986 Kampong, Utrecht (Hol)
1987 Bloemendaal (Hol)
1988-90 Uhlenhorst Mülheim (FRG)

WOMEN
1974 Harvetschuder Hamburg (FRG)
1976-82 Amsterdam (Hol)
1983-7 HGC Wassenaar (Hol)
1988-90 Amsterdam (Hol)

EUROPEAN INDOOR CUP
First contested by men's teams in 1974, and won every
time contested by FR Germany 1974, 1976, 1980, 1984,
1988.

HOCKEY ASSOCIATION CUP
English National Club Champions, now for the Nationwide
Anglia Cup. Winners:
1972-3 Hounslow
1974-5 Southgate
1976 Nottingham
1977 Slough
1978 Guildford
1979-81 Slough
1982 Southgate
1983 Neston
1984 East Grinstead
1985-8 Southgate
1989 Hounslow
1990 Havant

English National Inter-League
First held in 1975, and contested by the winners of all the
major English leagues. Now for the Poundstretcher
National League Cup, inaugurated in 1989.
Winners:
1975 Bedfordshire Eagles
1976 Slough
1977-8 Southgate
1979 Isca
1980-3 Slough
1984 Neston
1985-6 East Grinstead
1987 Slough
1988 Southgate
1989 Hounslow
1990 Havant

National Women's Club Champions
1979 Chelmsford
1980 Norton
1981 Sutton Coldfield
1982-3 Slough
1984 Sheffield
1985 Ipswich
1986 Slough
1987-9 Ealing
1990 Sutton Coldfield

National Women's League
1990 Slough

COUNTY CHAMPIONSHIPS
MEN – first held in 1957/8 season. Moved to December in
1985 and 1986, so those winners are shown as the
following year (i.e. second half of the season). Wins:
7 Middlesex	1959, 1961, 1977, 1981, 1988-90
4 Kent	1964-5, 1975, 1979
4 Wiltshire	1967-8, 1970, 1972
3 Hertfordshire	1960, 1974, 1976
3 Surrey	1963, 1973, 1986
3 Lancashire	1969, 1978, 1983
2 Worcestershire	1985, 1987
2 Buckinghamshire	1980, 1982

1 Lincolnshire 1958, Durham 1962, Cheshire 1966,
Staffordshire 1971, Yorkshire 1984

WOMEN – first held in 1968/9 season (*tied). Wins:
10 Lancashire	1969*, 1970, 1971*, 1973-4, 1976-7, 1979, 1985, 1989
3 Hertfordshire	1969*, 1971*, 1978
3 Leicestershire	1975*, 1980*, 1983
2 Suffolk	1980*, 1982
2 Staffordshire	1981, 1987
2 Middlesex	1984, 1986
2 Kent	1987-8

1 Essex 1972, Surrey 1975*

HORSE RACING

The Ancient Egyptians are believed to have participated in
horse racing more than 3000 years ago, and the sport
certainly formed part of the ancient Olympic Games.
Smithfield, in London, staged the first regular race
meetings in the 12th century and Britain's oldest race
course, on the Roodee at Chester, staged its first meeting
on 9 February 1540. The Jockey Club was formed in 1750,
and in 1752 the earliest recorded steeplechase took place
in Co. Cork, Ireland.

THE ENGLISH CLASSICS
Five races run from April to September each year for three-
year-olds.

1000 GUINEAS
The first classic of the English season, for fillies only,
carrying 9 stone. Raced over 1 mile at Newmarket and
was first run in 1814. It has been sponsored by General
Accident since 1984. *Post-war winners:*
Year	Winner	Jockey
1946	Hypericum	Doug Smith
1947	Imprudence	Rae Johnstone
1948	Queenpot	Gordon Richards
1949	Musidora	Edgar Britt
1950	Camaree	Rae Johnstone
1951	Belle of All	Gordon Richards
1952	Zabara	Ken Gethin
1953	Happy Laughter	Manny Mercer
1954	Festoon	Scobie Breasley

Year	Winner	Jockey
1955	Meld	Harry Carr
1956	Honeylight	Edgar Britt
1957	Rose Royal II	Charlie Smirke
1958	Bella Paola	Serge Boullenger
1959	Petite Etoile	Doug Smith
1960	Never Too Late	Roger Poincelet
1961	Sweet Solera	Bill Rickaby
1962	Abermaid	Bill Williamson
1963	Hula Dancer	Roger Poincelet
1964	Pourparler	Garnie Bougoure
1965	Night Off	Bill Williamson
1966	Glad Rags	Paul Cook
1967	Fleet	George Moore
1968	Caergwrle	Sandy Barclay
1969	Full Dress II	Ron Hutchinson
1970	Humble Duty	Lester Piggott
1971	Altesse Royale	Yves Saint-Martin
1972	Waterloo	Eddie Hide
1973	Mysterious	Geoff Lewis
1974	Highclere	Joe Mercer
1975	Nocturnal Spree	Johnny Roe
1976	Flying Water	Yves Saint-Martin
1977	Mrs McArdy	Eddie Hide
1978	Enstone Spark	Ernie Johnson
1979	One in a Million	Joe Mercer
1980	Quick As Lightning	Brian Rouse
1981	Fairy Footsteps	Lester Piggott
1982	On The House	John Reid
1983	Ma Biche	Freddy Head
1984	Pebbles	Philip Robinson
1985	Oh So Sharp	Steve Cauthen
1986	Midway Lady	Ray Cochrane
1987	Miesque	Freddy Head
1988	Ravinella	Gary Moore
1989	Musical Bliss	Walter Swinburn
1990	Salsabil	Willie Carson

Most wins

Jockey:
7 George Fordham – 1859 Mayonaise, 1861 Nemesis, 1865 Siberia, 1868 Formosa, 1869 Scottish Queen, 1881 Thebais, 1883 Hauteur
6 Frank Buckle – 1818 Corinne, 1820 Rowena, 1821 Zeal, 1822 Whizgig, 1823 Zinc, 1827 Arab
5 Jem Robinson – 1824 Cobweb, 1828 Zoe, 1830 Charlotte West, 1841 Potentia, 1844 Sorella
5 John Barnham Day – 1826 Problem, 1834 May-day, 1836 Destiny, 1837 Chapeau d'Espagne, 1840 Crucifix
Trainer:
9 Robert Robson – 1818 Corinne, 1819 Catgut, 1820 Rowena, 1821 Zeal, 1822 Whizgig, 1823 Zinc, 1825 Tontine, 1826 Problem, 1827 Arab
Owner: 8 4th Duke of Grafton – 1819 Catgut, 1820 Rowena, 1821 Zeal, 1822 Whizgig, 1823 Zinc, 1825 Tontine, 1826 Problem, 1827 Arab
Fastest time: 1min 36.85sec, Oh So Sharp 1985
Biggest winning margin: 20 lengths, Mayonaise 1859

2000 GUINEAS

First run at Newmarket in 1809, it is the other early-season classic. Run over 1 mile; colts carry 9st, and fillies (rarely entered) 8st 9lb. Seven fillies have won the race, the last Garden Path in 1944. Since 1984 sponsored by General Accident. *Post-war winners:*

Year	Winner	Jockey
1946	Happy Knight	Tommy Weston
1947	Tudor Minstrel	Gordon Richards
1948	My Babu	Charlie Smirke
1949	Nimbus	Charlie Elliott
1950	Palestine	Charlie Smirke
1951	Ki Ming	Scobie Breasley
1952	Thunderhead II	Roger Poincelet
1953	Nearula	Edgar Britt
1954	Darius	Manny Mercer
1955	Our Babu	Doug Smith
1956	Gilles de Retz	Frank Barlow
1957	Crepello	Lester Piggott
1958	Pall Mall	Doug Smith
1959	Taboun	George Moore
1960	Martial	Ron Hutchinson
1961	Rockavon	Norman Stirk
1962	Privy Councillor	Bill Rickaby
1963	Only For Life	Jimmy Lindley
1964	Baldric II	Bill Pyers
1965	Niksar	Duncan Keith
1966	Kashmir II	Jimmy Lindley
1967	Royal Palace	George Moore
1968	Sir Ivor	Lester Piggott
1969	Right Tack	Geoff Lewis
1970	Nijinsky	Lester Piggott
1971	Brigadier Gerard	Joe Mercer
1972	High Top	Willie Carson
1973	Mon Fils	Frankie Durr
1974	Nonoalco	Yves Saint-Martin
1975	Bolkonski	Gianfranco Dettori
1976	Wollow	Gianfranco Dettori
1977	Nebbiolo	Gabriel Curran
1978	Roland Gardens	Frankie Durr
1979	Tap On Wood	Steve Cauthen
1980	Known Fact	Willie Carson
1981	To-Agori-Mou	Greville Starkey
1982	Zino	Freddy Head
1983	Lomond	Pat Eddery
1984	El Gran Senor	Pat Eddery
1985	Shadeed	Lester Piggott
1986	Dancing Brave	Greville Starkey
1987	Don't Forget Me	Willie Carson
1988	Doyoun	Walter Swinburn
1989	Nashwan	Willie Carson
1990	Tirol	Michael Kinane

Most wins

Jockey:
9 Jem Robinson – 1825 Enamel, 1828 Cadland, 1831 Riddlesworth, 1833 Clearwell, 1834 Glencoe, 1835 Ibrahim, 1836 Bay Middleton, 1847 Conyngham, 1848 Flatchatcher

6 John Osborne 1857 Vedette, 1869 Pretender, 1871 Bothwell, 1872 Prince Charlie, 1875 Camballo, 1888 Ayrshire
5 Frank Buckle – 1810 Hephestion, 1820 Pindarrie, 1821 Reginald, 1822 Pastille, 1827 Turcoman
5 Charlie Elliott – 1923 Ellangowan, 1928 Flamingo, 1940 Djebel, 1941 Lambert Simnel, 1949 Nimbus
Trainer: 7 John Scott 1842 Meteor, 1843 Cotherstone, 1849 Nunnykirk, 1853 West Australian, 1856 Fazzoletto, 1860 The Wizard, 1862 The Marquis
Owner: 5 4th Duke of Grafton – 1820 Pindarrie, 1821 Reginald, 1822 Pastille, 1826 Dervise, 1827 Turcoman
5 – 5th Earl of Jersey 1831 Riddlesworth, 1834 Glencoe, 1835 Ibrahim, 1836 Bay Middleton, 1837 Achmet
Fastest time: 1min 35.8sec, My Babu 1948, 1min 35.84sec Tirol 1990 (fastest electronically timed)
Biggest winning margin: 8 lengths, Tudor Minstrel 1947

THE DERBY

The greatest of the Classics is raced each June over 1 mile 4 furlongs at Epsom Downs, except for 1915-8 and 1940-5, when the race was run at Newmarket. Since 1984 it has been sponsored by Ever Ready. Colts carry 9st, and fillies, if entered 8st 9lb. *Winners – fillies shown by #*

Year	Winner	Jockey
1780	Diomed	Sam Arnull
1781	Young Eclipse	Charles Hindley
1782	Assassin	Sam Arnull
1783	Saltram	Charles Hindley
1784	Sergeant	John Arnull
1785	Aimwell	Charles Hindley
1786	Noble	J.White
1787	Sir Peter Teazle	Sam Arnull
1788	Sir Thomas	William South
1789	Skyscraper	Sam Chifney, snr
1790	Rhadamanthus	John Arnull
1791	Eager	Matt Stephenson
1792	John Bull	Frank Buckle
1793	Waxy	Bill Clift
1794	Daedalus	Frank Buckle
1795	Spread Eagle	Anthony Wheatley
1796	Didelot	John Arnull
1797	(unamed colt)	John Singleton
1798	Sir Harry	Sam Arnull
1799	Archduke	John Arnull
1800	Champion	Bill Clift
1801	Eleanor #	John Saunders
1802	Tyrant	Frank Buckle
1803	Ditto	Bill Clift
1804	Hannibal	Bill Arnull
1805	Cardinal Beaufort	Denni Fitzpatrick
1806	Paris	John Shepherd
1807	Election	John Arnull
1808	Pan	Frank Collinson
1809	Pope	Tom Goodison
1810	Whalebone	Bill Clift
1811	Phantom	Frank Buckle
1812	Octavius	Bill Arnull
1813	Smolensko	Tom Goodison
1814	Blucher	Bill Arnull
1815	Whisker	Tom Goodison
1816	Prince Leopold	Will Wheatley
1817	Azor	Jem Robinson
1818	Sam	Sam Chifney, jnr
1819	Tiresias	Bill Clift
1820	Sailor	Sam Chifney, jnr
1821	Gustavus	Sam Day
1822	Moses	Tom Goodison
1823	Emilius	Frank Buckle
1824	Cedric	Jem Robinson
1825	Middleton	Jem Robinson
1826	Lapdog	George Dockeray
1827	Mameluke	Jem Robinson
1828	Cadland	Jem Robinson
1829	Frederick	John Forth
1830	Priam	Sam Day
1831	Spaniel	Will Wheatley
1832	St.Giles	Bill Scott
1833	Dangerous	Jem Chapple
1834	Plenipotentiary	Patrick Conolly
1835	Mundig	Bill Scott
1836	Bay Middleton	Jem Robinson
1837	Phosphorus	George Edwards
1838	Amato	Jim Chapple
1839	Bloomsbury	Sim Templeman
1840	Little Wonder	William MacDonald
1841	Coronation	Patrick Conolly
1842	Attila	Bill Scott
1843	Cotherstone	Bill Scott
1844	Orlando	Nat Flatman
1845	The Merry Monarch	Foster Bell
1846	Pyrrhus the First	Sam Day
1847	Cossack	Sim Templeman
1848	Surplice	Sim Templeman
1849	The Flying Dutchman	Charlie Marlow
1850	Voltigeur	Job Marson
1851	Teddington	Job Marson
1852	Daniel O'Rourke	Frank Butler
1853	West Australian	Frank Butler
1854	Andover	Alfred Day
1855	Wild Dayrell	Robert Sherwood
1856	Ellington	Tom Aldcroft
1857	Blink Bonny #	Jack Charlton
1858	Beadsman	John Wells
1859	Musjid	John Wells
1860	Thormanby	Harry Custance
1861	Kettledrum	Ralph Bullock
1862	Caractacus	John Parsons
1863	Macaroni	Tom Challoner
1864	Blair Athol	Jim Snowden
1865	Gladiateur	Harry Grimshaw
1866	Lord Lyon	Harry Custance
1867	Hermit	John Daley
1868	Blue Gown	John Wells
1869	Pretender	John Osborne
1870	Kingcraft	Tom French

Year	Horse	Jockey		Year	Horse	Jockey
1871	Favonius	Tom French		1928	Fellstead	Harry Wragg
1872	Cremorne	Charlie Maidment		1929	Trigo	Joe Marshall
1873	Doncaster	Fred Webb		1930	Blenheim	Harry Wragg
1874	Gearge Frederick	Harry Custance		1931	Cameronian	Freddie Fox
1875	Galopin	Jack Morris		1932	April the Fifth	Fred Lane
1876	Kisber	Charlie Maidment		1933	Hyperion	Tommy Weston
1877	Silvio	Fred Archer		1934	Windsor Lad	Charlie Smirke
1878	Sefton	Harry Constable		1935	Bahram	Freddie Fox
1879	Sir Bevys	George Fordham		1936	Mahmoud	Charlie Smirke
1880	Bend Or	Fred Archer		1937	Mid-day Sun	Michael Beary
1881	Iroquois	Fred Archer		1938	Bois Roussel	Charlie Elliott
1882	Shotover #	Tom Cannon		1939	Blue Peter	Eph Smith
1883	St.Blaise	Charlie Wood		1940	Pont l'Eveque	Sam Wragg
1884	St.Gatien	Charlie Wood		1941	Owen Tudor	Billy Nevett
	Harvester (dead-heat)	Sam Loates		1942	Watling Street	Harry Wragg
1885	Melton	Fred Archer		1943	Straight Deal	Tommy Carey
1886	Ormonde	Fred Archer		1944	Ocean Swell	Billy Nevett
1887	Merry Hampton	Jack Watts		1945	Dante	Billy Nevett
1888	Ayrshire	Fred Barrett		1946	Airborne	Tommy Lowrey
1889	Donovan	Tommy Loates		1947	Pearl Diver	George Bridgland
1890	Sainfoin	Jack Watts		1948	My Love	Rae Johnstone
1891	Common	George Barrett		1949	Nimbus	Charlie Elliott
1892	Sir Hugo	Fred Allsopp		1950	Galcador	Rae Johnstone
1893	Isinglass	Tommy Loates		1951	Arctic Prince	Charlie Spares
1894	Ladas	Jack Watts		1952	Tulyar	Charlie Smirke
1895	Sir Visto	Sam Loates		1953	Pinza	Gordon Richards
1896	Persimmon	Jack Watts		1954	Never Say Die	Lester Piggott
1897	Galtee More	Charlie Wood		1955	Phil Drake	Freddie Palmer
1898	Jeddah	Otto Madden		1956	Lavandin	Rae Johnstone
1899	Flying Fox	Morny Cannon		1957	Crepello	Lester Piggott
1900	Diamond Jubilee	Herbert Jones		1958	Hard Ridden	Charlie Smirke
1901	Volodyovski	Lester Reiff		1959	Parthia	Harry Carr
1902	Ard Patrick	Skeets Martin		1960	St.Paddy	Lester Piggott
1903	Rock Sand	Danny Maher		1961	Psidium	Roger Poincelet
1904	St.Amant	Kempton Cannon		1962	Larkspur	Neville Sellwood
1905	Cicero	Danny Maher		1963	Relko	Yves Saint-Martin
1906	Spearmint	Danny Maher		1964	Santa Claus	Scobie Breasley
1907	Orby	Johnny Reiff		1965	Sea Bird II	Pat Glennon
1908	Signorinetta #	Billy Bullock		1966	Charlottown	Scobie Breasley
1909	Minoru	Herbert Jones		1967	Royal Palace	George Moore
1910	Lemberg	Bernard Dillon		1968	Sir Ivor	Lester Piggott
1911	Sunstar	George Stern		1969	Blakeney	Ernie Johnson
1912	Tagalie #	Johnny Reiff		1970	Nijinsky	Lester Piggott
1913	Aboyeur	Edwin Piper		1971	Mill Reef	Geoff Lewis
1914	Durbar II	Matt MacGee		1972	Roberto	Lester Piggott
1915	Pommern	Steve Donoghue		1973	Morston	Eddie Hide
1916	Fifinella #	Joe Childs		1974	Snow Knight	Brian Taylor
1917	Gay Crusader	Steve Donaghue		1975	Grundy	Pat Eddery
1918	Gainsborough	Joe Childs		1976	Empery	Lester Piggott
1919	Grand Parade	Fred Templeman		1977	The Minstrel	Lester Piggott
1920	Spion Kop	Frank O'Neill		1978	Shirley Heights	Greville Starkey
1921	Humorist	Steve Donoghue		1979	Troy	Willie Carson
1922	Captain Cuttle	Steve Donoghue		1980	Henbit	Willie Carson
1923	Papyrus	Steve Donoghue		1981	Shergar	Walter Swinburn
1924	Sansovino	Tommy Weston		1982	Golden Fleece	Pat Eddery
1925	Manna	Steve Donoghue		1983	Teenoso	Lester Piggott
1926	Coronach	Joe Childs		1984	Secreto	Christy Roche
1927	Call Boy	Charlie Elliott		1985	Slip Anchor	Steve Cauthen

One of the greatest Derby winners: Sea Bird II, *ridden by*
Pat Glennon in 1965, when he won, easing up, by two
lengths from Meadow Court *with* I Say *third*
(Hulton-Deutsch)

1986	Shahrastani	Walter Swinburn
1987	Reference Point	Steve Cauthen
1988	Kahyasi	Ray Cochrane
1989	Nashwan	Willie Carson
1990	Quest For Fame	Pat Eddery

Most wins
Jockey: 9 Lester Piggott; 6 Jem Robinson, Steve
Donoghue; 5 John Arnull, Bill Clift, Frank Buckle, Fred
Archer; 4 Sam Arnull, Tom Goodison, Bill Scott, Jack
Watts, Charlie Smirke
Trainer: 7 Robert Robson 1793, 1802, 1809-10, 1815,
1817, 1823; John Porter 1868, 1882-3, 1886, 1890-1,
1899; Fred Darling 1922, 1925-6, 1931, 1938, 1940-1
Owner: 5 3rd Earl of Egremont 1782, 1804, 1806-7,
1826; HH Aga Khan III 1930, 1935-6, 1948 (half-share),
1952; 4 John Bowes 1835, 1843, 1852-3; Sir Joseph
Hawley 1851, 1858-9, 1868; 1st Duke of Westminster
1880, 1882, 1886, 1899; Sir Victor Sassoon 1953, 1957-
8, 1960
Fastest time: 2min 33.8sec Mahmoud 1936. The fastest
recorded stalls-started and electically timed Derby is 2m
33.84sec by Kahyasi in 1988
Biggest winning margin: 10 lengths, Shergar 1981

THE OAKS

Raced at Epsom, over 1 mile 4 furlongs for fillies only, all
of whom carry 9st. It was raced at Newmarket during
both World Wars. Since 1984 the race has been sponsored
by Gold Seal. Named after the Epsom home of the 12th
Earl of Derby, the first race was in 1779. *Post-war winners:*

Year	Winner	Jockey
1946	Steady Aim	Harry Wragg
1947	Imprudence	Rae Johnstone
1948	Masaka	Billy Nevett
1949	Musidora	Edgar Britt
1950	Asmena	Rae Johnstone
1951	Neasham Belle	Stan Clayton
1952	Frieze	Edgar Britt
1953	Ambiguity	Joe Mercer
1954	Sun Cap	Rae Johnstone
1955	Meld	Harry Carr
1956	Sicarelle	Freddie Palmer
1957	Carrozza	Lester Piggott
1958	Bella Paola	Max Garcia
1959	Petit Etoile	Lester Piggott
1960	Never Too Late	Roger Poincelet
1961	Sweet Solera	Bill Rickaby
1962	Monade	Yves Saint-Martin
1963	Noblesse	Garnie Bougoure
1964	Homeward Bound	Greville Starkey
1965	Long Look	Jack Purtell
1966	Valoris	Lester Piggott
1967	Pia	Eddie Hide
1968	La Lagune	Gérard Thiboeuf
1969	Sleeping Partner	John Gorton

1970	Lupe	Sandy Barclay
1971	Altesse Royale	Geoff Lewis
1972	Ginevra	Tony Murray
1973	Mysterious	Geoff Lewis
1974	Polygamy	Pat Eddery
1975	Juliette Marny	Lester Piggott
1976	Pawneese	Yves Saint-Martin
1977	Dunfermline	Willie Carson
1978	Fair Salinia	Greville Starkey
1979	Scintillate	Pat Eddery
1980	Bireme	Willie Carson
1981	Blue Wind	Lester Piggott
1982	Time Charter	Billy Newnes
1983	Sun Princess	Willie Carson
1984	Circus Plume	Lester Piggott
1985	Oh So Sharp	Steve Cauthen
1986	Midway Lady	Ray Cochrane
1987	Unite	Walter Swinburn
1988	Diminuendo	Steve Cauthen
1989	Aliysa	Walter Swinburn
1990	Salsabil	Willie Carson

Most wins

Jockey: 9 Frank Buckle – 1797 Niké, 1798 Bellisimma, 1799 Bellina, 1802 Scotia, 1803 Theophania, 1805 Meteora, 1817 Neva, 1818 Corinne, 1823 Zinc
6 Frank Butler – 1843 Poison, 1844 The Princess, 1849 Lady Evelyn, 1850 Rhedycina, 1851 Irish, 1852 Songstress;
6 Lester Piggott – as above

Trainer: 12 Robert Robson – 1802 Scotia, 1804 Pelisse, 1805 Meteora, 1807 Briseïis, 1808 Morel, 1809 Maid of Orleans, 1813 Music, 1815 Minuet, 1818 Corinne, 1822 Pastille, 1823 Zinc, 1825 Wings

Owner: 6 4th Duke of Grafton 1813 Music, 1815 Minuet, 1822 Pastille, 1823 Zinc, 1828 Turquoise, 1831 Oxygen

Fastest time: 2min 34.21sec Time Charter 1982

Biggest winning margin: 12 lengths, Sun Princess 1983

ST.LEGER

The oldest of the five Classics it was first held in 1776. It is run over a distance of 1 mile 6 furlongs 127 yards at Doncaster. Both colts and fillies enter; colts carry 9st, fillies 8st 11lb. During the First World War the race was held at Newmarket (1915-8) and during the Second World War at Thirsk (1940), Manchester (1941), Newmarket (1942- 4), and York (1945). Since 1984 the race has been sponsored by Holsten Pils. Because of damage to the Doncaster track the 1989 race was moved to Ayr, the first time an English classic had been held in Scotland. *Post-war winners:*

Year	Winner	Jockey
1946	Airborne	Tommy Lowrey
1947	Sayajirao	Edgar Britt
1948	Black Tarquin	Edgar Britt
1949	Ridge Wood	Michael Beary
1950	Scratch II	Rae Johnstone
1951	Talma II	Rae Johnstone
1952	Tulyar	Charlie Smirke
1953	Premonition	Eph Smith
1954	Never Say Die	Charlie Smirke

1955	Meld	Harry Carr
1956	Cambremer	Freddie Palmer
1957	Ballymoss	Tommy Burns
1958	Alcide	Harry Carr
1959	Cantelo	Eddie Hide
1960	St.Paddy	Lester Piggott
1961	Aurelius	Lester Piggott
1962	Hethersett	Harry Carr
1963	Ragusa	Garnie Bougoure
1964	Indiana	Jimmy Lindley
1965	Provoke	Joe Mercer
1966	Sodium	Frankie Durr
1967	Ribocco	Lester Piggott
1968	Ribero	Lester Piggott
1969	Intermezzo	Ron Hutchinson
1970	Nijinsky	Lester Piggott
1971	Athens Wood	Lester Piggott
1972	Boucher	Lester Piggott
1973	Peleid	Frankie Durr
1974	Bustino	Joe Mercer
1975	Bruni	Tony Murray
1976	Crow	Yves Saint-Martin
1977	Dunfermline	Willie Carson
1978	Julio Mariner	Eddie Hide
1979	Son of Love	Alain Lequeux
1980	Light Cavalry	Joe Mercer
1981	Cut Above	Joe Mercer
1982	Touching Wood	Paul Cook
1983	Sun Princess	Willie Carson
1984	Commanche Run	Lester Piggott
1985	Oh So Sharp	Steve Cauthen
1986	Moon Madness	Pat Eddery
1987	Reference Point	Steve Cauthen
1988	Minster Son	Willie Carson
1989	Michelozzo	Steve Cauthen

Most wins

Jockey:
9 Bill Scott – 1821 Jack Spigot, 1825 Memnon, 1828 The Colonel, 1829 Rowton, 1838 Don John, 1839 Charles the Twelfth, 1840 Launcelot, 1841 Satirist, 1846 Sir Tatton Sykes
8 John Jackson -1791 Young Traveller, 1794 Beningbrough, 1796 Ambrosia, 1798 Symmetry, 1805 Staveley, 1813 Altisidora, 1815 Filho da Puta, 1822 Theodore; 8 Lester Piggott, as above

Trainer: 16 John Scott 1827 Matilda, 1828 The Colonel, 1829 Rowton, 1832 Margrave, 1834 Touchstone, 1838 Don John, 1839 Charles the Twelfth, 1840 Launcelot, 1841 Satirist, 1845 The Baron, 1851 Newminster, 1853 West Australian, 1856 Warlock, 1857 Imperieuse, 1859 Gamester, 1862 The Marquis

Owner: 7 9th Duke of Hamilton 1786 Paragon, 1787 Spadille, 1788 Young Flora, 1792 Tartar, 1808 Petronius, 1809 Ashton, 1814 William

Fastest time: 3min 1.6sec Coronach, 1926 Windsor Lad 1934

Biggest winning margin: 12 lengths, Never Say Die 1954

Leading Jockeys at the five Classics

	Total	Derby	Oaks	2000	1000	Leger	Years
Lester Piggott	29	9	6	4	2	8	1954-85
Frank Buckle	27	5	9	5	6	2	1792-1827
Jem Robinson	24	6	2	9	5	2	1817-48
Fred Archer	21	5	4	4	2	6	1874-86
Bill Scott	19	4	3	3	-	9	1821-46
Jack Watts	19	4	4	2	4	5	1883-97
John Barham Day	16	-	5	4	5	2	1826-41
George Fordham	16	1	5	3	7	-	1859-83
Joe Childs	15	3	4	2	2	4	1912-33
Willie Carson	15	3	4	4	1	3	1972-90
Frank Butler	14	2	6	2	2	2	1843-53
Steve Donoghue	14	6	2	3	1	2	1915-37
Charlie Elliott	14	3	2	5	4	-	1923-49
Gordon Richards	14	1	2	3	3	5	1930-53

Leading Trainers at the five Classics

John Scott	40	5	8	7	4	16	1827-63
Robert Robson	34	7	12	6	9	-	1793-1827
Mat Dawson	28	6	5	5	6	6	1853-95
John Porter	23	7	3	5	2	6	1868-1900
Alec Taylor	21	3	8	4	1	5	1905-27
Fred Darling	19	7	2	5	2	3	1916-47
Noel Murless	19	3	5	2	6	3	1948-73

Leading Owners at the five Classics

4th Duke of Grafton	20	1	6	5	8	-	1813-31
17th Earl of Derby	20	3	2	2	7	6	1910-45
HH Aga Khan III	17	5	2	3	1	6	1924-57
6th Viscount Falmouth	16	2	4	3	4	3	1862-83

TRIPLE CROWN

The English Triple Crown of 2000 Guineas, Derby and St.Leger has been won by:
West Australian 1853, Gladiateur 1865, Lord Lyon 1866, Ormonde 1866, Common 1891, Isinglass 1893, Galtee More 1897, Flying Fox 1899, Diamond Jubilee 1900, Rock Sand 1903, Pommern 1915, Gay Crusader 1917, Gainsborough 1918, Bahram 1935, Nijinsky 1970.
The following horses have won the Fillies Triple Crown – 1000 Guineas, Oaks and St.Leger: Hannah 1871, Apology 1874, La Fléche 1892, Pretty Polly 1904, Sun Chariot 1942, Meld 1955, Oh So Sharp 1985
Four classics, all except the Derby, were won by: Formosa 1868 and Sceptre 1902.

PRINCIPAL GROUP ONE RACES IN ENGLAND

Pattern racing was introduced into Europe in 1971, with the major races classified into Groups 1, 2 and 3.

CORONATION CUP

Raced at Epsom each year, the day after the Derby. It is run over 1 mile 4 furlongs. First run 1902. Raced at Newbury 1915-6, Newmarket 1941, 1943-5.

Year	Winners since 1970	Jockey
1970	Caliban	Sandy Barclay
1971	Lupe	Geoff Lewis
1972	Mill Reef	Geoff Lewis
1973	Roberto	Lester Piggott
1974	Buoy	Joe Mercer
1975	Bustino	Joe Mercer
1976	Quiet Fling	Lester Piggott
1977	Exceller	Gérard Dubroeucq
1978	Crow	Pat Eddery
1979	Ile de Bourbon	John Reid
1980	Sea Chimes	Lester Piggott
1981	Master Willie	Phillip Waldron
1982	Easter Sun	Bruce Raymond
1983	Be My Native	Lester Piggott
1984	Time Charter	Steve Cauthen
1985	Rainbow Quest	Pat Eddery
1986	Saint Estephe	Pat Eddery
1987	Triptych	Tony Cruz
1988	Triptych	Steve Cauthen
1989	Sherriff's Star	Ray Cochrane
1990	In The Wings	Cash Asmussen

Most wins: 2 Pretty Polly 1905-6, The White Knight 1907-8, Petite Etoile 1960-1, Triptych, as above

ASCOT GOLD CUP

The highlight of the Royal Ascot meeting, the Gold Cup has been contested since 1807. It is the premier long distance race on the flat, run over 2 miles 4 furlongs. Between 1845-53 it was run as the Emperor's Plate. Held at Newmarket in 1917-8 (as the Newmarket Gold Cup), and in 1941-4.

Year	Winners since 1970	Jockey
1970	Precipice Wood	Jimmy Lindley
1971	Random Shot	Geoff Lewis
1972	Erimo Hawk	Pat Eddery
1973	Lassalle	Jimmy Lindley
1974	Ragstone	Ron Hutchinson
1975	Sagaro	Lester Piggott
1976	Sagaro	Lester Piggott
1977	Sagaro	Lester Piggott
1978	Shangamuzo	Greville Starkey
1979	Le Moss	Lester Piggott
1980	Le Moss	Joe Mercer
1981	Ardross	Lester Piggott
1982	Ardross	Lester Piggott
1983	Little Wolf	Willie Carson
1984	Gildoran	Steve Cauthen
1985	Gildoran	Brent Thomson
1986	Longboat	Willie Carson
1987	Paean	Steve Cauthen
1988	Sadeem	Greville Starkey
1989	Sadeem	Willie Carson
1990	Ashal	Richard Hills

Most wins: 3 Sagaro

KING'S STAND STAKES

The premier sprint race at the Royal Ascot meeting. It is run over 5 furlongs and was first held in 1862.

Year	Winners since 1970	Jockey
1970	Amber Rama	Yves St.Martin
1971	Swing Easy	Lester Piggott
1972	Sweet Revenge	Geoff Lewis
1973	Abergwaun	Lester Piggott
1974	Bay Express	Brian Taylor
1975	Flirting Around	Yves St.Martin
1976	Lochnager	Eddie Hide
1977	Godswalk	Lester Piggott
1978	Solinus	Lester Piggott
1979	Double Form	John Reid
1980	African Song	Pat Eddery
1981	Marwell	Walter Swinburn
1982	Fearless Lad	Eddie Hide
1983	Sayf El Arab	Taffy Thomas
1984	Habibti	Willie Carson
1985	Never So Bold	Lester Piggott
1986	Last Tycoon	Cash Asmussen
1987	Bluebird	Cash Asmussen
1988	Chilibang	Willie Carson
1989	Indian Ridge	Steve Cauthen
1990	Dayjur	Willie Carson

Most wins: 2 Golden Boss 1923-4, Gold Bridge 1933-4

CORAL ECLIPSE STAKES

First run in 1886. Raced over 1 mile 2 furlongs at Sandown Park each July. Run at Ascot 1946, Kempton Park 1973. Known as the Benson & Hedges Eclipse Stakes 1974-5, Coral since then.

Year	Winners since 1970	Jockey
1970	Connaught	Sandy Barclay
1971	Mill Reef	Geoff Lewis
1972	Brigadier Gerard	Joe Mercer
1973	Scottish Rifle	Ron Hutchinson
1974	Coup de Feu	Pat Eddery
1975	Star Appeal	Greville Starkey
1976	Wollow	Franco Dettori
1977	Artaius	Lester Piggott
1978	Gunner B	Joe Mercer
1979	Dickens Hill	Tony Murray
1980	Ela-Mana-Mou	Willie Carson
1981	Master Willie	Phillip Waldron
1982	Kalaglow	Greville Starkey
1983	Solford	Pat Eddery
1984	Sadlers Wells	Pat Eddery
1985	Pebbles	Steve Cauthen
1986	Dancing Brave	Greville Starkey
1987-8	Mtoto	Michael Roberts
1989	Nashwan	Willie Carson
1990	Elmaamul	Willie Carson

Most wins: 2 Buchan 1919-20, Polyphontes 1924-5, Mtoto, as above

CARROLL FOUNDATION JULY CUP

Run at Newmarket over 6 furlongs. First run 1876. Known as the William Hill July Cup 1978-83, Norcros July Cup 1984-8.

Year	Winners since 1970	Jockey
1970	Huntercombe	Sandy Barclay
1971	Realm	Brian Taylor
1972	Parsimony	Ron Hutchinson
1973	Thatch	Lester Piggott
1974	Saritamer	Lester Piggott
1975	Lianger	Yves St.Martin
1976	Lochnager	Eddie Hide
1977	Gentilhombre	Paul Cook
1978	Solinus	Lester Piggott
1979	Thatching	Lester Piggott
1980	Moorestyle	Lester Piggott
1981	Marwell	Walter Swinburn
1982	Sharpo	Pat Eddery
1983	Habibti	Willie Carson
1984	Chief Singer	Ray Cochrane
1985	Never So Bold	Steve Cauthen
1986	Green Desert	Walter Swinburn
1987	Ajdal	Walter Swinburn
1988	Soviet Star	Cash Asmussen
1989	Cadeaux Genereux	Paul Eddery

Most wins: 3 Sundridge 1902-4; 2 Spanish Prince 1912-3, Diadem 1919-20, Diomedes 1925-6, Bellacose 1935-6, Abernant 1949-50, Right Boy 1958-9

KING GEORGE VI & QUEEN ELIZABETH II DIAMOND STAKES

First run in 1951 it was originally known as the King George VI & Queen Elizabeth Festival of Britain Stakes. It became the King George VI & Queen Elizabeth Stakes in 1952 and the word 'Diamond' was added in 1975. Raced over 1 mile 4 furlongs at Ascot, it is one of the leading weight-for-age races in Europe.

Year	Winner	Jockey
1951	Supreme Court	Charlie Elliott
1952	Tulyar	Charlie Smirke
1953	Pinza	Gordon Richards
1954	Aureole	Eph Smith
1955	Vimy	Roger Poincelet
1956	Ribot	Enrico Camici
1957	Montaval	Freddie Palmer
1958	Ballymoss	Scobie Breasley
1959	Alcide	Willie Carr
1960	Aggressor	Jimmy Lindley
1961	Right Royal V	Roger Poincelet
1962	Match III	Yves Saint-Martin
1963	Ragusa	Georges Bougoure
1964	Nasram II	Bill Pyers
1965	Meadow Court	Lester Piggott
1966	Aunt Edith	Lester Piggott
1967	Busted	George Moore
1968	Royal Palace	Sandy Barclay
1969	Park Top	Lester Piggott
1970	Nijinsky	Lester Piggott
1971	Mill Reef	Geoff Lewis
1972	Brigadier Gerard	Joe Mercer
1973	Dahlia	Bill Pyers
1974	Dahlia	Lester Piggott
1975	Grundy	Pat Eddery
1976	Pawneese	Yves Saint-Martin
1977	The Minstrel	Lester Piggott
1978	Ile de Bourbon	John Reid
1979	Troy	Willie Carson
1980	Ela-Mana-Mou	Willie Carson
1981	Shergar	Walter Swinburn
1982	Kalaglow	Greville Starkey
1983	Time Charter	Joe Mercer
1984	Teenoso	Lester Piggott
1985	Petoski	Willie Carson
1986	Dancing Brave	Pat Eddery
1987	Reference Point	Steve Cauthen
1988	Mtoto	Michael Roberts
1989	Nashwan	Willie Carson

Most wins: 2 Dahlia

SWETTENHAM STUD SUSSEX STAKES

First run in 1841. Raced over 1 mile at Goodwood. Sponsored from 1985 by the Swettenham Stud (headed by Robert Sangster). For 3-year-olds only 1900-59, 3 & 4-year-olds 1960-74, 3-year-old upwards since 1975.

Year	Winners since 1970	Jockey
1970	Humble Duty	Duncan Keith
1971	Brigadier Gerard	Joe Mercer

Year	Winner	Jockey
1972	Sallust	Joe Mercer
1973	Thatch	Lester Piggott
1974	Aces of Aces	Jimmy Lindley
1975	Bolkonski	Franco Dettori
1976	Wollow	Franco Dettori
1977	Artaius	Lester Piggott
1978	Jaazeiro	Lester Piggott
1979	Kris	Joe Mercer
1980	Posse	Pat Eddery
1981	King's Lake	Pat Eddery
1982	On The House	John Reid
1983	Noalcoholic	George Duffield
1984	Chief Singer	Ray Cochrane
1985	Rousillon	Greville Starkey
1986	Sonic Lady	Walter Swinburn
1987	Soviet Star	Greville Starkey
1988	Warning	Pat Eddery
1989	Zilzal	Walter Swinburn

JUDDMONTE INTERNATIONAL STAKES

Inaugurated in 1972, it was known as the Benson & Hedges Gold Cup until 1985. From 1986-7 known as the Matchmaker International and International Stakes in 1988. The principal race of the three-day August meeting at York, it is run over 1 mile 2 furlongs.

Year	Winner	Jockey
1972	Roberto	Braulio Baeza
1973	Moulton	Geoff Lewis
1974	Dahlia	Lester Piggott
1975	Dahlia	Lester Piggott
1976	Wollow	Franco Dettori
1977	Relkino	Willie Carson
1978	Hawaiian Sound	Lester Piggott
1979	Troy	Willie Carson
1980	Master Willie	Phillip Waldron
1981	Beldale Flutter	Pat Eddery
1982	Assert	Pat Eddery
1983	Caerleon	Pat Eddery
1984	Cormorant Wood	Steve Cauthen
1985	Commanche Run	Lester Piggott
1986	Shardari	Walter Swinburn
1987	Triptych	Steve Cauthen
1988	Persian Heights	Pat Eddery
1989	Ile De Chypre	Tony Clark

YORKSHIRE OAKS

For 3-year-old fillies only. Held at York over 1 miles 4 furlongs. First run in 1849.

Year	Winners since 1970	Jockey
1970	Lupe	Sandy Barclay
1971	Fleet Wahine	Geoff Lewis
1972	Attica Meli	Geoff Lewis
1973	Mysterious	Geoff Lewis
1974	Dibidale	Willie Carson
1975	May Hill	Pat Eddery
1976	Sarah Siddons	Christy Roche
1977	Busaca	Pat Eddery
1978	Fair Salinia	Greville Starkey

1979	Connaught Bridge	Joe Mercer
1980	Shoot A Line	Lester Piggott
1981	Condessa	Declan Gillespie
1982	Awaasif	Lester Piggott
1983	Sun Princess	Willie Carson
1984	Circus Plume	Willie Carson
1985	Sally Brown	Walter Swinburn
1986	Untold	Greville Starkey
1987	Biny Pasha	Richard Quinn
1988	Diminuendo	Steve Cauthen
1989	Roseate Tern	Willie Carson

TATTERSALLS CHEVELEY PARK STAKES

A race for 2-year-old fillies. Run over the last 6 furlongs of the Bunbury Mile at Newmarket. First run in 1870. Tattersalls succeeded William Hill (1973-83) as sponsors in 1985.

Year	Winners since 1970	Jockey
1970	Magic Flute	Sandy Barclay
1971	Waterloo	Eddie Hide
1972	Jacinth	John Gorton
1973	Gentle Thoughts	Bill Pyers
1974	Cry Of Truth	John Gorton
1975	Pasty	Pat Eddery
1976	Durtal	Lester Piggott
1977	Sookera	Walter Swinburn
1978	Devon Ditty	Greville Starkey
1979	Mrs.Penny	John Matthias
1980	Marwell	Lester Piggott
1981	Woodstream	Pat Eddery
1982	Ma Biche	Freddy Head
1983	Desirable	Steve Cauthen
1984	Park Appeal	Declan Gillespie
1985	Embla	Angel Cordero
1986	Forest Flower	Tony Ives
1987	Ravinella	Gary Moore
1988	Pass the Peace	Richard Quinn
1989	Dead Certain	Cash Asmussen

TATTERSALLS MIDDLE PARK STAKES

A 6-furlong sprint for 2-year-olds run at Newmarket. First run in 1866 as the Middle Park Plate. Became Middle Park Stakes 1922. 1940 race at Nottingham and run as the New Middle Park Stakes. At one time the race was regarded as the 'Two-Year-Old's Championship', but in recent year's the quality of the fields have declined. Tattersalls became the race's sponsors in 1986.

Year	Winners since 1970	Jockey
1970	Brigadier Gerard	Joe Mercer
1971	Sharpen Up	Willie Carson
1972	Tudenham	Jimmy Lindley
1973	Habat	Pat Eddery
1974	Steel Heart	Lester Piggott
1975	Hittite Glory	Frankie Durr
1976	Tachypous	Geoff Lewis
1977	Formidable	Pat Eddery
1978	Junius	Lester Piggott
1979	Known Fact	Willie Carson

1980	Mattaboy	Lester Piggott
1981	Cajum	Lester Piggott
1982	Diesis	Lester Piggott
1983	Creag-An-Sgor	Steve Cauthen
1984	Bassenthwaite	Pat Eddery
1985	Stalker	Joe Mercer
1986	Mister Majestic	Ray Cochrane
1987	Gallic League	Steve Cauthen
1988	Mon Tresor	Michael Roberts
1989	Balla Cove	Steve Cauthen

DUBAI CHAMPION STAKES

Run at Newmarket over 1 mile 2 furlongs. First run in 1877. Dubai Champions Stakes from 1982.

Year	Winners since 1970	Jockey
1970	Lorenzaccio	Geoff Lewis
1971	Brigadier Gerard	Joe Mercer
1972	Brigadier Gerard	Joe Mercer
1973	Hurry Harriet	Jean Cruguet
1974	Giacometti	Lester Piggott
1975	Rose Bowl	Willie Carson
1976	Vitiges	Pat Eddery
1977	Flying Water	Yves Saint-Martin
1978	Swiss Maid	Greville Starkey
1979	Northern Baby	Philippe Paquet
1980	Cairn Rouge	Tony Murray
1981	Vayrann	Yves Saint-Martin
1982	Time Charter	Billy Newnes
1983	Cormorant Wood	Steve Cauthen
1984	Palace Music	Yves Saint-Martin
1985	Pebbles	Pat Eddery
1986	Triptych	Tony Cruz
1987	Triptych	Tony Cruz
1988	Indian Skimmer	Michael Roberts
1989	Legal Case	Ray Cochrane

Most wins: 2 Lemberg 1910-1, Orpheus 1920-1, Fairway 1928-9, Wychwood Abbot 1935-6, Hippius 1940-1, Dynamite 1951-2, Brigadier Gerard, Triptych

THREE CHIMNEYS DEWHURST STAKES

An end-of-season race for 2-year-olds at Newmarket, over 7 furlongs. It was first run in 1875 and was sponsored by William Hill 1973-86.

Year	Winners since 1970	Jockey
1970	Mill Reef	Geoff Lewis
1971	Crowned Prince	Lester Piggott
1972	Lunchtime	Pat Eddery
1973	Cellini	Lester Piggott
1974	Grundy	Pat Eddery
1975	Wollow	Franco Dettori
1976	The Minstrel	Lester Piggott
1977	Try My Best	Lester Piggott
1978	Tromos	John Lynch
1979	Monteverdi	Lester Piggott
1980	Storm Bird	Pat Eddery
1981	Wind and Wuthering	Philip Waldron
1982	Diesis	Lester Piggott

1983	El Gran Senor	Pat Eddery
1984	Kala Dancer	Geoff Baxter
1985	Huntingdale	Michael Hills
1986	Ajdal	Walter Swinburn
1987	Cancelled	
1988	Prince of Dance	Willie Carson
1989	Dashing Blade	John Matthias

MAJOR BRITISH HANDICAPS

WILLIAM HILL LINCOLN HANDICAP

The first big handicap of the season, it is raced over 1 mile at Doncaster in March. Formerly the Lincolnshire Handicap it was raced at Lincoln 1853-1964 except 1916 (Lingfield) and 1952-5 (Pontefract). It became the Lincoln Handicap in 1965 upon moving to its present venue. Irish Sweeps Lincoln Handicap 1969-78, race then sponsored by William Hill. Recent *winners:*

Year	Winner	Jockey
1978	Captain's Wings	Michael Wigham
1979	Fair Season	Greville Starkey
1980	King's Ride	Geoff Baxter
1981	Saher	Ray Cochrane
1982	King's Glory	Bryn Crossley
1983	Mighty Fly	Steve Cauthen
1984	Saving Mercy	Walter Swinburn
1985	Cataldi	Greville Starkey
1986	K-Battery	John Lowe
1987	Star of a Gunner	John Reid
1988	Cuvee Charlie	Mark Rimmer
1989	Fact Finder	Tyrone Williams
1990	Erichstar	Alan Munro

Most wins: 2 Ob 1906-7, Balmer 1957-8

LADBROKE CHESTER CUP

One of the oldest handicaps still in existence, the Chester Cup dates to 1824. Run over 2 miles 2 furlongs 97 yards. Not held 1983. Sponsored by Ladbroke from 1972. *Recent winners:*

Year	Winner	Jockey
1978	Sea Pigeon	Mark Birch
1979	Charlotte's Choice	Willie Carson
1980	Arapahos	Steve Cauthen
1981	Donegal Prince	Paddy Young
1982	Dawn Johnny	Walter Swinburn
1984	Contester	Geoff Baxter
1985	Morgan's Choice	Willie Carson
1986	Western Dancer	Paul Cook
1987	Just David	Michael Roberts
1988	Old Hubert	Myrddin Thomas
1989	Grey Salute	Pat Eddery
1990	Travelling Light	Alan Munro

Most wins: 2 Chivalrous 1822-3, Sea Pigeon 1977-8

ROYAL HUNT CUP

The principal handicap of the Royal Ascot meeting, it was first staged in 1843. Run over 1 mile. The 1941 race was at Newbury. *Recent winners:*

Year	Winner	Jockey
1978	Fear Naught	Michael Wigham
1979	Pipedreamer	Philip Waldron
1980	Tender Heart	Joe Mercer
1981	Teamwork	Greville Starkey
1982	Buzzard's Bay	Joe Mercer
1983	Mighty Fly	Steve Cauthen
1984	Hawkley	Tyrone Williams
1985	Come On The Blues	Chris Rutter
1986	Patriach	Richard Quinn
1987	Vague Shot	Steve Cauthen
1988	Governorship	John Reid
1989	True Panache	Pat Eddery
1990	Pontenuovo	Gary Bardwell

Most wins: 2 Master Vote 1947-8

GOODWOOD CUP

First run 1812. Over 2 miles 5 furlongs at Goodwood. *Recent winners:*

Year	Winner	Jockey
1977	Grey Baron	Geoff Lewis
1978	Tug Of War	Brian Rouse
1979	Le Moss	Joe Mercer
1980	Le Moss	Joe Mercer
1981	Ardross	Lester Piggott
1982	Heighlin	Steve Cauthen
1983	Little Wolf	Willie Carson
1984	Gildoran	Steve Cauthen
1985	Valuable Witness	Pat Eddery
1986	Longboat	Willie Carson
1987	Sergeyevich	Willie Carson
1988	Sadeem	Greville Starkey
1989	Mazzacano	Pat Eddery

Most wins: 2 Flint Jack 1922-3

TOTE EBOR HANDICAP

First run 1843. Over 1 mile 6 furlongs at York. Run at Pontefract over 1 mile 4 furlongs 1943-4. Johnnie Walker Ebor Handicap 1967-73, Terry's All Gold Ebor Handicap 1974-5, Tote from 1976. *Recent winners:*

Year	Winner	Jockey
1977	Move Off	Jimmy Bleasdale
1978	Totowah	Paul Cook
1979	Sea Pigeon	Jonjo O'Neill
1980	Shaftesbury	Greville Starkey
1981	Protection Racket	Mark Birch
1982	Another Sam	Brian Rouse
1983	Jupiter Island	Lester Piggott
1984	Crazy	Walter Swinburn
1985	Western Dancer	Paul Cook
1986	Primary	Greville Starkey
1987	Daarkom	Michael Roberts
1988	Kneller	Paul Eddery
1989	Sapience	Pat Eddery

LADBROKES AYR GOLD CUP

Run at Ayr over 6 furlongs. First run 1804. Burmah Castrol Gold Cup 1972-3, Ladbroke from 1974. *Recent winners:*

Year	Winner	Jockey
1977	Jon George	Bruce Raymond
1978	Vaigly Great	Greville Starkey
1979	Primula Boy	Bill Higgins
1980	Sparkling Boy	John Lowe
1981	First Movement	Mick Miller
1982	Famous Star	Paul Eddery
1983	Polly's Brother	Kevin Hodgson
1984	Able Albert	Mark Birch
1985	Camps Heath	Wendyll Woods
1986	Green Ruby	John Williams
1987	Not So Silly	Gary Bradwell
1988	So Careful	Nick Carlisle
1989	Joveworth	Jimmy Fortune

WILLIAM HILL CAMBRIDGESHIRE HANDICAP

With the Cesarewich it completes the Autumn Double. Run over 1 mile 1 furlong, it returned to the Newmarket July course in 1986 after a 45- year spell over the Rowley Mile course. First run 1839, as the Cambridgeshire Stakes until 1970. Run at Nottingham in 1940. Irish Sweeps Cambridgeshire Handicap 1971-7, William Hill since then. *Recent winners:*

Year	Winner	Jockey
1977	Sin Timon	Tony Kimberley
1978	Baronet	Brian Rouse
1979	Smartset	John Reid
1980	Baronet	Brian Rouse
1981	Braughing	Steve Cauthen
1982	Century City	Joe Mercer
1983	Sagamore	Taffy Thomas
1984	Leysh	John Lowe
1985	Tremblant	Pat Eddery
1986	Dallas	Ray Cochrane
1987	Balthus	Dean McKeown
1988	Quinland Terry	George Duffield
1989	Rambo's Hall	Dean McKeown

Most wins: 2 Hackler's Pride 1903-4, Christmas Daisy 1909-10, Sterope 1948-9, Prince de Galles 1969-70, Baronet, as above

TOTE CESAREWICH HANDICAP

The other half of the Autumn Double. Like the Cambridgeshire it was inaugurated in 1839 and is run at Newmarket, but over 2 miles 2 fulongs. *Recent winners:*

Year	Winner	Jockey
1977	Assured	Philip Waldron
1978	Centurion	John Matthias
1979	Sir Michael	Mark Rimmer
1980	Popsi's Joy	Lester Piggott
1981	Halsbury	Joe Mercer
1982	Mountain Lodge	Willie Carson
1983	Bajan Sunshine	Brian Rouse
1984	Tom Sharp	Steve Dawson
1985	Kayudee	Tony Murray
1986	Orange Hill	Richard Fox
1987	Private Audition	Gary Carter

1988	Nomadic Way	Willie Carson
1989	Double Dutch	Billy Newnes

THE IRISH CLASSICS

All Irish Classics are run at the Curragh, situated in County Kildare. The distances of all five races are the same as their English counterparts. *Winners since 1970:*

1000 GUINEAS *(First run 1922)*

1970	Black Satin	Ron Hutchinson
1971	Favoletta	Lester Piggott
1972	Pidget	Walter Swinburn, Snr.
1973	Cloonagh	Greville Starkey
1974	Gaily	Ron Hutchinson
1975	Miralla	Ryan Parnell
1976	Sarah Siddons	Christy Roche
1977	Lady Capulet	Tom Murphy
1978	More So	Christy Roche
1979	Godetia	Lester Piggott
1980	Cairn Rouge	Tony Murray
1981	Arctique Royale	Gabriel Curran
1982	Prince's Polly	Walter Swinburn, Jnr.
1983	L'Attrayante	Alain Badel
1984	Katies	Philip Robinson
1985	Al Bahathri	Tony Murray
1986	Sonic Lady	Walter Swinburn, Jnr.
1987	Forest Flower	Tony Ives
1988	Trusted Partner	Michael Kinane
1989	Ensconce	Ray Cochrane
1990	In The Groove	Steve Cauthen

2000 GUINEAS *(First run 1921)*

1970	Decies	Lester Piggott
1971	King's Company	Freddy Head
1972	Ballymore	Christy Roche
1973	Sharp Edge	Joe Mercer
1974	Furry Glen	George McGrath
1975	Grundy	Pat Eddery
1976	Northern Treasure	Gabriel Curran
1977	Pampapaul	Franco Dettori
1978	Jaazeiro	Lester Piggott
1979	Dickens Hill	Tony Murray
1980	Nikoli	Christy Roche
1981	King's Lake	Pat Eddery
1982	Dara Monarch	Michael Kinane
1983	Wassl	Tony Murray
1984	Sadlers Wells	George McGrath
1985	Triptych	Christy Roche
1986	Flash of Steel	Michael Kinane
1987	Don't Forget Me	Willie Carson
1988	Prince of Birds	Declan Gillespie
1989	Shaadi	Walter Swinburn, Jnr.
1990	Tirol	Pat Eddery

DERBY *(First run 1866)*

1970	Nijinsky	Liam Ward
1971	Irish Ball	Fredo Gilbert
1972	Steel Pulse	Bill Williamson

1973	Weaver's Hall	George McGrath
1974	English Prince	Yves Saint-Martin
1975	Grundy	Pat Eddery
1976	Malacate	Philippe Paquet
1977	The Minstrel	Lester Piggott
1978	Shirley Heights	Greville Starkey
1979	Troy	Willie Carson
1980	Tyrnavos	Tony Murray
1981	Shergar	Lester Piggott
1982	Assert	Christy Roche
1983	Shareef Dancer	Walter Swinburn, Jnr.
1984	El Gran Senor	Pat Eddery
1985	Law Society	Pat Eddery
1986	Shahrastani	Walter Swinburn, Jnr.
1987	Sir Harry Lewis	Steve Cauthen
1988	Kahyasi	Ray Cochrane
1989	Old Vic	Steve Cauthen
1990	Salsabil	Willie Carson

OAKS *(First run 1895)*

1970	Santa Tina	Lester Piggott
1971	Altesse Royale	Geoff Lewis
1972	Regal Exception	Maurice Philipperon
1973	Dahlia	Bill Pyers
1974	Dibidale	Willie Carson
1975	Juliette Marny	Lester Piggott
1976	Lagunette	Philippe Paquet
1977	Olwyn	John Lynch
1978	Fair Salinia	Greville Starkey
1979	Godetia	Lester Piggott
1980	Shoot A Line	Willie Carson
1981	Blue Wind	Walter Swinburn, Jnr.
1982	Swiftfoot	Willie Carson
1983	Give Thanks	Declan Gillespie
1984	Princess Pati	Pat Shanahan
1985	Helen Street	Willie Carson
1986	Colorspin	Pat Eddery
1987	Unite	Walter Swinburn, Jnr.
1988	Diminuendo	Steve Cauthen
dead heat:	Melodist	Walter Swinburn, Jnr.
1989	Aldaress	Michael Kinane

ST.LEGER *(First run 1915)*

1970	Allangrange	George McGrath
1971	Parnell	Alan Simpson
1972	Pidget	Thomas Burns
1973	Conor Pass	Peter Jarman
1974	Mistigri	Christy Roche
1975	Caucasus	Lester Piggott
1976	Meneval	Lester Piggott
1977	Transworld	Thomas Murphy
1978	M-Lolshan	Brian Taylor
1979	Niniski	Willie Carson
1980	Gonzales	Raymond Carroll
1981	Protection Racket	Brian Taylor
1982	Touching Wood	Paul Cook
1983	Mountain Lodge	Declan Gillespie
1984	Opale	Darrell McHargue

1985	Leading Counsel	Pat Eddery
1986	Authaal	Christy Roche
1987	Eurobird	Cash Asmussen
1988	Dark Lomond	Declan Gillespie
1989	Petite Ile	Ron Quinton

CARTIER MILLION
Ireland's richest race with total prizemoney of £11 million. The first ten horses are all guaranteed at least £10,000. Raced by two-year-olds over 7 furlongs at Phoenix Park.

Year	Winner	Jockey
1988	Corwyn Bay	Stephen Craine
1989	The Caretaker	Michael Kinane

THE FRENCH CLASSICS

POULE D'ESSAI DES POULICHES
The equivalent of the 1000 Guineas it is run at Longchamp over 1600 metres (1 mile). First run 1883. Held at Le Tremblay 1943, Maisons-Laffitte 1944-5.
Winners since 1970:

Year	Winner	Jockey
1970	Pampered Miss	Maurice Philipperon
1971	Bold Fascinator	Bill Williamson
1972	Mata Hari	Jean Cruguet
1973	Alles France	Yves Saint-Martin
1974	Dumka	Alain Lequeux
1975	Ivanjica	Freddy Head
1976	Riverqueen	Freddy Head
1977	Madelia	Yves Saint-Martin
1978	Dancing Maid	Freddy Head
1979	Three Troikas	Freddy Head
1980	Aryenne	Maurice Philipperon
1981	Ukraine Girl	Pat Eddery
1982	River Lady	Lester Piggott
1983	L'Attrayante	Alain Badel
1984	Masarika	Yves Saint-Martin
1985	Silvermine	Freddy Head
1986	Baiser Volé	Guy Guignard
1987	Miesque	Freddy Head
1988	Ravinella	Gary Moore
1989	Pearl Bracelet	Alfred Gilbert
1990	Houseproud	Pat Eddery

POULE D'ESSAI DES POULAINS
Also run at Longchamp over 1600 metres, it is the equivalent of the 2000 Guineas. First run 1883. Run at Auteuil 1940, Le Tremblay 1943, Maisons-Laffitte 1944-5.
Winners since 1970:

1970	Caro	Bill Williamson
1971	Zug	Jean-Claude Desaint
1972	Riverman	Jean-Claude Desaint
1973	Kalamoun	Henri Samani
1974	Moulines	Maurice Philipperon
1975	Green Dancer	Freddy Head
1976	Red Lord	Freddy Head
1977	Blushing Groom	Henri Samani
1978	Nishapour	Henri Samani

1979	Irish River	Maurice Philipperon
1980	In Fijar	Georges Doleuze
1981	Recitation	Greville Starkey
1982	Melyno	Yves Saint-Martin
1983	L'Emigrant	Cash Asmussen
1984	Siberian Express	Fredo Gibert
1985	No Pass No Sale	Yves Saint-Martin
1986	Fast Topaze	Cash Asmussen
1987	Soviet Star	Greville Starkey
1988	Blushing John	Freddy Head
1989	Kendor	Maurice Phillipperon
1990	Linamix	Freddy Head

PRIX DU JOCKEY CLUB

The French Derby, it was first run in 1836 Raced over 2400 metres (1miles 4 furlongs) at Chantilly. Raced at Longchamp 1919-20, 1941-2, 1945-7, Auteuil 1940, Le Trembay 1943-4. *Winners since 1970:*

1970	Sassafras	Yves Saint-Martin
1971	Rheffic	Bill Pyers
1972	Hard To Beat	Lester Piggott
1973	Roi Lear	Freddy Head
1974	Caracolero	Philippe Paquet
1975	Val de L'Orme	Freddy Head
1976	Youth	Freddy Head
1977	Crystal Palace	Gérard Dubroeucq
1978	Acamas	Yves Saint-Martin
1979	Top Ville	Yves Saint-Martin
1980	Policeman	Willie Carson
1981	Bikala	Serge Gorli
1982	Assert	Christy Roche
1983	Caerleon	Pat Eddery
1984	Darshaan	Yves Saint-Martin
1985	Mouktar	Yves Saint-Martin
1986	Bering	Gary Moore
1987	Natroun	Yves Saint-Martin
1988	Hours After	Pat Eddery
1989	Old Vic	Steve Cauthen
1990	Sanglamore	Pat Eddery

PRIX DE DIANE HERMES

The equivalent of the Oaks. It is run over 2100 metres (c.1 mile 2 furlongss) at Chantilly. First run 1843. Raced at Longchamp 1919-20, 1941-2, 1945-7, Le Trembay 1943-4. *Winners since 1970:*

1970	Sweet Mimosa	Bill Williamson
1971	Pistol Packer	Freddy Head
1972	Rescousse	Yves Saint-Martin
1973	Allez France	Yves Saint-Martin
1974	Highclere	Joe Mercer
1975	*No race*	
1976	Pawneese	Yves Saint-Martin
1977	Madelia	Yves Saint-Martin
1978	Reine de Saba	Freddy Head
1979	Dunette	Georges Doleuze
1980	Mrs.Penny	Lester Piggott
1981	Madam Gay	Lester Piggott
1982	Harbour	Freddy Head

1983	Escaline	Gary Moore
1984	Northern Trick	Cash Asmussen
1985	Lypharita	Lester Piggott
1986	Lacovia	Freddy Head
1987	Indian Skimmer	Steve Cauthen
1988	Restless Kar	Gérard Mosse
1989	Lady In Silver	Tony Cruz
1990	Rafha	Willie Carson

PRIX ROYAL OAK

Run over 3100 metres (c.1 mile 7 furlongs) at Longchamp. Rougly the equivalent of the St.Leger it was open only to 3-year-olds until 1978 but since then it has been open to 3-year-olds and upwards. First run 1869. Run at Le Tremblay 1943-4. *Winners since 1970:*

1970	Sassafras	Yves Saint-Martin
1971	Bourbon	Freddy Head
1972	Pleben	Marcel Depalmas
1973	Lady Berry	Marcel Depalmas
1974	Busiris	Freddy Head
1975	Henri Le Balafre	Henri Samani
1976	Exceller	Georges Dubroecq
1977	Rex Magan	Philippe Paquet
1978	Brave Johnny	Henri Samani
1979	Niniski	Willie Carson
1980	Gold River	Freddy Head
1981	Ardross	Lester Piggott
1982	Denel	Yves Saint-Martin
1983	Old Country	Pat Eddery
1984	Agent Double	Freddy Head
1985	Mersey	Jean-Luc Kessas
1986	El Cuite	Steve Cauthen
1987	Royal Gait	Alfred Gilbert
1988	Star Lift	Cash Asmussen
1989	Top Sunrise	Freddy Head

PRIX DE L'ARC DE TRIOMPHE

Europe's most prestigious race. It is run over 2400 metres (c. 1 mile 4 furlongs) at Longchamp on the first Sunday in October. It was first run in 1920. The 1943-4 races were at Le Tremblay over 2300m (c.1 mile 3 furlongs).

Year	*Winner*	*Jockey*
1920	Comrade	Frank Bullock
1921	Ksar	George Stern
1922	Ksar	Frank Bullock
1923	Parth	Frank O'Neill
1924	Massine	Fred Sharpe
1925	Priori	Marcel Allemand
1926	Biribi	Domingo Torterolo
1927	Mon Talisman	Charles Semblat
1928	Kantar	Arthur Esling
1929	Ortello	Paolo Caprioli
1930	Motrico	Marcel Fruhinsholtz
1931	Pearl Cap	Charles Semblat
1932	Motrico	Charles Semblat
1933	Crapom	Paolo Caprioli
1934	Brantôme	Charles Bouillon
1935	Samos	Wally Sibbritt

Steve Cauthen was champion jockey in the USA at the age of 17 in 1977. Since crossing the Atlantic he has been champion jockey in Britain three times (**All-Sport**)

1936	Corrida	Charlie Elliott
1937	Corrida	Charlie Elliott
1938	Eclair au Chocolat	Charles Bouillon
1941	La Pacha	Paul Francolon
1942	Djebel	Jacko Doyasbère
1943	Verso II	Guy Duforez
1944	Ardan	Jacko Doyasbère
1945	Nikellora	Rae Johnstone
1946	Caracalla	Charlie Elliott
1947	Le Paillon	Fernand Rochetti
1948	Migoli	Charlie Smirke
1949	Coronation	Roger Poincelet
1950	Tantième	Jacko Doyasbère
1951	Tantième	Jacko Doyasbère
1952	Nuccio	Roger Poincelet
1953	La Sorellina	Maurice Larraun
1954	Sica Boy	Rae Johnstone
1955	Ribot	Enrico Camici
1956	Ribot	Enrico Camici
1957	Oroso	Serge Boullenger
1958	Ballymoss	Scobie Breasley
1959	Saint Crespin	George Moore
1960	Puissant Chef	Max Garcia
1961	Molvedo	Enrico Camici
1962	Soltikoff	Marcel Depalmas
1963	Exbury	Jean Deforge
1964	Prince Royal II	Roger Poincelet
1965	Sea Bird II	Pat Glennon
1966	Bon Mot	Freddy Head
1967	Topyo	Bill Pyers
1968	Vaguely Noble	Bill Williamson
1969	Levmoss	Bill Williamson
1970	Sassafras	Yves Saint-Martin
1971	Mill Reef	Geoff Lewis
1972	San San	Freddy Head
1973	Rheingold	Lester Piggott
1974	Allez France	Yves Saint-Martin
1975	Star Appeal	Greville Starkey
1976	Ivanjica	Freddy Head
1977	Alleged	Lester Piggott
1978	Alleged	Lester Piggott
1979	Three Troikas	Freddy Head
1980	Detriot	Pat Eddery
1981	Gold River	Gary Moore
1982	Akiyda	Yves Saint-Martin
1983	All Along	Walter Swinburn
1984	Sagace	Yves Saint-Martin
1985	Rainbow Quest	Pat Eddery
1986	Dancing Brave	Pat Eddery
1987	Trempolino	Pat Eddery
1988	Tony Bin	John Reid
1989	Carroll House	Michael Kinane

Most wins

Horse: 2 Ksar, Motrico, Corrida, Tantième, Ribot, Alleged
Jockey: 4 Jacko Doyasbère, Freddy Head, Yves Saint-Martin, Pat Eddery
Trainer: 4 Charles Semblat 1942, 1944, 1946, 1949; Alec Head 1952, 1959, 1976, 1981; François Mathet 1950-1, 1970, 1982
Owner: 6 Marcel Boussac 1936-7, 1942, 1944, 1946, 1949
Fastest winning time: 2:26.3 Trempolino, 1987

CHAMPION JOCKEYS (FLAT)

The champion jockeys on the flat in Britain since 1900 have been:

Year	Champion	Winners
1900	Lester Reiff	143
1901	Otto Madden	130
1902	Willie Lane	170
1903	Otto Madden	154
1904	Otto Madden	161
1905	Elijah Wheatley	124
1906	Billy Higgs	149
1907	Billy Higgs	146
1908	Danny Maher	139
1909	Frank Wootton	165
1910	Frank Wootton	137
1911	Frank Wootton	187
1912	Frank Wootton	118
1913	Danny Maher	115
1914	Steve Donoghue	129
1915	Steve Donoghue	62
1916	Steve Donoghue	43
1917	Steve Donoghue	42
1918	Steve Donoghue	66
1919	Steve Donoghue	129
1920	Steve Donoghue	143
1921	Steve Donoghue	141
1922	Steve Donoghue	102
1923	Steve Donoghue	89
	Charlie Elliott	89
1924	Charlie Elliott	106
1925	Gordon Richards	118
1926	Tommy Weston	95
1927	Gordon Richards	164
1928	Gordon Richards	148
1929	Gordon Richards	135
1930	Freddy Fox	129
1931	Gordon Richards	145
1932	Gordon Richards	190
1933	Gordon Richards	259
1934	Gordon Richards	212
1935	Gordon Richards	217
1936	Gordon Richards	174
1937	Gordon Richards	216
1938	Gordon Richards	200
1939	Gordon Richards	155
1940	Gordon Richards	68
1941	Harry Wragg	71
1942	Gordon Richards	67
1943	Gordon Richards	65
1944	Gordon Richards	88
1945	Gordon Richards	104
1946	Gordon Richards	212
1947	Gordon Richards	269
1948	Gordon Richards	224
1949	Gordon Richards	261
1950	Gordon Richards	201
1951	Gordon Richards	227
1952	Gordon Richards	231
1953	Gordon Richards	191
1954	Doug Smith	129
1955	Doug Smith	168
1956	Doug Smith	155
1957	Scobie Breasley	173
1958	Doug Smith	165
1959	Doug Smith	157
1960	Lester Piggott	170
1961	Scobie Breasley	171
1962	Scobie Breasley	179
1963	Scobie Breasley	176
1964	Lester Piggott	140
1965	Lester Piggott	166
1966	Lester Piggott	191
1967	Lester Piggott	117
1968	Lester Piggott	139
1969	Lester Piggott	163
1970	Lester Piggott	162
1971	Lester Piggott	162
1972	Willie Carson	132
1973	Willie Carson	163
1974	Pat Eddery	148
1975	Pat Eddery	164
1976	Pat Eddery	162
1977	Pat Eddery	176
1978	Willie Carson	182
1979	Joe Mercer	164
1980	Willie Carson	165
1981	Lester Piggott	179
1982	Lester Piggott	188
1983	Willie Carson	159
1984	Steve Cauthen	130
1985	Steve Cauthen	195
1986	Pat Eddery	177
1987	Steve Cauthen	197
1988	Pat Eddery	183
1989	Pat Eddery	171

Most times champion:
26 Gordon Richards, as above
14 George Fordham 1855-63, 1865, 1867-9, 1871*
13 Fred Archer 1874-86
    Elnathan Flatman 1840-52
11 Lester Piggott, as above
10 Steve Donoghue, as above
* shared title

Sir Gordon Richards on Pinza *in the unsaddling ring after winning the 1953 Derby. The great jockey had just been knighted, and this was his first ever win in the race, at his 28th attempt* (**Popperfoto**)

Progressive records of most wins in a season since 1840:
50 Elnathan Flatman 1840
68 Elnathan Flatman 1841
81 Elnathan Flatman 1845
81 Elnathan Flatman 1846
89 Elnathan Flatman 1847
104 Elnathan Flatman 1848
108 George Fordham 1856
118 George Fordham 1859
146 George Fordham 1860
166 George Fordham 1862
172 Fred Archer 1875
207 Fred Archer 1876
218 Fred Archer 1877
229 Fred Archer 1878
232 Fred Archer 1883
241 Fred Archer 1884
246 Fred Archer 1885
259 Gordon Richards 1933
269 Gordon Richards 1947

Most career wins in Britain

Wins	Jockey	Years
4870	Gordon Richards	1921-54
4349	Lester Piggott	1948-85
3111	Doug Smith	1931-67
2967	Willie Carson	1962-89
2810	Joe Mercer	1950-85
2748	Fred Archer	1870-86
2699	Pat Eddery	1969-89
2591	Edward Hide	1951-85
2587	George Fordham	1850-84
2313	Eph Smith	1930-65
2161	Scobie Breasley	1950-68
2067	Bill Nevett	1924-56

LEADING TRAINERS *Since 1945*

		£
1945	Walter Earl	29,557
1946	Frank Butters	56,140
1947	Fred Darling	65,313
1948	Noel Murless	66,542
1949	Frank Butters	71,721
1950	Charles Semblat (Fra)	57,044
1951	Jack Jarvis	56,397
1952	Marcus Marsh	92,093
1953	Jack Jarvis	71,546
1954	Cecil Boyd-Rochfort	65,326
1955	Cecil Boyd-Rochfort	74,424
1956	Charles Elsey	61,621
1957	Noel Murless	116,898
1958	Cecil Boyd-Rochfort	84,186
1959	Noel Murless	145,727
1960	Noel Murless	118,327
1961	Noel Murless	95,972
1962	Dick Hern	70,206
1963	Paddy Prendergast (Ire)	125,294
1964	Paddy Prendergast (Ire)	128,102
1965	Paddy Prendergast (Ire)	75,323
1966	Vincent O'Brien (Ire)	123,848
1967	Noel Murless	256,899
1968	Noel Murless	141,508
1969	Arthur Budgett	105,349
1970	Noel Murless	199,524
1971	Ian Balding	157,488
1972	Dick Hern	206,767
1973	Noel Murless	132,984
1974	Peter Walwyn	206,445
1975	Peter Walwyn	382,527
1976	Henry Cecil	261,301
1977	Vincent O'Brien (Ire)	439,124
1978	Henry Cecil	382,812
1979	Henry Cecil	683,971
1980	Dick Hern	831,964
1981	Michael Stoute	723,786
1982	Henry Cecil	872,614
1983	Dick Hern	549,598
1984	Henry Cecil	551,939
1985	Henry Cecil	1,148,206
1986	Michael Stoute	1,269,933
1987	Henry Cecil	1,896,689
1988	Henry Cecil	1,186,122
1989	Henry Cecil	2,000,330

Most times leading trainer (since 1896): 12 Alec Taylor 1907, 1909-10, 1914, 1917-23, 1925; 9 Noel Murless, as above; 8 Frank Butters 1927-8, 1932, 1934-5, 1944, 1946, 1949; 8 Henry Cecil, as above; 6 Fred Darling 1926, 1933, 1940-2, 1947

LEADING OWNERS *Since 1945*

		£
1945	17th Earl of Derby	25,067
1946	HH Aga Khan III	24,118
1947	HH Aga Khan III	44,020
1948	HH Aga Khan III	46,393
1949	HH Aga Khan III	68,916
1950	Marcel Boussac	57,044
1951	Marcel Boussac	39,339
1952	HH Aga Khan III	92,518
1953	Sir Victor Sassoon	58,579
1954	HM The Queen	40,993
1955	Lady Zia Wernher	46,345
1956	Major Lionel Holliday	39,327
1957	HM The Queen	62,211
1958	John McShain	63,264
1959	Prince Aly Khan	100,668
1960	Sir Victor Sassoon	90,069
1961	Major Lionel Holliday	39,227
1962	Major Lionel Holliday	70,206
1963	Jim Mullion	68,882
1964	Mrs Howell Jackson	98,270
1965	Jean Ternynck	65,301
1966	Lady Zia Wernher	78,075
1967	Jim Joel	120,925
1968	Raymond Guest	97,075
1969	David Robinson	92,553

1970	Charles Engelhard	182,059
1971	Paul Mellon	138,786
1972	Mrs Jean Hislop	155,190
1973	Nelson Bunker Hunt	124,771
1974	Nelson Bunker Hunt	147,244
1975	Dr Carlo Vittadini	209,492
1976	Daniel Wildenstein	244,500
1977	Robert Sangster	348,023
1978	Robert Sangster	160,405
1979	Sir Michael Sobell	339,751
1980	Simon Weinstock	236,332
1981	HH Aga Khan IV	441,654
1982	Robert Sangster	397,749
1983	Robert Sangster	461,488
1984	Robert Sangster	395,901
1985	Sheikh Mohammed	1,082,502
1986	Sheikh Mohammad	830,121
1987	Sheikh Mohammad	1,232,240
1988	Sheikh Mohammad	1,143,343
1989	Sheikh Mohammad	1,296,148

Most times leading owner (since 1882): 13 HH Aga Khan III 1924, 1929-30, 1932, 1934-5, 1937, 1944, 1946-9, 1952; 6 17th Earl of Derby 1923, 1927-8, 1933, 1938, 1945; 5 Robert Sangster, as above; 5 Sheikh Mohammad, as above

LEADING MONEY WINNERS SEASON-BY-SEASON
The leading horses in terms of first prizemoney won each season in Britain since 1945 have been:

Year	Horse	£
1945	Sun Stream	13,685
1946	Airborne	20,345
1947	Migoli	17,215
1948	Black Tarquin	21,423
1949	Nimbus	30,236
1950	Palestine	21,583
1951	Supreme Court	36,016
1952	Tulyar	75,173
1953	Pinza	44,101
1954	Never Say Die	30,332
1955	Meld	42,562
1956	Ribot	23,727
1957	Crepello	32,257
1958	Ballymoss	38,686
1959	Petite Etoile	55,487
1960	St.Paddy	71,256
1961	Sweet Solera	36,988
1962	Hethersett	38,497
1963	Ragusa	66,011
1964	Santa Claus	72,067
1965	Sea Bird II	65,301
1966	Charlottown	78,075
1967	Royal Palace	92,998
1968	Sir Ivor	97,075
1969	Blakeney	63,108
1970	Nijinsky	159,681
1971	Mill Reef	121,913

1972	Brigadier Gerard	151,213
1973	Dahlia	79,230
1974	Dahlia	120,771
1975	Grundy	188,375
1976	Wollow	166,389
1977	The Minstrel	201,184
1978	Ile de Bourbon	136,012
1979	Troy	310,359
1980	Ela-Mana-Mou	236,332
1981	Shergar	295,654
1982	Kalaglow	242,304
1983	Sun Princess	221,356
1984	Secreto (USA)	227,680
1985	Oh So Sharp	311,576
1986	Dancing Brave	423,601
1987	Reference Point	683,029
1988	Mtoto	412,002
1989	Nashwan	772,045

All winners 3-year olds except the following: Ribot, Ballymoss, Brigadier Gerard, Dahlia (1974), Kalaglow

INTERNATIONAL CLASSIFICATION
The official Handicappers in Great Britain, Ireland and France have jointly compiled International Classifications each year from 1977. Racing in Italy and West Germany was added from 1985. These ratings are now produced for six categories: colts and fillies each at 2-y-o and 3-y-o, older male and older female. The highest rating overall has been achieved by the following horses each year:

1977	Alleged (Ire) 3-y-o 138
1978	Alleged (Ire) 4-y-o 140
1979	Three Troikas # (Fra) 3-y-o 137
1980	Moorestyle (UK) 3-y-o 131
1981	Shergar (UK) 3-y-o 140
1982	Golden Fleece (Ire) 3-y-o 134
1983	Shareef Dancer (UK) 3-y-o 133
1984	El Gran Senor (Ire) 3-y-o 138
1985	Slip Anchor (UK) 3-y-o 135
1986	Dancing Brave (UK) 3-y-o 141
1987	Reference Point (UK) 3-y-o 135
1988	Warning (UK) 3-y-o 133
1989	Old Vic (Ire) 3-y-o 134
	Zilzal (Fra) 3-y-o 134

fillies

RACEGOERS CLUB 'RACEHORSE OF THE YEAR' CHAMPIONSHIP
Introduced by the Racecourse Association in 1965, the Racegoers Club took over reponsibility for the award in 1978. Their members take part in a poll each year to decide their 'Horse of the Year'. *Winners:*

1965	Sea Bird II
1966	Charlottown
1967	Busted
1968	Sir Ivor
1969	Park Top
1970	Nijinsky

1971	Mill Reef		
1972	Brigadier Gerard		
1973-	4 Dahlia		
1975	Grundy		
1976	Pawneese		
1977	The Minstrel		
1978	Shirley Heights		
1979	Troy		
1980	Moorestyle		
1981	Shergar		
1982	Ardross		
1983	Habibti		
1984	Provideo		
1985	Pebbles		
1986	Dancing Brave		
1987	Reference Point		
1988	Mtoto		
1989	Nashwan		

NATIONAL HUNT RACING
(Steeplechase and hurdling in Britain)

GRAND NATIONAL

The most famous steeplechase in the world has been run annually at Aintree, Liverpool since 1847 with the exception of the war years. It was held at Gatwick in 1916-8. It was run at Aintree as the Grand Liverpool Steeple Chase 1839-42 and as the Liverpool and national Steeple Chase 1843-6. Also shown below are the winners of a preceding steeplechase run at a course in Maghull, some four miles from the present site at Aintree, in 1836-8. The current course takes in 30 fences over two circuits and is 4 miles 4 furlongs long. *Winners: (Amateur riders have their titles, e.g. Mr., Capt.). Weights are shown in stones and pounds.)*

Year	Winner	Weight	Jockey
1836	The Duke	-	-
1837	The Duke	12-0	Mr. Potts
1838	Sir William	12-0	Tom Oliver
1839	Lottery	12-0	Jem Mason
1840	Jerry	12-0	Mr. B.Bretherton
1841	Charity	12-0	H.N.Powell
1842	Gay Lad	12-0	Tom Oliver
1843	Vanguard	11-10	Tom Oliver
1844	Discount	10-12	H.Crickmere
1845	Cureall	11-5	Bill Loft
1846	Pioneer	11-12	W.Taylor
1847	Matthew	10-6	Denny Wynne
1848	Chandler	11-12	Capt. Josey Little
1849	Peter Simple	11-0	Tom Cunningham
1850	Abd-el-Kader	9-12	Chris Green
1851	Abd-el-Kader	10-4	T.Abbott
1852	Miss Mowbray	10-4	Mr. Alec Goodman
1853	Peter Simple	10-10	Tom Oliver
1854	Bourton	11-12	J.Tasker
1855	Wanderer	9-8	J.Hanlon
1856	Freetrader	9-6	George Stevens
1857	Emigrant	9-10	Charlie Boyce
1858	Little Charley	10-7	William Archer
1859	Half Caste	9-7	Chris Green
1860	Anatis	9-10	Mr. Tommy Pickernell
1861	Jealousy	9-12	Joe Kendall
1862	Huntsman	11-0	Harry Lamplugh
1863	Emblem	10-10	George Stevens
1864	Emblematic	10-6	George Stevens
1865	Alcibiade	11-4	Capt. Bee Coventry
1866	Salamnader	10-7	Mr. Alec Goodman
1867	Cortolvin	11-13	John Page
1868	The Lamb	10-7	Mr. George Ede
1869	The Colonel	10-7	George Stevens
1870	The Colonel	11-12	George Stevens
1871	The Lamb	11-4	Mr. Tommy Pickernell
1872	Casse Tête	10-0	John Page
1873	Disturbance	11-11	Mr.Maunsell Richardson
1874	Reugny	10-12	Mr.Maunsell Richardson
1875	Pathfinder	10-11	Mr. Tommy Pickernell
1876	Regal	11-3	Joe Cannon
1877	Austerlitz	10-8	Mr. Fred Hobson
1878	Shifnal	10-12	Jack Jones
1879	The Liberator	11-4	Mr. Garrett Moore
1880	Empress	10-7	Mr. Tommy Beasley
1881	Woodbrook	11-3	Mr. Tommy Beasley
1882	Seaman	11-6	Lord Manners
1883	Zoëdone	11-0	Count Graf Karl Kinsky
1884	Voluptuary	10-5	Mr. Ted Wilson
1885	Roquefort	11-0	Mr. Ted Wilson
1886	Old Joe	10-9	Tom Skelton
1887	Gamecock	11-0	Bill Daniels
1888	Playfair	10-7	George Mawson
1889	Frigate	11-5	Mr. Tommy Beasley
1890	Ilex	10-5	Arthur Nightingall
1891	Come Away	11-12	Mr. Harry Beasley
1892	Father O'Flynn	10-5	Capt. Roddy Owen
1893	Cloister	12-7	Bill Dollery
1894	Why Not	11-3	Arthur Nightingall
1895	Wild Man from Borneo	10-1	Mr. Joe Widger
1896	The Soarer	9-13	Mr. David Campbell
1897	Manifesto	11-3	Terry Kavanagh
1898	Drogheda	10-12	John Gourley
1899	Manifesto	12-7	George Williamson
1900	Ambush II	11-3	Algy Anthony
1901	Grudon	10-0	Arthur Nightingall
1902	Shannon Lass	10-1	David Read
1903	Drumcree	11-3	Percy Woodland
1904	Moifaa	10-7	Arthur Birch
1905	Kirkland	11-5	Tich Mason
1906	Ascetic's Silver	10-9	Hon.Aubrey Hastings
1907	Eremon	10-1	Alf Newey
1908	Rubio	10-5	Henry Bletsoe
1909	Lutteur III	10-11	George Parfrement
1910	Jenkinstown	10-5	Bob Chadwick
1911	Glenside	10-3	Mr. Jack Anthony
1912	Jerry M	12-7	Ernie Piggott
1913	Covertcoat	11-6	Percy Woodland
1914	Sunloch	9-7	William Smith

1915	Ally Sloper	10-6	Mr. Jack Anthony
1916	Vermouth	11-10	John Reardon
1917	Ballymacad	9-12	Ted Driscoll
1918	Poethlyn	11-6	Ernie Piggott
1919	Poethlyn	12-7	Ernie Piggott
1920	Troytown	11-9	Mr. Jack Anthony
1921	Shaun Spadah	11-7	Dick Rees
1922	Music Hall	11-8	Bilbie Rees
1923	Sergeant Murphy	11-3	Capt. Tuppy Bennett
1924	Master Robert	10-5	Bob Trudgill
1925	Double Chance	10-9	Major Jack Wilson
1926	Jack Horner	10-5	Billy Watkinson
1927	Sprig	12-4	Ted Leader
1928	Tipperary Tim	10-0	Mr. Bill Dutton
1929	Gregalach	11-4	Bob Everett
1930	Shaun Goilin	11-0	Tommy Cullinan
1931	Grakle	11-7	Bob Lyall
1932	Forbra	10-7	Jim Hamey
1933	Kellsboro' Jack	11-9	Dudley Williams
1934	Golden Miller	12-2	Gerry Wilson
1935	Reynoldstown	11-4	Mr. Frank Furlong
1936	Reynoldstown	12-2	Mr. Fulke Walwyn
1937	Royal Mail	11-13	Evan Williams
1938	Battleship	11-6	Bruce Hobbs
1939	Workman	10-6	Tim Hyde
1940	Bogskar	10-4	Mervyn Jones
1946	Lovely Cottage	10-8	Capt. Bobby Petre
1947	Caughoo	10-0	Eddie Dempsey
1948	Sheila's Cottage	10-7	Arthur Thompson
1949	Russian Hero	10-8	Leo McMorrow
1950	Freebooter	11-11	Jimmy Power
1951	Nickel Coin	10-1	Johnny Bullock
1952	Teal	10-12	Arthur Thompson
1953	Early Mist	11-2	Bryan Marshall
1954	Royal Tan	11-7	Bryan Marshall
1955	Quare Times	11-0	Pat Taaffe
1956	E.S.B.	11-3	Dave Dick
1957	Sundew	11-7	Fred Winter
1958	Mr. What	10-6	Arthur Freeman
1959	Oxo	10-13	Michael Scudamore
1960	Merryman II	10-12	Gerry Scott
1961	Nicolaus Silver	10-1	Bobby Beasley
1962	Kilmore	10-4	Fred Winter
1963	Ayala	10-0	Pat Buckley
1964	Team Spirit	10-3	Willie Robinson
1965	Jay Trump	11-5	Mr. Tommy Smith
1966	Anglo	10-0	Tim Norman
1967	Foinavon	10-0	John Buckingham
1968	Red Alligator	10-0	Brian Fletcher
1969	Highland Wedding	10-4	Eddie Harty
1970	Gay Trip	11-5	Pat Taaffe
1971	Specify	10-13	John Cook
1972	Well To Do	10-1	Graham Thorner
1973	Red Rum	10-5	Brian Fletcher
1974	Red Rum	12-0	Brian Fletcher
1975	L'Escargot	11-3	Tommy Carberry
1976	Rag Trade	10-12	John Burke
1977	Red Rum	11-8	Tommy Stack
1978	Lucius	10-9	Bob Davies
1979	Rubstic	10-0	Maurice Barnes
1980	Ben Nevis	10-12	Mr. Charlie Fenwick
1981	Aldaniti	10-13	Bob Champion
1982	Grittar	11-5	Mr. Dick Saunders
1983	Corbière	11-4	Ben De Haan
1984	Hallo Dandy	10-2	Neale Doughty
1985	Last Suspect	10-5	Hywel Davies
1986	West Tip	10-11	Richard Dunwoody
1987	Maori Venture	10-13	Steve Knight
1988	Rhyme'N Reason	10-11	Brendan Powell
1989	Little Polveir	10-3	Jimmy Frost
1990	Mr Frisk	10-6	Mr. Marcus Armytage

Most wins
Horse: 3 Red Rum, 2 Abd-el-Kader, Peter Simple, The Colonel, The Lamb, Manifesto, Reynoldstown, Poethlyn
Jockey: 5 George Stevens, 3 Tom Oliver, Mr. Tommy Pickernell, Mr. Tommy Beasley, Arthur Nightingall, Ernie Piggott, Mr. Jack Anthony, Brian Fletcher
Trainer: 4 Fred Rimell 1956, 1961, 1970, 1976
4 Aubrey Hastings 1906, 1915, 1917*, 1924
3 William Holman 1856, 1858, 1860
3 William Moore 1894, 1896, 1899
3 Tom Coulthwaite 1907, 1910, 1931
3 Vincent O'Brien 1953-5
3 Neville Crump 1948, 1952, 1960
3 Donald McCain 1973-4, 1977
3 Tim Forster 1972, 1980, 1985
* Gatwick race
Owner: 3 James Machell 1873-4, 1876; Sir Charles Assheton-Smith 1893, 1912-3; Noel Le Mare 1973-4, 1977
Fastest winning time: 8:47.8 Mr Frisk 1990
Record field: 66 in 1929
Richest prize: £70,870 by Mr Frisk in 1990

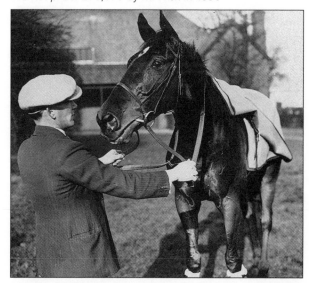

Golden Miller, *the greatest steeplechaser of his age, won the Cheltenham Gold Cup five times in succession, 1932-6, as well as the Grand National in 1934* (Hulton-Deutsch)

CHELTENHAM GOLD CUP

The Cheltenham Gold Cup is the most prestigious race on the National Hunt calendar in Britain. It was first held in 1924; the course has varied over the years but is now 3 miles 2 furlongs over 22 fences. Since 1980 the race has been sponsored by the Horserace Totalisator Board. There was no race in 1931, 1937, 1943-4. All horses now carry 12 stone.

Year	Winner	Jockey
1924	Red Splash	Dick Rees
1925	Ballinode	Ted Leader
1926	Koko	Tim Hamey
1927	Thrown In	Mr. Hugh Grosvenor
1928	Patron Saint	Dick Rees
1929	Easter Hero	Dick Rees
1930	Easter Hero	Tommy Cullinan
1932	Golden Miller	Ted Leader
1933	Golden Miller	Billy Stott
1934	Golden Miller	Gerry Wilson
1935	Golden Miller	Gerry Wilson
1936	Golden Miller	Evan Williams
1938	Morse Code	Danny Morgan
1939	Brendan's Cottage	George Owen
1940	Roman Hackle	Evan Williams
1941	Poet Prince	Roger Burford
1942	Médoc II	Frenchie Nicholson
1945	Red Rower	Davy Jones
1946	Prince Regent	Tim Hyde
1947	Fortina	Mr. Dick Black
1948	Cottage Rake	Aubrey Brabazon
1949	Cottage Rake	Aubrey Brabazon
1950	Cottage Rake	Aubrey Brabazon
1951	Silver Fame	Martin Molony
1952	Mont Tremblant	Dave Dick
1953	Knock Hard	Tim Molony
1954	Four Ten	Tommy Cusack
1955	Gay Donald	Tony Grantham
1956	Limber Hill	Jimmy Power
1957	Linwell	Michael Scudamore
1958	Kerstin	Stan Hayhurst
1959	Roddy Owen	Bobby Beasley
1960	Pas Seul	Bill Rees
1961	Saffron Tartan	Fred Winter
1962	Mandarin	Fred Winter
1963	Mill House	Willie Robinson
1964	Arkle	Pat Taaffe
1965	Arkle	Pat Taaffe
1966	Arkle	Pat Taaffe
1967	Woodland Venture	Terry Biddlecombe
1968	Fort Leney	Pat Taaffe
1969	What a Myth	Paul Kelleway
1970	L'Escargot	Tommy Carberry
1971	L'Escargot	Tommy Carberry
1972	Glencaraig Lady	Frank Berry
1973	The Dikler	Ron Barry
1974	Captain Christy	Bobby Beasley
1975	Ten Up	Tommy Carberry
1976	Royal Frolic	John Burke

Year	Winner	Jockey
1977	Davy Lad	Dessie Hughes
1978	Midnight Court	John Francome
1979	Alverton	Jonjo O'Neill
1980	Master Smudge	Richard Hoare
1981	Little Owl	Mr. Jim Wilson
1982	Silver Buck	Robert Earnshaw
1983	Bregawn	Graham Bradley
1984	Burrough Hill Lad	Phil Tuck
1985	Forgive'N'Forget	Martin Dwyer
1986	Dawn Run	Jonjo O'Neill
1987	The Thinker	Ridley Lamb
1988	Charter Party	Richard Dunwoody
1989	Desert Orchid	Simon Sherwood
1990	Norton's Coin	Graham McCourt

Most wins

Horse: 5 Golden Miller, 3 Cottage Rake, Arkle; 2 Easter Hero, L'Escargot

Jockey: 4 Pat Taafe, 3 Dick Rees, Aubrey Brabazon, Tommy Carberry

Trainer: 5 Tom Dreaper 1946, 1964-6, 1968; 4 Basil Briscoe 1932-5; Vincent O'Brien 1948-50, 1953; Fulke Walwyn 1952, 1962-3, 1973

Owner: 7 Miss Dorothy Paget 1932-6, 1940, 1952; 4 Anne, Duchess of Westminster 1964-6, 1975; 3 Frank Vickerman 1948-50

Fastest winning time: 6:23.4 Silver Fame 1951

CHAMPION HURDLE

The leading race in England for hurdlers, the Champion Hurdle was inaugurated in 1927. It is raced at Cheltenham during the Spring Festival meeting and is over two miles. Since 1978 it has been sponsored by Waterford Crystal. There was no race in 1931, 1943-4. The current weights are 11st 6lb for 4-year olds, 12st for older horses with a 5lb allowance for mares.

Year	Winner	Jockey
1927	Blaris	George Duller
1928	Brown Jack	Bilbie Rees
1929	Royal Falcon	Dick Rees
1930	Brown Tony	Tommy Cullinan
1932	Insurance	Ted Leader
1933	Insurance	Billy Stott
1934	Chenango	Danny Morgan
1935	Lion Courage	Gerry Wilson
1936	Victor Norman	Frenchie Nicholson
1937	Free Fare	Georges Pellerin
1938	Our Hope	Capt. Perry Harding
1939	African Sister	Keith Piggott
1940	Solford	Sean Magee
1941	Seneca	Ron Smyth
1942	Forestation	Ron Smyth
1945	Brains Trust	Fred Rimell
1946	Distel	Bobby O'Ryan
1947	National Spirit	Danny Morgan
1948	National Spirit	Ron Smyth
1949	Hatton's Grace	Aubrey Brabazon

Year	Winner	Jockey
1950	Hatton's Grace	Aubrey Brabazon
1951	Hatton's Grace	Tim Molony
1952	Sir Ken	Tim Molony
1953	Sir Ken	Tim Molony
1954	Sir Ken	Tim Molony
1955	Clair Soliel	Fred Winter
1956	Doorknocker	Harry Sprague
1957	Merry Deal	Grenville Underwood
1958	Bandalore	George Slack
1959	Fare Time	Fred Winter
1960	Another Flash	Bobby Beasley
1961	Eborneezer	Fred Winter
1962	Anzio	Willie Robinson
1963	Winning Fair	Mr. Alan Lillingston
1964	Magic Court	Pat McCarron
1965	Kirriemuir	Willie Robinson
1966	Salmon Spray	Johnny Haine
1967	Saucy Kit	Roy Edwards
1968	Persian War	Jimmy Uttley
1969	Persian War	Jimmy Uttley
1970	Persian War	Jimmy Uttley
1971	Bula	Paul Kelleway
1972	Bula	Paul Kelleway
1973	Comedy of Errors	Bill Smith
1974	Lanzarote	Richard Pitman
1975	Comedy of Errors	Ken White
1976	Night Nurse	Paddy Broderick
1977	Night Nurse	Paddy Broderick
1978	Monksfield	Tommy Kinane
1979	Monksfield	Dessie Hughes
1980	Sea Pigeon	Jonjo O'Neill
1981	Sea Pigeon	John Francome
1982	For Auction	Mr. Colin Magnier
1983	Gaye Brief	Richard Linley
1984	Dawn Run	Jonjo O'Neill
1985	See You Then	Steve Smith-Eccles
1986	See You Then	Steve Smith-Eccles
1987	See You Then	Steve Smith-Eccles
1988	Celtic Shot	Peter Scudamore
1989	Beech Road	Richard Guest
1990	Kribensis	Richard Dunwoody

Most wins

Horse: 3 Hatton's Grace, Sir Ken, Persian War, See You Then; 2 Insurance, National Spirit, Bula, Comedy of Errors, Night Nurse, Monksfield, Sea Pigeon
Jockey: 4 Tim Moloney, 3 Ron Smyth, Fred Winter, Jimmy Uttley, Steve Smith-Eccles
Trainer: 5 Peter Easterby 1967, 1976-7, 1980-1; 4 Vic Smyth 1941-2, 1947-8; Fred Winter 1971-2, 1974, 1988; 3 Vincent O'Brien 1949-51; Willie Stephenson 1952-4; Ryan Price 1955, 1959, 1961; Colin Davies 1968-70; Nicky Henderson 1985-7
Owner: 4 Miss Dorothy Paget 1932-3, 1940, 1946; 3 Mrs.Moya Keogh 1949-51; Maurice Kingsley 1952-4; Henry Alper 1968-70; Stype Wood Stud Ltd. 1985-7
Fastest winning time: 3:50.7 Kribensis 1990

OTHER PRINCIPAL NATIONAL HUNT RACES

TOTE/SCHWEPPES GOLD TROPHY

A handicap hurdle race, the Schweppes Gold Trophy was first run at Liverpool in 1963 but since 1964 has been run over two miles at Newbury. There was no race in 1969-70, 1974, 1978, 1981, 1983 and 1985-6. The Tote Gold Trophy from 1987.

Year	Winner	Weight	Jockey
1963	Rosyth	10-0	Josh Gifford
1964	Rosyth	10-2	Josh Gifford
1965	Elan	10-7	David Nicholson
1966	Le Vermontois	11-3	Josh Gifford
1967	Hill House	10-10	Josh Gifford
1968	Persian War	11-13	Jimmy Uttley
1971	Cala Mesquida	10-9	John Cook
1972	Good Review	10-9	Val O'Brien
1973	Indianapolis	10-6	John King
1975	Tammuz	10-13	Bill Smith
1976	Irish Fashion	10-4	Ron Barry
1977	True Lad	10-4	Tommy Stack
1979	Within the Law	11-4	Alan Brown
1980	Bootlaces	10-9	Paul Leach
1982	Donegal Prince	10-8	John Francome
1984	Ra Nova	10-6	Patrick Farrell
1987	Neblin	10-0	Stan Moore
1988	Jamesmead	10-0	Brendan Powell
1989	Grey Salute	11-5	Richard Dunwoody
1990	Deep Sensation	11-3	Richard Rowe

WHITBREAD GOLD CUP

The Whitbread Gold Cup has a special place in British National Hunt racing, as when inaugurated in 1957 it was the first race to attract major commercial sponsorship. Run at Sandown Park over 3 miles 5 furlongs 18 yards. The 1973 race was at Newcastle.

Year	Winner	Weight	Jockey
1957	Much Obliged	10-12	Henry East
1958	Taxidermist	10-8	John Lawrence
1959	Done Up	10-13	Harry Sprague
1960	Plummers Plain	10-0	Ron Harrison
1961	Pas Seul	12-0	Dave Dick
1962	Frenchman's Cove	11-3	Stan Mellor
1963	Hoodwinked	10-9	Paddy Buckley
1964	Dormant	9-7	Paddy Buckley
1965	Arkle	12-7	Pat Taaffe
1966	What a Myth	9-8	Paul Kelleway
1967	Mill House	11-11	David Nicholson
1968	Larbawn	10-9	Macer Gifford
1969	Larbawn	11-4	Josh Gifford
1970	Royal Toss	10-0	Richard Pitman
1971	Titus Oates	11-13	Ron Barry
1972	Grey Sombrero	9-10	Willie Shoemark
1973	Charlie Potheen	12-0	Ron Barry
1974	The Dikler	11-13	Ron Barry
1975	April Seventh	9-13	Stephen Knight
1976	Otter Way	10-10	John King

1977	Andy Pandy	10-12	John Burke
1978	Strombolus	10-0	Tommy Stack
1979	Diamond Edge	11-11	Bill Smith
1980	Royal Mail	11-5	Phillip Blacker
1981	Diamond Edge	11-7	Bill Smith
1982	Shady Deal	10-0	Richard Rowe
1983	Drumlargan	10-10	Mr. Frank Codd
1984	Special Cargo	11-2	Kevin Mooney
1985	By The Way	10-0	Robert Earnshaw
1986	Plundering	10-6	Simon Sherwood
1987	Lean Ar Aghaidh	9-10	Guy Landau
1988	Desert Orchid	11-11	Simon Sherwood
1989	Brown Windsor	10-0	Mark Bowlby
1990	Mr Frisk	10-5	Mr. Marcus Armytage

MACKESON GOLD CUP

Held annually at Cheltenham since 1960, with the exception of 1976 when it was run at Haydock Park. It is over 2 miles 4 furlongs.

Year	Winner	Weight	Jockey
1960	Fortria	12-8	Pat Taaffe
1961	Scottish Memories	10-7	Chris Finnegan
1962	Fortria	12-0	Pat Taaffe
1963	Richard of Bordeaux	10-5	Bobby Beasley
1964	Super Flash	10-5	Stan Mellor
1965	Dunkirk	12-7	Bill Rees
1966	Pawnbroker	11-9	Paddy Broderick
1967	Charlie Worcester	10-11	Josh Gifford
1968	Jupiter Boy	10-3	Eddie Harty
1969	Gay Trip	11-5	Terry Biddlecombe
1970	Chatham	10-3	Ken White
1971	Gay Trip	11-3	Terry Biddlecombe
1972	Red Candle	10-0	Jim Fox
1973	Skymas	10-5	Tommy Murphy
1974	Bruslee	10-7	Andy Turnell
1975	Clear Cut	10-9	Dennis Greaves
1976	Cancello	11-1	Dennis Atkins
1977	Bachelor's Hall	10-6	Martin O'Halloran
1978	Bawnogues	10-7	Craig Smith
1979	Man Alive	10-9	Ron Barry
1980	Bright Highway	11-1	Gerry Newman
1981	Henry Kissinger	10-13	Paul Barton
1982	Fifty Dollars More	11-0	Richard Linley
1983	Pounentes	10-6	Neale Doughty
1984	Half Free	11-10	Richard Linley
1985	Half Free	11-10	Richard Linley
1986	Very Promising	11-13	Richard Dunwoody
1987	Beau Ranger	10-2	Mark Perrett
1988	Pegwell Bay	11-2	Peter Scudamore
1989	Joint Sovereignty	10-4	Graham McCourt

HENNESSY COGNAC GOLD CUP

Run at Newbury over 3 miles 2 furlongs 82 yards. Inaugurated in 1957, and run at Cheltenham 1957-9.

Year	Winner	Weight	Jockey
1957	Mandarin	11-0	Gerry Madden
1958	Taxidermist	11-1	John Lawrence
1959	Kerstin	11-10	Stan Hayhurst
1960	Knucklecracker	11-1	Derek Ancil
1961	Mandarin	11-5	Willie Robinson
1962	Springbok	10-8	Gerry Scott
1963	Mill House	12-0	Willie Robinson
1964	Arkle	12-7	Pat Taaffe
1965	Arkle	12-7	Pat Taaffe
1966	Stalbridge Colonist	10-2	Stan Mellor
1967	Rondetto	10-1	Jeff King
1968	Man Of The West	10-0	Willie Robinson
1969	Spanish Steps	11-6	John Cooke
1970	Border Mask	11-1	David Mould
1971	Bighorn	10-11	David Cartwright
1972	Charlie Potheen	11-4	Richard Pitman
1973	Red Candle	10-4	Jim Fox
1974	Royal Marshall II	10-0	Graham Thorner
1975	April Seventh	11-2	Andy Turnell
1976	Zeta's Son	10-9	Ian Watkinson
1977	Bachelor's Hall	10-10	Martin O'Halloran
1978	Approaching	10-6	Bob Champion
1979	Fighting Fit	11-7	Richard Linley
1980	Bright Highway	11-6	Gerry Newman
1981	Diamond Edge	11-10	Bill Smith
1982	Bregawn	11-10	Graham Bradley
1983	Brown Chamberlin	11-8	John Francome
1984	Burrough Hill Lad	12-0	John Francome
1985	Galway Blaze	10-0	Mark Dwyer
1986	Broadheath	10-5	Paul Nicholls
1987	Playschool	10-8	Paul Nicholls
1988	Strands of Gold	10-0	Peter Scudamore
1989	Ghofar	10-0	Hywel Davies

KING GEORGE VI CHASE

The traditional Boxing Day fixture over 3 miles at Kempton Park, first run in 1947, brings together a small, but quality field of steeplechasers. Not held due to bad weather in 1961-2, 1967-8, 1970, 1981.

Year	Winner	Weight	Jockey
1947	Rowland Roy	11-13	Bryan Marshall
1948	Cottage Rake	12-6	Aubrey Brabazon
1949	Finnure	11-10	Dick Francis
1950	Manicou	11-8	Bryan Marshall
1951	Statecraft	11-11	Anthony Grantham
1952	Halloween	11-13	Fred Winter
1953	Galloway Braes	12-6	Robert Morrow
1954	Halloween	12-10	Fred Winter
1955	Limber Hill	11-13	James Power
1956	Rose Park	11-7	Michael Scudamore
1957	Mandarin	12-0	Gerry Madden
1958	Lochroe	11-7	Arthur Freeman
1959	Mandarin	11-5	Gerry Madden
1960	Saffron Tartan	11-7	Fred Winter
1963	Mill House	12-0	Willie Robinson
1964	Frenchman's Cove	11-7	Stan Mellor
1965	Arkle	12-0	Pat Taaffe
1966	Dormant	11-0	John King
1969	Titus Oates	11-10	Stan Mellor
1971	The Dikler	11-7	Barry Brogan

1972	Pendil	12-0	Richard Pitman
1974	Captain Christy	12-0	Bobby Coonan
1975	Captain Christy	12-0	Gerry Newman
1976	Royal Marshall	11-7	Graham Thorner
1977	Bachelor's Hall	11-7	Martin O'Halloran
1978	Gay Spartan	11-10	Tommy Carmody
1979	Silver Buck	11-10	Tommy Carmody
1980	Silver Buck	11-10	Tommy Carmody
1982	Wayward Lad	11-10	John Francome
1983	Wayward Lad	11-10	Robert Earnshaw
1984	Burrough Hill Lad	11-10	John Francome
1985	Wayward Lad	11-10	Graham Bradley
1986	Desert Orchid	11-10	Colin Brown
1987	Nupsala	11-10	Andre Pommier
1988	Desert Orchid	11-10	Simon Sherwood
1989	Desert Orchid	11-10	Richard Dunwoody

CHAMPION JOCKEYS (NATIONAL HUNT)

Prior to the 1925-6 season the championship was decided by winners in a calendar year. Since then it has been taken over the season. *Leading jockeys since 1945-6.*

Year	Champion	Winners
1944-45	Frenchie Nicholson	15
	Fred Rimell	15
1945-46	Fred Rimell	54
1946-47	Jack Dowdeswell	58
1947-48	Bryan Marshall	66
1948-49	Tim Molony	60
1949-50	Tim Molony	95
1950-51	Tim Molony	83
1951-52	Tim Molony	99
1952-53	Fred Winter	121
1953-54	Dick Francis	76
1954-55	Tim Molony	67
1955-56	Fred Winter	74
1956-57	Fred Winter	80
1957-58	Fred Winter	82
1958-59	Tim Brookshaw	83
1959-60	Stan Mellor	68
1960-61	Stan Mellor	118
1961-62	Stan Mellor	80
1962-63	Josh Gifford	70
1963-64	Josh Gifford	94
1964-65	Terry Biddlecombe	114
1965-66	Terry Biddlecombe	102
1966-67	Josh Gifford	122
1967-68	Josh Gifford	82
1968-69	Bob Davies	77
	Terry Biddlecombe	77
1969-70	Bob Davies	91
1970-71	Graham Thorner	74
1971-72	Bob Davies	89
1972-73	Ron Barry	125
1973-74	Ron Barry	94
1974-75	Tommy Stack	82
1975-76	John Francome	96
1976-77	Tommy Stack	97
1977-78	Jonjo O'Neill	149
1978-79	John Francome	95

The great popular favourite, Desert Orchid, *with over £500,000 prize money from 32 wins, 10 second places and six thirds in 62 races between 1983 and 1990* (All-Sport)

1979-80	Jonjo O'Neill	115
1980-81	John Francome	105
1981-82	John Francome	120
	Peter Scudamore	120
1982-83	John Francome	106
1983-84	John Francome	131
1984-85	John Francome	101
1985-86	Peter Scudamore	91
1986-87	Peter Scudamore	123
1987-88	Peter Scudamore	132
1988-89	Peter Scudamore	221
1989-90	Peter Scudamore	170

Most times champion (since 1900): 7 Gerry Wilson
1932/3-1937/8, 1940/1; John Francome, as above; 6 Tich
Mason 1901-2, 1904-7; Peter Scudamore (incl.one shared)
as above; 5 Bilbie Rees 1920-1, 1924-5, 1926/7; Billy Stott
1927/8-1931/2; Tim Moloney, as above
*Progressive record of most wins in a season/year (since
1900):*
53 Mr. H.S.Sidney (1900)
58 Tich Mason (1901)
67 Tich Mason (1902)
73 Tich Mason (1905)
76 W Payne (1911)

*Peter Scudamore smashed the record for most winners in
a National Hunt season, when he passed the previous
record of 149 on 6 Feb 1989 and went on to a total of
221 from 663 rides* **(All-Sport/Simon Bruty)**

78 I.Anthony (1912)
78 Jack Anthony (1922)
108 Bilbie Rees (1924)
121 Fred Winter (1952-3)
122 Josh Gifford (1966-7)
125 Ron Barry (1972-3)
149 Jonjo O'Neill (1977-8)
221 Peter Scudamore (1988-9)

Most wins in a National Hunt career

Wins	Jockey	Years
1233	Peter Scudamore	1978-90
1138	John Francome	1970-85
1035	Stan Mellor	1952-72
923	Fred Winter	1939-64
911	Bob Davies	1966-82
908	Terry Biddlecombe	1958-74
885	Jonjo O'Neill	1972-86
823	Ron Barry	1964-83

VINCENT O'BRIEN IRISH GOLD CUP

Ireland's richest steeplechase, first run at Leopardstown in
1987 over 3 miles

Year	Winner	Jockey
1987	Forgive'N'Forget	Mark Dwyer
1988	Playschool	Paul Nicholls
1989	Carvill's Hill	Ken Morgan
1990	Nick the Brief	Michael Lynch

NATIONAL HUNT CHAMPION HORSE OF THE YEAR

Awarded to the champion jumper annually, the voting is
along similar lines to that for the flat racehorse of the year.
Winners:

1965-6	Arkle
1966-7	Mill House
1967-8	Persian War
1968-9	Persian War
1969-70	Persian War
1970-1	Bula
1971-2	Bula
1972-3	Pendil
1973-4	Red Rum
1974-5	Comedy of Errors
1975-6	Night Nurse
1976-7	Night Nurse
1977-8	Midnight Court
1978-9	Monksfield
1979-8	Sea Pigeon
1980-1	Sea Pigeon
1981-2	Silver Buck
1982-3	Gaye Brief
1983-4	Dawn Run
1984-5	Borough Hill Lad
1985-6	Dawn Run
1986-7	Desert Orchid
1987-8	Desert Orchid
1988-9	Desert Orchid

HORSE RACING IN THE USA

THE TRIPLE CROWN
Like the English Classics, the three races that make up the American Triple Crown are for 3-year-olds only.

KENTUCKY DERBY
Raced at Churchill Downs, Louisville over 1 mile 2 furlongs (1 mile 4 furlongs 1875-95). *Winners since 1970:*

Year	Winner	Jockey
1970	Dust Commander	Mike Manganello
1971	Canonero	Gustavo Avila
1972	Riva Ridge	Ron Turcotte
1973	Secretariat	Ron Turcotte
1974	Cannonade	Angel Cordero, Jnr
1975	Foolish Pleasure	Jacinto Vasquez
1976	Bold Forbes	Angel Cordero, Jnr
1977	Seattle Slew	Jean Cruguet
1978	Affirmed	Steve Cauthen
1979	Spectacular Bid	Ron Franklin
1980	Genuine Risk	Jacinto Vasquez
1981	Pleasant Colony	Jorge Velasquez
1982	Gato Del Sol	Eddie Delahoussaye
1983	Sunny's Halo	Eddie Delahoussaye
1984	Swale	Laffit Pincay, Jnr
1985	Spend A Buck	Angel Cordero, Jnr
1986	Ferdinand	Willie Shoemaker
1987	Alysheba	Chris McCarron
1988	Winning Colors	Gary Stevens
1989	Sunday Silence	Pat Valenzuela
1990	Unbridled	Craig Perret

Most wins
Jockey: 5 Eddie Arcaro 1938, 1941, 1945, 1948, 1952; 5 Bill Hartack 1957, 1960, 1962, 1964, 1969
Trainer: 6 Ben Jones 1938, 1941, 1944, 1948-9, 1952
Owner: 8 Calumet Farm 1941, 1944, 1948-9, 1952, 1957-8, 1968
Fastest time: 1 min 59.4 sec Secretariat 1973

PREAKNESS STAKES
Raced at Pimlico, Baltimore, Maryland.over 1 mile 1.5 furlongs (1 mile 4 furlongs 1873-88, and at distances between 1m 70y and 1 mile 2 furlongs 1889-1925). *Winners since 1970:*

1970	Personality	Eddie Belmonte
1971	Canonero	Gustavo Avila
1972	Bee Bee Bee	Eddie Nelson
1973	Secretariat	Ron Turcotte
1974	Little Current	Miguel Rivera
1975	Master Derby	Darrell McHargue
1976	Elocutionist	John Lively
1977	Seattle Slew	Jean Cruguet
1978	Affirmed	Steve Cauthen
1979	Spectacular Bid	Ron Franklin
1980	Codex	Angel Cordero, Jnr
1981	Pleasant Colony	Jorge Velasquez
1982	Aloma's Ruler	Jack Kaenel
1983	Deputed Testamony	Don Miller jr
1984	Gate Dancer	Angel Cordero, Jnr

Sunday Silence *(below)* won both the Kentucky Derby and Preakness Stakes from Easy Goer, *but the order was reversed in the Belmont Stakes* (**All-Sport**)

1985	Tank's Prospect	Pat Day
1986	Snow Chief	Alex Solis
1987	Alysheba	Chris McCarron
1988	Risen Star	Eddie Delahoussaye
1989	Sunday Silence	Pat Valenzuela
1990	Summer Squall	Pat Day

Most wins
Jockey: 6 Eddie Arcaro 1941, 1948, 1950-1, 1955, 1957
Trainer: 7 Robert Wyndham Walden 1875, 1878-82, 1888
Owner: 5 George Lorillard 1878-82
Fastest time: 1 min 53.2 sec Tank's Prospect 1985

BELMONT STAKES

The oldest of the three Triple Crown races, it was first held in 1867. Run over 1 mile 4 furlongs at Belmont Park, New York. Raced at 1 mile 5 furlongs 1867-73 and at shorter distances 1890-25, until the current distance of 1 mile 4 furlongs from 1926 *Winners since 1970:*

1970	Echelon	John Rotz
1971	Pass Catcher	Walter Blum
1972	Riva Ridge	Ron Turcotte
1973	Secretariat	Ron Turcotte
1974	Little Current	Miguel Rivera
1975	Avatar	Willie Shoemaker
1976	Bold Forbes	Angel Cordero, Jnr
1977	Seattle Slew	Jean Cruguet
1978	Affirmed	Steve Cauthen
1979	Coastal	Ruben Hernandez
1980	Temperence Hill	Eddie Maple
1981	Summing	George Martens
1982	Conquistador Cielo	Laffit Pincay, Jnr
1983	Caveat	Laffit Pincay, Jnr
1984	Swale	Laffit Pincay, Jnr
1985	Creme Fraiche	Eddie Maple
1986	Danzig Connection	Chris McCarron
1987	Bet Twice	Craig Perrett
1988	Risen Star	Eddie Delahoussaye
1989	Easy Goer	Pat Day
1990	Go And Go	Michael Kinane

Most wins
Jockey: 6 Jimmy McLaughlin 1882-4, 1886-8; 6 Eddie Arcaro 1941-2, 1945, 1948, 1952, 1955
Trainer: 8 James Rowe Sr 1883-4, 1901, 1904, 1907-8, 1910, 1913
Owner: 5 Dwyer Bros 1883-4, 1886-8; 5 James R.Keene 1901, 1904, 1907-8, 1910; 5 William Woodward Sr (Belair Stud) 1930, 1932, 1935-6, 1939
Fastest time: 2 min 24.0 sec Secretariat 1973 (won by a record 31 lengths)

The following 11 horses have successfully won all legs of the Triple Crown:
1919 Sir Barton 1930 Gallant Fox 1935 Omaha 1937 War Admiral 1941 Whirlaway 1943 Count Fleet 1946 Assault 1948 Citation 1973 Secretariat 1977 Seattle Slew 1978 Affirmed

THE BREEDERS' CUP

The Breeders' Cup programme was founded in 1984 and administered by breeders with the aim of stimulating throughbred racing in the USA. The series offers more than $20 million annually, $10 million in the seven races run on the Breeders' Cup Event Day each November. The top purse, $3 million, is for the Breeders' Cup Classic ($1.35m to the winning owner). The purse for the Breeders' Cup Turf is $2 million, and the other races are each for $1 million. Various venues have been used, from the first meeting at Hollywood Park in 1984. Distances shown are those run in 1989 *Winners:*

BREEDERS' CUP SPRINT (6 furlongs)

1984	Ellio	Craig Perret
1985	Precisionist	Chris McCarron
1986	Smile	Jacinto Vasquez
1987	Very Subtle	Pat Valenzuela
1988	Gulch	Angel Cordero
1989	Dancing Spree	Angel Cordero

BREEDERS' CUP JUVENILE FILLIES (1 mile 110y)

1984	Outstandingly	Walter Guerra
1985	Twilight Ridge	Jorge Velasquez
1986	Brave Raj	Pat Valenzuela
1987	Epitome	Pat Day
1988	Open Mind	Angel Cordero
1989	Go For Wand	Randy Romero

BREEDERS' CUP DISTAFF (1 mile 1 furlong)

1984	Princess Rooney	Eddie Delahoussaye
1985	Life's Magic	Angel Cordero, Jnr
1986	Lady's Secret	Pat Day
1987	Sacahuista	Randy Romero
1988	Personal Ensign	Randy Romero
1989	Bayakoa	Laffit Pincay, Jnr

BREEDERS' CUP MILE

1984	Royal Heroine	Fernando Toro
1985	Cozzene	Walter Guerra
1986	Last Tycoon	Yves St.Martin
1987	Miesque	Freddy Head
1988	Miesque	Freddy Head
1989	Steinlen	Jose Santos

BREEDERS' CUP JUVENILE (1 mile 110y)

1984	Chief's Crown	Don MacBeth
1985	Tasso	Laffit Pincay, Jnr
1986	Capote	Laffit Pincay, Jnr
1987	Success Express	Jose Santos
1988	Is It True?	Laffit Pincay, Jnr
1989	Rhythm	Craig Perret

BREEDERS' CUP TURF (1.5 miles)

| 1984 | Lashkari | Yves St.Martin |
| 1985 | Pebbles | Pat Eddery |

1986	Manila	Jose Santos
1987	Theatrical	Pat Day
1988	Great Communicator	Ray Sibille
1989	Prized	Eddie Delahoussaye

BREEDERS' CUP CLASSIC
(1 mile 2 furlongs)

1984	Wild Again	Pat Day
1985	Proud Truth	Jorge Velasquez
1986	Skywalker	Laffit Pincay, Jnr
1987	Ferdinand	Willie Shoemaker
1988	Alysheba	Chris McCarron
1989	Sunday Silence	Chris McCarron

Most wins

Jockeys: 5 Laffit Pincay, Jnr; 4 Pat Day, Angel Cordero; 3 Chris McCarron, Jorge Velasquez, Jose Santos, Randy Romero
Trainer: 10 D.Wayne Lukas

ARLINGTON MILLION

A weight-for-age race for 3-year-olds and upwards run annually from 1981 at Arlington Park, Chicago.

1981	John Henry	Willie Shoemaker
1982	Perrault	Laffit Pincay, Jnr
1983	Tolomeo	Pat Eddery

1984	John Henry	Chris McCarron
1985	Teleprompter	Tony Ives
1986	Estrapade	Fernandez Toro
1987	Manila	Angel Cordero
1988	Mill Native	Cash Asmussen
1989	Steinlen	Jose Santos

WASHINGTON DC INTERNATIONAL

The Washington International was the idea of John D.Schapiro, the president of Laurel Racecourse in Maryland. The first International was at Laurel Park in October 1952 and was run over 1 mile 2 furlongs. The race showed a steady decline in international status in recent years, and Schapiro sold his interest in the track in 1984.

Most wins

Horse: 2 Bald Eagle (1959-60), Fort Marcy (1967, 1970), *Jockey:* 3 Lester Piggott (Sir Ivor 1968, Karabas 1969, Argument 1980); Manuel Ycaza (Bald Eagle 1959-60, Fort Marcy 1967)

Alysheba, the biggest money winner in history, retired after victory in the 1988 Breeders' Cup Classic (All-Sport)

ANNUAL US LEADING MONEY-WINNING HORSES
from 1946

Year	Leading horse	$
1946	Assault	424,195
1947	Armed	376,325
1948	Citation	709,470
1949	Ponder	321,825
1950	Noor	346,940
1951	Counterpoint	250,525
1952	Crafty Admiral	277,255
1953	Native Dancer	513,425
1954	Determine	328,700
1955	Nashua	752,550
1956	Needles	440,850
1957	Round Table	600,383
1958	Round Table	662,780
1959	Sword Dancer	537,004
1960	Bally Ache	455,045
1961	Carry Back	565,349
1962	Never Bend	402,969
1963	Candy Spots	604,481
1964	Gun Bow	580,100
1965	Buckpasser	568,096
1966	Buckpasser	669,078
1967	Damascus	817,941
1968	Forward Pass	546,674
1969	Arts and Letters	555,604
1970	Personality	444,049
1971	Riva Ridge	503,263
1972	Droll Roll	471,633
1973	Secretariat	860,404
1974	Chris Evert	551,063
1975	Foolish Pleasure	716,278
1976	Forego	491,701
1977	Seattle Slew	641,370
1978	Affirmed	901,541
1979	Spectacular Bid	1,279,334
1980	Temperance Hill	1,130,452
1981	John Henry	1,148,800
1982	Perrault	1,197,400
1983	All Along	2,138,963
1984	Slew O'Gold	2,627,944
1985	Spend A Buck	3,552,704
1986	Snow Chief	1,875,200
1987	Alysheba	2,511,156
1988	Alysheba	3,808,600
1989	Sunday Silence	4,578,454

ANNUAL US LEADING MONEY-WINNING JOCKEYS from 1946

1946	Ted Atkinson	1,036,825
1947	Doug Dodson	1,429,949
1948	Eddie Arcaro	1,686,230
1949	Steve Brooks	1,316,817
1950	Eddie Arcaro	1,410,160
1951	Willie Shoemaker	1,329,890
1952	Eddie Arcaro	1,859,591
1953	Willie Shoemaker	1,784,187
1954	Willie Shoemaker	1,876,760
1955	Eddie Arcaro	1,864,796
1956	Bill Hartack	2,343,955
1957	Bill Hartack	3,060,501
1958	Willie Shoemaker	2,961,693
1959	Willie Shoemaker	2,843,133
1960	Willie Shoemaker	2,123,961
1961	Willie Shoemaker	2,690,819
1962	Willie Shoemaker	2,916,844
1963	Willie Shoemaker	2,526,925
1964	Willie Shoemaker	2,649,553
1965	Braulio Baeza	2,582,702
1966	Braulio Baeza	2,951,022
1967	Braulio Baeza	3,088,888
1968	Braulio Baeza	2,835,108
1969	Jorge Velasquez	2,542,315
1970	Laffit Pincay Jr	2,626,526
1971	Laffit Pincay Jr	3,784,377
1972	Laffit Pincay Jr	3,225,827
1973	Laffit Pincay Jr	4,093,492
1974	Laffit Pincay Jr	4,251,060
1975	Braulio Baeza	3,695,198
1976	Angel Cordero Jr	4,709,500
1977	Steve Cauthen	6,151,750
1978	Darrel McHargue	6,029,885
1979	Laffit Pincay Jr	8,913,535
1980	Chris McCarron	7,663,300
1981	Chris McCarron	8,397,604
1982	Angel Cordero Jr	9,483,590
1983	Angel Cordero Jr	10,116,697
1984	Chris McCarron	12,045,813
1985	Laffit Pincay	13,353,299
1986	Jose Santos	11,329,297
1987	Jose Santos	12,375,433
1988	Jose Santos	14,877,298
1989	Jose Santos	13,838,389

Total Career Earnings (US Dollars)

Horses

Alysheba	6,679,242	1986-8
John Henry	6,597,947	1977-84
Sunday Silence	4,600,154	1988-9
Easy Goer	4,534,650	1988-9
Spend A Buck	4,220,669	1984-5
Creme Fraiche	4,024,727	1984-6

Chris McCarron (All-Sport)

Jockeys	Dollars	Wins	Years
Laffit Pincay	148,112,855	7327	1966-89
Angel Cordero Jr	145,166,215	6549	1960-89
Willie Shoemaker	123,375,524	8833	1949-90
Chris McCarron	118,606,116	5101	1974-89
Jorge Velasquez	107,994,513	6116	1965-89
Pat Day	88,863,765	4642	1972-89

Note the lower money of the past:

Johnny Longden	24,665,800	6032	1926-66

Most wins in a year

No	Jockey	Year	Rides
598	Kent Desormeaux	1989	2312
546	Chris McCarron	1974	2199
515	Sandy Hawley	1973	1925
487	Steve Cauthen	1977	2075
485	Willie Shoemaker	1953	1683

Trainers

Greatest season's earnings: $17,842,358 D.Wayne Lukas in 1988 from 318 winners.
Greatest career earnings: $85,200,235 D.Wayne Lukas 1977-90
Most wins in a year: 496 Jack Van Berg 1976
Most wins in a career: 5389 Jack Van Berg 1955-89

Eclipse Awards

From 1971 the annual polls conducted by the Throughbred Racing Associations, the *Daily Racing Form* and the National Turf Writers' Association have been combined to determine the recipients of the Eclipse Awards. *Overall Horse of the Year:*

1971   Ack Ack
1972-3 Secretariat
1974-6 Forego
1977   Seattle Slew
1978-9 Affirmed
1980   Spectacular Bid
1981   John Henry
1982   Conquistador Cielo
1983   All Along
1984   John Henry
1985   Spend A Buck
1986   Lady's Secret
1987   Ferdinand
1988   Alysheba
1989   Sunday Silence

Most wins in the Throughbred Racing Association Poll prior to 1971: 5 Kelso 1960-4, 2 Challedon 1940-1, Whirlaway 1941-2, Native Dancer 1952 (tie), 1954.

RACING IN AUSTRALIA

MELBOURNE CUP

The highlight of the racing season in Australia is the Melbourne Cup. Like Royal Ascot it is as much a social occasion as a race-day. Always held on the first Tuesday in November, it was inaugurated in 1861. The race is for 3- year-olds and upwards, and, since 1972 has been over 3200 metres of the Flemington racecourse in Victoria. Prior to then it was over the Imperial equivalent of two miles. Now sponsored by Fosters. *Post-war winners:*

Year	Winner	Jockey
1945	Rainbird	Billy Cook
1946	Russia	Darby Munro
1947	Hiraji	Jack Purtell
1948	Rimfire	Ray Neville
1949	Foxzami	W Fellows
1950	Comic Court	Pat Glennon
1951	Delta	Neville Sellwood
1952	Dalray	Bill Williamson
1953	Wodalla	Jack Purtell
1954	Rising Fast	Jack Purtell
1955	Toparoa	Neville Sellwood
1956	Evening Peal	G Podmore
1957	Straight Draw	Noel McGrowdie
1958	Baystone	Mel Schumacher
1959	Macdougal	Pat Glennon
1960	Hi Jinx	Bill Smith
1961	Lord Fury	Roy Selkrig
1962	Even Stevens	L Cole
1963	Gatum Gatum	Jim Johnson
1964	Polo Prince	R Taylor
1965	Light Fingers	Roy Higgins
1966	Galilee	Johnny Miller
1967	Red Handed	Roy Higgins
1968	Rain Lover	Jim Johnson
1969	Rain Lover	Jim Johnson
1970	Baghdad Note	E J Didham
1971	Silver Knight	Bruce Marshall
1972	Piping Lane	John Letts
1973	Gala Supreme	Frank Reys
1974	Think Big	Harry White
1975	Think Big	Harry White
1976	Van der Hum	R J Skelton
1977	Gold and Black	John Duggan
1978	Arwon	Harry White
1979	Hyperno	Harry White
1980	Beldale Ball	John Letts
1981	Just a Dash	Peter Cook
1982	Gurner's Lane	Mick Dittman
1983	Kiwi	Jimmy Cassidi
1984	Black Knight	Peter Cook
1985	What A Nuisance	P Hyland
1986	At Talaq	Michael Clarke
1987	Kensei	Larry Olsen
1988	Empire Rose	Tony Allan
1989	Tawrrific	Shane Dye

Most wins

Jockey: 4 Bobby Lewis (The Victory 1902, Patrobas 1915, Artilleryman 1919, Trivalve 1927); Harry White, as above
Trainer: 7 Bart Cummings 1965-7, 1974-5, 1977, 1979
Horse: 2 Archer 1861-2, Peter Pan 1932, 1934, Rain Lover 1968-9, Think Big 1974-5
Fastest winning time: 3:17.1 Tawrrific 1989

HURLING

Played at 15-a-side with stick and ball, hurling, the national game of Ireland, is of great antiquity. It was included in the Tailteann Games (instituted 1829 BC). It was outlawed in Ireland in 1367 by the statute of Kilkenny. The Irish Hurling Union was founded in 1879 and the rules standardized following the formation of the Gaelic Athletic Association in 1884.

All Ireland Championships

Played on the first Sunday in September each year the All-Ireland Final is the highlight of the hurling season. The final of this inter-county event takes place at Dublin's Croke Park and the winning team receives the McCarthy Cup. Contested annually from 1887, with the exception of the unfinished championship of 1888. *Wins:*

26 Cork	1890, 1892-4, 1902-3, 1919, 1926, 1928-9, 1931,1941-4, 1946, 1952-4, 1966, 1970, 1976-8, 1984, 1986
24 Kilkenny	1904-5, 1907, 1909, 1911-3, 1922, 1932-3, 1935, 1939, 1947, 1957, 1963, 1966-7, 1969, 1972, 1974-5, 1979, 1982-3
23 Tipperary	1887, 1895-6, 1898-1900, 1906, 1908, 1916, 1925, 1930, 1937, 1945, 1949-51, 1958, 1961-2, 1964-5, 1971, 1989
7 Limerick	1897, 1918, 1921, 1934, 1936, 1940, 1973
6 Dublin	1889, 1917, 1920, 1924, 1927, 1938
5 Wexford	1910, 1955-6, 1960, 1968
4 Galway	1923, 1980, 1987-8
2 Waterford	1948, 1959
2 Offaly	1981, 1985
1 Kerry	1891
1 London Irish	1901
1 Clare	1914
1 Laois	1915

Highest team score in a final: Tipperary 41 (4 goals, 29 points) Antrim 18 (3, 9) in 1989
Highest aggregate score in a final: 64 Cork 39 (6, 21) beat Wexford 25 (5, 10) in 1970
Most individual appearances: 10 Christy Ring (Cork and Munster) and John Doyle (Tipperary)

ICE HOCKEY

Played by teams of 6-a-side with stick and puck. It probably derives from bandy, played on ice-covered pitches, and the 1850s are usually cited for the advent of the puck in Canada, where the game has for long been the major sport. The first rules for Ice Hockey were drawn up by W.F.Robertson and R.F.Smith, students at McGill University, Montreal. The Ontario Hockey Association was formed in 1887.

The sport's governing body is the International Ice Hockey Federation (IIHF), founded in 1908 by Belgium, Bohemia, England, France and Switzerland. Membership reached 39 nations in 1989.

OLYMPIC GAMES

An Olympic sport from 1920, ice hockey was contested at the summer Games of 1920, but thereafter at the Winter Olympics. *Wins:*

7 USSR	1956, 1964, 1968, 1972, 1976, 1984, 1988
6 Canada	1920, 1924, 1928, 1932, 1948, 1952
2 USA	1960, 1980
1 Great Britain	1936

Most gold medals by an individual: 3 by the USSR players Vitaliy Davidov, Anatoliy Firssov, Viktor Kuzkin and Aleksandr Ragulin 1964-72; Vladislav Tretyak 1972-84.

WORLD CHAMPIONSHIPS

Held annually from 1930, except for the war years and in 1980. In Olympic years up to 1968 those championships were also recognised as the world championships. *Most wins:*

22 USSR	1954, 1956, 1963-71, 1973-5, 1978-9, 1981-3, 1986, 1989-90
19 Canada	1920, 1924, 1928, 1930-2, 1934-5, 1937-9, 1948, 1950-2, 1955, 1958-9, 1961
6 Czechoslovakia	1947, 1949, 1972, 1976-7, 1985
4 Sweden	1953, 1957, 1962, 1987
2 USA	1933, 1960
1 Great Britain	1936

Highest score in a world championship match: Australia beat New Zealand 58-0 at Perth, 14 Mar 1987.

EUROPEAN CHAMPIONSHIPS

Held annually, first in 1910. Now held concurrently with World Championships, but not from 1980 in Olympic years. *Champions:*

28 USSR	1954-6, 1958-60, 1963-70, 1973-5, 1978-83, 1985-7, 1989-90
15 Czechoslovakia	
Bohemia:	1911-2, 1914
Cs:	1922, 1925, 1929, 1933, 1947-9, 1961, 1971-2, 1976-7
9 Sweden	1921, 1923, 1928, 1932, 1951-3, 1957, 1962
4 Great Britain	1910, 1936-8
4 Switzerland	1926, 1935, 1939, 1950
2 Austria	1927, 1931
2 Germany	1930, 1934
1 Belgium	1913
1 France	1924

THE IIHF CANADA CUP

First held in 1979, this tournament is contested by the world's six best teams. *Winners:*
1979 Canada, 1981 USSR, 1984 Canada, 1987 Canada.

NATIONAL HOCKEY LEAGUE

Founded in 1917 in Montreal, succeeding the National Hockey Association. It is now contested by 21 teams from Canada and the USA, divided into two divisions within two conferences: Adams and Patrick Divisions in the Wales Conference; Norris and Smythe Divisions in the Campbell Conference. The top teams play-off annually for the Stanley Cup, which was first presented in 1893 by Lord Stanley of Preston, then Governor-General of Canada. From 1894 it was contested by amateur teams for the Canadian Championship. From 1910 it became the award for the winners of the professional league play-offs. *Year given is that of second half of season. There were two contests in 1896 and 1907, and in 1919 the series was unfinished due to an influenza outbreak.*

STANLEY CUP *wins:*

23 Montreal Canadiens 1916, 1924, 1930-1, 1944, 1946, 1953, 1956-60, 1965-6, 1968-9, 1971, 1973, 1976-9, 1986
11 Toronto Maple Leafs 1932, 1942, 1945, 1947-9, 1951, 1962-4, 1967
7 Detroit Red Wings 1936-7, 1943, 1950, 1952, 1954-5
6 Ottawa Senators 1909, 1911, 1920-1, 1923, 1927
5 Boston Bruins 1929, 1939, 1941, 1970, 1972
5 Edmonton Oilers 1984-5, 1987-8, 1990
4 Montreal Victorias 1895, 1896 (Dec), 1897-8
4 Montreal Wanderers 1906-8, 1910
4 New York Islanders 1980-3
3 Montreal AAA 1893-4, 1902
3 Ottawa Silver Seven 1903-5
3 New York Rangers 1928, 1933, 1940
3 Chicago Black Hawks 1934, 1938, 1961
2 Winnipeg Victorias 1896 (Feb), 1901
2 Quebec Bulldogs 1912-3
2 Montreal Maroons 1926, 1935
2 Philadelphia Flyers 1974-5
2 Montreal Shamrocks 1899, 1900
1 Kenora Thistles 1907 (Jan), Toronto Ontarios 1914, Vancouver Millionaires 1915, Seattle Metropolitans 1917, Toronto Arenas 1918, Toronto St Patricks 1922, Victoria Cougars 1925, Calgary Flames 1989.
Most finals: 31 Montreal Canadiens, 21 Toronto Maple Leafs, 18 Detroit Red Wings

The Conn Smythe Trophy for the most valuable player in the play-offs has been awarded annually from 1965. *Winners from 1980:*
1980 Bryan Trottier (NY Islanders)
1981 Butch Goring (NY Islanders)
1982 Mike Bossy (NY Islanders)
1983 Billy Smith (NY Islanders)
1984 Mark Messier (Edmonton)
1985 Wayne Gretzky (Edmonton)
1986 Patrick Roy (Montreal)
1987 Ron Hextall (Philadelphia)
1988 Wayne Gretzky (Edmonton)
1989 Al MacInnis (Calgary)
1990 Bill Ranford (Edmonton)

The only players to win it twice: Bobby Orr (Boston) 1970, 1972; Bernie Parent (Philadelphia) 1974-5, and Gretzky.

National League Career Scoring Leaders: *For regular season games, not including playoffs.*

Name	Goals	Assists	Points	Games	Years
Wayne Gretzky	677	1302	1979	847	1979-90
Gordie Howe	801	1049	1850	1767	1946-71
Marcel Dionne	731	1040	1771	1348	1971-89
Phil Esposito	717	873	1590	1282	1963-81
Stan Mitika	541	926	1467	1394	1958-80
John Bucyk	556	813	1369	1540	1955-78
Bryan Trottier	500	853	1353	1123	1975-90
Gilbert Perreault	512	814	1326	1191	1970-87
Guy Lafleur	536	755	1291	1028	1971-89
Alex Delvecchio	456	825	1281	1549	1951-74
Jean Ratelle	491	776	1267	1281	1960-81
Norm Ullman	490	739	1229	1410	1955-75
Other players with more than 550 goals					
Bobby Hull	610	560	1170	1063	
Mike Bossy	573	553	1126	752	1980-89

Most playoff points: 284 Wayne Gretzky (record 89 goals, 195 assists), 202 Jari Kurri (Edmonton) (92G, 110A), 174 Jean Béliveau (Montreal Can) (79G, 97A)

National League Season Scoring Records:
Goals	92	Wayne Gretzky (Edmonton Oilers) 1981/2
Assists	163	Wayne Gretzky (Edmonton Oilers) 1985/6
Points	215	Wayne Gretzky (Edmonton Oilers) 1985/6
NHL points	132	Montreal Canadiens 1976/7 (80 games, won 60, lost 8, tied 12)
Team goals	446	Edmonton Oilers 1983/4
Team assists	737	Edmonton Oilers 1985/6
Team points	1182	Edmonton Oilers 1983/4

National League Scoring Records in a Game:
Goals	7	Joe Malone for Quebec Bulldogs v Toronto St Patrick's, 31 Jan 1920
Assists	7	Billy Taylor for Detroit Red Wings v Chicago Black Hawks, 16 Mar 1947
	7	Wayne Gretzky for Edmonton Oilers v Washington, 15 Feb 1980
Points	10	Darryl Sittler (6 goals 4 assists) for Toronto Maple Leafs v Boston Bruins, 7 Feb 1976

Most points in a playoff game: 8 (3g/5a) Patrik Sundström for New Jersey Devils v Washington 22 Apr 1988, 8 (5g/3a) Mario Lemieux for Pittsburgh v Philadelphia 25 Apr 1989.
Team Goals	16	Montreal Canadiens beat Quebec Bulldogs 16-3, Quebec City, 3 Nov 1920
Team Aggregate	21	Montreal Canadiens beat Toronto St Patrick's 14-7, Montreal, 10 Jan 1930
	21	Edmonton Oilers beat Chicago Black Hawks 12-9, Chicago 11 Dec 1985

Wayne Gretzky

The phenomenal Gretzky has been scoring at a record pace since he entered the NHL. On 15 Oct 1989 he passed Gordie Howe's NHL scoring record of 1850 points in 10 years to Howe's 26. Gretzky's season by season record in regular season games – for Edmonton Oilers until 1987/8 and subsequently the Los Angeles Kings:

Season	Goals	Assists	Points
1979/80	51	86	137
1980/1	55	109	164
1981/2	92	120	212
1982/3	71	125	196
Season	Goals	Assists	Points
1983/4	87	118	205
1984/5	73	135	208
1985/6	52	163	215
1986/7	62	121	183
Season	Goals	Assists	Points
1987/8	40	109	149
1988/9	54	114	168
1989/90	40	102	142

In Stanley Cup play-offs his figures have been 89 goals, 195 assists, 284 points, to the end of the 1990 season.

Hart Trophy

Awarded annually from the 1923/4 season by the Professional Hockey Writers Association as the Most Valuable Player award of the NHL. Named after Cecil Hart, former manager-coach of the Montreal Canadiens. *Most wins:* 9 Wayne Gretzky (Edmonton) 1980-7, 1989; 6 Gordie Howe (Detroit) 1952-3, 1957-8, 1960, 1963; 3 Eddie Shore (Boston) 1933, 1936, 1938; 3 Bobby Orr (Boston) 1970-2; 3 Bobby Clarke (Philadelphia) 1973, 1975-6.

Other winners since 1970: 1974 Phil Esposito (Boston), 1977-8 Guy Lafleur (Montreal), 1979 Bryan Trottier (NY Islanders), 1988 Mario Lemieux (Pittsburgh), Mark Messier (Edmonton).

Art Ross Trophy

Awarded annually from 1947-8 to the NHL season's leading scorer. *Most wins:* 8 Wayne Gretzky (Edmonton) 1981-7, 1990; 6 Gordie Howe (Detroit) 1951-4, 1957, 1963; 5 Phil Esposito (Boston) 1969, 1971-4; 4 Stan Mikita (Chicago) 1964-5, 1967-8; 3 Bobby Hull (Chicago) 1960, 1962, 1966; 3 Guy Lafleur (Montreal Can) 1976-8.
Other winners since 1970: 1970 & 1975 Bobby Orr (Boston), 1979 Bryan Trottier (NY Islanders), 1980 Marcel Dionne (Los Angeles), 1988-9 Mario Lemieux (Pittsburgh).

James Norris Memorial Trophy

Awarded annually from the 1953-4 season to the league's leading defenseman.
Most wins: 8 Bobby Orr (Boston) 1968-75, 7 Doug Harvey (Montreal/NY Rangers) 1955-8, 1960-2; 3 Pierre Pilote (Chicago) 1963-5, 3 Denis Potvin (NY Islanders) 1976, 1978-9, 3 Ray Bourque (Boston) 1987-8, 1990.

Mario Lemieux (All-Sport)

Winners from 1980: 1980 Larry Robinson (Montreal), 1981 Randy Carlyle (Pittsburgh), 1982 Doug Wilson (Chicago), 1983-4 Rod Langway (Washington), 1985-6 Paul Coffey (Edmonton), 1987-8 Ray Bourque (Boston), 1989 Chris Chelios (Montreal), 1990 Ray Bourque (Boston).

World Hockey Association

Contested for seven seasons from 1972/3 to 1978/9 as a 12-team rival of the NHL. *Winners*

1973	NE Whalers
1974-5	Houston Aeros
1976	Winnipeg Jets
1977	Quebec Nordiques
1978-9	Winnipeg Jets

Adding WHA points to NHL points the leading scorers have been:
2358 Gordie Howe (975G/1383A), 2089 Wayne Gretzky (723/1366), 1808 Bobby Hull (913/895)

Women's World Championships

The first ever women's world championships were held in Canada in March 1990; Canada beat the USA 5-2.

ICE SKATING

Skating in a primitive form is over 2000 years old, but probably first became popular on frozen canals in the Netherlands some 300 years ago. The Dutch were the main exponents of speed skating over the next two hundred years. Figure skating originated in Britain and the first known skating club was the Edinburgh Skating Club, formed c.1742. The first recorded race was in the Fens in 1763 and the earliest artificial rink was opened in Baker Street, London, in 1842, although the surface was not of ice. The first artificial ice rink was opened at the Glaciarium, London, in 1876, three years before the foundation of the National Skating Association of Great Britain.

Ice skating may be divided into two: figure skating, on rinks of 60m x 30m, and speed skating. The world governing body for both is the International Skating Union (ISU), founded in 1892, and which now has its headquarters in Switzerland.

FIGURE SKATING

Note that in pairs and ice dance competitions the woman's name is conventionally listed first.

OLYMPIC GAMES

Ice skating was first included at the Olympic Games in 1908 in London, where events were held at Prince's Rink. The sport was included again in 1920 and at all Winter Games from 1924. *Winners:*

Men

1908 Ulrich Salchow (Swe)
1908* Nikolay Panin (USSR)
1920 Gillis Grafström (Swe)
1924 Gillis Grafström (Swe)
1928 Gillis Grafström (Swe)
1932 Karl Schäfer (Aut)
1936 Karl Schäfer (Aut)
1948 Richard Button (USA)
1952 Richard Button (USA)
1956 Hayes Alan Jenkins (USA)
1960 David Jenkins (USA)
1964 Manfred Schnelldorfer (FRG)
1968 Wolfgang Schwarz (Aut)
1972 Ondrej Nepela (Cs)
1976 John Curry (UK)
1980 Robin Cousins (UK)
1984 Scott Hamilton (USA)
1988 Brian Boitano (USA)
*Special figures competition

Women

1908 Madge Syers (née Cave) (UK)
1920 Magda Julin-Mauroy (Swe)
1924 Herma Planck-Szabó (Aut)
1928 Sonja Henie (Nor)
1932 Sonja Henie (Nor)
1936 Sonja Henie (Nor)
1948 Barbara Ann Scott (Can)
1952 Jeannette Altwegg (UK)
1956 Tenley Albright (USA)
1960 Carol Heiss (USA)
1964 Sjoukje Dijkstra (Hol)
1968 Peggy Fleming (USA)
1972 Beatrix Schuba (Aut)
1976 Dorothy Hamill (USA)
1980 Anett Pötzsch (GDR)
1984 Katarina Witt (GDR)
1988 Katarina Witt (GDR)

Pairs

1908 Anna Hübler/Heinrich Burger (Ger)
1920 Ludowika Jakobsson/Walter Jakobsson (Fin)
1924 Helene Engelmann/Alfred Berger (Aut)
1928 Andrée Joly/Pierre Brunet (Fra)
1932 Andrée Brunet (née Joly)/Pierre Brunet (Fra)
1936 Maxi Herber/Ernst Baier (Ger)
1948 Micheline Lannoy/Pierre Baugniet (Bel)
1952 Ria Falk/Paul Falk (FRG)
1956 Elisabeth Schwarz/Kurt Oppelt (Aut)
1960 Barbara Wagner/Robert Paul (Can)
1964 Lyudmila Belousova/Oleg Protopopov (USSR)
1968 Lyudmila Belousova/Oleg Protopopov (USSR)
1972 Irina Rodnina/Aleksey Ulanov (USSR)
1976 Irina Rodnina/Aleksandr Zaitsev (USSR)
1980 Irina Rodnina/Aleksandr Zaitsev (USSR)
1984 Yelena Valova/Oleg Vasilyev (USSR)
1988 Yekaterina Gordeyeva/Sergey Grinkov (USSR)

Ice Dance

1976 Lyudmila Pakhomova/Aleksandr Gorshkov (USSR)
1980 Natalya Linichuk/Gennadiy Karponosov (USSR)
1984 Jayne Torvill/Christopher Dean (GB)
1988 Natalya Bestemianova/Andrey Bukin (USSR)

Most gold medals: 3 Gillis Grafström, Sonja Henie, Irina Rodnina
Most medals: 4 Gillis Grafström, who also won a silver in 1932.
Oldest gold medallist: 38 yr 80 days Walter Jakobsson, pairs 1920
Youngest gold medallist: 15 yr 128 days Maxi Herber, pairs 1936
Best marks: Jayne Torvill and Christopher Dean were awarded a maximum nine sixes for artistic impression, as well as a further three sixes for technical merit, in the 1984 ice dancing free dance section.

WORLD CHAMPIONSHIPS

Held annually, first in St.Petersburg (now Leningrad) in 1896. The 1961 championships were cancelled after all the US team were killed in a plane crash. *Winners:*

Men

1896 Gilbert Fuchs (Ger)
1897 Gustav Hügel (Aut)
1898 Henning Grenander (Swe)
1899-1900 Gustav Hügel (Aut)
1901-5 Ulrich Salchow (Swe)
1906 Gilbert Fuchs (Ger)
1907-11 Ulrich Salchow (Swe)
1912-3 Fritz Kachler (Aut)
1914 Gösta Sandahl (Swe)
1922 Gillis Grafström (Swe)
1923 Fritz Kachler (Aut)
1924 Gillis Grafström (Swe)
1925-8 Willy Böckl (Aut)
1929 Gillis Grafström (Swe)
1930-6 Karl Schäfer (Aut)
1937-8 Felix Kaspar (Aut)
1939 Graham Sharp (UK)
1947 Hans Gerschwiler (Swi)
1948-52 Richard Button (USA)
1953-6 Hayes Alan Jenkins (USA)
1957-9 David Jenkins (USA)
1960 Alain Giletti (Fra)
1962 Donald Jackson (Can)
1963 Donald McPherson (Can)
1964 Manfred Schnelldorfer (FRG)
1965 Alain Calmat (Fra)
1966-8 Emmerich Danzer (Aut)
1969-70 Tim Wood (USA)
1971-3 Ondrej Nepela (Cs)
1974 Jan Hoffmann (GDR)
1975 Sergey Volkov (USSR)
1976 John Curry (UK)
1977 Vladimir Kovalyev (USSR)
1978 Charles Tickner (USA)
1979 Vladimir Kovalyev (USSR)
1980 Jan Hoffmann (GDR)
1981-4 Scott Hamilton (USA)
1985 Aleksandr Fadeyev (USSR)
1986 Brian Boitano (USA)
1987 Brian Orser (Can)
1988 Brian Boitano (USA)
1989-90 Kurt Browning (Can)
Most wins: 10 Ulrich Salchow, 7 Karl Schäfer, 5 Richard Button

Women

1906-7 Madge Syers (née Cave) (UK)
1908-11 Lily Kronberger (Hun)
1912-4 Opika von Méray Horvath (Hun)
1922-4 Herma Szabó (née Planck) (Aut)
1925-6 Herma Jaross (was Szabó) (Aut)
1927-36 Sonja Henie (Nor)
1937 Cecilia Colledge (UK)
1938-9 Megan Taylor (UK)
1947-8 Barbara Ann Scott (Can)
1949-50 Alena Vrzánová (Cs)
1951 Jeannette Altwegg (UK)
1952 Jacqueline du Bief (Fra)
1953 Tenley Albright (USA)
1954 Gundi Busch (FRG)
1955 Tenley Albright (USA)
1956-60 Carol Heiss (USA)
1962-4 Sjoukje Dijkstra (Hol)
1965 Petra Burka (Can)
1966-8 Peggy Fleming (USA)
1969-70 Gabriele Seyfert (GDR)
1971-2 Beatrix Schuba (Aut)
1973 Karen Magnussen (Can)
1974 Christine Errath (GDR)
1975 Dianne De Leeuw (Hol)
1976 Dorothy Hamill (USA)
1977 Linda Fratianne (USA)
1978 Anett Pötzsch (GDR)
1979 Linda Fratianne (USA)
1980 Anett Pötzsch (GDR)
1981 Denise Biellmann (Swi)
1982 Elaine Zayak (USA)
1983 Rosalynn Sumners (USA)
1984-5 Katarina Witt (GDR)
1986 Debbie Thomas (USA)
1987-8 Katarina Witt (GDR)
1989 Midori Ito (Jap)
1990 Jill Trenary (USA)
Most wins: 10 Sonja Henie, 6 Carol Heiss

Katarina Witt, the East German super-star, won six European, four World and two Olympic gold medals between 1982 and 1988 (**All-Sport/Simon Bruty**)

Pairs

1908 Anna Hübler/Heinrich Burger (Ger)
1909 Phyllis Johnson/James Johnson (UK)
1910 Anna Hübler/Heinrich Burger (Ger)
1911 Ludowika Eilers/Walter Jakobsson (Fin)
1912 Phyllis Johnson/James Johnson (UK)
1913 Helene Engelmann/Karl Mejstrick (Aut)
1914 Ludowika Eilers/Walter Jakobsson (Fin)
1922 Helene Engelmann/Alfred Berger (Aut)
1923 Ludowika Jakobsson (née Eilers)/Walter Jakobsson (Fin)
1924 Helene Engelmann/Alfred Berger (Aut)
1925 Herma Jaross/Ludwig Wrede (Aut)
1926 Andrée Joly/Pierre Brunet (Fra)
1927 Herma Jaross/Ludwig Wrede (Aut)
1928 Andrée Joly/Pierre Brunet (Fra)
1929 Lilly Scholz/Otto Kaiser (Aut)
1930 Andrée Brunet (née Joly)/Pierre Brunet (Fra)
1931 Emilia Rotter/László Szollás (Hun)
1932 Andrée Brunet/Pierre Brunet (Fra)
1933-5 Emilie Rotter/László Szollás(Hun)
1936-9 Maxi Herber/Ernst Baier (Ger)
1947-8 Micheline Lannoy/Pierre Baugniet (Bel)
1949 Andrea Kékesy/Ede Király (Hun)
1950 Karol Kennedy/Peter Kennedy (USA)
1951-2 Ria Falk (née Baran)/Paul Falk (FRG)
1953 Jennifer Nicks/John Nicks (UK)
1954-5 Frances Dafoe/Norris Bowden (Can)
1956 Elisabeth Schwarz/Kurt Oppelt (Aut)
1957-60 Barbara Wagner/Robert Paul (Can)
1962 Maria Jelinek/Otto Jelinek (Can)
1963-4 Marika Kilius/Hans-Jürgen Bäumler (FRG)
1965-8 Lyudmila Belousova/Oleg Protopopov (USSR)
1969-72 Irina Rodnina/Aleksey Ulanov (USSR)
1973-8 Irina Rodnina/Aleksandr Zaitsev (USSR)
1979 Tai Babilonia/Randy Gardner (USA)
1980 Marina Tcherkasova/Sergey Shakrai (USSR)
1981 Irina Vorobyeva/Igor Lissovsky (USSR)
1982 Sabine Baess/Tassilo Thierbach (GDR)
1983 Yelena Valova/Oleg Vasilyev (USSR)
1984 Barbara Underhill/Paul Martini (Can)
1985 Yelena Valova/Oleg Vasilyev (USSR)
1986-7 Yekaterina Gordeyeva/Sergey Grinkov (USSR)
1988 Yelena Valova/Oleg Vasilyev (USSR)
1989-90 Yekaterina Gordeyeva/Sergey Grinkov (USSR)
Most wins: 10 Irina Rodnina, 6 Aleksandr Zaitsev

Ice Dance

Although the first official world ice dance championships were in 1952, unofficial championships were staged in 1950 and 1951.
1950 Lois Waring/Michael McGean (USA)
1951 Jean Westwood/Lawrence Demmy (UK)
1952-5 Jean Westwood/Lawrence Demmy (UK)
1956 Pamela Weight/Paul Thomas (UK)
1957-8 June Markham/Courtney Jones (UK)
1959-60 Doreen Denny/Courtney Jones (UK)
1962-5 Eva Románová/Pavel Roman (Cs)

1966-9 Diana Towler/Bernard Ford (UK)
1970-4 Lyudmila Pakhomova/Aleksandr Gorshkov (USSR)
1975 Irina Moiseyeva/Andrey Minenkov (USSR)
1976 Lyudmila Pakhomova/Aleksandr Gorshkov (USSR)
1977 Irina Moiseyeva/Andrey Minenkov (USSR)
1978-9 Natalya Linichuk/Gennadiy Karponosov (USSR)
1980 Krisztina Regoczy/András Sallay (Hun)
1981-4 Jayne Torvill/Christopher.Dean (UK)
1985-8 Natalya Bestemianova/Andrey Bukin (USSR)
1989-90 Marina Klimova/Sergey Ponomarenko (USSR)
Most wins: 6 Lyudmila Pakhomova & Aleksandr Gorshkov

Best marks: Jayne Torvill and Christopher Dean were awarded 29 maximum sixes for ice dancing at the 1984 World Championships. This comprised seven in the compulsory dances, a perfect set of nine for artistic impression in both the set pattern and free dance sections and a further four sixes for technical merit in the latter.

SPEED SKATING

A standard outdoor speed skating circuit is 400 metres, with two lanes. The speed skaters race in pairs, the lanes crossing on the straights on either side of the track. Indoor speed skating is conducted on short tracks, the standard length being 111.12 metres, which can be laid out on a 60m x 30m skating or ice hockey rink.

OLYMPIC GAMES

Held at each Olympic Games from 1924 (for men) and 1960 (for women). Women's races had also been staged as demonstration events in 1932. *Winners:*

Men's 500 metres

1924 Charles Jewtraw (USA) 44.0
1928 Bernt Eversen (Nor) & Clas Thunberg (Fin) 43.4
1932 John Shea (USA) 43.4
1936 Ivar Ballangrud (Nor) 43.4
1948 Finn Helgesen (Nor) 43.1
1952 Kenneth Henry (USA) 43.2
1956 Yevgeniy Grischin (USSR) 40.2
1960 Yevgeniy Grischin (USSR) 40.2
1964 Terry McDermott (USA) 40.1
1968 Erhard Keller (FRG) 40.3
1972 Erhard Keller (FRG) 39.44
1976 Yevgeniy Kulikov (USSR) 39.17
1980 Eric Heiden (USA) 38.03
1984 Sergey Fokichev (USSR) 38.19
1988 Uwe-Jens Mey (GDR) 36.45

Men's 1000 metres

1976 Peter Mueller (USA) 1:19.32
1980 Eric Heiden (USA) 1:15.18
1984 Gaetan Boucher (Can) 1:15.80
1988 Nikolay Gulyayev (USSR) 1:13.03

Men's 1500 metres

1924 Clas Thunberg (Fin) 2:20.8
1928 Clas Thunberg (Fin) 2:21.1

1932 John Shea (USA) 2:57.5
1936 Charles Mathiesen (Nor) 2:19.2
1948 Sverre Farstad (Nor) 2:17.6
1952 Hjalmar Andersen (Nor) 2:20.4
1956 Yevgeniy Grischin (USSR) & Yuriy Mikhailov (USSR) 2:08.6
1960 Roald Aas (Nor) & Yevgeniy Grischin (USSR) 2:10.4
1964 Ants Antson (USSR) 2:10.3
1968 Cornelis Verkerk (Hol) 2:03.4
1972 Ard Schenk (Hol) 2:02.96
1976 Jan Egil Storholt (Nor) 1:59.38
1980 Eric Heiden (USA) 1:55.44
1984 Gaetan Boucher (Can) 1:58.36
1988 André Hoffmann (GDR) 1:52.06

Men's 5000 metres
1924 Clas Thunberg (Fin) 8:39.0
1928 Ivar Ballangrud (Nor) 8:50.5
1932 Irving Jaffee (USA) 9:40.8
1936 Ivar Ballangrud (Nor) 8:19.6
1948 Reidar Liaklev (Nor) 8:29.4
1952 Hjalmar Andersen (Nor) 8:10.6
1956 Boris Schilkov (USSR) 7:48.7
1960 Viktor Kositschkin (USSR) 7:51.3
1964 Knut Johannesen (Nor) 7:38.4
1968 Anton Maier (Nor) 7.22.4
1972 Ard Schenk (Hol) 7:23.61
1976 Sten Stensen (Nor) 7:24.48
1980 Eric Heiden (USA) 7:02.29
1984 Tomas Gustafsson (Swe) 7:12.28
1988 Tomas Gustafsson (Swe) 6:44.63

Men's 10 000 metres
1924 Julius Skutnabb (Fin) 18:04.8
1928 event cancelled after five races
1932 Irving Jaffee (USA) 19:13.6
1936 Ivar Ballangrud (Nor) 17:24.3
1948 Äke Seyffarth (Swe) 17:26.3
1952 Hjalmar Andersen (Nor) 16:45.8
1956 Sigvard Ericsson (Swe) 16:35.9
1960 Knut Johannesen (Nor) 15:46.6
1964 Jonny Nilsson (Swe) 15:50.1
1968 Johnny Höglin (Swe) 15:23.6
1972 Ard Schenk (Hol) 15:01.35
1976 Piet Kleine (Hol) 14:50.59
1980 Eric Heiden (USA) 14:28.13
1984 Igor Malkov (USSR) 14:39.90
1988 Tomas Gustafsson (Swe) 13:48.20

Men's all-round (aggregate)
1924 Clas Thunberg (Fin)

Women's 500 metres
1960 Helga Haase (GDR) 45.9
1964 Lidiya Skoblikova (USSR) 45.0
1968 Lyudmila Titova (USSR) 46.1
1972 Anne Henning (USA) 43.33
1976 Sheila Young (USA) 42.76
1980 Karin Enke (GDR) 41.78
1984 Christa Rothenburger (GDR) 41.02
1988 Bonnie Blair (USA) 39.10

In 1988 Tomas Gustafsson smashed the world record for 10 000 metres when he won his third Olympic gold medal (**All-Sport**)

Women's 1000 metres
1960 Klara Guseva (USSR) 1:34.1
1964 Lidiya Skoblikova (USSR) 1:33.2
1968 Carolina Geijssen (Hol) 1:32.6
1972 Monika Pflug (FRG) 1:31.40
1976 Tatyana Averina (USSR) 1:28.43
1980 Natalya Petruseva (USSR) 1:24.10
1984 Karin Enke (GDR) 1:21.61
1988 Christa Röthenburger (GDR) 1:17.65

Women's 1500 metres
1960 Lidiya Skoblikova (USSR) 2:25.2
1964 Lidiya Skoblikova (USSR) 2:22.6
1968 Kaija Mustonen (Fin) 2:22.4
1972 Dianne Holum (USA) 2:20.85
1976 Galina Stepanskaya (USSR) 2:16.58
1980 Annie Borckink (Hol) 2:10.95
1984 Karin Enke (GDR) 2:03.42
1988 Yvonne van Gennip (Hol) 2:00.68

Women's 3000 metres
1960 Lidiya Skoblikova (USSR) 5:14.3
1964 Lidiya Skoblikova (USSR) 5:14.9
1968 Johanna Schut (Hol) 4:56.2
1972 Christina Baas-Kaiser (Hol) 4:52.14
1976 Tatyana Averina (USSR) 4:45.19
1980 Björg Eva Jensen (Nor) 4:32.13
1984 Andrea Schöne (GDR) 4:27.79
1988 Yvonne van Gennip (Hol) 4:11.94

Women's 5000 metres
1988 Yvonne van Gennip (Hol) 7:14.13

Most Olympic Medals (G – Gold, S – Silver, B – Bronze)

MEN	G	S	B
7 Clas Thunberg (Nor)	5	1	1
7 Ivar Ballangrud (Nor)	4	2	1
5 Eric Heiden (USA)	5	-	-
5 Yevgeniy Grischin (USSR)	4	1	-
5 Knut Johannesen (Nor)	2	2	1

WOMEN			
8 Karin Enke/Kania (GDR)	3	4	1
6 Lidiya Skoblikova (USSR)	6	-	-
6 Andrea Schöne/Ehrig (GDR)	1	4	1

Eric Heiden, uniquely, won all five gold medals at one Games (1980).

WORLD CHAMPIONSHIPS
Held annually, first at Amsterdam in 1889. Officially recognised by the ISU from 1893. *Overall champions:*

Men
Contested over four distances: 500m, 1000m, 5000m and 10000m. Titles not awarded 1889-90, 1894, 1902-3, 1906-7.
1891 Joseph Donoghue (USA)

1893 Jaap Eden (Hol)
1895-6 Jaap Eden (Hol)
1897 Jack McCulloch (Can)
1898-9 Peder Østlund (Nor)
1900 Edvard Engelsaas (Nor)
1901 Franz Frederik Wathen (Fin)
1904 Sigurd Mathisen (Nor)
1905 Coen de Koning (Hol)
1908-9 Oscar Mathisen (Nor)
1910-1 Nikolay Strunnikov (Rus)
1912-4 Oscar Mathisen (Nor)
1922 Harald Ström (Nor)
1923 Clas Thunberg (Fin)
1924 Roald Larsen (Nor)
1925 Clas Thunberg (Fin)
1926 Ivar Ballangrud (Nor)

Yvonne van Gennip won three gold medals at the Winter Olympics in Calgary in 1988, setting world records at both 1500 and 3000 metres **(All-Sport)**

1927 Bernt Evensen (Nor)
1928-9 Clas Thunberg (Fin)
1930 Michael Staksrud (Nor)
1931 Clas Thunberg (Fin)
1932 Ivar Ballangrud (Nor)
1933 Hans Engnestangen (Nor)
1934 Bernt Evensen (Nor)
1935 Michael Staksrud (Nor)
1936 Ivar Ballangrud (Nor)
1937 Michael Staksrud (Nor)
1938 Ivar Ballangrud (Nor)
1939 Birger Wasenius (Fin)
1947 Lauri Parkkinen (Fin)
1948 Odd Lundberg (Nor)
1949 Kornel Pajor (Hun)
1950-2 Hjalmar Andersen (Nor)
1953 Oleg Goncharenko (USSR)
1954 Boris Schilkov (USSR)
1955 Sigvard Ericsson (Swe)
1956 Oleg Goncharenko (USSR)
1957 Knut Johannesen (Nor)
1958 Oleg Goncharenko (USSR)
1959 Juhani Järvinen (Fin)
1960 Boris Stenin (USSR)
1961 Henk van der Grift (Hol)
1962 Viktor Kosichkin (USSR)
1963 Jonny Nilsson (Swe)
1964 Knut Johannesen (Nor)
1965 Per Ivar Moe (Nor)
1966-7 Cornelis Verkerk (Hol)
1968 Anton Maier (Nor)
1969 Dag Fornaess (Nor)
1970-2 Ard Schenk (Hol)
1973 Göran Claesen (Swe)
1974 Sten Stensen (Nor)
1975 Harm Kuipers (Hol)
1976 Piet Kleine (Hol)
1977-9 Eric Heiden (USA)
1980 Hilbert van der Duim (Hol)
1981 Amund Sjøbrend (Nor)
1982 Hilbert van der Duim (Hol)
1983 Rolf Falk-Larssen (Nor)
1984 Oleg Bozyiev (USSR)
1985-6 Hein Vergeer (Hol)
1987 Nikolay Gulyayev (USSR)
1988 Eric Flaim (USA)
1989 Leo Visser (Hol)
1990 Johann-Olav Koss (Nor)

Most wins: 5 Oscar Mathisen, Clas Thunberg

Women
Contested over four distances: 500m, 1000m, 1500m and 3000m.
1936 Kit Klein (USA)
1937-8 Laila Schou Nilsen (Nor)
1939 Vernä Lesche (Fin)
1947 Vernä Lesche (Fin)

1948-50 Maria Isakova (USSR)
1951 Eevi Huttunen (Fin)
1952 Lidiya Selikhova (USSR)
1953 Khalida Schegoleyeva (USSR)
1954 Lidiya Selikhova (USSR)
1955 Rimma Zhukova (USSR)
1956 Sofiya Kondakova (USSR)
1957-8 Inga Artamonova (USSR)
1959 Tamara Rylova (USSR)
1960-1 Valentina Stenina (USSR)
1962 Inga Artamonova (USSR)
1963-4 Lidiya Skoblikova (USSR)
1965 Inga Artamonova (USSR)
1966 Valentina Stenina (USSR)
1967-8 Christina Kaiser (Hol)
1969 Lasma Kauniste (USSR)
1970 Atje Keulen-Deelstra (Hol)
1971 Nina Statkevich (USSR)
1972-4 Atje Keulen-Deelstra (Hol)
1975 Karin Kessow (GDR)
1976 Sylvia Burka (Can)
1977 Vera Bryndzey (USSR)
1978 Tatyana Averina (USSR)
1979 Beth Heiden (USA)
1980-1 Natalya Petruseva (USSR)
1982 Karin Enke (then Busch) (GDR)
1983 Andrea Schöne (GDR)
1984 Karin Enke (GDR)
1985 Andrea Schöne (GDR)
1986-8 Karin Kania (née Enke) (GDR)
1989 Constanze Moser (GDR)
1990 Jacqueline Börner (GDR)

Most wins: 5 Karin Kania, 4 Inga Artamonova, Atje Keulen-Deelstra

WORLD SPRINT CHAMPIONSHIPS
First held in 1970. Both men's and women's championships are contested over two distances: 500m and 1000m. *Overall winners:*

Men
1970 Valeriy Muratov (USSR)
1971 Erhard Keller (FRG)
1972 Leo Linkovesi (Fin)
1973 Valeriy Muratov (USSR)
1974 Per Bjørang (Nor)
1975 Aleksandr Safranov (USSR)
1976 Johan Granath (Swe)
1977-80 Eric Heiden (USA)
1981 Frode Rømming (Nor)
1982 Sergey Khlebnikov (USSR)
1983 Akira Kuroiwa (Jap)
1984 Gaetan Boucher (Can)
1985-6 Igor Zhelezovskiy (USSR)
1987 Akira Kuroiwa (Jap)
1988 Dan Jansen (USA)
1989 Igor Zhelezovskiy (USSR)

1990 Ki Tae-bae (SKo)
Most wins: 4 Eric Heiden

Women
1970 Lyudmila Titova (USSR)
1971 Ruth Schleiermacher (GDR)
1972 Monika Pflug (FRG)
1973 Sheila Young (USA)
1974 Leah Poulos (USA)
1975-6 Sheila Young (USA)
1977 Sylvia Burka (Can)
1978 Lyubov Sadchikova (USSR)
1979 Leah Muller (née Poulos) (USA)
1980-1 Karin Enke (GDR)
1982 Natalya Petruseva (USSR)
1983-4 Karin Enke (GDR)
1985 Christa Rothenburger (GDR)
1986-7 Karin Kania (née Enke) (GDR)
1988 Christa Rothenburger (GDR)
1989 Bonnie Blair (USA)
1990 Angela Hauck (GDR)

Most wins: 6 Karin Kania

WORLD CUP
Contested over a series of events during the winter, annualy from the 1985-6 season. *Winners:*
MEN

500 Metres
1986 Dan Jansen (USA)
1987 Nick Thometz (USA)
1988-90 Uwe-Jens Mey (GDR)

1000 Metres
1986 Dan Jansen (USA)
1987 Nick Thometz (USA)
1988 Dan Jansen (USA)
1989-90 Uwe-Jens Mey (GDR)

1500 Metres
1986 Michael Hadschieff (Aut)
1987 Hans Magnusson (Swe)
1988 André Hoffmann (GDR)
1989 Eric Flaim (USA)
1990 Johann-Olav Koss (Nor)

5000 & 10 000 Metres
1986 Dave Silk (USA)
1987 Geir Karlstad (Nor)
1988 Tomas Gustafsson (Swe)
1989 Gerard Kemkers (Hol)
1990 Bart Veldkamp (Hol)

WOMEN

500 Metres
1986 Christa Rothenburger (GDR)

1987 Bonnie Blair (USA)
1988 Christa Rothenburger (GDR)
1989 Christa Luding (née Rothenburger) (GDR)
1990 Angela Hauck (GDR) and Bonnie Blair (USA)

1000 Metres
1986 Karin Kania (GDR)
1987 Bonnie Blair (USA)
1988 Christa Rothenburger (GDR)
1989-90 Angela Hauck (GDR)

1500 Metres
1986 Annette Carlén (Swe)
1987 Yvonne van Gennip (Hol)
1988 Bonnie Blair (USA)
1989 Constanze Moser (GDR)
1990 Jacqueline Börner (GDR)

3000 Metres (and 5000 from 1989)
1986 Andrea Ehrig (GDR)
1987 Yvonne van Gennip (Hol)
1988 Gabi Zange (GDR)
1989 Heike Schalling (GDR)
1990 Gunda Kleeman (GDR)

WORLD SHORT TRACK CHAMPIONSHIPS
Held indoors over four distances: 500m, 1000m, 1500m and 3000m. Held unofficially 1978-80 and officially recognised by the ISU from 1981. *Winners:*

MEN
1978	Jim Lynch (Aus)
1979	Hiroshi Toda (Jap)
1980	Gaetan Boucher (Can)
1981	Benoit Baril (Can)
1982	Guy Daigneault (Can)
1983	Louis Grenier (Can)
1984	Guy Daigneault (Can)
1985	Toshinobu Kawai (Jap)
1986	Tatsuyoshi Isihara (Jap)
1987	Michel Daignault (Can) & Toshinobu Kawai (Jap)
1989	Michel Daignault (Can)
1990	Lee Joon-ho (SKo)

WOMEN
1978	Sarah Docter (Can)
1979	Sylvie Daigle (Can)
1980	Miyoshi Kato (Jap)
1981	Miyoshi Kato (Jap)
1982	Maryse Perreault (Can)
1983	Sylvie Daigle (Can)
1984	Mariko Kinoshita (Jap)
1985	Eiko Shishii (Jap)
1986	Bonnie Blair (USA)
1987	Eiko Shishii (Jap)
1989	Sylvie Daigle (Can)
1990	Sylvie Daigle (Can)

SPEED SKATING WORLD RECORDS

	min:sec	Name	Venue	Date
MEN				
500m	0:36.45	Uwe-Jens Mey GDR)	Calgary, Can	14 Feb 1988
	0:36.23u	Nick Thometz (USA)	Medeo, USSR	26 Mar 1987
1000m	1:12.58	Pavel Pegov (USSR)	Medeo, USSR	25 Mar 1983
	1:12.58	Igor Zhelezovskiy (USSR)	Heerenveen, Hol	25 Feb 1989
	1:12.05u	Nick Thometz (USA)	Medeo, USSR	27 Mar 1987
1500m	1:52.06	André Hoffmann	Calgary, Can	20 Feb 1988
3000m	3:57.52	Johann-Olav Koss (Nor)	Heerenveen, Hol	13 Mar 1990
	3:56.65u	Sergey Martyuk (USSR)	Medeo, USSR	11 Mar 1977
5000m	6:43.59	Geir Karlstad (Nor)	Calgary, Can	4 Dec 1987
10 000m	13:48.20	Tomas Gustafsson (Can)	Calgary, Can	21 Feb 1988
Sprint points	145.945	Igor Zhelezovskiy (USSR)	Heerenveen, Hol	25/26 Feb 1989
(500m, 1000m, 500m, 1000m)				
Points	161.158	André Hoffmann (GDR)	Davos, Swi	12/13 Mar 1983
(500m, 3000m, 1500m, 5000m)				
Overall points	159.356	Nikolay Gulyayev (USSR)	Heerenveen, Hol	14/15 Feb 1987
(500m, 5000m, 1500m, 10 000m)				
WOMEN				
500m	0:39.10	Bonnie Blair (USA)	Calgary, Can	22 Feb 1988
1000m	1:17.65	Christa Rothenburger (GDR)	Calgary, Can	26 Feb 1988
1500m	1:59.30	Karin Kania (née Enke) (GDR)	Medeo, USSR	22 Mar 1986
3000m	4:11.94	Yvonne van Gennip (Hol)	Calgary, Can	23 Feb 1988
5000m	7:14.13	Yvonne van Gennip (Hol)	Calgary, Can	28 Feb 1988
10 000m (u)	15:25.25	Yvonne van Gennip (Hol)	Heerenveen, Hol	19 Mar 1988
Sprint points	159.435	Bonnie Blair (USA)	Heerenveen, Hol	25/26 Feb 1989
(500m, 1000m, 500m, 1000m)				
Points	163.466	Karen Kania (GDR)	Karuizawa, Jap	22/23 Feb 1986
(500m, 1500m, 1000m, 3000m)				
Overall points	168.271	Karen Kania (GDR)	Medeo, USSR	21/22 Mar 1986
(500m, 3000m, 1500m, 5000m)				

u = *unofficial marks not ratified*
Note that marks set at Medeo (USSR) are assisted by high altitude (1691m above sea level)

WORLD SHORT TRACK SPEED SKATING RECORDS

	min:sec	Name	Venue	Date
MEN				
500m	0:44.46	Orazio Fagone (Ita)	Budapest, Hun	15 Jan 1988
1000m	1:31.80	Tsutomu Kawasaki (Jap)	Amsterdam	17 Mar 1990
1500m	2:25.25	Michel Daignault (Can)	Calgary, Can	22 Feb 1988
3000m	5:04.24	Tatsuyoshi Ishihara (Jap)	Amsterdam, Hol	17 Mar 1985
5000m relay	7:22.12	Netherlands	Budapest, Hun	17 Jan 1988
		(Jaco Mos, Richard Suyten, Peter van der Velde, Charles Veldhoven)		
WOMEN				
500m	0:47.77	Maria Cristina Sciolla (Ita)	Budapest, Hun	16 Jan 1988
1000m	1:39.00	Li Yan (Chn)	Calgary, Can	25 Feb 1988
1500m	2:34.85	Li Yan (Chn)	Calgary, Can	23 Feb 1988
3000m	5:18.33	Maria Rosa Candido (Ita)	Budapest, Hun	17 Jan 1988
3000m relay	4:45.88	Italy	Calgary, Can	24 Feb 1988
		(Mariarosa Candido, Gabriella Monteduro, Barbara Mussio, M.Cristina Sciolla)		

JUDO

The combat sport of judo developed from Japanese martial arts, especially from several different schools of ju-jitsu. Dr Jigoro Kano devised the modern sport from these and founded the Kodokan Judo, a training school, in 1882 at Shitaya. Efficiency classes in judo are divided into pupil (kyu) and master (dan) grades. The highest possible grade is 12th dan, awarded only to Jigoro Kano, the only Shihan (or doctor). Apart from him, the highest is the red belt awarded for 10th Dan to thirteen men.
Belt colours for Dan grades:
1st-5th Dan – black
6th-8th Dan – red and white
9th-11th Dan – red
12th Dan – white
The first judo club in Europe was The Budokwai, founded in London in 1918. The first All-Japan Championships were held in 1930. The International Judo Federation was formed in 1951, in which year the first European championships were held, and world championships were first held in 1956. Competitions are held at various weight limits; note that these changed in 1979.

OLYMPIC GAMES
When the Olympic Games were held in Tokyo in 1964 judo was added to the Olympic programme, initially at three weight categories. Judo was not included in 1968, but from 1972 has been on the programme at all Games. Women's demonstration events were introduced in 1988. *Winners:*

MEN
Open
1964 Anton Geesink (Hol)
1972 Willem Ruska (Hol)
1976 Haruki Uemura (Jap)
1980 Dietmar Lorenz (GDR)
1984 Yasuhiro Yamashita (Jap)
1988 *Not Held*

Over 95kg
1980 Angelo Parisi (Fra)
1984 Hitoshi Saito (Jap)
1988 Hitoshi Saito (Jap)

Over 93kg
1964 Isao Inokuma (Jap)
1972 Willem Ruska (Hol)
1976 Sergey Novikov (USSR)

Under 95kg
1980 Robert Van de Walle (Bel)
1984 Ha Hyoung-zoo (SKo)
1988 Aurelio Miguel (Bra)

Under 93kg
1972 Shota Chochoshvili (USSR)
1976 Kazuhiro Ninomiya (Jap)

Under 86kg
1980 Jürg Röthlisberger (Swi)
1984 Peter Seisenbacher (Aut)
1988 Peter Seisenbacher (Aut)

Under 80kg
1964 Isao Okano (Jap)
1972 Shinobu Sekine (Jap)
1976 Isamu Sonoda (Jap)

Under 78kg
1980 Shota Khabareli (USSR)
1984 Frank Weineke (FRG)
1988 Waldemar Legien (Pol)

Under 71kg
1980 Ezio Gamba (Ita)
1984 Ahn Byeong-kuen (SKo)
1988 Marc Alexandre (Fra)

Under 70kg
1964 Takehide Nakatani (Jap)
1972 Toyokazu Nomura (Jap)
1976 Vladimir Nevzorov (USSR)

Under 65kg
1980 Nikolay Solodukhin (USSR)
1984 Yoshiyuki Matsuoka (Jap)
1988 Lee Kyung-keun (SKo)

Under 63kg
1972 Takao Kawaguchi (Jap)
1976 Héctor Rodriguez (Cub)

Under 60kg
1980 Thierry Rey (Fra)
1984 Shinji Hosokawa (Jap)

1988 Kim Jae-yup (SKo)

Most titles: 2 Willem Ruska, Hitoshi Saito, Peter Seisenbacher

WOMEN
Winners at each category when women's judo was staged as a demonstration sport at Seoul in 1988:
48kg: Li Zhongyun (Chn)
52kg: Sharon Rendle (UK)
56kg: Suzanne Williams (Aus)
61kg: Diane Bell (UK)
66kg: Hikari Sasaki (Jap)
72kg: Ingrid Berghmans (Hol)
Over 72kg: Angelique Seriese (Hol)

WORLD CHAMPIONSHIPS
Winners:

Open
1956 Shokichi Natsui (Jap)
1958 Koji Sone (Jap)
1961 Anton Geesink (Hol)
1965 Isao Inokuma (Jap)
1967 Matsuo Matsunaga (Jap)
1969 Masatoshi Shinomaki (Jap)
1971 Masatoshi Shinomaki (Jap)
1973 Kazuhiro Ninomiya (Jap)
1975 Haruki Uemura (Jap)
1979 Sumio Endo (Jap)
1981 Yasuhiro Yamashita (Jap)
1983 Hitoshi Saito (Jap)
1985 Yoshimi Masaki (Jap)
1987 Naoya Ogawa (Jap)
1989 Naoya Ogawa (Jap)

Over 95kg
1979 Yasuhiro Yamashita (Jap)
1981 Yasuhiro Yamashita (Jap)
1983 Yasuhiro Yamashita (Jap)
1985 Cho Yong-chul (SKo)
1987 Grigoriy Vertichev (USSR)
1989 Naoya Ogawa (Jap)

Over 93kg
1965 Anton Geesink (Hol)
1967 Willem Ruska (Hol)
1969 Shuji Suma (Jap)
1971 Willem Ruska (Hol)
1973 Chonufuhe Tagaki (Jap)
1975 Sumio Endo (Jap)

Under 95kg
1979 Tengiz Khubuluri (USSR)
1981 Tengiz Khubuluri (USSR)

1983 Valeriy Divisenko (USSR)
1985 Hitoshi Sugai (Jap)
1987 Hitoshi Sugai (Jap)
1989 Koba Kurtanidze (USSR)

Under 93kg
1967 Nobuyuki Sato (Jap)
1969 Fumio Sasahara (Jap)
1971 Fumio Sasahara (Jap)
1973 Nobuyuki Sato (Jap)
1975 Jean-Luc Rouge (Fra)

Under 86kg
1979 Detlef Ultsch (GDR)
1981 Bernard Tchoullouyan (Fra)
1983 Detlef Ultsch (GDR)
1985 Peter Seisenbacher (Aut)
1987 Fabien Canu (Fra)
1989 Fabien Canu (Fra)

Under 80kg
1965 Isao Okano (Jap)
1967 Eiji Maruki (Jap)
1969 Isamu Sonoda (Jap)
1971 Shozo Fujii (Jap)
1973 Shozo Fujii (Jap)
1975 Shozo Fujii (Jap)

Under 78kg
1979 Shozo Fujii (Jap)
1981 Neil Adams (UK)
1983 Nobutoshi Hikage (Jap)
1985 Nobutoshi Hikage (Jap)
1987 Hirotaka Okada (Jap)
1989 Kim Byung-ju (SKo)

Under 71kg
1979 Kyoto Katsuki (Jap)
1981 Park Chong-hak (SKo)
1983 Hidetoshi Nakanishi (Jap)
1985 Ahn Byeong-kuen (SKo)
1987 Mike Swain (USA)
1989 Toshihiko Koga (Jap)

Under 70kg
1967 Hiroshi Minatoya (Jap)
1969 Hiroshi Minatoya (Jap)
1971 Hizashi Tsuzawa (Jap)
1973 Kazutoyo Nomura (Jap)
1975 Vladimir Nevzorov (USSR)

Under 65kg
1979 Nikolay Soludukhin (USSR)
1981 Katsuhiko Kashiwazaki (Jap)
1983 Nikolay Soludukhin (USSR)
1985 Yuriy Sokolov (USSR)
1987 Yosuke Yamamoto (Jap)
1989 Drago Becanovic (Yug)

Under 63kg
1965 Hiroshi Minatoya (Jap)
1967 Takosumi Shigeoka (Jap)
1969 Yoshio Sonoda (Jap)
1971 Takao Kawaguchi (Jap)
1973 Yoshiharu Minami (Jap)
1975 Yoshiharu Minami (Jap)

Under 60kg
1979 Thierry Ray (Fra)
1981 Yasuhiko Moriwaki (Jap)
1983 Khazret Tletseri (USSR)
1985 Shinji Hosokawa (Jap)
1987 Kim Jae-yup (SKo)
1989 Amiran Totikashvilli (USSR)

Most mrn's titles: 4 Yashiro
Yamashita, Shozo Fujii

WOMEN'S WORLD CHAMPIONSHIPS
First held in 1980. *Winners:*

Open
1980 Ingrid Berghmans (Bel)
1982 Ingrid Berghmans (Bel)
1984 Ingrid Berghmans (Bel)
1986 Ingrid Berghmans (Bel)
1987 Fengliang Gao (Chn)
1989 Estela Rodriguez (Cub)

Over 72kg
1980 Margarita de Cal (Ita)
1982 Natalina Lupino (Fra)
1984 Maria-Teresa Motta (Ita)
1986 Fengliang Gao (Chn)
1987 Fengliang Gao (Chn)

Under 72kg
1980 Jocelyne Triadou (Fra)
1982 Barbara Classen (FRG)
1984 Ingrid Berghmans (Bel)
1986 Irene de Kok (Hol)
1987 Irene de Kok (Hol)
1989 Ingrid Berghmans (Bel)

Under 66kg
1980 Edith Simon (Aut)
1982 Brigitte Deydier (Fra)
1984 Brigitte Deydier (Fra)
1986 Brigitte Deydier (Fra)
1987 Alexandra Schreiber (FRG)
1989 Emanuela Pierantozzi (Ita)

Under 61kg
1980 Anita Staps (Hol)
1982 Martine Rothier (Fra)
1984 Natasha Hernandez (Ven)

1986 Diane Bell (UK)
1987 Diane Bell (UK)
1989 Catherine Fleury (Fra)

Under 56kg
1980 Gerda Winklbauer (Aut)
1982 Béatrice Rodriguez (Fra)
1984 Ann-Maria Burns (USA)
1986 Ann Hughes (UK)
1987 Catherine Arnaud (Fra)
1989 Catherine Arnaud (Fra)

Under 52kg
1980 Edith Hrovat (Aut)
1982 Loretta Doyle (UK)
1984 Kaori Yamaguchi (Jap)
1986 Dominique Brun (Fra)
1987 Sharon Rendle (UK)
1989 Sharon Rendle (UK)

Under 48kg
1980 Jane Bridge (UK)
1982 Karen Briggs (UK)
1984 Karen Briggs (UK)
1986 Karen Briggs (UK)
1987 Zhang Yun Li (Chn)
1989 Karen Briggs (UK)

Most women's titles:
6 Ingrid Berghmans, 4 Karen Briggs, 3
Brigitte Deydier, Fengliang Gao

Karen Briggs maintains her supremacy at extra-light category of under 48 kilogram
(All-Sport/John Criching)

JIU-JITSU

Jiu-jitsu incorporates the martial arts skills of both body throws and kicking and punching techniques. The World Council of Jiu-Jitsu Organisations have staged biennial world championships from 1984. Team winners on each occasion, 1984, 1986 and 1988 have been Canada.

KARATE

Karate is a martial art developed in Japan, the name originating as recently as the 1930s. The techniques used, however, were devised from the sixth century Chinese art of Shaolin boxing 'kempo' and its development in Okinawa c.1500 into 'Tang Hand', whereby the island's inhabitants fought bare handed against armed Japanese oppressors. Tang Hand was introduced to Japan in the 1920s by Funakoshi Gichin, who adopted the word karate, meaning empty hand. The style he practised became known as Shotokan, now one of five major styles in Japan, the others being Wado-ryu, Gojo-ryu, Shito-ryu and Kyokushinkai, each placing different emphasis on technique, speed and power. Karate spread to the Western world from the 1950s, and the All-Japan Karate-do Organization (FAJKO), founded in 1964, staged the first multi-style world championships in 1970. Following this the World Union of Karate-do Organizations was created.

WORLD CHAMPIONSHIPS

First held in Tokyo in 1970, when there were team and individual championships. Women first competed in 1980. Kumite championships are now staged at different weight categories and there are also Kata (or sequence) events, whereby contestants do not fight each other but are marked for their routines. *Winners:*

Men's Team
1970 Japan
1972 France
1975 Great Britain
1977 Netherlands
1980 Spain
1982 Great Britain
1984 Great Britain
1986 Great Britain
1988 Great Britain

Men's Individual Kumite
No weight limit
1970 Kouji Wada (Jap)
1972 L.Watanabe-Taske (Bra)
1975 Kazusada Murakami (Jap)
1977 Otti Roethoff (Hol)
Under 60kg
1980 Ricardo Abad (Spa)
1982 Jukka-Pekka Väyrinen (Fin)
1984 Dirk Betzien (FRG)
1986 Hideto Nakano (Jap)
1988 Abdu Shaher (UK)
Under 65kg
1980 Toshiaki Maeda (Jap)
1982 Yuichi Suzuki (Jap)
1984 Ramon Malavé (Swe)

1986 Eizou Kondo (Jap)
1988 Tim Stephens (UK)
Under 70kg
1980 Damian Gonzales (Spa)
1982 Seiji Nishimura (Jap)
1984 Jim Collins (UK)
1986 Thierry Masci (Fra)
1988 Thierry Masci (Fra)
Under 75kg
1980 Sadao Tajima (Jap)
1982 Javier Gomez (Swi)
1984 Toon Stelling (Hol)
1986 K.Leeuwin (Hol)
1988 Kyo Hayashi (Jap)
Under 80kg
1980 T.Hill (USA)
1982 Pat McKay (UK)
1984 Pat McKay (UK)
1986 Jacques Tapol (Fra)
1988 Dudley Josepa (Hol)
Over 80kg
1980 Jean-Luc Montana (Fra)
1982 Jeff Thompson (UK)
1984 Jerome Atkinson (UK)
1986 Vic Charles (UK)
1988 Emmanuel Pinda (Fra)
Open
1980 Ricciardi (Ita)
1982 Hsiao Murase (Jap)
1984 Emmanuel Pinda (Fra)
1986 Karl Daggfeldt (Swe)
1988 *sanbon shobu*
　　José Manuel Egea (Spa)
　　ippon shobu
　　Claudio Guazzaroni (Ita)

Men's Individual Kata
1977 Keiji Okada (Jap)
1980 Keiji Okada (Jap)

1982 Masashi Koyama (Jap)
1984 Tsuguo Sakumoto (Jap)
1986 Tsuguo Sakumoto (Jap)
1988 Tsuguo Sakumoto (Jap)

Men's Team Kata
1986 Japan
1988 Japan

Women's Individual Kumite
Under 53kg
1982 Sophie Berger (Fra)
1984 Sophie Berger (Fra)
1986 Johanna Kauri (Fin)
1988 Yuko Hasama (Jap)
Under 60kg
1982 Yukari Yamakawa (Jap)
1984 Tomoko Kinishi (Jap)
1986 Ritva Virelius (Fin)
1988 A.Kimura (Jap)
Over 60kg
1982 Guus van Mourik (Hol)
1984 Guus van Mourik (Hol)
1986 Guus van Mourik (Hol)
1988 Guus van Mourik (Hol)

Women's Individual Kata
1980 Suzuko Okamura (Jap)
1982 Mie Nakayama (Jap)
1984 Mie Nakayama (Jap)
1986 Mie Nakayama (Jap)
1988 Yuki Mimura (Jap)

Women's Team Kata
1986 Taiwan
1988 Japan

KENDO

The Japanese martial art of swordsmanship, which was practised by the warrior class, the samurai. The earliest known reference to such arts in Japan was in 789 AD. Kendo is now practised with shiani, or bamboo swords.

WORLD CHAMPIONSHIPS

First held in 1970. *Winners:*
1970 Mitsuru Kobayashi (Jap)
1973 Tatsushi Sakuragi (Jap)
1976 Eijo Yoko (Jap)
1979 Hironori Yamada (Jap)
1982 Minoru Makita (Jap)
1985 Kunishide Koda (Jap)
1988 Isawu Okido (Jap)
Japan has won the team title at all seven championships.

LACROSSE

The name 'La Crosse', the French word for a crozier or staff, was given by French settlers in North America to the game played by Indians, and known by them as 'baggataway'. The Indians played on a very large pitch, some 500m long, their crosse or racket being a staff curved at one end into a rough circle, into which was fitted a net. The first non-Indian club was the Montreal Lacrosse Club, founded in 1839. The sport was introduced to Britain in 1867 by a party of Caughnawaga Indians. The first national body was the National Lacrosse Association, formed in Canada in 1867. The International Federation of Amateur Lacrosse (IFAL) was founded in 1928. Women were first reported to have played lacrosse in 1886 and the All-England Women's Lacrosse Association was formed in 1912. The women's game has evolved from the men's game and there are now considerable differences in the rules.
Men's lacrosse is played by teams of 10-a-side and women's principally by 12-a-side, although a major variant is the 6-a-side game.

Men's Lacrosse

WORLD CHAMPIONSHIPS

First held in 1967 in Toronto, *winners have been:*
USA 1967, 1974, 1982, 1986; Canada 1978.
The USA also won the pre-Olympic tournament in 1984. Their only loss at this level was by 16-17 to Canada in the 1978 final, after extra time, the only drawn game at this level.

OLYMPIC GAMES

Lacrosse was played at two Olympics, when the winners were: 1904 Shamrock (Can), 1908 Canada. It was also a demonstration sport in 1928, 1932 and 1948.

ENGLISH CLUB CHAMPIONSHIPS

Contested annually for the Iroquois Cup from 1890. *Most wins:*
17 Stockport 1897-1901, 1903, 1905, 1911-3, 1923-4, 1926, 1928, 1934, 1987, 1989
11 South Manchester 1890, 1895, 1904, 1906, 1909, 1933, 1966, 1971-3, 1980
10 Old Hulmeians 1907-8, 1910, 1914, 1932, 1949-50, 1962, 1964, 1968
10 Mellor 1935-7, 1948, 1963, 1965-7, 1969, 1988
7 Old Waconians 1938-9, 1947, 1951-3, 1955
6 Heaton Mersey 1927, 1954, 1958-60, 1986
6 Cheadle 1978-9, 1981, 1984-5, 1990
3 Boardman & Eccles 1922, 1929, 1961
3 Sheffield University 1977, 1982-3

Women's Lacrosse

WORLD CHAMPIONSHIPS

First held in 1969. *Winners:* 1969 GB, 1974 USA, 1978 Canada

WORLD CUP

First held 1982, replacing the World Championships. *Winners:* 1982 USA, 1986 Australia, 1989 USA.

MODERN PENTATHLON

This is the five sport discipline of cross-country riding, épée fencing, pistol shooting (at 25m), swimming (300m) and cross-country running (4000m). It has been included at every Olympic Games from 1912, and has been known as the military pentathlon. For many years the sport was dominated by members of the armed forces, who have been particularly able to pursue such diverse activities. Military lore explains the origin of the sport: a messenger has to travel across country on horseback, fighting his way through with sword and pistol; he then has to swim across a river, before finishing his journey on foot.
Each event is scored on points, determined either against the other competitors or against scoring tables. Note that the points scores given in the lists of champions are not necessarily comparable. Prior to 1954 the scoring was on the basis of places at each event.
The sport's governing body is L'Union Internationale de Pentathlon Moderne et Biathlon, the UIPMB. It was founded in 1948 as the UIPM, taking on the administration of biathlon (qv) in 1957.

OLYMPIC GAMES

Individual *winners:*
1912 Gösta Lilliehöök (Swe) 27
1920 Gustaf Dyrssen (Swe) 18
1924 Bo Lindman (Swe) 18
1928 Sven Thofelt (Swe) 47

1932 Johan Oxenstierna (Swe) 32
1936 Gotthardt Handrick (Ger) 31.5
1948 Willie Grut (Swe) 16
1952 Lars Hall (Swe) 32
1956 Lars Hall (Swe) 4843
1960 Ferenc Németh (Hun) 5024
1964 Ferenc Török (Hun) 5116
1968 Björn Ferm (Swe) 4964
1972 András Balczó (Hun) 5412
1976 Janusz Pyciak-Peciak (Pol) 5520
1980 Anatoliy Starostin (USSR) 5568
1984 Daniele Masala (Ita) 5469
1988 János Martinek (Hun) 5404

Team *winners (first held 1952):*
Hungary   1952, 1960, 1968, 1988
USSR   1956, 1964, 1972, 1980
Great Britain 1976
Italy   1984

Most gold medals: 3 András Balczó (Hun) individual 1972, team 1960 and 1968.
Most medals: 7 Pavel Lednev (USSR): individual 2nd 1976, 3rd 1968, 1972, 1980; team 1st 1972, 1980, 2nd 1968.
Greatest margin of victory: probably by Willie Grut in 1948 as he won three events and was placed fifth and eighth in the other two. On the present scoring system: 77 points András Balczó in 1972 over Boris Onischenko (USSR), who four years later was disqualified for using an illegal fencing weapon, which registered hits when no contact had occured with his opponent.

WORLD CHAMPIONSHIPS

Held annually from 1949 with the exception of Olympic years.

Individual *winners:*
1949 Tage Bjurefelt (Swe) 19
1950 Lars Hall (Swe) 19
1951 Lars Hall (Swe) 22
1953 Gábor Benedek (Hun) 22
1954 Björn Thofelt (Swe) 4634.5
1955 Konstantin Salnikov (USSR) 4453.5
1957 Igor Novikov (USSR) 4769
1958 Igor Novikov (USSR) 4924
1959 Igor Novikov (USSR) 4847
1961 Igor Novikov (USSR) 5217
1962 Eduards Dobnikov (USSR) 4647
1963 András Balczó (Hun) 5267
1965 András Balczó (Hun) 5302
1966 András Balczó (Hun) 5217
1967 András Balczó (Hun) 5056
1969 András Balczó (Hun) 5515
1970 Peter Kelemen (Hun) 5220
1971 Boris Onischenko (USSR) 5206
1973 Pavel Lednev (USSR) 5413
1974 Pavel Lednev (USSR) 5302
1975 Pavel Lednev (USSR) 5056

1977 Janusz Pyciak-Peciak (Pol) 5485
1978 Pavel Lednev (USSR) 5498
1979 Robert Nieman (USA) 5483
1981 Janusz Pyciak-Peciak (Pol) 5662
1982 Daniele Masala (Ita) 5680
1983 Anatoliy Starostin (USSR) 5506
1985 Attila Mizser (Hun) 5525
1986 Carlo Massullo (Ita) 5463*
1987 Joël Bouzou (Fra) 5462
1989 László Fabian (Hun) 5654

* original winner was Anatoliy Starostin (USSR) 5563, but he and 14 others were subsequently disqualified for illegal drugs use. The USSR also lost their women's team title.

Team *wins:*
12 USSR   1957-9, 1961-2, 1969, 1971, 1973-4, 1982-3, 1985
10 Hungary   1954-5, 1963, 1965-7, 1970, 1975, 1987, 1989
4 Sweden   1949-51, 1953
3 Poland   1977-8, 1981
1 USA 1979, Italy 1986

Relay – first held, for three-man teams, in 1989
1989 Hungary 5148

Most titles: 13 András Balczó (Hun) six individual, seven team including Olympics 1960-72.

WOMEN'S WORLD CHAMPIONSHIPS

First held in London in 1981.

Individual *winners:*
1981 Anne Ahlgren (Swe) 4975
1982 Wendy Norman (UK) 5311
1983 Lynn Chernobrywy (Can) 5328
1984 Svetlana Yakovleva (USSR) 5481
1985 Barbara Kotowska (Pol) 5336
1986 Irina Kiselyeva (USSR) 5323
1987 Irina Kiselyeva (USSR) 5406
1988 Dorota Idzi (Pol) 5308
1989 Lori Norwood (USA) 5315

Team *wins:*
3 Great Britain 1981-3
3 Poland 1985, 1988-9
2 USSR 1984, 1987
1 France 1986

Women's World Cup

This event which preceded the world championships.
Winners:
1978 Wendy Skipwith (UK)
1979 Kathy Taylor (UK)
1980 Wendy Norman (UK)
Team: Great Britain 1978-80

MOTOR CYCLING

The first known motor cycle race was on 20 September 1896 when eight competitors took part in a race from Paris to Nantes and back. The course covered 152 km (139 miles) and was won by M.Chevalier on a Michelin-Dion tricycle in 4 hr 10 min 37 sec. The first race for two-wheeled motor cycles was held over one mile (1.6 km) of an oval track at Sheen House, Richmond, Surrey on 29 Nov, 1897. The race was won by Charles Jarrott, riding a Fournier, in a time of 2 min 8 sec. The Auto-Cycle Union (ACU) is the governing body of the sport in Britain, and was founded in 1903. The world governing body, the Fédération Internationale Motorcycliste (FIM), was formed in 1904 under the title Fédération Internationale des Clubs Motorcyclistes.

WORLD CHAMPIONSHIPS

World Championships were instituted by the FIM in 1949 for 125, 250, 350 and 500 cc classes, as well as for sidecars. The 50 cc class was introduced in 1962 but was discontinued in 1983 to make way for the larger 80 cc class. In 1977-8 a Formula 750 class was contested. The 350cc class was discontinued at the end of the 1982 season. *Winners with make of bike ridden:*

50 cc

1962	Ernst Degner (FRG)	Suzuki
1963-4	Hugh Anderson (NZ)	Suzuki
1965	Ralph Bryans (Ire)	Honda
1966-8	Hans-Georg Anscheidt (FRG)	Suzuki
1969-70	Angel Nieto (Spa)	Derbi
1971	Jan de Vries (Hol)	Kreidler
1972	Angel Nieto (Spa)	Derbi
1973	Jan de Vries (Hol)	Kreidler
1974	Henk van Kessel (Hol)	Kreidler
1975	Angel Nieto (Spa)	Kreidler
1976-7	Angel Nieto (Spa)	Bultaco
1978	Ricardo Tormo (Spa)	Bultaco
1979-80	Eugenio Lazzarini (Ita)	Kreidler
1981	Ricardo Tormo (Spa)	Bultaco
1982	Stefan Dörflinger (Swi)	MBA
1983	Stefan Dörflinger (Swi)	Krauser Kreidler

80cc

1984	Stefan Dörflinger (Swi)	Zundapp
1985	Stefan Dörflinger (Swi)	Krauser
1986-8	Jorge Martinez (Spa)	Derbi
1989	Manuel Herreros (Spa)	Derbi

125cc

1949	Nello Pagani (Ita)	Mondial
1950	Bruno Ruffo (Ita)	Mondial
1951	Carlo Ubbiali (Ita)	Mondial
1952	Cecil Sandford (UK)	MV
1953	Werner Haas (FRG)	NSU
1954	Rupert Hollaus (Aut)	NSU
1955-6	Carlo Ubbiali (Ita)	MV
1957	Tarquinio Provini (Ita)	Mondial
1958-60	Carlo Ubbiali (Ita)	MV
1961	Tom Phillis (Aus)	Honda
1962	Luigi Taveri (Swi)	Honda
1963	Hugh Anderson (NZ)	Suzuki
1964	Luigi Taveri (Swi)	Honda
1965	Hugh Anderson (NZ)	Suzuki
1966	Luigi Taveri (Swi)	Honda
1967	Bill Ivy (UK)	Yamaha
1968	Phil Read (UK)	Yamaha
1969	Dave Simmonds (UK)	Kawasaki
1970	Dieter Braun (FRG)	Suzuki
1971-2	Angel Nieto (Spa)	Derbi
1973-4	Kent Andersson (Swe)	Yamaha
1975	Paolo Pileri (Ita)	Morbidelli
1976-7	Pier-Paolo Bianchi (Ita)	Morbidelli
1978	Eugenio Lazzarini (Ita)	MBA
1979	Angel Nieto (Spa)	Morbidelli
1980	Pier-Paolo Bianchi (Ita)	MBA
1981	Angel Nieto (Spa)	Minarelli
1982-4	Angel Nieto (Spa)	Garelli
1985	Fausto Gresini(Ita)	Garelli
1986	Luca Cadalora (Ita)	Garelli
1987	Fausto Gresini (Ita)	Garelli
1988	Jorge Martinez (Spa)	Derbi
1989	Alex Criville (Spa)	Cobas

250cc

1949	Bruno Ruffo (Ita)	Guzzi
1950	Dario Ambrosini (Ita)	Benelli
1951	Bruno Ruffo (Ita)	Guzzi
1952	Enrico Lorenzetti (Ita)	Guzzi
1953-4	Werner Haas (FRG)	NSU
1955	Herman Müller (FRG)	NSU
1956	Carlo Ubbiali (Ita)	MV
1957	Cecil Sandford (UK)	Mondial
1958	Tarquinio Provini (Ita)	MV
1959-60	Carlo Ubbiali (Ita)	MV
1961	Mike Hailwood (UK)	Honda
1962-3	Jim Redman (Rho)	Honda
1964-5	Phil Read (UK)	Yamaha
1966-7	Mike Hailwood (UK)	Honda
1968	Phil Read (UK)	Yamaha
1969	Kel Caruthers (Aus)	Benelli
1970	Rod Gould (UK)	Yamaha
1971	Phil Read (UK)	Yamaha
1972	Jarno Saarinen (Fin)	Yamaha
1973	Dieter Braun (FRG)	Yamaha
1974-6	Walter Villa (Ita)	Harley-Davidson
1977	Mario Lega (Ita)	Morbidelli
1978-9	Kork Ballington (SAf)	Kawasaki
1980-1	Anton Mang (FRG)	Kawasaki
1982	Jean-Louis Tournadre (Fra)	Yamaha
1983	Carlos Lavado (Ven)	Yamaha
1984	Christian Sarron (Fra)	Yamaha
1985	Freddie Spencer (USA)	Honda
1986	Carlos Lavado (Ven)	Yamaha
1987	Anton Mang (FRG)	Honda
1988-9	Sito Pons (Spa)	Honda

350cc

1949	Freddie Frith (UK)	Velocette
1950	Bob Foster (UK)	Velocette
1951-2	Geoff Duke (UK)	Norton
1953-4	Fergus Anderson (UK)	Guzzi
1955-6	Bill Lomas (UK)	Guzzi
1957	Keith Campbell (Aus)	Guzzi
1958-60	John Surtees (UK)	MV
1961	Gary Hocking (Rho)	MV
1962-5	Jim Redman (Rho)	Honda
1966-7	Mike Hailwood (UK)	Honda
1968-73	Giacomo Agostini (Ita)	MV
1974	Giacomo Agostini (Ita)	Yamaha
1975	Johnny Cecotto (Ven)	Yamaha
1976	Walter Villa (Ita)	Harley-Davidson
1977	Takazumi Katayama (Jap)	Yamaha
1978-9	Kork Ballington (SAf)	Kawasaki
1980	Jon Ekerold (SAf)	Yamaha
1981-2	Anton Mang (FRG)	Kawasaki

500cc

1949	Leslie Graham (UK)	AJS
1950	Umberto Masetti (Ita)	Gilera
1951	Geoff Duke (UK)	Norton
1952	Umberto Masetti (Ita)	Gilera
1953-55	Geoff Duke (UK)	Gilera
1956	John Surtees (GB)	MV
1957	Libero Liberati (Ita)	Gilera
1958-60	John Surtees (UK)	MV
1961	Gary Hocking (Rho)	MV
1962-65	Mike Hailwood (UK)	MV
1966-72	Giacomo Agostini (Ita)	MV
1973-4	Phil Read (UK)	MV
1975	Giacomo Agostini (Ita)	Yamaha
1976-7	Barry Sheene (UK)	Suzuki
1978-80	Kenny Roberts (USA)	Yamaha
1981	Marco Lucchinelli (Ita)	Suzuki
1982	Franco Uncini (Ita)	Suzuki
1983	Freddie Spencer (USA)	Honda
1984	Eddie Lawson (USA)	Yamaha
1985	Freddie Spencer (USA)	Honda
1986	Eddie Lawson (USA)	Yamaha
1987	Wayne Gardner (Aus)	Honda
1988	Eddie Lawson (USA)	Yamaha
1989	Eddie Lawson (USA)	Honda

750cc

1977	Steve Baker (USA)	Yamaha
1978	Johnny Cecotto (Ven)	Yamaha
1979	Patrick Pons (Fra)	Yamaha

Sidecar

1949-51	Eric Oliver (UK)	Norton
1952	Cyril Smith (UK)	Norton
1953	Eric Oliver (UK)	Norton
1954	Wilhelm Noll (FRG)	BMW
1955	Wilhelm Faust (FRG)	BMW
1956	Wilhelm Noll (FRG)	BMW
1957	Fritz Hillebrand (FRG)	BMW
1958-9	Walter Schneider (FRG)	BMW
1960	Helmut Fath (FRG)	BMW
1961-4	Max Deubel (FRG)	BMW
1965-6	Fritz Scheidegger (Swi)	BMW
1967	Klaus Enders (FRG)	BMW
1968	Helmut Fath (FRG)	URS
1969-70	Klaus Enders (FRG)	BMW
1971	Horst Owesle (FRG)	Munch
1972-3	Klaus Enders (FRG)	BMW
1974	Klaus Enders (FRG)	Busch BMW
1975	Rolf Steinhausen (FRG)	Konig
1976	Rolf Steinhausen (FRG)	Busch Konig
1977	George O'Dell (UK)	Yamaha
1978-9	Rolf Biland (Swi)	Yamaha
1980	Jock Taylor (UK)	Yamaha
1981	Rolf Biland (Swi)	Yamaha
1982	Werner Schwärzel (FRG)	Yamaha
1983	Rolf Biland (Swi)	Yamaha
1984-6	Egbert Streuer (Hol)	Yamaha
1987-9	Steve Webster (UK)	Yamaha

With his four world titles Eddie Lawson has the most world titles won by an American motorcyclist. His first Grand Prix race was on a Kawasaki at 250cc in 1981 and his first win at 500cc on a Yamaha in 1984. From that point he has been the supreme 500cc rider, world champion in 1984, 1986, 1988 and 1989, second in 1985 and third in 1987. He rode for Yamaha 1983-8 and for Honda 1989 **(All-Sport)**

Most titles (Solo)

Total	Rider	50cc	80	125	250	350	500	750	F1	Years
15	Giacomo Agostini (Ita)	-	-	-	-	7	8	-	-	1966-75
13	Angel Nieto (Spa)	6	-	7	-	-	-	-	-	1969-84
10	Mike Hailwood (UK)	-	-	-	3	2	4	-	1	1961-78
9	Carlo Ubbiali (Ita)	-	-	6	3	-	-	-	-	1951-60
8	Phil Read (UK)	-	-	1	4	-	2	-	1	1964-77
7	John Surtees (UK)	-	-	-	-	3	4	-	-	1956-60
6	Geoff Duke (UK)	-	-	-	-	2	4	-	-	1951-5
6	Jim Redman (Rho)	-	-	-	2	4	-	-	-	1962-5

Mike Hailwood and Phil Read are the only riders to have won world titles in four classes.

Most titles in each class

50cc 6 Angel Nieto, 3 Hans-Georg Anscheidt (FRG)
80cc 3 Jorge Martinez (Spa), 2 Stefan Dörflinger (Swi)
125cc 7 Angel Nieto, 6 Carlo Ubbiali (Ita)
250cc 4 Phil Read, 3 Mike Hailwood, Carlo Ubbiali, Walter Villa (Ita), Anton Mang (FRG)
350cc 7 Giacomo Agostini, 4 Jim Redman
500cc 8 Giacomo Agostini, 4 Geoff Duke, Mike Hailwood, John Surtees, Eddie Lawson (USA); 3 Kenny Roberts (USA)
750cc 1 Steve Baker (USA), Johnny Cecotto (Ven), Patrick Pons (Fra)
F1 5 Joey Dunlop (Ire), 2 Graeme Crosby (NZ)
Sidecar 6 Klaus Enders (FRG), 4 Rolf Biland (Swi), Max Deubel (FRG), Eric Oliver (UK); 3 Egbert Streuer (Hol), Steve Webster (UK)

Most Grand Prix wins

122 Giacomo Agostini (350cc- 54, 500cc- 68)
90 Angel Nieto (50cc- 27, 80cc- 1, 125cc- 62)
76 Mike Hailwood (125cc- 2, 250cc- 21, 350cc- 16, 500cc- 37)
52 Phil Read (125cc- 10, 250cc- 27, 350cc- 4, 500cc- 11)
Hailwood, Read, Jim Redman (Rho) and Charles Mortimer (UK) are the only riders to have won Grands Prix in four different classes.

Most Grand Prix wins in each class

50cc 27 Angel Nieto (Spa)
80cc 21 Jorge Martinez (Spa)
125cc 62 Angel Nieto (Spa)
250cc 33 Anton Mang (FRG)
350cc 54 Giacomo Agostini (Ita)
500cc 68 Giacomo Agostini (Ita)
Sidecar 52 Rolf Biland (Swi)

Fastest race: 1977 Belgian GP at Spa-Francorchamps, won by Barry Sheene (UK) on a 495cc Suzuki at an average speed of 217.37 km/h (135.07 mph)

WORLD ENDURANCE CHAMPIONSHIP

Inaugurated in 1980, it replaced the FIM Coupe d'Endurance. *Winners:*

1980	Marc Fontan & Hervé Moineau (Fra)	Honda
1981	Jean Lafond & Raymond Roche (Fra)	Kawasaki
1982	Jean-Claude Chemarin (Fra) & Jacques Cornu (Swi)	Kawasaki
1983	Richard Hubin (Bel) & Hervé Moineau (Fra)	Suzuki
1984-5	Gérard Coudray & Patrick Igoa (Fra)	Honda
1986	Patrick Igoa (Fra)	Honda
1987	Hervé Moineau (Fra)	Suzuki
1988	Hervé Moineau (Fra) & Thierry Crine (Fra)	Suzuki
1989	*Not held*	

TT FORMULA ONE WORLD CHAMPIONSHIP

Formula One, Two and Three World Championships were introduced in 1977. Formula Three was discontinued at the end of 1981, and Formula Two in 1986. The Formula One race at the Isle of Man TT forms a round in the championship. *Formula One winners:*

1977	Phil Read (UK)	Honda
1978	Mike Hailwood (UK)	Ducati
1979	Ron Haslam (UK)	Honda
1980-1	Graeme Crosby (NZ)	Suzuki
1982-6	Joey Dunlop (UK)	Honda
1987	Virginio Ferrari (Ita)	Yamaha
1988-9	Carl Fogarty (UK)	Honda

WORLD MANUFACTURERS' CHAMPIONSHIP

Most wins:
39 Yamaha/LCR Yamaha
125cc: 1967-8, 1973-4
250cc: 1964-5, 1968, 1970-4, 1977, 1982-4
350cc: 1973-7, 1980
500cc: 1974-5, 1986, 1988
Sidecar: 1977-89
37 MV Augusta
125cc: 1952-3, 1955-6, 1958-60
250cc: 1955-6, 1958-60
350cc: 1958-61, 1968-72,
500cc: 1956, 1958-65, 1967-73
28 Honda
50cc: 1965-6
125cc: 1961-2, 1964, 1966
250cc: 1961-3, 1966-7, 1985-9
350cc: 1962-7

500cc: 1966, 1983-5m 1987, 1989
19 BMW
    Sidecar: 1955-73
15 Suzuki
    50cc: 1962-4, 1967-8
    125cc: 1963, 1965, 1970
    500cc: 1976-82

ISLE OF MAN TT

In 1905 the Auto Cycle Club of the RAC held rehearsals for the 1906 International Cup Race on the Isle of Man, because road racing on the mainland was banned. It was so popular that it led to the first Tourist Trophy race being staged on 28 May 1907, won by Charlie Collier on a single-cylinder Matchless. The 15.8-mile St.John's course was used until 1911 when the 37 -mile Mountain course was used for the first time. The exact distance of the current Mountain circuit is 37.73 miles 60.72 km. The shorter Clypse course (10.79 miles 17.36 km) was introduced in 1954 to accomodate the return of sidecar racing, but it was unpopular with riders, and was abandoned at the end of 1959.

Senior TT

The most prestigious of all TT races. *Winners: (all UK riders unless otherwise stated)*

1911	Oscar Godfrey	Indian
1912	Frank Applebee	Scott
1913	Tim Wood	Scott
1914	Cyril Pullin	Rudge
1920	Tommy de la Hay	Sunbeam
1921	Howard Davies	AJS
1922	Alec Bennett (Ire)	Sunbeam
1923	Tom Sheard	Douglas
1924	Alec Bennett (Ire)	Norton
1925	Howard Davies	HRD
1926	Stanley Woods	Norton
1927	Alec Bennett (Ire)	Norton
1928-9	Charlie Dodson	Sunbeam
1930	Wal Handley	Rudge Whitworth
1931	Tim Hunt	Norton
1932-3	Stanley Woods	Norton
1934	Jimmy Guthrie	Norton
1935	Stanley Woods	Moto Guzzi
1936	Jimmy Guthrie	Norton
1937	Freddie Frith	Norton
1938	Harold Daniell	Norton
1939	Georg Meier (FRG)	BMW
1947	Harold Daniell	Norton
1948	Artie Bell	Norton
1949	Harold Daniell	Norton
1950-1	Geoff Duke	Norton
1952	Reg Armstrong (Ire)	Norton
1953-4	Ray Amm (S Rho)	Norton
1955	Geoff Duke	Gilera
1956	John Surtees	MV
1957	Bob McIntyre	Gilera
1958-60	John Surtees	MV
1961	Mike Hailwood	Norton
1962	Gary Hocking (S Rho)	MV
1963-5	Mike Hailwood	MV
1966-7	Mike Hailwood	Honda
1968-72	Giacomo Agostini (Ita)	MV
1973	Jack Findlay (Aus)	Suzuki
1974	Phil Carpenter	Yamaha
1975	Mick Grant	Kawasaki
1976	Tom Herron (Ire)	Yamaha
1977	Phil Read	Suzuki
1978	Tom Herron (Ire)	Suzuki
1979	Mike Hailwood	Suzuki
1980	Graeme Crosby (NZ)	Suzuki
1981	Mick Grant	Suzuki
1982	Norman Brown	Suzuki
1983-4	Rob McElnea	Suzuki
1985	Joey Dunlop (Ire)	Honda
1986	Roger Burnett	Honda
1987-8	Joey Dunlop (Ire)	Honda
1989	Steve Hislop	Honda
1990	Carl Fogarty	Honda

Winners of other major classes, since 1977:
Junior 250cc

1977	Charlie Williams	Yamaha
1978	Charles Mortimer	Yamaha
1979-80	Charlie Williams	Yamaha
1981	Steve Tonkin	Armstrong CCM
1982	Con Law	Waddon
1983	Con Law	EMC
1984	Graeme McGregor (Aus)	Yamaha
1985	Joey Dunlop (Ire)	Honda
1986	Steve Cull (Ire)	Honda
1987	Eddie Laycock (Ire)	EMC
1988	Joey Dunlop (Ire)	Honda
1989	Johnny Rea	Yamaha
1990	Ian Lougher	Yamaha

Formula I

1977	Phil Read	Honda
1978	Mike Hailwood	Ducati
1979	Alex George	Honda
1980	Mick Grant	Honda
1981	Graeme Crosby (NZ)	Suzuki
1982	Ron Haslam	Honda
1983-8	Joey Dunlop (Ire)	Honda
1989	Steve Hislop	Honda
1990	Carl Fogarty	Honda

Most TT wins

14 Mike Hailwood 1961-79, 13 Joey Dunlop (Ire) 1977-88, 10 Stan Woods 1923-39, Giacomo Agostini (Ita) 1966-75, 9 Siegfried Schauzu (FRG) 1967- 75, 8 Phil Read 1961-77, Charles Mortimer 1970-78, Charlie Williams 1973-80
TT lap record: 195.27 kmh/121.34 mph Steve Hislop (Honda) 4 June 1989
Three TT wins in one week
Mike Hailwood 1961 Senior, Lightweight 125, Lightweight 250
Mike Hailwood 1967 Senior, Junior, Lightweight 250
Joey Dunlop 1985 Senior, Junior, Formula One

Joey Dunlop 1988 Senior, Junior, Formula One
Steve Hislop 1989 Senior, Formula One, Supersport 600
Dual Senior/Junior TT winners in one year: Tim Hunt 1931,
Stan Woods 1932-3, Jimmy Guthrie 1934, Geoff Duke
1951, Ray Amm 1953, Bob McIntyre 1957, John Surtees
1958-9, Mike Hailwood 1967, Giacomo Agostini 1968-70,
1972, Joey Dunlop 1985, 1988

MOTO-CROSS

Also known as Scrambling, Moto-Cross is a specialised
branch of Motor Cycling. The first moto-cross race, over
an undulating course, with many climbs, drops, bends,
and on a dirt circuit, was at Camberley, Surrey in 1924.
While primarily a British sport, it went international in
1947 with the introduction of the Moto-Cross des
Nations, an annual team event for 500cc machines. The
Trophée des Nations, a team event for 250cc machines,
was introduced in 1961. A European Championship for
500cc machines was introduced in 1952 and for 250cc
machines in 1957. The 500cc class became the World
Championship in 1957and the 250cc event acquired
World Championship status in 1962. A 125cc event was
added in 1975, and a sidecar championship in 1980.

WORLD CHAMPIONS

500cc

1957	Bill Nilsson (Swe)	AJS
1958	René Baeten (Bel)	FN
1959	Sten Lundin (Swe)	Monark
1960	Bill Nilsson (Swe)	Husqvarna
1961	Sten Lundin (Swe)	Monark
1962-3	Rolf Tibblin (Swe)	Husqvarna
1964-5	Jeff Smith (UK)	BSA
1966-8	Paul Friedrichs (GDR)	CZ
1969-70	Bengt Aberg (Swe)	Husqvarna
1971-3	Roger de Coster (Bel)	Suzuki
1974	Heikki Mikkola (Fin)	Husqvarna
1975-6	Roger de Coster (Bel)	Suzuki
1977-8	Heikki Mikkola (Fin)	Yamaha
1979	Graham Noyce (UK)	Honda
1980-1	André Malherbe (Bel)	Honda
1982	Brad Lackey (USA)	Suzuki
1983	Håkan Carlqvist (Swe)	Yamaha
1984	André Malherbe (Bel)	Honda
1985-6	Dave Thorpe (UK)	Honda
1987	Georges Jobé (Nel)	Honda
1988	Eric Geboers (Bel)	Honda
1989	Dave Thorpe (UK)	Honda

250cc

1962-3	Torsten Hallman (Swe)	Husqvarna
1964	Joël Robert (Bel)	CZ
1965	Viktor Arbekov (USSR)	CZ
1966-7	Torsten Hallman (Swe)	Husqvarna

1968-9	Joël Robert (Bel)	CZ
1970	Joël Robert (Bel)	Suzuki
1973	Håkan Andersson (Swe)	Yamaha
1974	Gennadiy Moisseyev (USSR)	KTM
1975	Harry Everts (Bel)	Puch
1976	Heikki Mikkola (Fin)	Husqvarna
1977-8	Gennadiy Moisseyev (USSR)	KTM
1979	Håkan Carlqvist (Swe)	Husqvarna
1980	Georges Jobe (Bel)	Suzuki
1981	Neil Hudson (UK)	Yamaha
1982	Danny la Porte (USA)	Yamaha
1983	Georges Jobé (Bel)	Suzuki
1984-5	Heinz Kinigadner (Aut)	KTM
1986	Jacky Vimond (Fra)	Yamaha
1987	Eric Geboers (Bel)	Honda
1988-9	Jean-Michel Bayle (Fra)	Honda

125cc

1975-7	Gaston Rahier (Bel)	Suzuki
1978	Akira Watanabe (Jap)	Suzuki
1979-81	Harry Everts (Bel)	Suzuki
1982-3	Eric Geboers (Bel)	Suzuki
1984	Michèle Rinaldi (Ita)	Suzuki
1985	Pekka Vehkonen (Fin)	Cagira
1986	Dave Strijbos (Hol)	Cagira
1987-8	John Van Den Berg (Hol)	Yamaha
1989	Trampas Parker (USA)	KTM

Sidecar

1980	Reinhardt Bohler (FRG)	Yamaha
1981	Tom van Heugten (Hol)	Yamaha Wasp
1982-3	Erik Bollhalder (Swi)	Yamaha
1984-7	Hans Bachtöld (Swi)	EML Jumbo
1988	Christoph Hüsser (Lie)	KTM
1989	Christoph Hüsser (Lie)	KU 71

Most world titles
6 (all 250cc) Joël Robert (Bel) 1964, 1968-72

Moto-Cross Des Nations
1947-75 for five-man teams (best three to score). 1976-84
four man teams, at 500 cc. From 1985 the Coupe des
Nations, Trophée des Nations, and Moto Cross des Nations
have been merged into one three class (500, 250 and
125cc) competition. *Wins:*
15 Great Britain 1947, 1949-50, 1952-4, 1956-7, 1959-
              60, 1963-7
9 Belgium   1948, 1951, 1969, 1972-3, 1976-7,
              1979-80
9 USA   1981-9
7 Sweden   1955, 1958, 1961-2, 1970-1, 1974
2 USSR   1968, 1978
1 Czechoslovakia1975

Trophée des Nations
1961-75 for five-man teams (best three to score). From
1976-84 four-man teams, at 250cc. Merged with the
above event in 1985. *Wins:*

11 Belgium	1969-78, 1980
5 Sweden	1963-4, 1966-8
4 USA	1981-4
3 Great Britain	1961-2, 1965
1 USSR	1979

1965 – no result, meeting declared null and void

Coupe des Nations
At 125 cc *Winners:* Italy 1982, Belgium 1983, Netherlands 1984

TRIALS
Trials riding, the means of manipulating the cycle around a pre-determined course constituting many obstacles and natural hazards, has existed since the early days of motor cycling. The famous Scottish Six Days Trial, based around Edinburgh, was introduced in 1909, and the first International Six Days Trial took place in 1913. A World Championship was introduced in 1975.

World Champions
1975	Martin Lampkin (UK)	Bultaco
1976-8	Yrjö Vesterinen (Fin)	Bultaco
1979	Bernie Schreiber (USA)	Bultaco
1980	Ulf Karlsson (Swe)	Montesa
1981	Gilles Burgat (Fra)	SWM
1982-4	Eddy Lejeune (Bel)	Honda
1985-6	Thierry Michaud (Fra)	Fantic
1987	Jordi Tarres (Spa)	Beta
1988	Thierry Michaud (Fra)	Fantic
1989	Jordi Tarres (Spa)	Beta

Most titles: 3 Vesterinen, Lejeune, Michaud

MOTOR RACING

Following the birth of the motor car in the 19th century, it was inevitable that man would soon start racing. The first race involving motorised vehicles was believed to be the *La Vélocipède* 531km (19.3-mile) race in Paris on 20 April 1887, won by Count Jules Felix Philippe Albert de Dion de Malfiance driving a De Dion steam quadricycle. There is a claim, however, that a race took place in the United States in 1878, from Green Bay to Madison, Wisconsin, won by an Oshkosk steamer. The first 'real' motor car race was on 11-14 June 1895, a 1178 km (732 mile) race from Paris to Bordeaux and back. Grand Prix racing started with the 1906 French Grand Prix, and the World Drivers' Championship was instituted in 1950. The sport's international controlling body is the Fédération Internationale de l'Automobile (FIA), whose headquarters are in Paris.

WORLD CHAMPIONSHIP GRANDS PRIX
The FIA took a decision in 1949 to inaugurate a World Championship for Drivers in 1950 and the first World Championship race took place at Silverstone on 13 May 1950 when the Italian Giuseppe Farina won the British Grand Prix. A Constructors' Championship was instituted in 1958. From 1950 to 1960 the Indianapolis 500 formed part of the Championship. The following is a list of winners of all World Championship Grand Prix races.

Argentine Grand Prix
At Buenos Aires
1953	Alberto Ascari (Ita)	Ferrari
1954	Juan Manuel Fangio (Arg)	Maserati
1955	Juan Manuel Fangio (Arg)	Mercedes-Benz
1956	Juan Manuel Fangio (Arg)	Ferrari
	& Luigi Musso (Arg) (shared drive)	
1957	Juan Manuel Fangio (Arg)	Maserati
1958	Stirling Moss (UK)	Cooper
1960	Bruce McLaren (NZ)	Cooper
1972	Jackie Stewart (UK)	Tyrrell
1973	Emerson Fittipaldi (Bra)	Lotus
1974	Denny Hulme (NZ)	McLaren
1975	Emerson Fittipaldi (Bra)	McLaren
1977	Jody Scheckter (SAf)	Wolf
1978	Mario Andretti (USA)	Lotus
1979	Jacques Laffite (Fra)	Ligier
1980	Alan Jones (Aus)	Williams
1981	Nelson Piquet (Bra)	Brabham

Australian Grand Prix
At Adelaide
1985	Keke Rosberg (Fin)	Williams
1986	Alain Prost (Fra)	McLaren
1987	Gerhard Berger (Aut)	Ferrari
1988	Alain Prost (Fra)	McLaren
1989	Thierry Boutsen (Fra)	Williams

Austrian Grand Prix
At Zeltweg 1964, Österreichring 1970-87
1964	Lorenzo Bandini (Ita)	Ferrari
1970	Jacky Ickx (Bel)	Ferrari
1971	Jo Siffert (Swi)	BRM
1972	Emerson Fittipaldi (Bra)	Lotus
1973	Ronnie Peterson (Swe)	Lotus
1974	Carlos Reutemann (Arg)	Brabham
1975	Vittorio Brambilla (Ita)	March
1976	John Watson (UK)	Penske
1977	Alan Jones (Aus)	Shadow
1978	Ronnie Peterson (Swe)	Lotus
1979	Alan Jones (Aus)	Williams
1980	Jean-Pierre Jabouille (Fra)	Renault
1981	Jacques Laffite (Fra)	Ligier
1982	Elio de Angelis (Ita)	Lotus
1983	Alain Prost (Fra)	Renault
1984	Niki Lauda (Aut)	McLaren
1985-6	Alain Prost (Fra)	McLaren
1987	Nigel Mansell (UK)	Williams

Belgian Grand Prix
At Spa-Francorchamps 1950-6, 1958, 1960-8, 1970, 1983, 1985-9; Nivelles 1972, 1974; Zolder 1973, 1975-82, 1984
| 1950 | Juan Mauel Fangio (Arg) | Alfa-Romeo |

1951	Giuseppe Farina (Ita)	Alfa-Romeo
1952-3	Alberto Ascari (Ita)	Ferrari
1954	Juan Manuel Fangio (Arg)	Maserati
1955	Juan Manuel Fangio (Arg)	Mercedes-Benz
1956	Peter Collins (UK)	Ferrari
1958	Tony Brooks (UK)	Vanwall
1960	Jack Brabham (Aus)	Cooper
1961	Phil Hill (USA)	Ferrari
1962-5	Jim Clark (UK)	Lotus
1966	John Surtees (UK)	Ferrari
1967	Dan Gurney (USA)	Eagle
1968	Bruce McLaren (NZ)	McLaren
1970	Pedro Rodriguez (Mex)	BRM
1972	Emerson Fittipaldi (Bra)	Lotus
1973	Jackie Stewart (UK)	Tyrrell
1974	Emerson Fittipaldi (Bra)	McLaren
1975-6	Niki Lauda (Aut)	Ferrari
1977	Gunnar Nilsson (Swe)	Lotus
1978	Mario Andretti (USA)	Lotus
1979	Jody Scheckter (SAf)	Ferrari
1980	Didier Pironi (Fra)	Ligier
1981	Carlos Reutemann (Arg)	Williams
1982	John Watson (UK)	McLaren
1983	Alain Prost (Fra)	Renault
1984	Michele Alboreto (Ita)	Ferrari
1985	Ayrton Senna (Bra)	Lotus
1986	Nigel Mansell (UK)	Williams
1987	Alain Prost (Fra)	McLaren
1988-9	Ayrton Senna (Bra)	McLaren

Juan-Manuel Fangio, five times world champion between the ages of 40 and 46 (All-Sport)

Brazilian Grand Prix
At Interlagos, Sao Paulo 1973-7, 1979-80, 1990; Rio de Janeiro 1978, 1981-90

1973	Emerson Fittipaldi (Bra)	Lotus
1974	Emerson Fittipaldi (Bra)	McLaren
1975	Carlos Pace (Bra)	Brabham
1976	Niki Lauda (Aut)	Ferrari
1977-8	Carlos Reutemann (Arg)	Ferrari
1979	Jacques Laffite (Fra)	Ligier
1980	René Arnoux (Fra)	Renault
1981	Carlos Reutemann (Arg)	Williams
1982	Alain Prost (Fra)	Renault
1983	Nelson Piquet (Bra)	Brabham
1984-5	Alain Prost (Fra)	McLaren
1986	Nelson Piquet (Bra)	Williams
1987-8	Alain Prost (Fra)	McLaren
1989	Nigel Mansell (UK)	Ferrari
1990	Alain Prost (Fra)	Ferrari

British Grand Prix
At Silverstone 1950-4, 1956, 1958, 1960 and uneven years from 1963-87, then annually from 1988. Aintree 1955, 1957, 1959, 1961-2; Brands Hatch, even years from 1964-86.

1950	Giuseppe Farina (Ita)	Alfa-Romeo
1951	José Froilan Gonzalez (Arg)	Ferrari
1952-3	Alberto Ascari (Ita)	Ferrari
1954	José Froilan Gonzalez (Arg)	Ferrari

1955	Stirling Moss (UK)	Mercedes-Benz
1956	Juan Manuel Fangio (Arg)	Ferrari
1957	Stirling Moss (UK) &	
	Tony Brooks (UK)	Vanwall
1958	Peter Collins (UK)	Ferrari
1959-60	Jack Brabham (Aus)	Cooper
1961	Wolfgang von Trips (FRG)	Ferrari
1962-5	Jim Clark (UK)	Lotus
1966	Jack Brabham (Aus)	Brabham
1967	Jim Clark (UK)	Lotus
1968	Jo Siffert (Swi)	Lotus
1969	Jackie Stewart (UK)	Matra
1970	Jochen Rindt (Aut)	Lotus
1971	Jackie Stewart (UK)	Tyrrell
1972	Emerson Fittipaldi (Bra)	Lotus
1973	Peter Revson (USA)	McLaren
1974	Jody Scheckter (SAf)	Tyrrell
1975	Emerson Fittipaldi (Bra)	McLaren
1976	Niki Lauda (Aut)	Ferrari
1977	James Hunt (UK)	McLaren
1978	Carlos Reutemann (Arg)	Ferrari
1979	Clay Regazzoni (Swi)	Williams
1980	Alan Jones (Aus)	Williams
1981	John Watson (UK)	McLaren
1982	Niki Lauda (Aut)	McLaren
1983	Alain Prost (Fra)	Renault
1984	Niki Lauda (Aut)	McLaren
1985	Alain Prost (Fra)	McLaren
1986-7	Nigel Mansell (UK)	Williams
1988	Ayrton Senna (Bra)	McLaren
1989	Alain Prost (Fra)	McLaren

Canadian Grand Prix
At Mosport 1967, 1969, 1971-7; Mont Tremblant 1968, 1970; Montreal 1978-86, 1988-90

1967	Jack Brabham (Aus)	Brabham
1968	Denny Hulme (NZ)	McLaren
1969	Jacky Ickx (Bel)	Brabham
1970	Jacky Ickx (Bel)	Ferrari
1971-2	Jackie Stewart (UK)	Tyrrell
1973	Peter Revson (USA)	McLaren

1974	Emerson Fittipaldi (Bra)	McLaren
1976	James Hunt (UK)	McLaren
1977	Jody Scheckter (SAf)	Wolf
1978	Gilles Villeneuve (Can)	Ferrari
1979-80	Alan Jones (Aus)	Williams
1981	Jacques Laffite (Fra)	Ligier
1982	Nelson Piquet (Bra)	Brabham
1983	René Arnoux (Fra)	Ferrari
1984	Nelson Piquet (Bra)	Brabham
1985	Michele Alboreto (Ita)	Ferrari
1986	Nigel Mansell (UK)	Williams
1988	Ayrton Senna (Bra)	McLaren
1989	Thierry Boutsen (Bel)	Williams
1990	Ayrton Senna (Bra)	McLaren

Dutch Grand Prix

At Zandvoort

1952-3	Alberto Ascari (Ita)	Ferrari
1955	Juan Manuel Fangio (Arg)	Mercedes-Benz
1958	Stirling Moss (UK)	Vanwall
1959	Jo Bonnier (Swe)	BRM
1960	Jack Brabham (Aus)	Cooper
1961	Wolfgang von Trips (FRG)	Ferrari
1962	Graham Hill (UK)	BRM
1963-5	Jim Clark (UK)	Lotus
1966	Jack Brabham (Aus)	Brabham
1967	Jim Clark (UK)	Lotus
1968-9	Jackie Stewart (UK)	Matra
1970	Jochen Rindt (Aut)	Lotus
1971	Jacky Ickx (Bel)	Ferrari
1973	Jackie Stewart (UK)	Tyrrell
1974	Niki Lauda (Aut)	Ferrari
1975	James Hunt (UK)	Hesketh
1976	James Hunt (UK)	McLaren
1977	Niki Lauda (Aut)	Ferrari
1978	Mario Andretti (USA)	Lotus
1979	Alan Jones (Aus)	Williams
1980	Nelson Piquet (Bra)	Brabham
1981	Alain Prost (Fra)	Renault
1982	Didier Pironi (Fra)	Ferrari
1983	René Arnoux (Fra)	Ferrari
1984	Alain Prost (Fra)	McLaren
1985	Niki Lauda (Aut)	McLaren

European Grand Prix

Earlier Grand Prix races were designated 'European Grand Prix' but it was not until 1983 that it became a separate race. At Brands Hatch 1983, 1985; New Nürburgring 1984

1983	Nelson Piquet (Bra)	Brabham
1984	Alain Prost (Fra)	McLaren
1985	Nigel Mansell (UK)	Williams

French Grand Prix

At Rheims 1950-1, 1953-4, 1956, 1958-61, 1963, 1966; Rouen-les Essarts 1952, 1957, 1962, 1964, 1968; Clermont-Ferrand 1965, 1969-70, 1972; Le Mans 1967, Paul Ricard 1971, 1973, 1975-6, 1978, 1980, 1982-3,

1985-9; Dijon Prenois 1974, 1977, 1979, 1981, 1984

1950	Juan Manuel Fangio (Arg)	Alfa-Romeo
1951	Juan Manuel Fangio (Arg) &	
	Luigi Fagioli (Ita)	Alfa-Romeo
1952	Alberto Ascari (Ita)	Ferrari
1953	Mike Hawthorn (UK)	Ferrari
1954	Juan Manuel Fangio (Arg)	Mercedes-Benz
1956	Peter Collins (UK)	Ferrari
1957	Juan Manuel Fangio (Arg)	Maserati
1958	Mike Hawthorn (UK)	Ferrari
1959	Tony Brooks (UK)	Ferrari
1960	Jack Brabham (Aus)	Cooper
1961	Giancarlo Baghetti (Ita)	Ferrari
1962	Dan Gurney (USA)	Porsche
1963	Jim Clark (UK)	Lotus
1964	Dan Gurney (USA)	Brabham
1965	Jim Clark (UK)	Lotus
1966-7	Jack Brabham (Aus)	Brabham
1968	Jacky Ickx (Bel)	Ferrari
1969	Jackie Stewart (UK)	Matra
1970	Jochen Rindt (Aut)	Lotus
1971-2	Jackie Stewart (UK)	Tyrrell
1973-4	Ronnie Peterson (Swe)	Lotus
1975	Niki Lauda (Aut)	Ferrari
1976	James Hunt (UK)	McLaren
1977-8	Mario Andretti (USA)	Lotus
1979	Jean-Pierre Jabouille (Fra)	Renault
1980	Alan Jones (Aus)	Williams
1981	Alain Prost (Fra)	Renault
1982	René Arnoux (Fra)	Renault
1983	Alain Prost (Fra)	Renault
1984	Niki Lauda (Aut)	McLaren
1985	Nelson Piquet (Bra)	Brabham
1986-7	Nigel Mansell (UK)	Williams
1988-9	Alain Prost (Fra)	McLaren
1990	Alain Prost (Fra)	Ferrari

German Grand Prix

At Nürburgring 1951-4, 1956-8, 1961-9, 1971-6; Avus 1959, Hockenheim 1970, 1977-84, 1986-9; New Nürburgring 1985

1951-2	Alberto Ascari (Ita)	Ferrari
1953	Giuseppe Farina (Ita)	Ferrari
1954	Juan Manuel Fangio (Arg)	Mercedes-Benz
1956	Juan Manuel Fangio (Arg)	Ferrari
1957	Juan Manuel Fangio (Arg)	Maserati
1958	Tony Brooks (UK)	Vanwall
1959	Tony Brooks (UK)	Ferrari
1961	Stirling Moss (UK)	Lotus
1962	Graham Hill (UK)	BRM
1963-4	John Surtees (UK)	Ferrari
1965	Jim Clark (UK)	Lotus
1966	Jack Brabham (Aus)	Brabham
1967	Denny Hulme (NZ)	Brabham
1968	Jackie Stewart (UK)	Matra
1969	Jacky Ickx (Bel)	Brabham
1970	Jochen Rindt (Aut)	Lotus
1971	Jackie Stewart (UK)	Tyrrell
1972	Jacky Ickx (Bel)	Ferrari

1973	Jackie Stewart (UK)	Tyrrell
1974	Clay Regazzoni (Swi)	Ferrari
1975	Carlos Reutemann (Arg)	Brabham
1976	James Hunt (UK)	McLaren
1977	Niki Lauda (Aut)	Ferrari
1978	Mario Andretti (USA)	Lotus
1979	Alan Jones (Aus)	Williams
1980	Jacques Laffite (Fra)	Ligier
1981	Nelson Piquet (Bra)	Brabham
1982	Patrick Tambay (Fra)	Ferrari
1983	René Arnoux (Fra)	Ferrari
1984	Alain Prost (Fra)	McLaren
1985	Michele Alboreto (Ita)	Ferrari
1986-7	Nelson Piquet (Bra)	Williams
1988-9	Ayrton Senna (Bra)	McLaren

Hungarian Grand Prix
At Budapest

1986-7	Nelson Piquet (Bra)	Williams
1988	Ayrton Senna (Bra)	McLaren
1989	Nigel Mansell (UK)	Ferrari

Italian Grand Prix
At Monza 1950-79, 1981-9; Imola 1980

1950	Giuseppe Farina (Ita)	Alfa-Romeo
1951-2	Alberto Ascari (Ita)	Ferrari
1953	Juan Manuel Fangio (Arg)	Maserati
1954-5	Juan Manuel Fangio (Arg)	Mercedes-Benz
1956	Stirling Moss (UK)	Maserati
1957	Stirling Moss (UK)	Vanwall
1958	Tony Brooks (UK)	Vanwall
1959	Stirling Moss (UK)	Cooper
1960-1	Phil Hill (USA)	Ferrari
1962	Graham Hill (UK)	BRM
1963	Jim Clark (UK)	Lotus
1964	John Surtees (UK)	Ferrari
1965	Jackie Stewart (UK)	BRM
1966	Lodovico Scarfiotti (Ita)	Ferrari
1967	John Surtees (UK)	Honda
1968	Denny Hulme (NZ)	McLaren
1969	Jackie Stewart (UK)	Matra
1970	Clay Regazzoni (Swi)	Ferrari
1971	Peter Gethin (UK)	BRM
1972	Emerson Fittipaldi (Bra)	Lotus
1973-4	Ronnie Peterson (Swe)	Lotus
1975	Clay Regazzoni (Swi)	Ferrari
1976	Ronnie Peterson (Swe)	March
1977	Mario Andretti (USA)	Lotus
1978	Niki Lauda (Aut)	Brabham
1979	Jody Scheckter (SAf)	Ferrari
1980	Nelson Piquet (Bra)	Brabham
1981	Alain Prost (Fra)	Renault
1982	René Arnoux (Fra)	Renault
1983	Nelson Piquet (Bra)	Brabham
1984	Niki Lauda (Aut)	McLaren
1985	Alain Prost (Fra)	McLaren
1986-7	Nelson Piquet (Bra)	Williams
1988	Gerhard Berger (Aut)	Ferrari

1989	Alain Prost (Fra)	McLaren

Japanese Grand Prix
At Fuji 1976-7, Suzuka 1987-9

1976	Mario Andretti (USA)	Lotus
1977	James Hunt (UK)	McLaren
1987	Gerhard Berger (Aut)	Ferrari
1988	Ayrton Senna (Bra)	McLaren
1989	Alessandro Nannini (Ita)	Benetton

Las Vegas Grand Prix
At Caeser's Palace

1981	Alan Jones (Aus)	Williams
1982	Michele Alboreto (Ita)	Tyrrell

Mexican Grand Prix
At Mexico City

1963	Jim Clark (UK)	Lotus
1964	Dan Gurney (USA)	Brabham
1965	Richie Ginther (USA)	Honda
1966	John Surtees (UK)	Cooper
1967	Jim Clark (UK)	Lotus
1968	Graham Hill (UK)	Lotus
1969	Denny Hulme (NZ)	McLaren
1970	Jacky Ickx (Bel)	Ferrari
1986	Gerhard Berger (Aut)	Benetton
1987	Nigel Mansell (UK)	Williams
1988	Alain Prost (Fra)	McLaren
1989	Ayrton Senna (Bra)	McLaren
1990	Alain Prost (Fra)	Ferrari

Monaco Grand Prix
At Monte Carlo

1950	Juan Manuel Fangio (Arg)	Alfa-Romeo
1955	Maurice Trintignant (Fra)	Ferrari
1956	Stirling Moss (UK)	Maserati
1957	Juan Manuel Fangio (Arg)	Maserati
1958	Maurice Trintignant (Fra)	Cooper
1959	Jack Brabham (Aus)	Cooper
1960-1	Stirling Moss (UK)	Lotus
1962	Bruce McLaren (NZ)	Cooper
1963-5	Graham Hill (UK)	BRM
1966	Jackie Stewart (UK)	BRM
1967	Denny Hulme (NZ)	Brabham
1968-9	Graham Hill (UK)	Lotus
1970	Jochen Rindt (Aut)	Lotus
1971	Jackie Stewart (UK)	Tyrrell
1972	Jean-Pierre Beltoise (Fra)	BRM
1973	Jackie Stewart (UK)	Tyrrell
1974	Ronnie Peterson (Swe)	Lotus
1975-6	Niki Lauda (Aut)	Ferrari
1977	Jody Scheckter (SAf)	Wolf
1978	Patrick Depailler (Fra)	Tyrrell
1979	Jody Scheckter (SAf)	Ferrari
1980	Carlos Reutemann (Arg)	Williams
1981	Gilles Villeneuve (Can)	Ferrari
1982	Riccardo Patrese (Ita)	Brabham
1983	Keke Rosberg (Fin)	Williams

1984-6	Alain Prost (Fra)	McLaren
1987	Ayrton Senna (Bra)	Lotus
1988	Alain Prost (Fra)	McLaren
1989	Ayrton Senna (Bra)	McLaren
1990	Ayrton Senna (Bra)	McLaren

Moroccan Grand Prix
At Ain Diab, Casablanca

1958	Stirling Moss (UK)	Vanwall

Pescara Grand Prix
At Circuit Pescara

1957	Stirling Moss (UK)	Vanwall

Portuguese Grand Prix
At Oporto 1958, 1960; Monsanto 1959; Estoril 1984-9

1958	Stirling Moss (UK)	Vanwall
1959	Stirling Moss (UK)	Cooper
1960	Jack Brabham (Aus)	Cooper
1984	Alain Prost (Fra)	McLaren
1985	Ayrton Senna (Bra)	Lotus
1986	Nigel Mansell (UK)	Williams
1987-8	Alain Prost (Fra)	McLaren
1989	Gerhard Berger (Aut)	Ferrari

San Marino Grand Prix
At Imola

1981	Nelson Piquet (Bra)	Brabham
1982	Didier Pironi (Fra)	Ferrari
1983	Patrick Tambay (Fra)	Ferrari
1984	Alain Prost (Fra)	McLaren
1985	Elio de Angelis (Ita)	Lotus
1986	Alain Prost (Fra)	McLaren
1987	Nigel Mansell (UK)	Williams
1988-9	Ayrton Senna (Bra)	McLaren
1990	Riccardo Patrese (Ita)	Williams

South African Grand Prix
At East London 1962-3, 1965; Kyalami 1967-80, 1982-5

1962	Graham Hill (UK)	BRM
1963	Jim Clark (UK)	Lotus
1965	Jim Clark (UK)	Lotus
1967	Pedro Rodriguez (Mex)	Cooper
1968	Jim Clark (UK)	Lotus
1969	Jackie Stewart (UK)	Matra
1970	Jack Brabham (Aus)	Brabham
1971	Mario Andretti (USA)	Ferrari
1972	Denny Hulme (NZ)	McLaren
1973	Jackie Stewart (UK)	Tyrrell
1974	Carlos Reutemann (Arg)	Brabham
1975	Jody Scheckter (SAf)	Tyrrell
1976-7	Niki Lauda (Aut)	Ferrari
1978	Ronnie Peterson (Swe)	Lotus
1979	Gilles Villeneuve (Can)	Ferrari
1980	René Arnoux (Fra)	Renault
1982	Alain Prost (Fra)	Renault
1983	Riccardo Patrese (Ita)	Brabham
1984	Niki Lauda (Aut)	McLaren

1985	Nigel Mansell (UK)	Williams

Spanish Grand Prix
At Pedralbes 1951, 1954; Jarama 1968, 1970, 1972, 1974, 1976-9, 1981; Montjuich Park 1969, 1971, 1973, 1975; Jerez 1986-9

1951	Juan Manuel Fangio (Arg)	Alfa-Romeo
1954	Mike Hawthorn (UK)	Ferrari
1968	Graham Hill (UK)	Lotus
1969	Jackie Stewart (UK)	Matra
1970	Jackie Stewart (UK)	March
1971	Jackie Stewart (UK)	Tyrrell
1972-3	Emerson Fittipaldi (Bra)	Lotus
1974	Niki Lauda (Aut)	Ferrari
1975	Jochen Mass (FRG)	McLaren
1976	James Hunt (UK)	McLaren
1977-8	Mario Andretti (USA)	Lotus
1979	Patrick Depailler (Fra)	Ligier
1981	Gilles Villeneuve (Can)	Ferrari
1986	Ayrton Senna (Bra)	Lotus
1987	Nigel Mansell (UK)	Williams
1988	Alain Prost (Fra)	McLaren
1989	Ayrton Senna (Bra)	McLaren

Swedish Grand Prix
At Anderstorp

1973	Denny Hulme (NZ)	McLaren
1974	Jody Scheckter (SAf)	Tyrrell
1975	Niki Lauda (Aut)	Ferrari
1976	Jody Scheckter (SAf)	Tyrrell
1977	Jacques Lafitte (Fra)	Ligier
1978	Niki Lauda (Aut)	Brabham

Swiss Grand Prix
At Bremgarten, Berne 1950-4, Dijon (France) 1982

1950	Giuseppe Farina (Ita)	Alfa-Romeo
1951	Juan Manuel Fangio (Arg)	Alfa-Romeo
1952	Piero Taruffi (Ita)	Ferrari
1953	Alberto Ascari (Ita)	Ferrari
1954	Juan Manuel Fangio (Arg)	Mercedes-Benz
1982	Keke Rosberg (Fin)	Williams

United States Grand Prix
At Sebring 1959, Riverside 1960, Watkins Glen 1961-80, Phoenix 1989-90

1959	Bruce McLaren (NZ)	Cooper
1960	Stirling Moss (UK)	Lotus
1961	Innes Ireland (UK)	Lotus
1962	Jim Clark (UK)	Lotus
1963-5	Graham Hill (UK)	BRM
1966-7	Jim Clark (UK)	Lotus
1968	Jackie Stewart (UK)	Matra
1969	Jochen Rindt (Aut)	Lotus
1970	Emerson Fittipaldi (Bra)	Lotus
1971	François Cevert (Fra)	Tyrrell
1972	Jackie Stewart (UK)	Tyrrell
1973	Ronnie Peterson (Swe)	Lotus
1974	Carlos Reutemann (Arg)	Brabham

1975	Niki Lauda (Aut)	Ferrari
1976-7	James Hunt (UK)	McLaren
1978	Carlos Reutemann (Arg)	Ferrari
1979	Gilles Villeneuve (Can)	Ferrari
1980	Alan Jones (Aus)	Williams
1989	Alain Prost (Fra)	McLaren
1990	Ayrton Senna (Bra)	McLaren

United States Grand Prix East
At Detroit

1982	John Watson (UK)	McLaren
1983	Michele Alboreto (Ita)	Tyrrell
1984	Nelson Piquet (Bra)	Brabham
1985	Keke Rosberg (Fin)	Williams

| 1986-7 | Ayrton Senna (Bra) | Lotus |
| 1988 | Ayrton Senna (Bra) | McLaren |

United States Grand Prix West
At Long Beach 1976-8; Fir Park 1984

1976	Clay Regazzoni (Swi)	Ferrari
1977	Mario Andretti (USA)	Lotus
1978	Carlos Reutemann (Arg)	Ferrari
1979	Gilles Villeneuve (Can)	Ferrari
1980	Nelson Piquet (Fra)	Brabham
1981	Alan Jones (Aus)	Williams
1982	Niki Lauda (Aut)	McLaren
1983	John Watson (UK)	McLaren
1984	Keke Rosberg (Fin)	Williams

WORLD CHAMPIONS & RUNNERS-UP

Year	Winner	Points	Runner-up	Points
1950	Giuseppe Farina (Ita)	30	Juan Manuel Fangio (Arg)	27
1951	Juan Manuel Fangio (Arg)	31	Alberto Ascari (Ita)	25
1952	Alberto Ascari (Ita)	36	Giuseppe Farina (Ita)	24
1953	Alberto Ascari (Ita)	34.5	Juan Manuel Fangio (Arg)	28
1954	Juan Manuel Fangio (Arg)	42	José Froilán González (Arg)	$25^{1}/_{7}$
1955	Juan Manuel Fangio (Arg)	40	Stirling Moss (UK)	23
1956	Juan Manuel Fangio (Arg)	30	Stirling Moss (UK)	27
1957	Juan Manuel Fangio (Arg)	40	Stirling Moss (UK)	25
1958	Mike Hawthorn (UK)	42	Stirling Moss (UK)	41
1959	Jack Brabham (Aus)	31	Tony Brooks (UK)	27
1960	Jack Brabham (Aus)	43	Bruce McLaren (NZ)	34
1961	Phil Hill (USA)	34	Wolfgang von Trips (FRG)	33
1962	Graham Hill (UK)	42	Jim Clark (UK)	30
1963	Jim Clark (UK)	54	Graham Hill (UK) &	29
			Richie Ginther (USA)	29
1964	John Surtees (UK)	40	Graham Hill (UK)	39
1965	Jim Clark (UK)	54	Graham Hill (UK)	40
1966	Jack Brabham (Aus)	42	John Surtees (UK)	28
1967	Denny Hulme (NZ)	51	Jack Brabham (Aus)	46
1968	Graham Hill (UK)	48	Jackie Stewart (UK)	36
1969	Jackie Stewart (UK)	63	Jacky Ickx (Bel)	37
1970	Jochen Rindt (Aut)	45	Jacky Ickx (Bel)	40
1971	Jackie Stewart (UK)	62	Ronnie Peterson (Swe)	33
1972	Emerson Fittipaldi (Bra)	61	Jackie Stewart (UK)	45
1973	Jackie Stewart (UK)	71	Emerson Fittipaldi (Bra)	55
1974	Emerson Fittipaldi (Bra)	55	Clay Regazzoni (Swi)	52
1975	Niki Lauda (Aut)	64.5	Emerson Fittipaldi (Bra)	45
1976	James Hunt (UK)	69	Niki Lauda (Aut)	68
1977	Niki Lauda (Aut)	72	Jody Scheckter (SAf)	55
1978	Mario Andretti (USA)	64	Ronnie Peterson (Swe)	51
1979	Jody Scheckter (SAf)	51	Gilles Villeneuve (Can)	47
1980	Alan Jones (Aus)	67	Nelson Piquet (Bra)	54
1981	Nelson Piquet (Bra)	50	Carlos Reutemann (Arg)	49
1982	Keke Rosberg (Fin)	44	John Watson (UK) &	39
			Didier Pironi (Fra)	39
1983	Nelson Piquet (Bra)	59	Alain Prost (Fra)	57
1984	Niki Lauda (Aut)	72	Alain Prost (Fra)	71.5
1985	Alain Prost (Fra)	73	Michele Alboreto (Ita)	53
1986	Alain Prost (Fra)	72	Nigel Mansell (UK)	70
1987	Nelson Piquet (Bra)	73	Nigel Mansell (UK)	61
1988	Ayrton Senna (Bra)	90	Alain Prost (Fra)	87
1989	Alain Prost (Fra)	76	Ayrton Senna (Bra)	60

Most Grand Prix wins in a career (to end of 1989 season)

Wins	Driver	Career	Races	Points	Av.pts	Champs
39	Alain Prost (Fra)	1980-9	153	592.5	3.9	3
27	Jackie Stewart (UK)	1965-73	99	360	3.6	3
25	Jim Clark (UK)	1960-8	72	274	3.8	2
25	Niki Lauda (Aut)	1971-85	171	420	2.5	3
24	Juan Manuel Fangio (Arg)	1950-8	51	277.5	5.4	5
20	Nelson Piquet (Bra)	1978-89	172	410	2.4	3
20	Ayrton Senna (Bra)	1985-9	94	313	3.3	1
16	Stirling Moss (UK)	1951-61	66	186⁹/₁₄	2.8	-
15	Nigel Mansell (UK)	1985-9	132	250	1.9	-
14	Graham Hill (UK)	1958-75	176	289	1.6	2
14	Jack Brabham (Aus)	1955-70	126	261	2.1	3
14	Emerson Fittipaldi (Bra)	1970-80	144	281	2.0	2
13	Alberto Ascari (Ita)	1951-5	32	140¹/₇	4.4	2
12	Mario Andretti (USA)	1968-82	128	183	1.4	1
12	Carlos Reutemann (Arg)	1972-82	146	310	2.1	-
12	Alan Jones (Aus)	1975-86	116	206	1.8	1
10	James Hunt (UK)	1973-9	92	179	1.9	1
10	Ronnie Peterson (Swe)	1970-8	123	206	1.7	-
10	Jody Scheckter (SAf)	1972-80	112	255	2.3	1

Others to average more than 2.8 points per drive (Av.pts)

Giuseppe Farina (Ita)		1950-5	33	127.5	3.9
Mike Hawthorn (UK)		1953-8	45	127 9/14	2.8

Most Grand Prix starts: 192 Riccardo Patrese (Ita), 1977-89

Most wins in a season
8 Ayrton Senna (Bra) 1988; 7 Jim Clark (UK) 1963, Alain Prost (Fra) 1984, 1988; 6 Alberto Ascari (Ita) 1952, Juan Manuel Fangio (Arg) 1954, Jim Clark (UK) 1965, Jackie Stewart (UK) 1969, 1971, James Hunt (UK) 1976, Mario Andretti (USA) 1978, Nigel Mansell (UK) 1987, Ayrton Senna (Bra) 1989

Most successive wins: 9 Alberto Ascari (Ita) 1952-3, 5 Jack Brabham (Aus) 1960, Jim Clark (UK) 1965
Most pole positions: 42 Ayrton Senna, 33 Jim Clark (UK); 28 Juan Manuel Fangio (Arg); 24 Niki Lauda (Aut); Nelson Piquet (Bra)

Oldest
GP driver: 55 yr 292 days Louis Chiron (Mon) 1955 Monaco GP
GP winner: 53 yr 22 days Luigi Fagioli (Ita) 1951 French GP
GP points scorer: 53 yr 248 days Phillipe Etancelin (Fra) 1950 Italian GP (5th)
World champion: 46 yr 41 days Juan Manuel Fangio (Arg) 1957
Youngest
GP driver: 19 yr 182 days Mike Thackwell (NZ) 1980 Canadian GP
GP winner: 22yr 80 days Troy Ruttman (USA) 1952 Indianapolis 500
GP points scorer: 20 yr 113 days Ricardo Rodriguez (Mex) 1962 Belgian GP (4th)
World champion: 25 yr 273 days Emerson Fittipaldi (Bra) 1972

Ayrton Senna in his McLaren Honda. After his record eight Grand Prix wins in 1988 he added four more in 1989, although beaten by his teammate Alain Prost to the world title **(All-Sport)**

The most successful drivers

The leading drivers based on the following points system: 9 for winning the championship, 6 for coming 2nd, 4 for 3rd, 3 for 4th, 2 for 5th and 1 for finishing 6th in the championship (the same as the scoring system in the championship races each season) have been:

57 Juan Manuel Fangio (Arg)
53 Alain Prost (Fra)
44 Jackie Stewart (UK)
41 Niki Lauda (Aut)
40 Nelson Piquet (Bra)
38 Graham Hill (UK)
36 Stirling Moss (UK) *
34 Jack Brabham (Aus)
33 Jim Clark (UK)
31 Emerson Fittipaldi (Bra)
26 Alberto Ascari (Ita)
26 John Surtees (UK)
25 Denny Hulme (NZ)
25 Ayrton Senna (Bra)
23 Giuseppe Farina (Ita)
23 Jody Scheckter (SAf)
22 Carlos Reutemann (Arg) *
21 Mike Hawthorn (UK)
21 Jacky Ickx (Bel) *
* Indicates never won championship

CONSTRUCTORS' CHAMPIONSHIP

Year	Constructor	Points
1958	Vanwall	48
1959	Cooper-Climax	40
1960	Cooper-Climax	48
1961	Ferrari	45
1962	BRM	42
1963	Lotus-Climax	54
1964	Ferrari	45
1965	Lotus-Climax	54
1966	Brabham-Repco	42
1967	Brabham-Repco	63
1968	Lotus-Ford	62
1969	Matra-Ford	66
1970	Lotus-Ford	59
1971	Tyrrell-Ford	73
1972	Lotus-Ford	61
1973	Lotus-Ford	92
1974	McLaren-Ford	73
1975	Ferrari	72
1976	Ferrari	83
1977	Ferrari	95
1978	Lotus-Ford	86
1979	Ferrari	113
1980	Williams-Ford	120
1981	Williams-Ford	95
1982	Ferrari	74
1983	Ferrari	89
1984	McLaren-Porsche	143
1985	McLaren-TAG	90
1986	Williams-Honda	141
1987	Williams-Honda	137
1988	McLaren-Honda	199
1989	McLaren-Honda	141

Most wins: 8 Ferrari, 7 Lotus, 5 McLaren, 4 Williams, 2 Brabham, Cooper

Most Grand Prix wins

97	Ferrari	1951-89
80	McLaren	1968-89
79	Lotus	1960-87
42	Williams	1979-89
35	Brabham	1964-85
23	Tyrrell	1971-83
17	BRM	1959-72
16	Cooper	1958-67
15	Renault	1979-83
10	Alfa Romeo	1950-1

Most wins in a season
15 McLaren-Honda 1988; 12 McLaren-Porsche 1984; 10 McLaren-Honda 1989; 9 Williams-Honda 1987; 8 Lotus-Ford 1978; 7 Ferrari 1952-3, Lotus-Climax 1963, Tyrrell-Ford 1971, Lotus-Ford 1973
Most successive wins: 14 Ferrari 1952-3; 11 McLaren-Honda 1988; 9 Alfa Romeo 1950-1; 8 McLaren-Porsche 1984-5
Fastest average speed: 242.62 km/h (150.75 mph) 1971 Italian GP at Monza, won by Peter Gethin (UK) in a BRM. The fastest for a circuit in current use is 235.421 km/h (146.284 mph) by Nigel Mansell in a Williams-Honda at Zeltweg in the 1987 Austrian GP.
Slowest winning average speed: 98.68 km/h (61.33 mph) 1950 Monaco GP, Monte Carlo, won by Juan Manuel Fangio (Arg) in an Alfa Romeo.
Fastest Lap: 247.02 km/h (153.49 mph) Henri Pescarolo (Fra) March-Ford, 1971 Italian GP at Monza.
Qualfying lap record: 258.803 km/h (160.817 mph) Keke Rosberg (Fin) Williams-Honda, 1985 Britisg GP at Silverstone.

Longest races

805 km/500 miles Indianapolis 500, 1951-60
602 km/374 miles French GP (Rheims), 1951
555 km/345 miles Indianapolis 500, 1950 (shortened race)
508 km/316 miles Belgian GP (Spa) 1951-6

Longest circuit: 25.57 km/15.89 miles Pescara, Italy (1957 Pescara GP)
Shortest circuit: 3.14 km/1.95 miles Monte Carlo, France (1955-72 Monaco GP)

Most frequently used circuits

39 Monza, Italy 1950-89, 36 Monte Carlo, Monaco 1950-89, 24 Spa, Belgium 1950-89, 23 Silverstone, England 1950-89, 22 (Old) Nürburgring, FR Germany 1951-76, 20 Watkins Glen, USA 1961-80

INDIANAPOLIS 500

Held at the end of May each year, the Indianapolis 500 forms part of the Memorial Day celebrations. The race is held at the Indianapolis Raceway, Indiana, and covers 200 laps of the 2-mile oval shaped circuit. The first race was on 30 May 1911 and won by Ray Harroun in a Marmon Wasp. From 1950 to 1960 the race formed part of the World Driver's Championship, but very few European drivers competed in it.

The Borg-Warner Trophy has been awarded to the winner annually from 1936. It was introduced by Captain Eddie Rickenbacker, then owner of the Indianapolis Motor Speedway, and replaced the Wheeler-Shebler Trophy, presented from 1911 to 1935. The trophy, made of 80 lbs of sterling silver cost $10,000 originally and is now priceless. It displays the faces of all winners of the race from 1911. Winners personally keep a sterling silver miniature of the trophy, which is 5ft 9 in high plus a new base 1ft 6in high. *Winners since 1950: (all US unless otherwise stated).*

Year	Winner	Manufacturer	Av. speed (mph)
1950	Johnny Parsons	Kurtis Kraft-Offenhauser	124.002
1951	Lee Wallard	Kurtis Kraft-Offenhauser	126.244
1952	Troy Ruttmann	Kuzna-Offenhauser	128.922
1953	Bill Vukovich	Kurtis Kraft 500A-Offenhauser	128.740
1954	Bill Vukovich	Kurtis Kraft 500A-Offenhauser	130.840
1955	Bob Sweikert	Kurtis Kraft 500C-Offenhauser	128.209
1956	Pat Flaherty	Watson-Offenhauser	128.490
1957	Sam Hanks	Epperly-Offenhauser	135.601
1958	Jimmy Bryan	Epperly-Offenhauser	133.791
1959	Rodger Ward	Watson-Offenhauser	135.857
1960	Jim Rathmann	Watson-Offenhauser	138.767
1961	A.J.Foyt	Watson-Offenhauser	139.130
1962	Rodger Ward	Watson-Offenhauser	140.293
1963	Parnelli Jones	Watson-Offenhauser	143.137
1964	A.J.Foyt	Watson-Offenhauser	147.350
1965	Jim Clark (UK)	Lotus-Ford	150.686
1966	Graham Hill (UK)	Lola-Ford	144.317
1967	A.J.Foyt	Coyote-Ford	151.207
1968	Bobby Unser	Eagle-Offenhauser	152.882
1969	Mario Andretti	Hawk-Ford	156.867
1970	Al Unser	P.J.Colt-Ford	155.749
1971	Al Unser	P.J.Colt-Ford	157.735
1972	Mark Donohue	McLaren-Offenhauser	162.962
1973	Gordon Johncock	Eagle-Offenhauser	159.036
1974	Johnny Rutherford	McLaren-Offenhauser	158.589
1975	Bobby Unser	Eagle-Offenhauser	149.213
1976	Johnny Rutherford	McLaren-Offenhauser	148.725
1977	A.J.Foyt	Coyote-Ford	161.331
1978	Al Unser	Lola-Cosworth	161.363
1979	Rick Mears	Penske-Cosworth	158.899
1980	Johnny Rutherford	Chaparral-Cosworth	142.862
1981	Bobby Unser	Penske-Cosworth	139.085
1982	Gordon Johncock	Wildcat-Cosworth	162.062
1983	Tom Sneva	March-Cosworth	162.117
1984	Rick Mears	March-Cosworth	163.621
1985	Danny Sullivan	March-Cosworth	152.982
1986	Bobby Rahal	March-Cosworth	170.722
1987	Al Unser	March-Cosworth	162.175
1988	Rick Mears	Penske-Chevrolet	144.809
1989	Emerson Fittipaldi (Bra)	Penske-Chevrolet	167.581
1990	Arie Luyendyk (Hol)	Lola-Chevrolet	185.981

Most wins: 4 A.J.Foyt and Al Unser, as above; 3 Louis Meyer 1928, 1933, 1936; Mauri Rose 1941, 1947, 1948; Bobby Unser, Johnny Rutherford, Rick Mears – all as above

Fastest winning speed: 185.981 mph (299.299 km/h) Arie Luyendyk in a Lola-Chevrolet, 1990

Qualifying record speed for four laps: 225.301 mph (362.577 km/h) Emerson Fittipaldi in a Penske-Chevrolet, 1990

Single lap qualifying record: 225.575 mph (363.018 km/h) Emerson Fittipaldi, 1990

Al Unser equals the record in 1987 with a fourth win in the Indianapolis 500 (**All-Sport**)

TRANS-AM SERIES

Organised by the Sports Car Club of America (SCAA) the Trans-Am Series started in 1966 as the SCCA Trans-American Sedan Championship. It is a championship for high-performance mass-produced cars which are sold in the United States. Trans-Am races are basically 'sprint' events, with most distances around 100 miles.

Champions:
1966 Horst Kwech
1967 Jerry Titus
1968 Mark Donohue
1969 Mark Donohue
1970 Parnelli Jones
1971 Mark Donohue
1972 George Follmer
1973 Peter Gregg
1974 Peter Gregg
1975 John Greenwood
1976 George Follmer
1977 (Cat.1) Bob Tullius
     (Cat.2) Ludwig Heimrath
1978 (Cat.1) Bob Tullius
     (Cat.2) Greg Pickett
1979 (Cat.1) Gene Bothello
     (Cat.2) John Paul
1980 John Bauer
1981 Eppie Wietzes
1982 Elliott Forbes-Robinson
1983 David Hobbs
1984 Tom Gloy
1985 Wally Dallenbach Jr.
1986 Wally Dallenbach Jr.
1987 Scott Pruett
1988 Hurley Heywood
1989 Dorsey Schroeder

CART RACING

Championship Auto Racing Teams Inc. (CART) was founded in 1978 by Roger Penske and 'Pat' Patrick who broke away from the United States Auto Club (USAC) to form its own series of races. Indy Car racing (on oval speedways) has been in existence since 1909. Between 1909-55 the season-long championship was known as the AAA National Championship. It then became the USAC National Championship and since 1979, following the formation of CART, the CART National Championship. Since 1980 the series has been sponsored by PPG Industries and is known as the PPG Indy Car World Series. *Winners:*

AAA National Championship
1909 George Robertson
1910 Ray Harroun
1911 Ralph Mulford
1912 Ralph DePalma
1913 Earl Cooper
1914 Ralph DePalma
1915 Earl Cooper
1916 Dario Resta
1917 Earl Cooper
1918 Ralph Mulford
1919 Howard Wilcox
1920-1 Tommy Milton
1922 Jimmy Murphy
1923 Eddie Hearne
1924 Jimmy Murphy
1925 Peter DePaolo
1926 Harry Hartz

1927 Peter DePaolo
1928 Louie Meyer
1929 Louie Meyer
1930 Billy Arnold
1931 Louis Schneider
1932 Bob Carey
1933 Louie Meyer
1934 Bill Cummings
1935 Kelly Petillo
1936 Mauri Rose
1937 Wilbur Shaw
1938 Floyd Roberts
1939 Wilbur Shaw
1940-1 Rex Mays
1942-45 No racing
1946-8 Ted Horn
1949 Johnny Parsons
1950 Henry Banks
1951 Tony Bettenhausen, Sr
1952 Chuck Stevenson
1953 Sam Hanks
1954 Jimmy Bryan
1955 Bob Swikert

USAC National Championship
1956-7 Jimmy Bryan
1958 Tony Bettenhausen, Sr
1959 Rodger Ward
1960-1 A.J.Foyt
1962 Rodger Ward
1963-4 A.J.Foyt
1965-6 Mario Andretti
1967 A.J.Foyt
1968 Bobby Unser
1969 Mario Andretti
1970 Al Unser
1971-2 Joe Leonard
1973 Roger McCluskey

1974 Bobby Unser
1975 A.J.Foyt
1976 Gordon Johncock
1977-8 Tom Sneva
1979 A.J.Foyt

PPG Indy Car World Series
1979 Rick Mears
1980 Johnny Rutherford
1981-2 Rick Mears
1983 Al Unser
1984 Mario Andretti
1985 Al Unser
1986-7 Bobby Rahal
1988 Danny Sullivan
1989 Emerson Fittipaldi

Most wins: 7 A.J.Foyt, 4 Mario Andretti, 3 Earl Cooper, Louie Meyer, Ted Horn, Jimmy Bryan, Al Unser, Rick Mears

NASCAR CHAMPIONSHIP
The National Association for Stock Car Auto Racing, Inc. (NASCAR) was the brainchild of Virginian Bill France who formed the association in 1947. The first race sanctioned by NASCAR was over the Daytona Beach course on 15 February 1948. Early races were either over dirt tracks or beach circuits. Today they are run over enclosed circuits and NASCAR races are now among the most popular in the United States. The Winston Cup series was started in 1949 and was known as the Grand National series. It became the Winston Cup in 1970 following sponsorship by the R.J.Reynolds Tobacco Company.
Winners:
1949 Red Byron
1950 Bill Rexford
1951 Herb Thomas
1952 Tim Flock
1953 Herb Thomas
1954 Lee Petty
1955 Tim Flock
1956-7 Buck Baker
1958-9 Lee Petty
1960 Rex White
1961 Ned Jarrett
1962-3 Joe Weatherley
1964 Richard Petty
1965 Ned Jarrett
1966 David Pearson
1967 Richard Petty
1968-9 David Pearson

1970 Bobby Isaac
1971-2 Richard Petty
1973 Benny Parsons
1974-5 Richard Petty
1976-8 Cale Yarborough
1979 Richard Petty
1980 Dale Earnhardt
1981-2 Darrell Waltrip
1983 Bobby Allison
1984 Terry Labonte
1985 Darrell Waltrip
1986 Dale Earnhardt
1987 Dale Earnhardt
1988 Bill Elliott
1989 Rusty Wallace
Most wins: 7 Richard Petty, 3 Lee Petty, David Pearson, Cale Yarborough, Dale Earnhardt, Darrell Waltrip

NASCAR all-time leading money winners as at 1 January 1990
Darrell Waltrip	$10,048,041
Dale Earnhardt	9,751,388
Bill Elliott	9,182,039
Mario Andretti	7,261,803
Bobby Allison	7,244,822
Richard Petty	6,983,909
Rick Mears	6,814,932
Al Unser Sr	6,323,207
Bobby Rahal	6,289,469
Terry Labonte	5,849,561
Rusty Wallace	5,650,710
A.J.Foyt Jr	5,491,113
Al Unser Jr	5,456,001
Danny Sullivan	5,301,787
Cale Yarborough	5,093,933
Emerson Fittipaldi	5,005,691

DAYTONA 500
The Daytona 500, held at the Daytona International Speedway every February, is one of NASCAR's top events.
Winners:

Year	Winner	Manufacturer	Average speed	
1959	Lee Petty	Oldsmobile	218.05km/h	135.52mph
1960	Junior Johnson	Chevrolet	200.71km/h	124.74mph
1961	Marvin Panch	Pontiac	240.71km/h	149.60mph
1962	Fireball Roberts	Pontiac	245.42km/h	152.53mph
1963	Tiny Lund	Ford	243.88km/h	151.57mph
1964	Richard Petty	Plymouth	248.32km/h	154.33mph
1965	Fred Lorenzen	Ford	227.74km/h	141.54mph
1966	Richard Petty	Plymouth	258.45km/h	160.63mph
1967	Mario Andretti	Ford	236.41km/h	146.93mph
1968	Cale Yarborough	Mercury	230.49km/h	143.25mph
1969	LeeRoy Yarborough	Ford	254.14km/h	157.95mph
1970	Pepet Hamilton	Plymouth	240.71km/h	149.60mph
1971	Richard Petty	Plymouth	232.44km/h	144.46mph
1972	A.J.Foyt	Mercury	259.93km/h	161.55mph
1973	Richard Petty	Dodge	252.95km/h	157.21mph
1974	Richard Petty	Dodge	226.69km/h	140.89mph
1975	Benny Parsons	Chevrolet	247.22km/h	153.65mph
1976	David Pearson	Mercury	244.86km/h	152.18mph
1977	Cale Yarborough	Chevrolet	246.53km/h	153.22mph
1978	Bobby Allison	Ford	257.01km/h	159.73mph
1979	Richard Petty	Oldsmobile	231.66km/h	143.98mph
1980	Buddy Baker	Oldsmobile	285.76km/h	177.60mph
1981	Richard Petty	Buick	272.97km/h	169.65mph
1982	Bobby Allison	Buick	247.77km/h	153.99mph
1983	Cale Yarborough	Pontiac	250.97km/h	155.98mph
1984	Cale Yarborough	Chevrolet	242.94km/h	150.99mph
1985	Bill Elliott	Ford	277.18km/h	172.27mph
1986	Geoff Bodine	Chevrolet	238.33km/h	148.12mph
1987	Bill Elliott	Ford	283.60km/h	176.26mph
1988	Bobby Allison	Buick	221.29km/h	137.53mph
1989	Darrell Waltrip	Chevrolet	238.88km/h	148.47mph
1990	Derrike Cope	Chevrolet	266.76km/h	165.76mph

Most Wins: 7 Richard Petty, 4 Cale Yarborough, 3 Bobby Allison

LE MANS

The most famous of all sports car races, the Le Mans 24 Hour race was inaugurated on 26-27 May 1923, and won by André Lagache and René Leonard in a 3-litre Chenard & Walcker. The original Le Mans circuit at Sarthe, France, measured 17.26 km (10.73 miles) but the present circuit is 13.64km (8.48 miles). *Post-war winners:*

Year	Winner	Manufacturer	Av. speed km/h
1949	Luigi Chinetti (Ita)/Lord Peter Selsdon (UK)	Ferrari	132.418
1950	Louis Rosier/Jean-Louis Rosier (Fra)	Talbot-Lago	144.379
1951	Peter Walker/Peter Whitehead (UK)	Jaguar	150.466
1952	Hermann Lang/Karl Riess (FRG)	Mercedes-Benz	155.574
1953	Tony Rolt/Duncan Hamilton (UK)	Jaguar	170.335
1954	Froilan Gonzalez (Arg)/Maurice Trintignant (Fra)	Ferrari	164.386
1955	Mike Hawthorn/Ivor Bueb (UK)	Jaguar	172.308
1956	Ron Flockhart/Ninian Sanderson (UK)	Jaguar	168.120
1957	Ron Flockhart/Ivor Bueb (UK)	Jaguar	183.216
1958	Olivier Gendebien (Bel)/Phil Hill (USA)	Ferrari	170.912
1959	Carroll Shelby/Roy Salvadori (UK)	Aston Martin	181.162
1960	Olivier Gendebien/Paul Frère (Bel)	Ferrari	175.729
1961	Olivier Gendebien (Bel)/Phil Hill (USA)	Ferrari	186.526
1962	Olivier Gendebien (Bel)/Phil Hill (USA)	Ferrari	185.467
1963	Ludovico Scarfiotti/Lorenzo Bandini (Ita)	Ferrari	190.071

The start of the Le Mans 24 hour race in 1989 **(All-Sport/Darrell Ingham)**

1964	Jean Guichet (Fra)/Nino Vaccarella (Ita)	Ferrari	195.638
1965	Jochen Rindt (Aut)/Masten Gregory (USA)	Ferrari	194.879
1966	Chris Amon/Bruce McLaren (NZ)	Ford	201.795
1967	Dan Gurney/A.J.Foyt (USA)	Ford	218.033
1968	Pedro Rodriguez (Mex)/Lucien Bianchi (Bel)	Ford	185.536
1969	Jacky Ickx (Bel)/Jackie Oliver (UK)	Ford	208.250
1970	Hans Herrmann (FRG)/Richard Attwood (UK)	Porsche	191.992
1971	Helmut Marko (Aut)/Gijs van Lennep (Hol)	Porsche	222.304
1972	Henri Pescarolo (Fra)/Graham Hill (UK)	Matra-Simca	195.472
1973	Henri Pescarolo/Gérard Larrousse (Fra)	Matra-Simca	202.250
1974	Henri Pescarolo/Gérard Larrousse (Fra)	Matra-Simca	191.940
1975	Jacky Ickx (Bel)/Derek Bell (UK)	Mirage-Ford	191.480
1976	Jacky Ickx (Bel)/Gijs van Lennep (Hol)	Porsche	198.750
1977	Jacky Ickx (Bel)/Jürgen Barth (FRG)/Hurley Haywood (USA)	Porsche	194.802
1978	Jean-Pierre Jaussaud/Didier Pironi (Fra)	Renault Alpine	210.190
1979	Klaus Ludwig (FRG)/Bill Whittington (USA)/Don Whittington (USA)	Porsche	173.900
1980	Jean-Pierre Jaussaud/Jean Rondeau (Fra)	Rondeau-Ford	192.000
1981	Jacky Ickx (Bel)/Derek Bell (UK)	Porsche	201.060
1982	Jacky Ickx (Bel)/Derek Bell (UK)	Porsche	204.128
1983	Vern Schuppan (Aut)/ Hurley Haywood (USA)/Al Holbert (USA)	Porsche	210.330
1984	Klaus Ludwig (FRG)/Henri Pescarolo (Fra)	Porsche	204.180
1985	Klaus Ludwig (FRG)/Paulo Barillo (Ita)/'John Winter' (FRG)	Porsche	212.021
1986	Hans Stück (FRG)/Derek Bell (UK)/Al Holbert (USA)	Porsche	203.197
1987	Hans Stück (FRG)/Derek Bell (UK)/Al Holbert (USA)	Porsche	199.657
1988	Jan Lammers (Hol)/Johnny Dumfries (UK)/Andy Wallace (UK)	Jaguar	221.630
1989	Jochen Mass (FRG)/Manuel Reuter (FRG)/Stanley Dickens (Swe)	Mercedes	219.991
1990	John Nielsen (Den)/Martin Brundle (UK)/Price Cobb (USA)	Jaguar	204.070

Most wins: 6 Jacky Ickx, 5 Derek Bell, 4 Olivier Gendebien, Henri Pescarolo; 3 Woolf Barnato (UK) 1928-30, Luigi Chinetti (Ita/USA) 1932, 1934, 1949, Phil Hill
Most successful combinations: 3 wins Olivier Gendebien/Phil Hill, and Jacky Ickx/Derek Bell
Fastest winning speed: 222.304 kph Helmut Marko/Gijs van Lennep, 1971
Greatest distance covered: 5333.72 km/3314.22 miles Helmut Marko/Gijs van Lennep, 1971
Record for current circuit: 5332 km/3313.24 miles Jan Lammers/Johnny Dumfries/Andy Wallace, 1988
Most successful cars: 12 wins Porsche, 9 Ferrari, 7 Jaguar

WORLD SPORTS CAR CHAMPIONSHIP

Over the years the format, and car specification, has changed many times since its introduction in 1953. Between 1953-61 it was known as the Sports Car World Championship, with the title going to the leading manufacturer. The championship ended in 1961 and was revived in 1968 as a championship for competition sports cars and prototypes. With the distinction between competition and prototypes disappearing, a new Championship for Makes was introduced in 1972. In 1981, a championship for drivers was introduced for the first time, and it became known as the World Endurance Championship. The name was changed once more in 1986 when it became the Sports-Prototype World Championship, for both cars and drivers. Since 1985 the constructors' championship has been for teams. *Winners*

Cars
1953-4 Ferrari
1955 Mercedes-Benz
1956-8 Ferrari
1959 Aston Martin
1960-1 Ferrari
1968 Ford
1969-71 Porsche
1972 Ferrari
1973-4 Matra-Simca
1975 Alfa Romeo
1976-9 Porsche
1980 Lancia
1981-4 Porsche
1985 Rothmans-Porsche
1986 Brun Motorsport
1987-8 Silk Cut Jaguar
1989 Sauber Mercedes

Drivers
1981 Bob Garretson (USA)
1982-3 Jacky Ickx (Bel)
1984 Stefan Bellof (FRG)
1985-6 Derek Bell (UK) & Hans-Joachim Stück (FRG)
1987 Raul Boesel (Bra)
1988 Martin Brundle (UK)
1989 Jean-Louis Schlesser (Fra)

FORMULA TWO, FORMULA THREE and FORMULA 3000

Formula Two was introduced in 1947 to enable young drivers to gain experience ready for the step up to Formula One. Formula Three was created in the early 1950s for much the same reason. A European Formula Two championship was introduced in 1967 and a Formula Three championship followed in 1975. Both were discontinued in 1984, making way for the new European Formula 3000 Championship, later re-named the FIA Formula 3000 International Championship. Formula Three remains popular in Britain and championships have existed in various forms since 1966 when Harry Stiller won the Les Leston Championship. It was not until the introduction of the Vandervell British Formula Three Championship in 1979 that the event became unified.

European Formula Two champions

1967 Jacky Ickx (Bel)
1968 Jean-Pierre Beltoise (Fra)
1969 Johnny Servoz-Gavin (Fra)
1970 Clay Regazzoni (Swi)
1971 Ronnie Peterson (Swe)
1972 Mike Hailwood (UK)
1973 Jean-Pierre Jarier (Fra)
1974 Patrick Depailler (Fra)
1975 Jacques Laffite (Fra)
1976 Jean-Pierre Jabouille (Fra)
1977 René Arnoux (Fra)
1978 Bruno Giacomelli (Ita)
1979 Marc Surer (Swi)
1980 Brian Henton (UK)
1981 Geoff Lees (UK)
1982 Corrado Fabi (Ita)
1983 Jonathan Palmer (UK)
1984 Mike Thackwell (NZ)
(Discontinued)
Most race wins: 11 Jochen Rindt (Aut), Bruno Giacomelli (Ita); 9 Mike Thackwell (NZ), 7 Jean-Pierre Jarier (Fra), Jacques Laffite (Fra)

European Formula Three champions

1975 Larry Perkins (Aus)
1976 Riccardo Patrese (Ita)
1977 Piercarlo Ghinzani (Ita)
1978 Jan Lammers (Hol)
1979 Alain Prost (Fra)

1980 Michele Alboreto (Ita)
1981 Mauro Baldi (Ita)
1982 Oscar Larrauri (Arg)
1983 Pierluigi Martini (Ita)
1984 Ivan Capelli (Ita)
(Discontinued)
Most race wins: 11 Mauro Baldi (Ita), 8 Oscar Larrauri (Arg), Alain Prost (Fra); 7 Anders Olofsson (Swe), 6 John Nielsen (Den), Emanuele Pirro (Ita)

British Formula Three champions since 1979

1979 Chico Serra (Bra)
1980 Stefan Johansson (Swe)
1981 Jonathan Palmer (UK)
1982 Tommy Byrne (Ire)
1983 Ayrton Senna (Bra)
1984 Johnny Dumfries (UK)
1985 Mauricio Gugelmin (Bra)
1986 Andy Wallace (UK)

1987 Johnny Herbert (UK)
1988 J.J.Lehto (Fin)
1989 Allan McNish (UK)
Most race wins: 12 Ayrton Senna (Bra), 11 Andy Wallace (UK), 10 Johnny Dumfries (UK), 9 Martin Donnelly (UK), 8 Jonathan Palmer (UK), Martin Brundle (UK), J.J.Lehto (Fin)

FIA Formula 3000 Champions

1985 Christian Danner (FRG)
1986 Ivan Capelli (Ita)
1987 Stefano Modena (Ita)
1988 Roberto Moreno (Bra)
1989 Jean Alesi (Fra)
Most race wins: 5 Roberto Moreno (Bra), 4 Mike Thackwell (NZ), Emanuele Pirro (Ita), Christian Danner (FRG), Luis Perez Sala (Spa), Martin Donnelly (UK)

RALLYING

The first long-distance rally was from Peking, China, to Paris between 10 June–10 August 1907. It was won by Prince Scipione Borghese (Ita) driving an Itala. Since then many famous rallies have been staged. The most famous being the Monte Carlo Rally, instituted in 1911, when it was won by Henri Rougier (Fra) in a Tyrcat-Mery. The RAC International Rally of Great Britain (now known as the Lombard-RAC Rally) was first held in 1927 but it did not gain recognition as an international event by the FIA until 1951.

MONTE CARLO RALLY

Winners

1911	Henri Rougier (Fra)	Turcat-Mery
1912	J.Beutler	Berliet
1924	Jean Ledure	Bignan
1925	François Repusseau (Fra)	Renault 40 CV
1926	Hon.Victor Bruce/W.J.Brunell	AC Bristol
1927	Lefebvre (Fra)	Amilcar
1928	Jacques Bignan	Fiat
1929	Dr.Sprenger van Eijk	Graham-Paige
1930	Hector Petit	Licorne
1931	Donald Healey (UK)	Invicta
1932-3	M.Vasselle (Fra)	Hotchkiss
1934	Gas/Jean Trevoux (Fra)	Hotchkiss
1935	Christian Lahaye/R.Quatresous (Fra)	Renault Nervasport
1936	I.Zamfirescu/J.Quinlin	Ford
1937	René le Begue/J.Quinlin	Delahaye
1938	G Bakker Schut/Karel Ton	Ford
1939	Jean Trevoux/M.Lesurque (Fra)	Hotchkiss
1949	Jean Trevoux/M.Lesurque (Fra)	Hotchkiss
1950	Marcel Becquart/H.Secret (Fra)	Hotchkiss
1951	Jean Trevoux (Fra)/R.Crovetto	Delahaye
1952	Sidney Allard/G.Warburton (UK)	Allard P2
1953	Maurice Gatsonides/P.Worledge	Ford Zephyr
1954	Louis Chiron/C.Basadonna (Fra)	Lancia-Aurelia
1955	Per Malling/Gunnar Fadum (Swe)	Sunbeam-Talbot
1956	Ronnie Adams/F.E.A.Bigger (UK)	Jaguar Mk VII

1957	*No race due to Suez crisis*	
1958	Guy Monraisse/J.Feret (Fra)	Renault Dauphine
1959	Paul Coltelloni/P.Alexander	Citroen ID19
1960	Walter Schock/R.Moll	Mercedes 220SE
1961	Maurice Martin/R.Bateau (Fra)	Panhard PL17
1962	Erik Carlsson/Gunnar Haggbom (Swe)	Saab 96
1963	Erik Carlsson/Gunnar Palm (Swe)	Saab 96
1964	Paddy Hopkirk (Ire)/Henry Liddon	Mini-Cooper 'S'
1965	Timo Makinen (Fin)/Paul Easter	Mini-Cooper 'S'
1966	Pauli Toivonen (Fin)/Ensio Mikander	Citroen DS21
1967	Rauno Aaltonen (Fin)/Henry Liddon	Mini-Cooper 'S'
1968	Vic Elford/David Stone (UK)	Porsche 911T
1969-70	Björn Waldegård/Lars Helmer (Swe)	Porsche 911
1971	Ove Andersson (Swe)/David Stone (UK)	Alpine Renault A110
1972	Sandro Munari/Mario Manucci (Ita)	Lancia Fulvia
1973	Jean-Claude Andruet (Fra)/'Biche' (Michèle Petit)	Alpine Renault A110
1974	*No race due to fuel crisis*	
1975	Sandro Munari/Mario Manucci (Ita)	Lancia Stratos
1976	Sandro Munari/Silvio Maiga (Ita)	Lancia Stratos
1977	Sandro Munari/Mario Manucci (Ita)	Lancia Stratos
1978	Jean-Pierre Nicolas/Vincent Laverne (Fra)	Porsche Carrera 911
1979	Bernard Darniche/Alain Mahe (Fra)	Lancia Stratos
1980	Walter Röhrl/Christian Geistdorfer (FRG)	Fiat Abarth 131
1981	Jean Ragnotti/Jean-Marc André (Fra)	Renault 5 Turbo
1982-3	Walter Röhrl/Christian Geistdorfer (FRG)	Opel Ascona
1984	Walter Röhrl/Christian Geistdorfer (FRG)	Audi Quattro
1985	Ari Vatanen (Fin)/Terry Harryman (UK)	Peugeot 205 Turbo 16
1986	Henri Toivonen (Fin)/Sergio Cresto (Ita)	Lancia Delta S4
1987	Mikki Biasion/Tiziano Siviero (Ita)	Lancia Delta HF4
1988	Bruno Saby/Jean-Francois Fauchille (Fra)	Lancia Delta HF4
1989	Mikki Biasion/Tiziano Siviero (Ita)	Lancia Delta Integrale
1990	Didier Auriol/Bernard Occelli (Fra)	Lancia Delta Integrale 16

Most wins: 4 Sandro Munari (Ita), Walter Röhrl (FRG); 3 Jean Trevoux (Fra) 1939, 1949, 1951
Most successful co-driver: 4 wins Christian Geistdorfer (FRG), all with Walter Röhrl.

LOMBARD RAC RALLY
Winners since 1951:

1951	Ian Appleyard/Pat Appleyard (UK)	Jaguar XK120
1952	Godfrey Imhof/Mrs.B.Fleming (UK)	Allard Cadillac J2
1953	Ian Appleyard/Pat Appleyard (UK)	Jaguar XK120
1954	Johnny Wallwork/J.H.Brooks (UK)	Triumph TR2
1955	James Ray/Brian Horrock (UK)	Standard Ten
1956	Lyndon Sims, R.Jones/Tony Ambrose (UK)	Aston Martin DB2
1957	Not held due to Suez crisis	
1958	Peter Harper/Dr.E.W.Deane (UK)	Sunbeam Rapier
1959	Gerald Burgess/Sam Croft-Pearson(UK)	Ford Zephyr
1960	Erik Carlsson (Swe)/Stuart Turner (UK)	Saab 96
1961	Erik Carlsson (Swe)/John Brown (UK)	Saab 96
1962	Erik Carlsson (Swe)/David Stone (UK)	Saab 96
1963	Tom Trana/S.Lindström (Swe)	Volvo PV544
1964	Tom Trana/Gunnar Thermanius (Swe)	Volvo 122S
1965	Rauno Aaltonen (Fin)/Tony Ambrose (UK)	Mini-Cooper 'S'
1966	Bengt Soderström/Gunnar Palm (Swe)	Ford Cortina Lotus
1967	Not held due to foot and mouth outbreak	
1968	Simo Lampinen (Fin)/John Davenport (UK)	Saab 96 V4
1969-70	Harry Kallström (Fin)/Gunnar Haggbom (Swe)	Lancia Fulvia
1971	Stig Blomqvist/Arne Hertz (Swe)	Saab 96 V4

1972	Roger Clark/Tony Mason (UK)	Ford Escort RS
1973-5	Timo Mäkinen (Fin)/Henry Liddon (UK)	Ford Escort RS
1976	Roger Clark/Stuart Pegg (UK)	Ford Escort RS
1977	Björn Waldegård (Swe)/Hans Thorszelius	Ford Escort RS
1978-9	Hannu Mikkola (Fin)/Arne Hertz (Swe)	Ford Escort RS
1980	Henri Toivonen (Fin)/Paul White (UK)	Talbot Sunbeam Lotus
1981-2	Hannu Mikkola (Fin)/Arne Hertz (Swe)	Audi Quattro A1/A2
1983	Stig Blomqvist/Björn Cederberg (Swe)	Audi Quattro A2
1984	Ari Vatanen (Fin)/Terry Harryman (UK)	Peugeot 205 Turbo 16
1985	Henri Toivonen (Fin)/Neil Wilson (UK)	Lancia Delta S4
1986	Timo Salonen (Fin)/Seppo Harjanne (Fin)	Peugeot 205 Turbo
1987	Juha Kankkunen/Jiro Piironen (Fin)	Lancia Delta
1988	Markku Alén/Ilkka Kivimäki (Fin)	Lancia Delta
1989	Pentti Arikkala (Fin)/Ronan McNamee (Ire)	Mitsibushi

Most wins: 4 Hannu Mikkola (Fin); 3 Erik Carlsson (Swe), Timo Makinen (Fin)
Most successful co-drivers: 4 wins Arne Hertz (Swe); 3 wins Henry Liddon (UK)

SAFARI RALLY

The longest rally held annually is the Safari Rally, first raced in 1953 as the Coronation Safari in Kenya, Tanzania and Uganda but now restricted to Kenya. The race has covered up to 6234 km/3874 miles, as it did in 1971. No overall winner was declared in 1953, but the Class A prize went to Alan Dix and Jerry Larsen in their Volkswagen 1200.
Winners:

1954	D Marwaha/Vic Preston	Volkswagen 1200
1955	D Marwaha/Vic Preston	Ford Zephyr
1956	Eric Cecil/Tony Vickers	D.K.W.
1957	Arthur Burton/Angus Hofmann	Volkswagen 1200
1958	*No outright winner declared*	
1959-60	Bill Fritschy/Jack Ellis	Mercedes 219
1961	John Manussis/Bill Coleridge/David Beckett	Mercedes 220
1962	Tommy Fjastad/Bernhard Schneider	Volkswagen 1200
1963	Nick Nowicki/Paddy Cliff	Peugeot 404
1964	Peter Hughes/Billy Young	Ford Cortina GT
1965	Joginder Singh/Jaswant Singh (Ken)	Volvo PV544
1966-7	Bert Shankland/Chris Rothwell	Peugeot 404
1968	Nick Nowicki/Paddy Cliff	Peugeot 404
1969	Robin Hillyar/Jock Aird (UK)	Ford Taunus 20MRS
1970	Edgar Herrmann/Hans Schüller (FRG)	Datsun 1600SSS
1971	Edgar Herrmann/Hans Schüller (FRG)	Datsun 240Z
1972	Hannu Mikkola (Fin)/Gunnar Palm (Swe)	Ford Escort RS1600
1973	Shekhar Mehta/Lofty Drews (Ken)	Datsun 250Z
1974	Joginder Singh (Ken)/David Doig	Colt Galant 1600
1975	Ove Andersson/Arne Hertz (Swe)	Peugeot 504
1976	Joginder Singh (Ken)/David Doig	Mitsibushi Colt Lancer
1977	Björn Waldegård (Swe)/Hans Thorszelius	Ford Escort RS 1800
1978	Jean-Pierre Nicolas/Jean-Claude Lefebvre (Fra)	Peugeot 504 Coupe V6
1979-80	Shekhar Mehta/Mike Doughty (Ken)	Datsun 160J
1981-2	Shekhar Mehta/Mike Doughty (Ken)	Datsun Violet GT
1983	Ari Vartanen (Fin)/Terry Harryman (UK)	Opel Ascona 400
1984	Björn Waldegård (Swe)/Hans Thorszelius	Toyota Celica TCT
1985	Juha Kankkunen (Fin)/Fred Gallagher (UK)	Toyota Celica TCT
1986	Björn Waldegård (Swe)/Fred Gallagher (UK)	Toyota Celica Turbo
1987	Hannu Mikkola (Fin)/Arne Hertz (Swe)	Audi 200 Quattro
1988-9	Mikki Biasion/Tiziano Siviero (Ita)	Lancia Delta
1990	Björn Waldegård (Swe)/Fred Gallagher (UK)	Toyota Celica GT4

Most wins: 5 Shekhar Mehta, 4 Björn Waldegård, 3 Joginder Singh.
Most wins as co-driver: 4 Mike Doughty

WORLD RALLY CHAMPIONSHIPS

A World Championship for makes of car was inaugurated in 1968 and a driver's championship, known as the FIA Cup for Drivers was instituted in 1977; it became the official World Drivers' Championship in 1979. A championship for co-drivers was introduced in 1981. *Winners:*

Makes

1968 Ford (GB)	1979 Ford
1969 Ford (Europe)	1980 Fiat
1970 Porsche	1981 Talbot
1971 Alpine-Renault	1982 Audi
1972 Lancia	1983 Lancia
1973 Alpine-Renault	1984 Audi
1974-6 Lancia	1985-6 Peugeot
1977-8 Fiat	1987-9 Lancia

Drivers

1977 Sandro Munari (Ita)	1983 Hannu Mikkola (Fin)
1978 Markku Alén (Fin)	1984 Stig Blomqvist (Swe)
1979 Björn Waldegård (Swe)	1985 Timo Salonen (Fin)
1980 Walter Röhrl (FRG)	1986-7 Juha Kankkunen (Fin)
1981 Ari Vatanen (Fin)	1988-9 Mikki Biasion (Ita)
1982 Walter Röhrl (FRG)	

DRAG RACING

In this aspect of motor racing two cars (or bikes) race each other over a distance of a quarter of a mile (402.3m). The sport was developed in the 1930s in the USA. The sport's governing body in the USA, the National Hot Rod Association (NHRA) was founded in 1950.

Records

The lowest elapsed time recorded by a piston-engined dragster from a standing start to 440 yards is 4.909 seconds by Darrell Gwynn (USA) at Houston on 1 Mar 1990. The record for the highest terminal velocity reached at the end of a 440 yards run is 294.88 mph (474.55 km/h) by Gary Ormsby (USA) in the NHRA World Finals at Ennis, Texas on 7 Oct 1989. A women's world record for the lowest elapsed time was set by Shirley Muldowney at 4.974 sec at the NHRA Keystone Nationals at Reading, Pa. on 17 Sep 1989.

NHRA Winston Series

Each year drivers collect points in a series of races throughout North America, culminating in the annual Winston Finals. The most wins is 10 by Bob Glidden at Pro Stock, including five consecutively 1985-9. The élite competition is the Top Fuel class, at which recent winners have been:

1980 Shirley Muldowney
1981 Jeb Allen
1982 Shirley Muldowney
1983 Gary Beck
1984 Joe Amato
1985 Don Garlits
1986 Don Garlits
1987 Dick LaHaie
1988 Joe Amato
1989 Gary Ormsby

NHRA Winston Finals

Top Fuel winners, with (ET) and terminal speed (mph) reached from the inaugural Finals in 1965 have been:

Year	Driver	ET	mph
1965	Maynard Rupp	7.82	200.00
1966	Pete Robinson	7.27	203.16
1967	Bennie Osborn	7.03	223.88
1968	Bennie Osborn	7.05	211.76
1969	Steve Carbone	6.71	207.85
1970	Ronnie Martin	6.65	223.88
1971	Gerry Glynn	6.59	227.27
1972	Jim Walther	7.32	152.80
1973	Jerry Ruth	6.11	232.55
1974	Don Garlits	6.11	237.46
1975	Don Garlits	5.74	247.93
1976	Shirley Muldowney	5.94	248.61
1977	Dennis Baca	5.97	234.98
1978	Rob Bruins	5.98	247.58
1979	Don Garlits	6.36	237.46
1980	Shirley Muldowney	5.95	241.28
1981	Gary Beck	5.57	245.23
1982	Jim Barnard	5.92	233.16
1983	Shirley Muldowney	5.63	246.57
1984	Don Garlits	5.509	261.62
1985	Gary Beck	5.537	247.66
1986	Darryl Gwynn	5.36	
1987	Darryl Gwynn	5.138	276.32
1988	Joe Amato	6.818	202.79
1989	Gary Ormsby	4.919	291.26

NETBALL

Invented in the USA in 1891, netball is a women's 7-a-side game, developed from basketball. The first national association was that of New Zealand in 1924, followed by England in 1926. The International Federation of Women's Basketball and Netball Associations (IFWBNA) was formed in 1960.

WORLD CHAMPIONSHIPS

First held in 1963. *Winners:*
1963 Australia
1967 New Zealand
1971 Australia
1975 Australia
1979 Australia, New Zealand, Trinidad & Tobago
1983 Australia
1987 New Zealand

OLYMPIC GAMES

The first Olympic Games of the modern era were staged in Athens, Greece from the 6th to 15th April 1896. The driving force behind their revival was Pierre de Fredi, Baron de Coubertin, who was born in Paris in 1863. He believed in the Greek athletic ideal of perfection of mind and body, and his energies were devoted to achieving his dream of reintroducing the Olympic Games, which had been staged for more than a thousand years before their prohibition in AD 394. In 1889 de Coubertin was commissioned by the French government to form a universal sports association and he visited other European nations to gather information. He made public his views on 25 Nov 1892 at the Sorbonne in Paris. These led to the formation of the International Olympic Committee in 1894 and thence to the staging of the Olympic Games, which were opened in Athens on Easter Monday 1896.

Venues of Summer Games

1896 Athens	1952 Helsinki
1900 Paris	1956 Melbourne
1904 St Louis	1960 Rome
1906 Athens*	1964 Tokyo
1908 London	1968 Mexico City
1912 Stockholm	1972 Munich
1920 Antwerp	1976 Montreal
1924 Paris	1980 Moscow
1928 Amsterdam	1984 Los Angeles
1932 Los Angeles	1988 Seoul
1936 Berlin	1992 Barcelona
1948 London	

*Intercalated Games held as the tenth anniversary celebration of the 1896 Games. Results from these 1906 Games have been included in the records in this book. The record participation was in 1988 when there were 8465 competitors (6279 men, 2186 women) from a record 159 nations.

Venues of Winter Games

1924 Chamonix	1964 Innsbruck
1928 St Moritz	1968 Grenoble
1932 Lake Placid	1972 Sapporo
1936 Garmisch-Partenkirchen	1976 Innsbruck
1948 St Moritz	1980 Lake Placid
1952 Oslo	1984 Sarajevo
1956 Cortina d'Ampezzo	1988 Calgary
1960 Squaw Valley	1992 Albertville

From 1994, when they will be held in Lilliehammer, Norway the Winter Games will be held in the middle of the four-year cycle of the Summer Games.
The record participation was in 1988 when there were 1428 competitors (1113 men, 315 women) from a record 57 nations.

OLYMPIC RECORDS *See individual sports for champions at all events.*

Most medals
18 Larissa Latynina (USSR) Gymnastics 1956-64
15 Nikolay Andrianov (USSR) Gymnastics 1972-80
13 Eduardo Mangaiorotti (Ita) Fencing 1936-60
13 Takashi Ono (Jap) Gymnastics 1952-64
13 Boris Shakhlin (USSR) Gymnastics 1956-64
12 Sawao Kato (Jap) Gymnastics 1968-76
12 Paavo Nurmi (Fin) Athletics 1920-28

Most gold medals
10 Ray Ewry (USA) Athletics 1900-08
9 Larissa Latynina (USSR) Gymnastics 1956-64
9 Paavo Nurmi (Fin) Athletics 1920-28
9 Mark Spitz (USA) Swimming 1968-72
8 Sawao Kato (Jap) Gymnastics 1968-76

Most silver medals
6 Shirley Babashoff (USA) Swimming 1972-76
6 Aleksandr Ditaitin (USSR) Gymnastics 1976-80
6 Mikhail Voronin (USSR) Gymnastics 1968-72

Most bronze medals
6 Heikki Savolainen (Fin) Gymnastics 1928-52

Most Games winning medals
6 Aladár Gerevich (Hun) Fencing 1932-60

Most Games
MEN
8 Raimondo d'Inzeo (Ita) Equestrian 1948-76
8 Paul Elvström (Den) Yachting 1948-60, 1968-72, 1984-8
8 Durwood Knowles (UK/Bah) Yachting 1948-72, 1988
7 Ivan Ossier (Den) Fencing 1908-32, 1948
WOMEN
7 Kerstin Palm (Swe) Fencing 1964-88
6 Janice Lee Romary (née York) (USA) Fencing 1948-68
6 Lia Manoliu (Rom) Athletics 1952-72

Longest span of appearances
40 years Ivan Ossier (Den) Fencing 1908-48
40 years Magnus Konow (Nor) Yachting 1908-48
40 years Durwood Knowles (UK/Bah) Yachting 1948-88
40 years Paul Elvström (Den) Yachting 1948-88

Youngest medallists:
The unknown French boy who coxed the winning Netherlands rowing pair in 1900 was aged 7-10 years.
Next youngest medallists:
10y 215d Dimitrios Loundras (Gre) bronze Gymnastics 1896
12y 34d Inge Sörensen (Den) bronze Swimming 1936
12y 232d Noel Vandernotte (Fra) bronze Rowing 1936

Next youngest gold medallists:
13y 267d Marjorie Gestring (USA) Diving 1936
14y 12d Giorgio Cesana (Ita) Rowing 1906
Youngest gold medallist at Winter Games:
16y 260d William Fiske (USA) Bobsleigh 1928

Oldest medallists:
72y 279d Oscar Swahn (Swe) silver Shooting 1920
68y 194d Samuel Duvall (USA) silver Archery 1904
66y 154d Louis Noverraz (Swi) silver Yachting 1968

Oldest gold medallists:
64y 257d Oscar Swahn (Swe) Shooting 1912

64y 2d Galen Spencer (USA) Archery 1904
63y 244d Robert Williams (USA) Archery 1904
Oldest at Winter Games:
47yr 218d Giacomo Conti (Ita) Bobsleigh 1956

The only man to win gold medals in both Summer and Winter Games in Edward Eagan (USA), Boxing 1920 and Bobsleigh 1932.
The first woman to win a medal at both summer and winter Games was Christa Luding (née Rothenburger). She won speed skating gold at 500m in 1984 and 1000m in 1988 as well as the silver for 500m in 1988; in the 1988 summer Games she won the silver medal at sprint cycling.

Table of Olympic medal winners – Summer Games, 1896-1988

		Gold	Silver	Bronze	Total			Gold	Silver	Bronze	Total
1	USA	746	560	475	1781	41	India	8	3	3	14
2	USSR	395	323	299	1017	42	Ireland	4	4	5	13
3	Great Britain	174	223	207	604	43	Portugal	2	4	7	13
4	Germany[1]	157	207	207	571	44	North Korea[5]	2	5	5	12
5	France	153	167	177	497	45	Mongolia	0	5	6	11
6	Sweden	131	139	169	439	46	Ethiopia	5	1	4	10
7	GDR[2]	153	129	127	409	47	Pakistan	3	3	3	9
8	Italy	147	121	124	392	48	Uruguay	2	1	6	9
9	Hungary	124	112	136	372	49	Venezuela	1	2	5	8
10	Finland	97	75	110	282	50	Chile	0	6	2	8
11	Japan	87	75	82	244	51	Trinidad	1	2	4	7
12	Australia	71	67	87	225	52	Philippines	0	1	6	7
13	Romania	55	64	82	201	53	Morocco	3	1	2	6
14	Poland	40	56	95	191	54	Uganda	1	3	1	5
15	Canada	39	62	73	174	55	Tunisia	1	2	2	5
16	Switzerland	40	66	57	163	56	Colombia	0	2	3	5
17	Netherlands	43	47	63	153	57	Lebanon	0	2	2	4
18	Bulgaria	37	62	52	151	=58	Puerto Rico	0	1	3	4
19	Denmark	33	58	53	144	=58	Nigeria	0	1	3	4
20	Czechoslovakia	45	48	49	142	60	Peru	1	2	0	3
21	Belgium	35	48	42	125	61	Latvia[4]	0	2	1	3
22	Norway	42	33	33	108	=62	Taipei	0	1	2	3
23	Greece	22	39	39	100	=62	Ghana	0	1	2	3
24	Yugoslavia	26	29	28	83	=62	Thailand	0	1	2	3
25	Austria	19	26	34	79	65	Luxembourg	1	1	0	2
26	South Korea	19	22	29	70	66	Bahamas	1	0	1	2
27	China	20	19	21	60	67	Tanzania	0	2	0	2
28	Cuba	23	21	15	59	=68	Cameroun	0	1	1	2
29	New Zealand	26	6	23	55	=68	Haiti	0	1	1	2
30	South Africa[3]	16	15	21	52	=68	Iceland	0	1	1	2
31	Turkey	24	13	10	47	=71	Algeria	0	0	2	2
32	Argentina	13	18	13	44	=71	Panama	0	0	2	2
33	Mexico	9	12	18	39	=73	Zimbabwe	1	0	0	1
34	Brazil	7	9	20	36	=73	Surinam	1	0	0	1
35	Kenya	11	9	11	31	=75	Ivory Coast	0	1	0	1
36	Iran	4	11	15	30	=75	Singapore	0	1	0	1
37	Spain	4	12	8	24	=75	Sri Lanka	0	1	0	1
38	Jamaica	4	10	8	22	=75	Syria	0	1	0	1
39	Estonia[4]	6	6	9	21	=75	Costa Rica	0	1	0	1
40	Egypt	6	6	6	18	=75	Indonesia	0	1	0	1

	Gold	Silver	Bronze	Total			Gold	Silver	Bronze	Total
=75 Netherlands Antilles	0	1	0	1		=84 Zambia	0	0	1	1
=75 Senegal	0	1	0	1		=84 Djibouti	0	0	1	1
=75 Virgin Islands	0	1	0	1						
=84 Bermuda	0	0	1	1		[1] Germany 1896-1964. West Germany from 1968				
=84 Dominican Republic	0	0	1	1		[2] GDR. East Germany from 1968				
=84 Guyana	0	0	1	1		[3] South Africa up to 1960				
=84 Iraq	0	0	1	1		[4] Estonia and Latvia up to 1936				
=84 Niger	0	0	1	1		[5] North Korea from 1964				

Table of Olympic medal winners – Winter Games, 1924-88

		Gold	Silver	Bronze	Total				Gold	Silver	Bronze	Total
1	USSR	79	57	59	195		17	Japan	1	4	2	7
2	Norway	54	60	54	168		18	Hungary	0	2	4	6
3	USA	42	47	34	123		=19	Belgium	1	1	2	4
4	GDR[1]	39	36	35	110		=19	Poland	1	1	2	4
5	Finland	33	43	34	110		21	Yugoslavia	0	3	1	4
6	Austria	28	38	32	98		22	Spain	1	0	0	1
7	Sweden	36	25	31	92		23	North Korea[3]	0	1	0	1
8	Germany[2]	26	26	23	75		=24	Bulgaria	0	0	1	1
9	Switzerland	23	25	25	73		=24	Romania	0	0	1	1
10	Canada	14	13	17	44							
11	Netherlands	13	17	12	42							
12	France	13	10	16	39							
13	Italy	14	10	9	33							
14	Czechoslovakia	2	8	13	23							
15	Great Britain	7	4	10	21							
16	Liechtenstein	2	2	5	9							

Total includes all first, second and third place, including those events not on the current schedule.

[1] GDR. East Germany from 1968
[2] Germany, 1924-64, West Germany from 1968
[3] From 1964

ORIENTEERING

Cross-country running with the aid of map and compass, orienteering was invented by Major Ernst Killander in 1918 in Sweden. Their national federation, the Svenska Orienteringsförbundet, was formed in 1938. The International Orienteering Federation was established in 1961.

WORLD CHAMPIONSHIPS

First held in 1966 and staged biennially. *Winners:*

Men

1966 Åge Hadler (Nor)
1968 Karl Johansson (Swe)
1970 Stig Berge (Nor)
1972 Åge Hadler (Nor)
1974 Bernt Frilen (Swe)
1976 Egil Johansen (Nor)
1978 Egil Johansen (Nor)
1979 Øyvin Thon (Nor)
1981 Øyvin Thon (Nor)
1983 Morten Berglia (Nor)
1985 Kari Sallinen (Fin)
1987 Kent Olsson (Swe)
1989 Petter Thoresen (Nor)

Women

1966 Ulla Lindkvist (Swe)
1968 Ulla Lindkvist (Swe)
1970 Ingrid Hadler (Nor)
1972 Sarolta Monspart (Hun)
1974 Mona Norgaard (Den)
1976 Liisa Veijalainen (Fin)
1978 Anne Berit Eid (Nor)
1979 Outi Borgenstrom (Fin)
1981 Annichen Kringstad (Swe)
1983 Annichen Kringstad (Swe)
1985 Annichen Kringstad (Swe)
1987 Arja Hannus (Swe)
1989 Marita Skogum (Swe)

Men's Relay

Norway 1970, 1978, 1981, 1983, 1985, 1987, 1989
Sweden 1966, 1968, 1972, 1974, 1976, 1979

Women's Relay

Sweden 1966, 1970, 1974, 1976, 1981, 1983, 1985, 1989
Norway 1968, 1987
Finland 1972, 1978, 1979

PELOTA

Pelota is the generic name for a number of court games that are played, usually with gloves or baskets, although originally with the hands. *Longue paume* was played in France, having been introduced from Italy in the 13th century, and this developed into Real Tennis (qv), which was for long the French national game. When the game languished in the 17th century, it survived in the Basque country, straddling France and Spain, where the current game of Pelote Basque was developed. The Fédération Française de Pelote Basque was formed in 1921 and the Federacion Internacional de Pelota Vasca (FIPV) was founded in 1929 in Spain, where the sport is known as Pelota.

In the Basque country the traditional courts are known as trinquete, while usual in Latin America and Spain are courts of the fronton (enclosed stadium) variety, known in Basque as jai-alai, the name of the game in the USA and Latin America.

The chistera, used to propel the ball at great speed, was developed from a wicker fruit basket in the 1860s. Claims for the game to be the fastest of all ball games are reinforced by the highest ball velocity speed measured electronically at 302 km/h by José Ramon Areitio at Newport, Rhode Island in 1979.

WORLD CHAMPIONSHIPS

The FIVP stage world championships every four years, the first of which was in 1952, for a variety of events, including long and short court and trinquete court games. The most successful pair have been Roberto Elias and Juan Labat (Arg), who won the Trinquete Share in 1952, 1958, 1962 and 1966. Labat won seven world titles in all. The most wins in the long court game of Cesta Punta is three by Hamuy (Mex), with different partners, 1958, 1962 and 1966.

PETANQUE

Also known as 'boules', pétanque is derived from the ancient French game of Jeu Provençal, now differing from that game in that in the latter the bowls are delivered from a short run-up, whereas in pétanque they are delivered from a stationary position. The steel bowls (or boules) have a diameter of 7-8 cm and weigh 620-800 gm.

The Fédération Français de Pétanque et Jeu Provençal (FFPJP) was formed in 1945 and subsequently the Fédération Internationale (FIPJP). The British Pétanque Association was founded in 1974.

WORLD CHAMPIONSHIPS

First held in 1959. *Wins:*

10 France	1959, 1961, 1963, 1972, 1974, 1976-7, 1985, 1988-9	
4 Switzerland	1965-6, 1973, 1980	
3 Italy	1975, 1978-9	
2 Tunisia	1983, 1986	
2 Morocco	1984, 1987	
1 Algeria 1964, Spain 1971, Belgium 1981, Monaco 1982		

The first women's world championship was staged in 1988, when the winners were Thailand.

POLO

A four-a-side stick and ball game played on horseback. Polo originated in Central Asia, the earliest date given for such a game being 525 BC in Persia. The name of the game is derived from the Tibetan word 'pulu'. The British learnt of the game in India in the 1850s, and the earliest polo club of the modern era was the Cachar Club, founded in Assam in 1859. The game was first played in England in 1869 by the 10th Hussars, and in the USA in 1876.

The game's governing body is the Hurlingham Polo Association. Hurlingham, in London, first staged a match in 1874 and the club committee drew up the first set of English rules a year later.

Polo is played on the largest pitch of any game, with maximum length of 300 yards (274m) and width of 200 yards (182m) without boards, or 160 yards (146m with boards).

WORLD CHAMPIONSHIPS

Contested in 1989 in West Berlin, when the USA beat Great Britain 7-6 in the final. 3rd Argentina, 4th Chile.

WESTCHESTER CUP

The first international match was between Great Britain and the United States at Newport, Rhode Island in 1886 for an international trophy given by the Westchester Club. Last contested in 1939, the winners in this series were:
Great Britain 1886, 1900, 1902, 1914
United States 1909, 1911, 1913, 1921, 1924, 1927, 1930, 1936, 1939.
Contest for the Cup was revived in 1988, when the USA beat Australia by goal average in two games at Lexington, Kentucky.

High goal players

Polo games are often contested on a handicap basis, each

player being awarded a handicap measured in goals up to a maximum of ten, attained by the world's best players. In the history of the game 55 players have been awarded this handicap. A high goal player is one with a handicap of five, so a high goal team rates at 20 or more. The first match between two 40-goal teams, that is all players on the maximum, was played at Palermo, Buenos Aires, Argentina in 1975. The highest handicap ever attained by a woman is five by Claire Tomlinson in 1986.

CUP OF THE AMERICAS
Contested by Argentina and the USA. The US won the first two matches in 1928 and 1932, and the Argentinians have won all subsequent contests: 1936, 1950, 1966, 1969, 1979, 1980 and 1988.

OLYMPIC GAMES
Polo has been included at five Olympic Games. Winners:
1900 Foxhunters (UK/USA)
1908 Roehampton (UK)
1920 Great Britain
1924 Argentina
1936 Argentina

CHAMPION CUP
Britain's premier tournament from its inception in 1876 to 1939, when it was last played at Hurlingham. The teams with most wins were Freebooters 9, and Sussex 8.

BRITISH OPEN CHAMPIONSHIP
Played annually for the Cowdray Park Gold Cup at Cowdray Park, Midhurst, Sussex, this competition replaced the Champion Cup. *Winners:*

1956 Los Indios	1973-4 Stowell Park
1957 Windsor Park	1975 Greenhill Farm
1958 Cowdray Park	1976 Stowell Park
1959-60 Casarejo	1977 Foxcote
1961-2 Cowdray Park	1978 Stowell Park
1963 La Vulci	1979 Songhai
1964-5 Jersey Lilies	1980 Stowell Park
1966 Windsor Park	1981 Falcons
1967 Woolmer's Park	1982 Southfield
1968 Pimms	1983 Falcons
1969 Windsor Park	1984 Southfield
1970 Boca Raton	1985 Maple Leafs
1971-2 Pimms	1986-9 Tramontana

Most wins: 5 Stowell Park

POWERBOATING
Powerboat racing started in about 1900, and there are now a large number of categories of boats that race on either inland waters or offshore. A petrol engine had first been fitted in a boat by Jean Lenoir on the River Seine in 1865.

HARMSWORTH TROPHY
This perpetual trophy was presented by Sir Alfred Harmsworth (later Lord Northcliffe) in 1903. The race for the trophy was for many years the world's most prestigious powerboating event.
Winners:

Year	Boat	Driver	Speed km/h
1903	Napier I (Eng)	Dorothy Levitt	31.43
1904	Trefle-A-Quatre (Fra)	Emile Thubron	42.86
1905	Napier II (Eng)	Lord Montague	41.89
1906	Yarrow-Napier (Eng)	Lionel de Rothschild	24.91
1907	Dixie I (USA)	E.J.Schroeder	51.14
1908	Dixie II (USA)	E.J.Schroeder	50.45
1910	Dixie III (USA)	F.K.Burnham	58.00
1911	Dixie IV (USA)	F.K.Burnham	64.82
1912	Maple Leaf IV (Eng)	Tommy Sopwith	69.49
1913	Maple Leaf IV (Eng)	Tommy Sopwith	92.46
1920	Miss America I (USA)	Garfield Wood	98.99
1921	Miss America II (USA)	Garfield Wood	96.16
1926	Miss America V (USA)	Garfield Wood	98.359
1928	Miss America VII (USA)	Garfield Wood	95.474
1929	Miss America VIII (USA)	Garfield Wood	121.163
1930	Miss America IX (USA)	Garfield Wood	124.294
1932	Miss America X (USA)	Garfield Wood	126.315
1933	Miss America X (USA)	Garfield Wood	139.915
1949	Skip-A-Long (USA)	Stanley Dollar	151.737
1950	Slo-Mo-Shun IV (USA)	Stanley Sayres	162.029
1956	Shanty I (USA)	William Waggoner Jr	144.439
1959	Miss Supertest III (Can)	Bob Hayward	160.595
1960	Miss Supertest III (Can)	Bob Hayward	185.852
1961	Miss Supertest III (Can)	Bob Hayward	158.066

The series then lapsed, but was revised under a new formula in 1977 as the Harmsworth British & Commonwealth Trophy for Motorboats. *Winners:*

Year	Boat/Pilot
1977-8	Limit-Up (Eng)/Michael Doxford & Tim Powell
1979	Uno-Mint-Jewellery (Eng)/ Derek Pobjoy.

From 1980 to 1983 the Harmsworth Trophy was awarded on points for a series of offshore races. *Winning drivers:*

1980	Bill Elswick & Paul Clauser (USA)
1981	Paul Clauser (USA)
1982	Al Copeland & B.Sirios (USA)
1983	George Morales (USA)

In 1985 the Harmsworth trophy was contested by two-boat national teams at Formula Two for outboard engines:

1985	Jonathan Jones, Mark Wilson & John Hill (UK)
1986	Bill Seebold Jr (USA)

Not contested in 1987 and 1988, in 1989 the trophy was returned to world offshore competition and won by Stefano Casiraghi (Ita).

AMERICAN POWER BOAT ASSOCIATION GOLD CUP

The American Power Boat Association was formed in 1903, and held its first Gold Cup race on the Hudson River in 1904, when the winner was Standard, piloted by C.C.Riotto at an average speed of 39 km/h. *Winners (with average speed) from 1970:*

Year	Boat	Pilot	mph	km/h
1970	Miss Budweiser	Dean Chenoweth	101.848	163.908
1971	Miss Madison	Jim McCormick	101.522	163.384
1972	Atlas Van Lines	Bill Muncey	103.547	166.643
1973	Miss Budweiser	Dean Chenoweth	104.046	167.446
1974	Pay'N Pak	George Henley	112.056	180.337
1975	Pay'N Pak	George Henley	113.350	182.419
1976	Miss US	Tom d'Eath	108.021	173.843
1977	Atlas Van Lines	Bill Muncey	114.849	184.832
1978	Atlas Van Lines	Bill Muncey	104.448	167.330
1979	Atlas Van Lines	Bill Muncey	107.892	173.631
1980	Miss Budweiser	Dean Chenoweth	108.459	174.543
1981	Miss Budweiser	Dean Chenoweth	117.815	189.600
1982	Atlas Van Lines	Chip Hanauer	120.081	193.246
1983	Atlas Van Lines	Chip Hanauer	118.506	190.712
1984	Atlas Van Lines	Chip Hanauer	130.866	210.603
1985	Miller American	Chip Hanauer	121.612	195.710
1986	Miller American	Chip Hanauer	116.886	188.105
1987	Miller American	Chip Hanauer	127.745	205.580
1988	Circus Circus	Chip Hanauer	128.406	206.644
1989	Miss Budweiser	Tom D'Eath	131.388	211.443

Most wins: (pilot) 8 Bill Muncey 1956-7, 1961-2, 1972, 1977-9, 7 Chip Hanauer as above, 5 Garfield Wood 1917-21. (boat) 7 Atlas Van Lines as above.

COWES – TORQUAY OFFSHORE RACE

Instituted in 1961 by Sir Max Aitken of the Daily Express at first from Cowes to Torquay, but from 1968 including the return journey, for a distance of 320.4 km. *Winners:*

Year	Boat	Driver	Speed km/h
1961	Thunderbolt	Tommy Sopwith (UK)	40
1962	Tramontana	Jeffrey Quill (UK)	60
1963	A'Speranzella	Renato Levi (Ita)	66
1964	Surfrider	Charles Gardner (UK)	79
1965	Brave Moppie	Dick Bertram (USA)	63
1966	Ghost Rider	Jim Wynne (USA)	66
1967	Surfury	Charles Gardner (UK)	85
1968	Telstar	Tommy Sopwith (UK)	61
1969	The Cigarette	Don Aronow (USA)	107.3
1970	Miss Enfield 2	Tommy Sopwith (UK)	94.1
1971	Lady Nara	Ronny Bonelli (Ita)	63
1972	Aeromarine IX	Carlo Bonomi (Ita)	88
1973	Unowot	Don Shead (UK)	100
1974	Dry Martini	Carlo Bonomi (Ita)	107.7
1975	Uno Embassy	Don Shead (UK)	117.26
1976	I Like It Too	Charles Gill (UK)	112.5
1977	Yellowdrama III	Ken Cassir (UK)	120.91
1978	Kaama	Betty Cook (USA)	124.59
1979	Dry Martini II	Guido Nicolai (Ita)	102.54
1980	Satisfaction	Bill Elswick (USA)	128.16
1981	Rombo	Alberto Smania (Ita)	77.87
1982	Ego Rothmans	Renato della Valle (Ita)	105.59
1983	Ego Rothmans	Renato della Valle (Ita)	112.20
1984	Cinzano	Renato della Valle (Ita)	122.45
1985	Cinzano Bianco	Renato della Valle (Ita)	101.61
1986	Fresh and Clean	Giovanni Repossi (Ita)	119.31
1987	Rocky Euromarche	Jean-Pierre Fruitier (Fra)	127.33
1988	Cesa	Fabio Buzzi (Ita)	138.24
1989	Gancia dei Gancia	Stefano Casiraghi (Ita)	129.21

OLYMPIC GAMES

Motor boating was included in the 1908 Olympic Games. *Winners:*
Emile Thubron (Fra) won Class A in *Camille*; Thomas Thornycroft, Bernard Redwood and Captain Field-Richards won Classes B and C in *Gyrinus*.

FORMULA ONE WORLD CHAMPION

1982	Roger Jenkins (UK)
1983	Renato Molinari (Ita)
1984	Renato Molinari (Ita)
1985	Bob Spalding (UK)
1986	Gene Thibodaux (USA)
1987	Ben Robertson (USA) (just one race)

FORMULA TWO (FORMULA GRAND PRIX) WORLD CHAMPIONS

Inland circuit championships
1982-3 Michael Werner (FRG)
1984-5 John Hill (UK)

1986	Jonathan Jones (UK) and Buck Thornton (USA)
1987	Bill Seebold (USA)
1988	Chris Bush (USA)
1989	Jonathan Jones (UK)

OFFSHORE CLASS 1 WORLD CHAMPIONS

First held 1961. For 16 litre engines.
1966   Jim Wynne (USA)

1967 Don Aronow (USA)
1968 Vincenzo Balestrieri (Ita)
1969 Don Aronow (USA)
1970 Vincenzo Balestrieri (Ita)
1971 William Wishnick (USA)
1972 Bobby Rautboard (USA)
1973-4 Carlo Bonomi (Ita)
1975 Franz Wallace (Bra)
1976 Tom Gentry (USA)
1977 Betty Cook (USA)
1978 Francesco Cosentino (Ita)
1979 Betty Cook (USA)
1980 Michael Maynard (USA)
1981 Jerry Jacoby (USA)
1982 Renato della Valle (Ita)
1983 Tony Garcia (USA)
1984 Alberto Petri (Ita)
1985 Anthony Roberts (USA)
1986 Antonio Giofredi (Ita)
1987 Steve Curtis (UK)
1988 Fabio Buzzi (Ita)
1989 Stefano Casiraghi (Ita)

SPEED RECORDS

The Union Internationale Motonautique (UIM) recognise a large number of speed records for different categories of boats.

The fastest recognised for an outboard powered boat: 285.83 km/h in class (e) by P.R.Knight in a Lauterbach hull powered by a Chevrolet engine on Lake Ruataniwha, New Zealand, 1986.

The fastest speed recorded for a diesel (compression ignition) boat is 218.248 km/h by the hydroplane *Iveco World Leader* powered by an Aifo-Fiat engine, driven by Carlo Bonomi at Venice, Italy on 4 Apr 1985.

The fastest speed recorded by an electrically powered boat is 81.80 km/h by the hydroplane An Stradag driven by the Countess of Arran at Holme Pierrepont, Nottingham, England on 22 Nov 1989.

CLASS 2

For 8 litre engines.
1986 Luigi Radice (Ita)
1987 Peter Hidalgo (USA)
1988 Roger Fletcher (UK)
1989 Carlo Bonomi (Ita)

POWERLIFTING

From the many different lifts that have been practised by weightlifters and incorporated in tests of strength, powerlifting now recognises the squat, bench press and dead lift, all performed two-handed. The competitor is allowed three attempts at each lift and the best successful attempt on each lift is totalled. There are eleven weight categories for men and ten for women.

The sport of powerlifting was first contested at national level in Great Britain in 1958. The first US Championships were held in 1964. The International Powerlifting Federation was founded in 1972.

World Championships

First held for men as unofficial championships in 1971 and officially in 1973, and for women in 1980.

Champions from 1980: (totals given are the total of the three lifts in kilograms)

MEN

52kg
1980 Hideaki Inaba (Jap) 567.5
1981 Hideaki Inaba (Jap) 560
1982 Hideaki Inaba (Jap) 552.5
1983 Hideaki Inaba (Jap) 565
1984 Chuck Dunbar (USA) 532.5
1985 Hideaki Inaba (Jap) 562.5
1986 Hideaki Inaba (Jap) 577.5
1987 Hideaki Inaba (Jap) 587.5
1988 Hideaki Inaba (Jap) 560
1989 Hideaki Inaba (Jap) 560

56kg
1980 Precious McKenzie (NZ) 587.5
1981 Hiroyuki Isagawa (Jap) 577.5
1982 Lamar Gant (USA) 590
1983 Lamar Gant (USA) 575
1984 Lamar Gant (USA) 580
1985 Hiroyuki Isagawa (Jap) 562.5
1986 Hiroyuki Isagawa (Jap) 572.5
1987 Gerrard McNamara (Ire) 550
1988 Hiroyuki Isagawa (Jap) 585
1989 Hiroyuki Isagawa (Jap) 600

60kg
1980 Lamar Gant (USA) 705
1981 Lamar Gant (USA) 625
1982 Kullervo Lampela (Fin) 582.5
1983 Göran Henrysson (Swe) 605
1984 Göran Henrysson (Swe) 600
1985 Göran Henrysson (Swe) 605
1986 Lamar Gant (USA) 647.5
1987 Lamar Gant (USA) 677.5
1988 Lamar Gant (USA) 675
1989 Lamar Gant (USA) 650

67.5kg
1980 Rickey Crain (USA) 730
1981 Joe Bradley (USA) 732.5
1982 Stefan Nentis (Swe) 697.5
1983 Bob Wahl (USA) 705
1984 Dan Austin (USA) 722.5
1985 Eddie Pengelly (UK) 667.5
1986 Dan Austin (USA) 712.5
1987 Dan Austin (USA) 717.5
1988 Dan Austin (USA) 717.5
1989 Dan Austin (USA) 690

75kg
1980 Rick Gaugler (USA) 787.5
1981 Steve Alexander (USA) 752.5

1982	Rickey Crain (USA)	772.5
1983	Rickey Crain (USA)	762.5
1984	Gene Bell (USA)	762.5
1985	Eric Coppin (Bel)	765
1986	Rick Crilly (Can)	732.5
1987	Jarmo Virtanen (Fin)	802.5
1988	Jarmo Virtanen (Fin)	792.5
1989	Ausby Alexander (USA)	752.5

82.5kg

1980	Bill West (UK)	777.5
1981	Mike Bridges (USA)	945
1982	Mike Bridges (USA)	845
1983	Mike Bridges (USA)	807.5
1984	Ed Coan (USA)	875
1985	Jarmo Virtanen (Fin)	842.5
1986	Jarmo Virtanen (Fin)	850
1987	Gene Bell (USA)	822.5
1988	Hannu Malinen (Fin)	750
1989	Jarmo Virtanen (Fin)	827.5

90kg

1980	Vince Anello (USA) 867.5
1981	Walter Thomas (USA) 930
1982	Walter Thomas (USA) 857.5
1983	Kenneth Mattsson (Swe) 872.5
1984	Dennis Wright (USA) 840
1985	David Caldwell (UK) 832.5
1986	Jari Tahtinen (Fin) 822.5
1987	Sly Anderson (USA) 830
1988	Gene Bell (USA) 860
1989	George Herring (USA) 855

100kg

1980	Mark Dimiduk (USA)	922.5
1981	Jim Cash (USA)	922.5
1982	Kenneth Mattsson (Swe)	880
1983	Fred Hatfield (USA)	920
1984	Tony Stevens (UK)	915
1985	Tony Stevens (UK)	907.5
1986	Tony Stevens (UK)	882.5
1987	Conny Nilsson (Swe)	847.5
1988	Ed Coan (USA)	972.5
1989	Ed Coan (USA)	1015

110kg

1980	John Kuc (USA)	1000
1981	Reijo Kiviranta (Fin)	920
1982	Hannu Saarelainen (Fin)	887.5
1983	Steve Wilson (USA)	910
1984	Dave Jacoby (USA)	935
1985	Dave Jacoby (USA)	907.5
1986	Fred Hatfield (USA)	902.5
1987	Dave Jacoby (USA)	910
1988	Dave Jacoby (USA)	902.5
1989	John Neighbour (UK)	925

125kg

1981	Ernie Hackett (USA)	962.5
1982	John Gamble (USA)	907.5
1983	Lars Norén (Swe)	890
1984	Ab Wolders (Hol)	945
1985	Tom Henderson (USA)	935

1986	Lars Norén (Swe)	942.5
1987	John Neighbour (UK)	922.5
1988	Kyösti Vilmi (Fin)	930
1989	Kyösti Vilmi (Fin)	930

Over 125kg

1980	(over 110kg)	
	Doyle Kenady (USA)	1000
1981	Paul Wrenn (USA)	1027.5
1982	Tom Maggee (Can)	942.5
1983	Bill Kazmaier (USA)	975
1984	Lee Moran (USA)	977.5
1985	George Hechter (USA)	947.5
1986	Mike Hall (USA)	980
1987	Lars Norén (Swe)	1077.5
1988	Oders Wilson (USA)	1012.5
1989	Mike Hall (USA)	952.5

Most world titles:

15 Hideaki Inaba (Jap) 52kg 1974-83, 1985-9

14 Lamar Gant (USA) 56kg 1975-7, 1979, 1982-4;
60kg 1978, 1980-1, 1986-9

8 Larry Pacifico (USA) 90kg 1976; 100kg 1974-5, 1977-9; 110kg 1972-3

WOMEN

44kg

1980	Joan Fruth (USA)	275
1981	Donna Wicker (USA)	287.5
1982	Ginger Lord (USA)	300
1983	Cheryl Jones (USA)	317.5
1984	Cheryl Jones (USA)	347.5
1985	Cheryl Jones (USA)	350
1986	Judy Gedney (USA)	322.5
1987	Anna-Liisa Prinkkala (Fin)	332.5
1988	Hisako Yoshida (Jap)	335
1989	Anna-Liisa Prinkkala (Fin)	340

48kg

1980	Sue Roberts (Aus)	330
1981	Terry Dillard (USA)	340
1982	Terry Dillard (USA)	347.5
1983	Diana Rowell (USA)	355
1984	Majik Jones (USA)	390
1985	Bernadette Plouviez (Bel)	345
1986	Marie Vassart (Bel)	350
1987	Vuokko Viitasaari (Fin)	352.5
1988	Irma Ruler (Hol)	360
1989	Claudine Cognacq (Fra)	352.5

52kg

1980	Terry Dillard (USA)	347.5
1981	Sue Roberts (Aus)	370
1982	Sue Jordan (Aus)	365
1983	Kali Bogias (Can)	390
1984	Kali Bogias (Can)	392.5
1985	Sisi Dolman (Hol)	400
1986	Sisi Dolman (Hol)	400

1987	Mary Jeffrey (USA)	420
1988	Sisi Dolman (Hol)	410
1989	Sisi Dolman (Hol)	422.5

56kg

1980	Sue Elwyn (USA)	330
1981	Gayla Crain (USA)	395
1982	Julie Thomas (USA)	365
1983	Juli Thomas (USA)	440
1984	Vicky Steenrod (USA)	475
1985	Tina van Duyn-Woodley (Hol)	415
1986	Felecia Johnson (USA)	407.5
1987	Joy Burt (Can)	427.5
1988	Mary Jeffrey (USA)	440
1989	Mary Jeffrey (USA)	445

60kg

1980	Karen Gajda (USA)	405
1981	Eileen Todaro (USA)	387.5
1982	Ruth Shafer (USA)	450
1983	Ruth Shafer (USA)	500
1984	Diane Frantz (USA)	435
1985	Vicky Steenrod (USA)	502.5
1986	Rita Bass (UK)	420
1987	Vicky Steenrod (USA)	487.5
1988	Silvana Bollmann (FRG)	445
1989	Judith Auerbach (USA)	427.5

67.5kg

1980	Jennifer Reid (USA)	405
1981	Jennifer Weyland (USA)	467.5
1982	Angie Ross (USA)	435
1983	Linda Miller (Aus)	435
1984	Ruth Shafer (USA)	552.5
1985	Ruth Shafer (USA)	427.5
1986	Heidi Wittesch (Aus)	470
1987	Deborah McElroy (USA)	490
1988	Jackie Pierce (USA)	497.5
1989	Silvana Bollmann (FRG)	502.5

75kg

1980	Beverley Francis (Aus)	460
1981	Judith Oakes (UK)	462.5
1982	Beverley Francis (Aus)	497.5
1983	Pamela Matthews (Aus)	487.5
1984	Deborah McElroy-Patton (USA)	475
1985	Heidi Wittesch (Aus)	470
1986	Deborah Patton (USA)	462.5
1987	Terry Byland (USA)	477.5
1988	Heidi Wittesch (Aus)	522.5
1989	Liz Odendaal (Hol)	577.5

82.5kg

1980	Vicky Gagne (USA)	450
1981	Beverley Francis (Aus)	575
1982	Judith Oakes (UK)	502.5
1983	Beverley Francis (Aus)	577.5
1984	Beverley Francis (Aus)	557.5
1985	Beverley Francis (Aus)	565
1986	Juanita Trujillo (USA)	537.5
1987	Maggie Sandoval (USA)	522.5

1988	Judith Oakes (UK)	542.5
1989	Heidi Wittesch (Aus)	520

Over 82.5kg

1980	Ann Turbyne (USA)	502.5
1981	Wanda Sander (USA)	550

90kg

1982	Rebecca Waibler (FRG)	475
1983	Gael Mulhall (Aus)	525
1984	Annette Bohach (USA)	500
1985	Tore Eriksen (Nor)	465
1986	Lorraine Costango (USA)	550
1987	Jacqueline Pepper (UK)	462.5
1988	Lorraine Costanzo (USA)	605
1989	Heike Buch (FRG)	555

Over 90kg

1982	Annie McElroy (USA)	502.5
1983	Wanda Sander (USA)	522.5
1984	Annie McElroy (USA)	485
1985	Annie McElroy (USA)	527.5
1986	Annie McElroy (USA)	527.5
1987	Lorraine Costanzo (USA)	622.5
1988	Myrtle Augee (UK)	557.5
1989	Ulrike Herchenhein (FRG)	555

Most women's world titles:
6 Beverley Francis (Aus) 75kg 1980, 1982; 82.5kg 1981, 1983-5

WORLD RECORDS
all weights in kilograms

MEN
Class SQUAT

52kg	243	Hideaki Inaba (Jap)	1986
56kg	242.5	Hideaki Inaba (Jap)	1988
60kg	295	Joe Bradley (USA)	1980
67.5kg	300	Jessie Jackson (USA)	1987
75kg	328	Austy Alexander (USA)	1989
82.5kg	379.5	Mike Bridges (USA)	1982
90kg	375	Fred Hatfield (USA)	1980
100kg	422.5	Ed Coan (USA)	1989
110kg	393.5	Dan Wohleber (USA)	1981
125kg	412.5	David Waddington (USA)	1982
125+kg	445	Dwayne Fely (USA)	1982

Class BENCH PRESS

52kg	146.5	Joe Cunha (Jap)	1982
56kg	160.5	Hiroyaki Isagawa (Jap)	1989
60kg	180	Joe Bradley (USA)	1980
67.5kg	200	Kristoffer Hulecki (Swi)	1985
75kg	217.5	James Rouse (USA)	1980
82.5kg	240	Mike Bridges (USA)	1981
90kg	255	Mike McDonald (USA)	1980
100kg	261.5	Mike McDonald (USA)	1977
110kg	270	Jeffrey Magruder (USA)	1982
125kg	278.5	Tom Hardman (USA)	1982
125+kg	300	Bill Kazmeier (USA)	1981

Class DEAD LIFT

52kg	237.5	Hideaki Inaba (Jap)	1987
56kg	289.5	Lamar Gant (USA)	1982
60kg	310	Lamar Gant (USA)	1988
67.5kg	315	Daniel Austin (USA)	1989
75kg	333	Jarmo Virtanen (Fin)	1988
82.5kg	357.5	Veli Kumpuniemi (Fin)	1980
90kg	372.5	Walter Thomas (USA)	1982
100kg	378	Ed Coan (USA)	1989
110kg	395	John Kuc (USA)	1980
125kg	387.5	Lars Norén (Swe)	1987
125+kg	406	Lars Norén (Swe)	1988

Class TOTAL

52kg	587.5	Hideaki Inaba (Jap)	1987
56kg	625	Lamar Gant (USA)	1982
60kg	707.5	Joe Bradley (USA)	1982
67.5kg	762.5	Daniel Austin (USA)	1989
75kg	850	Rick Gaugler (USA)	1982
82.5kg	952.5	Mike Bridges (USA)	1982
90kg	937.5	Mike Bridges (USA)	1980
100kg	1032.5	Ed Coan (USA)	1989
110kg	1000	John Kuc (USA)	1980
125kg	1005	Ernie Hackett (USA)	1982
125+kg	1100	Bill Kazmaier (USA)	1981

WOMEN
Class SQUAT

44kg	142.5	Delcy Palk (USA)	1988
48kg	147.5	Keiko Nishio (Jap)	1987
52kg	173.5	Sisi Dolman (Hol)	1989
56kg	191	Mary Jeffrey (USA)	1989
60kg	200.5	Ruth Shafer (USA)	1983
67.5kg	230	Ruth Shafer (USA)	1984
75kg	225	Sumita Laha (Ind)	1989
82.5kg	230	Juanita Trujillo (USA)	1986
90kg	252.5	Lorraine Constanzo (USA)	1988
90+kg	262.5	Lorraine Constanzo (USA)	1987

Class BENCH PRESS

44kg	75	Teri Hoyt (USA)	1982
48kg	82.5	Michelle Evris (USA)	1981
52kg	95	Mary Ryan (USA)	1984
56kg	115	Mary Jeffrey (née Ryan) (USA)	1988
60kg	105.5	Judith Auerbach (USA)	1989
67.5kg	115	Heidi Wittesch (Aus)	1987
75kg	142.5	Liz Odendaal (Hol)	1989
82.5kg	150	Beverley Francis (Aus)	1981
90kg	130	Lorraine Constanzo (USA)	1988
90+kg	137.5	Myrtle Augee (UK)	1989

Class DEAD LIFT

44kg	165	Nancy Belliveau (Can)	1985
48kg	182.5	Majik Jones (USA)	1984
52kg	197.5	Diana Rowell (USA)	1984
56kg	200.5	Joy Burt (Can)	1989
60kg	213	Ruth Shafer (USA)	1983

67.5kg	244	Ruth Shafer (USA)	1984
75kg	230	Liz Odendaal (Hol)	1989
82.5kg	227.5	Vicky Gagne (USA)	1981
90kg	227.5	Lorraine Constanzo (USA)	1988
90+kg	237.5	Lorraine Constanzo (USA)	1987

Class	TOTAL		
44kg	352.5	Marie Vassart (Bel)	1985
48kg	390	Majik Jones (USA)	1984
52kg	427.5	Diana Rowell (USA)	1984
56kg	485	Mary Jeffrey (USA)	1988
60kg	502.5	Vicky Steenrod (USA)	1985
67.5kg	565	Ruth Shafer (USA)	1984
75kg	577.5	Liz Odendaal (Hol)	1989
82.5kg	577.5	Beverley Francis (Aus)	1983
90kg	607.5	Lorraine Constanzo (USA)	1988
90+kg	622.5	Lorraine Constanzo (USA)	1987

RACKETBALL

Two versions of the game exist. The initial game of Racquetball (US spelling), using handball courts 40ft by 20ft (12.2m by 6.1m), was invented in 1949 by Joe Sobek at the Greenwich YMCA, Connecticut, USA, originally as Paddle Rackets; he sawed half the handle off a tennis racquet. In the USA the International Racquetball Association was founded in 1968 by Bob Kendler (USA). Its name changed in 1980 to the American Amateur Raquetball Association (AARA). The sport now has more than ten million players in the USA.

The international governing body is The International Raquetball Federation (IRF).

Racketball (British spelling), using squash courts 32ft by 21ft (9.75m by 6.4m) was introduced in 1976, by Ian Wright, at Bexley SRC, Kent using a less bouncy ball than that used in the larger American courts. The British Racketball Association (BRA) was formed and staged inaugural British National Championships in 1984.

British Championships *Winners:*

Men	Women
1984 Denis Secher	1984 Greer Batty
1985 John Hakes	1985 Bett Dryhurst
1986 Murray Scott	1986 Bett Dryhurst
1987 Matthew Parker	1987 Bett Dryhurst
1988 Eric Sommers	1988 Kim Kelly
1989 Eric Sommers	1989 Kim Kelly

World Championships

The IRF has staged world championships biennially since 1982. Singles winners have been:

Men	Women
1982 Ed Andrews (USA)	1982 Cindy Baxter (USA)
1984 Ross Horney (Can)	1984 Mary Dee (USA)
1986 Egan Inoue (USA)	1986 Cindy Baxter (USA)
1988 Andy Roberts (USA)	1988 Heather Stupp (Can)

RACKETS

A racket and ball game for two or four players, derived as with other such games from various forms of hand ball games played in the Middle Ages. In England it was often played against walls of buildings, especially those of the Fleet Prison, London in the 18th century. An inmate Robert Mackay claimed the first world title in 1820.

The first closed court was the Prince's Club, built at Hans Place, London in 1853. The English governing body, the Tennis and Rackets Association was formed in 1907.

WORLD CHAMPIONS

Determined on a challenge basis, world champions have been:

1820	Robert Mackay (UK)
1825-34	Thomas Pittman (UK)
1834-8	John Pittman (UK)
1838-40	John Lamb (UK)
1840-6	vacant
1846-60	L.C.Mitchell (UK)
1860	Francis Erwood (UK)
1862-3	Sir William Hart-Dyke (UK)
1863-6	Henry Gray (UK)
1866-75	William Gray (UK)
1876-8	H.B. Fairs (UK)
1878-87	Joseph Gray (UK)
1887-1902	Peter Latham (UK)
1903-11	J.Jamsetji (Ind)
1911-3	Charles Williams (UK)
1913-28	Jock Souter (USA)
1929-35	Charles Williams (UK)
1937-47	David Milford (UK)
1947-54	James Dear (UK)
1954-71	Geoffrey Atkins (UK)
1972-3	William Surtees (USA)
1973-4	Howard Angus (UK)
1975-81	William Surtees (USA)
1981-4	John Prenn (UK)
1984-6	William Boone (UK)
1986-8	John Prenn (UK)
1988-	James Male (UK)

LACOSTE WORLD DOUBLES CHAMPIONSHIPS

First held in 1990 when James Male and John Prenn (UK) beat Neil Smith and Shannon Hazell (UK) over two legs.

BRITISH AMATEUR CHAMPIONSHIPS

Held annually, first in 1888 at singles and in 1890 at doubles.

Singles *Winners from 1969:*

1969	Charles Swallow
1970-1	Martin Smith
1972-5	Howard Angus
1976	William Boone

1977   Charles Hue Williams
1978   William Boone
1979-80 John Prenn
1981   William Boone
1982-3 John Prenn
1984-5 William Boone
1986   James Male (Dec 85)
1987   William Boone
1988   James Male
1989-90 William Boone

Most wins:
9 Edgar M.Baerlein 1903, 1905, 1908-11, 1920-1, 1923
8 Henry K.Foster 1894-1900, 1904
7 David Milford 1930, 1935-8, 1950-1
7 William Boone 1976, 1978, 1981, 1984-5, 1987-8 (?)
5 John Thompson 1954-5, 1957-9

Doubles *Winners from 1969:*
1969-71 Richard Gracey & Martin Smith
1972-3 Howard Angus & Charles Hue Williams
1974   Geoffrey Atkins & Charles Hue Williams
1975-7 William Boone & Tom Pugh
1978-9 Howard Angus & Andrew Milne
1980-4 William Boone & Randall Crawley (6 wins)
1985   John Prenn & Charles Hue Williams
1986   William Boone & Randall Crawley
1987   James Male & Rupert Owen-Browne
1988-90 John Prenn & James Male

Most wins: by the same pair:
10 David Milford & John Thompson 1948, 1950-2, 1954-9
by individuals with various partners:
11 David Milford also in 1938
11 John Thompson also in 1966
9 William Boone 1975-7, 1980-4, 1986
8 Henry K.Foster 1893-4, 1896-1900, 1903
8 Lord Aberdare (formerly the Hon.C.N.Bruce) 1921, 1924-8, 1930, 1934

BRITISH OPEN CHAMPIONSHIPS
Held irregularly for the Shepperd Cup 1929-71 on a challenge basis. From 1971 there has been an annual championship, held first as the Louis Roederer Open Invitation Tournament. From 1981 Celestion Loudspeakers have sponsored the sport and the event is now the Celestion Open Championship.

Sheppard Cup champions:
1929-30 Cyril Simpson
1932   Lord Aberdare
1933   Ian Akers-Douglas
1934   Albert Cooper
1936   David Milford
1946   James Dear
1951   James Dear
1954   Geoffrey Atkins
1959   John Thompson

1960   James Dear
1961   Geoffrey Atkins
1964   Geoffrey Atkins
1967   James Leonard
1970   Charles Swallow
1971   Martin Smith
1971   Howard Angus

Open Singles Champions:
1971-3 Howard Angus
1974   William Surtees
1975-6 Howard Angus
1977   John Prenn
1978   Howard Angus
1979   William Boone
1980-3 John Prenn
1984   William Boone
1985   John Prenn
1986   William Boone
1987-9 James Male
1990   Neil Smith

Open Doubles *winners (first held 1981)*
1981-5 William Boone & Randall Crawley
1986-90 John Prenn & James Male

OLYMPIC GAMES
Rackets was included in the 1908 Olympics, when gold medals were won at singles by Evan Noel (UK) and doubles by Vane Pennel and John Jacob Astor (UK).

REAL TENNIS

An indoor racket and ball game, which was first played as Jeu de paume in France in monastery cloisters in the 11th century. From the Middle Ages it was played by royalty, particularly by several Kings of France, where the game was extremely popular around 1600. It spread to other parts of Europe and was played by Henry VII and Henry VIII of England, but declined considerably in popularity in the 17th and 18th centuries.
The English governing body, the Tennis and Rackets Association was formed in 1907.

WORLD CHAMPIONS
The first recorded world champion is the oldest for any sport, the Frenchman Clergé from 1740.
Determined on a challenge basis, world champions have been:

Men's singles
c.1740-50 Clergé (Fra)
1765-85 Raymond Masson (Fra)
1785-1816 Joseph Barcellon (Fra)
1816-9 Marchesio (Ita)
1819-29 Philip Cox (UK)

1829-62 Edmond Barre (Fra)
1862-71 Edmund Tomkins (UK)
1871-85 George Lambert (UK)
1885-90 Tom Pettitt (USA)
1890-95 Charles Saunders (UK)
1895-1905 Peter Latham (UK)
1905-7 Cecil Fairs (UK)
1907-8 Peter Latham (UK)
1908-12 Cecil Fairs (UK)
1912-4 Fred Covey (UK)
1914-6 Jay Gould (USA)
1916-28 Fred Covey (UK)
1928-54 Pierre Etchebaster (Fra)
1955-7 James Dear (UK)
1957-9 Albert Johnson (UK)
1959-69 Northrup Knox (USA)
1969-72 G.H.'Pete' Bostwick (USA)
1972-5 Jimmy Bostwick (USA)
1976-81 Howard Angus (UK)
1981-7 Chris Ronaldson (UK)
1987- Wayne Davies (Aus)

Women's singles First played in 1985. *Winners:*
1985 Judy Clarke (Aus)
1987 Judy Clarke (Aus)
1989 Penny Fellows (UK)

Women's doubles First played in 1985. *Winners:*
1985 Judy Clarke & Annie Link (Aus)
1987 Lesley Ronaldson & Katrina Allen (UK)
1989 Alex Warren-Piper & Melissa Briggs (UK)

WORLD INVITATION TOURNAMENT
Men's singles
1987-8 Lachlan Deuchar (Aus)
1990 Lachlan Deuchar (Aus)
Men's Doubles
1988 Wayne Davies & Lachlan Deuchar (Aus)
1990 Wayne Davies & Lachlan Deuchar (Aus)
Women's Singles
1988 Sally Jones (UK)
1990 Alex Warren-Piper (UK).
Women's Doubles
1988 D.Barrabé & Penny Fellows (UK)
1990 Sally Jones & Alex Warren-Piper (UK)

OLYMPIC GAMES
The sport was included once in the Olympic Games, in 1908, when the title was won by Jay Gould (USA).

BRITISH AMATEUR CHAMPIONSHIPS
Held annually, first in 1888 at singles and in 1920 at doubles. *All winners from UK unless stated.*

Singles *Winners from 1965:*
1965 David Warburg
1966-80 Howard Angus
1981 Alan Lovell

1982 Howard Angus
1983-6 Alan Lovell
1987-9 Julian Snow
1990 James Male

Most wins:
16 Howard Angus 1966-80, 1982
13 Edgar M.Baerlein 1912, 1914, 1919-27, 1929-30
9 Eustace Miles 1899-1903, 1905-6, 1909-10

Doubles *Winners from 1967:*
1967-70 Howard Angus & David Warburg
1972-4 Howard Angus & David Warburg
1975 John Clench & Alan Lovell
1976 Howard Angus & David Warburg
1977-9 Alan Lovell & Andrew Windham
1980 Howard Angus & Richard Cooper
1981 Alan Lovell & Michael Dean
1982 Peter Seabrook & John Ward
1983-6 Alan Lovell & Michael Dean
1987 Julian Snow & James Male
1988 Alan Lovell & Michael Dean
1989-90 James Male & Michael Happell

Most wins:
by the same pair:
8 Howard Angus & David Warburg 1967-70, 1972-4, 1976
7 Edgar M.Baerlein & Lowther Lees 1929-31, 1934-7
by individuals with various partners:
11 Edgar M.Baerlein 1920-2, 1925, 1929-31, 1934-7
10 Lowther Lees 1926, 1928-31, 1934-7, 1946
10 Alan Lovell 1975, 1977-9, 1981, 1983-6, 1988

BRITISH OPEN CHAMPIONSHIPS
The Open championship on a challenge basis for the Prince's Club Shield (to 1976), has been won as follows:
(all winners from UK unless stated)

1931 Edgar Baerlein	1962 Ronald Hughes
1931 E.Ratcliffe	1967-8 Frank Willis
1932 W.A.Groom	1970 Howard Angus
1934-5 Lowther Lees	1972 Howard Angus
1938 James Dear	1975-6 Howard Angus
1950 Ronald Hughes	
1951 James Dear	
1956 James Dear	

The Open Invitation tournament was contested annually for the Field Trophy 1965-73; it was sponsored by Cutty Sark, 1974-8, then by Unigate, and the sponsors now are Rank Xerox with George Wimpey.

Open Singles *winners:*
1965 Ronald Hughes
1966-7 Frank Willis
1968 Howard Angus
1969 Frank Willis
1970 Howard Angus
1970 (Nov) Frank Willis

1971 Norwood Cripps
1972 Frank Willis
1973 Norwood Cripps
1974 Howard Angus
1975 Chris Ennis
1976-7 Howard Angus
1978 Chris Ronaldson
1979 Howard Angus
1980-5 Chris Ronaldson (two in 1980)
1986-9 Lachlan Deuchar (Aus)

Most wins: 8 Chris Ronaldson, Howard Angus

Open Doubles *winners: (first held 1971)*
1971 Ronald Hughes & Norwood Cripps
1972 Frank Willis & Chris Ennis
1973-5 Charles Swallow & Norwood Cripps
1976 Frank Willis & David Cull
1977-80 Norwood Cripps & Alan Lovell
    (5 wins, two in 1977)
1981 Chris Ronaldson & Michael Dean
1982 Norwood Cripps & Alan Lovell
1983 Chris Ronaldson & Michael Dean
1984-9 Wayne Davies & Lachlan Deuchar (Aus)

Women's Open Singles *(first held 1978)*
1978 Anna Moore
1979-81 Lesley Ronaldson
1982 Judy Clarke (Aus)
1983-6 Katrina Allen
1986 (Nov) Lesley Ronaldson
1987 Sally Jones
1988 Penny Fellows
1989 Sally Jones

Women's Open Doubles
1989 Sally Jones & Alex Warren-Piper

RODEO

Rodeo was developed from the 18th century fiestas of the early days of the North American cattle industry. Ranching skills, such as bronc busting, bull riding, steer wrestling and calf roping have become highly competitive activities in the professional rodeos held throughout the USA, Canada and Mexico.

The governing body is the Professional Rodeo Cowboys Association (PRCA), the name taken in 1974 by the Rodeo Cowboys Association, originally formed in 1936, and known as the Cowboys Turtles Association until 1945. Standard rodeo events are: bareback riding, saddle bronc riding, bull riding, calf roping and steer wrestling with three additional events also often contested: team roping, barrel racing and single-steer roping. In the first three riding events the object is to stay on for a minimum of eight seconds; in the others the object is to complete the task in the minimum time.

National Finals Rodeo

Each December the PRCA and Women's Professional Rodeo Association (WPRA) stage the National Finals Rodeo (NFR), which is the culmination of the season's rodeo events. The top 15 money-earning cowboys in each of six PRCA events and the top 15 WPRA barrel racers compete at the Finals. The first NFR was in 1959 at Dallas, Texas. Oklahoma City, Oklahoma hosted the Finals for 20 years before the event was moved to Las Vegas, Nevada in 1985. A record $2.2 million purse was offered for the 1989 Finals. *Most wins at each event:*

Saddle bronc riding: 6 Casey Tibbs 1949, 1951-4, 1959
Bareback bronc riding: 5 Joe Alexander 1971-5
                        5 Bruce Ford 1979-80, 1982-3, 1987
Bull riding: 8 Donnie Gay 1975-81, 1984; 7 Jim Shoulders 1951, 1954-9
Calf roping: 8 Dean Oliver 1955, 1958, 1960-4, 1969; Roy Cooper 1976-8, 1980-4
Steer wrestling: 6 Homer Pettigrew 1940, 1942-5, 1948
Team roping: 5 Jake Barnes & Clay O'Brien Cooper 1985-9
Single steer roping: 6 Everett Shaw 1945-6, 1948, 1951, 1959, 1962
All events: 16 Jim Shoulders 1949-59

All-Around Cowboy World Champions

Won annually by the cowboy who has won the most money in two or more different events. *Winners, with money won:*

1947	Todd Whatley	-
1948	Gerald Roberts	21,766
1949	Jim Shoulders	21,496
1950	Bill Linderman	30,715
1951	Casey Tibbs	29,104
1952	Harry Tompkins	30,934
1953	Bill Linderman	33,674
1954	Buck Rutherford	40,404
1955	Casey Tibbs	42,065
1956	Jim Shoulders	43,381
1957	Jim Shoulders	33,299
1958	Jim Shoulders	33,212
1959	Jim Shoulders	32,905
1960	Harry Tompkins	32,522
1961	Benny Reynolds	31,309
1962	Tom Nesmith	32,611
1963	Dean Oliver	31,329
1964	Dean Oliver	31,150
1965	Dean Oliver	33,163
1966	Larry Mahan	40,358
1967	Larry Mahan	51,996
1968	Larry Mahan	49,129
1969	Larry Mahan	57,726
1970	Larry Mahan	41,493
1971	Phil Lyne	49,245
1972	Phil Lyne	60,852
1973	Larry Mahan	64,447

1974	Tom Ferguson	66,929
1975	Leo Camarillo &	
	Tom Ferguson	50,300
1976	Tom Ferguson	87,908
1977	Tom Ferguson	76,730
1978	Tom Ferguson	103,734
1979	Tom Ferguson	96,272
1980	Paul Tierney	105,568
1981	Jimmie Cooper	105,862
1982	Chris Lybbert	123,709
1983	Roy Cooper	153,391
1984	Dee Pickett	122,618
1985	Lewis Feild	130,347
1986	Lewis Feild	166,042
1987	Lewis Feild	144,334
1988	Dave Appleton	121,546
1989	Ty Murray	134,806

Most wins: 6 Larry Mahan, Tom Ferguson
The leading career earnings winner is Roy Cooper with
$1,184,325 in 1975-89.

ROLLER HOCKEY

An adaptation of hockey and ice hockey, played as a five-
a-side game on roller skates. It was first known in Europe
as Rink Hockey. The Amateur Rink Hockey Association was
formed in Britain, originally c.1898, taking this name in
1908. The NHRA is affiliated to the Federation
Internationale de Roller Skating. The first European
Championships were held at Herne Bay, England in 1926.
Roller Hockey is to be staged as a demonstration sport at
the 1992 Olympic Games.

WORLD CHAMPIONSHIPS
First held in 1936. A biennial tournament, the World
Group A Championship was transferred to odd years from
1989.*Wins:*
12 Portugal	1947-50, 1952, 1956, 1958, 1960, 1962,	
	1968, 1974, 1982	
10 Spain	1951, 1954-5, 1964, 1966, 1970, 1972,	
	1976, 1980, 1989	
3 Italy	1953, 1986, 1988	
2 England	1936, 1939	
2 Argentina	1978, 1984	

EUROPEAN CHAMPIONSHIPS
Preceded the world championships, with which it was
amalgamated from 1936 to 1957. *Wins:*
16 Portugal	1947-50, 1952, 1956, 1959, 1961, 1963,
	1965, 1967, 1971, 1973, 1975, 1977, 1987
12 England	1926-32, 1934, 1936-9
9 Spain	1951, 1954-5, 1957, 1969, 1979, 1981,
	1983, 1985
1 Italy	1953

The first women's European championship was held in
1989 when the winners were the Netherlands.

ROLLER SKATING

The first ever roller skate had been invented by Joseph
Merlin of Belgium. He demonstrated it in 1760, but it was
not a success. The modern four-wheeled roller skate was
introduced by James Plympton in the USA in 1863. At first
it was used by ice skaters for practice, but soon developed
into a sport in its own right. The first roller rink in the USA
was opened by Plympton in 1866 at Newport, Rhode
Island. In Britain the National Skating Association assumed
control of roller skating in 1893 and staged the first
national championships the following year. The
International Roller Skating Federation (Fédération
Internationale de Patinage à Roulettes) was founded in
1924; it now has its headquarters in Lincoln, Nebraska.
In 1937 the first world championships were held for speed
skating (at Monza) and in the same year European
championships for figure skating were introduced (at
Stuttgart).

WORLD FIGURE SKATING CHAMPIONSHIPS
First held in 1947. *Winners (combined figures and free
skating):*

Men
1947 Donald Mounce (USA)
1949 Karl Peter (Swi)
1951-2 Freimut Stein (FRG)
1955-6 Franz Ningel (FRG)
1958-9 Karl-Heinz Losch (FRG)
1961-2 Karl-Heinz Losch (FRG)
1965 Hans Dahmen (FRG)
1966 Karl-Heinz Losch (FRG)
1967 Hans Dahmen (FRG)
1968 Jack Courtney (USA)
1970-2 Michael Obrecht (FRG)
1973 Randy Dayney (USA)
1974 Michael Obrecht (FRG)
1975 Leonardo Lienhard (Swi)
1976-8 Thomas Nieder (FRG)
1979-82 Michael Butzke (GDR)
1983 Joachim Helmle (FRG)
1984-5 Michele Biserni (Ita)
1986 Michele Tolomini (Ita)
1987-9 Sandro Guerra (Ita)

Most wins: 5 Karl-Heinz Losch

Women
1947 Ursula Wehrli (Swi)
1949 Franca Rio (Ita)
1951 Franca Rio (Ita)
1952 Lotte Cadenbach (FRG)
1955 Helene Kienzle (FRG)
1956 Rita Blumenberg (FRG)
1958 Marika Kilius (FRG)

1959 Ute Kitz (FRG)
1961 Marlies Fahse (FRG)
1962 Fränzi Schmidt (Swi)
1965-8 Astrid Bader (FRG)
1970 Christine Kreutzfeldt (FRG)
1971-2 Petra Häusler (FRG)
1973-5 Sigrid Mullenbach (FRG)
1976-8 Natalie Dunn (USA)
1979-81 Petra Schneider (née Ernert) (FRG)
1982-4 Claudia Bruppacher (FRG)
1985-7 Chiara Sartori (Ita)
1988-9 Rafaella Del Vinaccio (Ita)

Most wins: 4 Astrid Bader

Pairs
1947 Fernand Leemans & Elvire Collin (Bel)
1949 Ken Byrne & Jean Phethean (UK)
1951 Paul Falk & Ria Baran (FRG)
1952 Günther Koch & Sigrid Knake (FRG)
1955-6 Günther Koch & Sigrid Knake (FRG)
1958 Werner Mensching & Rita Blumenberg (FRG)
1959 Dieter Fingerle & Susu Schneider (FRG)
1961-2 Walther Hoffman & Maria Ludolph (FRG)
1965-7 Dieter Fingerle & Uta Keller (FRG)
1968 Jack Courtney & Sheryl Trueman (USA)
1970-2 Ronald Robovitsky & Gail Robovitsky (USA)
1973 Louis Stovel & Vicki Handyside (USA)
1974 Ron Sabo & Susan McDonald (USA)
1975-6 Ron Sabo & Darlene Waters (USA)
1977 Ray Chapatta & Karen Mejia (USA)
1978 Pat Jones & Rooie Coleman (USA)
1979 Ray Chapatta & Karen Mejia (USA)
1980-2 Paul Price & Tina Kniesley (USA)
1983-6 John Arishita & Tammy Jeru (USA)
1987-8 Fabio Trevisani & Monica Mezzadri (Ita)
1989 David DeMotte & Nicky Armstrong (USA)

Most wins: 4 Dieter Fingerle, John Arishtita & Tammy Jeru

The following skaters won world titles on both ice and rollers:
Ria and Paul Falk - roller pairs 1951, ice pairs 1951-2
Marika Kilius - roller 1958, ice pairs 1963-4

Dance
1947 Fred Ludwig & Barbara Gallagher (USA)
1949 Ken Byrne & Jean Phethean (UK)
1952 Ted Ellis & Marion Mercer (UK)
1955 Karl-Heinz Beyer & Marga Schäfer (FRG)
1956 Günther Koch & Sigrid Knake (FRG)
1958 Sydney Cooper & Patricia Cooper (UK)
1959 Peter Kwiet & Rita Paucka (FRG)
1961 Peter Kwiet & Rita Kwiet (née Paucka) (FRG)
1962 Brian Colclough & Patricia Colclough (UK)
1965 Brian Colclough & Patricia Colclough (UK)
1966-7 Hans-Jürgen Schamberger & Martha Schamberger
      (FRG)

1968 Donald Rudalawicz & Rita Smith (USA)
1970-1 Richard Horne & Jane Pankey (USA)
1972 Tom Straker & Bonnie Lambert (USA)
1973 James Stephens & Jane Puracchio (USA)
1974 Udo Donsdorf & Christine Henke (FRG)
1975-6 Kerry Cavazzi & Jane Puracchio (USA)
1977-9 Dan Littel & Florence Arsenault (USA)
1980 Torsten Carels & Gabriele Achenbach (GDR)
1981-2 Mark Howard & Cindy Smith (USA)
1983-4 David Golub & Angela Famiano (USA)
1985 Martin Hauss & Andrea Steudte (FRG)
1986 Scott Myers & Anna Danks (USA)
1987 Rolf Ferando & Lori Walsh (USA)
1988 Peter Wulf & Michaela Mitzlaff (FRG)
1989 Greg Goody & Jodee Viola (USA)

WORLD SPEED SKATING CHAMPIONSHIPS
First contested in 1937 for men and 1953 for women. Held on track or road, men's and women's events at distances from 300m to 10 000m.

Most titles won: (Track/Road)
MEN: 15 Giuseppe Cantarella (Ita) 7/8 1964-80, Giuseppe Cruciani (Ita) 8/7 1978-83
WOMEN: 18 Alberta Vianello (Ita) 8/10 1953-65, Annie Lambrechts (Bel) 1/17 1964-81

World Records
MEN – Track

	min:sec	
300m	0:25.248	O.Galliazzo (Ita) 1987
500m	0:41.233	G.De Persio (Ita) 1980
1000m	1:23.09	G.L.Botero (Col) 1988
1500m	2:07.770	G.De Persio (Ita) 1980
2000m	2:54.56	R.Klöss (FRG) 1988
3000m	4:21.764	G.De Persio (Ita) 1980
5000m	7:34.938	M.Giupponi (Ita) 1987
10 000m	15:14.876	O.Galliazzo (Ita) 1987
15 000m	23:07.868	O.Galliazzo (Ita) 1987
20 000m	30:52.792	P.Bomben (Ita) 1987
30 000m	47:42.820	T.Rossi (Ita) 1987
50 000m	1hr 20:17.736	T.Rossi (Ita) 1987

Road – where superior to track times:

300m	0:24.99	L.Antoniel (Ita) 1988
500m	0:40.910	P.Sarto (Ita) 1987
1000m	1:22.124	P.Sarto (Ita) 1987
2000m	2:51.333	G.De Persio (Ita) 1987
5000m	7:32.462	G.De Persio (Ita) 1987
10 000m	14:55.64	G.De Persio (Ita) 1988

WOMEN – Track

300m	0:26.986	S.De Cesaris (Ita) 1987
500m	0:44.404	S.De Cesaris (Ita) 1987
1000m	1:27.60	B.Fischer (FRG) 1988
1500m	2:14.644	M.Canafoglia (Ita) 1987
2000m	3:02.25	N.Malmström (FRG) 1988
3000m	4:38.464	M.Canafoglia (Ita) 1987
5000m	7:48.508	M.Canafoglia (Ita) 1987

10 000m	15:58.022	M.Canafoglia (Ita) 1987
15 000m	26:18.290	F.Monteverde (Ita) 1987
20 000m	32:53.970	A.Lambrechts (Bel) 1985
30 000m	49:15.906	A.Lambrechts (Bel) 1985
50 000m	1hr 21:26.942	A.Lambrechts (Bel) 1985

Road – where superior to track times

300m	0:26.794	M.Canafoglia (Ita) 1987
1500m	2:14.122	M.Canafoglia (Ita) 1987
15 000m	26:02.624	P.Biagini (Ita) 1987

ROWING

Rowing originates from ancient times but the sport in its present form dates to 1715 when Irish comedian Thomas Doggett instituted his famous race for scullers. There were many races at Walton in 1768, but the first known regatta was on the Thames at Ranelagh Gardens, Putney in 1775. The international governing body is the Fédération Internationale des Sociétés d'Aviron (FISA), founded in 1892, two years after the Belgian Federation of Rowing Clubs had staged a 'European Championship', with just one category of boat, the sculling outrigger. The winner over the 2800m course was Edouard Lescrauwaet (Bel). FISA held their first official European Championships in 1893. FISA had 67 member nations in 1989.

OLYMPIC GAMES

The first Olympic rowing competition was on the River Seine over a 1750m course in 1900, but in more recent times rowing courses have been on still waters. The standard length is now 2000m, but the course measured 2 miles (3219m) in 1904, 1.5 miles (2414m) in 1908 and 1883m in 1948. Weather and water conditions affect the times recorded. *Winners*

Men
Single Sculls
1900 Henri Barrelet (Fra) 7:35.6
1904 Frank Greer (USA) 10:08.5
1906 Gaston Delaplane (Fra) 5:53.4
1908 Harry Blackstaffe (UK) 9:26.0
1912 William Kinnear (UK) 7:47.6
1920 John Kelly Snr (USA) 7:35.0
1924 Jack Beresford Jr (UK) 7:49.2
1928 Henry Pearce (Aus) 7:11.0
1932 Henry Pearce (Aus) 7:44.4
1936 Gustav Schäfer (Ger) 8:21.5
1948 Mervyn Wood (Aus) 7:24.4
1952 Yuriy Tyukalov (USSR) 8:12.8
1956 Vyacheslav Ivanov (USSR) 8:02.5
1960 Vyacheslav Ivanov (USSR) 7:13.96
1964 Vyacheslav Ivanov (USSR) 8:22.51
1968 Henri Jan Wienese (Hol) 7:47.80
1972 Yuriy Malishev (USSR) 7:10.12
1976 Pertti Karppinen (Fin) 7:29.03
1980 Pertti Karppinen (Fin) 7:09.61
1984 Pertti Karpinnen (Fin) 7:00.24

1988 Thomas Lange (GDR) 6:49.86

Double Sculls
1904 John Mulcahy/William Varley (USA) 10:03.2
1920 Paul Costello/John Kelly Snr (USA) 7:09.0
1924 Paul Costello/John Kelly Snr (USA) 7:45.0
1928 Paul Costello/Charles McIlvaine (USA) 6:41.4
1932 William Garrett Gilmore/Kenneth Myers (USA) 7:17.4
1936 Jack Beresford/Leslie Southwood (UK) 7:20.8
1948 Richard Burnell/Herbert Bushnell (UK) 6:51.3
1952 Tranquilo Capozzo/Eduardo Guerrero (Arg) 7:32.2
1956 Aleksandr Berkutov/Yuriy Tyukalov (USSR) 7:24.0
1960 Václav Kozák/Pavel Schmidt (Cs) 6:47.50
1964 Boris Dubrovsky/Oleg Tyurin (USSR) 7:10.66
1968 Anatoliy Sass/Aleksandr Timoshinin (USSR) 6:51.82
1972 Gennadiy Korshikov/Aleksandr Timoshinin (USSR) 7:01.77
1976 Alf Hansen/Frank Hansen (Nor) 7:13.20
1980 Joachim Dreifke/Klaus Kröppelien (GDR) 6:24.33
1984 Bradley Lewis/Paul Enquist (USA) 6:36.87
1988 Ronald Florijn/Nicolaas Rienks (Hol) 6:21.13

Coxless Pairs
1904 Robert Farnam/Joseph Ryan (USA) 10:57.0
1908 John Fenning/Gordon Thomson (UK) 9:41.0
1924 Antonie Beijnen/Wilhelm Rösingh (Hol) 8:19.4
1928 Kurt Moeschter/Bruno Müller (Ger) 7:06.4
1932 Lewis Clive/Arthur Edwards (UK) 8:00.0
1936 Willie Eichorn/Hugo Strauss (Ger) 8:16.1
1948 George Laurie/John Wilson (UK) 7:21.1
1952 Charles Logg/Thomas Price (USA) 8:20.7
1956 James Fifer/Duvall Hecht (USA) 7:55.4
1960 Valentin Boreyko/Oleg Golovanov (USSR) 7:02.01
1964 George Hungerford/Roger Jackson (Can) 7:32.94
1968 Heinz-Jürgen Bothe/Jörg Lucke (GDR) 7:26.56
1972 Siegfried Brietzke/Wolfgang Mager (GDR) 6:53.16
1976 Bernd Landvoigt/Jörg Landvoigt (GDR) 7:23.31
1980 Bernd Landvoigt/Jörg Landvoigt (GDR) 6:48.01
1984 Petru Iosub/Valer Toma (Rom) 6:45.39
1988 Andrew Holmes/Steven Redgrave (UK) 6:36.84

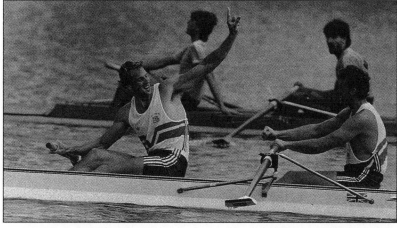

Steve Redgrave (left) and Andy Holmes after their Olympic victory in 1988
(All-Sport/Simon Bruty)

Coxed Pairs
1900 Minerva Amsterdam (Hol) 7:34.2
1906 Bucintoro (Ita) 4:23.0 (1000m)
1906 Bucintoro (Ita) 7:32.4 (1609m)
1920 Italy 7:56.0
1924 Switzerland 8:39.0
1928 Switzerland 7:42.6
1932 USA 8:25.8
1936 Germany 8:36.9
1948 Denmark 8:00.5
1952 France 8:28.6
1956 USA 8:26.1
1960 FR Germany 7:29.14
1964 USA 8:21.23
1968 Italy 8:04.81
1972 GDR 7:17.25
1976 GDR 7:58.99
1980 GDR 7:02.54
1984 Italy 7:05.99
1988 Italy 6:58.79

Quadruple Sculls
1976 GDR 6:18.65
1980 GDR 5:49.81
1984 FR Germany 5:57.55
1988 Italy 5:53.37

Coxless Fours
1904 Century BC, St.Louis (USA) 9:53.8
1908 Magdalen College, Oxford (UK) 8:34.0
1924 Great Britain 7:08.6
1928 Great Britain 6:36.0
1932 Great Britain 6:58.2
1936 Germany 7:01.8
1948 Italy 6:39.0
1952 Yugoslavia 7:16.0
1956 Canada 7:08.8
1960 USA 6:26.26
1964 Denmark 6:59.30
1968 GDR 6:39.18
1972 GDR 6:24.27
1976 GDR 6:37.42
1980 GDR 6:08.17
1984 New Zealand 6:03.48
1988 GDR 6:03.11

Coxed Fours
1900 Germania RC, Hamburg (Ger) 5:59.0*
1900 Cercle de l'Aviron (Fra) 7:11.0*
1906 Italy 8:13.0
1912 Germany 6:59.4
1920 Switzerland 6:54.0
1924 Switzerland 7:18.4
1928 Italy 6:47.8
1932 Germany 7:19.0
1936 Germany 7:16.2
1948 USA 6:50.3
1952 Czechoslovakia 7:33.4

1956 Italy 7:19.4
1960 FR Germany 6:39.12
1964 FR Germany 7:00.44
1968 New Zealand 6:45.62
1972 FR Germany 6:31.85
1976 USSR 6:40.22
1980 GDR 6:14.51
1984 Great Britain 6:18.64
1988 GDR 6:10.74
* Two finals were held in 1900

Eights
1900 Vesper BC (USA) 6:09.8
1904 Vesper BC (USA) 7:50.0
1908 Leander Club (UK) 7:52.0
1912 Leander Club (UK) 6:15.0
1920 USA 6:02.6
1924 USA 6:33.4
1928 USA 6:03.2
1932 USA 6:37.6
1936 USA 6:25.4
1948 USA 5:56.7
1952 USA 6:25.9
1956 USA 6:35.2
1960 Germany 5:57.18
1964 USA 6:18.23
1968 FR Germany 6:07.00
1972 New Zealand 6:08.94
1976 GDR 5:58.29
1980 GDR 5:49.05
1984 Canada 5:41.32
1988 FR Germany 5:46.05

Discontinued Events
76-Man Naval rowing boats (2000m)
1906 Varese (Ita) 10:45.0
17-Man Naval Rowing (3000m)
1906 Poros (Gre) 16:35.0
Coxed Fours Inriggers
1912 Denmark 7:47.0

Women *Women rowed over 1000m 1976-84, and over 2000m from 1988*
Single Sculls
1976 Christine Scheiblich (GDR)4:05.56
1980 Sanda Toma (Rom) 3:40.69
1984 Valeria Racila (Rom) 3:40.68
1988 Jutta Behrendt (GDR) 7:47.19

Double Sculls
1976 Svetla Otzetova/Zdravka Yordanova (Bul) 3:44.36
1980 Yelena Khlopsteva/Larisa Popova (USSR) 3:16.27
1984 Marioara Popescu/Elisabeta Oleniuc (Rom) 3:26.75
1988 Brigit Peter/Martina Schröter (GDR) 7:00.48

Coxless Pairs
1976 Stoyanka Grouitcheva/Siika Kelbetcheva (Bul)
        4:01.22

1980 Cornelia Klier/Ute Steindorf (GDR) 3:30.49
1984 Rodica Arba/Elena Horvat (Rom) 3:32.60
1988 Rodica Arba/Olga Homeghi (Rom) 7:28.13

Quadruple Sculls
1976 GDR 3:29.99
1980 GDR 3:15.32
1984 Romania 3:14.11
1988 GDR 6:21.06

Coxed Fours
1976 GDR 3:45.08
1980 GDR 3:19.27
1984 Romania 3:19.30
1988 GDR 6:56.00

Eights
1976 GDR 3:33.32
1980 GDR 3:03.32
1984 USA 2:59.80
1988 GDR 6:15.17

In the summaries that follow, the following abbreviations are used: 1x single sculls, 2x double sculls, 4x quadruple sculls, 4x+ quadruple sculls with coxswain, 2- coxless pairs, 2+ coxed pairs, 4- coxless fours, 4+ coxed fours, 8+ eights.

Most gold medals
3 John B.Kelly (USA) 1x 1920; 2x 1920, 1924
3 Paul Costello (USA) 2x 1920, 1924, 1928
3 Jack Beresford Jr (UK) 1x 1924; 4+ 1932; 2x 1936
3 Vyacheslav Ivanov (USSR) 1x 1956, 1960, 1964
3 Siegfried Brietzke (GDR) 2- 1972; 4- 1976, 1980
3 Pertti Karpinnen (Fin) 1x 1976, 1980, 1984

Most medals: (gold/silver/bronze)
5 (3/2/-) Jack Beresford Jr 1920-36 (at five different Games) The youngest Olympic medallist at any sport is an unknown French boy who coxed the winning Dutch pair in 1900; he was believed to have been between seven and ten years of age. The oldest Olympic medallist, also a winner, was Robert Zimonyi who coxed the US eights in 1964 at 46 yr 180 days. The oldest oarsman to win a gold medal was Guy Nickalls (UK) at 42 yr 170 days in the eights in 1908.

WORLD CHAMPIONSHIPS
The first World Championships were held at Lucerne in 1962. Women's events were first included in 1974.
Winners:

Men
Single Sculls
1962 Vyacheslav Ivanov (USSR)
1966 Don Spero (USA)
1970 Alberto Demiddi (Arg)
1974 Wolfgang Hönig (GDR)
1975 Peter-Michael.Kolbe (FRG)
1977 Joachim Dreifke (GDR)
1978 Peter-Michael Kolbe (FRG)
1979 Pertti Karppinen (Fin)
1981 Peter-Michael Kolbe (FRG)
1982 Rüdiger Reiche (GDR)
1983 Peter-Michael Kolbe (FRG)
1985 Pertti Karppinen (Fin)
1986 Peter-Michael Kolbe (FRG)
1987 Thomas Lange (GDR)
1989 Thomas Lange (GDR)

Double Sculls
1962 René Duhamel/Bernard Monnereau (Fra)
1966 Melchior Bürgin/Martin Studach (Swi)
1970 Jörgen Engelbrecht/Niels Secher (Den)
1974 Christof Kreuziger/Hans-Ulrich Schmied (GDR)
1975 Alf Hansen/Frank Hansen (Nor)
1977 Chris Baillieu/Michael Hart (UK)
1978-9 Alf Hansen/Frank Hansen (Nor)
1981 Klaus Kröppelien/Joachim Dreifke (GDR)
1982 Alf Hansen/Rolf Thorsen (Nor)
1983 Thomas Lange/Uwe Heppner (GDR)
1985 Thomas Lange/Uwe Heppner (GDR)
1986 Alberto Belgori/Igor Pescialli (Ita)
1987 Vasil Radeyev/Danatyl Yordanov (Bul)
1989 Lars Bjøness/Rol Bent Thorsen (Nor)

Coxless Pairs
1962 Dieter Bender/Günther Zumkeller (FRG)
1966 Peter Gorny/Werner Klatt (GDR)
1970 Peter Gorny/Werner Klatt (GDR)
1974-5 Bernd Landvoigt/Jörg Landvoigt (GDR)
1977 Vitaliy Yeliseyev/Aleksandr Kulagin (USSR)
1978-9 Bernd Landvoigt/Jörg Landvoigt (GDR)
1981 Yuriy Pimenov/Nikolay Pimenov (USSR)
1982 Magnus Grepperud/Sverre Loken (Nor)
1983 Carl Ertel/Ulf Sauerbrey (GDR)
1985-6 Nikolay Pimenov/Yuriy Pimenov (USSR)
1987 Andrew Holmes/Steven Redgrave (UK)
1989 Thomas Jung/Uwe Kellner (GDR)

Coxed Pairs
1962 FR Germany	1983 GDR
1966 Netherlands	1985 Italy
1970 Romania	1986 Great Britain
1974 USSR	1987 Italy
1975 GDR	1989 Italy
1977 Bulgaria	1981 Italy
1978 GDR	1982 Italy
1979 GDR	

Coxless Fours
1962 FR Germany	1981 USSR
1966 GDR	1982 Switzerland
1970 GDR	1983 FR Germany
1974-5 GDR	1985 FR Germany
1977 GDR	1986 USA
1978 USSR	1987 GDR
1979 GDR	1989 GDR

Coxed Fours

1962 FR Germany	1981-2 GDR
1966 GDR	1983 New Zealand
1970 FR Germany	1985 USSR
1974 GDR	1986-7 GDR
1975 USSR	1989 Romania
1977-9 GDR	

Quadruple Sculls

1974-5 GDR	1985 Canada
1977-9 GDR	1986-7 USSR
1981-2 GDR	1989 Romania
1983 FR Germany	

Eights

1962 FR Germany	1981 USSR
1966 FR Germany	1982-3 New Zealand
1970 GDR	1985 USSR
1974 USA	1986 Australia
1975 GDR	1987 USA
1977-9 GDR	1989 FR Germany

Women
Single Sculls
1974-5 Christine Scheiblich (GDR)
1977 Christine Scheiblich (GDR)
1978 Christine Hahn (née Scheiblich) (GDR)
1979 Sanda Toma (Rom)
1981 Sanda Toma (Rom)
1982 Irina Fetissova (USSR)
1983 Jutta Hampe (GDR)
1985 Cornelia Linse (GDR)
1986 Jutta Hampe (GDR)
1987 Magdalena Georgeyeva (Bul)
1989 Elisabeta Lipa (Rom)

Double Sculls
1974-5 Yelena Antonova/Galina Yermoleyeva (USSR)
1977 Anke Borchmann/Roswietha Zobelt (GDR)
1978 Svetla Otzetova/Zdravka Yordanova (Bul)
1979 Cornelia Linse/Heidi Westphal (GDR)
1981 Margarita Kokarevitha/Antonina Makhina (USSR)
1982 Yelena Braticko/Antonina Makhina (USSR)
1983 Jutta Scheck/Martina Schröter (GDR)
1985 Sylvia Schurabe/Martina Schröter (GDR)
1986 Sylvia Schurabe/Beate Schramm (GDR)
1987 Steska Madina/Violeta Ninova (Bul)
1989 Jana Sorgers/Beate Schramm (GDR)

Coxless Pairs
1974 Marilena Ghita/Cornelia Neascu (Rom)
1975 Sabine Dähne/Angelika Noack (GDR)
1977 Sabine Dähne/Angelika Noack (GDR)
1978-9 Cornelia Bugel/Ute Steindorf (GDR)
1981 Sigrid Anders/Iris Rudolph (GDR)
1982-3 Silvia Fröhlich/Marita Sandig (GDR)
1985 Rodica Arba/Elena Florea (Rom)
1986-7 Rodica Arba/Olga Homeghi (Rom)
1989 Kathrin Haaker/Judith Zeidler (GDR)

Quadruple Sculls

1974-5 GDR	1981-2 USSR
1977 GDR	1983 USSR
1978 Bulgaria	1985-7 GDR
1979 GDR	1989 GDR

Coxed Fours

1974-5 GDR	1983 GDR
1977-8 GDR	1985 GDR
1979 USSR	1986-7 Romania
1981-2 USSR	

Coxless Fours
1986 USA
1989 GDR

Eights

1974-5 GDR	1985-6 USSR
1977 GDR	1987 Romania
1978-9 USSR	1989 Romania
1981-3 USSR	

LIGHTWEIGHT WORLD CHAMPIONS

Men
Single Sculls
1974 William Belden (USA)
1975 Reto Wyss (Swi)
1976 Raimund Haberl (Aut)
1977 Reto Wyss (Swi)
1978 José Antonio Montosa (Spa)
1979 William Belden (USA)
1980 Christian Georg Wahrlich (FRG)
1981 Scott Roop (USA)
1982 Raimund Haberl (Aut)
1983-4 Bjarne Eltang (Den)
1985 Ruggero Verroca (Ita)
1986 Peter Antonie (Aus)
1987 Willem Van Belleghem (Bel)
1988 Alwin Otten (FRG)
1989 Frans Goebel (Hol)

Double Sculls
1978-9 Pal Bornick/Arne Gilje (Nor)
1980-4 Francesco Esposito/Ruggero Verroca (Ita)
1985 Luc Crispon/Thierry Renault (Fra)
1986 Carl Smith/Allan Whitwell (UK)
1987 Enrico Gandola/Giovanni Calabrese (Ita)
1988 Enrico Gandola/Francesco Esposito (Ita)
1989 Christoph Schmölzer/Walter Rantasa (Aut)

Coxless Fours

1974 Australia	1984 Spain
1975-7 France	1985 FR Germany
1978 Switzerland	1986 Italy
1979 United Kingdom	1987 FR Germany
1980-1 Australia	1988 Italy
1982 Italy	1989 FR Germany
1983 Spain	

Quadruple Sculls
1989 FR Germany

Eights
1974 USA	1981 Denmark
1975-6 FR Germany	1982 Italy
1977-8 United Kingdom	1983 Spain
1979 Spain	1984 Denmark
1980 United Kingdom	1985-9 Italy

Women
Single Sculls
1985 Adair Ferguson (Aus)
1986 Maria Sava (Rom)
1987 Magdalena Georgieva (Bul)
1988-9 Kris Karlson (USA)

Coxless Pairs
1987 Rodica Arba/Olga Homeghi (Rom)

Double Sculls
1985 Lin Clark/Beryl Crockford (UK)
1986 Chris Ernst/Cary Beth Sands (USA)
1987 Stefka Madina/Violeta Ninova (Bul)
1988 Laurien Vermuist/Ellen Meliesie (Hol)
1989 Cary Beth Sands/Kris Karlson (USA)

Coxed Fours
1985 FR Germany
1986 USA
1987 Romania

Coxless Fours
1988 China
1989 China

World Championships and Olympic Games
MOST GOLD MEDALS OVERALL

Men
6 Bernd & Jörg Landvoigt (GDR) 2- 1974-80
6 Joachim Dreifke (GDR) 1x 1977; 2x 1980-1, 4x 1974, 1978-9
6 Karl-Heinz Bussert (GDR) 4x 1976-9, 1981-2
6 Ulrich Diessner (GDR) 4+ 1977-80, 1982; 2+ 1983
6 Siegfried Brietzke & Wolfgang Mager (GDR) 2- 1972; 4- 1974-7, 1979
6 Giuseppe & Carmine Abbagnale (Ita) 2+ 1981-2, 1985, 1987-9
5 Pertti Karppinen (Fin) 1x 1976, 1979-80, 1984-5
5 Peter-Michael Kolbe (FRG) 1x 1975, 1978, 1981, 1983, 1986
5 Andreas Decker & Stefan Sempler (GDR) 4- 1974-7, 1979
5 Ulrich Karnatz (GDR) 8+ 1975-9
5 Gottfried Döhn (GDR) 4+ 1977-8, 1980; 8+ 1975-6
5 Alf Hansen (Nor) 2x 1975-6, 1978-9, 1982 (first four with his brother Frank)
5 Martin Winter (GDR) 4x 1977-8, 1980-2

5 Uwe Heppner (GDR) 2x 1983, 1985; 4x 1980-2
5 Andreas Gregor (GDR) cox 2+ 1983; 4+ 1977-8, 1980, 1982
5 Thomas Lange (GDR) 1x 1987-9, 2x 1983, 1985
5 Thomas Greiner (GDR) 4+ 1982, 2+ 1983, 4- 1987-9

Lightweight men
6 Ruggero Verroca (Ita) 1x 1985; 2x 1980-4
6 Francesco Esposito (Ita) 2x 1980-4 (all with Verroca), 1988 (with Enrico Gandola)

Women
6 Jutta Behrendt (née Hampe) 1x 1983, 1986, 1988; 4x 1985, 1987, 1989
5 Christine Hahn (née Schieblich) 1x 1974-8
5 Angelika Noack (GDR) 2- 1975, 1977; 4+ 1974, 1978, 1980
5 Yelena Terekhina (USSR) 8+ 1981-3, 1985-6

UNIVERSITY BOAT RACE
The Boat race between the Universities of Oxford and Cambridge is rowed annually on the River Thames from Putney to Mortlake over a distance of 6779km (4 miles 374 yards). It was first contested on 10 June 1829 from Hambledon Lock to Henley Bridge. From 1836 to 1842 it was rowed from Westminster to Putney, and in 1846, 1856 and 1863 from Mortlake to Putney; on all other occasions the present course has been used. Outrigged eights were first used in 1846.

To 1990 Cambridge lead in the series of 136 races with 69 wins to Oxford's 66. There were two races in 1849 and on 24 Mar 1877 there was the only dead-heat in the race's history.

Cambridge wins: 1836, 1839-41, 1845-6, 1849, 1856, 1858, 1860, 1870-4, 1876, 1879, 1884, 1886-9, 1899-1900, 1902-4, 1906-8, 1914, 1920-2, 1924-36, 1939, 1947-51, 1953, 1955-8, 1961-2, 1964, 1968-73, 1975, 1986

Oxford wins: 1829, 1842, 1849, 1852, 1854, 1857, 1859, 1861-9, 1875, 1878, 1880-3, 1885, 1890-8, 1901, 1905, 1909-13, 1923, 1937-8, 1946, 1952, 1954, 1959-60, 1963, 1965-7, 1974, 1976-85, 1987-90

Race record time: 16 min 45 sec Oxford 18 Mar 1984, an average speed of 24.28 km/h (15.09 mph)

Greatest margin: 20 lengths Cambridge 1900, apart from sinkings

Most successful individual: Boris Rankov (Oxford) rowed in six winning boats 1978-83

Most successful coach: Daniel Topolski of Oxford's ten successive wins 1976-85

Heaviest competitor: Chris Heathcote (Oxford, 1990) 110kg (243lb)

Heaviest crew: Oxford (1990) average weight: 94.5kg (208 lb)

Tallest competitor: Gavin Stewart (Oxford, 1987) 204.5cm (6ft 8 in)

Youngest competitor: Matthew Brittin (Cambridge, 1987) 18yr 208 days

Oldest competitor: Donald McDonald (Oxford, 1987) 31yr
The first woman to take part was Susan Brown, who
coxed the winning Oxford boats of 1981-2

HENLEY ROYAL REGATTA

Inaugurated in 1839. The course has varied slightly, but
has been about 1 mile 550 yards (2112m).

Diamond Sculls

Instituted in 1884 the Diamond Challenge Sculls at Henley
is regarded as the Blue Riband of amateur sculling.
Winners since 1970:
1970 Jochen Meissner (FRG)
1971 Alberto Demiddi (Arg)
1972 Aleksandr Timoshin (USSR)
1973-5 Sean Drea (Ire)
1976 Edward Hale (Aus)
1977-8 Tim Crooks (UK)
1979 Hugh Matheson (UK)
1980 Riccardo Ibarra (Arg)
1981-2 Chris Baillieu (UK)
1983 Steven Redgrave (UK)
1984 Chris Baillieu (UK)
1985 Steven Redgrave (UK)
1986 Bjarne Eltang (Den)
1987 Peter Michael Kolbe (FRG)
1988 Hamish McGlashan (Aus)
1989 Vaclav Chalupa (Cs)
1990 Eric Verdonk (NZ)
Most wins: 6 Stuart Mackenzie 1957-62, Guy Nickalls
(1888-91, 1893-4), A.A.Casamajor 1855-8, 1861,
J.Lowndes 1879-83; 4 Jack Beresford Jr 1920, 1924-6; 3
A.C.Dicker 1873-5, Frederick Kelly 1902-3, 1905, Sean
Drea, as above, Chris Baillieu, as above
Record time: 7 min 23 sec Vaclav Chalupa, 2 Jul 1989

Grand Challenge Cup

The oldest of all the Henley races, it dates to the first
Regatta in 1839. It is the world's premier open event for
eights. *Winners since 1970:*
1970 ASK Rostock (GDR)
1971 Tideway Scullers (UK)
1972 WMF Moscow (USSR)
1973-4 Trud Kolomna (USSR)
1975 Leander/Thames Tradesmen (UK)
1976 Thames Tradesmen (UK)
1977 University of Washington (USA)
1978 Trakia Club (Bul)
1979 Thames Tradesmen (UK)
1980 Charles River RA (USA)
1981 Oxford University/Thames Tradesmen (UK)
1982 Leander/London RC(UK)
1983 London RC/University of London (UK)
1984 Leander/London RC (UK)
1985 Harvard University (USA)
1986 Nautilus (UK)
1987 Soviet Army (USSR)
1988 Leander/Univeristy of London RC (UK)

1989-90 Hansa Dortmund RC (FRG)
Most wins: 27 Leander Club 1840, 1875, 1880, 1891-4,
1896, 1898-1901,1903-5, 1913, 1922, 1924-6, 1929,
1932, 1934, 1946, 1949, 1952-3
Most winning teams: 7 Guy Oliver Nickalls, 1920-2, 1924-
6, 1929
Record time: 5min 58sec Hansa Dortmund RC, 2 Jul 1989

The Nickalls family, Guy, his brother Vivian, and Guy's son,
Guy Oliver, had 43 Henley wins between them.

RUGBY LEAGUE

When the Rugby Union refused permission for players of
northern clubs to receive broken time for loss of wages,
22 clubs formed their own breakaway union and,
following a meeting at the George Hotel, Huddersfield in
1895, the Northern Union was formed. The number of
players per side was reduced from 15 to 13 in 1906 and
the union changed its name to the Northern Rugby
League in 1922. The word 'Northern' was dropped in
1980.

WORLD CUP/INTERNATIONAL CHAMPIONSHIP

Inaugurated in France in 1954, when Great Britain, France,
New Zealand and Australia played each other on a round-
robin basis. In 1975, when the competition was renamed
the International Championship, England and Wales
replaced Great Britain and the competition was played
world wide. The World Cup was discontinued after the
1977 championship but was revived in 1985 when one
match from each test series was designated a World Cup
game, with the leading two nations playing off in the final
in 1988.

	Winners	*Venue*
1954	Great Britain	France
1957	Australia	Australia
1960	Great Britain	England
1968	Australia	Australia/New Zealand
1970	Australia	England
1972	Great Britain	France
	Winners	*Venue*
1975	Australia	Worldwide
1977	Australia	Australia/New Zealand
1988	Australia	New Zealand (final)

Most wins: 6 Australia
Highest score: Papua New Guinea 12 Australia 62, at Port
Moresby, 4 Oct 1986

CHALLENGE CUP

Rugby League's premier knockout tournament in England,
the first final was at Leeds in 1897. The first Wembley final
was in 1929 and since 1933 the London stadium has been
the final's permanent venue, with the exception of the war
years.   *Winners:*

1897-8	Batley	1946	Wakefield Trinity
1899	Oldham	1947	Bradford Northern
1900	Swinton	1948	Wigan
1901	Batley	1949	Bradford Northern
1902	Broughton Rangers	1950	Warrington
1903-4	Halifax	1951	Wigan
1905	Warrington	1952	Workington Town
1906	Bradford	1953	Huddersfield
1907	Warrington	1954	Warrington
1908	Hunslet	1955	Barrow
1909	Wakefield Trinity	1956	St.Helens
1910	Leeds	1957	Leeds
1911	Broughton Rangers	1958-9	Wigan
1912	Dewsbury	1960	Wakefield Trinity
1913	Huddersfield	1961	St.Helens
1914	Hull	1962-3	Wakefield Trinity
1915	Huddersfield	1964	Widnes
1920	Huddersfield	1965	Wigan
1921	Leigh	1966	St.Helens
1922	Rochdale Hornets	1967	Featherstone Rovers
1923	Leeds	1968	Leeds
1924	Wigan	1969-70	Castleford
1925	Oldham	1971	Leigh
1926	Swinton	1972	St.Helens
1927	Oldham	1973	Featherstone Rovers
1928	Swinton	1974	Warrington
1929	Wigan	1975	Widnes
1930	Widnes	1976	St.Helens
1931	Halifax	1977-8	Leeds
1932	Leeds	1979	Widnes
1933	Huddersfield	1980	Hull Kingston Rovers
1934	Hunslet	1981	Widnes
1935	Castleford	1982	Hull
1936	Leeds	1983	Featherstone Rovers
1937	Widnes	1984	Widnes
1938	Salford	1985	Wigan
1939	Halifax	1986	Castleford
1941-2	Leeds	1987	Halifax
1943	Dewsbury	1988-90	Wigan
1944	Bradford Northern		
1945	Huddersfield		

Most wins: 11 Wigan, 10 Leeds, 7 Widnes, 6 Huddersfield; 5 St.Helens, Wakefield Trinity, Warrington, Halifax
Highest score (final): Wakefield Trinity 38 Hull 5 on 14 May 1960
Record aggregate (final): 52 pts Wigan 28 Hull 24 on 4 May 1985

Lance Todd Award

The Lance Todd Award goes to the Man of the Match in the Challenge Cup Final at Wembley as decided by a panel of Rugby League writers. The trophy is named after former New Zealand international Lance Todd who played for Wigan and later managed Salford. The first award was made in 1946. Recent winners:

1976 Geoff Pimblett (St.Helens)
1977 Steve Pitchford (Leeds)
1978 George Nicholls (St.Helens)
1979 Dave Topliss (Wakefield Trinity)
1980 Brian Lockwood (Hull Kingston Rovers)
1981 Mick Burke (Widnes)
1982 Eddie Cunningham (Widnes)
1983 David Hobbs (Featherstone Rovers)
1984 Joe Lydon (Widnes)
1985 Brett Kenny (Wigan)
1986 Bob Beardmore (Castleford)
1987 Graham Eadie (Halifax)
1988 Andy Gregory (Wigan)
1989 Ellery Hanley (Wigan)
1990 Andy Gregory (Wigan)

Warrington's Gerry Helme and Wigan's Andy Gregory are the only dual winners of the trophy

Ellery Hanley, captain of Wigan, with the Challenge Cup after his team's 27-0 win over St. Helens in 1989. Hanley won the Lance Todd Trophy as man of the match **(All-Sport)**

PREMIERSHIP TROPHY

The Premiership competition replaced the Championship Play-off, and was first contested at the end of the 1974-5 season. It is a knockout competition involving the top eight clubs in the first division with the champions playing the 8th club, 2nd club playing the 7th, and so on. The highest placed club has home advantage, and the final is played at a neutral venue. A 2nd Division Premiership was launched in 1987. Both Premiership finals are now played at Old Trafford, Manchester United FC.

Winners – Premiership Trophy

Figures in brackets indicates final league positions
1975 Leeds (3)
1976 St.Helens (5)
1977 St.Helens (2)
1978 Bradford Northern (2)
1979 Leeds (4)
1980 Widnes (2)
1981 Hull Kingston Rovers (3)
1982 Widnes (3)
1983 Widnes (5)
1984 Hull Kingston Rovers (1)
1985 St.Helens (2)
1986 Warrington (4)
1987 Wigan (1)
1988 Widnes (1)
1989 Widnes (1)
1990 Widnes (3)
Most wins: 6 Widnes, 3 St.Helens, 2 Hull Kingston Rovers, Leeds
Highest score (final): Warrington 38 Halifax 10 on 18 May 1986
Most appearances (final): 4 Keith Elwell (Widnes) 1978, 1980, 1982-3

Winners – 2nd Division Premiership

1987 Swinton (2)
1988 Oldham (1)
1989 Sheffield Eagles (3)
1990 Oldham (3)

Harry Sunderland Trophy

Named after former Australian team manager, broadcaster and journalist Harry Sunderland, the award is made to the Man of the Match in the Premiership Final (formerly the Championship Play-off). It was first awarded in 1965.
Recent winners:
1976 George Nicholls (St.Helens)
1977 Geoff Pimblett (St.Helens)
1978 Bob Haigh (Bradford Northern)
1979 Kevin Dick (Leeds)
1980 Mal Aspey (Widnes)
1981 Len Casey (Hull Kingston Rovers)
1982 Mick Burke (Widnes)
1983 Tony Myler (Widnes)
1984 John Dorahy (Hull Kingston Rovers)
1985 Harry Pinner (St.Helens)

1986 Les Boyd (Warrington)
1987 Joe Lydon (Wigan)
1988 David Hulme (Widnes)
1989 Alan Tait (Widnes)
1990 Alan Tait (Widnes)

Until Alan Tait in 1989-90, no player had won the trophy more than once. The only men to have won the Lance Todd and Harry Sunderland Trophies are:
Geoff Pimblett (St.Helens) 1976 LT, 1977 HS
George Nicholls (St.Helens) 1976 HS, 1978 LT
Mick Burke (Widnes) 1981 LT, 1982 HS
Joe Lydon (Widnes/Wigan) 1984 LT, 1987 HS

LEAGUE CHAMPIONSHIP

Twenty-two clubs formed the original Northern Union in 1895-6, won by Manningham. The 'league' then split into Yorkshire and Lancashire Senior Competitions until 1901-2 when 14 clubs broke away to form the Northern Rugby League. Two divisions were formed the following season. In 1905-6 the two divisions were merged into one and that is how they stayed (excepting the war years) until 1962-3 when two divisions were re-introduced. That lasted just two years, and the present two division system came into being in 1973-4. The title 'Rugby Football League' was adopted in 1922. Because not all clubs played each other twice, or at all in some cases, a Championship Play-off, involving the top four teams, was introduced in 1906-7. This remained unaltered (except during the war years) until 1962 when two divisions were re-introduced. But on the return to just one division in 1964-5 the play-off involved the top 16 teams. It was scrapped altogether at the end of the 1972-3 season.

Championship play-off wins:

9 Wigan 1909, 1922, 1926, 1934, 1946-7, 1950, 1952, 1960
7 Huddersfield 1912-3, 1915, 1929-30, 1949, 1962
6 St.Helens 1932, 1953, 1959, 1966, 1970-1
5 Hull 1920-1, 1936, 1956, 1958
4 Salford 1914, 1933, 1937, 1939
4 Swinton 1927-8, 1931, 1935
3 Leeds 1961, 1969, 1972
3 Oldham 1910-1, 1957
3 Warrington 1948, 1954-5
2 Halifax 1907, 1965; Hull KR 1923, 1925; Hunslet 1908, 1938; Wakefield Trinity 1967-8
1 Batley 1924, Dewsbury 1973, Leigh 1906, Workington Town 1951

Champions since 1973-4

Division One		Division Two	
1973/4	Salford	1973/4	Bradford Northern
1974/5	St.Helens	1974/5	Huddersfield
1975/6	Salford	1975/6	Barrow
1976/7	Featherstone Rovers	1976/7	Hull
1977/8	Widnes	1977/8	Leigh
1978/9	Hull Kingston Rovers	1978/9	Hull
1979/80	Bradford Northern	1979/80	Featherstone Rovers
1980/1	Bradford Northern	1980/1	York

Division One		Division Two	
1981/2	Leigh	1981/2	Oldham
1982/3	Hull	1982/3	Fulham
1983/4	Hull Kingston Rovers	1983/4	Barrow
1984/5	Hull Kingston Rovers	1984/5	Swinton
1985/6	Halifax	1985/6	Leigh
1986/7	Wigan	1986/7	Hunslet
1987/8	Widnes	1987/8	Oldham
1988/9	Widnes	1988/9	Leigh
1989/90	Wigan	1989/90	Hull KR

KNOCKOUT TROPHY

The knockout competition was first held in 1971-2. It was originally known as the Player's No.6 Trophy, and then the John Player Trophy until 1983, when it was renamed the John Player Special Trophy. It became the Regal Trophy in 1989. *Winners:*

1972	Halifax	1981	Warrington
1973	Leeds	1982	Hull
1974	Warrington	1983	Wigan
1975	Bradford Northern	1984	Leeds
1976	Widnes	1985	Hull Kingston Rovers
1977	Castleford	1986-7	Wigan
1978	Warrington	1988	St Helens
1979	Widnes	1989-90	Wigan
1980	Bradford Northern		

Wins: 5 Wigan, 3 Warrington, 2 Bradford Northern, Leeds, Widnes
Highest win (final): Warrington 27 Rochdale Hornets 16 on 9 Feb 1974
Most appearances (final): 6 Mick Adams, Keith Elwell, Eric Hughes (all Widnes) 1975-6, 1978-80, 1984

COUNTY CUPS

Both the Lancashire and Yorkshire County Challenge Cup competitions were first held in the 1905-6 season and are now early-season knock-out competitions. Wins:
Note, years indicate first half of season, in which the finals are usually played; in a few cases the final was actually played in the early months of the following year

Lancashire Cup

20 Wigan	1905, 1908-09, 1912, 1922, 1928, 1938, 1946-51, 1966, 1971, 1973, 1985-8
10 St Helens	1926, 1953, 1960-4, 1967-8, 1984
9 Oldham	1907, 1910, 1913, 1919, 1924, 1933, 1956-8
9 Warrington	1921, 1929, 1932, 1937, 1959, 1965, 1980, 1982, 1989
6 Widnes	1945, 1974-6, 1978-9
5 Salford	1931, 1934-6, 1972
4 Swinton	1925, 1927, 1939, 1969
4 Leigh	1952, 1955, 1970, 1981
3 Rochdale H	1911, 1914, 1918
2 Broughton R	1906, 1920
2 St Helens Recs	1923, 1930
2 Barrow	1954, 1983
1 Workington Town	1977

Yorkshire Cup

17 Leeds	1921, 1928, 1930, 1932, 1934-5, 1937, 1958, 1968, 1970, 1972-3, 1975-6, 1979-80, 1988
12 Huddersfield	1909, 1911, 1913-4, 1918-9, 1926, 1931, 1938, 1950, 1952, 1957
11 Bradford Northern	1940-1, 1943, 1945, 1948-9, 1953, 1965, 1978, 1987, 1989
9 Wakefield Trinity	1910, 1924, 1946-7, 1951, 1956, 1960-1, 1964
7 Hull Kingston Rovers	1920, 1929, 1966-7, 1971, 1974, 1985
5 Halifax	1908, 1944, 1954-5, 1963
5 Hull	1923, 1969, 1982-4
3 Hunslet	1905, 1907, 1962
3 York	1922, 1933, 1936
3 Dewsbury	1925, 1927, 1942
3 Castleford	1977, 1981, 1986
2 Featherstone Rovers	1939, 1959
1 Bradford	1906
1 Batley	1912

COUNTY LEAGUES

With the introduction of the two divisions in 1902-3 the Lancashire and Yorkshire Senior competitions were scrapped, but they re-appeared in 1907-8 as the Lancashire and Yorkshire Leagues. Club's results in the normal league, against teams from their own county, counted towards the appropriate County League. Both leagues were abandoned in 1970. *Most wins:*
Lancashire League: 18 Wigan 1909, 1911-5, 1921, 1923-4, 1926, 1941, 1946-7, 1950, 1952, 1959, 1962, 1970
Yorkshire League: 15 Leeds 1902, 1928, 1931, 1934-5, 1937-8, 1951, 1955, 1957, 1961, 1967-70

BBC 2 FLOODLIT TROPHY

A televised competition, broadcast by BBC2 on a Tuesday evening, it was open to clubs with adequate floodlighting. Eight clubs took part in the first year. The competition was abandoned in 1980 because of escalating costs. *Winners:*

1966-8	Castleford	1975	Salford
1969	Wigan	1976	St.Helens
1970	Leigh	1977	Castleford
1971	Leeds	1978	Hull Kingston Rovers
1972	St.Helens	1979	Widnes
1973	Leigh	1980	Hull
1974	Bramley		

Most wins: 4 Castleford, 2 Leigh, St.Helens

CHARITY SHIELD

Introduced in 1985, it is a pre-season match between the League champions and Challenge Cup winners. All matches 1985-8 played at the Douglas Bowl, Isle of Man. Since 1989 played at Anfield, Liverpool FC. *Winners:*

1985	Wigan
1986	Halifax
1987	Wigan
1988-9	Widnes

THE TOP TEAMS
Wins in major competitions by teams playing in the League in 1989-90. *As at May 1990*

	Chall Cup	Champ P-off	Prem Trophy	Div.2 Prem	KO Trophy	Flood Final	C'ty Cup	C'ty Lge.	Div 1	Div 2
Barrow	1	-	-	-	-	-	2	-	-	2
Batley	3	1	-	-	-	-	1	2	-	-
Bradford Northern	4	-	1	-	2	-	12	5	3	1
Bramley	-	-	-	-	-	1	-	-	-	-
Castleford	4	-	-	-	1	4	3	3	-	-
Dewsbury	2	1	-	-	-	-	3	1	-	1
Featherstone Rovers	3	-	-	-	-	-	2	-	1	1
Fulham	-	-	-	-	-	-	-	-	-	1
Halifax	5	2	-	-	1	-	5	6	2	-
Huddersfield Borough	6	7	-	-	-	-	12	11	-	1
Hull	2	5	-	-	1	1	5	4	1	2
Hull Kingston Rovers	1	2	2	-	1	1	7	2	3	1
Hunslet	2	2	-	-	-	-	3	3	-	2
Leeds	10	3	2	-	2	1	17	15	-	-
Leigh	2	1	-	-	-	2	4	-	1	3
Oldham	3	3	-	2	-	-	9	7	1	3
Rochdale Hornets	1	-	-	-	-	-	3	1	-	-
Runcorn H	-	-	-	-	-	-	-	1	-	-

(Lancashire League win as Liverpool Stanley)

	Chall Cup	Champ P-off	Prem Trophy	Div.2 Prem	KO Trophy	Flood Final	C'ty Cup	C'ty Lge.	Div 1	Div 2
Ryedale York	-	-	-	-	-	-	3	-	-	1
St.Helens	5	6	3	-	1	2	10	8	1	-
Salford	1	4	-	-	-	1	5	5	2	-
Sheffield Eagles	-	-	-	1	-	-	-	-	-	-
Swinton	3	4	-	1	-	-	4	5	2	1
Wakefield Town	5	2	-	-	-	-	9	7	-	1
Warrington	5	3	1	-	3	-	9	8	-	-
Whitehaven	-	-	-	-	-	-	-	-	-	-
Widnes	7	-	6	-	2	1	6	1	3	-
Wigan	11	9	1	-	5	1	20	18	2	-
Workington Town	1	1	-	-	-	-	1	-	-	-

No wins by Blackpool Borough, Carlisle, Chorley, Doncaster, Keighley, Nottingham City, Trafford B.

Outstanding teams – computed on the following points system for wins in:
Challenge Cup 5, Premiership/Championship 4, Regal/John Player Trophy 4, Division One title 2, Lancashire or Yorkshire Cup 1.

138 Wigan	58 Warrington	37 Hull KR
93 Leeds	46 Bradford N	36 Oldham
77 Widnes	43 Halifax	34 Swinton
76 St Helens	42 Wakefield T	30 Salford
70 Huddersfield	40 Hull	

SYDNEY PREMIERSHIP
The principal competition in Australia is the Sydney Premiership (sometimes referred to as the New South Wales Premiership), which culminates in the Grand Final each year. The winning team receives the Winfield Cup. The first Grand Final was in 1908. *Most wins:*
20 South Sydney 1908-9, 1914, 1918, 1925-9, 1931-2, 1950-1, 1953-5, 1967-8, 1970-1
15 St.George 1941, 1949, 1956-66, 1977, 1979
11 Balmain 1915-7, 1919-20, 1924, 1939, 1944, 1946-7, 1969
11 Eastern Suburbs 1911-3, 1923, 1935-7, 1940, 1945, 1974-5

Recent Winners
1980   Canterbury-Bankstown
1981-3 Parramatta
1984-5 Canterbury-Bankstown
1986   Parramatta
1987   Manly-Warringah
1988   Canterbury-Bankstown
1989   Canberra

RECORDS
All Matches
Biggest win: 119-2 Huddersfield v Swinton Park Rangers (Challenge Cup) 28 Feb 1914
Most tries in a match: 11 George Henry West (Hull Kingston Rovers) v Brookland Rovers (Challenge Cup) 4 Mar 1905
Most goals in a match: 22 Jim Sullivan (Wigan) v Flimby & Fothergill (Challenge Cup) 14 Feb 1925
Most points in a match: 53 (10 goals, 11 tries) George Henry West (Hull Kingston Rovers) – as above

Internationals

Most appearances: 60 Jim Sullivan (Wigan) Wales, GB & Other Nationalities, 1921-39
Most tries: 45 Mick Sullivan (Huddersfield, Wigan, St.Helens, York) GB & England 1954-63
Most goals: 160 Jim Sullivan
Most points: 329 Jim Sullivan
Biggest win: Australia 70 Papua New Guinea 8, Wagga Wagga, 20 Jul 1988

Season

Most tries: 80 Albert Rosenfeld (Huddersfield) 1913-4
Most goals: 221 David Watkins (Salford) 1972-3
Most points: 496 (194 goals, 36 tries) Lewis Jones (Leeds) 1956-7

Career

Most tries: 796 Brian Bevan (Warrington & Blackpool Borough) 1946-64
Most goals: 2,867 Jim Sullivan (Wigan) 1921-46
Most points: 6,220 (2575 goals, 358 tries, 4 drop goals) Neil Fox (Wakefield Trinity, Bradford Northern, Hull Kingston Rovers, York, Bramley, Huddersfield) 1956-79
Most appearances: 921 Jim Sullivan (Wigan) 1921-46
Most consecutive club appearances: 239 Keith Elwell (Widnes) May 1977- Sep 1982
Most consecutive games scoring points: 92 David Watkins (Salford) Aug 1972-Apr 1974

RUGBY UNION

The game of Rugby Union is traditionally said to have had its beginnings at Rugby School, when William Webb Ellis picked up the ball during a game of football in November 1823, and ran with it. The new 'handling' code of football developed and was played at Cambridge University in 1839. The first rugby club was formed at Guy's Hospital in 1843 and the Rugby Football Union (RFU) was founded in January 1871.
The International Rugby Football Board (IRFB) was founded in 1886. Members are: Australia, England, France, Ireland, New Zealand, Scotland, South Africa and Wales. The Federation International de Rugby Amateur (FIRA) held its first meeting in 1934, and membership reached 42 nations in 1989.

WORLD CUP

The inaugural World Cup was contested in Australia and New Zealand in 1987 by 16 national teams. The result of the final was New Zealand 29 France 9. The highest team score was New Zealand's 74-13 victory over Fiji at Christchurch on 27 May 1987. The most points in a match by an individual was 30 by Didier Camberabero (3 tries, 9 conversions) in France's 70-12 win over Zimbabwe at Auckland on 2 June 1987. The highest points scorer in the tournament was the New Zealand goalkicker, Grant Fox with 126 points in 6 games. Craig Green and John Kirwan (NZ) each scored six tries.

The second World Cup will be in Britain in 1991, with the final at Twickenham.

INTERNATIONAL CHAMPIONSHIP

First contested by England, Ireland, Scotland and Wales in 1884. France made it a 'Five Nations' tournament when they joined in 1910. Each country plays each other once during each season's championship. The championships of 1885, 1888-9, 1897-8 and 1972 were not completed for various reasons. *Winners (outright/shared wins)*

21/11 Wales	1893, 1900, 1902, 1905, 1906*, 1908-9, 1911, 1920*, 1922, 1931, 1932*, 1936, 1939*, 1947*, 1950, 1952, 1954*-5*, 1956, 1964*, 1965-6, 1969, 1970*, 1971, 1973*, 1975-6, 1978-9, 1988*
18/9 England	1883-4, 1886*, 1890*, 1892, 1910, 1912*, 1913-4, 1921, 1923-4, 1928, 1930, 1932*, 1934, 1937, 1939*, 1947*, 1953, 1954*, 1957-8, 1960*, 1963, 1973*, 1980
13/8 Scotland	1886*, 1887, 1890*, 1891, 1895, 1901, 1903-4, 1907, 1920*, 1925, 1926*-7*, 1929, 1933, 1938, 1964*, 1973*, 1984, 1986*, 1990
10/8 Ireland	1894, 1896, 1899, 1906*, 1912*, 1926*-7*, 1932*, 1935, 1939*, 1948-9, 1951, 1973*, 1974, 1982, 1983*, 1985
9/8 France	1954*, 1955*, 1959, 1960*, 1961-2, 1967-8, 1970*, 1973*, 1977, 1981, 1983*, 1986*, 1987, 1988*, 1989

* denotes shared win (note: there was a quintuple tie in 1973)

Grant Fox, the top scorer of Rugby Union's first World Cup
(All-Sport/Russell Cheyne)

Grand Slam
The beating of all other four countries during one season's championship has been achieved as follows:
8 Wales 1908-9*, 1911, 1950, 1952, 1971, 1976, 1978
8 England 1913-4, 1921, 1923-4, 1928, 1957, 1980
4 France 1968, 1977, 1981, 1987
3 Scotland 1925, 1984, 1990
1 Ireland 1948
* not including France, yet to enter

Triple Crown
The beating of the other three 'Home Countries' in one season's championship has been achieved as follows:
17 Wales   1893, 1900, 1902, 1905, 1908-9, 1911, 1950, 1952, 1965, 1969, 1971, 1976, 1977-9, 1988
15 England 1883-4, 1892, 1913-4, 1921, 1923-4, 1928, 1934, 1937, 1954, 1957, 1960, 1980
10 Scotland 1891, 1895, 1901, 1903, 1907, 1925, 1933, 1938, 1984, 1990
6 Ireland   1894, 1899, 1948-9, 1982, 1985

International Championship Records
TEAM
Highest score: Wales 49 France 14 at Swansea, 1 Jan 1910 (on present day scoring it would have been 59-16)
Most points in a season: 102 Wales 1975-6
Most tries in a season: 21 Wales 1909-10
INDIVIDUAL
Most points in a season: 54 (10 pen, 4 con, 4 dg) Jean-Patrick Lescarboura (Fra) 1984
Most tries in a season: 8 Cyril Lowe (Eng) 1913-14; Ian Smith (Sco) 1924-5
Most conversions in a season: 11 William Bancroft (Wal) 1908-9
Most penalty goals in a season: 16 Paul Thorburn (Wal) 1985-6
Most goals in a match: 9 (8 con, 1 pen) William Bancroft (Wales) v France, 1 Jan 1910
(con – conversion, pen – penalty goal, dg – drop goal)

The Nations' Records Against Each Other

ENGLAND	P	W	D	L
v Scotland	106	50	17	39
v Ireland	102	58	8	36
v Wales	95	37	12	46
v France	65	34	7	24
SCOTLAND				
v England	106	39	17	50
v Ireland	100	51	4	45
v Wales	94	40	2	52
v France	60	29	2	29
IRELAND				
v England	102	36	8	58
v Scotland	100	45	4	51
v Wales	92	32	5	55
v France	63	25	5	33
WALES				
v England	95	46	12	37
v Scotland	94	52	2	40
v Ireland	92	55	5	32
v France	63	36	3	24
FRANCE				
v England	65	24	7	34
v Ireland	63	32	5	26
v Wales	63	24	3	36
v Scotland	60	29	2	29

INTERNATIONAL RECORDS
The playing records of all major Rugby-playing nations is as follows as at June 1990. (For matches involving the nations in the International Championship see earlier)

ENGLAND	P	W	D	L
v New Zealand	15	3	-	12
v Australia	16	6	-	10
v South Africa	9	2	1	6
SCOTLAND	P	W	D	L
v New Zealand	15	-	2	13
v Australia	12	7	-	5
v South Africa	8	3	-	5
IRELAND	P	W	D	L
v Australia	12	6	-	6
v South Africa	10	1	1	8
v New Zealand	10	-	1	9
WALES	P	W	D	L
v Australia	13	8	-	5
v New Zealand	15	3	-	12
v South Africa	7	-	1	6
FRANCE	P	W	D	L
v New Zealand	26	5	-	21
v South Africa	19	3	4	12
v Australia	23	12	2	9
AUSTRALIA	P	W	D	L
v New Zealand	87	21	5	61
v South Africa	28	7	-	21
NEW ZEALAND	P	W	D	L
v South Africa	37	15	2	20

BLEDISLOE CUP
Contested by New Zealand and Australia, it was instigated in 1931 by Lord Bledisloe, the Governer-General of New Zealand. To spring 1990 New Zealand had 50 wins, Australia 16, and 4 matches were drawn.

INDIVIDUAL RECORDS

Leading cap winners   (as at 1 July 1990)
Figures in brackets indicates number of British Lions appearances.
81 (12) Mike Gibson (Ire) 1964-79
80 (17) Willie John McBride (Ire) 1962-75
78   Serge Blanco (France) 1980-90
70   Philippe Sella (Fra) 1982-90
69   Roland Bertranne (Fra) 1971-81
65 (4) Fergus Slattery (Ire) 1970-84

63		Michel Crauste (Fra) 1957-66
63		Benoit Dauga (Fra) 1964-72
63	(10)	Gareth Edwards (Wal) 1967-78
63	(8)	John P.R. Williams (Wal) 1969-81
60	(9)	Andy Irvine (Sco) 1972-82
59	(5)	Tom Kiernan (Ire) 1960-73
59	(1)	Phil Orr (Ire) 1976-87
59		Jean-Pierre Rives (Fra) 1975-84
57		Jean Condom (Fra) 1982-9
55		Colin Meads (NZ) 1957-71
55		Robert Paparemborde (Fra) 1975-83
55		Laurent Rodriguez (Fra) 1981-90
53	(1)	Jim Renwick (Sco) 1972-84
53	(12)	Graham Price (Wal) 1975-83
52	(6)	Jackie Kyle (Ire) 1947-58
52		Amédée Domenech (Fra) 1954-63
52		Colin Deans (Sco) 1978-87
52	(1)	Moss Keane (Ire) 1974-84
51		Jean Prat (Fra) 1945-55
51		Walter Spanghero (Fra) 1964-73
51	(5)	Gerald Davies (Wal) 1966-78
51	(8)	Ian McLachlan (Sco) 1969-79
51		Jean-Luc Joinel (Fra) 1977-87
51		Simon Poidevin (Aus) 1980-9
50		Michel Celeya (Fra) 1953-61
50		Sandy Carmichael (Sco) 1967-78

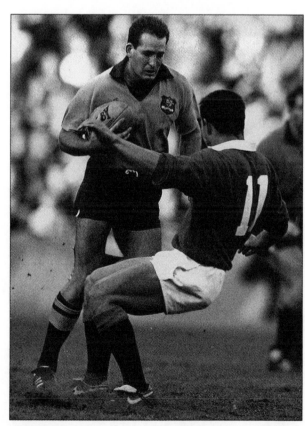

Try scorers supreme, but on this occasion David Campese appears to have the better of Rory Underwood
(All-Sport/Russell Cheyne)

Leading cap winners for other nations:
43 (1) Tony Neary (Eng) 1971-80
38   Frik Du Preez (SAf) 1960-71
38   Jan Ellis (SAf) 1965-76

Leading Points Scorers
508   Michael Lynagh (Aus) 1984-90
397*   Hugo Porta (Arg) 1974-88
367   Grant Fox (NZ) 1985-90
301   Andy Irvine (Sco/BL) 1972-82
283   Michael Kiernan (Ire) 1982-90
270   Naas Botha (SAf) 1980-9
265   Jean-Pierre Romeu (Fra) 1972-7
246   Ollie Campbell (Ire/BL) 1976-84
240   Dusty Hare (Eng/BL) 1974-84
227   Paul Thorburn (Wal) 1985-90
207   Don Clarke (NZ) 1956-64

BL = British Lions
* against International Board countries, 473 in all
internationals (49 matches)

Most points in a match: 30 Didier Camberabero, France v
Zimbabwe in a World Cup match on 2 June 1987

Leading Try Scorers
36 David Campese (Aus) 1982-90
32 Serge Blanco (Fra) 1980-90
25 John Kirwan (NZ) 1984-9
24 Ian Smith (Sco) 1924-33
23 Gerald Davies (Wal/BL) 1966-78
23 Christian Darrouy (Fra) 1957-67
22 Rory Underwood (Eng) 1984-90
22 Philippe Sella (Fra) 1982-90
20 Gareth Edwards (Wal) 1967-78

Most for the other nations:
Ireland : 15 George Stephenson 1920-30
South Africa: 15 Danie Gerber 1980-6
Most tries in a match: 5 George Lindsay, Scotland v Wales
at Raeburn Place, Edinburgh, 26 Feb 1887; Douglas
Lambert, England v France at Richmond, 5 Jan 1907

Other Records (All matches)
TEAM:
Highest score in any international: 106-4 New Zealand v
Japan at Tokyo, 1 Nov 1987
Record score for an international Tour match: 125-0 New
Zealand v Northern New South Wales at Quirindi,
Australia, 30 May 1962
Most points scored in a season: 1914 by Neath (Wales) in
1988/9
Most tries in a season: 345 by Neath (Wales) also in
1988/9
INDIVIDUAL
Most points in any international match: 34 Phil Bennett
(10 conversions, 2 tries, 2 penalty goals) v Japan at Tokyo,
24 Sep 1975

Most points scored in a career: 7337 Dusty Hare (Nottingham, Leicester, England, British Lions, and other representative matches) 1971-89

FIRA CHAMPIONSHIP
The first FIRA Championship was held in 1954 when three nations, France, Italy and Spain took part. It was not held again until 1965-66 and has been held annually ever since. The championships have been officially recognised only since 1973-74. The current compliment of nations are divided into two Groups, A and B. There was no championship in 1988. Instead, the 1989 championship encompassed two years, 1988-9. *Winners of Group A since 1974:*
11 France 1974, 1976, 1978-80, 1982, 1984-7, 1989
4 Romania 1975, 1977, 1981, 1983

Earlier winners:
France 1954, 1966-8, 1970-3
Romania 1969

HONG KONG SEVENS
Now sponsored by Cathay Pacific and the Hong Kong Bank, the first Hong Kong International sevens was held in 1976, with 12 teams taking part. Now, it is regarded as the most prestigious sevens tournament in the world.
Winners:

1976	Cantabrians	1984	Fiji
1977-8	Fiji	1985	Australia
1979	Australia	1986-7	New Zealand
1980	Fiji	1988	Australia
1981	Barbarians	1989	New Zealand
1982-3	Australia	1990	Fiji

BRITISH LIONS
The British Lions went on their first Tour in 1888, when they played a total of 35 matches in Australia and New Zealand. Since then there have been a further 21 Lions tours. *Complete record of all matches on each tour:*

Year	Country	P	W	D	L	F	A	Tour captain
1888	Australia	16	14	2	0	210	65	Robert Seddon (Eng)*
	New Zealand	19	13	4	2	82	33	
1891	South Africa	19	19	0	0	224	3	Bill MacLagan (Sco)
1896	South Africa	21	19	1	1	310	45	John Hammond (Eng)#
1899	Australia	21	18	0	3	333	90	Rev.Matthew Mullineaux (Eng)#
1903	South Africa	22	11	3	8	231	138	Mark Morrison (Sco)
1904	Australia	14	14	0	0	265	51	Darky Bedell-Sivright (Sco)
	New Zealand	5	2	1	2	22	33	
1908	Australia	9	7	0	2	139	48	Arthur Harding (Wal)
	New Zealand	17	9	1	7	184	153	
1910	South Africa	24	13	3	8	290	236	Dr.Tom Smyth (Ire)
1924	South Africa	21	9	3	9	175	155	Dr.Ronald Cove-Smith (Eng)
1930	New Zealand	21	15	0	6	420	205	Doug Prentice (Eng)
	Australia	7	5	0	2	204	113	
1938	South Africa	23	17	0	6	407	272	Sam Walker (Ire)
1950	New Zealand	23	17	1	5	420	162	Karl Mullen (Ire)
	Australia	6	5	0	1	150	52	
1955	South Africa	24	18	1	5	418	271	Robin Thompson (Ire)
1959	Australia	6	5	0	1	174	70	Ronnie Dawson (Ire)
	New Zealand	25	20	0	5	582	266	
1962	South Africa	24	15	4	5	351	208	Arthur Smith (Sco)
1966	Australia	8	7	1	0	202	48	Michael Campbell-Lamerton (Sco)
	New Zealand	25	15	2	8	300	281	
1968	South Africa	20	15	1	4	377	181	Tom Kiernan (Ire)
1971	Australia	2	1	0	1	25	27	John Dawes (Wal)
	New Zealand	24	22	1	1	555	204	
1974	South Africa	22	21	1	0	729	207	Willie John McBride (Ire)
1977	New Zealand	25	21	0	4	596	295	Phil Bennett (Wal)
	Fiji	1	0	0	1	21	25	
1980	South Africa	18	15	0	3	401	244	Billy Beaumont (Eng)
1983	New Zealand	18	12	0	6	478	276	Cieran Fitzgerald (Ire)
1989	Australia	12	11	0	1	360	192	Finlay Calder (Sco)

*Seddon lost his life in a drowning accident while sculling on the Hunter River, NSW, during the tour and was replaced by Andrew Stoddart (Eng), who also went on to captain England at cricket, the only man to achieve this double distinction.
Mullineaux and Hammond never played international rugby for one of the home countries

Test Summaries

BRITISH LIONS	P	W	D	L
v Australia	17	14	0	3
v New Zealand	32	24	3	5
v South Africa	40	14	6	20

British Lions Records

Biggest test win: 31-0 v Australia at Brisbane, 4 Jun 1966
Biggest test defeat: 6-38 by New Zealand at Auckland, 16 Jul 1983
Most caps: 17 Willie John McBride (Ire) 1962-74
Most internationals as captain: 6 Ronnie Dawson (Ire) 1959
Most points in internationals: 44 Phil Bennett (Wal) 1974-77
Most points in one international: 18 Tony Ward (Ire) v South Africa at Cape Town, 31 May 1980
Most tries in internationals: 6 Tony O'Reilly (Ire) 1955-9
Most tries in one international: 8 players have each scored two tries, the most recent being Gavin Hastings (Sco) against Australia in 1989
Most points on a tour: 188 Barry John (Wal) 1971 to Australia and New Zealand
Most tries on a tour: 22 Tony O'Reilly (Ire) 1959 to Australia and New Zealand
Most points in a tour match: 37 Alan Old (Eng) v South Western Districts at Mossel Bay, SAf, 29 May 1974
Most tries in a tour match: 6 David Duckham (Eng) v West Coast-Buller at Greymouth, NZ, 17 Jun 1971; 6 J.J.Williams (Wal) v South Western Districts at Mossel Bay SAF, 29 May 1974

'The King' – Barry John, who played in 25 internationals for Wales as fly half between 1966 and 1971. He scored a record 188 points on the Lions tour of 1971 (Hulton-Deutsch)

UNIVERSITY MATCH

The first match between the Universities of Oxford and Cambridge took place at The Parks, Oxford on 10 February 1872. It has been contested annually ever since, with the exception of the First World War years. During the second war, a special war-time series of matches was played. Cambridge staged the second match in 1873, the Oval 1874-80, Blackheath 1881-7, Queen's Club 1888-1921, and Twickenham thereafter. The years quoted are for the second half of the season, although the match is now played annually in December. *Wins:*

49 Cambridge	1873, 1877, 1880, 1886-9, 1892, 1896,1899-1900, 1905-6, 1913-14, 1920, 1923, 1926-9, 1935, 1937, 1939, 1946, 1948, 1953, 1955, 1957, 1959, 1961-4, 1968-9, 1973-7, 1979, 1981-5, 1988, 1990
46 Oxford	1872, 1876, 1878, 1882-5, 1890, 1894, 1897-8, 1901-2, 1904, 1907-8, 1910-2, 1921-2, 1924-5, 1930, 1932-4, 1938, 1947, 1949-52, 1956, 1958, 1960, 1965, 1967, 1970-2, 1978, 1980, 1986-7, 1989
13 Drawn	1874-5, 1879, 1881, 1891, 1893, 1895, 1903, 1909, 1931, 1936, 1954, 1966

War-time series: Between 1940-45 a total of 12 matches were played and the winners were:
9 Cambridge 1941 (2), 1942 (2), 1943 (3), 1944, 1944, 1945; 2 Oxford 1940, 1944; 1 Drawn 1945

COUNTY CHAMPIONSHIP

The English County Championship was introduced in 1889, when, after an unbeaten season, Yorkshire were declared the champions by the Rugby Union. The current system, the fifth, divides the counties into Northern Midland, London and South-Western divisions, with a promotion and relegation system, before the leading four counties play-off in semi-finals to decide which two meet in the final. Not held 1915-9, 1945-6 *Winners:*

First system
1889 Yorkshire
1890 Yorkshire

Second system
1891 Lancashire
1892-5 Yorkshire

Third system

	Winners	Runners-up
1896	Yorkshire	Surrey
1897	Kent	Cumberland
1898	Northumberland	Midlands
1899	Devon	Northumberland
1900	Durham	Devon
1901	Devon	Durham
1902	Durham	Gloucestershire
1903	Durham	Kent
1904	Kent	Durham

1905	Durham	Middlesex
1906	Devon	Durham
1907	Devon & Durham (shared)	
1908	Cornwall	Durham
1909	Durham	Cornwall
1910	Gloucestershire	Yorkshire
1911	Devon	Yorkshire
1912	Devon	Northumberland
1913	Gloucestershire	Cumberland
1914	Midlands	Durham
1920	Gloucestershire	Yorkshire

Fourth system

1921	Gloucestershire 31	Leicestershire 4
1922	Gloucestershire 19	North Midlands 0
1923	Somerset 8	Leicestershire 6
1924	Cumberland 14	Kent 3
1925	Leicestershire 14	Gloucestershire 6
1926	Yorkshire 15	Hampshire 14
1927	Kent 22	Leicestershire 12
1928	Yorkshire 12	Cornwall 8
1929	Middlesex 9 (after 8-8 draw)	Lancashire 8
1930	Gloucestershire 13	Lancashire 7
1931	Gloucestershire 10	Warwickshire 9
1932	Gloucestershire 9	Durham 3
1933	Hampshire 18	Lancashire 7
1934	East Midlands 10	Gloucestershire 0
1935	Lancashire 14	Somerset 0
1936	Hampshire 13	Northumberland 6
1937	Gloucestershire 5	East Midlands 0
1938	Lancashire 24	Surrey 12
1939	Warwickshire 8	Somerset 3
1947	Lancashire 14 (after 8-8 draw)	Gloucestershire 3
1948	Lancashire 5	Eastern Counties 0
1949	Lancashire 9	Gloucestershire 3
1950	Cheshire 5	East Midlands 0
1951	East Midlands 10	Middlesex 0
1952	Middlesex 9	Lancashire 6
1953	Yorkshire 11	East Midlands 3
1954	Middlesex 24	Lancashire 6
1955	Lancashire 14	Middlesex 8
1956	Middlesex 13	Devon 9
1957	Devon 12	Yorkshire 3
1958	Warwickshire 16	Cornwall 8
1959	Warwickshire 14	Gloucestershire 9
1960	Warwickshire 9	Surrey 6
1961	Cheshire 5 (after 0-0 draw)	Devon 3
1962	Warwickshire 11	Hampshire 6
1963	Warwickshire 13	Yorkshire 10
1964	Warwickshire 8	Lancashire 6
1965	Warwickshire 15	Durham 9
1966	Middlesex 6	Lancashire 0
1967	Surrey & Durham shared after 14-14 & 0-0 draws	
1968	Middlesex 9	Warwickshire 6
1969	Lancashire 11	Cornwall 9

1970	Staffordshire 11	Gloucestershire 9
1971	Surrey 14	Gloucestershire 3
1972	Gloucestershire 11	Warwickshire 6
1973	Lancashire 17	Gloucestershire 12
1974	Gloucestershire 22	Lancashire 12
1975	Gloucestershire 13	Eastern Counties 9
1976	Gloucestershire 24	Middlesex 9
1977	Lancashire 17	Middlesex 6
1978	North Midlands 10	Gloucestershire 7
1979	Middlesex 19	Northumberland 6
1980	Lancashire 21	Gloucestershire 15
1981	Northumberland 15	Gloucestershire 6
1982	Lancashire 7	North Midlands 3
1983	Gloucestershire 19	Yorkshire 7
1984	Gloucestershire 36	Somerset 18
1985	Middlesex 12	Notts, Lincs, Derbys 9
1986	Warwickshire 16	Kent 6
1987	Yorkshire 22	Middlesex 11
1988	Lancashire 23	Warwickshire 18
1989	Durham 13	Cornwall 9
1990	Lancashire 32	Middlesex 9

Most wins:
15 Gloucestershire, 14 Lancashire, 11 Yorkshire

JOHN PLAYER SPECIAL/PILKINGTON CUP

The RFU Knockout Competition for English club sides was inaugurated in the 1971/2 season and has been held annually since then. Sponsored by John Player 1971/2 to 1987/8 and by Pilkington from 1988/9. The final is at Twickenham. *Finals:*

1972	Gloucester 17	Moseley 6
1973	Coventry 27	Bristol 15
1974	Coventry 26	London Scottish 6
1975	Bedford 28	Rosslyn Park 12
1976	Gosforth 23	Rosslyn Park 14
1977	Gosforth 27	Waterloo 11
1978	Gloucester 6	Leicester 3
1979	Leicester 15	Moseley 12
1980	Leicester 21	London Irish 9
1981	Leicester 22	Gosforth 15
1982	Gloucester 12 shared with Moseley 12	
1983	Bristol 28	Leicester 22
1984	Bath 10	Bristol 9
1985	Bath 24	London Welsh 15
1986	Bath 25	Wasps 17
1987	Bath 19	Wasps 12
1988	Harlequins 28	Bristol 22
1989	Bath 10	Leicester 6
1990	Bath 48	Gloucester 6

Most wins: 6 Bath, 3 Leicester and Gloucester
Most successful clubs on a points system of 3 for a win, 2 for losing in the final and 1 for losing in the semi-finals:
18 Leicester, Bath; 12.5 Gloucester, 12 Coventry, 9 Bristol, 8.5 Moseley, 7 Gosforth and Harlequins

SCHWEPPES WELSH CUP

The Welsh Rugby Union Challenge Cup has been contested annually since the 1971/2 season. All finals have

been in Cardiff, at Arms Park, now the National Stadium.
Finals:

1972	Neath 15	Llanelli 9
1973	Llanelli 30	Cardiff 7
1974	Llanelli 12	Aberavon 10
1975	Llanelli 15	Aberavon 6
1976	Llanelli 15	Swansea 4
1977	Newport 16	Cardiff 15
1978	Swansea 13	Newport 9
1979	Bridgend 18	Pontypridd 12
1980	Bridgend 15	Swansea 9
1981	Cardiff 14	Bridgend 6
1982	Cardiff 12*	Bridgend 12
1983	Pontypool 18	Swansea 6
1984	Cardiff 24	Neath 19
1985	Llanelli 15	Cardiff 14
1986	Cardiff 28	Newport 21
1987	Cardiff 16	Swansea 15 (et)
1988	Llanelli 28	Neath 13
1989	Neath 14	Llanelli 13
1990	Neath 16	Bridgend 10

* won on most tries
Most wins: 6 Llanelli, 5 Cardiff
Most successful clubs on a points system for 3 for a win, 2 for losing in the final and 1 for losing in the semi-finals:
26 Llanelli, 25 Cardiff, 16 Bridgend, 15 Neath,
14 Swansea, 12 Aberavon, 8 Newport, 7 Pontypool

SCOTTISH CLUB CHAMPIONSHIP
The premier club competition in Scotland is the McEwans League, instituted 1974. There are currently seven divisions. *Division One winners:*

1974-8	Hawick
1979	Heriot's FP
1980	Gala
1982	Hawick
1983	Gala
1984-7	Hawick
1988-9	Kelso
1990	Melrose

Most wins: 10 Hawick

MIDDLESEX SEVENS
This leading Sevens tournament was inaugurated in 1926. The final of the knockout tournament is played at Twickenham and regularly attracts crowds in excess of 50,000. The winners receive the Russell Cargill Trophy.
Winners:

1926	Harlequins 25	St Mary's Hospital 3
1927	Harlequins 28	Blackheath 6
1928	Harlequins 19	Blackheath 8
1929	Harlequins 16	Rosslyn Park 9
1930	London Welsh 6	Blackheath 0
1931	London Welsh 9	Harlequins 5
1932	Blackheath 18	Harlequins 10
1933	Harlequins 23	Wasps 0
1934	Barbarians 6	Richmond 3*
1935	Harlequins 10	London Welsh 3
1936	Sale 18	Blackheath 6
1937	London Scottish 19	Old Merchant Taylors 3
1938	Metropolitan Police 13	London Scottish 3
1939	Cardiff 11	London Scottish 6
1940	St Mary's Hospital 14	OCTU Sandhurst 10
1941	Cambridge University 6	Welsh Guards 0
1942	St Mary's Hospital 8	RAF 6
1943	St Mary's Hospital 8	Middlesex Hospital 3
1944	St Mary's Hospital 15	RAF Jurby 5
1945	Nottingham 6	St Mary's Hospital 3
1946	St Mary's Hospital 13	Cardiff 3
1947	Rosslyn Park 12	Richmond 6
1948	Wasps 14	Harlequins 5
1949	Heriot's FP 16	London Scottish 6
1950	Rosslyn Park 16	Heriot's FP 0
1951	Richmond II 13	Wasps 10
1952	Wasps 12	St Thomas's Hospital 10
1953	Richmond 10	London Welsh 3
1954	Rosslyn Park 16	London Scottish 0
1955	Richmond 5	St Luke's College 0
1956	London Welsh 24	Emmanuel College, Cambridge 10
1957	St Luke's College 18	London Welsh 5
1958	Blackheath 16	Harlequins 3
1959	Loughborough Colls 3	London Welsh 0
1960	London Scottish 16	London Welsh 5
1961	London Scottish 20	Stewart's College FP 6
1962	London Scottish 18	Rosslyn Park 6
1963	London Scottish 15	Hawick 11
1964	Loughborough Colls 18	London Scottish 16
1965	London Scottish 15	Loughborough Colleges 8
1966	Loughborough Colls 29	Northampton 10
1967	Harlequins 14	Richmond 11
1968	London Welsh 16	Richmond 3
1969	St Luke's College 21	Edinburgh Wanderers 16
1970	Loughborough Colls 26	Edinburgh Wanderers 11
1971	London Welsh 18	Harlequins 9
1972	London Welsh 22	Public School Wanderers 18
1973	London Welsh 24	Public School Wanderers 22
1974	Richmond 34	London Welsh 16
1975	Richmond 24	Loughborough Colleges 8
1976	Loughborough Colls 21	Harlequins 20
1977	Richmond 26	Gosforth 16
1978	Harlequins 40	Rosslyn Park 12
1979	Richmond 24	London Scottish 10
1980	Richmond 34	Rosslyn Park 18
1981	Rosslyn Park 16	London Welsh 14
1982	Stewart's Melville FP 34	Richmond 12
1983	Richmond I 20	London Welsh 13
1984	London Welsh 34	Heriot's FP 18
1985	Wasps 25	Nottingham 6
1986	Harlequins 18	Nottingham 10
1987	Harlequins 22	Rosslyn Park 6
1988	Harlequins 20	Bristol 18
1989	Harlequins 18	Rosslyn Park 12
1990	Harlequins 26	Rosslyn Park 10

* after extra time

Most wins: 13 Harlequins, 9 Richmond, 8 London Welsh, 6 London Scottish, 5 St Mary's Hospital, Loughborough Colleges, 4 Rosslyn Park

NATIONAL MERIT TABLES

The RFU approved a plan in 1985 for the leading English clubs to form into two divisions known as Merit Tables 'A' and 'B'. Selected matches throughout the season were designated Merit Table matches, and an end-of-season league table was drawn up. A third Merit Table, C was added in 1986-7. They have since been renamed Leagues 1, 2 and 3.

Winners:	1	2	3
1985-6	Gloucester	Orrell	-
1986-7	Bath	Waterloo	Vale of Lune
1987-8	Leicester	Rosslyn Park	Wakefield
1988-9	Bath	Saracens	Plymouth Albion
1989-90	Wasps	Northampton	London Scottish

OLYMPIC GAMES

Rugby has been included in four Olympic celebrations, the first at Paris in 1900. Three teams took part in 1900 and 1924, and played on a round-robin basis, while just two teams entered in 1908 and 1920 with the one match deciding the gold medallists. *Winners:*
1900 France
1908 Australia
1920 USA
1924 USA

AUSTRALIA

Rugby was first played in Australia in 1829 and the first administrative body, the Southern Union, was formed in 1874. It was renamed the NSW Rugby Union in 1892. The first Australian rugby club was that of Sydney University, formed in 1864. New South Wales and Queensland are the predominant states for the game.

Sydney First Grade Premiership

First played in 1900. Wins (* Shared)
21 University 1901*, 1904, 1919-20, 1923-4, 1926-8, 1937, 1939, 1945, 1951, 1953-5, 1961-2, 1968, 1970, 1972
21 Randwick 1930, 1934, 1938, 1940, 1948, 1959, 1965-7, 1971, 1973-4, 1978-82, 1984, 1987-9
9 Eastern Suburbs 1903, 1913, 1921, 1931, 1941, 1944, 1946-7, 1969
8 Glebe 1900, 1901*, 1906-7, 1909, 1912, 1914, 1925*
6 Northern Suburbs 1933, 1935, 1960, 1963-4, 1975
6 Manly 1922, 1932, 1942-3, 1950, 1983
5 Gordon 1949, 1952, 1956, 1958, 1976
3 Newtown 1908, 1910-1
3 Parramatta 1977, 1985-6
2 Western Suburbs 1902, 1929
1 South Sydney 1905
1 Balmain 1925*
1 Drummoyne 1936
1 St.George 1957

NEW ZEALAND

Rugby was introduced into New Zealand in 1870. The first provincial union was that of Canterbury in 1879, and the New Zealand Rugby Football Union was founded in 1892.

Ranfurly Shield

The inter-provincial championship, first held in 1904. It is not a knockout competition, but one in which the champion state puts its title up for a challenge. *Winner and years when the title changed hands:*

1904 Wellington	1953 Canterbury
1905 Auckland	1956 Wellington
1913 Taranki	1957 Otago
1914 Wellington	1957 Taranaki
1920 Southland	1959 Southland
1921 Wellington	1959 Auckland
1922 Hawke's Bay	1960 North Auckland
1927 Wairarapa	1960 Auckland
1927 Manawhenua	1963 Wellington
1927 Canterbury	1963 Taranaki
1928 Wairarapa	1965 Auckland
1929 Southland	1966 Waikato
1930 Wellington	1966 Hawke's Bay
1931 Canterbury	1969 Canterbury
1934 Hawke's Bay	1971 Auckland
1934 Auckland	1971 North Auckland
1935 Canterbury	1972 Auckland
1935 Otago	1972 Canterbury
1937 Southland	1973 Marlborough
1938 Otago	1974 South Canterbury
1938 Southland	1974 Wellington
1947 Otago	1974 Auckland
1950 Canterbury	1976 Manawatu
1950 Wairarapa	1978 North Auckland
1950 South Canterbury	1979 Auckland
1950 North Auckland	1980 Waikato
1951 Waikato	1981 Wellington
1952 Auckland	1982 Canterbury
1952 Waikato	1985 Auckland
1953 Wellington	

Most successive defences: 33 Auckland 1985-90
Record attendance: 52,000 Auckland v Canterbury at Lancaster Park 1985

New Zealand National Championship

A season-long league championship inaugurated in 1976 involving 11 states in the first division. Each team plays every other once. There are also supplementary divisions enabling promotion to the first division.
Winners:

1976 Bay of Plenty	1983 Canterbury
1977 Canterbury	1984-5 Auckland
1978 Wellington	1986 Wellington
1979 Counties	1987-9 Auckland
1980 Manawatu	
1981 Wellington	
1982 Auckland	

SOUTH AFRICA

Rugby in South Africa, developed from a form of football known as 'Gog's game', was first played between civilian and military teams at Green Point Common, Cape Town, in 1862. The first union to be formed was Western Province in 1883 and the South African Rugby Board was founded in 1889.

Currie Cup

Inter-provincial tournament, first held 1889. Annual from 1968, prior to that it was mostly biennial, avoiding international tours. *Wins (* shared):*

29 Western Province 1889, 1892, 1894-5, 1897-8, 1904, 1906, 1908, 1914, 1920, 1925, 1927, 1929, 1932*, 1934*, 1936, 1947, 1954, 1959, 1964, 1966, 1979*, 1982-6, 1989*

17 Northern Transvaal 1946, 1956, 1968-9, 1971*, 1973-8, 1979*, 1980-1, 1987-8, 1989*

6 Transvaal 1922, 1939, 1950, 1952, 1971*, 1972

3 Griqualand West 1899, 1911, 1970

2 Border 1932*, 1934*

Highest score: Transvaal beat Far North 99-9 at Ellis Park, Johannesburg, 7 Jul 1973

SHINTY

This 12-a-side curved stick (the caman) and ball game is played almost exclusively in the Scottish Highlands. The pitch is up to 170 yards (155m) long and 80 yards (73m) wide, and the goals 10ft by 12ft (3.0 – 3.65m). The ball is about the size of a tennis ball and has a thick leather covering over a cork and worsted core.

The game's antecedents date back more than 2000 years to the ancient game of camanachd, meaning "the sport of the curved stick", and was brought to Scotland from Ireland with the Celtic immigration about 1400 years ago. The sport provided effective battle training, indeed it was probably a crude substitute for battle between clans. The present ruling body, the Camanachd Association was founded in 1893.

Camanachd Cup

The Camanachd Association Challenge Cup, instituted in 1896, is shinty's premier competition. *Most wins:*

28 Newtonmore	1907-10, 1929, 1931-2, 1936, 1947-8, 1950-1, 1955, 1957-9, 1967, 1970-2, 1975, 1977-9, 1981-2, 1985-6
19 Kyles Athletic	1904-6, 1920, 1922, 1924, 1927-8, 1935, 1956, 1962, 1965-6, 1968-9, 1974, 1976, 1980, 1983
11 Kingussie	1896, 1900, 1902-3, 1914, 1921, 1961, 1984, 1987-9

A record 11 winner's medals have been won by the Newtonmore players Johnnie Campbell, David Ritchie and Hugh Chisholm.

Highest score: 11-3 Newtonmore v. Furnace 1909

SHOOTING

The first shooting club, the Lucerne Shooting Guild (Switzerland) was formed around 1466 and the first recorded shooting match was at Zürich in 1472. The National Rifle Association of Great Britain was formed in 1860 and the Clay Bird Shooting Association was founded in 1903. The American National Rifle Association was formed in 1871. The international governing body for the sport, the Union International de Tir (UIT), was formed in Zürich in 1907.

OLYMPIC GAMES

Shooting has been part of the Olympic programme since the first Games in 1896; its inclusion possibly being as a result of the Games' founder, Baron Pierre de Coubertain, being an excellent shot. Separate events for women were first held in 1984 although they had competed alongside their male counterparts since 1968. In 1986 the ISU introduced new regulations for determining major championships and world records. The leading eight competitors at the end of the designated number of rounds take part in a final shoot-out round with the target sub-divided into tenths of a point for rifle and pistol shooting. For trap and skeet shooting each of the leading competitors has 25 extra shots. This new scoring system was introduced into the Olympic programme for the first time in 1988. *Winners:*

Free Pistol

60 shots from 50 metres

1896 Sumner Paine (USA) 442
1900 Conrad Röderer (Swi) 503
1906 Georgios Orphanidis (Gre) 221
1912 Alfred Lane (USA) 499
1920 Karl Frederick (USA) 496
1936 Torsten Ullmann (Swe) 559
1948 Edwin Vazquez Cam (Per) 545
1952 Huelet Benner (USA) 553
1956 Pentti Linnosvuo (Fin) 556
1960 Aleksey Gushchin (USSR) 560
1964 Väinö Markkanen (Fin) 560
1968 Grigoriy Kossykh (USSR) 562
1972 Ragnar Skanåkar (Swe) 567
1976 Uwe Potteck (GDR) 573
1980 Aleksandr Melentyev (USSR) 581
1984 Xu Haifeng (Chn) 566
1988 Sorin Babii (Rom) 660 (566+94)

Rapid Fire Pistol

Since 1948; 30 shots at five targets each at 25 metres. The shooter has 8 secs at each target in the first round, then 6 secs and then 4 secs. The set of 15 shots is then repeated.

1896 Jean Phrangoudis (Gre) 344
1900 Maurice Larrouy (Fra) 58
1906 Maurice Lecoq (Fra) 250

1908 Paul van Asbroeck (Bel) 490
1912 Alfred Lane (USA) 287
1920 Guilherme Paraense (Bra) 274
1924 Henry Bailey (USA) 18
1932 Renzo Morigi (Ita) 36
1936 Cornelius van Oyen (Ger) 36
1948 Károly Takács (Hun) 580
1952 Károly Takács (Hun) 579
1956 Stefan Petrescu (Rom) 587
1960 William McMillan (USA) 587
1964 Pentti Linnosvuo (Fin) 592
1968 Józef Zapedzki (Pol) 593
1972 Józef Zapedzki (Pol) 595
1976 Norbert Klaar (GDR) 597
1980 Corneliu Ion (Rom) 596
1984 Takeo Kamachi (Jap) 595
1988 Afanasi Kuzmin (USSR) 698 (598+100)

Small Bore Rifle – Prone

60 shots within two hours at a target with a bullseye
diameter of a mere 0.487in, and 50 metres away.
1908 A.A.Carnell (UK) 387
1912 Frederick Hird (USA) 194
1920 Lawrence Nuesslein (USA) 391
1924 Pierre Coquelin de Lisle (Fra) 398
1932 Bertil Rönnmark (Swe) 294
1936 Willy Rögeberg (Nor) 300
1948 Arthur Cook (USA) 599
1952 Iosif Sarbu (Rom) 400
1956 Gerald Ouellette (Can) 600*
1960 Peter Kohnke (FRG) 590
1964 László Hammerl (Hun) 597
1968 Jan Kurka (Cs) 598
1972 Li Ho-jun (NKo) 599
1976 Karlheinz Smieszek (FRG) 599
1980 Károly Varga (Hun) 599
1984 Edward Etzel (USA) 599

1988 Miroslav Varga (Cs) 703.9 (600+103.9)
* Record not allowed, range marginally short.

Small Bore Rifle – Three Positions

40 shots each from kneeling, standing and prone
positions at a target 50 metres away
1952 Erling Kongshaug (Nor) 1164
1956 Anatoliy Bogdanov (USSR) 1172
1960 Viktor Shamburkin (USSR) 1149
1964 Lones Wigger (USA) 1164
1968 Bernd Klingner (FRG) 1157
1972 John Writer (USA) 1166
1976 Lanny Bassham (USA) 1162
1980 Viktor Vlasov (USSR) 1173
1984 Malcolm Cooper (UK) 1173
1988 Malcolm Cooper (UK) 1279.3 (1180+99.3)

Running Game Target

30 shots at a 2in 10-ring target on a simulated boar that
does two runs across a 10-metre gap; one at 2.5 secs and
one at 5 secs
1900 Louis Debray (Fra) 20
1972 Yakov Zhelezniak (USSR) 569
1976 Aleksandr Gazov (USSR) 579
1980 Igor Sokolov (USSR) 589
1984 Li Yuwei (Chn) 587
1988 Tor Heiestad (Nor) 689 (591+98)

Trap

200 clay birds are released, one at a time, and at varying
angles. The shooter is allowed two shots at each clay.
1900 Roger de Barbarin (Fra) 17
1906 Gerald Merlin (UK)* 24
    Sidney Merlin (UK)** 15
1908 Walter Ewing (Can) 72
1912 James Graham (USA) 96
1920 Mark Arie (USA) 95

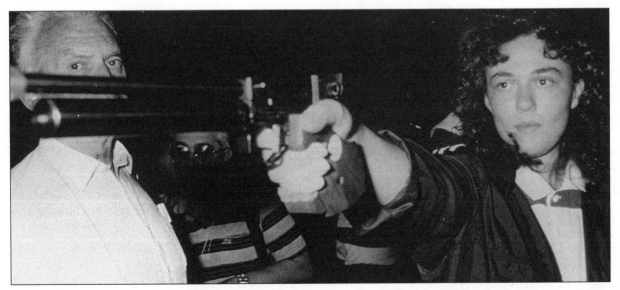

Jasna Sekaric set a world record for women's air pistol when she won the Olympic title in 1988 **(All-Sport/Pascal Rondeau)**

1924 Gyula Halasy (Hun) 98
1952 George Généreux (Can) 192
1956 Galliano Rossini (Ita) 195
1960 Ion Dumitrescu (Rom) 192
1964 Ennio Mattarelli (Ita) 198
1968 Bob Braithwaite (UK) 198
1972 Angelo Scalzone (Ita) 199
1976 Don Haldeman (USA) 190
1980 Luciano Giovanetti (Ita) 198
1984 Luciano Giovanetti (Ita) 192
1988 Dmitriy Monakov (USSR) 222 (197+25)
* single shot   ** double shot

Skeet
The shooter attempts to hit 200 clay targets which are released either one or two at a time. Unlike trap shooting he/she fires from eight different 'stations' and the birds are released from towers as opposed to ground level.
1968 Yevgeniy Petrov (USSR) 198
1972 Konrad Wirnhier (FRG) 195
1976 Josef Panácek (Cs) 198
1980 Hans Kjeld Rasmussen (Den) 196
1984 Matthew Dryke (USA) 198
1988 Axel Wegner (GDR) 222 (198+24)

Air Rifle
60 shots at 10 metres
1984 Philippe Heberle (Fra) 589
1988 Goran Maksimovic (Yug) 695.6 (594+101.6)

Air Pistol
60 shots at 10 metres
1988 Taniou Kiriakov (Bul) 687.9 (585+102.9)

WOMEN
Sport Pistol
60 shots at 10 metres
1984 Linda Thom (Can) 585
1988 Nino Salukvadze (USSR) 690 (591+99)

Air Rifle
40 shots at 10 metres
1984 Pat Spurgin (USA) 393
1988 Irina Chilova (USSR) 498.5 (395+103.5)

Air Pistol
40 shots at 10 metres
1988 Jasna Sekaric (Yug) 489.5 (389+100.5)

Small Bore Standard Rifle
60 shots at 10 metres
1984 Wu Xiaoxuan (Chn) 581
1988 Silvia Sperber (FRG) 685.6 (590+95.6)

Discontinued events
Free Rifle – three postions
120 shots from 300 metres
1896 Georgis Orphanidis (Gre)1583

1906 Gudbrand Skatteboe (Nor) 973
1908 Albert Helgerud (Nor) 909
1912 Paul Colas (Fra) 987
1920 Morris Fisher (USA) 996
1924 Morris Fisher (USA) 95
1948 Emil Grüning (Swi) 1120
1952 Anatoliy Bogdanov (USSR) 1123
1956 Vasiliy Borissov (USSR) 1138
1960 Hubert Hammerer (Aut) 1129
1964 Gary Anderson (USA) 1153
1968 Gary Anderson (USA) 1157
1972 Lones Wigger (USA) 1155

Free Rifle
1896 Pantelis Karasevdas (Gre) 2320: over 200m
1906 Marcel de Stadelhofen (Swi) 243: any position (300m)
1906 Gudbrand Skatteboe (Nor) prone (300m)
1906 Konrad Stäheli (Swi) kneeling (300m)
1906 Gudbrand Skatteboe (Nor) standing (300m)
1908 Jerry Millner (UK) 98: over 1000 yards

Free Rifle – Team
1906 Switzerland 4596
1908 Norway 5055
1912 Sweden 5655
1920 USA 4876
1924 USA 676

Military Rifle
1900 Emil Kellenberger (Swi) 930: three pos. (300m)
1900 Lars Madsen (Den) 305: standing (300m)
1900 Konrad Stäheli (Swi) 324: kneeling (300m)
1900 Achille Paroche (Fra) 332: prone (300m)
1906 Léon Moreaux (Fra) 187: stand or kneel (200m)
1906 Louis Richardet (Swi) 238: stand or kneel (300m)
1912 Sándor Prokopp (Hun) 97: three positions (300m)
1912 Paul Colas (Fra) 94: any position (600m)
1920 Otto Olsen (Nor) 60: prone (300m)
1920 Carl Osburn (USA) 56: standing (300m)
1920 Hugo Johansson (Swe) 59: prone (600m)

Military Rifle – Team
1900 Switzerland 4399: (300m)
1908 USA 2531: (200, 500, 600, 800, 900, 1000yd)
1912 USA 1687: (200, 400, 500, 600m)
1920 Denmark 266: standing (300m)
1920 USA 289: prone (300m)
1920 USA 287: prone (600m)
1920 USA 573: prone (300m & 600m)

Small Bore Rifle
1908 J.F.Fleming (UK) 24: moving target
1908 William Styles (UK) 45: disappearing target
1912 Wilhelm Carlberg (Swe) 242: disappearing target

Small Bore Rifle – Team
1908 United Kingdom 771: (50 & 100yd)
1912 Sweden 925: (25m)

1912 United Kingdom 762: (50m)
1920 USA 1899: (50m)

Live Pigeon Shooting
1900 Léon de Lunden (Bel) 21

Clay Pigeons – Team
1908 United Kingdom 407
1912 USA 532
1920 USA 547
1924 USA 363

Running Deer
1908 Oscar Swahn (Swe) 25 *
1908 Walter Winans (USA) 46 **
1912 Alfred Swahn (Swe) 41 *
1912 Åke Lundeberg (Swe) 79 **
1920 Otto Olsen (Nor) 43 *
1920 Ole Lilloe-Olsen (Nor) 82 **
1924 John Boles (USA) 40 *
1924 Ole Lilloe-Olsen (Nor) 76 **
* Single shot   ** Double shot

Running Deer – Team
1908 Sweden 86
1912 Sweden 151
1920 Norway 178 *
1920 Norway 343 **
1924 Norway 160 *
1924 United Kingdom 263 **
* Single shot   ** Double shot

Running Deer – Single and double shot
1952 John Larsen (Nor) 413
1956 Vitaliy Romanenko (USSR) 441

Military Revolver
1896 John Paine (USA) 442: (25m)
1906 Louis Richardet (Swi) 253: (20m)
1906 Jean Fouconnier (Fra) 219 (model 1873)

Duelling Pistol
1906 Léon Moreaux (Fra) 242: Over 20m
1906 Konstantinos Skarlatos (Gre) 133: Over 25m

Team Event
1900 Switzerland 2271
1908 USA 1914
1912 USA 1916 *
1912 Sweden 1145 **
1920 USA 2372 *
1920 USA 1310 **
* Over 50m   ** Over 30m

Most Olympic medals (G gold, S silver, B bronze)
Shooters to have won four or more gold medals:

Total	Name	G	S	B	Years
11	Carl Osburn (USA)	5	4	2	1912-24
8	Konrad Stäheli (Swi)	5	2	1	1900
8	Otto Olsen (Nor)	4	3	1	1920-4
7	Gudbrand Skatteboe (Nor)	4	3	-	1906-20
7	Willis Lee (USA)	5	1	1	1920
7	Lloyd Spooner (USA)	4	1	2	1920
7	Einer Liberg (Nor)	4	2	1	1908-24
6	Louis Richardet (Swi)	5	1	-	1900
6	Ole Lilloe-Olsen (Nor)	5	1	-	1920-4
6	Alfred Lane (USA)	5	-	1	1912-20
5	Morris Fisher (USA)	5	-	-	1920-4
Most by women					
2	Silvia Sperber (FRG)	1	1	-	1988
2	Wu Xiaoxuan (Chn)	1	-	1	1984
2	Jasna Sekaric (Yug)	1	-	1	1988

Most individual gold medals: 3 Gudbrand Skatteboe (Nor) 1906

Oscar Swahn (Swe) was aged 64 years 258 days when he won a gold medal in the team running deer event in 1912 to become the oldest gold medallist in Olympic history. He became the oldest ever Olympic competitor, and indeed medallist, in 1920 when he appeared in Sweden's silver medal winning team, again in the running deer event. He qualified for the 1924 Games, but illness prevented him competing.

WORLD RECORDS
Figures in brackets indicates score at end of regular competition + final shoot-out round score

MEN
Free Rifle (Three positions; 3 x 40 shots at 50m)
1283.4 (1183 + 100.4) Petr Kurka (Cs)   1988

Free Rifle (Prone; 60 shots at 50m)
704.9 (599 + 105.9) Petr Kurka (Cs)   1987
704.9 (598 + 106.9) Goran Maksimovic (Yug)   1988

Free Pistol (60 shots at 50m)
671 (579 + 92)   Sergey Pyzhyanov (USSR)   1990

Rapid Fire Pistol (60 shots at 25m)
698 (598 + 100)   Afanasiy Kuzmin (USSR)   1988

Running Game Target (60 shots at 50m with small bore rifle)
691 (594 + 97)   Sergey Luzov (USSR)   1986
691 (596 + 95)   Nikolay Lapin (USSR)   1987

Air Rifle (60 shots at 10m)
699.4 (596 + 103.4) Rajmond Debevec (Yug)   1990

Air Pistol (60 shots at 10m)
695.1 (593 + 102.1) Sergey Pyzhyanov (USSR) 1989

WOMEN
Standard Rifle (Three positions; 3 x 20 shots at 50m)
691.6 (587 + 104.6) Vessela Letcheva (Bul) 1987

Sport Pistol (60 shots at 25m)
695 (595 + 100)   Nino Salukvadze (USSR)   1987

Air Rifle (40 shots at 10m)
504 (399 + 105)   Vessela Letcheva (Bul)   1987

Air Pistol (40 shots at 10m)
492.4 (392 + 100.4)   Liselotte Breker (FRG)   1989

MIXED
Trap (200 targets)
224 (199 + 25)   Miroslav Bednarík (Cs)   1986

Skeet (200 targets)
224 (199 + 25)   Matthew Dryke (USA)   1986
224 (199 + 25)   Luca Scribani (Ita)   1988
224 (200 + 24)   Ribor Ole Rasmussen (Den) 1988

SKIING

The word ski was the Norwegian word for snow-shoe. The earliest ski, recovered from a peat bog in Sweden, has been dated as c.2500 BC. It is 1.1m long and c.20cm wide. Long skis. over 2m in length were used in Norway about 4000 years ago, and both long and short skis have been widely used in Scandinavian countries.

In modern times two main categories of skiing have evolved, Nordic, which encompasses cross-country and ski-jumping, and Alpine, which has downhill and slalom events. The first ski races were held in Norway and Australia in the 1850s and 1860s, after Søndre Nordheim had developed techniques and skis in the province of Telemark in Norway. The first national governing body was that of Norway, formed in 1883, public imagination being caught by the epic Greenland trek using skis of the great Norwegian explorer Fridtjof Nansen in 1888.

The technique of Alpine skiing was pioneered by the Austrian Mathias Zdarsky at the end of the 19th century and British enthusiasts developed winter sports and races, notably in Switzerland at the turn of the century. Sir Henry Lunn pioneered skiing holidays and his son Sir Arnold Lunn introduced the modern slalom event. The International Ski Federation (FIS) was founded in 1924 to succeed the International Skiing Commission, founded in Oslo in 1910.

See also *Biathlon* for the results of combined skiing and shooting.

ALPINE SKIING

OLYMPIC GAMES
Alpine skiing events were first included at the Olympic Games in 1936. *Winners:*

Men's Alpine Combination
Downhill and slalom
1936 Franz Pfnür (Ger)
1948 Henri Oreiller (Fra)
1988 Hubert Strolz (Aut)

Men's Downhill
1948 Henri Oreiller (Fra)
1952 Zeno Colò (Ita)
1956 Toni Sailer (Aut)
1960 Jean Vuarnet (Fra)
1964 Egon Zimmermann (Aut)
1968 Jean-Claude Killy (Fra)
1972 Bernhard Russi (Swi)
1976 Franz Klammer (Aut)
1980 Leonhard Stock (Aut)
1984 William Johnson (USA)
1988 Pirmin Zurbriggen (Swi)

Men's Giant Slalom
1952 Stein Eriksen (Nor)
1956 Toni Sailer (Aut)
1960 Roger Staub (Swi)
1964 François Bonlieu (Fra)
1968 Jean-Claude Killy (Fra)

1972 Gustavo Thoeni (Ita)
1976 Heini Hemmi (Swi)
1980 Ingemar Stenmark (Swe)
1984 Max Julen (Swi)
1988 Alberto Tomba (Ita)

Men's Slalom
1948 Edy Reinalter (Swi)
1952 Othmar Schneider (Aut)
1956 Toni Sailer (Aut)
1960 Ernst Hinterseer (Aut)
1964 Josef Stiegler (Aut)
1968 Jean-Claude Killy (Fra)
1972 Francisco Fernandez Ochoa
     (Spa)
1976 Piero Gros (Ita)
1980 Ingemar Stenmark (Swe)
1984 Phil Mahre (USA)
1988 Alberto Tomba (Ita)

Men's Super Giant Slalom
1988 Franck Riccard (Fra)

Women's Alpine Combination –
downhill and slalom
1936 Christel Cranz (Ger)
1948 Trude Beiser (Aut)
1988 Anita Wachter (Aut)

Women's Downhill
1948 Hedy Schlunegger (Swi)
1952 Trude Jochum (née Beiser) (Aut)

1956 Madeleine Berthod (Swi)
1960 Heidi Biebl (FRG)
1964 Christl Haas (Aut)
1968 Olga Pall (Aut)
1972 Marie-Thérèse Nadig (Swi)
1976 Rosi Mittermaier (FRG)
1980 Annemarie Moser-Pröll (Aut)
1984 Michela Figini (Swi)
1988 Marina Kiehl (FRG)

Women's Giant Slalom
1952 Andrea Mead-Lawrence (USA)
1956 Ossi Reichert (FRG)
1960 Yvonne Rüegg (Swi)
1964 Marielle Goitschel (Fra)
1968 Nancy Greene (Can)
1972 Marie-Thérèse Nadig (Swi)
1976 Kathy Kreiner (Can)
1980 Hanni Wenzel (Lie)
1984 Debbie Armstrong (USA)
1988 Vreni Schneider (Swi)

Women's Slalom
1948 Gretchen Fraser (USA)
1952 Andrea Mead-Lawrence (USA)
1956 Renée Colliard (Swi)
1960 Anne Heggtveit (Can)
1964 Christine Goitschel (Fra)
1968 Marielle Goitschel (Fra)
1972 Barbara Cochran (USA)
1976 Rosi Mittermaier (FRG)
1980 Hanni Wenzel (Lie)

1984 Paoletta Magoni (Ita)
1988 Vreni Schneider (Swi)

Women's Super Giant Slalom
1988 Sigrid Wolf (Aut)

Most Olympic medals
Four: Hanni Wenzel (Lie) two gold, a silver and a bronze 1976-80.
Three gold medals: Toni Sailer (Aut) 1956, Jean-Claude Killy (Fra) 1968.

WORLD CHAMPIONSHIPS
First held at downhill in 1931 at Mürren. Held annually 1931-9 and bienially post-war. Up to 1980 the Olympic Champions were also world champions, except in 1936 when separate championships were held. Listed for each event are post-war winners additional to those shown earlier as Olympic Champions, and those to have won most titles (including Olympics shown by *):

Men's Alpine Combination
1954 Stein Eriksen (Nor)
1956 Toni Sailer (Aut)
1958 Toni Sailer (Aut)
1960 Guy Périllat (Fra)
1962 Karl Schranz (Aut)
1964 Ludwig Leitner (FRG)
1966 Jean-Claude Killy (Fra)
1968 Jean-Claude Killy (Fra)
1970 Bill Kidd (USA)
1972 Gustavo Thoeni (Ita)
1974 Franz Klammer (Aut)
1976 Gustavo Thoeni (Ita)
1978 Andrea Wenzel (Lie)
1980 Phil Mahre (USA)
1982 Michel Vion (Fra)
1985 Pirmin Zurbriggen (Swi)
1987 Marc Girardelli (Lux)
1989 Marc Girardelli (Lux)

Most wins: 2 Anton Seelos (Aut) 1933, 1935; Emile Allais (Fra) 1937-8; Sailer, Killy, Thoeni, Girardelli.

Men's Downhill
1950 Zeno Colò (Ita)
1954 Christian Pravda (Aut)
1958 Toni Sailer (Aut)
1962 Karl Schranz (Aut)
1966 Jean-Claude Killy (Fra)
1970 Bernhard Russi (Swi)
1974 David Zwilling (Aut)
1978 Josef Walcher (Aut)

1982 Harti Weirather (Aut)
1985 Pirmin Zurbriggen (Swi)
1987 Peter Müller (Swi)
1989 Hansjörg Tauscher (FRG)

Most wins: 2 Walter Prager (Swi) 1931, 1933; each also one *: Colò, Sailer, Killy, Russi.

Men's Giant Slalom
1950 Zeno Colò (Ita)
1954 Stein Eriksen (Nor)
1958 Toni Sailer (Aut)
1962 Egon Zimmermann (Aut)
1966 Guy Périllat (Fra)
1970 Karl Schranz (Aut)
1974 Gustavo Thoeni (Ita)
1978 Ingemar Stenmark (Swe)
1982 Steve Mahre (USA)
1985 Markus Wasmaier (FRG)
1987 Pirmin Zurbriggen (Swi)
1989 Rudolf Nierlich (Aut)

Most wins (each also one *): 2 Eriksen, Sailer, Thoeni, Stenmark

Men's Slalom
1950 Georges Schneider (Swi)
1954 Stein Eriksen (Nor)
1958 Josef Rieder (Aut)
1962 Charles Bozon (Fra)
1966 Carlo Senoner (Ita)
1970 Jean-Noël Augert (Fra)
1974 Gustavo Thoeni (Ita)
1978 Ingemar Stenmark (Swe)

1982 Ingemar Stenmark (Swe)
1985 Jonas Nilsson (Swe)
1987 Frank Wörndl (FRG)
1989 Rudolf Nierlich (Aut)

Most wins: 3 Ingemar Stenmark (Swe) also 1980*

Men's Super Giant Slalom
1987 Pirmin Zurbriggen (Swi)
1989 Martin Hangl (Swi)

Women's Alpine Combination
1954 Ida Schöpfer (Swi)
1956 Madeleine Berthod (Swi)
1958 Frieda Dänzer (Swi)
1960 Anne Heggtveit (Can)
1962 Marielle Goitschel (Fra)
1964 Marielle Goitschel (Fra)
1966 Marielle Goitschel (Fra)
1968 Nancy Greene (Can)
1970 Michèle Jacot (Fra)
1972 Annemarie Pröll (Aut)
1974 Fabienne Serrat (Fra)
1976 Rosi Mittermaier (FRG)
1978 Annemarie Moser-Pröll (Aut)
1980 Hanni Wenzel (Lie)
1982 Erika Hess (Swi)
1985 Erika Hess (Swi)
1987 Erika Hess (Swi)
1989 Tamara McKinney (USA)

Marc Girardelli, world champion for Alpine combination and World Cup winner in 1989 **(All-Sport)**

Most wins: 5 Christl Cranz (Ger) 1934-5, 1937-9; 3 Marielle Goitschel, Erika Hess.

Women's Downhill
1950 Trude Beiser-Jochum (Aut)
1954 Ida Schöpfer (Swi)
1958 Lucille Wheeler (Can)
1962 Christl Haas (Aut)
1966 Erika Schinegger (Aut) #
1970 Annerösli Zyrd (Swi)
1974 Annemarie Moser-Pröll (Aut)
1978 Annemarie Moser-Pröll (Aut)
1982 Gerry Sorensen (Can)
1985 Michela Figini (Swi)
1987 Maria Walliser (Swi)
1989 Maria Walliser (Swi)

Most wins: 3 Christl Cranz (Ger) 1935, 1937, 1939; Moser-Pröll also 1980*
later declared as a man and gold went to Marielle Goitschel (Fra)

Women's Giant Slalom
1950 Dagmar Rom (Aut)
1954 Lucienne Schmitt (Fra)
1958 Lucille Wheeler (Can)
1962 Marianne Jahn (Aut)
1966 Marielle Goitschel (Fra)
1970 Betsy Clifford (Can)
1974 Fabienne Serrat (Fra)
1978 Maria Epple (FRG)
1982 Erika Hess (Swi)
1985 Diann Roffe (USA)
1987 Vreni Schneider (Swi)
1989 Vreni Schneider (Swi)

Most wins: 3 Schneider also 1988*

Women's Slalom
1950 Dagmar Rom (Aut)
1954 Trude Klecker (Aut)
1958 Inger Björnbakken (Nor)
1962 Marianne Jahn (Aut)
1966 Annie Famose (Fra)
1970 Ingrid Lafforgue (Fra)
1974 Hanni Wenzel (Lie)
1978 Lea Sölkner (Aut)
1982 Erika Hess (Swi)
1985 Perrine Pelen (Fra)
1987 Erika Hess (Swi)
1989 Mateja Svet (Yug)

Most wins: 4 Christl Cranz (Ger) 1934, 1937-9

Women's Super-giant Slalom
1987 Maria Walliser (FRG)

1989 Ulrike Maier (Aut)

Most wins at all events
Men 7 Toni Sailer (Aut), 6 Jean-Claude Killy (Fra)
Women 12 Christl Cranz (Ger) – and the 1936 Olympic combined; 7 Marielle Goitschel, 6 Erika Hess
All four titles have been won in one year by Sailer 1956 and Killy 1968.

WORLD CUP
Contested annually from 1967 over a series of events during the winter season. The year given is that of the second half of the season. *Winners:*

Men's Overall
1967-8 Jean-Claude Killy (Fra)
1969-70 Karl Schranz (Aut)
1971-3 Gustavo Thoeni (Ita)
1974 Piero Gros (Ita)
1975 Gustavo Thoeni (Ita)
1976-8 Ingemar Stenmark (Swe)
1979 Peter Lüscher (Swi)
1980 Andreas Wenzel (Lie)
1981-3 Phil Mahre (USA)
1984 Pirmin Zurbriggen (Swi)
1985-6 Marc Girardelli (Lux)
1987 Pirmin Zurbriggen (Swi)
1988 Pirmin Zurbriggen (Swi)
1989 Marc Girardelli (Lux)
1990 Pirmin Zurbriggen (Swi)
Most: 4 Thoeni, Zurbriggen; 3 Stenmark, Mahre, Zurbriggen, Girardelli

Men's Downhill
1967 Jean-Claude Killy (Fra)
1968 Gerhard Nenning (Aut)
1969 Karl Schranz (Aut)
1970 Karl Schranz (Aut) & Karl Cordin (Aut)
1971-2 Bernhard Russi (Swi)
1973-4 Roland Collombin (Swi)
1975-8 Franz Klammer (Aut)
1979-80 Peter Müller (Swi)
1981 Harti Weirather (Aut)
1982 Steve Podborski (Can) & Peter Müller (Swi)
1983 Franz Klammer (Aut)
1984 Urs Räber (Swi)
1985 Helmut Höhflehner (Aut)
1986 Peter Wirnsberger (Aut)
1987 Pirmin Zurbriggen (Swi)
1988 Pirmin Zurbriggen (Swi)
1989 Marc Girardelli (Lux)
1990 Helmut Höhflehner (Aut)

Most: 5 Klammer

Men's Giant Slalom
1967-8 Jean-Claude Killy (Fra)
1969 Karl Schranz (Aut)
1970 Gustavo Thoeni (Ita)
1971 Gustavo Thoeni (Ita) & Patrick Russel (Fra)
1972 Gustavo Thoeni (Ita)
1973 Hans Hinterseer (Aut)
1974 Piero Gros (Aut)
1975-6 Ingemar Stenmark (Swe)
1977 Heini Hemmi (Swi)
1978-81 Ingemar Stenmark (Swe)
1982-3 Phil Mahre (USA)
1984 Ingemar Stenmark (Swe)
1985 Marc Girardelli (Lux)
1986 Joel Gaspoz (Swi)
1987 Pirmin Zurbriggen (Swi)
1988 Alberto Tomba (Ita)
1989-90 Ole Christian Furuseth (Nor)
Most: 7 Stenmark

Men's Slalom
1967 Jean-Claude Killy (Fra)
1968 Dumeng Giovanoli (Swi)
1969 Alfred Matt (Aut), Alain Penz (Fra), Jean-Noël Augert (Fra), Patrick Russel (Fra)
1970 Patrick Russel & Alain Penz (Fra)
1971-2 Jean-Noël Augert (Fra)
1973-4 Gustavo Thoeni (Ita)
1975-81 Ingemar Stenmark (Swe)
1982 Phil Mahre (USA)
1983 Ingemar Stenmark (Swe)
1984-5 Marc Girardelli (Lux)
1986 Rok Petrovic (Yug)
1987 Bojan Krizaj (Yug)
1988 Alberto Tomba (Ita)
1989-90 Armin Bittner (FRG)
Most: 8 Stenmark

Men's Super Giant Slalom
1986 Markus Wasmeier (FRG)
1987-90 Pirmin Zurbriggen (Swi)
Most: 4 Zurbriggen

Women's Overall
1967-8 Nancy Greene (Can)
1969 Gertrud Gabl (Aut)
1970 Michèle Jacot (Fra)
1971-5 Annemarie Moser-Pröll (Aut)
1976 Rosi Mittermaier (FRG)
1977 Lise-Marie Morerod (Swi)
1978 Hanni Wenzel (Lie)
1979 Annemarie Moser-Pröll (Aut)
1980 Hanni Wenzel (Lie)

1981 Marie-Thérèse Nadig (Swi)
1982 Erika Hess (Swi)
1983 Tamara McKinney (USA)
1984 Erika Hess (Swi)
1985 Michela Figini (Swi)
1986-7 Maria Walliser (Swi)
1988 Michela Figini (Swi)
1989 Vreni Schneider (Swi)
1990 Petra Kronberger (Aut)
Most: 6 Moser-Pröll

Women's Downhill
1967 Marielle Goitschel (Fra)
1968 Isabelle Mir (Fra) &
    Olga Pall (Aut)
1969 Wiltrud Drexel (Aut)
1970 Isabelle Mir (Fra)
1971-5 Annemarie Moser-Pröll (Aut)
1976-7 Brigittte Habersatter-Totschnig
    (Aut)
1978-9 Annemarie Moser-Pröll (Aut)
1980-1 Marie-Thérèse Nadig (Swi)
1982 Cécile Gros-Gaudenier (Fra)
1983 Doris De Agostini (Swi)
1984 Maria Walliser (Swi)
1985 Michela Figini (Swi)
1986 Maria Walliser (Swi)
1987-9 Michela Figini (Swi)
1990 Katrin Gütensohn-Knopl (Aut
Most: 7 Annemarie Moser-Pröll (Aut),
4 Figini

Women's Giant Slalom
1967-8 Nancy Greene (Can)
1969 Marilyn Cochran (USA)

1970 Michèle Jacot &
    Françoise Macchi (Fra)
1971-2 Annemarie Moser-Pröll (Aut)
1973 Monika Kaserer (Aut)
1974 Hanni Wenzel (Lie)
1975 Annemarie Moser-Pröll (Aut)
1976-8 Lise-Marie Morerod (Swi)
1979 Christa Kinshoffer (Aut)
1980 Hanni Wenzel (Lie)
1981 Tamara McKinney (USA)
1982 Irene Epple (FRG)
1983 Tamara McKinney (USA)
1984 Erika Hess (Swi)
1985 Michela Figini (Swi) &
    Marina Kiehl (FRG)
1986 Vreni Schneider (Swi)
1987 Maria Walliser (Swi) &
    Vreni Schneider (Swi)
1988 Mateja Svet (Yug)
1989 Vreni Schneider (Swi)
1990 Anita Wachter (Aut)
Most: 3 Moser-Pröll, Morerod,
Schneider

Women's Slalom
1967 Marielle Goitschel &
    Annie Famose (Fra)
1968 Annie Famose (Fra)
1969 Gertrud Gabl (Aut)
1970 Ingrid Lafforgue (Fra)
1971 Britt Laforgue (Fra) &
    Betsy Clifford (Can)
1972 Britt Laforgue (Fra)
1973 Patricia Emonet (Fra)
1974 Christa Zechmeister (FRG)

1975-7 Lise-Marie Morerod (Swi)
1978 Hanni Wenzel (Lie)
1979 Regina Sackl (Aut)
1980 Perrine Pelen (Fra)
1981-3 Erika Hess (Swi)
1984 Tamara McKinney (USA)
1985 Erika Hess (Swi)
1986 Roswitha Steiner (Aut)
1987 Corinne Schmidhauser (Swi)
1988 Roswitha Steiner (Aut)
1989-90 Vreni Schneider (Swi)
Most: 4 Erika Hess

Women's Super Giant Slalom
1986 Marina Kiehl (FRG)
1987 Maria Walliser (Swi)
1988 Michela Figini (Swi)
1989-90 Carole Merle (Fra)

Most wins
The most wins in World Cup events is
86 by Ingemar Stenmark (Swe) 1974-
89. Franz Klammer (Aut) won a record
35 downhill races, 1974-85. Stenmark
won a men's record 13 World Cup
races in a season, 1979. The next
bests: Jean-Claude Killy (Fra) 12 in
1967, Pirmin Zurbriggen 11 in 1987.
The women's career record is 62 by
Annemarie Moser (Aut), 1970-9.

Nations' Cup
Awarded on the overall results for
men and women obtained in the
World Cup. Wins:
12 Austria 1969, 1973-82, 1990
7 Switzerland 1983-9
5 France 1967-8, 1970-2

Highest speed
The highest speed claimed for a skier
is 223.741 km/h by Michel Prufer
(Monaco) and the fastest by a woman
is 214.413 km/h by Tarja Mulari (Fin),
both at Les Arcs, France on 16 Apr
1988.

NORDIC SKIING

OLYMPIC GAMES
The first Winter Olympic Games, held
at Chamonix in 1924, included Nordic
skiing events, and they have been
included on the programme ever
since. *Winners:*

Men's 15km Cross-Country
Held at 18km 1924, 1936-52,

Vreni Schneider set a women's record of 14 World Cup wins and won all seven slalom races in 1989 (**All-Sport/David Cannon**)

19.7km 1928, 18.214km 1932. Now designated as classical style.
1924 Thorleif Haug (Nor) 1:14:31
1928 Johan Grøttumsbraaten (Nor) 1:37:01
1932 Sven Utterström (Swe) 1:23:07
1936 Erik-August Larsson (Swe) 1:14:38
1948 Martin Lundström (Swe) 1:13:50
1952 Hallgeir Brenden (Nor) 1:01:34
1956 Hallgeir Brenden (Nor) 49:39.0
1960 Haakon Brusveen (Nor) 51:55.5
1964 Eero Mäntyranta (Fin) 50:54.1
1968 Harald Grönningen (Nor) 47:54.2
1972 Sven-Åke Lundback (Swe) 45:28.24
1976 Nikolay Bayukov (USSR) 43:58.47
1980 Thomas Wassberg (Swe) 41:57.63
1984 Gunde Svan (Swe) 41:25.6
1988 Mikhail Devyatyarov (USSR) 41:18.9

Men's 30km Cross-Country
1956 Veikko Hakulinen (Fin) 1:44:06.0
1960 Sixten Jernberg (Swe) 1:51:03.9
1964 Eero Mäntyranta (Fin) 1:30:50.7
1968 Franco Nones (Ita) 1:35:39.2
1972 Vyacheslav Vedenin (USSR) 1:36:31.2
1976 Sergey Savelyev (USSR) 1:30:29.38
1980 Nikolay Zimyatov (USSR) 1:27:02.80
1984 Nikolay Zimyatov (USSR) 1:28:56.3
1988 Aleksey Prokurakov (USSR) 1:24:26.3

Men's 50km Cross-Country
1924 Thorleif Haug (Nor) 3:44:32
1928 Per-Erik Hedlund (Swe) 4:52:03
1932 Veli Saarinen (Fin) 4:28:00
1936 Elis Wiklund (Swe) 3:30:11
1948 Nils Karlsson (Swe) 3:47:48
1952 Veikko Hakulinen (Fin) 3:33:33
1956 Sixten Jernberg (Swe) 2:50:27
1960 Kalevi Hämäläinen (Fin) 2:59:06.3
1964 Sixten Jernberg (Swe) 2:43:52.6
1968 Ole Ellefsaeter (Nor) 2:28:45.8
1972 Pål Tyldum (Nor) 2:43:14.75
1976 Ivar Formo (Nor) 2:37:30.50
1980 Nikolay Zimyatov (USSR)

2:27:24.60
1984 Thomas Wassberg (Swe) 2:15:55.8
1988 Gunde Svan (Swe) 2:04:30.9

Men's 4 x 10km Cross-Country Relay
1936 Finland 2:41:33
1948 Sweden 2:32:08
1952 Finland 2:20:16
1956 USSR 2:15:30
1960 Finland 2:18:45.6
1964 Sweden 2:18:34.6
1968 Norway 2:08:33.5
1972 USSR 2:04:47.94
1976 Finland 2:07:59.72
1980 USSR 1:57:03.46
1984 Sweden 1:55:06.30
1988 Sweden 1:43:58.6

Men's Ski Jumping – 70 metre hill
1924 Jacob Tullin Thams (Nor)
1928 Alf Andersen (Nor)
1932 Birger Ruud (Nor)
1936 Birger Ruud (Nor)
1948 Petter Hugstedt (Nor)
1952 Arnfinn Bergmann (Nor)
1956 Anti Hyvärinen (Fin)
1960 Helmut Recknagel (GDR)
1964 Viekko Kankkänen (Fin)
1968 Jiri Raska (Cs)
1972 Yukio Kasaya (Jap)
1976 Hans-Georg Aschenbach (GDR)
1980 Toni Innauer (Aut)
1984 Jens Weissflog (GDR)
1988 Matti Nykänen (Fin)

Men's Ski Jumping – 90 metre hill
1964 Toralf Engan (Nor)
1968 Vladimir Byeloussov (USSR)
1972 Wojciech Fortuna (Pol)
1976 Karl Schnabl (Aut)
1980 Jouko Törmänen (Fin)
1984 Matti Nykänen (Fin)
1988 Matti Nykänen (Fin)

Men's Team Ski Jumping
1988 Finland

Men's Nordic Combined – Skiing and Jumping
1924 Thorleif Haug (Nor)
1928 Johan Grøttumsbraaten (Nor)
1932 Johan Grøttumsbraaten (Nor)
1936 Oddbjørn Hagen (Nor)
1948 Heikki Hasu (Fin)
1952 Simon Slåtvik (Nor)
1956 Sverre Stenersen (Nor)

1960 Georg Thoma (FRG)
1964 Tormod Knutsen (Nor)
1968 Franz Keller (FRG)
1972 Ulrich Wehling (GDR)
1976 Ulrich Wehling (GDR)
1980 Ulrich Wehling (GDR)
1984 Tom Sandberg (Nor)
1988 Hippolyt Kempf (Swi)

Men's Team Nordic Combined
1988 FR Germany

Women's 5km Cross-Country
1964 Klaudia Boyarskikh (USSR) 17:50.5
1968 Toini Gustafsson (Swe) 16:45.2
1972 Galina Kulakova (USSR) 17:00.50
1976 Helena Takalo (Fin) 15:48.69
1980 Raisa Smetanina (USSR) 15:06.92
1984 Marja-Liisa Hämäläinen (Fin) 17:04.0
1988 Marjo Matikainen (Fin) 15:04.0

Women's 10km Cross-Country
1952 Lydia Wideman (Fin) 41:40.0
1956 Lyubov Kozyryeva (USSR) 38:11.0
1960 Maria Gusakova (USSR) 39:46.6
1964 Klaudia Boyarskikh (USSR) 40:24.3
1968 Toini Gustafsson (Swe) 36:46.5
1972 Galina Kulakova (USSR) 34:17.8
1976 Raisa Smetanina (USSR) 30:13.41
1980 Barbara Petzold (GDR) 30:31.54
1984 Marja-Liisa Hämäläinen (Fin) 31:44.2
1988 Vida Ventsene (USSR) 30:08.3

Women's 20km Cross-Country
1984 Marja-Liisa Hämäläinen (Fin) 1:01:45.0
1988 Tamara Tikhonova (USSR) 55:53.6

Women's 4 x 5km Cross-Country Relay
1956 Finland 1:09:01.0
1960 Sweden 1:04:21.4
1964 USSR 59:20.2
1968 Norway 57:30.0
1972 USSR 48:46.15
1976 USSR 1:07:49.75
1980 GDR 1:02:11.10
1984 Norway 1:06:49.70
1988 USSR 59:51.1

Most Olympic medals *(G -Gold, S – Silver, B – Bronze)*

		G	S	B	Years
9	Sixten Jernberg (Swe)	4	3	2	1956-64
9	Raisa Smetanina (USSR)	3	5	1	1976-88
8	Galina Kulakova (USSR)	4	2	2	1968-80
7	Veikko Hakulinen (Fin)	3	3	1	1952-60
7	Eero Mäntyranta (Fin)	3	2	2	1960-8
6	Gunde Svan (Swe)	4	1	1	1984-8
6	Johan Grøttumsbraaten (Nor)	3	1	2	1924-32

Also four gold medals: Matti Nykänen (Fin) 1984-8, and a silver at 70m ski jumping 1984; Thomas Wassberg (Swe) 1980-8

Also three gold medals: Ulrich Wehling (GDR) 1972-80, Nikolay Zimyatov (USSR) 1984-8, Marja-Liisa Hämäläinen (Fin), who also won a bronze at the relay, all in 1984.

Gunde Svan (left) and Sixten Jernberg have been the most successful cross-country skiers at the world championships. The clothing has evolved from Jernberg's 1961 wear (Svan: All-Sport/ Jernberg: Hulton-Deutsch)

WORLD CHAMPIONSHIPS

After Nordic events had been included in the 1924 Olympics, the FIS organised annual competitions until 1937, when for the first time they were given official world championship status. Held annually until 1939, but biennially post-war. Up to 1980 the Olympic Champions were also world champions.

With the advent of new techniques, the men's cross-country races are now at 15km and 30km classical, and at 50km freestyle. From 1989 the 15km is now staged at both freestyle and classical.

Listed for each event are post-war winners additional to those shown earlier as Olympic Champions and those to have won most titles (including Olympics shown by *):

Men's 15km Cross-Country
1950 Karl Erik Åström (Swe)
1954 Veikko Hakulinen (Fin)
1958 Veikko Hakulinen (Fin)
1962 Assar Rönnlund (Swe)
1966 Gjermund Eggen (Nor)
1970 Lars-Göran Åslund (Swe)
1974 Magne Myrmo (Nor)
1978 Josef Luszczek (Pol)
1982 Oddvar Brå (Nor)
1985 Kari Härkänen (Fin)
1987 Marco Albarello (Ita)
1989 Gunde Svan (Swe)
Classical: Harri Kirvesniemi (Fin)
Most wins: 2 Johan Grøttumsbraaten (Nor) 1928*, 1931; Hallgeir Brendan 1952*, 1956*; Veikko Hakulinen; Gunde Svan 1984*.

Men's 30km Cross-Country
1954 Vladimir Kusin (USSR)
1958 Kalevi Hämäläinen (Fin)
1962 Eero Mäntyranta (Fin)
1966 Eero Mäntyranta (Fin)
1970 Vyacheslav Vedenin (USSR)
1974 Thomas Magnusson (Swe)
1978 Sergey Savelyev (USSR)
1982 Thomas Eriksson (Swe)
1985 Gunde Svan (Swe)
1987 Thomas Wassberg (Swe)
1989 Vladimir Smirnov (USSR)
Most wins: 3 Eero Mäntyranta (Fin) also 1964*

Men's 50km Cross-Country
1950 Gunnar Eriksson (Swe)
1954 Vladimir Kusin (USSR)
1958 Sixten Jernberg (Swe)
1962 Sixten Jernberg (Swe)
1966 Gjermund Eggen (Nor)
1970 Kalevi Oikarainen (Fin)
1974 Gerhard Grimmer (GDR)
1978 Sven-Åke Lundbäck (Swe)
1982 Thomas Wassberg (Swe)
1985 Gunde Svan (Swe)
1987 Maurilio De Zolt (Ita)
1989 Gunde Svan (Swe)
Most wins: 4 Sixten Jernberg (Swe) also 1956*, 1964*

Men's 4 x 10km Cross-Country Relay
Wins including Olympics (*):

10 Sweden 1933, 1950, 1958, 1962, 1978, 1987, 1989 and 3*

9 Finland 1934-5, 1938-9, 1954 and 4*

5 Norway 1937, 1966, 1982 tie, 1985 and 1*

5 USSR 1970, 1982 tie and 3*

1 GDR 1974

Men's Ski Jumping – 70 metre hill
1950 Hans Bjornstad (Nor)
1954 Matti Pietikäinen (Fin)
1958 Juhanni Kärkänen (Fin)
1962 Toralf Engan (Nor)
1966 Björn Wirkola (Nor)
1970 Gariy Napalkov (USSR)
1974 Hans-Georg Aschenbach (GDR)
1978 Mathias Buse (GDR)
1982 Armin Kogler (Aut)
1985 Jens Weissflog (GDR)
1987 Jiri Parma (Cs)
1989 Jens Weissflog (GDR)
Most wins: 5 Birger Ruud (Nor) 1931, 1932*, 1935, 1936*, 1937.

Men's Ski Jumping – 90 metre hill
1962 Helmut Recknagel (GDR)
1966 Björn Wirkola (Nor)
1970 Gariy Napalkov (USSR)
1974 Hans-Georg Aschenbach (GDR)
1978 Tapio Räisänen (Fin)
1982 Matti Nykänen (Fin)
1985 Per Bergerud (Nor)
1987 Andreas Felder (Aut)
1989 Jari Puikkonen (Fin)
Most wins: Matti Nykänen 1982, 1984*, 1988*

Men's Team Ski Jumping
1982 Norway
1985 Finland
1987 Finland
1989 Finland

Men's Nordic Combined
1950 Heikki Hasu (Fin)
1954 Sverre Stenersen (Nor)
1958 Paavo Korhonen (Fin)
1962 Arne Larsen (Nor)
1966 Georg Thoma (FRG)
1970 Ladislav Rygel (Cs)
1974 Ulrich Wehling (GDR)
1978 Konrad Winkler (GDR)
1982 Tom Sandberg (Nor)
1985 Hermann Weinbuch (FRG)
1987 Torbjørn Løkken (Nor)
1989 Einar Elden (Nor)

Most wins: 4 Johan Grøttumsbraaten (Nor) 1926, 1928*, 1931, 1932*; 4 Ulrich Wehling with 3*; 3 Oddbjørn Hagen (Nor) 1934-5, 1936*.

Men's Team Nordic Combined
1982 GDR
1985 FR Germany
1987 FR Germany
1989 Norway

Women's 5km Cross-Country
1962 Alevtina Koltschina (USSR)
1966 Alevtina Koltschina (USSR)
1970 Galina Kulakova (USSR)
1974 Galina Kulakova (USSR)
1978 Helena Takalo (Fin)
1982 Berit Aunli (Nor)
1985 Anette Bøe (Nor)
1987 Marjo Matikainen (Fin)
Most wins: 3 Galina Kulakova also 1972*

Women's 10km Cross-Country
1954 Lyubov Kozyryeva (USSR)
1958 Alevtina Koltschina (USSR)
1962 Alevtina Koltschina (USSR)
1966 Klaudia Boyarskikh (USSR)
1970 Alevtina Olyunina (USSR)
1974 Galina Kulakova (USSR)
1978 Zinaida Amosova (USSR)
1982 Berit Aunli (Nor)
1985 Anette Bøe (Nor)
1987 Anne Jahren (Nor)
1989 Yelena Vialbe (USSR)
classical: Marja-Liisa Kirvesniemi (Fin)
Most wins: 2 Kozyryeva also 1956*, Koltschina, Kulakova also 1972*

Women's 15km Cross-Country (Classical)
1989 Marjo Matikainen (Fin)

Women's 20km Cross-Country
1978 Zinaida Amosova (USSR)
1980 Veronika Hesse (GDR)
1982 Raisa Smetanina (USSR)
1985 Grete Nykkelmo (Nor)
1987 Maria-Elena Westin (Swe)

Women's 30km Cross-Country (freestyle)
1989 Yelena Vialbe (USSR)

Women's Cross-Country Relay 3 x 5km 1954-72, 4 x 5km from 1974
Wins including Olympics (*):
12 USSR   1954, 1958, 1962, 1966,

1970, 1974, 1985, 1987 and 4*

3 Finland 1978, 1989 and 1*

1 Sweden, Norway, GDR all *

Most wins at all events (individual/relay)
Men
10 (6/4) Gunde Svan (Swe) 1984-9
8 (5/3) Sixten Jernberg (Swe) 1956-64
7 (4/3) Thomas Wassberg (Swe) 1980-8
6 (6/-) Johan Grøttumsbraaten (Nor) 1926-32
6 (4/2) Veikko Hakulinen (Fin) 1952-60
6 (1/5) Klaes Karppinen (Fin) 1934-9

Women
9 (5/4) Galina Kulakova (USSR) 1970-80
8 (4/4) Alevtina Koltschina (USSR) 1958-66
6 (3/3) Raisa Smetanina (USSR) 1974-85

Most medals: 21 Raisa Smetanina, 17 Galina Kulakova
Most at one Championships: 5 Marjo Matikainen 1988

WORLD SKI-FLYING CHAMPIONSHIPS
Held separately from the Nordic World Championships in 1972 and biennially from 1973. *Winners:*
1972 Walter Steiner (Swi)
1973 Hans-Georg Aschenbach (GDR)
1975 Karel Kodejska (Cs)
1977 Walter Steiner (Swi)
1979 Armin Kogler (Aut)
1981 Jarri Puikkänen (Fin)
1983 Klaus Ostwald (GDR)
1985 Matti Nykänen (Fin)
1988 Gunnar Fidjestoel (Nor)
1990 Dieter Thoma (FRG)

WORLD CUP
Contested over a series of events during the winter season. *Winners:*

Men's Cross-Country World Cup
1979 Oddvar Brå (Nor)
1980 Juha Mieto (Fin)
1981 Aleksandr Zavialov (USSR)
1982 Bill Koch (USA)
1983 Aleksandr Zavialov (USSR)
1984 Gunde Svan (Swe)

1985 Gunde Svan (Swe)
1986 Gunde Svan (Swe)
1987 Torgny Mogren (Swe)
1988 Gunde Svan (Swe)
1989 Gunde Svan (Swe)
1990 Vegard Ulvang (Nor)

Women's Cross-Country World Cup

1979 Galina Kulakova (USSR)
1980 *Not held*
1981 Raisa Smetanina (USSR)
1982 Berit Aunli (Nor)
1983 Marja-Liisa Hämäläinen (Fin)
1984 Marja-Liisa Hämäläinen (Fin)
1985 Anette Bøe (Nor)
1986 Marjo Matikainen (Fin)
1987 Marjo Matikainen (Fin)
1988 Marjo Matikainen (Fin)
1989 Yelena Vialbe (USSR)
1990 Larisa Lasutina (USSR)

Ski Jumping World Cup

1980 Hubert Neupert (Aut)
1981 Armin Kogler (Aut)
1982 Armin Kogler (Aut)
1983 Matti Nykänen (Fin)
1984 Jens Weissflog (GDR)
1985 Matti Nykänen (Fin)
1986 Matti Nykänen (Fin)
1987 Vegaard Opaas (Nor)
1988 Matti Nykänen (Fin)
1989 Jan Boklöv (Swe)
1990 Ari-Pekka Nikkola (Fin)

Nordic Combination World Cup

1983 Espen Andersen (Nor)
1984 Tom Sandberg (Nor)
1985 Geir Andersen (Nor)
1986 Hermann Weinbuch (FRG)
1987 Torbjørn Løkken (Nor)
1988 Klaus Sulzenbacher (Aut)
1989 Trond Arne Bredesen (Nor)

1990 Klaus Sulzenbacher (Aut)

Ski jumping world records

MEN 194m Andreas Felder (Aut) at Planica, Yugoslavia 1987
WOMEN 110m Tiina Lehtola (Fin) at Ruka, Finland 29 Mar 1981

VASALOPP

The world's most famous long distance skiing race is the Vasalopp, contested annually since 1922 over a distance of 90km. This race commemorates the flight in 1521 of Gustav Vasa, later King Gustavus Eriksson, from Mora to Sälen in Sweden (85.8km). He was overtaken by speedy, loyal scouts on skis and persuaded to return and lead a rebellion and become king of Sweden. This famous race is always run on the first Sunday in March from Sälen to Mora, and about 12,000 men and women now contest the Vasalopp annually. The fastest recorded time is 3 hr 48 min 55 sec by Bengt Hassis (Swe) in 1986.
Most wins
8 Nils Karlsson (Swe) 1945-51, 1953
7 Janne Stefansson (Swe) 1962-6, 1968-9
4 Arthur Häggblad (Swe) 1933, 1935, 1937, 1940

WORLDLOPPET CUP

The Vasalopp is the longest of a series of great long distance (42-90km) races staged in various parts of the world which annually form the Worldloppet (11 races scheduled 1990-2). *Champions:*
1979-80 Matti Kuosku (Swe)
1981 Sven-Åke Lundbäck (Swe)
1982-3 Lars Frykberg (Swe)
1984 Bengt Hassis (Swe)
1985 Örjan Blomqvist (Swe)
1986 Konrad Hallenbarter (Swi)
1987-8 Anders Blomqvist (Swe)
1989 Örjan Blomqvist (Swe)

WOMEN (from 1989)
1989 Ellen Holcomb (USA)

Marjo Matikainen won a record five medals at cross-country events at the 1989 women's world championships
(All-Sport/Pascal Rondeau)

SLED DOG RACING

Racing between harnessed dog teams (usually huskies) had been practised by the Eskimos and Indians of the north of the North American continent and in Scandinavia, but the first formal record of a race was in 1908 when the All-Alaskan Sweepstakes were contested on a run of 408 miles (657 km) from Nome to Candle and back.

Sled dog racing was a demonstration sport at the 1932 Olympic Games, with two racas for twelve sled teams, seven dogs to a sled; winner on aggregate was Emile St Goddard (Can).

The International Sled Dog Racing Association was formed in 1966, with most races held at comparatively short distances, such as the World Championship races, first held in 1936 at 18 miles (29 km). Undoubtedly, however, the Iditarod now captures the greatest worldwide interest.

IDITAROD TRAIL

Raced annually since 1973 by dog teams, 1158 miles (1864 km) from Anchorage to Nome, Alaska. The inaugural winner Dick Wilmarth took 20 days 49 minutes and 41 seconds to complete the course, beating 33 other racers. In 1985 Libby Riddles became the first woman ever to win the race and she was followed by Susan Butcher the first to win in three successive years. *Winners – all USA:*

1973 Dick Wilmarth	1981-2 Rick Swenson
1974 Carl Huntington	1983 Rick Mackey
1975 Emmitt Peters	1984 Dean Osmar
1976 Gerald Riley	1985 Libby Riddles
1977 Rick Swenson	1986-8 Susan Butcher
1978 Rick Mackey	1989 Joe Runyan
1979 Rick Swenson	1990 Susan Butcher
1980 Joe May	

Most wins: 4 Rick Swenson, Susan Butcher
Record time: 11 days 1 hr 53min 23 sec Susan Butcher 1990

SNOOKER

Snooker was first played at Jubbulpore, India in 1875 when Colonel Neville Chamberlain (not to be confused wth the Prime Minister of the same name) insulted a fellow officer in the Devonshire Regiment by calling him a 'snooker' after missing an easy shot during a game of Black Pool which they were playing, but with extra coloured balls added. A 'snooker' was the name given to a new recruit at the Woolwich Military Academy at the time. The name stuck and their new game was called snooker. The Billiards Association was formed in 1885 and they recognised the sport's first set of rules in 1900.

EMBASSY WORLD PROFESSIONAL CHAMPIONSHIPS

The first world professional championship was organised in 1926-7 and was held continuously (except for the war years) until 1952 when the professional players and the governing body, the Billiards Association & Control Club, had a disagreement. A match between Horace Lindrum (Aus) and Clark McConachy (NZ) took place in 1952, and was accorded world championship status. The professional players, however, did not recognise this as the official championship and broke away to organise their own championship, known as the professional match-play championship. This ended in 1957 and it was not until its revival, albeit on a challenge basis, in 1964 that the world championship was held again.

It became a knockout event, similar to today's competition, in 1969. Current sponsors Embassy started their association with the championship in 1976 and all finals since 1977 have been played at the Crucible Theatre in Sheffield. Performances in world championships since 1974 have counted towards the ranking system. *Winners:*

1927-40 Joe Davis (Eng)
1946 Joe Davis (Eng)
1947 Walter Donaldson (Sco)
1948-9 Fred Davis (Eng)
1950 Walter Donaldson (Sco)
1951 Fred Davis (Eng)
1952 Horace Lindrum(Aus)
1952-6 # Fred Davis (Eng)
1957 # John Pulman (Eng)
1964-8* John Pulman (Eng)
1969 John Spencer (Eng)
1970 Ray Reardon (Wal)
1971 John Spencer (Eng)
1972 Alex Higgins (NI)
1973-6 Ray Reardon (Wal)
1977 John Spencer (Eng)
1978 Ray Reardon (Wal)
1979 Terry Griffiths (Wal)
1980 Cliff Thorburn (Can)
1981 Steve Davis (Eng)
1982 Alex Higgins (NI)
1983-4 Steve Davis (Eng)
1985 Dennis Taylor (NI)
1986 Joe Johnson (Eng)
1987-9 Steve Davis (Eng)
1990 Stephen Hendry (Sco)

Professional match-play championship
* between 1964 and 1968 John Pulman met, and beat, seven challengers: Fred Davis (3), Rex Williams (2), Freddie Van Rensburg, Eddie Charlton

The champions
Wins, and finishing as runners-up (R-U) or losing in the semi-finals (Semi):

	Win	R-U	Semi
Joe Davis	15	-	-
John Pulman	7	1	2
Ray Reardon	6	1	3
Fred Davis	3	6	6
Steve Davis	6	2	1
John Spencer	3	1	2
Walter Donaldson	2	3	2
Alex Higgins	2	2	3
Horace Lindrum	1	3	2

Cliff Thorburn	1	2	3
Dennis Taylor	1	1	3
Terry Griffiths	1	1	-
Joe Johnson	1	1	-
Stephen Hendry	1	-	1

(Professional match-play records excluded)

OTHER RANKING TOURNAMENTS
Currently scheduled as tournaments at which players can gather world ranking points.

BCE International
Traditionally the first ranking tournament of the season in Britain and the first event to be accorded ranking status after the world championship, in 1982. It started as the Jameson International in 1981, became the Goya Matchroom Trophy in 1985, the BCE International in 1986 and Fidelity Unit Trusts International in 1987-8 before reverting to BCE sponsorship in 1989. *Winners (Ranking from 1982):*
1981 Steve Davis (Eng)
1982 Tony Knowles (Eng)
1983-4 Steve Davis (Eng)
1985 Cliff Thorburn (Can)
1986 Neal Foulds (Eng)
1987-9 Steve Davis (Eng)

Rothman's Grand Prix
Previously known as the Professional Players Tournament, it became the Rothmans Grand Prix in 1984.

Winners (Ranking each year):
1982 Ray Reardon (Wal)
1983 Tony Knowles (Eng)
1984 Dennis Taylor (NI)
1985 Steve Davis (Eng)
1986 Jimmy White (Eng)
1987 Stephen Hendry (Sco)
1988-9 Steve Davis (Eng)

Mercentile Credit Classic
Mercentile succeeded Lada as sponsors of the Classic in 1985. Lada had, in turn, succeeded the event's first sponsors, Wilsons Brewery,in 1981. *Winners (Ranking from 1984):*
1980 (Jan) John Spencer (Eng)
1980 (Dec) Steve Davis (Eng)
1982 Terry Griffiths (Wal)
1984 Steve Davis (Eng)
1985 Willie Thorne (Eng)
1986 Jimmy White (Eng)
1987-8 Steve Davis (Eng)
1989 Doug Mountjoy (Wal)
1990 Steve James (Eng)

United Kingdom Open
First held at Blackpool in 1977 it was known as the United Kingdom Professional Championship until 1984 when it became open to overseas players. All finals since 1978 have been at the Preston Guildhall. Sponsors have been: Super Crystalate 1977, Corals 1978-85, Tennants 1986-88, Stormseal 1989. *Winners (Ranking from 1984):*
1977 Patsy Fagan (Ire)
1978 Doug Mountjoy (Wal)
1979 John Virgo (Eng)
1980-1 Steve Davis (Eng)
1982 Terry Griffiths (Wal)
1983 Alex Higgins (NI)
1984-7 Steve Davis (Eng)
1988 Doug Mountjoy (Wal)
1989 Stephen Hendry (Sco)

British Open
The British Open started as the British Gold Cup in 1980. Between 1981-4 it was known as the Yamaha International, and in 1985 it acquired the sponsorship of ICI Paints, who used their Dulux brand name. The sponsors in 1988 were MIM Britannia, in 1989 Anglian Windows and in 1990 Pearl Assurance. A ranking tournament since 1985. *Winners (Ranking from 1985):*
1980 Alex Higgins (NI)
1981-2 Steve Davis (Eng)
1983 Ray Reardon (Wal)
1984 Steve Davis (Eng)
1985 Silvino Francisco (SAf)
1986 Steve Davis (Eng)
1987 Jimmy White (Eng)
1988 Stephen Hendry (Sco)
1989 Tony Meo (Eng)
1990 Bob Chaperon (Can)

European Open
Held in 1989 at Deauville, and again in 1990 at Lyon, sponsored by Credit Lyonnais. *Winner:* 1989 and 1990 John Parrott (Eng)

Hong Kong Open
Held for the first time in 1989-90 it was the first ranking tournament to be held in the East. *Winner:* 1989 Mike Hallett (Eng)

555 Asian Open
Held for the first time in 1989, when after winning this tournament Stephen Hendry temporarily replaced Steve Davis at the top of the provisional world ranking list.

Dubai Duty Free Classic
Another of the ambitious overseas ranking tournaments launched in the 1989-90 season. *Winner:* 1989 Stephen Hendry (Sco)

Stephen Hendry, snooker's youngest world champion at 21 in 1990
(All-Sport/Pascal Rondeau)

OTHER TOURNAMENTS (NON-RANKING)

Pot Black
BBC Television's Pot Black was undoubtedly responsible for the growth of snooker in the 1970s. Although its single-frame format would not be acceptable in today's tournaments it, nevertheless, took the sport to millions via the television screen. Sadly the programme was discontinued in 1986. *Winners:*
1969 Ray Reardon (Wal)
1970-1 John Spencer (Eng)
1972-3 Eddie Charlton (Aus)
1974-5 Graham Miles (Eng)
1976 John Spencer (Eng)
1977 Perrie Mans (SAf)
1978 Doug Mountjoy (Wal)
1979 Ray Reardon (Wal)
1980 Eddie Charlton (Aus)
1981 Cliff Thorburn (Can)
1982-3 Steve Davis (Eng)
1984 Terry Griffiths (Wal)
1985 Doug Mountjoy (Wal)
1986 Jimmy White (Eng)

Benson & Hedges Masters
One of the most prestigious events after the World Professional Championship, and certainly the leading non-ranking tournament. Entry is by invitation only to 16 leading players. *Winners:*
1975 John Spencer (Eng)
1976 Ray Reardon (Wal)
1977 Doug Mountjoy (Wal)
1978 Alex Higgins (NI)
1979 Perrie Mans (SAf)
1980 Terry Griffiths (Wal)
1981 Alex Higgins (NI)
1982 Steve Davis (Eng)
1983 Cliff Thorburn (Can)
1984 Jimmy White (Eng)
1985-6 Cliff Thorburn (Can)
1987 Dennis Taylor (NI)
1988 Steve Davis (Eng)
1989-90 Stephen Hendry (Sco)

Benson & Hedges Irish Masters
Held at the Goff's Sales Ring in County Kildare, annually the last major championship before the World Championships. *Winners:*
1978 John Spencer (Eng)
1979 Doug Mountjoy (Wal)
1980-2 Terry Griffiths (Wal)

1983-4 Steve Davis (Eng)
1985-6 Jimmy White (Eng)
1987-8 Steve Davis (Eng)
1989 Alex Higgins (NI)
1990 Steve Davis (Eng)

World Cup
State Express sponsored the event from 1979-83. Guinness then had one year, when the event was moved to the second half of the season in 1984-85 before handing over to Car Care Plan in 1986. Since then sponsors have been: Tuborg 1987, Fersina Windows 1988-9, British Car Rental 1990. *Winners:*
1979 Wales
1980 Wales
1981 England
1982 Canada
1983 England
1985 All-Ireland
1986-7 All-Ireland 'A'
1988-9 England
1990 Canada

Scottish Masters
This early-season competition carries no ranking points as the field is limited to invited professionals only. Sponsored by Lang's 1981-7, not held in 1988, new sponsors, Regal, in 1989. *Winners:*
1981 Jimmy White (Eng)
1982-4 Steve Davis (Eng)
1985-6 Cliff Thorburn (Can)
1987 Joe Johnson (Eng)
1989 Stephen Hendry (Sco)

Everest World Match-play Championship
An invitation-only event restricted to the world's top 12 players based on the previous season's performances only. It was the first snooker competition, in 1988, to offer a £100,000 first prize. *Winners:*
1988 Steve Davis (Eng)
1989 Jimmy White (Eng)

Steve Davis's domination of ranking tournaments
Ranking tournament wins in the 1980s:
22 Steve Davis, 5 Ray Reardon, Stephen Hendry; 4 Jimmy White; 2 Tony Knowles, Cliff Thorburn, Dennis Taylor, Doug Mountjoy; 1 John Spencer, Terry Griffiths, Alex Higgins,

Joe Johnson, Neal Foulds, Willie Thorne, Silvino Francisco, Tony Meo, John Parrott, Mike Hallett.

WORLD RANKINGS
The World Professional Billiards & Snooker Association (1989 membership of 128 tournament players) published its first set of world rankings in 1976. A revised list is produced after the World Championship each year. *Top ranked players.*
1976-80 Ray Reardon (Wal)
1981 Cliff Thorburn (Can)
1982 Ray Reardon (Wal)
1983-9 Steve Davis (Eng)
1990 Stephen Hendry (Sco)

IBSF WORLD AMATEUR CHAMPIONSHIP
First held in Calcutta, India in 1963 it was a biennial event until 1984 when it became an annual competition. The championships are run by the International Billiards & Snooker Federation (1989 membership, 35 nations) which became the non-professional game's governing body in 1985. *Winners:*
1963 Gary Owen (Eng)
1966 Gary Owen (Eng)
1968 David Taylor (Eng)
1970 Jonathan Barron (Eng)
1972 Ray Edmonds (Eng)
1974 Ray Edmonds (Eng)
1976 Doug Mountjoy (Wal)
1978 Cliff Wilson (Wal)
1980 Jimmy White (Eng)
1982 Terry Parsons (Wal)
1984 O.B.Agrawal (Ind)
1985-6 Paul Mifsud (Malta)
1987 Darren Morgan (Wal)
1988 James Wattana (Tha)
1989 Ken Doherty (Ire)
Most wins: 2 Gary Owen, Ray Edmonds, Paul Mifsud
Highest break: 135 Brady Gollan (Can) 1988.

BREAKS
In recent years the compiling of a maximum 147 break under official conditions has become more common. The first man to compile a maximum was 'Murt' O'Donoghue(NZ) at Griffiths, New South Wales, Australia in 1934 and the first officially ratified

maximum was by Joe Davis in 1955. The first achieved in major tournaments were by John Spencer at Slough in 1979, when the table had oversized pockets, and by Steve Davis in the 1982 Lada Classic.

The first official maximum break by an amateur was by Geet Sethi (Ind) during his national championships on 21 February 1988.

The highest breaks in ranking tournaments have been:

147 Cliff Thorburn (1983 Embassy World Championship)
147 Willie Thorne (1987 Tennents UK Open)
147 Alain Robidoux (1989 ICI European Open)
145 Doug Mountjoy (1981 Embassy World Championship)
145 Dave Martin (1986 Dulux British Open)
144 Jimmy White (1986 Tennents UK Open)
143 Willie Thorne (1982 Embassy World Championship)
143 Bill Werbeniuk (1985 Embassy World Championship)
143 Rex Williams (1984 Lada Classic)
143 Nigel Gilbert (1989 Mercantile Credit Classic)
143 Darren Morgan (1989 Embassy World Championship – qualifying)

WOMEN'S WORLD OPEN CHAMPIONSHIP

The Women's Billiards Asociation. later the Billiards and Snooker Association, was founded in 1931, running the Women's Amateur Billiards Championship from 1931 and the Women's Amateur Snooker Championship from 1933. The first snooker world championship was held in 1976, in conjunction with the men's event at Middlesbrough. Women's world championships have subsequently been staged annually from 1980, except for 1982. The 1985-6 events being entitled Amateur Championships, the rest Open.

Winners:
1976 Vera Sleby (Eng)
1980 Lesley McIlraith (Aus)
1981 Vera Selby (Eng)
1983 Sue Foster (Eng)
1984 Stacey Hillyard (Eng)
1985-6 Allison Fisher (Eng)
1987 Ann-Marie Farren (Eng)
1988-90 Allison Fisher (Eng)

UK WOMEN'S CHAMPIONSHIPS

The UK Women's Open Championships were first held in 1986 and were won each year 1986-9 by Allison Fisher. The Women's Amateur Snooker Championships were first held in 1933. The most wins is eight by Maureen Baynton (née Barrett) 1954-6, 1961-2, 1964, 1966, 1968 and five by Vera Selby 1972-5, 1979.

SOFTBALL

Softball, invented by George Hancock of the Farragut Boat Club, Chicago in 1887, began as an indoor version of baseball. The game was originally known as 'kitten-ball' or 'mush-ball', the name softball being introduced by Walter Hakanson in 1926. The Amateur Softball Association of America was formed in 1933 and introduced US Championships for both men's and women's teams that year.

Played by nine-a-side teams, the game developed internationally following the formation in 1950 of the International Softball Federation (ISF). There are slow pitch and fast pitch varieties.

WORLD CHAMPIONSHIPS

World championships (fast pitch) for women were introduced in 1965 and for men a year later. Winners: (men's title shared in 1976)

MEN
USA   1966, 1968, 1976 (=), 1980, 1988
Canada   1972, 1976 (=)
New Zealand   1976 (=), 1984
WOMEN
Australia   1965
Japan   1970
USA   1974, 1978, 1986
New Zealand   1982

World Championship tournament records:
MEN
Most runs: 19 Marty Kernaghan(Can) 1988
Best average: .647 Clark Bosch (Can) 1988
Most strikeouts: 99 Kevin Herlihy (NZ) 1972
WOMEN
Most runs: 13 Kathy Elliott (USA) 1974
Best average: .550 Tamara Bryce (Pan) 1978
Most strikeouts: 76 Joan Joyce (USA) 1974

Junior world championships were first held in 1981.
Winners:
MEN 1981 Japan, 1985 NZ, 1989 NZ
WOMEN 1981 Japan, 1985 China, 1987 USA

The first ISF slow pitch championships were held in 1987, when the men's winners were the USA.

EUROPEAN CHAMPIONSHIPS
Women's winners: 1979-84 Netherlands, 1986-7 Italy, 1988 Netherlands

US NATIONAL FAST PITCH CHAMPIONS
Most annual Championships won:
MEN
10 Clearwater (Florida) Bombers 1950, 1954, 1956-7, 1960, 1962-3, 1966, 1968, 1973
7 Raybestos (Franklin) Cardinals, Stratford, Ct. 1955, 1958, 1969-70, 1972, 1976, 1983

WOMEN
20 Raybestos (Hi Ho) Brakettes, Stratford, Ct. 1958-60, 1963, 1966-8, 1971-8, 1980, 1982-3, 1985, 1988
9 Orange (Cal.) Lionettes 1950-2, 1955-6, 1962, 1965, 1969-70

US NATIONAL SLOW PITCH CHAMPIONS
Slow pitch championships were first held in 1953 for men and 1962 for women. *Most championships won:*
MEN
3 Skip Hogan A.C., Pittsburgh 1962, 1964-5; Joe Gatliff Auto Sales, Newport, Ky. 1956-7, 1963
Super slow pitch: 3 Howard's-Western Steer, Denver 1981, 1983-4, Steele's Silver Bullets, Grafton, Ohio 1985-7
WOMEN
5 Dots, Miami, Fla as Converse Dots 1969, Marks Brothers, N.Miami Dots 1974-5, Bob Hoffman Dots 1978-9; 4 Dana Gardens, Cincinnati 1962-4, 1966

SPEEDWAY

Dirt track racing on motorcycles in the United States has been traced back to 1902, and in England the first fully documented motorcycle track races were held at the Portman Road Ground in Ipswich in 1904. Modern speedway has developed from the 'short track' races held at the West Maitland Agricultural Show, New South Wales in 1923. The organiser of that meeting, Johnnie Hoskins brought the sport to Britain, where it evolved with small diameter track racing at Droylsden, Greater Manchester in 1927. The first meeting on a cinder track took place at High Beech, Essex the following year.

WORLD CHAMPIONSHIPS
The first World Championships, for individual riders, was held at Wembley, London in 1936. The team competition was introduced in 1960, and the Pairs in 1970. Two Pairs championships, in 1968 and 1969, had claimed the status of 'World' championship, but the governing body does not recognise these two events for record purposes. The Long Track championship was inaugurated in 1971. Ice Speedway world championships were instituted in 1966 with an individual competition; a team competition was added in 1979. *Winners:*

INDIVIDUAL
1936 Lionel Van Praag (Aus)
1937 Jack Milne (USA)
1938 Bluey Wilkinson (Aus)
1949 Tommy Price (Eng)
1950 Freddie Williams (Wal)
1951-2 Jack Young (Aus)
1953 Freddie Williams (Wal)
1954 Ronnie Moore (NZ)
1955 Peter Craven (Eng)
1956 Ove Fundin (Swe)
1957-8 Barry Briggs (NZ)
1959 Ronnie Moore (NZ)
1960-1 Ove Fundin (Swe)
1962 Peter Craven (Eng)
1963 Ove Fundin (Swe)
1964 Barry Briggs (NZ)
1965 Björn Knutsson (Swe)
1966 Barry Briggs (NZ)
1967 Ove Fundin (Swe)
1968-70 Ivan Mauger (NZ)
1971 Ole Olsen (Den)
1972 Ivan Mauger (NZ)
1973 Jerzy Szczakiel (Pol)
1974 Anders Michanek (Swe)
1975 Ole Olsen (Den)
1976 Peter Collins (Eng)
1977 Ivan Mauger (NZ)
1978 Ole Olsen (Den)
1979 Ivan Mauger (NZ)
1980 Michael Lee (Eng)
1981-2 Bruce Penhall (USA)
1983 Egon Müller (FRG)
1984-5 Erik Gundersen (Den)
1986-7 Hans Nielsen (Den)
1988 Erik Gundersen (Den)
1989 Hans Nielsen (Den)

Most successful riders

Name	1st	2nd	3rd
Ivan Mauger	6	3	1
Ove Fundin	5	3	3
Barry Briggs	4	3	3
Ole Olsen	3	1	2
Hans Nielsen	3	3	-
Erik Gundersen	3	1	-

Most appearances in finals: 18 Barry Briggs 1954-70, 1972

Ove Fundin
(Hulton-Deutsch)

PAIRS
Unofficial 1968-9
1968 Sweden (Ove Fundin/Torbjörn Harryson)
1969 New Zealand (Ivan Mauger/Bob Andrews)
1970 New Zealand (Ronnie Moore/Ivan Mauger)
1971 Poland (Jerzy Szczakiel/Andrzej Wyglenda)
1972 England (Ray Wilson/Terry Betts)
1973 Sweden (Anders Michanek/Tommy Jansson)
1974 Sweden (Anders Michanek/Soren Sjösten)
1975 Sweden (Anders Michanek/Tommy Jansson)
1976 England (John Louis/Malcolm Simmons)
1977 England (Peter Collins/Malcolm Simmons)
1978 England (Malcolm Simmons/Gordon Kennett)
1979 Denmark (Ole Olsen/Hans Nielsen)
1980 England (David Jessup/Peter Collins)
1981 USA (Bruce Penhall/Bobby Schwartz)
1982 USA (Dennis Sigalos/Bobby Schwartz)
1983 England (Kenny Carter/Peter Collins)
1984 England (Peter Collins/Chris Morton)
1985 Denmark (Erik Gundersen/Tommy Knudsen)
1986-9 Denmark (Hans Nielsen/Erik Gundersen)
Most wins (Team): 7 England, 6 Denmark, 4 Sweden
Most wins (Individual): 5 Erik Gundersen, 4 Peter Collins,
Hans Nielsen; 3 Anders Michanek, Malcolm Simmons
Maximum points (then 30/30) were scored by the winners
in 1971 and 1982.

TEAM
Wins
9 Great Britain/England
   GB 1968, 1971-3,
   England 1974-5, 1977, 1980, 1989
8 Denmark 1978, 1981, 1983-8

6 Sweden 1960, 1962-4, 1967, 1970
4 Poland 1961, 1965-6, 1969
1 Australia 1976, New Zealand 1979, USA 1982

Most wins by individual team members:
8 Hans Nielsen (Den) 1978, 1981, 1983-8
7 Erik Gundersen (Den) 1981, 1983-8
6 Ove Fundin (Swe) 1960, 1962-4, 1967, 1970
5 Peter Collins (GB/Eng) 1973-5, 1977, 1980
4 Malcolm Simmons (GB/Eng) 1973-5, 1977
4 Ivan Mauger (GB/NZ) 1968, 1971-2, 1979
4 Rune Sormander (Swe) 1960, 1962-4
4 Björn Knutsson (Swe) 1960, 1962-4
4 Gote Nordin (Swe) 1962-4, 1967

LONG TRACK
1971-2 Ivan Mauger (NZ)
1973 Ole Olsen (Den)
1974-6 Egon Müller (FRG)
1977 Anders Michanek (Swe)
1978 Egon Müller (FRG)
1979 Alois Weisbock (FRG)
1980 Karl Maier (FRG)
1981 Michael Lee (Eng)
1982 Karl Maier (FRG)
1983 Shawn Moran (USA)
1984 Erik Gundersen (Den)
1985 Simon Wigg (Eng)
1986 Erik Gundersen (Den)
1987-8 Karl Maier (FRG)
1989 Simon Wigg (Eng)

Most wins: 4 Egon Müller, Karl Maier
Most placings in first three: 7 Egon Müller and Karl Maier

WORLD ICE SPEEDWAY CHAMPIONSHIP
Individual winners:
1966 Gabdrahman Kadirov (USSR)
1967 Boris Samorodov (USSR)
1968-9 Gabdrahman Kadirov (USSR)
1970 Antonin Svaab (Cs)
1971-3 Gabdrahman Kadirov (USSR)
1974 Milan Spinka (Cs)
1975-8 Sergey Tarabanko (USSR)
1979-80 Anatoliy Bondarenko (USSR)
1981 Vladimir Lyubich (USSR)
1982-3 Sergey Kosakov (USSR)
1984 Erik Stenlund (Swe)
1985 Vladimir Suchov (USSR)
1986-7 Yuriy Ivanov (USSR)
1988 Erik Stenlund (Swe)
1989 Nikolay Nischenko (USSR)

Team wins
10 USSR 1979-84, 1986-9
1 Sweden 1985

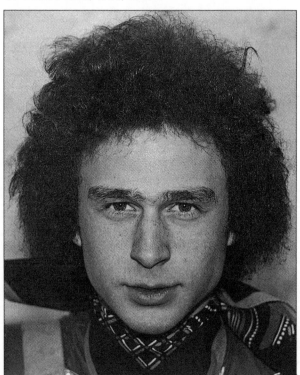

Hans Nielsen (Hulton-Deutsch)

Most world titles overall

	Total	Ind	Pairs	Team	L/T
Erik Gundersen (Den)	17	3	5	7	2
Hans Nielsen (Den)	15	3	4	8	-
Ivan Mauger (NZ)	14	6	2*	4	2
Ove Fundin (Swe)	12	5	1*	6	-
Peter Collins (Eng)	10	1	4	5	-
Ole Olsen (Den)	8	3	1	3	1
Malcolm Simmons (Eng)	7	-	3	4	-
Barry Briggs (NZ)	6	4	-	2	-
Bjorn Knutsson (Swe)	5	1	-	4	-
Tommy Knudsen (Den)	5	-	1	4	-

Including one unofficial pairs win

BRITISH SPEEDWAY LEAGUE

League racing was introduced to Britain in 1929, with a Southern League and a Northern Dirt Track League. The National League was founded in 1932. A second division was added 1936 and there was a third division in 1947-51. From 1957 there was again only one division. A rival league, the Provincial League came into being in 1960 and the two leagues merged in 1965 to form the British League. A second division was created in 1968. The new division was renamed the New National League in 1975, and since 1976 it has been known as the National League.
Winners

National League

1932	Wembley
1933	Belle Vue
1934	Belle Vue
1935	Belle Vue

	Division 1	Division 2
1936	Belle Vue	Southampton
1937	West Ham	Bristol
1938	New Cross	Hackney Wick
1939	Belle Vue	Newcastle
1946	Wembley	-

	Division 1	Division 2	Division 3
1947	Wembley	Middlesbrough	Eastbourne
1948	New Cross	Bristol	Exeter
1949	Wembley	Bristol	Stoke
1950	Wembley	Norwich	Oxford
1951	Wembley	Norwich	Poole
1952	Wembley	Poole	
1953	Wembley	Coventry	
1954	Wimbledon	Bristol	
1955	Southampton	Poole	
1956	Wimbledon	Swindon	
1957	Swindon		
1958	Wimbledon		
1959	Wimbledon		

	National League	Provincial League
1960	Wimbledon	Rayleigh

1961	Wimbledon	Poole
1962	Southampton	Poole
1963	Belle Vue	Wolverhampton
1964	Oxford	Newcastle

British League

1965	West Ham
1966	Halifax
1967	Swindon

	Division 1	Division 2
1968	Coventry	Belle Vue Colts
1969	Poole	Belle Vue Colts
1970	Belle Vue	Canterbury
1971	Belle Vue	Eastbourne
1972	Belle Vue	Crewe
1973	Reading	Boston
1974	Exeter	Birmingham

	British League	New National League
1975	Ipswich	Birmingham

	British League	National League
1976	Ipswich	Newcastle
1977	White City	Eastbourne
1978	Coventry	Canterbury
1979	Coventry	Mildenhall
1980	Reading	Rye House
1981	Cradley Heath	Middlesborough
1982	Belle Vue	Newcastle
1983	Cradley Heath	Newcastle
1984	Ipswich	Long Eaton
1985	Oxford	Ellesmere Port
1986	Oxford	Eastbourne
1987	Coventry	Eastbourne
1988	Coventry	Hackney
1989	Oxford	Poole

Most wins (Div.1): 10 Belle Vue, 8 Wembley, 7 Wimbledon, 5 Coventry

BRITISH LEAGUE RIDERS' CHAMPIONSHIP

1965-70 Barry Briggs (Swindon)
1971 Ivan Mauger (Belle Vue)
1972 Ole Olsen (Wolverhampton)
1973 Ivan Mauger (Exeter)
1974-5 Peter Collins (Belle Vue)
1976-8 Ole Olsen (Coventry)
1979 John Louis (Ipswich)
1980 Les Collins (Leicester)
1981-2 Kenny Carter (Halifax)
1983 Erik Gundersen (Cradley Heath)
1984 Chris Morton (Belle Vue)
1985 Erik Gundersen (Cradley Heath)
1986-7 Hans Nielsen (Oxford)
1988 Jan Pedersen (Cradley Heath)
1989 Shawn Moran (Belle Vue)

SQUASH

Squash rackets developed from rackets, being played with a softer ball, first at Harrow School in 1817 but it was not until the formation of the Squash Rackets Association in 1928 that the game grew in popularity world-wide. The first recognised champion was John Miskey, who won the US Amateur Championship in 1907, the year of formation of the United States Squash Racquets Association. The Women's Squash Rackets Association was founded in 1934, and the International Squash Rackets Federation (ISRF) was founded in 1967. The Women's International Squash Rackets Federation was formed in 1976.

WORLD OPEN CHAMPIONSHIP

The first World Open Championships were held in 1976. There were no championships in 1978 but since 1979 it has been an annual event for men, and a biennial event for women. *Winners:*

Men
1976-7 Geoff Hunt (Aus)
1979-80 Geoff Hunt (Aus)
1981-5 Jahangir Khan (Pak)
1986 Ross Norman (NZ)
1987 Jansher Khan (Pak)
1988 Jahangir Khan (Pak)
1989 Jansher Khan (Pak)
Most wins: 6 Jahangir Khan, 4 Geoff Hunt

Women
1976 Heather McKay (Aus)
1979 Heather McKay (Aus)
1981 Rhonda Thorne (Aus)
1983 Vicki Cardwell (Aus)
1985 Susan Devoy (NZ)
1987 Susan Devoy (NZ)
1989 Martine Le Moignan (UK)
Most wins: 2 Heather McKay, Susan Devoy

Women's Team
Great Britain 1979
Australia 1981, 1983
England 1985, 1987, 1989

WORLD AMATEUR/ISRF CHAMPIONSHIPS

First held in 1967 the championship became known as the ISRF World Championship in 1979 after the sport went open. Held every two years until 1985 *Winners:*
1967 Geoff Hunt (Aus)
1969 Geoff Hunt (Aus)
1971 Geoff Hunt (Aus)
1973 Cameron Nancarrow (Aus)
1975 Kevin Shawcross (Aus)
1977 Maqsood Ahmed (Pak)
1979 Jahangir Khan (Pak)
1981 Steve Bowditch (Aus)
1983 Jahangir Khan (Pak)
1985 Jahangir Khan (Pak)
Most wins: 3 Geoff Hunt, Jahangir Khan

Men's team
Held with the World Amateur/ISRF until 1985 and now separately
Australia 1967, 1969, 1971, 1973, 1989

Jansher Khan (All-Sport)

Pakistan 1977, 1981, 1983, 1985, 1987
Great Britain 1975, 1979

WORLD MASTERS

First held in 1979, it has not been held since 1984.

Men
1979 Qamar Zaman (Pak)
1980 Mohibullah Khan (Pak)
1981-4 Jahangir Khan (Pak)

Women
1984 Lucy Soutter (UK)

WORLD CUP

Held in 1984, when the mens winners were:
Singles: Jahangir Khan (Pak)
Pairs: Ross Thorne & Dean Williams (Aus)

BRITISH OPEN CHAMPIONSHIPS

First held in 1922 for women, and in 1930 for men, the British Open was regarded as the unofficial World Championship until the creation of the World Amateur Championship in 1967.
MEN
1930-1 Don Butcher (UK)
1932-7 Abdelfattah Amr Bey (Egy)
1938 James Dear (UK)
1946-9 Mahmoud Karim (Egy)
1950-5 Hashim Khan (Pak)
1956 Roshan Khan (Pak)
1957 Hashim Khan (Pak)
1958-61 Azam Khan (Pak)
1962 Mohibullah Khan (Pak)
1963-6 Abdelfattah Aboutaleb (Egy)
1967-8 Jonah Barrington (UK)
1969 Geoff Hunt (Aus)
1970-3 Jonah Barrington (UK)
1974 Geoff Hunt (Aus)
1975 Qamar Zaman (Pak)
1976-81 Geoff Hunt (Aus)
1982-90 Jahangir Khan (Pak)

Most wins: 9 Jahangir Khan, 8 Geoff Hunt, 7 Hashim Khan, 6 Abdelfattah Amr Bey, Jonah Barrington

WOMEN
1922 Joyce Cave (UK)
1922 Sylvia Huntsman(UK)

SQUASH 341

1923 Nancy Cave (UK)
1924 Joyce Cave (UK)
1925-6 Cecily Fenwick (UK)
1928 Joyce Cave (UK)
1929-30 Nancy Cave (UK)
1931 Cecily Fenwick (UK)
1932-4 Susan Noel (UK)
1934-9 Margot Lumb (UK)
1947-9 Joan Curry (UK)
1950-8 Janet Morgan (UK)
1960 Sheila Macintosh (UK)
1961 Fran Marshall (UK)
1962-5 Heather Blundell (Aus)
1966-77 Heather McKay
    (née Blundell) (Aus)
1978 Susan Newman (Aus)
1979 Barbara Wall (Aus)
1980-1 Vicki Hoffman (Aus)
1982-3 Vicki Cardwell (née Hoffman)
    (Aus)
1984-90 Susan Devoy (NZ)

Most wins: 16 Heather McKay, 9 Janet Morgan, 7 Susan Devoy, 6 Margot Lumb, 4 Vicki Cardwell (née Hoffman)

BRITISH AMATEUR CHAMPIONSHIP

Instituted in 1922. With the distinction between amateurs and professionals disappearing in 1979, the tournament came to an end.
Winners, all UK unless otherwise stated:
1922-3 Tommy Jameson
1924 Dugald Macpherson
1925 Victor Cazalet
1926 Jimmy Tomkinson
1927 Victor Cazalet
1928 Dugald McPherson
1929-30 Victor Cazalet
1931-3 Abdelfattah Amr Bey (Egy)
1934 Cyril Hamilton
1935-7 Abdelfattah Amr Bey (Egy)
1938 Kenneth Gandar Dower
1946-50 Norman Borrett
1951 Gavin Hildick-Smith
1952-3 Alan Fairbairn
1954 Roy Wilson
1955 Ibrahim Amin (Egy)
1956 Roy Wilson
1957-8 Nigel Broomfield
1959 Ibrahim Amin (Egy)
1960-1 Michael Oddy
1962 Ken Hiscoe (Aus)
1963-5 Aftab Jawaid (Pak)
1966-8 Jonah Barrington

1969 Geoff Hunt (Aus)
1970-1 Gogi Alauddin (Pak)
1972 Cameron Nancarrow (Aus)
1973-4 Mohibullah Khan (Pak)
1975 Kevin Shawcross (Aus)
1976 Bruce Brownlee (NZ)
1977-8 Gamal Awad (Egy)
1979 Jonathan Leslie
Most wins: 6 Abdelfattah Amr Bey, 5 Norman Borrett, 4 Victor Cazalet, 3 Aftab Jawaid

US OPEN
Inaugurated in 1986 as the US Professional (Softball) Championship.

Men
1986 Jahangir Khan (Pak)
1987 Jansher Khan (Pak)
1988 Jahangir Khan (Pak)
1989 Rodney Martin (Aus)

Women
1986 Lisa Opie (UK)
(Discontinued)

NORTH AMERICAN OPEN
Played with a harder ball, standard in North America where the courts are also narrower at 18' 6" to over 21'. First held 1953 after the amalgamation of the US and Canadian Open championships.
Winners:
1953 Henri Salaun (USA)
1954 Diehl Mateer Jr (USA)
1955-6 Hashim Khan (Pak)

1957 Roshan Khan (Pak)
1958 Diehl Mateer Jr (USA)
1959-60 Roshan Khan (Pak)
1961 Azam Khan (Pak)
1962 Hashim Khan (Pak)
1963-5 Mohibullah Khan (Pak)
1966 Ralph Howe (USA)
1967 Mohibullah Khan (Pak)
1968-73 Sharif Khan (Pak)
1974 Victor Niederhoffer (USA)
1975-81 Sharif Khan (Pak)
1982 Mike Desaulniers (Can)
1983 Mark Talbott (USA)
1984-5 Jahangir Khan (Pak)
1986 Mark Talbott (USA)
1987 Ned Edwards (USA)
1988 John Nimick (USA)
1989 Mark Talbott (USA)

Unbeaten Champions
Heather McKay (née Blundell) was unbeaten in women's squash from 1962 to 1980. She won 16 British Open titles and 14 consecutive Australian amateur titles 1960-73 before turning professional. After winning her second world title in 1979 she concentrated on a new sport – racquetball, and became the best player in Canada (to where she had moved in 1975) within a year. When Jahangir Khan lost to Ross Norman in the World Championship final at Toulouse, France, in November 1986, it was his first defeat since April 1981 when Geoff Hunt had beaten him in the final of the British Open.

Susan Devoy, the best woman squash player since the retirement of Heather McKay (All-Sport)

SURFING

Surfing was a traditional Polynesian activity, which has long been popular on suitable coast lines, such as off California, Hawaii or Australia. It was developed as a sporting activity in the 1950s and 1960s.

WORLD AMATEUR CHAMPIONSHIPS

First held in 1964. The only triple winner is Michael Novokov (Aus), who won men's Kneeboard titles in 1982, 1984 and 1986. *Open winners:*

MEN
1964 Bernard Farrelly (Aus)
1965 Felipe Pomar (Per)
1966 Robert 'Nat' Young (USA)
1968 Fred Hemmings (Haw)
1970 Ralph Arness (USA)
1972 Jimmy Blears (Haw)
1980 Mark Scott (Aus)
1982 Tommy Curren (USA)
1984 Scott Farnsworth (USA)
1986 Mark Sainsbury (Aus)
1988 Fabio Gouveia (Bra)

WOMEN
1964 Phyllis O'Donnell (Aus)
1965 Joyce Hoffmann (USA)
1966 Joyce Hoffmann (USA)
1968 Margo Godfrey (USA)
1970 Sharon Weber (Haw)
1972 Sharon Weber (Haw)
1980 Alisa Schwarzstein (USA)
1982 Jenny Gill (Aus)
1984 Janice Aragon (USA)
1986 Connie Nixon (Aus)
1988 Pauline Menczer (Aus)

WORLD PROFESSIONAL CHAMPIONSHIPS

First held in 1970. The Grand Prix circuit, organised by the Association of Surfing Professionals (ASP) since 1976, is held throughout the year. In 1989 there were 28 events in eight countries. The highest points are awarded for the Triple Crown events in Hawaii at the culmination of the tour. *Winners (year given from 1983 to 1987 is the first half of each May-April season):*

MEN
1970 Robert Young (Aus)
1971 Paul Neilsen (Aus)
1972 Jonathan Paarman (SAf)
1973 Ian Cairns (Aus)
1974 Reno Abellira (Haw)
1975 Mark Richards (Aus)
1976 Peter Townend (Aus)
1977 Shaun Tomson (SAf)
1978 Wayne Bartholomew (Aus)
1979 Mark Richards (Aus)
1980 Mark Richards (Aus)
1981 Mark Richards (Aus)
1982 Mark Richards (Aus)
1983 Tom Carroll (Aus)
1984 Tom Carroll (Aus)
1985 Tommy Curren (USA)
1986 Tommy Curren (USA)
1987 Damien Hardman (Aus)
1988 Barton Lynch (Aus)
1989 Martin Potter (UK)

WOMEN
1977 Margo Oberg (Haw)
1978 Lyne Boyer (Haw)
1979 Lyne Boyer (Haw)
1980 Margo Oberg (Haw)
1981 Margo Oberg (Haw)
1982 Debbie Beacham (USA)
1983 Kim Mearig (USA)
1984 Frieda Zamba (USA)
1985 Frieda Zamba (USA)
1986 Frieda Zamba (USA)
1987 Wendy Botha (SAf)
1988 Frieda Zamba (USA)
1989 Wendy Botha (SAf)

SWIMMING

Although swimming may have been popular in ancient times, it was not included in the Greek Olympic Games. The earliest references to swimming races were in Japan in 36 BC. In modern times competitive swimming was popularised in Britian from at least 1791. The first national swimming association was the Metropolitan Swimming Clubs Association, later to become the Amateur Swimming Association (ASA), founded in London in 1869. The first national champion was Tom Morris, who won a mile race in the Thames that year. Swimming has been held at every Olympic Games from the first in 1896. The international governing body for swimming, diving and water polo, the Fédération International de Natation Amateur (FINA) was founded in 1908.

WORLD RECORDS

World records for swimming were first recognised by FINA in 1908. At that time records for distances under 800m could be set in pools of any length over 25 yards, and it was possible for times to be taken in mid-course, and not just at the end of the pool. The range of distances proliferated, but was cut back in 1948 and in 1952, when, also, records for the breast-stroke and butterfly were separated. In 1957 FINA decreed that henceforth only times set in 50m or 55y pools would be accepted and no mid-pool times would be recognised. As short-course times are quicker (by c.0.7 sec. per turn), due to more turns, at some events it took a few years before the old records were surpassed. In 1968 Imperial distances were cut from the lists.

Records are shown for each of the currently recognised events, with the records at 15-year intervals from 1912 to 1987, with all records from then to 1990. Also listed are those swimmers to have set most records at each distance.
records set in short-course pools (up to 1957),
y mark made at the longer equivalent Imperial distance.

MEN

	min:sec	Name	Date

50 metres freestyle

1987	22.33	Matt Biondi (USA)	26 Jun 1986
	22.33	Matt Biondi (USA)	31 Mar 1987
	22.32	Tom Jager (USA)	13 Aug 1987
	22.23	Tom Jager (USA)	27 Mar 1988
	22.18	Peter Williams (SAf)	10 Apr 1988
	22.14	Matt Biondi (USA)	24 Sep 1988
	22.12	Tom Jager (USA)	20 Aug 1989
	21.98	Tom Jager (USA)	24 Mar 1990
	21.81	Tom Jager (USA)	24 Mar 1990
Most	3 Matt Biondi (USA)	22.33 – 22.14 1986-8	
	5 Tom Jager (USA)	22.32 – 21,81 1987-90	

100 metres freestyle

1912	1:01.6	Duke Kahanamoku (USA)	20 Jul 1912
1927	57.4 #	Johnny Weissmuller (USA)	17 Feb 1924
1942	56.4 #	Peter Fick (USA)	11 Feb 1936
1957	54.6	John Devitt (Aus)	28 Jan 1957
1972	51.22	Mark Spitz (USA)	3 Sep 1972
1987	48.74	Matt Biondi (USA)	24 Jun 1986
	48.42	Matt Biondi (USA)	10 Aug 1988
Most	4 Jim Montgomery (USA)	51.12 – 49.99 1975-6	
	4 Matt Biondi (USA)	49.24 – 48.42 1985-8	
	3 Duke Kahanamoku (USA)	61.6 – 60.4 1912-20	
	3 Mark Spitz (USA)	51.9 – 51.22 1970-2	

200 metres freestyle   (y = 220 yards)

1912	2:25.4y#	Charles Daniels (USA)	26 Mar 1909
1927	2:08.0 #	Johnny Weissmuller (USA)	5 Apr 1927
1942	2:07.2 #	Jack Medica (USA)	12 Apr 1935
1957	2:01.5 #	Dick Hanley (USA)	8 Mar 1957
1972	1:52.78	Mark Spitz (USA)	29 Aug 1972
1987	1:47.44	Michael Gross (FRG)	29 Jul 1984
	1:47.25	Duncan Armstrong (Aus)	19 Sep 1988
	1:46.69	Giorgio Lamberti (Ita)	15 Aug 1989
Most	9 Don Schollander (USA)	1:58.8 – 1:54.3 1963-8	
	5 Tsuyoshi Yamanaka (Jap)	2:03.0 – 2:00.4 1958-61	
	4 Mark Spitz (USA)	1:54.3 – 1:52.78 1969-72	
	4 Bruce Furniss (USA)	1:51.41 – 1:50.29 1975-6	
	4 Michael Gross (FRG)	1:48.28 – 1:47.44 1983-4	

400 metres freestyle   (y = 440 yards)

1912	5:21.6 #	Jack Hatfield (UK)	26 Sep 1912
1927	4:50.3 #	Arne Borg (Swe)	11 Sep 1925
1942	4:38.5 #	Bill Smith (USA)	13 May 1941
1957	4:25.9	Murray Rose (Aus)	12 Jan 1957
1972	4:00.11	Kurt Krumpholtz (USA)	4 Aug 1972
1987	3:47.80	Michael Gross (FRG)	27 Jun 1985
	3:47.38	Artur Wojdat (Pol)	25 Mar 1988
	3:46.95	Uwe Dassler (GDR)	23 Sep 1988
Most			
6 Vladimir Salnikov (USSR)		3:51.41 – 3:48.32 1979-83	
4 John Konrads (Aus)		4:25.9y – 4:15.9y 1958-60	
4 Tim Shaw (USA)		3:56.96 – 3:53.31 1974-5	

800 metres freestyle   (y = 880 yards)

1912	11:25.4y	Henry Taylor (UK)	21 Jul 1906
1927	10:22.2y	Johnny Weissmuller (USA)	27 Jul 1927
1942	9:50.9	Bill Smith (USA)	24 Jul 1941
1957	9:19.2y	George Breen (USA)	27 Oct 1956

Matt Biondi celebrates in 1988, when he won five gold medals, a silver and a bronze at the 1988 Olympics (All-Sport)

| 1972 | 8:23.8 | Brad Cooper (Aus) | 12 Jan 1972 |
| 1987 | 7:50.64 | Vladimir Salnikov (USSR) | 4 Jul 1986 |

Most
7 Steve Holland (Aus)	8:17.6 – 8:02.91 1973-6
4 Shozo Makino (Jap)	10:16.6 – 9:55.8 1931-5
4 Vladimir Salnikov (USSR)	7:56.43 – 7:50.64 1979-86

1500 metres freestyle

1912	22:00.0	George Hodgson (Can)	10 Jul 1912
1927	19:07.2	Arne Borg (Swe)	2 Sep 1927
1942	18:58.8	Tomikatsu Amano (Jap)	10 Aug 1938
1957	17:52.9	George Breen (USA)	5 Dec 1956
1972	15:52.58	Mike Burton (USA)	4 Sep 1972
1987	14:54.76	Vladimir Salnikov (USSR)	22 Feb 1983
	14:53.6	Glen Housman (Aus)	13 Dec 1989

(unratified due to timing malfunction)

Most
5 Arne Borg (Swe)	21:35.3 – 19:07.2 1923-7
5 Mike Burton (USA)	16:41.6 – 15:52.58 1966-72
4 Steve Holland (Aus)	15:37.8 – 15:10.59 1973-6

4 x 100 metres freestyle

1942	3:50.8 #	Yale University (USA)	18 Mar 1942
1957	3:46.8	Japan	6 Aug 1955
1972	3:26.42	USA	28 Aug 1972
1987	3:17.08	USA	17 Aug 1985
	3:16.53	USA	23 Sep 1988

(Chris Jacobs, Troy Dalbey, Tom Jager, Matt Biondi)

4 x 200 metres freestyle relay

1942	8:51.5	Japan	11 Aug 1936
1957	8:23.6	Australia	3 Dec 1956
1972	7:35.78	USA	31 Aug 1972
1987	7:15.69	USA	30 Jul 1984
	7:12.51	USA	21 Sep 1988

(Troy Dalbey, Matt Cetlinski, Doug Gjertsen, Matt Biondi)

100 metres backstroke

1912	1:15.6 #	Otto Fahr (Ger)	29 May 1912
1927	1:10.2 #	P.A.House (USA)	22 Mar 1927
1942	1:04.8 #	Adolph Kiefer (USA)	18 Jan 1936
1957	1:02.2	David Theile (Aus)	6 Dec 1956
1972	56.30	Roland Matthes (GDR)	4 Sep 1972
1987	55.19	Rick Carey (USA)	21 Aug 1983
	55.17	Igor Polyanskiy (USSR)	15 Mar 1988
	55.16	Igor Polyanskiy (USSR)	16 Mar 1988
	55.00	Igor Polyanskiy (USSR)	16 Jul 1988
	54.95	David Berkoff (USA)	12 Aug 1988
	54.91	David Berkoff (USA)	13 Aug 1988
	54.51	David Berkoff (USA)	24 Sep 1988

Most
8 Roland Matthes (GDR)	58.4 – 56.30 1967-72
4 Warren Kealoha (USA)	1:14.8 – 1:11.4 # 1920-6
4 Adolph Kiefer (USA)	1:07.0 #- 1:04.8 # 1935-6

200 metres backstroke

1912	2:48.4 #	Otto Fahr (Ger)	3 Apr 1912
1927	2:38.8 #	Walter Laufer (USA)	13 Jul 1926
1942	2:23.0 #	Adolph Kiefer (USA)	23 May 1941
1957	2:18.3 #	Gilbert Bozon (Fra)	26 Jun 1953

| 1972 | 2:02.82 | Roland Matthes (GDR) | 10 Jul 1972 |
| 1987 | 1:58.14 | Igor Polyanskiy (USSR) | 3 Mar 1985 |

Most
| 9 Roland Matthes (GDR) | 2:07.9 – 2:01.87 1967-73 |
| 4 Tom Stock (USA) | 2:16.0 – 2:10.9 1960-2 |

100 metres breaststroke   (* with butterfly stroke)

1912	1:17.8	Walther Bathe (Ger)	18 Dec 1910
1927	1:14.0 #	Walter Spence (USA)	28 Oct 1927
1942	1:07.3*#	Dick Hough (USA)	15 Apr 1939
1957	1:11.5	Vladimir Minashkin (USSR)	15 Sep 1957
1972	1:04.94	Nobutaka Taguchi (Jap)	30 Aug 1972
1987	1:01.65	Steven Lundquist (USA)	29 Jul 1984
	1:01.49	Adrian Moorhouse (UK)	15 Aug 1989
	1:01.49	Adrian Moorhouse (UK)	25 Jan 1990

Most
7 John Hencken (USA)	1:05.68 – 1:03.11 1972-6
6 Chet Jastremski (USA)	1:11.1 – 1:07.5 1961
5 Leonid Meshkov (USSR)	
	1:07.2*#- 1:06.5*# 1949-51
5 Steven Lundquist (USA)	1:02.62 – 1:01.65 1982-4

200 metres breaststroke   (* with butterfly stroke)

(u under-water swimming, permitted at breaststroke until 1957)

1912	3:00.8 #	Felicien Coubert (Bel)	2 Oct 1910
1927	2:48.0 #	Erich Rademacher (Ger)	11 Mar 1927
1942	2:36.8*#	Alfred Nakache (Fra)	6 Jul 1941
1957	2:31.0u#	Masaru Furukawa (Jap)	1 Oct 1955
1972	2:21.55	John Hencken (USA)	2 Sep 1972
1987	2:13.34	Victor Davis (Can)	2 Aug 1984
	2:12.90	Mike Barrowman (USA)	3 Aug 1989
	2:12.90	Nick Gillingham (UK)	18 Aug 1989
	2:12.89	Mike Barrowman (USA)	20 Aug 1989

Most
6 Joe Verdeur (USA)	2:35.6*#- 2:28.3*# 1946-50
5 John Hencken (USA)	2:22.79 – 2:18.21 1972-4
4 Masaru Furukawa (Jap)	
	2:36.6u#- 2:31.0u# 1954-5

100 metres butterfly

1957	1:01.0	Takashi Ishimoto (Jap)	14 Sep 1957
1972	54.27	Mark Spitz (USA)	31 Aug 1972
1987	52.84	Pablo Morales (USA)	24 Jun 1986

Most
7 Mark Spitz (USA)	56.3 – 54.27 1967-72
6 György Tumpek (Hun)	1:04.3# – 1:03.4 1953-7
5 Takashi Ishimoto (Jap)	1:01.5 – 1:00.1 1957-8

200 metres butterfly   (y = 220 yards)

1957	2:16.7 #	Bill Yorzyk (USA)	14 Apr 1956
1972	2:00.70	Mark Spitz (USA)	28 Aug 1972
1987	1:56.24	Michael Gross (FRG)	28 Jun 1986

Most
9 Mark Spitz (USA)	2:06.4 – 2:00.70 1967-72
6 Mike Troy (USA)	2:19.0 – 2:12.8 1959-60
5 Kevin Berry (Aus)	2:12.5y – 2:06.6 1962-4

200 metres individual medley

1972	2:07.17	Gunnar Larsson (Swe)	3 Sep 1972
1987	2:01.42	Alex Baumann (Can)	4 Aug 1984
	2:01.42	Alex Baumann (Can)	4 Mar 1986
	2:00.56	Tamás Darnyi (Hun)	23 Aug 1987

	2:00.17	Tamás Darnyi (Hun)	25 Sep 1988
	2:00.11	David Wharton (USA)	20 Aug 1989
Most	4 Alex Baumann (Can) 2:02.78 – 2:01.42 1981-6		

400 metres individual medley   (y = 440 yards)

1957	5:08.3 #	Vladimir Strouyanov (USSR)	17 Mar 1957
1972	4:30.81	Gary Hall (USA)	3 Aug 1972
1987	4:17.41	Alex Baumann (Can)	30 Jul 1984
	4:16.12	David Wharton (USA)	14 Aug 1987
	4:15.42	Tamás Darnyi (Hun)	19 Aug 1987
	4:14.75	Tamás Darnyi (Hun)	21 Sep 1988
Most	5 Gary Hall (USA) 4:43.3 – 4:30.81 1968-72		
	4 Ted Stickles (USA) 5:04.3 – 4:51.0y 1961-2		

4 x 100 metres medley relay

1957	4:14.8 #	USSR	14 Aug 1956
1972	3:48.16	USA	4 Sep 1972
1987	3:38.28	USA	18 Aug 1985
	3:36.93	USA	25 Sep 1988

(David Berkoff, Richard Schroeder, Matt Biondi, Chris Jacobs)

WOMEN
50 metres freestyle

1987	25.28	Tamara Costache (Rom)	23 Aug 1986
	24.98	Yang Wenyi (Chn)	11 Apr 1988
Most	4 Tamara Costache (Rom) 25.50 – 25.28 1986		

100 metres freestyle

1912	1:18.8	Fanny Durack (Aus)	21 Jul 1912
1927	1:10.0 #	Ethel Lackie (USA)	28 Jan 1926
1942	1:04.6 #	Willy den Ouden (Hol)	27 Feb 1936
1957	1:02.0	Dawn Fraser (Aus)	1 Dec 1956
1972	58.5	Shane Gould (Aus)	8 Jan 1972
1987	54.73	Kristin Otto (GDR)	19 Aug 1986
Most	11 Dawn Fraser (Aus) 1:04.5 – 58.9 1956-64		
	10 Kornelia Ender (GDR) 58.25 – 55.65 1973-6		

200 metres freestyle   (y = 220 yards)

1927	2:40.6y#	Martha Norelius (USA)	28 Feb 1926
1942	2:21.7 #	Ragnhild Hveger (Den)	11 Sep 1938
1957	2:18.5	Lorraine Crapp (Aus)	20 Oct 1956
1972	2:03.56	Shane Gould (Aus)	1 Sep 1972
1987	1:57.55	Heike Friedrich (GDR)	18 Jun 1986
Most	4 Dawn Fraser (Aus) 2:20.7 – 2:11.6y 1956-60		
	4 Kornelia Ender (GDR) 2:03.22 – 1:59.26 1974-6		

400 metres freestyle   (y = 440 yards)

1927	5:51.4y	Martha Norelius (USA)	23 Jan 1927
1942	5:00.1 #	Ragnhild Hveger (Den)	15 Sep 1940
1957	4:47.2	Lorraine Crapp (Aus)	20 Oct 1956
1972	4:19.04	Shane Gould (Aus)	30 Aug 1972
1987	4:06.28	Tracey Wickham (Aus)	24 Aug 1978
	4:05.45	Janet Evans (USA)	20 Dec 1987
	4:03.85	Janet Evans (USA)	22 Sep 1988
Most	8 Ragnhild Hveger (Den)5:14.2# – 5:00.1# 1937-40		
	5 Debbie Meyer (USA) 4:32.6 – 4:24.3 1967-70		
	4 Martha Norelius (USA)5:51.4y – 5:39.2# 1927-8		

800 metres freestyle   (y = 880 yards)

1927	12:17.8y#	Martha Norelius (USA)	31 Jul 1927
1942	10:52.5	Ragnhild Hveger (Den)	13 Aug 1941
1957	10:27.3	Mary Kok (Hol)	16 Feb 1957
1972	8:53.68	Keena Rothhammer (USA)	3 Sep 1972
1987	8:24.62	Tracey Wickham (Aus)	5 Aug 1978
	8:22.44	Janet Evans (USA)	28 Jul 1987
	8:19.53	Anke Möhring (GDR)	22 Aug 1987
	8:17.12	Janet Evans (USA)	22 Mar 1988
	8:16.22	Janet Evans (USA)	20 Aug 1989
Most	5 Debbie Meyer (USA) 9:35.8 – 9:10.4 1967-8		
	4 Ilsa Konrads (Aus) 10:17.7y -10:11.4y 1958-9		
	4 Petra Thümer (GDR) 8:40.68 – 8:35.04 1976-7		

1500 metres freestyle

1927	23:44.6	Martha Norelius (USA)	28 Jul 1927
1942	20:57.0	Ragnhild Hveger (Den)	20 Aug 1941
1957	20:03.1	Jans Koster (Hol)	27 Jul 1957
1972	17:00.6	Shane Gould (Aus)	12 Dec 1971
1987	16:04.49	Kim Lineham (USA)	19 Aug 1979
	16:00.73	Janet Evans (USA)	1 Aug 1987
	15:52.10	Janet Evans (USA)	26 Mar 1988
Most	5 Jenny Turrall (Aus) 16:49.9 – 16:33.94 1973-4		
	4 Debbie Meyer (USA) 18:11.1 – 17:19.9 1967-9		

4 x 100 metres freestyle

1942	4:27.6	Denmark	7 Aug 1938
1957	4:17.1	Australia	6 Dec 1956
1972	3:55.19	USA	30 Aug 1972
1987	3:40.57	GDR	19 Aug 1986

(Kristin Otto, Manuela Stellmach, Sabina Schulz, Heike Friedrich)

4 x 200 metres freestyle relay

1987	7:59.33	GDR	17 Aug 1986
	7:55.47	GDR	18 Aug 1987

(Manuela Stellmach, Astrid Strauss, Anke Möhring, Heike Friedrich)

100 metres backstroke

1927	1:22.0 #	Willy van den Turk (Hol)	10 Jul 1927
1942	1:10.9 #	Cor Kint (Hol)	22 Sep 1939
1957	1:12.9	Judy Grinham (UK)	5 Dec 1956
1972	1:05.6	Karen Muir (SAf)	6 Jul 1969
1987	1:00.59	Ina Kleber (GDR)	24 Aug 1984
Most	9 Ulrike Richter (GDR) 1:05.39 – 1:01.51 1973-6		
	4 Ria van Velsen (Hol) 1:12.3 – 1:10.9 1958-60		
	4 Lynn Burke (USA) 1:10.1 – 1:09.0 1960		

200 metres backstroke   (y = 220 yards)

1927	3:03.8 #	Sybil Bauer (USA)	9 Feb 1924
1942	2:38.8 #	Cor Kint (Hol)	29 Nov 1939
1957	2:38.5y	Lenie de Nijs (Hol)	17 May 1957
1972	2:19.19	Melissa Belote (USA)	4 Sep 1972
1987	2:08.60	Betsy Mitchell (USA)	27 Jun 1986
Most	10 Satoko Tanaka (Jap) 2:37.1 – 2:28.2 1959-63		
	4 Karen Muir (SAf) 2:27.1 – 2:23.8 1966-8		

100 metres breaststroke (* with butterfly stroke)

1927	1:28.8 #	Agnes Geraghty (USA)	13 Feb 1926
1942	1:20.2 #	Johanna Holzner (Ger)	13 Mar 1936
1957	1:16.9*#	Eva Szekely (Hun)	9 May 1951
1972	1:13.58	Cathy Carr (USA)	2 Sep 1972
1987	1:08.11	Sylvia Gerasch (GDR)	21 Aug 1986
	1:07.91	Silke Hörner (GDR)	21 Aug 1987
Most	6 Ute Geweniger (GDR) 1:10.20 – 1:08.51 1980-3		
	5 Catie Ball (USA)	1:15.6 – 1:14.2 1966-8	

200 metres breaststroke (y = 220 yards)

1927	3:16.6	Else Jacobsen (Den)	20 Aug 1927
1942	2:56.0 #	Maria Lenk (Bra)	8 Nov 1939
1957	2:46.4 #	Ada den Haan (Hol)	13 Nov 1956
1972	2:38.5	Catie Ball (USA)	26 Aug 1968
1987	2:27.40	Silke Hörner (GDR)	18 Aug 1986
	2:27.27	Allison Higson (Can)	29 May 1988
	2:26.71	Silke Hörner (GDR)	21 Sep 1988
Most	4 Ada den Haan (Hol)	2:46.4# – 2:51.3 1956-7	
	4 Galina Prozumenshikova (USSR)		
		2:47.7y-2:40.8 1964-6	

100 metres butterfly

1957	1:10.5	Atie Voorbij (Hol)	4 Aug 1957
1972	1:03.34	Mayumi Aoki (Jap)	1 Sep 1972
1987	57.93	Mary T.Meagher (USA)	16 Aug 1981
Most	6 Atie Voorbij (Hol)	1:13.7# – 1:10.5 1955-7	
	6 Kornelia Ender (GDR) 1:03.05 – 1:00.13 1973-6		

200 metres butterfly (y = 220 yards)

1957	2:38.1 #	Tineke Lagerberg (Hol)	19 Mar 1957
1972	2:15.57	Karen Moe (USA)	4 Sep 1972
1987	2:05.96	Mary T.Meagher (USA)	13 Aug 1981
Most	5 Rosemarie Kother (GDR)2:15.45 – 2:11.22 1973-6		
	5 Mary T.Meagher (USA)2:09.77 – 2:05.96 1979-81		
	4 Ada Kok (Hol)	2:25.8 – 2:21.0y 1965-7	
	4 Karen Moe (USA)	2:20.7 – 2:15.27 1970-2	

200 metres individual medley

1972	2:23.07	Shane Gould (Aus)	28 Aug 1972
1987	2:11.73	Ute Geweniger (GDR)	4 Jul 1981
Most	6 Ulrike Tauber (GDR)	2:18.97 – 2:15.85 1974-7	
	5 Claudia Kolb (USA)	2:27.8 – 2:23.5 1966-8	

400 metres individual medley

1957	5:38.9 #	Mary Kok (Hol)	2 Dec 1956
1972	5:02.97	Gail Neall (USA)	31 Aug 1972
1987	4:36.10	Petra Schneider (GDR)	1 Aug 1982
Most	6 Donna de Varona (USA)5:36.5 – 5:14.9 1960-4		
	5 Claudia Kolb (USA)	5:11.7 – 5:04.7 1967-8	
	4 Sylvia Ruuska (USSR)	5:46.6 – 5:40.2y 1958-9	
	4 Petra Schneider (GDR)4:39.96 – 4:36.10 1980-2		

4 x 100 metres medley relay

1957	4:53.1 #	Netherlands	8 Dec 1956
1972	4:20.75	USA	3 Sep 1972
1987	4:03.69	GDR	24 Aug 1984

(Ina Kleber, Sylvia Gerasch, Ines Geissler, Birgit Meineke)

Petra Schneider, whose world record for 400m individual medley remains the best eight years on (All-Sport)

Most world records at individual events

Including now obsolete distances the most world records set is:

MEN 32 Arne Borg (Swe) 1921-9; WOMEN 42 Ragnhild Hveger (Den) 1936-42.

The most for the currently recognised events:

(fr = freestyle, ba = backstroke, br = breaststroke, bu = butterfly, im = individual medley)

MEN

26	Mark Spitz (USA) 3 100fr, 4 200fr, 3 400fr, 7 100bu, 9 200bu 1967-72
17	Roland Matthes (GDR) 8 100ba, 9 200ba 1967-73
13	Vladimir Salnikov (USSR) 6 400fr, 4 800fr, 3 1500fr
12	John Konrads (Aus) 3 200fr, 4 400fr, 3 800fr, 2 1500fr
12	Don Schollander (USA) 9 200fr, 3 400fr 1963-8
12	John Hencken (USA) 7 100br, 5 200br 1972-6
10	Arne Borg (Swe) 3 400fr, 2 800fr, 5 1500fr 1922-7
10	Gary Hall (USA) 1 200ba, 1 200bu, 3 200im, 5 400im 1968-72
10	Steve Holland (Aus) 6 800fr, 4 1500fr 1973-6
10	Michael Gross (FRG) 4 200fr, 1 400fr, 1 100bu, 4 200bu 1983-6

WOMEN

23	Kornelia Ender (GDR) 10 100fr, 4 200fr, 1 100ba, 6 100bu, 2 200im 1973-6
15	Ragnhild Hveger (Den) 1 200fr, 8 400fr, 2 800fr, 3 1500fr, 1 200ba 1937-41
15	Dawn Fraser (Aus) 11 100fr, 4 200fr 1956-64
15	Debbie Meyer (USA) 1 200fr, 5 400fr, 5 800fr, 4 1500fr 1967-70
11	Claudia Kolb (USA) 5 200im, 5 400im, 1 100br 1964-8
11	Shane Gould (Aus) 2 100fr, 3 200fr, 2 400fr, 1 800fr, 2 1500fr, 1 200im 1971-2
11	Ulrike Richter (GDR) 9 100ba, 2 200ba 1973-6

Helene Madison (USA) 1930-2 and Shane Gould (Aus) 1971-2 set records at each freestyle distance: 100m, 200m, 400m, 800m and 1500m.

OLYMPIC GAMES

Olympic records are indicated by OR, or as listed at the end of each event if not set in a final. Events on the current programme are listed, followed by discontinued events.

MEN
50 metres freestyle
1988 Matt Biondi (USA) 22.14 OR

100 metres freestyle
1896 Alfréd Hajós (Hun) 1:22.2
1904 Zoltán von Halmay (Hun)
    1:02.08 (100y)
1906 Charles Daniels (USA) 1:13.4
1908 Charles Daniels (USA) 1:05.6
1912 Duke Kahanamoku (USA)
    1:03.4
1920 Duke Kahanamoku (USA)
    1:01.4
1924 Johnny Weissmuller (USA) 59.0
1928 Johnny Weissmuller (USA) 58.6
1932 Yasuji Miyazaki (Jap) 58.2
1936 Ferenc Csik (Hun) 57.6
1948 Walter Ris (USA) 57.3
1952 Clarke Scholes (USA) 57.4
1956 Jon Henricks (Aus) 55.4
1960 John Devitt (Aus) 55.2
1964 Don Schollander (USA) 53.4
1968 Mike Wenden (Aus) 52.2
1972 Mark Spitz (USA) 51.22
1976 Jim Montgomery (USA) 49.99
1980 Jörg Woithe (GDR) 50.40
1984 Rowdy Gaines (USA) 49.80
1988 Matt Biondi (USA) 48.63 OR

200 metres freestyle
1900 Frederick Lane (Aus) 2:25.2
1904 Charles Daniels (USA) 2:44.2
    (220y)
1968 Mike Wenden (Aus) 1:55.2
1972 Mark Spitz (USA) 1:52.78
1976 Bruce Furniss (USA) 1:50.29
1980 Sergey Koplyakov (USSR)
    1:49.81
1984 Michael Gross (FRG) 1:47.44
1988 Duncan Armstrong (Aus)
    1:47.25 OR

400 metres freestyle
1896 Paul Neumann (Aut) 8:12.6
    (500m)
1904 Charles Daniels (USA) 6:16.2
    (440y)
1906 Otto Scheff (Aut) 6:23.8
1908 Henry Taylor (UK) 5:36.8
1912 George Hodgson (Can) 5:24.4
1920 Norman Ross (USA) 5:26.8
1924 Johnny Weissmuller (USA)
    5:04.2
1928 Albeto Zorilla (Arg) 5:01.6
1932 Buster Crabbe (USA) 4:48.4
1936 Jack Medica (USA) 4:44.5
1948 William Smith (USA) 4:41.0

1952 Jean Boiteux (Fra) 4:30.7
1956 Murray Rose (Aus) 4:27.3
1960 Murray Rose (Aus) 4:18.3
1964 Don Schollander (USA) 4:12.2
1968 Mike Burton (USA) 4:09.0
1972 Brad Cooper (Aus) 4:00.27
1976 Brian Goodell (USA) 3:51.93
1980 Vladimir Salnikov (USSR)
    3:51.31
1984 George DiCarlo (USA) 3:51.23
1988 Uwe Dassler (GDR) 3:46.95 OR

1500 metres freestyle
1896 Alfréd Hajós (Hun) 18:22.2
    (1200m)
1900 John Jarvis (UK) 13:40.2
    (1000m)
1904 Emil Rausch (Ger) 27:18.2 (1
    Mile)
1906 Henry Taylor (UK) 28:28.0
1908 Henry Taylor (UK) 22:48.4
1912 George Hodgson (Can) 22:00.0
1920 Norman Ross (USA) 22:23.2
1924 Andrew Charlton (Aus) 20:06.6
1928 Arne Borg (Swe) 19:51.8
1932 Kusuo Kitamura (Jap) 19:12.4
1936 Noboru Terada (Jap) 19:13.7
1948 James McLane (USA) 19:18.5
1952 Ford Konno (USA) 18:30.0
1956 Murray Rose (Aus) 17:58.9
1960 John Konrads (Aus) 17:19.6
1964 Bob Windle (Aus) 17:01.7
1968 Mike Burton (USA) 16:38.9
1972 Mike Burton (USA) 15:52.58
1976 Brian Goodell (USA) 15:02.40
1980 Vladimir Salnikov (USSR)
    14:58.27 OR
1984 Michael O'Brien (USA) 15:05.20
1988 Vladimir Salnikov (USSR)
    15:00.40

100 metres backstroke
1904 Walter Brack (Ger) 1:16.8 (100y)
1908 Arno Bieberstein (Ger) 1:24.6
1912 Harry Hebner (USA) 1:21.2
1920 Warren Kealoha (USA) 1:15.2
1924 Warren Kealoha (USA) 1:13.2
1928 George Kojac (USA) 1:08.2
1932 Masaji Kiyokawa (Jap) 1:08.6
1936 Adolf Kiefer (USA) 1:05.9
1948 Allen Stack (USA) 1:06.4
1952 Yoshinobu Oyakawa (USA)
    1:05.4
1956 David Theile (Aus) 1:02.2
1960 David Theile (Aus) 1:01.9
1968 Roland Matthes (GDR) 58.7
1972 Roland Matthes (GDR) 56.58
1976 John Naber (USA) 55.49

1980 Bengt Baron (Swe) 56.53
1984 Rick Carey (USA) 55.79
1988 Daichi Suzuki (Jap) 55.05
OR: David Berkoff (USA) 54.51 (1988)

200 metres backstroke
1900 Ernst Hoppenberg (Ger) 2:47.0
1964 Jed Graef (USA) 2:10.3
1968 Roland Matthes (GDR) 2:09.6
1972 Roland Matthes (GDR) 2.02.82
1976 John Naber (USA) 1:59.19
1980 Sándor Wladár (Hun) 2:01.93
1984 Rick Carey (USA) 2:00.23
1988 Igor Polyanskiy (USSR) 1:59.37
OR Rick Carey (USA) 1:58.99 (1984)

100 metres breaststroke
1968 Don McKenzie (USA) 1:07.7
1972 Nobutaka Taguchi (Jap) 1:04.94
1976 John Hencken (USA) 1:03.11
1980 Duncan Goodhew (UK) 1:03.34
1984 Steve Lundquist (USA) 1:01.65
    OR
1988 Adrian Moorhouse (UK) 1:02.04

*Adrian Moorhouse, Olympic
champion and world record holder
for 100m breaststroke* (All-Sport)

200 metres breaststroke
1908 Frederick Holman (UK) 3:09.2
1912 Walter Bathe (Ger) 3:01.8
1920 Håken Malmroth (Swe) 3:04.4
1924 Robert Skelton (USA) 2:56.5
1928 Yoshiyuki Tsuruta (Jap) 2:48.8
1932 Yoshiyuki Tsuruta (Jap) 2:45.4
1936 Tetsuo Hamuro (Jap) 2:41.5
1948 Joseph Verdeur (USA) 2:39.3
1952 John Davies (Aus) 2:34.4
1956 Masaru Furukawa (Jap) 2:34.7
1960 William Mulliken (USA) 2:37.4
1964 Ian O'Brien (Aus) 2:27.8
1968 Felipe Munoz (Mex) 2:28.7
1972 John Hencken (USA) 2:21.55
1976 David Wilkie (UK) 2:15.11
1980 Robertas Zhulpa (USSR) 2:15.85
1984 Victor Davis (Can) 2:13.34 OR
1988 József Szabó (Hun) 2:13.52

100 metres butterfly
1968 Doug Russell (USA) 55.9
1972 Mark Spitz (USA) 54.27
1976 Matt Vogel (USA) 54.35
1980 Pär Arvidsson (Swe) 54.92
1984 Michael Gross (FRG) 53.08
1988 Anthony Nesty (Sur) 53.00 OR

200 metres butterfly
1956 William Yorzyk (USA) 2:19.3
1960 Mike Troy (USA) 2:12.8
1964 Kevin Berry (Aus) 2:06.6
1968 Carl Robie (USA) 2:08.7
1972 Mark Spitz (USA) 2:00.70
1976 Mike Bruner (USA) 1:59.23
1980 Sergey Fesenko (USSR) 1:59.76
1984 Jon Sieben (Aus) 1:57.04
1988 Michael Gross (FRG) 1:56.94 OR

200 metres individual medley
1968 Charles Hickcox (USA) 2:12.0
1972 Gunnar Larsson (Swe) 2:07.17
1984 Alex Baumann (Can) 2:01.42
1988 Tamás Darnyi (Hun) 2:00.17 OR

400 metres individual medley
1964 Richard Roth (USA) 4:45.4
1968 Charles Hickcox (USA) 4:48.4
1972 Gunnar Larsson (Swe) 4:31.98
1976 Rod Strachan (USA) 4:23.68
1980 Aleksandr Sidorenko (USSR)
    4:22.89
1984 Alex Baumann (Can) 4:17.41
1988 Tamás Darnyi (Hun) 4:14.75 OR

4x100 metres freestyle relay
1964 USA 3:33.2
1968 USA 3:31.7
1972 USA 3:26.42
1984 USA 3:19.03
1988 USA 3:16.53 OR

4x200 metres freestyle relay
1906 Hungary 16:52.4
1908 United Kingdom 10:55.6
1912 Australasia 10:11.6
1920 USA 10:04.4
1924 USA 9:53.4
1928 USA 9:36.2
1932 Japan 8:58.4
1936 Japan 8:51.5
1948 USA 8:46.0
1952 USA 8:31.1
1956 Australia 8:23.6
1960 USA 8:10.2
1964 USA 7:52.1
1968 USA 7:52.3
1972 USA 7:35.78

1976 USA 7:23.22
1980 USSR 7:23.50
1984 USA 7:15.69
1988 USA 7:12.51 OR

4x100 metres medley relay
1960 USA 4:05.4
1964 USA 3:58.4
1968 USA 3:54.9
1972 USA 3:48.16
1976 USA 3:42.22
1980 Australia 3:45.70
1984 USA 3:39.30
1988 USA 3:36.93 OR

Springboard diving
1908 Albert Zürner (Ger)
1912 Paul Günther (Ger)
1920 Louis Kuehn (USA)
1924 Albert White (USA)
1928 Peter Desjardins (USA)
1932 Michael Galitzen (USA)
1936 Richard Degener (USA)
1948 Bruce Harlan (USA)
1952 David Browning (USA)
1956 Robert Clotworthy (USA)
1960 Gary Tobian (USA)
1964 Kenneth Sitzberger (USA)
1968 Bernard Wrightson (USA)
1972 Vladimir Vasin (USSR)
1976 Philip Boggs (USA)

1980 Aleksandr Portnov (USSR)
1984 Greg Louganis (USA)
1988 Greg Louganis (USA)

Highboard platform diving
1904 George Sheldon (USA)
1906 Gottlob Walz (Ger)
1908 Hjalmar Johansson (Swe)
1912 Erik Adlerz (Swe)
1920 Clarence Pinkston (USA)
1924 Albert White (USA)
1928 Peter Desjardins (USA)
1932 Harold Smith (USA)
1936 Marshall Wayne (USA)
1948 Samuel Lee (USA)
1952 Samuel Lee (USA)
1956 Joaquin Capilla Pérez (Mex)
1960 Robert Webster (USA)
1964 Robert Webster (USA)
1968 Klaus Dibiasi (Ita)
1972 Klaus Dibiasi (Ita)
1976 Klaus Dibiasi (Ita)
1980 Falk Hoffmann (GDR)
1984 Greg Louganis (USA)
1988 Greg Louganis (USA)

WOMEN
50 metres freestyle
1988 Kristin Otto (GDR) 25.49 OR

100 metres freestyle
1912 Fanny Durack (Aus) 1:22.2
1920 Ethelda Bleibtrey (USA) 1:13.6
1924 Ethel Lackie (USA) 1:12.4
1928 Albina Osipowich (USA) 1:11.0
1932 Helene Madison (USA) 1:06.8
1936 Hendrika Mastenbroek (Hol)
    1:05.9
1948 Greta Andersen (Den) 1:06.3
1952 Katalin Szöke (Hun) 1:06.8
1956 Dawn Fraser (Aus) 1:02.0
1960 Dawn Fraser (Aus) 1:01.2
1964 Dawn Fraser (Aus) 59.5
1968 Jan Henne (USA) 1:00.0
1972 Sandra Neilson (USA) 58.59
1976 Kornelia Ender (GDR) 55.65
1980 Barbara Krause (GDR) 54.79 OR
1984 Nancy Hogshead (USA) &
    Carrie Steinseifer (USA) 55.92
1988 Kristin Otto (GDR) 54.93

200 metres freestyle
1968 Debbie Meyer (USA) 2:10.5
1972 Shane Gould (Aus) 2:03.56

Kristin Otto, with the six gold medals that she won at the 1988 Olympics **(All-Sport)**

1976 Kornelia Ender (GDR) 1:59.26
1980 Barbara Krause (GDR) 1:58.33
1984 Mary Wayte (USA) 1:59.23
1988 Heike Friedrich (GDR) 1:57.65
OR

400 metres freestyle
1920 Ethelda Bleibtrey (USA) 4:34.0
(300m)
1924 Martha Norelius (USA) 6:02.2
1928 Martha Norelius (USA) 5:42.8
1932 Helene Madison (USA) 5:28.5
1936 Hendrika Mastenbroek (Hol)
5:26.4
1948 Ann Curtis (USA) 5:17.8
1952 Valéria Gyenge (Hun) 5:12.1
1956 Lorraine Crapp (Aus) 4:54.6
1960 Chris Von Saltza (USA) 4:50.6
1964 Virginia Duenkel (USA) 4:43.3
1968 Debbie Meyer (USA) 4:31.8
1972 Shane Gould (Aus) 4:19.04
1976 Petra Thümer (GDR) 4:09.89
1980 Ines Diers (GDR) 4:08.76
1984 Tiffany Cohen (USA) 4:07.10
1988 Janet Evans (USA) 4:03.85 OR

800 metres freestyle
1968 Debbie Meyer (USA) 9:24.0
1972 Keena Rothhammer (USA)
8:53.68
1976 Petra Thümer (GDR) 8:37.14
1980 Michelle Ford (Aus) 8:28.90
1984 Tiffany Cohen (USA) 8:24.95
1988 Janet Evans (USA) 8:20.20 OR

100 metres backstroke
1924 Sybil Bauer (USA) 1:23.2
1928 Maria Braun (Hol) 1:22.0
1932 Eleanor Holm (USA) 1:19.4
1936 Nida Senff (Hol) 1:18.9
1948 Karen Harup (Den) 1:14.4
1952 Joan Harrison (SAf) 1:14.3
1956 Judy Grinham (UK) 1:12.9
1960 Lynn Burke (USA) 1:09.3
1964 Cathy Ferguson (USA) 1:07.7
1968 Kaye Hall (USA) 1:06.2
1972 Melissa Belote (USA) 1:05.78
1976 Ulrike Richter (GDR) 1:01.83
1980 Rica Reinisch (GDR) 1:00.86 OR
1984 Theresa Andrews (USA) 1:02.55
1988 Kristin Otto (GDR) 1:00.89

200 metres backstroke
1968 Pokey Watson (USA) 2:24.8
1972 Melissa Belote (USA) 2:19.19
1976 Ulrike Richter (GDR) 2:13.43
1980 Rica Reinisch (GDR) 2:11.77
1984 Jolanda de Rover (Hol) 2:12.38

1988 Krisztina Egerszegi (Hun)
2:09.29 OR

100 metres breaststroke
1968 Djurdjica Bjedov (Yug) 1:15.8
1972 Catherine Carr (USA) 1:13.58
1976 Hannelore Anke (GDR) 1:11.16
1980 Ute Geweniger (GDR) 1:10.22
1984 Petra Van Staveren (Hol)
1:09.88
1988 Tania Dangalakova (Bul) 1:07.95
OR

200 metres breaststroke
1924 Lucy Morton (UK) 3:33.2
1928 Hilde Schrader (Ger) 3:12.6
1932 Claire Dennis (Aus) 3:06.3
1936 Hideko Maehata (Jap) 3:03.6
1948 Petronella van Vliet (Hol) 2:57.2
1952 Eva Székely (Hun) 2:51.7
1956 Ursula Happe (FRG) 2:53.1
1960 Anita Lonsbrough (UK) 2:49.5
1964 Galina Prozumenshchikova
(USSR) 2:46.4
1968 Sharon Wichman (USA) 2:44.4
1972 Beverley Whitfield (Aus) 2:41.71
1976 Marina Koshevaya (USSR)
2:33.35
1980 Lina Kachushite (USSR) 2:29.54
1984 Anne Ottenbrite (Can) 2:30.38
1988 Silke Hörner (GDR) 2:26.71 OR

100 metres butterfly
1956 Shelley Mann (USA) 1:11.0
1960 Carolyn Schuler (USA) 1:09.5
1964 Sharon Stouder (USA) 1:04.7
1968 Lynette McClements (Aus)
1:05.0
1972 Mayumi Aoki (Jap) 1:03.34
1976 Kornelia Ender (GDR) 1:00.13
1980 Caren Metschuck (GDR)
1:00.42
1984 Mary T. Meagher (USA) 59.26
1988 Kristin Otto (GDR) 59.00 OR

200 metres butterfly
1968 Ada Kok (Hol) 2:24.7
1972 Karen Moe (USA) 2:15.57
1976 Andrea Pollack (GDR) 2:11.41
1980 Ines Geissler (GDR) 2:10.44
1984 Mary T.Meagher (USA) 2:06.90
OR
1988 Kathleen Nord (GDR) 2:09.51

200 metres individual medley
1968 Claudia Kolb (USA) 2:24.7
1972 Sharon Gould (Aus) 2:23.07
1984 Tracy Caulkins (USA) 2:12.64

1988 Daniela Hunger (GDR) 2:12.59
OR

400 metres individual medley
1964 Donna De Varona (USA) 5:18.7
1968 Claudia Kolb (USA) 5:08.5
1972 Gail Neall (Aus) 5:02.97
1976 Ulrike Tauber (GDR) 4:42.77
1980 Petra Schneider (GDR) 4:36.29
OR
1984 Tracy Caulkins (USA) 4:39.24
1988 Janet Evans (USA) 4:37.76

4x100 metres freestyle medley
1912 United Kingdom 5:52.8
1920 USA 5:11.6
1924 USA 4:58.8
1928 USA 4:47.6
1932 USA 4:38.0
1936 Netherlands 4:36.0
1948 USA 4:29.2
1952 Hungary 4:24.4
1956 Australia 4:17.1
1960 USA 4:08.9
1964 USA 4:03.8
1968 USA 4:02.5
1972 USA 3:55.19
1976 USA 3:44.82
1980 GDR 3:42.71
1984 USA 3:43.43
1988 GDR 3:40.63 OR

4x100 metres medley relay
1960 USA 4:41.1
1964 USA 4:33.9
1968 USA 4:28.3
1972 USA 4:20.75
1976 GDR 4:07.95
1980 GDR 4:06.67
1984 USA 4:08.34
1988 GDR 4:03.74 OR

Springboard diving
1920 Aileen Riggin (USA)
1924 Elizabeth Becker (USA)
1928 Helen Meany (USA)
1932 Georgia Coleman (USA)
1936 Marjorie Gestring (USA)
1948 Victoria Draves (USA)
1952 Pat McCormick (USA)
1956 Pat McCormick (USA)
1960 Ingrid Krämer (GDR)
1964 Ingrid Engel (née Krämer) (GDR)
1968 Sue Gossick (USA)
1972 Micki King (USA)
1976 Jennifer Chandler (USA)
1980 Irina Kalinina (USSR)
1984 Sylvie Bernier (Can)

1988 Gao Min (Chn)

Highboard platform diving
1912 Greta Johansson (Swe)
1920 Stefani Fryland-Clausen (Den)
1924 Caroline Smith (USA)
1928 Elizabeth Pinkston (USA)
1932 Dorothy Poynton (USA)
1936 Dorothy Hill (née Poynton) (USA)
1948 Victoria Draves (USA)
1952 Pat McCormick (USA)
1956 Pat McCormick (USA)
1960 Ingrid Krämer (GDR)
1964 Lesley Bush (USA)
1968 Milena Duchkova (Cs)
1972 Ulrika Knape (Swe)
1976 Elena Vaytsekhovskaya (USSR)
1980 Martina Jäschke (GDR)
1984 Zhou Jihong (Chn)
1988 Xu Yanmei (Chn)

Synchronised Swimming
Solo
1984 Tracie Ruiz (USA)
1988 Carolyn Waldo (Can)
Duet
1984 Candy Costie & Tracie Ruiz
   (USA)
1988 Michelle Cameron & Carolyn
   Waldo (Can)

Discontinued events – Men
50 yards freestyle
1904 Zoltán Halmay (Hun) 28.0
100 metres freestyle for sailors
1896 Ioannis Maiokinis (Gre) 2:20.4
200 metres obstacle event
1900 Frederick Lane (Aus) 2:38.4
400 metres breaststroke
1904 Georg Zacharias (Ger) 7:23.6
1912 Walter Bathe (Ger) 6:29.6
1920 Håkan Malmroth (Swe) 6:31.8
880 yards freestyle
1904 Emil Rausch (Ger) 13:11.4
4000 metres freestyle
1900 John Jarvis (UK) 58:24.0
Underwater swimming
1900 Charles de Vendeville (Fra)
Plunge for distance
1904 Paul Dickey (USA) 19.05m
200 metres team swimming
1900 Germany
4 x 50 yards relay
1904 New York AC (USA)
Plain high diving
1912 Erik Adlerz (Swe)
1920 Arvid Wallman (Swe)
1924 Richmond Eve (USA)

Most Olympic gold medals (individual/relay)

MEN
9	(4/5)	Mark Spitz (USA)	1968-72
6	(3/3)	Matt Biondi (USA)	1984-8
5	(4/1)	Charles Daniels (USA)	1904-8
5	(3/2)	Johnny Weissmuller (USA)	1924-8
5	(2/3)	Don Schollander (USA)	1964-8
4	(4/-)	Roland Matthes (GDR)	1968-72
4	(3/1)	Henry Taylor (UK)	1906-8
4	(3/1)	Murray Rose (Aus)	1956-60
4	(2/2)	John Naber (USA)	1976
4	(3/1)	Vladimir Salnikov (USSR)	1980-8
4	(4/-)	Greg Louganis (USA)	1984-8

WOMEN
6	(4/2)	Kristin Otto (GDR)	1988
4	(4/-)	Pat McCormick (USA)	1952-6
4	(3/1)	Dawn Fraser (Aut)	1956-64
4	(3/1)	Kornelia Ender (GDR)	1976

Spitz won a record seven gold medals at one Games, in 1972.

Most Olympic medals (gold/silver/bronze)

MEN
11	(9/1/1)	Mark Spitz (USA)	1968-72
8	(6/1/1)	Matt Biondi (USA)	1984-8
8	(5/1/2)	Charles Daniels (USA)	1904-8
8	(4/2/2)	Roland Matthes (GDR)	1968-72
8	(4/1/3)	Henry Taylor (UK)	1906-20

WOMEN
8	(4/4/-)	Dawn Fraser (Aut)	1956-64
8	(4/4/-)	Kornelia Ender (GDR)	1972-6
8	(2/6/-)	Shirley Babashoff (USA)	1972-6

Youngest gold medallist:
MEN	14yr 309d	Kusuo Kitamura (Jap) 1500m freestyle 1932
WOMEN	13yr 268d	Marjorie Gestring (USA) springboard diving 1936

Oldest gold medallist:
MEN	34yr 186d	Hjalmar Johansson (Swe) highboard diving 1908
WOMEN	30yr 41d	Ursula Happe (FRG) 200m breaststroke 1956

Youngest medallist:
MEN	14yr 10d	Nils Skoglund (Swe) 2nd highboard diving 1928
WOMEN	12yr 24d	Inge Sörensen (Den) 3rd 200m breaststroke 1936

WORLD CHAMPIONSHIPS
World Championships separate from the Olympic Games were first held in 1973, and are now staged every four years. Venues have been: 1973 Belgrade; 1975 Cali, Colombia; 1978 West Berlin; 1982 Guayaquil, Ecuador; 1986 Madrid. *Champions have been:*

MEN

50 metres freestyle
1986 Tom Jager (USA) 22.49

100 metres freestyle
1973 Jim Montgomery (USA) 51.70
1975 Andrew Coan (USA) 51.25
1978 David McCagg (USA) 50.24
1982 Jörg Woithe (GDR) 50.18
1986 Matt Biondi (USA) 48.94

200 metres freestyle
1973 Jim Montgomery (USA) 1:53.02
1975 Tim Shaw (USA) 1:51.04
1978 William Forrester (USA) 1:51.02
1982 Michael Gross (FRG) 1:49.84
1986 Michael Gross (FRG) 1:47.92

400 metres freestyle
1973 Rick DeMont (USA) 3:58.18
1975 Tim Shaw (USA) 3:54.88
1978 Vladimir Salnikov (USSR)
3:51.94
1982 Vladimir Salnikov (USSR)
3:51.30
1986 Rainer Henkel (FRG) 3:50.05

1500 metres freestyle
1973 Steve Holland (Aus) 15:31.85
1975 Tim Shaw (USA) 15:28.92
1978 Vladimir Salnikov (USSR)
15:03.99
1982 Vladimir Salnikov (USSR)
15:01.77
1986 Rainer Henkel (FRG) 15:05.31

4 x 100 metres freestyle
1973 USA 3:27.18
1975 USA 3:24.85
1978 USA 3:19.74
1982 USA 3:19.26
1986 USA 3:19.89

4 x 200 metres freestyle relay
1973 USA 7:33.22
1975 FRG 7:39.44
1978 USA 7:20.82
1982 USA 7:21.09
1986 GDR 7:15.91

100 metres backstroke
1973 Roland Matthes (GDR) 57.47
1975 Roland Matthes (GDR) 58.15
1978 Robert Jackson (USA) 56.36
1982 Dirk Richter (GDR) 55.95
1986 Igor Polyanski (USSR) 55.58

200 metres backstroke
1973 Roland Matthes (GDR) 2:01.87
1975 Zoltan Verraszto (Hun) 2:05.05
1978 Jesse Vassallo (USA) 2:02.16
1982 Rick Carey (USA) 2:00.82
1986 Igor Polyanski (USSR) 1:58.78

100 metres breaststroke
1973 John Hencken (USA) 1:04.02
1975 David Wilkie (UK) 1:04.26
1978 Walter Kusch (GDR) 1:03.56
1982 Steve Lundquist (USA) 1:02.75
1986 Victor Davis (Can) 1:02.71

200 metres breaststroke
1973 David Wilkie (UK) 2:19.28
1975 David Wilkie (UK) 2:18.23
1978 Nick Nevid (USA) 2:18.37
1982 Victor Davis (Can) 2:14.77
1986 József Szabó (Hun) 2:14.27

100 metres butterfly
1973 Bruce Robertson (Can) 55.69
1975 Greg Jagenburg (USA) 55.63
1978 Joe Bottom (USA) 54.30
1982 Matt Gribble (USA) 53.88
1986 Pablo Morales (USA) 53.54

200 metres butterfly
1973 Robin Backhaus (USA) 2:03.32
1975 William Forrester (USA) 2:01.95
1978 Michael Bruner (USA) 1:59.38
1982 Michael Gross (FRG) 1:58.85
1986 Michael Gross (FRG) 1:56.53

200 metres individual medley
1973 Gunnar Larsson (Swe) 2:08.36
1975 András Hargitay (Hun) 2:07.72
1978 Graham Smith (Can) 2:03.65
1982 Aleksey Sidorenko (USSR)
2:03.30
1986 Tamás Darnyi (Hun) 2:01.57

400 metres individual medley
1973 András Hargitay (Hun) 4:31.11
1975 András Hargitay (Hun) 4:32.57
1978 Jesse Vassallo (USA) 4:20.05
1982 Ricardo Prado (Bra) 4:19.78
1986 Tamás Darnyi (Hun) 4:18.98

4 x 100 metres medley relay
1973 USA 3:49.49
1975 USA 3:49.00
1978 USA 3:44.63
1982 USA 3:40.84
1986 USA 3:41.25

Springboard diving
1973 Phil Boggs (USA)
1975 Phil Boggs (USA)
1978 Phil Boggs (USA)
1982 Greg Louganis (USA)
1986 Greg Louganis (USA)

Highboard diving
1973 Klaus Dibiasi (Ita)
1975 Klaus Dibiasi (Ita)
1978 Greg Louganis (USA)
1982 Greg Louganis (USA)
1986 Greg Louganis (USA)

WOMEN
50 metres freestyle
1986 Tamara Costache (Rom) 25.28

100 metres freestyle
1973 Kornelia Ender (GDR) 57.54
1975 Kornelia Ender (GDR) 56.50
1978 Barbara Krause (GDR) 55.68
1982 Birgit Meineke (GDR) 55.79
1986 Kristin Otto (GDR) 55.05

200 metres freestyle
1973 Keena Rothhammer (USA)
2:04.99
1975 Shirley Babashoff (USA) 2:02.50
1978 Cynthia Woodhead (USA)
1:58.53
1982 Annemarie Verstappen (Hol)
1:59.53
1986 Heike Friedrich (GDR) 1:58.26

400 metres freestyle
1973 Heather Greenwood (USA)
4:20.28
1975 Shirley Babashoff (USA) 4:16.87
1978 Tracey Wickham (Aus) 4:06.28
1982 Carmela Schmidt (GDR) 4:08.98
1986 Heike Friedrich (GDR) 4:07.45

800 metres freestyle
1973 Novella Calligaris (Ita) 8:52.97
1975 Jenny Turrall (Aus) 8:44.75
1978 Tracey Wickham (Aus) 8:24.94
1982 Kim Lineham (USA) 8:27.48
1986 Astrid Strauss (GDR) 8:28.24

4 x 100 metres freestyle
1973 GDR 3:52.45
1975 GDR 3:49.37
1978 USA 3:43.43
1982 GDR 3:43.97
1986 GDR 3:40.57

4 x 200 metres freestyle relay
1986 GDR 7:59.33

100 metres backstroke
1973 Ulrike Richter (GDR) 1:05.42
1975 Ulrike Richter (GDR) 1:03.30
1978 Linda Jezek (USA) 1:02.55
1982 Kristin Otto (GDR) 1:01.30
1986 Betsy Mitchell (USA) 1:01.74

200 metres backstroke
1973 Melissa Belote (USA) 2:20.52
1975 Birgit Treiber (GDR) 2:15.46
1978 Linda Jezek (USA) 2:11.93
1982 Cornelia Sirch (GDR) 2:09.91
1986 Cornelia Sirch (GDR) 2:11.37

100 metres breaststroke
1973 Renate Vogel (GDR) 1:13.74
1975 Hannelore Anke (GDR) 1:12.72
1978 Yulia Bogdanova (USSR) 1:10.31
1982 Ute Geweniger (GDR) 1:09.14
1986 Sylvia Gerasch (GDR) 1:08.11

200 metres breaststroke
1973 Renate Vogel (GDR) 2:40.01
1975 Hannelore Anke (GDR) 2:37.25
1978 Lina Kachushite (USSR) 2:31.42
1982 Svetlana Varganova (USSR) 2:28.82
1986 Silke Horner (GDR) 2:27.40

100 metres butterfly
1973 Kornelia Ender (GDR) 1:02.53
1975 Kornelia Ender (GDR) 1:01.24
1978 Mary-Joan Pennington (USA) 1:00.20
1982 Mary T.Meagher (USA) 59.41
1986 Kornelia Gressler (GDR) 59.51

200 metres butterfly
1973 Rosemarie Kother (GDR) 2:13.76
1975 Rosemarie Kother (GDR) 2:13.82
1978 Tracy Caulkins (USA) 2:09.87
1982 Ines Geissler (GDR) 2:08.66
1986 Mary T.Meagher (USA) 2:08.41

200 metres individual medley
1973 Angela Hübner (GDR) 2:20.51
1975 Kathy Heddy (USA) 2:19.80
1978 Tracy Caulkins (USA) 2:14.07
1982 Petra Schneider (GDR) 2:11.79
1986 Kristin Otto (GDR) 2:15.56

400 metres individual medley
1973 Gudrun Wegner (GDR) 4:57.31
1975 Ulrike Tauber (GDR) 4:52.76
1978 Tracy Caulkins (USA) 4:40.83
1982 Petra Schneider (GDR) 4:36.10
1986 Kathleen Nord (GDR) 4:43.75

4 x 100 metres medley relay
1973 GDR 4:16.84
1975 GDR 4:14.74
1978 USA 4:08.21
1982 GDR 4:05.88
1986 GDR 4:04.82

Springboard diving
1973 Christine Kohler (GDR)
1975 Irina Kalinina (USSR)
1978 Irina Kalinina (USSR)
1982 Megan Neyer (USA)
1986 Min Gao (Chn)

Highboard diving
1973 Ulrike Knape (Swe)
1975 Janet Ely (USA)
1978 Irina Kalinina (USSR)
1982 Wendy Wyland (USA)
1986 Lin Chen (Chn)

Synchronised swimming solo
1973 Teresa Andersen (USA)
1975 Gail Buzonas (USA)
1978 Helen Vanderburg (Can)
1982 Tracie Ruiz (USA)
1986 Carolyn Waldo (Can)

Synchronised swimming duet
1973 Teresa Andersen & Gail Johnson (USA)
1975 Robin Curren & Amanda Norrish (USA)
1978 Michele Calkins & Helen Vanderburg (Can)
1982 Kelly Kryczka & Sharon Hambrook (Can)
1986 Carolyn Waldo & Michelle Cameron (Can)

Synchronised swimming team
1973 USA
1975 USA
1978 USA
1982 Canada
1986 Canada

Most gold medals: (individual/relay)
MEN
6 (2/4) Jim Montgomery (USA) 1973-5
5 (5/0) Greg Louganis (USA) 1978-86
5 (0/5) Rowdy Gaines (USA) 1978-82
WOMEN
8 (4/4) Kornelia Ender (GDR) 1973-5
7 (3/4) Kristin Otto (GDR) 1982-6

Most medals: (gold/silver/bronze)
MEN
8 (5/3/0) Rowdy Gaines (USA) 1978-82
WOMEN
10 (8/2/0) Kornelia Ender (GDR) 1973-5
9 (7/2/0) Kristin Otto (GDR) 1982-6
9 (2/5/2) Mary T.Meagher (USA) 1978-82

Most medals at one Championships (gold/silver/bronze)

MEN
7   (3/1/3)   Matt Biondi (USA) 1986
WOMEN
6   (5/1/0)   Tracy Caulkins (USA) 1978
6   (4/2/0)   Kristin Otto (GDR) 1986
6   (1/3/2)   Mary T.Meagher (USA) 1986

WORLD CUP
Held in 1979 only, when the USA won both men's and women's events.

WORLD CUP – DIVING
First held in 1979, it is now a team competition held biennially. *Team winners:*
1981 China
1983 China
1985 China
1987 USA
1989 China

EUROPEAN CUP
The European inter-nation competitions for men and women were first held in 1969. Staged biennially at first, they are now held annually in the winter in a 25m pool. *Winners:*
MEN
10 USSR 1971, 1975-6, 1979-83, 1987-8
3 GDR 1969, 1973, 1984
3 FRG 1985-6, 1989
WOMEN
15 GDR 1969, 1971, 1973, 1975, 1979-89
1 USSR 1976

EUROPEAN CHAMPIONSHIPS
First held in Budapest in 1926, and subsequently in 1927, 1931, 1934, 1938, 1947, at four-yearly intervals 1950-74, in 1977 and biennially from 1981. Winners since 1983, championship records if set before 1983, and swimmers to have won a particular event twice:

MEN
50 metres freestyle
1987 Jörg Woithe (GDR) 22.66
1989 Vladimir Tkachenko (USSR) 22.64

100 metres freestyle
1983 Per Johansson (Swe) 50.20
1985 Stéphane Caron (Fra) 50.20
1987 Sven Lodziewski (GDR) 49.79
1989 Giorgio Lamberti (Ita) 49.24
Most: 2 Istvan Barany (Hun) 1926, 1931; Alex Jany (Fra) 1947, 1950; Peter Nocke (FRG) 1974, 1977; Per Johansson (Swe) 1981, 1983

200 metres freestyle
1983 Michael Gross (FRG) 1:47.87
1985 Michael Gross (FRG) 1:47.95
1987 Anders Holmertz (Swe) 1:48.44
1989 Giorgio Lamberti (Ita) 1:46.69
Most: 2 Peter Nocke (FRG) 1974, 1977; Gross

400 metres freestyle
1983 Vladimir Salnikov (USSR) 3:49.80
1985 Uwe Dassler (GDR) 3:51.52
1987 Uwe Dassler (GDR) 3:48.95
1989 Artur Wojdat (Pol) 3:47.78
Most: 2 Arne Borg (Swe) 1926-7, Alex Jany (Fra) 1947, 1950; Dassler

1500 metres freestyle
1983 Vladimir Salnikov (USSR) 15:08.84
1985 Uwe Dassler (GDR) 15:08.56
1987 Rainer Henkel (FRG) 15:02.23
1989 Jörg Hoffmann (GDR) 15:01.52
Most: 3 Vladimir Salnikov (USSR) 1977, 1981, 1983; 2 Arne Borg (Swe) 1926-7

4 x 100 metres freestyle relay
1983 USSR 3:20.88
1985 FRG 3:22.18
1987 GDR 3:19.17
1989 FRG 3:19.68

4 x 200 metres freestyle relay
1983 FRG 7:20.40
1985 FRG 7:19.23
1987 FRG 7:13.10
1989 Italy 7:15.39

100 metres backstroke
1983 Dirk Richter (GDR) 56.10
1985 Igor Polyanskiy (USSR) 55.24
1987 Sergey Zabolotnov (USSR) 56.06
1989 Martin Lopez-Zubero (Spa) 56.44
Most: 2 Roland Matthes (GDR) 1970, 1974

200 metres backstroke
1983 Sergey Zabolotnov (USSR) 2:01.00
1985 Igor Polyanskiy (USSR) 1:58.50
1987 Sergey Zabolotnov (USSR) 1:59.35
1989 Stefano Battistelli (Ita) 1:59.96
Most: 2 Roland Matthes (GDR) 1970, 1974; Zabolotnov

100 metres breaststroke
1983 Robertas Zhulpa (USSR) 1:03.32
1985 Adrian Moorhouse (UK) 1:02.99
1987 Adrian Moorhouse (UK) 1:02.13
1989 Adrian Moorhouse (UK) 1:01.71 (1:01.49 ht)
Most: 3 Moorhouse, 2 Nikolay Pankin (USSR) 1970, 1974

200 metres breaststroke
1983 Adrian Moorhouse (UK) 2:17.49
1985 Dmitriy Volkov (USSR) 2:19.53
1987 József Szabó (Hun) 2:13.87

1989 Nick Gillingham (UK) 2:12.90
Most: 2 Erich Rademacher (Ger) 1926-7, Georgiy
    Prokopenko (USSR) 1962, 1966

100 metres butterfly
1983 Michael Gross (FRG) 54.00
1985 Michael Gross (FRG) 54.02
1987 Andrew Jameson (UK) 53.62
1989 Rafal Szukala (Pol) 54.47
Most: 2 Roger Pyttel (GDR) 1974, 1977; Gross

200 metres butterfly
1983 Michael Gross (FRG) 1:57.05
1985 Michael Gross (FRG) 1:56.65
1987 Michael Gross (FRG) 1:57.59
1989 Tamás Darnyi (Hun) 1:58.87
Most: 4 Gross 1981 and above; 2 Valentin Kuzmin (USSR)
    1962, 1966

200 metres individual medley
1983 Giovanni Franceshi (Ita) 2:02.48
1985 Tamás Darnyi (Hun) 2:03.23
1987 Tamás Darnyi (Hun) 2:00.56
1989 Tamás Darnyi (Hun) 2:01.03
Most: 3 Darnyi

400 metres individual medley
1983 Giovanni Franceshi (Ita) 4:20.41
1985 Tamás Darnyi (Hun) 4:20.70
1987 Tamás Darnyi (Hun) 4:15.42
1989 Tamás Darnyi (Hun) 4:15.25
Most: 3 Darnyi, 2 Sergey Fesenko (USSR) 1977, 1981

4 x 100 metres medley relay
1983 USSR 3:43.99
1985 FRG 3:43.59
1987 USSR 3:41.51
1989 USSR 3:41.44

Springboard diving
1983 Petar Georgiev (Bul)
1985 Nikolay Droschin (USSR)
1987 Albin Killat (FRG)
1989 Albin Killat (FRG)
Most: 2 Ewald Riebschlager (Ger) 1927, 1932; Killat

1m Springboard diving
1989 Edwin Jongejans (Hol)

Highboard diving
1983 David Ambarzumyan (USSR)
1985 Thomas Knuths (GDR)
1987 Georgiy Chogovadze (USSR)
1989 Georgiy Chogovadze (USSR)
Most: 2 Hans Luber (Ger) 1926-7, Brian Phelps (UK) 1958,
    1962; Klaus Dibiasi (Ita) 1966, 1974; Chogovadze

WOMEN
50 metres freestyle
1987 Tamara Costache (Rom) 25.50
1989 Catherine Plewinski (Fra) 25.63

100 metres freestyle
1983 Birgit Meineke (GDR) 55.18
1985 Heike Friedrich (GDR) 55.71
1987 Kristin Otto (GDR) 55.38
1989 Katrin Meissner (GDR) 55.38

200 metres freestyle
1983 Birgit Meineke (GDR) 1:59.45
1985 Heike Friedrich (GDR) 1:59.55
1987 Heike Friedrich (GDR) 1:58.95
1989 Manuela Stellmach (GDR) 1:58.93
Most: 2 Friedrich

400 metres freestyle
1983 Astrid Strauss (GDR) 4:08.07
1985 Astrid Strauss (GDR) 4:09.22
1987 Heike Friedrich (GDR) 4:06.39
1989 Anke Möhring (GDR) 4:05.84
Most: 2 Marie Braun (Hol) 1927, 1931; Strauss

800 metres freestyle
1983 Astrid Strauss (GDR) 8:32.12
1985 Astrid Strauss (GDR) 8:32.45
1987 Anke Möhring (GDR) 8:19.53
1989 Anke Möhring (GDR) 8:23.99
Most: 2 Strauss, Möhring

4 x 100 metres freestyle
1983 GDR 3:44.72
1985 GDR 3:44.48
1987 GDR 3:42.58
1989 GDR 3:42.46

4 x 200 metres freestyle relay
1983 GDR 8:02.27
1985 GDR 8:03.82
1987 GDR 7:55.47
1989 GDR 7:58.54

100 metres backstroke
1982 Ina Kleber (GDR) 1:01.79
1985 Birte Weigang (GDR) 1:02.16
1987 Kristin Otto (GDR) 1:01.86
1989 Kristin Otto (GDR) 1:01.86
Most: 2 Kleber 1981, 1983; Otto

200 metres backstroke
1983 Cornelia Sirch (GDR) 2:12.05
1985 Cornelia Sirch (GDR) 2:10.89
1987 Cornelia Sirch (GDR) 2:10.20
1989 Dagmar Hase (GDR) 2:12.46
Most: 3 Sirch

100 metres breaststroke
1983 Ute Geweniger (GDR) 1:08.51
1985 Sylvia Gerasch (GDR) 1:08.62
1987 Silke Hörner (GDR) 1:07.91
1989 Silke Börnicke (GDR) 1:09.55
Most: 2 Geweniger 1981, 1983

200 metres breaststroke
1983 Ute Geweniger (GDR) 2:30.64
1985 Tamara Bogomilova (Bul) 2:28.57
1987 Silke Hörner (GDR) 2:27.49
1989 Susanne Börnicke (GDR) 2:27.77
Most: 2 Galina Prozumeshikova/Stepanova (USSR) 1966,
  1970; Geweniger 1981, 1983

100 metres butterfly
1983 Ines Geissler (GDR) 1:00.31
1985 Kornelia Gressler (GDR) 59.46
1987 Kristin Otto (GDR) 59.52
1989 Catherine Plewinski (Fra) 59.08
Most: 2 Ada Kok (Hol) 1962, 1966

200 metres butterfly
1983 Cornelia Polit (GDR) 2:07.82
1985 Jacqueline Alex (GDR) 2:11.78
1987 Kathleen Nord (GDR) 2:08.85
1989 Kathleen Nord (GDR) 2:09.33
Most: 2 Nord

200 metres individual medley
1983 Ute Geweniger (GDR) 2:13.07
1985 Kathleen Nord (GDR) 2:16.07
1987 Cornelia Sirch (GDR) 2:15.04
1989 Daniela Hunger (GDR) 2:13.26
Most: 2 Ulrike Tauber (GDR) 1974, 1977; Geweniger 1981
  (2:12.64 rec), 1983

400 metres individual medley
1983 Kathleen Nord (GDR) 4:39.95
1985 Kathleen Nord (GDR) 4:47.08
1987 Noemi Lung (Rom) 4:40.21
1989 Daniela Hunger (GDR) 4:41.82
Rec: 1981 Petra Schneider (GDR) 4:39.30
Most: 2 Ulrike Tauber (GDR) 1974, 1977; Nord

4 x 100 metres medley relay
1983 GDR 4:05.79
1985 GDR 4:06.93
1987 GDR 4:04.05
1989 GDR 4:07.40

Springboard diving
1983 Brita Baldus (GDR)
1985 Zhanna Tsirulnikova (USSR)
1987 Daphne Jongejans (Hol)
1989 Marina Babkova (USSR)
Most: 2 Olga Jensch (née Jordan) (Ger) 1931, 1934; Mady
  Moreau (Fra) 1947, 1950

1m Springboard diving
1989 Irina Lachko (USSR)

Highboard diving
1983 Alla Lobankina (USSR)
1985 Anzyela Stasyulevich (USSR)
1987 Yelena Miroshina (USSR)
1989 Ute Wetzig (GDR)
Most: 2 Nicole Pelissard (Fra) 1947, 1950

Synchronised swimming solo
1983 Carolyn Wilson (UK)
1985 Carolyn Wilson (UK)
1987 Muriel Hermine (Fra)
1989 Khristina Falasinidi (USSR)
Most: 2 Wilson

Synchronised swimming duet
1983 Carolyn Wilson & Amanda Dodd (UK)
1985 Eva-Maria Edinger & Alexandra Worisch (Aut)
1987 Muriel Hermine & Karine Schuler (Fra)
1989 Karine Schuler & Marianne Aeschbacher (Fra)

Synchronised swimming team
1983 UK
1985 France
1987 France
1989 France

Most gold medals (individual/relay)
MEN
13   (8/5)   Michael Gross (FRG) 1981-5
WOMEN
11   4/7)   Heike Friedrich (GDR) 1985-9
9   (4/5)   Kristin Otto (GDR) 1983-9
8   (7/1   Ute Geweniger (GDR) 1981-3

Michael Gross won three individual events in both 1983 and 1985; in the latter he also swam on three winning FRG relay teams, for a record six golds at one Championships. With 13 gold medals, four silvers and a bronze he had a record 18 medals in the four Championships 1981-7.

A record five gold medals at one Championships have been won by three women: two individual and three relay for the GDR by Birgit Meineke in 1983 and Heike Friedrich in 1985; three individual and two relay for GDR by Kristin Otto in 1987.

Others to have won three individual events at one Championships: Arne Borg (Swe) 1927, Ian Black (UK) 1958, Gunnar Larsson (Swe) 1970, Ute Geweniger (GDR) 1981, Tamás Darnyi (Hun) 1987.

WORLD SHORT COURSE RECORDS – in 25m pools

Event	min:sec	Name	Date
MEN			
50m freestyle	21.76	Nils Rudolph (GDR)	11 Feb 1990
100m freestyle	48.2#	Michael Gross (FRG)	11 Feb 1988
	48.33	Tommy Werner (Swe)	19 Mar 1989
200m freestyle	1:43.64	Giorgio Lamberti (Ita)	11 Feb 1990
400m freestyle	3:40.81	Anders Holmertz (Swe)	3 Feb 1990
800m freestyle	7:38.75	Michael Gross (FRG)	8 Feb 1985
1500m freestyle	14:37.60	Vladimir Salnikov (USSR)	19 Dec 1982
4 x 50m freestyle relay	1:27.95	FR Germany	14 Feb 1988
4 x 100m freestyle relay	3:14.00	Sweden	19 Mar 1989
4 x 200m freestyle relay	7:05.17	FR Germany	9 Feb 1986
50m backstroke	25.06	Mark Tewksbury (Can)	2 Mar 1990
100m backstroke	53.69	Mark Tewksbury (Can)	2 Mar 1990
200m backstroke	1:56.60	Tamás Darnyi (Hun)	8 Feb 1987
50m breaststroke	27.15	Dmitriy Volkov (USSR)	30 Dec 1989
100m breaststroke	59.30	Dmitriy Volkov (USSR)	11 Feb 1990
200m breaststroke	2:08.82	Victor Davis (Can)	7 Feb 1987
50m butterfly	24.07	Marcel Gery (Can)	24 Feb 1990
100m butterfly	52.07	Marcel Gery (Can)	23 Feb 1990
200m butterfly	1:54.78	Michael Gross (FRG)	9 Feb 1985
200m individual medley	1:58.18	Pablo Morales (USA)	26 Apr 1987
400m individual medley	4:09.64	Alex Baumann (Can)	7 Mar 1987
4 x 50m medley relay	1:38.72	USA	14 Feb 1988
4 x 100m medley relay	3:36.66	University of Calgary (Can)	3 Mar 1990
WOMEN			
50m freestyle	24.81	Livia Copariu (Rom)	9 Apr 1989
100m freestyle	53.48	Livia Copariu (Rom)	9 Apr 1989
200m freestyle	1:56.35	Birgit Meineke (GDR)	7 Jan 1983
400m freestyle	4:02.05	Astrid Strauss (GDR)	8 Feb 1987
800m freestyle	8:15.34	Astrid Strauss (GDR)	6 Feb 1987
1500m freestyle	15:43.31	Petra Schneider (GDR)	10 Jan 1982
4 x 50m freestyle relay	1:42.13	FRG	13 Feb 1988
4 x 100m freestyle relay	3:38.77	GDR	12 Dec 1987
4 x 200m freestyle relay	7:58.74*	USA	10 Jan 1981
50m backstroke	28.91	Svenja Schlicht (FRG)	8 Feb 1987
100m backstroke	59.89	Betsy Mitchell (USA)	26 Apr 1987
200m backstroke	2:07.74	Cornelia Sirch (GDR)	9 Jan 1983
100m breaststroke	1:07.05	Silke Hörner (GDR)	8 Feb 1986
200m breaststroke	2:22.92	Susanne Börnike (GDR)	4 Feb 1989
50m butterfly	27.54	Jennifer Johnson (USA)	12 Feb 1984
	27.54	Christiane Sivert (GDR)	11 Feb 1990
100m butterfly	58.91*	Mary T.Meagher (USA)	3 Jan 1981
200m butterfly	2:05.65	Mary T.Meagher (USA)	2 Jan 1981
200m individual medley	2:10.60	Petra Schneider (GDR)	8 Jan 1982
400m individual medley	4:31.36	Noemi Lung (Rom)	31 Jan 1987
4 x 50m medley relay	1:54.37	GDR	14 Feb 1988
4 x 100m medley relay	4:02.85	GDR	8 Jan 1983

on relay first leg, * slower than the world long-course records (qv)

TABLE TENNIS

The origins of table tennis are uncertain, but sports goods manufacturers were selling equipment for the game in England in the 1880s. The use of a celluloid table tennis ball was pioneered by James Gibb. This ball, called 'Gossima', was manufactured by J.Jacques & Son, and it was probably Jacques who conceived the onomatopoeic name 'Ping Pong', by which the game was popularly known in the early part of this century. The use of pimpled rubber stuck on to a wooden bat was introduced around this time. A Ping Pong Association was formed in 1902, when the craze for the game was at a peak. This organisation was re-named the Table Tennis Association, but became defunct, before being re-constituted as the English Table Tennis Association in 1927.
The world governing body is the International Table Tennis Federation (ITTF), which was founded in 1926.

WORLD CHAMPIONSHIPS

European Championships were contested in December 1926, when the ITTF was formed, and the event was retrospectively designated as the World Championships. Subsequent championships were contested annually until 1957, except for the war years, and biennially from 1959. Note that two events are shown for 1933, and none for 1934, as the 1933-4 tournament was held in December 1933.

Swaythling Cup
The trophy for the men's team championship was given in 1926 by Lady Swaythling, mother of the Hon. Ivor Montagu, the first President of the ITTF. Matches are played over the best of nine singles, by teams of three. *Wins:*

12 Hungary	1926, 1928-31, 1933 (2), 1935, 1938, 1949, 1952, 1979
10 China	1961, 1963, 1965, 1971, 1975, 1977, 1981, 1983, 1985, 1987
7 Japan	1954-7, 1959, 1967, 1969
6 Czechoslovakia	1932, 1939, 1947-8, 1950-1
2 Sweden	1973, 1989
1 Austria 1936, USA 1937, England 1953	

Corbillon Cup
The Marcel Corbillon Cup was presented in 1934 by M.Corbillon, President of the French Table Tennis Association, for the winners of the women's team event. Matches are contested as the best of four singles and a doubles. *Wins:*

9 China	1965, 1975, 1977, 1979, 1981, 1983, 1985, 1987, 1989
8 Japan	1952, 1954, 1957, 1959, 1961, 1963, 1967, 1971
5 Romania	1950-1, 1953, 1955-6
3 Czechoslovakia	1935-6, 1938
2 Germany	1933, 1939

2 USA	1937, 1949
2 England	1947-8
1 USSR 1969, South Korea 1973	

Men's Singles:
Contested for the St. Bride Vase, presented in 1929 by the St. Bride Institute Table Tennis Club, London in recognition of the title won in 1929 by Fred Perry, later triple Wimbledon champion at lawn tennis. *Winners:*

1926 Roland Jacobi (Hun)
1928 Zoltán Mechlovits (Hun)
1929 Fred Perry (Eng)
1930 Viktor Barna (Hun)
1931 Miklós Szabados (Hun)
1932-5 Viktor Barna (Hun)
1936 Stanislav Kolár (Cs)
1937 Richard Bergmann (Aut)
1938 Bohumil Vána (Cs)
1939 Richard Bergmann (Aut)
1947 Bohumil Vána (Cs)
1948 Richard Bergmann (Eng)
1949 Johnny Leach (Eng)
1950 Richard Bergmann (Eng)
1951 Johnny Leach (Eng)
1952 Hiroji Satoh (Jap)
1953 Ferenc Sidó (Hun)
1954 Ichiro Ogimura (Jap)
1955 Toshiaki Tanaka (Jap)
1956 Ichiro Ogimura (Jap)
1957 Toshiaki Tanaka (Jap)
1959 Jung Kuo-tuan (Chn)
1961 Chuang Tse-tung (Chn)
1963 Chuang Tse-tung (Chn)
1965 Chuang Tse-tung (Chn)
1967 Nobuhiko Hasegawa (Jap)
1969 Shigeo Ito (Jap)
1971 Stellan Bengtsson (Swe)
1973 Hsi En-ting (Chn)
1975 István Jónyer (Hun)
1977 Mitsuru Kohno (Jap)
1979 Seiji Ono (Jap)
1981 Guo Yuehua (Chn)
1983 Guo Yuehua (Chn)
1985 Jiang Jialiang (Chn)
1987 Jiang Jialiang (Chn)
1989 Jan-Ove Waldner (Swe)

Most wins: 5 Viktor Barna, 4 Richard Bergmann

Women's Singles:
Contested for the G.Geist Prize, donated in 1931 by Dr.Gaspar Geist, President of the Hungarian Association. *Winners:*
1926 Mária Mednyánszky (Hun)
1928-31 Mária Mednyánszky (Hun)

1932-3 Anna Sipos (Hun)
1933 Marie Kettnerová (Cs)
1935 Marie Kettnerová (Cs)
1936 Ruth Aarons (USA)
1937 Ruth Aarons (USA) and Trudi Pritzi (Aut) *
1938 Trudi Pritzi (Aut)
1939 Vlasta Depetrisová (Cs)
1947-9 Gizi Farkas (Hun)
1950-5 Angelica Rozeanu (Rom)
1956 Tomi Okawa (Jap)
1957 Fujie Eguchi (Jap)
1959 Kimiyo Matsuzaki (Jap)
1961 Chiu Chung-hui (Chn)
1963 Kimiyo Matsuzaki (Jap)
1965 Naoko Fukazu (Jap)
1967 Sachiko Morisawa (Jap)
1969 Toshiko Kowada (Jap)
1971 Lin Hui-ching (Chn)
1973 Hu Yu-lan (Chn)
1975 Pak Yung-sun (NKo)
1977 Pak Yung-sun (NKo)
1979 Ge Xinai (Chn)
1981 Tong Ling (Chn)
1983 Cao Yanhua (Chn)
1985 Cao Yanhua (Chn)
1987 He Zhili (Chn)
1989 Qiao Hong (Chn)

* title left vacant, these were the finallists

Most wins: 6 Angelica Rozeanu, 5 Mária Mednyánszky

Men's Doubles
Contested for the Iran Cup, presented by the Shah of Iran in Paris in 1947. *Winners:*
1926 Roland Jacobi & Daniel Pécsi (Hun)
1928 Alfred Liebster & Robert Thum (Aut)
1929-32 Viktor Barna & Miklós Szabados (Hun)
1933 Viktor Barna & Sándor Glancz (Hun)
1933 Viktor Barna & Miklós Szabados (Hun)
1935 Viktor Barna & Miklós Szabados (Hun)
1936-7 Robert Blattner & James McClure (USA)
1938 James McClure & Sol Schiff (USA)
1939 Viktor Barna & Richard Bergmann (Eng)
1947 Adolf Slár & Bohumil Vána (Cs)
1948 Ladislav Stipek & Bohumil Vána (Cs)
1949 Ivan Andreadis & Frantisek Tokár (Cs)
1950 Ferenc Sidó & Ferenc Soós (Hun)
1951 Ivan Andreadis & Bohumil Vána (Cs)
1952 Norikazu Fujii & Tadaski Hayashi (Jap)
1953 József Kóczián & Ferenc Sidó (Hun)
1954 Zarko Dolinar & Vilim Harangozo (Yug)
1955 Ivan Andreadis & Ladislav Stipek (Cs)
1956 Ichiro Ogimura & Yoshio Tomita (Jap)
1957 Ivan Andreadis & Ladislav Stipek (Cs)
1959 Teruo Murakami & Ichiro Ogimura (Jap)
1961 Nobuyo Hoshino & Koji Kimura (Jap)
1963 Chang Shih-lin & Wang Chih-liang (Chn)

1965 Chuang Tse-tung & Hsu Yin-sheng (Chn)
1967 Hans Alser & Kjell Johansson (Swe)
1969 Hans Alser & Kjell Johansson (Swe)
1971 István Jonyer & Tibor Klampar (Hun)
1973 Stellan Bengtsson & Kjell Johansson (Swe)
1975 Gábor Gergely & István Jónyer (Hun)
1977 Li Zhenshi & Liang Geliang (Chn)
1979 Dragutin Surbek & Anton Stipancic (Yug)
1981 Cai Zhenhua & Li Zhenshi (Chn)
1983 Dragutin Surbek & Zoran Kalinic (Yug)
1985 Mikael Applegren & Ulf Carlsson (Swe)
1987 Chen Longcan & Wei Qinguang (Chn)
1989 Jörg Rosskopf & Steffen Fetzner (FRG)

Most wins: 8 Viktor Barna, 6 Miklós Szabados

Women's Doubles
Contested for the W.J.Pope Trophy. Mr Pope, Honorary Secretary of the ITTF 1947-50, presented the trophy in 1948. *Winners:*
1928 Erika Flamm (Aut) & Mária Mednyánszky (Hun)
1929 Erika Metzger & Mona Rüster (Ger)
1930-5 Mária Mednyánszky & Anna Sipos (Hun)
1936 Marie Kettnerová & Marie Smídová (Cs)
1937-8 Vlasta Depetrisová & Vera Votrubcová (Cs)
1939 Hilde Bussmann & Trudi Pritzi (Ger)
1947 Gizi Farkas (Hun) & Trudi Pritzi (Aut)
1948 Margaret Franks & Vera Thomas (Eng)
1949 Helen Elliot (Sco) & Gizi Farkas (Hun)
1950 Dora Beregi (Eng) & Helen Elliot (Sco)
1951 Diane Rowe & Rosalind Rowe (Eng)
1952 Shizuki Narahara & Tomi Nishimura (Jap)
1953 Gizi Farkas (Hun) & Angelica Rozeanu (Rom)
1954 Diane Rowe & Rosalind Rowe (Eng)
1955-6 Angelica Rozeanu & Ella Zeller (Rom)
1957 Livia Mosoczy & Agnes Simon (Hun)
1959 Taeko Namba & Kazuko Yamaizumi (Jap)
1961 Maria Alexandru & Geta Pitica (Rom)
1963 Kimiyo Matsuzaki & Masako Seki (Jap)
1965 Cheng Min-chih & Lin Hui-ching (Chn)
1967 Saeko Hirota & Sachiko Morisawa (Jap)
1969 Svetlana Grinberg & Zoya Rudnova (USSR)
1971 Cheng Min-chih & Lin Hui-ching (Chn)
1973 Maria Alexandru (Rom) & Miho Hamada (Jap)
1975 Maria Alexandru (Rom) & Shoko Takashima (Jap)
1977 Pak Yong-ok (NKo) & Yang Yin (Chn)
1979 Zhang Li & Zhang Deying (Chn)
1981 Zhang Deying & Cao Yanhua (Chn)
1983 Shen Jianping & Dai Lili (Chn)
1985 Dai Lili & Geng Lijuan (Chn)
1987 Yang Young-Ja & Hyun Jung-hwa (SKo)
1989 Qiao Hong & Deng Yaping (Chn)

Most wins: 7 Mária Mednyánszky, 6 Anna Sipos

Mixed Doubles
Contested for the Heydusek Prize, presented in 1948 by Zdenek Heydusek, Secretary of the Czechoslovak

Association. *Winners:*
1927-8 Zoltán Mechlovits & Mária Mednyánszky (Hun)
1929 István Kelen & Anna Sipos (Hun)
1930-1 Miklós Szabados & Mária Mednyánszky (Hun)
1932 Viktor Barna & Anna Sipos (Hun)
1933 István Kelen & Mária Mednyánszky (Hun)
1933 Miklós Szabados & Mária Mednyánszky (Hun)
1935 Viktor Barna & Anna Sipos (Hun)
1936 Miloslav Hamr & Trude Kleinová (Cs)
1937 Bohumil Vána & Vera Votrubcová (Cs)
1938 Lászlo Béllak (Hun) & Wendy Woodhead (Eng)
1939 Bohumil Vána & Vera Votrubcová (Cs)
1947 Ferenc Soós & Gizi Farkas (Hun)
1948 Richard Miles & Thelma Thall (USA)
1949-50 Ferenc Sidó & Gizi Farkas (Hun)
1951 Bohumil Vána (Cs) & Angelica Rozeanu (Rom)
1952-3 Ferenc Sidó (Hun) & Angelica Rozeanu (Rom)

1954 Ivan Andreadis (Cs) & Gizi Farkas (Hun)
1955 Kálmán Szepesi & Eva Kóczián (Hun)
1956 Erwin Klein & Leah Neuberger (USA)
1957 Ichiro Ogimura & Fujie Eguchi (Jap)
1959 Ichiro Ogimura & Fujie Eguchi (Jap)
1961 Ichiro Ogimura & Kimiyo Matsuzaki (Jap)
1963 Koji Kimura & Kazuko Ito (Jap)
1965 Koji Kimurra & Masako Seki (Jap)
1967 Nobuhiko Hasegawa & Noriko Yamanaka (Jap)
1969 Nobuhiko Hasegawa & Yasuka Konno (Jap)
1971 Chang Shih-ling & Lin Hui-ching (Chn)
1973 Liang Geliang & Li Li (Chn)
1975 Stanislav Gomozkov & Tatyana Ferdman (USSR)

The redoubtable Viktor Barna, photographed in 1947, 18 years after his first world title (Popperfoto)

1977 Jacques Secretin & Claude Bergeret (Fra)
1979 Liang Geliang & Ge Xinai (Chn)
1981 Xie Saike & Huang Junqun (Chn)
1983 Guo Yuehua & Ni Xialian (Chn)
1985 Cai Zhenhua & Cao Yanhua (Chn)
1987 Hui Jun & Geng Lijuan (Chn)
1989 Yoo Nam-kyu & Hyun Jung-hwa (SKo)

Most wins: 6 Mária Mednyánszky

Most individual world titles overall:
MEN: 15 Viktor Barna (Hun/Eng), 10 Miklós Szabados (Hun)
WOMEN: 18 Mária Mednyánszky (-Klucsik) (Hun), 12 Angelica Rozeanu (Rom), 11 Anna Sipos, (Hun), 10 Gizi Farkas (Hun)

OLYMPIC GAMES

Table Tennis was added to the Olympic programme for the first time in 1988. *Winners:*
Men's singles: Yoo Nam-kyu (SKo)
Men's doubles: Chen Longcan & Wei Qingguang (Chn)
Women's singles: Chen Jing (Chn)
Women's doubles: Hyun Jung-hwa & Yang Young-ja (SKo)

WORLD CUP

Held annually for men from 1980. *Winners:*
1980 Guo Yuehua (Chn)
1981 Tibor Klampar (Hun)
1982 Guo Yuehua (Chn)
1983 Mikael Appelgren (Swe)
1984 Jiang Jialiang (Chn)
1985 Chen Xinhua (Chn)
1986 Chen Longcan (Chn)
1987 Yi Teng (Chn)
1988 Andrzej Grubba (Pol)
1989 Ma Wenge (Chn)

From 1990 two new events have been introduced: the World Team Cup involving 16 men's and 12 women's teams, and a biennial World Doubles Cup.

EUROPEAN CHAMPIONSHIPS
Held biennially from 1958. Singles champions:

Men's singles
1958 Zoltán Berczik
1960 Zoltán Berczik
1962 Hans Alser (Swe)
1964 Kjell Johansson (Swe)
1966 Kjell Johansson (Swe)
1968 Dragutin Surbek (Yug)
1970 Hans Alser (Swe)
1974 Milan Orlowski (Cs)
1976 Jacques Secretin (Fra)
1978 Gábor Gergely (Hun)
1980 John Hilton (UK)

1982 Mikael Appelgren (Swe)
1984 Ulf Bengtsson (Swe)
1986 Jörgen Persson (Swe)
1988 Mikael Appelgren (Swe)
1990 Mikael Appelgren (Swe)

Women's singles
1958 Eva Kóczián (Hun)
1960 Eva Kóczián (Hun)
1962 Agnes Simon (FRG)
1964 Eva Földi (née Kóczián) (Hun)
1966 Maria Alexandru (Rom)
1968 Ilona Vostová (Cs)
1970 Zoya Rudnova (USSR)
1972 Zoya Rudnova (USSR)
1974 Judit Magos (Hun)
1976 Jull Hammersley (UK)
1978 Judit Magos (Hun)
1980 Valentina Popova (USSR)
1982 Bettina Vriesekoop (Hol)
1984 Valentina Popova (USSR)
1986 Csilla Bátorfi (Hun)
1988 Flyura Bulatova (USSR)
1990 Daniela Guergelcheva (Bul)

Men's team
10 Sweden	1964, 1966, 1968, 1970, 1972, 1974, 1980, 1986, 1988, 1990
4 Hungary	1958, 1960, 1978, 1982
2 Yugoslavia	1962, 1976
1 France	1984

Women's team
7 Hungary	1960, 1966, 1972, 1978, 1982, 1986, 1990
6 USSR	1970, 1974, 1976, 1980, 1984, 1988
2 England	1958, 1964
2 F.R.Germany	1962, 1968

ENGLISH OPEN CHAMPIONSHIPS
Instituted in 1921 this is the longest established national championship and has attracted many of the world's best players. Held annually to 1980, but biennially since then.
Most titles:
Men's singles: 6 Richard Bergmann (Aut/Eng) 1939-40, 1948, 1950, 1952, 1954; 5 Viktor Barna (Hun) 1933-5, 1937-8
Women's singles: 6 Maria Alexandru (Rom) 1963-4, 1970-2, 1974
Men's doubles: 7 Viktor Barna 1931, 1933-5, 1938-9, 1949
Women's doubles: 12 Diane Rowe (Eng) 1950-6, 1960, 1962-5 (first 6 with her twin Rosalind)
Mixed doubles: 8 Viktor Barna 1933-6, 1938, 1940, 1951, 1953
All events:
MEN 20 Viktor Barna (as above)
WOMEN 17 Diane Rowe (singles 1962, mixed 1952, 1954, 1956, 1960)

TAEKWONDO

Taekwondo is a martial art, with all activities based on defensive spirit, developed over 20 centuries in Korea. It was officially recognised as part of Korean tradition and culture in 1955. Thereafter the sport spread internationally so that it now has an estimated 22 million practitioners in the 115 countries which are members of the World Taekwondo Federation. This governing body was inaugurated following the first world championships in 1973 and recognised by the IOC in 1980. Taekwondo was played as an official sport at the 1983 Pan-American Games and at the 1984 Asian Games. It was a demonstration sport at the 1988 Olympic Games in Seoul and will be again in 1992. There are eight weight categories ranging from fin to heavyweight.

WORLD CHAMPIONSHIPS

These biennial championships were first held in Seoul in 1973, when they were organised by the Korea Taekwondo Association. Women's events were first staged unofficially in 1983, and have been included on the official programme from 1987. A record 63 nations were represented in 1985. *Champions at each weight category:*

MEN

Fin (50kg)
1975 Whang Soo-yong (SKo)
1977 Song Ki-yul (SKo)
1979 Lee Seung-kyung (SKo)
1982 José Cedeno (Ecu)
1983 Kwang Yeon-wang (SKo)
1985 Lee Sun-jang (SKo)
1987 Lim Sung-wook (SKo)
1989 Kwon Tae-ho (SKo)

Fly (54kg)
1975 Han You-keun (SKo)
1977 Ha Suk-kwang (SKo)
1979 Yang Ki-mo (SKo)
1982 Jeon Woong-hwan (SKo)
1983 Ko Jeong-ho (SKo)
1985 Kim Yeong-sik (SKo)
1987 Kang Chang-mo (SKo)
1989 Kim Chul-ho (SKo)

Bantam (58kg)
1975 Son Tae-whan (SKo)
1977 Kim Chong-ki (SKo)
1979 Kim Chong-ki (SKo)
1982 Kim Chong-ki (SKo)
1983 Han Hong-sik (SKo)
1985 Yoo Myung-sik (SKo)
1987 Yoo Myung-sik (SKo)
1989 Ham Jun (SKo)

Feather (64kg)
1975 Lee Gyeo-sung (SKo)
1977 Park Chung-ho (SKo)
1979 Yim Dai-taik (SKo)
1982 Jang Myeong-sam (SKo)
1983 Lee Jae-bong (SKo)
1985 Han Jae-koo (SKo)
1987 Lee Chian-hsiang (Tai)
1989 Jang Hyuk (SKo)

Light (70kg)
1973 Lee Ki-hyung (SKo)
1975 You Young-hab (SKo)
1977 Hwang Ming Der (Tai)
1979 Park Oh-sung (SKo)
1982 Park Oh-sung (SKo)
1983 Han Jae-ku (SKo)
1985 Park Bong-kwon (SKo)
1987 Yang Dae-seung (SKo)
1989 Yang Dae-seung (SKo)

Welter (76kg)
1975 Song Hur (SKo)
1977 You Young-hab (SKo)
1979 Oscar Mendiola (Mex)
1982 Park Cheon-jae (SKo)
1983 Yilmaz Helvacioglu (Tur)
1985 Chung Kook-hyun (SKo)
1987 Chung Kook-hyun (SKo)
1989 Lee Hyun-suk (SKo)

Light-middle
1979 Rainer Müller (FRG)
1982 Chung Kook-hyun (SKo)
1983 Chung Kook-hyun (SKo)

Middle (83kg)
1975 Yang Young-kwan (SKo)
1977 Song Hur (SKo)
1979 Kim Sang-chun (SKo)
1982 Kim Sang-chun (SKo)
1983 Lee Dong-joon (SKo)
1985 Lee Dong-joon (SKo)
1987 Lee Kye-haeng (SKo)
1989 Jeong Yong-suk (SKo)

Light-heavy
1979 Chung Chan (SKo)
1982 Ha Yong-seong (SKo)
1983 Fargas Inreno (Spa)

Heavy (over 83kg)
1973 Kim Jeong-tae (SKo)
1975 Choi Jeong-do (SKo)
1977 Ahn Jang-shik (SKo)
1979 Sjef Vos (Hol)
1982 Dirk Jung (FRG)
1983 Jang Seung-hwa (SKo)
1985 Hendrik Meijer (Hol)
1987 Michael Arndt (FRG)
1989 Amr Khairy Mahmoud (Egy)
Most wins: 4 Chung Kook-hyun, 3 Kim Chong-ki

WOMEN

Fin (43kg)
1987 Jang Ei-suk (SKo)
1989 Chin Yu-fang (Tai)

Fly (47kg)
1987 Pai Yun-yao (Tai)
1989 Weon Sun-jin (SKo)

Bantam (51kg)
1987 Tennur Yerlhsu (Tur)
1989 Jung Nam-suk (SKo)

Feather (55kg)
1987 Kim So-young (SKo)
1989 Kim So-young (SKo)

Light (60kg)
1987 Lee Eun-young (SKo)
1989 Lee Eun-young (SKo)

Welter (65kg)
1987 Coral Bistuer (Spa)
1989 Anita Silsby (USA)

Middle (70kg)
1987 Margaretha De Jongh (Hol)
1989 Lydia Zele (USA)

Heavy (over 70kg)
1987 Lynette Love (USA)
1989 Jung Wan-sook (SKo)

OLYMPIC GAMES

1988 gold medallists:

MEN

50kg	Kwon Tae-ho (SKo)
54kg	Ha Tae-kyung (SKo)
58kg	Ji Yong-suk (SKo)
64kg	Chang Myung-sam (SKo)
70kg	Park Bong-kwon (SKo)
76kg	Chung Kook-hyun (SKo)
83kg	Lee Kye-haeng (SKo)
Over 83kg	Jimmy Kim (USA)

WOMEN

43kg	Chin Yu-fang (Tai)
47kg	Choo Nan-yool (SKo)
51kg	Chen Yi-an (Tai)
55kg	Annemette Christensen (Den)
60kg	Dana Hee (USA)
65kg	Arlene Limas (USA)
70kg	Kim Hyun-hee (SKo)
Over 70kg	Lynette Love (USA)

TENNIS

Lawn Tennis evolved from Real Tennis and while accounts of various forms of 'Field Tennis' were recorded in the 18th century, the real 'father' of lawn tennis is regarded as Major Wingfield who showed off his new game, which he called Sphairistike, at a Christmas party at a country house at Nantcwlyd, Wales, in 1873. He patented the game in 1874. The Marylebone Cricket Club were responsible in revising Wingfield's initial rules and in 1877 the All England Croquet Club added the name Lawn Tennis to their title.

WIMBLEDON CHAMPIONSHIPS

The All-England Championships at Wimbledon are regarded as the most prestigious championships in the world. They were first held in 1877 and, until 1922, were organised on a challenge round basis, in which the defending champion met the winner of an all comers tournament in the final. *Winners:*

Men's singles

1877 Spencer Gore (UK)
1878 Frank Hadow (UK)
1879-80 Rev.John Hartley (UK)
1881-6 William Renshaw (UK)
1887 Herbert Lawford (UK)
1888 Ernest Renshaw (UK)
1889 William Renshaw (UK)
1890 Willoughby Hamilton (UK)
1891-2 Wilfred Baddeley (UK)
1893-4 Joshua Pim (UK)
1895 Wilfred Baddeley (UK)
1896 Harold Mahoney (UK)
1897-1900 Reginald Doherty (UK)
1901 Arthur Gore (UK)
1902-6 Lawrence Doherty (UK)
1907 Norman Brookes (Aus)
1908-9 Arthur Gore (UK)
1910-3 Tony Wilding (NZ)
1914 Norman Brookes (Aus)
1919 Gerald Patterson (Aus)
1920-1 Bill Tilden (USA)
1922 Gerald Patterson (Aus)
1923 William Johnston (USA)
1924 Jean Borotra (Fra)
1925 René Lacoste (Fra)
1926 Jean Borotra (Fra)
1927 Henri Cochet (Fra)
1928 René Lacoste (Fra)
1929 Henri Cochet (Fra)
1930 Bill Tilden (USA)
1931 Sidney Wood (USA)
1932 Ellsworth Vines (USA)
1933 Jack Crawford (Aus)
1934-6 Fred Perry (UK)
1937-8 Donald Budge (USA)
1939 Bobby Riggs (USA)
1946 Yvon Petra (Fra)
1947 Jack Kramer (USA)
1948 Bob Falkenburg (USA)
1949 Ted Schroeder (USA)
1950 Budge Patty (USA)
1951 Dick Savitt (USA)
1952 Frank Sedgman (Aus)
1953 Vic Seixas (USA)
1954 Jaroslav Drobny (Egy)
1955 Tony Trabert (USA)
1956-7 Lew Hoad (Aus)
1958 Ashley Cooper (Aus)
1959 Alex Olmedo (USA)
1960 Neale Fraser (Aus)
1961-2 Rod Laver (Aus)
1963 Chuck McKinley (USA)
1964-5 Roy Emerson (Aus)
1966 Manuel Santana (Spa)
1967 John Newcombe (Aus)
1968-9 Rod Laver (Aus)
1970-1 John Newcombe (Aus)
1972 Stan Smith (USA)
1973 Jan Kodes (Cs)
1974 Jimmy Connors (USA)
1975 Arthur Ashe (USA)
1976-80 Björn Borg (Swe)
1981 John McEnroe (USA)
1982 Jimmy Connors (USA)
1983-4 John McEnroe (USA)
1985-6 Boris Becker (FRG)
1987 Pat Cash (Aus)
1988 Stefan Edberg (Swe)
1989 Boris Becker (FRG)
1990 Stefan Edberg (Swe)
Most wins (pre-1922):
7 William Renshaw 1881-6, 1889
(post-1922): 5 Björn Borg 1976-80

Women's singles

Note: see end of Tennis section for cross-reference list of women's maiden and married names.
1884-5 Maud Watson (UK)
1886 Blanche Bingley (UK)
1887-8 Lottie Dod (UK)
1889 Blanche Hillyard (UK)
1890 Helene Rice (UK)
1891-3 Lottie Dod (UK)
1894 Blanche Hillyard (UK)
1895-6 Charlotte Cooper (UK)
1897 Blanche Hillyard (UK)
1898 Charlotte Cooper (UK)
1899-1900 Blanche Hillyard (UK)
1901 Charlotte Sterry (UK)
1902 Muriel Robb (UK)
1903-4 Dorothea Douglass (UK)
1905 May Sutton (USA)
1906 Dorothea Douglass (UK)
1907 May Sutton (USA)
1908 Charlotte Sterry (UK)
1909 Dora Boothby (UK)
1910-1 Dorothea Lambert Chambers (UK)
1912 Ethel Larcombe (UK)
1913-4 Dorothea Lambert Chambers (UK)
1919-23 Suzanne Lenglen (Fra)
1924 Kathleen McKane (UK)
1925 Suzanne Lenglen (Fra)
1926 Kathleen Godfree (UK)
1927-9 Helen Wills (USA)
1930 Helen Moody (USA)
1931 Cilly Aussem (Ger)
1932-3 Helen Moody (USA)
1934 Dorothy Round (UK)
1935 Helen Moody (USA)
1936 Helen Jacobs (USA)
1937 Dorothy Round (UK)
1938 Helen Moody (USA)
1939 Alice Marble (USA)
1946 Pauline Betz (USA)
1947 Margaret Osborne (USA)
1948-50 Louise Brough (USA)
1951 Doris Hart (USA)
1952-4 Maureen Connolly (USA)
1955 Louise Brough (USA)
1956 Shirley Fry (USA)
1957-8 Althea Gibson (USA)
1959-60 Maria Bueno (Bra)
1961 Angela Mortimer (UK)
1962 Karen Susman (USA)
1963 Margaret Smith (Aus)
1964 Maria Bueno (Bra)
1965 Margaret Smith (Aus)
1966-8 Billie Jean King (USA)
1969 Ann Jones (UK)
1970 Margaret Court (Aus)
1971 Evonne Goolagong (Aus)
1972-3 Billie Jean King (USA)
1974 Chris Evert (USA)
1975 Billy Jean King (USA)
1976 Chris Evert (USA)
1977 Virginia Wade (UK)
1978-9 Martina Navrátilová (Cs)
1980 Evonne Cawley (Aus)

1981 Chris Evert Lloyd (USA)
1982-7 Martina Navrátilová (US)
1988-9 Steffi Graf (FRG)
1990 Martina Navrátilová (US)
Most wins (pre-1922): 7 Dorothea Lambert Chambers (née Douglass) 1903-4, 1906, 1910-1, 1913-4
(post-1922): 9 Martina Navrátilová 1978-9, 1982-7, 1990; 8 Helen Moody (née Wills) 1927-30, 1932-3, 1935, 1938

Men's doubles
1879 L.R.Erskine & Herbert Lawford (UK)
1880-1 Ernest Renshaw & William Renshaw (UK)
1882 Rev.John Hartley & R.T.Richardson (UK)
1883 C.W.Grinstead & C.E.Welldon (UK)
1884-6 Ernest Renshaw & William Renshaw (UK)
1887 Patrick Bowes-Lyon & Herbert Wilberforce (UK)
1888-9 Ernest Renshaw & William Renshaw (UK)
1890 Joshua Pim & Frank Stoker (UK)
1891 Herbert Baddeley & Wilfred Baddeley (UK)
1892 Harry Barlow & Ernest Lewis (UK)
1893 Joshua Pim & Frank Stoker (UK)
1894-6 Herbert Baddeley & Wilfred Baddeley (UK)
1897-1901 Lawrence Doherty & Reginald Doherty (UK)
1902 Frank Riseley & Sidney Smith (UK)

1903-5 Lawrence Doherty & Reginald Doherty (UK)
1906 Frank Riseley & Sidney Smith (UK)
1907 Norman Brookes (Aus) & Anthony Wilding (NZ)
1908 Josiah Ritchie (UK) & Anthony Wilding (NZ)
1909 Arthur Gore & Roper Barrett (UK)
1910 Josiah Ritchie (UK) & Anthony Wilding (NZ)
1911 Max Decugis & André Gobert (Fra)
1912-3 Charles Dixon & Roper Barrett (UK)
1914 Norman Brookes (Aus) & Anthony Wilding (NZ)
1919 Pat O'Hara Wood & Ronald Thomas (Aus)
1920 Charles Garland & Richard Williams (USA)
1921 Randolph Lycett & Max Woosnam (UK)
1922 James Anderson (Aus) & Randolph Lycett (UK)
1923 Leslie Godfree & Randolph Lycett (UK)
1924 Frank Hunter & Vincent Richards (USA)
1925 Jean Borotra & René Lacoste (Fra)
1926 Jacques Brugnon & Henri Cochet (Fra)
1927 Frank Hunter & William Tilden (USA)
1928 Jacques Brugnon & Henri Cochet (Fra)
1929-30 William Allison & John Van Ryn (USA)
1931 George Lott & John Van Ryn (USA)
1932-3 Jean Borotra & Jacques Brugnon (Fra)
1934 George Lott & Lester Stoefen (USA)
1935 Jack Crawford & Adrian Quist (Aus)

Jack Kramer leaps the net after his 6-1,6-3,6-2 win over Tom Brown to take the 1947 Wimbledon title. He went on to lead the way for professional tennis **(Popperfoto)**

Ken Rosewall (left) and Lew Hoad, both at the age of 17 in 1952, at the outset of their remarkable careers
(Hulton-Deutsch)

1936 Pat Hughes & Raymond Tuckey (UK)
1937-8 Don Budge & Gene Mako (USA)
1939 Ellwood Cooke & Bobby Riggs (USA)
1946 Tom Brown & Jack Kramer (USA)
1947 Bob Falkenburg & Jack Kramer (USA)
1948 John Bromwich & Frank Sedgman (Aus)
1949 Ricardo Gonzales & Frank Parker (USA)
1950 John Bromwich & Adrian Quist (Aus)
1951-2 Ken McGregor & Frank Sedgman (Aus)
1953 Lew Hoad & Ken Rosewall (Aus)
1954 Rex Hartwig & Mervyn Rose (Aus))
1955 Rex Hartwig & Lew Hoad (Aus)
1956 Lew Hoad & Ken Rosewall (Aus)
1957 Gardnar Mulloy & Budge Patty (USA)
1958 Sven Davidson & Ulf Schmidt (Swe)
1959 Roy Emerson & Neale Fraser (Aus)
1960 Rafael Osuna (Mex) & Dennis Ralston (USA)
1961 Roy Emerson & Neale Fraser (Aus)
1962 Bob Hewitt & Fred Stolle (Aus)
1963 Rafael Osuna & Antonio Palafox (Mex)
1964 Bob Hewitt & Fred Stolle (Aus)
1965 John Newcombe & Tony Roche (Aus)
1966 Ken Fletcher & John Newcombe (Aus)
1967 Bob Hewitt & Frew McMillan (SAf)
1968-70 John Newcombe & Tony Roche (Aus)

1971 Roy Emerson & Rod Laver (Aus)
1972 Bob Hewitt & Frew McMillan (SAf)
1973 Jimmy Connors (USA) & Ilie Nastase (Rom)
1974 John Newcombe & Tony Roche (Aus)
1975 Vitas Gerulaitis & Sandy Mayer (USA)
1976 Brian Gottfried (USA) & Raúl Ramirez (Mex)
1977 Ross Case & Geoff Masters (Aus)
1978 Bob Hewitt & Frew McMillan (SAf)
1979 Peter Fleming & John McEnroe (USA)
1980 Pete McNamara & Paul McNamee (Aus)
1981 Peter Fleming & John McEnroe (USA)
1982 Peter McNamara & Paul McNamee (Aus)
1983-4 Peter Fleming & John McEnroe (USA)
1985 Heinz Günthardt (Swi) & Balázs Taróczy (Hun)
1986 Joakim Nyström & Mats Wilander (Swe)
1987-8 Ken Flach & Robert Seguso (USA)
1989 John Fitzgerald (Aus) & Anders Järryd (Swe)
1990 Rick Leach & Jim Pugh (USA)
Most wins: 8 Lawrence & Reginald Doherty 1897-1901, 1903-5

Women's doubles
1913 Winifred McNair & Dora Boothby (UK)
1914 Agnes Morton (UK) & Elizabeth Ryan (USA)
1919-23 Suzanne Lenglen (Fra) & Elizabeth Ryan (USA)

1924 Hazel Wightman & Helen Wills (USA)
1925 Suzanne Lenglen (Fra) & Elizabeth Ryan (USA)
1926 Mary Browne & Elizabeth Ryan (USA)
1927 Helen Wills & Elizabeth Ryan (USA)
1928 Peggy Saunders & Phyllis Watson (UK)
1929 Peggy Michell & Phyllis Watson (UK)
1930 Helen Moody (née Wills) & Elizabeth Ryan (USA)
1931 Dorothy Barron & Phyllis Mudford (UK)
1932 Doris Metaxa (Fra) & Josane Sigart (Bel)
1933-4 Simone Mathieu (Fra) & Elizabeth Ryan (USA)
1935-6 Freda James & Kay Stammers (UK)
1937 Simone Mathieu (Fra) & Billie Yorke (UK)
1938-9 Sarah Fabyan & Alice Marble (USA)
1946 Louise Brough & Margaret Osborne (USA)
1947 Doris Hart & Pat Todd (USA)
1948-50 Louise Brough & Margaret Du Pont (USA)
1951-3 Shirley Fry & Doris Hart (USA)
1954 Louise Brough & Margaret Du Pont (USA)
1955 Angela Mortimer & Anne Shilcock (UK)
1956 Angela Buxton (UK) & Althea Gibson (USA)
1957 Althea Gibson & Darlene Hard (USA)
1958 Maria Bueno (Bra) & Althea Gibson (USA)
1959 Jean Arth & Darlene Hard (USA)
1960 Maria Bueno (Bra) & Darlene Hard (USA)
1961 Karen Hantze & Billie Jean Moffitt (USA)
1962 Billie Jean Moffit & Karen Susman (USA)
1963 Maria Bueno (Bra) & Darlene Hard (USA)
1964 Margaret Smith & Lesley Turner (Aus)
1965 Maria Bueno (Bra) & Billie Jean Moffitt (USA)
1966 Maria Bueno (Bra) & Nancy Richey (USA)
1967-8 Rosemary Casals & Billie Jean King (USA)
1969 Margaret Court & Judy Tegart (Aus)
1970-1 Rosemary Casals & Billie Jean King (USA)
1972 Billie Jean King (USA) & Betty Stove (Hol)
1973 Rosemary Casals & Billie Jean King (USA)
1974 Evonne Goolagong (Aus) & Peggy Michel (USA)
1975 Ann Kiyomura (USA) & Kazuko Sawamatsu (Jap)
1976 Chris Evert (USA) & Martina Navrátilová (Cs)
1977 Helen Cawley (Aus) & Joanne Russell (USA)
1978 Kerry Reid & Wendy Turnbull (Aus)
1979 Billie Jean King (USA) & Martina Navrátilová (Cs)
1980 Kathy Jordan & Anne Smith (USA)
1981-4 Martina Navrátilová & Pam Shriver (USA)
1985 Kathy Jordan (USA) & Elizabeth Smylie (Aus)
1986 Martina Navrátilová & Pam Shriver (USA)
1987 Claudia Kohde-Kilsch (FRG) & Helena Sukova (Cs)
1988 Steffi Graf (FRG) & Gabriela Sabatini (Arg)
1989-90 Jana Novotná & Helena Suková (Cs)
Most wins: 12 Elizabeth Ryan 1914, 1919-23, 1925-7, 1930, 1933-4

Mixed doubles
1913 Hope Crisp & Agnes Tuckey (UK)
1914 James Parke & Ethel Larcombe (UK)
1919 Randolph Lycett (UK) & Elizabeth Ryan (USA)
1920 Gerald Patterson (Aus) & Suzanne Lenglen (Fra)
1921 Randolph Lycett (UK) & Elizabeth Ryan (USA)
1922 Pat O'Hara Wood (USA) & Suzanne Lenglen (Fra)

1923 Randolph Lycett (UK) & Elizabeth Ryan (USA)
1924 Brian Gilbert & Kathleen McKane (UK)
1925 Jean Borotra & Suzanne Lenglen (Fra)
1926 Leslie Godfree & Kathleen Godfree (UK)
1927 Frank Hunter & Elizabeth Ryan (USA)
1928 Pat Spence (SAf) & Elizabeth Ryan (USA)
1929 Frank Hunter & Helen Wills (USA)
1930 Jack Crawford (Aus) & Elizabeth Ryan (USA)
1931 George Lott & Anna Harper (USA)
1932 Enrique Maier (Spa) & Elizabeth Ryan (USA)
1933 Gottfried von Cramm & Hilda Krahwinkel (Ger)
1934 Ryuki Miki (Jap) & Dorothy Round (UK)
1935-6 Fred Perry & Dorothy Round (UK)
1937-8 Don Budge & Alice Marble (USA)
1939 Bobby Riggs & Alice Marble (USA)
1946 Tom Brown & Louise Brough (USA)
1947-8 John Bromwich (Aus) & Louise Brough (USA)
1949 Eric Sturgess & Sheila Summers (SAf)
1950 Eric Sturgess (SAf) & Louise Brough (USA)
1951-2 Frank Sedgman (Aus) & Doris Hart (USA)
1953-5 Vic Seixas & Doris Hart (USA)
1956 Vic Seixas & Shirley Fry (USA)
1957 Mervyn Rose (Aus) & Darlene Hard (USA)
1958 Bob Howe & Lorraine Coghlan (Aus)
1959-60 Rod Laver (Aus) & Darlene Hard (USA)
1961 Fred Stolle & Lesley Turner (Aus)
1962 Neale Fraser (Aus) & Margaret Du Pont (USA)
1963 Ken Fletcher & Margaret Smith (Aus)
1964 Fred Stolle & Lesley Turner (Aus)
1965-6 Ken Fletcher & Margaret Smith (Aus)
1967 Owen Davidson (Aus) & Billie Jean King (USA)
1968 Ken Fletcher & Margaret Court (Aus)
1969 Fred Stolle (Aus) & Ann Jones (UK)
1970 Ilie Nastase (Rom) & Rosemary Casals (USA)
1971 Owen Davidson (Aus) & Billie Jean King (USA)
1972 Ilie Nastase (Rom) & Rosemary Casals (USA)
1973-4 Owen Davidson (Aus) & Billie Jean King (USA)
1975 Marty Riessen (USA) & Margaret Court (Aus)
1976 Tony Roche (Aus) & Françoise Durr (Fra)
1977 Bob Hewitt & Greer Stevens (SAf)
1978 Frew McMillan (SAf) & Betty Stove (Hol)
1979 Bob Hewitt & Greer Stevens (SAf)
1980 John Austin & Tracy Austin (USA)
1981 Frew McMillan (SAf) & Betty Stove (Hol)
1982 Kevin Curren (SAf) & Anne Smith (USA)
1983-4 John Lloyd (UK) & Wendy Turnbull (Aus)
1985 Paul McNamee (Aus) & Martina Navrátilová (USA)
1986 Ken Flach & Kathy Jordan (USA)
1987 Jeremy Bates & Jo Durie (UK)
1988 Sherwood Stewart & Zina Garrison (USA)
1989 Jim Pugh (USA) & Jana Novotná (Cs)
1990 Rick Leach & Zina Garrison (USA)
Most wins (Men): 4 Vic Seixas 1953-6, Owen Davidson 1967, 1971, 1973-4, Ken Fletcher 1963, 1965-6, 1968 (Women): 7 Elizabeth Ryan 1919, 1921, 1923, 1927-8, 1930, 1932

Most Wimbledon titles

	Total	Singles	Doubles	Mixed	Years
Billie Jean King (USA)	20	6	10	4	1961-79
Elizabeth Ryan (USA)	19	-	12	7	1914-34
Martina Navrátilová (Cs/USA)	17	9	7	1	1976-90
Suzanne Lenglen (Fra)	15	6	6	3	1919-25
Lawrence Doherty (UK)	13	5	8	-	1897-1905
Louise Brough (USA)	13	4	5	4	1946-55

Most successful singles players

From the abolition of the challenge round in 1922, the leading players on the following points basis: 8 for winning the tournament, 4 for losing in the final, 2 for losing semi-finalists and 1 for losing quarter finalists have been:

MEN

Points	Name	Won	F	SF	QF	Years
46	Björn Borg	5	1	-	2	1973-81
45	Jimmy Connors	2	4	5	3	1972-87
41	Rod Laver	4	2	-	1	1959-71
37	John McEnroe	3	2	2	1	1977-89
33	Jean Borotra	2	3	2	1	1924-31
32	Boris Becker	3	2	-	-	1985-90
29	John Newcombe	3	1	-	1	1966-74
27	Henri Cochet	2	1	3	1	1925-33
27	Fred Perry	3	-	1	1	1931-6
24	Jaroslav Drobny	1	2	3	2	1946-55
23	Roy Emerson	2	-	1	5	1959-70
22	Stefan Edberg	2	1	1	-	1987-90

Note: Bill Tilden had two wins 1920-1 in challenge round days plus 14 points (1 win, 2 sf) 1927-30.

Jimmy Connors reached the top of world tennis in 1974, when he won Wimbledon, US and Australian Opens, and still ranked in the world top ten 15 years later in 1989
(All-Sport/Simon Bruty)

WOMEN

88	Martina Navrátilová	9	2	3	2	1975-90
75	Billie Jean King	6	3	5	5	1962-83
68	Helen Wills/Moody	8	1	-	-	1924-38
66	Chris Evert	3	7	7	-	1972-89
51	Louise Brough	4	3	3	1	1946-57
41	Margaret Smith/Court	3	2	4	1	1961-75
36	Maria Bueno	3	2		4	1958-68
35	Helen Jacobs	1	5	2	3	1929-39
28	Doris Hart	1	3	3	2	1946-55
27	Evonne Goolagong/Cawley	2	3	3	1	1971-80
26*	Suzanne Lenglen	3	-	1	-	1922-5
26	Ann Haydon/Jones	1	1	6	2	1958-69
24	Dorothy Round	2	1	-	4	1931-7
24	Maureen Connolly	3	-	-	-	1952-4
23	Kitty McKane/Godfree	2	1	1	1	1923-7
23	Margaret Osborne/Du Pont	1	2	2	3	1946-58
22	Steffi Graf	2	1	1	-	1987-90
20	Virginia Wade	1	-	3	6	1967-83

* also three wins 1919-21
Most appearances in finals: 10 Navrátilová and Evert, 9 King
Most semi-finals: 17 Evert, 14 King, 13 Navrátilová, 11 Connors (men's record)

Prior to 1922, there was a challenge round in which the defending champion played against the winner of the all-comers tournament. The most successful players were as follows: *(W = winner, RU = runner-up, losing in challenge round final, AC = winning all-comers tournament)*

Name	W	RU	AC
MEN			
William Renshaw	7	1	2
Lawrence Doherty	5	1	2
Reginald Doherty	4	1	1
Tony Wilding	4	1	1
Arthur W.Gore	3	3	4
Wilfred Baddeley	3	3	3
Herbert Lawford	1	5	5
WOMEN			
Dorothea Douglass (later Mrs Lambert Chambers)	7	4	4
Blanche Bingley/Hillyard	6	6	8
Charlotte Cooper/Sterry	5	5	6
Lottie Dod	5	-	2

UNITED STATES CHAMPIONSHIPS

An American championship, open to all comers, was held at Staten Island in September 1880 and won by Englishman O.E.Woodhouse. The first official US Championships were in 1881, following the formation of the US National Lawn Tennis Association. These were contested annually by amateurs until 1969, the year after the sport went open. In 1968 and 1969, however, there were two Championships, the Amateur and Open events. Since 1970 there has only been an Open competition. Played at Flushing Meadow, New York since 1978, previously at a variety of venues, notably the West Side Club, Forest Hills, New York since the 1920s. *Winners:*

Men's singles
Challenge Round basis 1884-1911
1881-7 Richard Sears (USA)
1888-9 Henry Slocum Jr (USA)
1890-2 Oliver Campbell (USA)
1893-4 Robert Wrenn (USA)
1895 Fred Hovey (USA)
1896-7 Robert Wrenn (USA)
1898-1900 Malcolm Whitman (USA)
1901-2 William Larned (USA)
1903 Lawrence Doherty (UK)
1904 Holcombe Ward (USA)
1905 Beals Wright (USA)
1906 William Clothier (USA)
1907-11 William Larned (USA)
1912-3 Maurice McLoughlin (USA)
1914 Norris Williams (USA)
1915 William Johnston (USA)
1916 Norris Williams (USA)
1917-8 Lindley Murray (USA)
1919 William Johnston (USA)
1920-5 Bill Tilden (USA)
1926-7 René Lacoste (Fra)
1928 Henri Cochet (Fra)
1929 Bill Tilden (USA)
1930 John Doeg (USA)
1931-2 Ellsworth Vines (USA)
1933-4 Fred Perry (UK)
1935 Wilmer Allison (USA)
1936 Fred Perry (UK)
1937-8 Donald Budge (USA)
1939 Bobby Riggs (USA)
1940 Donald McNeil (USA)
1941 Bobby Riggs (USA)

1942 Ted Schroeder (USA
1943 Joseph Hunt (USA)
1944-5 Frank Parker (USA)
1946-7 Jack Kramer (USA)
1948-9 Ricardo Gonzales (USA)
1950 Arthur Larsen (USA)
1951-2 Frank Sedgman (USA)
1953 Tony Trabert (USA)
1954 Vic Seixas (USA)
1955 Tony Trabert (USA)
1956 Ken Rosewall (Aus)
1957 Malcolm Anderson (Aus)
1958 Ashley Cooper (Aus)
1959-60 Neale Fraser (Aus)
1961 Roy Emerson (Aus)
1962 Rod Laver (Aus)
1963 Raphael Osuna (Mex)
1964 Roy Emerson (Aus)
1965 Manuel Santana (Spa)
1966 Fred Stolle (Aus)
1967 John Newcombe (Aus)
1968 Arthur Ashe (USA)
Open Arthur Ashe (USA)
1969 Stan Smith (USA)
Open Rod Laver (Aus)
1970 Ken Rosewall (Aus)
1971 Stan Smith (USA)
1972 Ilie Nastase (Rom)
1973 John Newcombe (Aus)
1974 Jimmy Connors (USA)
1975 Manuel Orantes (Spa)
1976 Jimmy Connors (USA)
1977 Guillermo Vilas (Arg)
1978 Jimmy Connors (USA)
1979-81 John McEnroe (USA)
1982-3 Jimmy Connors (USA)
1984 John McEnroe (USA)
1985-7 Ivan Lendl (Cs)
1988 Mats Wilander (Swe)
1989 Boris Becker (FRG)

Most wins: 7 Richard Sears, Bill
Larned, Bill Tilden

Women's singles
Challenge Round basis 1887-1918
1887 Ellen Hansell (USA)
1888-9 Bertha Townsend (USA)
1890 Ellen Roosevelt (USA)
1891-2 Mabel Cahill (USA)
1893 Aline Terry (USA)
1894 Helen Helwig (USA)
1895 Juliette Atkinson (USA)
1896 Elisabeth Moore (USA)
1897-8 Juliette Atkinson (USA)
1899 Marion Jones (USA)
1900 Myrtle McAteer (USA)
1901 Elisabeth Moore (USA)

Steffi Graf not only won the Grand Slam of singles titles in 1988, but added the Olympic gold medal **(All-Sport/BobMartin)**

1902 Marion Jones (USA)
1903 Elisabeth Moore (USA)
1904 May Sutton (USA)
1905 Elisabeth Moore (USA)
1906 Helen Homans (USA)
1907 Evelyn Sears (USA)
1908 Maud Bargar-Wallach
1909-11 Hazel Hotchkiss (USA)
1912-4 Mary Browne (USA)
1915-8 Molla Bjurstedt (USA(
1919 Hazel Wightman (née Hotchkiss)
1920-2 Molla Mallory (née Bjurstedt)
1923-5 Helen Wills (USA)
1926 Molla Mallory (USA)
1927-9 Helen Wills (USA)
1930 Betty Nuthall (UK)
1931 Helen Moody (née Wills)
1932-5 Helen Jacobs (USA)
1936 Alice Marble (USA)
1937 Anita Lizana (Chl)
1938-40 Alice Marble (USA)
1941 Sarah Cooke (USA)
1942-4 Pauline Betz (USA)
1945 Sarah Cooke (USA)
1946 Pauline Betz (USA)
1947 Louise Brough (USA)
1948-50 Margaret Du Pont (USA)
1951-3 Maureen Connolly (USA)
1954-5 Doris Hart (USA)
1956 Shirley Fry (USA)
1957-8 Althea Gibson (USA)
1959 Maria Bueno (Bra)
1960-1 Darlene Hard (USA)
1962 Margaret Smith (Aus)
1963-4 Maria Bueno (Bra)
1965 Margaret Smith (Aus)
1966 Maria Bueno (Bra)
1967 Billie Jean King (USA)
1968 Margaret Court (Aus)
Open Virginia Wade (UK)
1969 Margaret Court (Aus)
Open Margaret Court (Aus)
1970 Margaret Court (Aus)
1971-2 Billie Jean King (USA)
1973 Margaret Court (Aus)
1974 Billie Jean King (USA)
1975-8 Chris Evert (USA)
1979 Tracy Austin (USA)
1980 Chris Evert Lloyd (USA)
1981 Tracy Austin (USA)
1982 Chris Evert Lloyd (USA)
1983-4 Martina Navrátilová (USA)
1985 Hanna Mandlíková (Cs)
1986-7 Martina Navrátilová (USA)
1988-9 Steffi Graf (FRG)

Most wins:
7 Molla Mallory (née Bjurstedt), Helen Moody (née Wills)

Men's doubles *Winners from 1946*
1946 Gardnar Mulloy & William Talbert (USA)
1947 Jack Kramer & Ted Schroeder (USA)
1948 Gardnar Mulloy & William Talbert (USA)
1949 John Bromwich & William Sidwell (Aus)
1950 John Bromwich & Frank Sedgman (Aus)
1951 Ken McGregor & Frank Sedgman (Aus)
1952 Mervin Rose (Aus) & Vic Seixas (USA)
1953 Rex Hartwig & Mervyn Rose (Aus)
1954 Vic Seixas & Tony Trabert (USA)
1955 Kosei Kano & Atsushi Miyagi (Jap)
1956 Lew Hoad & Ken Rosewall (Aus)
1957 Ashley Cooper & Neale Fraser (Aus)
1958 Alex Olmedo & Ham Richardson (USA)
1959-60 Roy Emerson & Neale Fraser (Aus)
1961 Charles McKinley & Dennis Ralston (USA)
1962 Antonio Palafox & Rafael Osuna (Mex)
1963-4 Charles McKinley & Dennis Ralston (USA)
1965-6 Roy Emerson & Fred Stolle (Aus)
1967 John Newcombe & Tony Roche (Aus)
1968 Bob Lutz & Stan Smith (USA)
Open Bob Lutz & Stan Smith (USA)
1969 Dick Crealy & Allan Stone (Aus)
Open Ken Rosewall & Fred Stolle (Aus)
1970 Pierre Barthes (Fra) & Nikki Pilic (Yug)
1971 John Newcombe (Aus) & Roger Taylor (UK)
1972 Cliff Drysdale (SAf) & Roger Taylor (UK)
1973 Owen Davidson & John Newcombe (Aus)
1974 Bob Lutz & Stan Smith (USA)
1975 Jimmy Connors (USA) & Ilie Nastase (Rom)
1976 Tom Okker (Hol) & Marty Riessen (USA)
1977 Bob Hewitt & Frew McMillan (SAf)
1978 Bob Lutz & Stan Smith (USA)
1979 Peter Fleming & John McEnroe (USA)
1980 Bob Lutz & Stan Smith (USA)
1981 Peter Fleming & John McEnroe (USA)
1982 Kevin Curren (SAf) & Steve Denton (USA)
1983 Peter Fleming & John McEnroe (USA)
1984 John Fitzgerald (Aus) & Tomás Smid (Cs)
1985 Ken Flach & Robert Seguso (USA)
1986 Andrés Gómez (Ecu) & Slobodan Zivojinovic (Yug)
1987 Stefan Edberg & Anders Järryd (Swe)
1988 Sergio Casal & Emilio Sánchez (Spa)
1989 John McEnroe (USA) & Mark Woodforde (Aus)
Most wins by one pair: 5 Richard Sears & James Dwight 1882-4, 1886-7
By player: 6 Richard Sears (also won with Joseph Clark 1885), 6 Holcombe Ward 1899-1901 (with Dwight Davis), 1904-6 (with Beals Wright); 5 Bill Tilden 1918, 1921-2 (with Vincent Richards), 1923 (with Brian Norton), 1927 (with Francis Hunter); 5 Vincent Richards, also with Norris Williams 1925-6; 5 George Lott Jr 1928 (with John Hennessy), 1929-30 (with John Doeg), 1933-4 (with Lester Stoefen)

Women's doubles *Winners from 1946*
1942-50 Louise Brough & Margaret Osborne (USA)
1951-4 Shirley Fry & Doris Hart (USA)
1955-7 Louise Brough & Margaret Du Pont (USA)

1958-9 Jean Arth & Darlene Hard (USA)
1960 Maria Bueno (Bra) & Darlene Hard (USA)
1961 Darlene Hard (USA) & Lesley Turner (Aus)
1962 Maria Bueno (Bra) & Darlene Hard (USA)
1963 Robyn Ebbern & Margaret Smith (Aus)
1964 Karen Susman & Billie Jean Moffitt (USA)
1965 Nancy Richey & Carole Graebner (USA)
1966 Maria Bueno (Bra) & Nancy Richey (USA)
1967 Rosemary Casals & Billie Jean King (USA)
1968 Maria Bueno (Bra) & Margaret Court (Aus)
Open Maria Bueno (Bra) & Margaret Court (Aus)
1969 Margaret Court (Aus) & Virginia Wade (UK)
Open Françoise Durr (Fra) & Darlene Hard (USA)
1970 Margaret Court & Judy Dalton (Aus)
1971 Rosemary Casals (USA) & Judy Dalton (Aus)
1972 Françoise Durr (Fra) & Betty Stove (Hol)
1973 Margaret Court (Aus) & Virginia Wade (UK)
1974 Rosemary Casals & Billie Jean King (USA)
1975 Margaret Court (Aus) & Virginia Wade (UK)
1976 Linda Boshoff & Ilana Kloss (SAf)
1977 Martina Navrátilová (Cs) & Betty Stove (Hol)
1978 Billie Jean King (USA) & Martina Navrátilová (Cs)
1979 Betty Stove (Hol) & Wendy Turnbull (Aus)
1980 Billie Jean King (USA) & Martina Navrátilová (Cs)
1981 Kathy Jordan & Anne Smith (USA)
1982 Rosemary Casals (USA) & Wendy Turnbull (Aus)
1983-4 Martina Navrátilová & Pam Shriver (USA)
1985 Claudia Kohde-Kilsch (FRG) & Helena Suková (Cs)
1986-7 Martina Navrátilová & Pam Shriver (USA)
1988 Gigi Fernandez & Robin White (USA)
1989 Martina Navrátilová (USA) & Hana Mandlíková (Aus)

Most wins by one pair: 12 Louise Brough & Margaret Du Pont (née Osborne), as above;
By player: 13 Margaret Du Pont also 1941 (with Sarah Cooke), 12 Louise Brough, 8 Martina Navrátilová, 7 Juliette Atkinson 1894-5 (with Helen Helwig), 1896 (with Elisabeth Moore), 1897-8 (with Kathleen Atkinson), 1901 (with Myrtle McAteer), 1902 (with Marion Jones); 7 Margaret Court (née Smith), 6 Hazel Wightman (née Hotchkiss) 1909-10 (with Edith Rotch), 1911, 1915 (with Eleonora Sears), 1924, 1928 (with Helen Wills)

Mixed doubles *Winners from 1946*
1943-6 William Talbert & Margaret Osborne (USA)
1947 John Bromwich (Aus) & Louise Brough (USA)
1948 Tom Brown & Louise Brough (USA)
1949 Eric Sturgess (SAf) & Louise Brough (USA)

1950 Ken McGregor (Aus) & Margaret Du Pont (USA)
1951-2 Frank Sedgman (Aus) & Doris Hart (USA)
1953-5 Vic Seixas & Doris Hart (USA)
1956 Ken Rosewall (Aus) & Margaret Du Pont (USA)
1957 Kurt Nielsen (Den) & Althea Gibson (USA)
1958-60 Neale Fraser (Aus) & Margaret Du Pont (USA)
1961 Robert Mark & Margaret Smith (Aus)
1962 Fred Stolle & Margaret Smith (Aus)
1963 Ken Fletcher & Margaret Smith (Aus)
1964 John Newcombe & Margaret Smith (Aus)
1965 Fred Stolle & Margaret Smith (Aus)
1966 Owen Davidson (Aus) & Donna Fales (USA)
1967 Owen Davidson (Aus) & Billie Jean King (USA)
1968 Peter Curtis (UK) & Mary-Ann Eisel (USA)
1969 Paul Sullivan & Patty Hogan (USA)
Open Marty Riessen (USA) & Margaret Court (née Smith) (Aus)
1970 Marty Riessen (USA) & Margaret Court (Aus)
1971 Owen Davidson (Aus) & Billie Jean King (USA)
1972 Marty Riessen (USA) & Margaret Court (Aus)
1973 Owen Davidson (Aus) & Billie Jean King (USA)
1974 Geoff Masters (Aus) & Pam Teeguarden (USA)
1975 Dick Stockton & Rosemary Casals (USA)
1976 Phil Dent (Aus) & Billie Jean King (USA)
1977-8 Frew McMillan (SAf) & Betty Stove (Hol)
1979 Bob Hewitt & Greer Stevens (SAf)
1980 Marty Riessen & Wendy Turnbull (USA)
1981-2 Kevin Curren (SAf) & Anne Smith (USA)
1983 John Fitzgerald & Elizabeth Sayers (Aus)
1984 Tom Gullikson (USA) & Manuela Maleeva (Bul)
1985 Heinz Günthardt (Swi) & Martina Navrátilová (USA)
1986 Sergio Casal (Spa) & Raffaella Reggi (Ita)
1987 Emilio Sánchez (Spa) & Martina Navrátilová (USA)
1988 Jim Pugh (USA) & Jana Novotná (Cs)
1989 Shelby Cannon & Robin White (USA)

Most wins by one pair: 4 William Talbert & Margaret Osborne 1943-6
By woman: 9 Margaret Du Pont (née Osborne) as above, 8 Margaret Court (née Smith), 6 Hazel Wightman (née Hotchkiss) 1909, 1911, 1920 (with Wallace Johnson), 1910 (with Joseph Carpenter), 1915 (with Harry Johnson), 1918 (with Irving Wright)
By man: Edwin Fischer 1894-6, 1898; Wallace Johnson 1907, 1909, 1911, 1920; Bill Tilden 1913-4, 1922-3; William Talbert 1943-6; Owen Davidson 1966-7, 1971, 1973; Marty Riessen 1969-70, 1972, 1980

Most United States titles	*Total*	*Singles*	*Doubles*	*Mixed*	*Years*
Margaret Du Pont (USA)	25	3	13	9	1941-60
Margaret Court (Aus)	22	7	7	8	1961-75*
Louise Brough (USA)	17	1	12	4	1942-57
Bill Tilden (Aus)	16	7	5	4	1913-29
Hazel Wightman (USA)	16	4	6	6	1909-28
Sarah Cooke (USA)	15	2	9	4	1930-45
Martina Navrátilová (Cs/USA)	14	4	8	2	1977-89

* *including both Amateur and Open Championships 1968-9*

FRENCH CHAMPIONSHIPS

The French Championships were first held in 1891 but they remained 'closed', open only to members of French clubs, until 1925 when they became a fully international event. They have always been held on hard courts, and at the Stade Roland Garros since 1928. *All champions from 1925 for singles and from 1946 for doubles:*

Men's singles

1925 René Lacoste (Fra)
1926 Henri Cochet (Fra)
1927 René Lacoste (Fra)
1928 Henri Cochet (Fra)
1929 René Lacoste (Fra)
1930 Henri Cochet (Fra)
1931 Jean Borotra (Fra)
1932 Henri Cochet (Fra)
1933 Jack Crawford (Aus)
1934 Gottfried Von Cramm (Ger)
1935 Fred Perry (UK)
1936 Gottfried Von Cramm (Ger)]
1937 Henner Henkel (Ger)
1938 Donald Budge (USA)
1939 Donald McNeill (USA)
1946 Marcel Bernard (Fra)
1947 József Asboth (Hun)
1948-9 Frank Parker (USA)
1950 Budge Patty (USA)
1951-2 Jaroslav Drobny (Egy)
1953 Ken Rosewall (Aus)
1954-5 Tony Trabert (USA)
1956 Lew Hoad (Aus)
1957 Sven Davidson (Swe)
1958 Mervyn Rose (Aus)
1959-60 Nicola Pietrangeli (Ita)
1961 Manuel Santana (Spa)
1962 Rod Laver (Aus)
1963 Roy Emerson(Aus)
1964 Manuel Santana (Spa)
1965 Fred Stolle (Aus)
1966 Tony Roche (Aus)
1967 Roy Emerson (Aus)
1968 Ken Rosewall (Aus)
1969 Rod Laver (Aus)
1970-1 Jan Kodes (Cs)
1972 Andrés Gimeno (Spa)
1973 Ilie Nastase (Rom)
1974-5 Björn Borg (Swe)
1976 Adriano Panatta (Ita)
1977 Guillermo Vilas (Arg)
1978-81 Björn Borg (Swe)
1982 Mats Wilander (Swe)
1983 Yannick Noah (Fra)
1984 Ivan Lendl (Cs)
1985 Mats Wilander (Swe)
1986-7 Ivan Lendl (Cs)
1988 Mats Wilander (Swe)
1989 Michael Chang (USA)
1990 Andrés Gómez (Ecu)

Most wins: 6 Björn Borg

Women's singles

1925-6 Suzanne Lenglen (Fra)
1927 Kea Bouman (Hol)
1928-30 Helen Wills Moody (USA)
1931 Cilly Aussem (Ger)
1932 Helen Moody (USA)
1933-4 Margaret Scriven (UK)
1935-7 Hilde Sperling (Ger)
1938-9 Simone Mathieu (Fra)
1946 Margaret Osborne (USA)
1947 Pat Todd (USA)
1948 Nelly Landry (Fra)
1949 Margaret Du Pont
      (née Osborne) (USA)
1950 Doris Hart (USA)
1951 Shirley Fry (USA)
1952 Doris Hart (USA)
1953-4 Maureen Connolly (USA)
1955 Angela Mortimer (UK)
1956 Althea Gibson (USA)
1957 Shirley Bloomer (UK)
1958 Zsuzsi Körmöczy (Hun)
1959 Christine Truman (UK)

1960 Darlene Hard (USA)
1961 Ann Haydon (UK)
1962 Margaret Smith (Aus)
1963 Lesley Turner (Aus)
1964 Margaret Smith (Aus)
1965 Lesley Turner (Aus)
1966 Ann Jones (née Haydon) (UK)
1967 Françoise Durr (Fra)
1968 Nancy Richey (USA)
1969 Margaret Court (née Smith)
      (Aus)
1970 Margaret Court (Aus)
1971 Evonne Goolagong (Aus)
1972 Billie Jean King (USA)
1973 Margaret Court (Aus)
1974-5 Chris Evert (USA)
1976 Sue Barker (UK)
1977 Mimi Jausovec (Yug)
1978 Virginia Ruzici (Rom)
1979-80 Chris Evert Lloyd (USA)
1981 Hana Mandlíková (Cs)
1982 Martina Navrátilová (USA)
1983 Chris Evert Lloyd (USA)
1984 Martina Navrátilová (USA)
1985-6 Chris Evert Lloyd (USA)
1987-8 Steffi Graf (FRG)
1989 Arantxa Sánchez (Spa)
1990 Monica Seles (Yug)
Most wins: 7 Chris Evert Lloyd

Chris Evert retired in 1989, having won a record 157 tournaments and 1304 matches in her professional career (All-Sport)

Men's doubles
1946 Marcel Bernard & Yvon Petra (Fra)
1947 Eustace Fannin & Eric Sturgess (SAf)
1948 Lennart Bergelin (Swe) & Jaroslav Drobny (Cs)
1949 Richard Gonzales & Frank Parker (USA)
1950 William Talbert & Tony Trabert (USA)
1951-2 Ken McGregor & Frank Sedgman (Aus)
1953 Lew Hoad & Ken Rosewall (Aus)
1954-5 Vic Seixas & Tony Trabert (USA)
1956 Don Candy (Aus) & Robert Perry (USA)
1957 Mal Anderson & Ashley Cooper (Aus)
1958 Ashley Cooper & Neale Fraser (Aus)
1959 Nicola Pietrangeli & Orlando Sirola (Ita)
1960 Roy Emerson & Neale Fraser (Aus)
1961 Roy Emerson & Rod Laver (Aus)
1962 Roy Emerson & Neale Fraser (Aus)
1963 Roy Emerson (Aus) & Manuel Santana (Spa)
1964 Roy Emerson & Ken Fletcher (Aus)
1965 Roy Emerson & Fred Stolle (Aus)
1966 Clark Graebner & Dennis Ralston (USA)
1967 John Newcombe & Tony Roche (Aus)
1968 Ken Rosewall & Fred Stolle (Aus)
1969 John Newcombe & Tony Roche (Aus)
1970 Ilie Nastase & Ion Tiriac (Rom)
1971 Arthur Ashe & Marty Riessen (USA)
1972 Bob Hewitt & Frew McMillan (SAf)
1973 John Newcombe (Aus) & Tom Okker (Hol)
1974 Dick Crealy (Aus) & Onny Parun (NZ)
1975 Brian Gottfried (USA) & Raúl Ramirez (Mex)
1976 Fred McNair & Sherwood Stewart (USA)
1977 Brian Gottfried (USA) & Raúl Ramirez (Mex)
1978 Gene Mayer & Hank Pfister (USA)
1979 Sandy Mayer & Gene Mayer (USA)
1980 Victor Amaya & Hank Pfister (USA)
1981 Heinz Günthardt (Swi) & Balázs Taróczy (Hun)
1982 Sherwood Stewart & Ferdi Taygan (USA)
1983 Anders Järryd & Hans Simonsson (Swe)
1984 Henri Leconte & Yannick Noah (Fra)
1985 Mark Edmondson & Kim Warwick (Aus)
1986 John Fitzgerald (Aus) & Tomás Smid (Cs)
1987 Anders Järryd (Swe) & Robert Seguso (USA)
1988 Andrés Gómez (Ecu) & Emilio Sánchez (Spa)
1989 Jim Grabb & Patrick McEnroe (USA)
1990 Sergio Casal & Emilio Sánchez (Spa)
Most wins: 6 Roy Emerson, 5 Jean Borotra, 1925, 1929 (with René Lacoste), 1928, 1934 (with Jacques Brugnon), 1936 (with Marcel Bernard); 5 Jacques Brugnon 1927, 1930, 1932 (with Henri Cochet), 1928, 1934 (with Borotra)

Women's doubles
1946-7 Louise Brough & Margaret Osborne (USA)
1948 Doris Hart & Pat Todd (USA)
1949 Louise Brough & Margaret Du Pont (née Osborne) (USA)
1950-3 Shirley Fry & Doris Hart (USA)
1954 Maureen Connolly (USA) & Nell Hopman (Aus)
1955 Beverley Fleitz & Darlene Hard (USA)
1956 Angela Buxton (UK) & Althea Gibson (USA)
1957 Shirley Bloomer (UK) & Darlene Hard (USA)
1958 Yola Ramirez & Rosa Reyes (Mex)
1959 Sandra Reynolds & Renée Schuurman (SAf)
1960 Maria Bueno (Bra) & Darlene Hard (USA)
1961 Sandra Reynolds & Renée Schuurman (SAf)
1962 Sandra Price (née Reynolds) & Renée Schuurman (SAf)
1963 Ann Jones (UK) & Renée Schuurman (SAf)
1964-5 Margaret Smith & Lesley Turner (Aus)
1966 Margaret Smith & Judy Tegart (Aus)
1967 Françoise Durr (Fra) & Gail Sheriff (Aus)
1968-9 Françoise Durr (Fra) & Ann Jones (UK)
1970-1 Françoise Durr & Gail Chanfreau (Fra)
1972 Billie Jean King (USA) & Betty Stove (Hol)
1973 Margaret Court (Aus) & Virginia Wade (UK)
1974 Chris Evert (USA) & Olga Morozova (USSR)
1975 Chris Evert (USA) & Martina Navrátilová (Cs)
1976 Fiorella Bonicelli (Uru) & Gail Lovera (Fra)
1977 Regina Marsikova (Cs) & Pam Teeguarden (USA)
1978 Mimi Jausovec (Yug) & Virginia Ruzici (Rom)
1979 Betty Stove (Hol) & Wendy Turnbull (Aus)
1980 Kathy Jordan & Anne Smith (USA)
1981 Ros Fairbank & Tanya Harford (SAf)
1982 Martina Navrátilová & Anne Smith (USA)
1983 Ros Fairbank (SAf) & Candy Reynolds (USA)
1984-5 Martina Navrátilová & Pam Shriver (USA)
1986 Martina Navrátilová (USA) & Andrea Temesvári (Hun)
1987-8 Martina Navrátilová & Pam Shriver (USA)
1989 Larissa Savchenko & Natalya Zvereva (USSR)
1990 Jana Novotná & Helena Suková (Cs)
Most wins: 6 Simone Mathieu (Fra) 1933-4 (with Elizabeth Ryan), 1936-8 (with Billie Yorke), 6 Martina Navrátilová

Mixed doubles
1946 Budge Patty & Pauline Betz (USA)
1947 Eric Sturgess & Sheila Summers (SAf)
1948 Jaroslav Drobny (Cs) & Pat Todd (USA)
1949 Eric Sturgess & Sheila Summers (SAf)
1950 Enrique Morea (Arg) & Barbara Scofield (USA)
1951-2 Frank Sedgman (Aus) & Doris Hart (USA)
1953 Vic Seixas & Doris Hart (USA)
1954 Lew Hoad (Aus) & Maureen Connolly (USA)
1955 Gordon Forbes (SAf) & Darlene Hard (USA)
1956 Luis Ayala (Chl) & Thelma Long (Aus)
1957 Jan Javorsky & Vera Puzejová (Cs)
1958 Nicola Pietrangeli (Ita) & Shirley Bloomer (UK)
1959 Billy Knight (UK) & Yola Ramirez (Mex)
1960 Bob Howe (Aus) & Maria Bueno (Bra)
1961 Rod Laver (Aus) & Darlene Hard (USA)
1962 Bob Howe (Aus) & Renée Schuurman (SAf)
1963-5 Ken Fletcher & Margaret Smith (Aus)
1966 Frew McMillan & Annette Van Zyl (SAf)
1967 Owen Davidson (Aus) & Billie Jean King (USA)
1968 Jean-Claude Barclay & Françoise Durr (Fra)
1969 Marty Riessen (USA) & Margaret Court (née Smith) (Aus)
1970 Bob Hewitt (SAf) & Billie Jean King (USA)
1971 Jean-Claude Barclay & Françoise Durr (Fra)

1972 Kim Warwick & Evonne Goolagong (Aus)
1973 Jean-Claude Barclay & Françoise Durr (Fra)
1974 Ivan Molina (Col) & Martina Navrátilová (Cs)
1975 Thomaz Koch (Bra) & Fiorella Bonicelli Uru)
1976 Kim Warwick (Aus) & Ilana Kloss (SAf)
1977 John McEnroe & Mary Carillo (USA)
1978 Pavel Slozil & Renata Tomanova (Cs)
1979 Bob Hewitt (SAf) & Wendy Turnbull (Aus)
1980 Bill Martin & Anne Smith (USA)
1981 Jimmy Arias & Andrea Jaeger (USA)
1982 John Lloyd (UK) & Wendy Turnbull (Aus)

1983 Eliot Teltscher & Barbara Jordan (USA)
1984 Dick Stockton & Anne Smith (USA)
1985 Heinz Günthardt (Swi) & Martina Navrátilová (USA)
1986 Ken Flach & Kathy Jordan (USA)
1987 Emilio Sánchez (Spa) & Pam Shriver (USA)
1988 Jorge Lozano (Mex) & Lori McNeill (USA)
1989 Tom Nijssen & Manon Bollegraf (Hol)
1990 Jorge Lozano & Arantxa Sánchez (Spa)

Most wins (Men): 3 Ken Fletcher, Jean-Claude Barclay
(Women): 4 Margaret Court (née Smith)

Most French titles

	Total	Singles	Doubles	Mixed	Years
Margaret Court (Aus)	13	5	4	4	1962-73
Martina Navrátilová (Cs/USA)	11	2	7	2	1974-88
Simone Mathieu (Fra)	10	2	6	2	1933-9
Doris Hart (USA)	10	2	5	3	1948-53
Henri Cochet (Fra)	9	4	3	2	1926-30
Françoise Durr (Fra)	9	1	5	3	1967-73
Chris Evert Lloyd (USA)	9	7	2	-	1974-86

AUSTRALIAN CHAMPIONSHIPS

The first Australasian championships were held in 1905, and it was not until 1925 that the title changed to its present style. New Zealand twice hosted the championship, in 1906 and 1912. There were two championships in 1977 because the event was moved from early-season (January) to December. It reverted to a January date in 1987, which meant there was no championship in 1986. *Post-war winners:*

Men's singles

1946 John Bromwich (Aus)
1947 Dinny Pails (Aus)
1948 Adrian Quist (Aus)
1949-50 Frank Sedgman (Aus)
1951 Dick Savitt (USA)
1952 Ken McGregor (Aus)
1953 Ken Rosewall (Aus)
1954 Mervyn Rose (Aus)
1955 Ken Rosewall (Aus)
1956 Lew Hoad (Aus)
1957-8 Ashley Cooper (Aus)
1959 Alex Olmedo (USA)
1960 Rod Laver (Aus)
1961 Roy Emerson (Aus)
1962 Rod Laver (Aus)
1963-7 Roy Emerson (Aus)
1968 Bill Bowrey (Aus)
1969 Rod Laver (Aus)
1970 Arthur Ashe (USA)
1971-2 Ken Rosewall (Aus)
1973 John Newcombe (Aus)
1974 Jimmy Connors (USA)
1975 John Newcombe (Aus)
1976 Mark Edmondson (Aus)

1977 Roscoe Tanner (USA)
     Vitas Gerulaitis (USA)
1978-9 Guillermo Vilas (Arg)
1980 Brian Teacher (USA)
1981-2 Johan Kriek (SAf)
1983-4 Mats Wilander (Swe)
1985 Stefan Edberg (Swe)
1987 Stefan Edberg (Swe)
1988 Mats Wilander (Swe)
1989-90 Ivan Lendl (Cs)

Most wins: 6 Roy Emerson, 4 Jack Crawford (Aus) 1931-3, 1935; Ken Rosewall

Women's singles

1946-8 Nancye Bolton (Aus)
1949 Doris Hart (USA)
1950 Louise Brough (USA)
1951 Nancye Bolton (Aus)
1952 Thelma Long (Aus)
1953 Maureen Connolly (USA)
1954 Thelma Long (Aus)
1955 Beryl Penrose (Aus)
1956 Mary Carter (Aus)
1957 Shirley Fry (USA)
1958 Angela Mortimer (UK)
1959 Mary Reitano (Aus)
1960-6 Margaret Smith (Aus)
1967 Nancy Richey (USA)
1968 Billie Jean King (USA)
1969 Margaret Court (née Smith) (Aus)
1970-1 Margaret Court (Aus)
1972 Virginia Wade (UK)
1973 Margaret Court (Aus)
1974-5 Evonne Goolagong (Aus)

1976 Evonne Cawley (née Goolagong) (Aus)
1977 Kerry Reid (Aus)
    Evonne Cawley (Aus)
1978 Christine O'Neill (Aus)
1979 Barbara Jordan (USA)
1980 Hana Mandlíková (Cs)
1981 Martina Navrátilová (USA)
1982 Chris Evert Lloyd (USA)
1983 Martina Navrátilová (USA)
1984 Chris Evert Lloyd (USA)
1985 Martina Navrátilová (USA)
1987 Hana Mandlíková (Cs)
1988-90 Steffi Graf (FRG)

Most wins: 11 Margaret Court (née Smith), 6 Nancye Bolton (née Wynne) 1937, 1940, 1946-8, 1951; 5 Daphne Akhurst 1925-6, 1928-30

Men's doubles
1946-50 John Bromwich & Adrian Quist (Aus)
1951-2 Ken McGregor & Frank Sedgman (Aus)
1953 Lew Hoad & Ken Rosewall (Aus)
1954 Rex Hartwig & Mervyn Rose (Aus)
1955 Vic Seixas & Tony Trabert (USA)
1956 Lew Hoad & Ken Rosewall (Aus)
1957 Neale Fraser & Lew Hoad (Aus)
1958 Ashley Cooper & Neale Fraser (Aus)
1959-61 Rod Laver & Robert Mark (Aus)
1962 Roy Emerson & Neale Fraser (Aus)
1963-4 Bob Hewitt & Fred Stolle (Aus)
1965 John Newcombe & Tony Roche (Aus)
1966 Roy Emerson & Fred Stolle (Aus)
1967 John Newcombe & Tony Roche (Aus)
1968 Dick Crealy & Allan Stone (Aus)
1969 Roy Emerson & Rod Laver (Aus)
1970 Bob Lutz & Stan Smith (USA)
1971 John Newcombe & Tony Roche (Aus)
1972 Owen Davidson & Ken Rosewall (Aus)
1973 Mal Anderson & John Newcombe (Aus)
1974 Ross Case & Geoff Masters (Aus)
1975 John Alexander & Phil Dent (Aus)
1976 John Newcombe & Tony Roche (Aus)
1977 Arthur Ashe (USA) & Tony Roche (Aus)
    Ray Ruffels & Allan Stone (Aus)
1978 Wojtek Fibak (Pol) & Kim Warwick (Aus)
1979 Peter McNamara & Paul McNamee (Aus)
1980-1 Mark Edmondson & Kim Warwick (Aus)
1982 John Alexander & John Fitzgerald (Aus)
1983 Mark Edmonson & Paul McNamee (Aus)
1984 Mark Edmondson (Aus) & Sherwood Stewart (USA)
1985 Paul Annacone (USA) & Christo Van Rensburg (SAf)
1987 Stefan Edberg & Anders Järryd (Swe)
1988-9 Rick Leach & Jim Pugh (USA)
1990 Pieter Aldrich & Dannie Visser (SAf)

Most wins by one pair: 8 John Bromwich & Adrian Quist 1938-40, 1946-50
By player: 10 Adrian Quist 1936-7 (with Don Turnbull),

and 8 with John Bromwich.

Women's doubles
1946 Mary Bevis & Joyce Fitch (Aus)
1947-9 Nancye Bolton & Thelma Long (Aus)
1950 Louise Brough & Doris Hart (USA)
1951-2 Nancye Bolton & Thelma Long (Aus)
1953 Maureen Connolly & Julie Sampson (USA)
1954 Mary Hawton (née Bevis) & Beryl Penrose (Aus)
1955 Mary Hawton & Beryl Penrose (Aus)
1956 Mary Hawton & Thelma Long (Aus)
1957 Shirley Fry & Althea Gibson (USA)
1958 Mary Hawton & Thelma Long (Aus)
1959 Sandra Reynolds & Renée Schuurman (SAf)
1960 Maria Bueno (Bra) & Christine Truman (UK)
1961 Mary Reitano & Margaret Smith (Aus)
1962-3 Robyn Ebbern & Margaret Smith (Aus)
1964 Judy Tegart & Lesley Turner (Aus)
1965 Margaret Smith & Lesley Turner (Aus)
1966 Carole Graebner & Nancy Richey (USA)
1967 Judy Tegart & Lesley Turner (Aus)
1968 Karen Krantzcke & Kerry Melville (Aus)
1969 Margaret Court (née Smith) & Judy Tegart (Aus)
1970 Margaret Court & Judy Dalton (née Tegart) (Aus)
1971 Margaret Court & Evonne Goolagong (Aus)
1972 Helen Gourlay & Kerry Harris (Aus)
1973 Margaret Court (Aus) & Virginia Wade (UK)
1974-5 Evonne Goolagong (Aus) & Peggy Michel (USA)
1976 Evonne Cawley (née Goolagong) & Helen Gourlay (Aus)
1977 Diane Fromholtz & Helen Gourlay (Aus)
    Evonne Cawley & Helen Cawley (Aus) shared the December title with Ramona Guerrant (USA) & Kerry Reid (née Melville) (Aus). Final not played
1978 Betsy Nagelsen (USA) & Renata Tomanova (Cs)
1979 Judith Chaloner (NZ) & Dianne Evers (Aus)
1980 Betsy Nagelsen (USA) & Martina Navrátilová (Cs)
1981 Kathy Jordan & Anne Smith (USA)
1982-5 Martina Navrátilová & Pam Shriver (USA)
1987-9 Martina Navrátilová & Pam Shriver (USA)
1990 Helena Suková & Jana Novotná (Cs)

Most wins by one pair: 10 Nancye Bolton (née Wynne) & Thelma Long (née Coyne) 1936-40, 1947-9, 1951-2; 7 Martina Navrátilová & Pam Shriver
By player: 12 Thelma Long, also 1956, 1958 (with Mary Hawton); 10 Nancye Bolton, 8 Margaret Court (née Smith), 8 Martina Navrátilová, 7 Pam Shriver

Mixed doubles
1946-8 Colin Long & Nancye Bolton (Aus)
1949-50 Frank Sedgman (Aus) & Doris Hart (USA)
1951-2 George Worthington & Thelma Long (Aus)
1953 Rex Hartwig (Aus) & Julie Sampson (USA)
1954 Rex Hartwig & Thelma Long (Aus)
1955 George Worthington & Thelma Long (Aus)
1956 Neale Fraser & Beryl Penrose (Aus)
1957 Mal Anderson & Fay Muller (Aus)

1958 Bob Howe & Mary Hawton (Aus)
1959 Robert Mark (Aus) & Sandra Reynolds (SAf)
1960 Trevor Fancutt (SAf) & Jan Lehane (Aus)
1961 Bob Hewitt & Jan Lehane (Aus)
1962 Fred Stolle & Lesley Turner (Aus)
1963-4 Ken Fletcher & Margaret Smith (Aus)
1965 John Newcombe & Margaret Smith (Aus) shared title with Owen Davidson & Robyn Ebbern (Aus). Final not played.
1966 Tony Roche & Judy Tegart (Aus)
1967 Owen Davidson & Lesley Turner (Aus)

1968 Dick Crealy (Aus) & Billie Jean King (USA)
1969 Marty Riessen (USA) & Margaret Court (née Smith) (Aus) shared title with Fred Stolle (Aus) & Ann Jones (UK). Final not played.
1970-85 not held
1987 Sherwood Stewart & Zina Garrison (USA)
1988-9 Jim Pugh (USA) & Jana Novotná (Cs)

Most wins by one pair: 4 Harry Hopman & Nell Hopman (née Hall) 1930, 1936-7, 1939; 4 Colin Long & Nancye Bolton (née Wynne) 1940, 1946-8

Most Australian titles

	Total	Singles	Doubles	Mixed	Years
Margaret Court (Aus)	21	11	8	2	1960-73
Nancye Bolton (Aus)	20	6	10	4	1936-51
Thelma Long (Aus)	18	2	12	4	1936-58
Daphne Akhurst (Aus)	13	5	4	4	1924-30
Adrian Quist (Aus)	13	3	10	-	1936-50
Best record by a non-Australian:					
Martina Navrátilová	10	3	7	-	1980-89

THE ALL TIME GREATS

A summary of the most titles won by players in the four Grand Slam events – Wimbledon, US Open, French Championship, and Australian Championship, first for each tournament and then analysed by singles and doubles.

	Total	Wimb.	US	French	Aus	Singles	Doubles	Mixed
Margaret Court (Aus) *	66	10	22	13	21	26	21	19
Martina Navrátilová (Cs/USA)	52	17	14	11	10	18	29	5
Billie Jean King (USA)	39	20	13	4	2	12	16	11
Margaret Du Pont (USA)	37	7	25	5	-	6	21	10
Louis Brough (USA)	35	13	17	3	2	6	21	8
Doris Hart (USA)	35	10	11	10	4	6	14	15
Helen Wills-Moody (USA)	31	12	13	6	-	19	9	3
Roy Emerson (Aus)	28	5	6	8	9	12	16	-
Elizabeth Ryan (USA)	26	19	3	4	-	-	17	9
John Newcombe (Aus) *	25	9	6	3	7	7	17	1

* Court's totals include both US Amateur and Open Championships 1968-9. Not included are the undecided Australian mixed doubles finals: two for Court, one for Newcombe.

The most Grand Slam tournament doubles wins by one pair
20 Louise Brough & Margaret Du Pont 1942-57
20 Martina Navrátilová & Pam Shriver 1981-9

GRAND SLAM
To achieve the Grand Slam is to simultaneously hold the titles of the four major tournaments as above. Originally one had to win all four in the same year to claim the Grand Slam. The following players have achieved this feat: (Single years indicates all four titles won in one year)

Men's Singles
Donald Budge (USA) 1937/8, 1938
Rod Laver (Aus) 1962
Rod Laver (Aus) 1969

Women's Singles
Maureen Connolly (USA) 1952/3, 1953
Margaret Court (Aus) 1969/70, 1970, 1970/1
Martina Navrátilová (USA) 1983/4
Steffi Graf (FRG) 1988, 1988/9
The first three each won six successive Grand Slam tournaments, Graf won five.

Men's Doubles
Frank Sedgman (Aus) 1950/1, 1951, 1951/2
Ken McGregor (Aus) 1951, 1951/2

Women's Doubles
Louise Brough (USA) 1949/50
Maria Bueno (Bra) 1960
Martina Navrátilová (USA) 1983/4, 1984, 1984/5, 1985/6, 1986/7
Pam Shriver (USA) 1983/4, 1984, 1984/5, 1986/7
Navrátilová and Shriver won a record eight successive Grand Slam tournaments together 1983-5

Mixed Doubles
Margaret Smith (Aus) 1962/3, 1963, 1963/4
Ken Fletcher (Aus) 1963, 1963/4
Owen Davidson (Aus) 1966/7, 1967
Billie Jean King (USA) 1967/8

DAVIS CUP
The American player Dwight F. Davis donated a cup in 1900 to be contested by national teams. Up to 1971 the winning nation accepted a challenge from the country winning a knockout competition. But since 1972 the entire competition has been on a knockout basis with countries divided into zonal groups with a promotion and relegation system into the World Group of 16 nations who play-off for the Cup. There was no competition in 1901 and 1910, or during the war years. Each match is contested over two pairs of singles and a doubles. *Finals:*

	Winners	Runners-Up	
1900	USA	British Isles	3-0
1902	USA	British Isles	3-2
1903	British Isles	USA	4-1
1904	British Isles	Belgium	5-0
1905	British Isles	USA	5-0
1906	British Isles	USA	5-0
1907	Australasia	British Isles	3-2
1908	Australasia	USA	3-2
1909	Australasia	USA	5-0
1911	Australasia	USA	5-0
1912	British Isles	Australasia	3-2
1913	USA	British Isles	3-2
1914	Australasia	USA	3-2
1919	Australasia	British Isles	4-1
1920	USA	Australasia	5-0
1921	USA	Japan	5-0
1922	USA	Australasia	4-1
1923	USA	Australia	4-1
1924	USA	Australia	5-0
1925	USA	France	5-0
1926	USA	France	4-1
1927	France	USA	3-2
1928	France	USA	4-1
1929	France	USA	3-2
1930	France	USA	4-1
1931	France	Great Britain	3-2
1932	France	USA	3-2
1933	Great Britain	France	3-2
1934	Great Britain	USA	4-1
1935	Great Britain	USA	5-0
1936	Great Britain	Australia	3-2
1937	USA	Great Britain	4-1
1938	USA	Australia	3-2
1939	Australia	USA	3-2
1946	USA	Australia	5-0
1947	USA	Australia	4-1
1948	USA	Australia	5-0
1949	USA	Australia	4-1
1950	Australia	USA	4-1
1951	Australia	USA	3-2
1952	Australia	USA	4-1
1953	Australia	USA	3-2
1954	USA	Australia	3-2
1955	Australia	USA	5-0
1956	Australia	USA	5-0
1957	Australia	USA	3-2
1958	USA	Australia	3-2
1959	Australia	USA	3-2
1960	Australia	Italy	4-1
1961	Australia	Italy	5-0
1962	Australia	Mexico	5-0
1963	USA	Australia	3-2
1964	Australia	USA	3-2
1965	Australia	Spain	4-1
1966	Australia	India	4-1
1967	Australia	Spain	4-1
1968	USA	Australia	4-1
1969	USA	Romania	5-0
1970	USA	F.R.Germany	5-0
1971	USA	Romania	3-2
1972	USA	Romania	3-2
1973	Australia	USA	5-0
1974	South Africa	India	w/o
1975	Sweden	Czechoslovakia	3-2
1976	Italy	Chile	4-1
1977	Australia	Italy	3-1
1978	USA	Great Britain	4-1
1979	USA	Italy	5-0
1980	Czechoslovakia	Italy	4-1
1981	USA	Argentina	3-1
1982	USA	France	4-1
1983	Australia	Sweden	3-2
1984	Sweden	USA	4-1
1985	Sweden	F.R.Germany	3-2
1986	Australia	Sweden	3-2
1987	Sweden	India	5-0
1988	F.R.Germany	Sweden	4-1
1989	F.R.Germany	Sweden	3-2

Wins: 28 USA, 26 Australia/Australasia, 9 British Isles/Great Britain, 6 France, 4 Sweden, 2 F.R.Germany, 1 Czechoslovakia, Italy, South Africa
Most times played for winning team: 8 Roy Emerson (Aus) 1959-62, 1964-7; 7 Bill Tilden (USA) 1920-6

Most Davis Cup Appearances

	Rubbers	Wins	Singles	Doubles	Win%	Years
Nicola Pietrangeli (Ita)	163	120	78/109	42/54	73.6	1954-72
Ilie Nastase (Rom)	146	110	74/96	36/50	75.3	1966-85
Jacques Brichant (Bel)	120	71	52/79	19/41	59.2	1949-65
Manuel Santana (Spa)	119	91	69/85	22/34	76.5	1958-73
Thomaz Koch (Bra)	118	75	46/77	29/41	63.6	1962-81

Best win percentage of those to have played more than 100 matches

Gottfried von Cramm (Ger)	102	82	58/69	24/33	80.4	1932-53

Most appearances and most wins for Great Britain:

Mike Sangster	65	43	29/48	14/17	66.2	1960-8
Fred Perry	52	45	34/38	11/14	86.5	1931-6

Singles and doubles figures show wins/matches played

Best records in Davis Cup Finals/Challenge Rounds *10 or more wins*

Bill Tilden (USA)	28	21	17/22	4/6	75.0	1920-30
Roy Emerson (Aus)	18	15	11/12	4/6	83.3	1959-62, 1964-7
Norman Brookes (Aus)	22	15	9/14	6/8	68.2	1907-09, 1911-12, 1914, 1919-20
Henri Cochet (Fra)	20	14	11/14	3/6	70.0	1926-33
Stan Smith (USA)	16	12	6/8	6/8	75.0	1968-73, 1978-9
William Johnston (USA)	16	13	11/14	2/2	81.2	1920-7
Lawrence Doherty (UK)	12	12*	7/7	4/4	100.0	1902-06
John McEnroe (USA)	13	11	9/10	2/3	84.6	1978-9, 1981-2, 1984
Rod Laver (Aus)	12	10	8/10	2/2	83.3	1959-62, 1973

* including a walk-over

WIGHTMAN CUP

The former American player Hazel Wightman (née Hotchkiss) donated the trophy in 1920 to be contested by national female teams. However, none showed any interest until 1923 when the USA and Great Britain played for the trophy. Since then all Wightman Cup matches have been between the two nations. The format was five singles and two doubles. In 1990, with the decline in British tennis standards and after four 7-0 US wins in the previous five matches, a decision was taken to suspend the event. *Wins:*

51 USA 1923, 1926-7, 1929, 1931-9, 1946-57, 1959, 1961-7, 1969-73, 1976-7, 1979-89

10 Great Britain 1924-5, 1928, 1930, 1958, 1960, 1968, 1974-5, 1978

The United States 'whitewashed' Great Britain 14 times by inflicting a 7-0 defeat upon them. The years in which they performed the feat were: 1923, 1946-7, 1949-50, 1952-4*, 1977, 1979, 1981, 1985-6, 1988-9

* In 1954 the USA won all six matches played.

Great Britain's best results were 6-1 wins in 1924 and 1974

Most Wightman Cup appearances

	Rubbers	Wins	Years
Virginia Wade (UK)	56	19	1965-85
Chris Evert Lloyd (USA)	38	34*	1971-85
Ann Jones (UK)	32	16	1957-75
Helen Moody (USA)	30	21	1923-38
Helen Jacobs (USA)	30	19	1927-39

* won all her 26 singles

Others with 20 or more wins:

Billie Jean King (USA)	26	21	1961-78
Doris Hart (USA)	24	22	1946-55
Louise Brough (USA)	22	22	1946-57

FEDERATION CUP

An international women's team competition played on a knockout basis at one venue each year. It was first held in 1963. *Winners:*

1963 USA
1964-5 Australia
1966-7 USA
1968 Australia
1969 USA
1970-1 Australia
1972 South Africa
1973-4 Australia
1975 Czechoslovakia
1976-82 USA
1983-5 Czechoslovakia
1986 USA
1987 F.R.Germany
1988 Czechoslovakia
1989 USA

Wins: 13 USA; 7 Australia; 5 Czechoslovakia; 1 South Africa, FR Germany

Most appearances: Virginia Wade (UK) played in a record 100 rubbers (56 singles, 44 doubles) 1967-83, winning 66 (36 singles, 30 doubles).

Chris Evert Lloyd won her first 29 singles in the competition 1977-86. In all she won 40/42 singles, 16/18 doubles 1977-89. Margaret Court won all her 20 singles matches for Australia 1963-71.

WORLD TEAM CUP

Formerly known as the Nations Cup, it is an eight-nation men's team event. First held in Kingston, Jamaica, in 1975 it was not held the next two years but was revived in 1977. *Winners:*
1975 USA
1978 Spain
1979 Australia
1980 Argentina
1981 Czechoslovakia
1982 USA
1983 Spain
1984-5 USA
1986 France
1987 Czecholsovakia
1988 Sweden
1989 FR Germany
1990 Yugoslavia
Most wins: 4 USA

MEN'S GRAND PRIX MASTERS

Throughout the season various tournaments count towards the Masters and points are gained according to performances. The value of points available per tournament is geared to the stature of the tournament. At the end of the season the leading 16 players play-off for the Masters singles title, and eight pairs play-off for the doubles title. There was no event in 1977 because the date of the final was switched from December to the following January. There were two tournaments in 1986 because it reverted back to a December final. *Winners:*

Singles
1970 Stan Smith (USA)
1971-3 Ilie Nastase (Rom)
1974 Guillermo Vilas (Arg)
1975 Ilie Nastase (Rom)
1976 Manuel Orantes (Spa)
1978 Jimmy Connors (USA)
1979 John McEnroe (USA)
1980-1 Björn Borg (Swe)
1982-3 Ivan Lendl (Cs)
1984-5 John McEnroe (USA)
1986-7 Ivan Lendl (Cs)
1988 Boris Becker (FRG)
1989 Stefan Edberg (Swe)

Most wins:
4 Ilie Nastase, Ivan Lendl
Jimmy Connors qualified for the play-offs for a record 14 years 1972-85.

Doubles
1970 Arthur Ashe & Stan Smith (USA)
1971-4 Not held
1975 Juan Gisbert & Manuel Orantes (Spa)
1976 Fred McNair & Sherwood Stewart (USA)
1978 Bob Hewitt & Frew McMillan (SAf)

1979-85 Peter Fleming & John McEnroe (USA)
1986 Stefan Edberg & Anders Järryd (Swe) (two wins)
1987 Miloslav Mecir & Tomás Smid (Cs)
1988 Rick Leach & Jim Pugh (USA)
1989 Patrick McEnroe & Jim Grabb (USA)

Most wins: 7 John McEnroe & Peter Fleming

WOMEN'S INTERNATIONAL SERIES

As with the men, so women have had an International championship played after a season-long series of tournaments. *Winners: (see also Virginia Slims/Avon Series below)*

SINGLES
1977-8 Chris Evert (USA)
1979* Martina Navrátilová (Cs)
1980* Tracy Austin (USA)
1981 Tracy Austin (USA)
1982 Martina Navrátilová (USA)
1983* Martina Navrátilová (USA)
1984* Martina Navrátilová (USA)

DOUBLES
1977 Françoise Durr (Fra) & Virginia Wade (UK)
1978 Billie Jean King (USA) & Martina Navrátilová (Cs)
1979* Billie Jean King (USA) & Martina Navrátilová (Cs)
1980* Rosemary Casals (USA) & Wendy Turnbull (Aus)
1981 Martina Navrátilová (Cs) & Pam Shriver (USA)
1982 Martina Navrátilová & Pam Shriver (USA)
1983* Martina Navrátilová & Pam Shriver (USA)
1984* Martina Navrátilová & Pam Shriver (USA)
* *played the following year*

VIRGINIA SLIMS/AVON SERIES

From 1971 there was an annual series of Virginia Slims tournaments, with a Championships as the climax. Avon Products took over the sponsorship 1979-82, with Virginia Slims back again in 1983 when their initial series ran for 15 months to March 1984. From 1983 the Virginia Slims final has been the one women's match played over the best of five sets. *Championship winners (the Doubles event has not been staged each year):*

Singles
1971 Billie Jean King (USA)
1972-3 Chris Evert (USA)
1974 Evonne Goolagong (Aus)
1975 Chris Evert (USA)
1976 Evonne Cawley (née Goolagong) (Aus)
1977 Chris Evert (USA)
1978-9 Martina Navrátilová (Cs)
1980 Tracy Austin (USA)
1981 Martina Navrátilová (Cs)
1982 Sylvia Hanika (FRG)
1983-5* Martina Navrátilová (USA)
1986 Martina Navrátilová (USA)
1987 Steffi Graf (FRG)

Ivan Lendl, the biggest money-winner in men's tennis (**All-Sport**)

1988 Gabriela Sabatini (Arg)
1989 Steffi Graf (FRG)

Doubles
1971 Rosemary Casals & Bille Jean King (USA)
1973 Rosemary Casals (USA) & Margaret Court (Aus)
1974 Rosemary Casals & Billlie Jean King (USA)
1979 Françoise Durr (Fra) & Betty Stove (Hol)
1980 Billie Jean King (USA) & Martina Navrátilová (Cs)
1981 Martina Navrátilová (Cs) & Pam Shriver (USA)
1982 Martina Navrátilová & Pam Shriver (USA)
1984* Martina Navrátilová & Pam Shriver (USA)
1985* Hana Mandlíková (Cs) & Wendy Turnbull (Aus)
1986-9 Martina Navrátilová & Pam Shriver (USA)
* played the following year

WORLD CHAMPIONSHIP TENNIS
World Championship Tennis Incorporated (WCT) was founded in 1967 to promote professional tennis. Following a series of qualifying tournaments a finals tournament was held annually for men from 1971.
Winners:
1971-2 Ken Rosewall (Aus)
1973 Stan Smith (USA)
1974 John Newcombe (Aus)
1975 Arthur Ashe (USA)
1976 Björn Borg (Swe)
1977 Jimmy Connors (USA)
1978 Vitas Gerulaitis (USA)
1979 John McEnroe (USA)
1980 Jimmy Connors (USA)
1981 John McEnroe (USA)
1982 Ivan Lendl (Cs)
1983-4 John McEnroe (USA)
1985 Ivan Lendl (Cs)
1986 Anders Järryd (Swe)
1987 Miloslav Mecir (Cs)
1988 Boris Becker (FRG)
1989 John McEnroe (USA)

WCT DOUBLES
Introduced in 1973, *winners have been:*
1973 Bob Lutz & Stan Smith (USA)
1974 Bob Hewitt & Frew McMillan (SAf)
1975 Brian Gottfried (USA) & Raúl Ramirez (Mex)
1976 Wojtek Fibak (Pol) & Tom Okker (Hol)
1977 Vijay Amritraj (Ind) & Dick Stockton (USA)
1978 Wojtek Fibak (Pol) & Tom Okker (Hol)
1979 Peter Fleming & John McEnroe (USA)
1980 Brian Gottfried (USA) & Raúl Ramirez (Mex)
1981 Peter McNamara & Paul McNamee (Aus)
1982-3 Heinz Günthardt (Swi) & Balázs Taróczy (Hun)
1984 Pavel Slozil & Tomás Smid (Cs)
1985 Ken Flach & Robert Seguso (USA)
1986 Heinz Günthardt (Swi) & Balázs Taróczy (Hun)
1986# Stefan Edberg & Anders Järryd (Swe)
1990 Rick Leach & Jim Pugh (USA)
brought forward from January to December

ITF WORLD CHAMPIONS
A panel of former champions decide annually who are the International Tennis Federation's World Champions.
Winners since the inauguration of the award in 1978 have been:

Men
1978-80 Björn Borg (Swe)
1981 John McEnroe (USA)
1982 Jimmy Connors (USA)
1983-4 John McEnroe (USA)
1985-7 Ivan Lendl (Cs)
1988 Mats Wilander (Swe)
1989 Boris Becker (FRG)

Women
1978 Chris Evert (USA)
1979 Martina Navrátilová (Cs)
1980-1 Chris Evert Lloyd (USA)
1982-6 Martina Navrátilová (USA)
1987-9 Steffi Graf (FRG)

THE MONEY WINNERS
Players to have won the most prize money – as at the end of 1989:

Men
Ivan Lendl	$15,626,336
John McEnroe	10,887,456
Jimmy Connors	8,094,670
Mats Wilander	7,123,221
Stefan Edberg	6,637,795
Boris Becker	6,572,705
Guillermo Vilas	4,897,967
Björn Borg	3,607,206

Women
Martina Navrátilová	$15,343,813
Chris Evert	8,896,195
Steffi Graf	5,251,345
Hana Mandlíková	3,291,186
Pam Shriver	4,272,521
Helena Suková	2,910,382
Wendy Turnbull	2,748,624
Gabriela Sabatini	2,680,646

OLYMPIC GAMES
Lawn Tennis was included in the Olympic Games from 1896 to 1924 and as a demonstration sport in 1968. Following the staging of an international tournament at the 1984 Games, at which the singles winners were Stefan Edberg (Swe) and Steffi Graf (FRG), Tennis was re-introduced to the Olympics in 1988. *Champions:*

Men's Singles
1896 John Boland (UK/Ire)
1900 Hugh Doherty (UK)
1904 Beals Wright (USA)

1906 Max Decugis (Fra)
1908(a) Josiah Ritchie (UK)
1908(b) Arthur Gore (UK)
1912(a) Charles Winslow (SAf)
1912(b) André Gobert (Fra)
1920 Louis Raymond (SAf)
1924 Vince Richards (USA)
1988 Miloslav Mecir (Cs)

Men's Doubles

1896 John Boland (Ire) & Fritz Traun (Ger)
1900 Reginald & Hugh Doherty (UK)
1904 Beals Wright & Edgar Leonard (USA)
1906 Max Decugis & Maurice Germot (Fra)
1908(a) George Hillyard & Reginald Doherty (UK)
1908(b) Arthur Gore & Herbert Roper Barrett (UK)
1912(a) Charles Winslow & Harold Kitson (SAf)
1912(b) André Gobert & Maurice Germot (Fra)
1920 Oswald Turnbull & Max Woosnam (UK)
1924 Vince Richards & Frank Hunter (UK)
1988 Ken Flach & Robert Seguso (USA)

Women's Singles

1900 Charlotte Cooper (UK)
1906 Esmée Simiriotou (Gre)
1908(a) Dorothea Lambert Chambers (UK)
1908(b) Gwendoline Eastlake-Smith (UK)
1912(a) Marguerite Broquedis (Fra)
1912(b) Edith Hannam (UK)
1920 Suzanne Lenglen (Fra)
1924 Helen Wills (USA)
1988 Steffi Graf (FRG)

Women's Doubles

1920 Winifred McNair & Kathleen McKane (UK)
1924 Hazel Wightman & Helen Wills (USA)
1988 Pam Shriver & Zina Garrison (USA)

Mixed Doubles

1900 Reginald Doherty & Charlotte Cooper (UK)
1906 Max and Marie Decugis (Fra)
1912(a) Heinrich Schomburgk & Dora König (Ger)
1912(b) Percy Dixon & Edith Hannam (UK)
1920 Max Decugis & Suzanne Lenglen (Fra)
1924 Norris Williams & Hazel Wightman (USA)
(a) Outdoor (b) Indoor

Most medals: 6 Max Decugis (Fra) a record 4 gold, 1 silver and 1 bronze 1900-20; 5 Kathleen McKane (UK) 1 gold, 2 silver, 2 bronze, 1920-4

MAIDEN NAMES/MARRIED NAMES

	Maiden Name	Married Name
Chris	Evert	Lloyd, now Mill
Mary	Bevis	Hawton
Blanche	Bingley	Hillyard
Molly	Bjurstedt	Mallory
Mary	Carter	Reitano

Charlotte	Cooper	Sterry
Thelma	Coyne	Long
Evonne	Goolagong	Cawley
Helen	Gourlay	Cawley
Karen	Hantze	Susman
Ann	Haydon	Jones
Hazel	Hotchkiss	Wightman
Dorothea	Lambert-Chambers	Douglass
Kathleen	McKane	Godfree
Kerry	Melville	Reid
Billie Jean	Moffitt	King
Sarah	Palfrey	Fabyan, then Cooke
Margaret	Osborne	Du Pont
Vera	Puzejová	Suková
Peggy	Saunders	Michel
Elizabeth	Sayers	Smyllie
Gail	Sherriff	Chanfreau, then Lovera
Margaret	Smith	Court
Judy	Tegart	Dalton
Helen	Wills	Moody
Nancye	Wynne	Bolton

TRAMPOLINING

Trampolining has formed part of circus acts for many years but it only started to attract interest as a sport after the design of trampolines similar to modern day ones, by George Nissen in the United States in 1936. The first official trampolining tournament took place in the United States in 1947.

WORLD CHAMPIONSHIPS

Instituted in 1964 they have been held biennially since 1968. *Winners*

Men's Individual

1964 Danny Millman (USA)
1965 George Irwin (USA)
1966 Wayne Miller (USA)
1967-8 Dave Jacobs (USA)
1970 Wayne Miller (USA)
1972 Paul Luxon (UK)
1974 Richard Tisson (Fra)
1976 Richard Tisson (Fra) & Yevgeniy Yanes (USSR)
1978 Yevgeniy Yanes (USSR)
1980 Stewart Matthews (UK)
1982 Carl Furrer (UK)
1984 Lionel Pioline (Fra)
1986 Lionel Pioline (Fra)
1988 Vadim Krasnochapka (USSR)

Men's synchronised pairs

1965 Gary Irwin & Frank Smith (USA)
1966 Wayne Miller & David Jacobs (USA)
1967 Hartmut Riehler & Kurt Treiter (FRG)
1968 Klaus Forster & Michael Budenberg (FRG)

1970 Don Waters & Gary Smith (USA)
1972 Paul Luxon & Robert Hughes (UK)
1974 Robet Nealy & Jim Cartledge (USA)
1976 Yevgeniy Yakovenko & Yevgeniy Yanes (USSR)
1978 Yevgeniy Yanes & Vladimir Zhadoyev (USSR)
1980 Stewart Matthews & Carl Furrer (UK)
1982 Stuart Ransom & Mark Calderon (USA)
1984 Igor Bogachev & Vadim Krasnochapka (USSR)
1986 Igor Bogachev & Vadim Krasnochapka (USSR)
1988 Igor Bogachev & Vadim Krasnochapka (USSR)

Men's tumbling
1965 Frank Schmitz (USA)
1966 Frank Fortier (USA)
1976 Jim Bertz (USA)
1978 Jim Bertz (USA)
1980 Kevin Eckberg (USA)
1982 Steve Elliott (USA)
1984 Steve Elliott (USA)
1986 Jerry Hardy (USA)
1988 Pascal Eouzan (Fra)

Men's double mini trampoline
1976 Ron Merriott (USA)
1978 Stuart Ransom (USA)
1980 Derrick Lotz (SAf)
1982 Brett Austine (Aus)
1984 Brett Austine (Aus)
1986 Brett Austine (Aus)
1988 Adrian Wareham (Aus)

Women's individual
1964-8 Judy Wills (USA)
1970 Renee Ransom (USA)
1972 Alexandra Nicholson (USA)
1974 Alexandra Nicholson (USA)
1976 Svetlana Levina (USSR)
1978 Tatyana Anisimova (USSR)
1980 Ruth Keller (Swi)
1982 Ruth Keller (Swi)
1984 Sue Shotton (UK)
1986 Tatyana Lushina (USSR)
1988 Khoperla Rusudum (USSR)
Most wins: 5 Judy Wills

Women's synchronised pairs
1966-7 Judy Wills & Nancy Smith (USA)
1968 Ute Czech & Agathe Jarosch (FRG)
1970 Jennifer Liebenberg & Lucia Odendaal (SAf)
1972 Marilyn Stieg & Bobby Grant (USA)
1974 Ute Scheile & Petra Wenzel (FRG)
1976 Svetlana Levina & Olga Starikova (USSR)
1978 Ute Luxon & Ute Scheile (FRG)
1980 Gabriele Bahr & Beate Kruswicki (FRG)
1982 Jacqueline de Ruiter & Marjo van Dierman (Hol)
1984 Kirsty McDonald & Sue Shotton (UK)
1986 Yelena Merkulova & Tatyana Lushina (USSR)
1988 Yelena Kolomiets & Khoperla Rusudum (USSR)

Women's tumbling
1965-6 Judy Wills (USA)
1976 Tracey Long (USA)
1978 Nancy Quattrochi (USA)
1980 Tracy Contour (USA)
1982 Jill Hollembeak (USA)
1984 Jill Hollembeak (USA)
1986 Jill Hollembeak (USA)
1988 Megan Cunningham (USA)

Women's double mini trampoline
1976 Leigh Hennessy (USA)
1978 Leigh Hennessy (USA)
1980 Beth Fairchild (USA)
1982 Christine Tough (Can)
1984 Gabi Dreier (FRG)
1986 Bettina Lehmann (FRG)
1988 Liz Jensen (Aus)

WORLD CUP
Held annually from 1980, except 1988. *Most titles at each discipline:*
Men's Individual: 3 Carl Furrer (UK) 1980-1, 1983
Women's Individual: 3 Sue Shotton (UK) 1981, 1983, 1986, Andrea Holmes (UK) 1984-5, 1987
Men's Synchro: 2 John Hansen & Anders Christiansen (Den) 1982, 1985; Lionel Pioline & Daniel Pean (Fra) 1983-4
Women's Synchro: 3 Gabriel Bahr & Beate Kruswicki (FRG) 1983-5

TRIATHLON

The triathlon combines long distance swimming, cycling and running. A group of Americans first established the sport in 1974. Their efforts led to the first Hawaii 'Ironman', which was contested by 15 intrepid sportsmen, of whom 12 finished, on 18 Feb 1978.

The growth in popularity of the event can be seen from the numbers of contestants in the 'Ironman', from 15 in its first two years to 108 in 1980, 326 in 1981, 580 and 850 in the two held in 1982, to reach 1000 in 1984.

After earlier abortive attempts to found a worldwide governing body, L'Union Internationale de Triathlon (UIT) was founded at Avignon in 1989, and this organisation staged the first official World Championships in Avignon on 6 Aug 1989.

WORLD CHAMPIONSHIPS
The first official championships were contested at Avignon, France 1989 by national teams of five men and five women over the internationally regulated distances of 1.5km swim (actually the event was held in the river Rhône, and the distance extended to compensate for the flow, but at 2.2km it was overestimated), 40km cycle ride and 10km run. *Winners:*
MEN: Mark Allen (USA) 1:58:46
WOMEN: Erin Baker (NZ) 2:10:01

HAWAII IRONMAN

Contestants first swim 2.4 miles (3.8km), then cycle 112 miles (180km) and finally run a full marathon of 26 miles 385 yards (42.195km). The 1978-80 course was in Oahu, from 1981 it has been in Kona, Hawaii. *Winners:*

MEN
1978	Gordon Haller (USA) 11:46:58
1979	Tom Warren (USA) 11:15:56
1980	Dave Scott (USA) 9:24:33
1981	John Howard (USA) 9:38:29
1982 (Feb)	Scott Tinley (USA) 9:19:41
1982 (Oct)	Dave Scott (USA) 9:08:23
1983	Dave Scott (USA) 9:05:57
1984	Dave Scott (USA) 8:54:30
1985	Scott Tinley (USA) 8:50:54
1986	Dave Scott (USA) 8:28:37
1987	Dave Scott (USA) 8:34:13
1988	Scott Molina (USA) 8:31:00
1989	Mark Allen (USA) 8:09:16

Mark Allen was supreme in triathlon in 1989, when he won the inaugural world title, his first Hawaii Ironman, and his sixth Nice victory (All-Sport)

WOMEN
1979	Lyn Lemaire (USA) 12:55:38
1980	Robin Beck (USA) 11:21:24
1981	Linda Sweeney (USA) 12:00:32
1982 (Feb)	Kathleen McCartney (USA) 11:09:40
1982 (Oct)	Julie Leach (USA) 10:54:08
1983	Sylviane Puntous (Can) 10:43:36
1984	Sylviane Puntous (Can) 10:25:13
1985	Joanne Ernst (USA) 10:25:22
1986	Paula Newby-Fraser (Zim) 9:49:14*
1987	Erin Baker (NZ) 9:35:25
1988	Paula Newby-Fraser (Zim) 9:01:01
1989	Paula Newby-Fraser (Zim) 9:00:56

* Sylviane Puntous was disqualified after finishing in 9:47:49.

The fastest time ever recorded over the Ironman distances is 8:01:32 by Dave Scott (USA) at Lake Biwa, Japan on 30 Jul 1989.

EUROPEAN CHAMPIONSHIPS

First contested, over the same distances as in Hawaii, European Championships have subsequently been held at shorter distance categories as well.

Ironman
MEN
1985	Gregor Stam (Hol) 8:56:55
1986	Scott Tinley (USA) 8:27:46
European	Magnus Lönnqvist (Fin) 8:40:11
1987	Axel Keonders (Hol) 8:36:22
1988	Not held
1989	Axel Koenders (Hol) 8:26:58

WOMEN
1984	Sarah Springman (UK)
1985	Erin Baker (NZ) 9:26:30
European	Sarah Springman (UK) 10:18:53
1986	Erin Baker (NZ) 9:27:36
European	Sarah Springman (UK) 9:59:49
1987	Sarah Coope (UK) 9:48:17
1989	Sarah Coope (UK) 9:33:20

Middle distance – *2.5km swim, 80km cycle, 20km run*
MEN
1985	Peter Zijerveld (Hol) 4:10:05
1987	Glenn Cook (UK) 3:57:19
1988	Rob Barel (Hol) 3:44:50
1989	*Not held*

WOMEN
1985	Lieve Paulus (Bel) 4:45:19
1987	Sarah Coope (UK) 4:28:38
1988	Sarah Coope (UK) 4:15:42

Short distance
MEN
1985	Rob Barel (Hol) 2:37:42
1986	Rob Barel (Hol) 1:59:50
1987	Rob Barel (Hol) 1:58:12
1988	Rob Barel (Hol) 1:50:23
1989	Yves Cordier (Fra)

WOMEN
1985	Erin Baker (NZ) 2:51:18
European	Alexandra Kremer (FRG) 3:06:02
1986	Lieve Paulus (Bel) 2:17:10
1987	Sarah Coope (UK) 2:17:03
1988	Sarah Springman (UK) 2:04:53
1989	Simone Mortier (Fra) 2:16:59

'WORLD CHAMPIONSHIP' TRIATHLON at Nice
Contested annually from 1982 over shorter distances than the 'Ironman': 3.2km swim, 120km cycle, 32km run from 1982-7. In 1988 the swim distance was changed to 4000m. *Winners:*
MEN
1982	Mark Allen (USA) 6:33:52
1983	Mark Allen (USA) 6:04:51
1984	Mark Allen (USA) 6:05:23
1985	Mark Allen (USA) 5:53:13
1986	Mark Allen (USA) 5:46:10
1987	Richard Wells (NZ) 5:59:53
1988	Rob Barel (Hol) 6:05:06
1989	Mark Allen (USA) 5:54:31
1990	Mark Allen (USA) 5:50:52

WOMEN
1982	Lyn Brooks (USA) 7:40:44
1983	Linda Buchanan (USA) 7:06:03
1984	Colleen Cannon (USA) 7:05:15
1985	Erin Baker (NZ) 6:37:21
1986	Linda Buchanan (USA) 6:50:56*
1987	Kirsten Hanssen (USA) 6:54:27
1988	Erin Baker (NZ) 6:27:06
1989	Paula Newby-Fraser (Zim) 6:49:43
1990	Paula Newby-Fraser (Zim) 6:36:19

* Erin Baker was disqualified after finishing in 6:40:26

TUG-OF-WAR

The term 'Tug-of-War' is thought to have originated in England in the 19th century. Such a trial of strength and skill, involving two teams of eight pulling against each other on opposite ends of a long, thick rope is believed to be of great antiquity.

The first rules were framed by the New York AC in 1879 and the sport was included in the Olympic Games from 1900 until 1920. In Britain tug-of-war was administered by the Amateur Athletic Association, and championships held in conjunction with the AAAs until 1970, but a separate organisation, the Tug-of-War Association, was formed in 1958. The world governing body is the International Tug-of-War Federation.

OLYMPIC GAMES
Winners:
1900 Sweden/Denmark
1904 Milwaukee AC (USA)
1906 Germany
1908 City Police (UK)
1912 Sweden
1920 Great Britain

WORLD CHAMPIONSHIPS
European Championships for men were first held in 1965, and these were followed by World Championships for men in 1975 and for women in 1986. There are categories depending on the total weight of the team. *World champions*
MEN
720kg
England 1975-8, 1980, 1982
Ireland 1984, 1986, 1988
Switzerland 1985

640kg
England 1975-6, 1978, 1980, 1986, 1988
Ireland 1982, 1984
Switzerland 1985

560kg
Switzerland 1982, 1985
England 1984, 1988
Ireland 1986

Catchweight (no weight specification)
England 1984

WOMEN
520 & 560kg 1986 and 1988 Sweden

The most successful team has been the Sheen Farmers, who competed for England, winning at 640kg in 1975-6 and at 720kg 1977-8 and 1980.
World Championships are now held biennially.

EUROPEAN CHAMPIONS

MEN
720kg
England 1965-5, 1968-74, 1979, 1981, 1987

640kg
England 1968, 1971-2, 1974, 1983
Wales 1969
Northern Ireland 1970
Sweden 1973
Netherlands 1979
Switzerland 1981, 1989
Ireland 1987
560kg
England 1979

Ireland 1987
Switzerland 1989

WOMEN
560kg: 1987 Sweden
520kg: 1987 Sweden

In England the Wood Treatment team (formerly the Bosley Farmers) from Cheshire won 20 consecutive catchweight titles 1959-78, as well as two world (1975-6) and ten European titles at 720kg

VOLLEYBALL

The game was invented, originally as "Mintonette" in 1895 by William G.Morgan, director of physical training at the YMCA, Holyoke, Massachussets, USA. His aim was to provide a more recreational, non-contact game than basketball, which had been invented just four years earlier by James Naismith, whom Morgan had met while a student at Springfield YMCA. The number of players per side was fixed at six in 1918.

Volleyball was first played at an international games, at the 1913 Far Eastern Games in Manila, Philippines. The International Volleyball Federation (FIVB) was formed in 1947 and world championships first held in 1949, with the game introduced to the Olympics in 1964. It is now one of the most widely practised game in the world, with 175 members of the FIVB in 1989.

They shall not pass – the Soviet Union men defend against the South Koreans at the Olympics (All-Sport)

OLYMPIC CHAMPIONS
Held for men and women at all Olympics from 1964.

	MEN	WOMEN
1964	USSR	Japan
1968	USSR	USSR
1972	Japan	USSR
1976	Poland	Japan
1980	USSR	USSR
1984	USA	China
1988	USA	USSR

Most medals:
MEN 2 gold, 1 bronze Yuriy Poyarkov (USSR) 1964-72
1 gold, 1 silver, 1 bronze Katsutoshi Nekoda (Jap) 1964-72
WOMEN 2 gold, 2 silver Inna Ryskal (USSR) 1964-76

WORLD CHAMPIONS
First held 1949, then every four years from 1952.
MEN
6 USSR   1949, 1952, 1960, 1962, 1978, 1982
2 Czechoslovakia   1956, 1966
1 GDR 1970, Poland 1974, USA 1986
WOMEN
4 USSR   1952, 1956, 1960, 1970
3 Japan   1962, 1967, 1974
2 China   1982, 1986
1 Cuba   1978

WORLD CUP
Held every four years from 1965 (men) and 1973
(women). *Wins:*
MEN:
3 USSR   1965, 1977, 1981
1 GDR 1969, USA 1985, Cuba 1989
WOMEN:
2 China   1981, 1985
1 USSR 1973, Japan 1977, Cuba 1989

EUROPEAN CHAMPIONSHIPS
First held in 1948 for men and 1949 for women. Now
held biennially. *Wins:*
MEN
11 USSR 1950-1, 1967, 1971, 1975, 1977, 1979, 1981,
1983, 1985, 1987
3 Czechoslovakia   1948, 1955, 1958
1 Romania 1963, Italy 1989
WOMEN
12 USSR 1949-51, 1958, 1963, 1967, 1971, 1975, 1977,
1979, 1983, 1985, 1989
1 Czechoslovakia 1955, Bulgaria 1981, GDR 1987

BEACH VOLLEYBALL
World Championships were first held at Ipanema Beach,
Rio de Janeiro, Brazil in February 1987. Winners of the
doubles event were Sinjin Smith and Randy Stoklos (USA).
They won again in 1988 and 1990. In 1989 there were no
world championships but a world series was held and won
by Karch Kiraly & Steve Timmons (USA).

WATER POLO

Played by teams of 7-a-side (from squads of 11). Originally
known as 'football in the water' it was developed in
Britain from 1869. The first rules were drafted in 1876 and
the sport was first given official recognition by the
Amateur Swimming Association in Great Britain in 1885. It
has been an Olympic event since 1900, and came under
the aegis of FINA after swimming's governing body was
founded in 1908. The first women's International
competition was in 1978. Governed by FINA (see
swimming).

OLYMPIC GAMES
The first two winning teams were club sides: Osborne
Swimming Club, Manchester, representing Great Britain in
1900 and New York AC in 1904. Wins:
6 Hungary   1932, 1936, 1952, 1956, 1964, 1976
4 Great Britain 1900, 1908, 1912, 1920
3 Yugoslavia   1968, 1984, 1988
2 Italy   1948, 1960
2 USSR   1972, 1980
1 USA (New York AC) 1904, France 1924, Germany 1928.

Individuals to have won three gold medals:
George Wilkinson (UK) 1900-12, Paul Radmilovic &
Charles Smith (UK) 1908-20, Deszö Gyarmati & György
Kárpáti (Hun) 1952-64. Gyarmati won most medals,
adding silver in 1948 and bronze in 1960.

WORLD CHAMPIONSHIPS
First held at the world swimming championships in 1973.
Winners:
MEN
1973 Hungary
1975 USSR
1978 Italy
1982 USSR
1986 Yugoslavia
WOMEN
1986 Australia

FINA WORLD CUP
First held in 1979. *Winners:*
MEN
1979 Hungary
1981 USSR
1983 USSR
1985 FR Germany
1987 Yugoslavia
1989 Yugoslavia
WOMEN – winners of unoffficial championships:
1979 USA
1981 Canada
1988 Netherlands

EUROPEAN CHAMPIONS
MEN

10 Hungary	1926-7, 1931, 1934, 1938, 1954, 1958, 1962, 1974, 1977
5 USSR	1966, 1970, 1983, 1985, 1987
2 FR Germany	1981, 1989
1 Italy	1947,
1 Netherlands	1950

WOMEN

3 Netherlands	1985, 1987, 1989

A European Nation's Cup, played between nations on a home and away basis commenced in 1990.

WATER SKIING

Water-skiing, as practised today, was pioneered in the 1920s, particularly by Ralph Samuelson on Lake Pepin, Minnesota, USA. The sport's origins, however, can be traced back hundreds of years through people walking on planks and aquaplaning. The development of the motor boat to tow skiers was clearly the key factor in the sport's growth.

The world governing body is the World Water Ski Union (WWSU), first formed as the Union Internationale de Ski Nautique in Geneva in 1946. World championships were instituted in 1949.

WORLD CHAMPIONSHIPS
First held at Juan Les Pins, France in 1949 and now staged biennially. *Winners:*

Men's Overall
1949 Christian Jourdan (Fra) &
      Guy de Clercq (Bel)
1950 Dick Pope Jr (USA)
1953 Alfredo Mendoza (USA)
1955 Alfredo Mendoza (USA)
1957 Joe Cash (USA)
1959 Chuck Stearns (USA)
1961 Bruno Zaccardi (Ita)
1963 Billy Spencer (USA)
1965 Roland Hillier (USA)
1967 Mike Suyderhoud (USA)
1969 Mike Suyderhoud (USA)
1971 George Athans (Can)
1973 George Athans (Can)
1975 Carlos Suarez (Ven)
1977 Mike Hazelwood (UK)
1979 Joel McClintock (Can)
1981 Sammy Duvall (USA)
1983 Sammy Duvall (USA)
1985 Sammy Duvall (USA)
1987 Sammy Duvall (USA)
1989 Patrice Martin (Fra)

Sammy Duval (All-Sport)

Men's Slalom

1949	Christian Jourdan (Fra)
1950	Dick Pope Jr (USA)
1953	Charles Blackwell (Can)
1955	Alfredo Mendoza (USA)
1957	Joe Cash (USA)
1959	Chuck Stearns (USA)
1961	Jimmy Jackson (USA)
1963	Billy Spencer (USA)
1965	Roland Hillier (USA)
1967	Tito Antunano (Mex)
1969	Victor Palomo (Spa)
1971	Mike Suyderhoud (USA)
1973	George Athans (Can)
1975	Roby Zucchi (Ita)
1977	Bob LaPoint (USA)
1979	Bob LaPoint (USA)
1981	Andy Mapple (UK)
1983	Bob LaPoint (USA)
1985	Patrice Martin (Fra)
1987	Bob LaPoint (USA)
1989	Andy Mapple (UK)

Men's Tricks

Pierre Gouin (Fra)
Jack Andresen (USA)
Warren Witherall (USA)
Scotty Scott (USA)
Mike Amsbury (USA)
Philippe Logut (Fra)
Jean Marie Muller (Fra)
Billy Spencer (USA)
Ken White (USA)
Alan Kempton (USA)
Bruce Cockburn (Aus)
Ricky McCormick (USA)
Wayne Grimditch (USA)
Wayne Grimditch (USA)
Carlos Suarez (Ven)
Patrice Martin (Fra)
Cory Pickos (USA)
Cory Pickos (USA)
Bob LaPoint (USA)
Patrice Martin (Fra)
Aymeric Benet (Fra)

Men's Jumping

Guy de Clercq (Bel)
Guy de Clercq (Bel)
Alfredo Mendoza (USA)
Alfredo Mendoza (USA)
Joe Mueller (USA)
Buster McCalla (USA)
Larry Penacho (USA)
Jimmy Jackson (USA)
Larry Penacho (USA)
Alan Kempton (USA)
Wayne Grimditch (USA)
Mike Suyderhoud (USA)
Ricky McCormick (USA)
Ricky McCormick (USA)
Mike Suyderhoud (USA)
Mike Hazelwood (UK)
Mike Hazelwood (UK)
Sammy Duvall (USA)
Geoff Carrington (Aus)
Sammy Duvall (USA)
Geoff Carrington (Aus)

Women's Overall

1949	Willa Worthington (USA)
1950	Willa McGuire* (USA)
1953	Leah Marie Rawls (USA)
1955	Willa McGuire (USA)
1957	Marina Doria (Swi)
1959	Vickie Van Hook (USA)
1961	Sylvie Hulsemann (Lux)
1963	Jeanette Brown (USA)
1965	Liz Allan (USA)
1967	Jeanette Stewart-Wood (UK)
1969	Liz Allan (USA)
1971	Christy Weir (USA)
1973	Lisa St John (USA)
1975	Liz Shetter (née Allan) (USA)
1977	Cindy Todd (USA)
1979	Cindy Todd (USA)
1981	Karin Roberge (USA)
1983	Ana Maria Carrasco (Ven)
1985	Karen Neville (Aus)
1987	Deena Brush (USA)
1989	Deena Mapple (née Brush) (USA)

Women's Slalom

1949	Willa Worthington (USA)
1950	Evie Wolford (USA)
1953	Evie Wolford (USA)
1955	Willa McGuire (USA)
1957	Marina Doria (Swi)
1959	Vickie Van Hook (USA)
1961	Janelle Kirkley (USA)
1963	Jeanette Brown (USA)
1965	Barbara Cooper-Clack (USA)
1967	Liz Allan (USA)
1969	Liz Allan (USA)
1971	Christy Freeman (USA)
1973	Sylvie Maurial (Fra)
1975	Liz Shetter (USA)
1977	Cindy Todd (USA)
1979	Pattsie Messner (USA)
1981	Cindy Todd (USA)
1983	Cindy Todd (USA)
1985	Camille Duvall (USA)
1987	Kim Laskoff (USA)
1989	Kim Laskoff (USA)

Women's Tricks

Madeleine Boutellier (Fra)
Willa McGuire* (USA)
Leah Marie Rawls (USA)
Marina Doria (Swi)
Marina Doria (Swi)
Piera Castelvetri (Ita)
Sylvie Hulsemann (Lux)
Guyonne Dalle (Fra)
Dany Duflot (Fra)
Dany Duflot (Fra)
Liz Allan (USA)
Willi Stahle (Hol)
Maria Victoria Carrasco (Ven)
Maria Victoria Carrasco (Ven)
Maria Victoria Carrasco (Ven)
Natalya Rumyantseva (USSR)
Ana Maria Carrasco (Ven)
Natalya Ponomaryeva (USSR)*
Judy McClintock (Can)
Natalya Rumyantseva (USSR)
Tawn Larsen (USA)

Women's Jumping

Willa Worthington (USA)
Johnette Kirkpatrick (USA)
Sandra Swaney (USA)
Willa McGuire (USA)
Nancie Rideout (USA)
Nancie Rideout (USA)
Renate Hansluvka (Aut)
Renate Hansluvka (Aut)
Liz Allan (USA)
Jeanette Stewart-Wood (UK)
Liz Allan (USA)
Christy Weir (USA)
Liz Shetter (née Allan) (USA)
Liz Shetter (USA)
Linda Giddens (USA)
Cindy Todd (USA)
Deena Brush (USA)
Cindy Todd (USA)
Deena Brush (USA)
Deena Brush (USA)
Deena Mapple (née Brush) (USA)

* McGuire née Worthington, Ponomaryeva née Rumyantseva

Deena Brush, overall world champion in 1987. She retained her title in 1989 after her marriage to British star Andy Mapple
(All-Sport)

Most wins
Overall: MEN 4 Sammy Duvall; WOMEN 3 Willa McGuire (née Worthington), Liz Shetter (née Allan).
Individual: MEN: 5 Bob LaPoint; WOMEN: 8 Liz Shetter (née Allan)
Liz Allan is the only water skier to win all four titles in one year, 1969.
Team: Title won by the USA at all 17 championships 1957-89.

EUROPEAN CHAMPIONSHIPS
Held annually since 1947. *Overall champions:*

Men
1947 Claude de Clercq (Bel)
1948 Jean-Pierre Mussat (Fra)
1949 Christian Jourdan (Fra) &
       Guy de Clercq (Bel)
1950-2 Claude de Clercq (Bel)
1953 Guy Vermeersch (Bel)
1954 Marc Flachard (Fra)
1955 Simon Khoury (Leb)
1956 Franco Carraro (Ita)
1957-8 Jean Marie Muller (Fra)
1959-61 Bruno Zaccardi (Ita)
1962-3 Maxime Vazeille (Fra)
1964 Mario Pozzini (Ita)
1965 Jean-Jacques Pottier (Fra)
1966 Bruno Zaccardi (Ita)
1967 Jean Michel Jamin (Fra)
1968 Roby Zucchi (Ita)
1969 Jean-Yves Parpette
1970-1 Roby Zucchi (Ita)
1972 Paul Seaton (UK)
1973 Lars Björk (Swe)
1974-5 Paul Seaton (UK)
1976-7 Mike Hazelwood (UK)
1978-83 Mike Hazelwood (UK)
1984-5 Patrice Martin (Fra)
1985 Patrice Martin (Fra)
1986 Mike Hazelwood (UK)
1987-9 Andrea Alessi (Ita)

Women
1947 Maggy Savard (Fra)
1950 Monique Girod (Swz)

1951-2 Jacqueline Marcour (Fra)
1953-6 Marina Doria (Swi)
1957 Jacqueline Keller (Fra)
1958-60 Piera Castelvetri (Ita)
1961 Sylvie Hulsemann (Lux)
1962-3 Renate Hansluvka (Aut)
1964 Dany Duflot (Fra)]
1965 Renate Hansluvka (Aut)
1966 Sylvie Hulsemann (Lux)
1967 Jeanette Stewart-Wood (UK)
1968 Sylvie Hulsemann (Lux)
1969 Eliane Borter (Swz)
1970-1 Sylvie Maurial (Fra)
1972 Willi Stahle (Hol)
1973 Sylvie Maurial (Fra)
1974-5 Willi Stahle (Hol)
1976 Chantal Escot (Fra)
1977 Chantal Escot-Amade (Fra)
1978-9 Anita Carlman (Swe)
1980 Marlon van Dijk (Hol)
1981 Anita Carlman (Swe)
1982 Natalya Rumyantseva (USSR)
1983 Anita Carlman (Swe)
1984 Natalya Ponomaryeva (née Rumyantseva) (USSR)
1985 Helena Kjellander (Swe)
1986 Philippa Roberts (UK)
1987 Natalya Rumyantseva (USSR)
1988 Helena Kjellander (Swe)
1989 Natalya Rumyantseva (USSR)

Most wins: MEN 9 Mike Hazelwood, 4 Claude de Clercq, Bruno Zaccardi
WOMEN: 4 Marina Doria, Anita Carlman, Natalya Rumyantseva

WORLD CUP

For men's teams, first held 1980. *Wins:*
2 Great Britain 1980, 1984
2 USA 1982, 1986
1 France 1988

EUROPEAN CUP

For men's teams, first held 1980. *Wins:*
4 Great Britain 1983, 1987-9
2 Italy 1980, 1986
2 Sweden 1984-5
1 France 1982

WORLD RECORDS

MEN
Slalom 3 buoys on a 10.25m line: Andy Mapple (UK) Poynton Beach, USA 29 Mar 1989
Tricks 10990 points Cory Pickos (USA) Wapakenetka, USA 15 Jul 1989
Jump 62.4m Sammy Duvall (USA) Shreveport, USA 24 Jul 1988

WOMEN
Slalom 5 buoys on a 11.25m line: Jennifer Leachman (USA) Fort Worth, USA 29 Aug 1988
Tricks 8460 points Tawn Larsen (USA) Sparta, USA 29 Aug 1988
Jump 47.5m Deena Mapple (née Brush) (USA) Charlotte, USA 9 Jul 1988

WORLD BAREFOOT Water Skiing Championships

The first person reported to water ski barefoot was Dick Pope Jr in Florida in 1947. World barefoot championships, which have been dominated by Australians, were first held in 1978; events are wake slalom, tricks, start methods (not in 1988) and jump. *Overall winners:*

Year	Men	Women
1978	Brett Wing (Aus)	Colleen Wilkinson (Aus)
1980	Brett Wing (Aus)	Kim Lampard (Aus)
1982	Brett Wing (Aus)	Kim Lampard (Aus)
1985	Mike Seipel (USA)	Kim Lampard (Aus)
1986	Mike Seipel (USA)	Kim Lampard (Aus)
1988	Rick Powell (USA)	Lori Powell (USA)

Brett Wing won all five titles in 1980.
Team: Championship won by Australia on all five occasions 1978-86 and USA in 1988.

Barefoot world jump records

MEN: 22.1m Brett Sands (Aus) 1989,
WOMEN: 14.5m Debbie Pugh (Aus) 1989.

WORLD SKI RACING CHAMPIONSHIPS

First held in 1979. I*ndividual winners:*

Year	Men	Women
1979	Wayne Ritchie (Aus)	Bronwyn Wright (Aus)
1983	Danny Bartels (Bel)	Liz Hobbs (UK)
1984	Danny Bartels (Bel)	Liz Hobbs (UK)
1985	Mark Pickering (Aus)	Debbie Nordblad (USA)
1988	Stephen Moore (UK)	Tanya Williams (Aus)
1989	Ian Dipple (Aus)	Marsha Fitzgerald (USA)

Team USA 1979, 1984, 1988, 1989; Australia 1979, 1983, 1985

In 1986 Stephen Moore (UK) won the inaugural ski racing World Cup, winning all three races. The World Cup and the World Championships now take place in alternate years.

The fastest speed recorded on water skis is 230.26 km/h by Christopher Massey (Aus) on the Hawkesbury River, New South Wales, Australia in 1983.

The official barefoot speed record over a quarter-mile course is 192.08 km/h by Scott Pelaton (USA) at Chowchilla, California, USA in 1983. The fastest by a woman is 118.56 km/h by Karen Toms (Aus) on the Hawkesbury River, Salisbury, New South Wales in 1984.

WEIGHTLIFTING

Strength testing by lifting heavy weights is an ancient sport and competitions for lifting weights of stone were included in the ancient Olympic Games. Just five years after a world championship competition was held in 1891, weightlifting was included in the first of the modern Olympic Games. The events were for one-arm and two-arm lifts. During the couple of centuries preceding that, professional strongmen had demonstrated awesome feats of strength, but some of the advertised weights may be doubted.

Modern weightlifting, as included on the Olympic programme, is a combination of strength and skill. There are two standard lifts: the snatch, which is a one-movement lift from the floor to an extended arm position above the head; and the jerk, which is a two movement lift, the clean from floor to shoulders, and then the jerk itself from the shoulders to a fully extended arm position above the head. Competitors have up to three attempts at each weight, and three referees determine whether lifts are correct. Until 1972 the press was also included as a standard lift, but it was then dropped due to the difficulties involved in judging it. There are ten bodyweight categories for lifters.

The world governing body, the Interntional Weightlifting Federation (IWF) was formed in 1920 as the Fédération Haltérophile Internationale.

World and Olympic Champions

Although the IWF first ran world championships at Tallinn, Estonia in 1922, they have subsequently recognised 18 championships held from those in Vienna, Austria in 1898 to 1920. Championships were held again in 1923, but not again until 1937 and 1938. They have been held annually from 1946 (except for 1967), with the Olympic Games recognised as the official championships during those years. Olympic Games weightlifting was contested at one-hand jerk and two-hand jerk with no weight categories in 1896, 1904 and 1906. Weight categories were introduced at the 1920 Olympic Games and have expanded over the years. From 1920 to 1946 there were five: 60kg, 67.5kg, 75kg, 82.5kg, over 82.5kg. Further additions have been: 56kg 1947, 90kg 1951, 52kg and 110kg 1969, 100kg 1977, with the super-heavyweights now over 110kg. Somewhat confusingly, the heavyweight class was thus over 82.5kg until 1950, over 90kg until 1968, and at the 110kg limit when the super-heavyweight class was introduced in 1969. At the 1920 Olympics three lifts were totalled, with one-hand snatch added to the one- and two-handed jerk. In 1924 two additional lifts were added, two-hands press and snatch. From 1928 to 1972 the results were decided on the aggregate of press, snatch and jerk, and from the 1973 World Championships on snatch and jerk.

a) Most World and Olympic (*) titles 1896-1924
6 Josef Grafl (Aut) 67.5+kg 1910; 80+kg 1908-11, 1913
4 Josef Steinbach (Aut) overall 1904, 1905, 80kg+ 1905;

one-hand jerk 1906*
4 Leopold Hennermüller (Aut) 67.5kg 1910, 80kg 1911 (twice), 1913
4 Emil Kliment (Aut) 60kg 1910, 1911 (twice), 1913
b) World and Olympic Champions (*) from 1928
Olympic Games 1964 to 1984 also recognised as World Championships; 1988 was not.
Totals are shown in kilograms; 1928-72 three lifts, since 1973 two lifts.

52kg *Formerly Flyweight*
1969 Vladimir Krishchisin (USSR) 337.5
1970 Sandor Holczreiter (Hun) 342.5
1971 Zygmunt Smalcerz (Pol) 340
1972* Zygmunt Smalcerz (Pol) 337.5
1973 Mohammed Nassiri (Irn) 240
1974 Mohammed Nassiri (Irn) 232.5
1975 Zygmunt Smalcerz (Pol) 237.5
1976* Aleksandr Voronin (USSR) 242.5
1977 Aleksandr Voronin (USSR) 247.5
1978 Kanybek Osmonalyev (USSR) 240
1979 Kanybek Osmonalyev (USSR) 242.5
1980* Kanybek Osmonalyev (USSR) 245
1981 Kanybek Osmonalyev (USSR) 247.5
1982 Stefan Leletko (Pol) 250
1983 Neno Terziiski (Bul) 260
1984* Zeng Guoqiang (Chn) 235
1985 Sevdalin Marinov (Bul) 252.5
1986 Sevdalin Marinov (Bul) 257.5
1987 Sevdalin Marinov (Bul) 262.5
1988* Sevdalin Marinov (Bul) 270
1989 Ivan Ivanov (Bul) 272.5

56kg *Formerly Bantamweight*
1947 Joseph de Pietro (USA) 300
1948* Joseph de Pietro (USA) 307.5
1949 Mahmoud Namdjou (Irn) 315
1950 Mahmoud Namdjou (Irn) 310
1951 Mahmoud Namdjou (Irn) 317.5
1952* Ivan Udodov (USSR) 315
1953 Ivan Udodov (USSR) 315
1954 Bakir Farhutdinov (USSR) 315
1955 Vladimir Stogov (USSR) 335
1956* Charles Vinci (USA) 342.5
1957 Vladimir Stogov (USSR) 345
1958 Vladimir Stogov (USSR) 342.5
1959 Vladimir Stogov (USSR) 332.5
1960* Charles Vinci (USA) 345
1961 Vladimir Stogov (USSR) 345
1962 Yoshinobu Miyake (Jap) 352.5
1963 Aleksey Vakhonin (USSR) 345
1964* Aleksey Vakhonin (USSR) 357.5
1965 Imre Földi (Hun) 360
1966 Aleksey Vakhonin (USSR) 362.5
1968* Mohammad Nassiri (Irn) 367.5

1969 Mohammed Nassiri (Irn) 360
1970 Mohammed Nassiri (Irn) 362.5
1971 Gennadiy Chetin (USSR) 370
1972* Imre Földi (Hun) 377.5
1973 Atanas Kirov (USSR) 257.5
1974 Atanas Kirov (USSR) 255
1975 Atanas Kirov (USSR) 255
1976* Norair Nurikyan (Bul) 262.5
1977 Jiro Hosotani (Jap) 252.5
1978 Daniel Nunez (Cub) 260
1979 Anton Kodiabashev (Bul) 267.5
1980* Daniel Nunez (Cub) 275
1981 Anton Kodiabashev (Bul) 272.5
1982 Anton Kodiabashev (Bul) 280
1983 Oksen Mirzoyan (USSR) 292.5
1984* Wu Shude (Chn) 267.5
1985 Neno Terziiski (Bul) 280
1986 Mitko Grablev (Bul) 290
1987 Neno Terziiski (Bul) 287.5
1988* Oksen Mirzoyan (USSR) 292.5
   (Mitko Grablev (Bul) 297.5 disqualified after positive
   drugs test)
1989 Hafis Suleimanov (USSR) 287.5

60kg *Formerly featherweight*
1928* Franz Andrysek (Aut) 287.5
1932* Raymond Suvigny (Fra) 287.5
1936* Anthony Terlazzo (USA) 312.5
1937 Georg Liebsch (Ger) 297.5
1938 Georg Liebsch (Ger) 305
1946 Arvid Andersson (Swe) 320
1947 Robert Higgins (USA) 310
1948* Mahmoud Fayad (Egy) 332.5
1949 Mahmoud Fayad (Egy) 332.5
1950 Mahmoud Fayad (Egy) 327.5
1951 Sayed Gouda (Egy) 310
1952* Rafael Chimiskyan (USSR) 337.5
1953 Nikolay Saksonov (USSR) 337.5
1954 Rafael Chimiskyan (USSR) 350
1955 Rafael Chimiskyan (USSR) 350
1956* Isaac Berger (USA) 352.5
1957 Yevgeniy Minayev (USSR) 362.5
1958 Isaac Berger (USA) 372.5
1959 Marian Zielinski (Pol) 365
1960* Yevgeniy Minayev (USSR) 372.5
1961 Isaac Berger (USA) 367.5
1962 Yevgeniy Minayev (USSR) 362.5
1963 Yoshinobu Miyake (Jap) 375
1964* Yoshinobu Miyake (Jap) 397.5
1965 Yoshinobu Miyake (Jap) 385
1966 Yoshinobu Miyake (Jap) 387.5
1968* Yoshinobu Miyake (Jap) 392.5
1969 Yoshiyuki Miyake (Jap) 385
1970 Mieczyslaw Nowak (Pol) 392.5
1971 Yoshiyuki Miyake (Jap) 387.5
1972* Norair Nurikyan (Bul) 402.5
1973 Dito Shanidze (USSR) 272.5
1974 Georgi Todorov (Bul) 280

1975 Georgi Todorov (Bul) 285
1976* Nikolay Kolesnikov (USSR) 285
1977 Nikolay Kolesnikov (USSR) 280
1978 Nikolay Kolesnikov (USSR) 270
1979 Marek Severyn (USSR) 290
1980* Viktor Mazin (USSR) 290
1981 Beloslav Manolov (Bul) 302.5
1982 Yurik Sarkisyan (USSR) 302.5
1983 Yurik Sarkisyan (USSR) 312.5
1984* Chen Weiqiang (Chn) 282.5
1985 Neum Shalamanov (Bul) 322.5
1986 Neum Shalamanov (Bul) 335
1987 Stefan Topurov (Bul) 315
1988* Naim Suleymanoglou# (Tur) 342.5
1989 Naim Suleymanoglou (Tur) 317.5

formerly Naim Suleimanov or Neum Shalamanov

67.5kg *Formerly Lightweight*
1928* Kurt Helbig (Ger) 322.5
   & Hans Haas (Aut) 322.5
1932* René Duverger (Fra) 325
1936* Anwar Mohammed Mesbah (Egy) 342.5
   & Robert Fein (Aut) 342.5
1937 Anthony Terlazzo (USA) 357.5
1938 Anthony Terlazzo (USA) 350
1946 Stanley Stanczyk (USA) 367.5
1947 Peter George (USA) 352.5
1948* Ibrahim Shams (Egy) 360
1949 Ibrahim Shams (Egy) 352.5
1950 Joseph Pitman (USA) 352.5
1951 Ibrahim Shams (Egy) 342.5
1952* Tommy Kono (USA) 362.5
1953 Peter George (USA) 370
1954 Dmitriy Ivanov (USSR) 367.5
1955 Nikolay Kostilyev (USSR) 382.5
1956* Igor Rybak (USSR) 380
1957 Viktor Bushuyev (USSR) 380
1958 Viktor Bushuyev (USSR) 390
1959 Viktor Bushuyev (USSR) 385
1960* Viktor Bushuyev (USSR) 397.5
1961 Waldemar Baszanowski (Pol) 402.5
1962 Vladimir Kaplunov (USSR) 415
1963 Marian Zielinski (Pol) 417.5
1964* Waldemar Baszanowski (Pol) 432.5
1965 Waldemar Baszanowski (Pol) 427.5
1966 Yevgeniy Katsura (USSR) 437.5
1968* Waldemar Baszanowski (Pol) 437.5
1969 Waldemar Baszanowski (Pol) 445
1970 Zbigniew Kaczmarek (Pol) 440
1971 Zbigniew Kaczmarek (Pol) 440
1972* Mukharbi Kirzhinov (USSR) 460
1973 Mukharbi Kirzhinov (USSR) 305
1974 Pyotr Korol (USSR) 305
1975 Pyotr Korol (USSR) 312.5
1976* Pyotr Korol (USSR) 305
1977 Roberto Urrutia (Cub) 315
1978 Yanko Rusev (Bul) 310

1979 Yanko Rusev (Bul) 332.5
1980* Yanko Rusev (Bul) 342.5
1981 Joachim Kunz (GDR) 340
1982 Piotr Mandra (Pol) 325
1983 Joachim Kunz (GDR) 340
1984* Yao Jingyuan (Chn) 320
1985 Mikhail Petrov (Bul) 335
1986 Mikhail Petrov (Bul) 342.5
1987 Mikhail Petrov (Bul) 350
1988* Joachim Kunz (GDR) 340
  (Angel Guenchev (Bul) 362.5 disqualified after
  positive drugs test)
1989 Israil Militosyan (USSR) 347.5

75kg *Formerly Middleweight*
1928* Roger Francois (Fra) 335
1932* Rudolf Ismayr (Ger) 345
1936* Khadr El Touni (Egy) 387.5
1937 John Terpak (USA) 352.5
1938 Adolf Wagner (Ger) 367.5
1946 Khadr El Touni (Egy) 377.5
1947 Stanley Stanczyk (USA) 405
1948* Frank Spellman (USA) 390
1949 Khadr El Touni (Egy) 397.5
1950 Khadr El Touni (Egy) 400
1951 Peter George (USA) 395
1952* Peter George (USA) 400
1953 Tommy Kono (USA) 407.5
1954 Peter George (USA) 405
1955 Peter George (USA) 405
1956* Fyodor Bogdanovskiy (USSR) 420
1957 Tommy Kono (USA) 420
1958 Tommy Kono (USA) 430
1959 Tommy Kono (USA) 425
1960* Aleksandr Kurinov (USSR) 437.5
1961 Aleksandr Kurinov (USSR) 435
1962 Aleksandr Kurinov (USSR) 422.5
1963 Aleksandr Kurinov (USSR) 437.5
1964* Hans Zdrazila (Cs) 445
1965 Viktor Kurentsov (USSR) 437.5
1966 Viktor Kurentsov (USSR) 450
1968* Viktor Kurentsov (USSR) 475
1969 Viktor Kurentsov (USSR) 467.5
1970 Viktor Kurentsov (USSR) 462.5
1971 Vladimir Kanygin (USSR) 477.5
1972* Yordan Bikov (Bul) 485
1973 Nedelcho Kolev (Bul) 337.5
1974 Nedelcho Kolev (Bul) 335
1975 Peter Wenzel (GDR) 335
1976* Yordan Mitkov (Bul) 335
1977 Yurik Vardanyan (USSR) 345
1978 Roberto Urrutia (Cub) 347.5
1979 Roberto Urrutia (Cub) 345
1980* Asen Zlatev (Bul) 360
1981 Yanko Rusev (Bul) 360
1982 Yanko Rusev (Bul) 365
1983 Alexander Varbanov (Bul) 370
1984* Karl-Heinz Radschinsky (FRG) 340

1985 Alexander Varbanov (Bul) 370
1986 Alexander Varbanov (Bul) 377.5
1987 Borislav Gydikov (Bul) 375
1988* Borislav Gydikov (Bul) 375
1989 Altjamurat Orazdurdyev (USSR) 362.5

82.5kg *Formerly Light-Heavyweight*
1928* Said Nosseir (Egy) 355
1932* Louis Hostin (Fra) 372.5
1936* Louis Hostin (Fra) 372.5
1937 Fritz Haller (Aut) 375
1938 John Davis (USA) 387.5
1946 Grigoriy Novak (USSR) 425
1947 John Terpak (USA) 387.5
1948* Stanley Stanczyk (USA) 417.5
1949 Stanley Stanczyk (USA) 412.5
1950 Stanley Stanczyk (USA) 420
1951 Stanley Stanczyk (USA) 402.5
1952* Trofim Lomakin (USSR) 417.5
1953 Arkadiy Vorobyev (USSR) 430
1954 Tommy Kono (USA) 435
1955 Tommy Kono (USA) 435
1956* Tommy Kono (USA) 447.5
1957 Trofim Lomakin (USSR) 450
1958 Trofim Lomakin (USSR) 440
1959 Rudolf Plyukfelder (USSR) 457.5
1960* Ireneusz Palinski (Pol) 442.5
1961 Rudolf Plyukfelder (USSR) 450
1962 Gyözö Veres (Hun) 460
1963 Gyözö Veres (Hun) 477.5
1964* Rudolf Plyukfelder (USSR) 475
1965 Norbert Osimek (Pol) 472.5
1966 Vladimir Belyayev (USSR) 485
1968* Boris Syelitskiy (USSR) 485
1969 Masashi Ohuchi (Jap) 487.5
1970 Gennadiy Ivanchenko (USSR) 505
1971 Boris Pavlov (USSR) 495
1972* Leif Jensen (Nor) 507.5
1973 Vladimir Rizhenkov (USSR) 350
1974 Trendafil Stoychev (Bul) 350
1975 Valeriy Shariy (USSR) 357.5
1976* Valeriy Shariy (USSR) 365
1977 Gennadiy Bessonov (USSR) 352.5
1978 Yurik Vardanyan (USSR) 377.5
1979 Yurik Vardanyan (USSR) 370
1980* Yurik Vardanyan (USSR) 400
1981 Yurik Vardanyan (USSR) 392.5
1982 Asen Zlatev (Bul) 400
1983 Yurik Vardanyan (USSR) 392.5
1984* Petre Becheru (Rom) 355
1985 Yurik Vardanyan (USSR) 397.5
1986 Asen Zlatev (Bul) 405
1987 László Barsi (Hun) 390
1988* Israil Arsamakov (USSR) 377.5
1989 Kiril Kounev (Bul) 385

82.5+kg *Heavyweight*
1928* Josef Strassberger (Ger) 372.5

The Bulgarian soldier Blagoi Blagoyev, world champion at 90kg weight limit from 1981 to 1983 (All-Sport)

1932* Jaroslav Skobla (Cs) 380
1936* Josef Manger (Aut) 410
1937 Josef Manger (Ger) 420
1938 Josef Manger (Ger) 410
1946 John Davis (USA) 435
1947 John Davis (USA) 455
1948* John Davis (USA) 452.5
1949 John Davis (USA) 442.5
1950 John Davis (USA) 462.5

90kg *Formerly Middle-heavyweight*
1951 Norbert Schemansky (USA) 427.5
1952* Norbert Schemansky (USA) 445
1953 Norbert Schemansky (USA) 442.5
1954 Arkadiy Vorobyev (USSR) 460
1955 Arkadiy Vorobyev (USSR) 455
1956* Arkadiy Vorobyev (USSR) 462.5
1957 Arkadiy Vorobyev (USSR) 470
1958 Arkadiy Vorobyev (USSR) 465
1959 Louis Martin (UK) 445
1960* Arkadiy Vorobyev (USSR) 472.5
1961 Ireneusz Palinski (Pol) 475
1962 Louis Martin (UK) 480
1963 Louis Martin (UK) 480
1964* Vladimir Golovanov (USSR) 487.5
1965 Louis Martin (UK) 487.5
1966 Geza Toth (Hun) 487.5
1968* Kaarlo Kangasniemi (Fin) 517.5
1969 Kaarlo Kangasniemi (Fin) 515
1970 Vasiliy Kolotov (USSR) 537.5
1971 David Rigert (USSR) 542.5
1972* Andon Nikolov (Bul) 525
1973 David Rigert (USSR) 365
1974 David Rigert (USSR) 387.5
1975 David Rigert (USSR) 377.5
1976* David Rigert (USSR) 382.5
1977 Sergey Poltoratskiy (USSR) 375
1978 Rolf Milser (FRG) 377.5
1979 Gennadiy Bessonov (USSR) 380
1980* Peter Baczako (Hun) 377.5
1981 Blagoi Blagoyev (Bul) 405
1982 Blagoi Blagoyev (Bul) 415
1983 Blagoi Blagoyev (Bul) 417.5
1984* Nicu Vlad (Rom) 392.5
1985 Anatoliy Khrapatiy (USSR) 395
    & Viktor Solodov (USSR) 395
1986 Anatoliy Khrapatiy (USSR) 412.5
1987 Anatoliy Khrapatiy (USSR) 417.5
1988* Anatoliy Khrapatiy (USSR) 412.5
1989 Anatoliy Khrapatiy (USSR) 415

90kg+ *Heavyweight*
1951 John Davis (USA) 432.5
1952* John Davis (USA) 460
1953 Douglas Hepburn (Can) 467.5
1954 Norbert Schemansky (USA) 487.5
1955 Paul Anderson (USA) 512.5
1956* Paul Anderson (USA) 500

1957 Aleksey Medvedev (USSR) 500
1958 Aleksey Medvedev (USSR) 485
1959 Yuriy Vlasov (USSR) 500
1960* Yuriy Vlasov (USSR) 537.5
1961 Yuriy Vlasov (USSR) 525
1962 Yuriy Vlasov (USSR) 540
1963 Yuriy Vlasov (USSR) 557.5
1964* Leonid Zhabotinskiy (USSR) 572.5
1965 Leonid Zhabotinskiy (USSR) 552.5
1966 Leonid Zhabotinskiy (USSR) 567.5
1968* Leonid Zhabotinskiy (USSR) 572.5

100kg
1977 Anatoliy Kozlov (USSR) 367.5
1978 David Rigert (USSR) 390
1979 Pavel Sirchin (USSR) 385
1980* Otto Zaremba (Cs) 395
1981 Viktor Sots (USSR) 407.5
1982 Viktor Sots (USSR) 422.5
1983 Pavel Kuznyetsov (USSR) 422.5
1984* Rolf Milser (FRG) 385
1985 Sandor Szanyi (Hun) 415
1986 Nicu Vlad (Rom) 437.5
1987 Pavel Kuznyetsov (USSR) 422.5
1988* Pavel Kuznyetsov (USSR) 425
1989 Petar Stefanov (Bul) 415

110kg *Formerly Heavyweight*
1969 Robert Bednarski (USA) 555
1970 Jan Talts (USSR) 565
1971 Yuriy Kozin (USSR) 552.5
1972* Jan Talts (USSR) 580
1973 Pavel Pervushin (USSR) 385
1974 Valeriy Ustyuzhin (USSR) 380
1975 Valentin Khristov (Bul) 417.5
1976* Yuriy Zaitsev (USSR) 385
1977 Valentin Khristov (Bul) 405
1978 Yuriy Zaitsev (USSR) 402.5
1979 Sergey Arakelov (USSR) 410
1980* Leonid Taranenko (USSR) 422.5
1981 Valeriy Kravchuk (USSR) 415
1982 Sergey Arakelov (USSR) 427.5
1983 Vyacheslav Klokov (USSR) 440
1984* Norberto Oberburger (Ita) 390
1985 Yuriy Zakharevich (USSR) 422.5
1986 Yuriy Zakharevich (USSR) 447.5
1987 Yuriy Zakharevich (USSR) 445
1988* Yuriy Zakharevich (USSR) 455
1989 Stefan Botev (Bul) 427.5

110kg+ *Formerly Super-heavyweight*
1969 Joseph Dube (USA) 577.5
1970 Vasiliy Alekseyev (USSR) 612.5
1971 Vasiliy Alekseyev (USSR) 635
1972* Vasiliy Alekseyev (USSR) 640
1973 Vasiliy Alekseyev (USSR) 402.5
1974 Vasiliy Alekseyev (USSR) 425
1975 Vasiliy Alekseyev (USSR) 427.5

1976* Vasiliy Alekseyev (USSR) 440
1977 Vasiliy Alekseyev (USSR) 430
1978 Jürgen Heuser (GDR) 417.5
1979 Sultan Rakhmanov (USSR) 430
1980* Sultan Rakhmanov (USSR) 440
1981 Anatoliy Pisarenko (USSR) 425
1982 Anatoliy Pisarenko (USSR) 445
1983 Anatoliy Pisarenko (USSR) 450
1984* Dean Lukin (Aus) 412.5
1985 Antonio Krastev (Bul) 437.5
1986 Antonio Krastev (Bul) 460
1987 Aleksandr Kurlovich (USSR) 472.5
1988* Aleksandr Kurlovich (USSR) 462.5
1989 Aleksandr Kurlovich (USSR) 460

MOST TITLES

Olympic Games: ten men have won two gold medals. The most medals is four by Norbert Schemansky (USA) gold 90kg 1952, silver 82+kg 1948, bronze 90+kg 1960, 1964.

World and Olympic:

8 John Davis (USA) 1938-52
8 Tommy Kono (USA) 1952-9
8 Vasiliy Alekseyev (USSR) 1970-7
7 Arkadiy Vorobyev (USSR) 1953-60

David Rigert was the supreme champion of the 1970s at middle-heavyweight (All-Sport)

7 Yurik Vardanyan (USSR) 1977-85
6 Stanley Stanczyk (Pol) 1946-51
6 Peter George (USA) 1947-55
6 Yoshinobu Miyake (Jap) 1962-8
6 David Rigert (USSR) 1971-8

Gold medals are also awarded at World Championships for each lift. The lifters to have won the most gold medals overall have been: P – press, S – snatch, J – jerk, T – Total

No.	Name	P	S	J	T
22	Vasiliy Alekseyev (USSR)	2	5	7	8
20	Yurik Vardanyan (USSR)	-	6	7	7
17	David Rigert (USSR)	1	5	5	6
15	Yanko Rusev (Bul)	-	5	5	5

WORLD CUP

Awarded on a points basis to the best lifter at an annual gala, attended by the world's best, who qualify from a worldwide series of events.

Year	World Cup winner	Gala winner
1980	György Szalai (Hun)	Janos Solyomvari (Hun)
1981	Yanko Rusev (Bul)	Blagoi Blagoyev (Bul)
1982	Blagoi Blagoyev (Bul)	Blagoi Blagoyev (Bul)
1983	Blagoi Blagoyev (Bul)	Oksen Mirzoyan (USSR)
1984	Naim Suleimanov (Bul)	Naim Suleimanov (Bul)
1985	Neum Shalamanov* (Bul)	Neum Shalamanov (Bul)
1986	Neum Shalamanov (Bul)	Asen Zlatev (Bul)
1987	Mikhail Petrov (Bul)	Mikhail Petrov (Bul)

| 1988 | Stefan Botev (Bul) | Stefan Botev (Bul) |
| 1989 | Liu Shoubin (Chn) | Liu Shoubin (Chn) |

* Change of name from Naim Suleimanov

WORLD WEIGHTLIFTING RECORDS

Bodyweight

Class	Lift	kg	Name and country	Date
52kg	Snatch	120	Sevdalin Marinov (Bul)	1988
	Jerk	155	Ivan Ivanov (Bul)	1989
	Total	272.5	Ivan Ivanov (Bul)	1989
56kg	Snatch	134.5	Liu Shoubin (China)	1989
	Jerk	171	Neno Terziiski (Bul)	1987
	Total	300	Neum Shalamanov (Bul)	1984
60kg	Snatch	152.5	Naim Suleymanoglu (Tur) #	1988
	Jerk	190	Naim Suleymanoglu (Tur) #	1988
	Total	342.5	Naim Suleymanoglu (Tur) #	1988
67.5kg	Snatch	160	Israil Militosyan (USSR)	1989
		162.5u	Kim Men-nam (Nko)	1990
	Jerk	200.5	Mikhail Petrov (Bul)	1987
	Total	355	Mikhail Petrov (Bul)	1987
75kg	Snatch	170	Angel Guenchev (Bul)	1987
	Jerk	215.5	Alexander Varbanov (Bul)	1987
	Total	382.5	Alexander Varbanov (Bul)	1988
82.5kg	Snatch	183	Asen Zlatev (Bul)	1986
	Jerk	225	Asen Zlatev (Bul)	1986
	Total	405	Yurik Vardanyan (USSR)	1984
90kg	Snatch	195.5	Blagoi Blagoyev (Bul)	1983
	Jerk	235	Anatoliy Khrapatiy (USSR)	1988
	Total	422.5	Viktor Solodov (USSR)	1984
100kg	Snatch	200.5	Nicu Vlad (Rom)	1986
	Jerk	242.5	Aleksandr Popov (USSR)	1988
	Total	440	Yuriy Zakharevich (USSR)	1983
110kg	Snatch	210	Yuriy Zakharevich (USSR)	1988
	Jerk	250.5	Yuriy Zakharevich (USSR)	1988
	Total	455	Yuriy Zakharevich (USSR)	1988
110kg+	Snatch	216	Antonio Krastev (Bul)	1987
	Jerk	266	Leonid Taranenko (USSR)	1988
	Total	475	Leonid Taranenko (USSR)	1988

# formerly Suleimanov/Shalanov of Bulgaria
u = unofficial

How the super-heavyweight jerk record has progressed.
The record at the end of each decade:

161.5	Charles Rigoulet (Fra)	1925
167.5	Arnold Luhäär (Estonia)	1937
177.5	John Davis (USA)	1948
197.5	Juri Vlasov (USSR)	1959
220.5	Robert Bednarski (USA)	1968
256	Vasiliy Alekseyev (USSR)	1977
266	Leonid Taranenko (USSR)	1988

Most improvements:		from		to	
31 Vasiliy Alekseyev (USSR)		221.5kg 1970		256kg	1977
9 Juri Vlasov (USSR)		197.5kg 1959		215.5kg	1964
6 Norbert Schemansky (USA)		185kg	1952	192.5kg	1954
6 Leonid Zhabotinsky (USSR)		213kg	1964	220kg	1968

WOMEN'S WEIGHTLIFTING

WORLD RECORDS

World records can only be set at World Championships: 1987 at Daytona Beach, Florida, USA; 1988 at Jakarta, Indonesia; 1989 at Manchester, UK.

Bodyweight

Class	Lift	kg	Name and country	Date
44kg	Snatch	72.5	Xing Fen (Chn)	1989
	Jerk	92.5	Xing Fen (Chn)	1989
	Total	165	Xing Fen (Chn)	1989
48kg	Snatch	75	Huang Xiaoyu (Chn)	1987
	Jerk	97.5	Huang Xiaoyu (Chn)	1989
	Total	172.5	Huang Xiaoyu (Chn)	1989
52kg	Snatch	80	Peng Liping (Chn)	1988
	Jerk	107.5	Peng Liping (Chn)	1989
	Total	185	Peng Liping (Chn)	1989
56kg	Snatch	82.5	Ma Na (Chn)	1988
	Jerk	107.5	Wu Haiqing (Chn)	1990
	Total	190	Wu Haiqing (Chn)	1990
60kg	Snatch	87.5	Ma Na (Chn)	1989
	Jerk	115	Camelia Nikolova (Bul)	1989
	Total	202.5	Camelia Nikolova (Bul)	1989
67.5kg	Snatch	97.5	Guo Qiuxiang (Chn)	1989
	Jerk	122.5	Guo Qiuxiang (Chn)	1989
	Total	220	Guo Qiuxiang (Chn)	1989
75kg	Snatch	102.5	Milena Trendafilova (Bul)	1990
	Jerk	135	Milena Trendafilova (Bul)	1990
	Total	237.5	Milena Trendafilova (Bul)	1990
82.5kg	Snatch	102.5	Li Hongling (Chn)	1989
	Jerk	137.5	Li Hongling (Chn)	1989
	Total	240	Li Hongling (Chn)	1989
82.5kg+	Snatch	110	Karyn Marshall (USA)	1990
	Jerk	142.5	Li Yajuan (Chn)	1990
	Total	242.5	Li Yajuan (Chn)	1990

WORLD CHAMPIONS

44kg
1987 Cai Jun (Chn) 145
1988 Xing Fen (Chn) 147.5
1989 Xing Fen (Chn) 165

48kg
1987 Huang Xiaoyu (Chn) 170
1988 Huang Xiaoyu (Chn) 165
1989 Huang Xiaoyu (Chn) 172.5

52kg
1987 Yan Zangqun (Chn) 157.5
1988 Peng Liping (Chn) 175
1989 Peng Liping (Chn) 185

56kg
1987 Cui Aihong (Chn) 160
1988 Ma Na (Chn) 180
1989 Xing Liwei (Chn) 180

60kg
1987 Zeng Xinling (Chn) 180
1988 Jing Yang (Chn) 195
1989 Ma Na (Chn) 202.5

67.5kg
1987 Gao Lijuan (Chn) 180
1988 Guo Qiuxiang (Chn) 210
1989 Guo Qiuxiang (Chn) 220

75kg
1987 Li Hongling (Chn) 210
1988 Li Hongling (Chn) 212.5
1989 Milena Trendafilova (Bul) 220

82.5kg
1987 Karyn Marshall (USA) 220
1988 Li Yanxia (Chn) 215
1989 Li Hongling (Chn) 240

82.5+kg
1987 Han Changmei (Chn) 210
1988 Han Changmei (Chn) 232.5
1989 Han Changmei (Chn) 242.5

WRESTLING

Wrestling was part of the Ancient Olympics, and wall drawings from nearly 6000 years ago depict it as taking place long before then. Wrestling was included in the first Modern Olympics in 1896, sixteen years before the formation of the International Amateur Wrestling Association (FILA). The two forms of wrestling at international level are Freestyle and Greco-Roman. The principle difference between the two is that use of the legs is completely prohibited in the Greco-Roman style. Holds below the waist are also prohibited in this style of wrestling.

OLYMPIC GAMES
A heavyweight division of Greco-Roman wrestling was included in the first modern Olympics. Freestyle wrestling was introduced in 1904. *Winners:*

FREESTYLE
48kg – Light-flyweight
1904 Robert Curry (USA)
1972 Roman Dmitriyev (USSR)
1976 Hasan Isaev (Bul)
1980 Claudio Pollio (Ita)
1984 Robert Weaver (USA)
1988 Takashi Kobayashi (Jap)

52kg – Flyweight
Limit 115lb/52.16kg in 1904
1904 George Mehnert (USA)
1948 Lennart Viitala (Fin)
1952 Hasan Gemici (Tur)
1956 Mirian Tsalkalamanidze (USSR)
1960 Ahmet Bilek (Tur)
1964 Yoshikatsu Yoshida (Jap)
1968 Shigeo Nakata (Jap)
1972 Kiyomi Kato (Jap)
1976 Yuji Takada (Jap)

1980 Anatoliy Beloglazov (USSR)
1984 Saban Trstena (Yug)
1988 Mitsuru Sato (Jap)

57kg – Bantamweight
Limits: 125lb/56.70kg 1904, 119lb/54kg 1908, 56kg 1924-36
1904 Isidor Niflot (USA)
1908 George Mehnert (USA)
1924 Kustaa Pihlajamäki (Fin)
1928 Kaarlo Mäkinen (Fin)
1932 Robert Pearce (USA)
1936 Odön Zombori (Hun)
1948 Nasuh Akar (Tur)
1952 Shohachi Ishii (Jap)
1956 Mustafa Dagistanli (Tur)
1960 Terrence McCann (USA)
1964 Yojiro Uetake (Jap)
1968 Yojiro Uetake (Jap)
1972 Hideaki Yanagida (Jap)
1976 Vladimir Yumin (USSR)
1980 Sergey Beloglazov (USSR)
1984 Hideaki Tomiyama (Jap)
1988 Sergey Beloglazov (USSR)

62kg – Featherweight
Limits: 135lb/61.24kg 1904, 133lb/60.3kg 1908, 60kg 1920, 61kg 1924-36, 63kg 1964-8
1904 Benjamin Bradshaw (USA)
1908 George Dole (USA)
1920 Charles Ackerly (USA)
1924 Robin Reed (USA)
1928 Allie Morrison (USA)
1932 Hermanni Pihlajamäki (Fin)
1936 Kustaa Pihlajamäki (Fin)
1948 Gazanfer Bilge (Tur)
1952 Bayram Sit (Tur)
1956 Shozo Sasahara (Jap)
1960 Mustafa Dagistanli (Tur)
1964 Osamu Watanabe (Jap)
1968 Masaaki Kaneko (Jap)
1972 Zagalav Abdulbekov (USSR)
1976 Yang Jung-mo (SKo)
1980 Magomedgasan Abushev (USSR)
1984 Randy Lewis (USA)
1988 John Smith (USA)

68kg – Lightweight
Limits: 145lb/65.77kg 1904, 146.75 lb/66.6kg 1908, 67.5kg 1920, 66kg 1924-36, 67kg 1948-60, 70kg 1964-8
1904 Otto Roehm (USA)
1908 George de Relwyskow (UK)
1920 Kalle Anttila (Fin)
1924 Russell Vis (USA)
1928 Osväld Käpp (Est)
1932 Charles Pacôme (Fra)
1936 Károly Kárpáti (Hun)
1948 Celâl Atik (Tur)

1952 Olle Anderberg (Swe)
1956 Emamali Habibi (Irn))
1960 Shelby Wilson (USA)
1964 Enyu Valtschev (Bul) *
1968 Abdollah Movahed Ardabili (Irn)
1972 Dan Gable (USA)
1976 Pavel Pinigin (USSR)
1980 Saipulla Absaidov (USSR)
1984 You In-tak (SKo)
1988 Arsen Fadzeyev (USSR)
* competed as Dimov in 1960

The medal ceremony for freestyle wrestling, 57kg class, at the 1988 Olympics. 1st Sergey Beloglazov, 2nd Askari Mohammadian, 3rd Noh Kyung-sun **(All-Sport)**

74kg – Welterweight
Limits: 158lb/71.67kg 1904; 72kg 1924-36, 73kg 1948-60, 78kg 1964-8
1904 Charles Erickson (USA)
1924 Hermann Gehri (Swi)
1928 Arvo Haavisto (Fin)
1932 Jack Van Bebber (USA)
1936 Frank Lewis (USA)
1948 Yasar Dogu (Tur)
1952 William Smith (USA)
1956 Mitsuo Ikeda (Jap)
1960 Douglas Blubaugh (USA)
1964 Ismail Ogan (Tur)
1968 Mahmut Atalay (Tur)
1972 Wayne Wells (USA)

1976 Jiichiro Date (Jap)
1980 Valentin Raitchev (Bul)
1984 David Schultz (USA)
1988 Ken Monday (USA)

82kg – Middleweight
Limits: 161lb/73kg 1908, 165 lb/75kg 1920, 79kg 1924-60, 87kg 1964-8
1908 Stanley Bacon (UK)
1920 Eino Leino (Fin)
1924 Fritz Hagmann (Swi)
1928 Ernst Kyburz (Swi)
1932 Ivar Johansson (Swe)
1936 Emile Poilvé (Fra)
1948 Glen Brand (USA)
1952 David Tsimakuridze (USSR)
1956 Nikolai Stanchev (Bul)
1960 Hasan Güngör (Tur)
1964 Prodan Gardschev (Bul)
1968 Boris Gurevich (USSR)
1972 Levan Tediashvili (USSR)
1976 John Peterson (USA)
1980 Ismail Abilov (Bul)
1984 Mark Schultz (USA)
1988 Han Myung-woo (SKo)

90kg – Light-heavyweight
Limits: 82.5kg, 1920, 87kg 1924-60, 97kg 1964-8
1920 Anders Larsson (Swe)
1924 John Spellman (USA)
1928 Thure Sjöstedt (Swe)
1932 Peter Mehringer (USA)
1936 Knut Fridell (Swe)
1948 Henry Wittenberg (USA)
1952 Wiking Palm (Swe)
1956 Gholam Reza Takhti (Irn)
1960 Ismet Atli (Tur)
1964 Aleksandr Medved (USSR)
1968 Ahmet Ayik (Tur)
1972 Ben Peterson (USA)
1976 Levan Tediashvili (USSR)
1980 Sanasar Oganesyan (USSR)
1984 Ed Banach (USA)
1988 Makharbek Khadartsev (USSR)

100kg – Heavyweight
Limits: over 158lb/71.60kg 1904, over 73kg, 1908, over 82.5kg 1920, over 87kg 1924-60, over 97kg 1964-8
1904 Bernhuff Hansen (USA)
1908 George O'Kelly (UK)
1920 Robert Roth (Swi)
1924 Harry Steel (USA)
1928 Johan Richthoff (Swe)
1932 Johan Richthoff (Swe)
1936 Kristjan Palusalu (Est)
1948 Gyula Bóbis (Hun)
1952 Arsen Mekokishvili (USSR)
1956 Hamit Kaplan (Tur)

1960 Wilfried Dietrich (FRG)
1964 Aleksandr Ivanitskiy (USSR)
1968 Aleksandr Medved (USSR)
1972 Ivan Yarygin (USSR)
1976 Ivan Yarygin (USSR)
1980 Ilya Mate (USSR)
1984 Lou Banach (USA)
1988 Vasile Puscasu (Rom)

Over 100kg – Super-heavyweight
1972 Aleksandr Medved (USSR
1976 Soslan Andiyev (USSR)
1980 Soslan Andiyev (USSR)
1984 Bruce Baumgartner (USA)
1988 David Gobedzhishvilli (USSR)

GRECO ROMAN
48kg – Light-flyweight
1972 Gheorghe Berceanu (Rom)
1976 Aleksey Schumakov (USSR)
1980 Zaksylik Ushkempirov (USSR)
1984 Vincenzo Maenza (Ita)
1988 Vincenzo Maenza (Ita)

52kg – Flyweight
1948 Pietro Lombardi (Ita)
1952 Boris Gurevich (USSR)
1956 Nikolay Solovyov (USSR)
1960 Dumitru Pirvulescu (Rom)
1964 Tsutomu Hanahara (Jap)
1968 Petar Kirov (Bul)
1972 Petar Kirov (Bul)
1976 Vitaliy Konstantinov (USSR)
1980 Vakhtang Blagidze (USSR)
1984 Atsuji Miyahara (Jap)
1988 Jon Rønningen (Nor)

57kg – Bantamweight
Limits: 58kg 1924-8, 56kg 1932-6
1924 Eduard Pütsep (Est)
1928 Kurt Leucht (Ger)
1932 Jakob Brendel (Ger)
1936 Márton Lörincz (Hun)
1948 Kurt Pettersén (Swe)
1952 Imre Hódos (Hun)
1956 Konstantin Vyrupayev (USSR)
1960 Oleg Karavayev (USSR)
1964 Masamitsu Ichiguchi (Jap)
1968 János Varga (Hun)
1972 Rustem Kazakov (USSR)
1976 Pertti Ukkola (Fin)
1980 Shamil Serikov (USSR)
1984 Pasquale Passarelli (FRG)
1988 András Sike (Hun)

62kg – Featherweight
Limits: 60kg 1912-20, 62kg 1924-8, 1948-60, 61kg 1932-6, 63kg 1964-8

Aleksandr Medved (centre) has won his third successive Olympic gold medal. Bulgarian silver medallist Osman Douraliev (left) shakes hands with Chris Taylor (USA), the heaviest man ever to compete at the Olympics, he weighed between 182 and 190kg (401-419lbs) **(Hulton-Deutsch)**

1912 Kaarlo Koskelo (Fin)
1920 Oskari Friman (Fin)
1924 Kalle Antila (Fin)
1928 Voldemar Väli (Est)
1932 Giovanni Gozzi (Ita)
1936 Yasar Erkan (Tur)
1948 Mehmet Oktav (Tur)
1952 Yakov Punkin (USSR)
1956 Rauno Mäkinen (Fin)
1960 Müzahir Sille (Tur)

1964 Imre Polyák (Hun)
1968 Roman Rurua (USSR)
1972 Georgi Markov (Bul)
1976 Kazimierz Lipién (Pol)
1980 Stylianos Migiakis (Gre)
1984 Kim Weon-kee (SKo)
1988 Kamandar Madzhidov (USSR)

68kg – Lightweight
Limits: 75kg 1906, 66.6kg 1908, 67.5kg 1912-28, 66kg

1932-6, 67kg 1948-60, 70kg 1964-8
1906 Rudolf Watzl (Aut)
1908 Enrico Porro (Ita)
1912 Eemil Väre (Fin)
1920 Eemil Väre (Fin)
1924 Oskari Friman (Fin)
1928 Lajos Keresztes (Hun)
1932 Erik Malmberg (Swe)
1936 Lauri Koskela (Fin)
1948 Gustaf Freij (Swe)
1952 Schazam Safin (USSR)
1956 Kyösti Lehtonen (Fin)
1960 Avtandil Koridze (USSR)
1964 Kazim Ayvaz (Tur)
1968 Munji Mumemura (Jap)
1972 Shamil Khisamutdinov (USSR)
1976 Suren Nalbandyan (USSR)
1980 Stefan Rusu (Rom)
1984 Vlado Lisjak (Yug)
1988 Levon Dzhulfalakyan (USSR)

74kg – Welterweight
Limits: 72kg 1932-36, 73kg 1948-60, 78kg 1964-8
1932 Ivar Johansson (Swe)
1936 Rudolf Svedberg (Swe)
1948 Gösta Andersson (Swe)
1952 Miklós Szilvási (Hun)
1956 Mithat Bayrak (Tur)
1960 Mithat Bayrak (Tur)
1964 Anatoliy Kolesov (USSR)
1968 Rudolf Vesper (GDR)
1970 Vitezslav Mácha (Cs)
1976 Anatoliy Bykov (USSR)
1980 Ferenc Kocsis (Hun)
1984 Jouko Salomaki (Fin)
1988 Kim Young-nam (SKo)

82kg – Middleweight
Limits: 85kg 1906, 73kg 1908, 75kg 1912-28, 79kg 1932-60, 87kg 1964-8
1906 Verner Weckman (Fin)
1908 Frithiof Mårtensson (Fin)
1912 Claes Johansson (Swe)
1920 Carl Westergren (Swe)
1924 Edvard Westerlund (Fin)
1928 Väinö Kokkinen (Fin)
1932 Väinö Kokkinen (Fin)
1936 Ivar Johansson (Swe)
1948 Axel Grönberg (Swe)
1952 Axel Grönberg (Swe)
1956 Givy Kartoziya (USSR)
1960 Dimiter Dobrev (Bul)
1964 Branislav Simic (Yug)
1968 Lothar Metz (GDR)
1972 Csaba Hegedüs (Hun)
1976 Momir Petkovic (Yug)
1980 Gennadiy Korban (USSR)
1984 Ion Draica (Rom)

1988 Mikhail Mamiashvili (USSR)

90kg – Light-heavyweight
Limits: 93kg 1908, 82.5kg 1912-28, 87kg 1932-60, 97kg 1964-8
1908 Verner Weckman (Fin)
1912 No winner – Anders Ahlgren (Swe) and Ivan Böhling (Fin) fought out a draw after nine hours
1920 Claes Johansson (Swe)
1924 Carl Westergren (Swe)
1928 Ibrahim Moustafa (Egy)
1932 Rudolf Svensson (Swe)
1936 Axel Cadier (Swe)
1948 Karl-Eric Nilsson (Swe)
1952 Kelpo Gröndahl (Fin)
1956 Valentin Nikolayev (USSR)
1960 Tevfik Kis (Tur)
1964 Boyan Radev (Bul)
1968 Boyan Radev (Bul)
1972 Valeriy Rezantsev (USSR)
1976 Valeriy Rezantsev (USSR)
1980 Norbert Növényi (Hun)
1984 Steven Fraser (USA)
1988 Atanas Komchev (Bul)

100kg – Heavyweight
Limits: open 1896,over 85kg 1906, over 93kg, 1908, over 82.5kg 1912-28, over 81kg 1932-60, over 91kg 1964-8
1896 Carl Schuhmann (Ger)
1906 Sören Jensen (Den)
1908 Richárd Weisz (Hun)
1912 Yrjö Saarela (Fin)
1920 Adolf Lindfors (Fin)
1924 Henri Deglane (Fra)
1928 Rudolf Svensson (Swe)
1932 Carl Westergren (Swe)
1936 Kristjan Palusalu (Est)
1948 Ahmet Kirecci (Tur)
1952 Johannes Kotkas (USSR)
1956 Anatoliy Parfenov (USSR)
1960 Ivan Bogdan (USSR)
1964 István Kozma (Hun)
1968 István Kozma (Hun)
1972 Nicolae Martinescu (Rom)
1976 Nikolay Balboshin (USSR)
1980 Georgi Raikov (Bul)
1984 Vasile Andrei (Rom)
1988 Andrzej Wronski (Pol)

Over 100kg – Super-heavyweight
1972 Anatoliy Roschin (USSR)
1976 Aleksandr Kolchinsky (USSR)
1980 Aleksandr Kolchinsky (USSR)
1984 Jeffrey Blatnick (USA)
1988 Aleksandr Karelin (USSR)

Discontinued event – 3-class winners
1906 Søren Marinus Jensen (Den)

WORLD CHAMPIONSHIPS

Unofficial world championships for Greco-Roman wrestling were held at Vienna in 1904, with further such championships held on 14 occasions (including five in 1911!) prior to the first official world championships, held in Helsinki in 1921. There was a further Greco-Roman world championship in 1922 but no more until 1950, since when they have been held regularly, and now annually in non-Olympic years. The first Freestyle championships were held at Helsinki in 1951. Olympic champions are automatically world champions in Olympic years. The current weight limits have been standard since 1969, variations are shown for each category. Winners since 1950:

FREESTYLE

Results shown below for 1953 are for unofficial championships

48kg – Light-flyweight
1969-71 Ebrahim Javadi (Irn)
1973 Roman Dmitriyev (USSR)
1974-5 Hasan Isaev (Murselov) (Bul)
1977 Anatoliy Beloglazov (USSR)
1978-9 Sergey Kornilayev (USSR)
1981-2 Sergey Kornilayev (USSR)
1983 Kim Chol-hwan (SKo)
1985 Kim Chol-hwan (SKo)
1986-7 Li Yae-sik (NKo)
1989 Kim Jong-shin (SKo)

52kg – Flyweight
1951 Ali Yücel (Tur)
1953 Georgiy Saydov (USSR)
1954 Hüseyin Akbas (Tur)
1957 Mehmet Kartal (Tur)
1959 Ali Aliyev (USSR)
1961-2 Ali Aliyev (USSR)
1963 Kemal Yanilmaz (Tur)
1965 Yoshikatsu Yoshida (Jap)
1966 Jang Chang-sun (SKo)
1967 Shigeo Nakata (Jap)
1969 Richard Sanders (USA)
1970 Ali Riza (Tur)
1971 Mohamad Ghorbani (Irn)
1973 Ebrahim Javadi (Irn)
1974-5 Yuji Takada (Jap)
1977 Yuji Takada (Jap)
1978 Anatoliy Beloglazov (USSR)
1979 Yuji Takada (Jap)
1981 Toshio Asakura (Jap)
1982 Hartmut Reich (GDR)
1983 Valentin Jordanov (Bul)
1985 Valentin Jordanov (Bul)
1986 Kim Yong-sik (NKo)
1987 Valentin Jordanov (Bul)
1989 Valentin Jordanov (Bul)

57kg – Bantamweight
1951 Nasuh Akar (Tur)
1953 Hüseyin Akbas (Tur)
1954 Mustafa Dagistanli (Tur)
1957 Hüseyin Akbas (Tur)
1959 Hüseyin Akbas (Tur)
1961 Mohamad Saifpour Sabadi (Irn)
1962 Hüseyin Akbas (Tur)
1963 Aidyn Ibragimov (USSR)
1965 Tomiaki Fukada (Jap)
1966-7 Ali Aliyev (USSR)
1969 Tamadichi Tanaka (Jap)
1970-1 Hideaki Yanagida (Jap)
1973 Mohsen Farahvashi (Irn)
1974 Vladimir Yumin (USSR)
1975 Masao Arai (Jap)
1977 Tadashi Sasaki (Jap)
1978-9 Hideaki Tomiyama (Jap)
1981 Sergey Beloglazov (USSR)
1982 Anatoliy Beloglazov (USSR)
1983 Sergey Beloglazov (USSR)
1985-7 Sergey Beloglazov (USSR)
1989 Kim Sik-seung (NKo)

62kg – Featherweight
Limit: 63kg 1962-7
1951 Haydar Zafer (Tur)
1953 Norair Musyegyan (USSR)
1954 Shozo Sasahara (Jap)
1957 Mustafa Dagistanli (Tur)
1959 Mustafa Dagistanli (Tur)
1961 Vladimir Rubashvili (USSR)
1962-3 Osamu Watanabe (Jap)
1965 Mohamad Saifpour Sabadi (Irn)
1966-7 Masaki Kaneko (Jap)
1969 Takeo Morita (Jap)
1970 Shamseddin Seyed-Abassy (Irn)
1971 Zagalav Abdulbekov (USSR)
1973 Zagalav Abdulbekov (USSR)
1974-5 Zeveg Oidov (Mgl)
1977-9 Vladimir Yumin (USSR)
1981 Simeon Sjeterev (Bul)
1982 Sergeiy Beloglazov (USSR)
1983 Viktor Alekseyev (USSR)
1985 Viktor Alekseyev (USSR)
1986 Hasar Isayev (USSR)
1987 John Smith (USA)
1989 John Smith (USA)

68kg – Lightweight
Limits: 67kg 1951-61, 70kg 1962-7
1951 Olle Anderberg (Swe)
1953 Viktor Sinyavskiy (UUSSR)
1954 Djahanbakte Tovfighe (Irn)
1957 Alimbek Bestayev (USSR)
1959 Viktor Sinyavskiy (USSR)
1961 Mohamad-Ali Sanatkaram (Irn)
1962 Enyu Valtschev (Bul)

1963 Iwao Horiuchi (Jap)
1965-7 Abdollah Movahed (Irn)
1969-70 Abdollah Movahed (Irn)
1971 Dan Gable (USA)
1973 Lloyd Keaser (USA)
1974 Nasrulla Nasrullayev (USSR)
1975 Pavel Pinigin (USSR)
1977-8 Pavel Pinigin (USSR)
1979 Mikhail Kharachura (USSR)
1981 Saipulla Absaidov (USSR)
1982 Mikhail Kharachura (USSR)
1983 Arsen Fadzeyev (USSR)
1985-7 Arsen Fadzeyev (USSR)
1989 Boris Budayev (USSR)

74kg – Welterweight
Limits: 73kg 1951-61, 78kg 1962-7
1951 Celál Atik (Tur)
1953 Ismail Ogan (Tur)
1954 Vakhtang Balavadze (USSR)
1957 Vakhtang Balavadze (USSR)
1959 Emamali Habibi (Irn)
1961-2 Emamali Habibi (Irn)
1963 Guliko Sagaradze (USSR)
1965 Guliko Sagaradze (USSR)
1966 Mahmut Atalay (Tur)
1967 Daniel Robin (Fra)
1969 Zarbeg Beriashvili (USSR)
1970 Wayne Wells (USA)
1971 Yuriy Gusov (USSR)
1973 Mansour Barzegar (Irn)
1974-5 Ruslan Ashuraliyev (USSR)
1977 Stan Dziedzic (USA)
1978-9 Leroy Kemp (USA)
1981 Martin Knosp (FRG)
1982 Leroy Kemp (USA)
1983 Dave Schultz (USA)
1985-6 Raúl Cascaret (Cubs)
1987 Adlan Vareyev (USSR)
1989 Ken Monday (USA)

82kg – Middleweight
Limits: 79kg 1951-61, 87kg 1962-7
1951 Haydar Zafer (Tur)
1953 Hasan Güngör (Tur)
1954 Abbas Zandi (Irn)
1957 Nabi Sorouri (Irn)
1959 Georgiy Chirtladze (USSR)
1961-2 Mansour Mehdizadeh (Irn)
1963 Prodan Gardschev (Bul)
1965 Mansour Mehdizadeh (Irn)
1966 Prodan Gardschev (Bul)
1967 Boris Gurevich (USSR)
1969 Fred Fozzard (USA)
1970 Yuriy Shakhmuradov (USSR)
1971 Levan Tediashvili (USSR)
1973 Vasiliy Sulzhin (USSR)
1974 Viktor Novozhilov (USSR)

1975 Adolf Seger (FRG)
1977 Adolf Seger (FRG)
1978 Magomed Aratsilov (USSR)
1979 István Kovács (Hun)
1981 Chris Campbell (USA)
1982-3 Tejmuraj Dzogolyev (USSR)
1985 Mark Schultz (USA)
1986 Vladimir Modosyan (USSR)
1987 Mark Schultz (USA)
1989 Elmadi Zhabraylov (USSR)

90kg – Light-heavyweight
Limits: 87kg 1951-61, 97kg 1962-7
1951 Yasar Dogu (Tur)
1953 Anatoliy Albul (USSR)
1954 August Englas (USSR)
1957 Petro Sirakov (Bul)
1959 Golam Reza Takhti (Irn)
1961 Golam Reza Takhti (Irn)
1962-3 Aleksandr Medved (USSR)
1965 Ahmet Ayik (Tur)
1966 Aleksandr Medved (USSR)
1967 Ahmet Ayik (Tur)
1969 Boris Gurevich (USSR)
1970 Gennadiy Strakhov (USSR)
1971 Rusi Petrov (Bul)
1973-5 Levan Tediashvili (USSR)
1977 Anatoliy Prokopchuk (USSR)
1978 Uwe Neupert (GDR)
1979 Khasan Ortsyev (USSR)
1981 Sanasar Oganesyan (USSR)
1982 Uwe Neupert (GDR)
1983 Piotr Nanev (USSR)
1985 Bill Sherr (USA)
1986-7 Macharbek Khadartsev (USSR)
1989 Macharbek Khadartsev (USSR)

100kg – Heavyweight
Limits: over 87kg 1951-61, over 97kg 1962-7
1951 Bertil Antonsson (Swe)
1953 Lyutvi Akhmedov (Bul)
1954 Arsen Mekokishvili (USSR)
1957 Hamit Kaplan (Tur)
1959 Lyutvi Ahmedov (Bul)
1961 Wilfried Dietrich (FRG)
1962-3 Aleksandr Ivanitskiy (USSR)
1965-6 Aleksandr Ivanitskiy (USSR)
1967 Aleksandr Medved (USSR)
1969 Shota Lomidze (USSR)
1970 Vladimir Gulyutkin (USSR)
1971 Shota Lomidze (USSR)
1973 Ivan Yarygin (USSR)
1974 Vladimir Gulyutkin (USSR)
1975 Khorloo Baianmunkh (Mgl)
1977 Aslanbek Bisultanov (USSR)
1978 Harald Büttner (GDR)
1979 Ilya Mate (USSR)
1981 Roland Gehrke (GDR)

1982 Ilya Mate (USSR)
1983 Aslan Khadartzev (USSR)
1985 Levy Khabelov (USSR)
1986 Aslan Khadartzev (USSR)
1987 Levy Khabelov (USSR)
1989 Akhmed Atanov (USSR)

Over 100kg – Super-heavyweight
1969-71 Aleksandr Medved (USSR)
1973 Soslan Andiyev (USSR)
1974 Ladislav Simon (Rom)
1975 Soslan Andiyev (USSR)
1977 Soslan Andiyev (USSR)
1979 Salman Khasimikov (USSR)
1981-3 Salman Khasimikov (USSR)
1985 David Gobedyichviliy (USSR)
1986 Bruce Baumgartner (USA)
1987 Aslan Khadartzev (USSR)
1989 Ali Reza Soleimani (Ira)

GRECO ROMAN
48kg – Light-flyweight
1969-70 Gheorghe Berceanu (Rom)
1971 Vladimir Zubkov (USSR)
1973-5 Vladimir Zubkov (USSR)
1977 Aleksey Shumakov (USSR)
1978 Constantin Alexandru (Rom)
1981 Zaksylik Ushkempirov (USSR)
1982 Temur Kazarashvili (USSR)
1983 Bratan Tsenov (Bul)
1985-7 Magyatdin Allakhverdyev (USSR)
1989 Oleg Kucherenko (USSR)

52kg – Flyweight
1950 Bengt Johansson (Swe)
1953 Boris Gurevich (USSR)
1955 Ignazio Fabra (Ita)
1958 Boris Gurevich (USSR)
1961 Armais Sayadov (USSR)
1962 Sergey Rybalko (USSR)
1963 Borivoje Vukov (Yug)
1965 Sergey Rybalko (USSR)
1966 Angel Kerezov (Bul)
1967 Vladimir Bakulin (USSR)
1969 Aluzadeh Firuz (Irn)
1970-1 Petar Kirov (Bul)
1973 Nicu Ginga (Rom)
1974 Peter Kirov (USSR)
1975 Vitaliy Konstantinov (USSR)
1977 Nicu Ginga (Rom)
1978 Vakhtang Blagidze (USSR)
1979 Lajos Rácz (Hun)
1981 Vakhtang Blagidze (USSR)
1982-3 Benyur Pashayan (USSR)
1985 Jan Rønningen (Nor)
1986 Sergey Dyudyayev (USSR)
1987 Pedro Roque (Cuba)
1989 Aleksandr Ignatenko (USSR)

57kg – Bantamweight
1950 Ali Mahmoud Hassan (Egy)
1953 Artyem Teryan (USSR)
1955 Vladimir Stashevich (USSR)
1958 Oleg Karavayev (USSR)
1961 Oleg Karavayev (USSR)
1962 Masamitsu Ichiguchi (Jap)
1963 János Varga (Hun)
1965 Ion Cernea (Rom)
1966 Fritz Stange (FRG)
1967 Ion Baciu (Rom)
1969 Rustem Kazakov (USSR)
1970 János Varga (Hun)
1971 Rustem Kazakov (USSR)
1973 Jozef Lipien (Pol)
1974-5 Farhat Mustafin (USSR)
1977 Pertti Ukkola (Fin)
1978-9 Shamil Serikov (USSR)
1981 Pasquale Passarelli (FRG)
1982 Piotr Michalik (Pol)
1983 Masaki Eto (Jap)
1985 Stojan Balov (Bul)
1986 Emil Ivanov (Bul)
1987 Patrice Mourier (Fra)
1989 Emil Ivanov (Bul)

62kg – Featherweight
Limit: 63kg 1962-7
1950 Olle Anderberg (Swe)
1953 Olle Anderberg (Swe)
1955 Imre Polyák (Hun)
1958 Imre Polyák (Hun)
1961 Hamid Mustafa (Egy)
1962 Imre Polyák (Hun)
1963 Gennadiy Sapunov (USSR)
1965 Yuriy Grigoryev (USSR)
1966-7 Roman Rurua (USSR)
1969 Roman Rurua (USSR)
1970 Hideo Fujimoto (Jap)
1971 Georgi Markov (Bul)
1973-4 Kazimierz Lipien (Pol)
1975 Nelson Davidyan (USSR)
1977 László Réczi (Hun)
1978 Boris Kramarenko (USSR)
1979 István Tóth (Hun)
1981 István Tóth (Hun)
1982 Ryszard Swierad (Pol)
1983 Hannu Lahtinen (Fin)
1985 Zhivko Vangelov (Bul)
1986 Kamandar Madzhidov (USSR)
1987 Zhivko Vangelov (Bul)
1989 Kamandar Madzhidov (USSR)

68kg – Lightweight
Limit: 67kg 1950-61, 70kg 1962-7
1950 József Gál (Hun)
1953 Gustav Freij (Swe)
1955 Grigoriy Gamarnik (USSR)

1958 Riza Dogan (Tur)
1961 Avtandil Koridze (USSR)
1962 Kazim Ayvaz (Tur)
1963 Stevan Horvat (Yug)
1965 Gennadiy Supanov (USSR)
1966 Stevan Horvat (Yug)
1967 Eero Tapio (Fin)
1969 Simion Popescu (Rom)
1970 Roman Rurua (USSR)
1971 Sreten Damjanovic (Yug)
1973 Shamil Khisamutdinov (USSR)
1974 Nelson Davidyan (USSR)
1975 Shamil Khisamutdinov (USSR)
1977 Heinz-Helmut Wehling (GDR)
1978 Stefan Rusu (Rom)
1979 Andrzej Supron (Pol)
1981-2 Gennadiy Yermilov (USSR)
1983 Tapio Sipilä (Fin)
1985 Stefan Negrisan (Rom)
1986 Levon Dzhulfalakyan (USSR)
1987 Aslautdin Abeyev (USSR)
1989 Claudio Passarelli (GDR)

74kg – Welterweight
Limit: 73kg 1950-61, 78kg 1962-7
1950 Matti Simanainen (Fin)
1953 Gurgen Chatvorjan (USSR)
1955 Vladimir Maneyev (USSR)
1958 Kazim Ayvaz (Tur)
1961 Valeriu Bularca (Rom)
1962-3 Anatoliy Kolesov (USSR)
1965 Anatoliy Kolesov (USSR)
1966-7 Viktor Igumenov (USSR)
1969-71 Viktor Igumenov (USSR)
1973 Ivan Kolev (Bul)
1974 Viteslav Mácha (Cs)
1975 Anatoliy Bykov (USSR)
1977 Viteslav Mácha (Cs)
1978 Arif Niftulayev (USSR)
1979 Ferenc Kocsis (Hun)
1981 Aleksandr Kudryavtsev (USSR)
1982 Stefan Rusu (Rom)
1983 Mikhail Mamiashvili (USSR)
1985-6 Mikhail Mamiashvili (USSR)
1987 Jouko Salomäki (Fin)
1989 Daulet Turlykhanov (USSR)

82kg – Middleweight
Limit: 79kg 1950-61, 97kg 1962-7
1950 Axel Grönberg (Swe)
1953 Givy Kartoziya (USSR)
1955 Givy Kartoziya (USSR)
1958 Riza Dogan (Tur)
1961 Vasiliy Zenin (USSR)
1962-3 Tevfik Kis (Tur)
1965 Roman Bogdanov (USSR)
1966 Valentin Olenik (USSR)
1967 László Sillai (Hun)

1969 Petar Krumov (Bul)
1970 Anatoliy Nazarenko (USSR)
1971 Csaba Hegedüs (Hun)
1973 Leonid Liberman (USSR)
1974-5 Anatoliy Nazarenko (USSR)
1977 Vlademir Cheboskarov (USSR)
1978 Ion Draica (Rom)
1979 Gennadiy Korban (USSR)
1981 Gennadiy Korban (USSR)
1982-3 Temur Abkhasava (USSR)
1985 Bogdan Daras (Pol)
1986 No medal awarded – both Bogdan Karas. (Pol) &
     Tibor Komaromi (Hun) disqualified
1987 Tibor Komaromi (Hun)
1989 Tibor Komaromi (Hun)

90kg – Light-heavyweight
Limit: 87kg 1950-61, 97kg 1962-7
1950 Muharrem Candas (Tur)
1953 August Englas (USSR)
1955 Valentin Nikolayev (USSR)
1958 Rostom Abashidze (USSR)
1961 György Gurics (Hun)
1962-3 Rostom Abashidze (USSR)
1965 Valeriy Anisimov (USSR)
1966 Boyan Radev (Bul)
1967 Nikolay Yakovenko (USSR)
1969 Aleksandr Yurkevich (USSR)
1970-1 Valeriy Rezantsev (USSR)
1973-5 Valeriy Rezantsev (USSR)
1977 Frank Andersson (Swe)
1978 Stojan Nikolov (Bul)
1979 Frank Andersson (Swe)
1981 Igor Kanygin (USSR)
1982 Frank Andersson (Swe)
1983 Igor Kanygin (USSR)
1985 Michael Houk (USA)
1986 Andrzej Malina (Pol)
1987 Vladimir Popov (USSR)
1989 Maik Bullmann (GDR)

100kg – Heavyweight
Limits: over 87kg 1950-61, over 97kg 1962-7
1950 Bertil Antonsson (Swe)
1953 Bertil Antonsson (Swe)
1955 Aleksandr Mazur (USSR)
1958 Ivan Bogdan (USSR)
1961 Ivan Bogdan (USSR)
1962 István Kozma (Hun)
1963 Anatoliy Rochin (USSR)
1965 Nikolay Shmakov (USSR)
1966-7 István Kozma (Hun)
1969 Nikolay Yakovenko (USSR)
1970-1 Per Svensson (Swe)
1973-4 Nikolay Balboshin (USSR)
1975 Kamen Lozanov (Bul)
1977-9 Nikolay Balboshin (USSR)
1981 Mikhail Saladze (USSR)

1982 Roman Wroclawski (Pol)
1983 Andrej Dmitrov (Bul)
1985 Andrej Dmitrov (Bul)
1986 Tamás Gáspár (Hun)
1987 Guram Gedekhauri (USSR)
1989 Gerhard Himmel (FRG)

Over 100kg – Super-heavyweight
1969-70 Anatoliy Roshin (USSR)
1971 Alexandr Tomov (Bul)
1973-5 Alexandr Tomov (Bul)
1977 Nikolai Dinev (Bul)
1978 Aleksandr Kolinchskiy (USSR)
1979 Alexandr Tomov (Bul)
1981 Refik Memisevic (Yug)
1982 Nikolai Dinev (Bul)
1983 Yevgeniy Artioshin (USSR)
1985 Igor Rostozotskiy (USSR)
1986 Tomas Johansson (Swe)
1987 Igor Rostorotskiy (USSR)
1989 Aleksandr Karelin (USSR)

MOST WORLD & OLYMPIC TITLES

10 Aleksandr Medved (USSR) Freestyle: 97kg 1962-4, 1966; over 97kg 1967-8, over 100kg 1969-72
8 Sergey Beloglazov (USSR) Freestyle: 57kg 1980-1, 1983, 1985-8; 62kg 1982
7 Valeriy Rezantsev (USSR) Greco Roman: 90kg 1970-6
6 Abdollah Movahed (Irn) Freestyle: 70/68kg 1965-70
6 Levan Tediashvili (USSR) Freestyle: 82kg 1971-2; 90kg 1973-6
6 Nikolay Balboshin (USSR) Greco Roman: 100kg 1973-4, 1976, 1977-9
6 Soslan Andiyev (USSR) Freestyle: over 100kg 1973, 1975-8, 1980
5 Ali Aliev (USSR) Freestyle: 52kg 1959, 1961-2; 57kg 1966-7
5 Aleksandr Ivanitskiy (USSR) Freestyle: over 97kg 1962-6
5 István Kozma (Hun) Greco-Roman: over 97kg 1962, 1964, 1966-8
5 Viktor Igumenov (USSR) Greco Roman: 78kg 1966-7, 74kg 1969-71
5 Roman Rurua (USSR) Greco Roman: 63/62kg 1966-69, 68kg 1970
5 Petar Kirov (Bul) Greco-Roman: 52kg 1968, 1970-2, 1974
5 Alexandr Tomov (Bul) Greco-Roman over 100kg 1971, 1973-5, 1979
5 Yuji Takada (Jap) Freestyle: 52kg 1974-7, 1979
5 Arsen Fadzeyev (USSR) Freestyle 68kg 1983, 1985-9

YACHTING

Yachting originated in the 16th and 17th centuries in the Netherlands, then the world's greatest maritime power. The first known yacht race for pleasure was in September 1661 when Charles II challenged the Duke of York to a race over a 23-mile stretch of the River Thames from Greenwich to Gravesend. The sport became popular towards the end of the 19th century, nearly 150 years after the formation of the world's first yacht club, the Water Club of Cork, Ireland in 1720.

AMERICA'S CUP

One of the most famous of all sporting trophies, the Cup was donated by the Royal Yacht Squadron for a race around the Isle of Wight in 1851. The American schooner America won the race and took the trophy to the United States. The New York Yacht club then offered it as a challenge trophy but, despite many challenges over the years, the cup stayed in American hands until 1983 when it temporarily became Australian property.

Year	Winning boat	Winning skipper	Score	Challenger
1870	Magic	Andrew Comstock	-	Cambria (Eng)
1871	Columbia & Sappho	Nelson Comstock Sam Greenwood	4-1	Livonia (Eng)
1876	Madeleine	Josephus Williams	2-0	Countess of Dufferin (Can)
1881	Mischief	Nathaniel Clock	2-0	Atalanta (Can)
1885	Puritan	Aubrey Crocker	2-0	Genesta (Eng)
1886	Mayflower	Martin Stone	2-0	Galatea (Eng)
1887	Volunteer	Henry Haff	2-0	Thistle (Sco)
1893	Vigilant	William Hansen	3-0	Valkyrie II (Eng)
1895	Defender	Henry Haff	3-0	Valkyrie III (Eng)
1899	Columbia	Charlie Barr	3-0	Shamrock (Eng)
1901	Columbia	Charlie Barr	3-0	Shamrock II (Eng)
1903	Reliance	Charlie Barr	3-0	Shamrock III (Eng)
1920	Resolute	Charles Adams	3-2	Shamrock IV (Eng)

1930	Enterprise	Harold Vanderbilt	4-0	Shamrock V (Eng)
1934	Rainbow	Harold Vanderbilt	4-2	Endeavour (Eng)
1937	Ranger	Harold Vanderbilt	4-0	Endeavour II (Eng)
1958	Columbia	Briggs Cunningham	4-0	Sceptre (Eng)
1962	Weatherly	Emil Mosbacher Jr	4-1	Gretel (Aus)
1964	Constellation	Bob Bavier Jr	4-0	Sovereign (Eng)
1967	Intrepid	Emil Mosbacher Jr	4-0	Dame Pattie (Aus)
1970	Intrepid	Bill Ficker	4-1	Gretel II (Aus)
1974	Courageous	Ted Hood	4-0	Southern Cross (Aus)
1977	Courageous	Ted Turner	4-0	Australia (Aus)
1980	Freedom	Dennis Conner	4-1	Australia (Aus)
1983	Australia II	John Bertrand	4-3	Liberty (USA)
1987	Stars & Stripes	Dennis Conner	4-0	Kookaburra III (Aus)
1988	Stars & Stripes	Dennis Conner	2-0	New Zealand (NZ)

* *Stars and Stripes* accepted a special challenge from *New Zealand* (skippered by David Barnes) in a best-of-three series in 1988. After a successful defence the American Supreme Court ruled that Conner's use of the catamaran against the New Zealand monohull had violated the Deed of Gift governing the race. However this decision was reversed by the New York Appeals Court in 1989 and the legal battle ended in 1990 in favour of Conner.
Most times winning skipper: 3 Charlie Barr, Harold Vanderbilt, Dennis Conner; 2 Henry Haff, Emil Mosbacher Jr
Most times skippered challenger: 3 Jim Hardy 1970, 1974, 1980

Dennis Conner at the helm of Stars & Stripes *in the 1988 races for the America's Cup* (All-Sport)

ADMIRAL'S CUP

The Royal Ocean Racing Club donated the trophy in 1957 to encourage yachtsmen from abroad to race in English waters. Up to three boats per nation are allowed to enter and in 1975, 1977 and 1979, a record 19 nations competed. The biennial series of six races (five until 1987), combining inshore and offshore racing, take place in the English Channel, at Cowes, in the Solent, and culminating with the Fastnet Race (established in 1925), 605 miles (975 km) from Cowes, round the Fastnet Rock off the south-west coast of Ireland and back. *Winners:*

9 UK 1957, 1959, 1963, 1965, 1971, 1975, 1977, 1981, 1989
3 FR Germany 1973, 1983, 1985
2 USA 1961, 1969; Australia 1967, 1979
1 New Zealand 1987

OLYMPIC GAMES

Yachting did not make its Olympic debut until 1900. It should have been included in the first modern Olympics programme four years earlier, but bad weather prevented any competition. The classes of competition have varied over the years, with the champions at current classes shown first, followed by winning teams at the discontinued events.

Soling

1972 USA (Harry Melges, William Bentsen, William Allen)
1976 Denmark (Poul Jensen, Valdemar Bandolowski, Erik H.Hansen)
1980 Denmark (Poul Jensen, Valdemar Bandolowski, Erik H.Hansen)
1984 USA (Robert Haines Jr, Edward Trevelyan, Roderick Davis)
1988 GDR (Jochen Schümann, Thomas Flach, Bernd Jäkel)

Finn – Olympic monotype

Classes: 12-foot and 18-foot (2-handed) dinghies in 1920, Meulan 1924, International 12-foot 1928, Snowbird 1932, International Olympia 1936, Firefly 1948. Finn from 1952.
1920 Franciscus Hin/Johannes Hin(Hol) 12-foot
1920 Francis Richards/T.Hedburg(UK) 18-foot
1924 Léon Huybrechts (Bel)
1928 Sven Thorell (Swe)
1932 Jacques Lebrun (Fra)
1936 Daniel Kagchelland (Hol)
1948 Paul Elvstrøm (Den)
1952 Paul Elvstrøm (Den)
1956 Paul Elvstrøm (Den)
1960 Paul Elvstrøm (Den)
1964 Willi Kuhweide (FRG)
1968 Valentin Mankin (USSR)
1972 Serge Maury (Fra)
1976 Jochen Schümann (GDR)
1980 Esko Rechardt (Fin)
1984 Russell Coutts (NZ)
1988 José-Luis Doreste (Spa)

470 class

1976 Frank Hübner/Harro Bode (FRG)
1980 Marcos Soares/Eduardo Penido (Bra)
1984 Luis Doreste/Roberto Molina (Spa)
1988 Thierry Peponnet/Luc Pillot (Fra)

Flying Dutchman

Sharpie class in 1956
1956 Peter Mander/John Cropp (NZ)
1960 Peder Lunde Jr/Björn Bergvall (Nor)
1964 Helmer Pedersen/Earle Wells (NZ)
1968 Rodney Pattisson/Iain Macdonald-Smith (UK)
1972 Rodney Pattisson/Christopher Davies (UK)
1976 Jörg Diesch/Eckert Diesch (FRG)
1980 Alejandro Abascal/Miguel Noguer (Spa)
1984 Jonathan McKee/William Carl Buchan (USA)
1988 Jørgen Bojsen-Møller/Christian Grønberg (Den)

Star

1932 Gilbert Gray/Andrew Libano Jr (USA)
1936 Peter Bischoff/Hans-Joachim Weise (Ger)
1948 Hilary Smart/Paul Smart (USA)
1952 Agostino Straulino/Nicolo Rode (Ita)
1956 Herbert Williams/Lawrence Low (USA)
1960 Timir Pinegin/Fyodor Shutkov (USSR)
1964 Durward Knowles/Cecil Cooke (Bah)
1968 Lowell North/Peter Barrett (USA)
1972 David Forbes/John Anderson (Aus)
1980 Valentin Mankin/Aleksandr Muzychenko (USSR)
1984 Bill Buchan/Stephen Erickson (USA)
1988 Michael McIntyre/Bryn Vaile (UK)

Tornado

1976 Reg White/John Osborn (UK)
1980 Alexandre Welter/Lars Björkström (Bra)
1984 Rex Sellers/Christopher Timms (NZ)
1988 Jean-Yves Le Deroff/Nicolas Henard (Fra)

Boardsailing (Windglider)

1984 Stephan van den Berg (Hol)
1988 Bruce Kendall (NZ)

Women's 470 class

1988 Allison Jolly/Lynne Jewell (USA)

Most individual gold medals: 4 Paul Elvstrøm

DISCONTINUED EVENTS

Swallow
1948 Stewart Morris/David Bond (UK)
Tempest
1972 Valentin Mankin/Vitaliy Dyrdyra (USSR)
1976 John Albrechtson/Ingvar Hansson (Swe)
Dragon
1948 Norway
1952 Norway
1956 Sweden
1960 Greece

1964 Denmark
1968 USA
1972 Australia
5.5 metres
1952 USA
1956 Sweden
1960 USA
1964 Australia
1968 Sweden
6 metres
1908 Great Britain
1912 France
1920 Norway
1924 Norway
1928 Norway
1932 Sweden
1936 Great Britain
1948 USA
1952 USA
6 metres (1907 rating)
1920 Belgium
6.5 metres
1920 Netherlands
7 metres
1908 Great Britain
1920 Great Britain
8 metres
1908 Great Britain
1912 Norway
1920 Norway
1924 Norway
1928 France
1932 USA
1936 Italy
8 metres (1907 rating)
1920 Norway
10 metres
1912 Sweden
1920 Norway (1907 rating)
1920 Norway (1919 rating)
12 metres
1908 Great Britain
1912 Norway
1920 Norway (1907 rating)
1920 Norway (1919 rating)
30 square metres
1920 Sweden
40 square metres
1920 Sweden

Tonnage categories in 1900

1/2 Ton	France
1/2 -1 Ton	France
1-2 Ton	Switzerland
2-3 Ton	Great Britain
3-10 Ton	France
10-20 Ton	France
Open	Great Britain

THE WHITBREAD ROUND THE WORLD RACE

The longest race in the world, it was inaugurated in August 1973, and is organised by the Royal Naval Sailing Association. Held quadrennially, the distance is 26,180 nautical miles (increased to 32,000 in 1990), starting and finishing at Portsmouth, England and rounding the Cape of Good Hope and Cape Horn. Conducted as a handicap race, with various classes. In the following list the handicap winner is shown first, followed by the fastest yacht that year; Flyer II and Steinlager 2 won both.

Year	Winning skipper	Yacht	Time
1974	Ramon Carlin (Mex)	Sayula II	152d 9h 00m
	Chay Blyth (UK)	Great Britain II	144d 10 hr
1978	Cornelis van Rietschoten (Hol)	Flyer	136d 5hr
	Rob James (UK)	Great Britain II	134d 12hr
1982	Cornelis van Rietschoten (Hol)	Flyer II	120d 6h 35m
1986	Lionel Pean (Fra)	L'Esprit d'Equipe	132d 0h 16m
	Pierre Fehlmann (Swi)	UBS Switzerland	117d 14h 32m
1990	Peter Blake (NZ)	Steinlager 2	128d 9h 40m

A world record for single-handed non-stop sailing around the world was set in the Vendée Globe Challenge, 109 days 8 hrs, 48 mins 50 secs by Titouan Lamazou (Fra) in the 60-ft sloop Ecureuil d'Aquitaine from Les Sables d'Olonne, France and back, 26 Nov 1989 to 15 Mar 1990.

SINGLE HANDED TRANSATLANTIC RACE

Held every four years from Plymouth to Newport, Rhode Island, approximately 3000 miles (4825 km), the race was named the Observer Single-Handed Transatlantic Race (OSTAR) 1960-84. When The Observer were succeeded as sponsors by the Carlsberg brewing company the 1988 race was known as C-STAR. The race was the idea of Colonel 'Blondie' Hasler, who finished second in the inaugural race. There is now a size limit for the boats of 18.3m (60 ft), but the largest contestant was the 71.9m four-master Club Mediterranée, sailed to second place in 1976 by Alain Colas (Fra). Monohulls won the first three races and in 1976, trimarans all the others, as the average speed of the winner has risen from 3.09 knots in 1960 to 11.23 knots in 1988.

Year	Winner	Yacht	Time
1960	Francis Chichester (UK)	Gypsy Moth III	40d 12hr 30min
1964	Eric Tabarly (Fra)	Pen Duick II	27d 3hr 56min
1968	Geoffrey Williams (UK)	Sir Thomas Lipton	25d 20hr 33min
1972	Alain Colas (Fra)	Pen Duick IV	20d 13hr 15min
1976	Eric Tabarly (Fra)	Pen Duick VI	23d 20hr 12min
1980	Phil Weld (USA)	Moxie	17d 23hr 12min
1984	Yvon Fauconnier (Fra)	Umupro Jardin V	16d 6hr 00min
1988	Philippe Poupon (Fra)	Fleury Michon	10d 9hr 15min

BOARDSAILING

Boardsailing (often called Windsurfing, which is a trade name) was pioneered as a sport by Henry Hoyle Schweitzer and Jim Drake in California, USA, in 1968, but the origin of boardsailing dates back to 1958 when 12-year-old Peter Chilvers of England devised the first prototype sailboard. The sport became popular in the 1970s and a world championship was instituted in 1973. Boardsailing was included in the Olympic Games for the first time in 1984.

SPEED RECORDS

The highest speed reached under sail on water by any craft over a 500m timed run is by the boardsailer Pascal Maka (Fra) at 42.91 knots (79.47 km/h) at Saintes Maries de-le-Mer, Camargue, France on 27 Feb 1990. The women's record was set at the same venue by Brigitte Giminez (Fra) who achieved a speed of 39.13 knots (72.51 km/k) on 28 Oct 1989.

SPORTSMEN OF THE YEAR

BBC Sports Personality of the Year

First awarded in 1954, winners of this prestigious annual award for British sports men and women have been:

1954 Chris Chataway (athletics)
1955 Gordon Pirie (athletics)
1956 Jim Laker (cricket)
1957 Dai Rees (golf)
1958 Ian Black (swimming)
1959 John Surtees (motorcycling)
1960 David Broome (show jumping)
1961 Stirling Moss (motor racing)
1962 Anita Lonsbrough (swimming)
1963 Dorothy Hyman (athletics)
1964 Mary Rand (athletics)
1965 Tommy Simpson (cycling)
1966 Bobby Moore (football)
1967 Henry Cooper (boxing)
1968 David Hemery (athletics)
1969 Ann Jones (tennis)
1970 Henry Cooper (boxing)
1971 Princess Anne (equestrianism)
1972 Mary Peters (athletics)
1973 Jackie Stewart (motor racing)
1974 Brendan Foster (athletics)
1975 David Steele (cricket)
1976 John Curry (ice skating)
1977 Virginia Wade (tennis)
1978 Steve Ovett (athletics)
1979 Sebastian Coe (athletics)
1980 Robin Cousins (ice skating)
1981 Ian Botham (cricket)
1982 Daley Thompson (athletics)
1983 Steve Cram (athletics)
1984 Jayne Torvill & Christopher Dean (ice dancing)
1985 Barry McGuigan (boxing)
1986 Nigel Mansell (motor racing)
1987 Fatima Whitbread (athletics)
1988 Steve Davis (snooker)
1989 Nick Faldo (golf)

Sports Writers Sports men and women of the Year

Voted annually by the British sports writers. *Winners:*

Year	Man	Woman
1975	David Wilkie (swimming)	Lucinda Prior-Palmer (equestrian)
1976	James Hunt (motor racing)	Gillian Gilks (badminton)
1977	Barry Sheene (motor cycling)	Virginia Wade (tennis)
1978	Daley Thompson (athletics)	Sharron Davies (swimming)
1979	Sebastian Coe (athletics)	Caroline Bradley (show jumping)
1980	Sebastian Coe (athletics)	Sharron Davies (swimming)
1981	Sebastian Coe (athletics)	Jayne Torvill (ice skating)
1982	Daley Thompson (athletics)	Wendy Norman (modern pentathlon)
1983	Steve Cram (athletics)	Jo Durie (tennis)
1984	Seb Coe (athletics)	Tessa Sanderson (athletics)
1985	Steve Cram (athletics)	Virginia Holgate (equestrianism)
1986	Lloyd Honeyghan (boxing)	Fatima Whitbread (athletics)
1987	Nick Faldo (golf)	Fatima Whitbread (athletics)
1988	Sandy Lyle (golf)	Liz McColgan (athletics)
1989	Nick Faldo (golf)	Yvonne Murray (athletics)

Sports Illustrated Sportsman of the Year

The great American magazine has awarded this title annually since 1954 to the sports man or woman who 'symbolizes in character and performance the ideals of sportsmanship'. Nationality US unless shown. *Winners:*

1954 Roger Bannister (UK, T & F, miler)
1955 Johnny Podres (baseball)
1956 Bobby Joe Morrow (T & F, sprinter)
1957 Stan Musial (baseball)
1958 Rafer Johnson (T & F, decathlon)
1959 Ingemar Johansson (Swe, boxing)
1960 Arnold Palmer (golf)
1961 Jerry Lucas (basketball)
1962 Terry Baker (football)
1963 Pete Rozelle (NFL commissioner)
1964 Ken Venturi (golf)
1965 Sanford Koufax (baseball)
1966 Jim Ryun (T & F, miler)
1967 Carl Yastrzemski (basketball)
1968 Bill Russell (basketball)
1969 Tommy Seaver (baseball)
1970 Bobby Orr (Can, ice hockey)
1971 Lee Trevino (golf)
1972 Billie Jean King (tennis) & John Wooden (basketball coach)
1973 Jackie Stewart (UK, motor racing)
1974 Muhammad Ali (boxing)
1975 Pete Rose (baseball)
1976 Chris Evert (tennis)
1977 Steve Cauthen (horse racing)
1978 Jack Nicklaus (golf)
1979 Willie Stargell (baseball) & Terry Bradshaw (football)
1980 US Olympic ice hockey team
1981 Ray Leonard (boxing)
1982 Wayne Gretzky (Can, ice hockey)
1983 Mary Decker (T & F, distance running)

1984 Edwin Moses (T & F, 400m hurdler) & Mary Lou Retton (gymnastics)
1985 Kareem Abdul-Jabbar (basketball)
1986 Joe Paterno (football coach)
1987 'Athletes who care'
1988 Orel Hershiser (baseball)
1989 Greg LeMond (cycling)
T& F = track and field athletics

James E.Sullivan Memorial Trophy

This annual award was instituted in the USA in 1930 in memory of James E.Sullivan, president of the AAU 1906-14, for the 'amateur athlete, who, by performance, example and good influence did the most to advance the cause of good sportsmanship during the year'. *Winners:*
1930 Bobby Jones (golf)
1931 Bernie Berlinger (T & F, decathlon)
1932 Jim Bausch (T & F, decathlon)
1933 Glenn Cunningham (T & F, miler)
1934 Bill Bonthron (T & F, miler)
1935 Lawson Little (golf)
1936 Glenn Morris (T & F, decathlon)
1937 Don Budge (tennis)
1938 Don Lash (T & F, distance)
1939 Joe Burk (rowing)
1940 Greg Rice (T & F, distance)
1941 Leslie MacMitchell (T & F, miler)
1942 Cornelius Warmerdam (T & F, pole vault)
1943 Gilbert Dodds (T & F, miler)
1944 Ann Curtis (swimming)
1945 Felix 'Doc' Blanchard (football)
1946 Arnold Tucker (football etc.)
1947 John Kelly Jr (rowing)
1948 Bob Mathias (T & F, decathlon)
1949 Dick Button (ice skating)
1950 Fred Wilt (T & F, distance)
1951 Bob Richards (T & F, pole vault)
1952 Horace Ashenfelter (T & F, steeplechaser)
1953 Dr Sammy Lee (diving)
1954 Mal Whitfield (T & F, half-miler)
1955 Harrison Dillard (T & F, hurdler)
1956 Patricia McCormick (diving)
1957 Bobby Joe Morrow (T & F, sprinter)
1958 Glenn Davis (T & F, 400m hurdles)
1959 Parry O'Brien (T & F, shot putter)
1960 Rafer Johnson (T & F, decathlon)
1961 Wilma Rudolph (T & F, sprinter)
1962 Jim Beatty (T & F, miler)
1963 John Pennel (T & F, pole vault)
1964 Don Schollander (swimming)
1965 Bill Bradley (basketball)
1966 Jim Ryun (T & F, miler)
1967 Randy Matson (T & F, shot putter)
1968 Debbie Meyer (swimming)
1969 Bill Toomey (T & F, decathlon)
1970 John Kinsella (swimming)
1971 Mark Spitz (swimming)
1972 Frank Shorter (T & F, marathon)
1973 Bill Walton (basketball)
1974 Rick Wohlhuter (T & F, half-miler)
1975 Tim Shaw (swimming)
1976 Bruce Jenner (T & F, decathlon)
1977 John Naber (swimming)
1978 Tracy Caulkins (swimming)
1979 Kurt Thomas (gymnastics)
1980 Eric Heiden (speed skating)
1981 Carl Lewis (T & F, sprinter/long jump)
1982 Mary Decker (T & F, distance)
1983 Edwin Moses (T & F, 400m hurdles)
1984 Greg Louganis (diving)
1985 Joan Benoit Samuelson (T & F, marathon)
1986 Jackie Joyner-Kersee (T & F, heptathlon)
1987 Jim Abbott (baseball)
1988 Florence Griffith-Joyner (T & F, sprinter)
1989 Janet Evans (swimming)

Jesse Owens International Trophy

Presented annually to the international athlete who best personifies the qualities of the great Olympian, who won four gold medals in 1936. *Winners:*
1981 Eric Heiden (USA, speed skating)
1982 Sebastian Coe (UK, athletics)
1983 Mary Slaney (USA, athletics)
1984 Edwin Moses (USA, athletics)
1985 Carl Lewis (USA, athletics)
1986 Saïd Aouita (Mor, athletics)
1987 Greg Louganis (USA, diving)
1988 Ben Johnson (Can, athletics)
1989 Florence Griffith-Joyner (USA, athletics)
1990 Roger Kingdom (USA, athletics)

L'Equipe Champion des Champions

The French sports daily newspaper *L'Equipe* has selected the following as its world sports man or woman of the year:
1976 Alberto Juantorena (Cub, athletics)
1977 Rosemarie Ackermann (GDR, athletics)
1978 Henry Rono (Ken, athletics)
1979 Sebastian Coe (UK, athletics)
1980 Eric Heiden (USA, ice skating)
1981 Sebastian Coe (UK, athletics)
1982 Paolo Rossi (Ita, football)
1983 Carl Lewis (USA, athletics)
1984 Carl Lewis (USA, athletics)
1985 Sergey Bubka (USSR, athletics)
1986 Diego Maradona (Arg, football)
1987 Ben Johnson (Can, athletics)
1988 Florence Griffith-Joyner (USA, athletics)
1989 Greg LeMond (USA, cycling)

PAN-AMERICAN GAMES

The Pan-American Games are multi-sport competitions open to athletes from North, Central and South American nations. They have been held every four years from 1951, when the Games were opened in Buenos Aires by the Argentinian President, Juan Peron, in front of a 100,000 crowd. They were originally planned for 1942, but delayed due to the outbreak of war.

27 sports were contested at the last Games in Indianapolis in 1987, all 23 Olympic summer sports with the addition of baseball, roller skating, softball and taekwondo. 34 nations are affiliated to the controlling body, the Pan-American Sports Organization.

Venues
1951 Buenos Aires, Argentina
1955 Mexico City, Mexico
1959 Chicago, USA
1963 Sao Paulo, Brazil
1967 Winnipeg, Canada
1971 Cali, Colombia
1975 Mexico City, Mexico
1979 San Juan, Puerto Rico
1983 Caracas, Venezuela
1987 Indianapolis, USA
1991 Havana, Cuba

Track and Field Athletics

Games best performances prior to 1991

MEN	min sec	name	year
100 metres	10.06	Leandro Peñalver (Cub)	1983
200 metres	19.86	Don Quarrie (Jam)	1971
400 metres	44.45	Ronnie Ray (USA)	1975
800 metres	1:46.3 m	James Robinson (USA)	1979
	1:46.31	Agberto Guimarães (Bra)	1983
1500 metres	3:40.5 m	Don Paige (USA)	1979
5000 metres	13:31.40	Arturo Barrios (Mex)	1987
10000 metres	28:20.37	Bruce Bickford (USA)	1987
Marathon	2hr 12:42	Jorge Gonzalez (PR)	1983
3000m steeple	8:23.26	Adauto Domingues (Bra)	1987
110m hurdles	13.20	Renaldo Nehemiah (USA)	1979
400m hurdles	48.49	Winthrop Graham (Jam)	1987
4x100m relay	38.31	USA	1975
4x400m relay	2:59.54	USA	1987
20km walk	1hr 24:50	Carlos Mercenario (Mex)	1987
50km walk	3hr 58:54	Martin Bermudez (Mex)	1987

	metres		
High jump	2.32	Javier Sotomayor (Cub)	1987
Pole vault	5.71	Mike Tully (USA)	1987
Long jump	8.75	Carl Lewis (USA)	1987
Triple jump	17.89	João Carlos de Oliveira (Bra)	1975
Shot	20.22	Dave Laut (USA)	1979
Discus	67.32	Luis M.Delis (Cub)	1983
Hammer	77.24	Jud Logan (USA)	1987
Javelin (old)	84.16	Duncan Atwood (USA)	1979
(new)	78.68	Duncan Atwood (USA)	1987
Decathlon	8024 pts	Bruce Jenner (USA)	1975

WOMEN	min sec		
100 metres	11.05	Evelyn Ashford (USA) (in semi)	1979
200 metres	22.24w	Evelyn Ashford (USA) (& 22.45 in semi)	1979
400 metres	50.12	Ana F.Quirot (Cub) (in heat)	1987
800 metres	1:59.06	Ana F.Quirot (Cub)	1987
1500 metres	4:05.7 m	Mary Decker (USA)	1979
3000 metres	8:53.6 m	Jan Merrill (USA)	1979
10000 metres	33:00.00	Marty Cooksey (USA)	1987
Marathon	2hr 52:06	Maricarmen Cardemas (Mex)	1987
100m hurdles	12.81	LaVonna Martin (USA)	1987
400m hurdles	54.23	Judi Brown King (USA)	1987
4x100m relay	42.90	USA	1975
4x400m relay	3:23.35	USA	1987

	metres		
High Jump	1.96	Coleen Sommer (USA)	1987

	metres		
Long jump	7.45	Jackie Joyner (USA)	1987
Shot	19.34	Maria Sarria (Cub)	1983
Discus	65.58	Maritza Marten (Cub)	1987
Javelin	63.76	Maria C.Colon (Cub)	1983
Heptathlon	6184 pts	Cindy Greiner (USA)	1987

w = wind assisted mark

Most individual event wins:
4 Osvaldo Suarez (Arg) 5000m 1955, 1963; 10000m 1955, 1959
4 João Carlos de Oliveira (Bra) long jump and triple jump 1975 and 1979

Swimming

Games best performances prior to 1991

Event	min:sec	name		year
MEN				
50m freestyle	22.55	Tom Williams (USA)		1987
100m freestyle	50.07	Rowdy Gaines (USA)	(in heat)	1983
200m freestyle	1:49.89	Bruce Hayes (USA)		1983
400m freestyle	3:53.01	Brian Goodell (USA)		1979
1500m freestyle	15:20.90	Alex Kostich (USA))		1987
4 x 100m freestyle relay	3:21.41	USA		1983
4 x 200m freestyle relay	7:23.63	USA		1983
100m backstroke	55.19	Rick Carey (USA)		1983
200m backstroke	1:59.34	Rick Carey (USA)		1983
100m breaststroke	1:02.28	Steve Lundquist (USA)		1983
200m breaststroke	2:19.31	Steve Lundquist (USA)		1983
100m butterfly	53.89	Anthony Nesty (Surinam)		1987
200m butterfly	1:58.85	Craig Beardsley (USA)		1983
200m individual medley	2:03.29	Jesse Vasallo (USA)		1979
400m individual medley	4:21.43	Ricardo Prado (Bra)		1983
4 x 100m medley relay	3:40.42	USA		1983
WOMEN				
100m freestyle	56.22	Cynthia Woodhead (USA)		1979
200m freestyle	1:58.43	Cynthia Woodhead (USA)		1979
400m freestyle	4:10.56	Cynthia Woodhead (USA)		1979
800m freestyle	8:34.72	Tami Bruce (USA)		1987
4 x 100m freestyle relay	3:45.82	USA		1979
4 x 200m freestyle relay	8:13.34	USA		1987
100m backstroke	1:01.86	Silvia Poll (CRC)	(relay 1st leg)	1987
200m backstroke	2:13.65	Katie Welch (USA		1987
100m breaststroke	1:10.63	Anne Ottenbrite (Can)		1983
200m breaststroke	2:35.53	Kathy Bald (Can)		1983
100m butterfly	1:00.53	Jill Sterkel (USA)		1979
200m butterfly	2:09.77	Mary T.Meagher (USA)		1983
200m individual medley	2:16.11	Tracy Caulkins (USA)		1979
400m individual medley	4:46.05	Tracy Caulkins (USA)		1979
4 x 100m medley relay	4:12.99	USA		1983

1987 Games – leading nations at all sports

Nation	gold	silver	bronze
USA	168	118	83
Cuba	75	52	48
Canada	30	57	75
Brazil	14	14	33
Argentina	12	14	27
Mexico	9	11	18
Puerto Rico	3	6	20
Venezuela	3	11	12
Colombia	3	8	13
Jamaica	2	3	8

During the 1987 Games the USA collected its 1000th gold medal and 2000th medal from all Pan-American Games.

Most individual event wins:
MEN: 4 Steve Furniss (USA) 200m and 400m ind. medley 1971 and 1975
WOMEN: 4 Cynthia Woodhead (USA)100m, 200m and 400m freestyle 1979, 200m freestyle 1983
4 Tracy Caulkins (USA) 200m and 400m ind. medley 1979 and 1983

MISCELLANEOUS GAMES

Asian Games

The first Asian Games were held at New Delhi, India on 8-11 Mar 1951, when ten nations took part. These multi-sport Games have since 1954 been held at four-yearly intervals. 11 nations took part in 1951 and this number had grown to a record 29 nations in 1982.

A predecessor of the Asian Games were the Far Eastern Games, first held in 1913 in Manila, with China, the Phillipines and two Japanese athletes taking part. These Games were held every two years to 1927 and then in 1930 and 1934.

Venues: 1951 New Delhi, 1954 Manila, 1958 Tokyo, 1962 Djakarta, 1966 Bangkok, 1970 Bangkok, 1974 Teheran, 1978 Bangkok, 1982 New Delhi, 1986 Seoul, 1990 Beijing.

Central American and Caribbean Games

First held in 1926 in Mexico City, and at four-yearly intervals ever since except for 1942. The 15th Games were staged in Guatemala City in 1990.

Pan-Arab Games

These Games were instituted by decree of the Arab League in 1951, and first held in 1953. Thereafter they were staged every four years until 1965, but then a gap until 1985 (at 18 sports).

South East Asia Games

First held in Bangkok, Thialand in 1959, they have subsequently been held bienially except for 1963. At the 15th Games in 1989 in Kuala Lumpur, Malaysia 24 sports were contested, including, amongst more familiar ones, the regional sports of sepak takrwa and silat olahraga, a martial art.

World Games

A four-yearly international championship for sports not on the Olympic programme, the World Games were first held at Santa Clara, USA in 1981. Subsequent festivals have been held in London (UK) 1985 and Karlsruhe (FRG) in 1989. At the latter the following 17 sports were contested: artistic cycling, bodybuilding, bowling, field archery, fistball, karate, korfball, life-saving, netball, pétanque, roller hockey, roller skating (figure and speed), sub-aqua, taekwando, trampolining and tumbling, tug-of-war, water skiing. Various other sports were also demonstrated.

World Student Games

The 'Universiade' or World Student Games, organised by the Féderation Internationale du Sport Universitaire (FISU), is well established as one of the world's most important sports meetings, although it has been somewhat under-regarded in the UK and perhaps in the USA.

The first 'International Universities' Games was held in Warsaw, organised by the Conféderation Internationale des Étudiants (CIE). From 1951 to 1962 rival Games were staged by FISU and the UIE. The latter, Communist inspired, were known as the World Youth Games from 1954 and these had the higher standards. From 1963, however, the Games merged and are now held biennially. Ten sports are usually included at the summer Games: association football, athletics, basketball, fencing, gymnastics, judo, swimming, tennis, volleyball and water polo.

The 1989 Games were due to be held in São Paulo, Brazil, but these had to be abandoned. Duisburg, FRG, staged four leading sports: athletics, men's basketball, fencing and rowing.

Venues (from 1951-61: U – UIE, F – FISU)
1924 Warsaw, 1927 Rome, 1928 Paris, 1930 Darmstadt, 1933 Turin, 1935 Budapest, 1937 Paris, 1939 Monaco, 1947 Paris, 1949 Budapest, 1951 Berlin (U) & Luxembourg (F), 1953 Bucharest (U) & Dortmund (F), 1954 Budapest (U), 1955 Warsaw (U) & San Sebastian (F), 1957 Moscow (U) & Paris (F), 1959 Vienna (U) & Turin (F), 1961 Sofia (F), 1962 Helsinki (U), 1963 Porto Alegre, 1965 Budapest, 1967 Tokyo, 1970 Turin, 1973 Moscow, 1975 Rome (unofficial), 1977 Sofia, 1979 Mexico City, 1981 Bucharest, 1983 Edmonton, 1985 Kobe, 1987 Zagreb, 1989 Duisburg. Scheduled next: 1991 Sheffield, 1993 Buffalo.

Winter sports are staged at the Winter Universiade, of which the 14th was at Sofia, Bulgaria in 1989 and the next will be at Sapporo, Japan in 1991 and at Zakopane, Poland in 1993. There are also separate World University Championships at various other sports.

INDEX OF SPORTS AND MAJOR EVENTS

The index contains all the sports included in this book, with cross-references to alternative names. It also includes various competitions, but excludes most of those that are, by their name, obviously included in their respective sports.